Volume 2

Mathematics II

Custom Edition for Utah School Districts

Randall I. Charles
Basia Hall
Dan Kennedy
Laurie E. Bass
Allan E. Bellman
Sadie Chavis Bragg
William G. Handlin
Art Johnson
Stuart J. Murphy
Grant Wiggins

PEARSON

Acknowledgments appear on page Z61, which constitutes an extension of this copyright page.

Taken from:

High School Math 2014 Common Core Integrated Math 2 Write-In Student Edition Volume 1
Copyright © 2014 by Pearson Education, Inc.
Published by Pearson Education, Inc.
One Lake Street, Upper Saddle River, New Jersey 07458

High School Math 2014 Common Core Integrated Math 2 Write-In Student Edition Volume 2
Copyright © 2014 by Pearson Education, Inc.
Published by Pearson Education, Inc.

Precalculus: Graphical, Numerical, Algebraic, Eighth Edition
By Franklin D. Demana, Bert K. Waits, Gregory D. Foley, Daniel Kennedy
Copyright © 2011 by Pearson Education, Inc.
Published by Addison-Wesley
501 Boylston Street, Suite 900, Boston, MA 02116

Pearson Learning Solutions, 501 Boylston Street, Suite 900, Boston, MA 02116
A Pearson Education Company
www.pearsoned.com

Printed in the United States of America

6 7 8 9 10 V011 18 17 16 15 14

000200010271817052

AH

PEARSON

ISBN 10: 1-269-54674-0
ISBN 13: 978-1-269-54674-4

From the **Authors**

Welcome

Math is a powerful tool with far-reaching applications throughout your life. We have designed a unique and engaging program that will enable you to tap into the power of mathematics and mathematical reasoning. This award-winning program has been developed to align fully to the Common Core State Standards.

Developing mathematical understanding and problem-solving abilities is an ongoing process—a journey both inside and outside the classroom. This course is designed to help make sense of the mathematics you encounter in and out of class each day and to help you develop mathematical proficiency.

You will learn important mathematical principles. You will also learn how the principles are connected to one another and to what you already know. You will learn to solve problems and learn the reasoning that lies behind your solutions. You will also develop the key mathematical practices of the Common Core State Standards.

Each chapter begins with the "big ideas" of the chapter and some essential questions that you will learn to answer. Through this question-and-answer process you will develop your ability to analyze problems independently and solve them in different applications.

Your skills and confidence will increase through practice and review. Work through the problems so you understand the concepts and methods presented and the thinking behind them. Then do the exercises. Ask yourself how new concepts relate to old ones. Make the connections!

Everyone needs help sometimes. You will find that this program has built-in opportunities, both in this text and online, to get help whenever you need it.

The problem-solving and reasoning habits and problem-solving skills you develop in this program will serve you in all your studies and in your daily life. They will prepare you for future success not only as a student, but also as a member of a changing technological society.

Best wishes,

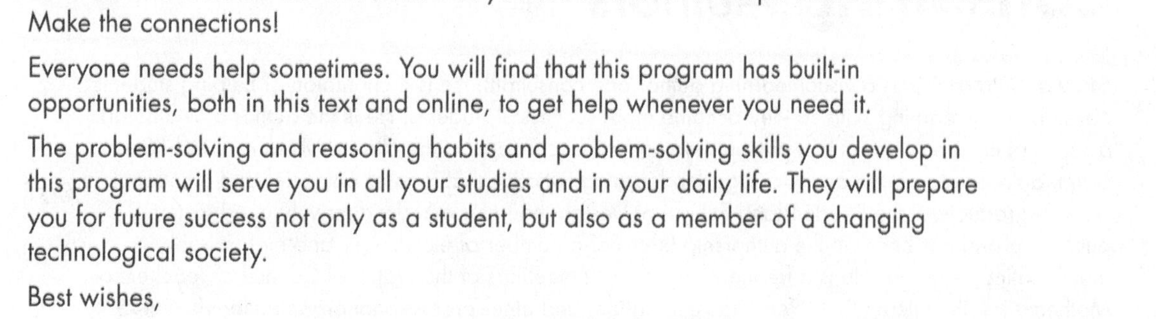

Series *Authors*

Randall I. Charles, Ph.D., is Professor Emeritus in the Department of Mathematics at San Jose State University, San Jose, California. He began his career as a high school mathematics teacher, and he was a mathematics supervisor for five years. Dr. Charles has been a member of several NCTM committees including the writing team for the Curriculum Focal Points. He is the former Vice President of the National Council of Supervisors of Mathematics. Much of his writing and research has been in the area of problem solving. He has authored more than 90 mathematics textbooks for kindergarten through college.

Dan Kennedy, Ph.D., is a classroom teacher and the Lupton Distinguished Professor of Mathematics at the Baylor School in Chattanooga, Tennessee. A frequent speaker at professional meetings on the subject of mathematics education reform, Dr. Kennedy has conducted more than 50 workshops and institutes for high school teachers. He is coauthor of textbooks in calculus and precalculus, and from 1990 to 1994 he chaired the College Board's AP Calculus Development Committee. He is a 1992 Tandy Technology Scholar and a 1995 Presidential Award winner.

Basia Hall currently serves as Manager of Instructional Programs for the Houston Independent School District. With 33 years of teaching experience, Ms. Hall has served as a department chair, instructional supervisor, school improvement facilitator, and professional development trainer. She has developed curricula for Algebra 1, Geometry, and Algebra 2 and co-developed the Texas state mathematics standards. A 1992 Presidential Awardee, Ms. Hall is past president of the Texas Association of Supervisors of Mathematics and is a state representative for the National Council of Supervisors of Mathematics (NCSM).

Consulting *Authors*

Stuart J. Murphy is a visual learning author and consultant. He is a champion of helping students develop visual learning skills so they become more successful students. He is the author of MathStart, a series of children's books that presents mathematical concepts in the context of stories, and *I See I Learn*, a Pre-Kindergarten and Kindergarten learning initiative that focuses on social and emotional skills. A graduate of the Rhode Island School of Design, he has worked extensively in educational publishing and has been on the authorship teams of a number of elementary and high school mathematics programs. He is a frequent presenter at meetings of the National Council of Teachers of Mathematics, the International Reading Association, and other professional organizations.

Grant Wiggins, Ed.D., is the President of Authentic Education in Hopewell, New Jersey. He earned his B.A. from St. John's College in Annapolis and his Ed.D. from Harvard University Dr. Wiggins consults with schools, districts, and state education departments on a variety of reform matters; organizes conferences and workshops; and develops print materials and web resources on curricular change. He is perhaps best known for being the coauthor, with Jay McTighe, of *Understanding by Design®* and *The Understanding by Design® Handbook*[1], the award-winning and highly successful materials on curriculum published by ASCD®. His work has been supported by the Pew Charitable Trusts, the Geraldine R. Dodge Foundation, and the National Science Foundation.

[1] ASCD®, publisher of the "Understanding by Design® Handbook" co-authored by Grant Wiggins and registered owner of the trademark "Understanding by Design®", has not authorized or sponsored this work and is in no way affiliated with Pearson or its products.

Program *Authors*

Algebra Topics

Allan E. Bellman, Ph.D., is an Associate Professor of Mathematics Education at the University of Mississippi. He previously taught at the University of California, Davis for 12 years and in public school in Montgomery County, Maryland for 31. He has been an instructor for both the Woodrow Wilson National Fellowship Foundation and the Texas Instruments' T^3 program. Dr. Bellman has expertise in the use of technology in education and assessment-driven instruction and speaks frequently on these topics. He is a recipient of the Tandy Award for Teaching Excellence and has twice been listed in Who's Who Among America's Teachers.

Sadie Chavis Bragg, Ed.D., is Senior Vice President of Academic Affairs and professor of mathematics at the Borough of Manhattan Community College of the City University of New York. She is a past president of the American Mathematical Association of Two-Year Colleges (AMATYC). In recognition for her service to the field of mathematics locally, statewide, nationally, and internationally, she was awarded AMATYC's most prestigious award, The Mathematics Excellence Award for 2010. Dr. Bragg has coauthored more than 60 mathematics textbooks for kindergarten through college.

William G. Handlin, Sr., is a classroom teacher and Department Chair of Mathematics and former Department Chair of Technology Applications at Spring Woods High School in Houston, Texas. Awarded Life Membership in the Texas Congress of Parents and Teachers for his contributions to the well-being of children, Mr. Handlin is also a frequent workshop and seminar leader in professional meetings.

Geometry Topics

Laurie E. Bass is a classroom teacher at the 9–12 division of the Ethical Culture Fieldston School in Riverdale, New York. A classroom teacher for more than 30 years, Ms. Bass has a wide base of teaching experiences, ranging from Grade 6 through Advanced Placement Calculus. She was the recipient of a 2000 Honorable Mention for the Radio Shack National Teacher Awards. She has been a contributing writer for a number of publications, including software-based activities for the Algebra 1 classroom. Among her areas of special interest are cooperative learning for high school students and geometry exploration on the computer. Ms. Bass is a frequent presenter at local, regional, and national conferences.

Art Johnson, Ed.D., is a professor of mathematics education at Boston University. He is a mathematics educator with 32 years of public school teaching experience, a frequent speaker and workshop leader, and the recipient of a number of awards: the Tandy Prize for Teaching Excellence, the Presidential Award for Excellence in Mathematics Teaching, and New Hampshire Teacher of the Year. He was also profiled by the Disney Corporation in the American Teacher of the Year Program. Dr. Johnson has contributed 18 articles to NCTM journals and has authored over 50 books on various aspects of mathematics.

Using **Your Book** *with Success*

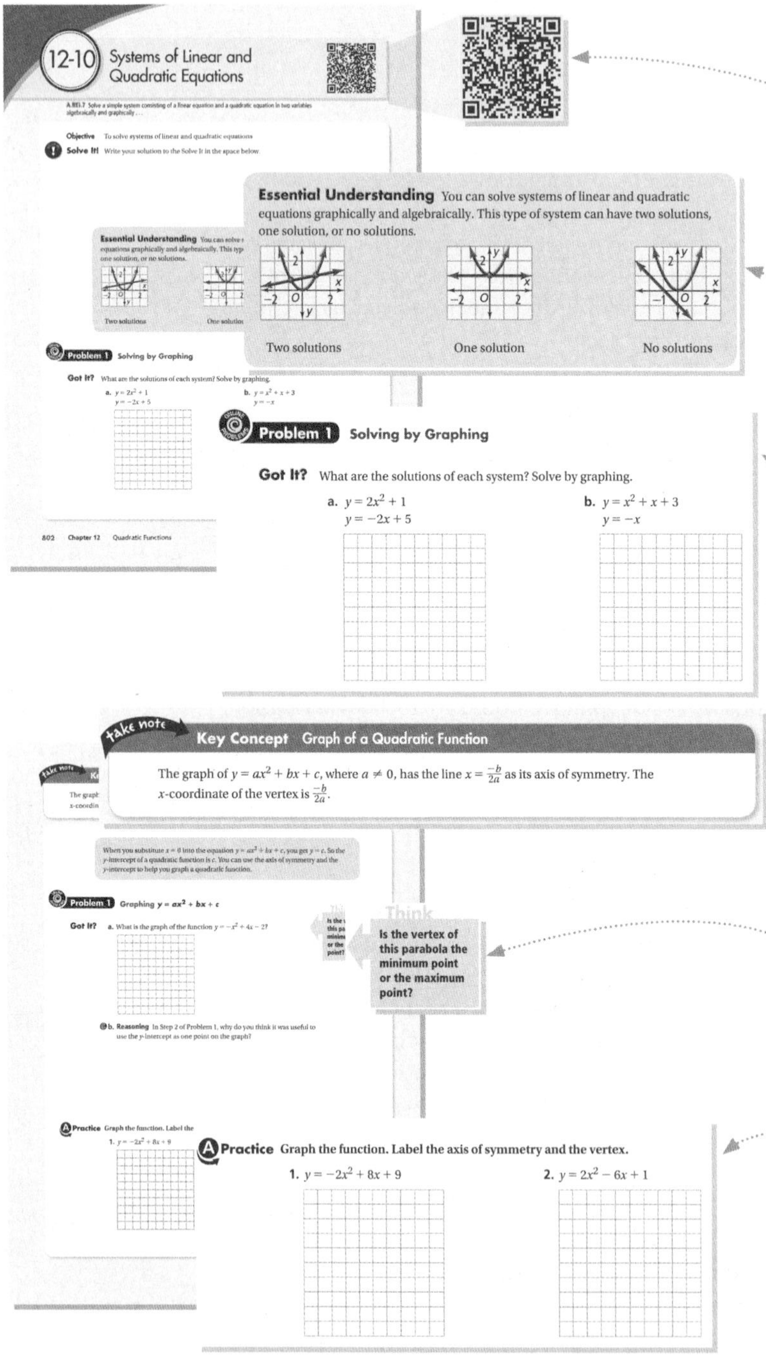

- You will find a QR code on the lesson openers. Each code links to a unique instructional video developed by **Virtual Nerd**™.
- The **Essential Understanding** presents the key concept of the lesson and connects to the Big Ideas that are introduced in the Chapter Opener.
- After working through the Problem in the Interactive Digital Path, you complete a **Got It?** exercise in your book. For exercises that require graphing, a blank grid is provided.
- You can use the instructional summaries in the **Take Note** boxes to review concepts when completing homework or studying for an assessment.
- The **Think** and **Plan** boxes suggest questions to help you make sense of the problem and develop a solution plan.
- Each **Got It?** exercise is followed by additional exercises that focus on the same math concept and skill. You complete these exercises in your book.

At the end of each lesson is a **Lesson Check** that you complete in your book. The Do you know HOW? section focuses on skills and the Do you UNDERSTAND? section targets your understanding of the math concepts related to the skills.

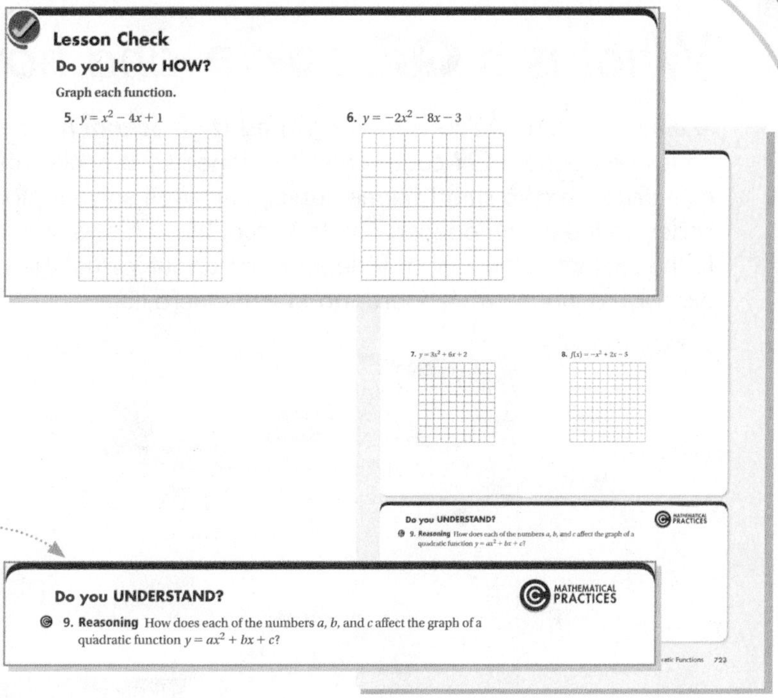

Lesson Check

Do you know HOW?

Graph each function.

5. $y = x^2 - 4x + 1$

6. $y = -2x^2 - 8x - 3$

Do you UNDERSTAND? MATHEMATICAL PRACTICES

9. **Reasoning** How does each of the numbers a, b, and c affect the graph of a quadratic function $y = ax^2 + bx + c$?

Each lesson ends with **More Practice and Problem Solving** Exercises. You will complete these exercises in your homework notebook or on a separate sheet of paper.

The exercises with the **Common Core logo** help you become more proficient with the Standards for Mathematical Practice. Those with **STEM** logo provide practice with science, technology, or engineering topics.

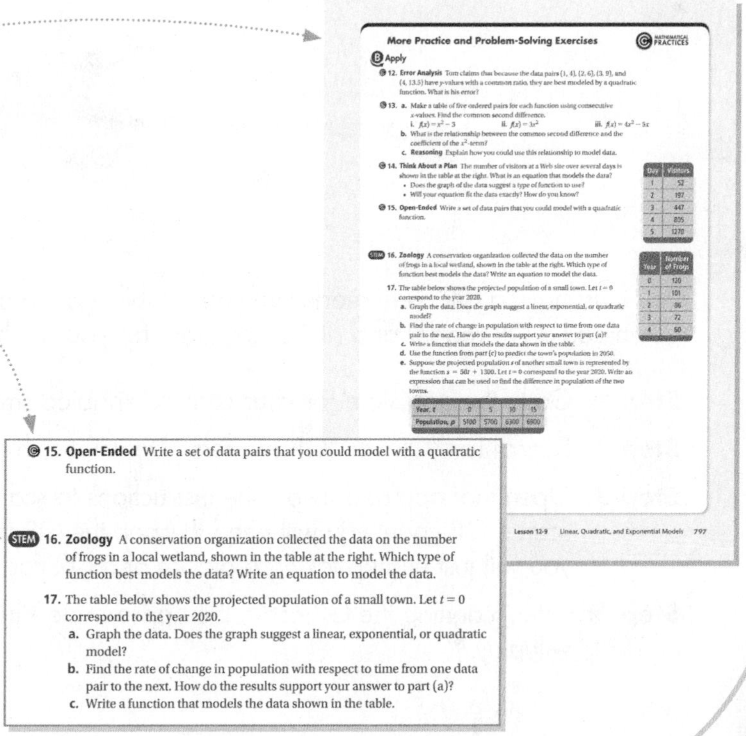

More Practice and Problem-Solving Exercises

15. **Open-Ended** Write a set of data pairs that you could model with a quadratic function.

STEM 16. **Zoology** A conservation organization collected the data on the number of frogs in a local wetland, shown in the table at the right. Which type of function best models the data? Write an equation to model the data.

17. The table below shows the projected population of a small town. Let $t = 0$ correspond to the year 2020.
    a. Graph the data. Does the graph suggest a linear, exponential, or quadratic model?
    b. Find the rate of change in population with respect to time from one data pair to the next. How do the results support your answer to part (a)?
    c. Write a function that models the data shown in the table.

What is a **QR code** *and how do I use it?*

A unique feature of Pearson's ***Integrated High School Mathematics*** is the QR code on lesson openers. QR codes can be scanned by any electronic device with a camera, such as a smart phone, tablet, and even some laptop computers. The QR codes on the lesson openers link to Virtual Nerd™ tutorial videos that directly relate to the content in the lesson. To learn more about Virtual Nerd tutorial videos and its exclusive dynamic whiteboard, go to virtualnerd.com.

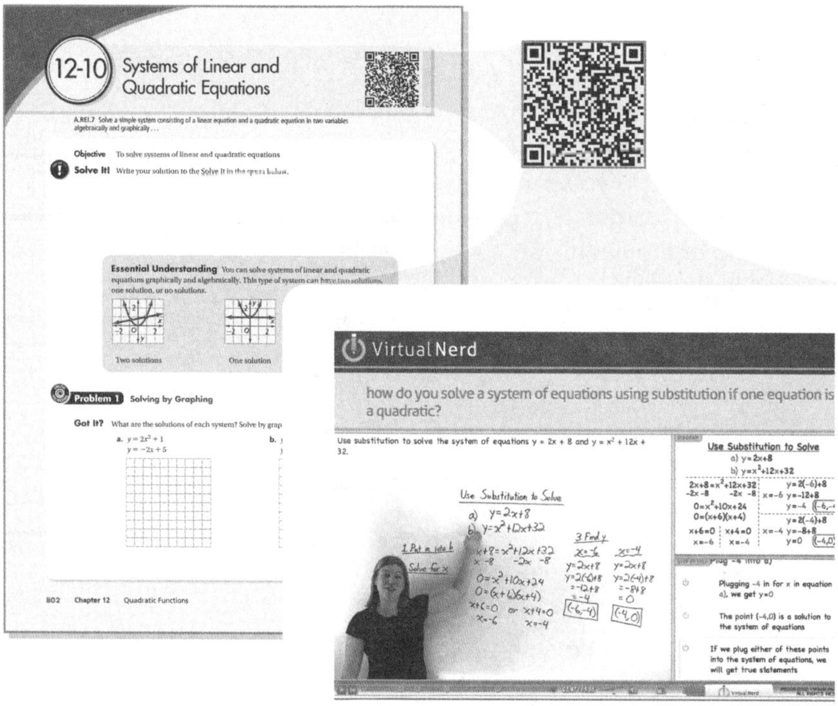

You must have a QR code reader on your mobile device or computer. You can download a QR reader app at the app store for your mobile device.

Step 1: Go to the app store for your camera-enabled smart phone or tablet.

Step 2: Search for "QR" or "QR readers". Download the QR reader app.

Step 3: Open that app and follow the instructions to scan. Whenever you want to scan a QR code, you will need to open the QR reader app first, otherwise you will just end up taking a picture of a QR code.

Step 4: After scanning the QR code, the appropriate Virtual Nerd tutorial video will play.

What **Resources** *can I use when studying?*

Pearson's ***Integrated High School Mathematics*** offers a range of resources that you can use out of class.

Student Worktext Your book is more than a textbook. Not only does it have important summaries of key math concepts and skills, it will also have your worked-out solutions to the *Got It?* and *Practice* exercises and your own notes for each lesson or problem. Use your book to:

- Refer back to your worked-out solutions and notes.
- Review the key concepts of each lesson by rereading the *Essential Understanding* and *Take Note* boxes.
- Access video tutorials of the concepts addressed in the lesson by scanning the QR codes.

Pearson SuccessNet You have full access to all of the resources on Pearson SuccessNet, including the **Interactive Digital Path** where you will find all of the *Solve Its!* and Problems presented in class. Revisit the animated, stepped-out problems presented in-class to clarify and solidify your math knowledge. Additional resources available to you include:

- Interactive Student Worktext
- Homework Video Tutors in English and Spanish
- Online Glossary with audio in English and Spanish
- MathXL for School Interactive Math Practice
- Math Tools and Online Manipulatives
- Multilingual Handbook
- Assessments with immediate feedback

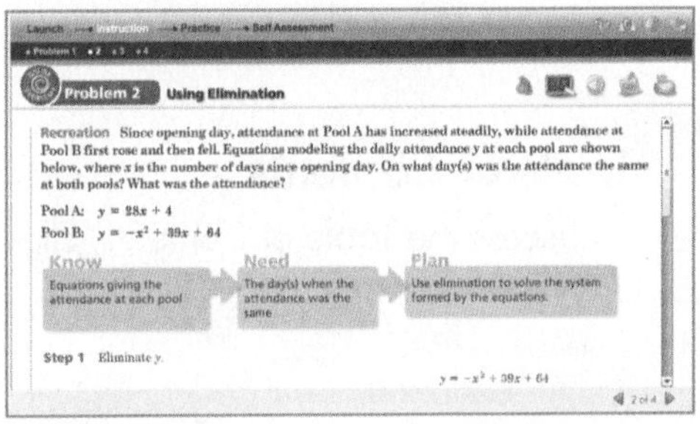

Mobile eText You may wish to access your student book on the go, either online or offline via download. Pearson's ***Integrated High School Mathematics*** also offers you a complete mobile etext of the Student Worktext.

- Use the notes, highlight, and bookmark features to personalize your eText.
- Watch animated problem videos with step-by-step instruction for every lesson.

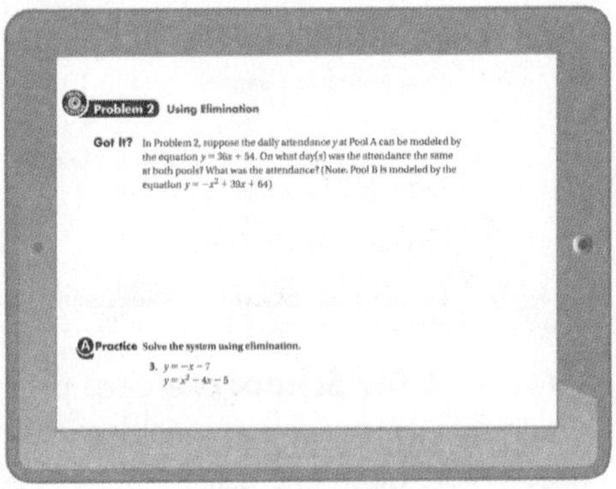

Pearson SuccessNet

Pearson SuccessNet is the gateway to all of the digital components of the program. You can use the online content to review the day's lesson, complete lessons independently, get help with your homework assignments, and prepare for and/or take an assessment. You will be given a username and password to log into www.pearsonsuccessnet.com.

The Homepage

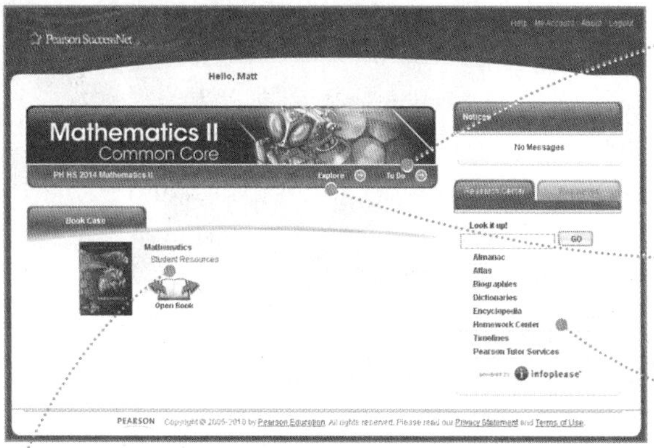

The **To Do** tab contains a list of assignments that you need to complete. You can also access your gradebook and review past assignments.

The **Explore** tab provides you access to the Table of Contents and all of the digital content for the program.

You can also access the following student resources: Practice Worksheets, Homework Video Tutors, and a Multilingual Handbook

Your eText includes links to animated lesson videos, highlighting and note taking tools, and a visual glossary with audio.

Table of Contents

To access the Table of Contents, click on *Explore* from your Homepage.

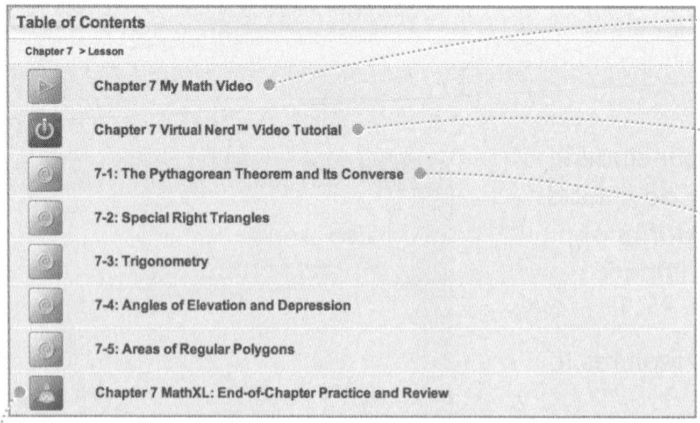

Student-developed videos bring real-life context to mathematics.

Step-by-step video tutorials offer additional support.

Digital lessons include access to animated problems, math tools, homework exercises, and self-assessments.

MathXL for School exercises provide additional practice. Examples and tutorials support every problem, and instant feedback is provided as you complete each exercise.

Interactive Digital Path

To access the **Interactive Digital Path**, click on the appropriate lesson from the Table of Contents.

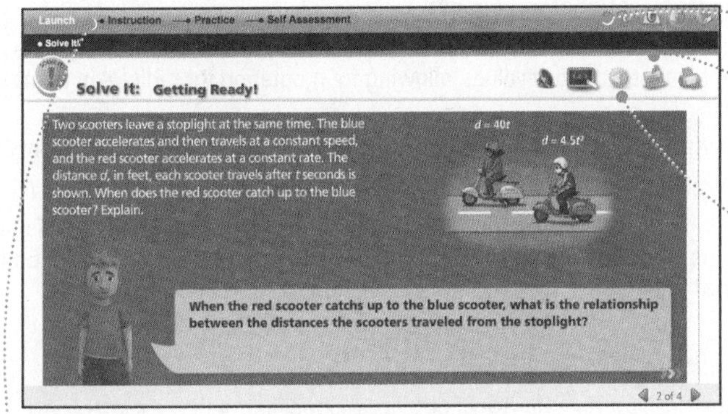

Math Tools help you explore and visualize concepts.

You'll find opportunities to review formulas, properties, and other key concepts.

Interactive Glossary is available in English and Spanish with audio.

Every lesson includes the following:

Launch: Interactive lesson opener connects the math to real-world applications.

Instruction: All lesson problems are stepped out with detailed instruction. You can complete the subsequent *Got It?* exercises in your Student Worktext.

Practice: Exercises from your Student Worktext are available for view.

Self-Assessment: You can take the self-check lesson quiz, and then check your answers on the second screen.

MathXL for School

To access *MathXL for School*, click on the Chapter Review and Practice link from the Table of Contents.

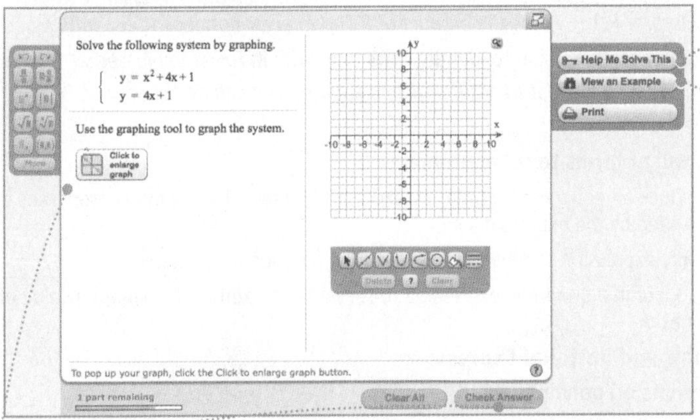

Select **Help Me Solve This** for an interactive step-by-step tutorial.

Select **View an Example** to see a similar worked out problem.

Input your answer and select **Check Answer** to get immediate feedback. After completing the exercise, a new exercise automatically regenerates, so you have unlimited practice opportunities.

Common Core *State Standards*

Mathematics II

Number and Quantity

The Real Number System

Extend the properties of exponents to rational exponents.

N.RN.1 Explain how the definition of the meaning of rational exponents follows from extending the properties of integer exponents to those values, allowing for a notation for radicals in terms of rational exponents.

N.RN.2 Rewrite expressions involving radicals and rational exponents using the properties of exponents.

Use properties of rational and irrational numbers.

N.RN.3 Explain why the sum or product of rational numbers is rational; that the sum of a rational number and an irrational number is irrational; and that the product of a nonzero rational number and an irrational number is irrational.

Quantities

Reason quantitatively and use units to solve problems.

N.Q.2 Define appropriate quantities for the purpose of descriptive modeling.★

The Complex Number System

Perform arithmetic operations with complex numbers.

N.CN.1 Know there is a complex number i such that $i^2 = -1$, and every complex number has the form $a + bi$ with a and b real.

N.CN.2 Use the relation $i^2 = -1$ and the commutative, associative, and distributive properties to add, subtract, and multiply complex numbers.

Use complex numbers in polynomial identities and equations.

N.CN.7 Solve quadratic equations with real coefficients that have complex solutions.

Algebra

Seeing Structure in Expressions

Interpret the structure of expressions

A.SSE.1 Interpret expressions that represent a quantity in terms of its context.★

A.SSE.1b Interpret complicated expressions by viewing one or more of their parts as a single entity. *For example, interpret* $P(1 + r)^n$ *as the product of P and a factor not depending on P.*★

A.SSE.2 Use the structure of an expression to identify ways to rewrite it. *For example, see* $x^4 - y^4$ *as* $(x^2)^2 - (y^2)^2$*, thus recognizing it as a difference of squares that can be factored as* $(x^2 - y^2)(x^2 + y^2)$.

Write expressions in equivalent forms to solve problems

A.SSE.3 Choose and produce an equivalent form of an expression to reveal and explain properties of the quantity represented by the expression.★

A.SSE.3a Factor a quadratic expression to reveal the zeros of the function it defines.★

A.SSE.3b Complete the square in a quadratic expression to reveal the maximum or minimum value of the function it defines.★

Arithmetic with Polynomials and Rational Expressions

Perform arithmetic operations on polynomials

A.APR.1 Understand that polynomials form a system analogous to the integers, namely, they are closed under the operations of addition, subtraction, and multiplication; add, subtract, and multiply polynomials.

Creating Equations★

Create equations that describe numbers or relationships

A.CED.1 Create equations and inequalities in one variable and use them to solve problems. *Include equations arising from linear and quadratic functions, and simple rational and exponential functions.*★

A.CED.2 Create equations in two or more variables to represent relationships between quantities; graph equations on coordinate axes with labels and scales.★

A.CED.4 Rearrange formulas to highlight a quantity of interest, using the same reasoning as in solving equations. *For example, rearrange Ohm's law $V = IR$ to highlight resistance R.*★

Reasoning with Equations and Inequalities

Understand solving equations as a process of reasoning and explain the reasoning

A.REI.1 Explain each step in solving a simple equation as following from the equality of numbers asserted at the previous step, starting from the assumption that the original equation has a solution. Construct a viable argument to justify a solution method.

Solve equations and inequalities in one variable

A.REI.4 Solve quadratic equations in one variable.

A.REI.4a Use the method of completing the square to transform any quadratic equation in x into an equation of the form $(x - p)^2 = q$ that has the same solutions. Derive the quadratic formula from this form.

A.REI.4b Solve quadratic equations by inspection (e.g., for $x^2 = 49$), taking square roots, completing the square, the quadratic formula and factoring, as appropriate to the initial form of the equation. Recognize when the quadratic formula gives complex solutions and write them as $a \pm bi$ for real numbers a and b.

Solve systems of equations

A.REI.7 Solve a simple system consisting of a linear equation and a quadratic equation in two variables algebraically and graphically. *For example, find the points of intersection between the line $y = -3x$ and the circle $x^2 + y^2 = 3$.*

Functions

Interpreting Functions

Interpret functions that arise in applications in terms of the context

F.IF.4 For a function that models a relationship between two quantities, interpret key features of graphs and tables in terms of the quantities, and sketch graphs showing key features given a verbal description of the relationship. *Key features include: intercepts; intervals where the function is increasing, decreasing, positive, or negative; relative maximums and minimums; symmetries; end behavior; and periodicity.*★

F.IF.5 Relate the domain of a function to its graph and, where applicable, to the quantitative relationship it describes. *For example, if the function h(n) gives the number of person-hours it takes to assemble n engines in a factory, then the positive integers would be an appropriate domain for the function.*★

F.IF.6 Calculate and interpret the average rate of change of a function (presented symbolically or as a table) over a specified interval. Estimate the rate of change from a graph.★

Analyze functions using different representations

F.IF.7 Graph functions expressed symbolically and show key features of the graph, by hand in simple cases and using technology for more complicated cases.★

F.IF.7a Graph linear and quadratic functions and show intercepts, maxima, and minima.★

Analyze functions using different representations

F.IF.7.b Graph square root, cube root, and piecewise-defined functions, including step functions and absolute value functions.

F.IF.7.e Graph exponential and logarithmic functions, showing intercepts and end behavior, and trigonometric functions, showing period, midline, and amplitude.

F.IF.8 Write a function defined by an expression in different but equivalent forms to reveal and explain different properties of the function.

F.IF.8a Use the process of factoring and completing the square in a quadratic function to show zeros, extreme values, and symmetry of the graph, and interpret these in terms of a context.

F.IF.9 Compare properties of two functions each represented in a different way (algebraically, graphically, numerically in tables, or by verbal descriptions).

Building Functions

Build a function that models a relationship between two quantities

F.BF.1 Write a function that describes a relationship between two quantities.★

F.BF.1a Determine an explicit expression, a recursive process, or steps for calculation from a context.

F.BF.1b Combine standard function types using arithmetic operations. *For example, build a function that models the temperature of a cooling body by adding a constant function to a decaying exponential, and relate these functions to the model.*

Build new functions from existing functions

F.BF.3 Identify the effect on the graph of replacing $f(x)$ by $f(x) + k$, $k\,f(x)$, $f(kx)$, and $f(x + k)$ for specific values of k (both positive and negative); find the value of k given the graphs. Experiment with cases and illustrate an explanation of the effects on the graph using technology. *Include recognizing even and odd functions from their graphs and algebraic expressions for them.*

Geometry

Similarity, Right Triangles, and Trigonometry

Understand similarity in terms of similarity transformations

G.SRT.1 Verify experimentally the properties of dilations given by a center and a scale factor:

G.SRT.1a A dilation takes a line not passing through the center of the dilation to a parallel line, and leaves a line passing through the center unchanged.

G.SRT.1b The dilation of a line segment is longer or shorter in the ratio given by the scale factor.

G.SRT.2 Given two figures, use the definition of similarity in terms of similarity transformations to decide if they are similar; explain using similarity transformations the meaning of similarity for triangles as the equality of all corresponding pairs of angles and the proportionality of all corresponding pairs of sides.

G.SRT.3 Use the properties of similarity transformations to establish the AA criterion for two triangles to be similar.

Prove theorems involving similarity

G.SRT.4 Prove theorems about triangles. *Theorems include: a line parallel to one side of a triangle divides the other two proportionally, and conversely; the Pythagorean Theorem proved using triangle similarity.*

G.SRT.5 Use congruence and similarity criteria for triangles to solve problems and to prove relationships in geometric figures.

Define trigonometric ratios and solve problems involving right triangles

G.SRT.6 Understand that by similarity, side ratios in right triangles are properties of the angles in the triangle, leading to definitions of trigonometric ratios for acute angles.

G.SRT.7 Explain and use the relationship between the sine and cosine of complementary angles.

G.SRT.8 Use trigonometric ratios and the Pythagorean Theorem to solve right triangles in applied problems.★

Geometric Measurement and Dimension

Explain volume formulas and use them to solve problems

G.GMD.1 Give an informal argument for the formulas for the circumference of a circle, area of a circle, volume of a cylinder, pyramid, and cone. *Use dissection arguments, Cavalieri's principle, and informal limit arguments.*

G.GMD.3 Use volume formulas for cylinders, pyramids, cones, and spheres to solve problems.★

Statistics and Probability

Interpreting Categorical and Quantitative Data

Summarize, represent, and interpret data on two categorical and quantitative variables

S.ID.6 Represent data on two quantitative variables on a scatter plot, and describe how the variables are related.

S.ID.6a Fit a function to the data; use functions fitted to data to solve problems in the context of the data. *Use given functions or choose a function suggested by the context. Emphasize linear, quadratic, and exponential models.*

S.ID.6.b Informally assess the fit of a function by plotting and analyzing residuals.

Conditional Probability and the Rules of Probability

Understand independence and conditional probability and use them to interpret data

S.CP.1 Describe events as subsets of a sample space (the set of outcomes) using characteristics (or categories) of the outcomes, or as unions, intersections, or complements of other events ("or," "and," "not").

S.CP.2 Understand that two events *A* and *B* are independent if the probability of *A* and *B* occurring together is the product of their probabilities, and use this characterization to determine if they are independent.

S.CP.3 Understand the conditional probability of *A* given *B* as *P*(*A* and *B*)/*P*(*B*), and interpret independence of *A* and *B* as saying that the conditional probability of *A* given *B* is the same as the probability of *A*, and the conditional probability of *B* given *A* is the same as the probability of *B*.

S.CP.4 Construct and interpret two-way frequency tables of data when two categories are associated with each object being classified. Use the two-way table as a sample space to decide if events are independent and to approximate conditional probabilities.

S.CP.5 Recognize and explain the concepts of conditional probability and independence in everyday language and everyday situations.

Use the rules of probability to compute probabilities of compound events in a uniform probability model

S.CP.6 Find the conditional probability of *A* given *B* as the fraction of *B*'s outcomes that also belong to *A*, and interpret the answer in terms of the model.

S.CP.7 Apply the Addition Rule, $P(A \text{ or } B) = P(A) + P(B) - P(A \text{ and } B)$, and interpret the answer in terms of the model.

BIGideas

These Big Ideas are the organizing ideas for the study of important areas of mathematics: algebra, geometry, and statistics.

Algebra

Properties

- In the transition from arithmetic to algebra, attention shifts from arithmetic operations (addition, subtraction, multiplication, and division) to the use of the *properties* of these operations.
- All of the facts of arithmetic and algebra follow from certain properties.

Variable

- Quantities are used to form expressions, equations, and inequalities.
- An expression refers to a quantity but does not make a statement about it. An equation (or an inequality) is a statement about the quantities it mentions.
- Using variables in place of numbers in equations (or inequalities) allows the statement of relationships among numbers that are unknown or unspecified.

Equivalence

- A single quantity may be represented by many different expressions.
- The facts about a quantity may be expressed by many different equations (or inequalities).

Solving Equations & Inequalities

- Solving an equation is the process of rewriting the equation to make what it says about its variable(s) as simple as possible.
- Properties of numbers and equality can be used to transform an equation (or inequality) into equivalent, simpler equations (or inequalities) in order to find solutions.
- Useful information about equations and inequalities (including solutions) can be found by analyzing graphs or tables.
- The numbers and types of solutions vary predictably, based on the type of equation.

Proportionality

- Two quantities are *proportional* if they have the same ratio in each instance where they are measured together.
- Two quantities are *inversely proportional* if they have the same product in each instance where they are measured together.

Function

- A function is a relationship between variables in which each value of the input variable is associated with a unique value of the output variable.
- Functions can be represented in a variety of ways, such as graphs, tables, equations, or words. Each representation is particularly useful in certain situations.
- Some important families of functions are developed through transformations of the simplest form of the function.
- New functions can be made from other functions by applying arithmetic operations or by applying one function to the output of another.

Modeling

- Many real-world mathematical problems can be represented algebraically. These representations can lead to algebraic solutions.
- A function that models a real-world situation can be used to make estimates or predictions about future occurrences.

Statistics and Probability

Data Collection and Analysis

- Sampling techniques are used to gather data from real-world situations. If the data are representative of the larger population, inferences can be made about that population.
- Biased sampling techniques yield data unlikely to be representative of the larger population.
- Sets of numerical data are described using measures of central tendency and dispersion.

Data Representation

- The most appropriate data representations depend on the type of data—quantitative or qualitative, and univariate or bivariate.
- Line plots, box plots, and histograms are different ways to show distribution of data over a possible range of values.

Probability

- Probability expresses the likelihood that a particular event will occur.
- Data can be used to calculate an experimental probability, and mathematical properties can be used to determine a theoretical probability.
- Either experimental or theoretical probability can be used to make predictions or decisions about future events.
- Various counting methods can be used to develop theoretical probabilities.

Geometry

Visualization

- Visualization can help you see the relationships between two figures and help you connect properties of real objects with two-dimensional drawings of these objects.

Transformations

- Transformations are mathematical functions that model relationships with figures.
- Transformations may be described geometrically or by coordinates.
- Symmetries of figures may be defined and classified by transformations.

Measurement

- Some attributes of geometric figures, such as length, area, volume, and angle measure, are measurable. Units are used to describe these attributes.

Reasoning & Proof

- Definitions establish meanings and remove possible misunderstanding.
- Other truths are more complex and difficult to see. It is often possible to verify complex truths by reasoning from simpler ones using deductive reasoning.

Similarity

- Two geometric figures are similar when corresponding lengths are proportional and corresponding angles are congruent.
- Areas of similar figures are proportional to the squares of their corresponding lengths.
- Volumes of similar figures are proportional to the cubes of their corresponding lengths.

Coordinate Geometry

- A coordinate system on a line is a number line on which points are labeled, corresponding to the real numbers.
- A coordinate system in a plane is formed by two perpendicular number lines, called the *x*- and *y*-axes, and the quadrants they form. The coordinate plane can be used to graph many functions.
- It is possible to verify some complex truths using deductive reasoning in combination with the distance, midpoint, and slope formulas.

8 Proving Theorems About Triangles

Chapter 8

Geometry

Congruence
Prove geometric theorems
Make geometric constructions

Geometry

Similarity, Right Triangles, and Trigonometry
Prove theorems involving similarity

Circles
Understand and apply theorems about circles

9

Proving Theorems About Quadrilaterals

Chapter 9

Geometry

Congruence

Prove geometric theorems

Geometry

Similarity, Right Triangles, and Trigonometry

Prove theorems involving similarity

10

Similarity

Chapter 10

Geometry

Congruence
Make geometric constructions

Similarity, Right Triangles, and Trigonometry
Understand similarity in terms of similarity transformations
Prove theorems involving similarity

Geometry

Expressing Geometric Properties with Equations
Use coordinates to prove simple geometric theorems algebraically

11

Right Triangles and Trigonometry

Chapter 11

Geometry

Congruence
Prove geometric theorems
Make geometric constructions

Geometry

Similarity, Right Triangles, and Trigonometry
Prove theorems involving similarity

Circles
Understand and apply theorems about circles

12

Circles

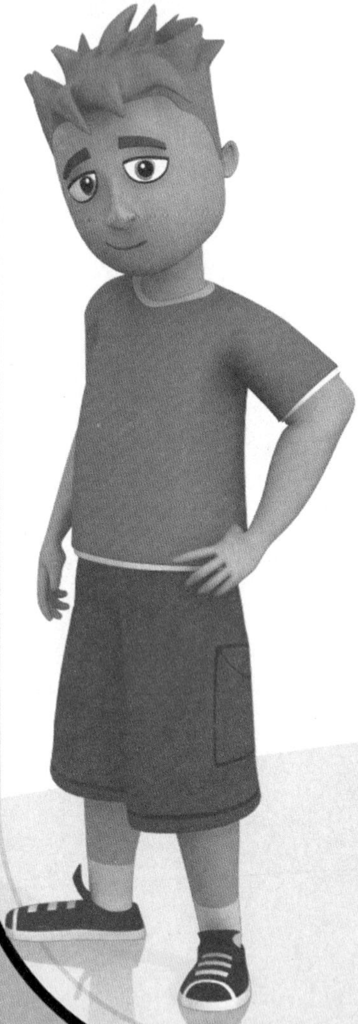

Chapter 12

Geometry

Circles

Understand and apply theorems about circles

Find arc lengths and areas of sectors of circles

13

Surface Area and Volume

Chapter 13

Number and Quantity

Quantities

Reason quantitatively and use units to solve problems

Geometry

Geometric Measurement and Dimension

Explain volume formulas and use them to solve problems

Modeling with Geometry

Apply geometric concepts in modeling situations

14

Probability

Chapter 14

Statistics and Probability

Conditional Probability and the Rules of Probability

Understand independence and conditional probability and use them to interpret data

Use the rules of probability to compute probabilities of compound events in a uniform probability model

Statistics and Probability

Using Probability to Make Decisions

Use probability to evaluate outcomes of decisions

H

Honors Appendix

CHAPTER 8

Get Ready!

Basic Constructions

Use a compass and straightedge for each construction.

1. Construct the perpendicular bisector of a segment.
2. Construct the bisector of an angle.

The Midpoint Formula and Distance Formula

Find the coordinates of the midpoints of the sides of $\triangle ABC$. Then find the lengths of the three sides of the triangle.

3. $A(5, 1), B(-3, 3), C(1, -7)$
4. $A(-1, 2), B(9, 2), C(-1, 8)$
5. $A(-2, -3), B(2, -3), C(0, 3)$

Finding the Negation

Write the negation of each statement.

6. The team won.
7. It is not too late.
8. $m\angle R > 60$

Slope

Find the slope of the line passing through the given points.

9. $A(9, 6), B(8, 12)$
10. $C(3, -2), D(0, 6)$
11. $E(-3, 7), F(-3, 12)$

Looking Ahead Vocabulary

12. The *distance* between your home and your school is the length of the shortest path connecting them. How might you define the *distance between a point and a line* in geometry?
13. Consider the *midpoint* of a segment. What do you think a *midsegment* of a triangle is?
14. If two parties are happening at the same time, they are *concurrent.* What would it mean for three lines to be *concurrent*?

CHAPTER 8

Proving Theorems About Triangles

Big Ideas

1 Coordinate Geometry
Essential Question How do you use coordinate geometry to find relationships within triangles?

2 Measurement
Essential Question How do you solve problems that involve measurements of triangles?

3 Reasoning and Proof
Essential Question How do you write indirect proofs?

Domains

- Congruence
- Similarity, Right Triangles, and Trigonometry
- Mathematical Practice: Construct viable arguments

Interactive Digital Path

Log in to **pearsonsuccessnet.com** and click on Interactive Digital Path to access the Solve Its and animated Problems.

Chapter Preview

Vocabulary

English/Spanish Vocabulary Audio Online:

English	Spanish
altitude of a triangle, *p. 555*	altura de un triángulo
centroid, *p. 553*	centroid
circumcenter, *p. 545*	circuncentro
concurrent, *p. 545*	concurrente
equidistant, *p. 537*	equidistante
incenter, *p. 548*	incentro
indirect proof, *p. 562*	prueba indirecta
median, *p. 553*	mediana
midsegment of a triangle, *p. 529*	segmento medio de un triángulo
orthocenter, *p. 556*	ortocentro

8-1 Midsegments of Triangles

G.CO.10 Prove theorems about triangles . . . the segment joining midpoints of two sides of a triangle is parallel to the third side and half the length . . . Also **G.SRT.5**

Objective To use properties of midsegments to solve problems

Solve It! Write your solution to the Solve It in the space below.

In the Solve It, $\overline{LN}$ is a midsegment of $\triangle ABC$. A **midsegment of a triangle** is a segment connecting the midpoints of two sides of the triangle.

Essential Understanding There are two special relationships between a midsegment of a triangle and the third side of the triangle.

take note

Theorem 22 Triangle Midsegment Theorem

Theorem	If . . .	Then . . .
If a segment joins the midpoints of two sides of a triangle, then the segment is parallel to the third side and is half as long.	D is the midpoint of $\overline{CA}$ and E is the midpoint of $\overline{CB}$	$\overline{DE} \parallel \overline{AB}$ and $DE = \frac{1}{2}AB$

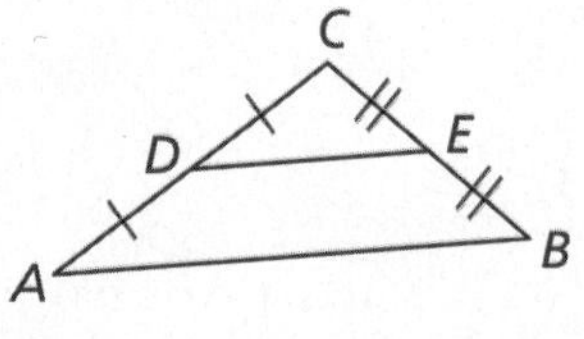

You will prove Theorem 22 in Lesson 9-8.

Here's Why It Works You can verify that the Triangle Midsegment Theorem works for a particular triangle. Use the following steps to show that $\overline{DE} \parallel \overline{AB}$ and that $DE = \frac{1}{2}AB$ for a triangle with vertices at $A(4, 6)$, $B(6, 0)$, and $C(0, 0)$, where D and E are the midpoints of $\overline{CA}$ and $\overline{CB}$.

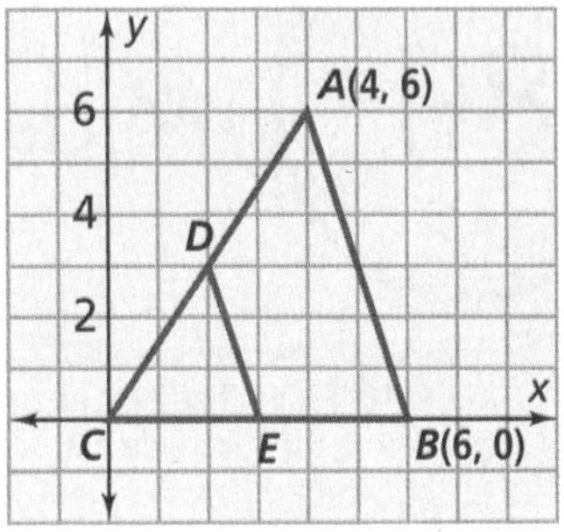

Step 1 Use the Midpoint Formula, $M = \left(\frac{x_1 + x_2}{2}, \frac{y_1 + y_2}{2}\right)$, to find the coordinates of D and E.

The midpoint of $\overline{CA}$ is $D\left(\frac{0+4}{2}, \frac{0+6}{2}\right) = D(2, 3)$.

The midpoint of $\overline{CB}$ is $E\left(\frac{0+6}{2}, \frac{0+0}{2}\right) = E(3, 0)$.

Step 2 To show that the midsegment $\overline{DE}$ is parallel to the side $\overline{AB}$, find the slope, $m = \frac{y_2 - y_1}{x_2 - x_1}$, of each segment.

$$\text{slope of } \overline{DE} = \frac{0-3}{3-2} = \frac{-3}{1} = -3$$

$$\text{slope of } \overline{AB} = \frac{0-6}{6-4} = \frac{-6}{2} = -3$$

The slopes of $\overline{DE}$ and $\overline{AB}$ are equal, so $\overline{DE}$ and $\overline{AB}$ are parallel.

Step 3 To show $DE = \frac{1}{2}AB$, use the Distance Formula, $d = \sqrt{(x_2 - x_1)^2 + (y_2 - y_1)^2}$, to find DE and AB.

$$DE = \sqrt{(3-2)^2 + (0-3)^2} = \sqrt{1+9} = \sqrt{10}$$

$$AB = \sqrt{(6-4)^2 + (0-6)^2} = \sqrt{4+36} = \sqrt{40} = 2\sqrt{10}$$

Since $\sqrt{10} = \frac{1}{2}(2\sqrt{10})$, you know that $DE = \frac{1}{2}AB$.

ONLINE PROBLEMS

Problem 1 Identifying Parallel Segments

Got It? **a.** In $\triangle XYZ$, A is the midpoint of $\overline{XY}$, B is the midpoint of $\overline{YZ}$, and C is the midpoint of $\overline{ZX}$. What are the three pairs of parallel segments?

b. Reasoning What is $m\angle VUO$ in the figure below? Explain your reasoning.

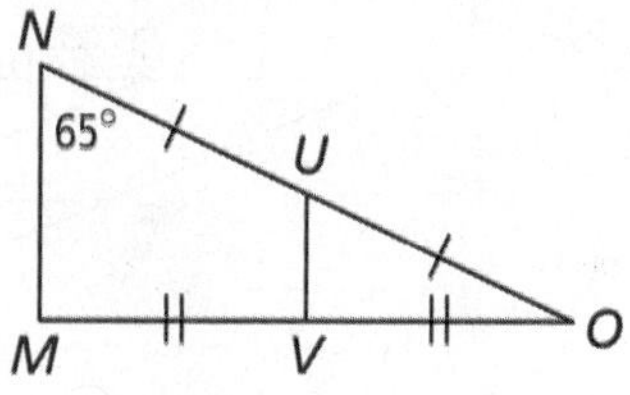

Think

What is the relationship between the 65° angle and $\angle VUO$?

Practice

1. Identify three pairs of parallel segments in the diagram.

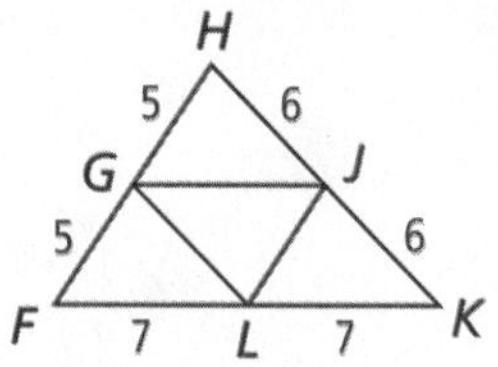

2. Name the segment that is parallel to $\overline{GE}$.

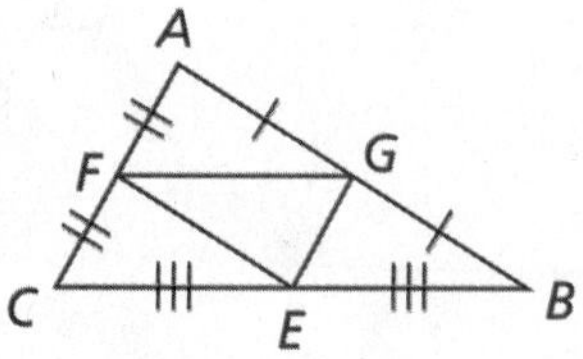

Problem 2 Finding Lengths

Got It? In the figure at the right, $AD = 6$ and $DE = 7.5$. What are the lengths of $\overline{DC}$, $\overline{AC}$, $\overline{EF}$, and $\overline{AB}$?

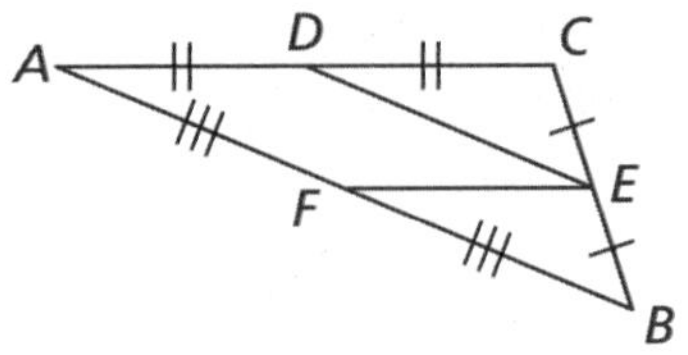

A Practice **Algebra** **Find the value of x.**

3.

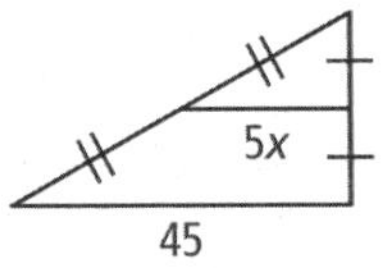

4.

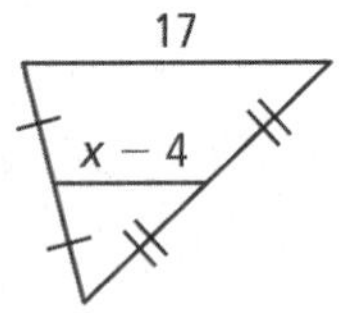

You can use the Triangle Midsegment Theorem to find lengths of segments that might be difficult to measure directly.

Problem 3 Using a Midsegment of a Triangle

Got It? $\overline{CD}$ is a bridge being built over a lake, as shown in the figure below. What is the length of the bridge?

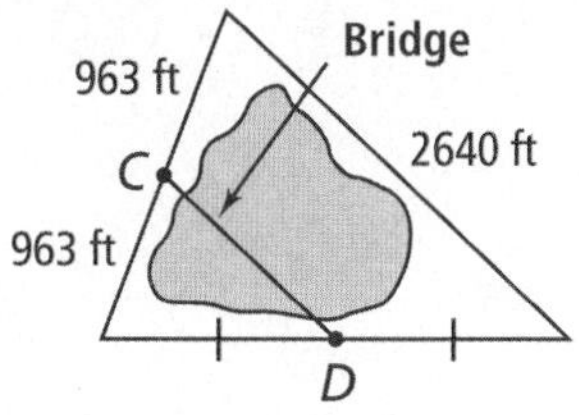

Think

Which theorem will help you solve this problem?

Practice 5. **Surveying** A surveyor needs to measure the distance PQ across the lake. Beginning at point S, she locates the midpoints of $\overline{SQ}$ and $\overline{SP}$ at M and N. She then measures $\overline{NM}$. What is PQ?

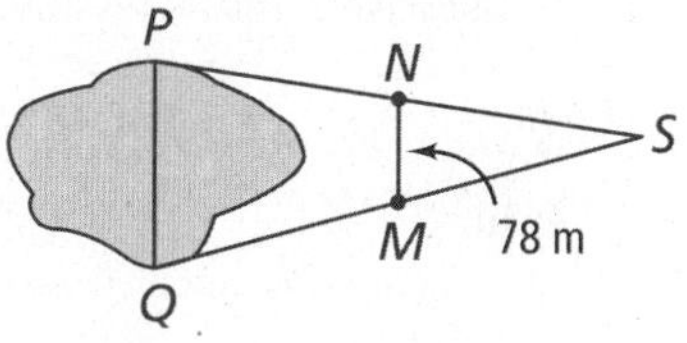

Lesson Check

Do you know HOW?

Use the figure at the right for Exercises 6–8.

6. Which segment is parallel to $\overline{JK}$?

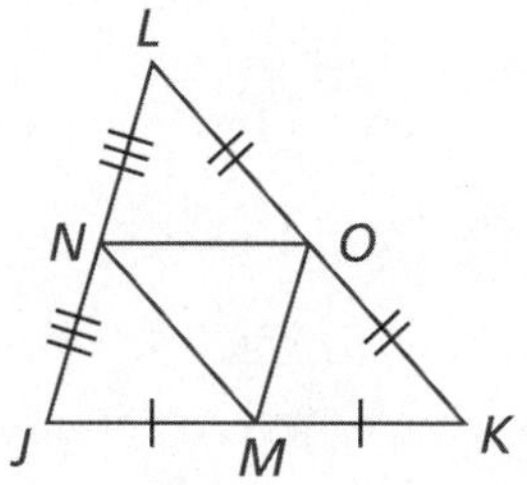

7. If $LK = 46$, what is NM?

8. If $JK = 5x + 20$ and $NO = 20$, what is the value of x?

Do you UNDERSTAND?

MATHEMATICAL PRACTICES

9. Vocabulary How does the term *midsegment* describe the segments discussed in this lesson?

10. Reasoning If two noncollinear segments in the coordinate plane have slope 3, what can you conclude?

11. Error Analysis A student sees this figure and concludes that $\overline{PL} \parallel \overline{NO}$. What is the error in the student's reasoning?

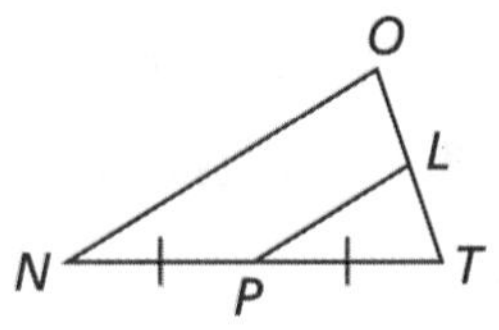

More Practice and Problem-Solving Exercises

MATHEMATICAL PRACTICES

B Apply

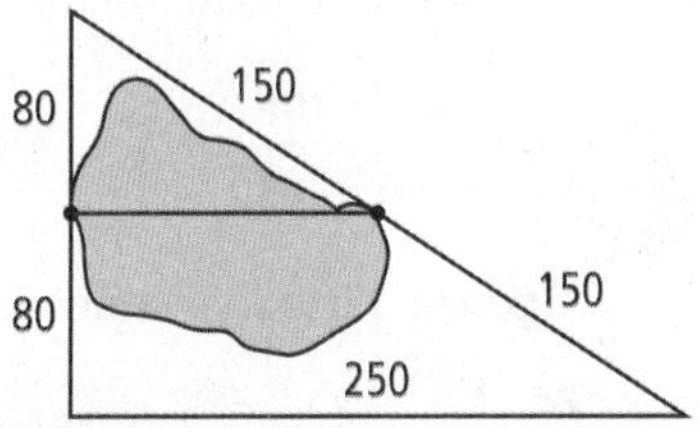

12. Kayaking You want to paddle your kayak across a lake. To determine how far you must paddle, you pace out a triangle, counting the number of strides, as shown.

a. If your strides average 3.5 ft, what is the length of the longest side of the triangle?

b. What distance must you paddle across the lake?

13. Architecture The triangular face of the Rock and Roll Hall of Fame in Cleveland, Ohio, is isosceles. The length of the base is 229 ft 6 in. Each leg is divided into four congruent parts by the red segments. What is the length of the white segment? Explain your reasoning.

14. Think About a Plan Draw $\triangle ABC$. Construct another triangle so that the three sides of $\triangle ABC$ are the midsegments of the new triangle.

- Can you visualize or sketch the final figure?
- Which segments in your final construction will be parallel?

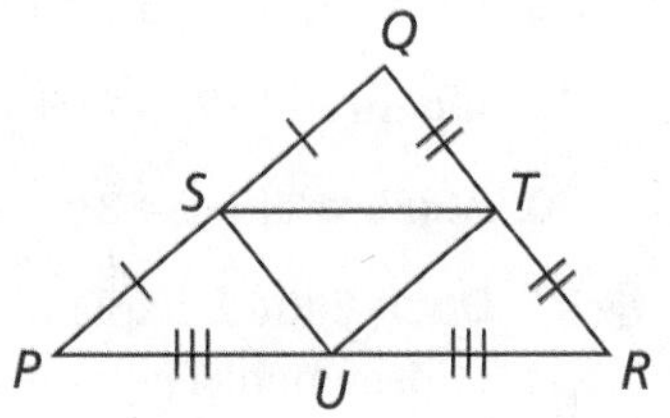

15. Writing In the figure at the right, $m\angle QST = 40$. What is $m\angle QPR$? Explain how you know.

16. Coordinate Geometry The coordinates of the vertices of a triangle are $E(1, 2)$, $F(5, 6)$, and $G(3, -2)$.

a. Find the coordinates of H, the midpoint of $\overline{EG}$, and J, the midpoint of $\overline{FG}$.

b. Show that $\overline{HJ} \parallel \overline{EF}$.

c. Show that $HJ = \frac{1}{2}EF$.

X is the midpoint of $\overline{UV}$. Y is the midpoint of $\overline{UW}$.

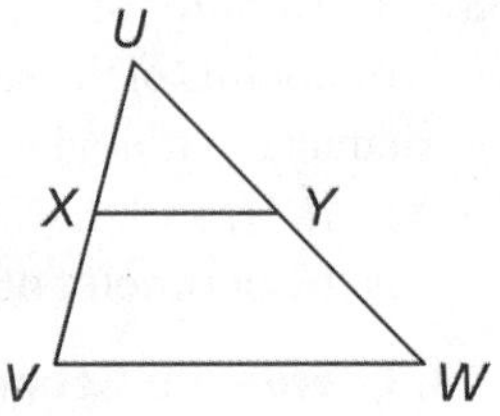

17. If $m\angle UXY = 60$, find $m\angle V$.

18. If $m\angle W = 45$, find $m\angle UYX$.

19. If $XY = 50$, find VW.

20. If $VW = 110$, find XY.

$\overline{IJ}$ is a midsegment of $\triangle FGH$. $IJ = 7$, $FH = 10$, and $GH = 13$. Find the perimeter of each triangle.

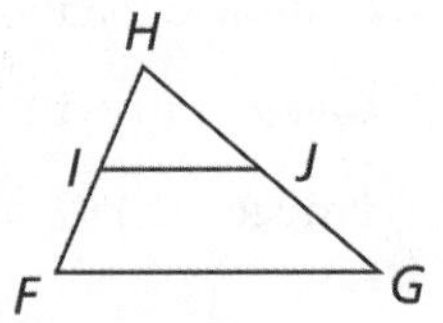

21. $\triangle IJH$

22. $\triangle FGH$

23. Kite Design You design a kite to look like the one at the right. Its diagonals measure 64 cm and 90 cm. You plan to use ribbon, represented by the rectangle, to connect the midpoints of its sides. How much ribbon do you need?

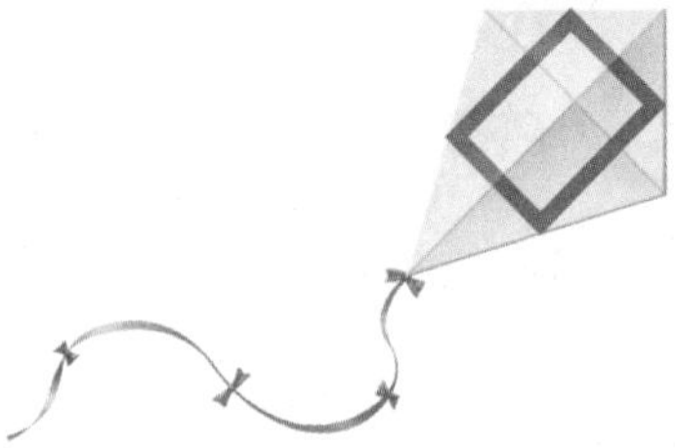

Ⓐ 77 cm

Ⓑ 122 cm

Ⓒ 154 cm

Ⓓ 308 cm

Algebra Find the value of each variable.

24.

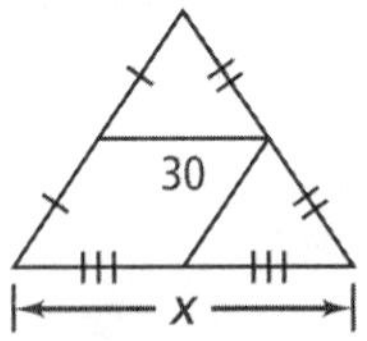

25.

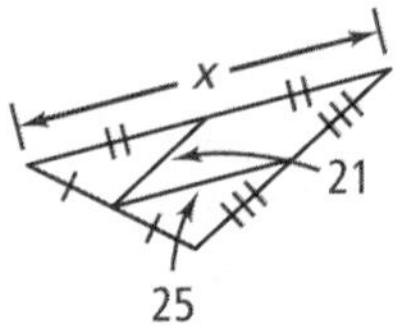

26.

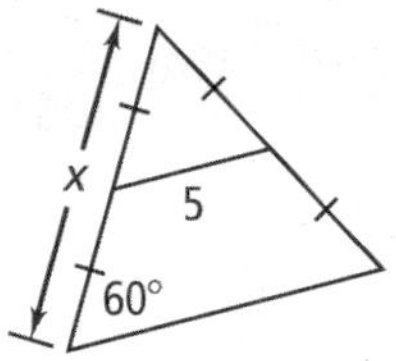

27.

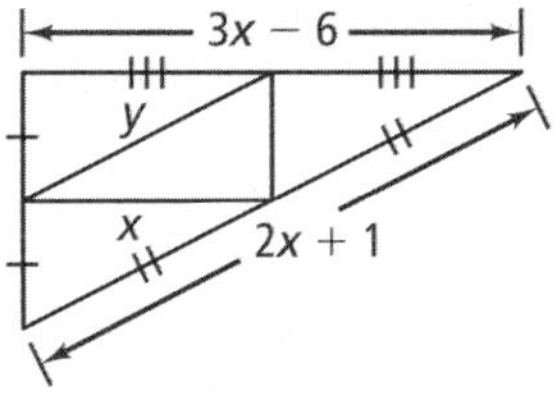

Use the figure at the right for Exercises 28–30.

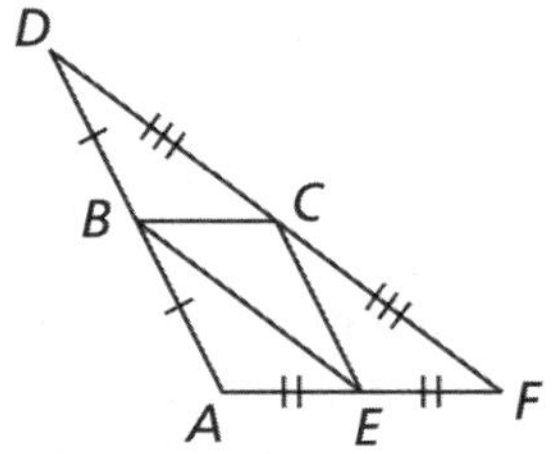

28. $DF = 24$, $BC = 6$, and $DB = 8$. Find the perimeter of $\triangle ADF$.

29. Algebra If $BE = 2x + 6$ and $DF = 5x + 9$, find DF.

30. Algebra If $EC = 3x - 1$ and $AD = 5x + 7$, find EC.

31. Open-Ended Explain how you could use the Triangle Midsegment Theorem as the basis for this construction: Draw $\overline{CD}$. Draw point A not on $\overline{CD}$. Construct $\overline{AB}$ so that $\overline{AB} \parallel \overline{CD}$ and $AB = \frac{1}{2}CD$.

Challenge

32. Reasoning In the diagram at the right, K, L, and M are the midpoints of the sides of $\triangle ABC$. The vertices of the three small red triangles are the midpoints of the sides of $\triangle KBL$, $\triangle AKM$, and $\triangle MLC$. The perimeter of $\triangle ABC$ is 24 cm. What is the perimeter of the shaded region?

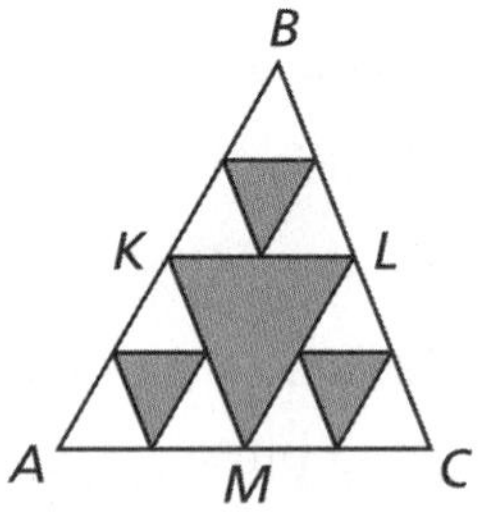

33. Coordinate Geometry In $\triangle GHJ$, $K(2, 3)$ is the midpoint of $\overline{GH}$, $L(4, 1)$ is the midpoint of $\overline{HJ}$, and $M(6, 2)$ is the midpoint of $\overline{GJ}$. Find the coordinates of G, H, and J.

Proof 34. Complete the Prove statement and then write a proof.

Given: In $\triangle VYZ$, S, T, and U are midpoints.

Prove: $\triangle YST \cong \triangle TUZ \cong \triangle SVU \cong$ __?__

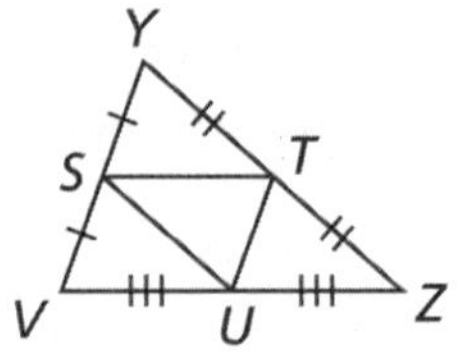

8-2 Perpendicular and Angle Bisectors

G.CO.9 Prove theorems about lines and angles . . . points on a perpendicular bisector of a line segment are exactly those equidistant from the segment's endpoints. Also **G.CO.12, G.SRT.5**

Objective To use properties of perpendicular bisectors and angle bisectors

Solve It! Write your solution to the Solve It in the space below.

In the Solve It, you thought about the relationships that must exist in order for a bulletin board to hang straight. You will explore these relationships in this lesson.

Essential Understanding There is a special relationship between the points on the perpendicular bisector of a segment and the endpoints of the segment.

In the diagram below, $\overleftrightarrow{CD}$ is the perpendicular bisector of $\overline{AB}$. $\overleftrightarrow{CD}$ is perpendicular to $\overline{AB}$ at its midpoint. In the diagram on the right, $\overline{CA}$ and $\overline{CB}$ are drawn to complete $\triangle CAD$ and $\triangle CBD$.

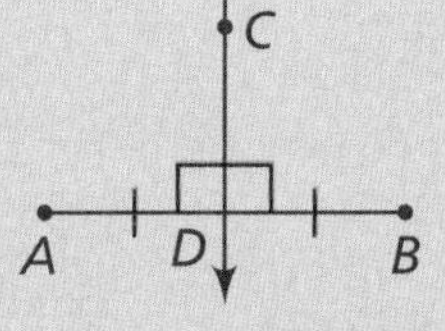

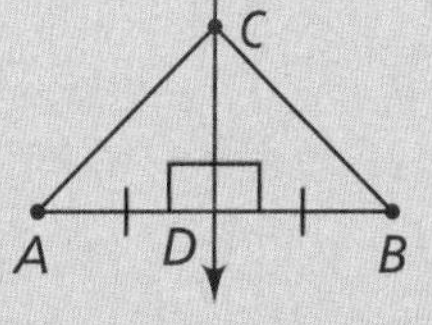

You should recognize from your work in Chapter 7 that $\triangle CAD \cong \triangle CBD$. So you can conclude that $\overline{CA} \cong \overline{CB}$, or that $CA = CB$. A point is **equidistant** from two objects if it is the same distance from the objects. So point C is equidistant from points A and B.

This suggests a proof of Theorem 23, the Perpendicular Bisector Theorem. Its converse is also true and is stated as Theorem 24.

take note

Theorem 23 Perpendicular Bisector Theorem

Theorem	If . . .	Then . . .
If a point is on the perpendicular bisector of a segment, then it is equidistant from the endpoints of the segment.	$\overleftrightarrow{PM} \perp \overline{AB}$ and $MA = MB$	$PA = PB$

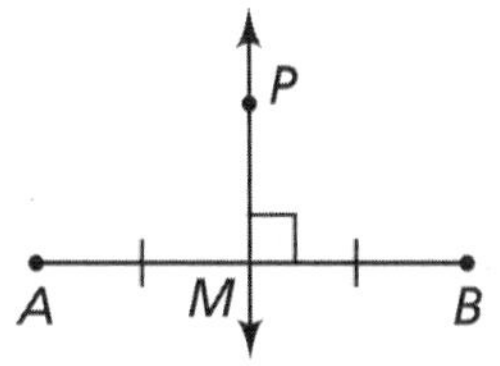

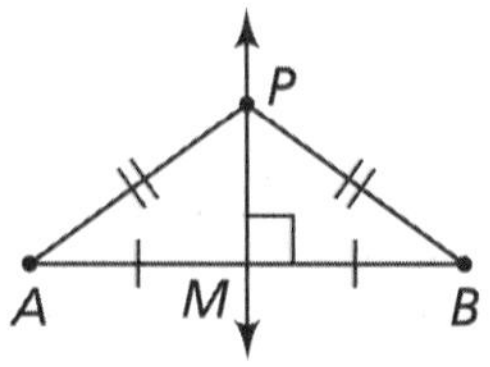

You will prove Theorem 23 in Exercise 26.

Theorem 24 Converse of the Perpendicular Bisector Theorem

Theorem	If . . .	Then . . .
If a point is equidistant from the endpoints of a segment, then it is on the perpendicular bisector of the segment.	$PA = PB$	$\overleftrightarrow{PM} \perp \overline{AB}$ and $MA = MB$

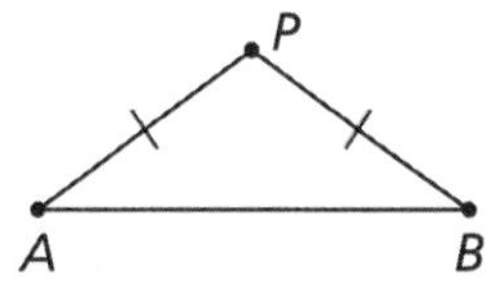

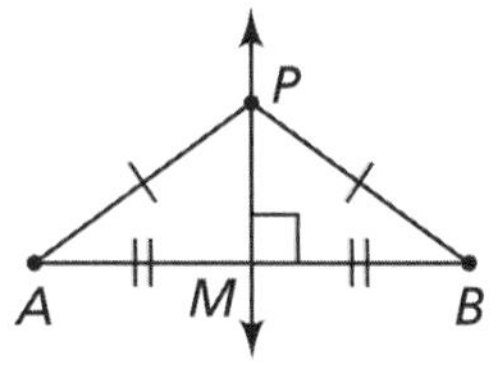

You will prove Theorem 24 in Exercise 27.

ONLINE PROBLEMS

Problem 1 Using the Perpendicular Bisector Theorem

Got It? What is the length of $\overline{QR}$?

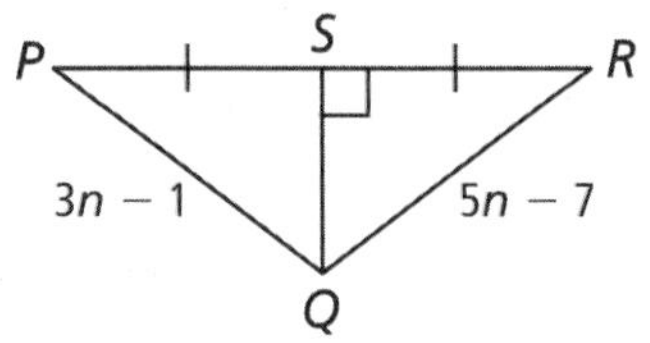

A Practice **Use the figure at the right for Exercises 1 and 2.**

1. What is the relationship between $\overline{MB}$ and $\overline{JK}$?

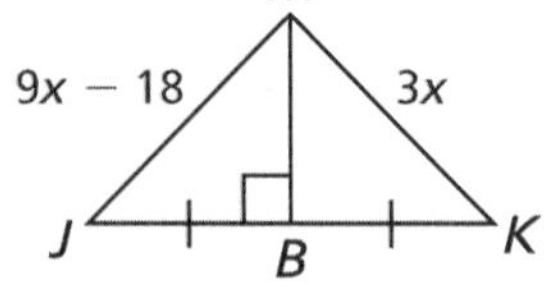

2. Find JM.

Problem 2 Using a Perpendicular Bisector

Plan

How do you find points that are equidistant from two given points?

Got It? **a.** Suppose the director from Problem 2 wants the T-shirt stand to be equidistant from the paddle boats and the Spaceship Shoot. What are the possible locations?

b. Reasoning Can you place the T-shirt stand so that it is equidistant from the paddle boats, the Spaceship Shoot, and the Rollin' Coaster? Explain.

Practice **3. Reading Maps** Use the map of a part of Manhattan. Is St. Vincent's Hospital equidistant from Village Kids Nursery School and Legacy School? How do you know?

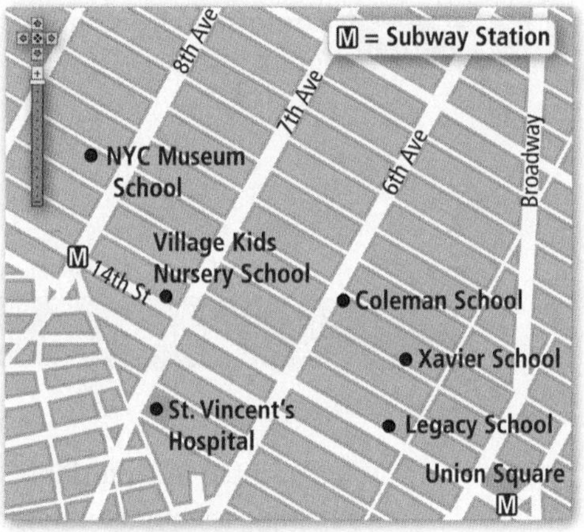

4. Writing On a piece of paper, mark a point H for home and a point S for school. Describe how to find the set of points equidistant from H and S.

Essential Understanding There is a special relationship between the points on the bisector of an angle and the sides of the angle.

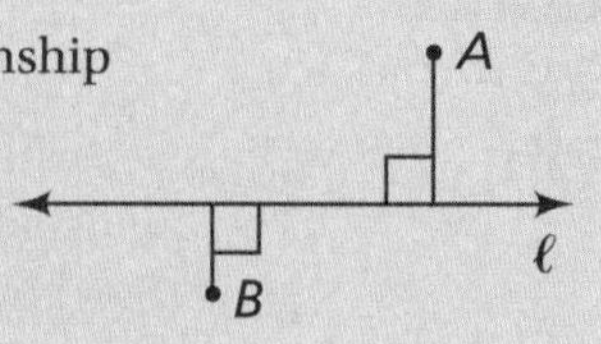

The **distance from a point to a line** is the length of the perpendicular segment from the point to the line. This distance is also the length of the shortest segment from the point to the line. You will prove this in Lesson 8-6. In the figure at the right, the distances from A to ℓ and from B to ℓ are represented by the red segments.

In the diagram, $\overrightarrow{AD}$ is the bisector of $\angle CAB$. If you measure the lengths of the perpendicular segments from D to the two sides of the angle, you will find that the lengths are equal. Point D is equidistant from the sides of the angle.

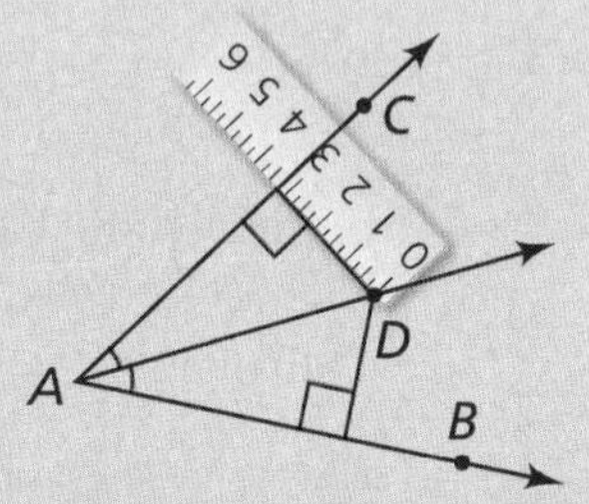

take note

Theorem 25 Angle Bisector Theorem

Theorem	If . . .	Then . . .
If a point is on the bisector of an angle, then the point is equidistant from the sides of the angle.	$\overrightarrow{QS}$ bisects $\angle PQR$, $\overline{SP} \perp \overrightarrow{QP}$, and $\overline{SR} \perp \overrightarrow{QR}$	$SP = SR$

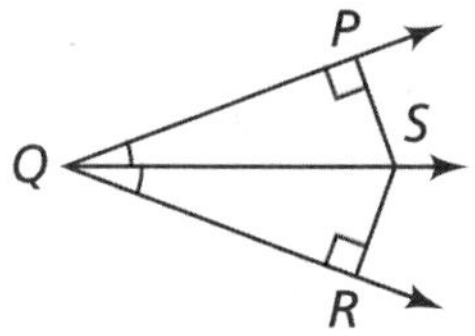

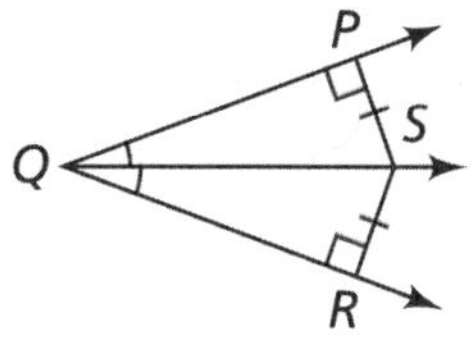

You will prove Theorem 25 in Exercise 28.

Theorem 26 Converse of the Angle Bisector Theorem

Theorem	If . . .	Then . . .
If a point in the interior of an angle is equidistant from the sides of the angle, then the point is on the angle bisector.	$\overline{SP} \perp \overrightarrow{QP}$, $\overline{SR} \perp \overrightarrow{QR}$, and $SP = SR$	$\overrightarrow{QS}$ bisects $\angle PQR$

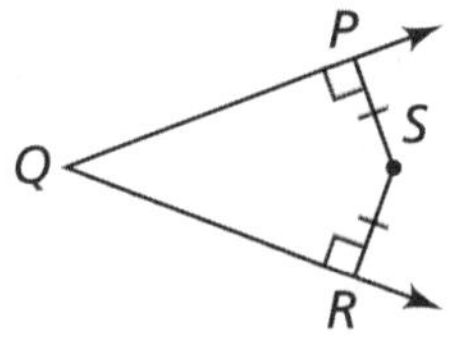

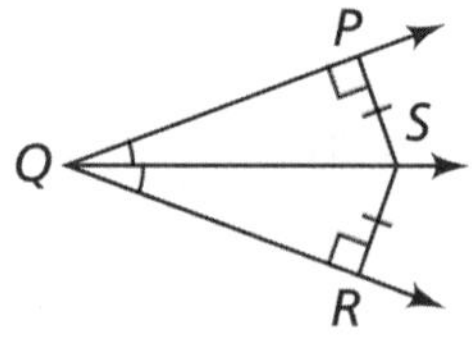

You will prove Theorem 26 in Exercise 29.

Problem 3 Using the Angle Bisector Theorem

Got It? What is the length of $\overline{FB}$?

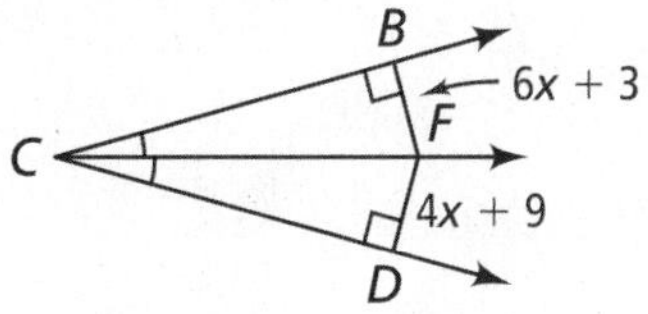

Think

How can you use the expression for *FD* to check your answer?

Practice **5.** Find $m\angle KHL$ and $m\angle FHL$.

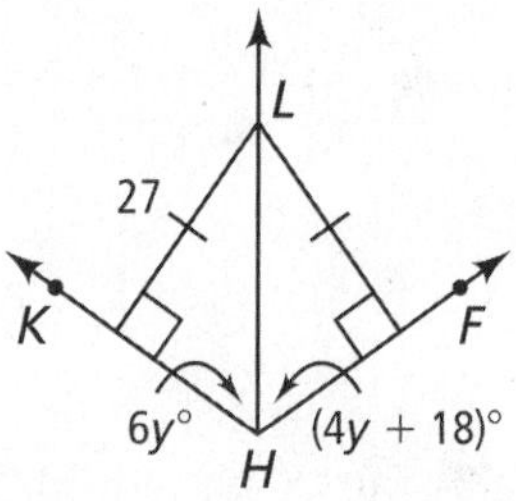

6. Algebra Find x, JK, and JM.

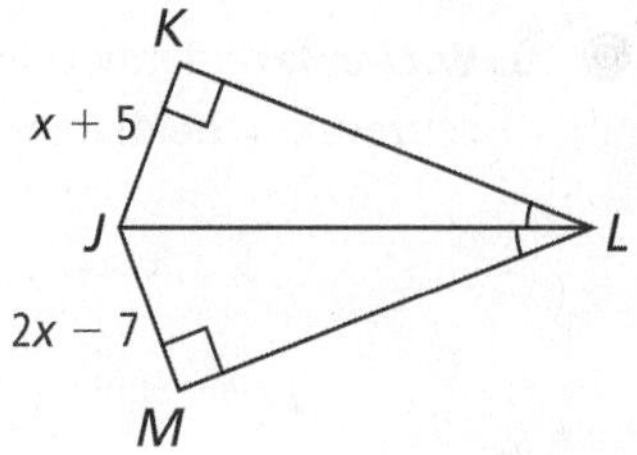

Lesson Check

Do you know HOW?

Use the figure at the right for Exercises 7–9.

7. What is the relationship between $\overline{AC}$ and $\overline{BD}$?

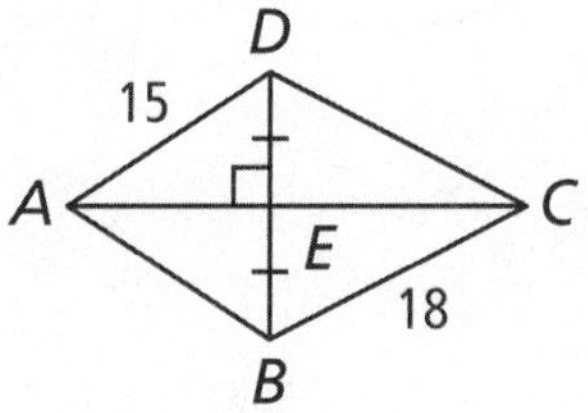

8. What is the length of $\overline{AB}$?

9. What is the length of $\overline{DC}$?

Do you UNDERSTAND?

MATHEMATICAL PRACTICES

10. Vocabulary Draw a line and a point not on the line. Draw the segment that represents the distance from the point to the line.

11. Writing Point P is in the interior of $\angle LOX$. Describe how you can determine whether P is on the bisector of $\angle LOX$ without drawing the angle bisector.

More Practice and Problem-Solving Exercises

MATHEMATICAL PRACTICES

B Apply

Algebra Use the figure at the right for Exercises 12–16.

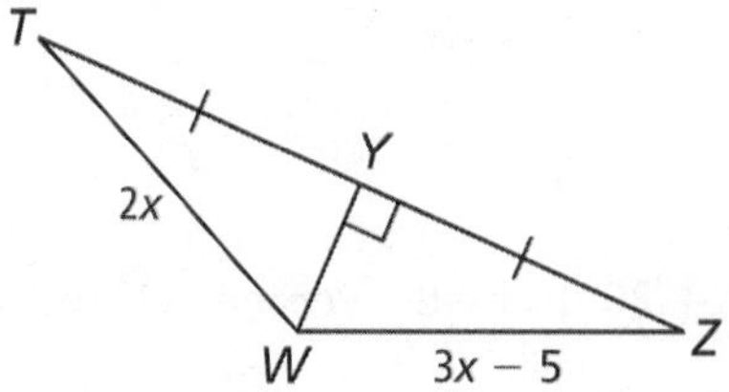

12. Find the value of x.

13. Find TW.

14. Find WZ.

15. What kind of triangle is $\triangle TWZ$? Explain.

16. If R is on the perpendicular bisector of $\overline{TZ}$, then R is ____?____ from T and Z, or ____?____ = ____?____.

17. Think About a Plan In the diagram at the right, the soccer goalie will prepare for a shot from the player at point P by moving out to a point on $\overline{XY}$. To have the best chance of stopping the ball, should the goalie stand at the point on $\overline{XY}$ that lies on the perpendicular bisector of $\overline{GL}$ or at the point on $\overline{XY}$ that lies on the bisector of $\angle GPL$? Explain your reasoning.

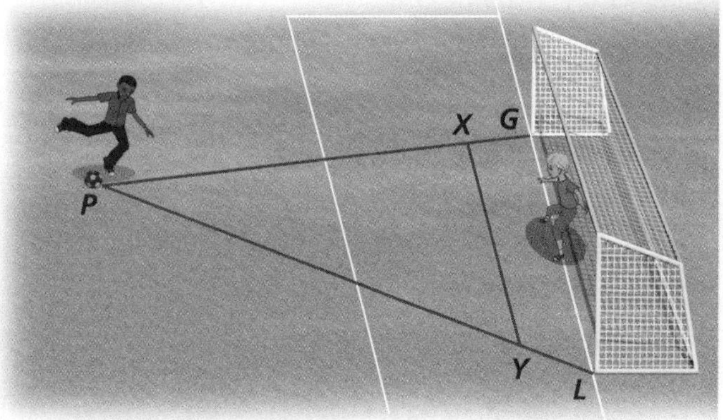

- How can you draw a diagram to help?
- Would the goalie want to be the same distance from G and L or from $\overline{PG}$ and $\overline{PL}$?

18. a. Constructions Draw $\angle CDE$. Construct the angle bisector of the angle.
b. Reasoning Use the converse of the Angle Bisector Theorem to justify your construction.

19. a. Constructions Draw $\overline{QR}$. Construct the perpendicular bisector of $\overline{QR}$ to construct $\triangle PQR$.
b. Reasoning Use the Perpendicular Bisector Theorem to justify that your construction is an isosceles triangle.

20. Write Theorems 23 and 24 as a single biconditional statement.

21. Write Theorems 25 and 26 as a single biconditional statement.

22. Error Analysis To prove that $\triangle PQR$ is isosceles, a student began by stating that since Q is on the segment perpendicular to $\overline{PR}$, Q is equidistant from the endpoints of $\overline{PR}$. What is the error in the student's reasoning?

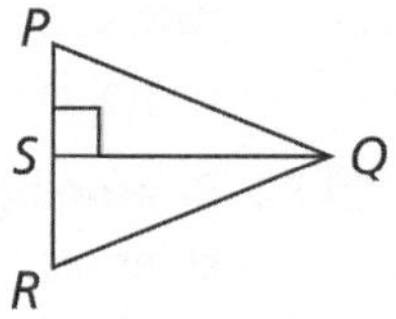

Writing **Determine whether A must be on the bisector of $\angle TXR$. Explain.**

23.

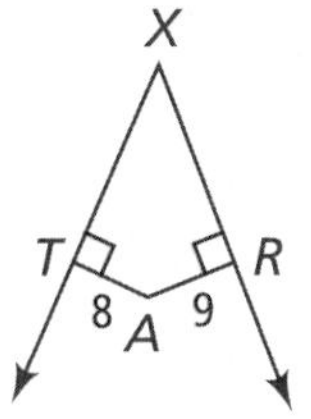

24.

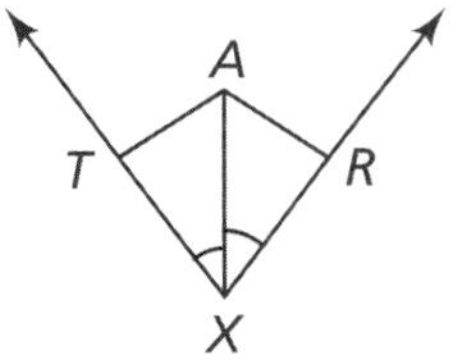

25.

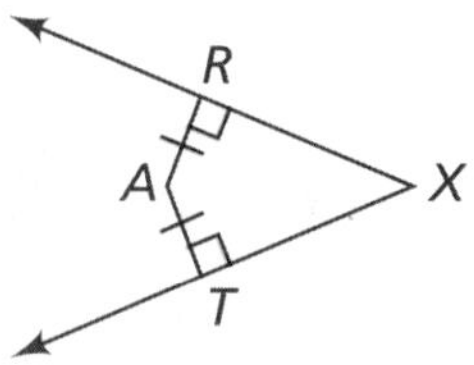

Proof **26.** Prove the Perpendicular Bisector Theorem.

Given: $\overleftrightarrow{PM} \perp \overline{AB}$, $\overleftrightarrow{PM}$ bisects $\overline{AB}$

Prove: $AP = BP$

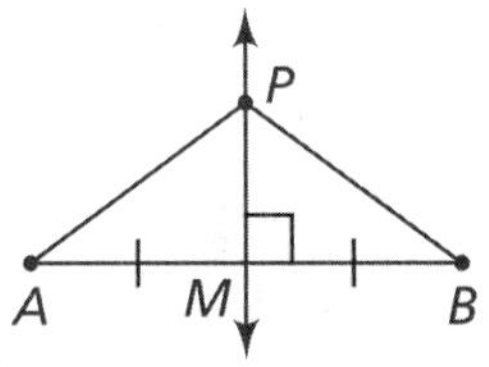

Proof **27.** Prove the Converse of the Perpendicular Bisector Theorem.

Given: $PA = PB$, with $\overline{PM} \perp \overline{AB}$ at M.

Prove: P is on the perpendicular bisector of $\overline{AB}$.

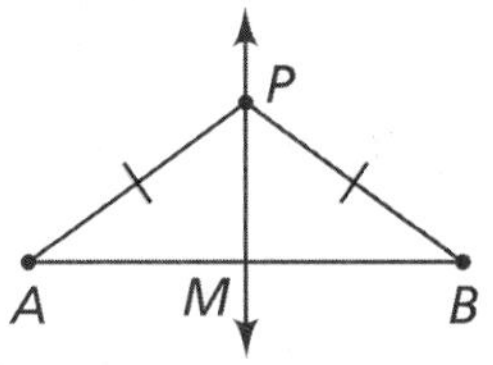

Proof **28.** Prove the Angle Bisector Theorem.

Given: $\overrightarrow{QS}$ bisects $\angle PQR$, $\overline{SP} \perp \overrightarrow{QP}$, $\overline{SR} \perp \overrightarrow{QR}$

Prove: $SP = SR$

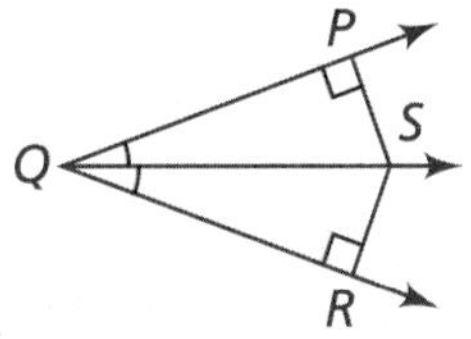

Proof **29.** Prove the Converse of the Angle Bisector Theorem.

Given: $\overline{SP} \perp \overrightarrow{QP}$, $\overline{SR} \perp \overrightarrow{QR}$, $SP = SR$

Prove: $\overrightarrow{QS}$ bisects $\angle PQR$.

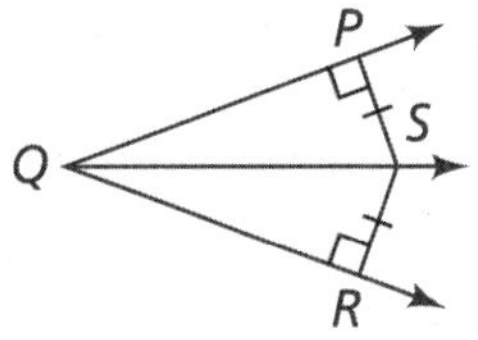

30. Coordinate Geometry Use points $A(6, 8)$, $O(0, 0)$, and $B(10, 0)$.

a. Write equations of lines ℓ and m such that $\ell \perp \overleftrightarrow{OA}$ at A and $m \perp \overleftrightarrow{OB}$ at B.

b. Find the intersection C of lines ℓ and m.

c. Show that $CA = CB$.

d. Explain why C is on the bisector of $\angle AOB$.

Challenge

31. A, B, and C are three noncollinear points. Describe and sketch a line in plane ABC such that points A, B, and C are equidistant from the line. Justify your response.

32. Reasoning M is the intersection of the perpendicular bisectors of two sides of $\triangle ABC$. Line ℓ is perpendicular to plane ABC at M. Explain why a point E on ℓ is equidistant from A, B, and C. (*Hint:* See Lesson 1-1, Exercise 30. Explain why $\triangle EAM \cong \triangle EBM \cong \triangle ECM$.)

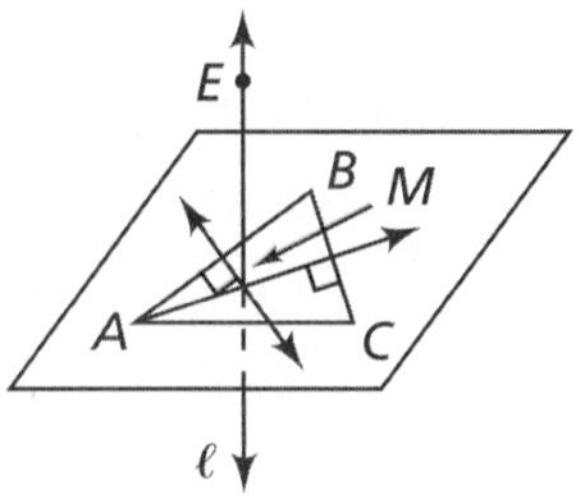

8-3 Bisectors in Triangles

G.CO.10 Prove theorems about triangles . . . Also **G.C.3**

Objective To identify properties of perpendicular bisectors and angle bisectors

Solve It! Write your solution to the Solve It in the space below.

In the Solve It, the three lines you drew intersect at one point, the center of the circle. When three or more lines intersect at one point, they are **concurrent.** The point at which they intersect is the **point of concurrency.**

Essential Understanding For any triangle, certain sets of lines are always concurrent. Two of these sets of lines are the perpendicular bisectors of the triangle's three sides and the bisectors of the triangle's three angles.

take note

Theorem 27 Concurrency of Perpendicular Bisectors Theorem

Theorem

The perpendicular bisectors of the sides of a triangle are concurrent at a point equidistant from the vertices.

Diagram

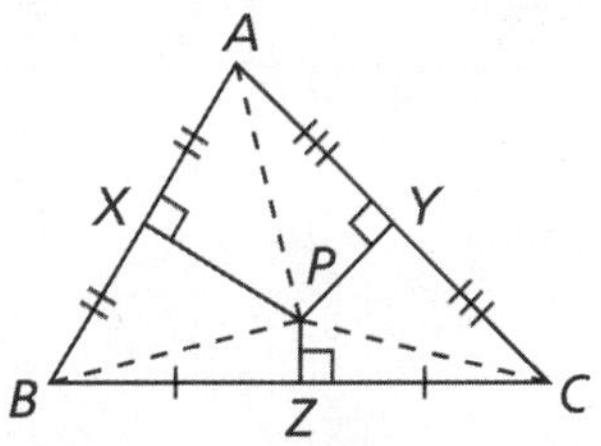

Symbols

Perpendicular bisectors $\overline{PX}$, $\overline{PY}$, and $\overline{PZ}$ are concurrent at P.

$PA = PB = PC$

The point of concurrency of the perpendicular bisectors of a triangle is called the **circumcenter of the triangle.**

Since the circumcenter is equidistant from the vertices, you can use the circumcenter as the center of the circle that contains each vertex of the triangle. You say the circle is **circumscribed about** the triangle.

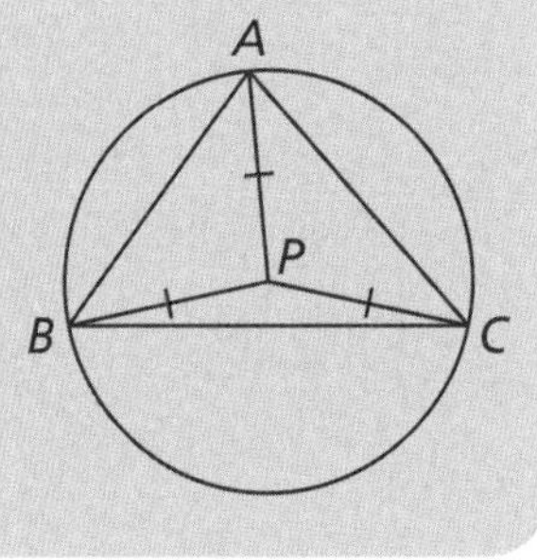

Proof Proof of Theorem 27

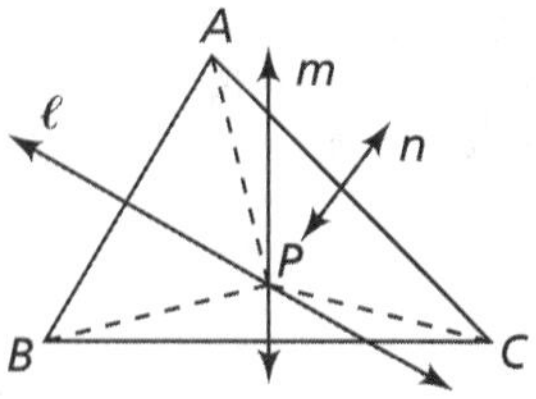

Given: Lines ℓ, m, and n are the perpendicular bisectors of the sides of $\triangle ABC$. P is the intersection of lines ℓ and m.

Prove: Line n contains point P, and $PA = PB = PC$.

Proof: A point on the perpendicular bisector of a segment is equidistant from the endpoints of the segment. Point P is on ℓ, which is the perpendicular bisector of $\overline{AB}$, so $PA = PB$. Using the same reasoning, since P is on m, and m is the perpendicular bisector of $\overline{BC}$, $PB = PC$. Thus, $PA = PC$ by the Transitive Property. Since $PA = PC$, P is equidistant from the endpoints of $\overline{AC}$. Then, by the Converse of the Perpendicular Bisector Theorem, P is on line n, the perpendicular bisector of $\overline{AC}$.

The circumcenter of a triangle can be inside, on, or outside a triangle.

Acute triangle

Right triangle

Obtuse triangle

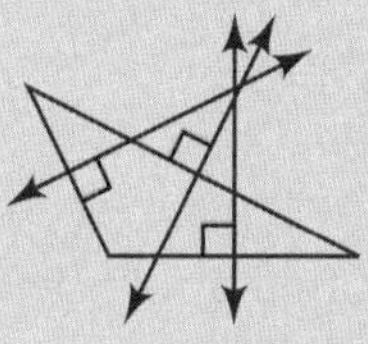

Problem 1 Finding the Circumcenter of a Triangle

Got It? What are the coordinates of the circumcenter of the triangle with vertices $A(2, 7)$, $B(10, 7)$, and $C(10, 3)$?

A Practice **1. Coordinate Geometry** Find the coordinates of the circumcenter of the triangle.

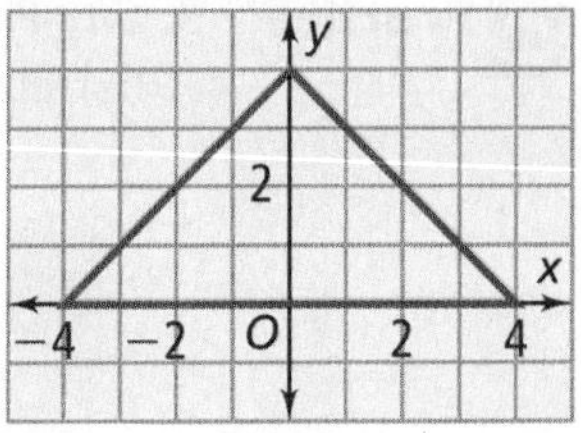

2. Coordinate Geometry Find the coordinates of the circumcenter of the triangle with vertices $A(-4, 5)$, $B(-2, 5)$, and $C(-2, -2)$.

Problem 2 Using a Circumcenter

Think

How do you find a point equidistant from three points?

Got It? **In Problem 2, the town planner wants to place a bench equidistant from the three trees in the park. Where should he place the bench?**

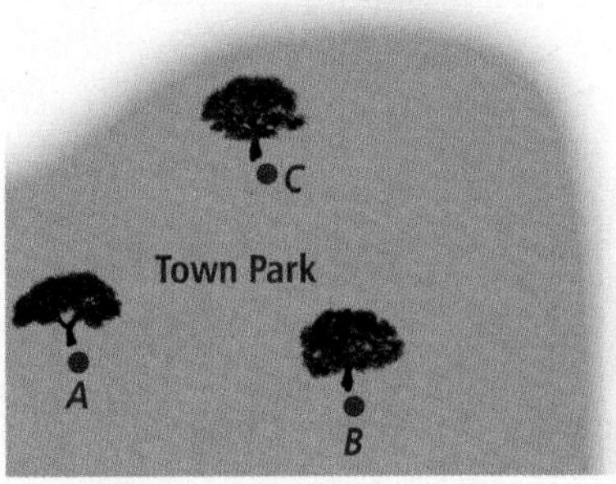

Practice 3. **City Planning** Show where town officials should place a recycling barrel so that it is equidistant from the lifeguard chair, the snack bar, and the volleyball court. Explain.

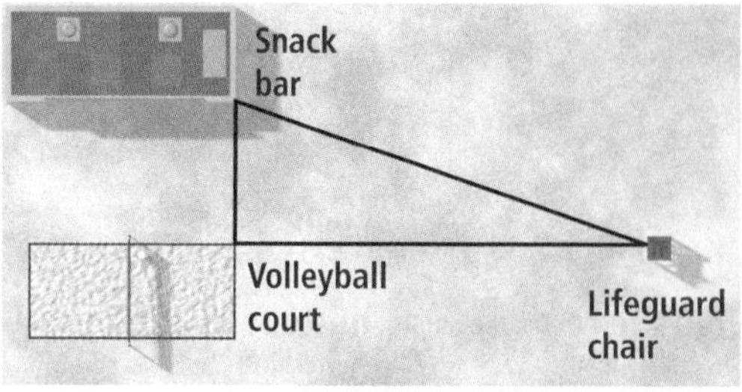

take note

Theorem 28 Concurrency of Angle Bisectors Theorem

Theorem

The bisectors of the angles of a triangle are concurrent at a point equidistant from the sides of the triangle.

Diagram

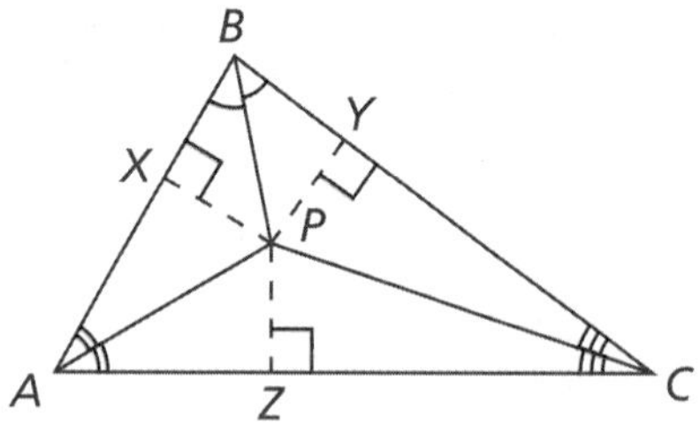

Symbols

Angle bisectors $\overline{AP}$, $\overline{BP}$, and $\overline{CP}$ are concurrent at P.

$PX = PY = PZ$

You will prove Theorem 28 in Exercise 17.

The point of concurrency of the angle bisectors of a triangle is called the **incenter of the triangle**. For any triangle, the incenter is always inside the triangle. In the diagram, points X, Y, and Z are equidistant from P, the incenter of $\triangle ABC$. P is the center of the circle that is **inscribed in** the triangle.

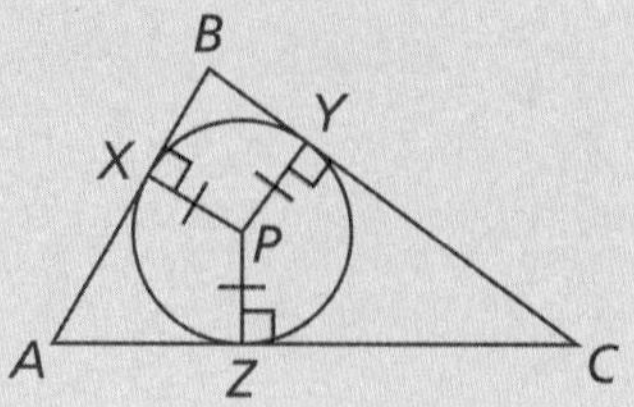

Problem 3 Identifying and Using the Incenter of a Triangle

Think

Which segments in the diagram are congruent?

Got It? a. $QN = 5x + 36$ and $QM = 2x + 51$. What is QO?

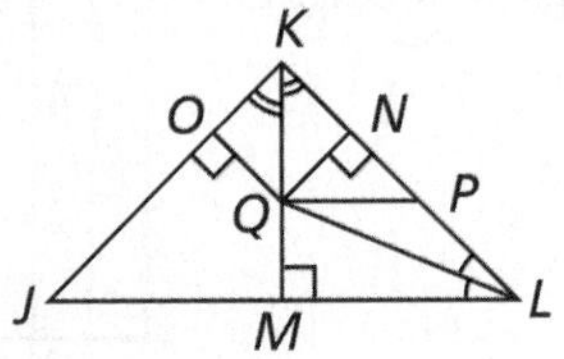

b. Reasoning Is it possible for QP to equal 50? Explain.

Practice 4. Name the point of concurrency of the angle bisectors.

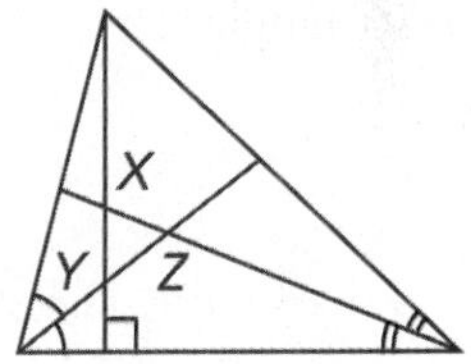

5. Find the value of x.

$RS = 4(x - 3) + 6$ and $RT = 5(2x - 6)$.

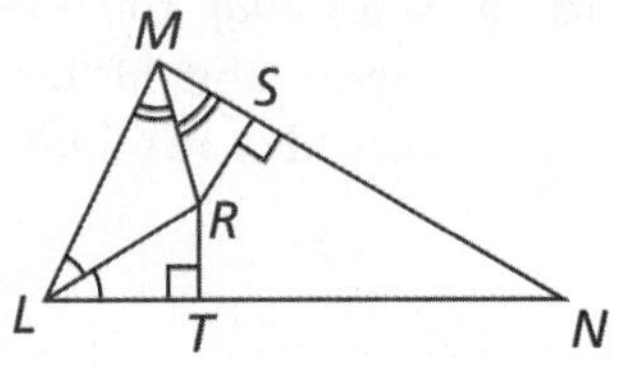

Lesson Check

Do you know HOW?

6. What are the coordinates of the circumcenter of the triangle at the right?

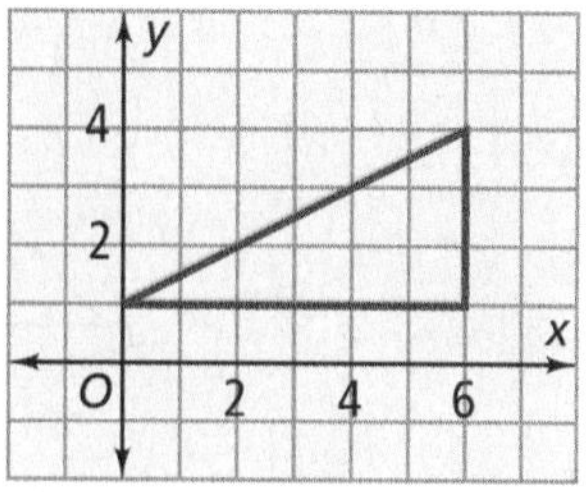

7. In the figure at the right, $TV = 3x - 12$ and $TU = 5x - 24$. What is the value of x?

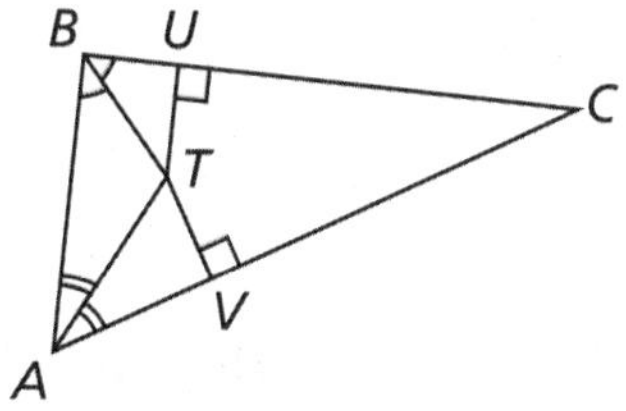

Do you UNDERSTAND?

MATHEMATICAL PRACTICES

8. Vocabulary A triangle's circumcenter is outside the triangle. What type of triangle is it?

9. Reasoning You want to find the circumcenter of a triangle. Why do you only need to find the intersection of two of the triangle's perpendicular bisectors, instead of all three?

10. Error Analysis Your friend sees the triangle at the right and concludes that $CT = CP$. What is the error in your friend's reasoning?

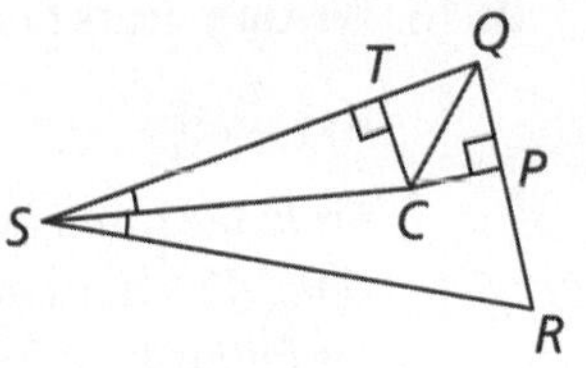

11. Compare and Contrast How are the circumcenter and incenter of a triangle alike? How are they different?

More Practice and Problem-Solving Exercises

MATHEMATICAL PRACTICES

B Apply

12. Think About a Plan In the figure at the right, P is the incenter of isosceles $\triangle RST$. What type of triangle is $\triangle RPT$? Explain.

- What segments determine the incenter of a triangle?
- What do you know about the base angles of an isosceles triangle?

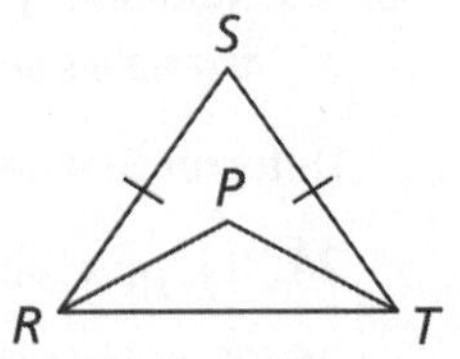

Constructions **Draw a triangle that fits the given description. Then construct the inscribed circle and the circumscribed circle. Describe your method.**

13. right triangle, $\triangle DEF$

14. obtuse triangle, $\triangle STU$

15. Algebra In the diagram at the right, G is the incenter of $\triangle DEF$, $m\angle DEF = 60$, and $m\angle EFD = 2 \cdot m\angle EDF$. What are $m\angle DGE$, $m\angle DGF$, and $m\angle EGF$?

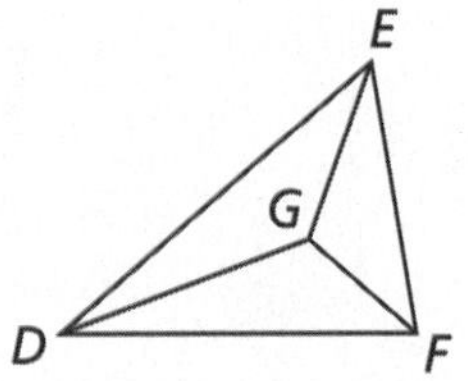

16. Writing Ivars found an old piece of paper inside an antique book.

It read,

From the spot I buried Olaf's treasure, equal sets of paces did I measure; each of three directions in a line, there to plant a seedling Norway pine. I could not return for failing health; now the hounds of Haiti guard my wealth. —*Karl*

After searching Caribbean islands for five years, Ivars found an island with three tall Norway pines. How might Ivars find where Karl buried Olaf's treasure?

Proof **17.** Use the diagram at the right to prove the Concurrrency of Angle Bisectors Theorem.

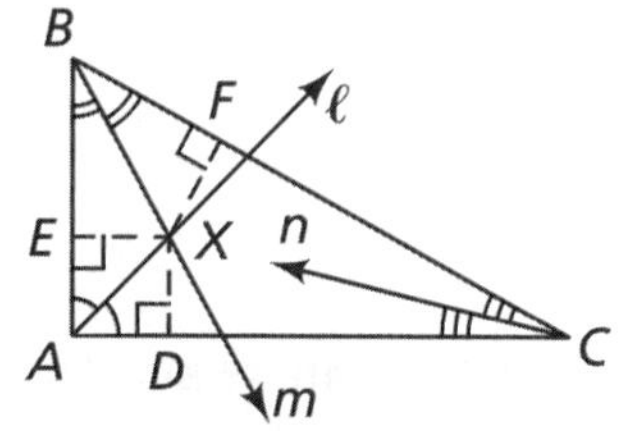

Given: Rays ℓ, m, and n are bisectors of the angles of $\triangle ABC$. X is the intersection of rays ℓ and m, $\overline{XD} \perp \overline{AC}$, $\overline{XE} \perp \overline{AB}$, and $\overline{XF} \perp \overline{BC}$.

Prove: Ray n contains point X, and $XD = XE = XF$.

18. Noise Control You are trying to talk to a friend on the phone in a busy bus station. The buses are so loud that you can hardly hear. Referring to the figure at the right, should you stand at P or C to be as far as possible from all the buses? Explain.

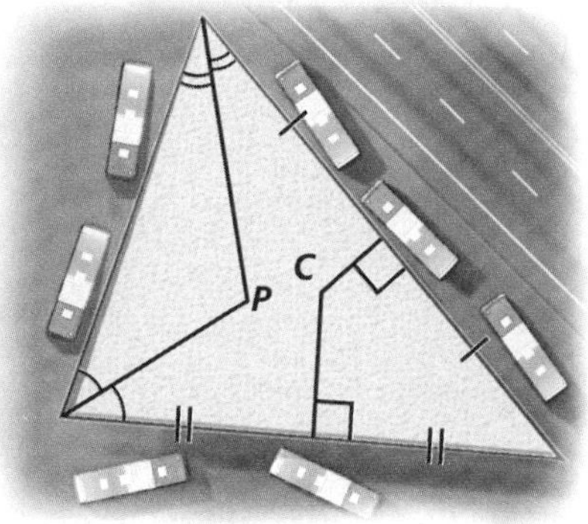

Reasoning Determine whether each statement is *true* or *false*. If the statement is false, give a counterexample.

19. The incenter of a triangle is equidistant from all three vertices.

20. The incenter of a triangle always lies inside the triangle.

21. You can circumscribe a circle about any three points in a plane.

22. If point C is the circumcenter of $\triangle PQR$ and the circumcenter of $\triangle PQS$, then R and S must be the same point.

Challenge

23. Reasoning Explain why the circumcenter of a right triangle is on one of the triangle's sides.

Determine whether each statement is *always, sometimes,* or *never* true. Explain.

24. It is possible to find a point equidistant from three parallel lines in a plane.

25. The circles inscribed in and circumscribed about an isosceles triangle have the same center.

8-4 Medians and Altitudes

G.CO.10 Prove theorems about triangles . . . the medians of a triangle meet at a point. Also G.SRT.5

Objective To identify properties of medians and altitudes of a triangle

Solve It! Write your solution to the Solve It in the space below.

In the Solve It, the last set of segments you drew are the triangle's medians. A **median of a triangle** is a segment whose endpoints are a vertex and the midpoint of the opposite side.

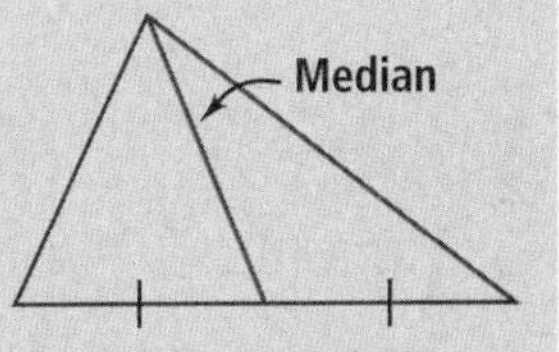

Essential Understanding A triangle's three medians are always concurrent.

take note

Theorem 29 Concurrency of Medians Theorem

The medians of a triangle are concurrent at a point that is two thirds the distance from each vertex to the midpoint of the opposite side.

$DC = \frac{2}{3}DJ \quad EC = \frac{2}{3}EG \quad FC = \frac{2}{3}FH$

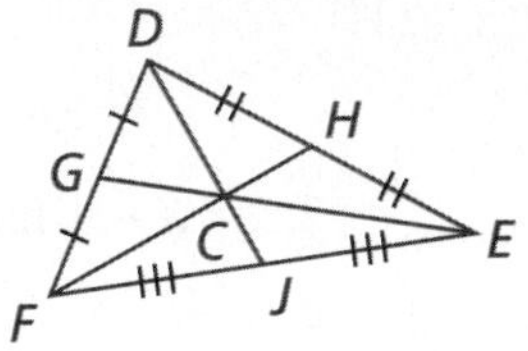

You will prove Theorem 29 in Lesson 9-8.

In a triangle, the point of concurrency of the medians is the **centroid of the triangle**. The point is also called the *center of gravity* of a triangle because it is the point where a triangular shape will balance. For any triangle, the centroid is always inside the triangle.

Problem 1 Finding the Length of a Median

Got It? **a.** If $ZA = 9$, what is the length of $\overline{ZC}$?

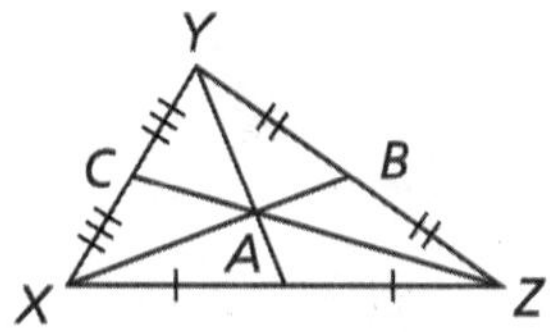

b. Reasoning What is the ratio of ZA to AC? Explain.

Practice In $\triangle TUV$, Y is the centroid.

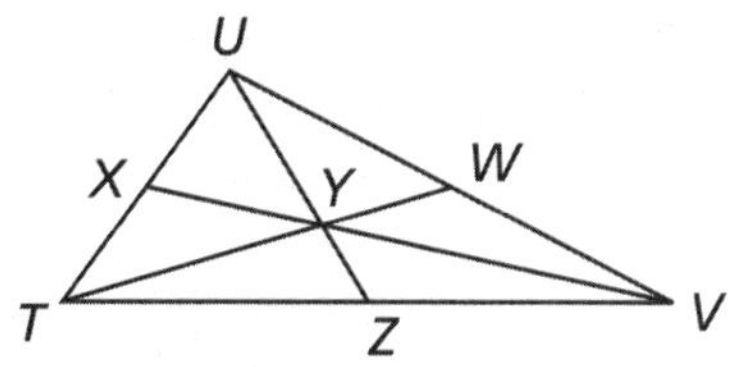

1. If $YU = 3.6$, find ZY and ZU.

2. If $VX = 9$, find VY and YX.

An **altitude of a triangle** is the perpendicular segment from a vertex of the triangle to the line containing the opposite side. An altitude of a triangle can be inside or outside the triangle, or it can be a side of the triangle.

Problem 2 Identifying Medians and Altitudes

Plan

How do you determine whether a segment is an altitude or a median?

Got It? **For $\triangle ABC$, is each segment a *median*, an *altitude*, or *neither*? Explain.**

a. $\overline{AD}$

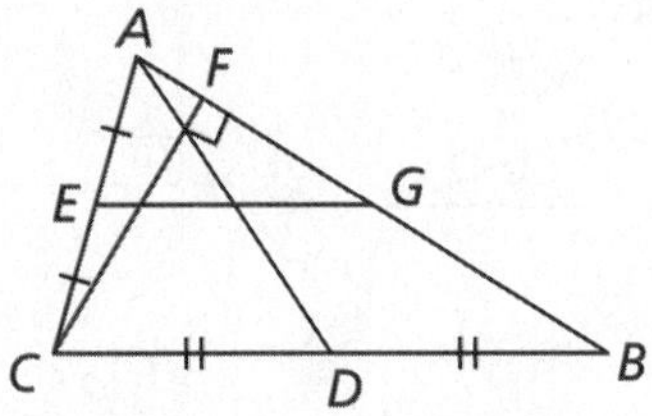

b. $\overline{EG}$

c. $\overline{CF}$

Practice **For $\triangle ABC$, is the red segment a *median*, an *altitude*, or *neither*? Explain.**

3.

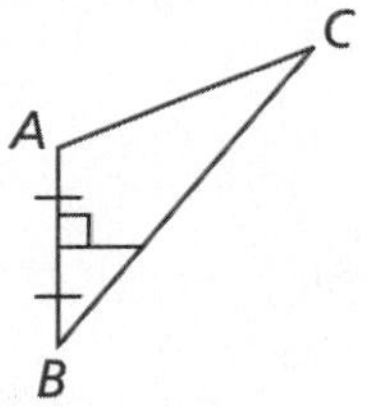

4.

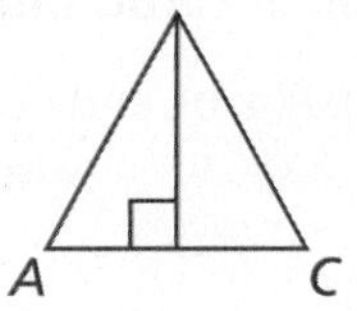

take note

Theorem 30 Concurrency of Altitudes Theorem

The lines that contain the altitudes of a triangle are concurrent.

You will prove Theorem 30 in Lesson 9-8.

The lines that contain the altitudes of a triangle are concurrent at the **orthocenter of the triangle**. The orthocenter of a triangle can be inside, on, or outside the triangle.

Acute triangle | Right triangle | Obtuse triangle

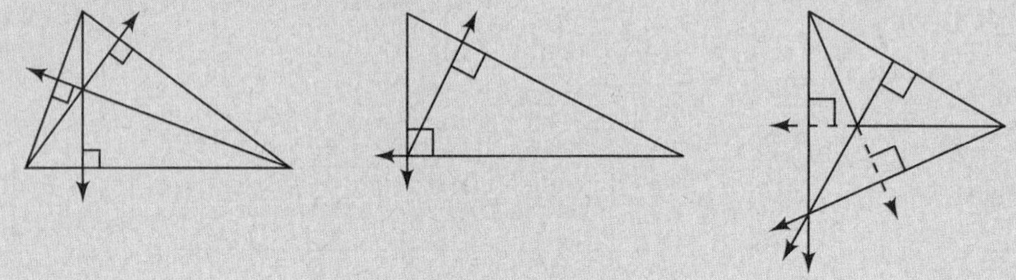

Problem 3 Finding the Orthocenter

Got It? $\triangle DEF$ has vertices $D(1, 2)$, $E(1, 6)$, and $F(4, 2)$. What are the coordinates of the orthocenter of $\triangle DEF$?

Think
Which two altitudes of $\triangle DEF$ should you choose?

Practice **Coordinate Geometry** **In Exercises 5 and 6, find the coordinates of the orthocenter of $\triangle ABC$ with the given vertices.**

5. $A(0, 0)$, $B(4, 0)$, and $C(4, 2)$

6. $A(0, -2)$, $B(4, -2)$, and $C(-2, -8)$

take note

Concept Summary Special Segments and Lines in Triangles

Perpendicular Bisectors	Angle Bisectors	Medians	Altitudes

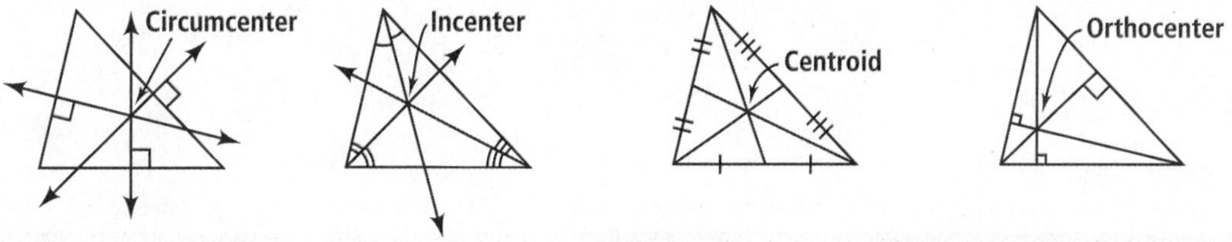

Lesson Check

Do you know HOW?

Use $\triangle ABC$ for Exercises 7–10.

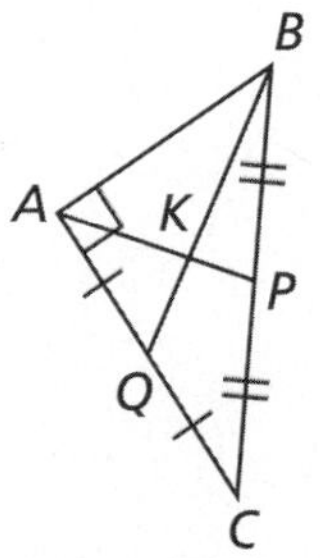

7. Is $\overline{AP}$ a *median* or an *altitude*?

8. If $AP = 18$, what is KP?

9. If $BK = 15$, what is KQ?

10. Which two segments are altitudes?

Do you UNDERSTAND?

MATHEMATICAL PRACTICES

11. Error Analysis Your classmate says she drew $\overline{HJ}$ as an altitude of $\triangle ABC$. What error did she make?

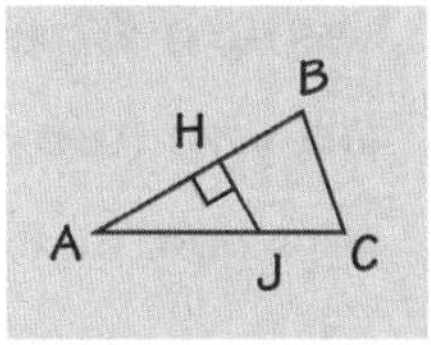

12. Reasoning Does it matter which two altitudes you use to locate the orthocenter of a triangle? Explain.

13. Reasoning The orthocenter of $\triangle ABC$ lies at vertex A. What can you conclude about $\overline{BA}$ and $\overline{AC}$? Explain.

More Practice and Problem-Solving Exercises

MATHEMATICAL PRACTICES

B Apply

Name the centroid.

14.

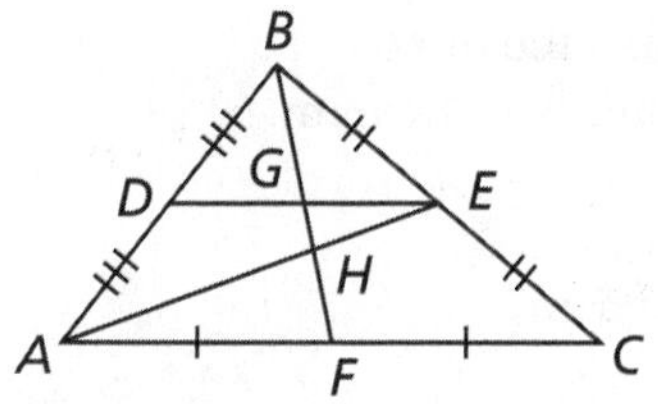

15.

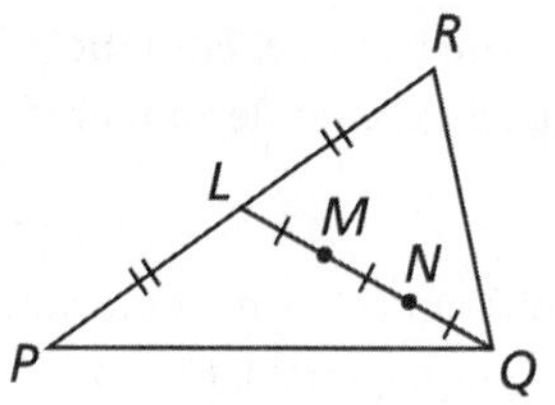

Name the orthocenter of $\triangle XYZ$.

16.

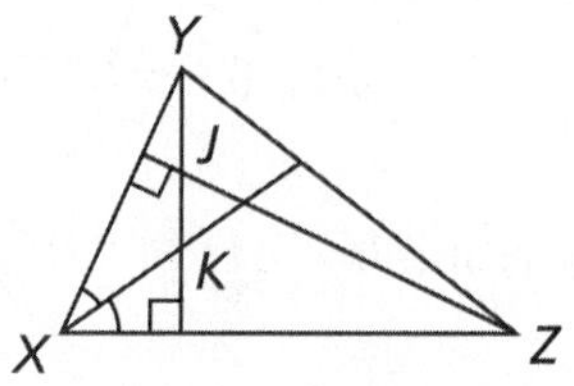

17.

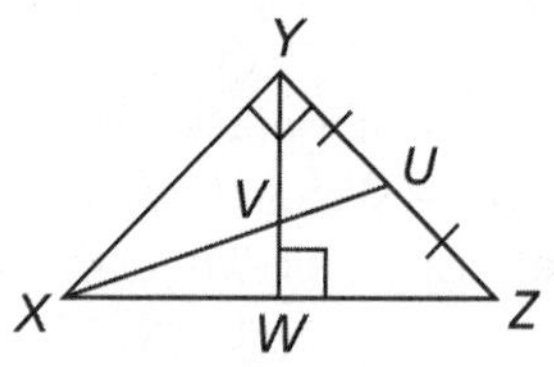

18. Think About a Plan In the diagram at the right, $\overline{QS}$ and $\overline{PT}$ are altitudes and $m\angle R = 55$. What is $m\angle POQ$?

- What does it mean for a segment to be an altitude?
- What do you know about the sum of the angle measures in a triangle?
- How do you sketch overlapping triangles separately?

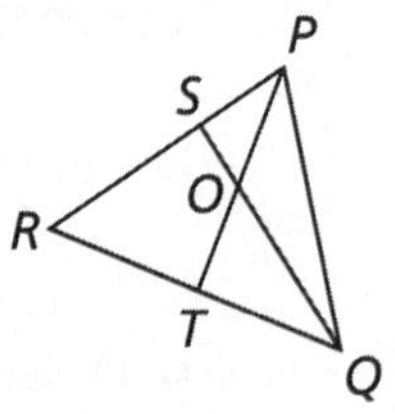

Constructions **Draw a triangle that fits the given description. Then construct the centroid and the orthocenter.**

19. acute scalene triangle, $\triangle LMN$

20. obtuse isosceles triangle, $\triangle RST$

In Exercises 21–24, name each segment.

21. a median in $\triangle ABC$

22. an altitude in $\triangle ABC$

23. a median in $\triangle BDC$

24. an altitude in $\triangle AOC$

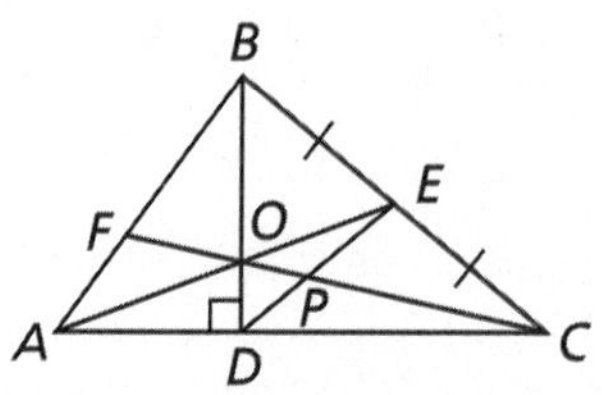

25. Reasoning A centroid separates a median into two segments. What is the ratio of the length of the shorter segment to the length of the longer segment?

Paper Folding The figures below show how to construct altitudes and medians by paper folding. Refer to them for Exercises 26 and 27.

Folding an Altitude

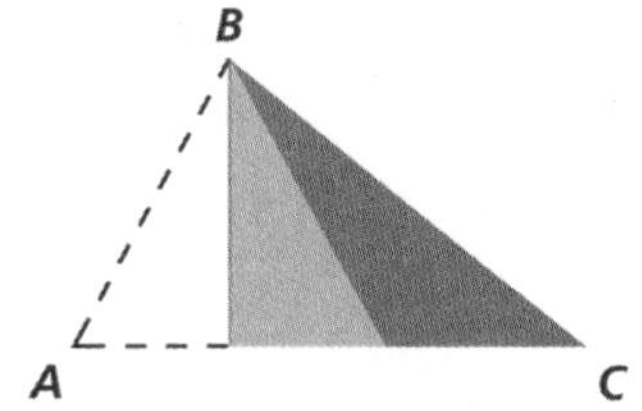

Fold the triangle so that a side $\overline{AC}$ overlaps itself and the fold contains the opposite vertex *B*.

Folding a Median

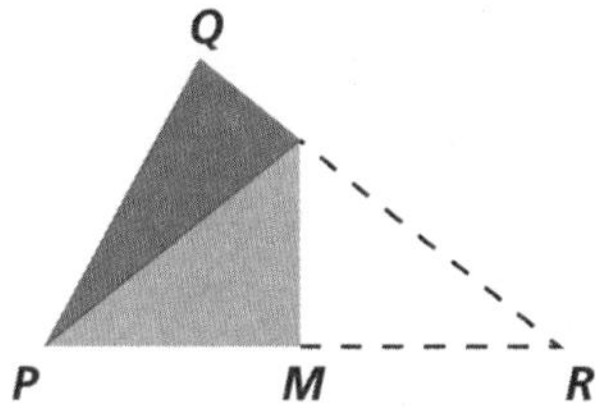

Fold one vertex *R* to another vertex *P*. This locates the midpoint *M* of a side.

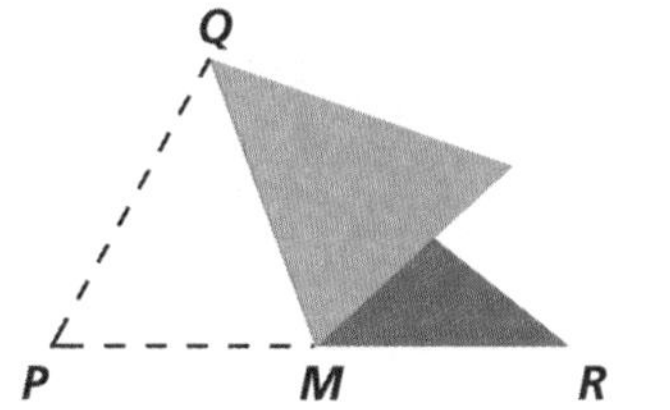

Unfold the triangle. Then fold it so that the fold contains the midpoint *M* and the opposite vertex *Q*.

26. Cut out a large triangle. Fold the paper carefully to construct the three medians of the triangle and demonstrate the Concurrency of Medians Theorem. Use a ruler to measure the length of each median and the distance of each vertex from the centroid.

27. Cut out a large acute triangle. Fold the paper carefully to construct the three altitudes of the triangle and demonstrate the Concurrency of Altitudes Theorem.

28. In the figure at the right, *C* is the centroid of $\triangle DEF$. If $GF = 12x^2 + 6y$, which expression represents *CF*?

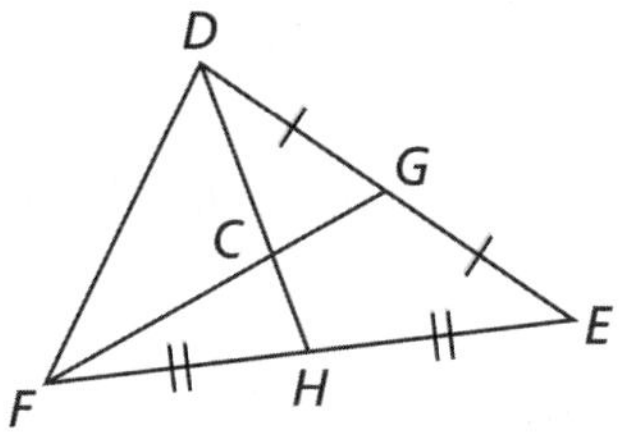

(A) $6x^2 + 3y$

(B) $8x^2 + 4y$

(C) $4x^2 + 2y$

(D) $8x^2 + 3y$

29. Reasoning What type of triangle has its orthocenter on the exterior of the triangle? Draw a sketch to support your answer.

30. Writing Explain why the median to the base of an isosceles triangle is also an altitude.

31. Coordinate Geometry $\triangle ABC$ has vertices $A(0, 0)$, $B(2, 6)$, and $C(8, 0)$. Complete the following steps to verify the Concurrency of Medians Theorem for $\triangle ABC$.

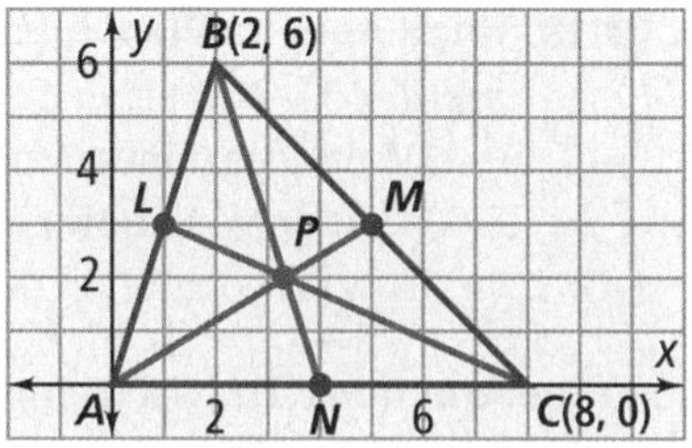

a. Find the coordinates of midpoints *L*, *M*, and *N*.

b. Find equations of $\overleftrightarrow{AM}$, $\overleftrightarrow{BN}$, and $\overleftrightarrow{CL}$.

c. Find the coordinates of *P*, the intersection of $\overleftrightarrow{AM}$ and $\overleftrightarrow{BN}$. This point is the centroid.

d. Show that point *P* is on $\overleftrightarrow{CL}$.

e. Use the Distance Formula to show that point *P* is two-thirds of the distance from each vertex to the midpoint of the opposite side.

Challenge

32. Constructions *A*, *B*, and *O* are three noncollinear points. Construct point *C* such that *O* is the orthocenter of $\triangle ABC$. Describe your method.

33. Reasoning In an isosceles triangle, show that the circumcenter, incenter, centroid, and orthocenter can be four different points, but all four must be collinear.

***A, B, C,* and *D* are points of concurrency for the triangle. Determine whether each point is a *circumcenter, incenter, centroid,* or *orthocenter*. Explain.**

34.

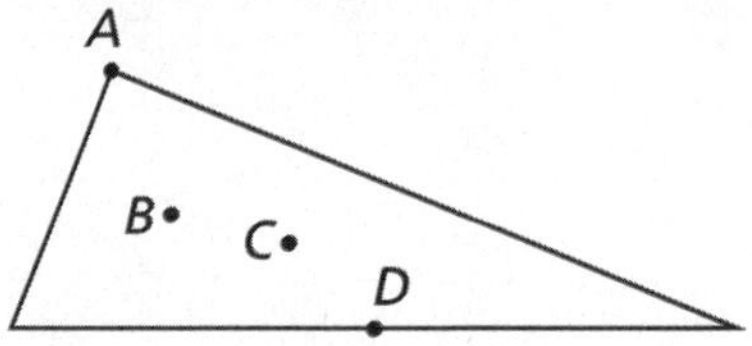

35.

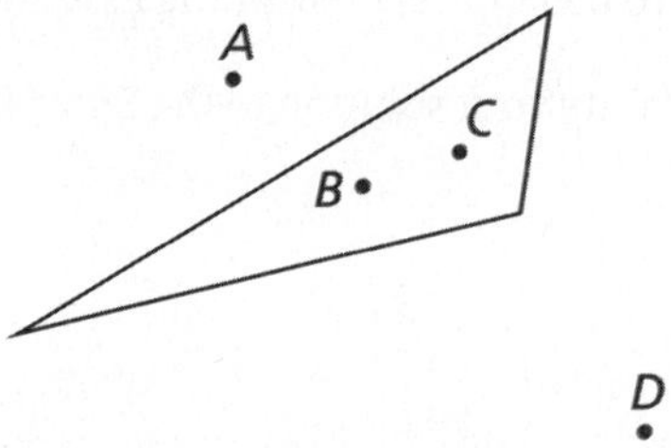

36. History In 1765, Leonhard Euler proved that, for any triangle, three of the four points of concurrency are collinear. The line that contains these three points is known as Euler's Line. Use Exercises 34 and 35 to determine which point of concurrency does not necessarily lie on Euler's Line.

8-5 Indirect Proof

G.CO.10 Prove theorems about triangles . . .

Objective To use indirect reasoning to write proofs

Solve It! Write your solution to the Solve It in the space below.

In the Solve It, you can conclude that a square must contain a certain number if you can eliminate the other three numbers as possibilities. This type of reasoning is called indirect reasoning. In **indirect reasoning,** all possibilities are considered and then all but one are proved false. The remaining possibility must be true.

Essential Understanding You can use indirect reasoning as another method of proof.

A proof involving indirect reasoning is an **indirect proof.** Often in an indirect proof, a statement and its negation are the only possibilities. When you see that one of these possibilities leads to a conclusion that contradicts a fact you know to be true, you can eliminate that possibility. For this reason, indirect proof is sometimes called *proof by contradiction.*

take note

Key Concept Writing an Indirect Proof

Step 1 State as a temporary assumption the opposite (negation) of what you want to prove.

Step 2 Show that this temporary assumption leads to a contradiction.

Step 3 Conclude that the temporary assumption must be false and that what you want to prove must be true.

In the first step of an indirect proof you assume as true the opposite of what you want to prove.

Problem 1 Writing the First Step of an Indirect Proof

Got It? Suppose you want to write an indirect proof of each statement. As the first step of the proof, what would you assume?

a. $\triangle BOX$ is not acute.

b. At least one pair of shoes you bought cost more than $25.

Practice **Write the first step of an indirect proof of the given statement.**

1. At least one angle is obtuse.

2. $m\angle 2 > 90$

To write an indirect proof, you have to be able to identify a contradiction.

Problem 2 Identifying Contradictions

Think

How do you know that two statements contradict each other?

Got It? a. Which two statements contradict each other?

I. $\triangle XYZ$ is acute.

II. $\triangle XYZ$ is scalene.

III. $\triangle XYZ$ is equiangular.

b. Reasoning Statements I and II below contradict each other. Statement III is the negation of Statement I. Are Statements II and III equivalent? Explain your reasoning.

I. $\triangle ABC$ is scalene.

II. $\triangle ABC$ is equilateral.

III. $\triangle ABC$ is not scalene.

Practice **Identify the two statements that contradict each other.**

3. **I.** Each of the two items that Val bought costs more than $10.

II. Val spent $34 for the two items.

III. Neither of the two items that Val bought costs more than $15.

4. **I.** In right $\triangle ABC$, $m\angle A = 60$.

II. In right $\triangle ABC$, $\angle A \cong \angle C$.

III. In right $\triangle ABC$, $m\angle B = 90$.

Problem 3 Writing an Indirect Proof

Got It? **Given:** $7(x + y) = 70$ and $x \neq 4$.

Prove: $y \neq 6$

Plan

What statement should be negated to begin the proof?

A Practice

5. Developing Proof Fill in the blanks to prove the following statement. If the Yoga Club and Go Green Club together have fewer than 20 members and the Go Green Club has 10 members, then the Yoga Club has fewer than 10 members.

Given: The total membership of the Yoga Club and the Go Green Club is fewer than 20. The Go Green Club has 10 members.

Prove: The Yoga Club has fewer than 10 members.

Proof: Assume temporarily that the Yoga Club has 10 or more members.

This means that together the two clubs have

a. ________________ members. This contradicts the given

information that **b.** ________________________________.

The temporary assumption is false. Therefore, it is true that

c. ____.

6. Developing Proof Fill in the blanks to prove the following statement. In a given triangle, $\triangle LMN$, there is at most one right angle.

Given: $\triangle LMN$

Prove: $\triangle LMN$ has at most one right angle.

Proof: Assume temporarily that $\triangle LMN$ has more than one **a.** ________________. That is, assume that both $\angle M$ and $\angle N$ are **b.** ________________. If $\angle M$ and $\angle N$ are both right angles, then $m\angle M = m\angle N =$ **c.** ________________. By the Triangle Angle-Sum Theorem, $m\angle L + m\angle M + m\angle N =$ **d.** ________. Use substitution to write the equation $m\angle L +$ **e.** ________ $+$ **f.** ________ $= 180$. When you solve for $m\angle L$, you find that $m\angle L =$ **g.** ________. This means that there is no $\triangle LMN$, which contradicts the given statement. So the temporary assumption that $\triangle LMN$ has **h.** ________________ must be false. Therefore, $\triangle LMN$ has **i.** ________________.

Lesson Check

Do you know HOW?

7. Suppose you want to write an indirect proof of the following statement. As the first step of the proof, what would you assume?

Quadrilateral *ABCD* has four right angles.

8. Write a statement that contradicts the following statement. Draw a diagram to support your answer.

Lines *a* and *b* are parallel.

Do you UNDERSTAND?

MATHEMATICAL PRACTICES

9. **Error Analysis** A classmate began an indirect proof as shown at the right. Explain and correct your classmate's error.

~~Given: $\triangle ABC$~~
~~Prove: $\angle A$ is obtuse.~~
~~Assume temporarily that $\angle A$ is acute.~~

More Practice and Problem-Solving Exercises

MATHEMATICAL PRACTICES

B Apply

10. **History** Use indirect reasoning to eliminate all but one of the following answers. In what year was George Washington born?

(A) 1492 (B) 1732 (C) 1902 (D) 2002

11. **Think About a Plan** Write an indirect proof.

Given: $\angle 1 \not\cong \angle 2$

Prove: $\ell \nparallel p$

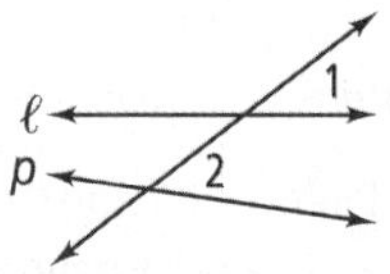

- What assumption should be the first step of your proof?
- In the figure, what type of angle pair do $\angle 1$ and $\angle 2$ form?

Write the first step of an indirect proof of the given statement.

12. If a number n ends in 5, then it is not divisible by 2.

13. If point X is on the perpendicular bisector of $\overline{AB}$, then $\overline{XB} \cong \overline{XA}$.

14. If a transversal intersects two parallel lines, then alternate exterior angles are congruent.

15. **Reasoning** Identify the two statements that contradict each other.

I. The orthocenter of $\triangle JRK$ is on the triangle.

II. The centroid of $\triangle JRK$ is inside the triangle.

III. $\triangle JRK$ is an obtuse triangle.

Write an indirect proof.

Proof **16.** Use the figure at the right.

Given: $\triangle ABC$ with $BC > AC$

Prove: $\angle A \not\cong \angle B$

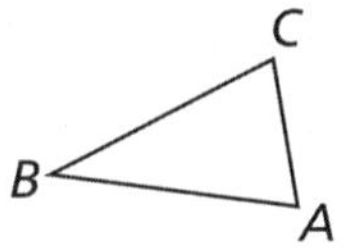

Proof **17. Given:** $\triangle XYZ$ is isosceles.

Prove: Neither base angle is a right angle.

Writing For Exercises 18 and 19, write a convincing argument that uses indirect reasoning.

STEM **18. Chemistry** Ice is forming on the sidewalk in front of Toni's house. Show that the temperature of the sidewalk surface must be 32°F or lower.

19. Show that an obtuse triangle cannot contain a right angle.

20. Error Analysis Your friend wants to prove indirectly that $\triangle ABC$ is equilateral. For a first step, he writes, "Assume temporarily that $\triangle ABC$ is scalene." What is wrong with your friend's statement? How can he correct himself?

21. Literature In Arthur Conan Doyle's story "The Sign of the Four," Sherlock Holmes talks to his friend Watson about how a culprit enters a room that has only four entrances: a door, a window, a chimney, and a hole in the roof.

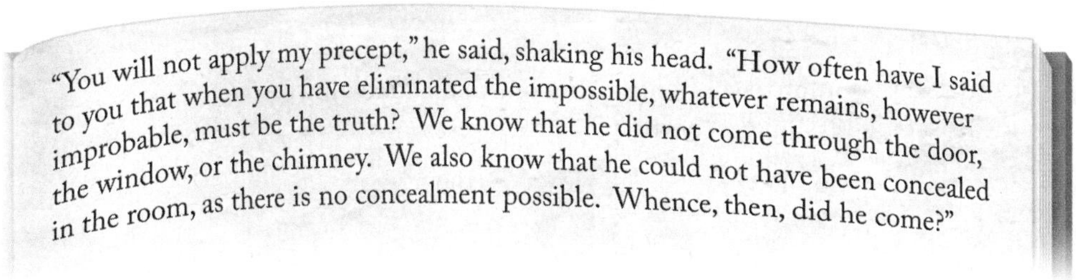
"You will not apply my precept," he said, shaking his head. "How often have I said to you that when you have eliminated the impossible, whatever remains, however improbable, must be the truth? We know that he did not come through the door, the window, or the chimney. We also know that he could not have been concealed in the room, as there is no concealment possible. Whence, then, did he come?"

How did the culprit enter the room? Explain.

Proof **22.** Prove Theorem 9, the Converse of the Corresponding Angles Theorem. (*Hint:* Use the Triangle Angle-Sum Theorem.)

Challenge

Use the figure at the right for Exercises 23 and 24.

Proof **23. Given:** $\triangle ABC$ is scalene, $m\angle ABX = 36$, $m\angle CBX = 36$
Prove: $\overline{XB}$ is not perpendicular to $\overline{AC}$.

Proof **24. Given:** $\triangle ABC$ is scalene, $m\angle ABX = 36$, $m\angle CBX = 36$
Prove: $\overline{AX} \not\cong \overline{XC}$

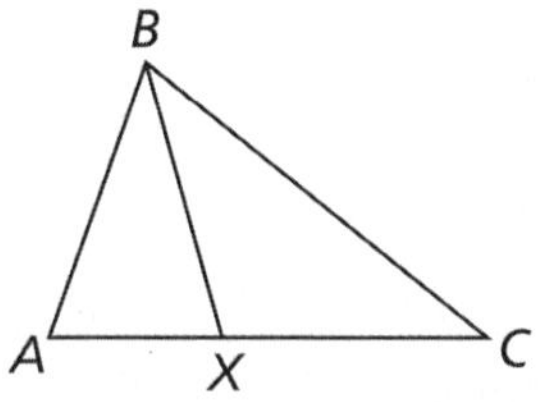

8-6 Inequalities in One Triangle

G.CO.10 Prove theorems about triangles . . .

Objective To use inequalities involving angles and sides of triangles

Solve It! Write your solution to the Solve It in the space below.

In the Solve It, you explored triangles formed by various lengths of board. You may have noticed that changing the angle formed by two sides of the sandbox changes the length of the third side.

Essential Understanding The angles and sides of a triangle have special relationships that involve inequalities.

take note

Property **Comparison Property of Inequality**

If $a = b + c$ and $c > 0$, then $a > b$.

Proof of the Comparison Property of Inequality

Given: $a = b + c, c > 0$
Prove: $a > b$

Statements	Reasons
1) $c > 0$	**1)** Given
2) $b + c > b + 0$	**2)** Addition Property of Inequality
3) $b + c > b$	**3)** Identity Property of Addition
4) $a = b + c$	**4)** Given
5) $a > b$	**5)** Substitution

The Comparison Property of Inequality allows you to prove the following corollary to the Triangle Exterior Angle Theorem, which states that the measure of each exterior angle of a triangle equals the sum of the measure of its two remote interior angles.

take note

Corollary Corollary to the Triangle Exterior Angle Theorem

Corollary	If . . .	Then . . .
The measure of an exterior angle of a triangle is greater than the measure of each of its remote interior angles.	$\angle 1$ is an exterior angle. 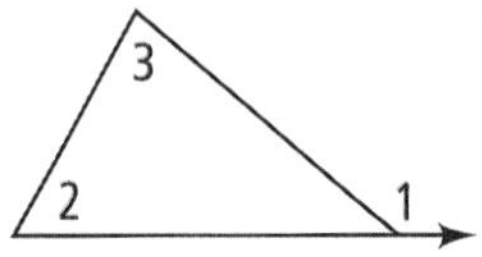	$m\angle 1 > m\angle 2$ and $m\angle 1 > m\angle 3$

Proof Proof of the Corollary

Given: $\angle 1$ is an exterior angle of the triangle.
Prove: $m\angle 1 > m\angle 2$ and $m\angle 1 > m\angle 3$.

Proof: By the Triangle Exterior Angle Theorem, $m\angle 1 = m\angle 2 + m\angle 3$. Since $m\angle 2 > 0$ and $m\angle 3 > 0$, you can apply the Comparison Property of Inequality and conclude that $m\angle 1 > m\angle 2$ and $m\angle 1 > m\angle 3$.

ONLINE PROBLEMS

Problem 1 Applying the Corollary

Got It? Why is $m\angle 5 > m\angle C$?

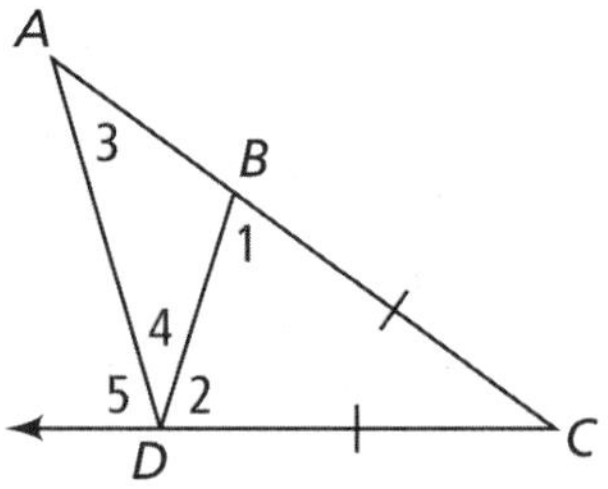

A Practice Explain why $m\angle 1 > m\angle 2$.

1.

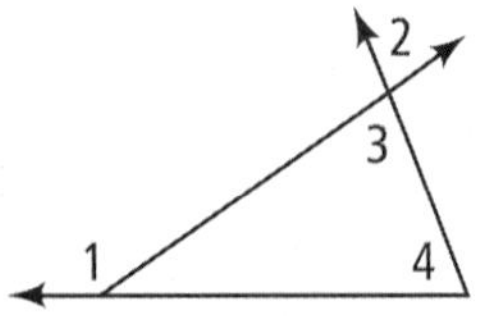

2.

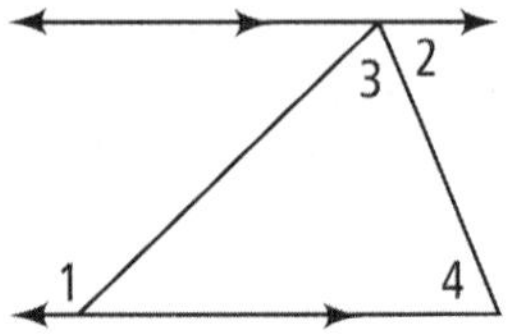

You can use the corollary to the Triangle Exterior Angles theorem to prove the following theorem.

take note

Theorem 31

Theorem	If . . .	Then . . .
If two sides of a triangle are not congruent, then the larger angle lies opposite the longer side.	$XZ > XY$	$m\angle Y > m\angle Z$

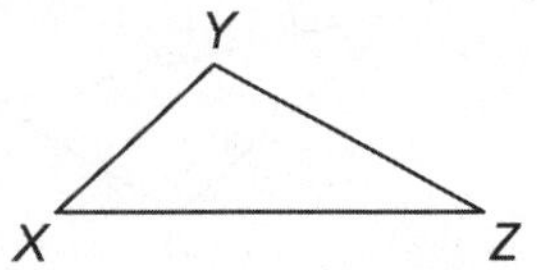

You will prove Theorem 31 in Exercise 23.

Problem 2 Using Theorem 31

Got It? Suppose the landscape architect from Problem 2 wants to place a drinking fountain at the corner with the second-largest angle. Which two streets form the corner with the second-largest angle?

A Practice **For Exercises 3 and 4, list the angles of each triangle in order from smallest to largest.**

3.

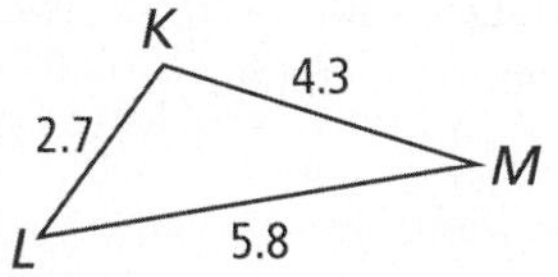

4. $\triangle ABC$, where $AB = 8$, $BC = 5$, and $CA = 7$

Theorem 32 below is the converse of Theorem 31. The proof of Theorem 32 relies on indirect reasoning.

take note

Theorem 32

Theorem	If . . .	Then . . .
If two angles of a triangle are not congruent, then the longer side lies opposite the larger angle.	$m\angle A > m\angle B$	$BC > AC$

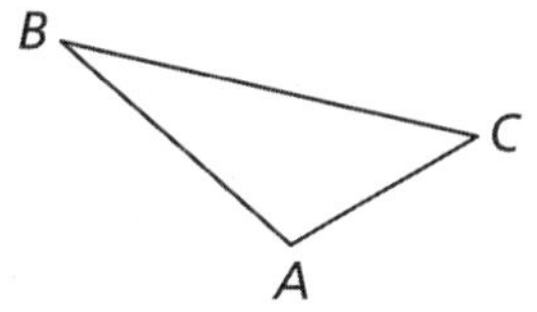

Proof Indirect Proof of Theorem 32

Given: $m\angle A > m\angle B$
Prove: $BC > AC$

Step 1 Assume temporarily that BC is not greater than AC. That is, assume temporarily that either $BC < AC$ or $BC = AC$.

Step 2 If $BC < AC$, then $m\angle A < m\angle B$ (Theorem 31). This contradicts the given fact that $m\angle A > m\angle B$. Therefore, $BC < AC$ must be false.

If $BC = AC$, then $m\angle A = m\angle B$ (Isosceles Triangle Theorem). This also contradicts $m\angle A > m\angle B$. Therefore, $BC = AC$ must be false.

Step 3 The temporary assumption $BC \ngtr AC$ is false, so $BC > AC$.

ONLINE PROBLEMS

Problem 3 Using Theorem 32

Got It? **Reasoning** In the figure below, $m\angle S = 24$ and $m\angle O = 130$. Which side of $\triangle SOX$ is the shortest side? Explain your reasoning.

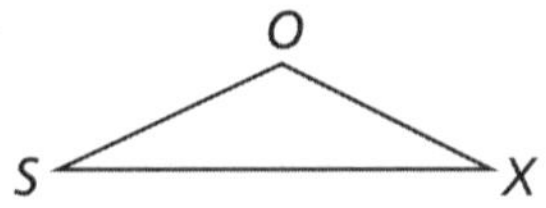

Plan

How do you use the angle measures to order the side lengths?

Practice **For Exercises 5 and 6, list the sides of each triangle in order from shortest to longest.**

5.

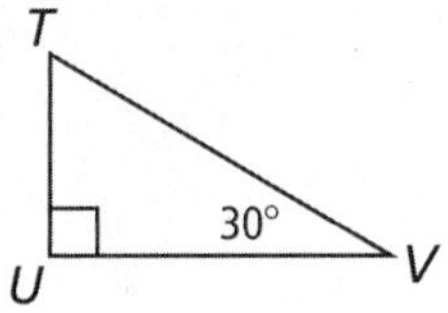

6. $\triangle DEF$, with $m\angle D = 20$, $m\angle E = 120$, and $m\angle F = 40$

For three segments to form a triangle, their lengths must be related in a certain way. Notice that only one of the sets of segments below can form a triangle. The sum of the smallest two lengths must be greater than the greatest length.

take note

Theorem 33 Triangle Inequality Theorem

The sum of the lengths of any two sides of a triangle is greater than the length of the third side.

$XY + YZ > XZ$ $\quad$ $YZ + XZ > XY$ $\quad$ $XZ + XY > YZ$

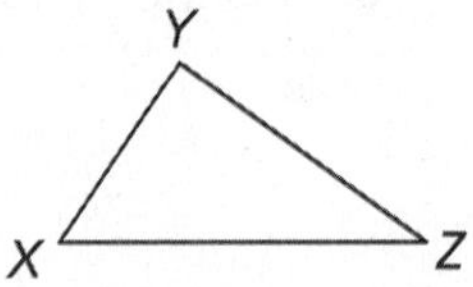

You will prove Theorem 33 in Exercise 28.

Problem 4 Using the Triangle Inequality Theorem

Got It? Can a triangle have sides with the given lengths? Explain.

a. 2 m, 6 m, and 9 m

Think
How can you determine if the lengths can form a triangle?

b. 4 yd, 6 yd, and 9 yd

Practice **Can a triangle have sides with the given lengths? Explain.**

7. 2 in., 3 in., 6 in.

8. 11 cm, 12 cm, 15 cm

Problem 5 Finding Possible Side Lengths

Got It? A triangle has side lengths of 4 in. and 7 in. What is the range of possible lengths for the third side?

Practice **Algebra** **The lengths of two sides of a triangle are given. Find the range of possible lengths for the third side.**

9. 18 m, 23 m

10. 20 km, 35 km

Lesson Check

Do you know HOW?

Use $\triangle ABC$ for Exercises 11 and 12.

11. Which side is the longest?

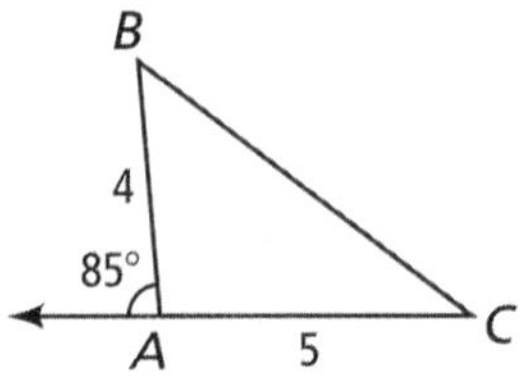

12. Which angle is the smallest?

13. Can a triangle have sides of lengths 4, 5, and 10? Explain.

Do you UNDERSTAND?

MATHEMATICAL PRACTICES

14. Error Analysis A friend tells you that she drew a triangle with perimeter 16 and one side of length 8. How do you know she made an error in her drawing?

15. **Reasoning** Is it possible to draw a right triangle with an exterior angle measuring 88? Explain your reasoning.

More Practice and Problem-Solving Exercises

MATHEMATICAL PRACTICES

B Apply

16. **Think About a Plan** You are setting up a study area where you will do your homework each evening. It is triangular with an entrance on one side. You want to put your computer in the corner with the largest angle and a bookshelf on the longest side. Where should you place your computer? On which side should you place the bookshelf? Explain.
    - What type of triangle is shown in the figure?
    - Once you find the largest angle of a triangle, how do you find the longest side?

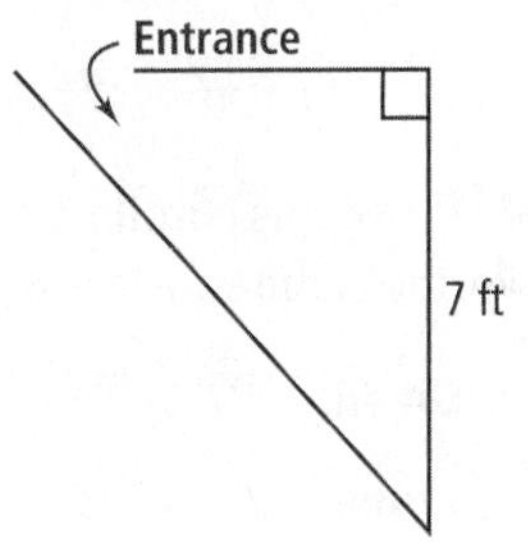

17. **Algebra** Find the longest side of $\triangle ABC$, with $m\angle A = 70$, $m\angle B = 2x - 10$, and $m\angle C = 3x + 20$.

18. **Writing** You and a friend compete in a scavenger hunt at a museum. The two of you walk from the Picasso exhibit to the Native American gallery along the dashed red line. When he sees that another team is ahead of you, your friend says, "They must have cut through the courtyard." Explain what your friend means.

19. **Error Analysis** Your family drives across Kansas on Interstate 70. A sign reads, "Wichita 90 mi, Topeka 110 mi." Your little brother says, "I didn't know that it was only 20 miles from Wichita to Topeka." Explain why the distance between the two cities does not have to be 20 mi.

Reasoning Determine which segment is shortest in each diagram.

20. 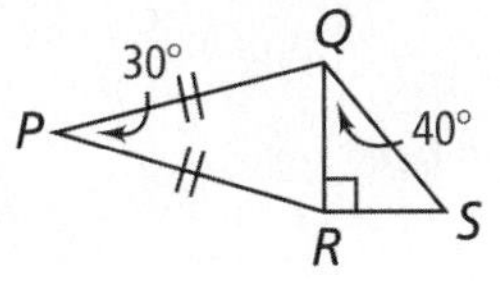

21. 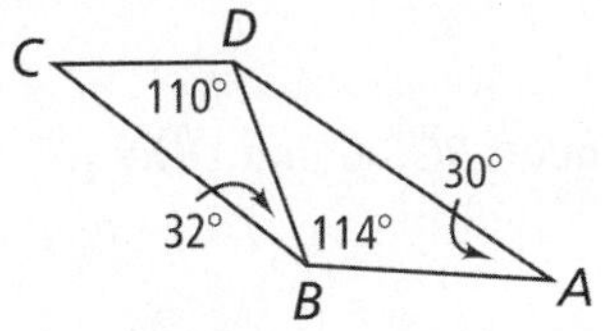

22. 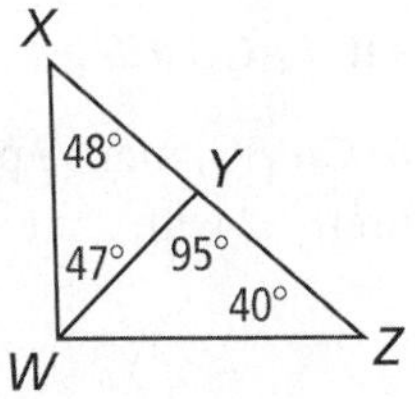

23. **Developing Proof** Fill in the blanks for a proof of Theorem 31: If two sides of a triangle are not congruent, then the larger angle lies opposite the longer side.

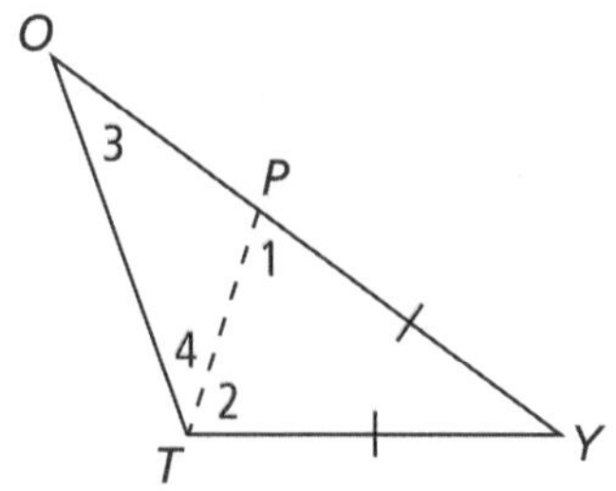

Given: $\triangle TOY$, with $YO > YT$

Prove: a. ___?___ > b. ___?___

Mark P on $\overline{YO}$ so that $\overline{YP} \cong \overline{YT}$. Draw $\overline{TP}$.

Statements	Reasons
1) $\overline{YP} \cong \overline{YT}$	1) Ruler Postulate
2) $m\angle 1 = m\angle 2$	2) c. ___?___
3) $m\angle OTY = m\angle 4 + m\angle 2$	3) d. ___?___
4) $m\angle OTY > m\angle 2$	4) e. ___?___
5) $m\angle OTY > m\angle 1$	5) f. ___?___
6) $m\angle 1 > m\angle 3$	6) g. ___?___
7) $m\angle OTY > m\angle 3$	7) h. ___?___

Proof 24. Prove this corollary to Theorem 32: The perpendicular segment from a point to a line is the shortest segment from the point to the line.

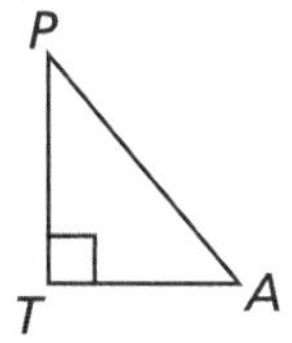

Given: $\overline{PT} \perp \overline{TA}$

Prove: $PA > PT$

Challenge

25. **Probability** A student has two straws. One is 6 cm long and the other is 9 cm long. She picks a third straw at random from a group of four straws whose lengths are 3 cm, 5 cm, 11 cm, and 15 cm. What is the probability that the straw she picks will allow her to form a triangle? Justify your answer.

For Exercises 26 and 27, x and y are integers such that $1 < x < 5$ and $2 < y < 9$.

26. The sides of a triangle are 5 cm, x cm, and y cm. List all possible (x, y) pairs.

27. **Probability** What is the probability that you can draw an isosceles triangle that has sides 5 cm, x cm, and y cm, with x and y chosen at random?

Proof 28. Prove the Triangle Inequality Theorem: The sum of the lengths of any two sides of a triangle is greater than the length of the third side.

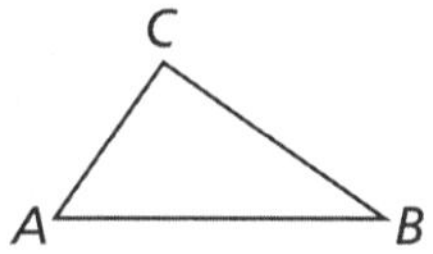

Given: $\triangle ABC$

Prove: $AC + CB > AB$

(*Hint:* On $\overrightarrow{BC}$, mark a point D not on $\overline{BC}$, so that $DC = AC$. Draw $\overline{DA}$ and use Theorem 32 with $\triangle ABD$.)

8-7 Inequalities in Two Triangles

G.CO.10 Prove theorems about triangles . . .

Objective To apply inequalities in two triangles

Solve It! Write your solution to the Solve It in the space below.

In the Solve It, the hands of the clock and the segment labeled x form a triangle. As the time changes, the shape of the triangle changes, but the lengths of two of its sides do not change.

Essential Understanding In triangles that have two pairs of congruent sides, there is a relationship between the included angles and the third pair of sides.

When you close a door, the angle between the door and the frame (at the hinge) gets smaller. The relationship between the measure of the hinge angle and the length of the opposite side is the basis for the SAS Inequality Theorem, also known as the Hinge Theorem.

take note

Theorem 34 The Hinge Theorem (SAS Inequality Theorem)

Theorem	If . . .	Then . . .
If two sides of one triangle are congruent to two sides of another triangle, and the included angles are not congruent, then the longer third side is opposite the larger included angle.	$m\angle A > m\angle X$	$BC > YZ$

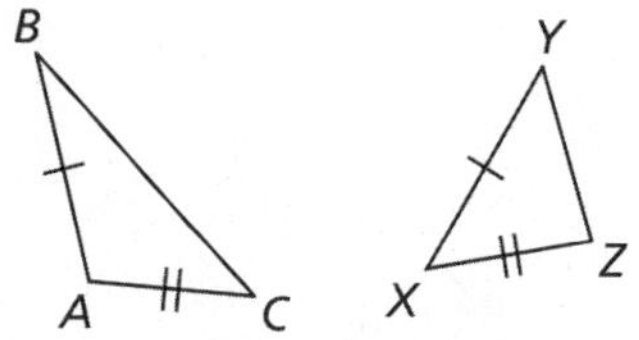

You will prove Theorem 34 in Exercise 21.

Problem 1 Using the Hinge Theorem

Got It? **a.** What inequality relates LN and OQ in the figure at the right?

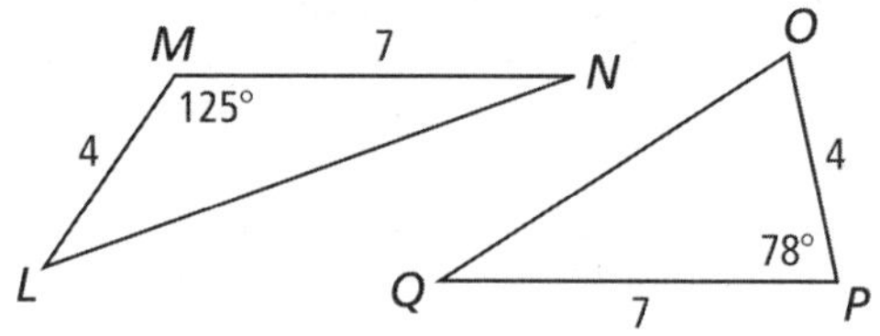

b. Reasoning In $\triangle ABC$, $AB = 3$, $BC = 4$, and $CA = 6$. In $\triangle PQR$, $PQ = 3$, $QR = 5$, and $RP = 6$. How can you use indirect reasoning to explain why $m\angle P > m\angle A$?

Practice **Write an inequality relating the given side lengths. If there is not enough information to reach a conclusion, write *no conclusion*.**

1. LM and KL

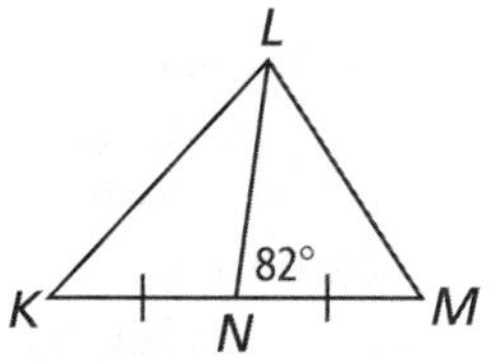

2. YZ and UV

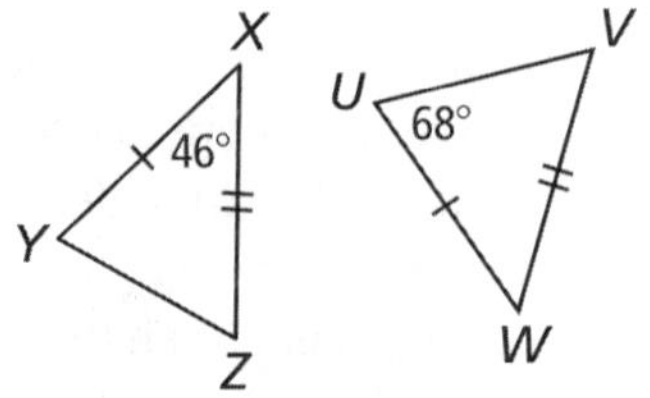

Problem 2 Applying the Hinge Theorem

Got It? The diagram below shows a pair of scissors in two different positions. In which position is the distance between the tips of the two blades greater? Use the Hinge Theorem to justify your answer.

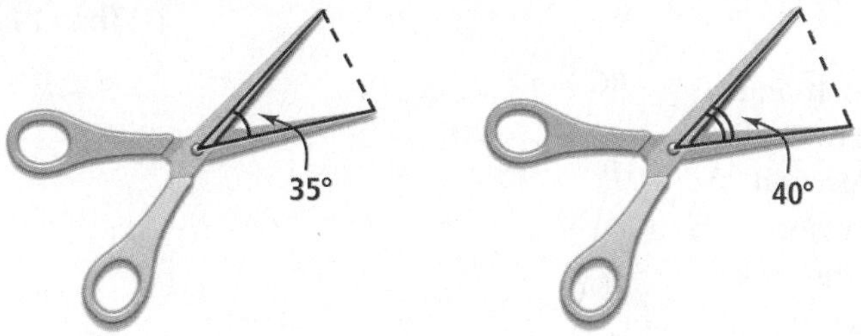

Think

What does not change about both pairs of scissors in the diagram?

Practice 3. The diagram below shows a robotic arm in two different positions. In which position is the tip of the robotic arm closer to the base? Use the Hinge Theorem to justify your answer.

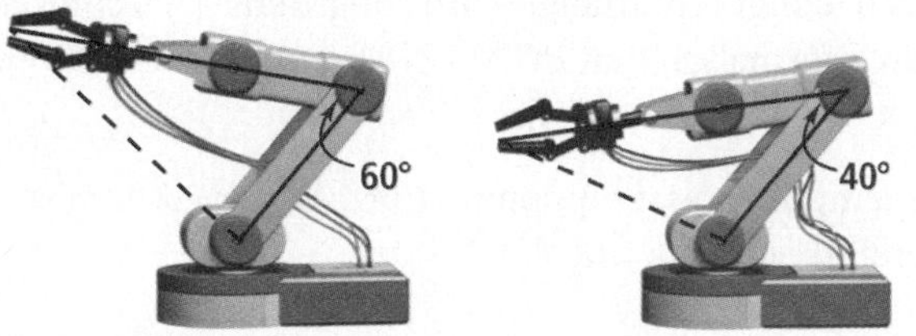

The Converse of the Hinge Theorem is also true. The proof of the converse is an indirect proof.

take note

Theorem 35 Converse of the Hinge Theorem (SSS Inequality)

Theorem	If . . .	Then . . .
If two sides of one triangle are congruent to two sides of another triangle, and the third sides are not congruent, then the larger included angle is opposite the longer third side.	$BC > YZ$	$m\angle A > m\angle X$

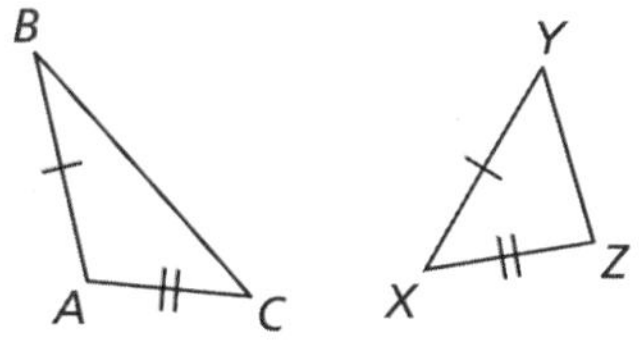

Proof Indirect Proof of the Converse of the Hinge Theorem (SSS Inequality)

Given: $\overline{AB} \cong \overline{XY}$, $\overline{AC} \cong \overline{XZ}$, $BC > YZ$

Prove: $m\angle A > m\angle X$

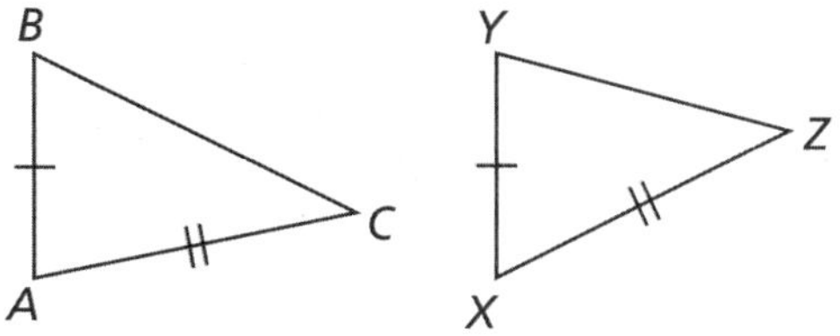

Step 1 Assume temporarily that $m\angle A \ngtr m\angle X$. This means either $m\angle A < m\angle X$ or $m\angle A = m\angle X$.

Step 2 If $m\angle A < m\angle X$, then $BC < YZ$ by the Hinge Theorem. This contradicts the given information that $BC > YZ$. Therefore, the assumption that $m\angle A < m\angle X$ must be false.

If $m\angle A = m\angle X$, then $\triangle ABC \cong \triangle XYZ$ by SAS. If the two triangles are congruent, then $BC = YZ$ because corresponding parts of congruent triangles are congruent. This contradicts the given information that $BC > YZ$. Therefore, the assumption that $m\angle A = m\angle X$ must be false.

Step 3 The temporary assumption that $m\angle A \ngtr m\angle X$ is false. Therefore, $m\angle A > m\angle X$.

ONLINE PROBLEMS

Problem 3 Using the Converse of the Hinge Theorem

Got It? What is the range of possible values for x in the figure at the right?

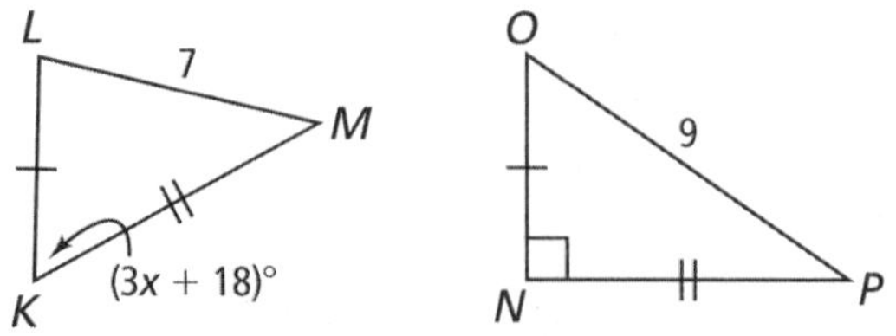

Practice **Algebra** Find the range of possible values for each variable.

4. 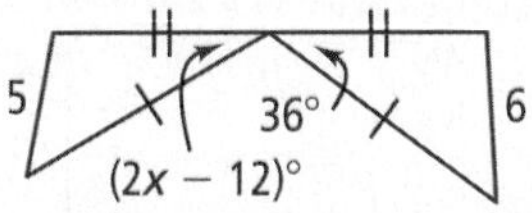

5. 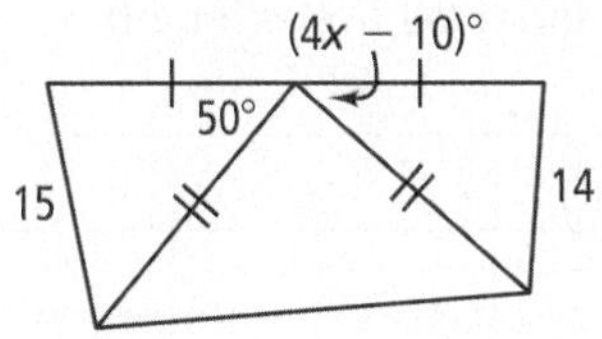

Problem 4 Proving Relationships in Triangles

Got It? **Given:** $m\angle MON = 80$, O is the midpoint of $\overline{LN}$

Prove: $LM > MN$

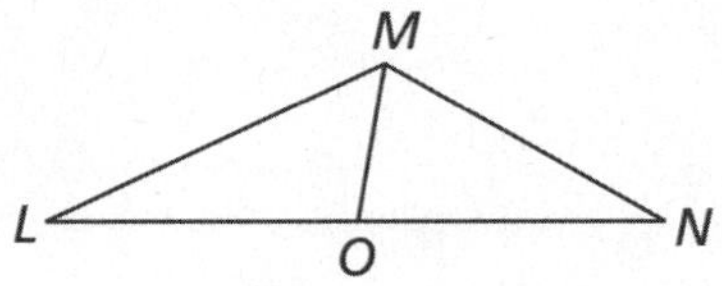

Think

How can you find the measure of $\angle MOL$?

Practice

6. **Developing Proof** Complete the following proof.

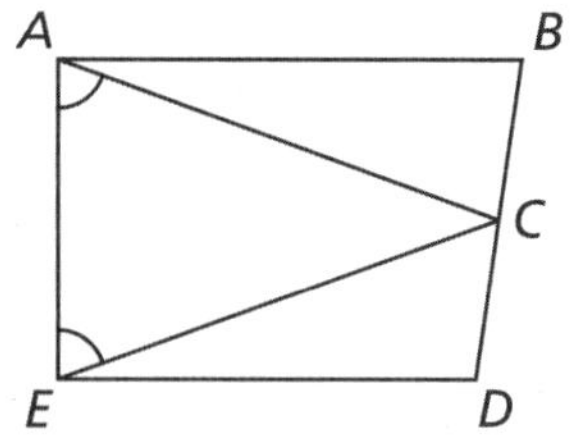

Given: C is the midpoint of $\overline{BD}$, $m\angle EAC = m\angle AEC$, $m\angle BCA > m\angle DCE$

Prove: $AB > ED$

Statements	Reasons
1) $m\angle EAC = m\angle AEC$	1) Given
2) $AC = EC$	2) a. ____________
3) C is the midpoint of $\overline{BD}$.	3) b. ____________
4) $\overline{BC} \cong \overline{CD}$	4) c. ____________
5) d. ____________	5) $\cong$ segments have = length.
6) $m\angle BCA > m\angle DCE$	6) e. ____________
7) $AB > ED$	7) f. ____________

Lesson Check

Do you know HOW?

Write an inequality relating the given side lengths or angle measures.

7. FD and BC

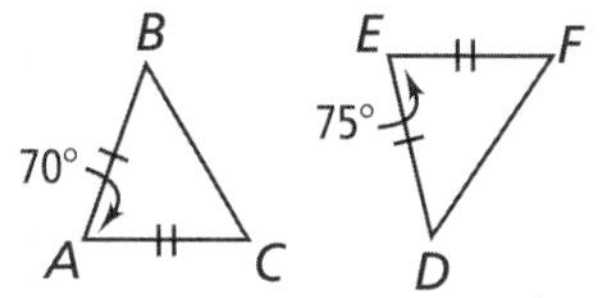

8. $m\angle UST$ and $m\angle VST$

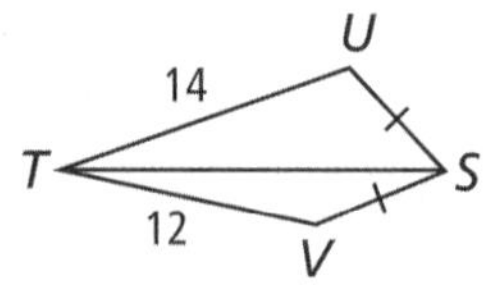

Do you UNDERSTAND?

MATHEMATICAL PRACTICES

9. **Vocabulary** Explain why *Hinge Theorem* is an appropriate name for Theorem 34.

10. **Error Analysis** From the figure at the right, your friend concludes that $m\angle BAD > m\angle BCD$. How would you correct your friend's mistake?

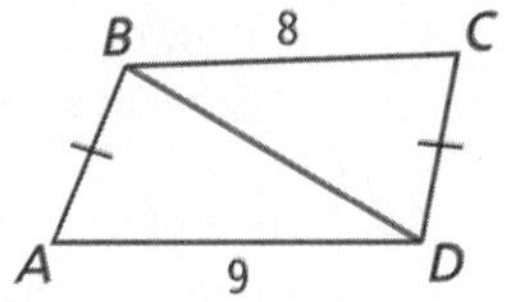

11. **Compare and Contrast** How are the Hinge Theorem and the SAS Congruence Postulate similar?

More Practice and Problem-Solving Exercises

MATHEMATICAL PRACTICES

B Apply

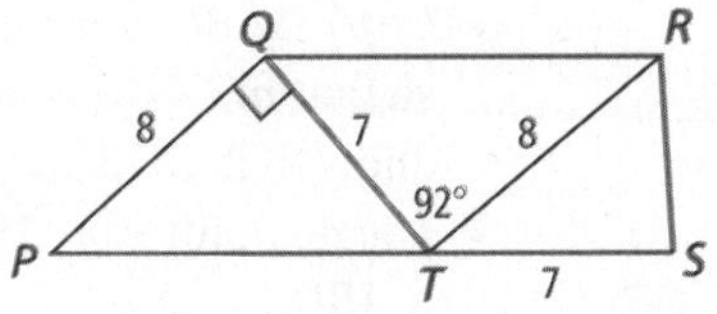

Copy and complete with > or <. Explain your reasoning.

12. PT ■ QR

13. $m\angle QTR$ ■ $m\angle RTS$

14. PT ■ RS

15. a. **Error Analysis** Your classmate draws the figure at the right. Explain why the figure cannot have the labeled dimensions.

b. **Open-Ended** Describe a way you could change the dimensions to make the figure possible.

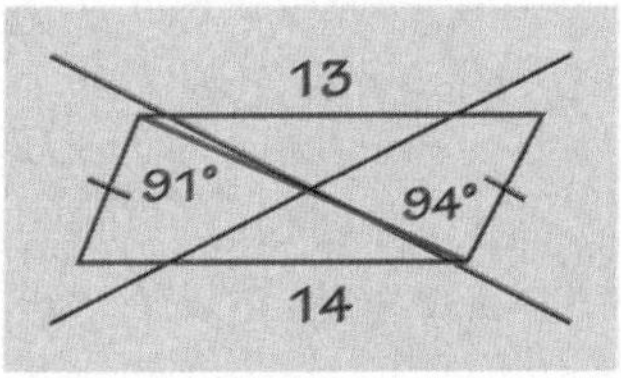

16. Reasoning The legs of a right isosceles triangle are congruent to the legs of an isosceles triangle with an 80° vertex angle. Which triangle has a greater perimeter? How do you know?

17. Think About a Plan Ship A and Ship B leave from the same point in the ocean. Ship A travels 150 mi due west, turns 65° toward north, and then travels another 100 mi. Ship B travels 150 mi due east, turns 70° toward south, and then travels another 100 mi. Which ship is farther from the starting point? Explain.

- How can you use the given angle measures?
- How does the Hinge Theorem help you to solve this problem?

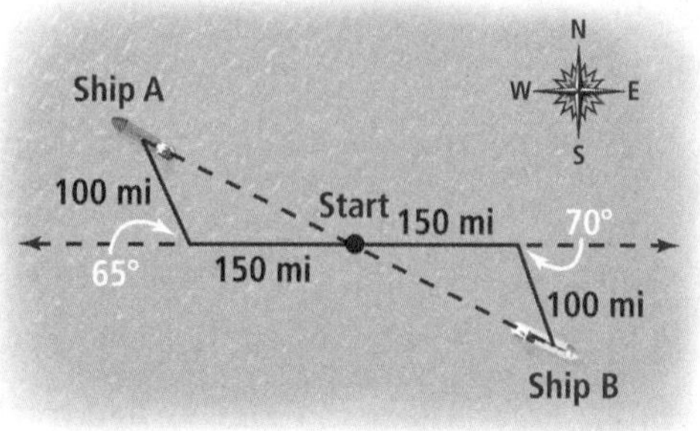

18. Which of the following lists the segment lengths in order from least to greatest?

(A) *CD, AB, DE, BC, EF*

(B) *EF, DE, AB, BC, CD*

(C) *BC, DE, EF, AB, CD*

(D) *EF, BC, DE, AB, CD*

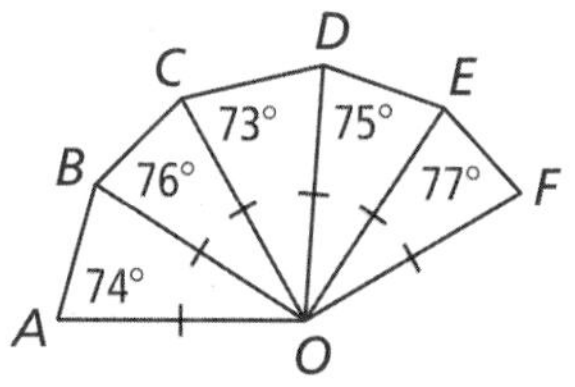

Proof 19. Use the figure at the right.

Given: $\triangle ABE$ is isosceles with vertex $\angle B$, $\triangle ABE \cong \triangle CBD$, $m\angle EBD > m\angle ABE$

Prove: $ED > AE$

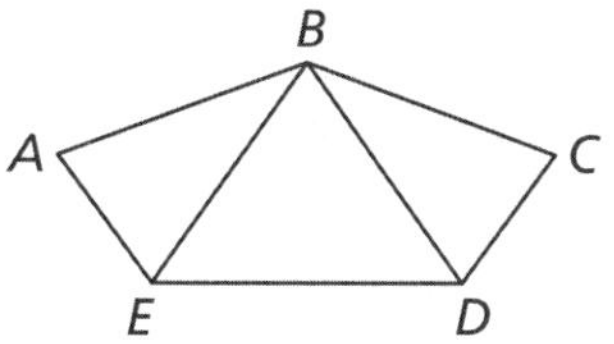

Challenge

20. Coordinate Geometry $\triangle ABC$ has vertices $A(0, 7)$, $B(-1, -2)$, $C(2, -1)$, and $O(0, 0)$. Show that $m\angle AOB > m\angle AOC$.

Proof 21. Use the plan below to complete a proof of the Hinge Theorem: If two sides of one triangle are congruent to two sides of another triangle and the included angles are not congruent, then the longer third side is opposite the larger included angle.

Given: $\overline{AB} \cong \overline{XY}$, $\overline{BC} \cong \overline{YZ}$, $m\angle B > m\angle Y$

Prove: $AC > XZ$

Plan for proof:

- Copy $\triangle ABC$. Locate point D outside $\triangle ABC$ so that $m\angle CBD = m\angle ZYX$ and $BD = YX$. Show that $\triangle DBC \cong \triangle XYZ$.
- Locate point F on $\overline{AC}$, so that $\overline{BF}$ bisects $\angle ABD$.
- Show that $\triangle ABF \cong \triangle DBF$ and that $\overline{AF} \cong \overline{DF}$.
- Show that $AC = FC + DF$.
- Use the Triangle Inequality Theorem to write an inequality that relates DC to the lengths of the other sides of $\triangle FCD$.
- Relate DC and XZ.

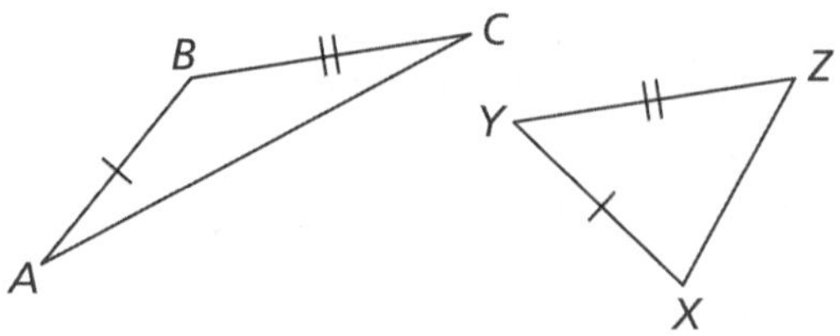

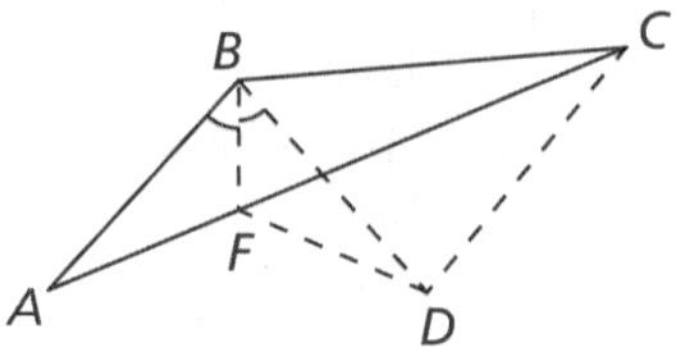

8 Chapter Review

MathXL® for School
Go to pearsonsuccessnet.com

8-1 Midsegments of Triangles

Quick Review

A **midsegment of a triangle** is a segment that connects the midpoints of two sides. A midsegment is parallel to the third side and is half as long.

Example

Algebra Find the value of x.

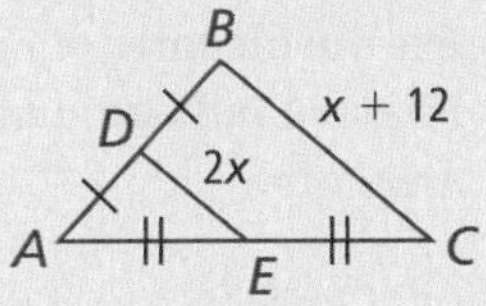

$\overline{DE}$ is a midsegment because D and E are midpoints.

$DE = \frac{1}{2}BC$	△ Midsegment Theorem
$2x = \frac{1}{2}(x + 12)$	Substitute.
$4x = x + 12$	Multiply each side by 2.
$3x = 12$	Subtract x from each side.
$x = 4$	Divide each side by 3.

Exercises

Algebra Find the value of x.

1.

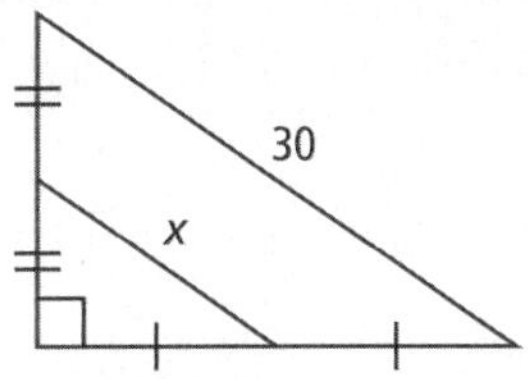

2.

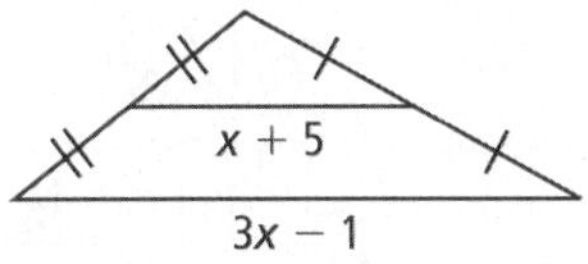

3. $\triangle ABC$ has vertices $A(0, 0)$, $B(2, 2)$, and $C(5, -1)$. Find the coordinates of L, the midpoint of $\overline{AC}$, and M, the midpoint of $\overline{BC}$. Verify that $\overline{LM} \parallel \overline{AB}$ and $LM = \frac{1}{2}AB$.

8-2 Perpendicular and Angle Bisectors

Quick Review

The **Perpendicular Bisector Theorem** together with its converse states that P is equidistant from A and B if and only if P is on the perpendicular bisector of $\overline{AB}$.

The **distance from a point to a line** is the length of the perpendicular segment from the point to the line.

The **Angle Bisector Theorem** together with its converse states that P is equidistant from the sides of an angle if and only if P is on the angle bisector.

Example

In the figure, $QP = 4$ and $AB = 8$. Find QR and CB.

Q is on the bisector of $\angle ABC$, so $QR = QP = 4$. B is on the perpendicular bisector of $\overline{AC}$, so $CB = AB = 8$.

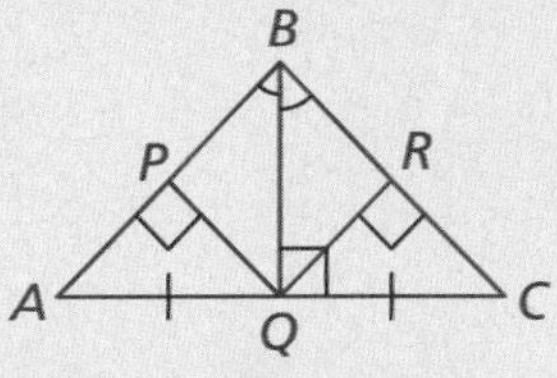

Exercises

4. **Writing** Describe how to find all the points on a baseball field that are equidistant from second base and third base.

In the figure, $m\angle DBE = 50$. Find each of the following.

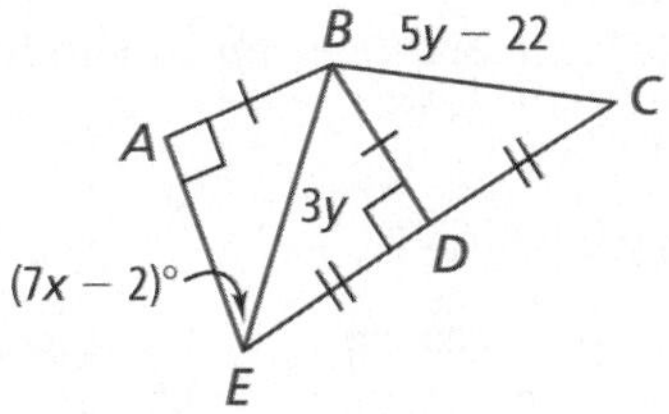

5. $m\angle BED$
6. $m\angle BEA$
7. x
8. y
9. BE
10. BC

8-3 Bisectors in Triangles

Quick Review

When three or more lines intersect in one point, they are **concurrent.**

- The point of concurrency of the perpendicular bisectors of a triangle is the **circumcenter of the triangle.**
- The point of concurrency of the angle bisectors of a triangle is the **incenter of the triangle.**

Example

Identify the incenter of the triangle.

The incenter of a triangle is the point of concurrency of the angle bisectors. $\overline{MR}$ and $\overline{LQ}$ are angle bisectors that intersect at *Z*. So, *Z* is the incenter.

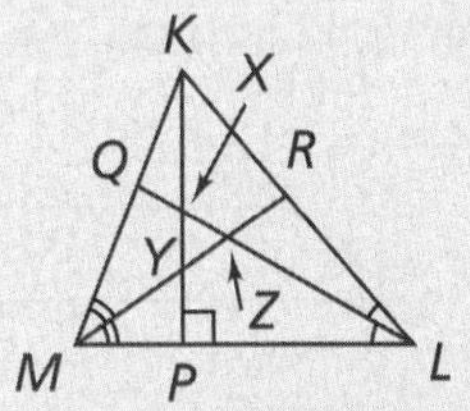

Exercises

Find the coordinates of the circumcenter of $\triangle DEF$.

11. $D(6, 0)$, $E(0, 6)$, $F(-6, 0)$

12. $D(0, 0)$, $E(6, 0)$, $F(0, 4)$

13. $D(5, -1)$, $E(-1, 3)$, $F(3, -1)$

14. $D(2, 3)$, $E(8, 3)$, $F(8, -1)$

***P* is the incenter of $\triangle XYZ$. Find the indicated angle measure.**

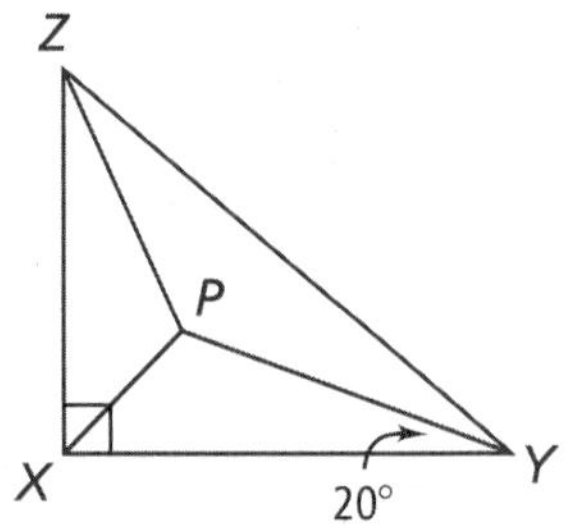

15. $m\angle PXY$

16. $m\angle XYZ$

17. $m\angle PZX$

8-4 Medians and Altitudes

Quick Review

A **median of a triangle** is a segment from a vertex to the midpoint of the opposite side. An **altitude of a triangle** is a perpendicular segment from a vertex to the line containing the opposite side.

- The point of concurrency of the medians of a triangle is the **centroid of the triangle.** The centroid is two thirds the distance from each vertex to the midpoint of the opposite side.
- The point of concurrency of the altitudes of a triangle is the **orthocenter of the triangle.**

Example

If $PB = 6$, what is SB?

S is the centroid because $\overline{AQ}$ and $\overline{CR}$ are medians. So, $SB = \frac{2}{3}PB = \frac{2}{3}(6) = 4$.

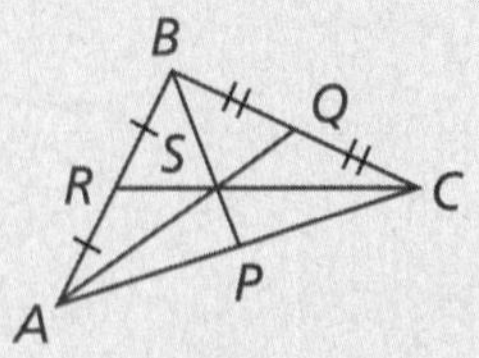

Exercises

Determine whether $\overline{AB}$ is a *median*, an *altitude*, or *neither*. Explain.

18.

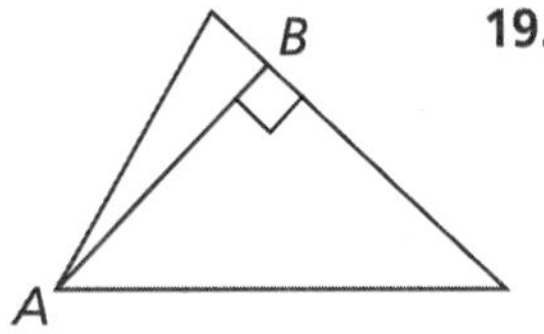

19.

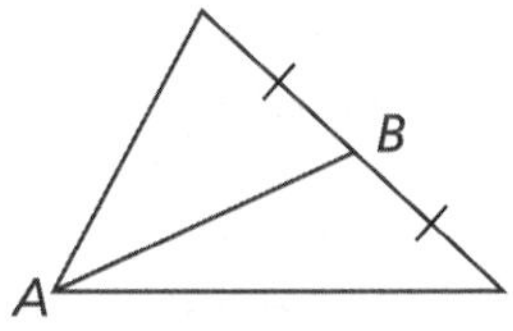

20. $\triangle PQR$ has medians $\overline{QM}$ and $\overline{PN}$ that intersect at *Z*. If $ZM = 4$, find QZ and QM.

$\triangle ABC$ has vertices $A(2, 3)$, $B(-4, -3)$, and $C(2, -3)$. Find the coordinates of each point of concurrency.

21. centroid

22. orthocenter

8-5 Indirect Proof

Quick Review

In an **indirect proof**, you first assume temporarily the opposite of what you want to prove. Then you show that this temporary assumption leads to a contradiction.

Example

Which two statements contradict each other?

I. The perimeter of $\triangle ABC$ is 14.
II. $\triangle ABC$ is isosceles.
III. The side lengths of $\triangle ABC$ are 3, 5, and 6.

An isosceles triangle can have a perimeter of 14.

The perimeter of a triangle with side lengths 3, 5, and 6 is 14.

An isosceles triangle must have two sides of equal length. Statements II and III contradict each other.

Exercises

Write a convincing argument that uses indirect reasoning.

23. The product of two numbers is even. Show that at least one of the numbers must be even.

24. Two lines in the same plane are not parallel. Show that a third line in the plane must intersect at least one of the two lines.

25. Show that a triangle can have at most one obtuse angle.

26. Show that an equilateral triangle cannot have an obtuse angle.

27. The sum of three integers is greater than 9. Show that one of the integers must be greater than 3.

8-6 and 8-7 Inequalities in Triangles

Quick Review

For any triangle,

- the measure of an exterior angle is greater than the measure of each of its remote interior angles
- if two sides are not congruent, then the larger angle lies opposite the longer side
- if two angles are not congruent, then the longer side lies opposite the larger angle
- the sum of any two side lengths is greater than the third

The **Hinge Theorem** states that if two sides of one triangle are congruent to two sides of another triangle, and the included angles are not congruent, then the longer third side is opposite the larger included angle.

Example

Which is greater, BC or AD?

$\overline{BA} \cong \overline{CD}$ and $\overline{BD} \cong \overline{DB}$, so $\triangle ABD$ and $\triangle CDB$ have two pairs of congruent corresponding sides. Since $60 > 45$, you know $BC > AD$ by the Hinge Theorem.

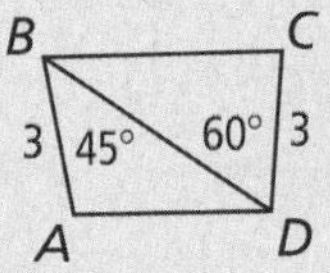

Exercises

28. In $\triangle RST$, $m\angle R = 70$ and $m\angle S = 80$. List the sides of $\triangle RST$ in order from shortest to longest.

Is it possible for a triangle to have sides with the given lengths? Explain.

29. 5 in., 8 in., 15 in.

30. 10 cm, 12 cm, 20 cm

31. The lengths of two sides of a triangle are 12 ft and 13 ft. Find the range of possible lengths for the third side.

Use the figure below. Complete each statement with $>$, $<$, or $=$.

32. $m\angle BAD$ ■ $m\angle ABD$

33. $m\angle CBD$ ■ $m\angle BCD$

34. $m\angle ABD$ ■ $m\angle CBD$

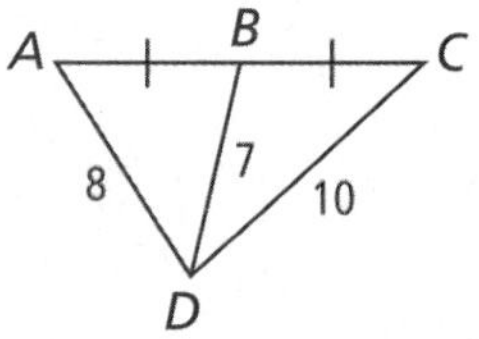

8 *Pull It* All Together

PERFORMANCE TASK

ASSESSMENT

Estimating the Length of a Hiking Trail

A group of hikers plan to hike from the campground lookout tower to the hut. To challenge the group, the leader gives them the diagram below. (All distances are given in kilometers.) The dashed line shows the trail they will take, but the distances along the trail are unknown.

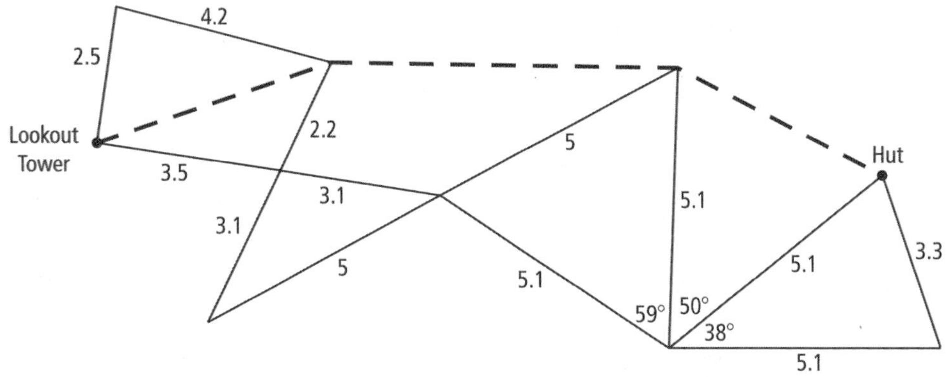

The group must determine the best lower bound and the best upper bound for the length of the trail. To do this, they are allowed to use the Triangle Inequality Theorem and the Hinge Theorem.

Task Description

Find a range in kilometers for the length of the trail.

- Do you need to draw any additional segments in the diagram to help you estimate the length of the trail?
- The trail from the lookout tower to the hut includes three segments. How can you find a range for each segment? How do these ranges lead you to determine the lower and upper bounds for the length of the trail?

CHAPTER 9

Get Ready!

Properties of Parallel Lines

Algebra **Use properties of parallel lines to find the value of *x*.**

1.

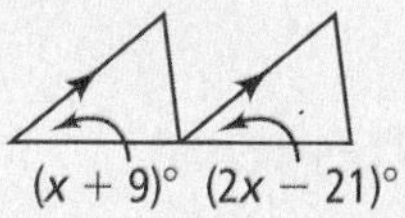

2.

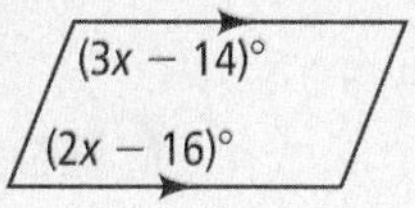

3.

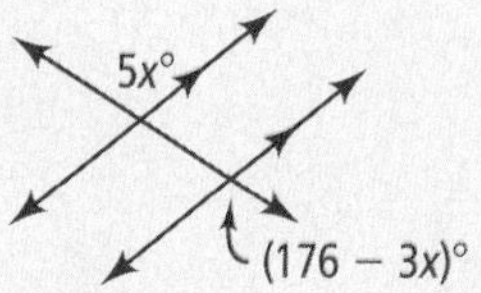

Proving Lines Parallel

Algebra **Determine whether $\overline{AB}$ is parallel to $\overline{CD}$.**

4.

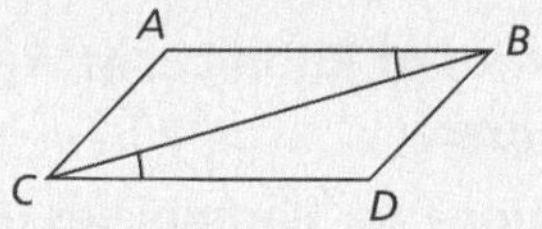

5.

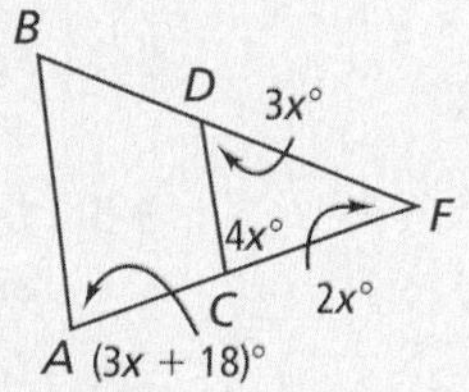

6.

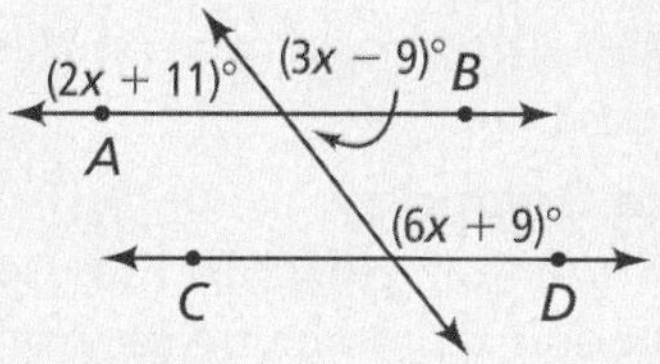

Using Slope to Determine Parallel and Perpendicular Lines

Algebra **Determine whether each pair of lines is *parallel, perpendicular,* or *neither.***

7. $y = -2x; y = -2x + 4$ **8.** $y = -\frac{3}{5}x + 1; y = \frac{5}{3}x - 3$ **9.** $2x - 3y = 1; 3x - 2y = 8$

Proving Triangles Congruent

Determine the postulate or theorem that makes each pair of triangles congruent.

10.

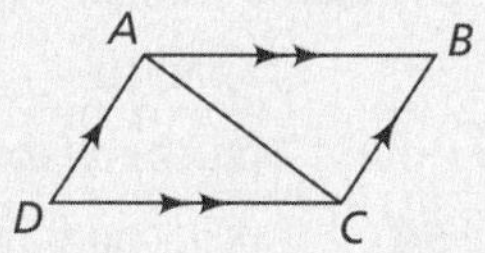

11.

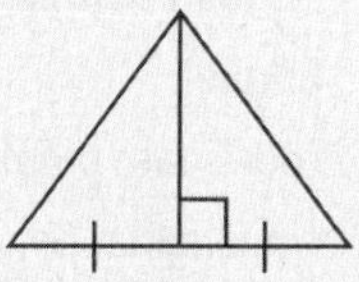

12.

Looking Ahead Vocabulary

13. You know the meaning of *equilateral.* What do you think an *equiangular* polygon is?

14. When a team wins two *consecutive* gold medals, it means they have won two gold medals in a row. What do you think two *consecutive* angles in a quadrilateral means?

CHAPTER 9

Proving Theorems About Quadrilaterals

Big Ideas

1 Measurement
Essential Question How can you find the sum of the measures of polygon angles?

2 Reasoning and Proof
Essential Question How can you classify quadrilaterals?

3 Coordinate Geometry
Essential Question How can you use coordinate geometry to prove general relationships?

© Domains

- Congruence
- Similarity, Right Triangles, and Trigonometry
- Expressing Geometric Properties with Equations

Chapter Preview

9-1 The Polygon Angle-Sum Theorems
9-2 Properties of Parallelograms
9-3 Proving That a Quadrilateral Is a Parallelogram
9-4 Properties of Rhombuses, Rectangles, and Squares
9-5 Conditions for Rhombuses, Rectangles, and Squares
9-6 Trapezoids and Kites
9-7 Applying Coordinate Geometry
9-8 Proofs Using Coordinate Geometry

Vocabulary

English/Spanish Vocabulary Audio Online:

English	Spanish
coordinate proof, *p. 649*	prueba de coordenadas
equiangular polygon, *p. 594*	polígono equiángulo
equilateral polygon, *p. 594*	polígono equilátero
isosceles trapezoid, *p. 636*	trapecio isósceles
kite, *p. 640*	cometa
midsegment of a trapezoid, *p. 638*	segmento medio de un trapecio
parallelogram, *p. 600*	paralelogramo
rectangle, *p. 619*	rectángulo
regular polygon, *p. 594*	polígono regular
rhombus, *p. 619*	rombo
trapezoid, *p. 636*	trapecio

Interactive Digital Path

Log in to **pearsonsuccessnet.com** and click on Interactive Digital Path to access the Solve Its and animated Problems.

9-1 The Polygon Angle-Sum Theorems

G.CO.9 Prove theorems about lines and angles . . . Also **G.SRT.5**

Objectives To find the sum of the measures of the interior angles of a polygon
To find the sum of the measures of the exterior angles of a polygon

Solve It! Write your solution to the Solve It in the space below.

The Solve It is related to a formula for the sum of the interior angle measures of a polygon. (In this textbook, a polygon is convex unless otherwise stated.)

Essential Understanding The sum of the interior angle measures of a polygon depends on the number of sides the polygon has.

By dividing a polygon with n sides into $(n-2)$ triangles, you can show that the sum of the interior angle measures of any polygon is a multiple of 180.

take note

Theorem 36 Polygon Angle-Sum Theorem

The sum of the measures of the interior angles of an n-gon is $(n-2)180$.

Problem 1 Finding a Polygon Angle Sum

Got It? **a.** What is the sum of the interior angle measures of a 17-gon?

b. **Reasoning** The sum of the interior angle measures of a polygon is 1980. How can you find the number of sides in the polygon?

Practice **Find the sum of the interior angle measures of each polygon.**

1. 35-gon

2. 20-gon

An **equilateral polygon** is a polygon with all sides congruent.

An **equiangular polygon** is a polygon with all angles congruent.

A **regular polygon** is a polygon that is both equilateral and equiangular.

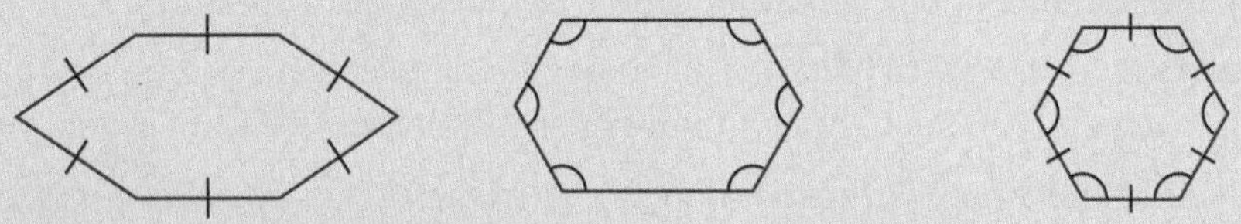

take note

Corollary to the Polygon Angle-Sum Theorem

The measure of each interior angle of a regular n-gon is $\frac{(n-2)180}{n}$.

You will prove the Corollary to the Polygon Angle-Sum Theorem in Exercise 36.

Problem 2 Using the Polygon Angle-Sum Theorem

Got It? What is the measure of each interior angle in a regular nonagon?

Think How does the word *regular* help you answer the question?

A Practice Find the measure of one interior angle in each regular polygon.

3. 

4. 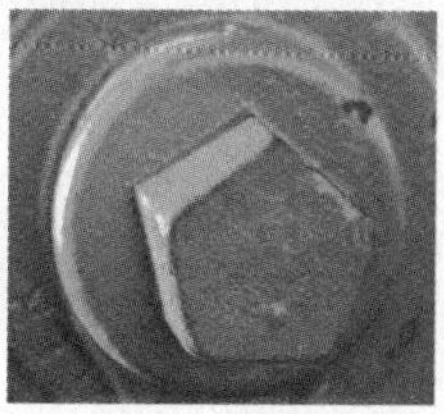

Problem 3 Using the Polygon Angle-Sum Theorem

Got It? What is $m\angle G$ in quadrilateral $EFGH$?

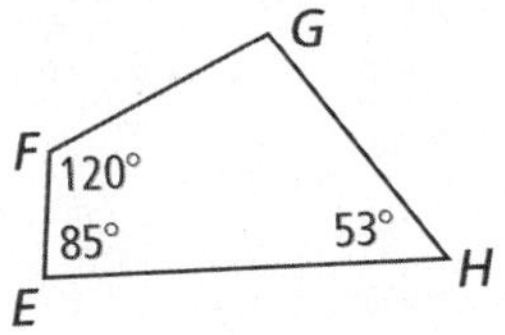

Think

What is the sum of the measures of the angles of a quadrilateral?

A Practice **Algebra** In Exercises 5 and 6, find the missing angle measures.

5. 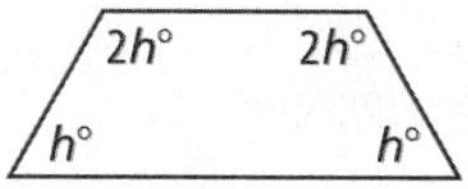

6. 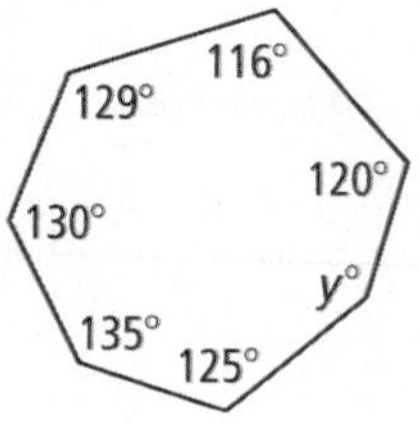

You can draw exterior angles at any vertex of a polygon. The figures below show that the sum of the measures of the exterior angles, one at each vertex, is 360.

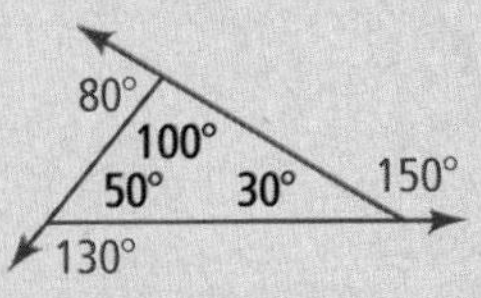

80 + 150 + 130 = 360

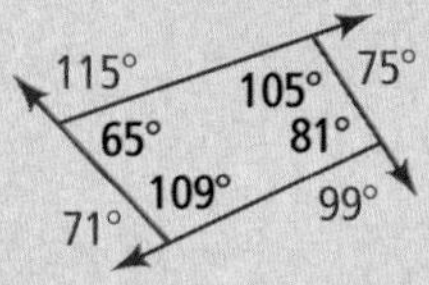

115 + 75 + 99 + 71 = 360

take note

Theorem 37 **Polygon Exterior Angle-Sum Theorem**

The sum of the measures of the exterior angles of a polygon, one at each vertex, is 360.

For the pentagon, $m\angle 1 + m\angle 2 + m\angle 3 + m\angle 4 + m\angle 5 = 360$.

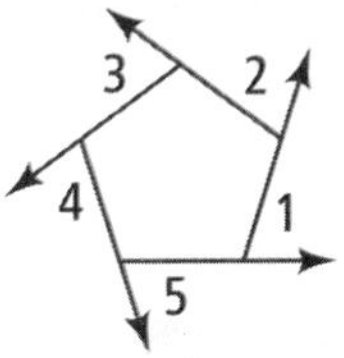

You will prove Theorem 37 in Exercise 32.

ONLINE PROBLEMS

Problem 4 Finding an Exterior Angle Measure

Got It? What is the measure of an exterior angle of a regular nonagon?

A Practice **Find the measure of an exterior angle of each regular polygon.**

7. 36-gon

8. 100-gon

Lesson Check

Do you know HOW?

9. What is the sum of the interior angle measures of an 11-gon?

10. What is the sum of the measures of the exterior angles of a 15-gon?

11. Find the measures of an interior angle and an exterior angle of a regular decagon.

Do you UNDERSTAND?

MATHEMATICAL PRACTICES

12. Vocabulary Can you draw an equiangular polygon that is not equilateral? Explain.

13. Reasoning Which angles are the exterior angles for $\angle 1$? What do you know about their measures? Explain.

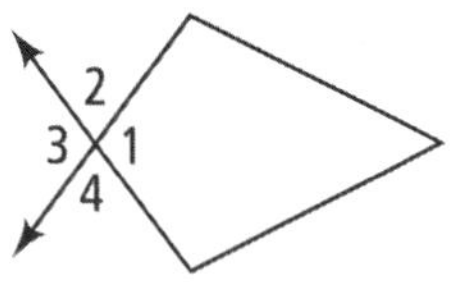

14. Error Analysis Your friend says that she measured an interior angle of a regular polygon as 130. Explain why this result is impossible.

More Practice and Problem-Solving Exercises

MATHEMATICAL PRACTICES

B Apply

The sum of the interior angle measures of a polygon with *n* sides is given. Find *n*.

15. 180 **16.** 1080 **17.** 1980 **18.** 2880

19. Open-Ended Sketch an equilateral polygon that is not equiangular.

20. Stage Design A theater-in-the-round allows for a play to have an audience on all sides. The diagram at the right shows a platform constructed for a theater-in-the-round stage. What type of regular polygon is the largest platform? Find the measure of each numbered angle.

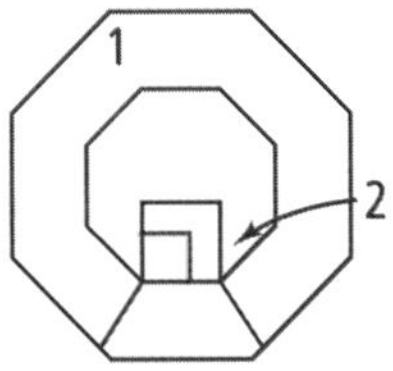

21. Think About a Plan A triangle has two congruent interior angles and an exterior angle that measures 100. Find two possible sets of interior angle measures for the triangle.

- How can a diagram help you?
- What is the sum of the angle measures in a triangle?

Algebra **Find the value of each variable.**

22.

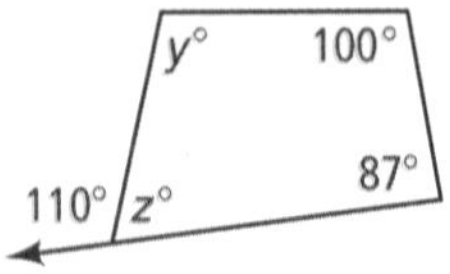

23.

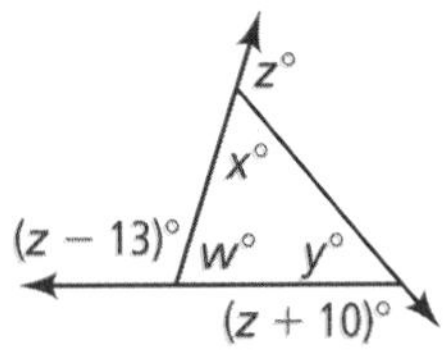

24.

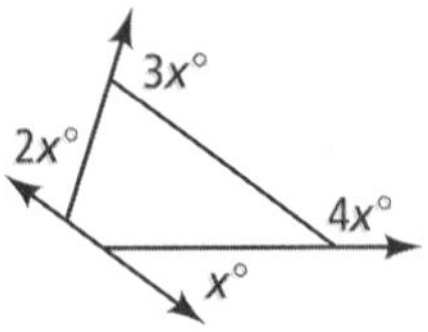

The measure of an exterior angle of a regular polygon is given. Find the measure of an interior angle. Then find the number of sides.

25. 72 **26.** 36 **27.** 18 **28.** 30 **29.** x

Packaging The gift package at the right contains fruit and cheese. The fruit is in a container that has the shape of a regular octagon. The fruit container fits in a square box. A triangular cheese wedge fills each corner of the box.

30. Find the measure of each interior angle of a cheese wedge.

31. Reasoning Show how to rearrange the four pieces of cheese to make a regular polygon. What is the measure of each interior angle of the polygon?

32. Algebra A polygon has n sides. An interior angle of the polygon and an adjacent exterior angle form a straight angle.

a. What is the sum of the measures of the n straight angles?
b. What is the sum of the measures of the n interior angles?
c. Using your answers above, what is the sum of the measures of the n exterior angles?
d. What theorem do the steps above prove?

33. Reasoning Your friend says she has another way to find the sum of the interior angle measures of a polygon. She picks a point inside the polygon, draws a segment to each vertex, and counts the number of triangles. She multiplies the total by 180, and then subtracts 360 from the product. Does her method work? Explain.

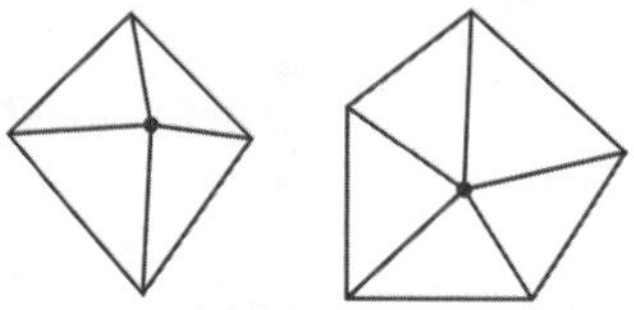

34. Algebra The measure of an interior angle of a regular polygon is three times the measure of an exterior angle of the same polygon. What is the name of the polygon?

Challenge

35. Probability Find the probability that the measure of an interior angle of a regular n-gon is a positive integer when n is an integer and $3 \leq n \leq 12$.

36. a. In the Corollary to the Polygon Angle-Sum Theorem, explain why the measure of an interior angle of a regular n-gon is given by the formulas $\frac{180(n-2)}{n}$ and $180 - \frac{360}{n}$.

b. Use the second formula to explain what happens to the measures of the interior angles of regular n-gons as n becomes a large number. Explain also what happens to the polygons.

37. *ABCDEFGHJK* is a regular decagon. A ray bisects $\angle C$, and another ray bisects $\angle D$. The two rays intersect in the decagon's interior. Find the measure of the acute angles formed by the intersecting rays.

9-2 Properties of Parallelograms

G.CO.11 Prove theorems about parallelograms. Theorems include: opposite sides are congruent, opposite angles are congruent, the diagonals of a parallelogram bisect each other . . . Also **G.SRT.5**

Objectives To use relationships among sides and angles of parallelograms
To use relationships among diagonals of parallelograms

Solve It! Write your solution to the Solve It in the space below.

A **parallelogram** is a quadrilateral with both pairs of opposite sides parallel. In the Solve It, you made some conjectures about the characteristics of a parallelogram. In this lesson, you will verify whether your conjectures are correct.

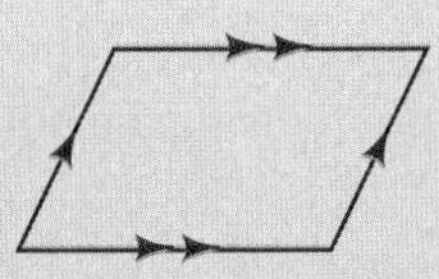

Essential Understanding Parallelograms have special properties regarding their sides, angles, and diagonals.

In a quadrilateral, **opposite sides** do not share a vertex and **opposite angles** do not share a side.

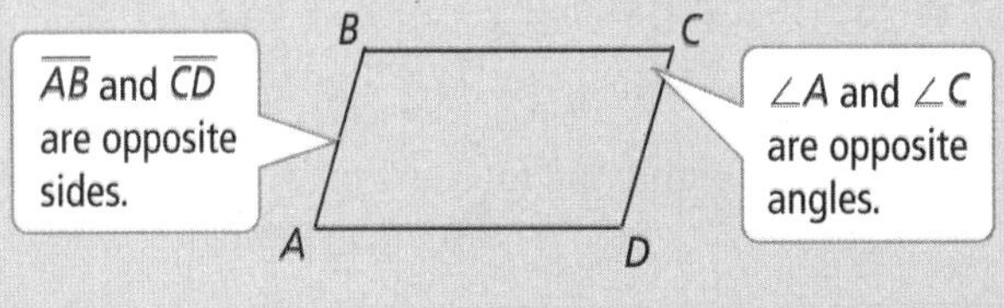

You can abbreviate *parallelogram* with the symbol ▱ and *parallelograms* with the symbol ▱s. You can use what you know about parallel lines and transversals to prove some theorems about parallelograms.

take note

Theorem 38

Theorem	If . . .	Then . . .
If a quadrilateral is a parallelogram, then its opposite sides are congruent.	*ABCD* is a ▱ 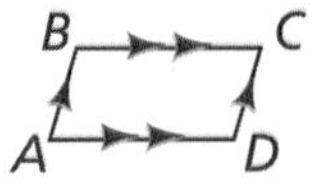	$\overline{AB} \cong \overline{CD}$ and $\overline{BC} \cong \overline{DA}$ 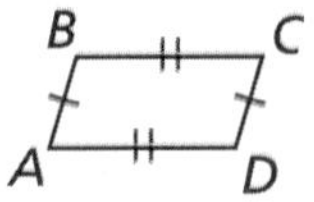

Proof Proof of Theorem 38

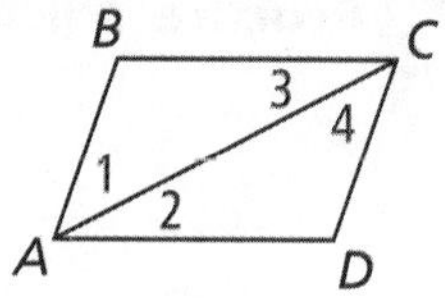

Given: $\square ABCD$

Prove: $\overline{AB} \cong \overline{CD}$ and $\overline{BC} \cong \overline{DA}$

Statements	Reasons
1) $ABCD$ is a parallelogram.	**1)** Given
2) $\overline{AB} \parallel \overline{CD}$ and $\overline{BC} \parallel \overline{DA}$	**2)** Definition of parallelogram
3) $\angle 1 \cong \angle 4$ and $\angle 3 \cong \angle 2$	**3)** If lines are $\parallel$, then alt. int. $\angle$s are $\cong$.
4) $\overline{AC} \cong \overline{AC}$	**4)** Reflexive Property of $\cong$
5) $\triangle ABC \cong \triangle CDA$	**5)** ASA
6) $\overline{AB} \cong \overline{CD}$ and $\overline{BC} \cong \overline{DA}$	**6)** Corresp. parts of $\cong \triangle$s are $\cong$.

Angles of a polygon that share a side are **consecutive angles**. In the diagram, $\angle A$ and $\angle B$ are consecutive angles because they share side $\overline{AB}$.

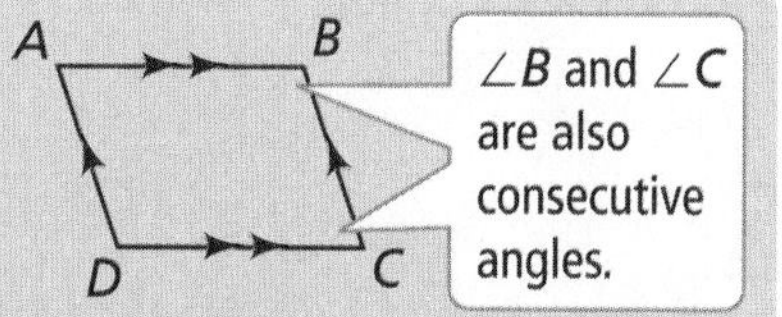

The theorem below uses the fact that consecutive angles of a parallelogram are same-side interior angles of parallel lines.

take note

Theorem 39

Theorem	If . . .	Then . . .
If a quadrilateral is a parallelogram, then its consecutive angles are supplementary.	$ABCD$ is a $\square$ 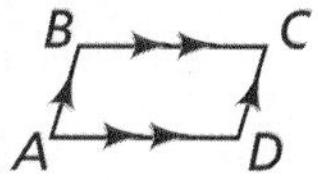	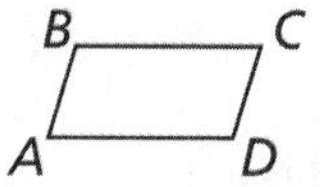 $m\angle A + m\angle B = 180$ $m\angle B + m\angle C = 180$ $m\angle C + m\angle D = 180$ $m\angle D + m\angle A = 180$

You will prove Theorem 39 in Exercise 23.

Problem 1 Using Consecutive Angles

Got It? Suppose you adjust the lamp in Problem 1 so that $m\angle S = 86$. What is $m\angle R$ in $\square PQRS$?

Think

What is the relationship between $\angle R$ and $\angle S$?

A Practice **Algebra** Find the value of x in each parallelogram.

1. 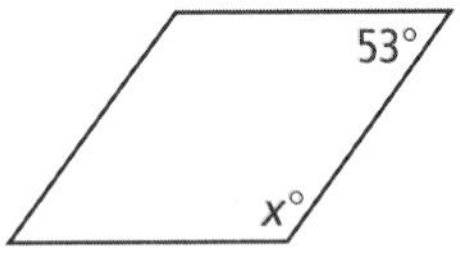

2. 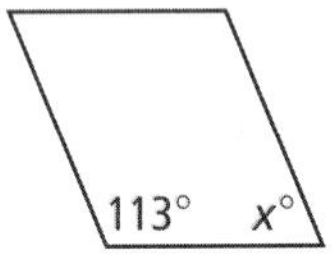

Parallelograms have some other special properties.

take note

Theorem 40

Theorem	If . . .	Then . . .
If a quadrilateral is a parallelogram, then its opposite angles are congruent.	$ABCD$ is a ▱ 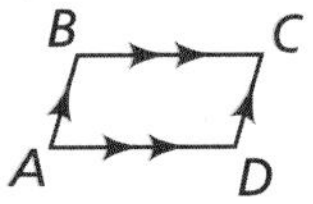	$\angle A \cong \angle C$ and $\angle B \cong \angle D$ 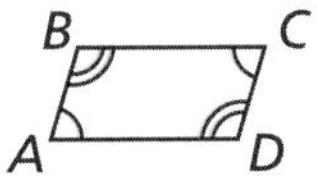

Theorem 41

Theorem	If . . .	Then . . .
If a quadrilateral is a parallelogram, then its diagonals bisect each other.	$ABCD$ is a ▱ 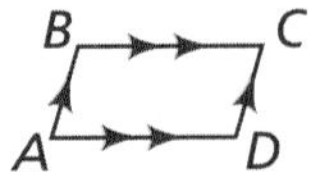	$\overline{AE} \cong \overline{CE}$ and $\overline{BE} \cong \overline{DE}$ 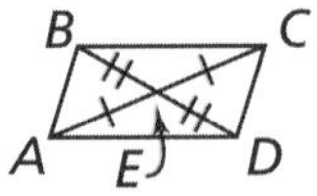

You will prove Theorem 41 in Exercise 3.

A proof of Theorem 40 in Problem 2 uses the consecutive angles of a parallelogram and the fact that supplements of the same angle are congruent.

Problem 2 Using Properties of Parallelograms in a Proof

Got It? Use the diagram at the right.

Given: $\square ABCD$, $\overline{AK} \cong \overline{MK}$
Prove: $\angle BCD \cong \angle CMD$

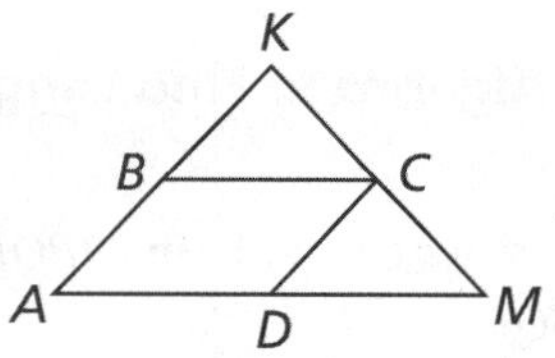

Think

What kind of triangle is $\triangle AKM$?

Practice 3. **Developing Proof** Complete this two-column proof of Theorem 41.

Given: $\square ABCD$
Prove: $\overline{AC}$ and $\overline{BD}$ bisect each other at E.

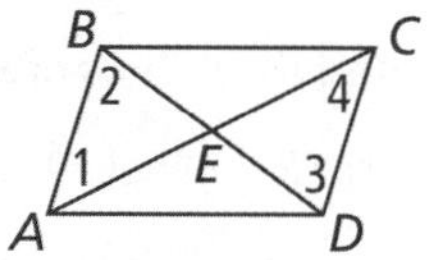

Statements	Reasons
1) $ABCD$ is a parallelogram.	**1)** Given
2) $\overline{AB} \parallel \overline{DC}$	**2) a.** __________
3) $\angle 1 \cong \angle 4$; $\angle 2 \cong \angle 3$	**3) b.** __________
4) $\overline{AB} \cong \overline{DC}$	**4) c.** __________
5) d. __________	**5)** ASA
6) $\overline{AE} \cong \overline{CE}$; $\overline{BE} \cong \overline{DE}$	**6) e.** __________
7) f. __________	**7)** Definition of bisector

You can use Theorem 41 to find unknown lengths in parallelograms.

Problem 3 Using Algebra to Find Lengths

Got It? **a.** Find the values of x and y in $\square PQRS$ at the right. What are PR and SQ?

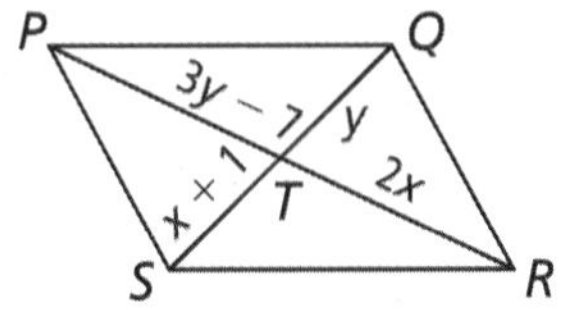

b. Reasoning In Problem 3, does it matter which variable you solve for first? Explain.

Practice **Algebra** Find the values of x and y in $\square PQRS$.

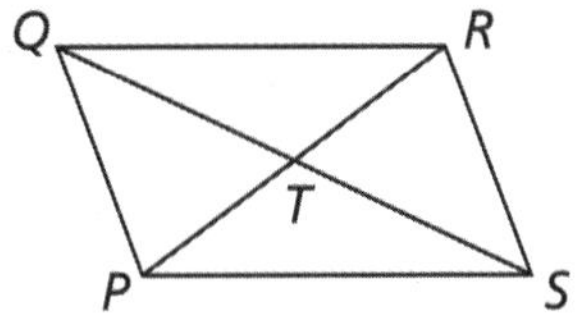

4. $PT = 2x$, $TR = y + 4$, $QT = x + 2$, $TS = y$

5. $PT = x + 2$, $TR = y$, $QT = 2x$, $TS = y + 3$

You will use parallelograms to prove the following theorem.

take note

Theorem 42

Theorem	If . . .	Then . . .
If three (or more) parallel lines cut off congruent segments on one transversal, then they cut off congruent segments on every transversal.	$\overleftrightarrow{AB} \parallel \overleftrightarrow{CD} \parallel \overleftrightarrow{EF}$ and $\overline{AC} \cong \overline{CE}$ 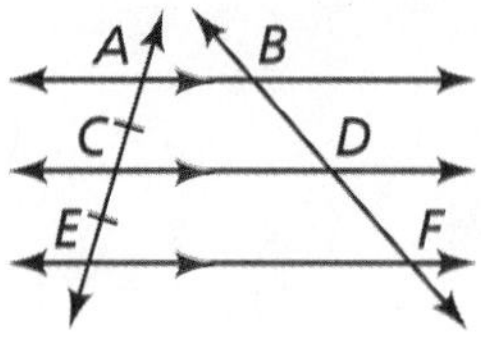	$\overline{BD} \cong \overline{DF}$ 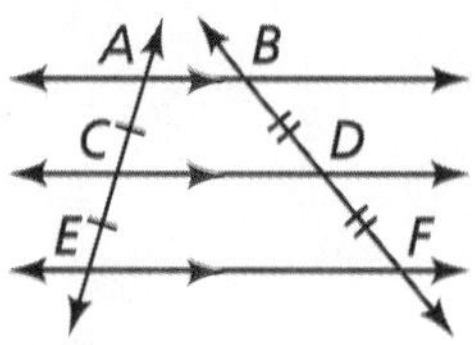

You will prove Theorem 42 in Exercise 34.

Problem 4 Using Parallel Lines and Transversals

Got It? Use the figure in Problem 4, shown at the right. If $EF = FG = GH = 6$ and $AD = 15$, what is CD?

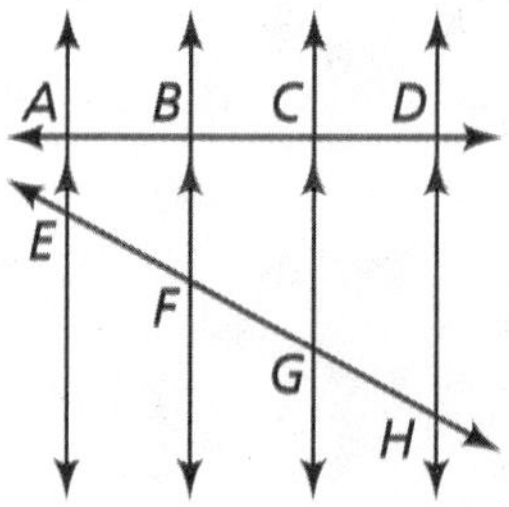

Practice In the figure, $PQ = QR = RS$. Find each length.

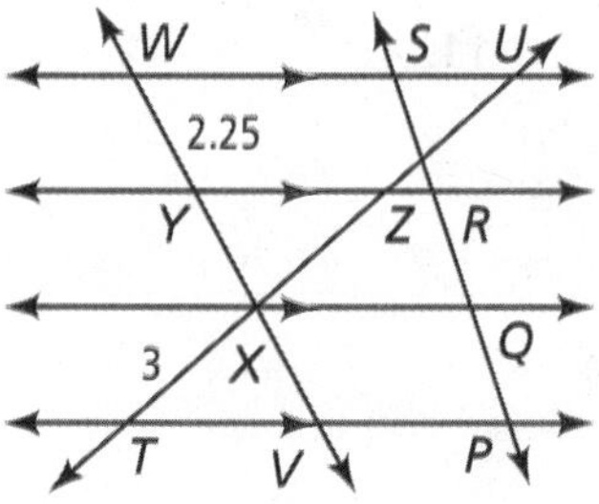

6. ZU

7. WV

Lesson Check

Do you know HOW?

For Exercises 8–11, use the diagram of $\square ABCD$ to find each value.

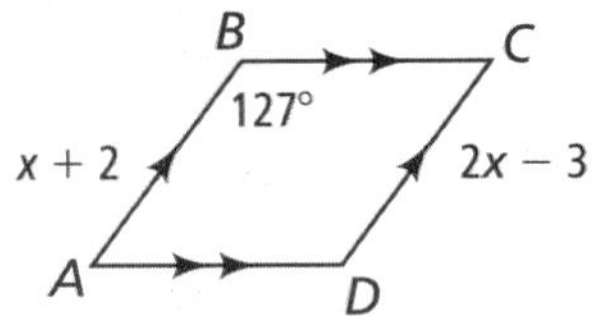

8. $m\angle A$

9. $m\angle D$

10. x

11. AB

12. What are *ED* and *FD* in the figure at the right?

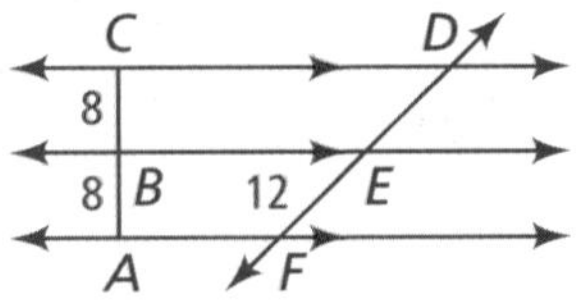

Do you UNDERSTAND?

MATHEMATICAL PRACTICES

13. Reasoning If you know one angle measure of a parallelogram, how do you find the other three angle measures? Explain.

14. Compare and Contrast What is the difference between a quadrilateral and a parallelogram?

15. Error Analysis Your classmate says that $QV = 10$. Explain why the statement may not be correct.

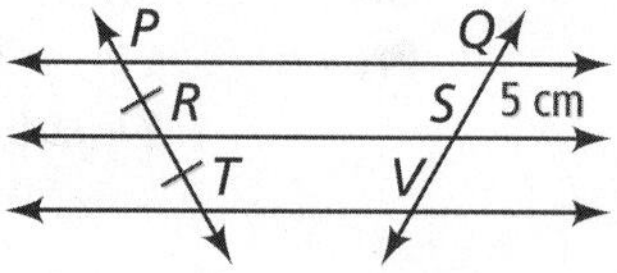

More Practice and Problem-Solving Exercises

MATHEMATICAL PRACTICES

B Apply

Algebra **Find the value(s) of the variable(s) in each parallelogram.**

16.

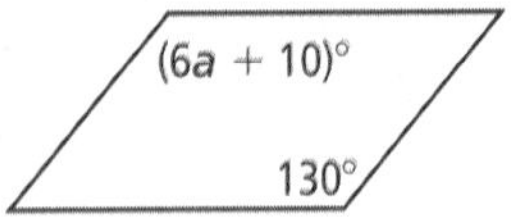

17.

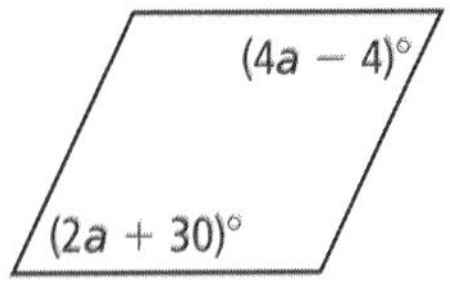

18.

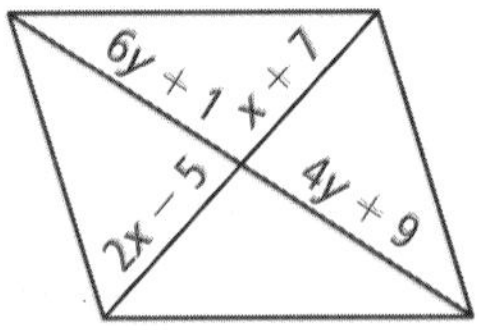

19. Think About a Plan What are the values of x and y in the parallelogram?

- How are the angles related?
- Which variable should you solve for first?

Algebra **Find the value of a. Then find each side length or angle measure.**

20.

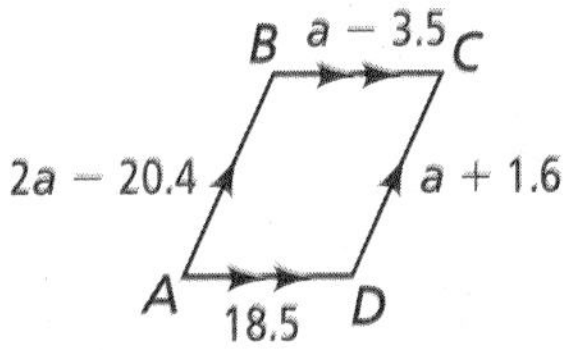

21.

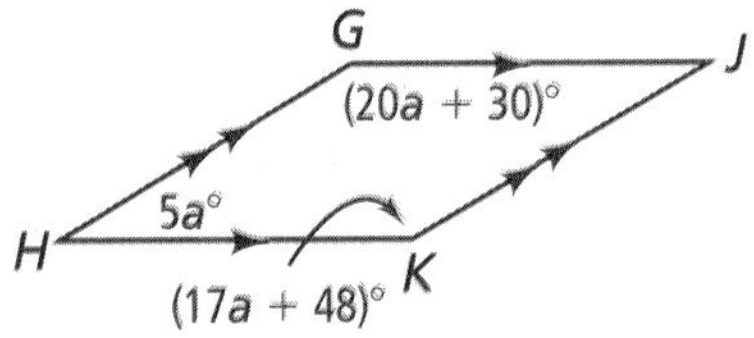

22. Studio Lighting A pantograph is an expandable device shown at the right. Pantographs are used in the television industry in positioning lighting and other equipment. In the photo, points D, E, F, and G are the vertices of a parallelogram. ▱$DEFG$ is one of many parallelograms that change shape as the pantograph extends and retracts.

a. If $DE = 2.5$ ft, what is FG?

b. If $m\angle E = 129$, what is $m\angle G$?

c. What happens to $m\angle D$ as $m\angle E$ increases or decreases? Explain.

Proof **23. Prove Theorem 39.**

Given: ▱$ABCD$

Prove: $\angle A$ is supplementary to $\angle B$.
$\angle A$ is supplementary to $\angle D$.

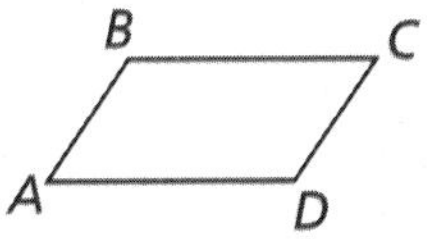

Proof **In the figure at the right, $\overline{GS}$ and $\overline{EH}$ intersect at point N. Use the diagram at the right to complete Exercises 24–26.**

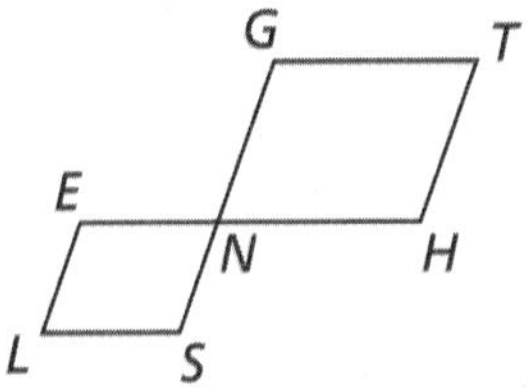

24. Given: ▱$LENS$ and ▱$NGTH$
Prove: $\angle L \cong \angle T$

25. Given: ▱$LENS$ and ▱$NGTH$
Prove: $\overline{LS} \parallel \overline{GT}$

26. Given: ▱$LENS$ and ▱$NGTH$
Prove: $\angle E$ is supplementary to $\angle T$.

Proof **In the figure at the right, points *S*, *Y*, and *T* are collinear, and points *T*, *Z*, and *W* are collinear. Use the figure for Exercises 27 and 28.**

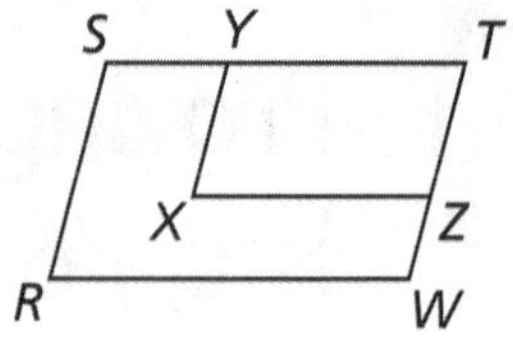

27. Given: $\square RSTW$ and $\square XYTZ$
Prove: $\angle R \cong \angle X$

28. Given: $\square RSTW$ and $\square XYTZ$
Prove: $\overline{XY} \parallel \overline{RS}$

Find the measures of the numbered angles for each parallelogram.

29.

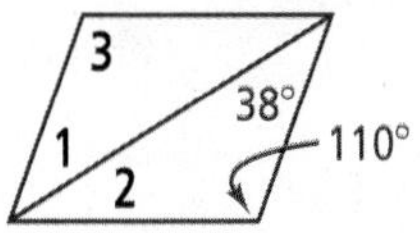

30.

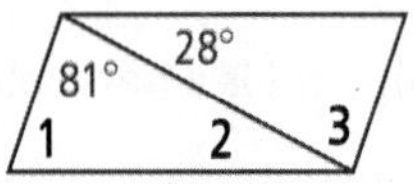

31.

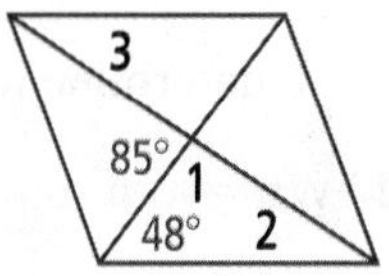

32. Algebra The perimeter of $\square ABCD$ is 92 cm. AD is 7 cm more than twice AB. Find the lengths of all four sides of $\square ABCD$.

Challenge

33. Writing Is there an SSSS congruence theorem for parallelograms? Explain.

Proof **34.** Prove Theorem 42. Use the diagram at the right.

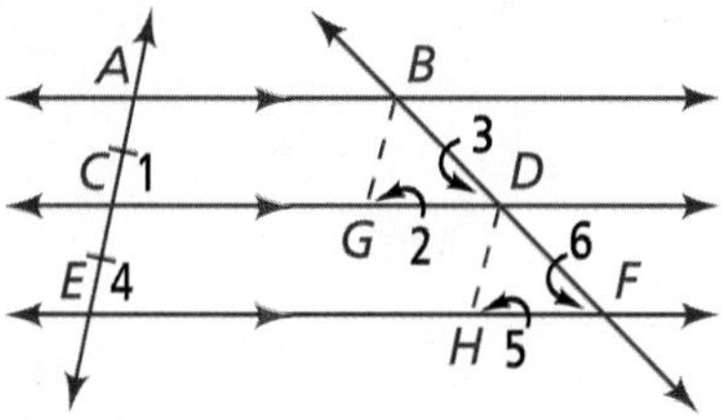

Given: $\overleftrightarrow{AB} \parallel \overleftrightarrow{CD} \parallel \overleftrightarrow{EF}$, $\overline{AC} \cong \overline{CE}$
Prove: $\overline{BD} \cong \overline{DF}$
(*Hint:* Draw lines through B and D parallel to $\overleftrightarrow{AE}$ and intersecting $\overleftrightarrow{CD}$ at G and $\overleftrightarrow{EF}$ at H.)

35. Measurement Explain how to separate a blank card into three strips that are the same height by using lined paper, a straightedge, and Theorem 42.

9-3 Proving That a Quadrilateral Is a Parallelogram

G.CO.11 Prove theorems about parallelograms . . . the diagonals of a parallelogram bisect each other . . .
Also **G.SRT.5**

Objective To determine whether a quadrilateral is a parallelogram

Solve It! Write your solution to the Solve It in the space below.

In the Solve It, you used angle properties to show that lines are parallel. In this lesson, you will apply the same properties to show that a quadrilateral is a parallelogram.

Essential Understanding You can decide whether a quadrilateral is a parallelogram if its sides, angles, and diagonals have certain properties.

In Lesson 9-2, you learned theorems about the properties of parallelograms. In this lesson, you will learn the converses of those theorems. That is, if a quadrilateral has certain properties, then it must be a parallelogram. Theorem 43 is the converse of Theorem 38.

take note

Theorem 43

Theorem	If . . .		Then . . .
If both pairs of opposite sides of a quadrilateral are congruent, then the quadrilateral is a parallelogram.	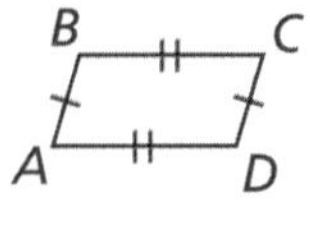	$\overline{AB} \cong \overline{CD}$ $\overline{BC} \cong \overline{DA}$	$ABCD$ is a ▱ 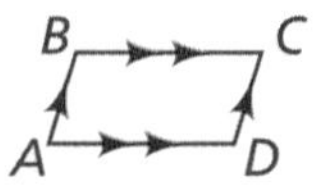

You will prove Theorem 43 in Exercise 15.

Theorems 44 and 45 are the converses of Theorems 39 and 40, respectively. They use angle relationships to conclude that a quadrilateral is a parallelogram.

take note

Theorem 44

Theorem

If an angle of a quadrilateral is supplementary to both of its consecutive angles, then the quadrilateral is a parallelogram.

If . . .

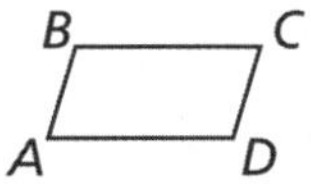

$m\angle A + m\angle B = 180$

$m\angle A + m\angle D = 180$

Then . . .

ABCD is a ▱

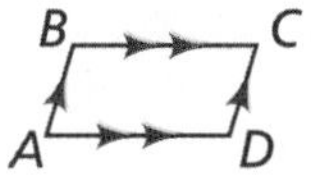

You will prove Theorem 44 in Exercise 16.

Theorem 45

Theorem

If both pairs of opposite angles of a quadrilateral are congruent, then the quadrilateral is a parallelogram.

If . . .

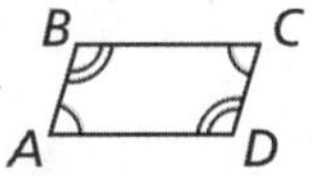

$\angle A \cong \angle C$

$\angle B \cong \angle D$

Then . . .

ABCD is a ▱

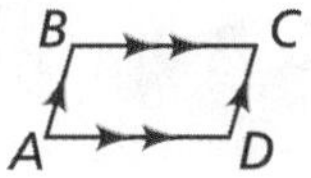

You will prove Theorem 45 in Exercise 13.

You can use algebra together with Theorems 43, 44, and 45 to find segment lengths and angle measures that assume that a quadrilateral is a parallelogram.

ONLINE PROBLEMS

Problem 1 Finding Values for Parallelograms

Got It? Use the diagram below. For what values of *x* and *y* must *EFGH* be a parallelogram?

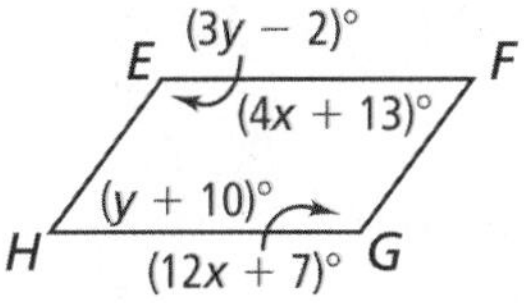

Plan

What theorem should you use?

A Practice **Algebra** **In Exercises 1 and 2, for what values of x and y must *ABCD* be a parallelogram?**

1. 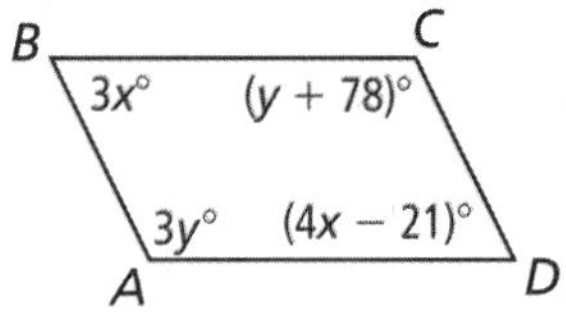

2. 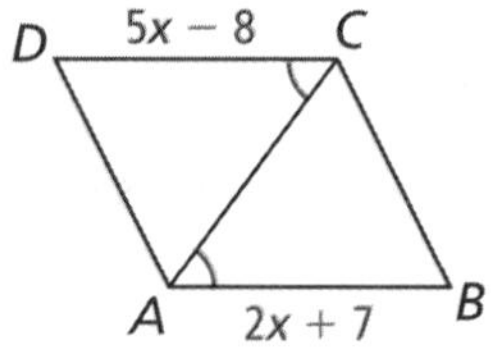

You know that the converses of Theorems 38, 39, and 40 are true. Using what you have learned, you can show that the converse of Theorem 41 is also true.

take note

Theorem 46

Theorem	If . . .		Then . . .
If the diagonals of a quadrilateral bisect each other, then the quadrilateral is a parallelogram.	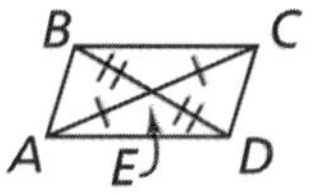	$\overline{AE} = \overline{CE}$ $\overline{BE} = \overline{DE}$	*ABCD* is a ▱ 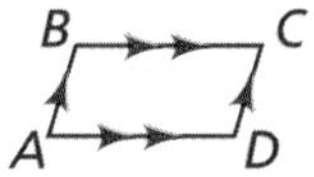

Proof Proof of Theorem 46

Given: $\overline{AC}$ and $\overline{BD}$ bisect each other at E.

Prove: *ABCD* is a parallelogram.

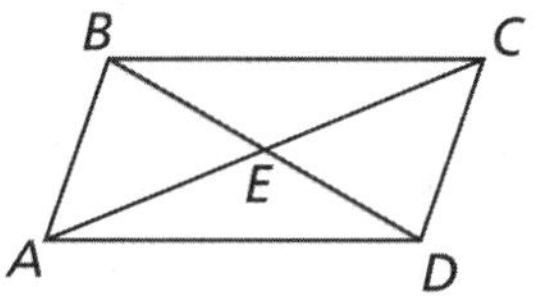

$\overline{AC}$ and $\overline{BD}$ bisect each other at E.
Given

$\angle AEB \cong \angle CED$
Vertical ∠s are ≅.

$\overline{AE} \cong \overline{CE}$, $\overline{BE} \cong \overline{DE}$
Def. of segment bisector

$\angle BEC \cong \angle DEA$
Vertical ∠s are ≅.

$\triangle AEB \cong \triangle CED$
SAS

$\triangle BEC \cong \triangle DEA$
SAS

$\angle BAE \cong \angle DCE$
Corresp. parts of ≅ △s are ≅.

$\angle ECB \cong \angle EAD$
Corresp. parts of ≅ △s are ≅.

$\overline{AB} \parallel \overline{CD}$
If alternate interior ∠s ≅, then lines are ∥.

$\overline{BC} \parallel \overline{AD}$
If alternate interior ∠s ≅, then lines are ∥.

ABCD is a parallelogram.
Def. of parallelogram

Theorem 47 suggests that if you keep two objects of the same length parallel, such as cross-country skis, then the quadrilateral formed by connecting their endpoints is always a parallelogram.

take note

Theorem 47

Theorem	If . . .		Then . . .
If one pair of opposite sides of a quadrilateral is both congruent and parallel, then the quadrilateral is a parallelogram.	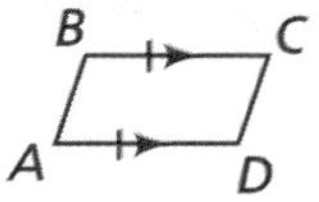	$\overline{BC} \cong \overline{DA}$ $\overline{BC} \parallel \overline{DA}$	$ABCD$ is a ▱ 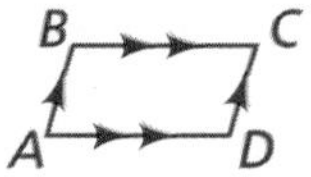

You will prove Theorem 47 in Exercise 14.

Problem 2 Deciding Whether a Quadrilateral Is a Parallelogram

Think

How do you decide if you have enough information?

Got It? Can you prove that the quadrilateral is a parallelogram based on the given information? Explain.

a. Given: $\overline{EF} \cong \overline{GD}$, $\overline{DE} \parallel \overline{FG}$

Prove: $DEFG$ is a parallelogram.

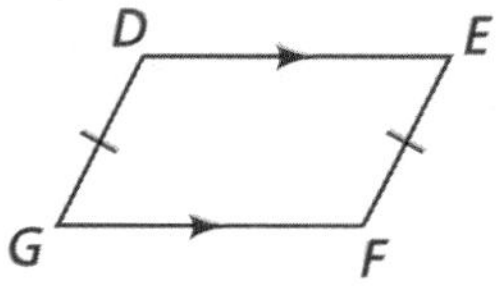

b. Given: $\angle ALN \cong \angle DNL$, $\angle ANL \cong \angle DLN$

Prove: $LAND$ is a parallelogram.

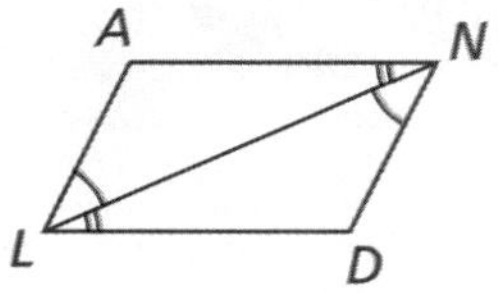

Practice **Algebra Can you prove that the quadrilateral is a parallelogram based on the given information? Explain.**

3.

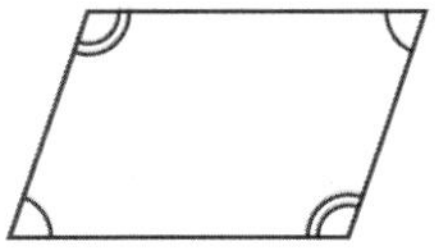

4.

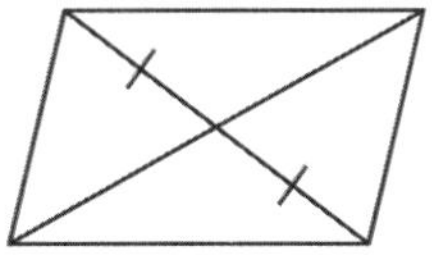

Problem 3 Identifying Parallelograms

Got It? **Reasoning** What is the maximum height that the vehicle lift can elevate the truck? Explain.

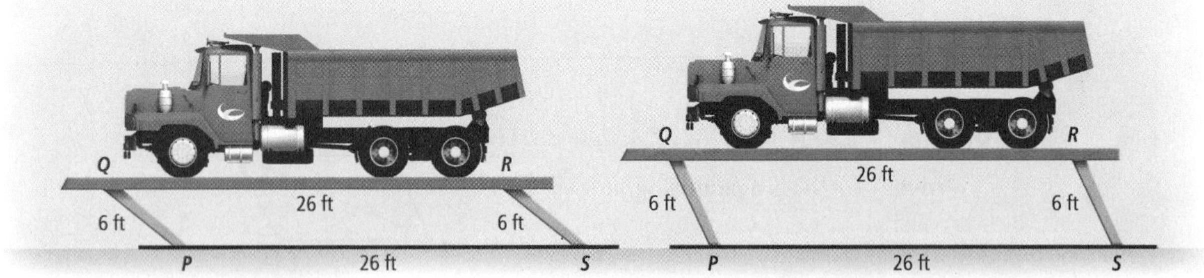

Practice **5. Fishing** Quadrilaterals are formed on the side of this fishing tackle box by the adjustable shelves and connecting pieces. Explain why the shelves are always parallel to each other no matter what their position is.

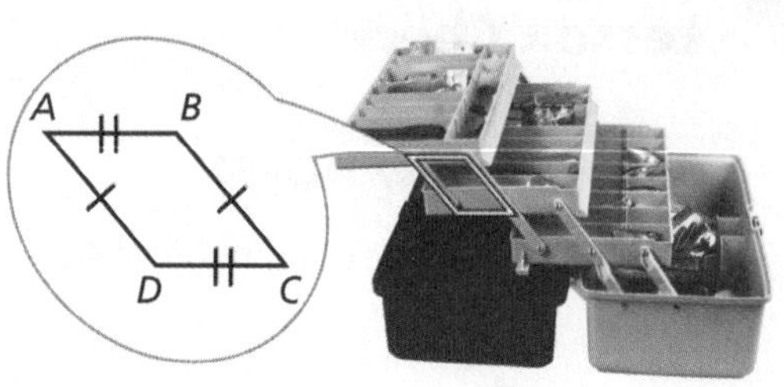

take note

Concept Summary Proving That a Quadrilateral Is a Parallelogram

Method	Source	Diagram
Prove that both pairs of opposite sides are parallel.	Definition of parallelogram	
Prove that both pairs of opposite sides are congruent.	Theorem 43	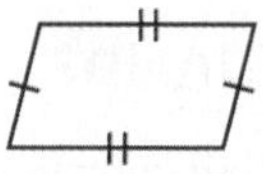
Prove that an angle is supplementary to both of its consecutive angles.	Theorem 44	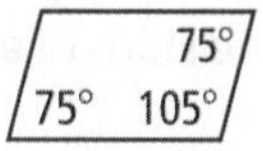
Prove that both pairs of opposite angles are congruent.	Theorem 45	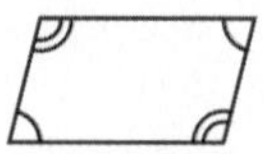
Prove that the diagonals bisect each other.	Theorem 46	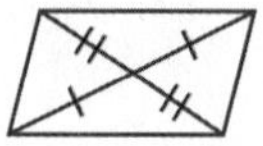
Prove that one pair of opposite sides is congruent and parallel.	Theorem 47	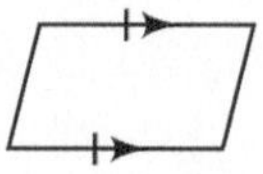

Lesson Check

Do you know HOW?

6. For what value of y must *LMNP* be a parallelogram?

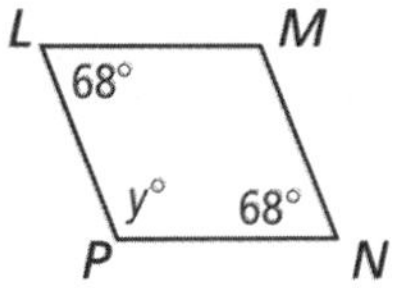

For Exercises 7 and 8, is the given information enough to prove that *ABCD* is a parallelogram? Explain.

7.

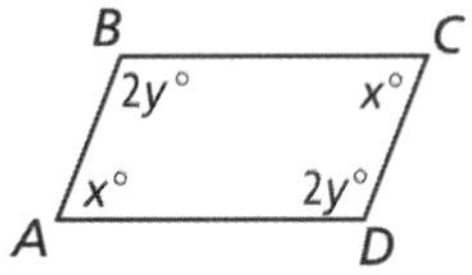

8.

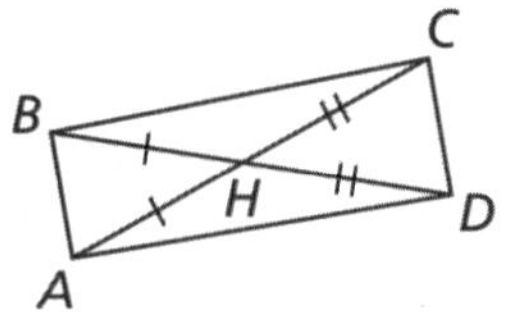

Do you UNDERSTAND?

MATHEMATICAL PRACTICES

9. Vocabulary Explain why you can now write a biconditional statement regarding opposite sides of a parallelogram.

10. Compare and Contrast How is Theorem 46 in this lesson different from Theorem 41 in the previous lesson? In what situations should you use each theorem? Explain.

11. Error Analysis Your friend says, "If a quadrilateral has a pair of opposite sides that are congruent and a pair of opposite sides that are parallel, then it is a parallelogram." What is your friend's error? Explain.

More Practice and Problem-Solving Exercises

MATHEMATICAL PRACTICES

B Apply

12. Writing Combine each of Theorems 38, 39, 40, and 41 with its converse from this lesson into biconditional statements.

13. Developing Proof Complete this two-column proof of Theorem 45.

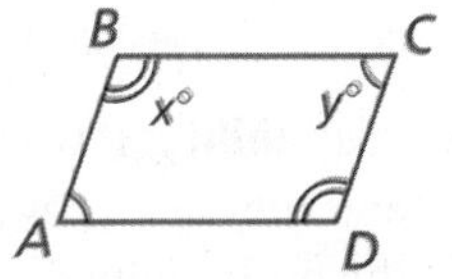

Given: $\angle A \cong \angle C$, $\angle B \cong \angle D$

Prove: $ABCD$ is a parallelogram.

Statements	Reasons
1) $x + y + x + y = 360$	1) The sum of the measures of the angles of a quadrilateral is 360.
2) $2(x + y) = 360$	2) a. ?
3) $x + y = 180$	3) b. ?
4) $\angle A$ and $\angle B$ are supplementary. $\angle A$ and $\angle D$ are supplementary.	4) Definition of supplementary
5) c. ? $\parallel$? , ? $\parallel$?	5) d. ?
6) $ABCD$ is a parallelogram.	6) e. ?

14. Think About a Plan Prove Theorem 47.

Proof **Given:** $\overline{BC} \parallel \overline{DA}$, $\overline{BC} \cong \overline{DA}$

Prove: $ABCD$ is a parallelogram.

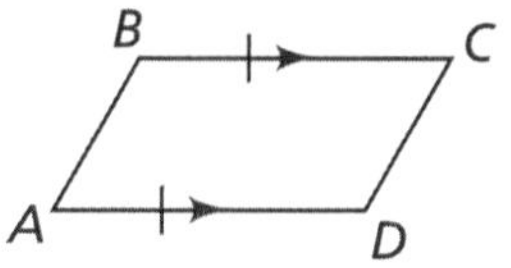

- How can drawing diagonals help you?
- How can you use triangles in this proof?

Proof **15.** Prove Theorem 43.

Given: $\overline{AB} \cong \overline{CD}$, $\overline{BC} \cong \overline{DA}$

Prove: $ABCD$ is a parallelogram.

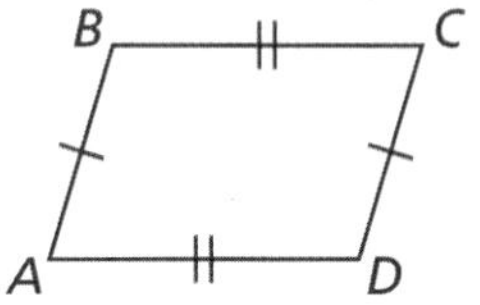

Proof **16.** Prove Theorem 44.

Given: $\angle A$ is supplementary to $\angle B$.
$\angle A$ is supplementary to $\angle D$.

Prove: $ABCD$ is a parallelogram.

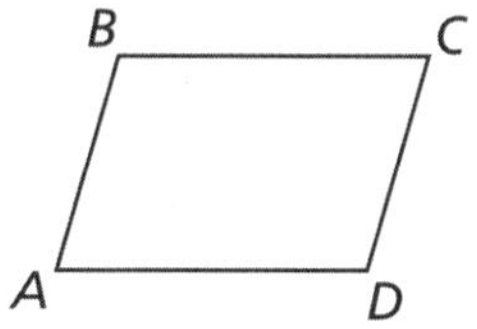

Algebra For what values of the variables must *ABCD* be a parallelogram?

17.

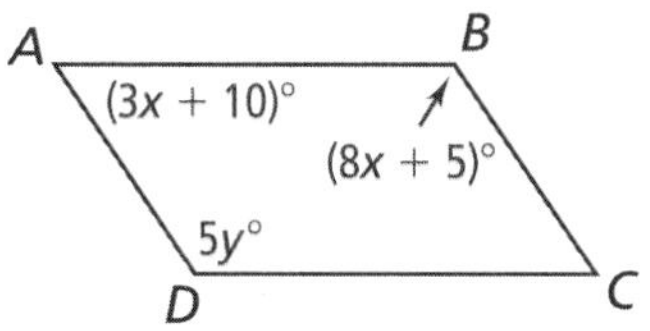

18.

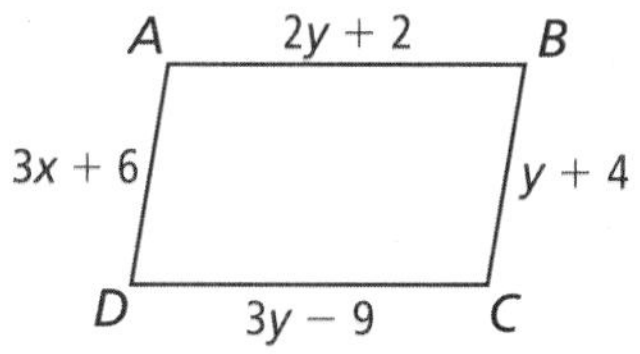

19.

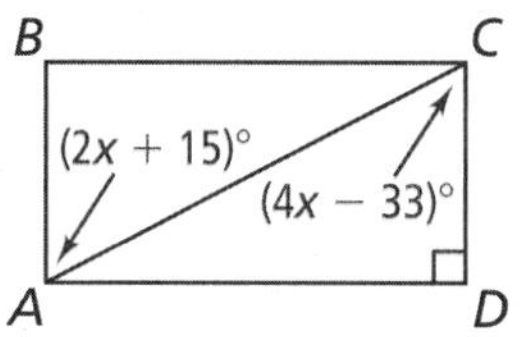

Proof **20. Given:** $\triangle TRS \cong \triangle RTW$

Prove: $RSTW$ is a parallelogram.

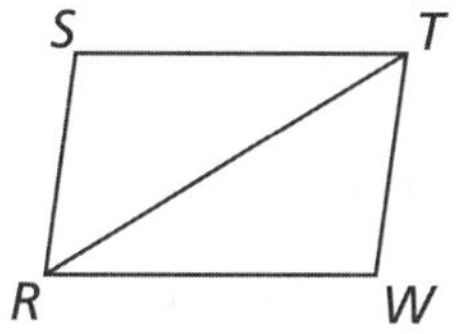

21. Open-Ended Sketch two noncongruent parallelograms $ABCD$ and $EFGH$ such that $\overline{AC} \cong \overline{EG}$ and $\overline{BD} \cong \overline{FH}$.

Challenge

Proof **22. Construction** In the figure at the right, point D is constructed by drawing two arcs. One has center C and radius AB. The other has center B and radius AC. Prove that $\overline{AM}$ is a median of $\triangle ABC$.

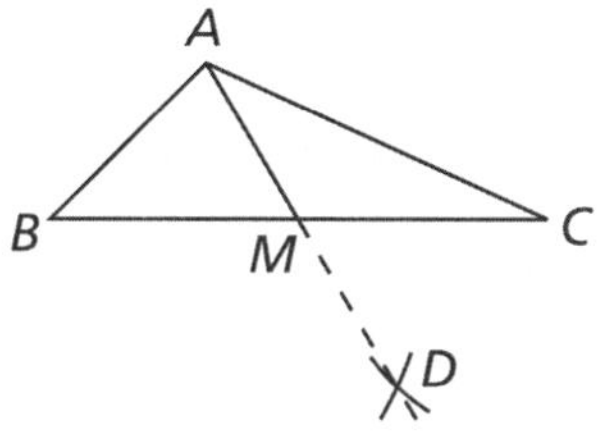

23. Probability If two opposite angles of a quadrilateral measure 120 and the measures of the other angles are multiples of 10, what is the probability that the quadrilateral is a parallelogram?

9-4 Properties of Rhombuses, Rectangles, and Squares

G.CO.11 Prove theorems about parallelograms . . . rectangles are parallelograms with congruent diagonals.
Also **G.SRT.5**

Objectives To define and classify special types of parallelograms
To use properties of diagonals of rhombuses and rectangles

Solve It! Write your solution to the Solve It in the space below.

In the Solve It, you formed a special type of parallelogram with characteristics that you will study in this lesson.

Essential Understanding The parallelograms in the Take Note box below have basic properties about their sides and angles that help identify them. The diagonals of these parallelograms also have certain properties.

take note

Key Concept Special Parallelograms

Definition	Diagram
A **rhombus** is a parallelogram with four congruent sides.	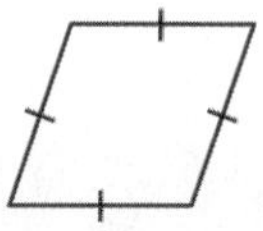
A **rectangle** is a parallelogram with four right angles.	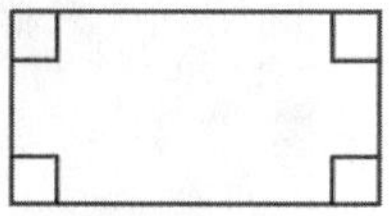
A **square** is a parallelogram with four congruent sides and four right angles.	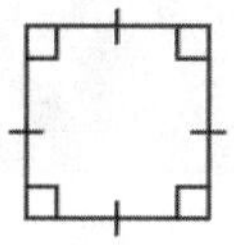

The Venn diagram at the right shows the relationships among special parallelograms.

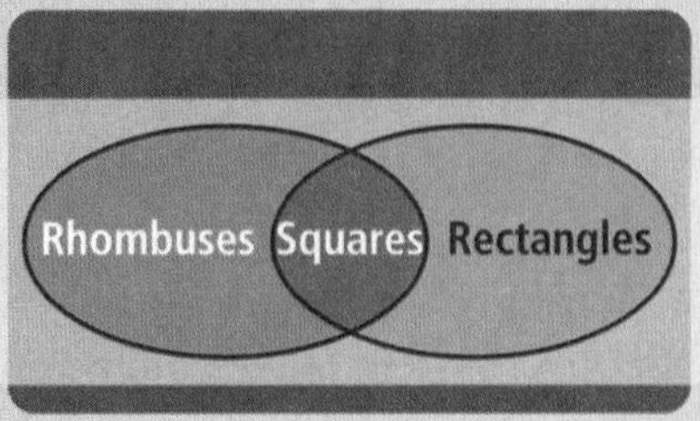

Problem 1 Classifying Special Parallelograms

Got It? Is ▱*EFGH* in Problem 1 a rhombus, a rectangle, or a square? Explain.

Think
How do you decide whether *EFGH* is a rhombus, rectangle, or square?

A Practice **Decide whether the parallelogram is a rhombus, a rectangle, or a square. Explain.**

1.

2.

take note

Theorem 48

Theorem

If a parallelogram is a rhombus, then its diagonals are perpendicular.

If . . .

ABCD is a rhombus

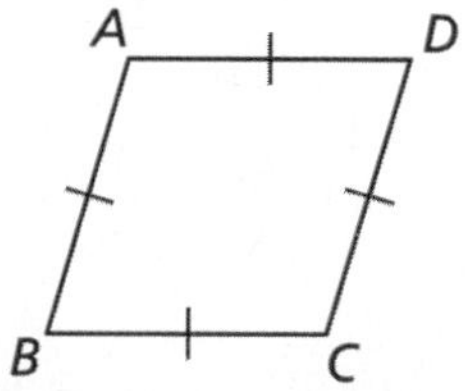

Then . . .

$\overline{AC} \perp \overline{BD}$

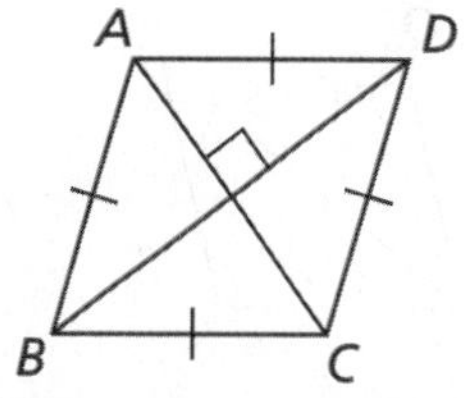

Theorem 49

Theorem

If a parallelogram is a rhombus, then each diagonal bisects a pair of opposite angles.

If . . .

ABCD is a rhombus

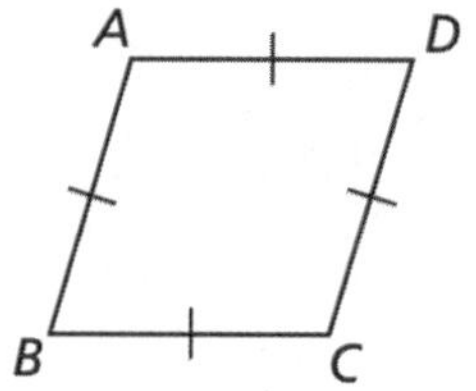

Then . . .

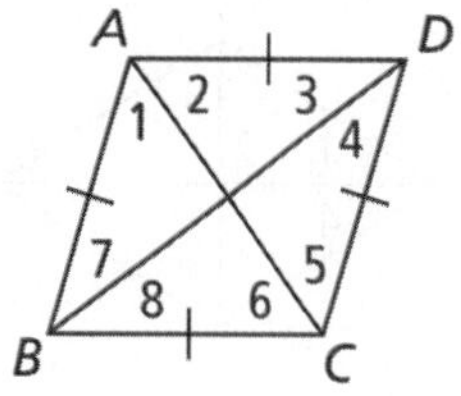

$\angle 1 \cong \angle 2$
$\angle 3 \cong \angle 4$
$\angle 5 \cong \angle 6$
$\angle 7 \cong \angle 8$

You will prove Theorem 49 in Exercise 34.

Proof **Proof of Theorem 48**

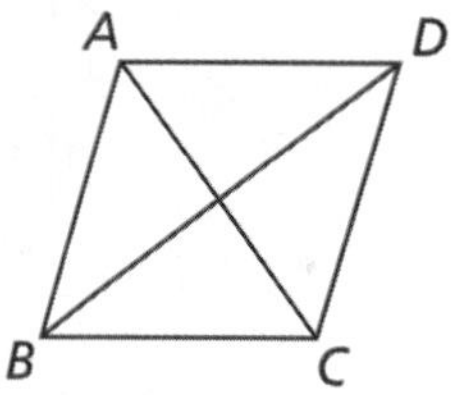

Given: *ABCD* is a rhombus.

Prove: The diagonals of *ABCD* are perpendicular.

Statements	Reasons
1) *A* and *C* are equidistant from *B* and *D*; *B* and *D* are equidistant from *A* and *C*.	**1)** All sides of a rhombus are ≅.
2) *A* and *C* are on the perpendicular bisector of $\overline{BD}$; *B* and *D* are on the perpendicular bisector of $\overline{AC}$.	**2)** Converse of the Perpendicular Bisector Theorem
3) $\overline{AC} \perp \overline{BD}$	**3)** Through two points, there is one unique line perpendicular to a given line.

You can use Theorems 48 and 49 to find angle measures in a rhombus.

Problem 2 Finding Angle Measures

Got It? What are the measures of the numbered angles in rhombus $PQRS$?

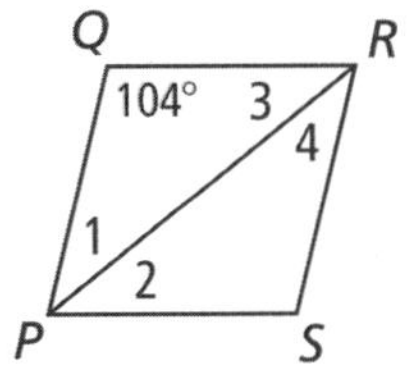

Think

What type of triangle is $\triangle PQR$?

A Practice **Find the measures of the numbered angles in each rhombus.**

3.

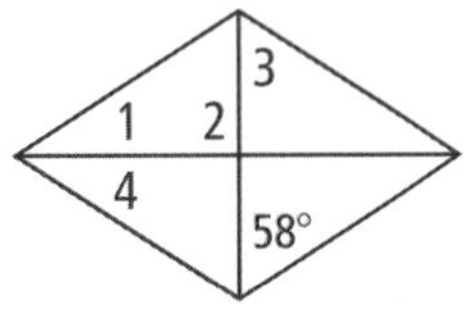

4.

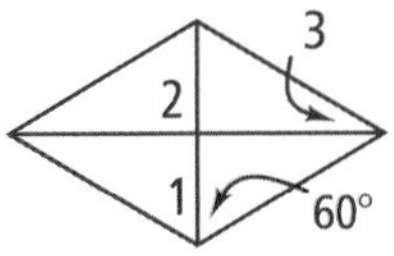

The diagonals of a rectangle also have a special property.

take note

Theorem 50

Theorem	If . . .	Then . . .
If a parallelogram is a rectangle, then its diagonals are congruent.	$ABCD$ is a rectangle 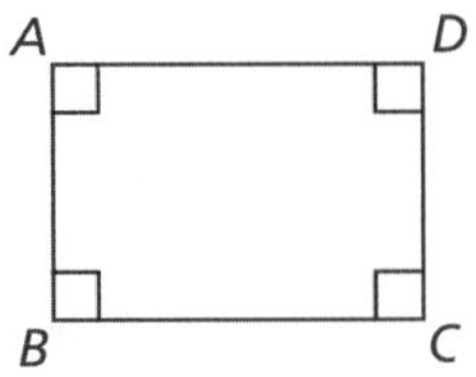	$\overline{AC} \cong \overline{BD}$ 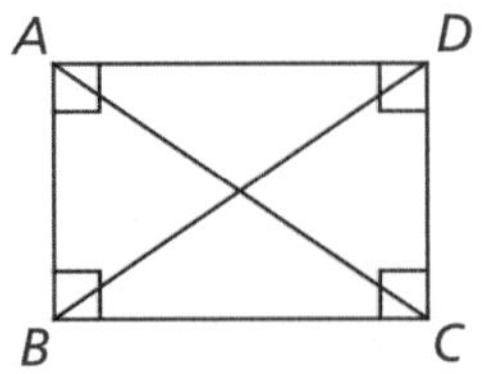

You will prove Theorem 50 in Exercise 30.

Problem 3 Finding Diagonal Length

Got It? **a.** If $LN = 4x - 17$ and $MO = 2x + 13$, what are the lengths of the diagonals of rectangle *LMNO*?

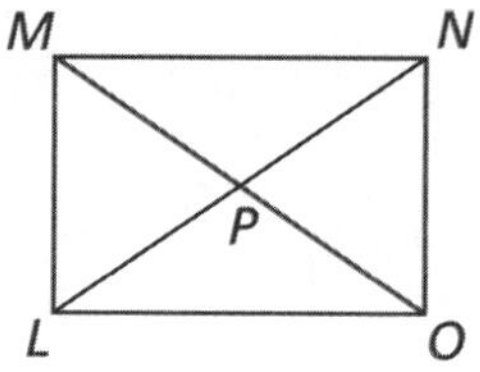

b. Reasoning What type of triangle is $\triangle PMN$? Explain.

Practice **Algebra** *LMNP* **is a rectangle. Find the value of** x **and the length of each diagonal.**

5. $LN = 5x - 8$ and $MP = 2x + 1$

6. $LN = 3x + 1$ and $MP = 8x - 4$

Lesson Check

Do you know HOW?

Is each parallelogram a rhombus, rectangle, or square? Explain.

7.

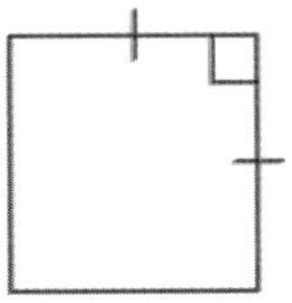

8.

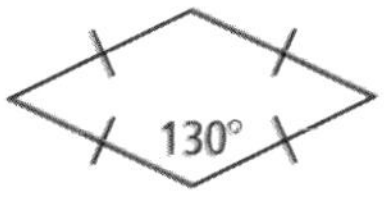

9. What are the measures of the numbered angles in the rhombus?

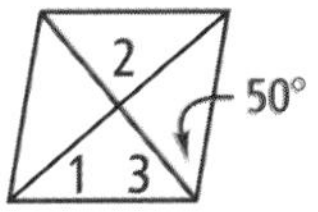

10. Algebra *JKLM* is a rectangle. If $JL = 4x - 12$ and $MK = x$, what is the value of x? What is the length of each diagonal?

Do you UNDERSTAND?

MATHEMATICAL PRACTICES

11. Vocabulary Which special parallelograms are equiangular? Which special parallelograms are equilateral?

12. Error Analysis Your class needs to find the value of x for which $\square DEFG$ is a rectangle. A classmate's work is shown at the right. What is the error? Explain.

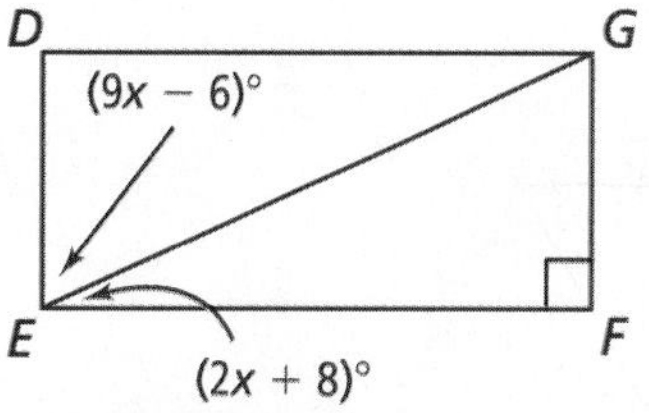

~~$2x + 8 = 9x - 6$~~
~~$14 = 7x$~~
~~$2 = x$~~

More Practice and Problem-Solving Exercises

MATHEMATICAL PRACTICES

B Apply

Determine the most precise name for each quadrilateral.

13.

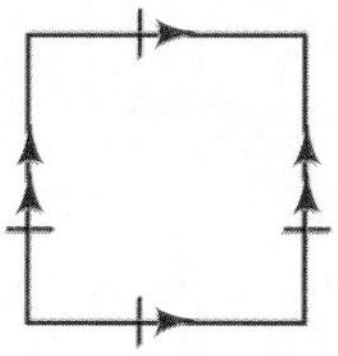

14.

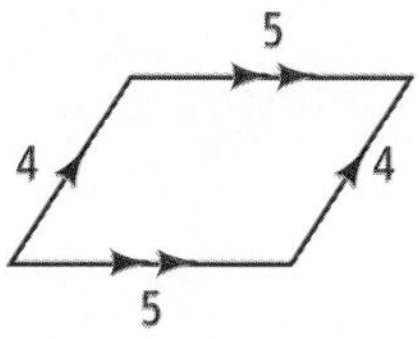

15.

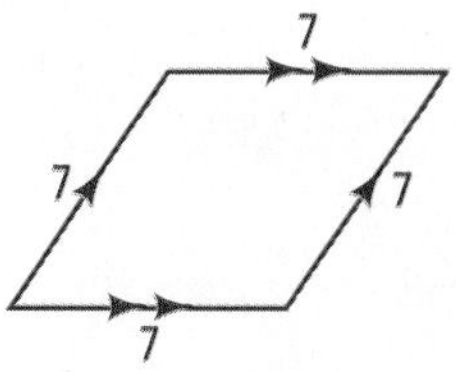

16.

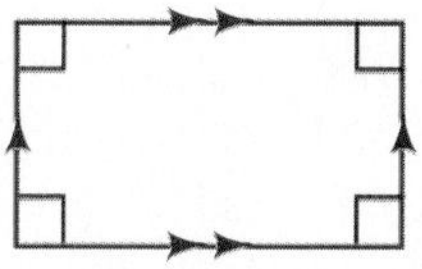

List the quadrilaterals that have the given property. Choose among *parallelogram, rhombus, rectangle,* and *square.*

17. All sides are ≅.

18. Opposite sides are ≅.

19. Opposite sides are ∥.

20. Opposite ∠s are ≅.

21. All ∠s are right ∠s.

22. Consecutive ∠s are supplementary.

23. Diagonals bisect each other.

24. Diagonals are ≅.

25. Diagonals are ⊥.

26. Each diagonal bisects opposite ∠s.

Algebra Find the values of the variables. Then find the side lengths.

27. rhombus

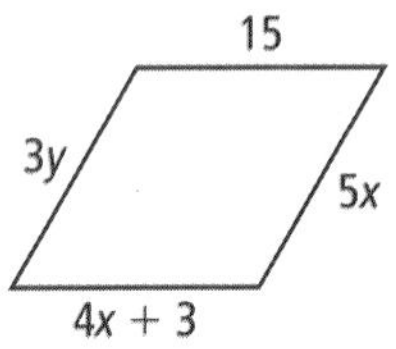

28. square

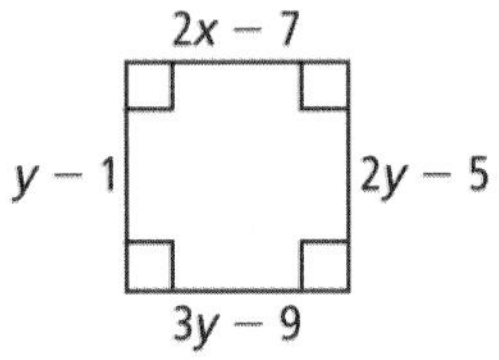

29. Think About a Plan Write a proof.

Proof

Given: Rectangle *PLAN*

Prove: $\triangle LTP \cong \triangle NTA$

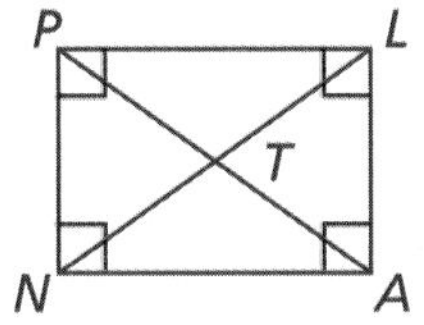

- What do you know about the diagonals of rectangles?
- Which triangle congruence postulate or theorem can you use?

30. Developing Proof Complete the flow proof of Theorem 50.

Given: *ABCD* is a rectangle.

Prove: $\overline{AC} \cong \overline{BD}$

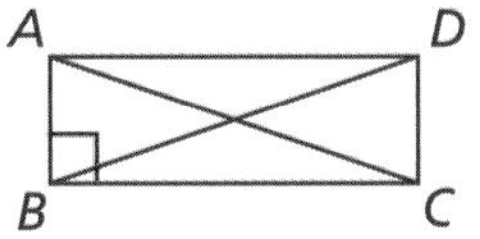

ABCD is a rectangle.
a. ?

ABCD is a ▱.
b. ?

e. ?
Opposite sides of a ▱ are ≅.

$\overline{BC} \cong \overline{BC}$
c. ?

∠*ABC* and ∠*DCB* are right ∠s.
d. ?

∠*ABC* ≅ ∠*DCB*
g. ?

f. ?
SAS

$\overline{AC} \cong \overline{BD}$
h. ?

Algebra **Find the value(s) of the variable(s) for each parallelogram.**

31. $RZ = 2x + 5$, $SW = 5x - 20$

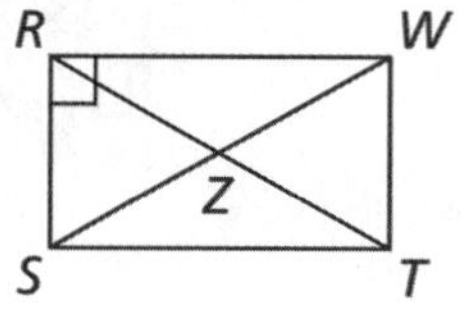

32. $m\angle 1 = 3y - 6$

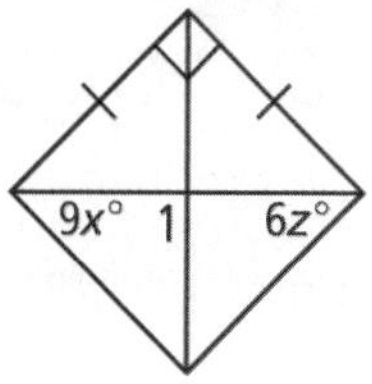

33. $BD = 4x - y + 1$

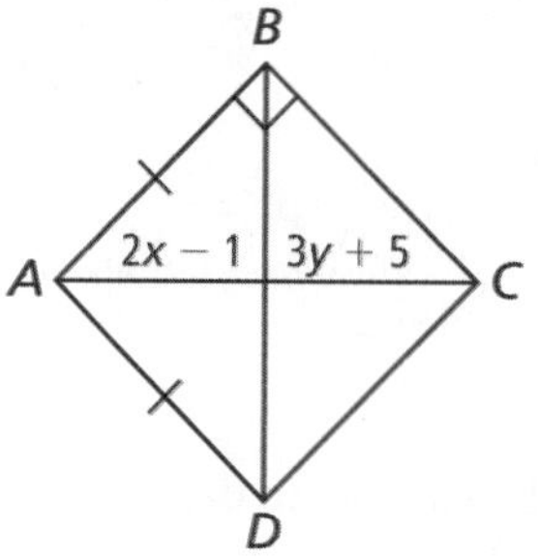

34. Prove Theorem 49.
Proof
Given: $ABCD$ is a rhombus.

Prove: $\overline{AC}$ bisects $\angle BAD$ and $\angle BCD$.

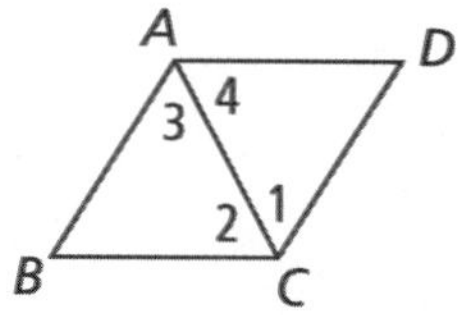

35. Writing Summarize the properties of squares that follow from a square being (a) a parallelogram, (b) a rhombus, and (c) a rectangle.

36. Algebra Find the angle measures and the side lengths of the rhombus at the right.

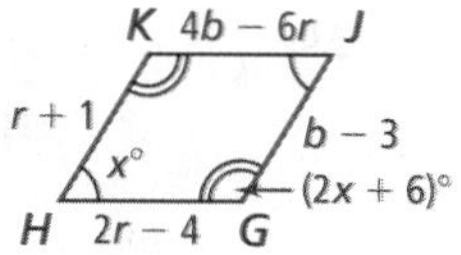

37. Open-Ended On graph paper, draw a parallelogram that is neither a rectangle nor a rhombus.

Algebra ***ABCD*** **is a rectangle. Find the length of each diagonal.**

38. $AC = 2(x - 3)$ and $BD = x + 5$

39. $AC = 2(5a + 1)$ and $BD = 2(a + 1)$

40. $AC = \frac{3y}{5}$ and $BD = 3y - 4$

41. $AC = \frac{3c}{9}$ and $BD = 4 - c$

Challenge

Algebra **Find the value of** ***x*** **in the rhombus.**

42.

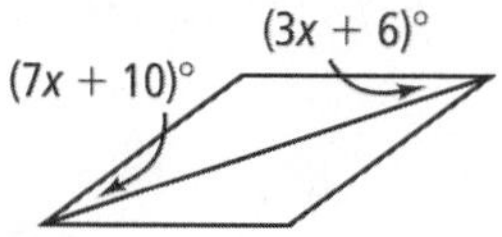

43.

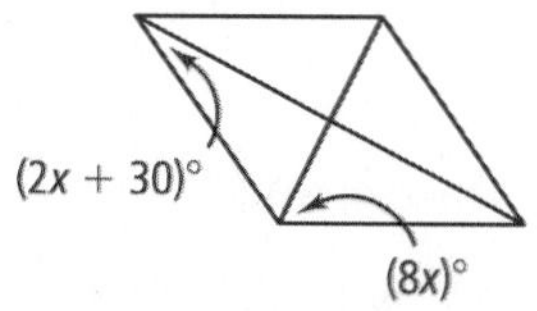

9-5 Conditions for Rhombuses, Rectangles, and Squares

G.CO.11 Prove theorems about parallelograms . . . rectangles are parallelograms with congruent diagonals. Also **G.SRT.5**

Objective To determine whether a parallelogram is a rhombus or rectangle

Solve It! Write your solution to the Solve It in the space below.

Essential Understanding You can determine whether a parallelogram is a rhombus or a rectangle based on the properties of its diagonals.

take note

Theorem 51

Theorem	If . . .	Then . . .
If the diagonals of a parallelogram are perpendicular, then the parallelogram is a rhombus.	$ABCD$ is a ▱ and $\overline{AC} \perp \overline{BD}$ 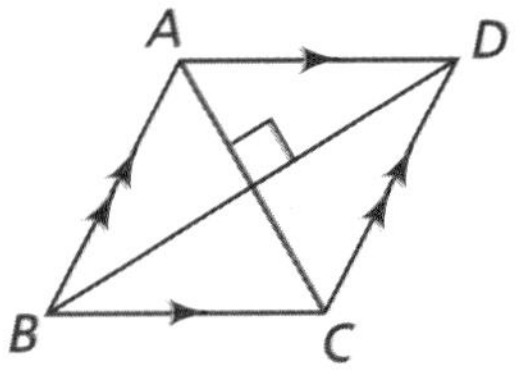	$ABCD$ is a rhombus 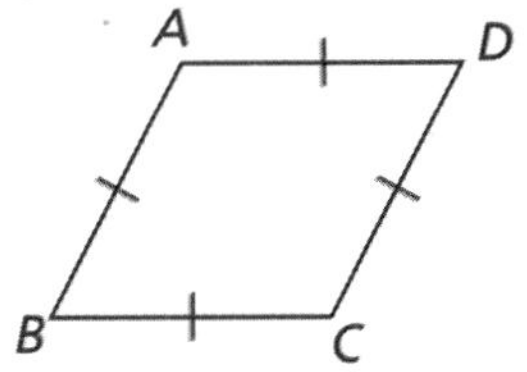

Proof Proof of Theorem 51

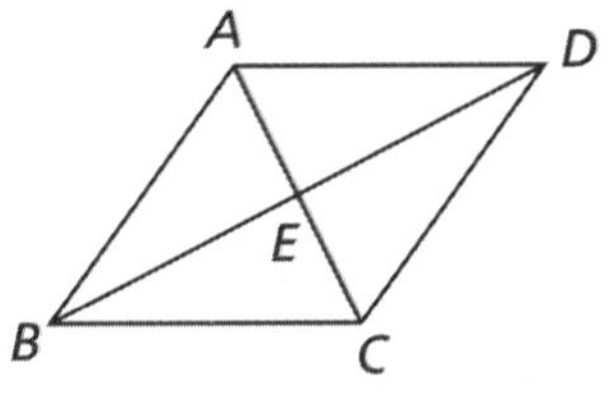

Given: $ABCD$ is a parallelogram, $\overline{AC} \perp \overline{BD}$
Prove: $ABCD$ is a rhombus.

Since $ABCD$ is a parallelogram, $\overline{AC}$ and $\overline{BD}$ bisect each other, so $\overline{BE} \cong \overline{DE}$. Since $\overline{AC} \perp \overline{BD}$, $\angle AED$ and $\angle AEB$ are congruent right angles. By the Reflexive Property of Congruence, $\overline{AE} \cong \overline{AE}$.

So $\triangle AEB \cong \triangle AED$ by SAS. Corresponding parts of congruent triangles are congruent, so $\overline{AB} \cong \overline{AD}$. Since opposite sides of a parallelogram are congruent, $\overline{AB} \cong \overline{DC} \cong \overline{BC} \cong \overline{AD}$. By definition, $ABCD$ is a rhombus.

take note

Theorem 52

Theorem

If one diagonal of a parallelogram bisects a pair of opposite angles, then the parallelogram is a rhombus.

If . . .

ABCD is a ▱, $\angle 1 \cong \angle 2$, and $\angle 3 \cong \angle 4$

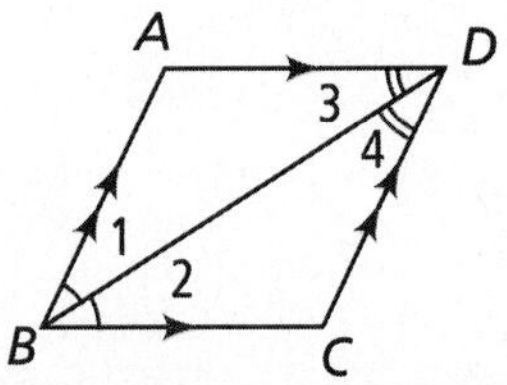

Then . . .

ABCD is a rhombus

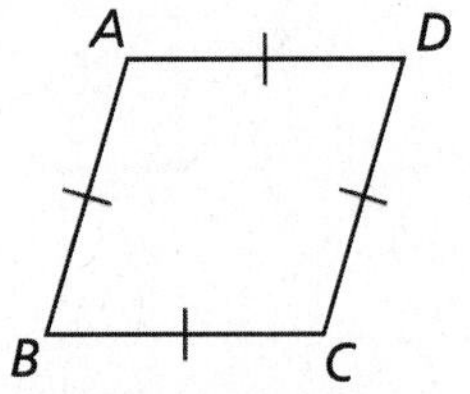

You will prove Theorem 52 in Exercise 21.

Theorem 53

Theorem

If the diagonals of a parallelogram are congruent, then the parallelogram is a rectangle.

If . . .

ABCD is a ▱, and $\overline{AC} \cong \overline{BD}$

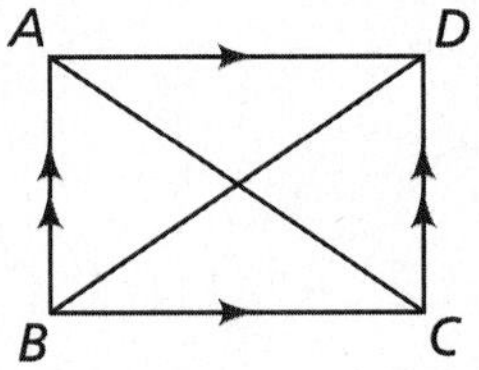

Then . . .

ABCD is a rectangle

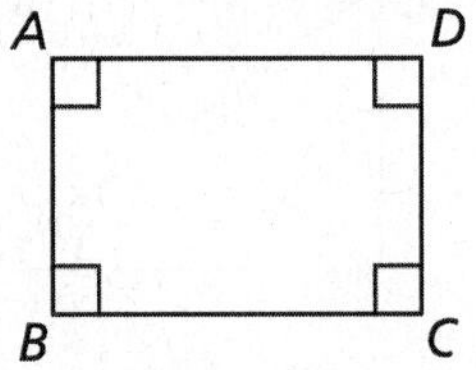

You will prove Theorem 53 in Exercise 22.

You can use Theorems 51, 52, and 53 to classify parallelograms. Notice that if a parallelogram is both a rectangle and a rhombus, then it is a square.

ONLINE PROBLEMS

Problem 1 Identifying Special Parallelograms

Think

How can you determine whether a figure is a special parallelogram?

Got It? **a.** A parallelogram has angle measures of 20, 160, 20, and 160. Can you conclude that it is a rhombus, a rectangle, or a square? Explain.

b. Reasoning Suppose the diagonals of a quadrilateral bisect each other. Can you conclude that it is a rhombus, a rectangle, or a square? Explain.

Practice **Can you conclude that the parallelogram is a rhombus, a rectangle, or a square? Explain.**

1. 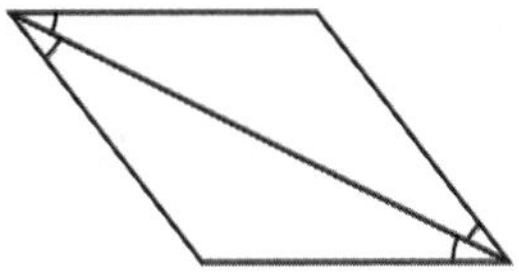

2. 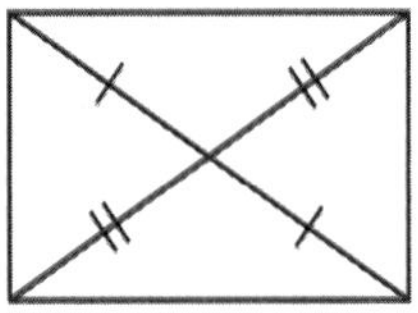

Problem 2 Using Properties of Special Parallelograms

Got It? For what value of y is $\square DEFG$ a rectangle?

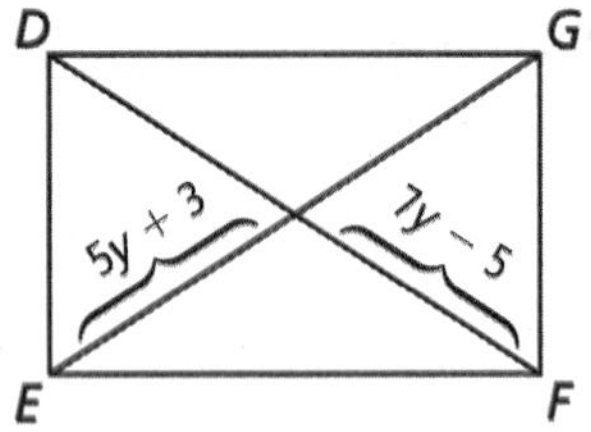

Think
What do you know about the diagonals of a rectangle?

Practice **For what value of x is the figure the given special parallelogram?**

3. rhombus

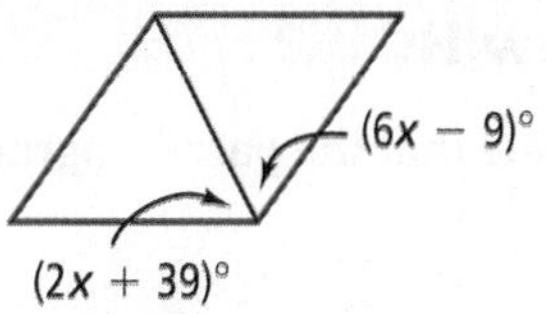

4. rectangle

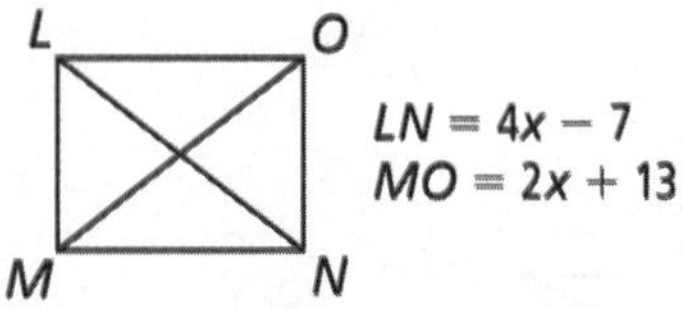

Problem 3 Using Properties of Parallelograms

Got It? Can you adapt the method described in Problem 3 to stake off a square play area? Explain.

Practice **5. Carpentry** A carpenter is building a bookcase. How can the carpenter use a tape measure to check that the bookshelf is rectangular? Justify your answer and name any theorems used.

Lesson Check

Do you know HOW?

Can you conclude that the parallelogram is a rhombus, a rectangle, or a square? Explain.

6. 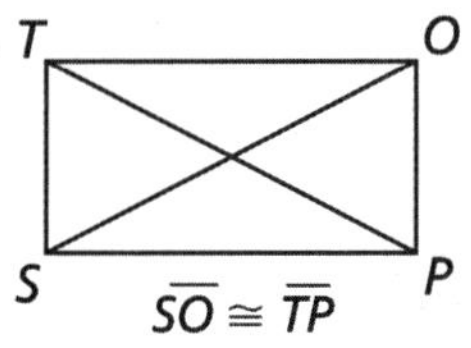

7. 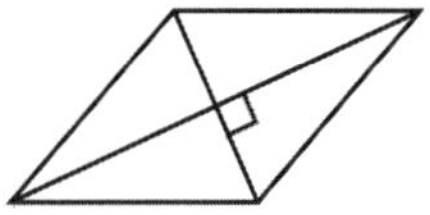

For what value of x is the figure the given special parallelogram?

8. rhombus

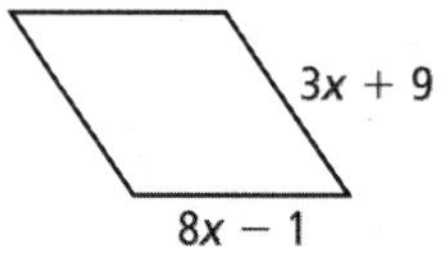

9. rectangle

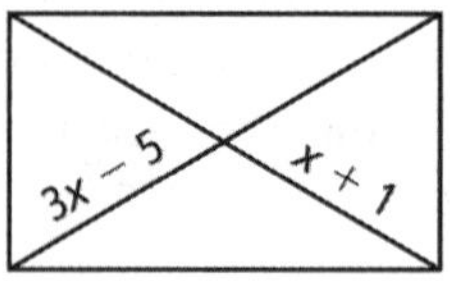

Do you UNDERSTAND?

MATHEMATICAL PRACTICES

10. Name all of the special parallelograms that have each property.

a. Diagonals are perpendicular.

b. Diagonals are congruent.

c. Diagonals are angle bisectors.

d. Diagonals bisect each other.

e. Diagonals are perpendicular bisectors of each other.

11. Error Analysis Your friend says, "A parallelogram with perpendicular diagonals is a rectangle." What is your friend's error? Explain.

12. Reasoning When you draw a circle and two of its diameters and connect the endpoints of the diameters, what quadrilateral do you get? Explain.

More Practice and Problem-Solving Exercises

MATHEMATICAL PRACTICES

B Apply

13. Hardware You can use a simple device called a turnbuckle to "square up" structures that are parallelograms. For the gate pictured at the right, you tighten or loosen the turnbuckle on the diagonal cable so that the rectangular frame will keep the shape of a parallelogram when it sags. What are two ways you can make sure that the turnbuckle works? Explain.

14. Reasoning Suppose the diagonals of a parallelogram are both perpendicular and congruent. What type of special quadrilateral is it? Explain your reasoning.

Algebra For what value of x is the figure the given special parallelogram?

15. rectangle

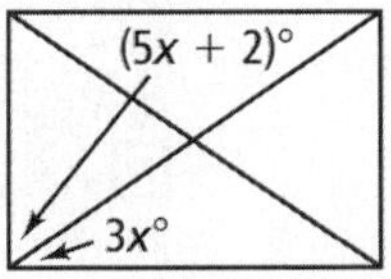

16. rhombus

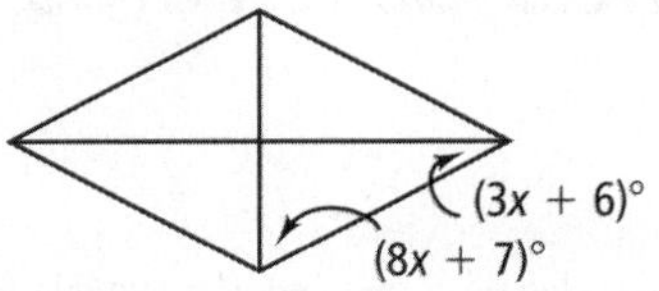

17. rectangle

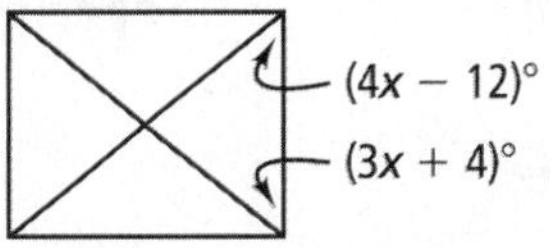

Open-Ended Given two segments with lengths a and b ($a \neq b$), what special parallelograms meet the given conditions? Show each sketch.

18. Both diagonals have length a.

19. The two diagonals have lengths a and b.

20. One diagonal has length a, and one side of the quadrilateral has length b.

Proof **21.** Prove Theorem 52.

Given: $ABCD$ is a parallelogram. $\overline{AC}$ bisects $\angle BAD$ and $\angle BCD$.

Prove: $ABCD$ is a rhombus.

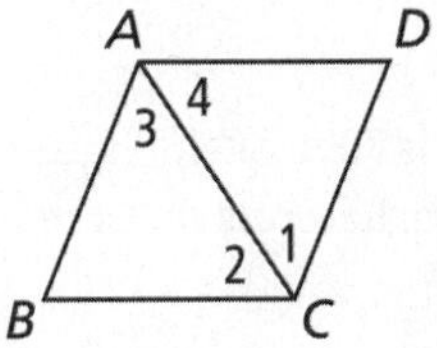

Proof **22.** Prove Theorem 53.

Given: $\square ABCD$, $\overline{AC} \cong \overline{BD}$

Prove: $ABCD$ is a rectangle.

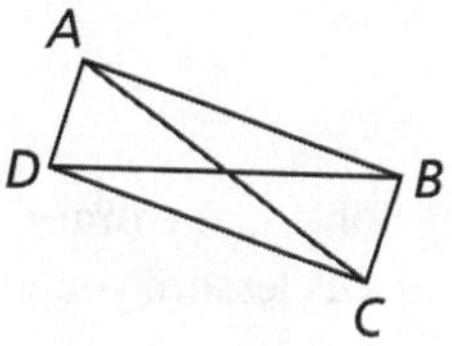

Think About a Plan Explain how to construct each figure given its diagonals.

- What do you know about the diagonals of each figure?
- How can you apply constructions to what you know about the diagonals?

23. parallelogram

24. rectangle

25. rhombus

Challenge

Determine whether the quadrilateral can be a parallelogram. Explain.

26. The diagonals are congruent, but the quadrilateral has no right angles.

27. Each diagonal is 3 cm long and two opposite sides are 2 cm long.

28. Two opposite angles are right angles, but the quadrilateral is not a rectangle.

Proof **29.** In Theorem 52, replace "a pair of opposite angles" with "one angle." Write a paragraph that proves this new statement to be true, or give a counterexample to prove it to be false.

9-6 Trapezoids and Kites

G.SRT.5 Use congruence . . . criteria . . . to solve problems and to prove relationships in geometric figures.
Also **G.CO.9**

Objective To verify and use properties of trapezoids and kites

Solve It! Write your solution to the Solve It in the space below.

In the Solve It, the orange and green regions are trapezoids. The entire figure is a kite. In this lesson, you will learn about these special quadrilaterals that are not parallelograms.

Essential Understanding The angles, sides, and diagonals of a trapezoid have certain properties.

A **trapezoid** is a quadrilateral with exactly one pair of parallel sides. The parallel sides of a trapezoid are called **bases**. The nonparallel sides are called **legs**. The two angles that share a base of a trapezoid are called **base angles**. A trapezoid has two pairs of base angles.

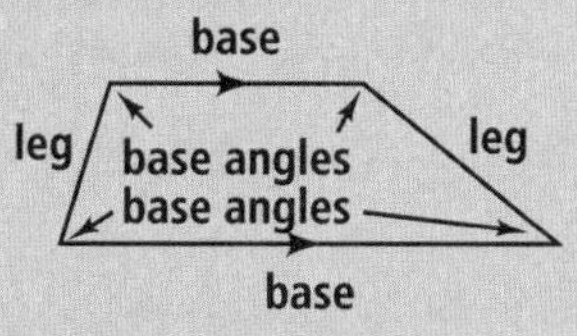

An **isosceles trapezoid** is a trapezoid with legs that are congruent. *ABCD* at the right is an isosceles trapezoid. The angles of an isosceles trapezoid have some unique properties.

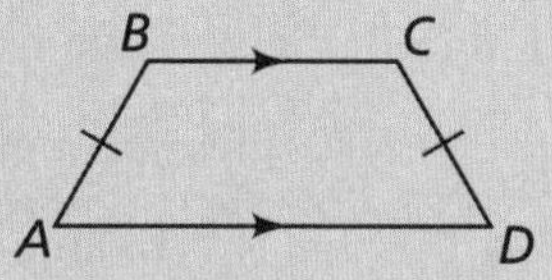

take note

Theorem 54

Theorem	If . . .	Then . . .
If a quadrilateral is an isosceles trapezoid, then each pair of base angles is congruent.	*TRAP* is an isosceles trapezoid with bases $\overline{RA}$ and $\overline{TP}$ 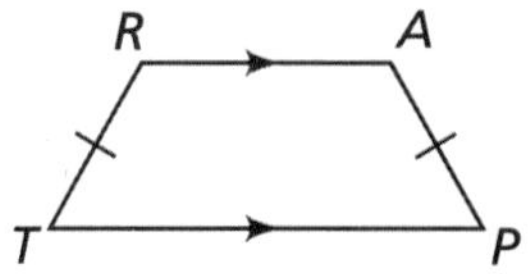	$\angle T \cong \angle P$, $\angle R \cong \angle A$ 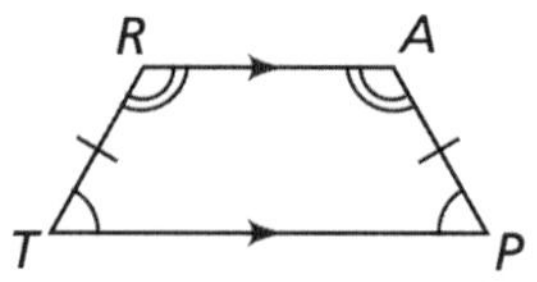

You will prove Theorem 54 in Exercise 35.

Problem 1 Finding Angle Measures in Trapezoids

Think

What do you know about the angles of an isosceles trapezoid?

Got It? **a.** In the diagram, *PQRS* is an isosceles trapezoid and $m\angle R = 106$. What are $m\angle P$, $m\angle Q$, and $m\angle S$?

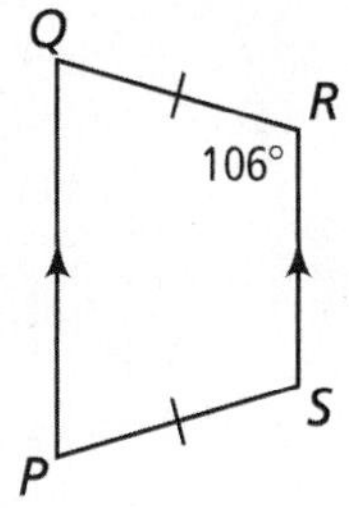

b. Reasoning In Problem 1, if *CDEF* were not an isosceles trapezoid, would $\angle C$ and $\angle D$ still be supplementary? Explain.

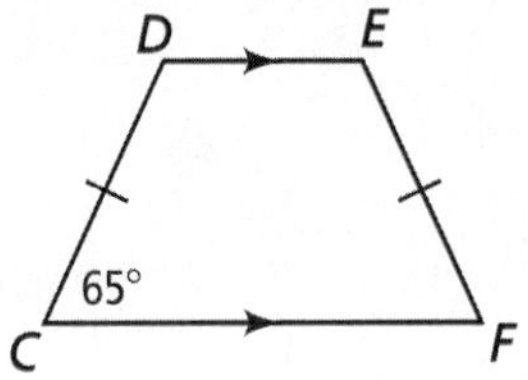

Practice **Find the measures of the numbered angles in each isosceles trapezoid.**

1.

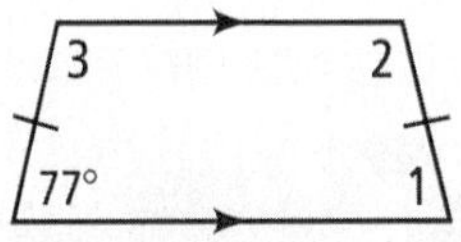

2.

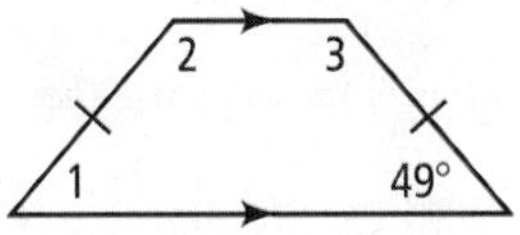

Problem 2 Finding Angle Measures in Isosceles Trapezoids

Got It? A fan like the one in Problem 2 has 15 angles meeting at the center. What are the measures of the base angles of the trapezoids in its second ring?

A Practice **Find the measures of the numbered angles in each isosceles trapezoid.**

3.

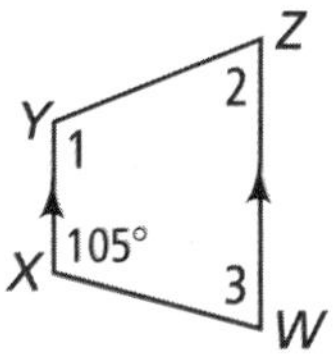

4.

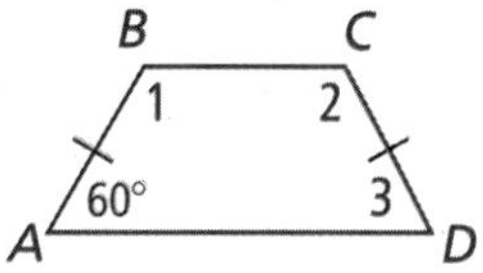

take note

Theorem 55

Theorem	If . . .	Then . . .
If a quadrilateral is an isosceles trapezoid, then its diagonals are congruent.	*ABCD* is an isosceles trapezoid 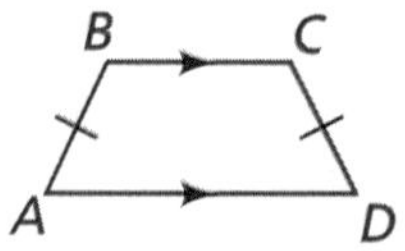	$\overline{AC} \cong \overline{BD}$ 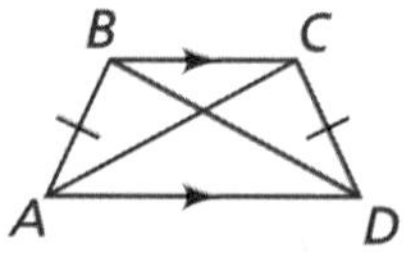

You will prove Theorem 55 in Exercise 43.

In Lesson 8-1, you learned about midsegments of triangles. Trapezoids also have midsegments. The **midsegment of a trapezoid** is the segment that joins the midpoints of its legs. The midsegment has two unique properties.

take note

Theorem 56 Trapezoid Midsegment Theorem

Theorem	If . . .	Then . . .
If a quadrilateral is a trapezoid, then (1) the midsegment is parallel to the bases, and (2) the length of the midsegment is half the sum of the lengths of the bases.	*TRAP* is a trapezoid with midsegment $\overline{MN}$ 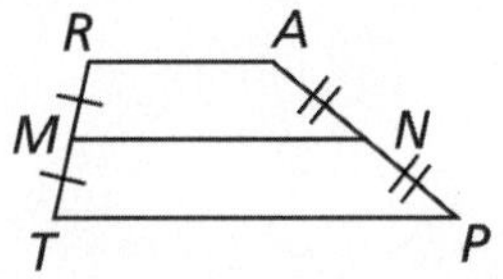	(1) $\overline{MN} \parallel \overline{TP}$, $\overline{MN} \parallel \overline{RA}$, and (2) $MN = \frac{1}{2}\left(TP + RA\right)$

You will prove Theorem 56 in Lesson 9-8.

ONLINE PROBLEMS

Problem 3 Using the Midsegment of a Trapezoid

Think
How can you check your answer?

Got It? a. **Algebra** $\overline{MN}$ is the midsegment of trapezoid *PQRS*. What is *x*? What is *MN*?

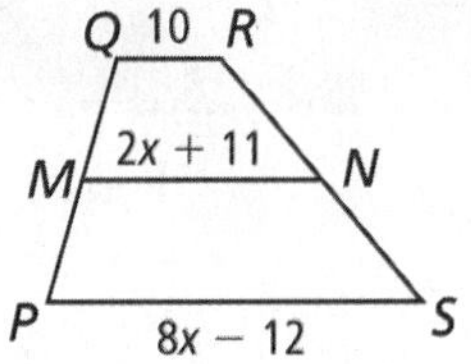

b. **Reasoning** How many midsegments can a triangle have? How many midsegments can a trapezoid have? Explain.

Practice Find *EF* in each trapezoid.

5.

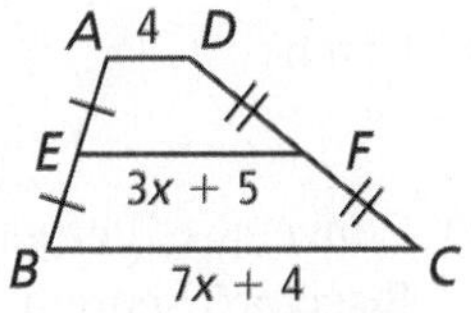

6. 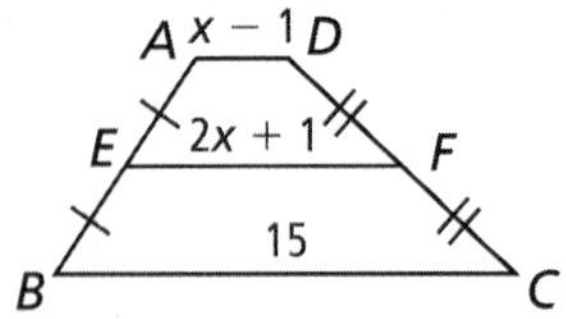

A **kite** is a quadrilateral with two pairs of consecutive sides congruent and no opposite sides congruent.

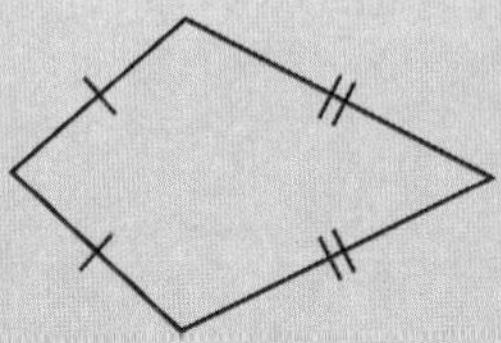

Essential Understanding The angles, sides, and diagonals of a kite have certain properties.

take note

Theorem 57

Theorem	If . . .	Then . . .
If a quadrilateral is a kite, then its diagonals are perpendicular.	*ABCD* is a kite 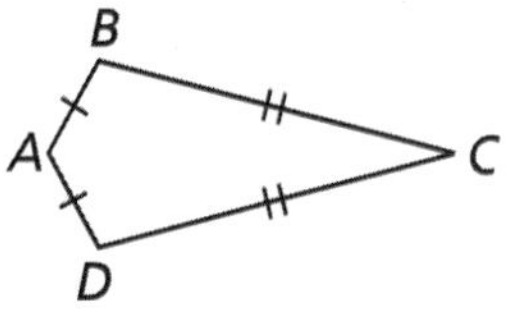	$\overline{AC} \perp \overline{BD}$ 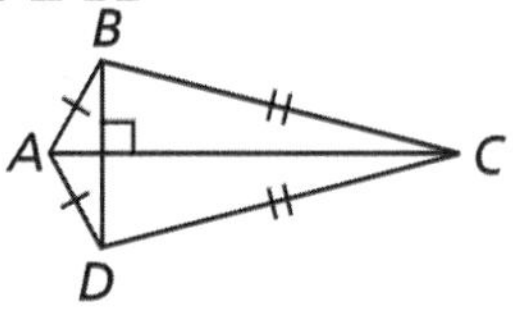

Proof Proof of Theorem 57

Given: Kite *ABCD* with $\overline{AB} \cong \overline{AD}$ and $\overline{CB} \cong \overline{CD}$

Prove: $\overline{AC} \perp \overline{BD}$

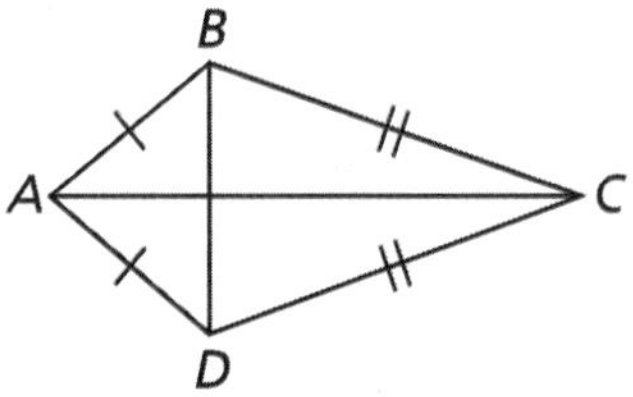

Statements	Reasons
1) Kite *ABCD* with $\overline{AB} \cong \overline{AD}$ and $\overline{CB} \cong \overline{CD}$	**1)** Given
2) *A* and *C* lie on the perpendicular bisector of $\overline{BD}$.	**2)** Converse of Perpendicular Bisector Theorem
3) $\overline{AC}$ is the perpendicular bisector of $\overline{BD}$.	**3)** Two points determine a line.
4) $\overline{AC} \perp \overline{BD}$	**4)** Definition of perpendicular bisector

Problem 4 Finding Angle Measures in Kites

Got It? Quadrilateral *KLMN* is a kite. What are $m\angle 1$, $m\angle 2$, and $m\angle 3$?

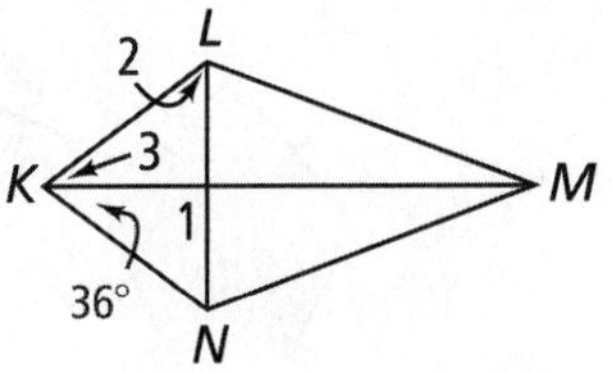

Practice Find the measures of the numbered angles in each kite.

7.

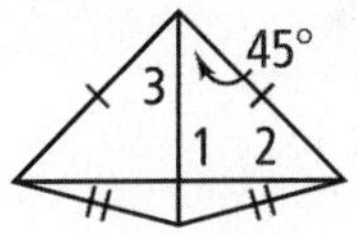

8.

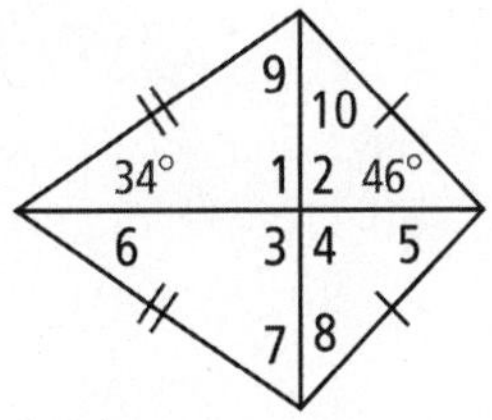

Concept Summary Relationships Among Quadrilaterals

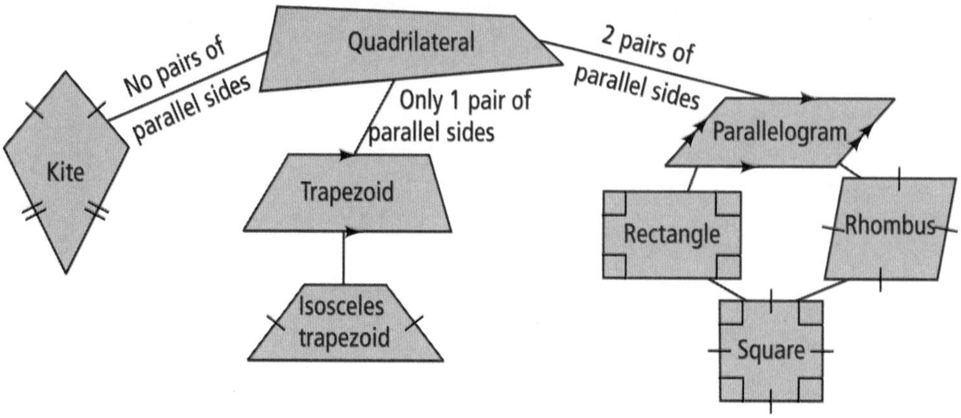

Lesson Check

Do you know HOW?

What are the measures of the numbered angles?

9.

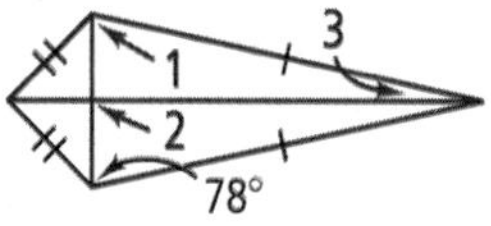

10.

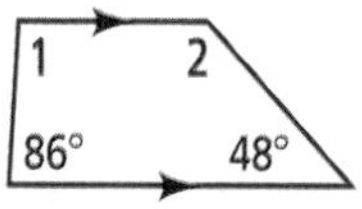

11. What is the length of the midsegment of a trapezoid with bases of lengths 14 and 26?

Do you UNDERSTAND?

MATHEMATICAL PRACTICES

12. Vocabulary Is a kite a parallelogram? Explain.

13. Compare and Contrast How is a kite similar to a rhombus? How is it different? Explain.

14. Error Analysis Since a parallelogram has two pairs of parallel sides, it certainly has one pair of parallel sides. Therefore, a parallelogram must also be a trapezoid. What is the error in this reasoning? Explain.

More Practice and Problem-Solving Exercises

MATHEMATICAL PRACTICES

B Apply

15. Open-Ended Sketch two noncongruent kites such that the diagonals of one are congruent to the diagonals of the other.

16. Think About a Plan The perimeter of a kite is 66 cm. The length of one of its sides is 3 cm less than twice the length of another. Find the length of each side of the kite.

- Can you draw a diagram?
- How can you write algebraic expressions for the lengths of the sides?

17. Reasoning If *KLMN* is an isosceles trapezoid, is it possible for $\overline{KM}$ to bisect $\angle LMN$ and $\angle LKN$? Explain.

Algebra **Find the value of the variable in each isosceles trapezoid.**

18.

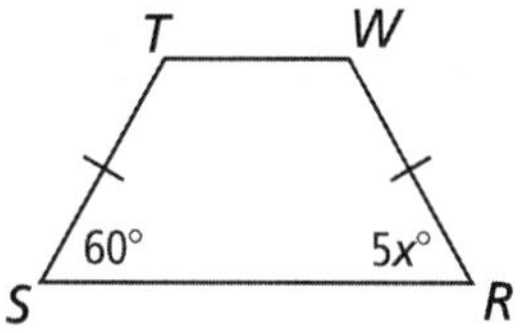

19.

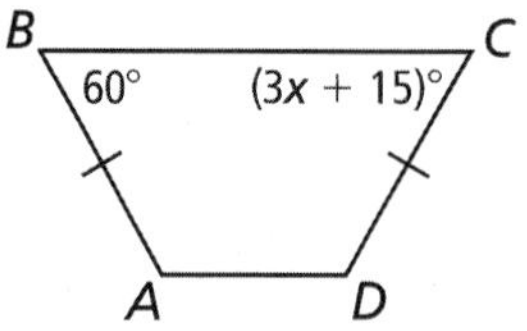

20.

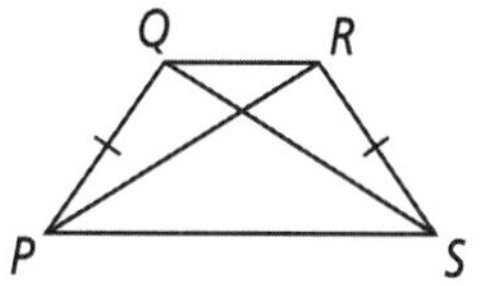

$QS = x + 5$
$RP = 3x + 3$

Algebra **Find the lengths of the segments with variable expressions.**

21.

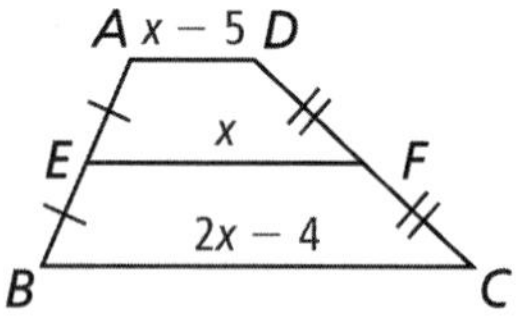

22.

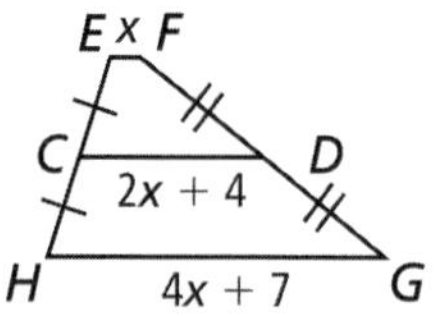

23.

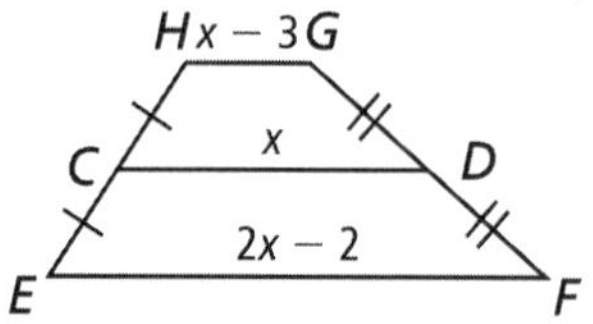

Algebra **Find the value(s) of the variable(s) in each kite.**

24.

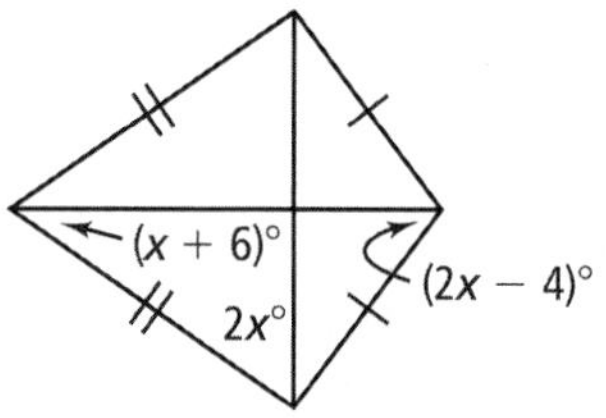

25.

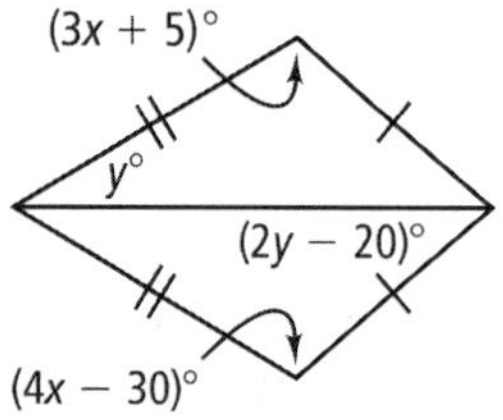

26.

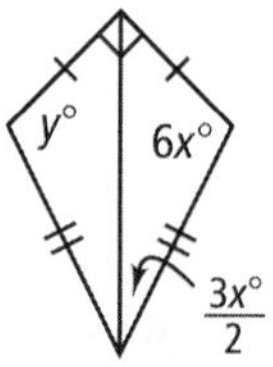

STEM **Bridge Design** **The beams of the bridge at the right form quadrilateral *ABCD*. $\triangle AED \cong \triangle CDE \cong \triangle BEC$ and $m\angle DCB = 120$.**

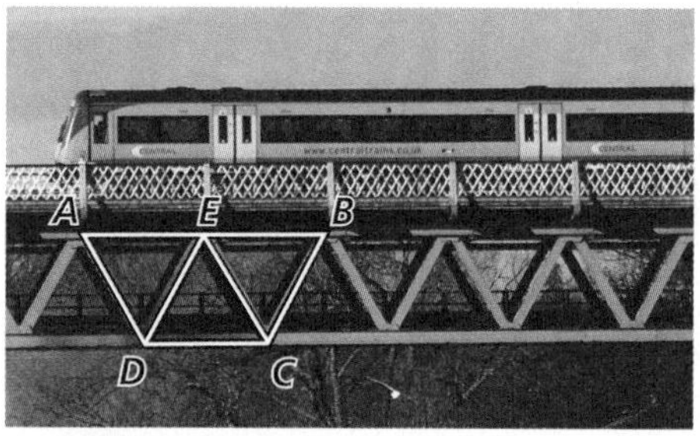

27. Classify the quadrilateral. Explain your reasoning.

28. Find the measures of the other interior angles of the quadrilateral.

Reasoning **Can two angles of a kite be as follows? Explain.**

29. opposite and acute

30. consecutive and obtuse

31. opposite and supplementary

32. consecutive and supplementary

33. opposite and complementary

34. consecutive and complementary

35. Developing Proof The plan suggests a proof of Theorem 54. Write a proof that follows the plan.

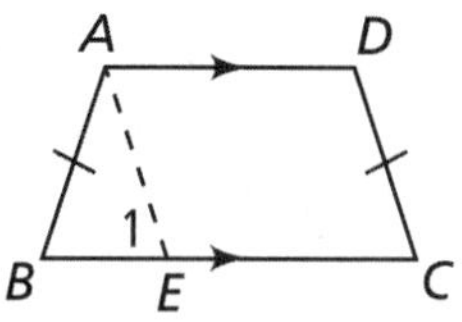

Given: Isosceles trapezoid *ABCD* with $\overline{AB} \cong \overline{DC}$

Prove: $\angle B \cong \angle C$ and $\angle BAD \cong \angle D$

Plan: Begin by drawing $\overline{AE} \parallel \overline{DC}$ to form parallelogram *AECD* so that $\overline{AE} \cong \overline{DC} \cong \overline{AB}$. $\angle B \cong \angle C$ because $\angle B \cong \angle 1$ and $\angle 1 \cong \angle C$. Also, $\angle BAD \cong \angle D$ because they are supplements of the congruent angles, $\angle B$ and $\angle C$.

Proof **36.** Prove the converse of Theorem 54: If a trapezoid has a pair of congruent base angles, then the trapezoid is isosceles.

Name each type of special quadrilateral that can meet the given condition. Make sketches to support your answers.

37. exactly one pair of congruent sides

38. two pairs of parallel sides

39. four right angles

40. adjacent sides that are congruent

41. perpendicular diagonals

42. congruent diagonals

Proof **43.** Prove Theorem 55.

Given: Isosceles trapezoid *ABCD* with $\overline{AB} \cong \overline{DC}$

Prove: $\overline{AC} \cong \overline{DB}$

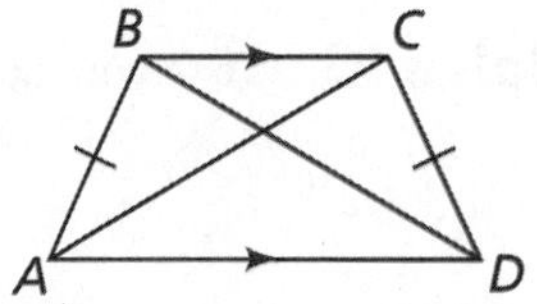

Proof **44.** Prove the converse of Theorem 55: If the diagonals of a trapezoid are congruent, then the trapezoid is isosceles.

Proof **45.** **Given:** Isosceles trapezoid *TRAP* with $\overline{TR} \cong \overline{PA}$

Prove: $\angle RTA \cong \angle APR$

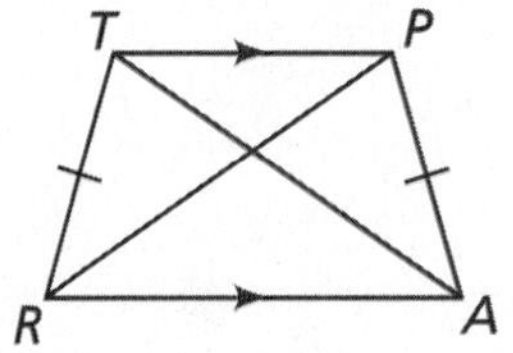

Proof **46.** Prove that the angles formed by the noncongruent sides of a kite are congruent. (*Hint:* Draw a diagonal of the kite.)

Determine whether each statement is *true* or *false*. Justify your response.

47. All squares are rectangles.

48. A trapezoid is a parallelogram.

49. A rhombus can be a kite.

50. Some parallelograms are squares.

51. Every quadrilateral is a parallelogram.

52. All rhombuses are squares.

Challenge

Proof **53.** **Given:** Isosceles trapezoid *TRAP* with $\overline{TR} \cong \overline{PA}$; $\overline{BI}$ is the perpendicular bisector of $\overline{RA}$, intersecting $\overline{RA}$ at *B* and $\overline{TP}$ at *I*.

Prove: $\overline{BI}$ is the perpendicular bisector of $\overline{TP}$.

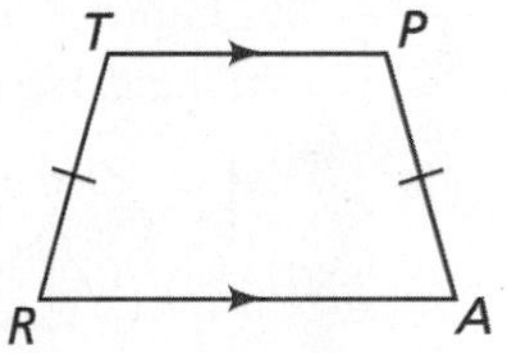

For a trapezoid, consider the segment joining the midpoints of the two given segments. How are its length and the lengths of the two parallel sides of the trapezoid related? Justify your answer.

54. the two nonparallel sides

55. the diagonals

56. $\overleftrightarrow{BN}$ is the perpendicular bisector of $\overline{AC}$ at *N*. Describe the set of points, *D*, for which *ABCD* is a kite.

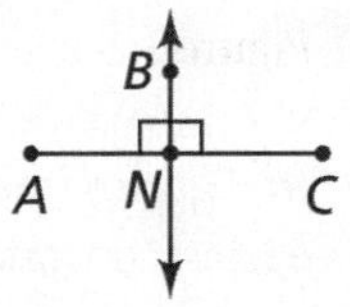

9-7 Applying Coordinate Geometry

G.CO.11 Prove theorems about parallelograms. Theorems include: opposite sides are congruent . . . Also G.CO.10

Objective To name coordinates of special figures by using their properties

Solve It! Write your solution to the Solve It in the space below.

In the Solve It, you found coordinates of a point and named it using numbers for the x- and y-coordinates. In this lesson, you will learn to use variables for the coordinates.

Essential Understanding You can use variables to name the coordinates of a figure. This allows you to show that relationships are true for a general case.

In Chapter 8, you learned about the segment joining the midpoints of two sides of a triangle. Here are three possible ways to place a triangle and its midsegment.

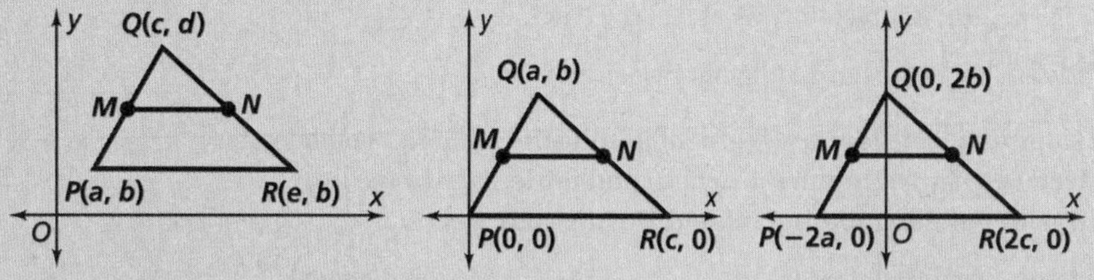

Figure 1 **Figure 2** **Figure 3**

Figure 1 does not use the axes, so it requires more variables. Figures 2 and 3 have good placement. In Figure 2, the midpoint coordinates are $M\left(\frac{a}{2}, \frac{b}{2}\right)$ and $N\left(\frac{a+c}{2}, \frac{b}{2}\right)$. In Figure 3, the coordinates are $M(-a, b)$ and $N(c, b)$. You can see that Figure 3 is the easiest to work with.

To summarize, to place a figure in the coordinate plane, it is usually helpful to place at least one side on an axis or to center the figure at the origin. For the coordinates, try to anticipate what you will need to do in the problem. Then multiply the coordinates by the appropriate number to make your work easier.

Problem 1 Naming Coordinates

Got It? What are the coordinates of the vertices of each figure?

a. *RECT* is a rectangle with height a and length $2b$. The y-axis bisects $\overline{EC}$ and $\overline{RT}$.

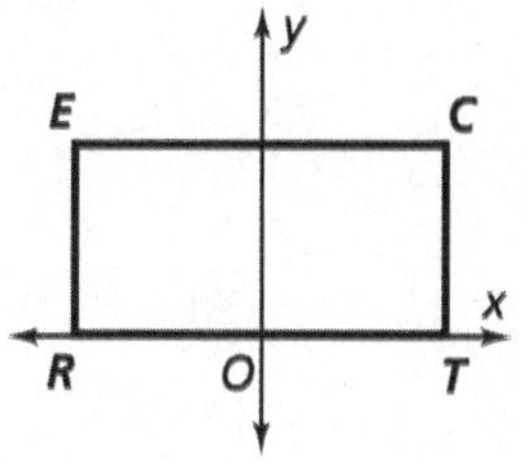

b. *KITE* is a kite where $IE = 2a$, $KO = b$, and $OT = c$. The x-axis bisects $\overline{IE}$.

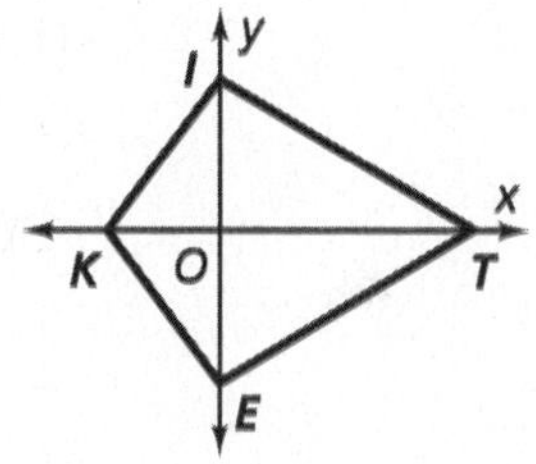

Practice **Algebra** **What are the coordinates of the vertices of each figure?**

1. parallelogram where S is a units from the origin and Z is b units from the origin

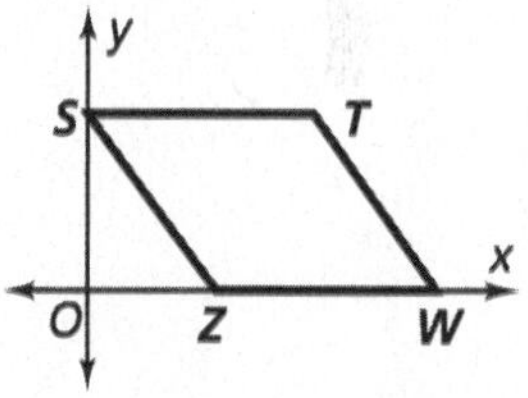

2. isosceles trapezoid with base centered at the origin, with base $2a$ and $OR = c$

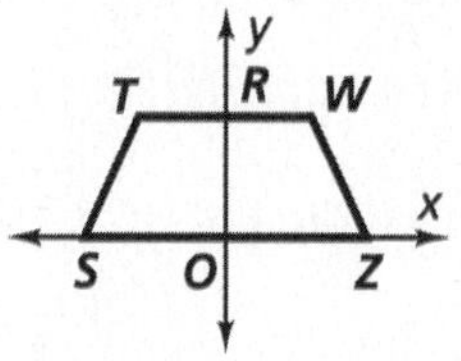

Problem 2 Using Variable Coordinates

Got It? a. **Reasoning** In Problem 2, explain why the x-coordinate of B is the sum of $2a$ and $2b$.

b. The diagram below shows a trapezoid with the base centered at the origin. Is the trapezoid isosceles? Explain.

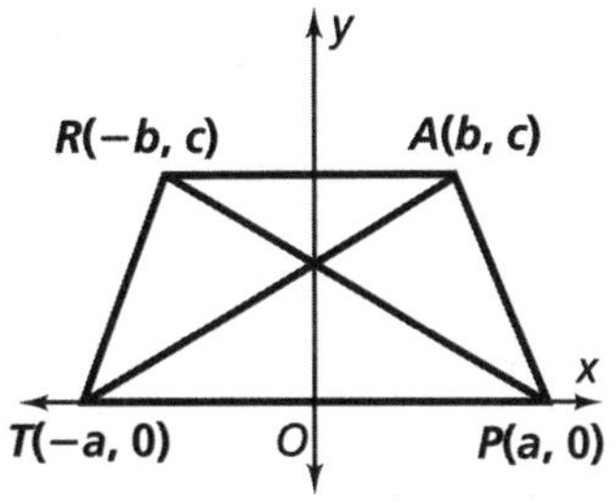

Plan

Which formula should you use to show that the trapezoid is isosceles?

Practice 3. The diagram at the right shows a parallelogram. Without using the Distance Formula, determine whether the parallelogram is a rhombus. How do you know?

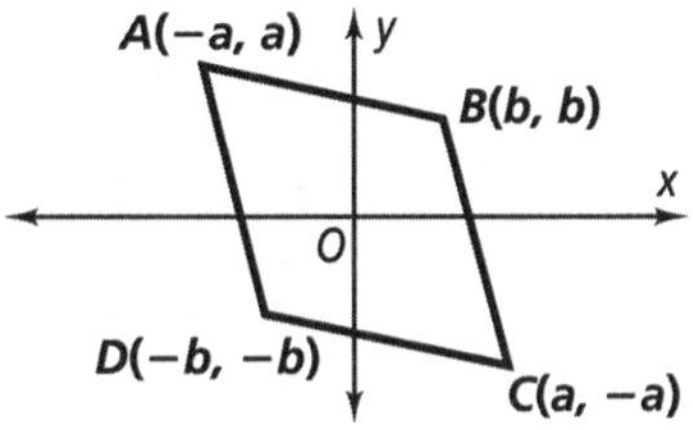

You can use coordinate geometry and algebra to prove theorems in geometry. This kind of proof is called a **coordinate proof.** Sometimes it is easier to show that a theorem is true by using a coordinate proof rather than a standard deductive proof. It is useful to write a plan for a coordinate proof. Problem 3 shows you how.

Problem 3 Planning a Coordinate Proof

Think

What conditions must be proved for the Triangle Midsegment Theorem?

Got It? Plan a coordinate proof of the Triangle Midsegment Theorem (Theorem 22).

Practice 4. Plan a coordinate proof to show that the midpoints of the sides of an isosceles trapezoid form a rhombus.

a. Name the coordinates of isosceles trapezoid *TRAP* at the right, with bottom base length $4a$, top base length $4b$, and $EG = 2c$. The y-axis bisects the bases.

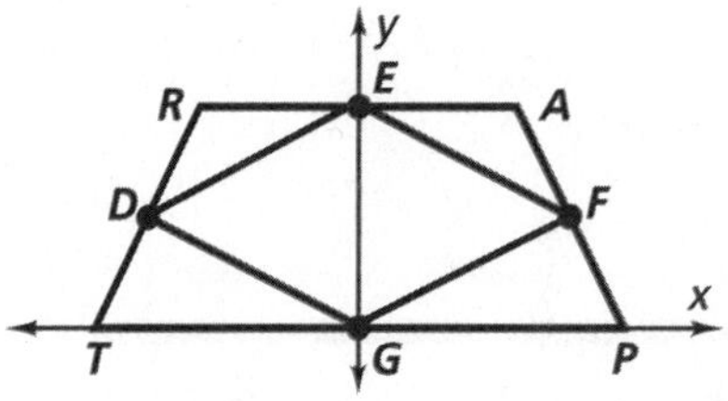

b. Write the *Given* and *Prove* statements.

c. How will you find the coordinates of the midpoints of each side?

d. How will you determine whether *DEFG* is a rhombus?

Lesson Check

Do you know HOW?

Use the diagram at the right.

5. In $\square KLMO$, $OM = 2a$. What are the coordinates of K and M?

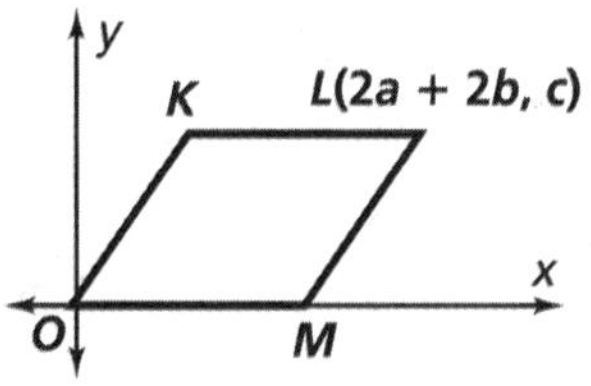

6. What are the slopes of the diagonals of *KLMO*?

7. What are the coordinates of the point of intersection of $\overline{KM}$ and $\overline{OL}$?

Do you UNDERSTAND?

MATHEMATICAL PRACTICES

8. Reasoning How do variable coordinates generalize figures in the coordinate plane?

9. Reasoning A vertex of a quadrilateral has coordinates (a, b). The x-coordinates of the other three vertices are a or $-a$, and the y-coordinates are b or $-b$. What kind of quadrilateral is the figure?

10. Error Analysis A classmate says the endpoints of the midsegment of the trapezoid in Problem 3 are $\left(\frac{b}{2}, \frac{c}{2}\right)$ and $\left(\frac{d+a}{2}, \frac{c}{2}\right)$. What is your classmate's error? Explain.

More Practice and Problem-Solving Exercises

MATHEMATICAL PRACTICES

B Apply

11. Open-Ended Place a general quadrilateral in the coordinate plane.

12. Reasoning A rectangle *LMNP* is centered at the origin with $M(r, -s)$. What are the coordinates of *P*?

Give the coordinates for point *P* without using any new variables.

13. isosceles trapezoid

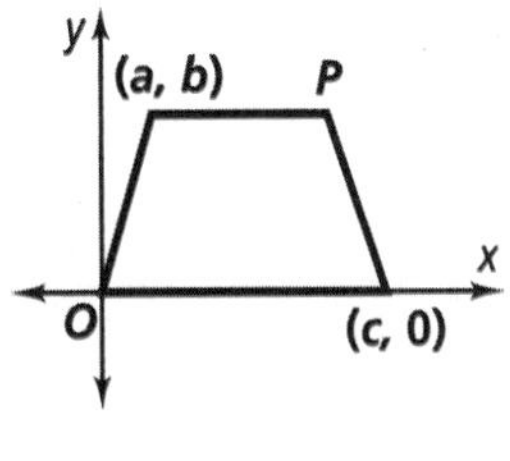

14. trapezoid with a right ∠

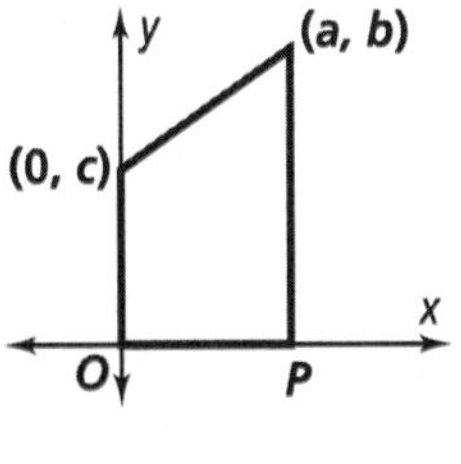

15. kite

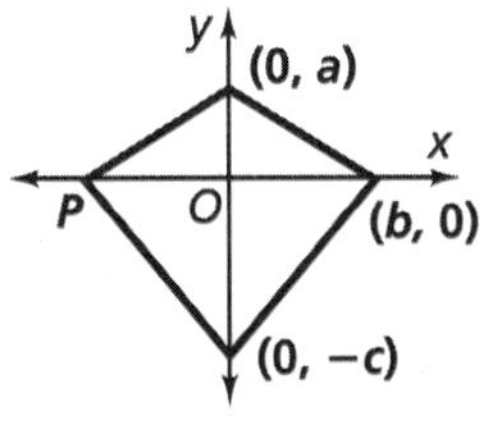

16. a. Draw a square whose diagonals of length $2b$ lie on the x- and y-axes.
b. Give the coordinates of the vertices of the square.
c. Compute the length of a side of the square.
d. Find the slopes of two adjacent sides of the square.
e. Writing Do the slopes show that the sides are perpendicular? Explain.

17. Make two drawings of an isosceles triangle with base length $2b$ and height $2c$.
a. In one drawing, place the base on the x-axis with a vertex at the origin.
b. In the second, place the base on the x-axis with its midpoint at the origin.
c. Find the lengths of the legs of the triangle as placed in part (a).
d. Find the lengths of the legs of the triangle as placed in part (b).
e. How do the results of parts (c) and (d) compare?

18. W and Z are the midpoints of $\overline{OR}$ and $\overline{ST}$, respectively. In parts (a)–(c), find the coordinates of W and Z.

a.

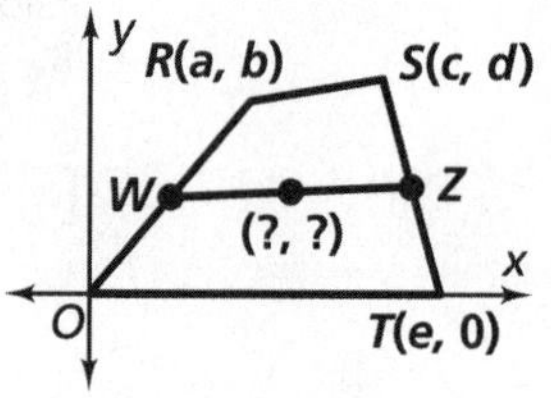

b.

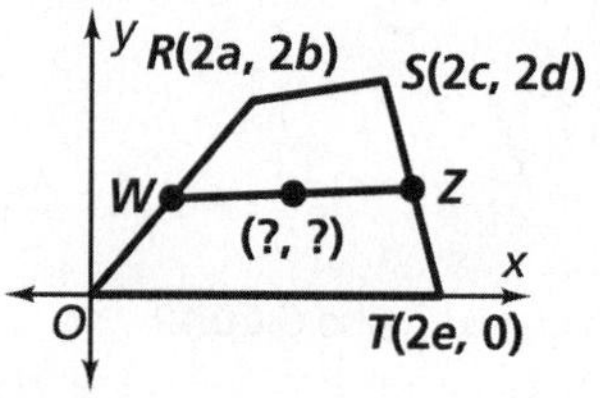

c.

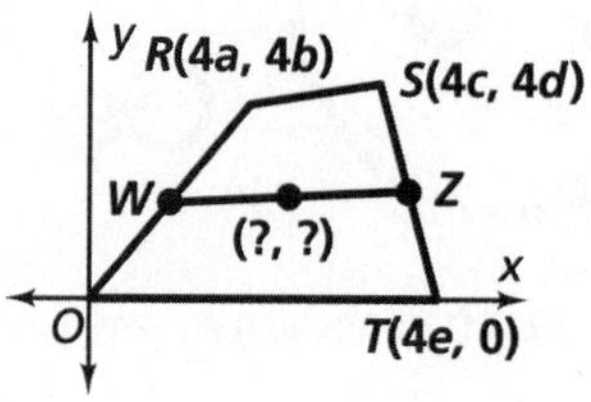

d. You are to plan a coordinate proof involving the midpoint of $\overline{WZ}$. Which of the figures (a)–(c) would you prefer to use? Explain.

Plan the coordinate proof of each statement.

19. **Think About a Plan** The opposite sides of a parallelogram are congruent (Theorem 38).
- How will you place the parallelogram in a coordinate plane?
- What formulas will you need to use?

20. The diagonals of a rectangle bisect each other.

21. The consecutive sides of a square are perpendicular.

Classify each quadrilateral as precisely as possible.

22. $A(b, 2c)$, $B(4b, 3c)$, $C(5b, c)$, $D(2b, 0)$

23. $E(a, b)$, $F(2a, 2b)$, $G(3a, b)$, $H(2a, -b)$

24. $O(0, 0)$, $P(t, 2s)$, $Q(3t, 2s)$, $R(4t, 0)$

25. $O(0, 0)$, $L(-e, f)$, $M(f - e, f + e)$, $N(f, e)$

26. What property of a rhombus makes it convenient to place its diagonals on the x- and y-axes?

STEM 27. **Marine Archaeology** Marine archaeologists sometimes use a coordinate system on the ocean floor. They record the coordinates of points where artifacts are found. Assume that each diver searches a square area and can go no farther than b units from the starting point. Draw a model for the region one diver can search. Assign coordinates to the vertices without using any new variables.

Challenge

Here are coordinates for eight points in the coordinate plane ($q > p > 0$). $A(0, 0)$, $B(p, 0)$, $C(q, 0)$, $D(p + q, 0)$, $E(0, q)$, $F(p, q)$, $G(q, q)$, $H(p + q, q)$. Which four points, if any, are the vertices for each type of figure?

28. parallelogram
29. rhombus
30. rectangle
31. square
32. trapezoid
33. isosceles trapezoid

9-8 Proofs Using Coordinate Geometry

G.CO.11 Prove theorems about parallelograms . . . Also **G.CO.10**

Objective To prove theorems using figures in the coordinate plane

Solve It! Write your solution to the Solve It in the space below.

In the Solve It, the coordinates of the points include variables. In this lesson, you will use coordinates with variables to write coordinate proofs.

Essential Understanding You can prove geometric relationships using variable coordinates for figures in the coordinate plane.

Problem 1 Writing a Coordinate Proof

Got It? **Reasoning** Refer to the proof in Problem 1. What is the advantage of using coordinates $O(0, 0)$, $E(0, 2b)$, and $F(2a, 0)$ rather than $O(0, 0)$, $E(0, b)$, and $F(a, 0)$?

Think
What is the advantage of placing the legs of the right triangle on the axes?

Practice **Developing Proof** **Complete the following coordinate proof.**

1. The medians drawn to the congruent sides of an isosceles triangle are congruent.

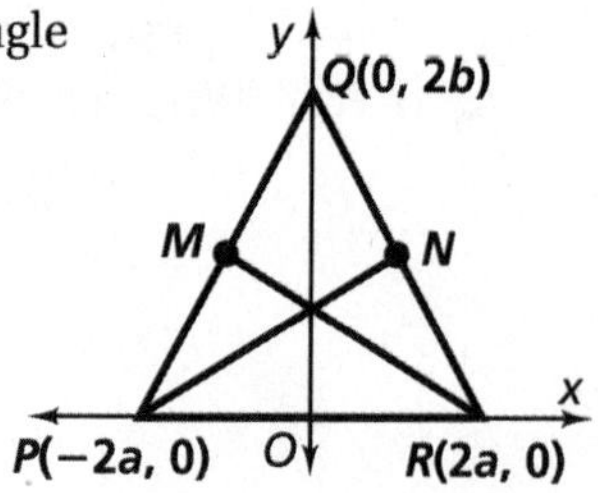

Given: $\triangle PQR$ with $\overline{PQ} \cong \overline{RQ}$, M is the midpoint of $\overline{PQ}$, N is the midpoint of $\overline{RQ}$

Prove: $\overline{PN} \cong \overline{RM}$

a. What are the coordinates of M and N?

b. What are PN and RM?

c. Explain why $\overline{PN} \cong \overline{RM}$.

In the previous lesson, you wrote a plan for the proof of the Trapezoid Midsegment Theorem. Now you will write the full coordinate proof.

Problem 2 Writing a Coordinate Proof

Got It? Write a coordinate proof of the Triangle Midsegment Theorem (Theorem 22).

Think
How will you place the triangle in the coordinate plane and assign coordinates?

A Practice **Developing Proof** Complete the following coordinate proof.

2. The diagonals of an isosceles trapezoid are congruent.

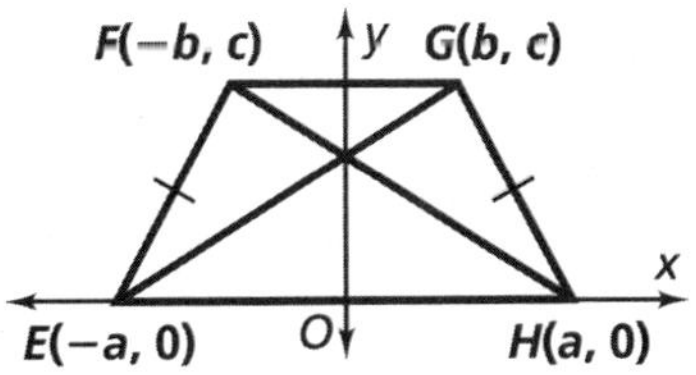

Given: Trapezoid *EFGH* with $\overline{EF} \cong \overline{GH}$

Prove: $\overline{EG} \cong \overline{FH}$

a. Find *EG*.

b. Find *FH*.

c. Explain why $\overline{EG} \cong \overline{FH}$.

Lesson Check

Do you know HOW?

3. Use coordinate geometry to prove that the diagonals of a rectangle are congruent.

a. Place rectangle *PQRS* in the coordinate plane with *P* at (0, 0).

b. What are the coordinates of *Q*, *R*, and *S*?

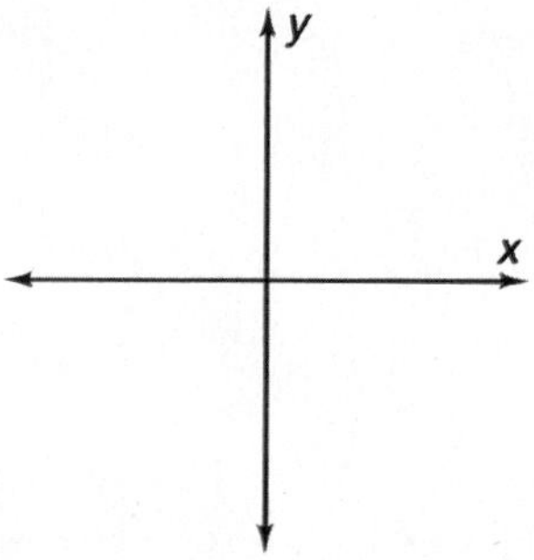

c. Write the *Given* and *Prove* statements.

d. Write a coordinate proof.

Do you UNDERSTAND?

MATHEMATICAL PRACTICES

4. Reasoning Describe a good strategy for placing the vertices of a rhombus for a coordinate proof.

5. **Error Analysis** Your classmate places a trapezoid on the coordinate plane. What is the error?

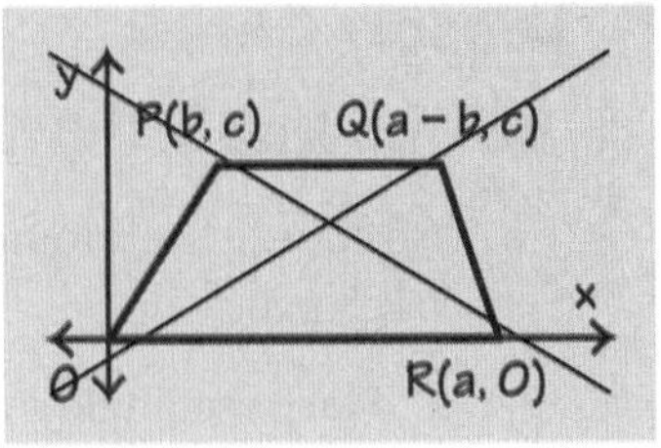

More Practice and Problem-Solving Exercises

MATHEMATICAL PRACTICES

B Apply

Tell whether you can reach each type of conclusion below using coordinate methods. Give a reason for each answer.

6. $\overline{AB} \cong \overline{CD}$
7. $\overline{AB} \parallel \overline{CD}$
8. $\overline{AB} \perp \overline{CD}$
9. $\overline{AB}$ bisects $\overline{CD}$.
10. $\overline{AB}$ bisects $\angle CAD$.
11. $\angle A \cong \angle B$
12. $\angle A$ is a right angle.
13. $AB + BC = AC$
14. $\triangle ABC$ is isosceles.
15. Quadrilateral $ABCD$ is a rhombus.
16. $\overline{AB}$ and $\overline{CD}$ bisect each other.
17. $\angle A$ is the supplement of $\angle B$.
18. $\overline{AB}$, $\overline{CD}$, and $\overline{EF}$ are concurrent.

Proof 19. **Flag Design** The flag design at the right is made by connecting the midpoints of the sides of a rectangle. Use coordinate geometry to prove that the quadrilateral formed is a rhombus.

20. **Open-Ended** Give an example of a statement that you think is easier to prove with a coordinate geometry proof than with a proof method that does not require coordinate geometry. Explain your choice.

Use coordinate geometry to prove each statement.

21. **Think About a Plan** If a parallelogram is a rhombus, its diagonals are perpendicular (Theorem 48).
    - How will you place the rhombus in a coordinate plane?
    - What formulas will you need to use?

22. The altitude to the base of an isosceles triangle bisects the base.

23. If the midpoints of a trapezoid are joined to form a quadrilateral, then the quadrilateral is a parallelogram.

24. One diagonal of a kite divides the kite into two congruent triangles.

Proof **25.** You learned in Theorem 29 that the centroid of a triangle is two thirds the distance from each vertex to the midpoint of the opposite side. Complete the steps to prove this theorem.

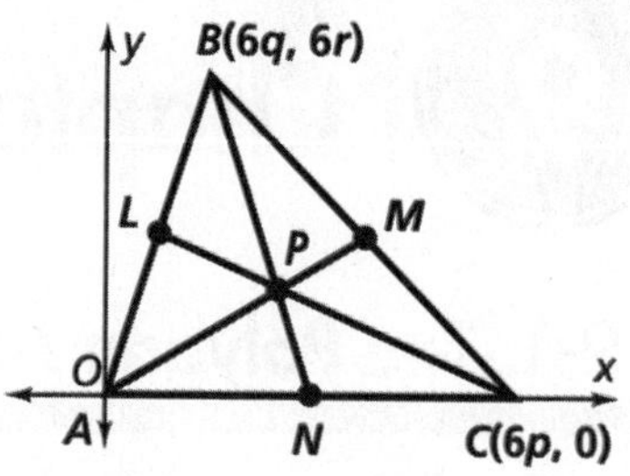

a. Find the coordinates of points L, M, and N, the midpoints of the sides of $\triangle ABC$.

b. Find equations of $\overleftrightarrow{AM}$, $\overleftrightarrow{BN}$, and $\overleftrightarrow{CL}$.

c. Find the coordinates of point P, the intersection of $\overleftrightarrow{AM}$ and $\overleftrightarrow{BN}$.

d. Show that point P is on $\overleftrightarrow{CL}$.

e. Use the Distance Formula to show that point P is two thirds the distance from each vertex to the midpoint of the opposite side.

Proof **26.** Complete the steps to prove Theorem 30. You are given $\triangle ABC$ with altitudes p, q, and r. Show that p, q, and r intersect at a point (called the orthocenter of the triangle).

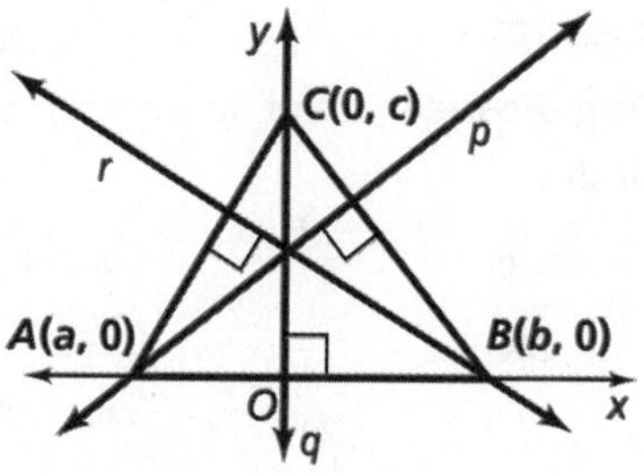

a. The slope of $\overline{BC}$ is $\frac{c}{-b}$. What is the slope of line p?

b. Show that the equation of line p is $y = \frac{b}{c}(x - a)$.

c. What is the equation of line q?

d. Show that lines p and q intersect at $\left(0, \frac{-ab}{c}\right)$.

e. The slope of $\overline{AC}$ is $\frac{c}{-a}$. What is the slope of line r?

f. Show that the equation of line r is $y = \frac{a}{c}(x - b)$.

g. Show that lines r and q intersect at $\left(0, \frac{-ab}{c}\right)$.

h. What are the coordinates of the orthocenter of $\triangle ABC$?

Challenge

27. Multiple Representations Use the diagram at the right.

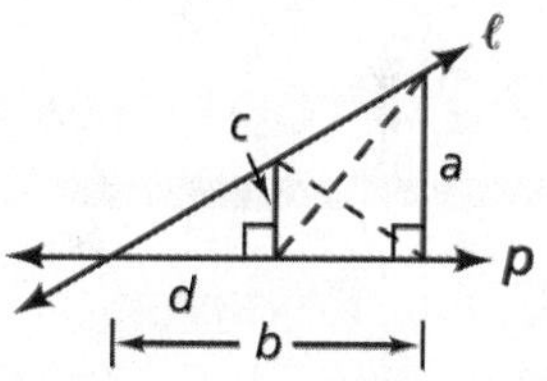

a. Explain using area why $\frac{1}{2}ad = \frac{1}{2}bc$ and therefore $ad = bc$.

b. Find two ratios for the slope of ℓ. Use these two ratios to show that $ad = bc$.

Proof **28. Prove:** If two lines are perpendicular, the product of their slopes is -1.

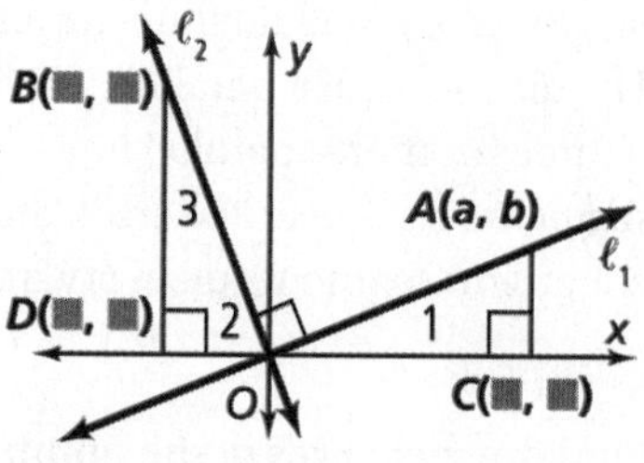

a. Two nonvertical lines, ℓ_1 and ℓ_2, intersect as shown at the right. Find the coordinates of C.

b. Choose coordinates for D and B. (*Hint:* Find the relationship between $\angle 1$, $\angle 2$, and $\angle 3$. Then use congruent triangles.)

c. Complete the proof that the product of slopes is -1.

9 Chapter Review

MathXL® for School
Go to pearsonsuccessnet.com

9-1 The Polygon Angle-Sum Theorems

Quick Review

The sum of the measures of the interior angles of an n-gon is $(n-2)180$. The measure of one interior angle of a regular n-gon is $\frac{(n-2)180}{n}$. The sum of the measures of the exterior angles of a polygon, one at each vertex, is 360.

Example

Find the measure of an interior angle of a regular 20-gon.

Measure $= \frac{(n-2)180}{n}$	Corollary to the Polygon Angle-Sum Theorem
$= \frac{(20-2)180}{20}$	Substitute.
$= \frac{18 \cdot 180}{20}$	Simplify.
$= 162$	

The measure of an interior angle is 162.

Exercises

Find the measure of an interior angle and an exterior angle of each regular polygon.

1. hexagon
2. 16-gon
3. pentagon
4. What is the sum of the exterior angles for each polygon in Exercises 1–3?

Find the measure of the missing angle.

5.
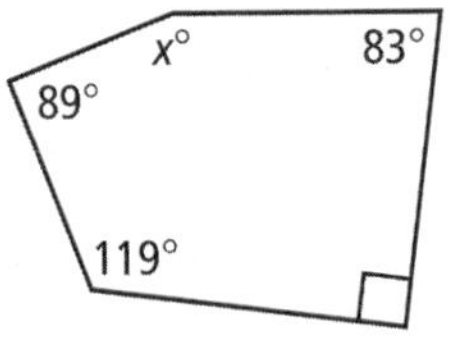

6.
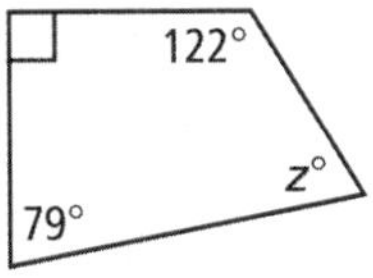

9-2 Properties of Parallelograms

Quick Review

Opposite sides and **opposite angles** of a **parallelogram** are congruent. **Consecutive angles** in a parallelogram are supplementary. The diagonals of a parallelogram bisect each other. If three (or more) parallel lines cut off congruent segments on one transversal, then they cut off congruent segments on every transversal.

Example

Find the measures of the numbered angles in the parallelogram.

Since consecutive angles are supplementary, $m\angle 1 = 180 - 56$, or 124. Since opposite angles are congruent, $m\angle 2 = 56$ and $m\angle 3 = 124$.

Exercises

Find the measures of the numbered angles for each parallelogram.

7.
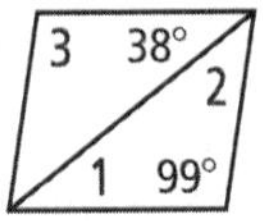

8.
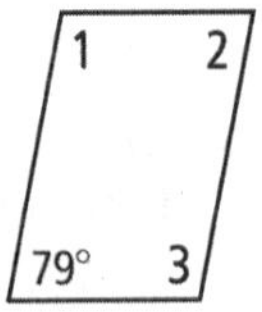

9.
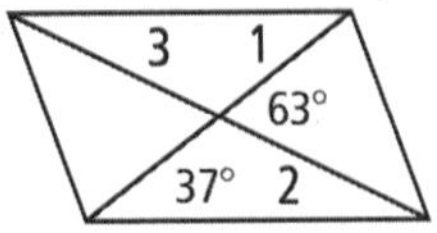

10.

Find the values of x and y in ▱ $ABCD$.

11. $AB = 2y$, $BC = y + 3$, $CD = 5x - 1$, $DA = 2x + 4$
12. $AB = 2y + 1$, $BC = y + 1$, $CD = 7x - 3$, $DA = 3x$

9-3 Proving That a Quadrilateral Is a Parallelogram

Quick Review

A quadrilateral is a parallelogram if any one of the following is true.

- Both pairs of opposite sides are parallel.
- Both pairs of opposite sides are congruent.
- Consecutive angles are supplementary.
- Both pairs of opposite angles are congruent.
- The diagonals bisect each other.
- One pair of opposite sides is both congruent and parallel.

Example

Must the quadrilateral be a parallelogram?

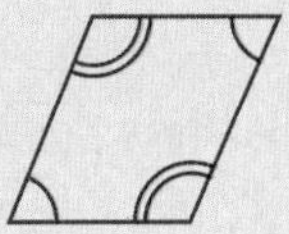

Yes, both pairs of opposite angles are congruent.

Exercises

Determine whether the quadrilateral must be a parallelogram.

13.

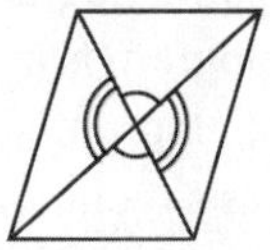

14.

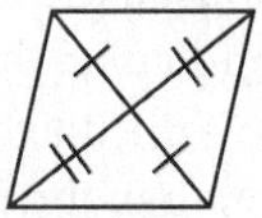

Algebra Find the values of the variables for which *ABCD* must be a parallelogram.

15.

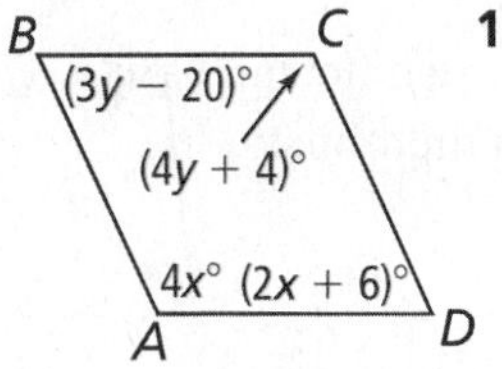

16.

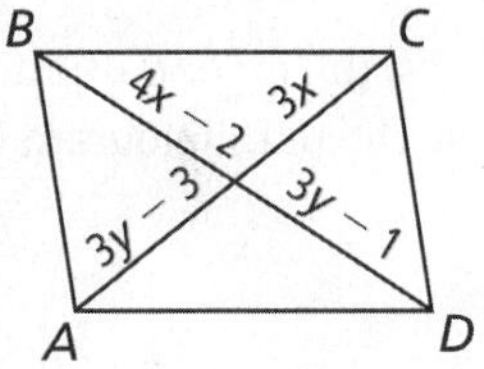

9-4 Properties of Rhombuses, Rectangles, and Squares

Quick Review

A **rhombus** is a parallelogram with four congruent sides.

A **rectangle** is a parallelogram with four right angles.

A **square** is a parallelogram with four congruent sides and four right angles.

The diagonals of a rhombus are perpendicular. Each diagonal bisects a pair of opposite angles.

The diagonals of a rectangle are congruent.

Example

What are the measures of the numbered angles in the rhombus?

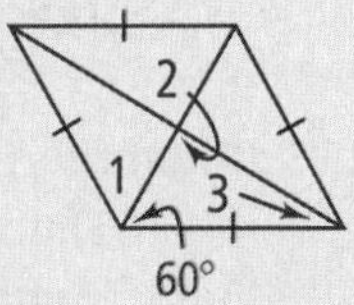

$m\angle 1 = 60$ Each diagonal of a rhombus bisects a pair of opposite angles.

$m\angle 2 = 90$ The diagonals of a rhombus are ⊥.

$60 + m\angle 2 + m\angle 3 = 180$ Triangle Angle-Sum Thm.

$60 + 90 + m\angle 3 = 180$ Substitute.

$m\angle 3 = 30$ Simplify.

Exercises

Find the measures of the numbered angles in each special parallelogram.

17.

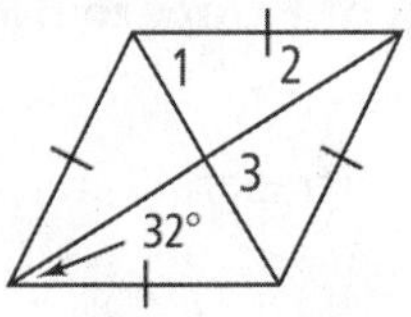

18.

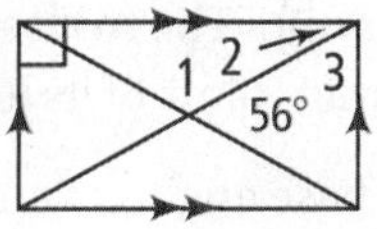

Determine whether each statement is *always, sometimes,* or *never* true.

19. A rhombus is a square.

20. A square is a rectangle.

21. A rhombus is a rectangle.

22. The diagonals of a parallelogram are perpendicular.

23. The diagonals of a parallelogram are congruent.

24. Opposite angles of a parallelogram are congruent.

9-5 Conditions for Rhombuses, Rectangles, and Squares

Quick Review

If one diagonal of a parallelogram bisects two angles of the parallelogram, then the parallelogram is a rhombus. If the diagonals of a parallelogram are perpendicular, then the parallelogram is a rhombus. If the diagonals of a parallelogram are congruent, then the parallelogram is a rectangle.

Example

Can you conclude that the parallelogram is a rhombus, rectangle, or square? Explain.

Yes, the diagonals are perpendicular, so the parallelogram is a rhombus.

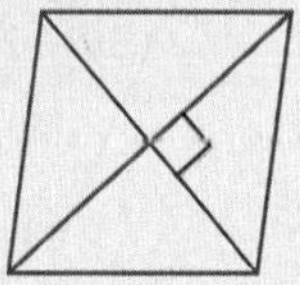

Exercises

Can you conclude that the parallelogram is a rhombus, rectangle, or square? Explain.

25.

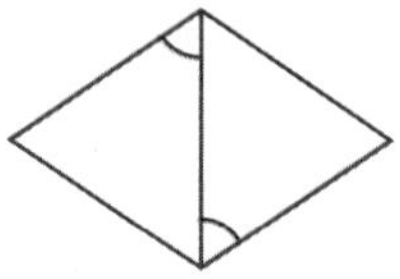

26.

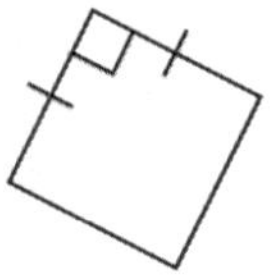

For what value of x is the figure the given parallelogram? Justify your answer.

27. Rhombus

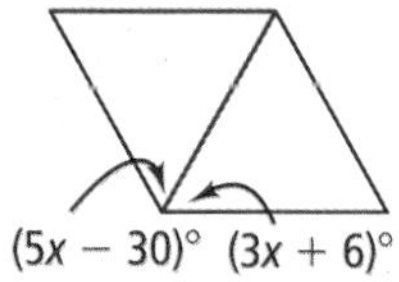

28. Rectangle

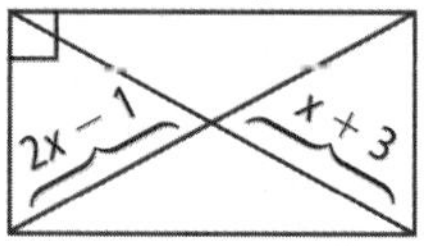

9-6 Trapezoids and Kites

Quick Review

The parallel sides of a **trapezoid** are its **bases** and the nonparallel sides are its **legs**. Two angles that share a base of a trapezoid are **base angles** of the trapezoid. The **midsegment of a trapezoid** joins the midpoints of its legs.

The base angles of an isosceles trapezoid are congruent.

The diagonals of an isosceles trapezoid are congruent.

The diagonals of a kite are perpendicular.

Example

***ABCD* is an isosceles trapezoid. What is $m\angle C$?**

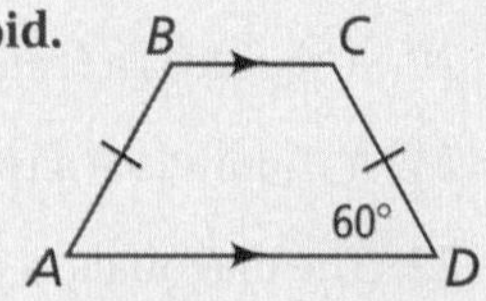

Since $\overline{BC} \parallel \overline{AD}$, $\angle C$ and $\angle D$ are same-side interior angles.

$m\angle C + m\angle D = 180$	Same-side interior angles are supplementary.
$m\angle C + 60 = 180$	Substitute.
$m\angle C = 120$	Subtract 60 from each side.

Exercises

Find the measures of the numbered angles in each isosceles trapezoid.

29.

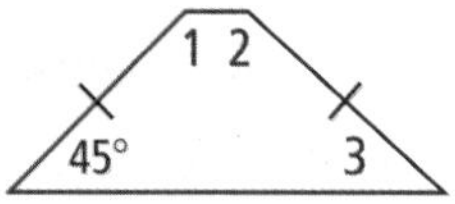

30.

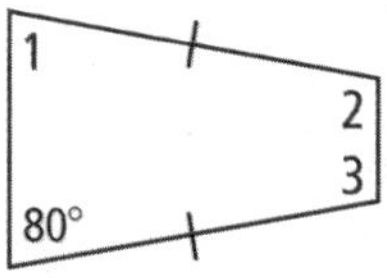

Find the measures of the numbered angles in each kite.

31.

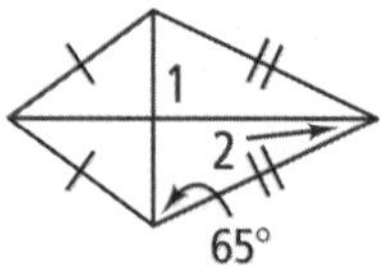

32.

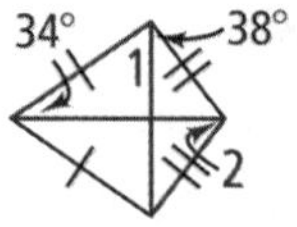

33. Algebra A trapezoid has base lengths of $(6x - 1)$ units and 3 units. Its midsegment has a length of $(5x - 3)$ units. What is the value of x?

9-7 and 9-8
Applying Coordinate Geometry and Proofs Using Coordinate Geometry

Quick Review

When placing a figure in the coordinate plane, it is usually helpful to place at least one side on an axis. Use variables when naming the coordinates of a figure in order to show that relationships are true for a general case.

Example

Rectangle *PQRS* has length a and width $4b$. The x-axis bisects $\overline{PS}$ and $\overline{QR}$. What are the coordinates of the vertices?

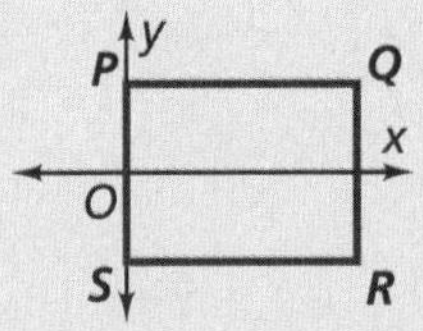

Since the width of *PQRS* is $4b$ and the x-axis bisects $\overline{PS}$ and $\overline{QR}$, all the vertices are $2b$ units from the x-axis. $\overline{PS}$ is on the y-axis, so $P = (0, 2b)$ and $S = (0, -2b)$. The length of *PQRS* is a, so $Q = (a, 2b)$ and $R = (a, -2b)$.

Exercises

34. In rhombus *FLPS*, the axes form the diagonals. If $SL = 2a$ and $FP = 4b$, what are the coordinates of the vertices?

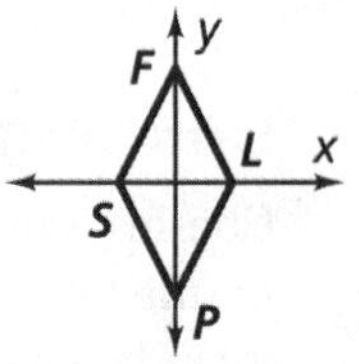

35. The figure at the right is a parallelogram. Give the coordinates of point *P* without using any new variables.

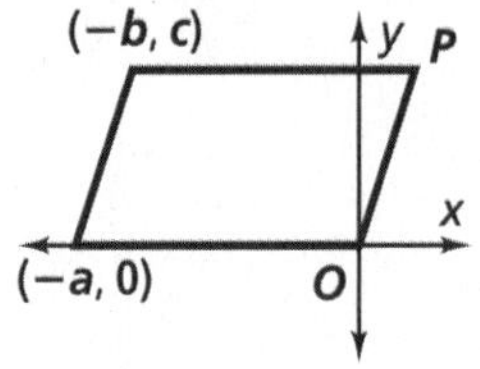

36. Use coordinate geometry to prove that the quadrilateral formed by connecting the midpoints of a kite is a rectangle.

9 Pull It All Together

PERFORMANCE TASK

Building a Kite

ASSESSMENT

Charles is building a paper kite. He needs another dowel to make the vertical support for the frame. He gives his friend Amy the measurements below but neglects to include the length of the support.

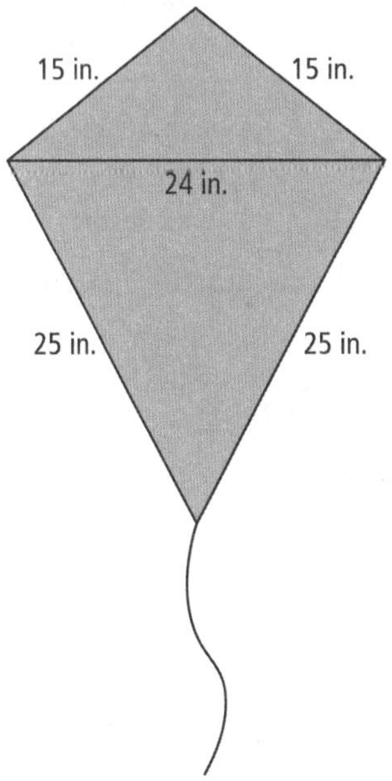

Task Description

Find the length of the vertical support for this kite and the area of the paper used to make the kite.

- What is true about the diagonals of a kite? How can you use this information to find the length of the vertical support?
- How can you find the kite's area by decomposing the kite into smaller figures?

CHAPTER 10

Get Ready!

Properties of Parallel Lines

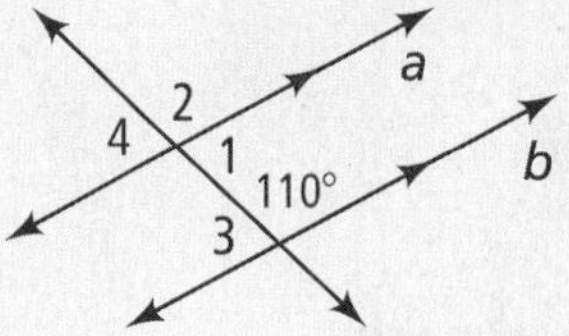

Use the diagram at the right. Find the measure of each angle. Justify your answer.

1. $\angle 1$ **2.** $\angle 2$ **3.** $\angle 3$ **4.** $\angle 4$

Naming Congruent Parts

$\triangle PAC \cong \triangle DHL$. **Complete each congruence statement.**

5. $\overline{PC} \cong$ _?_ **6.** $\angle H \cong$ _?_ **7.** $\angle PCA \cong$ _?_ **8.** $\triangle HDL \cong$ _?_

Triangle Congruence

Write a congruence statement for each pair of triangles. Explain why the triangles are congruent.

9.

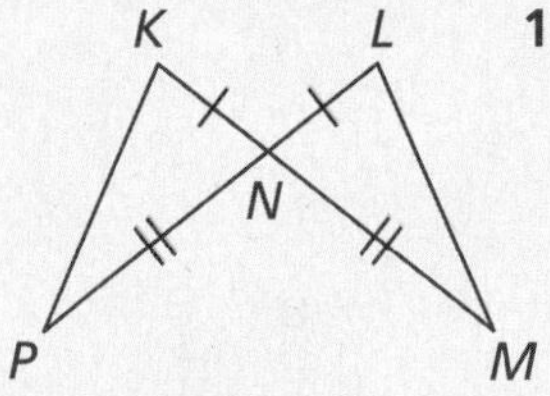

10.

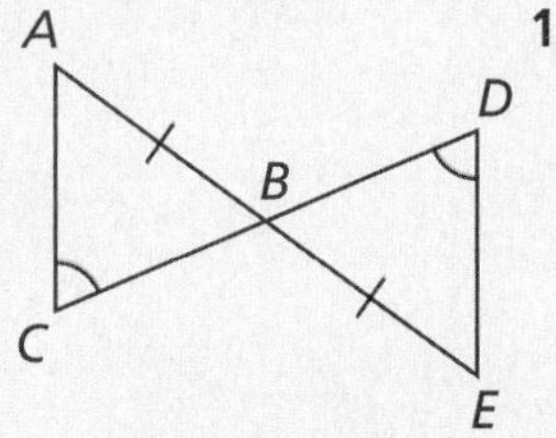

11.

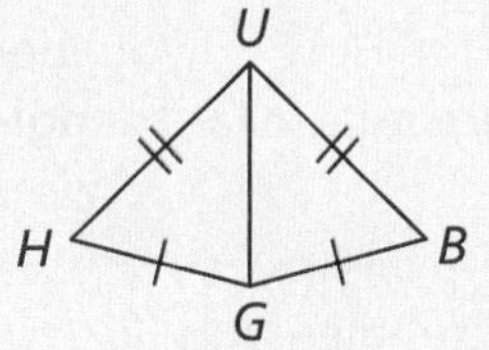

Midsegments of Triangles

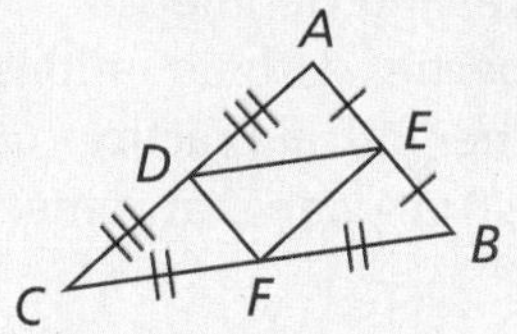

Use the diagram at the right for Exercises 12–13.

12. If $BC = 12$, then $BF =$ _?_ and $DE =$ _?_.

13. If $EF = 4.7$, then $AD =$ _?_ and $AC =$ _?_.

VOCABULARY Looking Ahead Vocabulary

14. An artist sketches a person. She is careful to draw the different parts of the person's body in *proportion*. What does *proportion* mean in this situation?

15. Siblings often look *similar* to each other. How might two geometric figures be *similar*?

16. A road map has a *scale* on it that tells you how many miles are equivalent to a distance of 1 inch on the map. How would you use the *scale* to estimate the distance between two cities on the map?

CHAPTER 10

Similarity

Big Ideas

1 Similarity
Essential Question How do you use proportions to find side lengths in similar polygons?

2 Reasoning and Proof
Essential Question How do you show two triangles are similar?

3 Visualization
Essential Question How do you identify corresponding parts of similar triangles?

Domains

- Similarity, Right Triangles, and Trigonometry
- Expressing Geometric Properties with Equations
- Mathematical Practice: Construct viable arguments

Interactive Digital Path

Log in to **pearsonsuccessnet.com** and click on Interactive Digital Path to access the Solve Its and animated Problems.

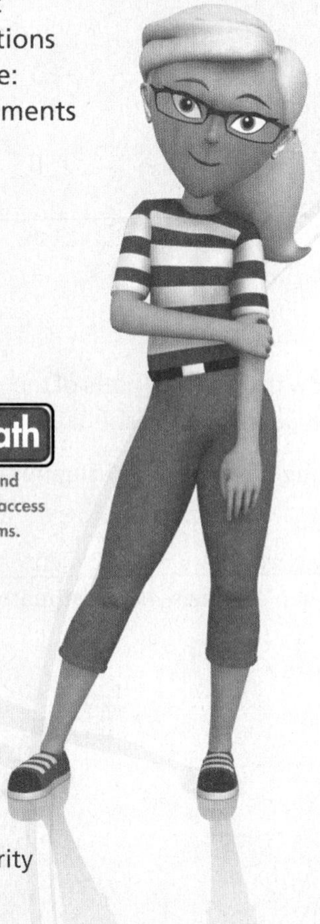

Chapter Preview

Vocabulary

English/Spanish Vocabulary Audio Online:

English	Spanish
dilation, *p. 723*	dilatación
extremes of a proportion, *p. 670*	valores extremos de una proporción
geometric mean, *p. 701*	media geométrica
indirect measurement, *p. 694*	medición indirecta
means of a proportion, *p. 670*	valores medios de una proporción
proportion, *p. 670*	proporción
ratio, *p. 667*	razón
scale drawing, *p. 682*	dibujo a escala
scale factor, *p. 678, 723*	factor de escala
similar, *p. 678, 733*	semejante
similar polygons, *p. 678*	polígonos semejantes

10-1 Ratios and Proportions

Prepares for **G.SRT.5** Use . . . similarity criteria for triangles to solve problems and to prove relationships in geometric figures. Also **N.Q.2**

Objective To write ratios and solve proportions

Solve It! Write your solution to the Solve It in the space below.

In the Solve It, you compared two quantities for four years.

Essential Understanding You can write a *ratio* to compare two quantities.

A **ratio** is a comparison of two quantities by division. You can write the ratio of two numbers a and b, where $b \neq 0$, in three ways: $\frac{a}{b}$, $a : b$, and a to b. You usually express a and b in the same unit and write the ratio in simplest form.

Problem 1 Writing a Ratio

Got It? A bonsai tree is 18 in. wide and stands 2 ft tall. What is the ratio of the width of the bonsai to its height?

Think
How can you write the width and the height using the same units?

Practice **Write the ratio of the first measurement to the second measurement.**

1. length of a tennis racket: 2 ft 4 in.

   length of a table tennis paddle: 10 in.

2. diameter of a table tennis ball: 40 mm

   diameter of a tennis ball: 6.8 cm

Problem 2 Dividing a Quantity Into a Given Ratio

Got It? The measures of two supplementary angles are in the ratio 1 : 4. What are the measures of the angles?

Practice **3. Baseball** A baseball team played 154 regular season games. The ratio of the number of games they won to the number of games they lost was $\frac{5}{2}$. How many games did they win? How many games did they lose?

4. The measures of two supplementary angles are in the ratio 5 : 7. What is the measure of the larger angle?

An **extended ratio** compares three (or more) numbers. In the extended ratio $a : b : c$, the ratio of the first two numbers is $a : b$, the ratio of the last two numbers is $b : c$, and the ratio of the first and last numbers is $a : c$.

Problem 3 Using an Extended Ratio

Got It? The lengths of the sides of a triangle are in the extended ratio 4 : 7 : 9. The perimeter is 60 cm. What are the lengths of the sides?

Think
How do you use the extended ratio to write the equation?

A Practice **5.** The lengths of the sides of a triangle are in the extended ratio 6 : 7 : 9. The perimeter of the triangle is 88 cm. What are the lengths of the sides?

6. The measures of the angles of a triangle are in the extended ratio 4 : 3 : 2. What is the measure of the largest angle?

Essential Understanding If two ratios are equivalent, you can write an equation stating that the ratios are equal. If the equation contains a variable, you can solve the equation to find the value of the variable.

An equation that states that two ratios are equal is called a **proportion.** The first and last numbers in a proportion are the **extremes.** The middle two numbers are the **means.**

extremes (2 and 6)

$2 : 3 = 4 : 6$

means (3 and 4)

extremes → $\frac{2}{3} = \frac{4}{6}$ ← means

take note

Key Concept Cross Products Property

Words	Symbols	Example
In a proportion, the product of the extremes equals the product of the means.	If $\frac{a}{b} = \frac{c}{d}$, where $b \neq 0$ and $d \neq 0$, then $ad = bc$.	$\frac{2}{3} = \frac{4}{6}$ $2 \cdot 6 = 3 \cdot 4$ $12 = 12$

Here's Why It Works Begin with $\frac{a}{b} = \frac{c}{d}$, where $b \neq 0$ and $d \neq 0$.

$bd \cdot \frac{a}{b} = \frac{c}{d} \cdot bd$ Multiply each side of the proportion by *bd*.

$\frac{\cancel{b}d}{1} \cdot \frac{a}{\cancel{b}} = \frac{c}{\cancel{d}} \cdot \frac{b\cancel{d}}{1}$ Divide the common factors.

$ad = bc$ Simplify.

Problem 4 Solving a Proportion

Got It? What is the solution of each proportion?

a. $\frac{9}{2} = \frac{a}{14}$

b. $\frac{15}{m + 1} = \frac{3}{m}$

Practice Algebra Solve each proportion.

7. $\frac{y}{10} = \frac{15}{25}$

8. $\frac{n + 4}{8} = \frac{n}{4}$

Using the Properties of Equality, you can rewrite proportions in equivalent forms.

take note

Key Concept Properties of Proportions

a, b, c, and d do not equal zero.

Property	How to Apply It
(1) $\frac{a}{b} = \frac{c}{d}$ is equivalent to $\frac{b}{a} = \frac{d}{c}$.	Write the reciprocal of each ratio. $\frac{2}{3} = \frac{4}{6}$ becomes $\frac{3}{2} = \frac{6}{4}$.
(2) $\frac{a}{b} = \frac{c}{d}$ is equivalent to $\frac{a}{c} = \frac{b}{d}$.	Switch the means. $\frac{2}{3} = \frac{4}{6}$ becomes $\frac{2}{4} = \frac{3}{6}$.
(3) $\frac{a}{b} = \frac{c}{d}$ is equivalent to $\frac{a+b}{b} = \frac{c+d}{d}$.	In each ratio, add the denominator to the numerator. $\frac{2}{3} = \frac{4}{6}$ becomes $\frac{2+3}{3} = \frac{4+6}{6}$.

ONLINE PROBLEMS

Problem 5 Writing Equivalent Proportions

Got It? For parts (a) and (b), use the proportion $\frac{x}{6} = \frac{y}{7}$. What ratio completes the equivalent proportion? Justify your answer.

a. $\frac{6}{x} = \frac{\blacksquare}{\blacksquare}$

b. $\frac{\blacksquare}{\blacksquare} = \frac{y+7}{7}$

c. Reasoning Explain why $\frac{6}{x-6} = \frac{7}{y-7}$ is an equivalent proportion to $\frac{x}{6} = \frac{y}{7}$. (Assume $x \neq 6$ and $y \neq 7$.)

Practice In the diagram, $\frac{a}{b} = \frac{3}{4}$. Complete each statement. Justify your answer.

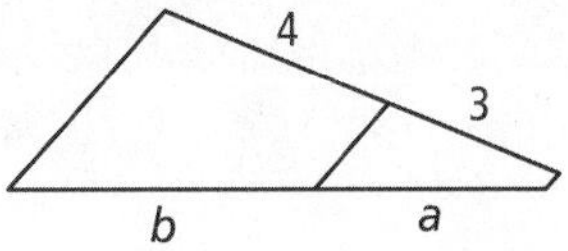

9. $4a = \blacksquare$

10. $\frac{a + b}{b} = \frac{\blacksquare}{\blacksquare}$

Lesson Check

Do you know HOW?

11. A cell phone is 84 mm long and 46 mm wide. What is the ratio of the width to the length?

12. Two angle measures are in the ratio 5 : 9. Write expressions for the two angle measures in terms of the variable x.

13. What is the solution of the proportion $\frac{20}{z} = \frac{5}{3}$?

14. For $\frac{a}{7} = \frac{13}{b}$ complete each equivalent proportion.

a. $\frac{a}{\blacksquare} = \frac{7}{\blacksquare}$

b. $\frac{a-7}{7} = \frac{\blacksquare}{\blacksquare}$

c. $\frac{7}{a} = \frac{\blacksquare}{\blacksquare}$

Do you UNDERSTAND?

MATHEMATICAL PRACTICES

15. **Vocabulary** What is the difference between a ratio and a proportion?

16. **Open-Ended** The lengths of the sides of a triangle are in the extended ratio 3 : 6 : 7. What are two possible sets of side lengths, in inches, for the triangle?

17. **Error Analysis** What is the error in the solution of the proportion shown at the right?

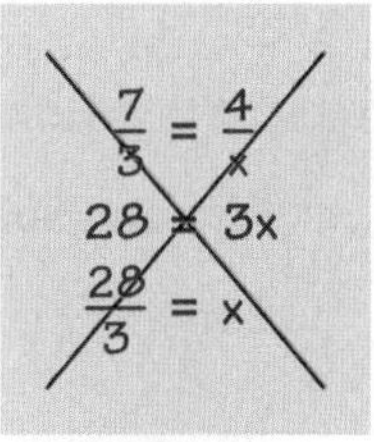

18. What is a proportion that has means 6 and 18 and extremes 9 and 12?

More Practice and Problem-Solving Exercises

MATHEMATICAL PRACTICES

B Apply

Coordinate Geometry Use the graph. Write each ratio in simplest form.

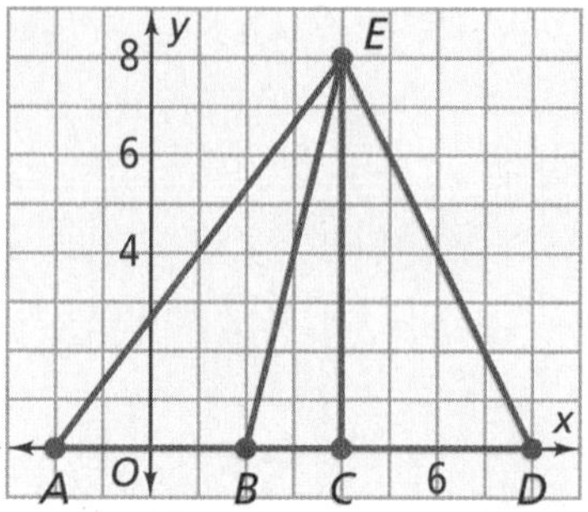

19. $\frac{AC}{BD}$ **20.** $\frac{AE}{EC}$ **21.** slope of $\overline{EB}$ **22.** slope of $\overline{ED}$

23. Think About a Plan The area of a rectangle is 150 in.^{2}. The ratio of the length to the width is 3 : 2. Find the length and the width.
- What is the formula for the area of a rectangle?
- How can you use the given ratio to write expressions for the length and width?

Art To draw a face, you can sketch the head as an oval and then lightly draw horizontal lines to help locate the eyes, nose, and mouth. You can use the extended ratios shown in the diagrams to help you place the lines for an adult's face or for a baby's face.

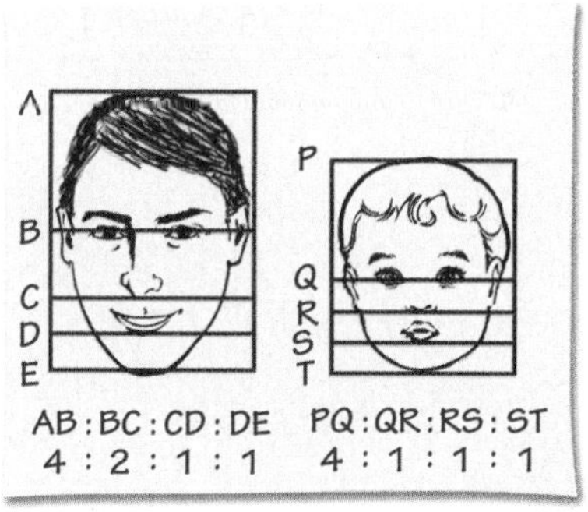

24. If $AE = 72$ cm in the diagram, find AB, BC, CD, and DE.

25. You draw a baby's head as an oval that is 21 in. from top to bottom.
a. How far from the top should you place the line for the eyes?
b. Suppose you decide to make the head an adult's head. How far up should you move the line for the eyes?

Algebra Solve each proportion.

26. $\frac{1}{7y - 5} = \frac{2}{9y}$

27. $\frac{4a + 1}{7} = \frac{2a}{3}$

28. $\frac{5}{x + 2} = \frac{3}{x + 1}$

29. $\frac{2b - 1}{4} = \frac{b - 2}{12}$

30. The ratio of the length to the width of a rectangle is 9 : 4. The width of the rectangle is 52 mm. Write and solve a proportion to find the length.

31. Open-Ended Draw a quadrilateral that satisfies this condition: The measures of the consecutive angles are in the extended ratio 4 : 5 : 4 : 7.

32. Reasoning The means of a proportion are 4 and 15. List all possible pairs of positive integers that could be the extremes of the proportion.

33. Writing Describe how to use the Cross Products Property to determine whether $\frac{10}{26} = \frac{16}{42}$ is a true proportion.

34. Reasoning Explain how to use two different properties of proportions to change the proportion $\frac{3}{4} = \frac{12}{16}$ into the proportion $\frac{12}{3} = \frac{16}{4}$.

Complete each statement. Justify your answer.

35. If $4m = 9n$, then $\frac{m}{n} = \frac{■}{■}$.

36. If $\frac{30}{t} = \frac{18}{r}$, then $\frac{t}{r} = \frac{■}{■}$.

37. If $\frac{a+5}{5} = \frac{b+2}{2}$, then $\frac{a}{5} = \frac{■}{■}$.

38. If $\frac{a}{b} = \frac{c}{d}$, then $\frac{a+b}{c+d} = \frac{■}{■}$.

39. If $\frac{a}{b} = \frac{c}{d}$, then $\frac{a+c}{b+d} = \frac{■}{■}$.

40. If $\frac{a}{b} = \frac{c}{d}$, then $\frac{a+2b}{b} = \frac{■}{■}$.

Challenge

Algebra Use properties of equality to justify each property of proportions.

41. $\frac{a}{b} = \frac{c}{d}$ is equivalent to $\frac{b}{a} = \frac{d}{c}$.

42. $\frac{a}{b} = \frac{c}{d}$ is equivalent to $\frac{a}{c} = \frac{b}{d}$.

43. $\frac{a}{b} = \frac{c}{d}$ is equivalent to $\frac{a+b}{b} = \frac{c+d}{d}$.

10-2 Similar Polygons

G.SRT.5 Use . . . similarity criteria for triangles to solve problems and to prove relationships in geometric figures.

Objective To identify and apply similar polygons

Solve It! Write your solution to the Solve It in the space below.

Similar figures have the same shape but not necessarily the same size. You can abbreviate *is similar to* with the symbol ~.

Essential Understanding You can use ratios and proportions to decide whether two polygons are similar and to find unknown side lengths of similar figures.

take note

Key Concept Similar Polygons

Define	Diagram	Symbols
Two polygons are **similar polygons** if corresponding angles are congruent and if the lengths of corresponding sides are proportional.	$ABCD \sim GHIJ$ 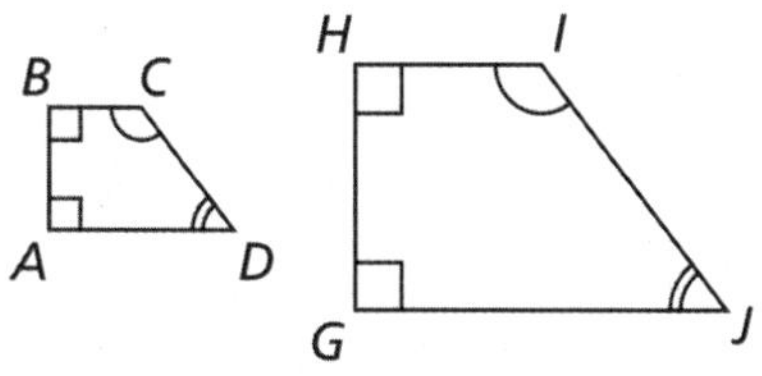	$\angle A \cong \angle G$ $\angle B \cong \angle H$ $\angle C \cong \angle I$ $\angle D \cong \angle J$ $\frac{AB}{GH} = \frac{BC}{HI} = \frac{CD}{IJ} = \frac{AD}{GJ}$

You write a similarity statement with corresponding vertices in order, just as you write a congruence statement. When three or more ratios are equal, you can write an **extended proportion.** The proportion $\frac{AB}{GH} = \frac{BC}{HI} = \frac{CD}{IJ} = \frac{AD}{GJ}$ is an extended proportion.

A **scale factor** is the ratio of corresponding linear measurements of two similar figures. The ratio of the lengths of corresponding sides $\overline{BC}$ and $\overline{YZ}$, or more simply stated, the ratio of corresponding sides, is $\frac{BC}{YZ} = \frac{20}{8} = \frac{5}{2}$. So the scale factor of $\triangle ABC$ to $\triangle XYZ$ is $\frac{5}{2}$, or 5 : 2.

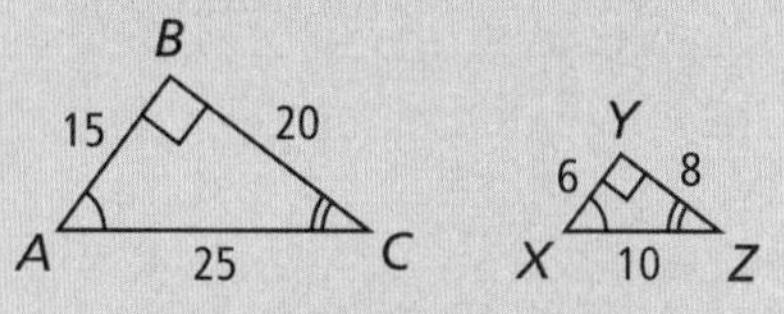

$\triangle ABC \sim \triangle XYZ$

Problem 1 Understanding Similarity

Got It? *DEFG* ~ *HJKL*

a. What are the pairs of congruent angles?

b. What is the extended proportion for the ratios of the lengths of corresponding sides?

Think

How can you use the similarity statement to write ratios of corresponding sides?

Practice **List the pairs of congruent angles and the extended proportion that relates the corresponding sides for the similar polygons.**

1. *RSTV* ~ *DEFG*

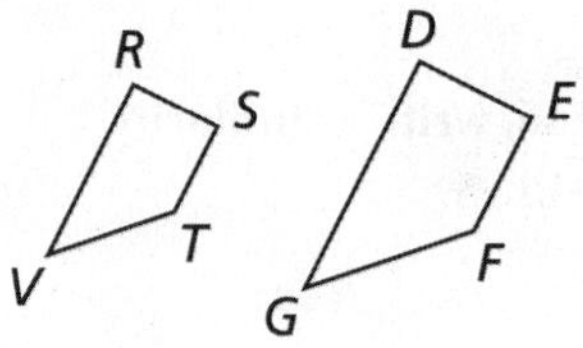

2. *KLMNP* ~ *HGFDC*

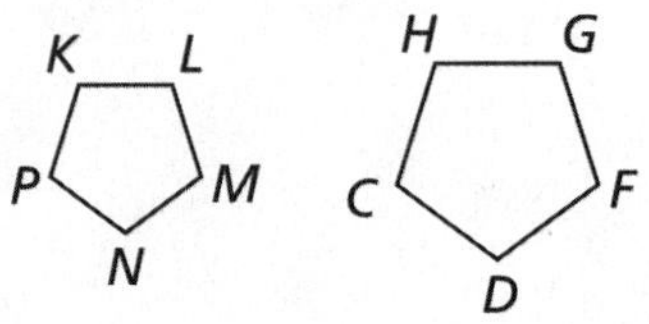

Problem 2 Determining Similarity

Think

How do you identify corresponding sides?

Got It? Are the polygons similar? If they are, write a similarity statement and give the scale factor.

a.

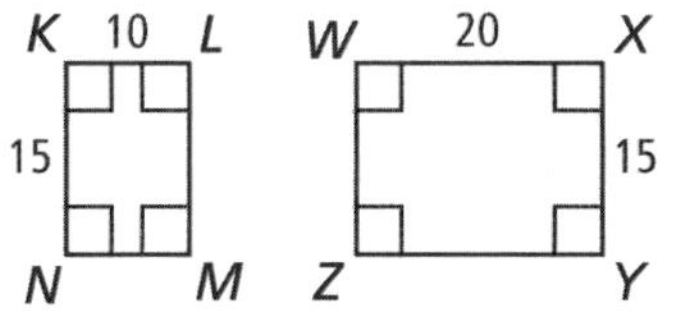

b.

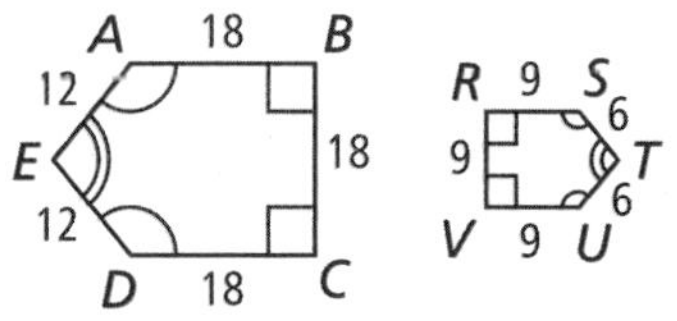

A Practice **Determine whether the polygons are similar. If so, write a similarity statement and give the scale factor. If not, explain.**

3.

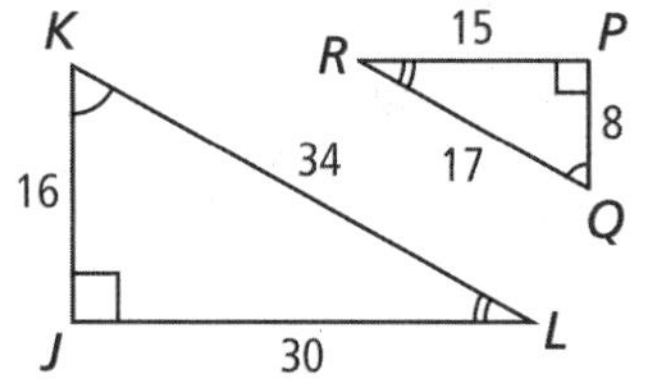

4.

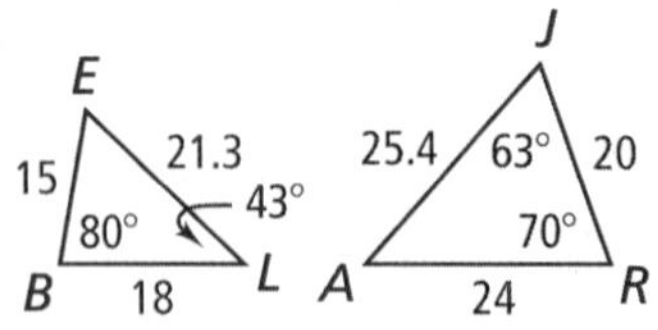

Problem 3 Using Similar Polygons

Got It? Use the diagram in Problem 3. $ABCD \sim EFGD$ What is the value of y?

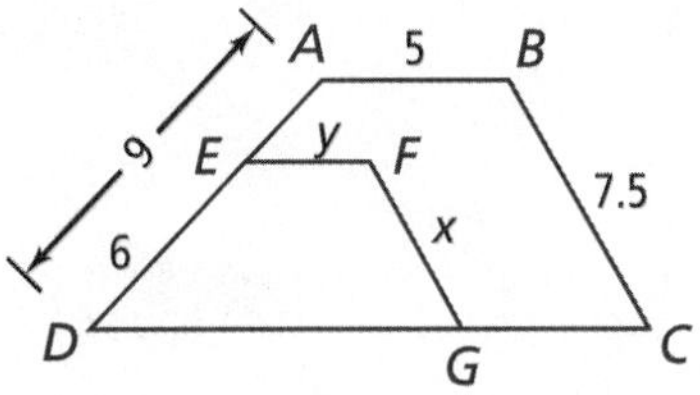

Practice Algebra The polygons are similar. Find the value of each variable.

5.

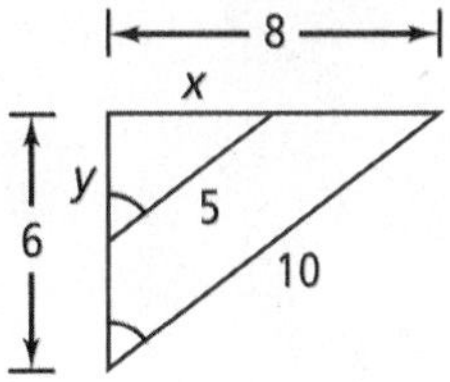

6.

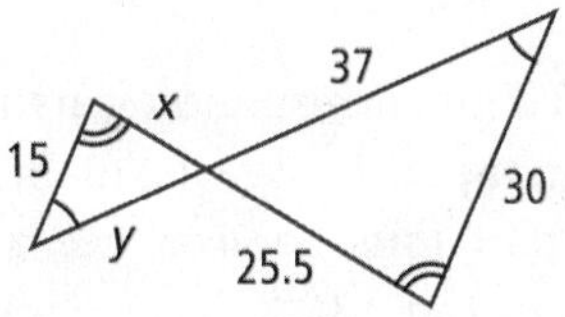

Problem 4 Using Similarity

Got It? A poster design is 6 in. high by 10 in. wide. What are the dimensions of the largest enlarged poster that will fit in a space 3 ft high by 4 ft wide?

Practice **STEM**

7. Web Page Design The space allowed for the mascot on a school's Web page is 120 pixels wide by 90 pixels high. Its digital image is 500 pixels wide by 375 pixels high. What is the largest image of the mascot that will fit on the Web page?

8. Art The design for a mural is 16 in. wide and 9 in. high. What are the dimensions of the largest possible complete mural that can be painted on a wall 24 ft wide by 14 ft high?

In a **scale drawing**, all lengths are proportional to their corresponding actual lengths. The **scale** is the ratio that compares each length in the scale drawing to the actual length. The lengths used in a scale can be in different units. For example, a scale might be written as 1 cm to 50 km, 1 in. = 100 mi, or 1 in. : 10 ft.

You can use proportions to find the actual dimensions represented in a scale drawing.

Problem 5 Using a Scale Drawing

Got It? **a.** Use the scale drawing in Problem 5. What is the actual height of the towers above the roadway?

b. **Reasoning** The Space Needle in Seattle is 605 ft tall. A classmate wants to make a scale drawing of the Space Needle on an $8\frac{1}{2}$ in.-by-11 in. sheet of paper. He decides to use the scale 1 in. = 50 ft. Is this a reasonable scale? Explain.

A Practice

STEM

9. **Architecture** You want to make a scale drawing of New York City's Empire State Building using the scale 1 in. = 250 ft. If the building is 1250 ft tall, how tall should you make the building in your scale drawing?

10. **Cartography** A cartographer is making a map of Pennsylvania. She uses the scale 1 in. = 10 mi. The actual distance between Harrisburg and Philadelphia is about 95 mi. How far apart should she place the two cities on the map?

Lesson Check

Do you know HOW?

JDRT ~ *WHYX*. Complete each statement.

11. $\angle D \cong$ ________

12. $\frac{RT}{YX} = \frac{■}{WX}$

13. Are the polygons similar? If they are, write a similarity statement and give the scale factor.

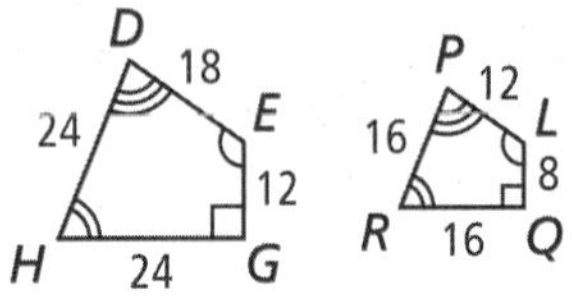

14. $\triangle FGH \sim \triangle MNP$. What is the value of x?

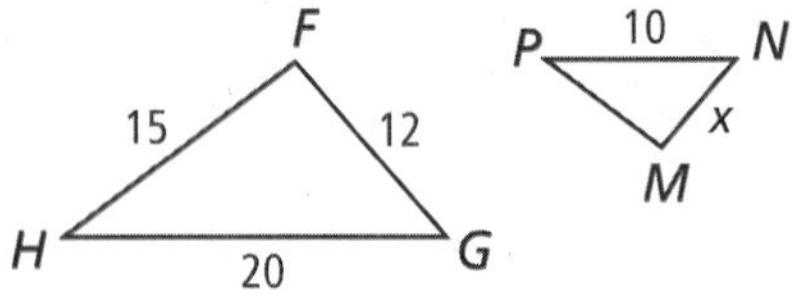

Do you UNDERSTAND?

MATHEMATICAL PRACTICES

15. Vocabulary What does the scale on a scale drawing indicate?

16. **Error Analysis** The polygons at the right are similar. Which similarity statement is *not* correct? Explain.

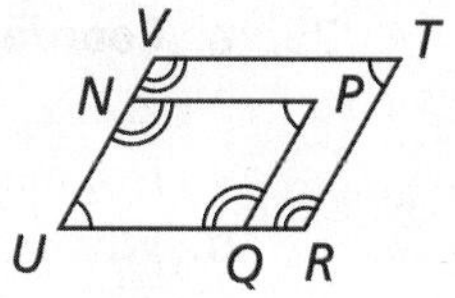

A. $TRUV \sim NPQU$ **B.** $RUVT \sim QUNP$

17. **Reasoning** Is similarity reflexive? Transitive? Symmetric? Justify your reasoning.

18. The triangles at the right are similar. What are three similarity statements for the triangles?

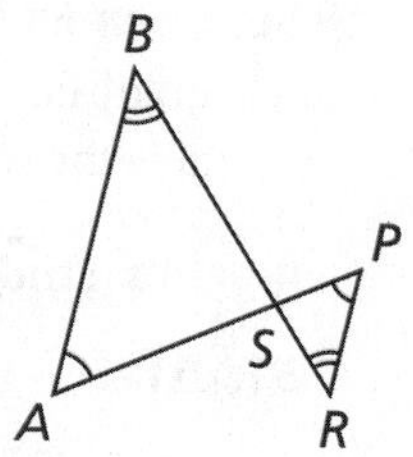

More Practice and Problem-Solving Exercises

MATHEMATICAL PRACTICES

B Apply

In the diagram at the right, $\triangle DFG \sim \triangle HKM$. Find each of the following.

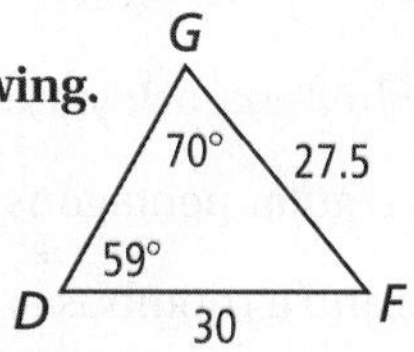

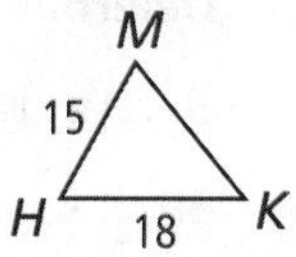

19. the scale factor of $\triangle HKM$ to $\triangle DFG$

20. $m\angle K$

21. $\frac{GD}{MH}$

22. MK

23. GD

24. **Flags** A company produces a standard-size U.S. flag that is 3 ft by 5 ft. The company also produces a giant-size flag that is similar to the standard-size flag. If the shorter side of the giant-size flag is 36 ft, what is the length of its longer side?

25. a. Coordinate Geometry What are the measures of $\angle A$, $\angle ABC$, $\angle BCD$, $\angle CDA$, $\angle E$, $\angle F$, and $\angle G$? Explain.

b. What are the lengths of $\overline{AB}$, $\overline{BC}$, $\overline{CD}$, $\overline{DA}$, $\overline{AE}$, $\overline{EF}$, $\overline{FG}$, and $\overline{AG}$?

c. Is $ABCD$ similar to $AEFG$? Justify your answer.

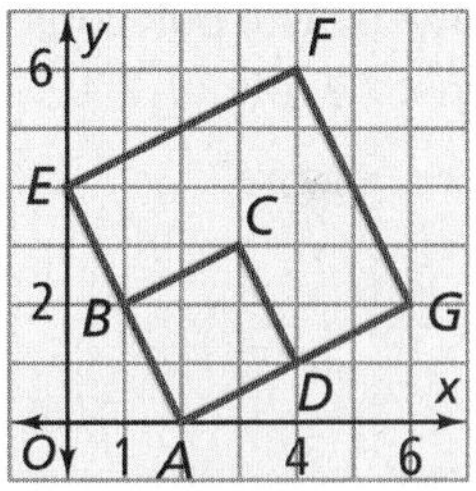

26. Think About a Plan The Davis family is planning to drive from San Antonio to Houston. About how far will they have to drive?

- How can you find the distance between the two cities on the map?
- What proportion can you set up to solve the problem?

27. Reasoning Two polygons have corresponding side lengths that are proportional. Can you conclude that the polygons are similar? Justify your reasoning.

28. Writing Explain why two congruent figures must also be similar. Include scale factor in your explanation.

29. $\triangle JLK$ and $\triangle RTS$ are similar. The scale factor of $\triangle JLK$ to $\triangle RTS$ is 3 : 1. What is the scale factor of $\triangle RTS$ to $\triangle JLK$?

30. Open-Ended Draw and label two different similar quadrilaterals. Write a similarity statement for each and give the scale factor.

Algebra Find the value of *x*. Give the scale factor of the polygons.

31. $\triangle WLJ \sim \triangle QBV$

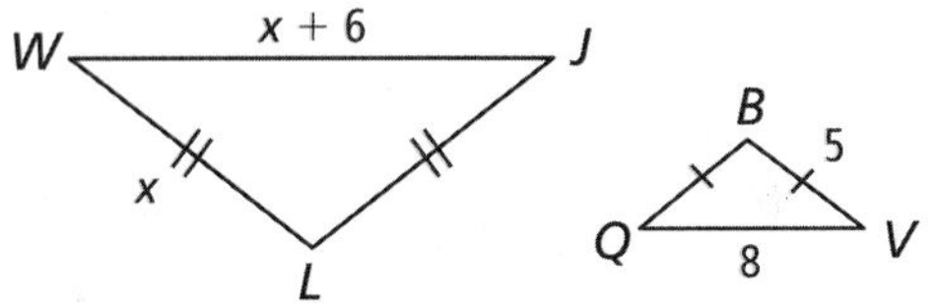

32. $GKNM \sim VRPT$

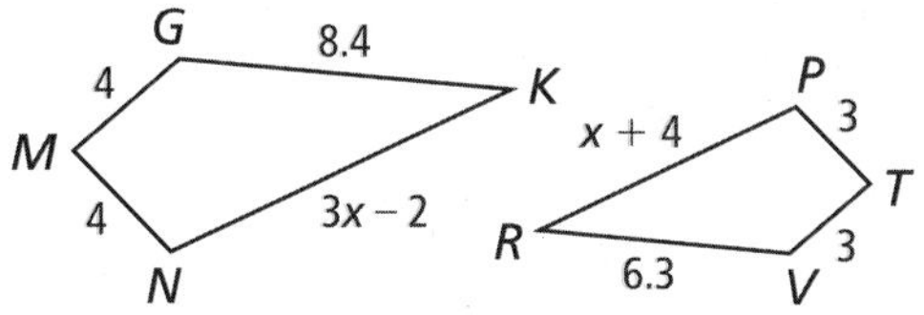

Sports Choose a scale and make a scale drawing of each rectangular playing surface.

33. A soccer field is 110 yd by 60 yd.

34. A volleyball court is 60 ft by 30 ft.

35. A tennis court is 78 ft by 36 ft.

36. A football field is 360 ft by 160 ft.

Determine whether each statement is always, sometimes, or never true.

37. Any two regular pentagons are similar.

38. A hexagon and a triangle are similar.

39. A square and a rhombus are similar.

40. Two similar rectangles are congruent.

STEM **41. Architecture** The scale drawing at the right is part of a floor plan for a home. The scale is 1 cm = 10 ft. What are the actual dimensions of the family room?

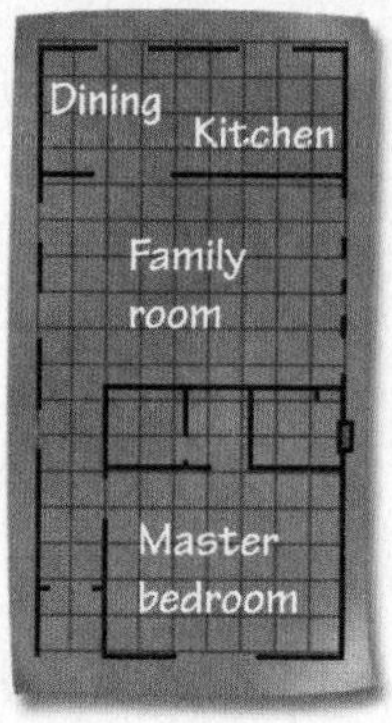

Challenge

42. The lengths of the sides of a triangle are in the extended ratio 2 : 3 : 4. The perimeter of the triangle is 54 in.

a. The length of the shortest side of a similar triangle is 16 in. What are the lengths of the other two sides of this triangle?

b. Compare the ratio of the perimeters of the two triangles to their scale factor. What do you notice?

43. In rectangle $BCEG$, $BC : CE = 2 : 3$. In rectangle $LJAW$, $LJ : JA = 2 : 3$. Show that $BCEG \sim LJAW$.

44. Prove the following statement: If $\triangle ABC \sim \triangle DEF$ and $\triangle DEF \sim \triangle GHK$, then $\triangle ABC \sim \triangle GHK$.

10-3 Proving Triangles Similar

G.SRT.5 Use . . . similarity criteria for triangles to solve problems and to prove relationships in geometric figures. Also **G.GPE.5**

Objectives To use the AA ~ Postulate and the SAS ~ and SSS ~ Theorems
To use similarity to find indirect measurements

Solve It! Write your solution to the Solve It in the space below.

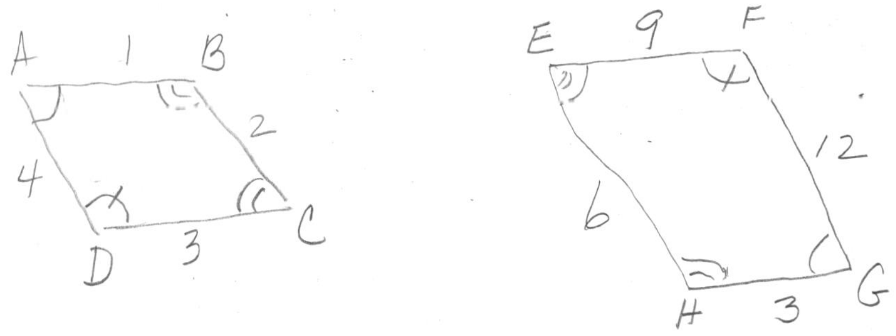

ABCD ~ GHEF

$\frac{1}{3} = \frac{2}{6} = \frac{3}{4} = \frac{4}{12}$ sides are proportional

In the Solve It, you determined whether the two triangles are similar. That is, you needed information about all three pairs of angles and all three pairs of sides. In this lesson, you'll learn an easier way to determine whether two triangles are similar.

Essential Understanding You can show that two triangles are similar when you know the relationships between only two or three pairs of corresponding parts.

take note

Postulate 5 Angle-Angle Similarity (AA ~) Postulate

Postulate	If . . .	Then . . .
If two angles of one triangle are congruent to two angles of another triangle, then the triangles are similar.	$\angle S \cong \angle M$ and $\angle R \cong \angle L$	$\triangle SRT \sim \triangle MLP$

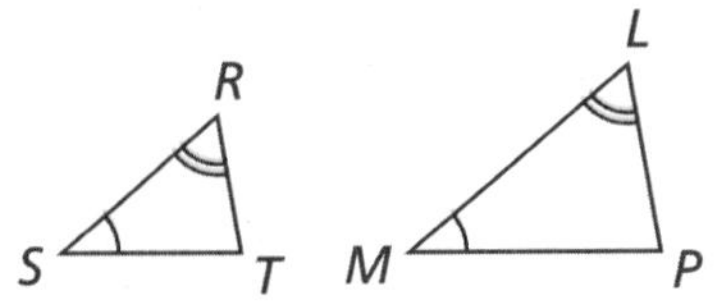

Problem 1 Using the AA ~ Postulate

Got It? Are the two triangles similar? How do you know?

a.

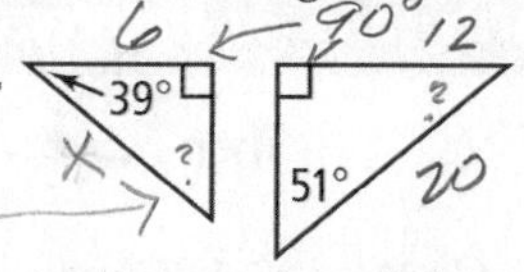

$90° = 90°$

$? = 180 - 39 - 90$

$? = 51$ △'s are similar, AA~ Post

$\frac{6}{12} = \frac{x}{20}$ Solve by cross-multiply

b.

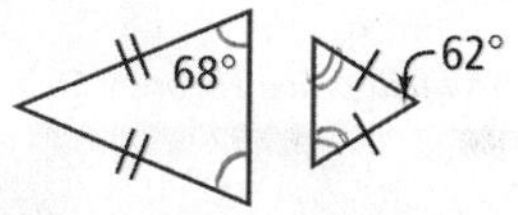

$180 - 68 - 68 = ?$ — not similar

$? = 44$ No ≅ ∠'s

> **What do you need to show that the triangles are similar?**

A Practice **Determine whether the triangles are similar. If so, write a similarity statement and name the postulate you used. If not, explain.**

1.

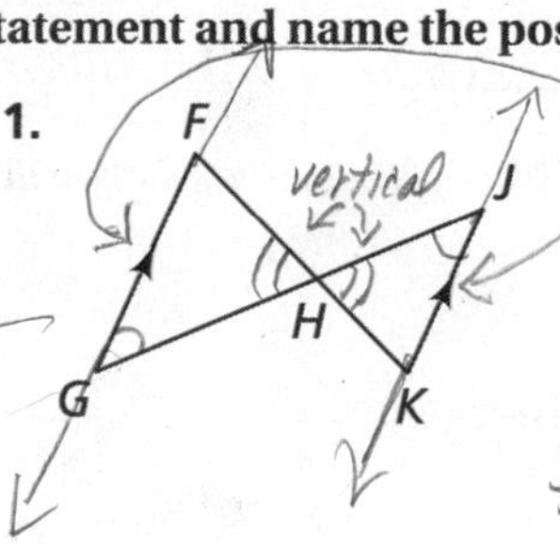

Parallel sides

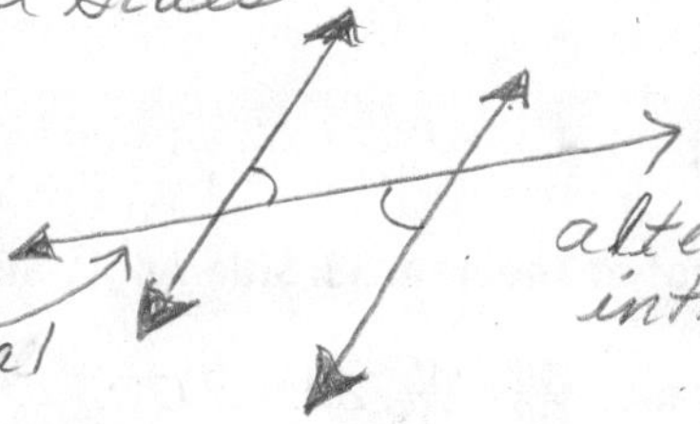

∠G ≅ ∠J ∠FHG ≅ ∠JHK

★ Alt. Int. ∠'s Vertical

△FHG ~ △KHJ

similarity statement

2.

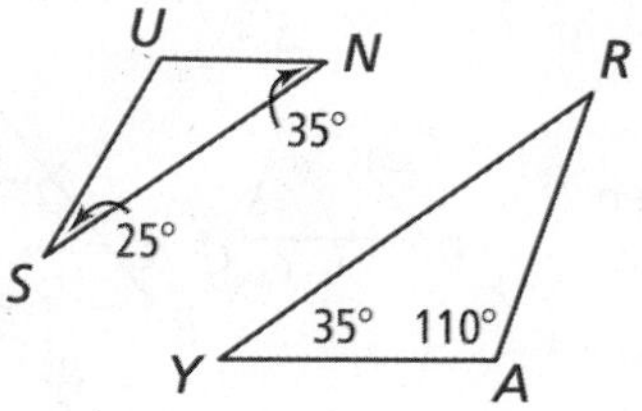

Here are two other ways to determine whether two triangles are similar.

take note

Theorem 58 Side-Angle-Side Similarity (SAS ~) Theorem

Theorem	If . . .	Then . . .
If an angle of one triangle is congruent to an angle of a second triangle, and the sides that include the two angles are proportional, then the triangles are similar.	$\frac{AB}{QR} = \frac{AC}{QS}$ and $\angle A \cong \angle Q$	$\triangle ABC \sim \triangle QRS$

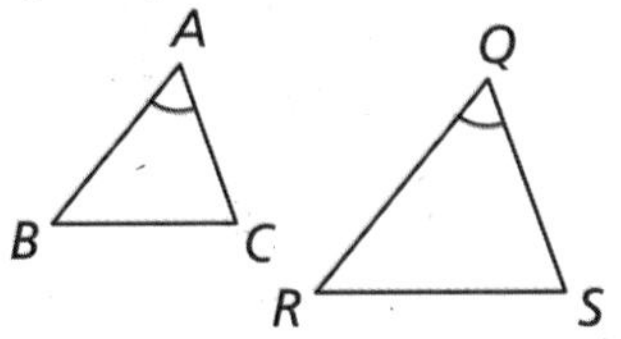

You will prove Theorem 58 in Exercise 32.

Theorem 59 Side-Side-Side Similarity (SSS ~) Theorem

Theorem	If . . .	Then . . .
If the corresponding sides of two triangles are proportional, then the triangles are similar.	$\frac{AB}{QR} = \frac{AC}{QS} = \frac{BC}{RS}$	$\triangle ABC \sim \triangle QRS$

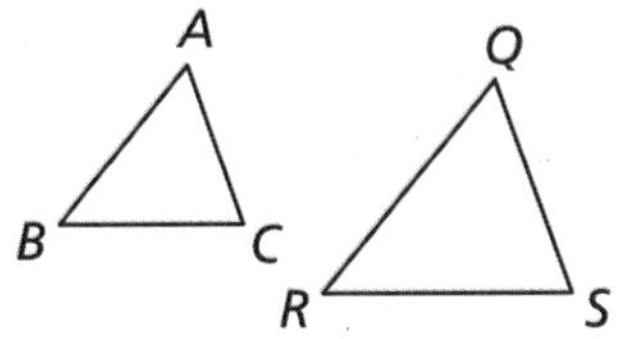

You will prove Theorem 59 in Exercise 33.

Proof Proof of Theorem 58: Side-Angle-Side Similarity Theorem

Given: $\frac{AB}{QR} = \frac{AC}{QS}$, $\angle A \cong \angle Q$

Prove: $\triangle ABC \sim \triangle QRS$

Plan for Proof: Choose X on $\overline{RQ}$ so that $QX = AB$. Draw $\overleftrightarrow{XY} \parallel \overline{RS}$. Show that $\triangle QXY \sim \triangle QRS$ by the AA ~ Postulate. Then use the proportion $\frac{QX}{QR} = \frac{QY}{QS}$ and the given proportion $\frac{AB}{QR} = \frac{AC}{QS}$ to show that $AC = QY$. Then prove that $\triangle ABC \cong \triangle QXY$. Finally, prove that $\triangle ABC \sim \triangle QRS$ by the AA ~ Postulate.

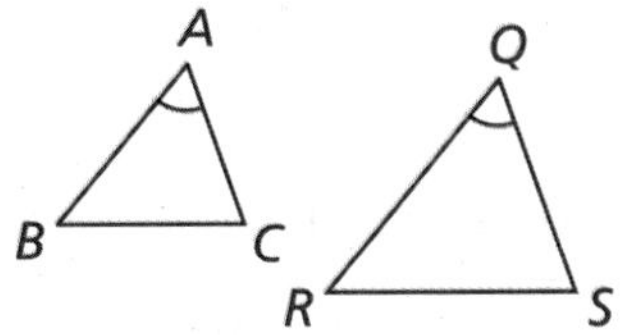

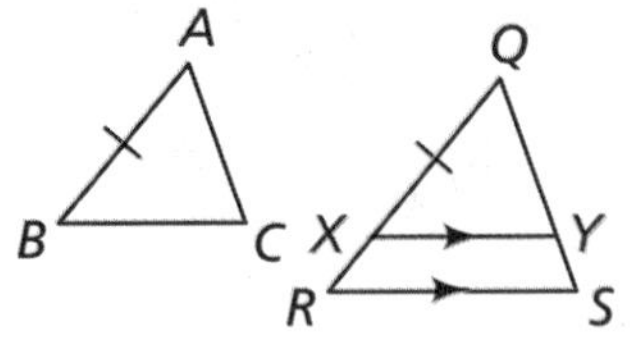

Problem 2 Verifying Triangle Similarity

Got It? Are the triangles similar? If so, write a similarity statement for the triangles and explain how you know the triangles are similar.

a.

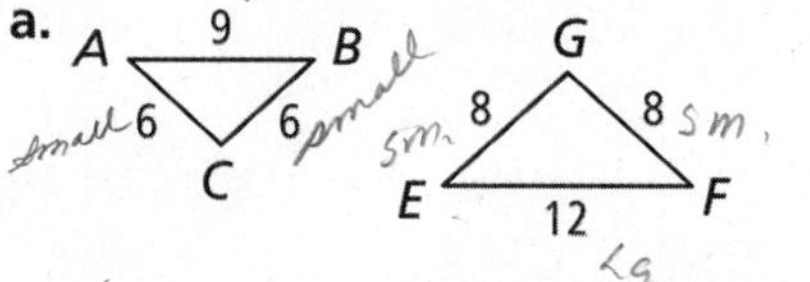

use SSS~similar post

$\triangle ABC \sim \triangle EFG$

$\frac{6}{8} = \frac{6}{8} = \frac{9}{12}$ = 72 yes

b.

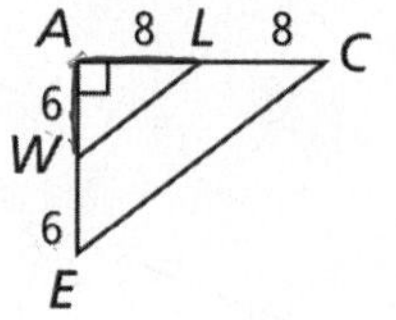

SAS ~ Post.

$\angle A \cong \angle A$

$\frac{6}{12} = \frac{8}{16}$ → 96 = 96 Similar

SAS ~ Post
$\triangle AWL \sim \triangle AEC$

Practice **Determine whether the triangles are similar. If so, write a similarity statement and name the postulate or theorem you used. If not, explain.**

3.

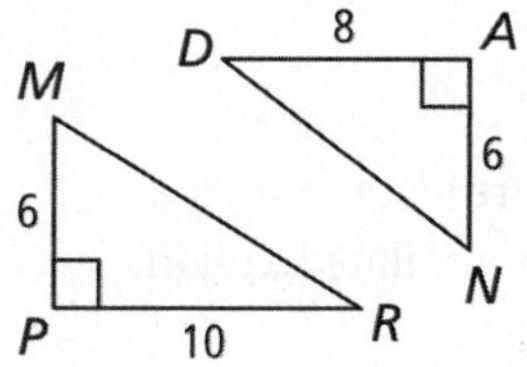

SSS ~ Postulate

4.

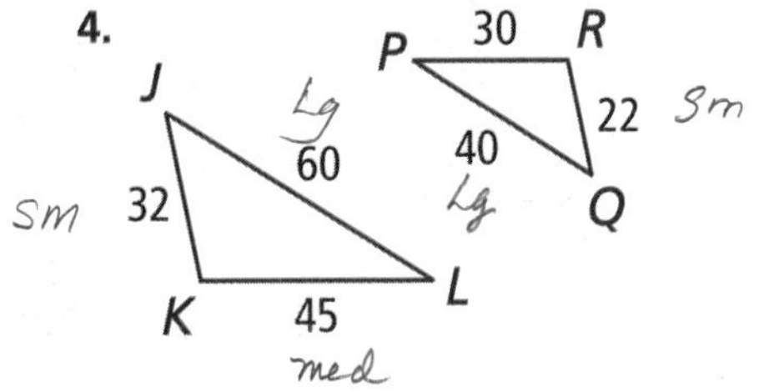

$\frac{60}{40} = \frac{45}{30} = \frac{32}{22}$

1800 1800 960 = 990 = not Similar

Problem 3 Proving Triangles Similar

Proof

Got It? a. **Given:** $\overline{MP} \parallel \overline{AC}$

Prove: $\triangle ABC \sim \triangle PBM$

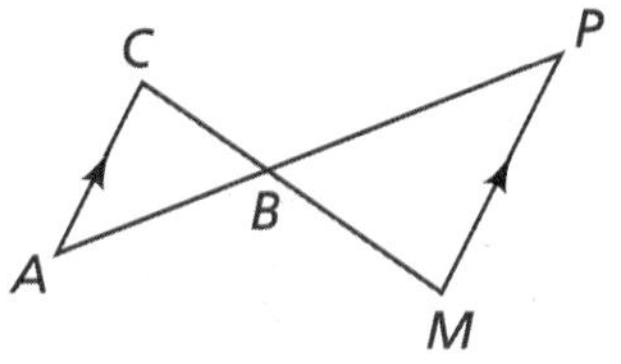

b. Reasoning For the figure above, suppose you are given only that $\frac{CA}{PM} = \frac{CB}{MB}$. Could you prove that the triangles are similar? Explain.

Practice

Proof **5. Given:** $\angle ABC \cong \angle ACD$

Prove: $\triangle ABC \sim \triangle ACD$

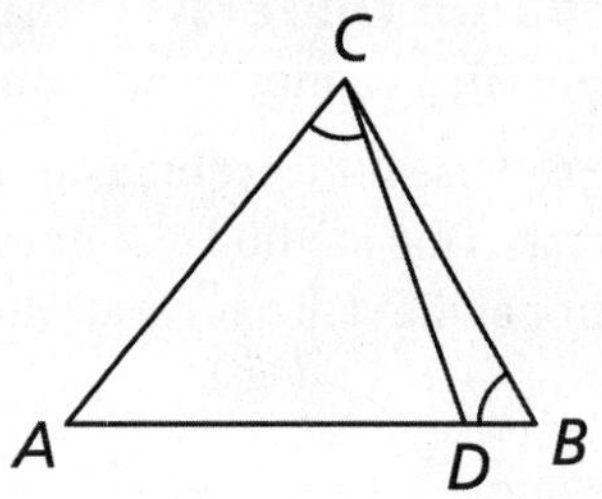

Proof **6. Given:** $PR = 2NP$, $PQ = 2MP$

Prove: $\triangle MNP \sim \triangle QRP$

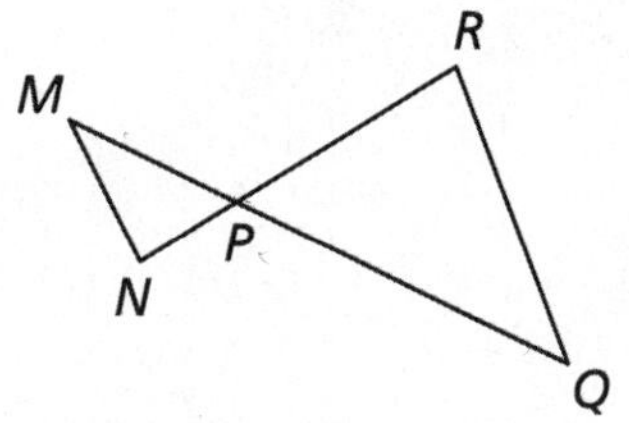

Essential Understanding Sometimes you can use similar triangles to find lengths that cannot be measured easily using a ruler or other measuring device.

You can use **indirect measurement** to find lengths that are difficult to measure directly. One method of indirect measurement uses the fact that light reflects off a mirror at the same angle at which it hits the mirror.

Problem 4 Finding Lengths in Similar Triangles

Got It? **Reasoning** Why is it important that the ground be flat to use the method of indirect measurement illustrated in Problem 4? Explain.

Practice 7. **Indirect Measurement** Explain why the triangles are similar. Then find the distance represented by x.

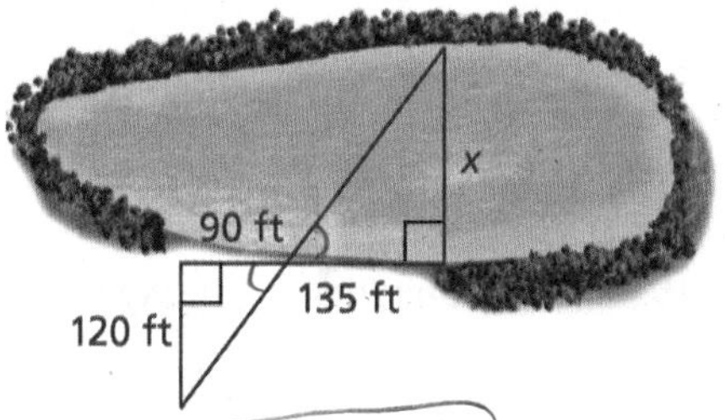

$\measuredangle 90° = \measuredangle 90°$

true because $\triangle \sim \triangle$ →

$\frac{90}{135} = \frac{120}{x} = \frac{16,200}{90} = \frac{90x}{90} = \boxed{180 = x}$

Both triangles are similar by the AA ∼ Post.
90° = 90° and vertical ∡'s

8. **Washington Monument** At a certain time of day, a 1.8-m-tall person standing next to the Washington Monument casts a 0.7-m shadow. At the same time, the Washington Monument casts a 65.8-m shadow. How tall is the Washington Monument?

Lesson Check

Do you know HOW?

Are the triangles similar? If yes, write a similarity statement and explain how you know they are similar.

9.

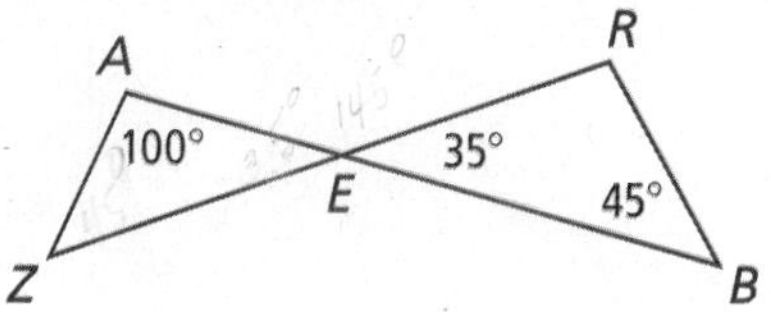

10.

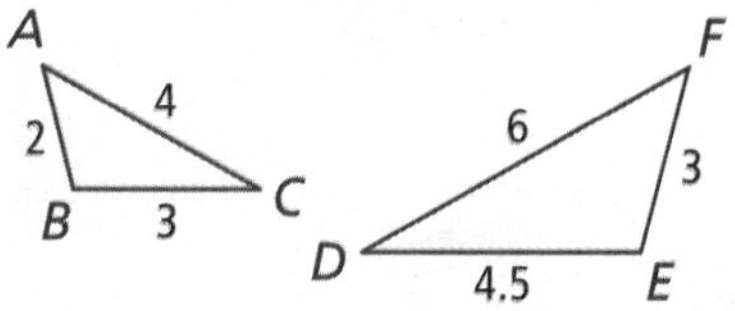

11.

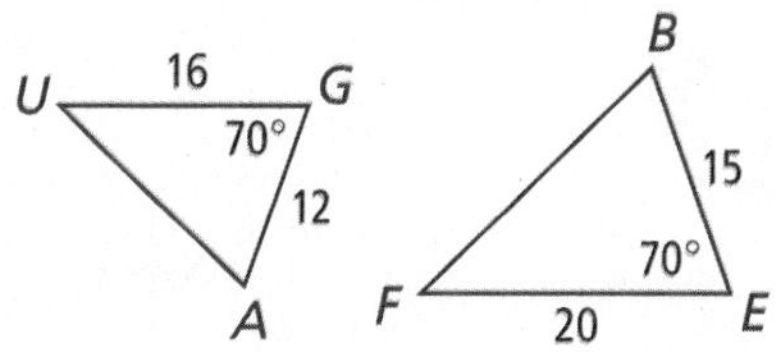

Do you UNDERSTAND?

MATHEMATICAL PRACTICES

12. Vocabulary How could you use indirect measurement to find the height of the flagpole at your school?

13. Error Analysis Which solution for the value of x in the figure at the right is *not* correct? Explain.

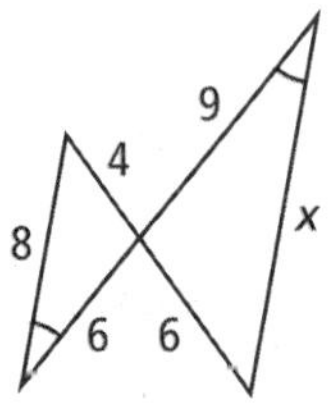

A.

$$\frac{4}{8} = \frac{8}{x}$$
$$4x = 72$$
$$x = 18$$

B.

$$\frac{8}{x} = \frac{4}{6}$$
$$48 = 4x$$
$$12 = x$$

14. a. Compare and Contrast How are the SAS Similarity Theorem and the SAS Congruence Postulate alike? How are they different?

b. How are the SSS Similarity Theorem and the SSS Congruence Postulate alike? How are they different?

More Practice and Problem-Solving Exercises

MATHEMATICAL PRACTICES

B Apply

Can you conclude that the triangles are similar? If so, state the postulate or theorem you used and write a similarity statement. If not, explain.

15.

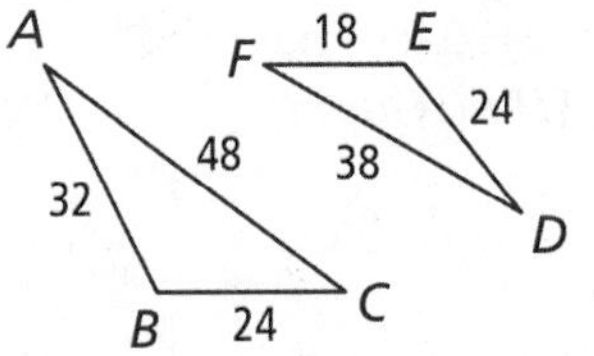

16.

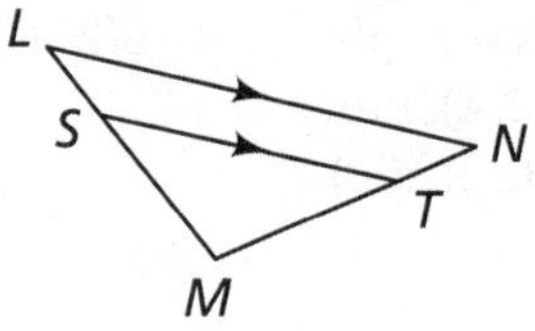

17.

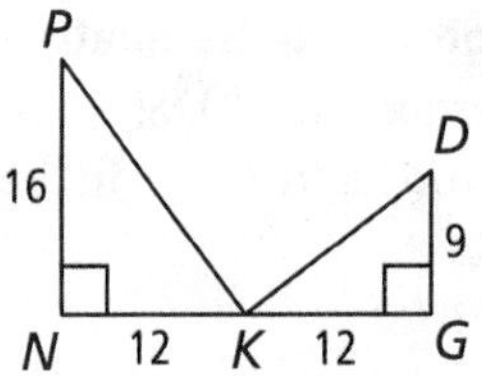

18. a. Are two isosceles triangles always similar? Explain.

b. Are two right isosceles triangles always similar? Explain.

19. Think About a Plan On a sunny day, a classmate uses indirect measurement to find the height of a building. The building's shadow is 12 ft long and your classmate's shadow is 4 ft long. If your classmate is 5 ft tall, what is the height of the building?

- Can you draw and label a diagram to represent the situation?
- What proportion can you use to solve the problem?

20. Indirect Measurement A 2-ft vertical post casts a 16-in. shadow at the same time a nearby cell phone tower casts a 120-ft shadow. How tall is the cell phone tower?

Algebra **For each pair of similar triangles, find the value of x.**

21.

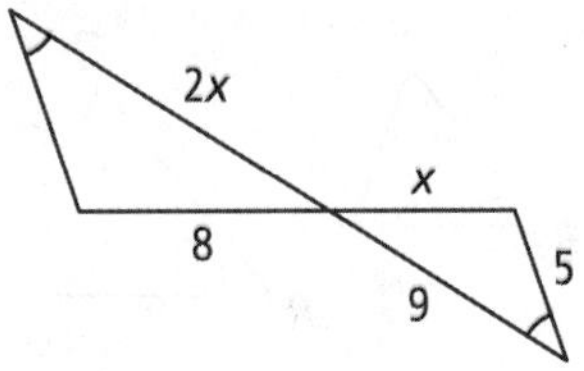

22.

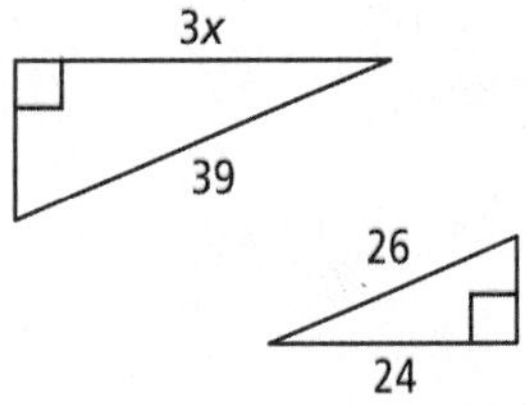

23.

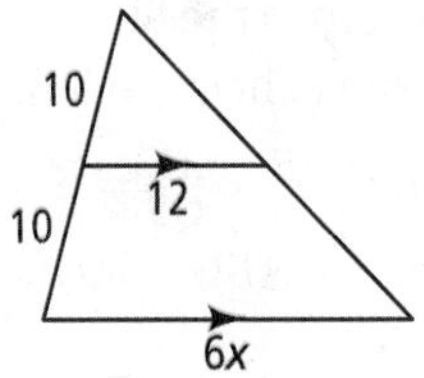

24. Given: $\overline{PQ} \perp \overline{QT}$, $\overline{ST} \perp \overline{TQ}$, $\frac{PQ}{ST} = \frac{QR}{TV}$

Proof

Prove: $\triangle VKR$ is isosceles.

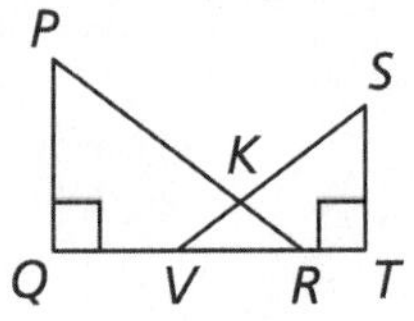

25. Given: $\overline{AB} \parallel \overline{CD}$, $\overline{BC} \parallel \overline{DG}$

Proof

Prove: $AB \cdot CG = CD \cdot AC$

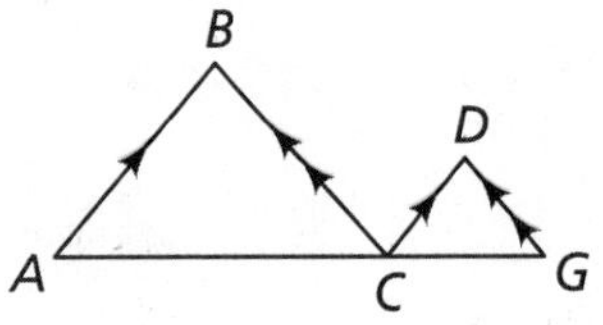

26. Reasoning Does any line that intersects two sides of a triangle and is parallel to the third side of the triangle form two similar triangles? Justify your reasoning.

27. Constructions Draw any $\triangle ABC$ with $m\angle C = 30$. Use a straightedge and compass to construct $\triangle LKJ$ so that $\triangle LKJ \sim \triangle ABC$.

28. **Reasoning** In the diagram at the right, $\triangle PMN \sim \triangle SRW$. $\overline{MQ}$ and $\overline{RT}$ are altitudes. The scale factor of $\triangle PMN$ to $\triangle SRW$ is 4 : 3. What is the ratio of $\overline{MQ}$ to $\overline{RT}$? Explain how you know.

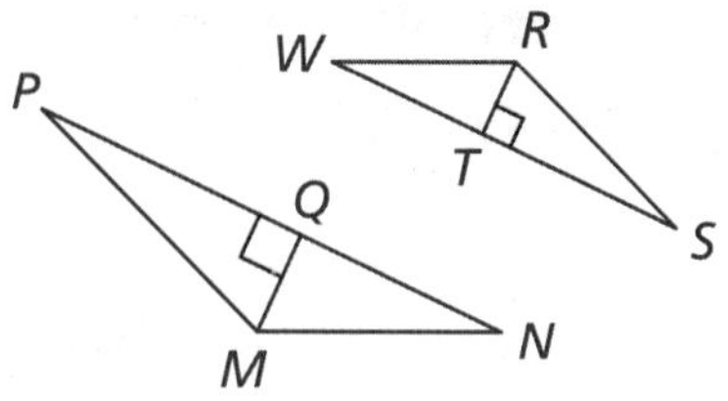

29. **Coordinate Geometry** $\triangle ABC$ has vertices $A(0, 0)$, $B(2, 4)$, and $C(4, 2)$. $\triangle RST$ has vertices $R(0, 3)$, $S(-1, 5)$, and $T(-2, 4)$. Prove that $\triangle ABC \sim \triangle RST$. (*Hint:* Graph $\triangle ABC$ and $\triangle RST$ in the coordinate plane.)
Proof

Challenge

30. Write a proof of the following: Any two nonvertical parallel lines have equal slopes.
Proof

Given: Nonvertical lines ℓ_1 and ℓ_2, $\ell_1 \parallel \ell_2$, $\overline{EF}$ and $\overline{BC}$ are $\perp$ to the x-axis

Prove: $\frac{BC}{AC} = \frac{EF}{DF}$

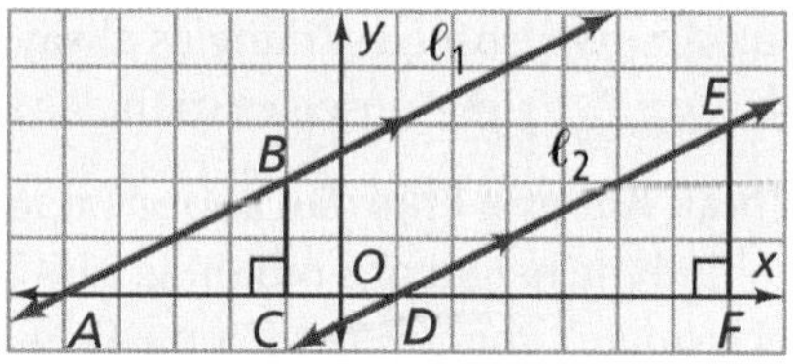

31. Use the diagram in Exercise 30. Prove: Any two nonvertical lines with equal slopes are parallel.
Proof

32. Prove the Side-Angle-Side Similarity Theorem (Theorem 58).
Proof

Given: $\frac{AB}{QR} = \frac{AC}{QS}$, $\angle A \cong \angle Q$

Prove: $\triangle ABC \sim \triangle QRS$

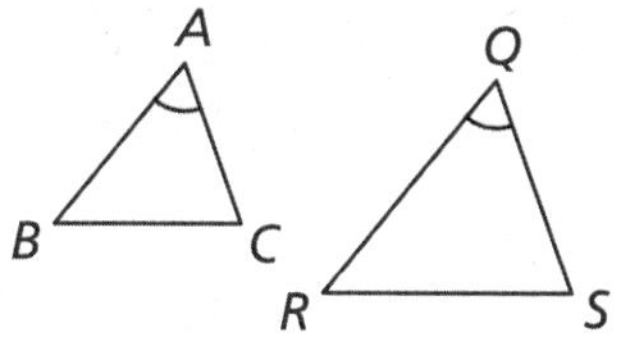

33. **Proof** Prove the Side-Side-Side Similarity Theorem (Theorem 59).
Proof

Given: $\frac{AB}{QR} = \frac{AC}{QS} = \frac{BC}{RS}$

Prove: $\triangle ABC \sim \triangle QRS$

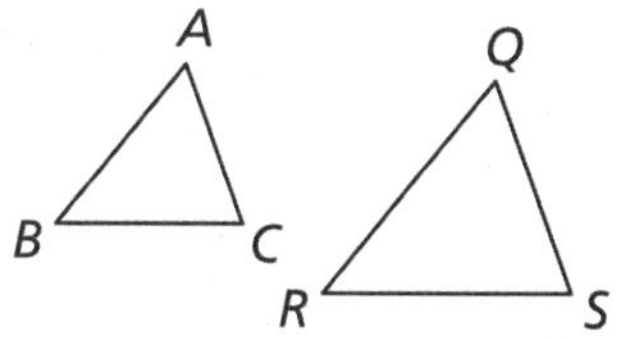

10-4 Similarity in Right Triangles

G.SRT.5 Use . . . similarity criteria for triangles to solve problems and to prove relationships in geometric figures. Also **G.GPE.5, G.GPE.6**

Objective To find and use relationships in similar right triangles

Solve It! Write your solution to the Solve It in the space below.

In the Solve It, you looked at three similar right triangles. In this lesson, you will learn new ways to think about the proportions that come from these similar triangles. You began with three separate, nonoverlapping triangles in the Solve It. Now you will see the two smaller right triangles fitting side by side to form the largest right triangle.

Essential Understanding When you draw the *altitude to the hypotenuse* of a right triangle, you form three pairs of similar right triangles.

take note

Theorem 60

Theorem	If . . .	Then . . .
The altitude to the hypotenuse of a right triangle divides the triangle into two triangles that are similar to the original triangle and to each other.	$\triangle ABC$ is a right triangle with right $\angle ACB$, and $\overline{CD}$ is the altitude to the hypotenuse	$\triangle ABC \sim \triangle ACD$ $\triangle ABC \sim \triangle CBD$ $\triangle ACD \sim \triangle CBD$

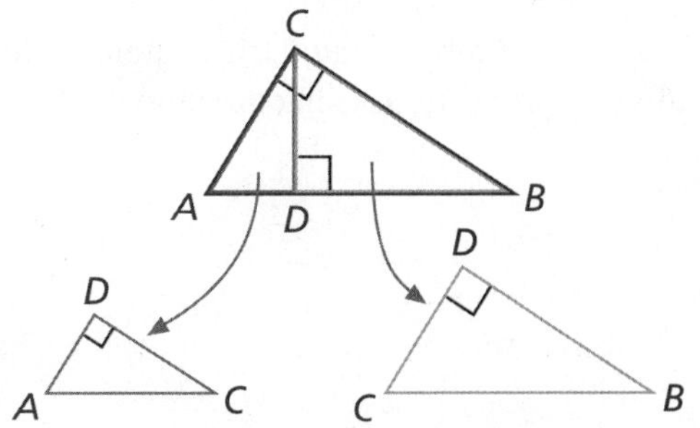

Proof Proof of Theorem 60

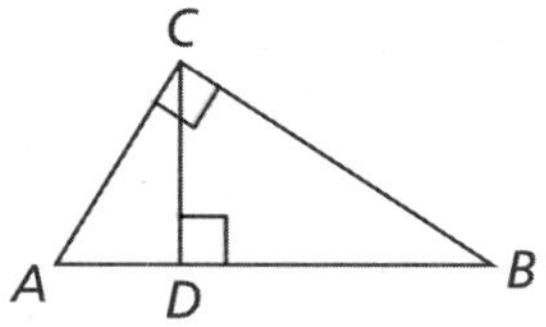

Given: Right $\triangle ABC$ with right $\angle ACB$ and altitude $\overline{CD}$
Prove: $\triangle ACD \sim \triangle ABC$, $\triangle CBD \sim \triangle ABC$, $\triangle ACD \sim \triangle CBD$

Statements	Reasons
1) $\angle ACB$ is a right angle.	**1)** Given
2) $\overline{CD}$ is an altitude.	**2)** Given
3) $\overline{CD} \perp \overline{AB}$	**3)** Definition of altitude
4) $\angle ADC$ and $\angle CDB$ are right angles.	**4)** Definition of $\perp$
5) $\angle ADC \cong \angle ACB$, $\angle CDB \cong \angle ACB$	**5)** All right $\angle$s are $\cong$.
6) $\angle A \cong \angle A$, $\angle B \cong \angle B$	**6)** Reflexive Property of $\cong$
7) $\triangle ACD \sim \triangle ABC$, $\triangle CBD \sim \triangle ABC$	**7)** AA $\sim$ Postulate
8) $\angle ACD \cong \angle B$	**8)** Corresponding $\angle$s of $\sim \triangle$s are $\cong$.
9) $\angle ADC \cong \angle CDB$	**9)** All right $\angle$s are $\cong$.
10) $\triangle ACD \sim \triangle CBD$	**10)** AA $\sim$ Postulate

Problem 1 Identifying Similar Triangles

Got It? **a.** What similarity statement can you write relating the three triangles in the diagram?

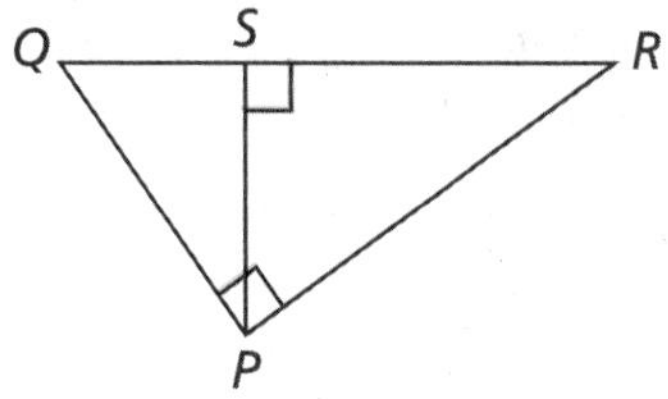

Plan
What will help you see the corresponding vertices?

b. Reasoning From the similarity statement in part (a), write two different proportions using the ratio $\frac{SR}{SP}$.

A Practice **Write a similarity statement relating the three triangles in each diagram.**

1\. 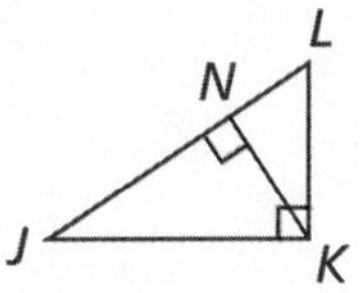

2\. 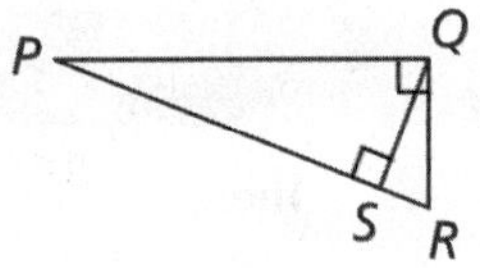

Proportions in which the means are equal occur frequently in geometry. For any two positive numbers a and b, the **geometric mean** of a and b is the positive number x such that $\frac{a}{x} = \frac{x}{b}$.

Problem 2 Finding the Geometric Mean

Got It? What is the geometric mean of 4 and 18?

Plan
How do you use the definition of *geometric mean*?

A Practice **Algebra** **Find the geometric mean of each pair of numbers.**

3. 5 and 125

4. 4 and 49

In part (b) of the Got it for Problem 1, you used a pair of similar triangles to write a proportion with a geometric mean.

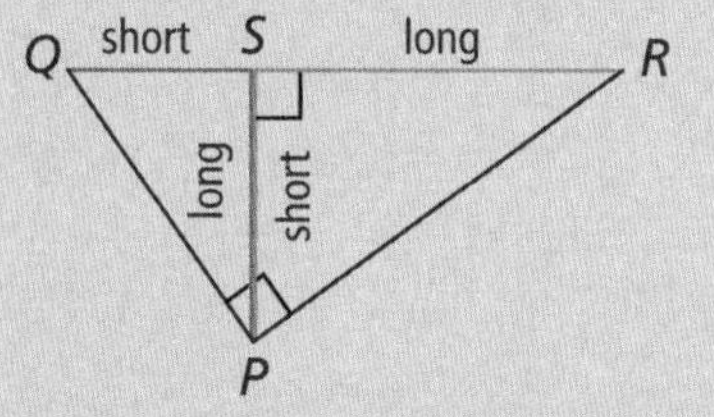

$\triangle SQP \sim \triangle SPR$

$$\frac{\text{short leg}}{\text{short leg}} = \frac{\text{long leg}}{\text{long leg}}$$

$$\frac{SQ}{SP} = \frac{SP}{SR}$$

SP is the geometric mean of *SQ* and *SR*.

This illustrates the first of two important corollaries of Theorem 60.

take note

Corollary 1 to Theorem 60

Corollary

The length of the altitude to the hypotenuse of a right triangle is the geometric mean of the lengths of the segments of the hypotenuse.

If . . .

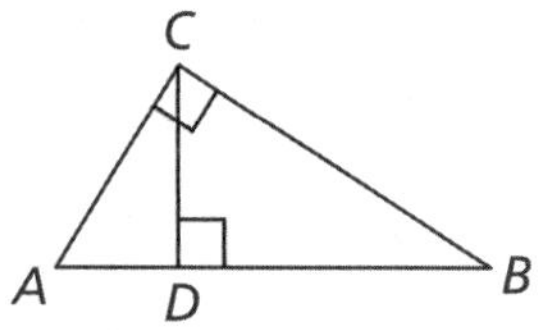

Then . . .

$$\frac{AD}{CD} = \frac{CD}{DB}$$

Example

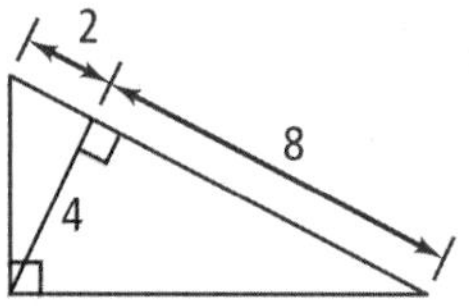

Segments of hypotenuse → $\frac{2}{4} = \frac{4}{8}$ ← Altitude to hypotenuse

You will prove Corollary 1 in Exercise 34.

take note

Corollary 2 to Theorem 60

Corollary

The altitude to the hypotenuse of a right triangle separates the hypotenuse so that the length of each leg of the triangle is the geometric mean of the length of the hypotenuse and the length of the segment of the hypotenuse adjacent to the leg.

If . . .

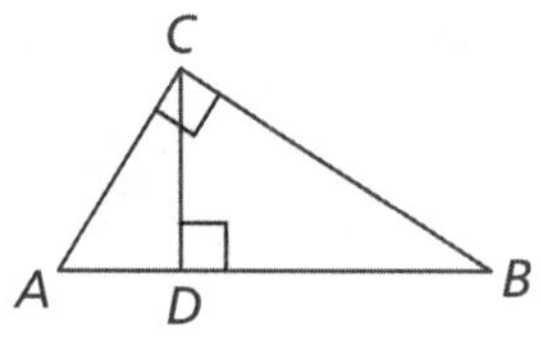

Then . . .

$$\frac{AB}{AC} = \frac{AC}{AD}$$

$$\frac{AB}{CB} = \frac{CB}{DB}$$

Example

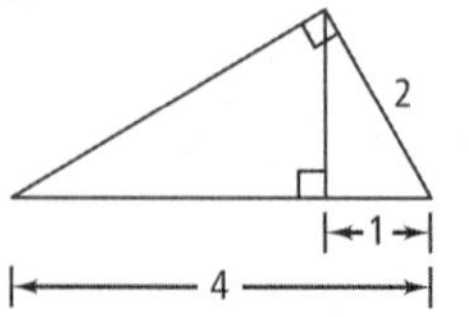

Hypotenuse → $\frac{4}{2} = \frac{2}{1}$ ← Leg; ← Segment of hypotenuse adjacent to leg

You will prove Corollary 2 in Exercise 35.

The corollaries to Theorem 60 give you ways to write proportions using lengths in right triangles without thinking through the similar triangles. To help remember these corollaries, consider the diagram and these properties.

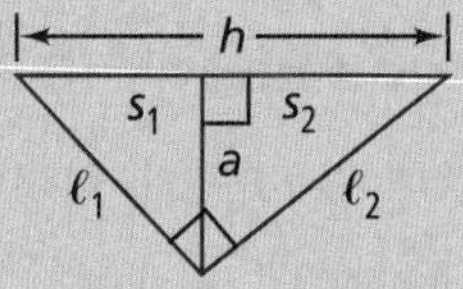

Corollary 1

$\frac{s_1}{a} = \frac{a}{s_2}$

Corollary 2

$\frac{h}{\ell_1} = \frac{\ell_1}{s_1}, \frac{h}{\ell_2} = \frac{\ell_2}{s_2}$

Problem 3 Using the Corollaries

Plan

How do you decide which corollary to use?

Got It? What are the values of x and y?

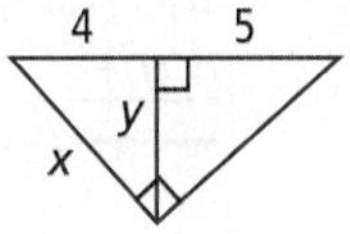

Practice Algebra Solve for x and y.

5.

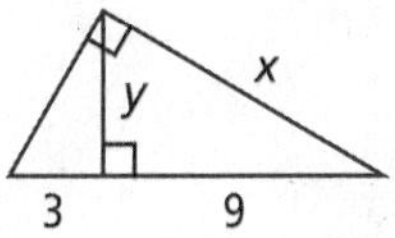

6.

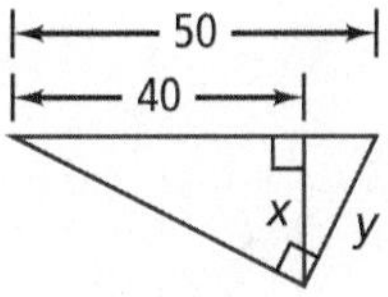

Lesson Check

Do you know HOW?

Find the geometric mean of each pair of numbers.

7. 4 and 9

8. 4 and 12

Use the figure to complete each proportion.

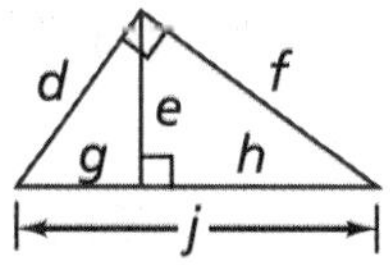

9. $\frac{g}{e} = \frac{e}{\blacksquare}$

10. $\frac{j}{d} = \frac{d}{\blacksquare}$

11. $\frac{\blacksquare}{f} = \frac{f}{\blacksquare}$

12. $\frac{j}{\blacksquare} = \frac{\blacksquare}{g}$

Do you UNDERSTAND?

MATHEMATICAL PRACTICES

13. Vocabulary Identify the following in $\triangle RST$.

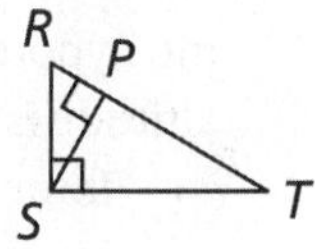

a. the hypotenuse

b. the segments of the hypotenuse

c. the segment of the hypotenuse adjacent to leg $\overline{ST}$

14. Error Analysis A classmate wrote an incorrect proportion to find x. Explain and correct the error.

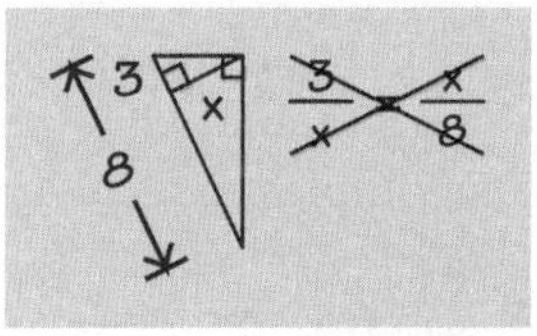

More Practice and Problem-Solving Exercises

MATHEMATICAL PRACTICES

B Apply

15. a. The altitude to the hypotenuse of a right triangle divides the hypotenuse into segments 2 cm and 8 cm long. Find the length of the altitude to the hypotenuse.

b. Use a ruler to make an accurate drawing of the right triangle in part (a).

c. Writing Describe how you drew the triangle in part (b).

Algebra Find the geometric mean of each pair of numbers.

16. 1 and 1000

17. 5 and 1.25

18. $\sqrt{8}$ and $\sqrt{2}$

19. $\frac{1}{2}$ and 2

20. $\sqrt{28}$ and $\sqrt{7}$

21. Reasoning A classmate says the following statement is true: The geometric mean of positive numbers a and b is $\sqrt{ab}$. Do you agree? Explain.

22. Think About a Plan The altitude to the hypotenuse of a right triangle divides the hypotenuse into segments with lengths in the ratio 1 : 2. The length of the altitude is 8. How long is the hypotenuse?

- How can you use the given ratio to help you draw a sketch of the triangle?
- How can you use the given ratio to write expressions for the lengths of the segments of the hypotenuse?
- Which corollary to Theorem 60 applies to this situation?

23. Archaeology To estimate the height of a stone figure, Anya holds a small square up to her eyes and walks backward from the figure. She stops when the bottom of the figure aligns with the bottom edge of the square and the top of the figure aligns with the top edge of the square. Her eye level is 1.84 m from the ground. She is 3.50 m from the figure. What is the height of the figure to the nearest hundredth of a meter?

24. Reasoning Suppose the altitude to the hypotenuse of a right triangle bisects the hypotenuse. How does the length of the altitude compare with the lengths of the segments of the hypotenuse? Explain.

The diagram shows the parts of a right triangle with an altitude to the hypotenuse. For the two given measures, find the other four. Use simplest radical form.

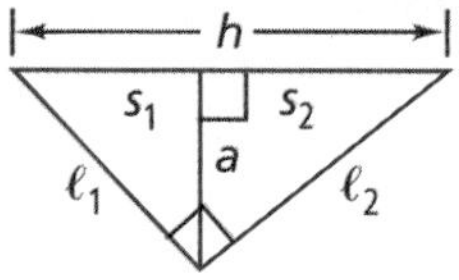

25. $h = 2$, $s_1 = 1$ **26.** $a = 6$, $s_1 = 6$ **27.** $h = 6$, $s_2 = 3$ **28.** $s_1 = 2$, $h = 4$

29. Coordinate Geometry $\overline{CD}$ is the altitude to the hypotenuse of right $\triangle ABC$. The coordinates of A, D, and B are (4, 2), (4, 6), and (4, 7), respectively. Find all possible coordinates of point C.

Algebra Find the value of x.

30.

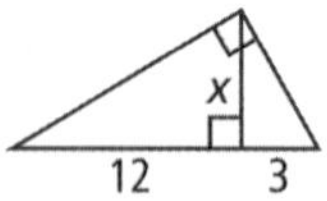

31.

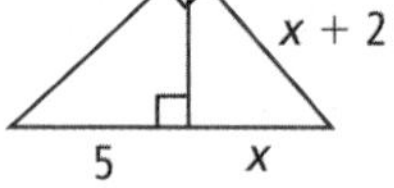

32.

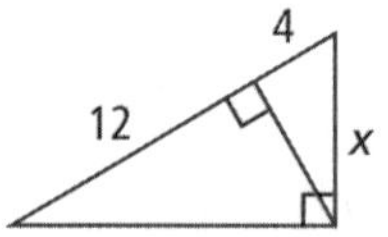

33.

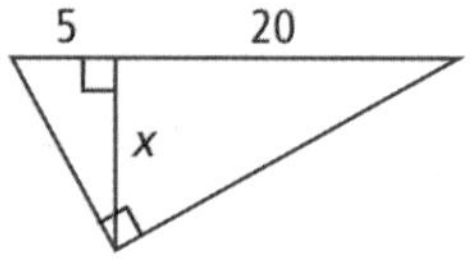

Use the figure at the right for Exercises 34 and 35.

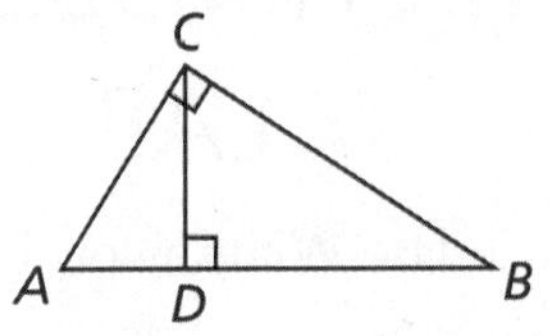

34. Prove Corollary 1 to Theorem 60. **Proof**

Given: Right $\triangle ABC$ with altitude to the hypotenuse $\overline{CD}$

Prove: $\frac{AD}{CD} = \frac{CD}{DB}$

35. Prove Corollary 2 to Theorem 60. **Proof**

Given: Right $\triangle ABC$ with altitude to the hypotenuse $\overline{CD}$

Prove: $\frac{AB}{AC} = \frac{AC}{AD}$, $\frac{AB}{BC} = \frac{BC}{DB}$

36. Given: Right $\triangle ABC$ with altitude $\overline{CD}$ to the hypotenuse $\overline{AB}$. **Proof**

Prove: The product of the slopes of perpendicular lines, where neither line is vertical is -1.

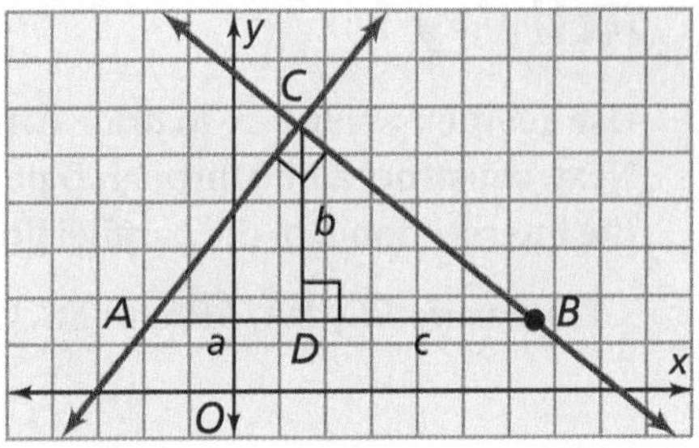

Challenge

37. a. Consider the following conjecture: The product of the lengths of the two legs of a right triangle is equal to the product of the lengths of the hypotenuse and the altitude to the hypotenuse. Draw a figure for the conjecture. Write the *Given* information and what you are to *Prove*.

b. Reasoning Is the conjecture true? Explain.

38. a. In the diagram, $c = x + y$. Use Corollary 2 to Theorem 60 to write two more equations involving a, b, c, x, and y.

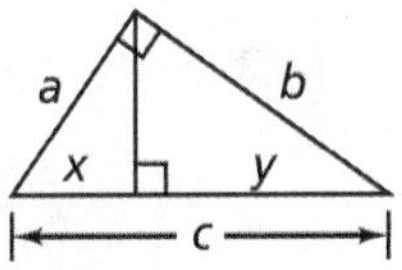

b. The equations in part (a) form a system of three equations in five variables. Reduce the system to one equation in three variables by eliminating x and y.

c. State in words what the one resulting equation tells you.

39. Given: In right $\triangle ABC$, $\overline{BD} \perp \overline{AC}$, and $\overline{DE} \perp \overline{BC}$. **Proof**

Prove: $\frac{AD}{DC} = \frac{BE}{EC}$

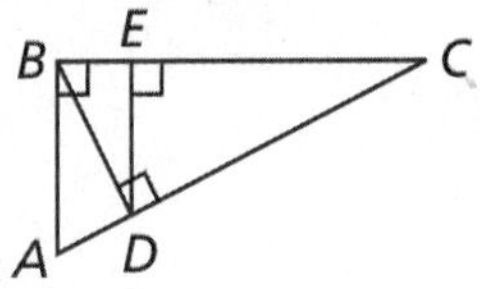

TECHNOLOGY LAB

Use With Lesson 10-5

Exploring Proportions in Triangles

G.CO.12 Make formal geometric constructions with a variety of tools and methods . . . Also prepares for **G.SRT.4**

Activity 1

MATHEMATICAL PRACTICES

Use geometry software to draw $\triangle ABC$. Construct point D on $\overline{AB}$. Next, construct a line through D parallel to $\overline{AC}$. Then construct the intersection E of the parallel line with $\overline{BC}$.

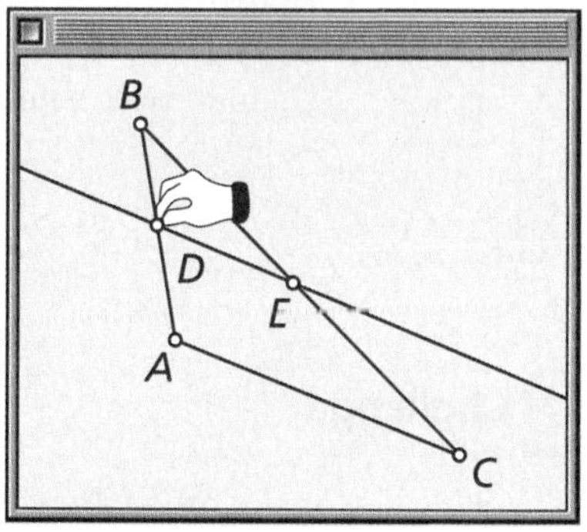

1. Measure $\overline{BD}$, $\overline{DA}$, $\overline{BE}$, and $\overline{EC}$. Calculate the ratios $\frac{BD}{DA}$ and $\frac{BE}{EC}$.

2. Manipulate $\triangle ABC$ and observe $\frac{BD}{DA}$ and $\frac{BE}{EC}$. What do you notice?

3. Make a conjecture about the four segments formed by a line parallel to one side of a triangle intersecting the other two sides.

Activity 2

Use geometry software to construct $\triangle ADE$ with vertices $A(3, 3)$, $D(-1, 0)$, and $E(5, 1)$.

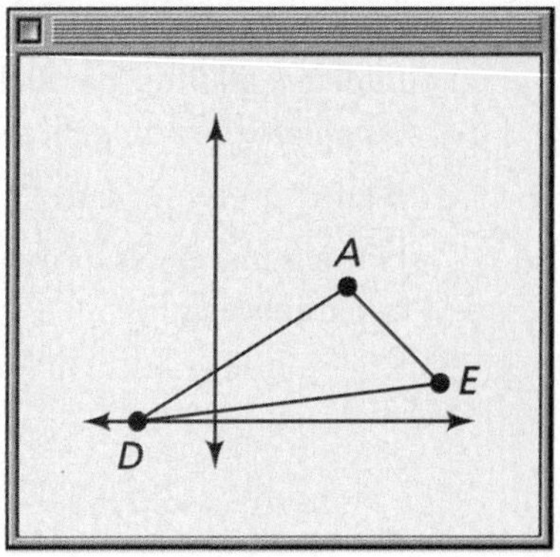

4. Measure $\overline{AD}$, $\overline{AE}$, and $\overline{DE}$.

5. Suppose you draw $\overline{BC}$ so that it partitions $\triangle ADE$ and $AB = \frac{2}{3}AD$ and $\overline{CB} \parallel \overline{DE}$. Describe how you could approximate the coordinates of points B and C.

6. Now use the geometry software to draw $\overline{BC}$ and manipulate the segment to most closely find the points B and C. What are the coordinates of points B and C?

Exercises

7. Construct $\overleftrightarrow{AB} \parallel \overleftrightarrow{CD} \parallel \overleftrightarrow{EF}$. Then construct two transversals that intersect all three parallel lines. Measure $\overline{AC}$, $\overline{CE}$, $\overline{BD}$, and $\overline{DF}$. Calculate the ratios $\frac{AC}{CE}$ and $\frac{BD}{DF}$. Manipulate the locations of A and B and observe $\frac{AC}{CE}$ and $\frac{BD}{DF}$. Make a conjecture about the segments of the transversals formed by the three parallel lines intersecting two transversals.

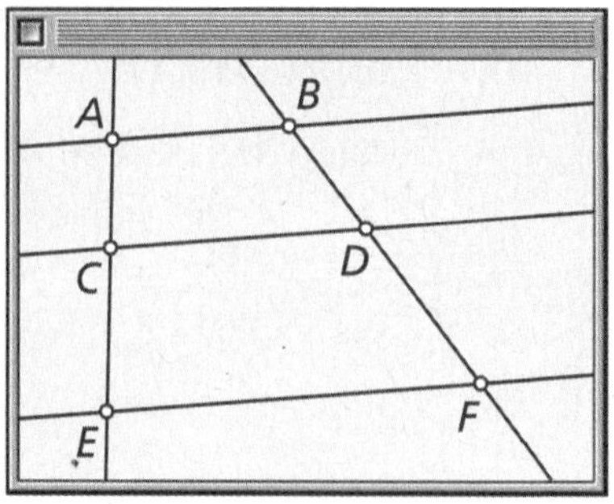

8. Suppose four or more parallel lines intersect two transversals. Make a conjecture about the segments of the transversals.

10-5 Proportions in Triangles

G.SRT.4 Prove theorems about triangles . . . a line parallel to one side of a triangle divides the other two proportionally . . .

Objective To use the Side-Splitter Theorem and the Triangle-Angle-Bisector Theorem

Solve It! Write your solution to the Solve It in the space below.

Side Splitter th.

if $\overleftrightarrow{RS} \parallel \overleftrightarrow{XY}$

then . . .

$\triangle QRS \sim \triangle QXY$

and

$\frac{XR}{RQ} = \frac{YS}{SQ}$

$\frac{a}{b} = \frac{c}{d}$

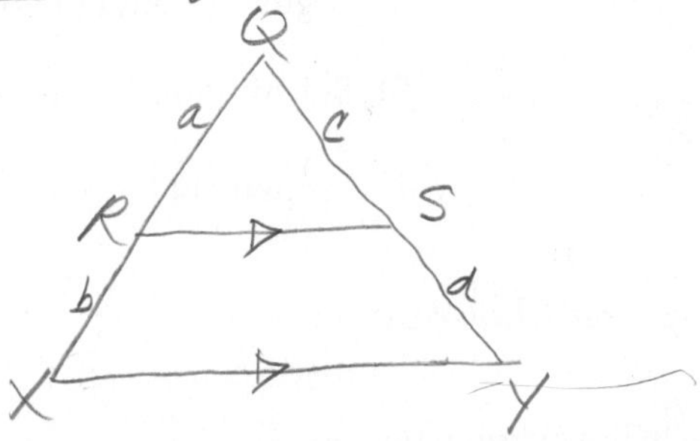

The Solve It involves parallel lines cut by two transversals that intersect. In this lesson, you will learn how to use proportions to find lengths of segments formed by parallel lines that intersect two or more transversals.

Essential Understanding When two or more parallel lines intersect other lines, proportional segments are formed.

take note

Theorem 61 Side-Splitter Theorem

Theorem	If . . .	Then . . .
If a line is parallel to one side of a triangle and intersects the other two sides, then it divides those sides proportionally.	$\overleftrightarrow{RS} \parallel \overleftrightarrow{XY}$ 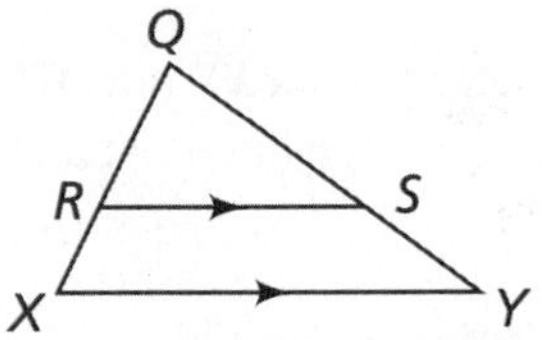	$\frac{XR}{RQ} = \frac{YS}{SQ}$

12x10 120
27X

Proof Proof of Theorem 61: Side-Splitter Theorem

Given: $\triangle QXY$ with $\overleftrightarrow{RS} \parallel \overleftrightarrow{XY}$

Prove: $\frac{XR}{RQ} = \frac{YS}{SQ}$

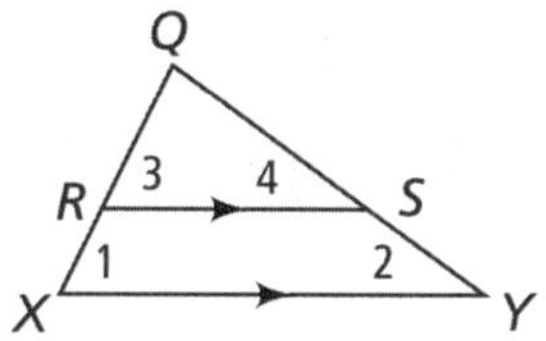

Statements	Reasons
1) $\overleftrightarrow{RS} \parallel \overleftrightarrow{XY}$	**1)** Given
2) $\angle 1 \cong \angle 3, \angle 2 \cong \angle 4$	**2)** If lines are $\parallel$, then corresponding $\angle$s are $\cong$.
3) $\triangle QXY \sim \triangle QRS$	**3)** AA $\sim$ Postulate
4) $\frac{XQ}{RQ} = \frac{YQ}{SQ}$	**4)** Corresponding sides of $\sim$ $\triangle$s are proportional.
5) $XQ = XR + RQ, YQ = YS + SQ$	**5)** Segment Addition Postulate
6) $\frac{XR + RQ}{RQ} = \frac{YS + SQ}{SQ}$	**6)** Substitution Property
7) $\frac{XR}{RQ} = \frac{YS}{SQ}$	**7)** Property of Proportions (3)

ONLINE PROBLEMS

Problem 1 Using the Side-Splitter Theorem

Plan

How can you use the parallel lines in the diagram?

Got It? **a.** What is the value of a in the diagram below?

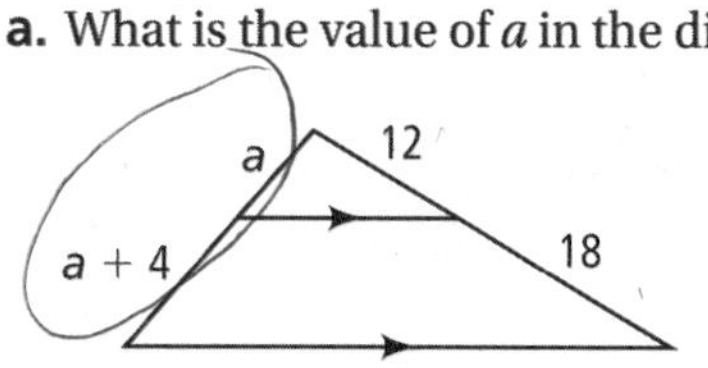

$\frac{a}{(a+4)} = \frac{12}{18}$

$12(a+4) = 18a$

$12a + 48 = 18a$

$-12a \quad -12a$

$\frac{48}{6} = \frac{6a}{6}$

$8 = a$

b. Reasoning In $\triangle XYZ$, $\overline{RS}$ joins $\overline{XY}$ and $\overline{YZ}$ with R on $\overline{XY}$ and S on $\overline{YZ}$, and $\overline{RS} \parallel \overline{XZ}$. If $\frac{YR}{RX} = \frac{YS}{SZ} = 1$, what must be true about RS? Justify your reasoning.

Practice Algebra Solve for x.

1.

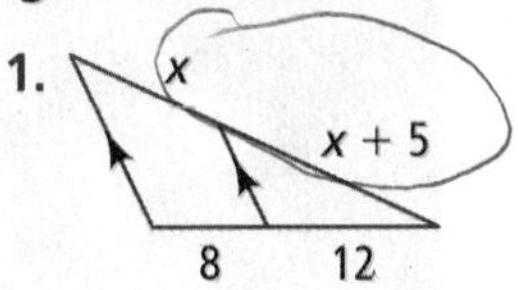

2.

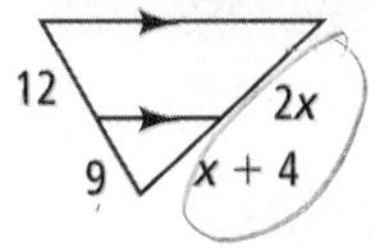

$\frac{x}{x+5} = \frac{8}{12}$

$8(x+5) = 12x$

$8x + 40 = 12x$
$-8x \quad -8x$

$\frac{40}{4} = \frac{4x}{4}$

$x = 10$

$\frac{2x}{(x+4)} = \frac{12}{9}$

$12x + 48 = 18x$
$-12x \quad -12x$

$\frac{48}{6} = \frac{6x}{6}$

$x = 8$

take note

Corollary — Corollary to the Side-Splitter Theorem

Corollary	If . . .	Then . . .
If three parallel lines intersect two transversals, then the segments intercepted on the transversals are proportional.	$a \parallel b \parallel c$	$\frac{AB}{BC} = \frac{WX}{XY}$

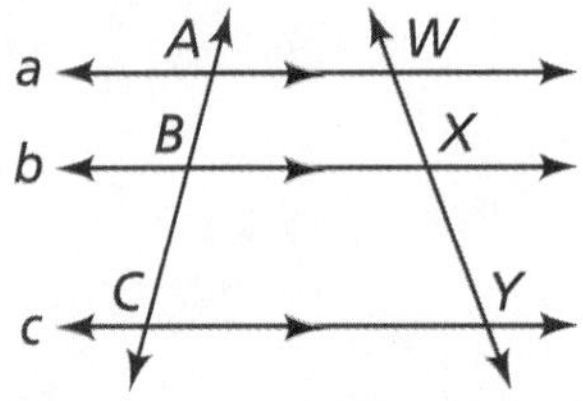

You will prove the Corollary to Theorem 61 in Exercise 36.

Problem 2 Finding a Length

Got It? In the figure in Problem 2, what is the length of Site C along the road?

Plan
What information does the diagram give you?

all ∡'s add to 180°
Exterior ∡ Th.
∡a = ∡b + ∡c
linear Pair
∡a + ∡d = 180°

all angles are equal = 60°

Practice **3. Marine Biology** Use the information shown on the auger shell. What is the value of y?

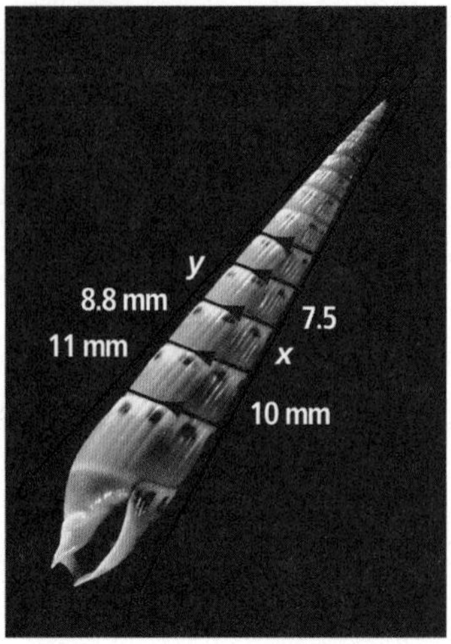

4. Algebra Solve for x.

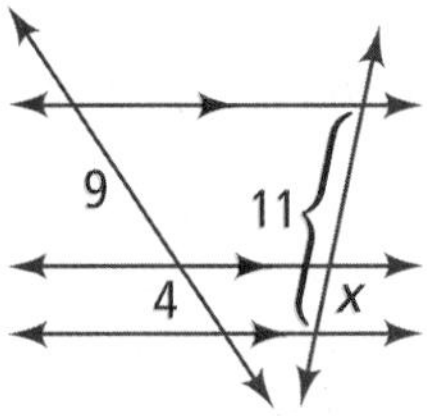

Essential Understanding The bisector of an angle of a triangle divides the opposite side into two segments with lengths proportional to the sides of the triangle that form the angle.

take note

Theorem 62 Triangle-Angle-Bisector Theorem

Theorem	If . . .	Then . . .
If a ray bisects an angle of a triangle, then it divides the opposite side into two segments that are proportional to the other two sides of the triangle.	$\overrightarrow{AD}$ bisects $\angle CAB$ 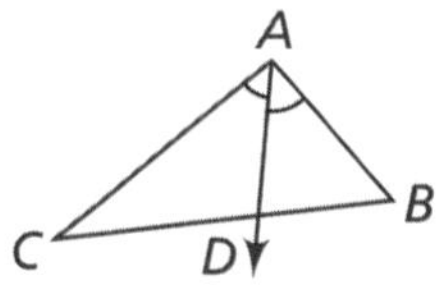	$\frac{CD}{DB} = \frac{CA}{BA}$

You will prove the Triangle-Angle-Bisector Theorem in Exercise 37.

Problem 3 Using the Triangle-Angle-Bisector Theorem

Got It? What is the value of y?

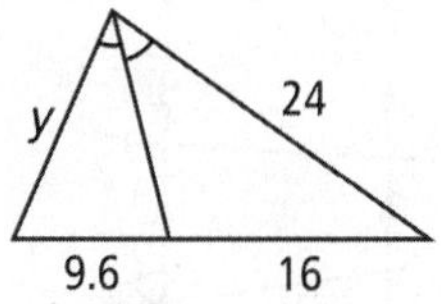

Practice 5. **Algebra** Solve for x.

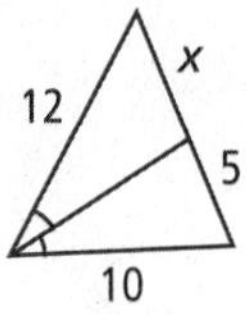

6. The lengths of the sides of a triangle are 5 cm, 12 cm, and 13 cm. Find the lengths, to the nearest tenth, of the segments into which the bisector of each angle divides the opposite side.

Lesson Check

Do you know HOW?

Use the figure to complete each proportion.

7. $\frac{a}{b} = \frac{\blacksquare}{e}$

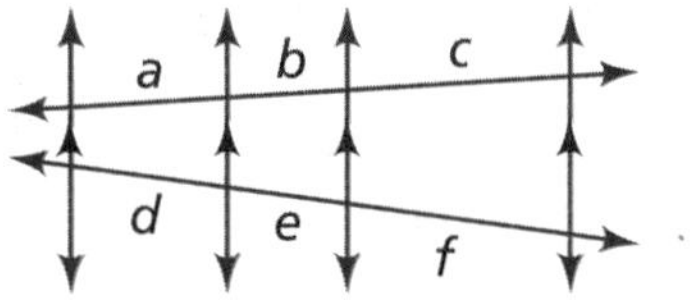

8. $\frac{b}{\blacksquare} = \frac{e}{f}$

9. $\frac{a}{b+c} = \frac{\blacksquare}{e+f}$

What is the value of x in each figure?

10. 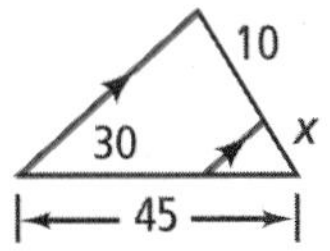

11. 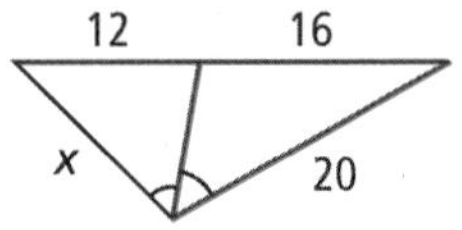

Do you UNDERSTAND?

MATHEMATICAL PRACTICES

12. **Compare and Contrast** How is the Corollary to the Side-Splitter Theorem related to Theorem 42: If three (or more) parallel lines cut off congruent segments on one transversal, then they cut off congruent segments on every transversal?

13. Compare and Contrast How are the Triangle-Angle-Bisector Theorem and Corollary 1 to Theorem 60 alike? How are they different?

14. Error Analysis A classmate says you can use the Side-Splitter Theorem to find both x and y in the diagram. Explain what is wrong with your classmate's statement.

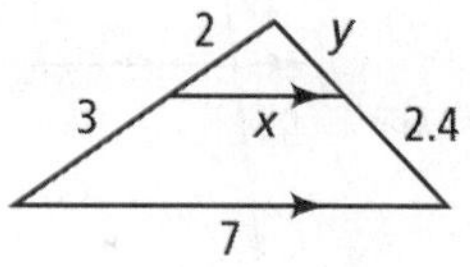

More Practice and Problem-Solving Exercises

MATHEMATICAL PRACTICES

B Apply

Use the figure at the right to complete each proportion. Justify your answer.

15. $\frac{RS}{■} = \frac{JR}{KJ}$

16. $\frac{KJ}{JP} = \frac{KS}{■}$

17. $\frac{QL}{PM} = \frac{SQ}{■}$

18. $\frac{PT}{■} = \frac{TQ}{KQ}$

19. $\frac{KL}{LW} = \frac{■}{MW}$

20. $\frac{■}{KP} = \frac{LQ}{KQ}$

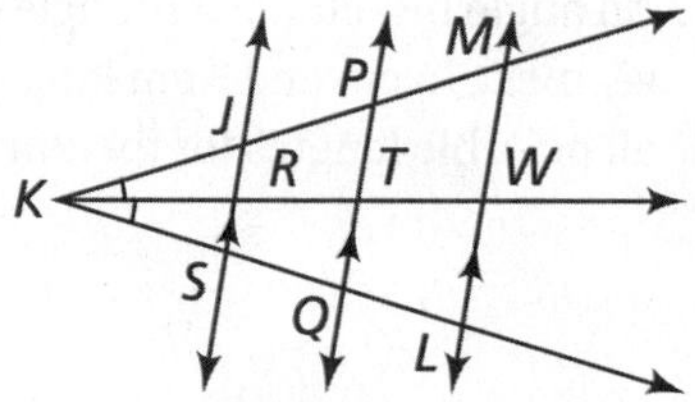

STEM Urban Design **In Washington, D.C., E. Capitol Street, Independence Avenue, C Street, and D Street are parallel streets that intersect Kentucky Avenue and 12th Street.**

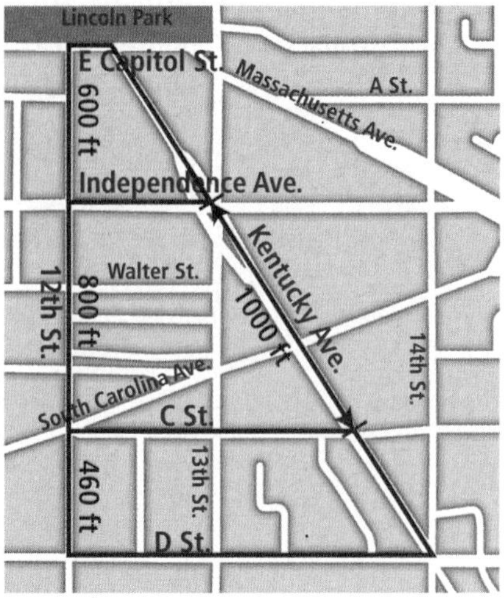

21. How long (to the nearest foot) is Kentucky Avenue between C Street and D Street?

22. How long (to the nearest foot) is Kentucky Avenue between E. Capitol Street and Independence Avenue?

Algebra **Solve for x.**

23.

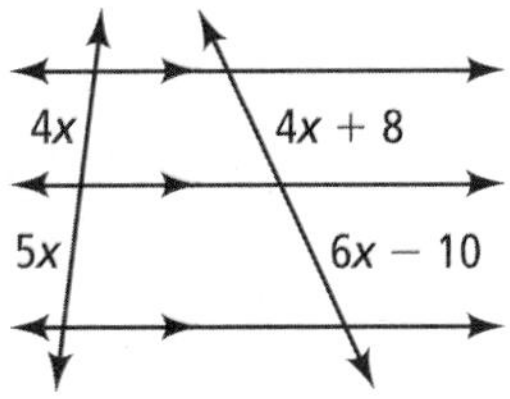

24.

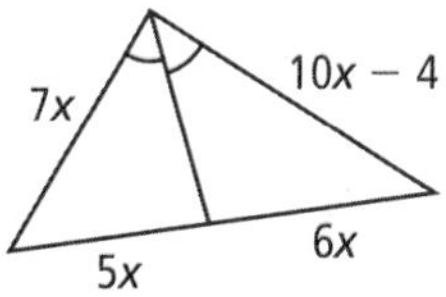

25.

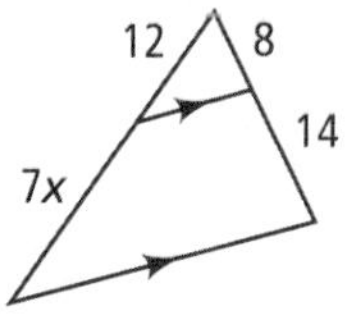

26. Think About a Plan The perimeter of the triangular lot at the right is 50 m. The surveyor's tape bisects an angle. Find the lengths x and y.

- How can you use the perimeter to write an equation in x and y?
- What other relationship do you know between x and y?

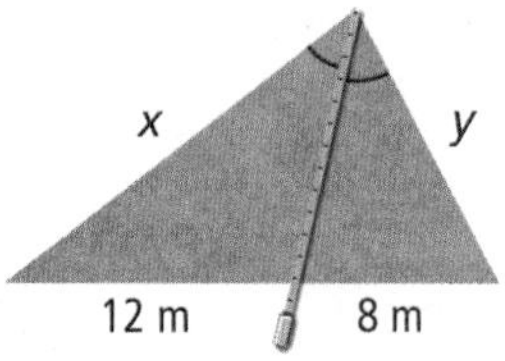

27. Prove the Converse of the Side-Splitter Theorem: If a line divides two sides of a triangle proportionally, then it is parallel to the third side.

Proof

Given: $\frac{XR}{RQ} = \frac{YS}{SQ}$

Prove: $\overline{RS} \parallel \overline{XY}$

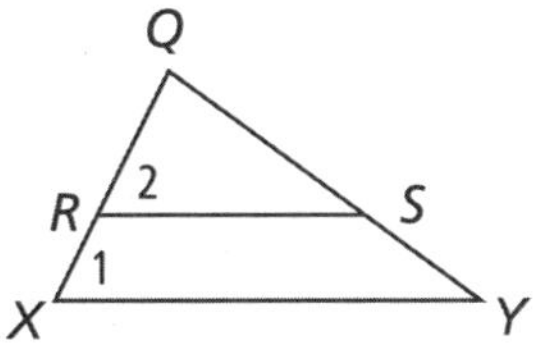

Determine whether the red segments are parallel. Explain each answer. You can use the theorem proved in Exercise 27.

28.

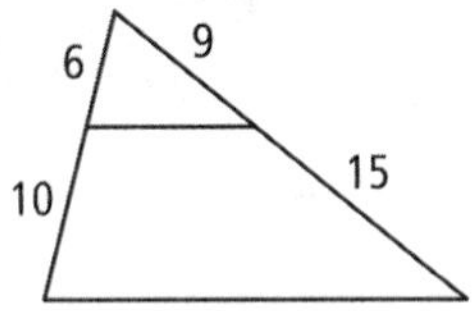

29.

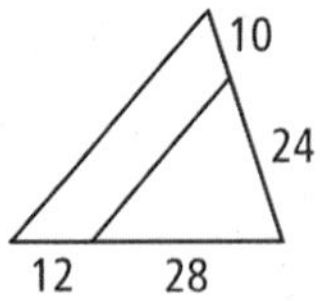

30.

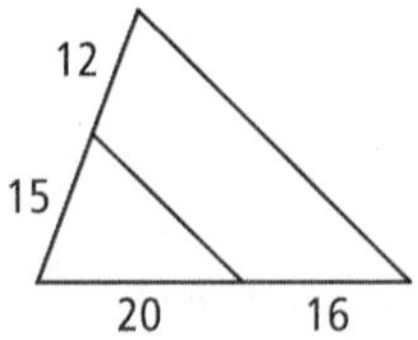

31. An angle bisector of a triangle divides the opposite side of the triangle into segments 5 cm and 3 cm long. A second side of the triangle is 7.5 cm long. Find all possible lengths for the third side of the triangle.

32. Open-Ended In a triangle, the bisector of an angle divides the opposite side into two segments with lengths 6 cm and 9 cm. How long could the other two sides of the triangle be? (*Hint:* Make sure the three sides satisfy the Triangle Inequality Theorem.)

33. Reasoning In $\triangle ABC$, the bisector of $\angle C$ bisects the opposite side. What type of triangle is $\triangle ABC$? Explain your reasoning.

Algebra Solve for x.

34.

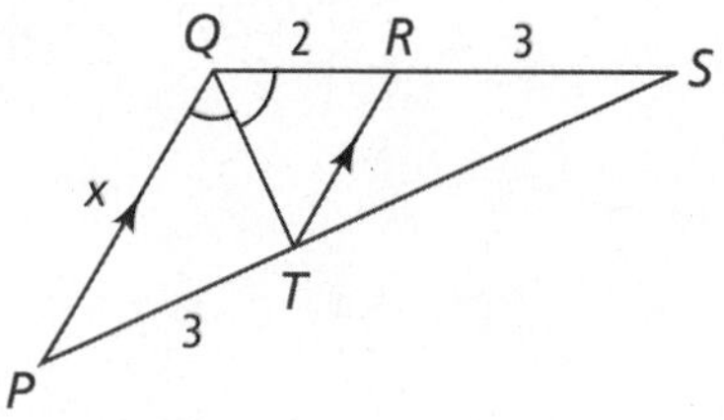

35.

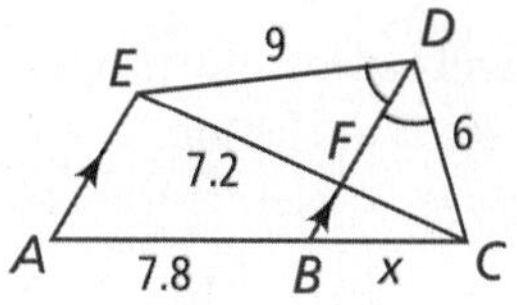

36. Prove the Corollary to the Side-Splitter Theorem. In the diagram from the statement of the theorem, draw the auxiliary line $\overleftrightarrow{CW}$ and label its intersection with b as point P.

Proof

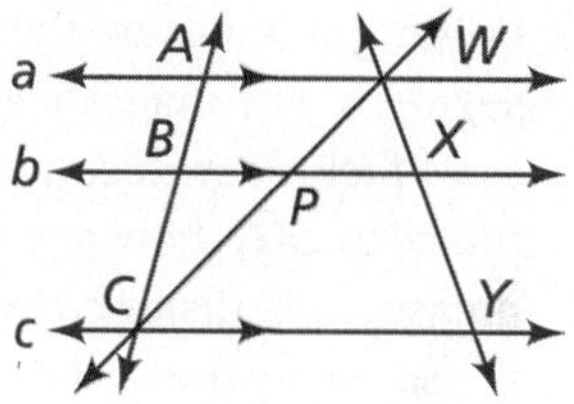

Given: $a \parallel b \parallel c$

Prove: $\frac{AB}{BC} = \frac{WX}{XY}$

37. Prove the Triangle-Angle-Bisector Theorem. In the diagram from the statement of the theorem, draw the auxiliary line $\overleftrightarrow{BE}$ so that $\overleftrightarrow{BE} \parallel \overline{DA}$. Extend $\overline{CA}$ to meet $\overleftrightarrow{BE}$ at point F.

Proof

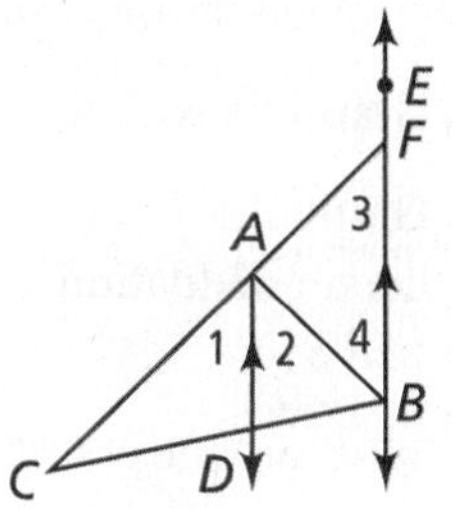

Given: $\overleftrightarrow{AD}$ bisects $\angle CAB$.

Prove: $\frac{CD}{DB} = \frac{CA}{BA}$

Challenge

38. Use the definition in part (a) to prove the statements in parts (b) and (c).

a. Write a definition for a midsegment of a parallelogram.

b. A parallelogram midsegment is parallel to two sides of the parallelogram.

c. A parallelogram midsegment bisects the diagonals of a parallelogram.

39. State the converse of the Triangle-Angle-Bisector Theorem. Give a convincing argument that the converse is true or a counterexample to prove that it is false.

40. In $\triangle ABC$, the bisectors of $\angle A$, $\angle B$, and $\angle C$ cut the opposite sides into lengths a_1 and a_2, b_1 and b_2, and c_1 and c_2, respectively, labeled in order counterclockwise around $\triangle ABC$. Find the perimeter of $\triangle ABC$ for each set of values.

a. $b_1 = 16, b_2 = 20, c_1 = 18$

b. $a_1 = \frac{5}{3}, a_2 = \frac{10}{3}, b_1 = \frac{15}{4}$

ACTIVITY LAB

Use With Lesson 10-6

Exploring Dilations

G.SRT.1.b The dilation of a line segment is . . . given by the scale factor. Also **G.SRT.1.a**

In this activity, you will explore the properties of dilations. A dilation is defined by a center of dilation and a scale factor.

Activity 1

To dilate a segment by a scale factor n with center of dilation at the origin, you measure the distance from the origin to each point on the segment. The diagram at the right shows the dilation of GH by the scale factor 3 with center of dilation at the origin. To locate the dilation image of $\overline{GH}$, draw rays from the origin through points G and H. Then measure the distance from the origin to G. Next, find the point along the same ray that is 3 times that distance. Label the point G'. Now dilate the endpoint H similarly. Draw $\overline{G'H'}$.

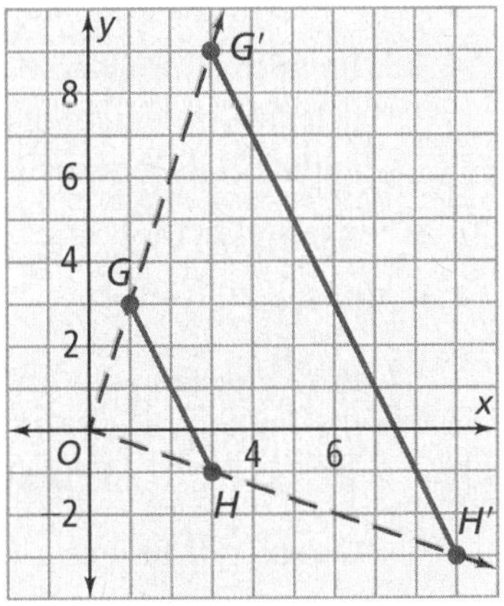

1. Graph $\overline{RS}$ with $R(1, 4)$ and $S(2, -1)$. What is the length of $\overline{RS}$?
2. Graph the dilations of the endpoints of $\overline{RS}$ by scale factor 2 and center of dilation at the origin. Label the dilated endpoints R' and S'.
3. What are the coordinates of R' and S'?
4. Graph $\overline{R'S'}$.

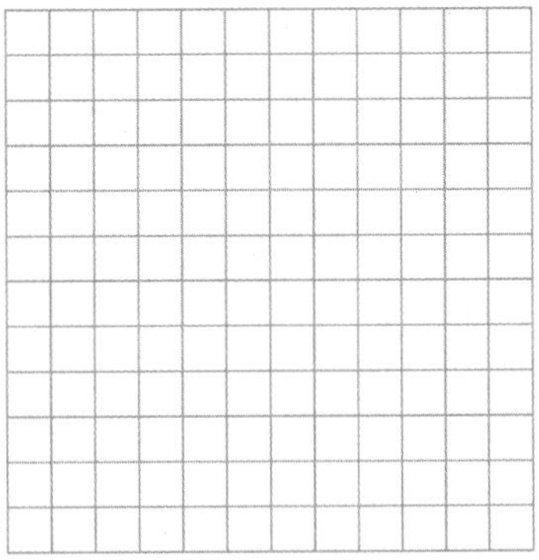

5. What is $R'S'$?
6. How do the lengths of $\overline{RS}$ and $\overline{R'S'}$ compare?

7. Graph the dilation of $\overline{RS}$ by scale factor $\frac{1}{2}$ with center of dilation at the origin. Label the dilation $\overline{R''S''}$.

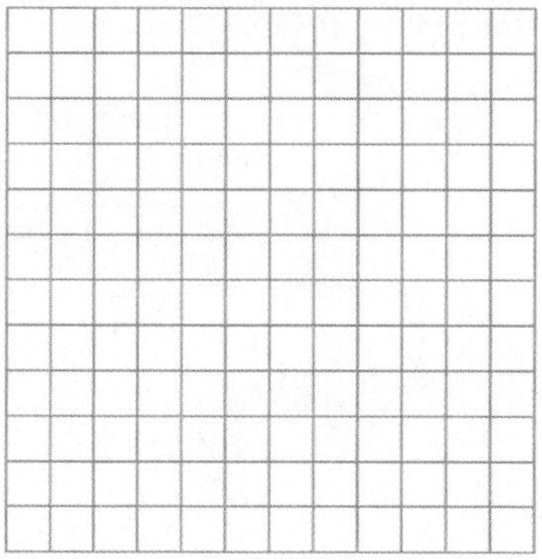

8. What is $R''S''$?

9. How do the lengths of $\overline{R'S'}$ and $\overline{R''S''}$ compare?

10. What can you conjecture about the length of a line segment that has been dilated by scale factor n?

Activity 2

11. Graph $L'M'N'P'$, the dilation of $LMNP$ with scale factor 3 and center of dilation at the origin. What are the coordinates of L', M', N', and P'?

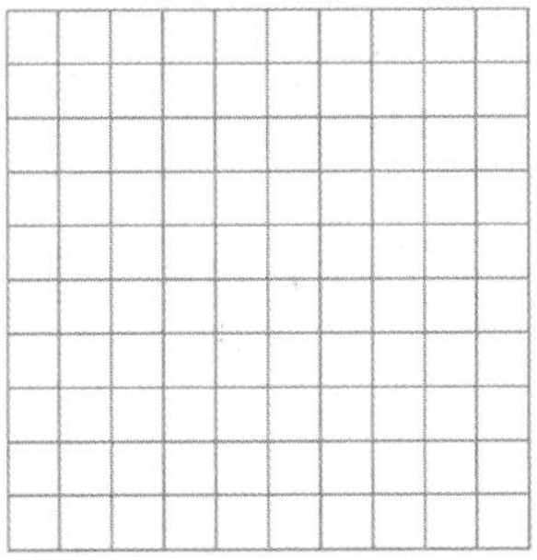

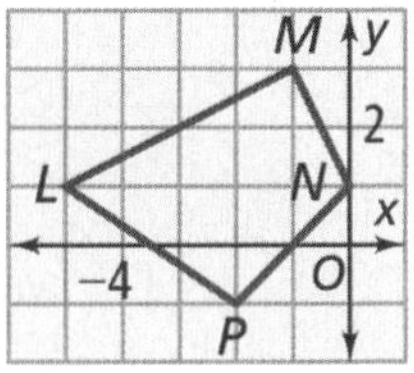

12. How are the coordinates of the vertices of $LMNP$ and $L'M'N'P'$ related?

13. Compare the shape, size, and orientation of the preimage $LMNP$ with the image $L'M'N'P'$. What conjecture can you make about the properties of dilations?

10-6 Dilations

G.SRT.1.a A dilation takes a line not passing through the center of the dilation to a parallel line . . .
Also **G.SRT.1.b**

Objective To understand dilation images of figures

Solve It! Write your solution to the Solve It in the space below.

In the Solve It, you looked at how the pupil of an eye changes in size, or *dilates*. In this lesson, you will learn how to dilate geometric figures.

Essential Understanding You can use a scale factor to make a larger or smaller copy of a figure that is similar to the original figure.

take note

Key Concept Dilation

A **dilation** with **center of dilation** C and **scale factor** n, $n > 0$, can be written as $D_{(n,\, C)}$. A dilation is a transformation with the following properties.

- The image of C is itself (that is, $C' = C$).
- For any other point R, R' is on $\overrightarrow{CR}$ and $CR' = n \cdot CR$, or $n = \frac{CR'}{CR}$.
- Dilations preserve angle measure.

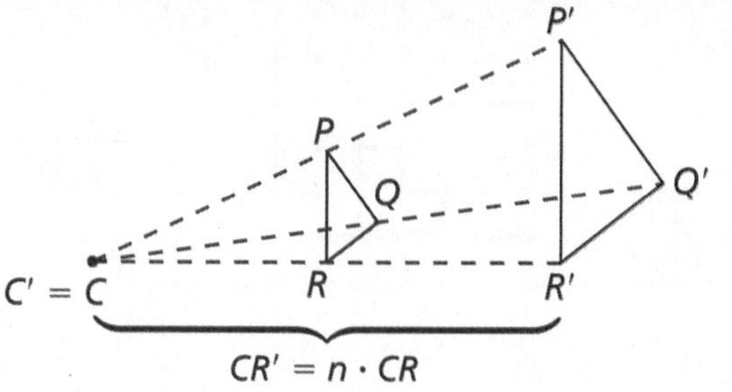

The scale factor n of a dilation is the ratio of a length of the image to the corresponding length in the preimage, with the image length always in the numerator. For the figure shown above, $n = \frac{CR'}{CR} = \frac{R'P'}{RP} = \frac{P'Q'}{PQ} = \frac{Q'R'}{QR}$.

A dilation is an **enlargement** if the scale factor n is greater than 1. The dilation is a **reduction** if the scale factor n is between 0 and 1.

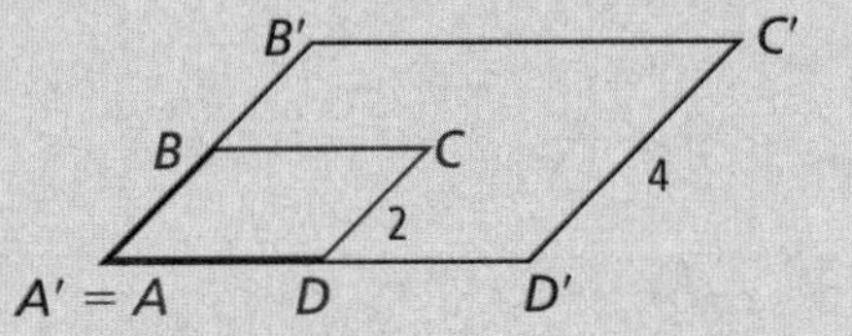

Enlargement
center A, scale factor 2

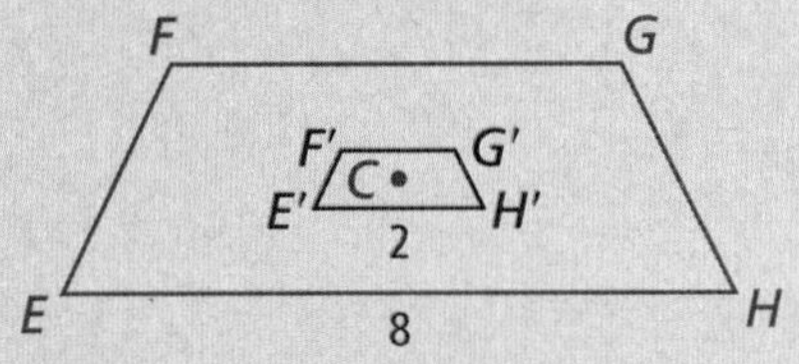

Reduction
center C, scale factor $\frac{1}{4}$

Problem 1 Finding a Scale Factor

Got It? Is $D_{(n,\,O)}(JKLM) = J'K'L'M'$ an enlargement or a reduction? What is the scale factor n of the dilation?

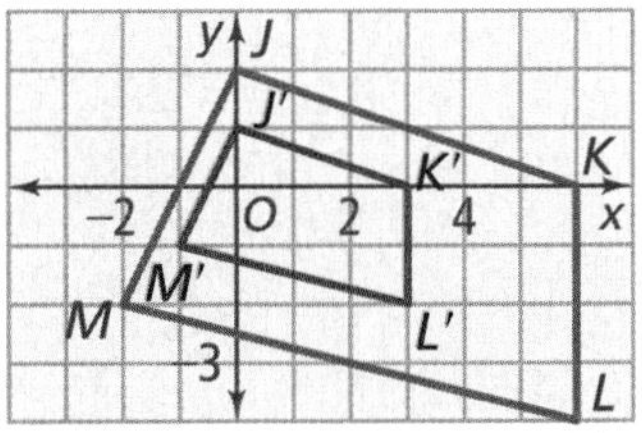

Practice **The red figure is a dilation image of the blue figure. The labeled point is the center of dilation. Tell whether the dilation is an enlargement or a reduction. Then find the scale factor of the dilation.**

1.

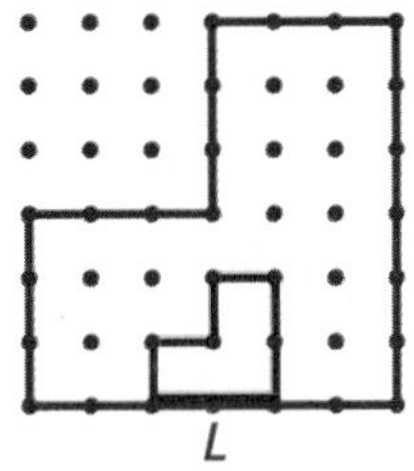

2.

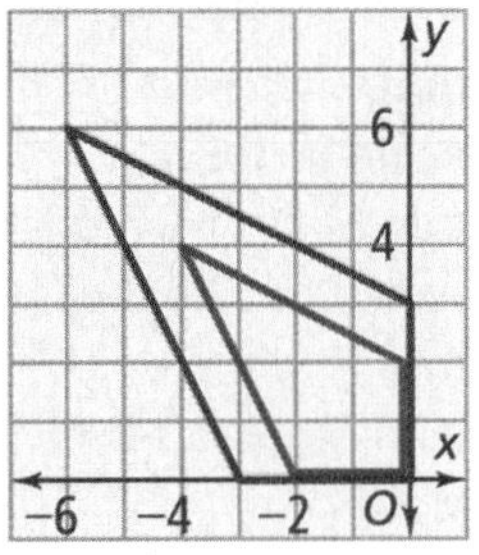

In the Got It for Problem 1, you looked at a dilation of a figure drawn in the coordinate plane. In this book, all dilations of figures in the coordinate plane have the origin as the center of dilation. So you can find the dilation image of a point $P(x, y)$ by multiplying the coordinates of P by the scale factor n. A dilation of scale factor n with center of dilation at the origin can be written as

$$D_n(x, y) = (nx, ny)$$

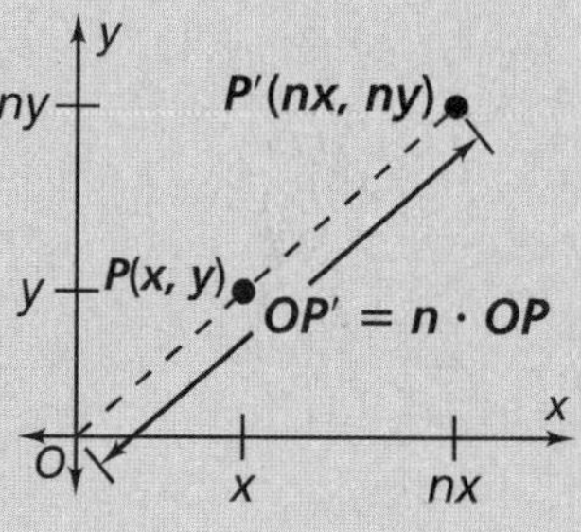

Problem 2 Finding a Dilation Image

Think
Will the vertices of the triangle move closer to (0, 0) or farther from (0, 0)?

Got It? **a.** What are the coordinates of the vertices of $D_{\frac{1}{2}}(\triangle PZG)$?

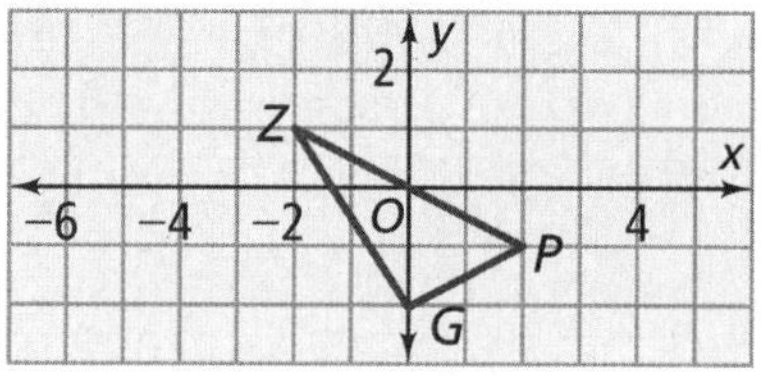

b. Reasoning How are $\overline{PZ}$ and $\overline{P'Z'}$ related? How are $\overline{PG}$ and $\overline{P'G'}$, and $\overline{GZ}$ and $\overline{G'Z'}$ related? Use these relationships to make a conjecture about the effects of dilations on lines.

Practice **Find the images of the vertices of $\triangle PQR$ for each dilation. Graph the image.**

3. $D_3(\triangle PQR)$

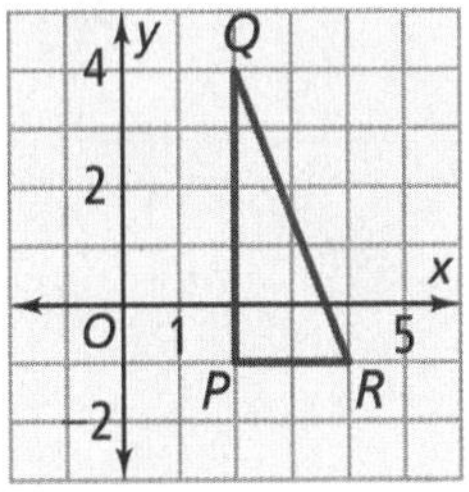

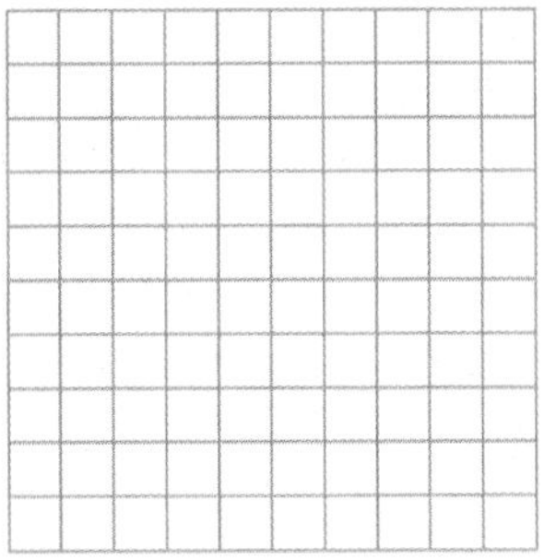

4. $D_{\frac{3}{4}}(\triangle PQR)$

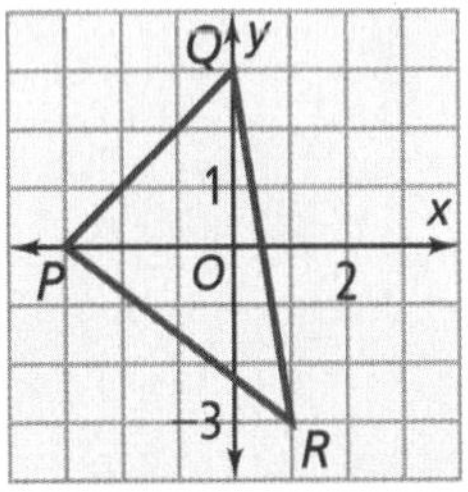

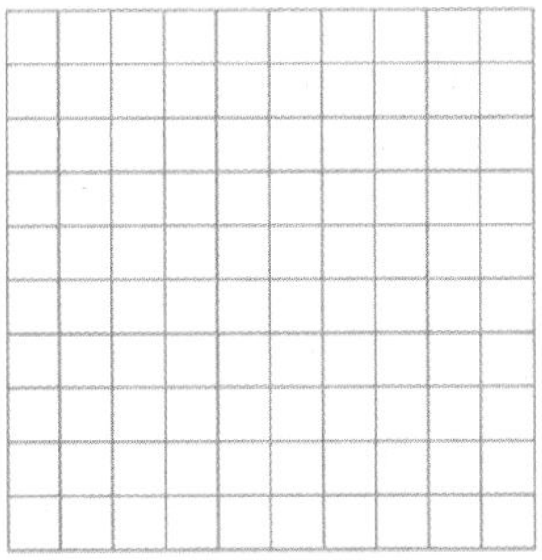

Dilations and scale factors help you understand real-world enlargements and reductions, such as images seen through a microscope or on a computer screen.

Problem 3 Using a Scale Factor to Find a Length

Got It? The height of a document on your computer screen is 20.4 cm. When you change the zoom setting on your screen from 100% to 25%, the new image of your document is a dilation of the previous image with scale factor 0.25. What is the height of the new image?

Think
What does a scale factor of 0.25 tell you?

Practice **Magnification** **You look at each object described in Exercises 5 and 6 under a magnifying glass. Find the actual dimension of each object.**

5. The image of an ant is 7 times the ant's actual size and has a length of 1.4 cm.

6. The image of a capital letter N is 6 times the letter's actual size and has a height of 1.68 cm.

Lesson Check

Do you know HOW?

7. The red figure is a dilation image of the blue figure with center of dilation *C*. Is the dilation an enlargement or a reduction? What is the scale factor of the dilation?

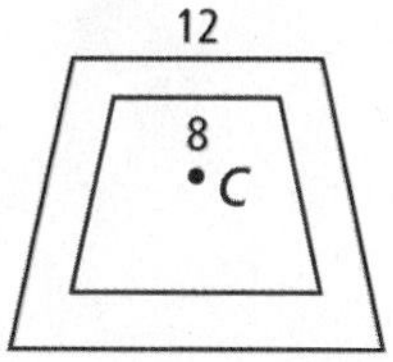

Find the image of each point.

8. $D_2(1, -5)$

9. $D_{\frac{1}{2}}(0, 6)$

10. $D_{10}(0, 0)$

Do you UNDERSTAND?

MATHEMATICAL PRACTICES

11. Vocabulary Describe the scale factor of a reduction.

12. Error Analysis The red figure is a dilation image of the blue figure for a dilation with center A. Two students made errors when asked to find the scale factor. Explain and correct their errors.

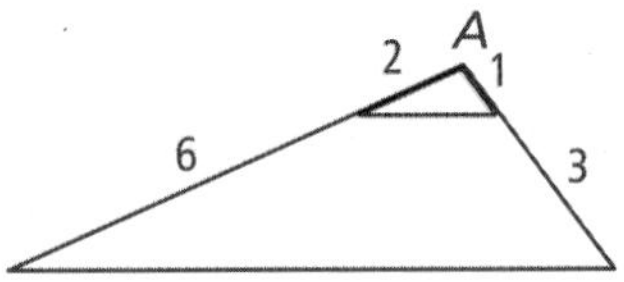

a.

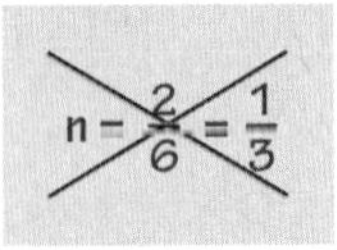

b.

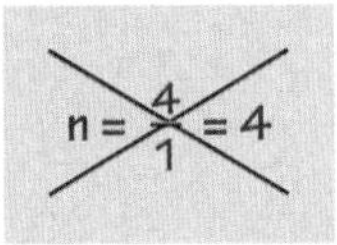

More Practice and Problem-Solving Exercises

MATHEMATICAL PRACTICES

B Apply

Find the image of each point for the given scale factor.

13. $L(-3, 0); D_5(L)$

14. $N(-4, 7); D_{0.2}(N)$

15. $A(-6, 2); D_{1.5}(A)$

16. $F(3, -2); D_{\frac{1}{3}}(F)$

17. $B\left(\frac{5}{4}, -\frac{3}{2}\right); D_{\frac{1}{10}}(B)$

18. $Q\left(6, \frac{\sqrt{3}}{2}\right); D_{\sqrt{6}}(Q)$

Use the graph at the right. Find the vertices of the image of *QRTW* for a dilation with center (0, 0) and the given scale factor.

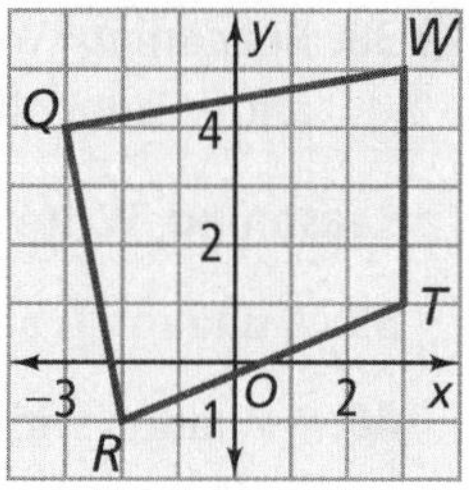

19. $\frac{1}{4}$ **20.** 0.6 **21.** 0.9 **22.** 10 **23.** 100

24. Compare and Contrast Compare the definition of scale factor of a dilation to the definition of scale factor of two similar polygons. How are they alike? How are they different?

25. Think About a Plan The diagram at the right shows $\triangle LMN$ and its image $\triangle L'M'N'$ for a dilation with center P. Find the values of x and y. Explain your reasoning.

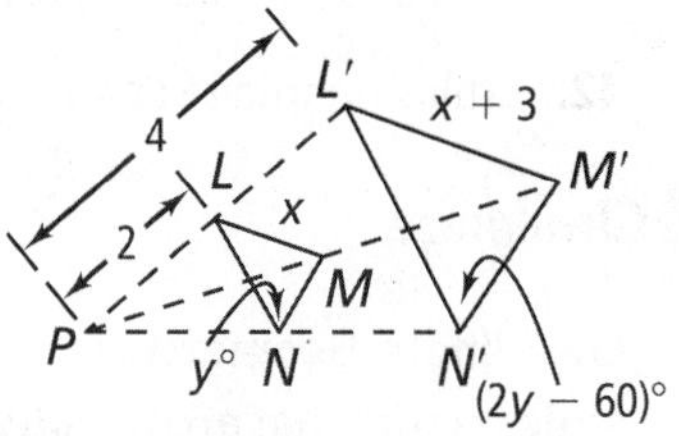

- What is the relationship between $\triangle LMN$ and $\triangle L'M'N'$?
- What is the scale factor of the dilation?
- Which variable can you find using the scale factor?

26. Writing An equilateral triangle has 4-in. sides. Describe its image for a dilation with center at one of the triangle's vertices and scale factor 2.5.

Coordinate Geometry **Graph *MNPQ* and its image *M'N'P'Q'* for a dilation with center (0, 0) and the given scale factor.**

27. $M(1, 3), N(-3, 3), P(-5, -3), Q(-1, -3); 3$

28. $M(2, 6), N(-4, 10), P(-4, -8), Q(-2, -12); \frac{1}{4}$

29. Open-Ended Use the dilation command in geometry software or drawing software to create a design that involves repeated dilations, such as the one shown at the right. The software will prompt you to specify a center of dilation and a scale factor. Print your design and color it. Feel free to use other transformations along with dilations.

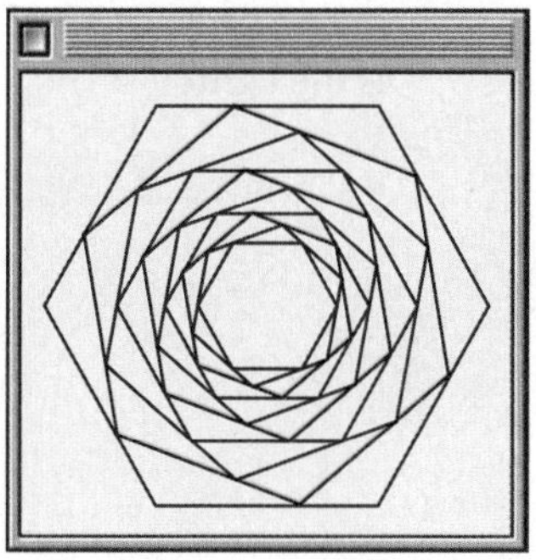

30. Copy Reduction Your picture of your family crest is 4.5 in. wide. You need a reduced copy for the front page of the family newsletter. The copy must fit in a space 1.8 in. wide. What scale factor should you use on the copy machine to adjust the size of your picture of the crest?

A dilation maps $\triangle HIJ$ onto $\triangle H'I'J'$. Find the missing values.

31. $HI = 8$ in. $H'I' = 16$ in.
$IJ = 5$ in. $I'J' = ■$ in.
$HJ = 6$ in. $H'J' = ■$ in.

32. $HI = 7$ cm $H'I' = 5.25$ cm
$IJ = 7$ cm $I'J' = ■$ cm
$HJ = ■$ cm $H'J' = 9$ cm

33. $HI = ■$ ft $H'I' = 8$ ft
$IJ = 30$ ft $I'J' = ■$ ft
$HJ = 24$ ft $H'J' = 6$ ft

Copy $\triangle TBA$ and point *O* for each of Exercises 34–37. Draw the dilation image $\triangle T'B'A'$.

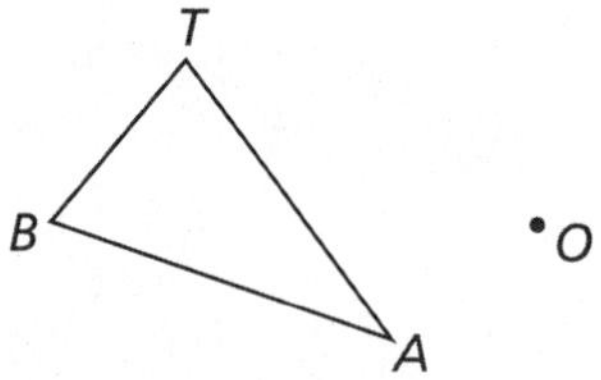

34. $D_{(2,\,O)}(\triangle TBA)$ **35.** $D_{(3,\,B)}(\triangle TBA)$

36. $D_{(\frac{1}{3},\,T)}(\triangle TBA)$ **37.** $D_{(\frac{1}{2},\,O)}(\triangle TBA)$

38. Reasoning You are given $\overline{AB}$ and its dilation image $\overline{A'B'}$ with A, B, A', and B' noncollinear. Explain how to find the center of dilation and scale factor.

Reasoning Write *true* or *false* for Exercises 39–42. Explain your answers.

39. A dilation is an isometry.

40. A dilation with a scale factor greater than 1 is a reduction.

41. For a dilation, corresponding angles of the image and preimage are congruent.

42. A dilation image cannot have any points in common with its preimage.

Challenge

Coordinate Geometry In the coordinate plane, you can extend dilations to include scale factors that are negative numbers. For Exercises 43 and 44, use $\triangle PQR$ with vertices $P(1, 2)$, $Q(3, 4)$, and $R(4, 1)$.

43. Graph $D_{3}(\triangle PQR)$.

44. **a.** Graph $D_{-1}(\triangle PQR)$.

b. Explain why the dilation in part (a) may be called a *reflection through a point*. Extend your explanation to a new definition of point symmetry.

45. Shadows A flashlight projects an image of rectangle $ABCD$ on a wall so that each vertex of $ABCD$ is 3 ft away from the corresponding vertex of $A'B'C'D'$. The length of $\overline{AB}$ is 3 in. The length of $\overline{A'B'}$ is 1 ft. How far from each vertex of $ABCD$ is the light?

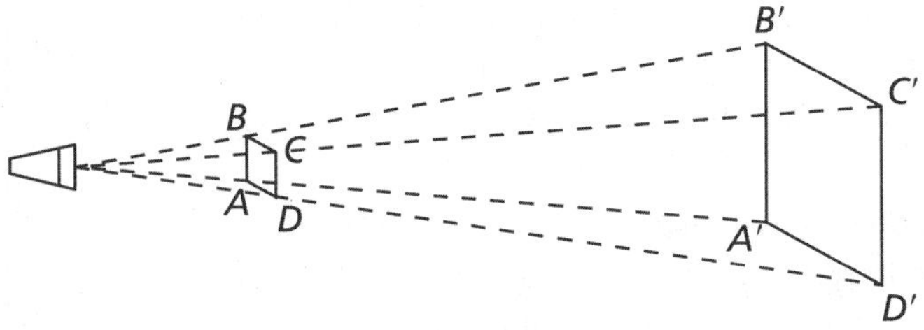

10-7 Similarity Transformations

G.SRT.2 Given two figures, use the definition of similarity in terms of similarity transformations to decide if they are similar . . . Also **G.SRT.3**

Objective To identify similarity transformations and verify properties of similarity

Solve It! Write your solution to the Solve It in the space below.

In the Solve It, you used a composition of a rigid motion and a dilation to describe the mapping from $\triangle ABC$ to $\triangle A'B'C'$.

Essential Understanding You can use compositions of rigid motions and dilations to help you understand the properties of similarity.

Problem 1 Drawing Transformations

Got It? Reasoning $\triangle LMN$ has vertices $L(-4, 2)$, $M(-3, -3)$, and $N(-1, 1)$. Suppose the triangle is translated 4 units right and 2 units up and then dilated by a scale factor of 0.5 with center of dilation at the origin. Sketch the resulting image of the composition of transformations.

Practice $\triangle MAT$ has vertices $M(6, -2)$, $A(4, -5)$, and $T(1, -2)$. For each of the following, sketch the image of the composition of transformations.

1. rotation of 180° about the origin followed by a dilation by a scale factor of 1.5

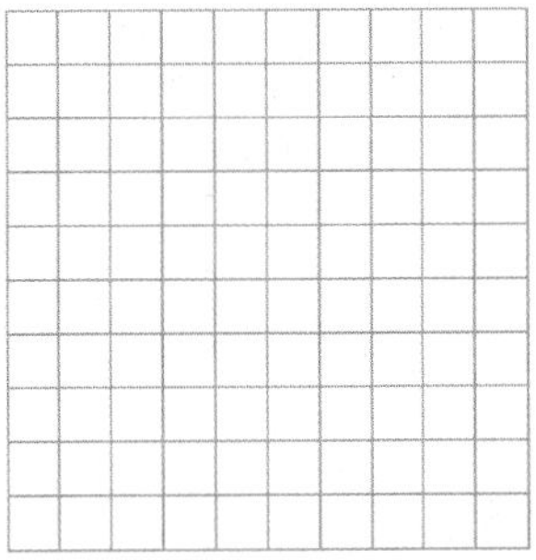

2. translation 6 units up followed by a reflection across the *y*-axis and then a dilation by a scale factor of 2

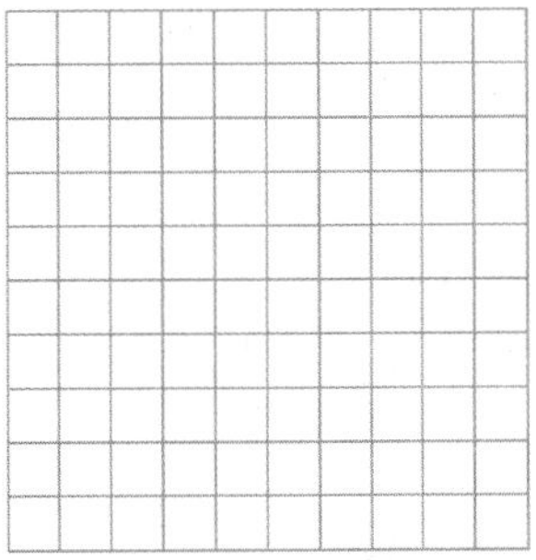

Problem 2 Describing Transformations

Got It? What is a composition of rigid motions and a dilation that maps trapezoid *ABCD* to trapezoid *MNHP*?

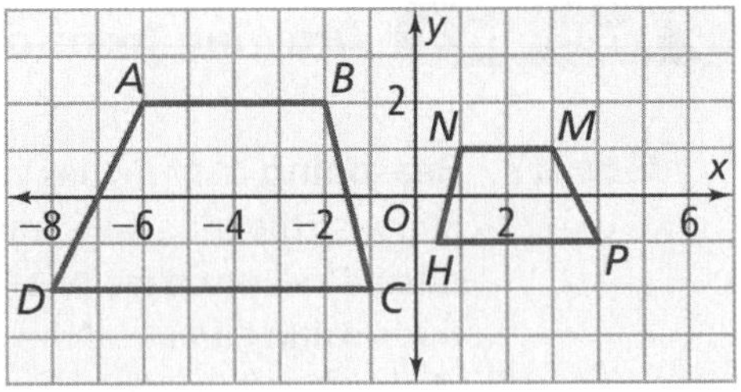

Practice **For each graph, describe the composition of transformations that maps $\triangle FGH$ to $\triangle QRS$.**

3.

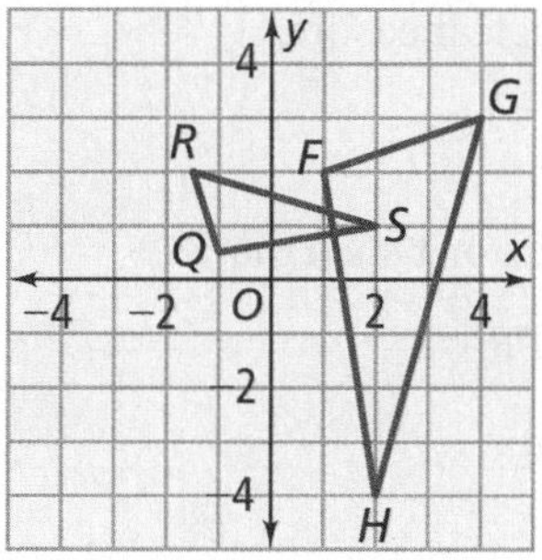

4.

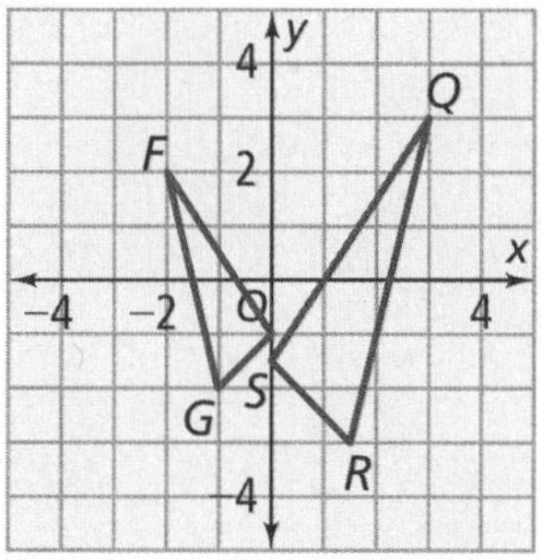

Notice that the figures in Problems 1 and 2 appear to have the same shape but different sizes. Compositions of rigid motions and dilations map preimages to similar images. For this reason, they are called **similarity transformations.** Similarity transformations give you another way to think about similarity.

take note

Key Concept Similar Figures

Two figures are **similar** if and only if there is a similarity transformation that maps one figure onto the other.

Here's Why It Works Consider the composition of a rigid motion and a dilation shown at the right.

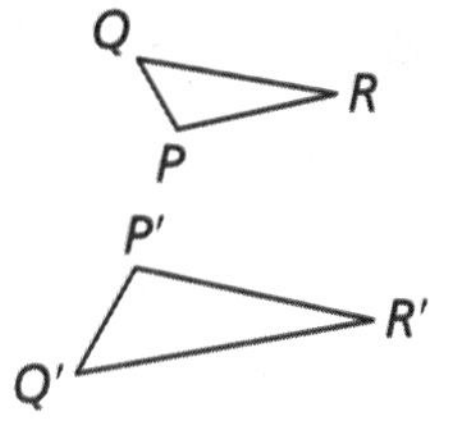

Because rigid motions and dilations preserve angle measure, $m\angle P = m\angle P'$, $m\angle Q = m\angle Q'$, and $m\angle R = m\angle R'$. So corresponding angles are congruent.

Because there is a dilation, there is some scale factor k such that:

$$P'Q' = kPQ \qquad Q'R' = kQR \qquad P'R' = kPR$$

$$k = \frac{P'Q'}{PQ} \qquad k = \frac{Q'R'}{QR} \qquad k = \frac{P'R'}{PR}$$

So $\frac{P'Q'}{PQ} = \frac{Q'R'}{QR} = \frac{P'R'}{PR}$.

Problem 3 Finding Similarity Transformations

Think

Does it matter what the center of dilation is?

Got It? Is there a similarity transformation that maps $\triangle JKL$ to $\triangle RST$? If so, identify the similarity transformation and write a similarity statement. If not, explain.

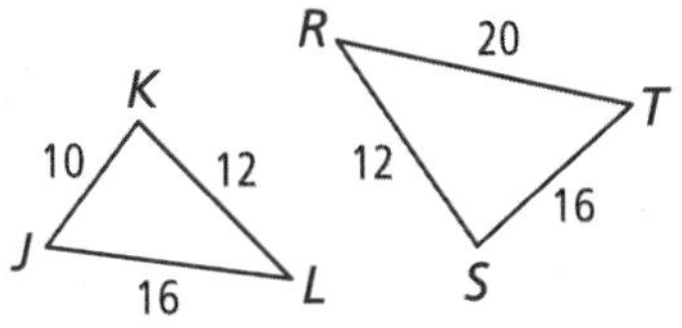

Practice **For each pair of figures in Exercises 5 and 6, determine if there is a similarity transformation that maps one figure onto the other. If so, identify the similarity transformation and write a similarity statement. If not, explain.**

5.

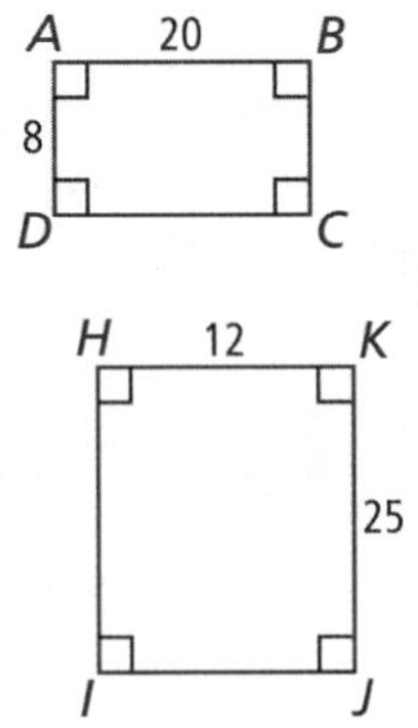

6.

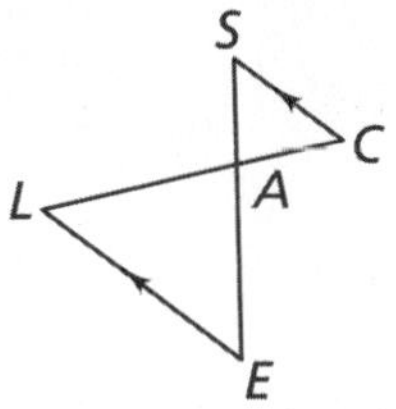

Similarity transformations provide a powerful general approach to similarity. In Problem 3, you used similarity transformations to verify the AA Postulate for triangle similarity. Another advantage to the transformational approach to similarity is that you can apply it to figures other than polygons.

Problem 4 Determining Similarity

Got It? Are the figures below similar? Explain.

How can you determine whether two figures are similar if you have no information about side lengths or angle measures?

Practice **For each pair of figures in Exercises 7 and 8, determine whether or not the figures are similar. Explain your reasoning.**

7.

8.

Lesson Check

Do you know HOW?

Use the diagram at the right for Exercises 9 and 10.

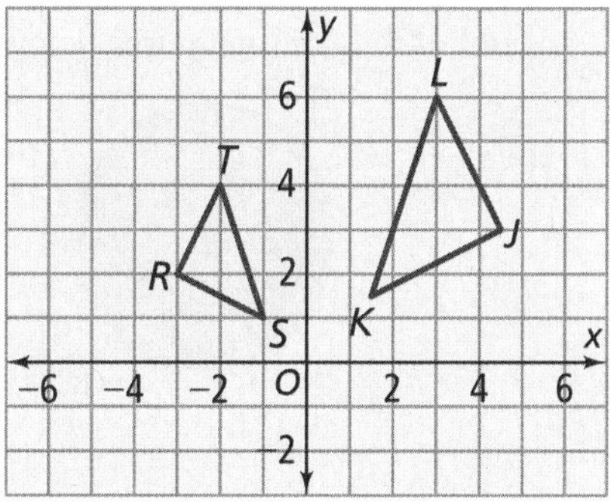

9. What is a similarity transformation that maps $\triangle RST$ to $\triangle JKL$?

10. What are the coordinates of $(D_{\frac{1}{4}} \circ r_{(180^\circ,\, O)})(\triangle RST)$?

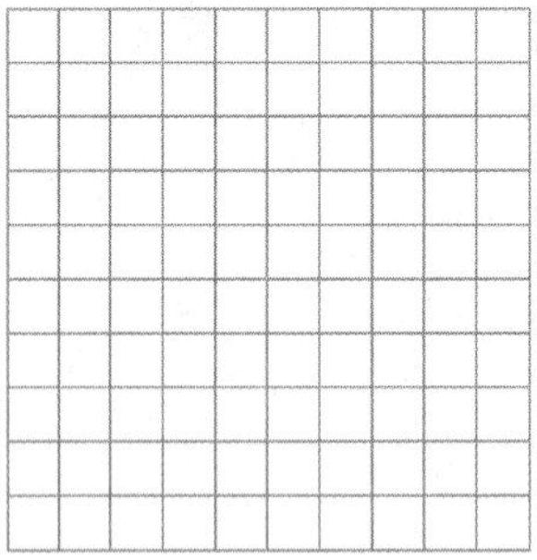

Do you UNDERSTAND?

MATHEMATICAL PRACTICES

11. Vocabulary Describe how the word *dilation* is used in areas outside of mathematics. How do these applications relate the mathematical definition?

12. Open-Ended For $\triangle TUV$ at the right, give the vertices of a similar triangle after a similarity transformation that uses at least 1 rigid motion.

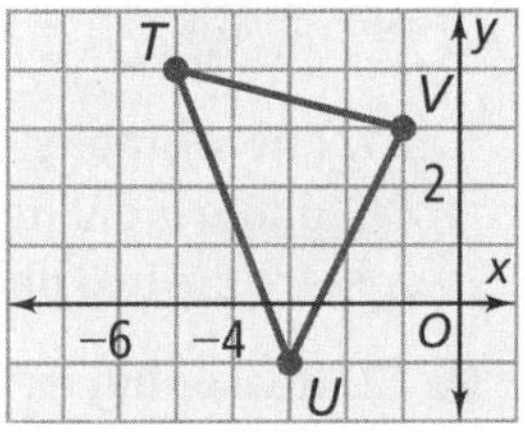

More Practice and Problem-Solving Exercises

MATHEMATICAL PRACTICES

B Apply

13. Writing Your teacher used geometry software program to plot $\triangle ABC$ with vertices $A(2, 1)$, $B(6, 1)$, and $C(6, 4)$. Then he used a similarity transformation to plot $\triangle DEF$ with vertices $D(-4, -2)$, $E(-12, -2)$, and $F(-12, -8)$. The corresponding angles of the two triangles are congruent. How can the Distance Formula be used to verify that the lengths of the corresponding sides are proportional? Verify that the figures are similar.

14. Think About a Plan Suppose that $\triangle JKL$ is formed by connecting the midpoints of $\triangle ABC$. Is $\triangle AJL$ similar to $\triangle ABC$? Explain.

- How are the side lengths of $\triangle AJL$ related to the side lengths of $\triangle ABC$?
- Can you find a similarity transformation that maps $\triangle AJL$ to $\triangle ABC$? Explain.

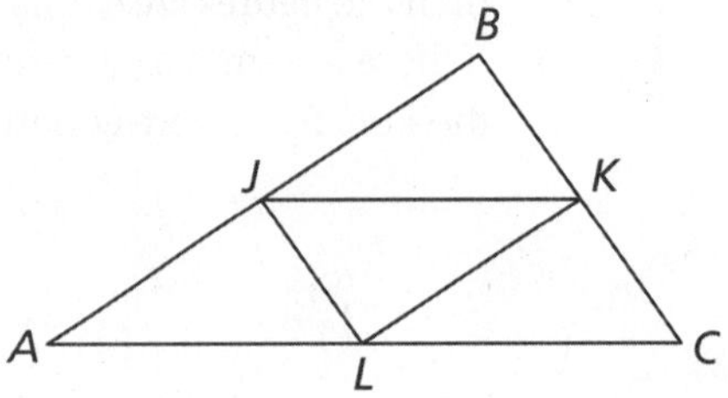

15. Writing What properties are preserved by rigid motions but not by similarity transformations?

Determine whether each statement is *always, sometimes,* or *never* true.

16. There is a similarity transformation between two rectangles.

17. There is a similarity transformation between two squares.

18. There is a similarity transformation between two circles.

19. There is a similarity transformation between a right triangle and an equilateral triangle.

20. Indirect Measurement A surveyor wants to use similar triangles to determine the distance across a lake as shown at the right.

a. Are the two triangles in the figure similar? Justify your reasoning.

b. What is the distance d across the lake?

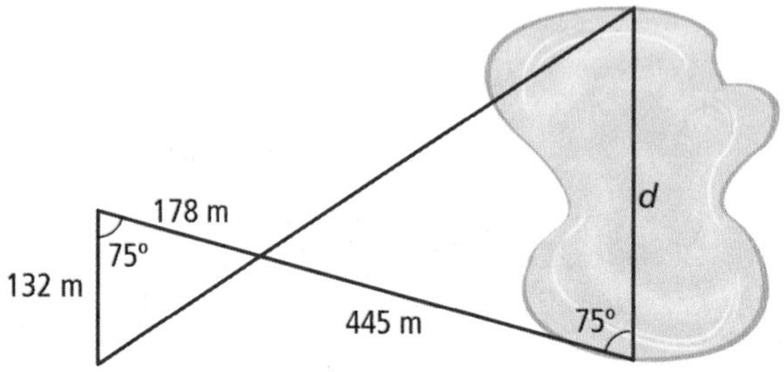

21. Photography A 4-in. by 6-in. rectangular photo is enlarged to fit an 8-in. by 10-in. frame. Are the two photographs similar? Explain.

22. Reasoning Is a rigid motion an example of a similarity transformation? Explain your reasoning and give an example.

23. Art A printing company enlarges a banner for a graduation party by a scale factor of 8.

a. What are the dimensions of the larger banner?

b. How can the printing company be sure that the enlarged banner is similar to the original?

Challenge

24. If $\triangle ABC$ has vertices given by $A(u, v)$, $B(w, x)$, and $C(y, z)$, and $\triangle NOP$ has vertices given by $N(5u, -4v)$, $O(5w, -4x)$, and $P(5y, -4z)$, is there a similarity transformation that maps $\triangle ABC$ to $\triangle NOP$? Explain.

25. Overhead Projector When Mrs. Sheldon places a transparency on the screen of the overhead projector, the projector shows an enlargement of the transparency on the wall. Does this situation represent a similarity transformation? Explain.

26. Reasoning Tell whether each statement below is *true* or *false.*

a. In order to show that two figures are similar, it is sufficient to show that there is a similarity transformation that maps one figure to the other.

b. If there is a similarity transformation that maps one figure to another figure, then the figures are similar.

c. If there is a similarity transformation that maps one figure to another figure, then the figures are congruent.

10 Chapter Review

MathXL® for School
Go to pearsonsuccessnet.com

10-1 Ratios and Proportions

Quick Review

A **ratio** is a comparison of two quantities by division. A **proportion** is a statement that two ratios are equal. The **Cross Products Property** states that if $\frac{a}{b} = \frac{c}{d}$, where $b \neq 0$ and $d \neq 0$, then $ad = bc$.

Example

What is the solution of $\frac{x}{x+3} = \frac{4}{6}$?

$6x = 4(x + 3)$	Cross Products Property
$6x = 4x + 12$	Distributive Property
$2x = 12$	Subtract $4x$ from each side.
$x = 6$	Divide each side by 2.

Exercises

1. A high school has 16 math teachers for 1856 math students. What is the ratio of math teachers to math students?

2. The measures of two complementary angles are in the ratio 2 : 3. What is the measure of the smaller angle?

Algebra **Solve each proportion.**

3. $\frac{x}{7} = \frac{18}{21}$

4. $\frac{6}{11} = \frac{15}{2x}$

5. $\frac{x}{3} = \frac{x+4}{5}$

6. $\frac{8}{x+9} = \frac{2}{x-3}$

10-2 and 10-3 Similar Polygons and Proving Triangles Similar

Quick Review

Similar polygons have congruent corresponding angles and proportional corresponding sides. You can prove triangles similar with limited information about congruent corresponding angles and proportional corresponding sides.

Postulate or Theorem	What You Need
Angle-Angle (AA ~)	two pairs of ≅ angles
Side-Angle-Side (SAS ~)	two pairs of proportional sides and the included angles ≅
Side-Side-Side (SSS ~)	three pairs of proportional sides

Example

Is △*ABC* similar to △*RQP*? How do you know?

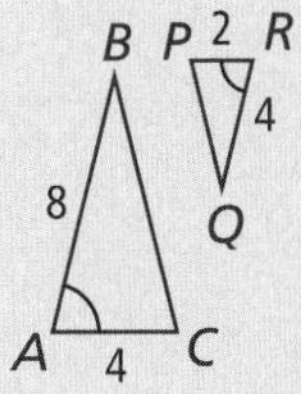

You know that $\angle A \cong \angle R$. $\frac{AB}{RQ} = \frac{AC}{RP} = \frac{2}{1}$, so the triangles are similar by the SAS ~ Theorem.

Exercises

The polygons are similar. Write a similarity statement and give the scale factor.

7.

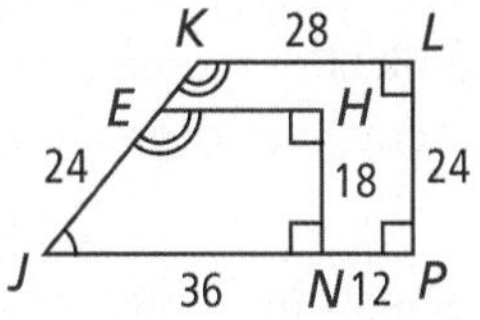

8.

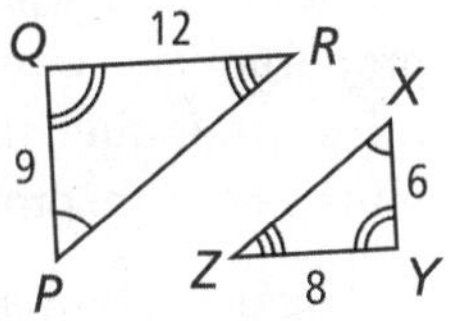

9. City Planning The length of a rectangular playground in a scale drawing is 12 in. If the scale is 1 in. = 10 ft, what is the actual length?

10. Indirect Measurement A 3-ft vertical post casts a 24-in. shadow at the same time a pine tree casts a 30-ft shadow. How tall is the pine tree?

Are the triangles similar? How do you know?

11.

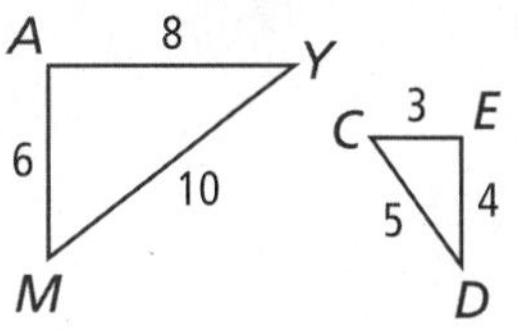

12.

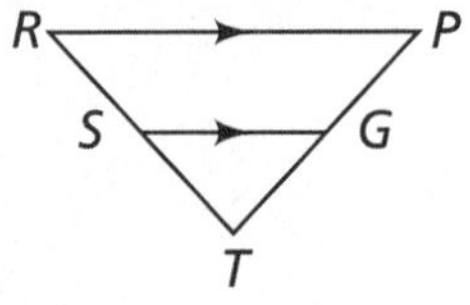

10-4 Similarity in Right Triangles

Quick Review

$\overline{CD}$ is the altitude to the hypotenuse of right $\triangle ABC$.

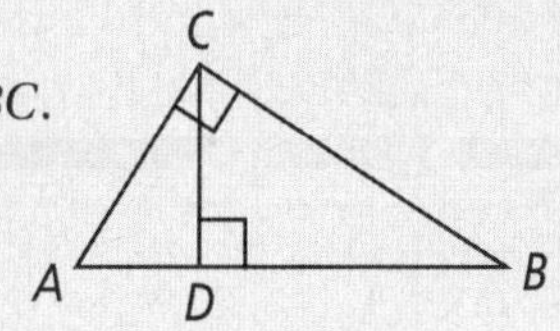

- $\triangle ABC \sim \triangle ACD$, $\triangle ABC \sim \triangle CBD$, and $\triangle ACD \sim \triangle CBD$
- $\frac{AD}{CD} = \frac{CD}{DB}$, $\frac{AB}{AC} = \frac{AC}{AD}$, and $\frac{AB}{CB} = \frac{CB}{DB}$

Example

What is the value of x?

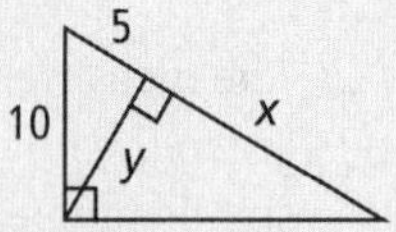

$\frac{5+x}{10} = \frac{10}{5}$	Write a proportion.
$5(5 + x) = 100$	Cross Products Property
$25 + 5x = 100$	Distributive Property
$5x = 75$	Subtract 25 from each side.
$x = 15$	Divide each side by 5.

Exercises

Find the geometric mean of each pair of numbers.

13. 9 and 16

14. 5 and 12

Algebra **Find the value of each variable. Write your answer in simplest radical form.**

15.

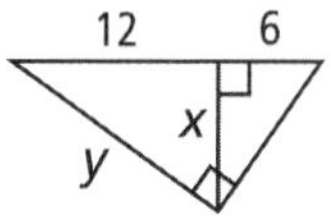

16.

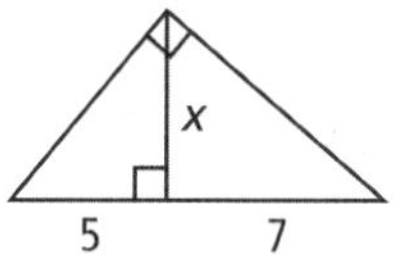

17.

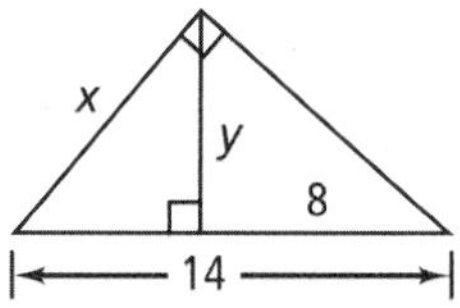

18.

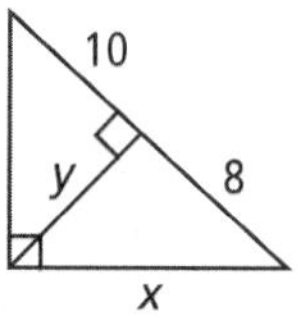

10-5 Proportions in Triangles

Quick Review

Side-Splitter Theorem and Corollary

If a line parallel to one side of a triangle intersects the other two sides, then it divides those sides proportionally. If three parallel lines intersect two transversals, then the segments intercepted on the transversals are proportional.

Triangle-Angle-Bisector Theorem

If a ray bisects an angle of a triangle, then it divides the opposite side into two segments that are proportional to the other two sides of the triangle.

Example

What is the value of x?

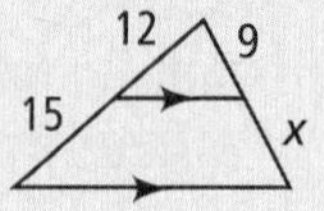

$\frac{12}{15} = \frac{9}{x}$	Write a proportion.
$12x = 135$	Cross Products Property
$x = 11.25$	Divide each side by 12.

Exercises

Algebra **Find the value of x.**

19.

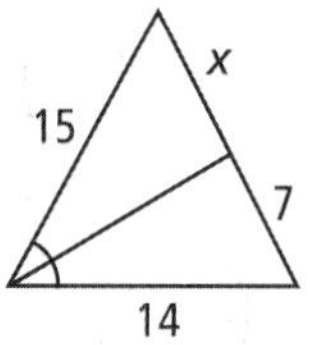

20.

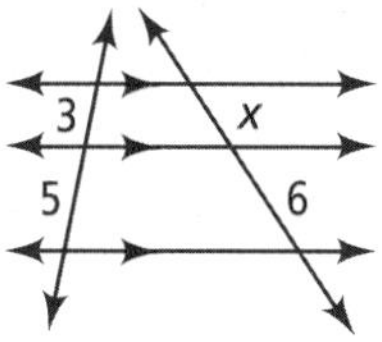

21.

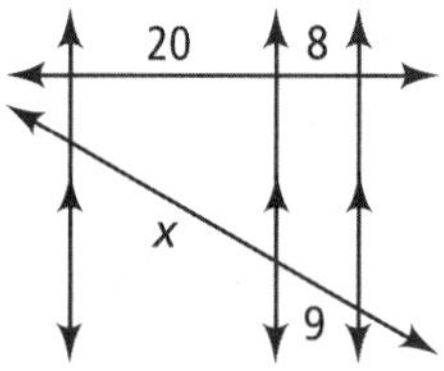

22.

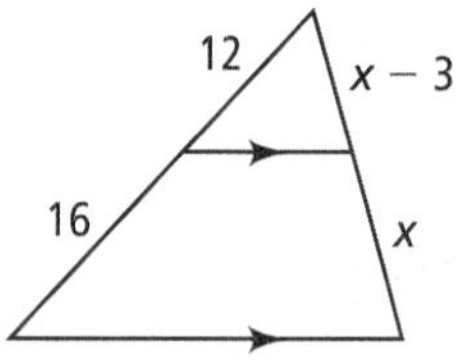

23.

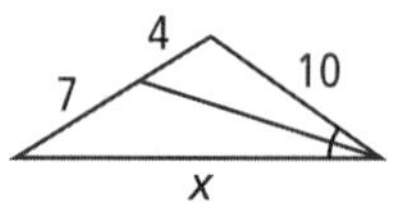

24.

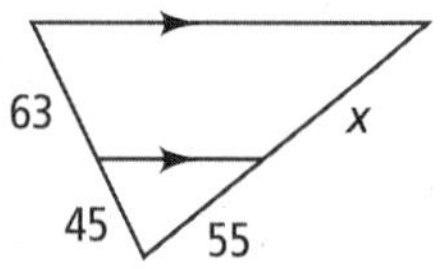

10-6 Dilations

Quick Review

The diagram shows a **dilation** with center *C* and scale factor *n*. The preimage and image are similar.

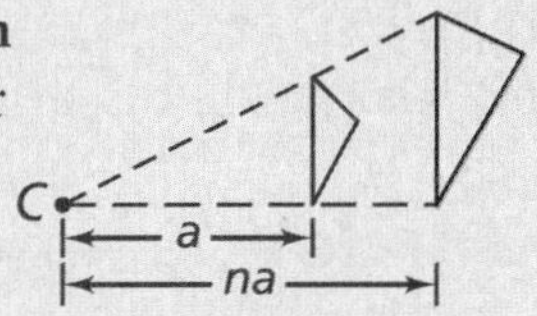

Example

The blue figure is a dilation image of the black figure. The center of dilation is *A*. Is the dilation an enlargement or a reduction? What is the scale factor?

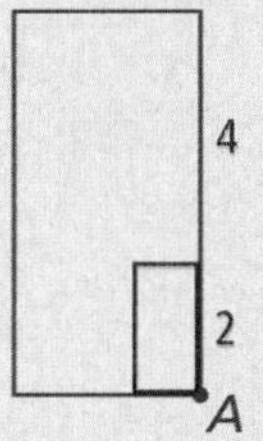

The image is smaller than the preimage, so the dilation is a reduction. The scale factor is $\frac{\text{image length}}{\text{original length}} = \frac{2}{2+4} = \frac{2}{6}$, or $\frac{1}{3}$.

Exercises

25. The red figure is a dilation image of the blue figure. The center of dilation is *O*. Tell whether the dilation is an enlargement or a reduction. Then find the scale factor.

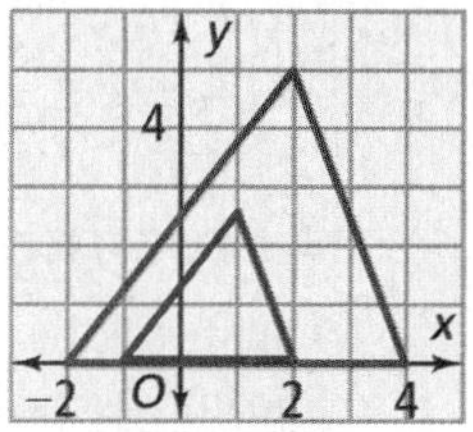

Graph the polygon with the given vertices. Then graph its image for a dilation with center (0, 0) and the given scale factor.

26. $M(-3, 4), A(-6, -1), T(0, 0), H(3, 2)$; scale factor 5

27. $F(-4, 0), U(5, 0), N(-2, -5)$; scale factor $\frac{1}{2}$

28. A dilation maps $\triangle LMN$ onto $\triangle L'M'N'$. $LM = 36$ ft, $LN = 26$ ft, $MN = 45$ ft, and $L'M' = 9$ ft. Find $L'N'$ and $M'N'$.

10-7 Similarity Transformations

Quick Review

Two figures are similar if and only if there is a similarity transformation that maps one figure onto the other.

When a figure is transformed by a composition of rigid motions and dilations, the corresponding angles of the image and preimage are congruent, and the ratios of corresponding sides are proportional.

Example

Is $\triangle JKL$ similar to $\triangle DCX$? If so, write a similarity transformation rule. If not, explain why not.

$\triangle JKL$ can be rotated and then translated so that *J* and *D* coincide and $\overline{JK}$ and $\overline{CD}$ are collinear. Then if $\triangle JKL$ is dilated by scale factor $\frac{4}{5}$, then $\triangle JKL$ will coincide with $\triangle DCX$. So $\triangle JKL$ is similar to $\triangle DCX$, and the similarity transformation is a rotation, followed by a translation, followed by a dilation of scale factor $\frac{4}{5}$.

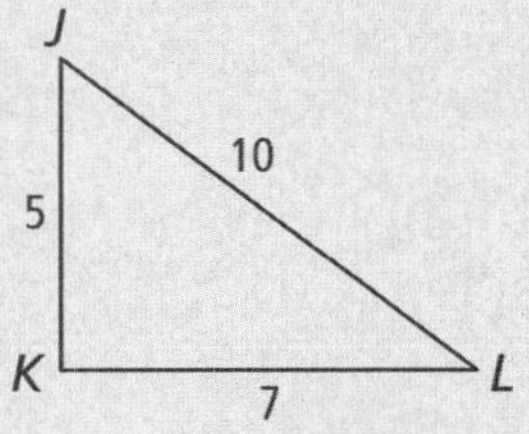

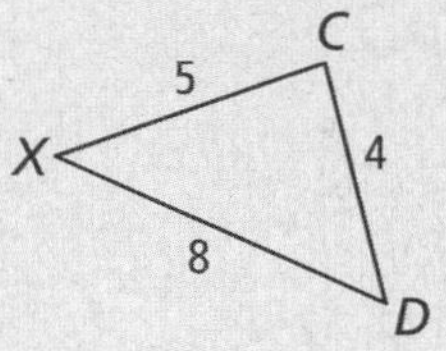

Exercises

29. ▱*GHJK* has vertices $G(-3, -1), H(-3, 2)$ $J(4, 2)$, and $K(4, -1)$. Draw ▱*GHJK* and its image when you apply the composition $D_2 \circ R_{x\text{-axis}}$.

30. Writing Suppose that you have an 8-in. by 12-in. photo of your friends and a 2-in. by 6-in. copy of the same picture. Are the two photos similar figures? How do you know?

31. Reasoning A model airplane has an overall length that is $\frac{1}{20}$ the actual plane's length, and an overall height that is $\frac{1}{18}$ the actual plane's height. Are the model airplane and the actual airplane similar figures? Explain.

32. Determine whether the figures at the right are similar. If so, write the similarity transformation rule. If not, explain.

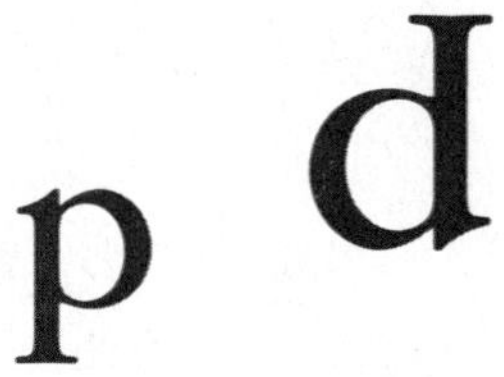

10 Pull It All Together

PERFORMANCE TASK

Adjusting a Graphing Calculator Window

ASSESSMENT

Lillian graphs the functions $y = 2x + 3$ and $y = -\frac{1}{2}x + 1$ on her graphing calculator. She knows the lines are perpendicular, but they do not appear to be on the screen.

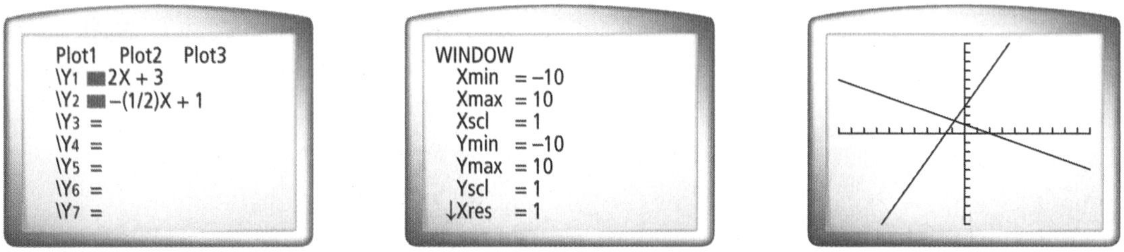

The screens above are the same shape as Lillian's graphing calculator screen. The **window** screen shows the interval of the x-axis (from **Xmin** to **Xmax**) and the y-axis (from **Ymin** to **Ymax**) for the viewing screen.

Lillian wants to adjust the values of **Xmin** and **Xmax** so that the graph of the lines is not skewed.

Task Description

Determine the values of Xmin and Xmax that Lillian should use for the viewing screen.

- What are the dimensions of the calculator screen in centimeters?
- How can similar figures help you solve the problem?

CHAPTER 11

Get Ready!

Solving Proportions

Algebra **Solve for x. If necessary, round answers to the nearest thousandth.**

1. $0.2734 = \frac{x}{17}$ **2.** $0.5858 = \frac{24}{x}$ **3.** $0.8572 = \frac{5271}{x}$ **4.** $0.5 = \frac{x}{3x + 5}$

Proving Triangles Similar

Name the postulate or theorem that proves each pair of triangles similar.

5. $\overline{CD} \parallel \overline{AB}$

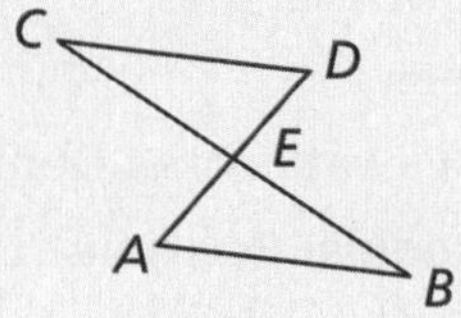

6.

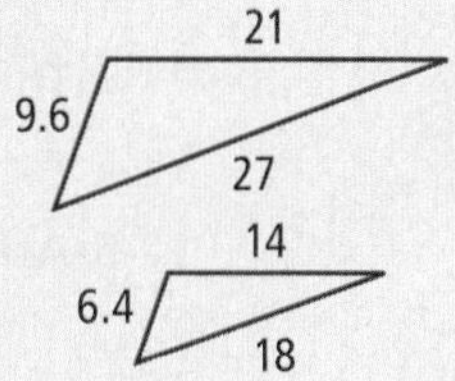

7. $\overline{JK} \perp \overline{ML}$

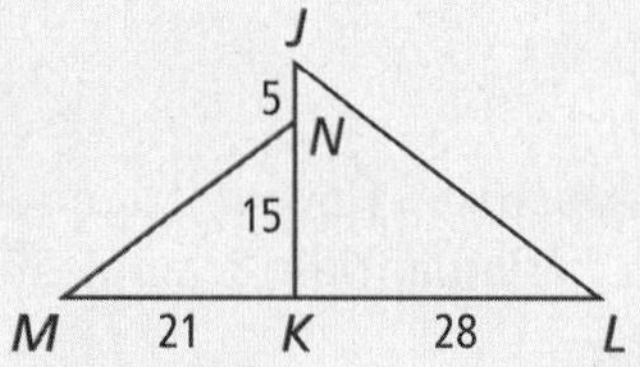

Similarity in Right Triangles

Algebra **Find the value of x in $\triangle ABC$ with right $\angle C$ and altitude $\overline{CD}$.**

8.

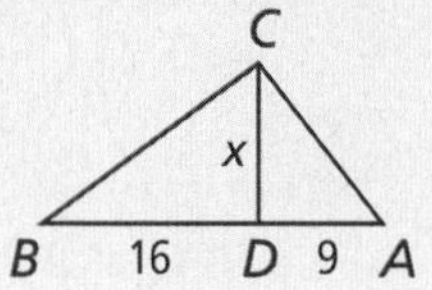

9.

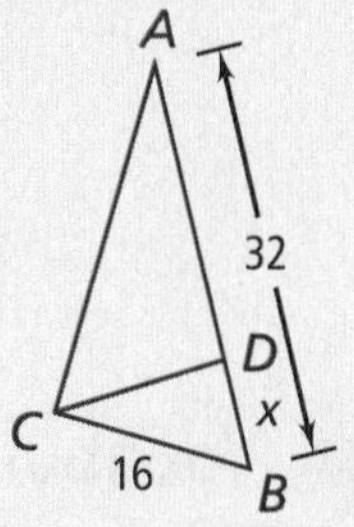

10.

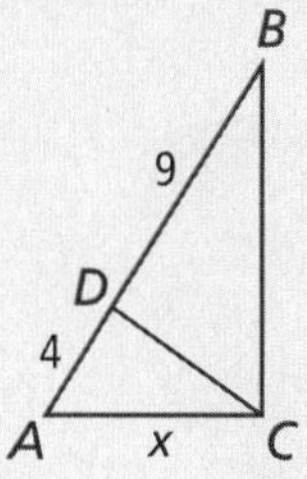

11.

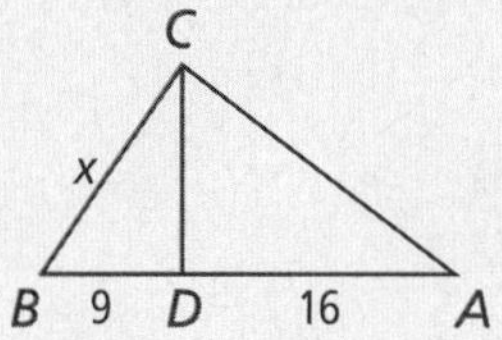

Looking Ahead Vocabulary

12. People often describe the height of a mountain as its *elevation*. How might you describe an *angle of elevation* in geometry?

13. You see the prefix *tri-* in many words, such as *triad, triathlon, trilogy*, and *trimester*. What does the prefix indicate in these words? What geometric figure do you think is associated with the phrase *trigonometric ratio*? Explain.

CHAPTER 11

Right Triangles and Trigonometry

Big Ideas

1 Measurement

Essential Question: How do you find a side length or angle measure in a right triangle?

2 Similarity

Essential Question: How do trigonometric ratios relate to similar right triangles?

Domains

- Similarity, Right Triangles, and Trigonometry
- Modeling with Geometry

Chapter Preview

Interactive Digital Path

Log in to **pearsonsuccessnet.com** and click on Interactive Digital Path to access the Solve Its and animated Problems.

Vocabulary

English/Spanish Vocabulary Audio Online:

English	Spanish
angle of depression, *p. 777*	ángulo de depresión
angle of elevation, *p. 777*	ángulo de elevación
apothem, *p. 784*	apotema
cosine, *p. 768*	coseno
Pythagorean triple, *p. 746*	tripleta de Pitágoras
radius of a regular polygon, *p. 784*	radio de un polígono regular
sine, *p. 768*	seno
tangent, *p. 768*	tangente

11-1 The Pythagorean Theorem and Its Converse

G.SRT.8 Use . . . the Pythagorean Theorem to solve right triangles in applied problems. Also **G.SRT.4**

Objective To use the Pythagorean Theorem and its converse

Solve It! Write your solution to the Solve It in the space below.

The equations in the Solve It demonstrate an important relationship in right triangles called the Pythagorean Theorem. This theorem is named for Pythagoras, a Greek mathematician who lived in the 500s B.C. We now know that the Babylonians, Egyptians, and Chinese were aware of this relationship before its discovery by Pythagoras. There are many proofs of the Pythagorean Theorem. You will see one proof in this lesson and others later in the book.

Essential Understanding If you know the lengths of any two sides of a right triangle, you can find the length of the third side by using the Pythagorean Theorem.

take note

Theorem 63 Pythagorean Theorem

Theorem	If . . .	Then . . .
If a triangle is a right triangle, then the sum of the squares of the lengths of the legs is equal to the square of the length of the hypotenuse.	$\triangle ABC$ is a right triangle 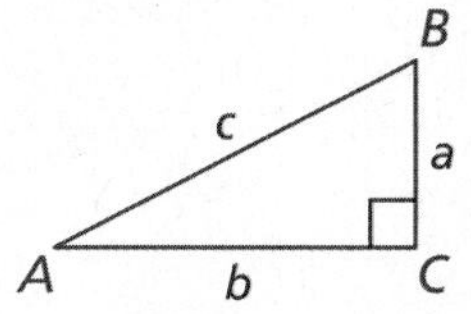	$(\text{leg}_1)^2 + (\text{leg}_2)^2 = (\text{hypotenuse})^2$ $a^2 + b^2 = c^2$

You will prove Theorem 63 in Exercise 33.

A **Pythagorean triple** is a set of nonzero whole numbers a, b, and c that satisfy the equation $a^2 + b^2 = c^2$. Below are some common Pythagorean triples.

3, 4, 5   5, 12, 13   8, 15, 17   7, 24, 25

If you multiply each number in a Pythagorean triple by the same whole number, the three numbers that result also form a Pythagorean triple. For example, the Pythagorean triples 6, 8, 10, and 9, 12, 15 each result from multiplying the numbers in the triple 3, 4, 5 by a whole number.

ONLINE PROBLEMS Problem 1 Finding the Length of the Hypotenuse

Got It? **a.** The legs of a right triangle have lengths 10 and 24. What is the length of the hypotenuse?

b. Do the side lengths in part (a) form a Pythagorean triple? Explain.

A Practice **1. Algebra** Find the value of x.

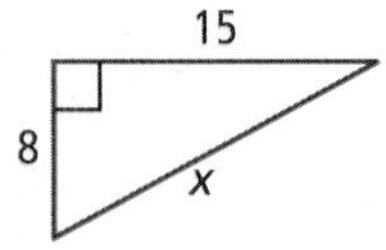

2. Do the numbers 4, 5, 6 form a Pythagorean triple? Explain.

Problem 2 Finding the Length of a Leg

Got It? The hypotenuse of a right triangle has length 12. One leg has length 6. What is the length of the other leg? Express your answer in simplest radical form.

Practice **Algebra** Find the value of x. Express your answer in simplest radical form.

3.

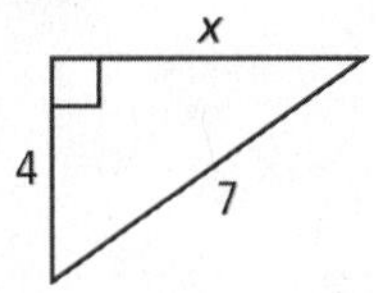

4.

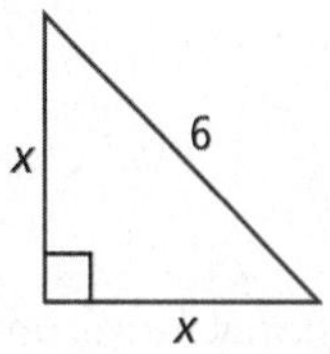

Problem 3 Finding Distance

Got It? The size of a computer monitor is the length of its diagonal. You want to buy a 19-in. monitor that has a height of 11 in. What is the width of the monitor? Round to the nearest tenth of an inch.

Think
How do you know when to use a calculator?

A Practice

5. Home Maintenance A painter leans a 15-ft ladder against a house. The base of the ladder is 5 ft from the house. To the nearest tenth of a foot, how high on the house does the ladder reach?

6. A walkway forms one diagonal of a square playground. The walkway is 24 m long. To the nearest meter, how long is a side of the playground?

You can use the Converse of the Pythagorean Theorem to determine whether a triangle is a right triangle.

take note

Theorem 64 Converse of the Pythagorean Theorem

Theorem	If . . .	Then . . .
If the sum of the squares of the lengths of two sides of a triangle is equal to the square of the length of the third side, then the triangle is a right triangle.	$a^2 + b^2 = c^2$ 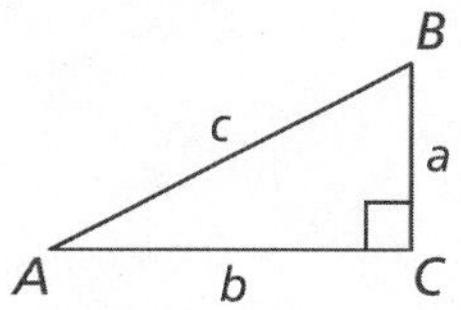	$\triangle ABC$ is a right triangle

You will prove Theorem 64 in Exercise 36.

ONLINE PROBLEMS

Problem 4 Identifying a Right Triangle

Got It? **a.** A triangle has side lengths 16, 48, and 50. Is the triangle a right triangle? Explain.

Plan
How do you know where each of the side lengths goes in the equation?

b. Reasoning Once you know which length represents the hypotenuse, does it matter which length you substitute for a and which length you substitute for b? Explain.

Practice **Is the triangle a right triangle? Explain.**

7. 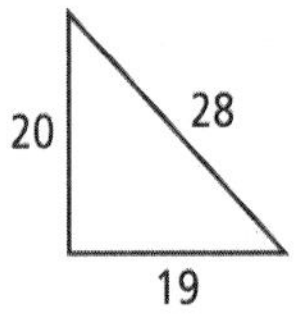

8. 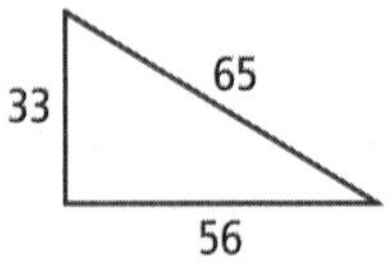

The theorems below allow you to determine whether a triangle is acute or obtuse. These theorems relate to the Hinge Theorem, which states that the longer side is opposite the larger angle and the shorter side is opposite the smaller angle.

take note

Theorem 65

Theorem	If . . .	Then . . .
If the square of the length of the longest side of a triangle is greater than the sum of the squares of the lengths of the other two sides, then the triangle is obtuse.	$c^2 > a^2 + b^2$ 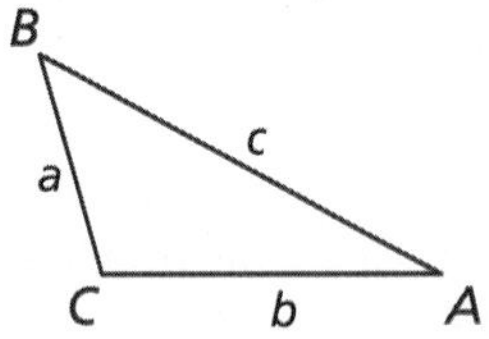	$\triangle ABC$ is obtuse

You will prove Theorem 65 in Exercise 37.

take note

Theorem 66

Theorem	If . . .	Then . . .
If the square of the length of the longest side of a triangle is less than the sum of the squares of the lengths of the other two sides, then the triangle is acute.	$c^2 < a^2 + b^2$ 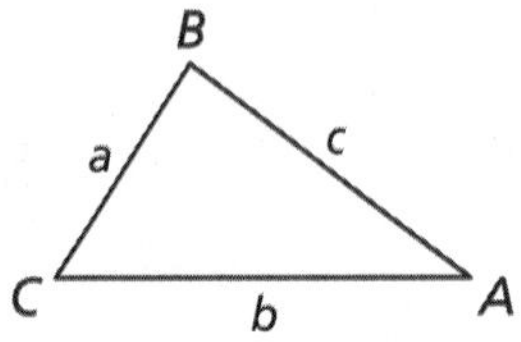	$\triangle ABC$ is acute

You will prove Theorem 66 in Exercise 38.

Problem 5 Classifying a Triangle

Got It? Is a triangle with side lengths 7, 8, and 9 *acute, obtuse,* or *right*?

Plan

What information do you need?

A Practice **The lengths of the sides of a triangle are given. Classify each triangle as *acute, obtuse,* or *right.***

9. 0.3, 0.4, 0.6

10. $\sqrt{11}$, $\sqrt{7}$, 4

Lesson Check

Do you know HOW?

What is the value of x in simplest radical form?

11.

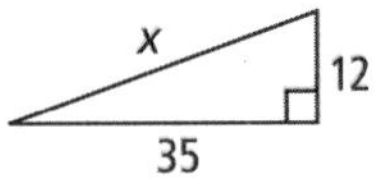

12.

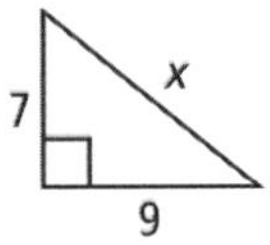

13.

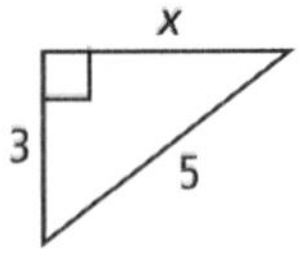

14.

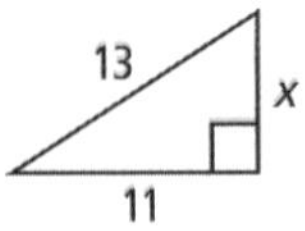

Do you UNDERSTAND?

MATHEMATICAL PRACTICES

15. Vocabulary Describe the conditions that a set of three numbers must meet in order to form a Pythagorean triple.

16. Error Analysis A triangle has side lengths 16, 34, and 30. Your friend says it is not a right triangle. Look at your friend's work and describe the error.

$$16^2 + 34^2 \stackrel{?}{=} 30^2$$
$$256 + 1156 \stackrel{?}{=} 900$$
$$1412 \neq 900$$

More Practice and Problem-Solving Exercises

MATHEMATICAL PRACTICES

B Apply

17. Think About a Plan You want to embroider a square design. You have an embroidery hoop with a 6 in. diameter. Find the largest value of x so that the entire square will fit in the hoop. Round to the nearest tenth.

- What does the diameter of the circle represent in the square?
- What do you know about the sides of a square?
- How do the side lengths of the square relate to the length of the diameter?

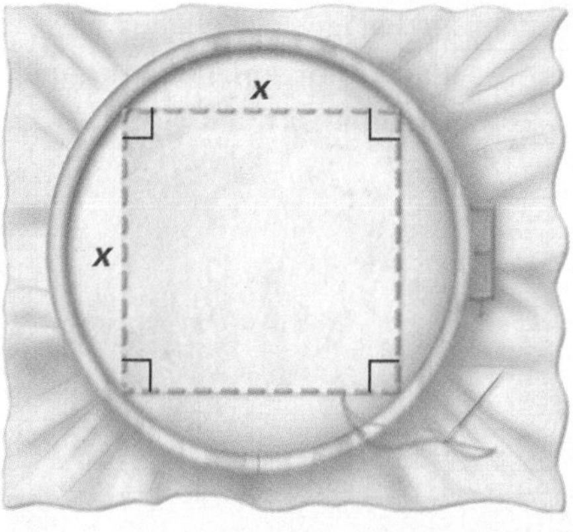

18. In parallelogram $RSTW$, $RS = 7$, $ST = 24$, and $RT = 25$. Is $RSTW$ a rectangle? Explain.

Proof 19. Coordinate Geometry You can use the Pythagorean Theorem to prove the Distance Formula. Let points $P(x_1, y_1)$ and $Q(x_2, y_2)$ be the endpoints of the hypotenuse of a right triangle.

a. Write an algebraic expression to complete each of the following: $PR = \underline{?}$ and $QR = \underline{?}$.

b. By the Pythagorean Theorem, $PQ^2 = PR^2 + QR^2$. Rewrite this statement by substituting the algebraic expressions you found for PR and QR in part (a).

c. Complete the proof by taking the square root of each side of the equation that you wrote in part (b).

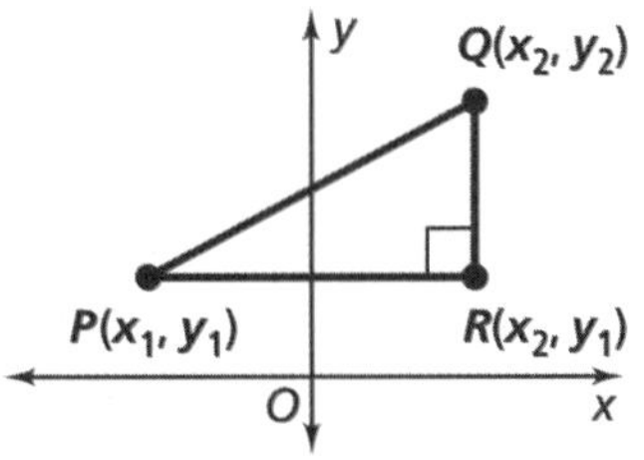

Algebra **Find the value of x. If your answer is not an integer, express it in simplest radical form.**

20. 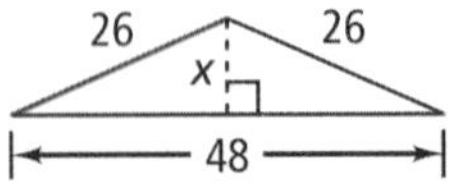

21. 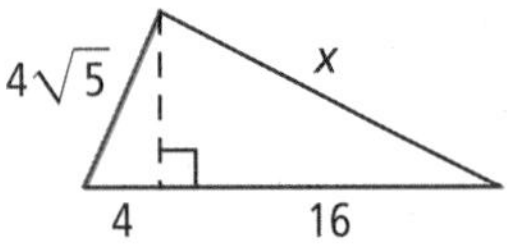

22. 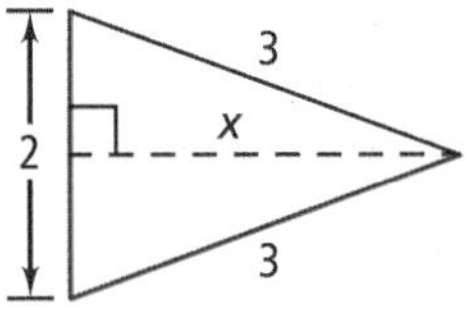

For each pair of numbers, find a third whole number such that the three numbers form a Pythagorean triple.

23. 20, 21 **24.** 14, 48 **25.** 13, 85 **26.** 12, 37

Open-Ended **Find integers j and k such that (a) the two given integers and j represent the side lengths of an acute triangle and (b) the two given integers and k represent the side lengths of an obtuse triangle.**

27. 4, 5 **28.** 2, 4 **29.** 6, 9

30. 5, 10 **31.** 6, 7 **32.** 9, 12

Proof 33. Prove the Pythagorean Theorem.

Given: $\triangle ABC$ is a right triangle.
Prove: $a^2 + b^2 = c^2$
(*Hint:* Begin with proportions suggested by Theorem 60 or its corollaries.)

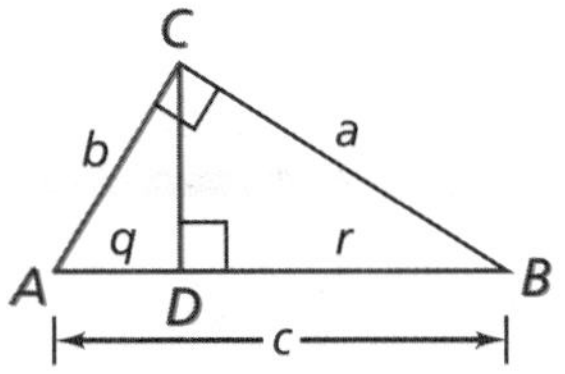

STEM 34. Astronomy The Hubble Space Telescope orbits 600 km above Earth's surface. Earth's radius is about 6370 km. Use the Pythagorean Theorem to find the distance x from the telescope to Earth's horizon. Round your answer to the nearest ten kilometers. (Diagram is not to scale.)

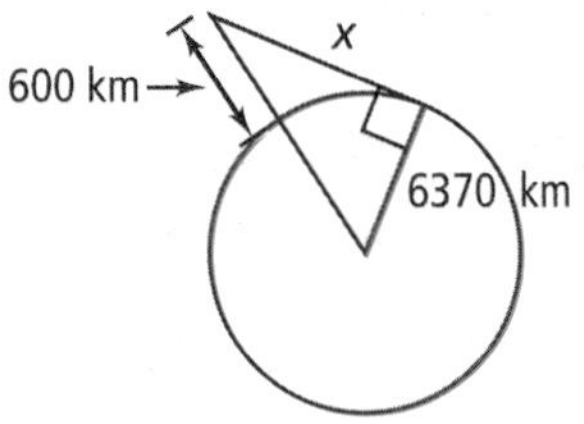

35. Prove that if the slopes of two lines ℓ_1 and ℓ_2 have product -1, then the lines are perpendicular. Use parts (a)-(c) to write a coordinate proof.

a. First, argue that neither line can be horizontal nor vertical.

b. Then, tell why the lines must intersect. (*Hint:* Use indirect reasoning.)

c. Place the lines in the coordinate plane. Choose a point on ℓ_1 and find a related point on ℓ_2. Complete the proof.

Challenge

Proof 36. Use the plan and write a proof of Theorem 64 (Converse of the Pythagorean Theorem).

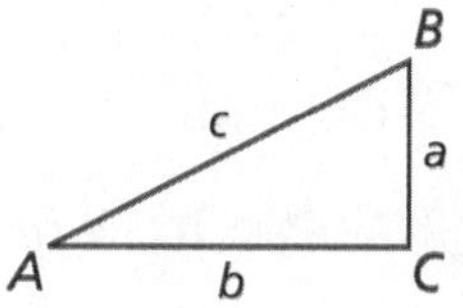

Given: $\triangle ABC$ with sides of length a, b, and c, where $a^2 + b^2 = c^2$

Prove: $\triangle ABC$ is a right triangle.

Plan: Draw a right triangle (not $\triangle ABC$) with legs of lengths a and b. Label the hypotenuse x. By the Pythagorean Theorem, $a^2 + b^2 = x^2$. Use substitution to compare the lengths of the sides of your triangle and $\triangle ABC$. Then prove the triangles congruent.

Proof 37. Use the plan and write a proof of Theorem 65.

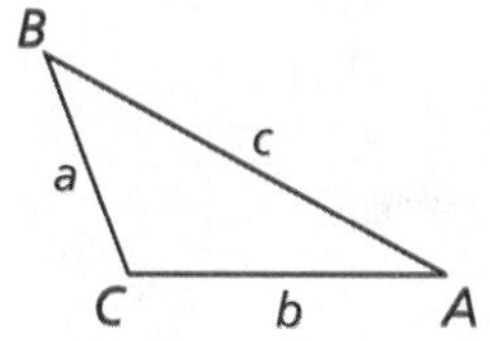

Given: $\triangle ABC$ with sides of length a, b, and c, where $c^2 > a^2 + b^2$

Prove: $\triangle ABC$ is an obtuse triangle.

Plan: Draw a right triangle (not $\triangle ABC$) with legs of lengths a and b. Label the hypotenuse x. By the Pythagorean Theorem, $a^2 + b^2 = x^2$. Use substitution to compare lengths c and x. Then use the Converse of the Hinge Theorem to compare $\angle C$ to the right angle.

Proof 38. Prove Theorem 66.

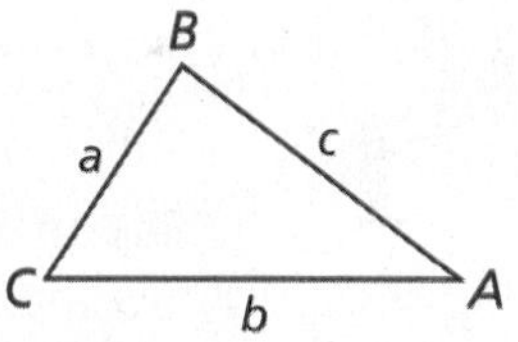

Given: $\triangle ABC$ with sides of length a, b, and c, where $c^2 < a^2 + b^2$

Prove: $\triangle ABC$ is an acute triangle.

11-2 Special Right Triangles

G.SRT.8 Use . . . the Pythagorean Theorem to solve right triangles in applied problems.

Objective To use the properties of 45°-45°-90° and 30°-60°-90° triangles

Solve It! Write your solution to the Solve It in the space below.

The Solve It involves triangles with angles 45°, 45°, and 90°.

Essential Understanding Certain right triangles have properties that allow you to use shortcuts to determine side lengths without using the Pythagorean Theorem.

The acute angles of a right isosceles triangle are both 45° angles. Another name for an isosceles right triangle is a 45°-45°-90° triangle. If each leg has length x and the hypotenuse has length y, you can solve for y in terms of x.

$x^2 + x^2 = y^2$ Use the Pythagorean Theorem.

$2x^2 = y^2$ Simplify.

$x\sqrt{2} = y$ Take the positive square root of each side.

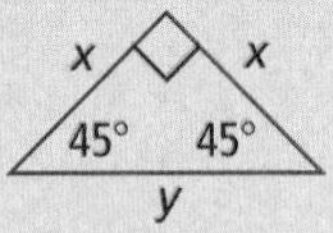

You have just proved the following theorem.

take note

Theorem 67 45°-45°-90° Triangle Theorem

In a 45°-45°-90° triangle, both legs are congruent and the length of the hypotenuse is $\sqrt{2}$ times the length of a leg.

hypotenuse $= \sqrt{2} \cdot$ leg

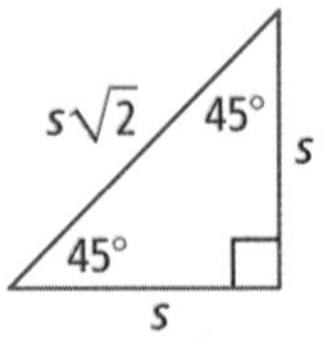

Problem 1 Finding the Length of the Hypotenuse

Got It? What is the length of the hypotenuse of a 45°-45°-90° triangle with leg length $5\sqrt{3}$?

Practice **Find the value of each variable. If your answer is not an integer, express it in simplest radical form.**

1.

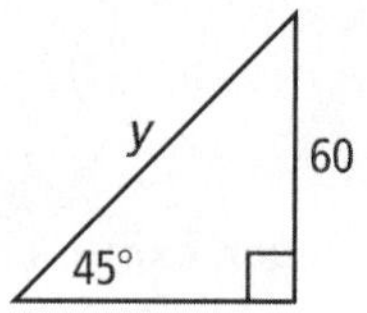

2.

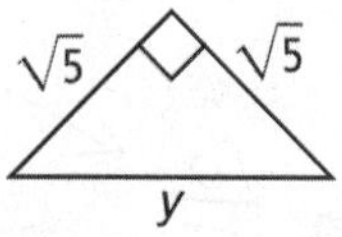

Problem 2 Finding the Length of a Leg

Got It? **a.** The length of the hypotenuse of a 45°-45°-90° triangle is 16. What is the length of one leg?

(handwritten: "it is meant just x")

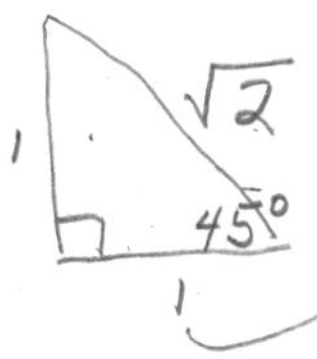

$\frac{x}{1} = \frac{16}{\sqrt{2}} = \frac{16\sqrt{2}}{2} = \boxed{8\sqrt{2}}$

b. Reasoning In Problem 2, why can you multiply $\frac{6}{\sqrt{2}}$ by $\frac{\sqrt{2}}{\sqrt{2}}$?

Practice **Find the value of each variable. If your answer is not an integer, express it in simplest radical form.**

3.

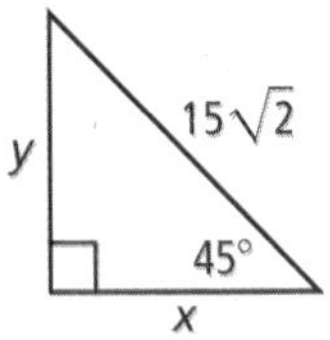

$\frac{x}{x} = \frac{15\sqrt{2}}{\sqrt{2}}$ $15 =$

4.

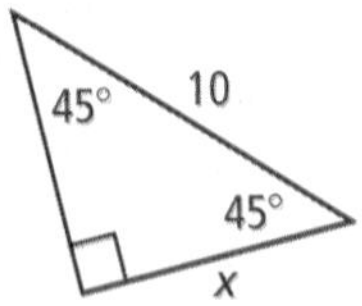

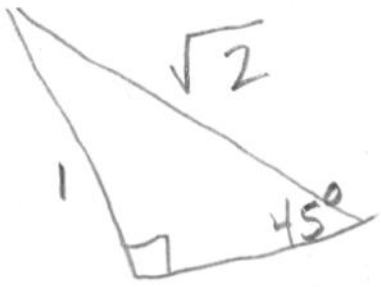

$\frac{x}{1} = \frac{10}{\sqrt{2}}$ $\boxed{x = 5\sqrt{2}}$ ← Rationalize the denominator

Conjugate (fancy word for 1)

$\frac{10}{\sqrt{2}} = \frac{10}{\sqrt{2}} \cdot \frac{\sqrt{2}}{\sqrt{2}} = \frac{10\sqrt{2}}{\sqrt{4}} = \frac{10\sqrt{2}}{2}$ (technically 1) → $\boxed{5\sqrt{2}}$

Copy Paste Delete

$\frac{10}{\sqrt{2}} = \frac{10\sqrt{2}}{2} = \boxed{5\sqrt{2}}$

Copy radical
paste to top
Delete radical sign

When you apply the 45°-45°-90° Triangle Theorem to a real-life example, you can use a calculator to evaluate square roots.

Problem 3 Finding Distance

Got It? You plan to build a path along one diagonal of a 100 ft-by-100 ft square garden. To the nearest foot, how long will the path be?

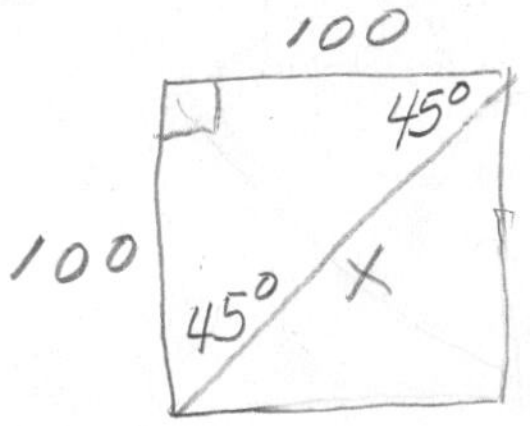

It is an isosoles

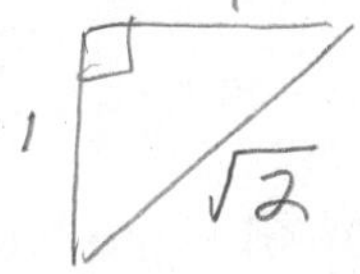

$\frac{x}{\sqrt{2}} = \frac{100}{1} = 100\sqrt{2} = x$

Practice 5. **Dinnerware Design** What is the side length of the smallest square plate on which a 20-cm chopstick can fit along a diagonal without any overhang? Round your answer to the nearest tenth of a centimeter.

6. **Aviation** The four blades of a helicopter meet at right angles and are all the same length. The distance between the tips of two adjacent blades is 36 ft. How long is each blade? Round your answer to the nearest tenth of a foot.

Another type of special right triangle is a 30°-60°-90° triangle.

take note

Theorem 68 30°-60°-90° Triangle Theorem

In a 30°-60°-90° triangle, the length of the hypotenuse is twice the length of the shorter leg. The length of the longer leg is $\sqrt{3}$ times the length of the shorter leg.

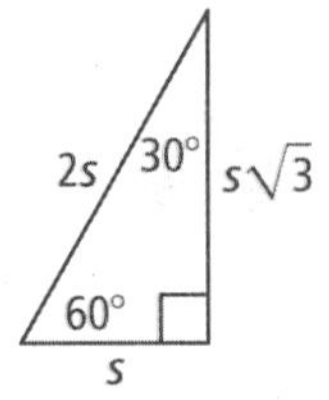

hypotenuse = 2 • shorter leg

longer leg = $\sqrt{3}$ • shorter leg

Proof Proof of Theorem 68: 30°-60°-90° Triangle Theorem

For equilateral $\triangle WXZ$, altitude $\overline{WY}$ bisects $\angle W$ and is the perpendicular bisector of $\overline{XZ}$. So, $\overline{WY}$ divides $\triangle WXZ$ into two congruent 30°-60°-90° triangles.

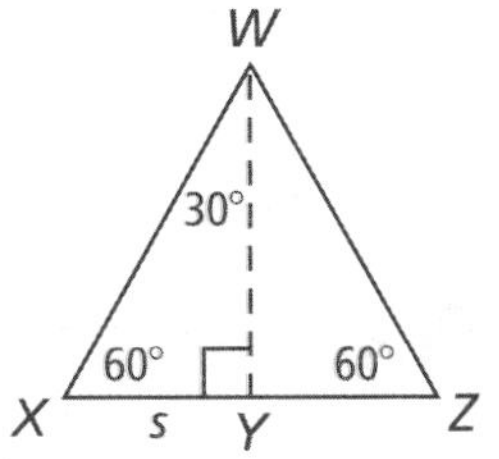

Thus, $XY = \frac{1}{2}XZ = \frac{1}{2}XW$, or $XW = 2XY = 2s$.

$XY^2 + YW^2 = XW^2$	Use the Pythagorean Theorem.
$s^2 + YW^2 = (2s)^2$	Substitute *s* for *XY* and 2*s* for *XW*.
$YW^2 = 4s^2 - s^2$	Subtract s^2 from each side.
$YW^2 = 3s^2$	Simplify.
$YW = s\sqrt{3}$	Take the positive square root of each side.

You can also use the 30°-60°-90° Triangle Theorem to find side lengths.

Problem 4 Using the Length of One Side

Got It? What is the value of *f* in simplest radical form?

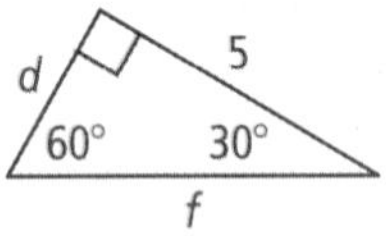

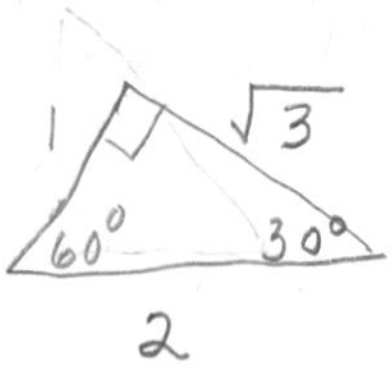

Think How can you write an equation that relates the longer leg to the hypotenuse?

$\frac{f}{2} = \frac{5}{\sqrt{3}}$ $\quad \frac{10}{\sqrt{3}} = \frac{f\sqrt{3}}{\sqrt{3}}$ $\quad = \frac{10\sqrt{3}}{3} = f$

$\frac{d}{1} = \frac{5}{\sqrt{3}}$

$d = \frac{5\sqrt{3}}{3}$

Practice **Algebra** In Exercises 7–8, find the value of each variable. If your answer is not an integer, express it in simplest radical form.

7.

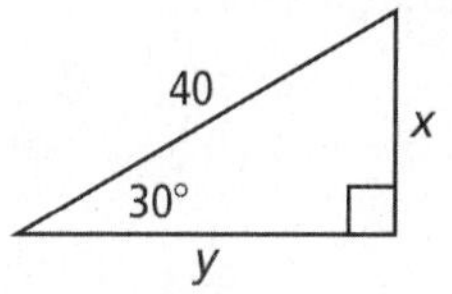

8.

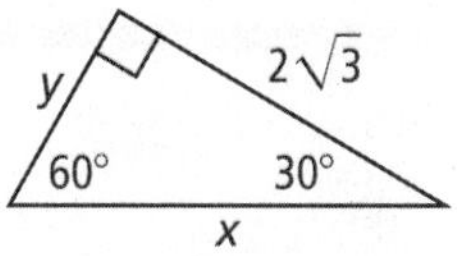

Problem 5 Applying the 30°-60°-90° Triangle Theorem

Got It? Suppose the sides of the pendant, from Problem 5, are 18 mm long. What is the height of the pendant to the nearest tenth of a millimeter?

Plan
How does knowing the shape of the pendant help?

Practice STEM

9. Architecture An escalator lifts people to the second floor of a building, 25 ft above the first floor. The escalator rises at a 30° angle. To the nearest foot, how far does a person travel from the bottom to the top of the escalator?

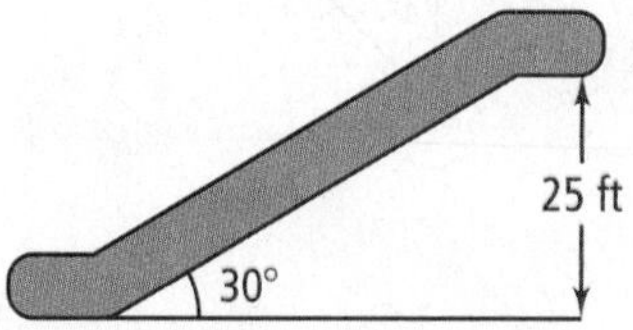

STEM **10. City Planning** A rectangular park has a walkway that joins opposite corners. A triangle formed from two sides of the park and the walkway is a 30°-60°-90° triangle. If the shorter side of the park measures 150 feet, what is the length of the walkway?

Lesson Check

Do you know HOW?

What is the value of x? If your answer is not an integer, express it in simplest radical form.

11.

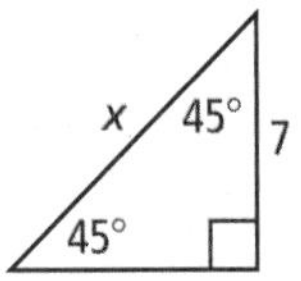

12.

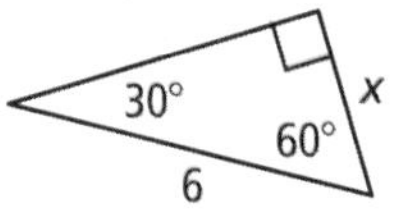

13.

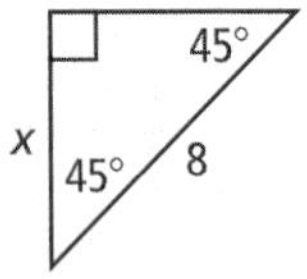

14.

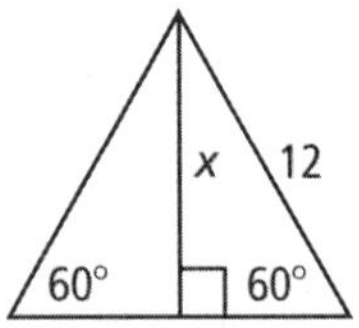

Do you UNDERSTAND?

MATHEMATICAL PRACTICES

15. **Error Analysis** Sandra drew the triangle at the right. Rika said that the labeled lengths are not possible. With which student do you agree? Explain.

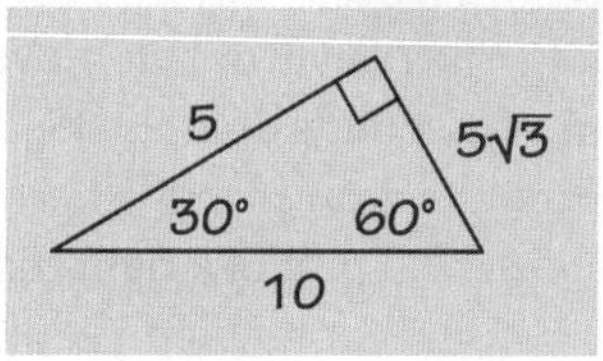

16. **Reasoning** A test question asks you to find two side lengths of a 45°-45°-90° triangle. You know that the length of one leg is 6, but you forgot the special formula for 45°-45°-90° triangles. Explain how you can still determine the other side lengths. What are they?

More Practice and Problem-Solving Exercises

MATHEMATICAL PRACTICES

B Apply

Algebra Find the value of each variable. If your answer is not an integer, express it in simplest radical form.

17.

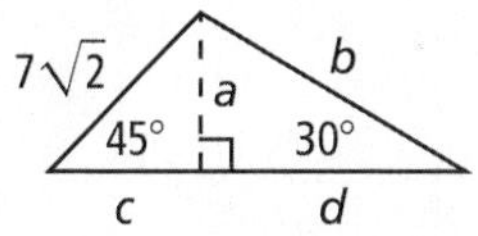

18.

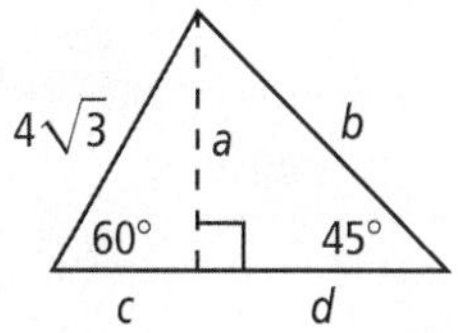

19.

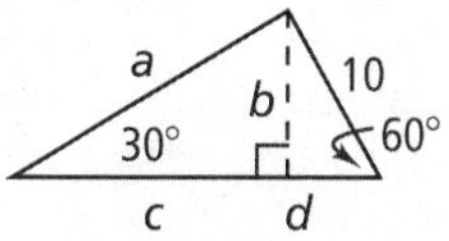

20.

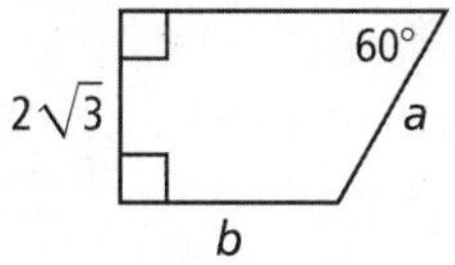

21.

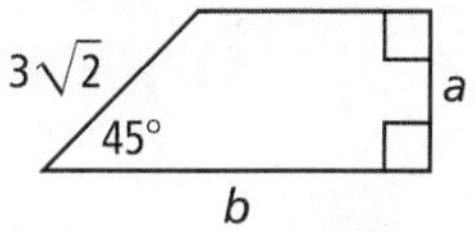

22.

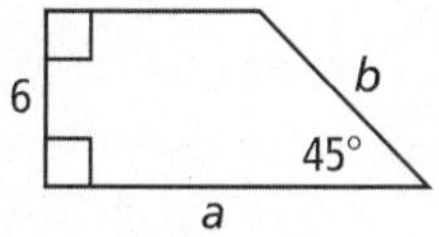

23. **Think About a Plan** A farmer's conveyor belt carries bales of hay from the ground to the barn loft. The conveyor belt moves at 100 ft/min. How many seconds does it take for a bale of hay to go from the ground to the barn loft?
- Which part of a right triangle does the conveyor belt represent?
- You know the speed. What other information do you need to find time?
- How are minutes and seconds related?

24. **House Repair** After heavy winds damaged a house, workers placed a 6-m brace against its side at a 45° angle. Then, at the same spot on the ground, they placed a second, longer brace to make a 30° angle with the side of the house.
   a. How long is the longer brace? Round to the nearest tenth of a meter.
   b. About how much higher does the longer brace reach than the shorter brace?

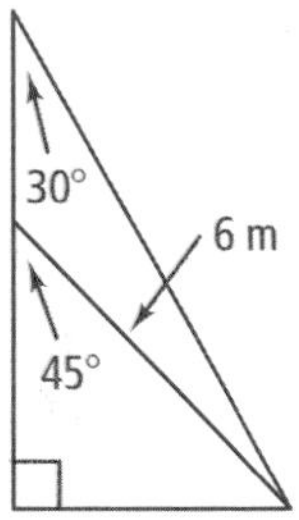

25. **Open-Ended** Write a real-life problem that you can solve using a 30°-60°-90° triangle with a 12-ft hypotenuse. Show your solution.

26. **Constructions** Construct a 30°-60°-90° triangle using a segment that is the given side.
   a. the shorter leg b. the hypotenuse c. the longer leg

Challenge

27. **Geometry in 3 Dimensions** Find the length d, in simplest radical form, of the diagonal of a cube with edges of the given length.
   a. 1 unit b. 2 units c. s units

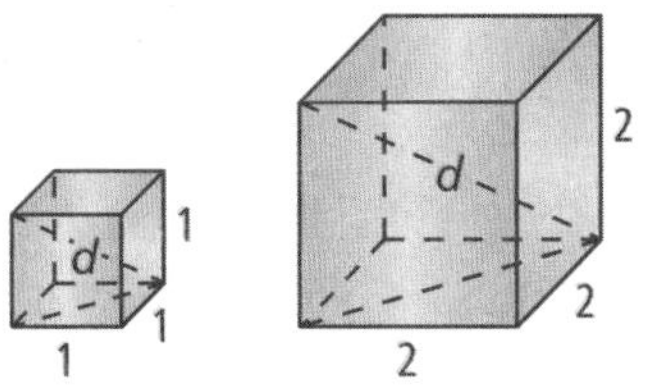

TECHNOLOGY LAB

Use With Lesson 11-3

Exploring Trigonometric Ratios

G.SRT.6 Understand that by similarity, side ratios in right triangles are properties of the angles in the triangle, . . .

Construct

Use geometry software to construct $\overrightarrow{AB}$ and $\overrightarrow{AC}$ so that $\angle A$ is acute. Through a point D on $\overrightarrow{AB}$, construct a line perpendicular to $\overrightarrow{AB}$ that intersects $\overrightarrow{AC}$ in point E.

Moving point D changes the size of $\triangle ADE$. Moving point C changes the size of $\angle A$.

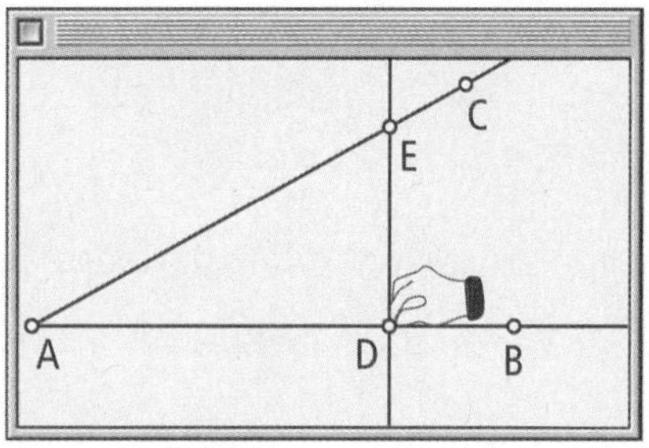

Exercises

1. • Measure $\angle A$ and find the lengths of the sides of $\triangle ADE$.

• Calculate the ratio $\frac{\text{leg opposite } \angle A}{\text{hypotenuse}}$, which is $\frac{ED}{AE}$.

• Move point D to change the size of $\triangle ADE$ without changing $m\angle A$.

What do you observe about the ratio as the size of $\triangle ADE$ changes?

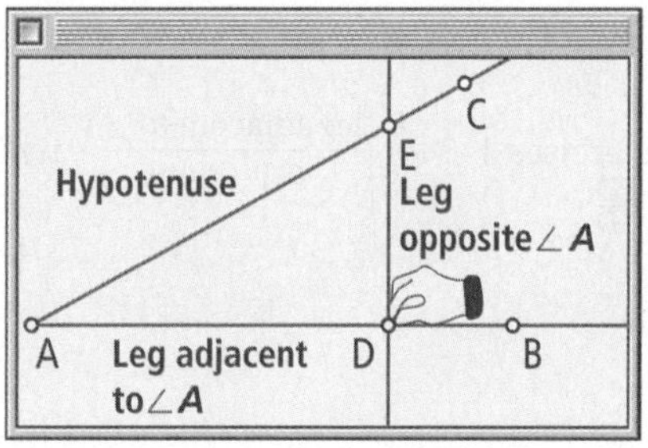

2. • Move point C to change $m\angle A$.

a. What do you observe about the ratio as $m\angle A$ changes?

b. What value does the ratio approach as $m\angle A$ approaches 0? As $m\angle A$ approaches 90?

3. • Make a table that shows values for $m\angle A$ and the ratio $\frac{\text{leg opposite } \angle A}{\text{hypotenuse}}$. In your table, include 10, 20, 30, . . ., 80 for $m\angle A$.

• Compare your table with a table of trigonometric ratios.

Do your values for $\frac{\text{leg opposite } \angle A}{\text{hypotenuse}}$ match the values in one of the columns of the table? What is the name of this ratio in the table?

Extend

4. Repeat Exercises 1–3 for $\frac{\text{leg adjacent to } \angle A}{\text{hypotenuse}}$, which is $\frac{AD}{AE}$, and $\frac{\text{leg opposite } \angle A}{\text{leg adjacent to } \angle A}$, which is $\frac{ED}{AD}$.

5. • Choose a measure for $\angle A$ and determine the ratio $r = \frac{\text{leg opposite } \angle A}{\text{hypotenuse}}$. Record $m\angle A$ and this ratio.

• Manipulate the triangle so that $\frac{\text{leg adjacent to } \angle A}{\text{hypotenuse}}$ has the same value r. Record this $m\angle A$ and compare it with your first value of $m\angle A$.

• Repeat this procedure several times. Look for a pattern in the two measures of $\angle A$ that you found for different values of r.

Make a conjecture.

11-3 Trigonometry

G.SRT.8 Use trigonometric ratios . . . to solve right triangles in applied problems. Also **G.SRT.7, F.TF.8**

Objective To use the sine, cosine, and tangent ratios to determine side lengths and angle measures in right triangles

Solve It! Write your solution to the Solve It in the space below.

Essential Understanding If you know certain combinations of side lengths and angle measures of a right triangle, you can use ratios to find other side lengths and angle measures.

Any two right triangles that have a pair of congruent acute angles are similar by the AA Similarity Postulate. Similar right triangles have equivalent ratios for their corresponding sides called **trigonometric ratios**.

take note

Key Concept Trigonometric Ratios

sine of $\angle A = \dfrac{\text{length of leg opposite } \angle A}{\text{length of hypotenuse}} = \dfrac{a}{c}$

cosine of $\angle A = \dfrac{\text{length of leg adjacent to } \angle A}{\text{length of hypotenuse}} = \dfrac{b}{c}$

tangent of $\angle A = \dfrac{\text{length of leg opposite } \angle A}{\text{length of leg adjacent to } \angle A} = \dfrac{a}{b}$

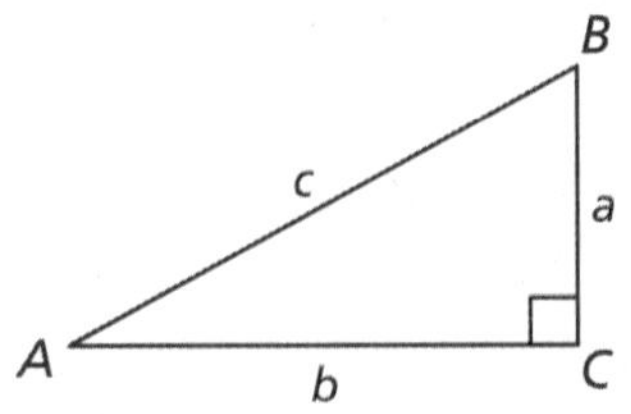

You can abbreviate the ratios as

$\sin A = \dfrac{\text{opposite}}{\text{hypotenuse}}$, $\cos A = \dfrac{\text{adjacent}}{\text{hypotenuse}}$, and $\tan A = \dfrac{\text{opposite}}{\text{adjacent}}$.

Problem 1 Writing Trigonometric Ratios

Think
How do the sides relate to $\angle G$?

Got It? What are the sine, cosine, and tangent ratios for $\angle G$?

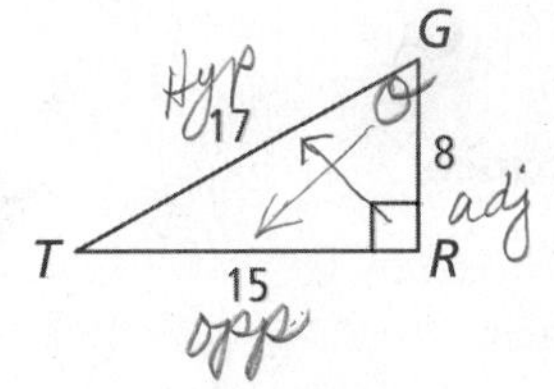

Soh Cah Toa

$\sin G = \frac{15}{17}$

$\frac{O}{H} = \frac{15}{17}$

$\cos G = \frac{8}{17}$

$\frac{A}{H} = \frac{8}{17}$

$\tan G = \frac{15}{8}$

$\frac{O}{a} = \frac{15}{8}$

Practice Write the ratios for sin *M*, cos *M*, and tan *M*.

1.

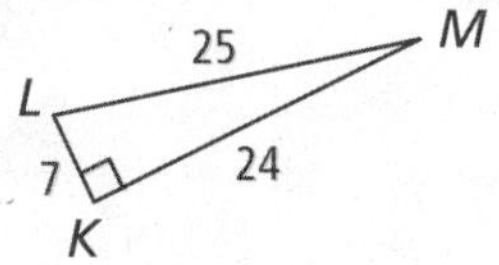

2.

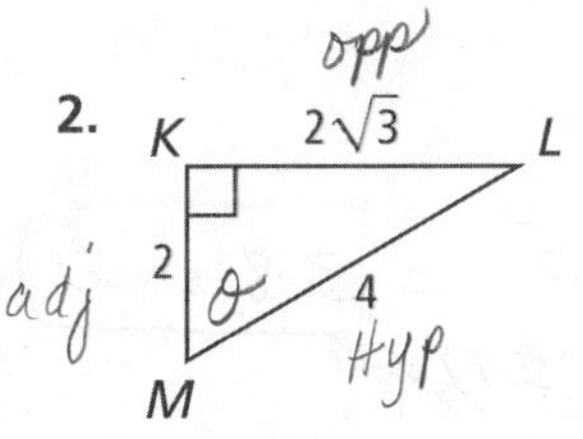

$\sin M = \frac{2\sqrt{3}}{4} = \frac{1\sqrt{3}}{2}$

$\frac{O}{H}$

Can't change inside the radical but outside #'s can change

$\cos M = \frac{2}{4} = \frac{1}{2}$

$\frac{A}{H}$

Toa

$\frac{O}{a} = \frac{2\sqrt{3}}{2} = \sqrt{3}$

In Chapter 10, you used similar triangles to measure distances indirectly. You can also use trigonometry for indirect measurement.

Problem 2 Using a Trigonometric Ratio to Find Distance

Got It? For parts (a)–(c), find the value of w to the nearest tenth.

a.

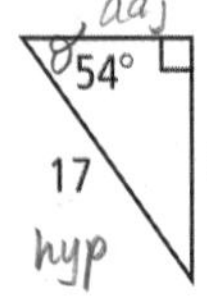

when you only know 1 side you need to use Trig.

Soh Cah Toa

$\sin\theta = \frac{opp}{Hyp}$

$\sin(54) = \frac{w}{17}$

$17 \cdot \sin(54) = W$

$13.8 = w$

variable on top... multiply denom. to other side

b.

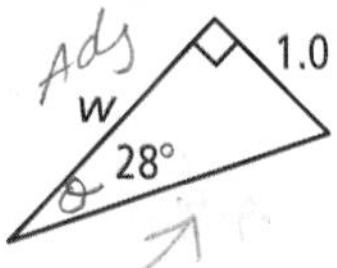

hyp is not given

Soh Cah Toa

$\tan\theta = \frac{opp}{adj}$

$\tan(28°) = \frac{1}{W}$ → variable on bottom, switch places w/ Trig function

$W = \frac{1}{\tan(28)}$ put in calculator

$W = 1.9$

c.

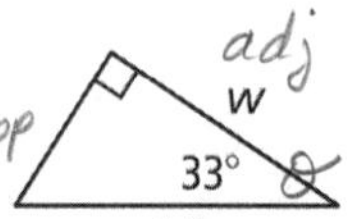

Soh Cah Toa

$\cos\theta = \frac{Adj}{Hyp}$

$4.5 \cdot \cos(33) = \frac{w}{4.5} \cdot 4.5$

$= 3.8 = w$ (3.77)

d. A section of Filbert Street in San Francisco rises at an angle of about 17°. If you walk 150 ft up this section, what is your vertical rise? Round to the nearest foot.

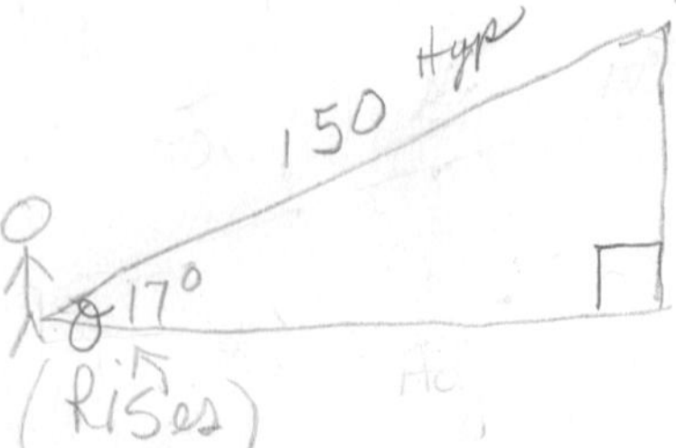

This angle doesn't rise it goes down

Soh Cah Toa

$\sin\theta = \frac{o}{h}$

$150 \cdot \sin(17°) = \frac{m}{150} \cdot 150$

$43.85 \approx 44 \text{ ft} = M$

A Practice 3. **Find the value of x. Round to the nearest tenth.**

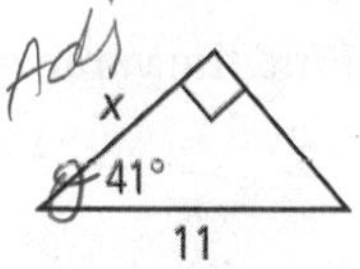

4. **Public Transportation** An escalator in the subway station has a vertical rise of 195 ft 9.5 in., and rises at an angle of 10.4°. How long is the escalator? Round to the nearest foot.

If you know the sine, cosine, or tangent ratio for an angle, you can use an inverse ($\sin^{-1}$, $\cos^{-1}$, or $\tan^{-1}$) to find the measure of the angle.

Problem 3 Using Inverses

Got It? a. Use the figure below. What is $m\angle Y$ to the nearest degree?

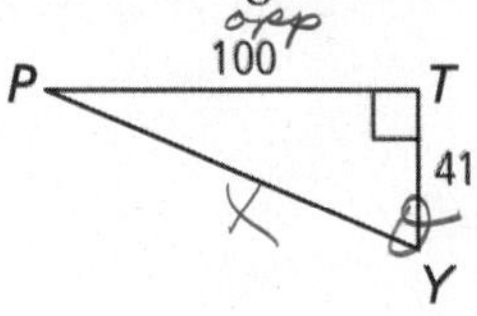

Think

When should you use an inverse?

b. Reasoning Suppose you know the lengths of all three sides of a right triangle. Does it matter which trigonometric ratio you use to find the measure of any of the three angles? Explain.

Practice **Find the value of x. Round to the nearest degree.**

5.

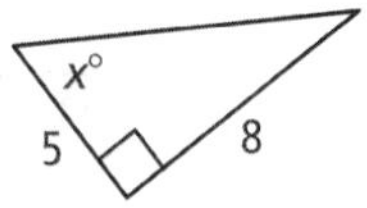

6.

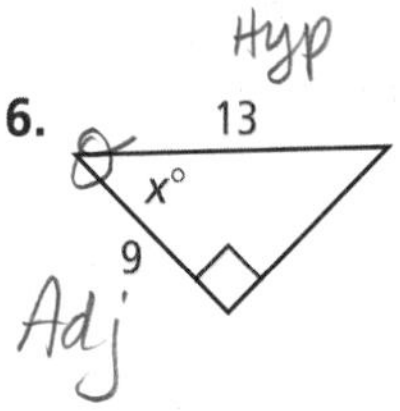

Soh Cah Toa

$\cos\theta = \frac{adj}{Hyp}$

$\cos\theta = \frac{9}{13}$

$\theta = \cos^{-1}\left(\frac{9}{13}\right)$

$\theta = 46°$

Lesson Check

Do you know HOW?

Write each ratio.

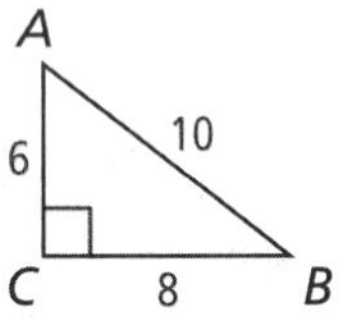

7. sin A

8. cos A

9. tan A

10. sin B

11. cos B

12. tan B

What is the value of x? Round to the nearest tenth.

13.

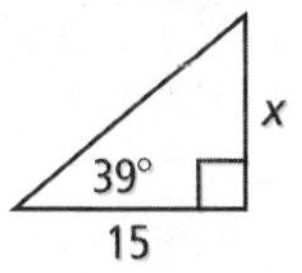

14.

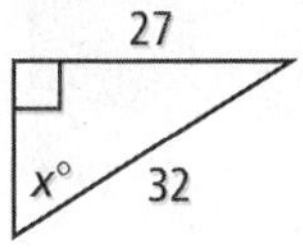

Do you UNDERSTAND?

MATHEMATICAL PRACTICES

15. Vocabulary Some people use SOH-CAH-TOA to remember the trigonometric ratios for sine, cosine, and tangent. Why do you think that word might help? (*Hint*: Think of the first letters of the ratios.)

16. Error Analysis A student states that $\sin A > \sin X$ because the lengths of the sides of $\triangle ABC$ are greater than the lengths of the sides of $\triangle XYZ$. What is the student's error? Explain.

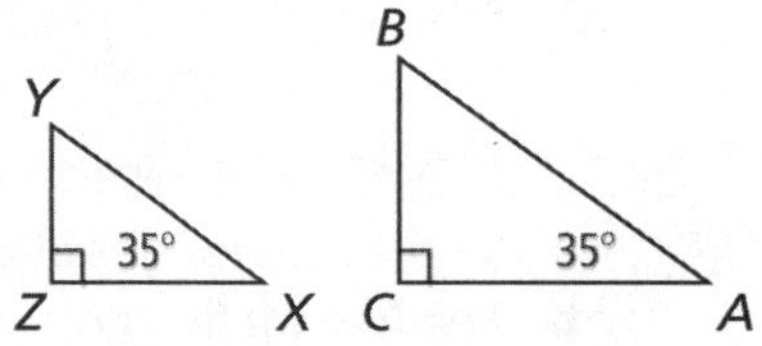

More Practice and Problem-Solving Exercises

MATHEMATICAL PRACTICES

B Apply

17. The lengths of the diagonals of a rhombus are 2 in. and 5 in. Find the measures of the angles of the rhombus to the nearest degree.

18. Think About a Plan Carlos plans to build a grain bin with a radius of 15 ft. The recommended slant of the roof is 25°. He wants the roof to overhang the edge of the bin by 1 ft. What should the length x be? Give your answer in feet and inches.

- What is the position of the side of length x in relation to the given angle?
- What information do you need to find a side length of a right triangle?
- Which trigonometric ratio could you use?

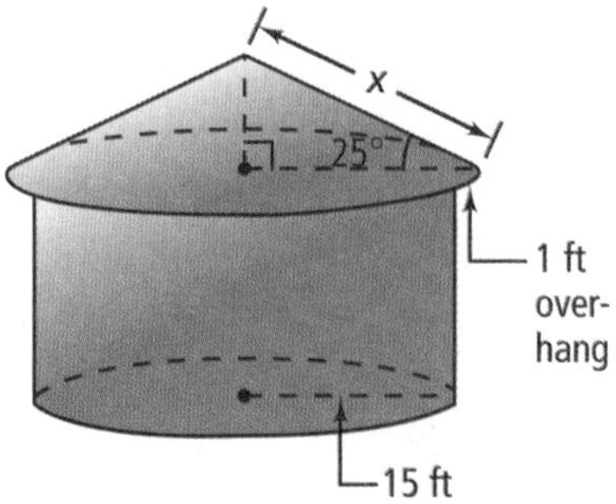

An *identity* is an equation that is true for all the allowed values of the variable. Use what you know about trigonometric ratios to show that each equation is an identity.

19. $\tan X = \frac{\sin X}{\cos X}$ **20.** $\sin X = \cos X \cdot \tan X$ **21.** $\cos X = \frac{\sin X}{\tan X}$

Find the values of w and then x. Round lengths to the nearest tenth and angle measures to the nearest degree.

22.

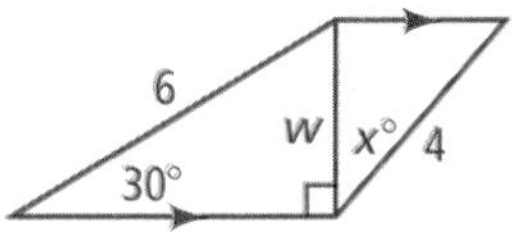

23.

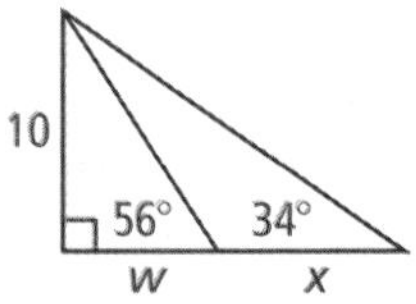

24.

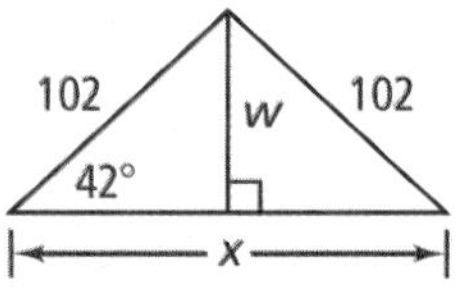

STEM 25. Pyramids All but two of the pyramids built by the ancient Egyptians have faces inclined at 52° angles. Suppose an archaeologist discovers the ruins of a pyramid. Most of the pyramid has eroded, but the archaeologist is able to determine that the length of a side of the square base is 82 m. How tall was the pyramid, assuming its faces were inclined at 52°? Round your answer to the nearest meter.

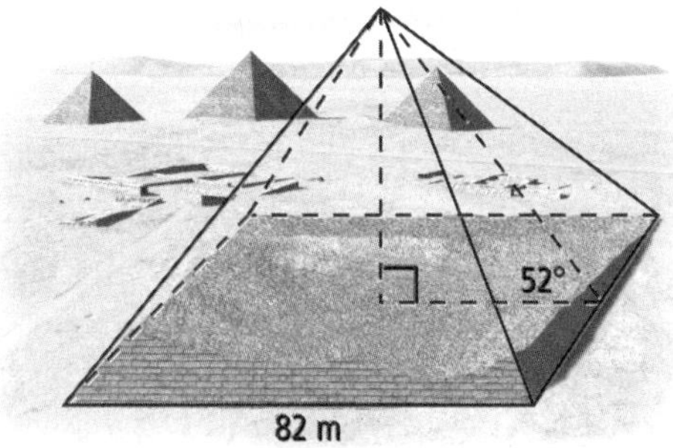

26. a. In $\triangle ABC$ at the right, how does $\sin A$ compare to $\cos B$? Is this true for the acute angles of other right triangles?

b. Reading Math The word *cosine* is derived from the words *complement's sine*. Which angle in $\triangle ABC$ is the complement of $\angle A$? Of $\angle B$?

c. Explain why the derivation of the word *cosine* makes sense.

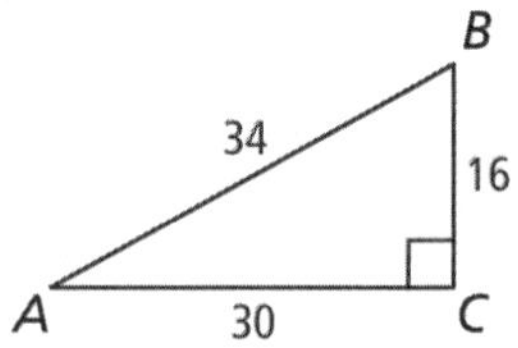

Proof **27.** For right $\triangle ABC$ with right $\angle C$, prove each of the following.

a. $\sin A < 1$ **b.** $\cos A < 1$

28. a. Writing Explain why $\tan 60° = \sqrt{3}$. Include a diagram with your explanation.

b. Make a Conjecture How are the sine and cosine of a 60° angle related? Explain.

The sine, cosine, and tangent ratios each have a reciprocal ratio. The reciprocal ratios are cosecant (csc), secant (sec), and cotangent (cot). Use $\triangle ABC$ and the definitions below to write each ratio.

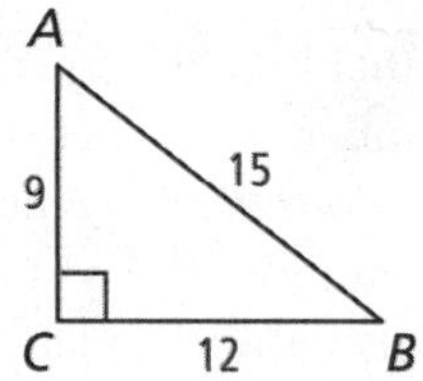

$\csc X = \frac{1}{\sin X}$ $\sec X = \frac{1}{\cos X}$ $\cot X = \frac{1}{\tan X}$

29. $\csc A$ **30.** $\sec A$ **31.** $\cot A$

32. $\csc B$ **33.** $\sec B$ **34.** $\cot B$

35. Graphing Calculator Use the **table** feature of your graphing calculator to study $\sin X$ as X gets close to (but not equal to) 90. In the **y=** screen, enter $Y1 = \sin X$.

a. Use the **tblset** feature so that X starts at 80 and changes by 1. Access the **table**. From the table, what is $\sin X$ for $X = 89$?

b. Perform a "numerical zoom-in." Use the **tblset** feature, so that X starts with 89 and changes by 0.1. What is $\sin X$ for $X = 89.9$?

c. Continue to zoom in numerically on values close to 90. What is the greatest value you can get for $\sin X$ on your calculator? How close is X to 90? Does your result contradict what you are asked to prove in Exercise 27a?

d. Use right triangles to explain the behavior of $\sin X$ found above.

36. a. Reasoning Does $\tan A + \tan B = \tan(A + B)$ when $A + B < 90$? Explain.

b. Does $\tan A - \tan B = \tan(A - B)$ when $A - B > 0$? Use part (a) and indirect reasoning to explain.

Challenge

Verify that each equation is an identity by showing that each expression on the left simplifies to 1.

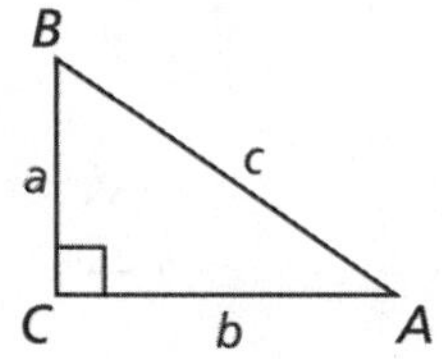

37. $(\sin A)^2 + (\cos A)^2 = 1$ **38.** $(\sin B)^2 + (\cos B)^2 = 1$

39. $\frac{1}{(\cos A)^2} - (\tan A)^2 = 1$ **40.** $\frac{1}{(\sin A)^2} - \frac{1}{(\tan A)^2} = 1$

In Exercises 41–43, the value of one trigonometric ratio is given. Find the value of the other trigonometric ratio using the identities from Exercises 19 and 37.

41. $\sin x = \frac{12}{13}$; $\cos x$

42. $\cos x = \frac{3}{4}$; $\sin x$

43. $\sin x = \frac{3}{5}$; $\tan x$

44. Show that $(\tan A)^2 - (\sin A)^2 = (\tan A)^2 \cdot (\sin A)^2$ is an identity.

STEM **45. Astronomy** The Polish astronomer Nicolaus Copernicus devised a method for determining the sizes of the orbits of planets farther from the sun than Earth. His method involved noting the number of days between the times that a planet was in the positions labeled A and B in the diagram. Using this time and the number of days in each planet's year, he calculated c and d.

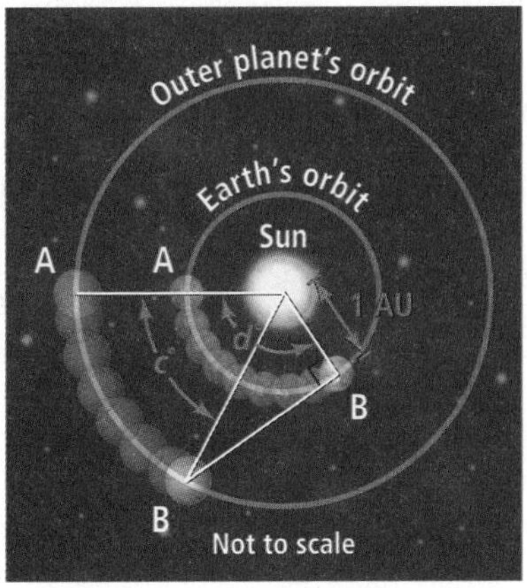

a. For Mars, $c = 55.2$ and $d = 103.8$. How far is Mars from the sun in astronomical units (AU)? One astronomical unit is defined as the average distance from Earth to the center of the sun, about 93 million miles.

b. For Jupiter, $c = 21.9$ and $d = 100.8$. How far is Jupiter from the sun in astronomical units?

11-4 Angles of Elevation and Depression

G.SRT.8 Use trigonometric ratios . . . to solve right triangles in applied problems.

Objective To use angles of elevation and depression to solve problems

Solve It! Write your solution to the Solve It in the space below.

The angles in the Solve It are formed below the horizontal black pipe. Angles formed above and below a horizontal line have specific names.

Suppose a person on the ground sees a hang glider at a 38° angle above a horizontal line. This angle is the **angle of elevation.**

At the same time, the person in the hang glider sees the person on the ground at a 38° angle below a horizontal line. This angle is the **angle of depression.**

Notice that the angle of elevation is congruent to the angle of depression because they are alternate interior angles.

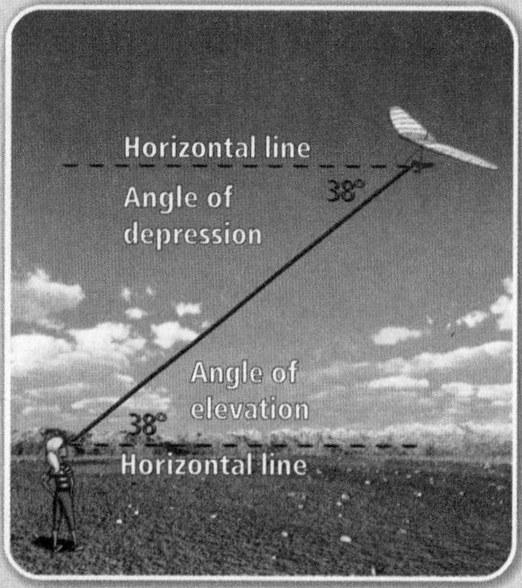

Essential Understanding You can use the angles of elevation and depression as the acute angles of right triangles formed by a horizontal distance and a vertical height.

Problem 1 Identifying Angles of Elevation and Depression

Plan
How can you tell if it is an angle of elevation or depression?

Got It? Use the diagram in Problem 1. What is a description of the angle as it relates to the situation shown?

a. $\angle 2$

b. $\angle 3$

Practice **Describe each angle as it relates to the situation in the diagram.**

1. $\angle 2$

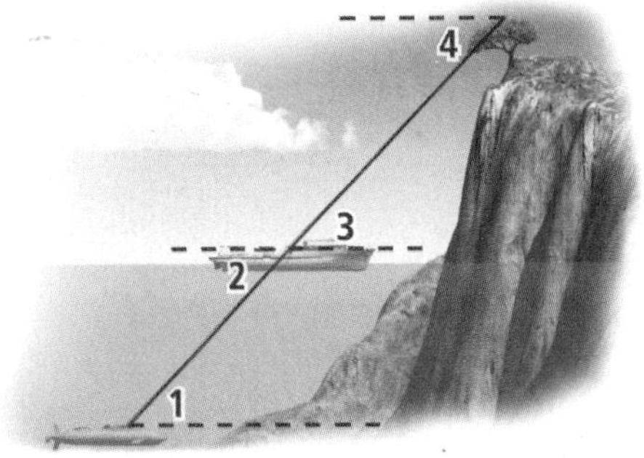

∡1 = Elev
∡2 = depression
∡3 = Elev
∡4 = Dep

2. $\angle 5$

Soh Cah Toa

Problem 2 Using the Angle of Elevation

Think

Why does your eye level matter here?

Got It? You sight a rock climber on a cliff at a 32° angle of elevation. Your eye level is 6 ft above the ground and you are 1000 ft from the base of the cliff. What is the approximate height of the rock climber from the ground?

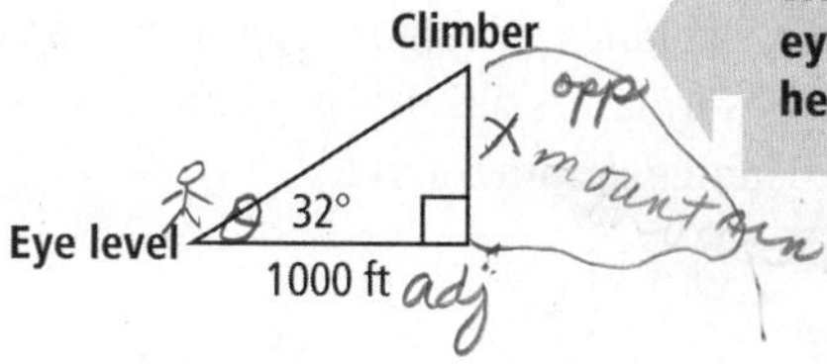

$\tan \theta = \frac{opp}{adj}$

$1000\ \theta(32) = \frac{x}{1000}\ 1000$

625

$+ 6$ eye level $= \boxed{631 ft = x}$

Practice Find the value of x. Round to the nearest tenth of a unit.

3.

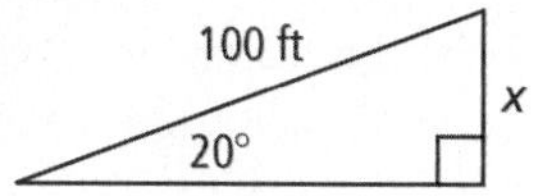

STEM **4. Meteorology** A meteorologist measures the angle of elevation of a weather balloon as 41°. A radio signal from the balloon indicates that it is 1503 m from his location. To the nearest meter, how high above the ground is the balloon?

Problem 3 Using the Angle of Depression

Got It? An airplane pilot sights a life raft at a 26° angle of depression. The airplane's altitude is 3 km. What is the airplane's horizontal distance d from the raft?

altitude = height

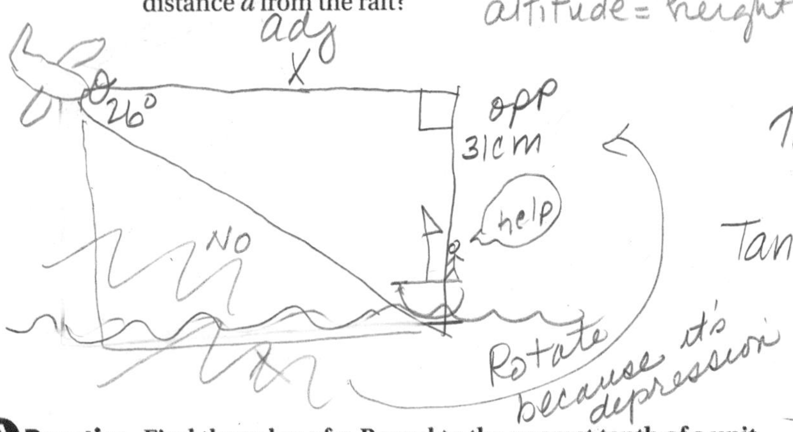

Soh Cah Toa

$\tan\theta = \frac{opp}{adj}$

$\tan(26) = \frac{3}{X}$

switch

$X = \frac{3}{\tan(26)}$

$X = 6$ Km

Practice Find the value of x. Round to the nearest tenth of a unit.

5.

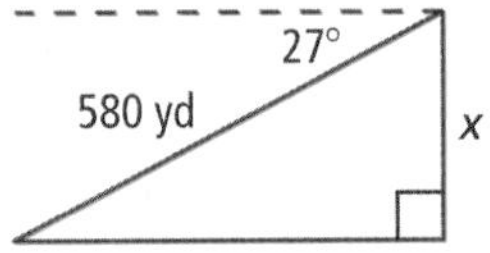

6. **Indirect Measurement** A tourist looks out from the crown of the Statue of Liberty, approximately 250 ft above the ground. The tourist sees a ship coming into the harbor and measures the angle of depression as 18°. Find the distance from the base of the statue to the ship to the nearest foot.

Lesson Check

Do you know HOW?

What is a description of each angle as it relates to the diagram?

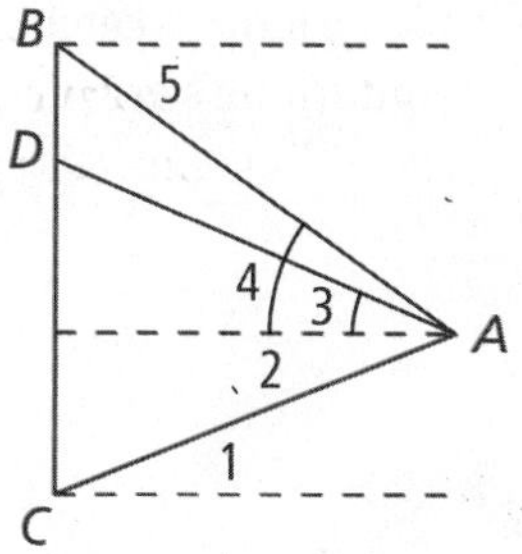

7. ∠1

8. ∠2

9. ∠3

10. ∠4

11. ∠5

12. What are two pairs of congruent angles in the diagram? Explain why they are congruent.

Do you UNDERSTAND?

MATHEMATICAL PRACTICES

13. Vocabulary How is an angle of elevation formed?

14. Error Analysis A homework question says that the angle of depression from the bottom of a house window to a ball on the ground is 20°. At the right is your friend's sketch of the situation. Describe your friend's error.

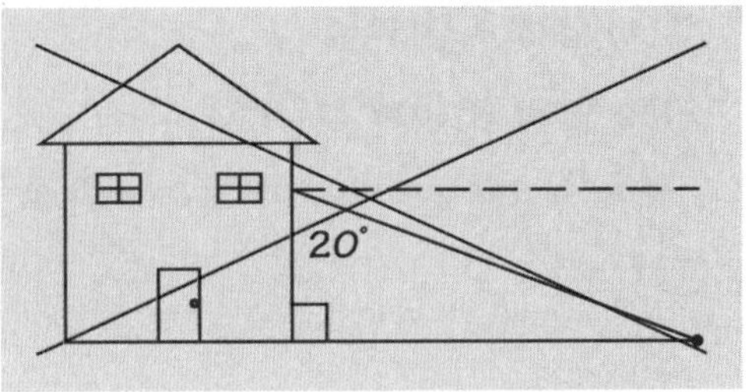

More Practice and Problem-Solving Exercises

MATHEMATICAL PRACTICES

B Apply

15. Flagpole The world's tallest unsupported flagpole is a 282-ft-tall steel pole in Surrey, British Columbia. The shortest shadow cast by the pole during the year is 137 ft long. To the nearest degree, what is the angle of elevation of the sun when the flagpole casts its shortest shadow?

16. Think About a Plan Two office buildings are 51 m apart. The height of the taller building is 207 m. The angle of depression from the top of the taller building to the top of the shorter building is 15°. Find the height of the shorter building to the nearest meter.

- How can a diagram help you?
- How does the angle of depression from the top of the taller building relate to the angle of elevation from the top of the shorter building?

Algebra The angle of elevation *e* from *A* to *B* and the angle of depression *d* from *B* to *A* are given. Find the measure of each angle.

17. e: $(7x - 5)°$, d: $4(x + 7)°$

18. e: $(3x + 1)°$, d: $2(x + 8)°$

19. e: $(x + 21)°$, d: $3(x + 3)°$

20. e: $5(x - 2)°$, d: $(x + 14)°$

21. Writing A communications tower is located on a plot of flat land. The tower is supported by several guy wires. Assume that you are able to measure distances along the ground, as well as angles formed by the guy wires and the ground. Explain how you could estimate each of the following measurements.

a. the length of any guy wire

b. how high on the tower each wire is attached

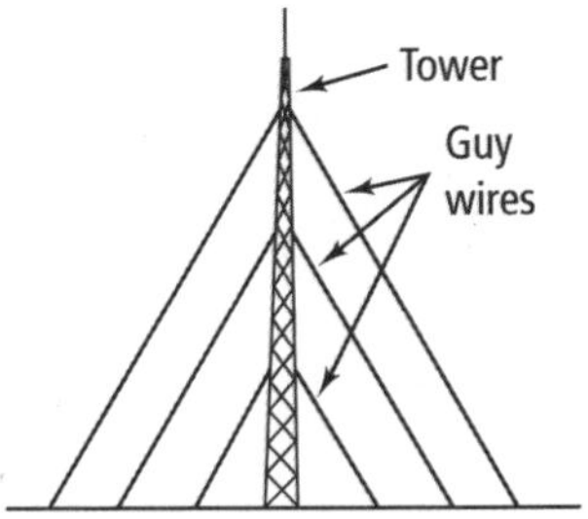

Flying **An airplane at a constant altitude a flies a horizontal distance d toward you at velocity v. You observe for time t and measure its angles of elevation $\angle E_1$ and $\angle E_2$ at the start and end of your observation. Find the missing information.**

22. $a = \blacksquare$ mi, $v = 5$ mi/min, $t = 1$ min, $m\angle E_1 = 45$, $m\angle E_2 = 90$

23. $a = 2$ mi, $v = \blacksquare$ mi/min, $t = 15$ s, $m\angle E_1 = 40$, $m\angle E_2 = 50$

24. $a = 4$ mi, $d = 3$ mi, $v = 6$ mi/min, $t = \blacksquare$ min, $m\angle E_1 = 50$, $m\angle E_2 = \blacksquare$

25. Aerial Television A blimp provides aerial television views of a football game. The television camera sights the stadium at a 7° angle of depression. The altitude of the blimp is 400 m. What is the line-of-sight distance from the television camera to the base of the stadium? Round to the nearest hundred meters.

Challenge

26. Firefighting A firefighter on the ground sees fire break through a window near the top of the building. The angle of elevation to the windowsill is 28°. The angle of elevation to the top of the building is 42°. The firefighter is 75 ft from the building and her eyes are 5 ft above the ground. What roof-to-windowsill distance can she report by radio to firefighters on the roof?

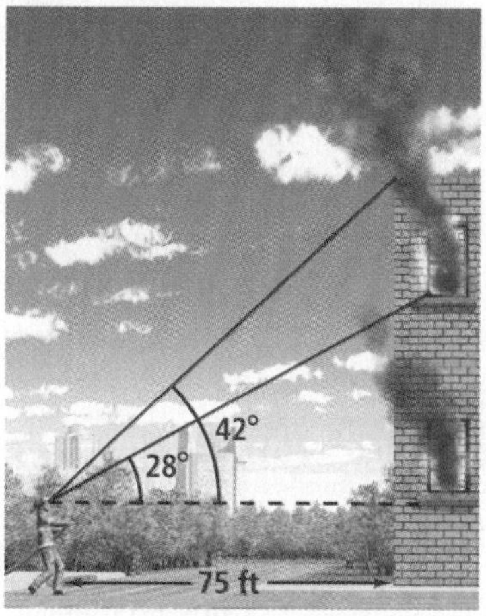

27. Geography For locations in the United States, the relationship between the latitude ℓ and the greatest angle of elevation a of the sun at noon on the first day of summer is $a = 90° - \ell + 23.5°$. Find the latitude of your town. Then determine the greatest angle of elevation of the sun for your town on the first day of summer.

11-5 Areas of Regular Polygons

G.CO.13 Construct . . . a regular hexagon inscribed in a circle. Also **A.SSE.1.b**

Objective To find the area of a regular polygon

Solve It! Write your solution to the Solve It in the space below.

The Solve It involves the area of a polygon. You can use trigonometric ratios and special right triangles to investigate properties of regular polygons.

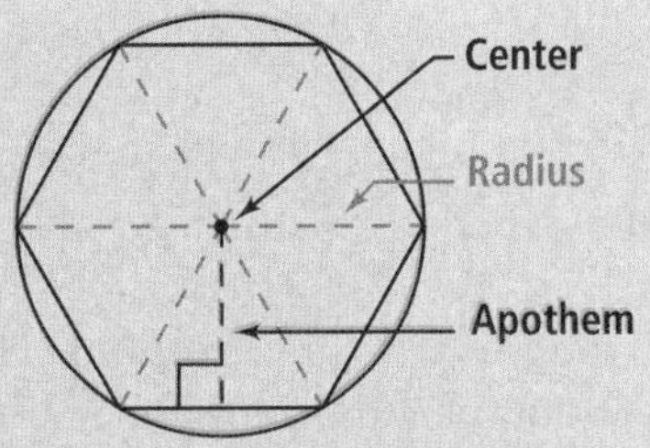

Essential Understanding The area of a regular polygon is related to the distance from the center to a side.

You can circumscribe a circle about any regular polygon. The center of a regular polygon is the center of the circumscribed circle. The **radius of a regular polygon** is the distance from the center to a vertex. The **apothem** is the perpendicular distance from the center to a side.

Problem 1 Finding Angle Measures

Think
How do you know the radii make isosceles triangles?

Got It? Below, a portion of a regular octagon has radii and an apothem drawn. What is the measure of each numbered angle?

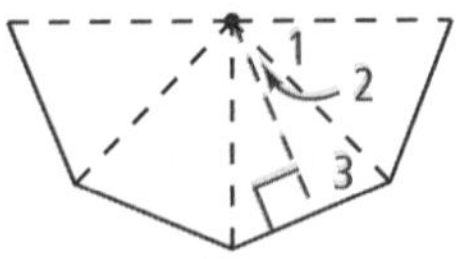

Practice **Each regular polygon has radii and apothem as shown. Find the measure of each numbered angle.**

1. 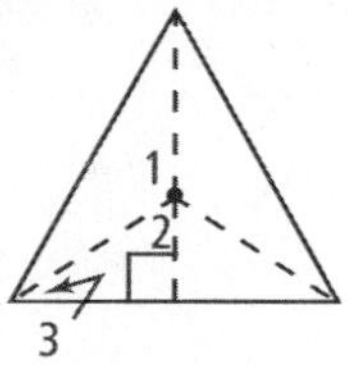

2. 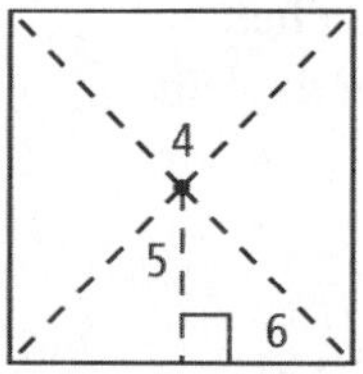

take note

Postulate 6

If two figures are congruent, then their areas are equal.

Suppose you have a regular n-gon with side s. The radii divide the figure into n congruent isosceles triangles. By Postulate 5, the areas of the isosceles triangles are equal. Each triangle has a height of a and a base of length s, so the area of each triangle is $\frac{1}{2}as$.

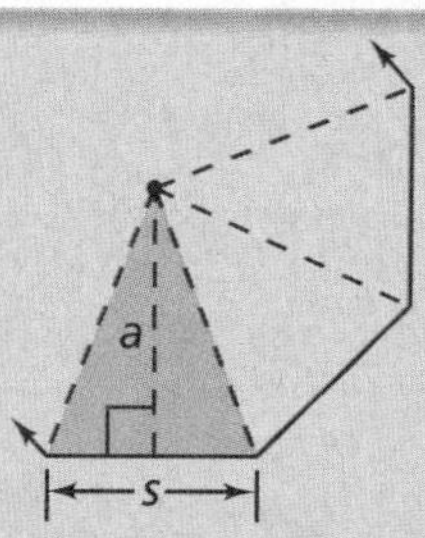

Since there are n congruent triangles, the area of the n-gon is $A = n \cdot \frac{1}{2}as$. The perimeter p of the n-gon is the number of sides n times the length of a side s, or ns. By substitution, the area can be expressed as $A = \frac{1}{2}ap$.

Theorem 69 Area of a Regular Polygon

The area of a regular polygon is half the product of the apothem and the perimeter.

$A = \frac{1}{2}ap$

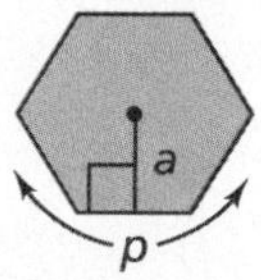

Problem 2 Finding the Area of a Regular Polygon

Got It? **a.** What is the area of a regular pentagon with an 8-cm apothem and 11.6-cm sides?

Plan

What do you know about the regular pentagon?

b. Reasoning If the side of a regular polygon is reduced to half its length, how does the perimeter of the polygon change? Explain.

Practice **Find the area of each regular polygon with the given apothem a and side length s. Round to the nearest square unit.**

3. 7-gon, $a = 29.1$ ft, $s = 28$ ft

4. nonagon, $a = 27.5$ in., $s = 20$ in.

Problem 3 Using Special Triangles to Find Area

Got It? The side of a regular hexagon is 16 ft. What is the area of the hexagon? Round your answer to the nearest square foot.

Practice 5. **Art** You are painting a mural of colored equilateral triangles. The radius of each triangle is 12.7 in. What is the area of each triangle to the nearest square inch?

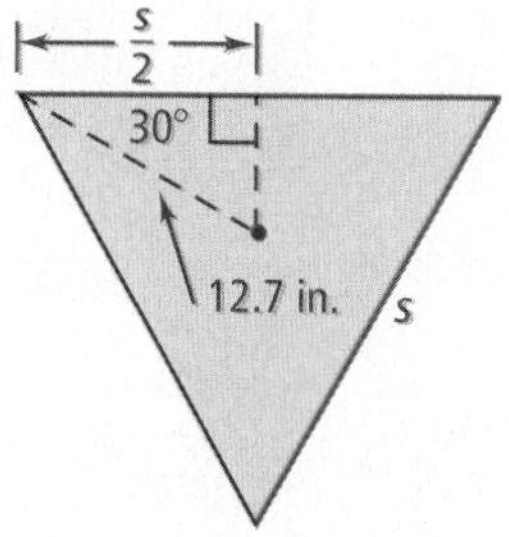

6. Find the area of the equilateral triangle. Leave your answer in simplest radical form.

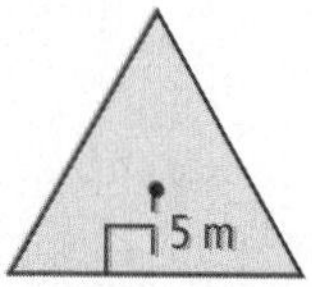

Lesson Check

Do you know HOW?

What is the area of each regular polygon? Round your answer to the nearest tenth.

7.

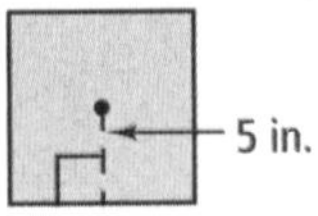

8.

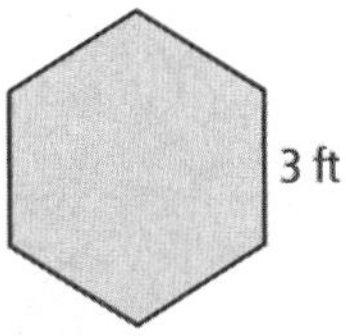

9.

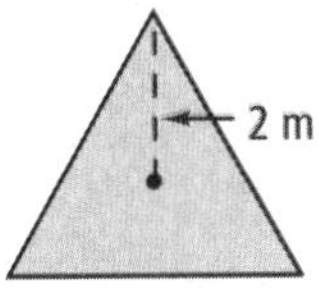

10.

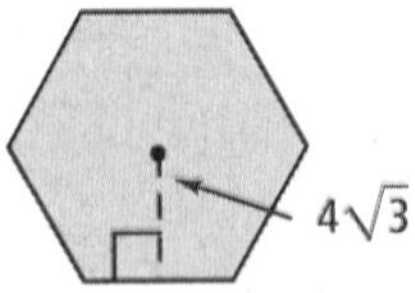

Do you UNDERSTAND?

MATHEMATICAL PRACTICES

11. **Vocabulary** What is the difference between a radius and an apothem?

12. What is the relationship between the side length and the apothem in each figure?

a. a square

b. a regular hexagon

c. an equilateral triangle

13. **Error Analysis** Your friend says you can use special triangles to find the apothem of any regular polygon. What is your friend's error? Explain.

More Practice and Problem-Solving Exercises

MATHEMATICAL PRACTICES

B Apply

Find the measures of the angles formed by (a) two consecutive radii and (b) a radius and a side of the given regular polygon.

14. pentagon **15.** octagon **16.** nonagon **17.** dodecagon

STEM **18. Satellites** One of the smallest space satellites ever developed has the shape of a pyramid. Each of the four faces of the pyramid is an equilateral triangle with sides about 13 cm long. What is the area of one equilateral triangular face of the satellite? Round your answer to the nearest whole number.

19. Think About a Plan The gazebo in the photo is built in the shape of a regular octagon. Each side is 8 ft long, and the enclosed area is about 309 ft^2. What is the length of the apothem?

- How can you *draw a diagram* to help you solve the problem?
- How can you use the area of a regular polygon formula?

20. A regular hexagon has perimeter 120 m. Find its area.

21. The area of a regular polygon is 36 $in.^2$. Find the length of a side if the polygon has the given number of sides. Round your answer to the nearest tenth.

a. 3 **b.** 4 **c.** 6

d. Estimation Suppose the polygon is a pentagon. What would you expect the length of a side to be? Explain.

22. A portion of a regular decagon has radii and an apothem drawn. Find the measure of each numbered angle.

23. Writing Explain why the radius of a regular polygon is greater than the apothem.

24. Constructions Use a compass to draw a circle.

a. Construct two perpendicular diameters of the circle.

b. Construct diameters that bisect each of the four right angles.

c. Connect the consecutive points where the diameters intersect the circle. What regular polygon have you constructed?

d. Use your construction to construct a square inscribed in a circle.

Find the perimeter and area of each regular polygon. Round to the nearest tenth, as necessary.

25. a square with vertices at $(-1, 0)$, $(2, 3)$, $(5, 0)$ and $(2, -3)$

26. an equilateral triangle with two vertices at $(-4, 1)$ and $(4, 7)$

27. a hexagon with two adjacent vertices at $(-2, 1)$ and $(1, 2)$

28. To find the area of an equilateral triangle, you can use the formula $A = \frac{1}{2}bh$ or $A = \frac{1}{2}ap$. A third way to find the area of an equilateral triangle is to use the formula $A = \frac{1}{4}s^2\sqrt{3}$. Verify the formula $A = \frac{1}{4}s^2\sqrt{3}$ in two ways as follows:

a. Find the area of Figure 1 using the formula $A = \frac{1}{2}bh$.

b. Find the area of Figure 2 using the formula $A = \frac{1}{2}ap$.

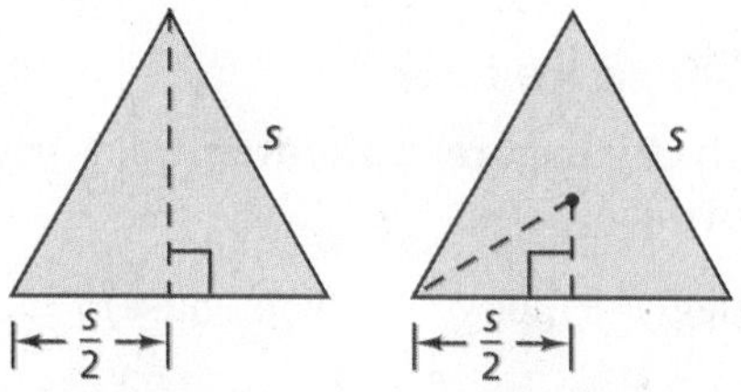

Figure 1 **Figure 2**

Proof 29. For Problem 1 in this lesson, write a proof that the apothem bisects the vertex angle of an isosceles triangle formed by two radii.

Challenge

Proof 30. Prove that the bisectors of the angles of a regular polygon are concurrent and that they are, in fact, radii of the polygon. (*Hint*: For regular *n*-gon *ABCDE*. . ., let *P* be the intersection of the bisectors of $\angle ABC$ and $\angle BCD$. Show that $\overline{DP}$ must be the bisector of $\angle CDE$.)

31. Coordinate Geometry A regular octagon with center at the origin and radius 4 is graphed in the coordinate plane.

a. Since V_2 lies on the line $y = x$, its *x*- and *y*-coordinates are equal. Use the Distance Formula to find the coordinates of V_2 to the nearest tenth.

b. Use the coordinates of V_2 and the formula $A = \frac{1}{2}bh$ to find the area of $\triangle V_1OV_2$ to the nearest tenth.

c. Use your answer to part (b) to find the area of the octagon to the nearest whole number.

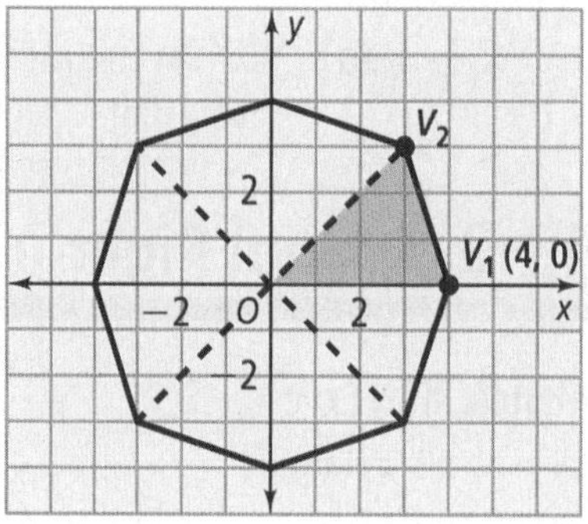

11 Chapter Review

MathXL® for School
Go to pearsonsuccessnet.com

11-1 The Pythagorean Theorem and Its Converse

Quick Review

The **Pythagorean Theorem** holds true for any right triangle.

$(\text{leg}_1)^2 + (\text{leg}_2)^2 = (\text{hypotenuse})^2$

$a^2 + b^2 = c^2$

The Converse of the Pythagorean Theorem states that if $a^2 + b^2 = c^2$, where c is the greatest side length of a triangle, then the triangle is a right triangle.

Example

What is the value of x?

$a^2 + b^2 = c^2$	Pythagorean Theorem
$x^2 + 12^2 = 20^2$	Substitute.
$x^2 = 256$	Simplify.
$x = 16$	Take the positive square root.

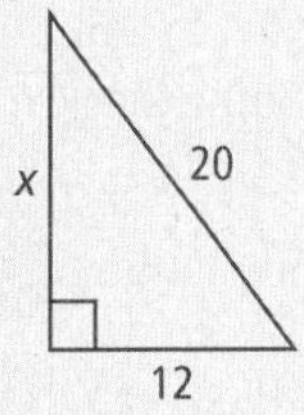

Exercises

Find the value of x. If your answer is not an integer, express it in simplest radical form.

1.

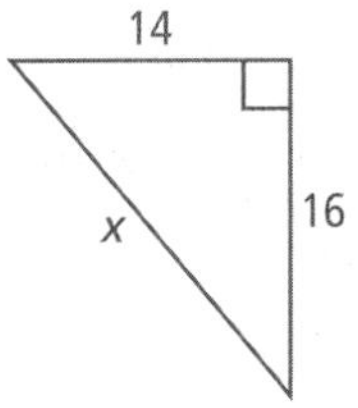

2.

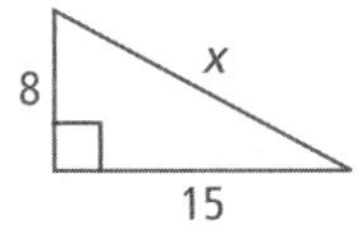

3.

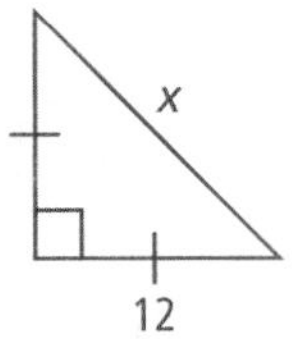

4.

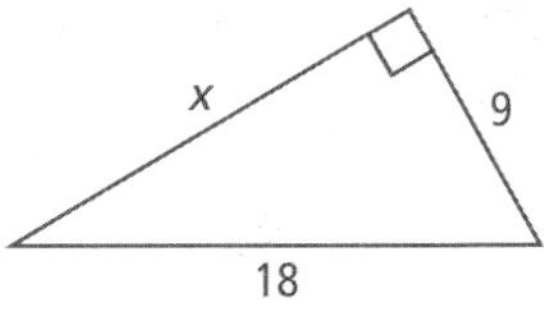

11-2 Special Right Triangles

Quick Review

45°-45°-90° Triangle

hypotenuse = $\sqrt{2}$ • leg

30°-60°-90° Triangle

hypotenuse = 2 • shorter leg

longer leg = $\sqrt{3}$ • shorter leg

Example

What is the value of x?

The triangle is a 30°-60°-90° triangle, and x represents the length of the longer leg.

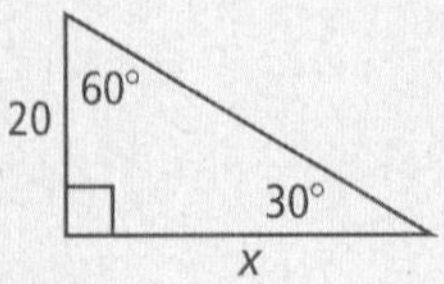

longer leg = $\sqrt{3}$ • shorter leg

$x = 20\sqrt{3}$

Exercises

Find the value of each variable. If your answer is not an integer, express it in simplest radical form.

5.

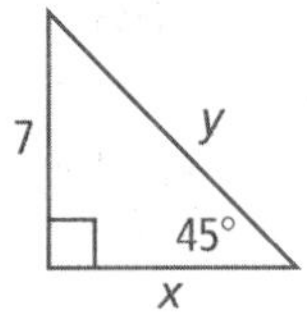

6.

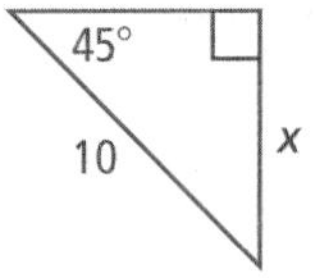

7.

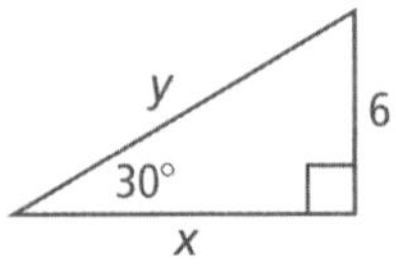

8.

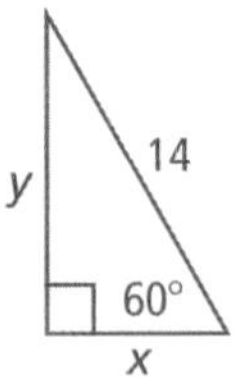

9. A square garden has sides 50 ft long. You stretch a hose from one corner of the garden to another corner along the garden's diagonal. To the nearest tenth, how long is the hose?

11-3 and 11-4
Trigonometry and Angles of Elevation and Depression

Quick Review

In right $\triangle ABC$, C is the right angle.

$$\sin A = \frac{\text{leg opposite } \angle A}{\text{hypotenuse}}$$

$$\cos A = \frac{\text{leg adjacent to } \angle A}{\text{hypotenuse}}$$

$$\tan A = \frac{\text{leg opposite } \angle A}{\text{leg adjacent to } \angle A}$$

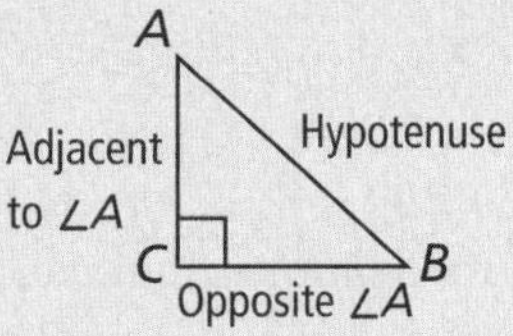

Example

What is FE to the nearest tenth?

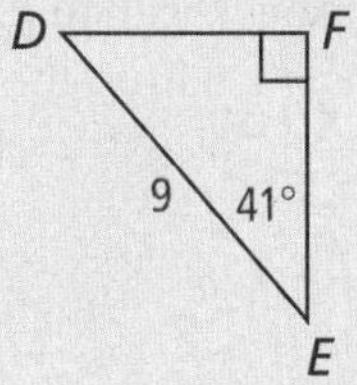

You know the length of the hypotenuse, and $\overline{FE}$ is the side adjacent to $\angle E$.

$\cos 41° = \frac{FE}{9}$ Use cosine.

$FE = 9(\cos 41°)$ Multiply each side by 9.

$FE \approx 6.8$ Use a calculator.

Exercises

Express sin A, cos A, and tan A as ratios.

10.

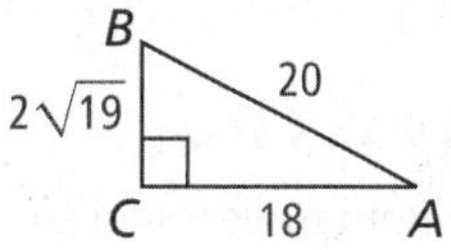

11.

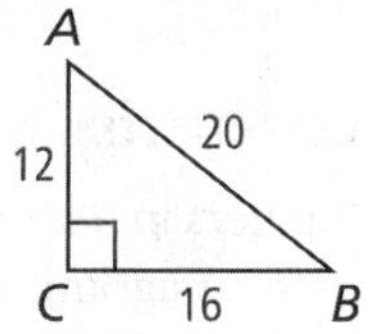

Find the value of x to the nearest tenth.

12.

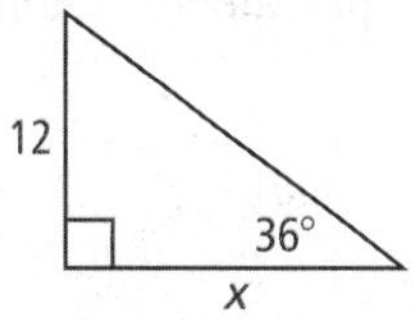

13.

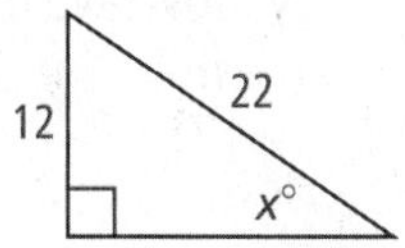

14. While flying a kite, Linda lets out 45 ft of string and anchors it to the ground. She determines that the angle of elevation of the kite is 58°. What is the height of the kite from the ground? Round to the nearest tenth.

11-5 Areas of Regular Polygons

Quick Review

The **center of a regular polygon** C is the center of its circumscribed circle. The **radius** r is the distance from the center to a vertex. The **apothem** a is the perpendicular distance from the center to a side. The area of a regular polygon with apothem a and perimeter p is $A = \frac{1}{2}ap$.

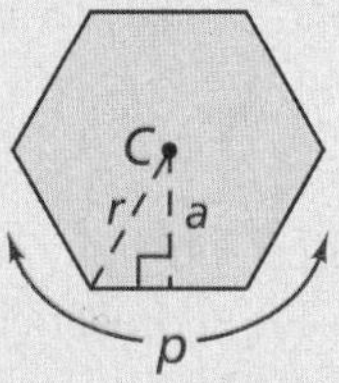

Example

What is the area of a regular hexagon with apothem 17.3 mm and perimeter 120 mm?

$A = \frac{1}{2}ap$ Use the area formula.

$= \frac{1}{2}(17.3)(120) = 1038$ Substitute and simplify.

The area of the hexagon is 1038 mm^2.

Exercises

Find the area of each regular polygon. If your answer is not an integer, leave it in simplest radical form.

15.

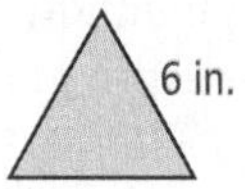

16.

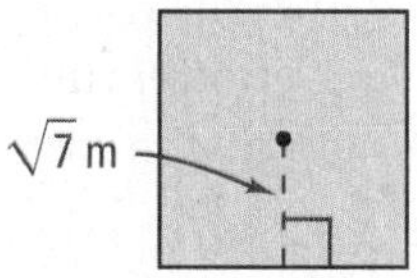

17. What is the area of a regular hexagon with a perimeter of 240 cm?

18. What is the area of a square with radius 7.5 m?

Sketch each regular polygon with the given radius. Then find its area to the nearest tenth.

19. triangle; radius 4 in.

20. square; radius 8 mm

21. hexagon; radius 7 cm

Pull It All Together

PERFORMANCE TASK

ASSESSMENT

Locating a Forest Fire

Rangers in the two lookout towers at a state forest notice a plume of smoke, as shown in the diagram. The towers are 2000 ft apart. One ranger observes the smoke at an angle of 54°. The other ranger observes it an angle of 30°. Both angles are measured from the line that connects the two towers. When the rangers call to report the fire, they must give the fire department the approximate distance from their lookout tower to the fire.

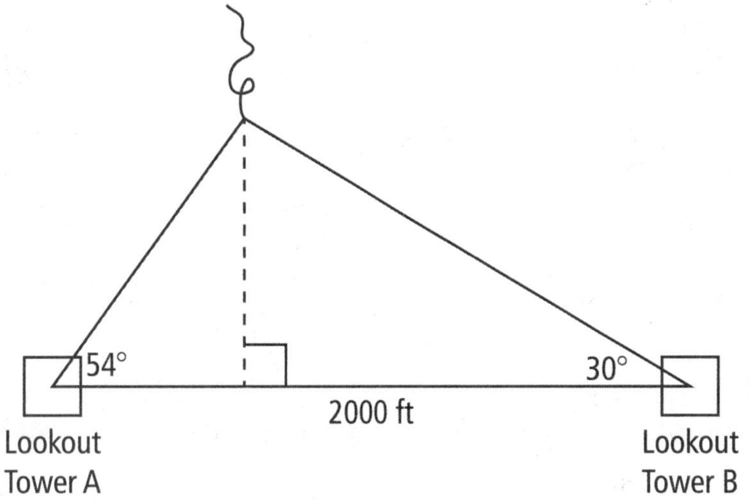

Task Description

Find the distance from each lookout tower to the fire.

- The dashed vertical line segment divides the distance between the lookout towers into two parts. What expressions can you use to represent the lengths of the parts?
- What expression represents the length of the dashed vertical line segment?

CHAPTER 12

Get Ready!

Solving Equations

Algebra Solve for x.

1. $\frac{1}{2}(x + 42) = 62$ **2.** $(5 + 3)8 = (4 + x)6$ **3.** $(9 + x)2 = (12 + 4)3$

Isosceles and Equilateral Triangles

Algebra Find the value of x.

4.

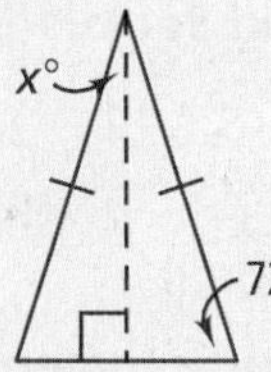

5.

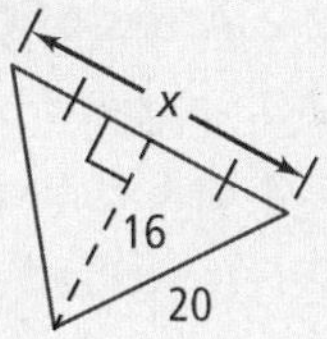

6.

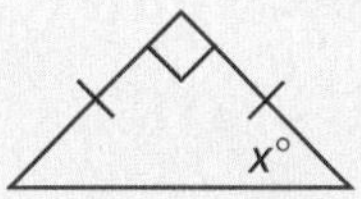

7.

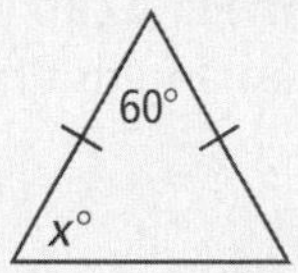

The Pythagorean Theorem

Algebra Find the value of x. Leave your answer in simplest radical form.

8.

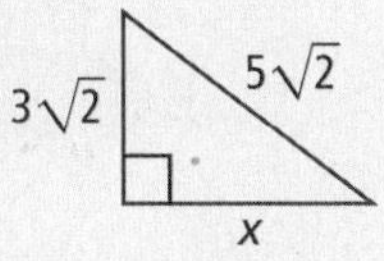

9.

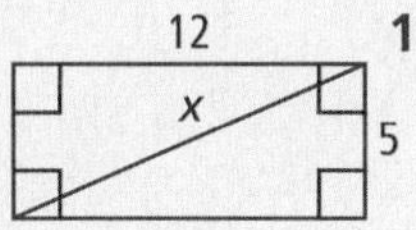

10.

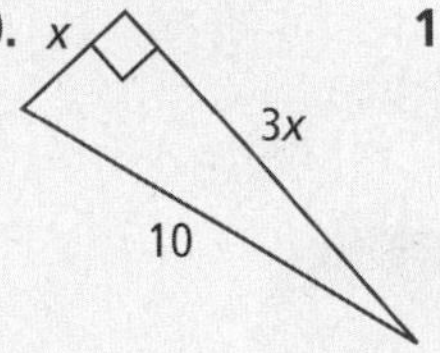

11.

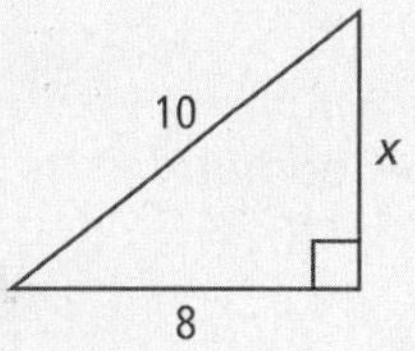

Looking Ahead Vocabulary

12. When you are in a conversation and you go off on a *tangent*, you are leading the conversation away from the main topic. What do you think a line that is *tangent* to a circle might look like?

13. You learned how to *inscribe* a triangle in a circle in Chapter 9. What do you think an *inscribed* angle is?

14. A defensive player *intercepts* a pass when he catches the football before it reaches the intended receiver. On a circle, what might an *intercepted* arc of an angle be?

CHAPTER 12

Circles

Big Ideas

1 Reasoning and Proof

Essential Question: How can you prove relationships between angles and arcs in a circle?

2 Measurement

Essential Question: When lines intersect a circle or within a circle, how do you find the measures of resulting angles, arcs, and segments?

Domains

- Circles
- Modeling with Geometry

Chapter Preview

Interactive Digital Path

Log in to **pearsonsuccessnet.com** and click on Interactive Digital Path to access the Solve Its and animated Problems.

Vocabulary

English/Spanish Vocabulary Audio Online:

English	Spanish
central angle, *p. 797*	ángulo central
chord, *p. 828*	cuerda
concentric circles, *p. 800*	círculos concéntricos
diameter, *p. 797*	diámetro
inscribed angle, *p. 839*	ángulo inscrito
intercepted arc, *p. 839*	arco interceptor
major arc, *p. 797*	arco mayor
minor arc, *p. 797*	arco menor
secant, *p. 849*	secante
sector of a circle, *p. 809*	sector de un círculo
segment of a circle, *p. 810*	segmento de un círculo
tangent to a circle, *p. 818*	tagente de un círculo

12-1 Circles and Arcs

G.C.1 Prove . . . all circles are similar. Also **G.C.2, G.C.5**

Objectives To find the measures of central angles and arcs
To find the circumference and arc length

Solve It! Write your solution to the Solve It in the space below.

In a plane, a **circle** is the set of all points equidistant from a given point called the **center**. You name a circle by its center. Circle P ($\odot P$) is shown below.

A **diameter** is a segment that contains the center of a circle and has both endpoints on the circle. A **radius** is a segment that has one endpoint at the center and the other endpoint on the circle. **Congruent circles** have congruent radii. A **central angle** is an angle whose vertex is the center of the circle.

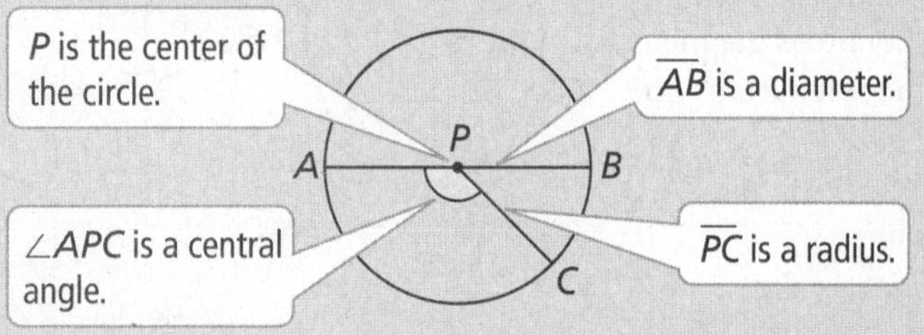

Essential Understanding You can find the length of part of a circle's circumference by relating it to an angle in the circle.

An arc is a part of a circle. One type of arc, a **semicircle**, is half of a circle. A **minor arc** is smaller than a semicircle. A **major arc** is larger than a semicircle. You name a minor arc by its endpoints and a major arc or a semicircle by its endpoints and another point on the arc.

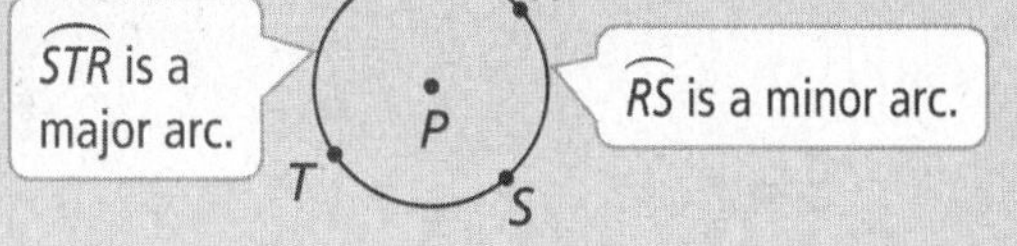

Problem 1 Naming Arcs

Think

How can you identify the minor arcs?

Got It? **a.** What are the minor arcs of $\odot A$?

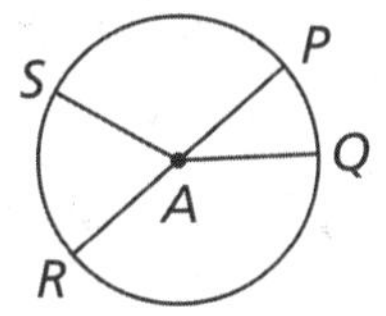

b. What are the semicircles of $\odot A$?

c. What are the major arcs of $\odot A$ that contain point Q?

A Practice Name the following in $\odot O$.

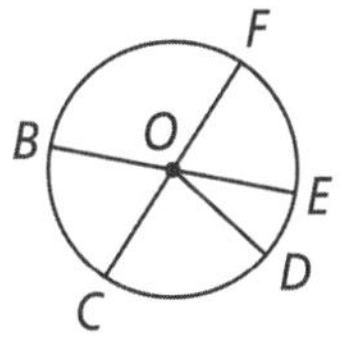

1. the major arcs

2. the semicircles

---

take note

Key Concept Arc Measure

Arc Measure

The measure of a minor arc is equal to the measure of its corresponding central angle.

The measure of a major arc is the measure of the related minor arc subtracted from 360.

The measure of a semicircle is 180.

Example

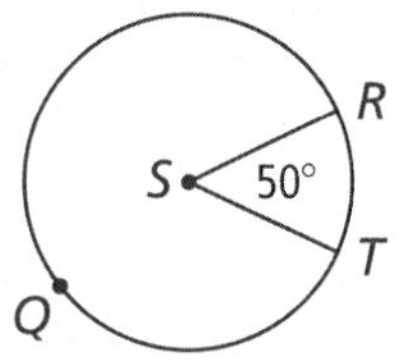

$m\widehat{RT} = m\angle RST = 50$

$m\widehat{TQR} = 360 - m\widehat{RT}$

$= 310$

Adjacent arcs are arcs of the same circle that have exactly one point in common. You can add the measures of adjacent arcs just as you can add the measures of adjacent angles.

take note

Postulate 7 Arc Addition Postulate

The measure of the arc formed by two adjacent arcs is the sum of the measures of the two arcs.

$m\widehat{ABC} = m\widehat{AB} + m\widehat{BC}$

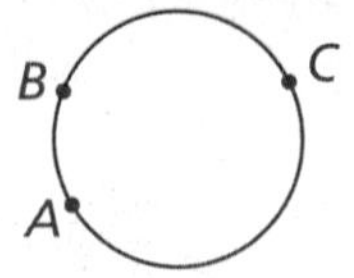

Problem 2 Finding the Measures of Arcs

Got It? What is the measure of each arc in $\odot C$?

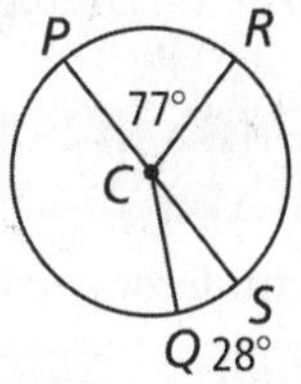

a. $m\overparen{PR}$

b. $m\overparen{RS}$

c. $m\overparen{PRQ}$

d. $m\overparen{PQR}$

Practice Find the measure of each arc in $\odot P$.

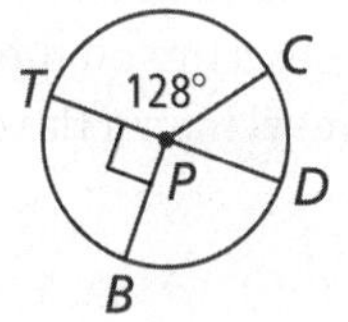

3. $\overparen{CBD}$

4. $\overparen{BCD}$

The **circumference** of a circle is the distance around the circle. The number **pi** (π) is the ratio of the circumference of a circle to its diameter.

take note

Theorem 70 Circumference of a Circle

The circumference of a circle is π times the diameter.

$C = \pi d$ or $C = 2\pi r$

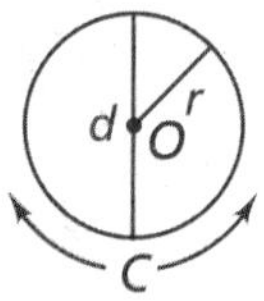

The number π is irrational, so you cannot write it as a terminating or repeating decimal. To approximate π, you can use 3.14, $\frac{22}{7}$, or the π key on your calculator.

Many properties of circles deal with ratios that stay the same no matter what size the circle is. This is because all circles are similar to each other. To see this, consider the circles at the right. There is a translation that maps circle O so that it shares the same center with circle P.

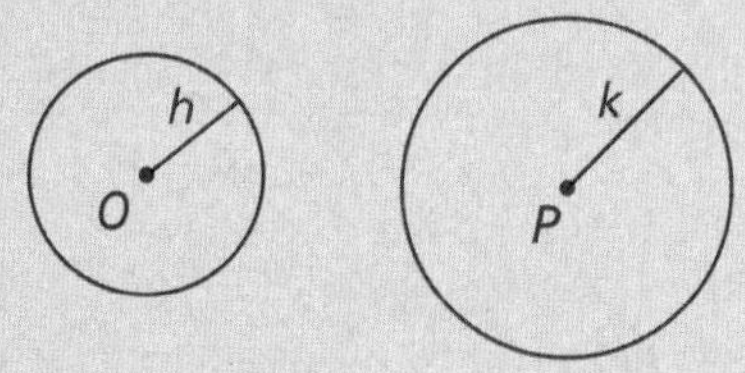

There also exists a dilation with scale factor $\frac{k}{h}$ that maps circle O to circle P. A translation followed by a dilation is a similarity transformation. Because a similarity transformation maps circle O to circle P, the two circles are similar.

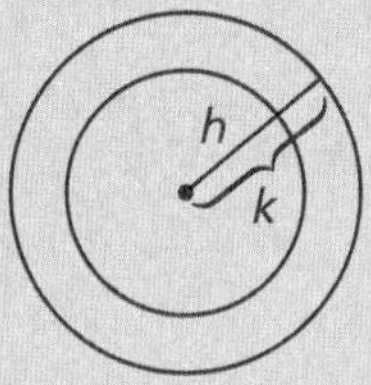

Concentric circles

Coplanar circles that have the same center are called **concentric circles**.

ONLINE PROBLEMS

Problem 3 Finding a Distance

Got It? **a.** A car has a circular turning radius of 16.1 ft. The distance between the two front tires is 4.7 ft. How much farther does a tire on the outside of the turn travel than a tire on the inside?

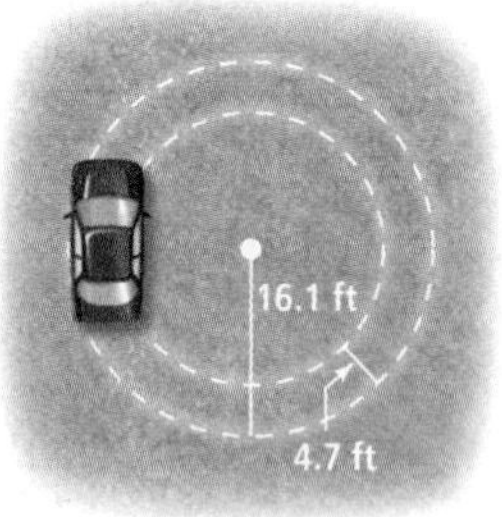

Plan

What do you need to find?

b. Reasoning Suppose the radius of $\odot A$ is equal to the diameter of $\odot B$. What is the ratio of the circumference of $\odot A$ to the circumference of $\odot B$? Explain.

Practice **5.** Find the circumference of this circle. Leave your answer in terms of π.

6. The wheel of a compact car has a 25-in. diameter. The wheel of a pickup truck has a 31-in. diameter. To the nearest inch, how much farther does the pickup truck wheel travel in one revolution than the compact car wheel?

The measure of an arc is in degrees, while the **arc length** is a fraction of the circumference.

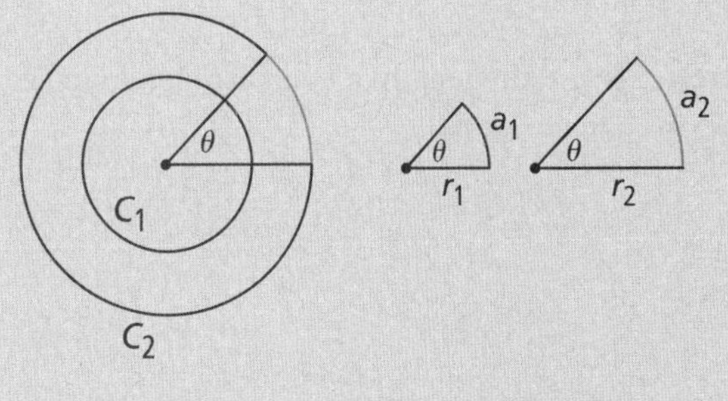

Consider the arcs shown at the right. Since the circles are concentric, there is a dilation that maps C_1 to C_2. The same dilation maps the slice of the small circle to the slice of the large circle. Since corresponding lengths of similar figures are proportional,

$$\frac{r_1}{r_2} = \frac{a_1}{a_2}$$

$$r_1 a_2 = r_2 a_1$$

$$a_1 = r_1 \cdot \frac{a_2}{r_2}$$

This means that the arc length a_1 is equal to the radius r_1 times some number. So for a given central angle, the length of the arc it intercepts depends only on the radius.

An arc of 60° represents $\frac{60}{360}$, or $\frac{1}{6}$, of the circle. So its arc length is $\frac{1}{6}$ of the circumference. This observation suggests the following theorem.

take note

Theorem 71 Arc Length

The length of an arc of a circle is the product of the ratio $\frac{\text{measure of the arc}}{360}$ and the circumference of the circle.

$$\text{length of } \widehat{AB} = \frac{m\widehat{AB}}{360} \cdot 2\pi r$$
$$= \frac{m\widehat{AB}}{360} \cdot \pi d$$

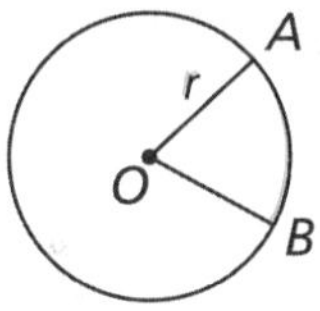

ONLINE PROBLEMS

Problem 4 Finding Arc Length

Got It? What is the length of a semicircle with radius 1.3 m? Leave your answer in terms of π.

A Practice **Find the length of each arc shown in red. Leave your answer in terms of π.**

7.

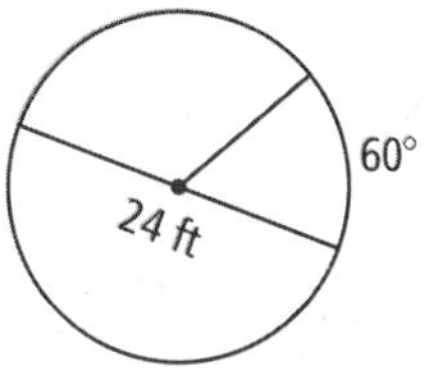

8.

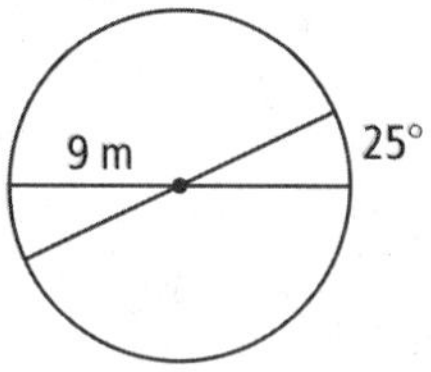

Lesson Check

Do you know HOW?

Use $\odot P$ at the right to answer each question. For Exercises 13 and 14, leave your answers in terms of π.

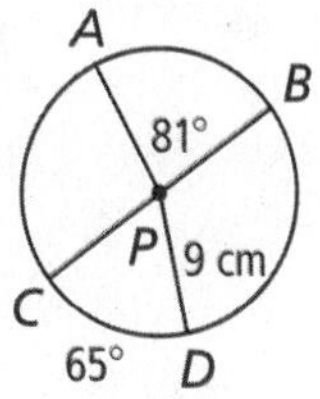

9. What is the name of a minor arc?

10. What is the name of a major arc?

11. What is the name of a semicircle?

12. What is $m\overset{\frown}{AB}$?

13. What is the circumference of $\odot P$?

14. What is the length of $\overset{\frown}{BD}$?

Do you UNDERSTAND?

MATHEMATICAL PRACTICES

15. Vocabulary What is the difference between the measure of an arc and arc length? Explain.

16. Error Analysis Your class must find the length of $\widehat{AB}$. A classmate submits the following solution. What is the error?

$$\text{Length of } \widehat{AB} = \frac{m\widehat{AB}}{360} \cdot 2\pi r$$
$$= \frac{110}{360} \cdot 2\pi(4)$$
$$= \frac{22}{9}\pi \text{ m}$$

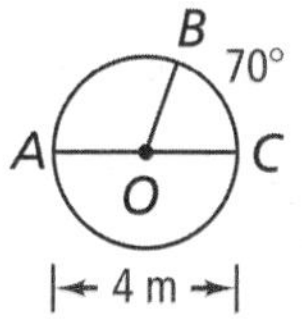

More Practice and Problem-Solving Exercises

MATHEMATICAL PRACTICES

B Apply

17. Think About a Plan Nina designed a semicircular arch made of wrought iron for the top of a mall entrance. The nine segments between the two concentric semicircles are each 3 ft long. What is the total length of wrought iron used to make this structure? Round your answer to the nearest foot.

- What do you know from the diagram?
- What formula should you use to find the amount of wrought iron used in the semicircular arches?

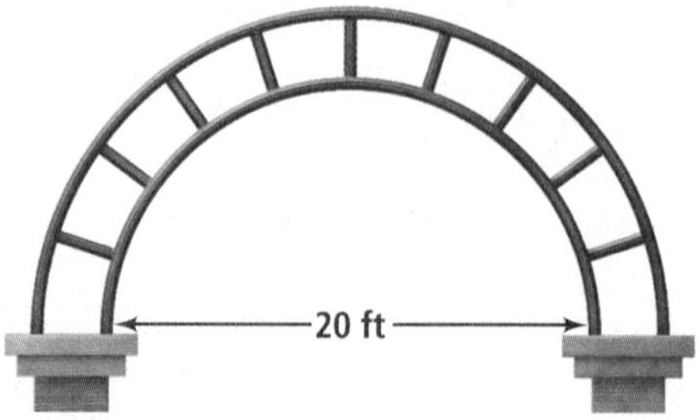

Find each indicated measure for $\odot O$.

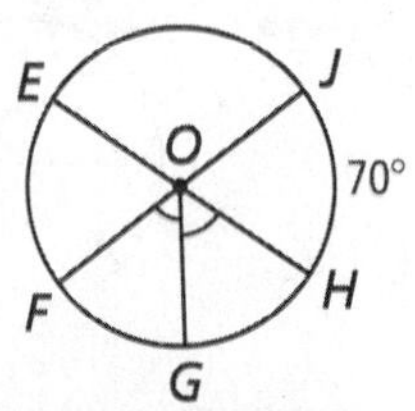

18. $m\angle EOF$ **19.** $m\overset{\frown}{EJH}$ **20.** $m\overset{\frown}{FH}$

21. $m\angle FOG$ **22.** $m\overset{\frown}{JEG}$ **23.** $m\overset{\frown}{HFJ}$

24. Pets A hamster wheel has a 7-in. diameter. How many feet will a hamster travel in 100 revolutions of the wheel?

STEM **25. Traffic** Five streets come together at a traffic circle, as shown at the right. The diameter of the circle traveled by a car is 200 ft. If traffic travels counterclockwise, what is the approximate distance from East St. to Neponset St.?

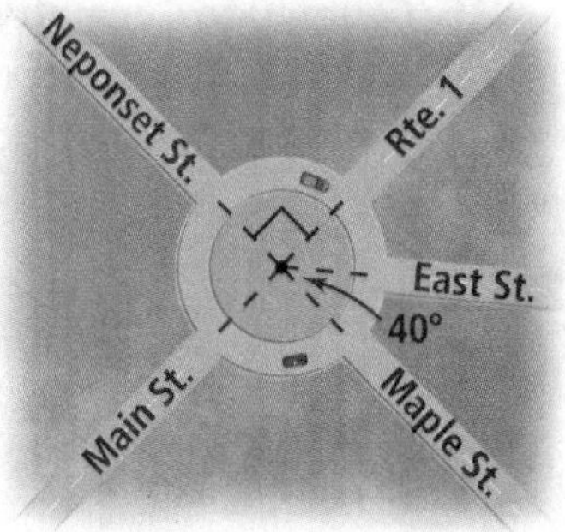

(A) 227 ft (C) 454 ft

(B) 244 ft (D) 488 ft

26. Writing Describe two ways to find the arc length of a major arc if you are given the measure of the corresponding minor arc and the radius of the circle.

27. Time Hands of a clock suggest an angle whose measure is continually changing. How many degrees does a minute hand move through during each time interval?

a. 1 min **b.** 5 min **c.** 20 min

Algebra Find the value of each variable.

28.

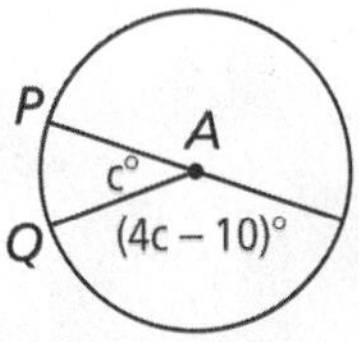

29.

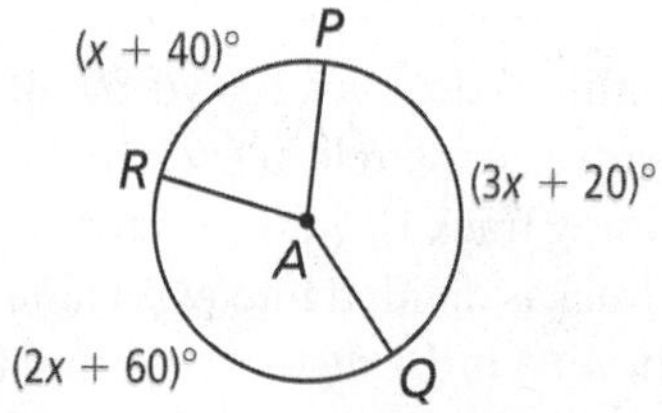

30. Landscape Design A landscape architect is constructing a curved path through a rectangular yard. The curved path consists of two 90° arcs. He plans to edge the two sides of the path with plastic edging. What is the total length of plastic edging he will need? Round your answer to the nearest meter.

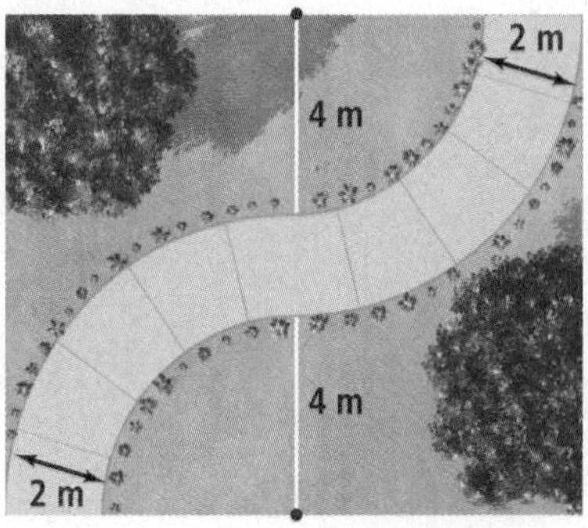

31. Reasoning Suppose the radius of a circle is doubled. How does this affect the circumference of the circle? Explain.

32. A 60° arc of $\odot A$ has the same length as a 45° arc of $\odot B$. What is the ratio of the radius of $\odot A$ to the radius of $\odot B$?

Find the length of each arc shown in red. Leave your answer in terms of π.

33.

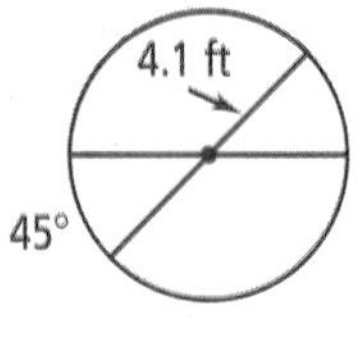

34.

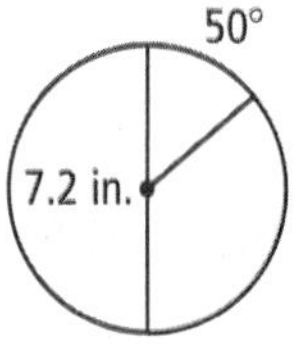

35.

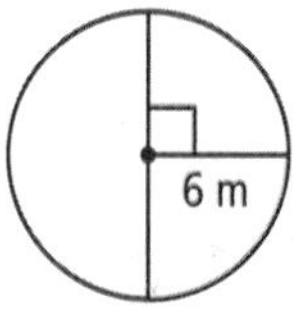

36. Coordinate Geometry Find the length of a semicircle with endpoints (1, 3) and (4, 7). Round your answer to the nearest tenth.

37. In $\odot O$, the length of $\overset{\frown}{AB}$ is 6π cm and $m\overset{\frown}{AB}$ is 120. What is the diameter of $\odot O$?

Challenge

38. The diagram below shows two concentric circles. $\overline{AR} \cong \overline{RW}$. Show that the length of $\overset{\frown}{ST}$ is equal to the length of $\overset{\frown}{QR}$.

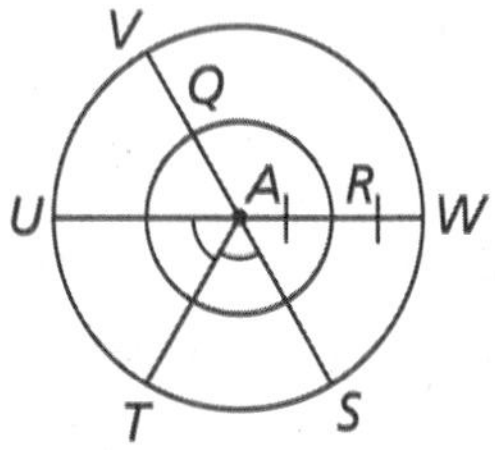

39. Given: $\odot P$ with $\overline{AB} \parallel \overline{PC}$
Proof **Prove:** $m\overset{\frown}{BC} = m\overset{\frown}{CD}$

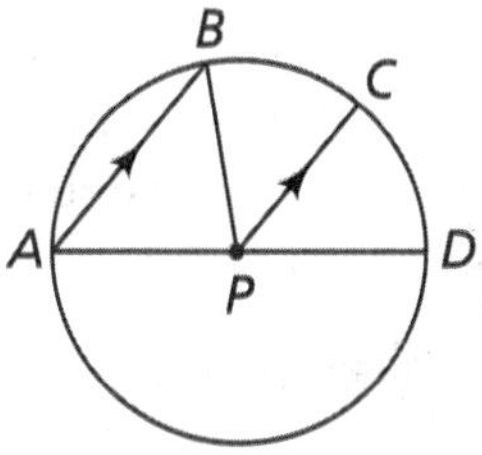

40. Sports An athletic field is a 100 yd-by-40 yd rectangle, with a semicircle at each of the short sides. A running track 10 yd wide surrounds the field. If the track is divided into eight lanes of equal width, what is the distance around the track along the inside edge of each lane?

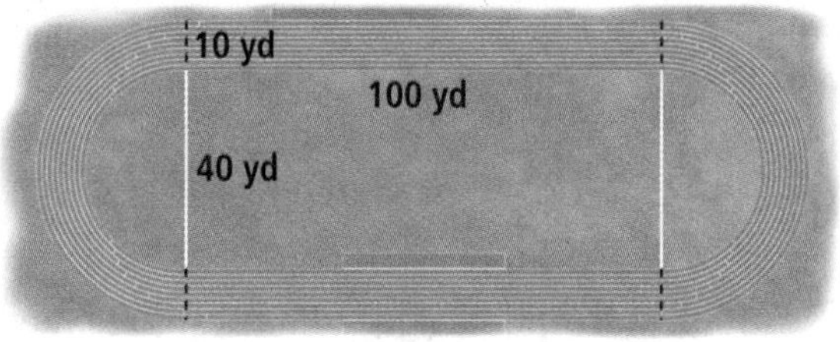

12-2 Areas of Circles and Sectors

G.C.5 Derive using similarity the fact that the length of the arc intercepted by an angle is proportional to the radius . . . derive the formula for the area of a sector.

Objective To find the areas of circles, sectors, and segments of circles

Solve It! Write your solution to the Solve It in the space below.

In the Solve It, you explored the area of a circle.

Essential Understanding You can find the area of a circle when you know its radius. You can use the area of a circle to find the area of part of a circle formed by two radii and the arc the radii form when they intersect with the circle.

take note

Theorem 72 Area of a Circle

The area of a circle is the product of π and the square of the radius.

$A = \pi r^2$

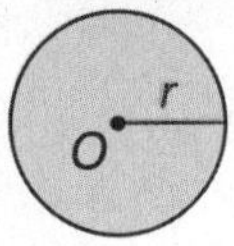

Problem 1 Finding the Area of a Circle

Think
What do you need in order to use the area formula?

Got It? **a.** What is the area of a circular wrestling region with a 42-ft diameter?

b. Reasoning If the radius of a circle is halved, how does its area change? Explain.

Practice **Find the area of the circle. Leave your answer in terms of π.**

1.

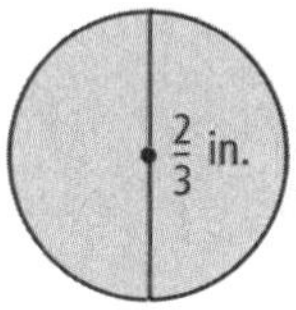

STEM **2. Agriculture** Some farmers use a circular irrigation method. An irrigation arm acts as the radius of an irrigation circle. How much land is covered with an irrigation arm of 300 ft?

A **sector of a circle** is a region bounded by an arc of the circle and the two radii to the arc's endpoints. You name a sector using one arc endpoint, the center of the circle, and the other arc endpoint.

The area of a sector is a fractional part of the area of a circle. The area of a sector formed by a 60° arc is $\frac{60}{360}$, or $\frac{1}{6}$, of the area of the circle.

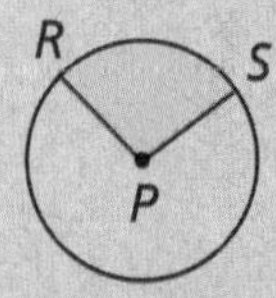

Sector *RPS*

take note

Theorem 73 Area of a Sector of a Circle

The area of a sector of a circle is the product of the ratio $\frac{\text{measure of the arc}}{360}$ and the area of the circle.

$$\text{Area of sector } AOB = \frac{m\overset{\frown}{AB}}{360} \cdot \pi r^2$$

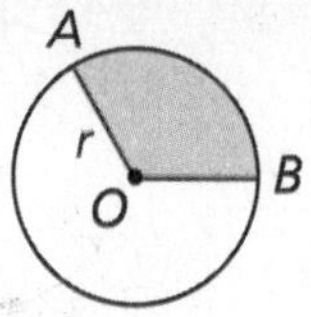

Problem 2 Finding the Area of a Sector of a Circle

Got It? A circle has a radius of 4 in. What is the area of a sector bounded by a 45° minor arc? Leave your answer in terms of π.

Think
What fraction of a circle's area is the area of a sector formed by a 45° arc?

Practice 3. Find the area of each shaded sector of the circle. Leave your answer in terms of π.

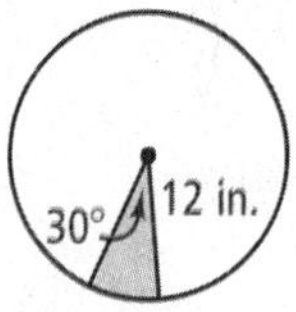

4. Find the area of sector *TOP* in $\odot O$ using the given information. Leave your answer in terms of π.

$d = 16$ in., $m\overset{\frown}{PT} = 135$

A part of a circle bounded by an arc and the segment joining its endpoints is a **segment of a circle**.

To find the area of a segment for a minor arc, draw radii to form a sector. The area of the segment equals the area of the sector minus the area of the triangle formed.

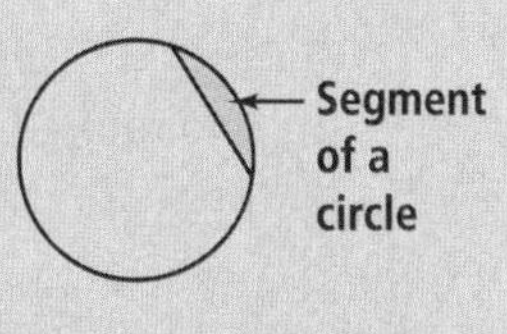

take note

Key Concept Area of a Segment

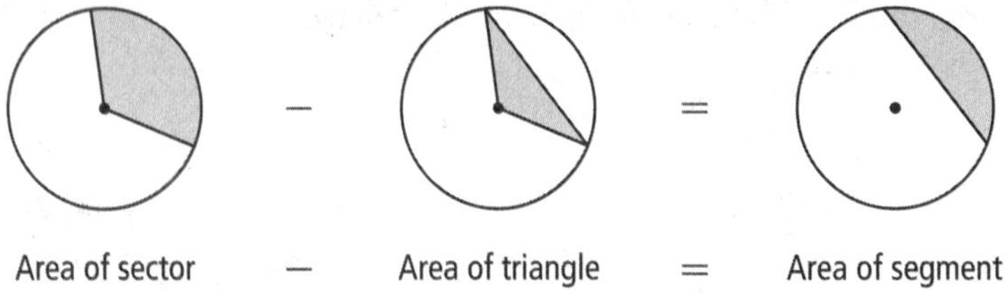

Problem 3 Finding the Area of a Segment of a Circle

Got It? What is the area of the shaded segment shown at the right? Round your answer to the nearest tenth.

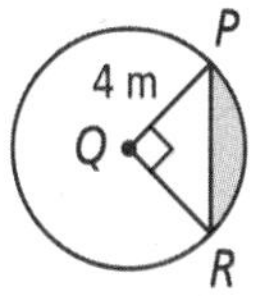

Practice **Find the area of each shaded segment. Round your answer to the nearest tenth.**

5.

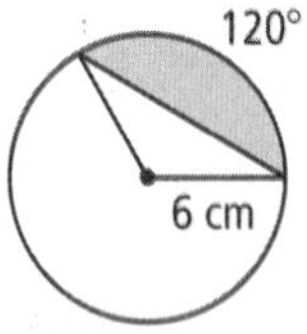

6.

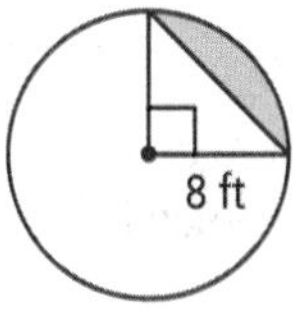

Lesson Check

Do you know HOW?

7. What is the area of a circle with diameter 16 in.? Leave your answer in terms of π.

Find the area of the shaded region of the circle. Leave your answer in terms of π.

8.

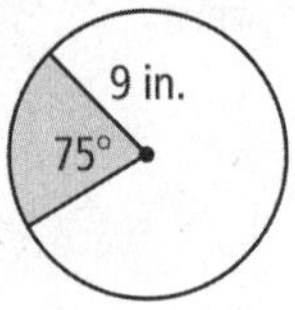

9.

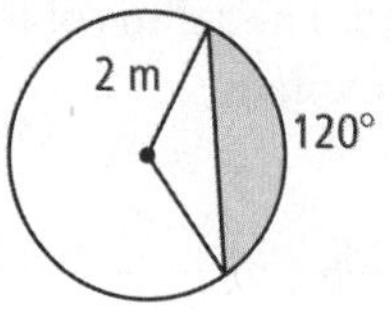

Do you UNDERSTAND?

MATHEMATICAL PRACTICES

10. Vocabulary What is the difference between a sector of a circle and a segment of a circle?

11. Reasoning Suppose a sector of $\odot P$ has the same area as a sector of $\odot O$. Can you conclude that $\odot P$ and $\odot O$ have the same area? Explain.

12. Error Analysis Your class must find the area of a sector of a circle determined by a 150° arc. The radius of the circle is 6 cm. What is your classmate's error? Explain.

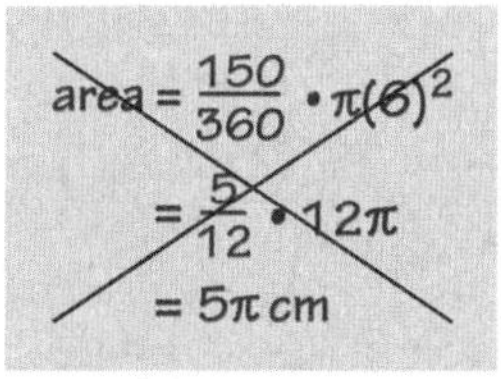

More Practice and Problem-Solving Exercises

MATHEMATICAL PRACTICES

B Apply

Find the area of the shaded region. Leave your answer in terms of π and in simplest radical form.

13.

14.

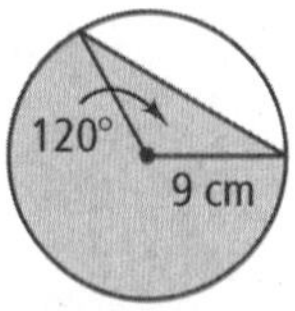

15.

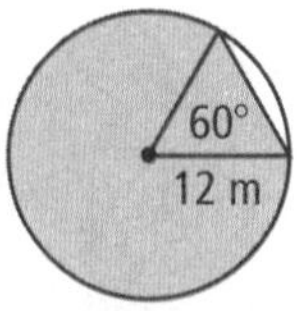

16.

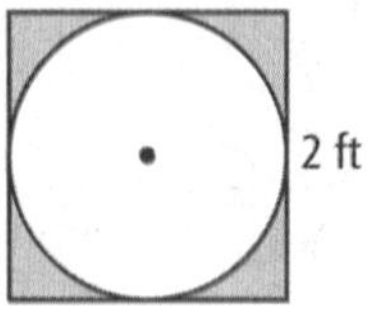

17.

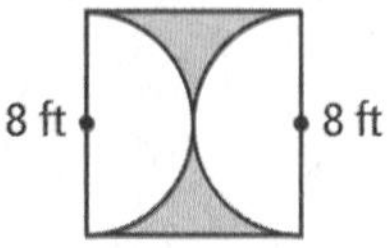

18.

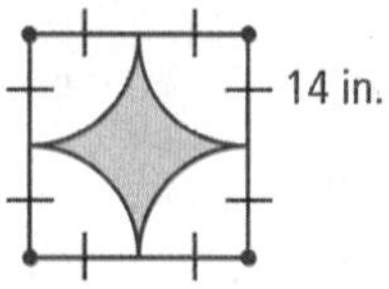

19. Transportation A town provides bus transportation to students living beyond 2 mi of the high school. What area of the town does *not* have the bus service? Round to the nearest tenth.

20. Design A homeowner wants to build a circular patio. If the diameter of the patio is 20 ft, what is its area to the nearest whole number?

21. Think About a Plan A circular mirror is 24 in. wide and has a 4-in. frame around it. What is the area of the frame?
- How can you *draw a diagram* to help solve the problem?
- What part of a circle is the width?
- Is there more than one area to consider?

STEM **22. Industrial Design** Refer to the diagram of the regular hexagonal nut. What is the area of the hexagonal face to the nearest millimeter?

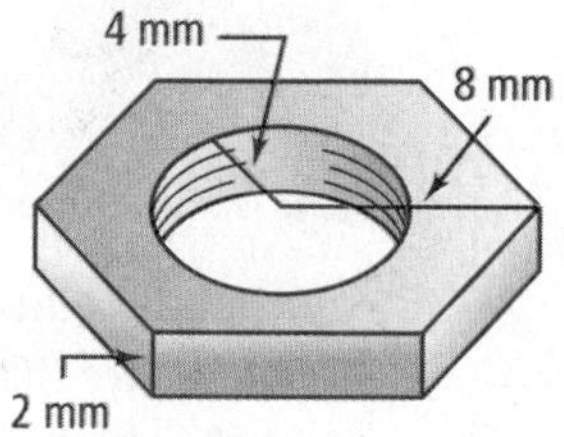

23. Reasoning $\overline{AB}$ and $\overline{CD}$ are diameters of $\odot O$. Is the area of sector AOC equal to the area of sector BOD? Explain.

24. A circle with radius 12 mm is divided into 20 sectors of equal area. What is the area of one sector to the nearest tenth?

25. The circumference of a circle is 26π in. What is its area? Leave your answer in terms of π.

26. In a circle, a 90° sector has area 36π in.^{2}. What is the radius of the circle?

27. Open-Ended Draw a circle and a sector so that the area of the sector is 16π cm^2. Give the radius of the circle and the measure of the sector's arc.

28. A method for finding the area of a segment determined by a minor arc is described in this lesson.

a. Writing Describe two ways to find the area of a segment determined by a major arc.

b. If $m\widehat{AB} = 90$ in a circle of radius 10 in., find the areas of the two segments determined by $\widehat{AB}$.

Find the area of the shaded segment to the nearest tenth.

29.

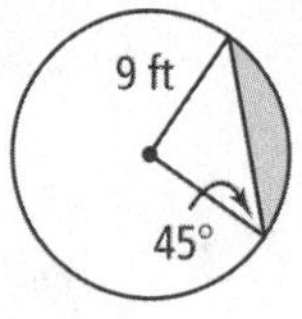

30.

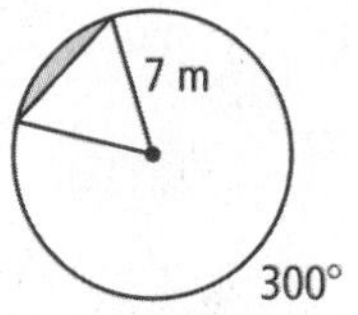

31.

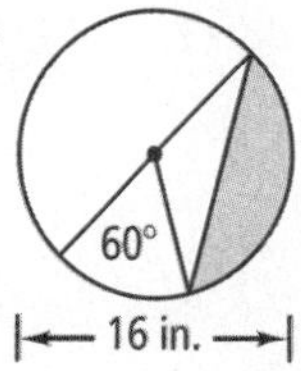

Challenge

Find the area of the shaded region. Leave your answer in terms of π.

32.

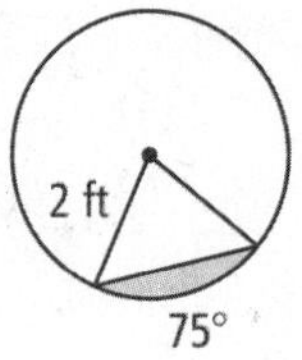

33.

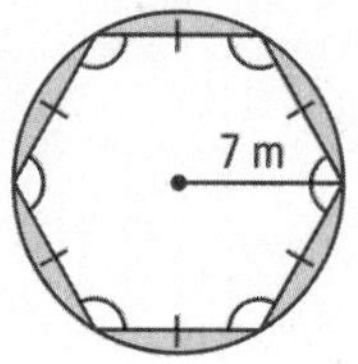

34.

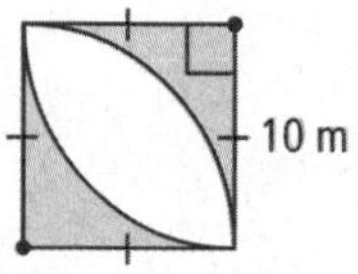

35. **Recreation** An 8 ft-by-10 ft floating dock is anchored in the middle of a pond. The bow of a canoe is tied to a corner of the dock with a 10-ft rope, as shown in the picture below.

a. Sketch a diagram of the region in which the bow of the canoe can travel.

b. What is the area of that region? Round your answer to the nearest square foot.

36. $\odot O$ at the right is inscribed in square $ABCD$ and circumscribed about square $PQRS$. Which is smaller, the blue region or the red region? Explain.

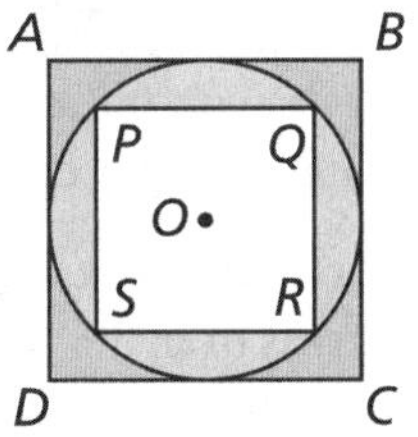

37. Circles T and U each have radius 10, and $TU = 10$. Find the area of the region that is contained inside both circles. (*Hint:* Think about where T and U must lie in a diagram of $\odot T$ and $\odot U$.)

ACTIVITY LAB

Use With Lesson 12-2

Circles and Radians

G.C.5 Derive using similarity the fact that the length of the arc intercepted by an angle is proportional to the radius . . . derive the formula for the area of a sector.

Angles can be measured in degrees or *radians*. Radians are measures based on arc length.

Activity 1

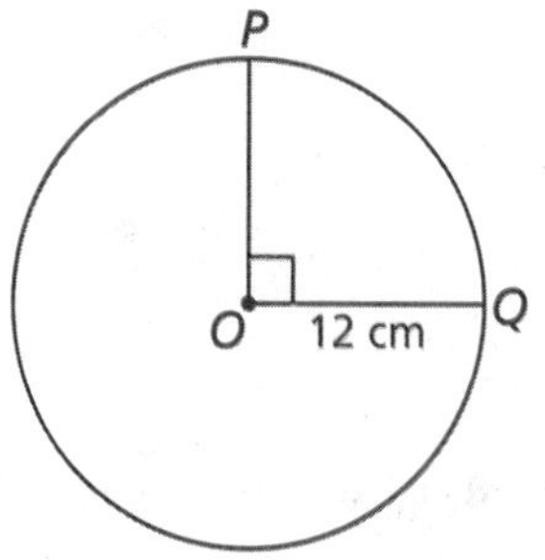

Circle O has a radius of 12 cm and $m\angle POQ = 90$.

1. Find the length of $\overset{\frown}{PQ}$. Write your answer in terms of π.

2. Find the ratio of the arc length to the radius of circle P. This is the radian measure of $\angle POQ$.

The **radian measure** of a central angle of a circle is the ratio of the arc length of the intercepted arc to the radius of the circle.

$$\text{radian measure} = \frac{\text{arc length}}{\text{radius}}$$

One radian is equal to the measure of the central angle whose intercepted arc has a length equal to the radius of the circle.

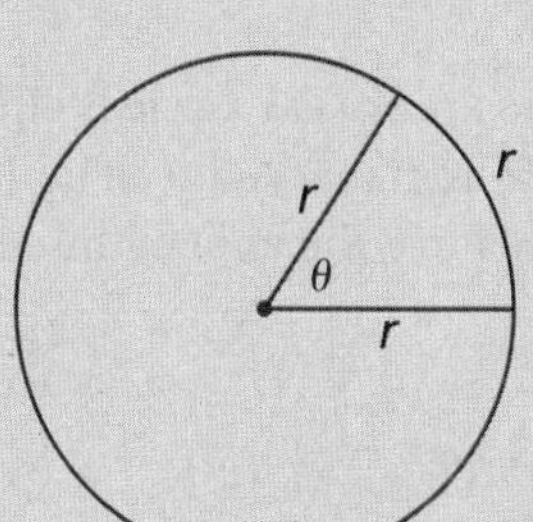

$\theta = 1$ radian

In Lesson 12-2, you learned how to find the area of the sector of a circle using proportions and the area of the circle. In Activity 2, you will derive a formula for the area of a sector when the central angle is given in radians.

Activity 2

Consider the circle below with a central angle of θ radians and radius r.

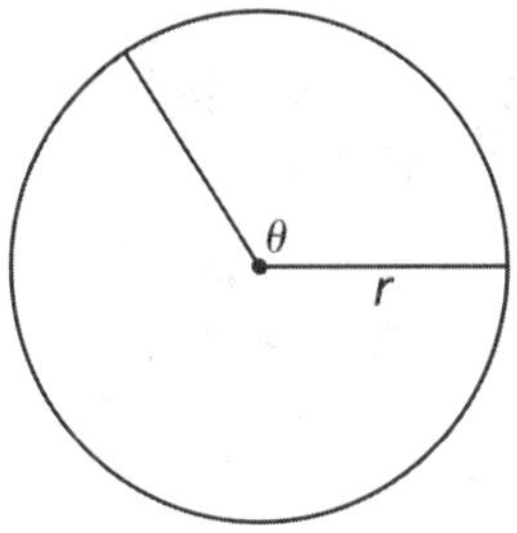

3. Write an expression for the area of the circle.

4. What is the angle measure, in radians, of a 360° central angle of the circle?

5. Write an expression for the ratio of θ to the radian measure of a 360° central angle.

6. The ratio of the area of the sector, x, to the area of the circle is equal to the ratio of the measure of the central angle θ to 2π radians. Write an equation that shows this proportional relationship. Then solve for x, the area of the sector.

Exercises

In Exercises 7–9, find the area of each sector with given radius and central angle. Round to the nearest tenth.

7. $r = 9$ in., $m\angle\theta = 0.9$ radian

8. $r = 4.5$ ft, $m\angle\theta = 1.6$ radians

9. $r = 15$ mm, $m\angle\theta = 2$ radians

10. a. How many degrees are in 2π radians?

b. How many radians are in 180 degrees?

c. Reasoning How can you convert angle measures from degrees to radians? How can you convert angle measures from radians to degrees?

12-3 Tangent Lines

G.C.2 Identify and describe relationships among inscribed angles, radii, and chords . . . the radius of a circle is perpendicular to the tangent where the radius intersects the circle. Also G.C.4

Objective To use properties of a tangent to a circle

Solve It! Write your solution to the Solve It in the space below.

In the Solve It, you drew lines that touch a circle at only one point. These lines are called tangents. This use of the word *tangent* is related to, but different from, the tangent ratio in right triangles that you studied in Chapter 11.

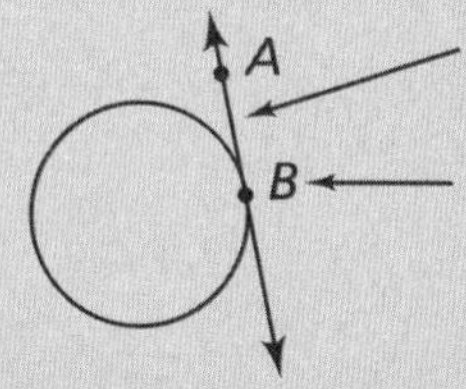

A **tangent to a circle** is a line in the plane of the circle that intersects the circle in exactly one point.

The point where a circle and a tangent intersect is the **point of tangency**.

$\overrightarrow{BA}$ is a tangent ray and $\overline{BA}$ is a tangent segment.

Essential Understanding A radius of a circle and the tangent that intersects the endpoint of the radius on the circle have a special relationship.

take note

Theorem 74

Theorem	If . . .	Then . . .
If a line is tangent to a circle, then the line is perpendicular to the radius at the point of tangency.	$\overleftrightarrow{AB}$ is tangent to $\odot O$ at P 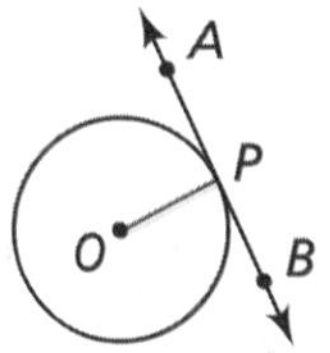	$\overleftrightarrow{AB} \perp \overline{OP}$ 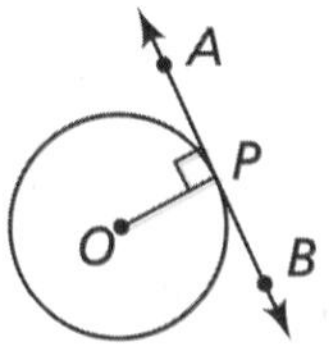

Proof **Indirect Proof of Theorem 74**

Given: n is tangent to $\odot O$ at P.
Prove: $n \perp \overline{OP}$

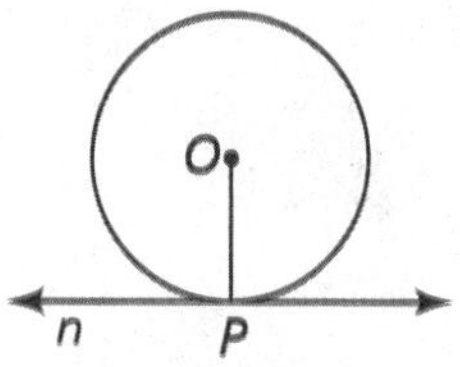

Step 1 Assume that n is not perpendicular to $\overline{OP}$.

Step 2 If line n is not perpendicular to $\overline{OP}$, then, for some other point L on n, $\overline{OL}$ must be perpendicular to n. Also there is a point K on n such that $\overline{LK} \cong \overline{LP}$ because perpendicular lines form congruent adjacent angles. $\overline{OL} = \overline{OL}$. So, $\triangle OLK \cong \triangle OLP$ by SAS.

Since corresponding parts of congruent triangles are congruent, $\overline{OK} \cong \overline{OP}$. So K and P are both on $\odot O$ by the definition of a circle. For two points on n to also be on $\odot O$ contradicts the given fact that n is tangent to $\odot O$ at P. So the assumption that n is not perpendicular to $\overline{OP}$ must be false.

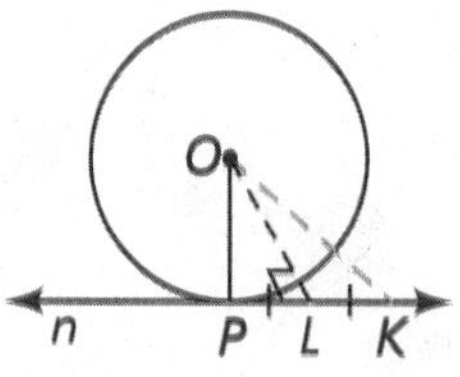

Step 3 Therefore, $n \perp \overline{OP}$ must be true.

Problem 1 Finding Angle Measures

Got It? **a.** $\overline{ED}$ is tangent to $\odot O$. What is the value of x?

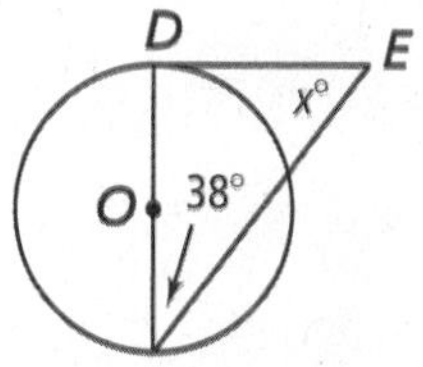

b. Reasoning Consider a quadrilateral like the one in Problem 1. Write a formula you could use to find the measure of any angle x formed by two tangents when you know the measure of the central angle c whose radii intersect the tangents.

A Practice **Algebra** **Lines that appear to be tangent are tangent. *O* is the center of each circle. What is the value of *x*?**

1. 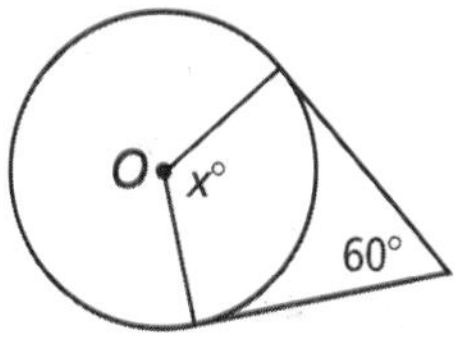

2. 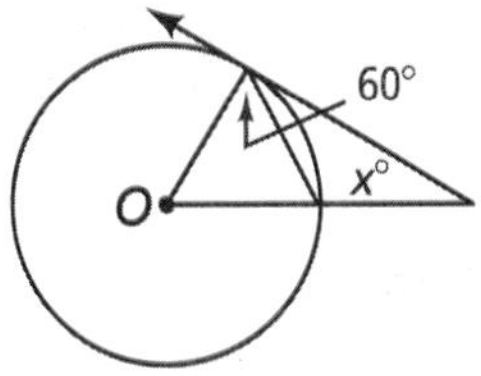

Problem 2 Finding Distance

Got It? What is the distance to the horizon that a person can see on a clear day from an airplane 2 mi above Earth? Earth's radius is about 4000 mi.

Practice **STEM** **Earth Science** **The circle at the right represents Earth. The radius of Earth is about 6400 km. Find the distance d to the horizon that a person can see on a clear day from each of the following heights h above Earth. Round your answer to the nearest tenth of a kilometer.**

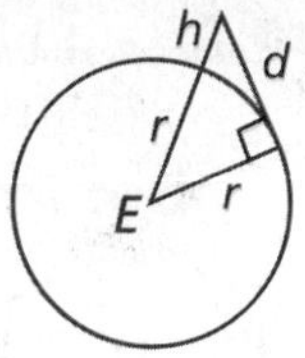

3. 1 km

4. 2500 m

Theorem 75 is the converse of Theorem 74. You can use it to prove that a line or segment is tangent to a circle. You can also use it to construct a tangent to a circle.

take note

Theorem 75

Theorem	If . . .	Then . . .
If a line in the plane of a circle is perpendicular to a radius at its endpoint on the circle, then the line is tangent to the circle.	$\overleftrightarrow{AB} \perp \overline{OP}$ at P 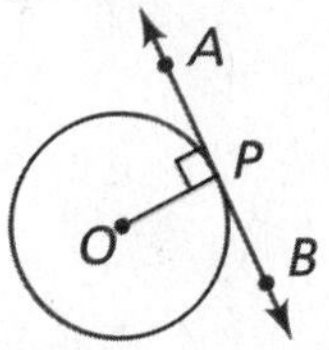	$\overleftrightarrow{AB}$ is tangent to $\odot O$

You will prove Theorem 75 in Exercise 26.

Problem 3 Finding a Radius

Got It? What is the radius of $\odot O$?

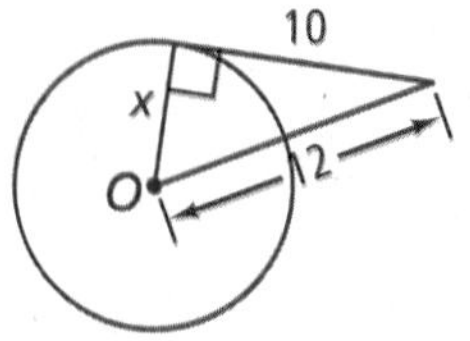

Think
Why does the value *x* appear on each side of the equation?

A Practice **Algebra** In each circle, what is the value of x, to the nearest tenth?

5.

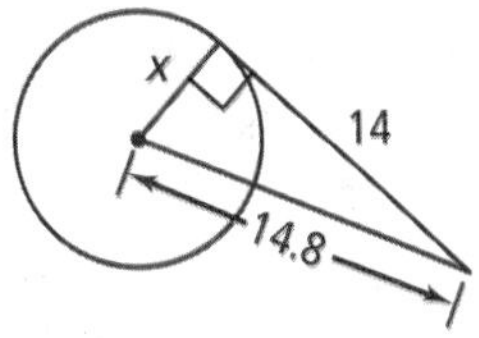

6.

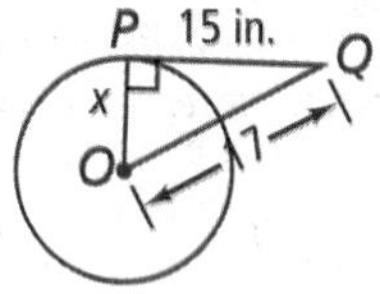

Problem 4 Identifying a Tangent

Got It? Is $\overline{ML}$ tangent to $\odot N$ at L? Explain.

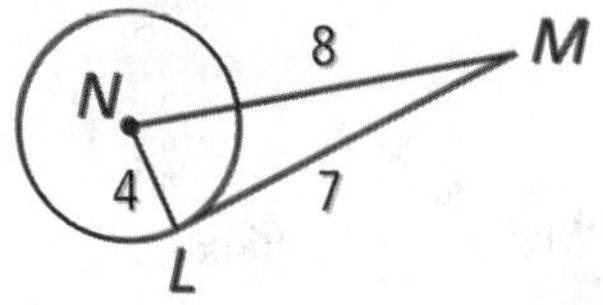

A Practice **Determine whether a tangent is shown in each diagram. Explain.**

7.

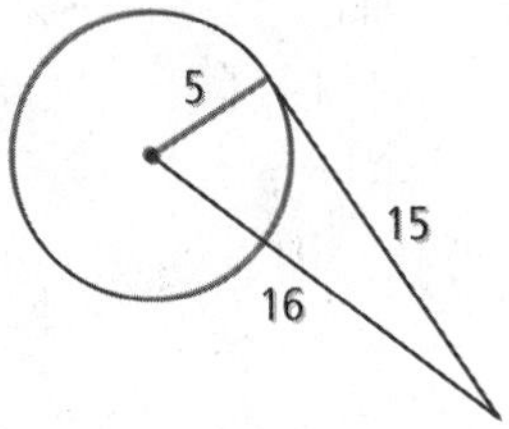

8.

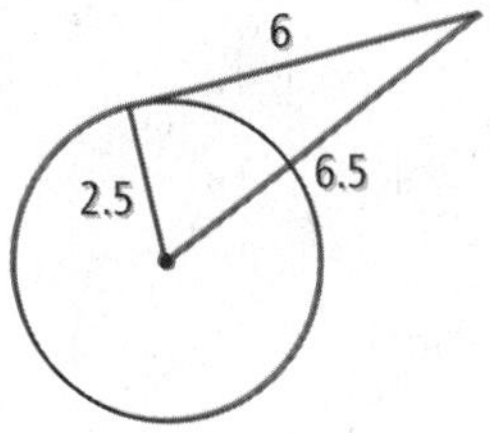

In the Solve It, you made a conjecture about the lengths of two tangents from a common endpoint outside a circle. Your conjecture may be confirmed by the following theorem.

take note

Theorem 76

Theorem	If . . .	Then . . .
If two tangent segments to a circle share a common endpoint outside the circle, then the two segments are congruent.	$\overline{BA}$ and $\overline{BC}$ are tangent to $\odot O$ 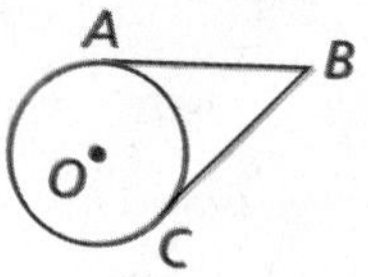	$\overline{BA} \cong \overline{BC}$

You will prove Theorem 76 in Exercise 19.

In the figure at the right, the sides of the triangle are tangent to the circle. The circle is *inscribed* in the triangle. The triangle is *circumscribed about* the circle.

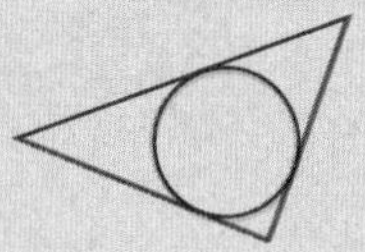

Problem 5 Circles Inscribed in Polygons

Got It? $\odot O$ is inscribed in $\triangle PQR$, which has a perimeter of 88 cm. What is the length of $\overline{QY}$?

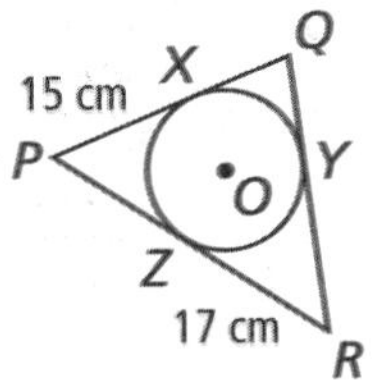

Plan

How does knowing the pairs of congruent segments help?

Practice Each polygon circumscribes a circle. What is the perimeter of each polygon?

9.

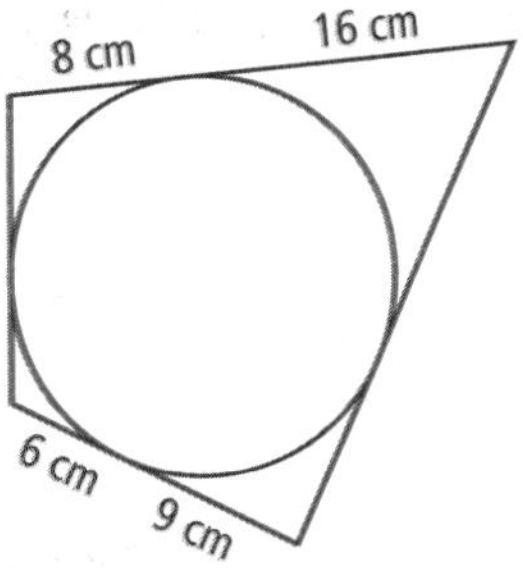

10.

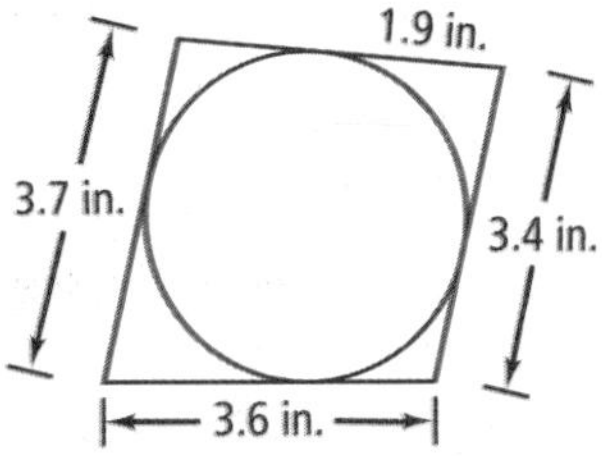

Lesson Check

Do you know HOW?

Use the figure at the right for Exercises 11–13.

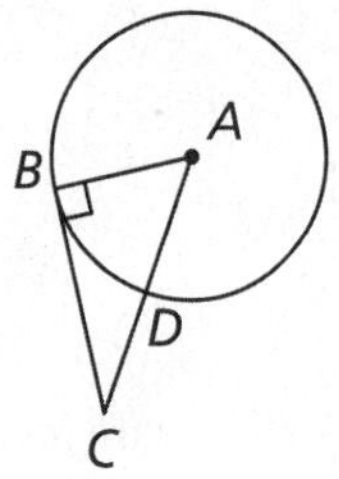

11. If $m\angle A = 58$, what is $m\angle ACB$?

12. If $AC = 10$ and $BC = 8$, what is the radius?

13. If $AC = 12$ and $BC = 9$, what is the radius?

Do you UNDERSTAND?

MATHEMATICAL PRACTICES

14. Vocabulary How are the phrases *tangent ratio* and *tangent of a circle* used differently?

15. Error Analysis A classmate insists that $\overline{DF}$ is a tangent to $\odot E$. Explain how to show that your classmate is wrong.

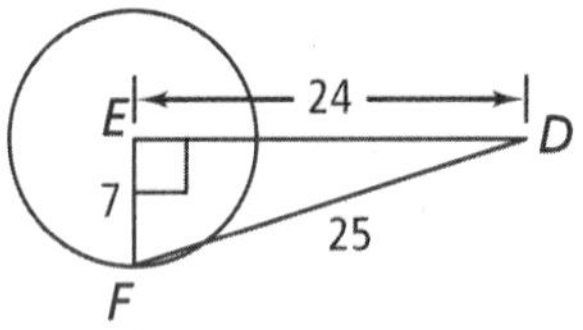

More Practice and Problem-Solving Exercises

MATHEMATICAL PRACTICES

B Apply

STEM **16. Solar Eclipse** Common tangents to two circles may be *internal* or *external.* If you draw a segment joining the centers of the circles, a common internal tangent will intersect the segment. A common external tangent will not. For this cross-sectional diagram of the sun, moon, and Earth during a solar eclipse, use the terms above to describe the types of tangents of each color.

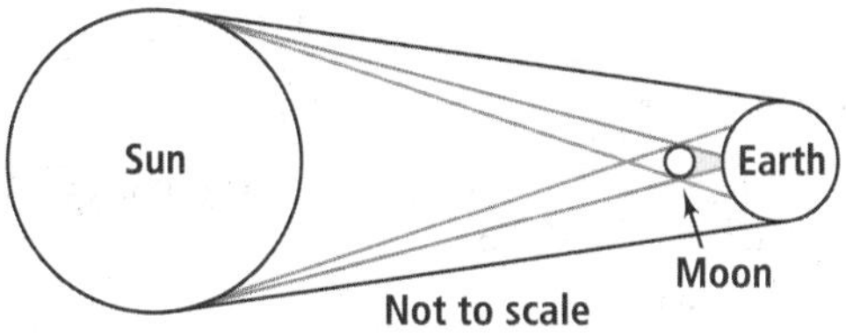

a. red **b.** blue **c.** orange

d. Which tangents show the extent on Earth's surface of total eclipse? Of partial eclipse?

17. Reasoning A nickel, a dime, and a quarter are touching as shown. Tangents are drawn from point A to both sides of each coin. What can you conclude about the four tangent segments? Explain.

18. Think About a Plan Leonardo da Vinci wrote, "When each of two squares touch the same circle at four points, one is double the other." Explain why the statement is true.

- How will drawing a sketch help?
- Are both squares inside the circle?

Proof 19. Prove Theorem 76.

Given: $\overline{BA}$ and $\overline{BC}$ are tangent to $\odot O$ at A and C, respectively.

Prove: $\overline{BA} \cong \overline{BC}$

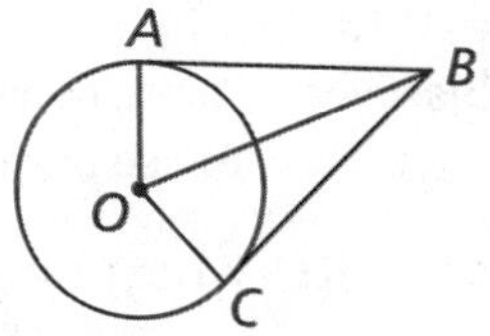

Proof 20. Given: $\overline{BC}$ is tangent to $\odot A$ at D.

$\overline{DB} \cong \overline{DC}$

Prove: $\overline{AB} \cong \overline{AC}$

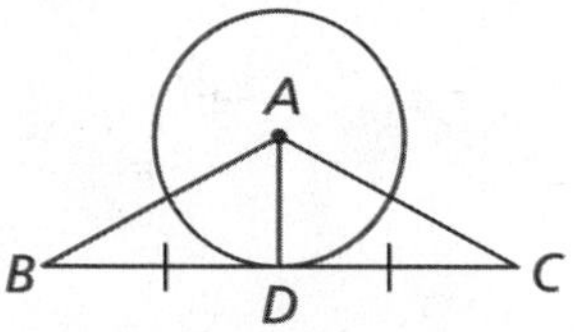

Proof 21. Given: $\odot A$ and $\odot B$ with common tangents $\overline{DF}$ and $\overline{CE}$

Prove: $\triangle GDC \sim \triangle GFE$

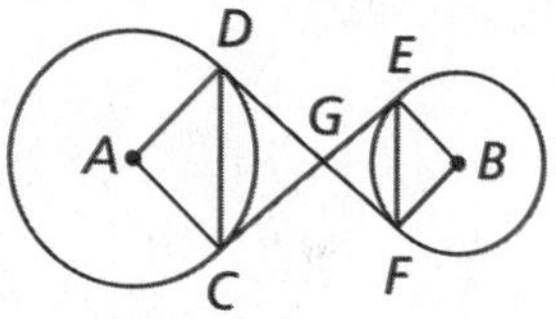

22. a. A belt fits snugly around the two circular pulleys. $\overline{CE}$ is an auxiliary line from E to $\overline{BD}$, and $\overline{CE} \parallel \overline{BA}$. What type of quadrilateral is $ABCE$? Explain.

b. What is the length of $\overline{CE}$?

c. What is the distance between the centers of the pulleys to the nearest tenth?

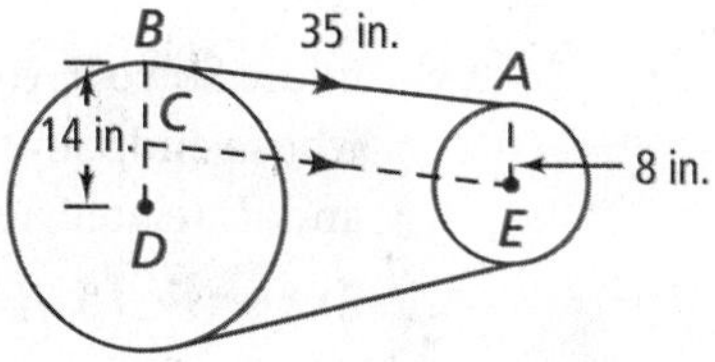

23. $\overline{BD}$ and $\overline{CK}$ at the right are diameters of $\odot A$. $\overline{BP}$ and $\overline{QP}$ are tangents to $\odot A$. What is $m\angle CDA$?

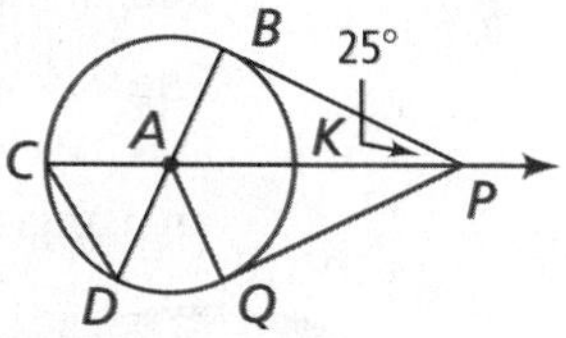

24. Constructions Draw a circle. Label the center T. Locate a point on the circle and label it R. Construct a tangent to $\odot T$ at R.

25. Coordinate Geometry Graph the equation $x^2 + y^2 = 9$. Then draw a segment from (0, 5) tangent to the circle. Find the length of the segment.

Challenge

Proof 26. Write an indirect proof of Theorem 75.

Given: $\overleftrightarrow{AB} \perp \overline{OP}$ at P.

Prove: $\overleftrightarrow{AB}$ is tangent to $\odot O$.

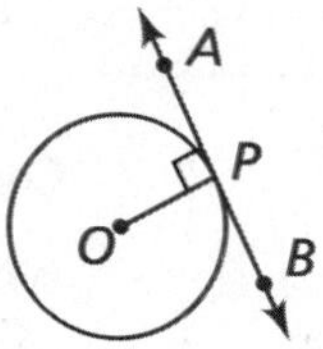

27. Two circles that have one point in common are *tangent circles*. Given any triangle, explain how to draw three circles that are centered at each vertex of the triangle and are tangent to each other.

12-4 Chords and Arcs

G.C.2 Identify and describe relationships among inscribed angles, radii, and chords . . .

Objectives To use congruent chords, arcs, and central angles
To use perpendicular bisectors to chords

Solve It! Write your solution to the Solve It in the space below.

In the Solve It, you found the length of a **chord**, which is a segment whose endpoints are on a circle. The diagram shows the chord $\overline{PQ}$ and its related arc, $\widehat{PQ}$.

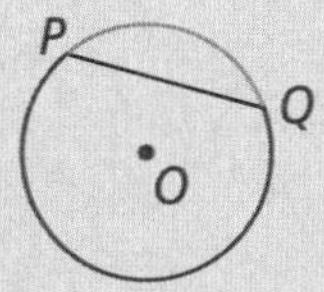

Essential Understanding You can use information about congruent parts of a circle (or congruent circles) to find information about other parts of the circle (or circles).

The following theorems and their converses confirm that if you know that chords, arcs, or central angles in a circle are congruent, then you know the other two parts are congruent.

take note

Theorem 77 and Its Converse

Theorem

Within a circle or in congruent circles, congruent central angles have congruent arcs.

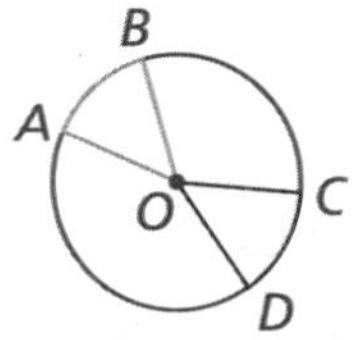

Converse

Within a circle or in congruent circles, congruent arcs have congruent central angles.

If $\angle AOB \cong \angle COD$, then $\widehat{AB} \cong \widehat{CD}$.
If $\widehat{AB} \cong \widehat{CD}$, then $\angle AOB \cong \angle COD$.

You will prove Theorem 77 and its converse in Exercises 17 and 33.

take note

Theorem 78 and Its Converse

Theorem

Within a circle or in congruent circles, congruent central angles have congruent chords.

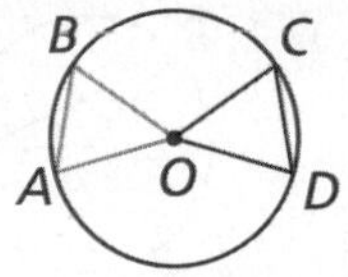

Converse

Within a circle or in congruent circles, congruent chords have congruent central angles.

If $\angle AOB \cong \angle COD$, then $\overline{AB} \cong \overline{CD}$.
If $\overline{AB} \cong \overline{CD}$, then $\angle AOB \cong \angle COD$.

You will prove Theorem 78 and its converse in Exercises 18 and 34.

Theorem 79 and Its Converse

Theorem

Within a circle or in congruent circles, congruent chords have congruent arcs.

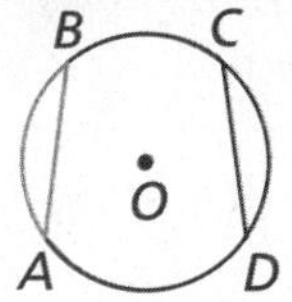

Converse

Within a circle or in congruent circles, congruent arcs have congruent chords.

If $\overline{AB} \cong \overline{CD}$, then $\overset{\frown}{AB} \cong \overset{\frown}{CD}$.
If $\overset{\frown}{AB} \cong \overset{\frown}{CD}$, then $\overline{AB} \cong \overline{CD}$.

You will prove Theorem 79 and its converse in Exercises 19 and 35.

ONLINE PROBLEMS

Problem 1 Using Congruent Chords

Got It? **Reasoning** Use the diagram in Problem 1, shown below. Suppose you are given $\odot O \cong \odot P$ and $\angle OBC \cong \angle PDF$. How can you show $\angle O \cong \angle P$? From this, what else can you conclude?

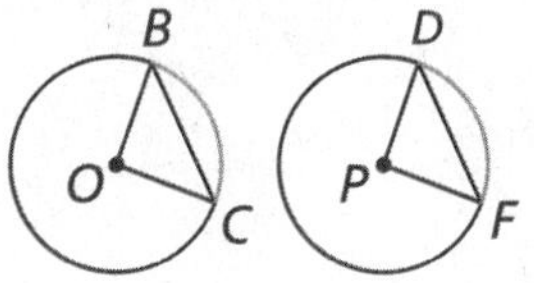

Think

Why is it important that the circles are congruent?

Practice In Exercises 1 and 2, the circles are congruent. What can you conclude?

1. 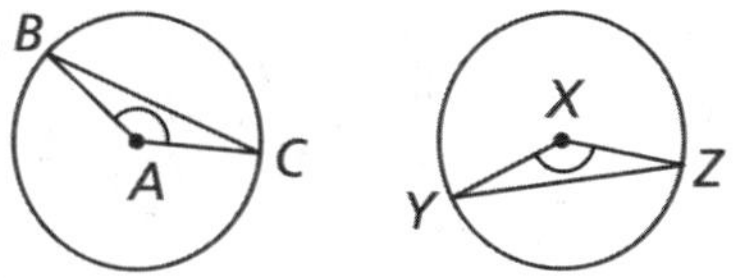

2. 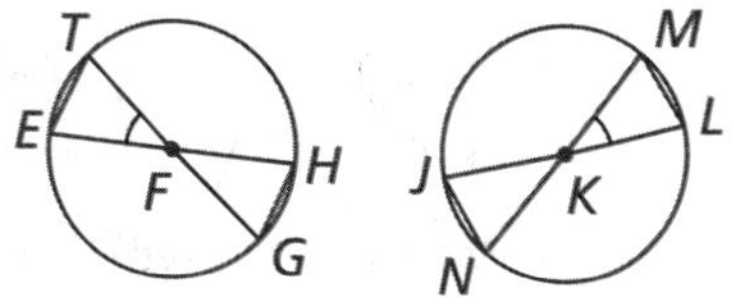

take note

Theorem 80 and Its Converse

Theorem

Within a circle or in congruent circles, chords equidistant from the center or centers are congruent.

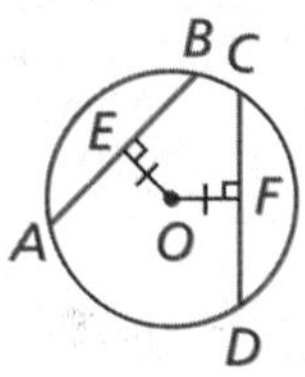

Converse

Within a circle or in congruent circles, congruent chords are equidistant from the center (or centers).

If $OE = OF$, then $\overline{AB} \cong \overline{CD}$.
If $\overline{AB} \cong \overline{CD}$, then $OE = OF$.

You will prove the converse of Theorem 80 in Exercise 36.

Proof **Proof of Theorem 80**

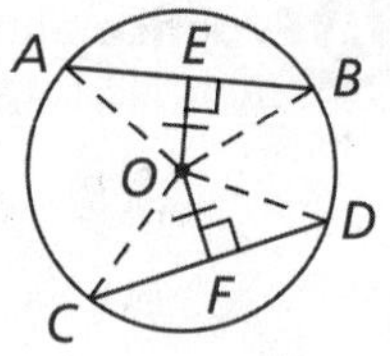

Given: $\odot O$, $\overline{OE} \cong \overline{OF}$, $\overline{OE} \perp \overline{AB}$, $\overline{OF} \perp \overline{CD}$

Prove: $\overline{AB} \cong \overline{CD}$

Statements	Reasons
1) $\overline{OA} \cong \overline{OB} \cong \overline{OC} \cong \overline{OD}$	**1)** Radii of a circle are congruent.
2) $\overline{OE} \cong \overline{OF}$, $\overline{OE} \perp \overline{AB}$, $\overline{OF} \perp \overline{CD}$	**2)** Given
3) $\angle AEO$ and $\angle CFO$ are right angles.	**3)** Def. of perpendicular segments
4) $\triangle AEO \cong \triangle CFO$	**4)** HL Theorem
5) $\angle A \cong \angle C$	**5)** Corres. parts of $\cong$ ⚠ are $\cong$.
6) $\angle B \cong \angle A$, $\angle C \cong \angle D$	**6)** Isosceles Triangle Theorem
7) $\angle B \cong \angle D$	**7)** Transitive Property of Congruence
8) $\angle AOB \cong \angle COD$	**8)** If two ∠s of a $\triangle$ are $\cong$ to two ∠s of another $\triangle$, then the third ∠s are $\cong$.
9) $\overline{AB} \cong \overline{CD}$	**9)** $\cong$ central angles have $\cong$ chords.

ONLINE PROBLEMS

Problem 2 Finding the Length of a Chord

Got It? What is the value of x? Justify your answer.

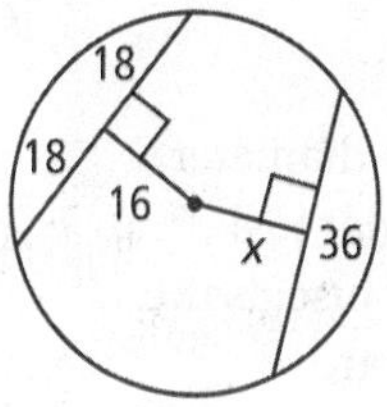

Plan

What information can you gather from the chords?

A Practice Find the value of x.

3.

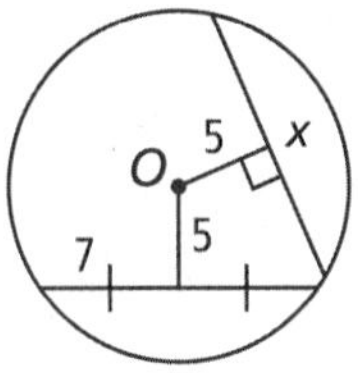

4.

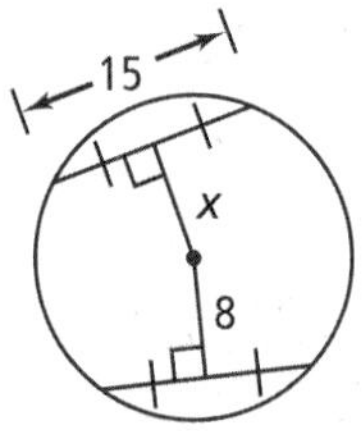

The Converse of the Perpendicular Bisector Theorem from Lesson 8-2 has special applications to a circle and its diameters, chords, and arcs.

take note

Theorem 81

Theorem	If . . .	Then . . .
In a circle, if a diameter is perpendicular to a chord, then it bisects the chord and its arc.	$\overline{AB}$ is a diameter and $\overline{AB} \perp \overline{CD}$ 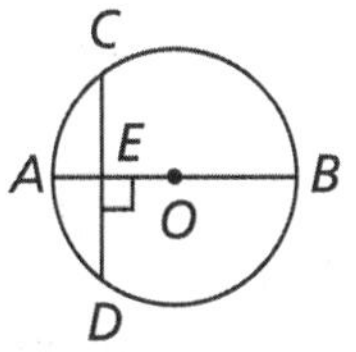	$\overline{CE} \cong \overline{ED}$ and $\overset{\frown}{CA} \cong \overset{\frown}{AD}$ 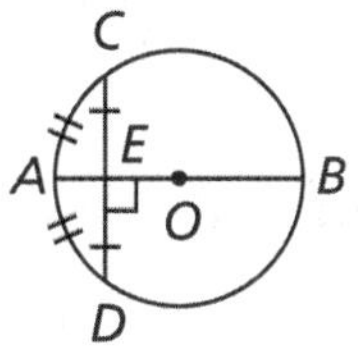

You will prove Theorem 81 in Exercise 20.

Theorem 82

Theorem	If . . .	Then . . .
In a circle, if a diameter bisects a chord (that is not a diameter), then it is perpendicular to the chord.	$\overline{AB}$ is a diameter and $\overline{CE} \cong \overline{ED}$ 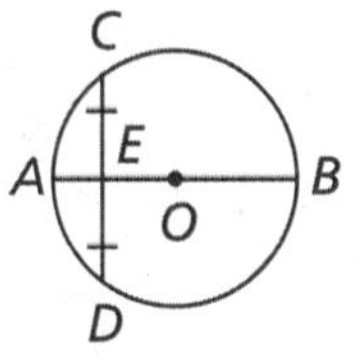	$\overline{AB} \perp \overline{CD}$ 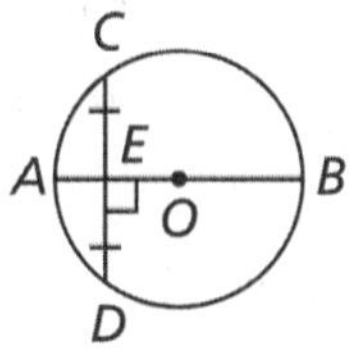

take note

Theorem 83

Theorem	If . . .	Then . . .
In a circle, the perpendicular bisector of a chord contains the center of the circle.	$\overline{AB}$ is the perpendicular bisector of chord $\overline{CD}$ 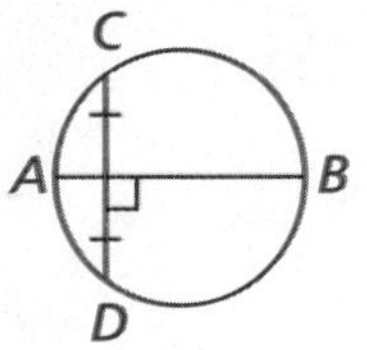	$\overline{AB}$ contains the center of $\odot O$ 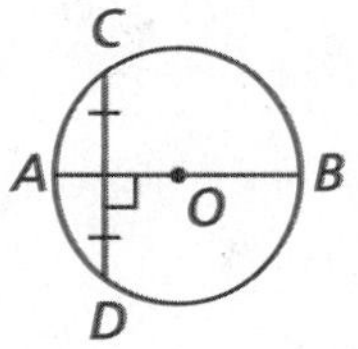

You will prove Theorem 83 in Exercise 31.

Proof **Proof of Theorem 82**

Given: $\odot O$ with diameter $\overline{AB}$ bisecting $\overline{CD}$ at E
Prove: $\overline{AB} \perp \overline{CD}$

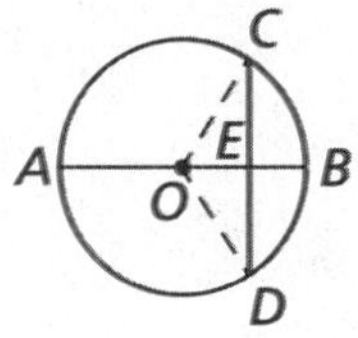

Proof: $OC = OD$ because the radii of a circle are congruent. $CE = ED$ by the definition of *bisect*. Thus, O and E are both equidistant from C and D. By the Converse of the Perpendicular Bisector Theorem, both O and E are on the perpendicular bisector of $\overline{CD}$. Two points determine one line or segment, so $\overline{OE}$ is the perpendicular bisector of $\overline{CD}$. Since $\overline{OE}$ is part of $\overline{AB}$, $\overline{AB} \perp \overline{CD}$.

ONLINE PROBLEMS

Problem 3 Using Diameters and Chords

Got It? Trace a coin. What is its radius?

A Practice 5. In the diagram at the right, $\overline{GH}$ and $\overline{KM}$ are perpendicular bisectors of the chords they intersect. What can you conclude about the center of the circle? Justify your answer.

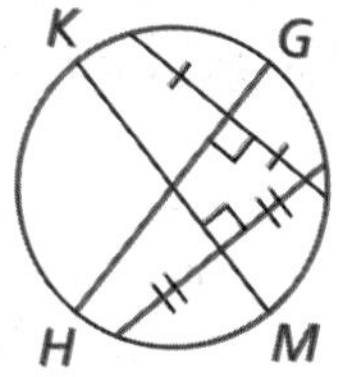

6. In $\odot O$, $\overline{AB}$ is a diameter of the circle and $\overline{AB} \perp \overline{CD}$. What conclusions can you make?

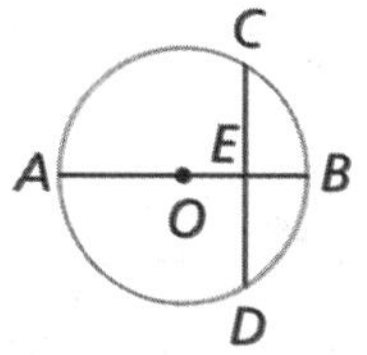

Problem 4 Finding Measures in a Circle

Got It? Reasoning In part (B) of Problem 4, how does the auxiliary $\overline{BA}$ make it simpler to solve for y?

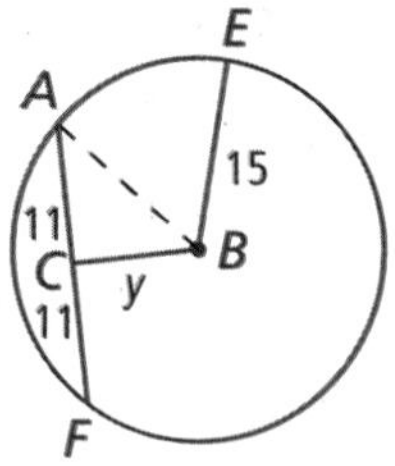

Practice **Algebra** Find the value of x to the nearest tenth.

7.

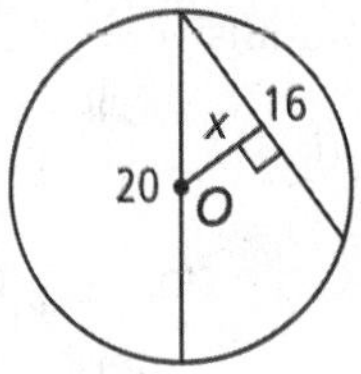

8.

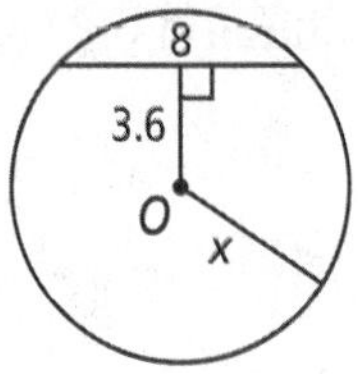

Lesson Check

Do you know HOW?

In $\odot O$, $m\overparen{CD} = 50$ and $\overline{CA} \cong \overline{BD}$.

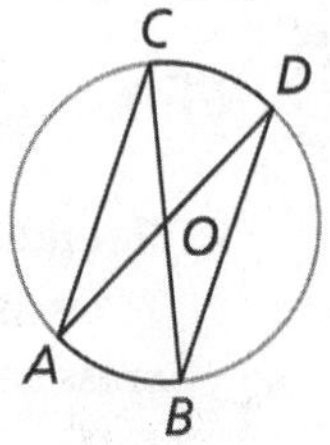

9. What is $m\overparen{AB}$? How do you know?

10. What is true of $\overparen{CA}$ and $\overparen{BD}$? Why?

11. Since $CA = BD$, what do you know about the distance of $\overline{CA}$ and $\overline{BD}$ from the center of $\odot O$?

Do you UNDERSTAND?

MATHEMATICAL PRACTICES

12. Vocabulary Is a radius a chord? Is a diameter a chord? Explain your answers.

13. Error Analysis What is the error in the diagram?

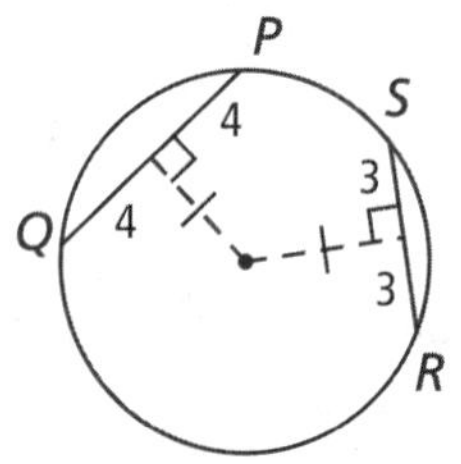

More Practice and Problem-Solving Exercises

MATHEMATICAL PRACTICES

B Apply

14. Geometry in 3 Dimensions In the figure at the right, sphere O with radius 13 cm is intersected by a plane 5 cm from center O. Find the radius of the cross section $\odot A$.

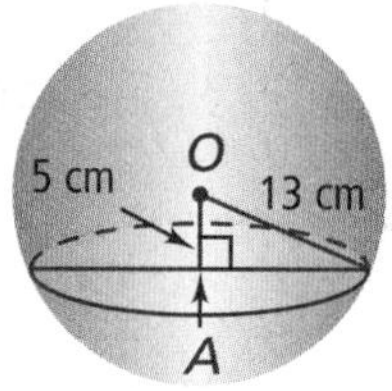

15. Geometry in 3 Dimensions A plane intersects a sphere that has radius 10 in., forming the cross section $\odot B$ with radius 8 in. How far is the plane from the center of the sphere?

16. Think About a Plan Two concentric circles have radii of 4 cm and 8 cm. A segment tangent to the smaller circle is a chord of the larger circle. What is the length of the segment to the nearest tenth?

- How will you start the diagram?
- Where is the best place to position the radius of each circle?

Proof **17.** Prove Theorem 77.

Given: $\odot O$ with $\angle AOB \cong \angle COD$
Prove: $\overset{\frown}{AB} \cong \overset{\frown}{CD}$

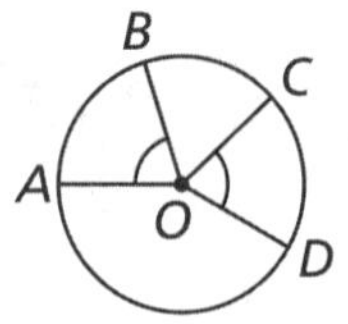

Proof **18.** Prove Theorem 78.

Given: $\odot O$ with $\angle AOB \cong \angle COD$
Prove: $\overline{AB} \cong \overline{CD}$

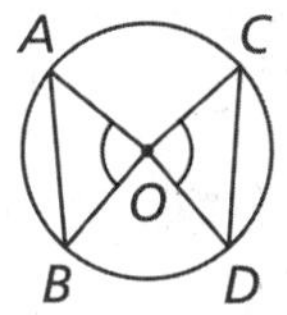

Proof **19.** Prove Theorem 79.

Given: $\odot O$ with $\overline{AB} \cong \overline{CD}$
Prove: $\overset{\frown}{AB} \cong \overset{\frown}{CD}$

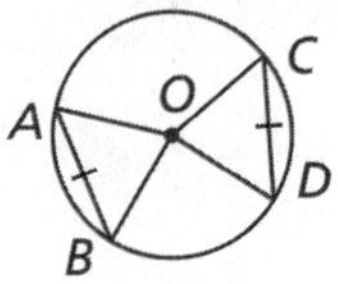

Proof **20.** Prove Theorem 81.

Given: $\odot O$ with diameter $\overline{ED} \perp \overline{AB}$ at C
Prove: $\overline{AC} \cong \overline{BC}$, $\overset{\frown}{AD} \cong \overset{\frown}{BD}$

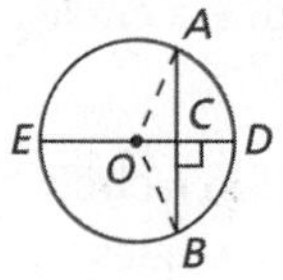

$\odot A$ and $\odot B$ are congruent. $\overline{CD}$ is a chord of both circles.

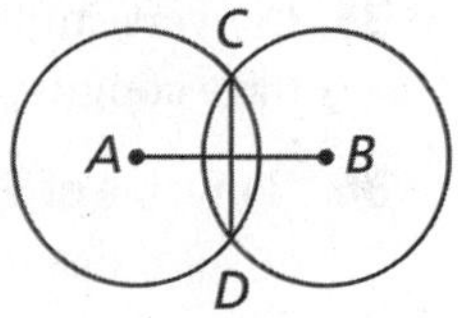

21. If $AB = 8$ in. and $CD = 6$ in., how long is a radius?

22. If $AB = 24$ cm and a radius $= 13$ cm, how long is $\overline{CD}$?

23. If a radius $= 13$ ft and $CD = 24$ ft, how long is $\overline{AB}$?

24. Construction Use Theorem 78 to construct a regular octagon.

25. In the diagram at the right, the endpoints of the chord are the points where the line $x = 2$ intersects the circle $x^2 + y^2 = 25$. What is the length of the chord? Round your answer to the nearest tenth.

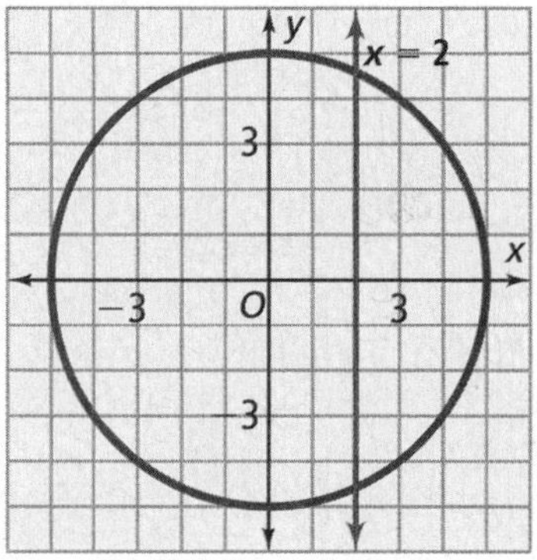

26. Construction Use a circular object such as a can or a saucer to draw a circle. Construct the center of the circle.

27. Writing Theorems 77 and 78 both begin with the phrase "within a circle or in congruent circles." Explain why the word *congruent* is essential for both theorems.

Find $m\overset{\frown}{AB}$. (*Hint:* You will need to use trigonometry in Exercise 30.)

28.

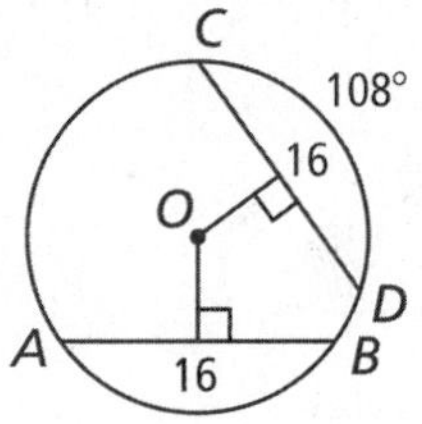

29.

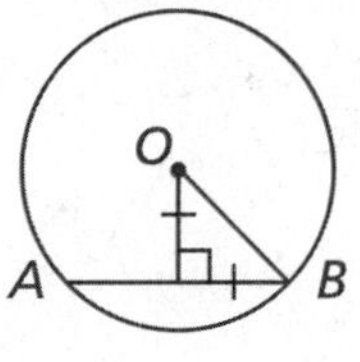

30.

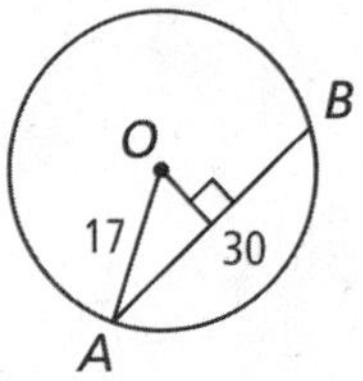

Proof **31.** Prove Theorem 83.

Given: ℓ is the $\perp$ bisector of $\overline{WY}$.
Prove: ℓ contains the center of $\odot X$.

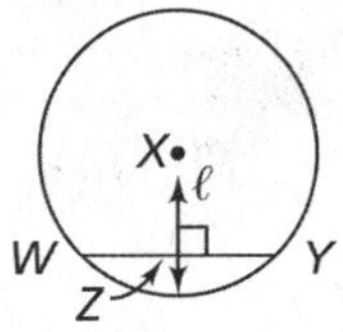

Proof **32. Given:** $\odot A$ with $\overline{CE} \perp \overline{BD}$
Prove: $\overset{\frown}{BC} \cong \overset{\frown}{DC}$

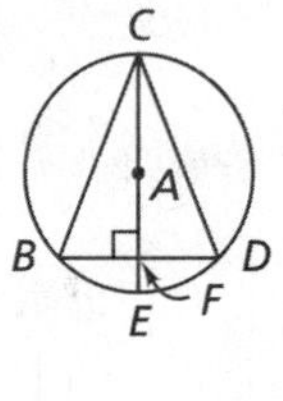

Challenge

Proof **Prove each of the following.**

33. Converse of Theorem 77: Within a circle or in congruent circles, congruent arcs have congruent central angles.

34. Converse of Theorem 78: Within a circle or in congruent circles, congruent chords have congruent central angles.

35. Converse of Theorem 79: Within a circle or in congruent circles, congruent arcs have congruent chords.

36. Converse of Theorem 80: Within a circle or congruent circles, congruent chords are equidistant from the center (or centers).

Proof **37.** If two circles are concentric and a chord of the larger circle is tangent to the smaller circle, prove that the point of tangency is the midpoint of the chord.

12-5 Inscribed Angles

G.C.2 Identify and describe relationships among inscribed angles, radii, and chords . . . Also G.C.3, G.C.4

Objectives To find the measure of an inscribed angle
To find the measure of an angle formed by a tangent and a chord

Solve It! Write your solution to the Solve It in the space below.

An angle whose vertex is on the circle and whose sides are chords of the circle is an **inscribed angle**. An arc with endpoints on the sides of an inscribed angle, and its other points in the interior of the angle, is an **intercepted arc**. In the diagram, inscribed $\angle C$ intercepts $\widehat{AB}$.

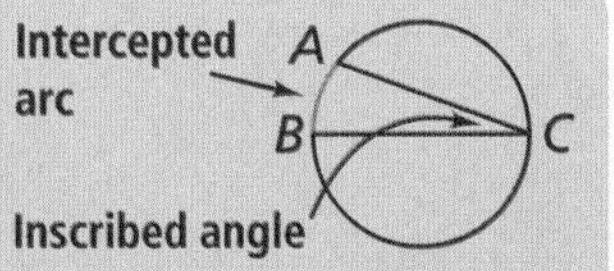

Essential Understanding Angles formed by intersecting lines have a special relationship to the arcs the intersecting lines intercept. In this lesson, you will study arcs formed by inscribed angles.

take note

Theorem 84 Inscribed Angle Theorem

The measure of an inscribed angle is half the measure of its intercepted arc.

$$m\angle B = \frac{1}{2} m\widehat{AC}$$

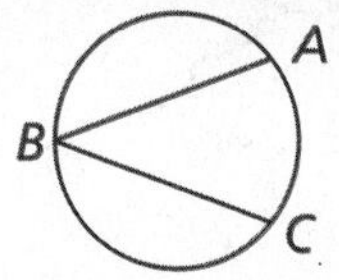

To prove Theorem 84, there are three cases to consider.

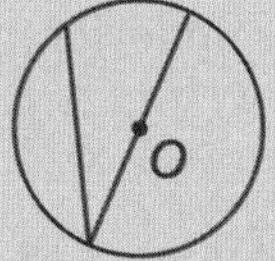

I: The center is on a side of the angle.

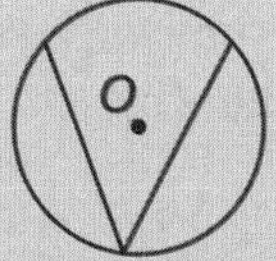

II: The center is inside the angle.

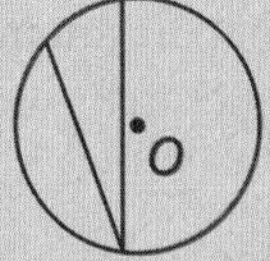

III: The center is outside the angle.

The following is a proof of Case I. You will prove Case II and Case III in Exercises 19 and 20.

Proof Proof of Theorem 84, Case I

Given: $\odot O$ with inscribed $\angle B$ and diameter $\overline{BC}$

Prove: $m\angle B = \frac{1}{2}m\widehat{AC}$

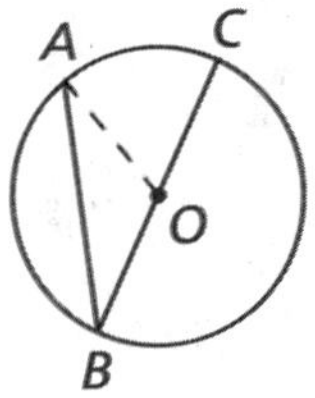

Draw radius $\overline{OA}$ to form isosceles $\triangle AOB$ with $OA = OB$ and, hence, $m\angle A = m\angle B$ (Isosceles Triangle Theorem).

$m\angle AOC = m\angle A + m\angle B$	Triangle Exterior Angle Theorem
$m\widehat{AC} = m\angle AOC$	Definition of measure of an arc
$m\widehat{AC} = m\angle A + m\angle B$	Substitute.
$m\widehat{AC} = 2m\angle B$	Substitute and simplify.
$\frac{1}{2}m\widehat{AC} = m\angle B$	Divide each side by 2.

ONLINE PROBLEMS

Problem 1 Using the Inscribed Angle Theorem

Got It? **a.** In $\odot O$, what is $m\angle A$?

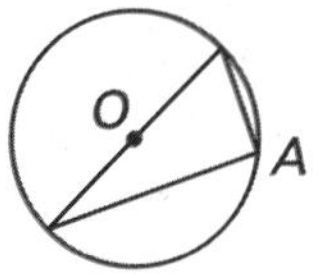

Plan

What is the intercepted arc of each angle?

b. What are $m\angle A$, $m\angle B$, $m\angle C$, and $m\angle D$?

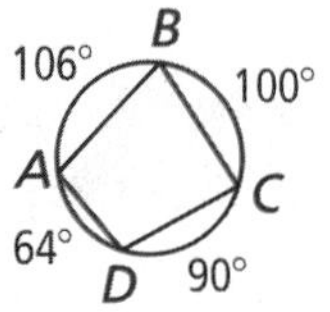

c. What do you notice about the sums of the measures of the opposite angles in the quadrilateral in part (b)?

Practice **Find the value of each variable. For each circle, the dot represents the center.**

1.

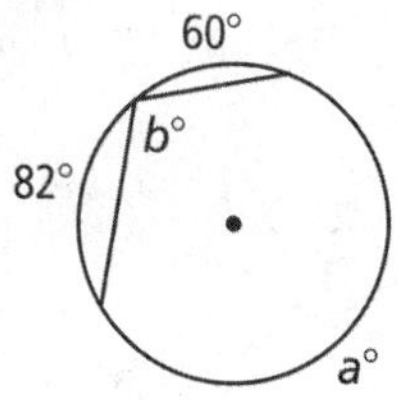

2.

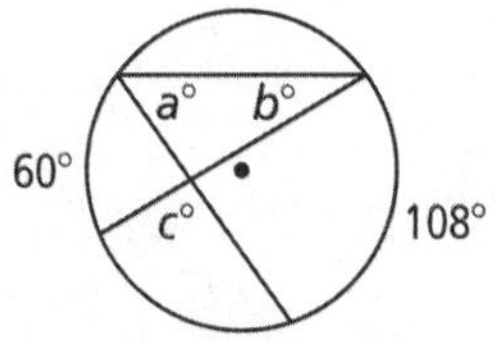

You will use three corollaries to the Inscribed Angle Theorem to find measures of angles in circles. The first corollary may confirm an observation you made in the Solve It.

take note

Corollaries to Theorem 84 The Inscribed Angle Theorem

Corollary 1

Two inscribed angles that intercept the same arc are congruent.

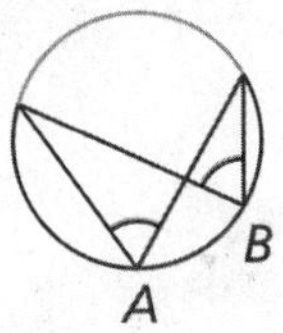

Corollary 2

An angle inscribed in a semicircle is a right angle.

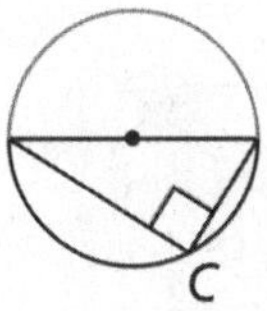

Corollary 3

The opposite angles of a quadrilateral inscribed in a circle are supplementary.

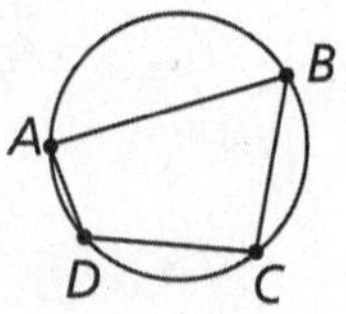

You will prove these corollaries in Exercises 24–26.

Problem 2 Using Corollaries to Find Angle Measures

Got It? In the diagram at the right, what is the measure of each numbered angle?

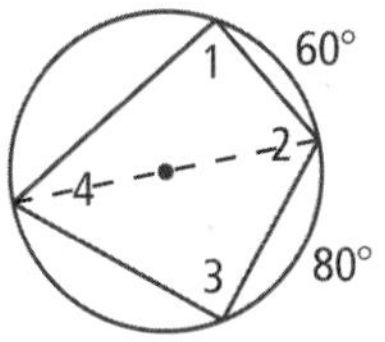

Think

What does the auxiliary line represent in the diagram?

Practice **Find the value of each variable. For each circle, the dot represents the center.**

3.

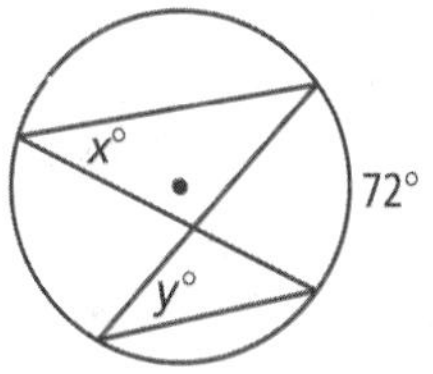

4.

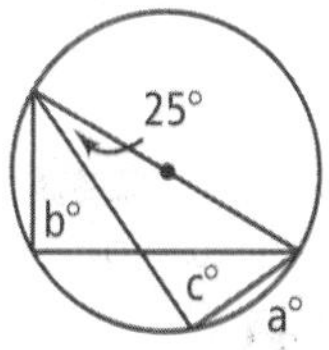

The following diagram shows point *A* moving along the circle until a tangent is formed. From the Inscribed Angle Theorem, you know that in the first three diagrams $m\angle A$ is $\frac{1}{2}m\,\widehat{BC}$. As the last diagram suggests, this is also true when *A* and *C* coincide.

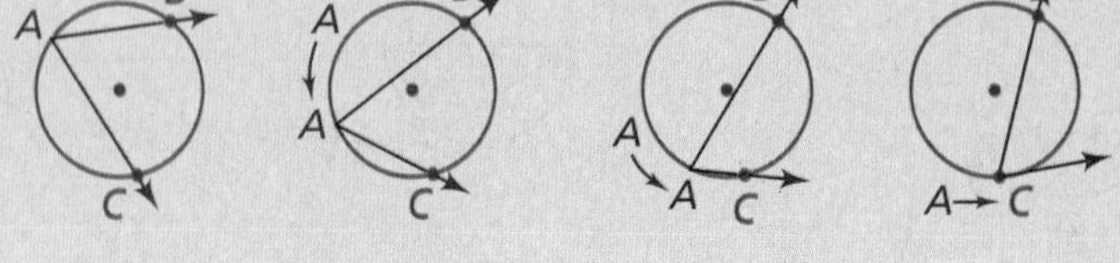

take note

Theorem 85

The measure of an angle formed by a tangent and a chord is half the measure of the intercepted arc.

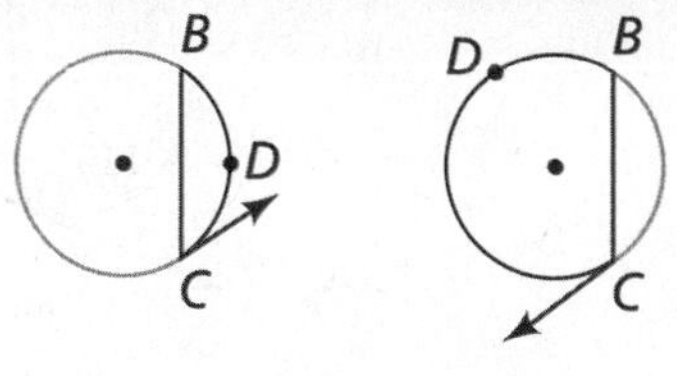

$m\angle C = \frac{1}{2} m\widehat{BDC}$

You will prove Theorem 85 in Exercise 27.

Problem 3 Using Arc Measure

Got It? **a.** In the diagram at the right, $\overline{KJ}$ is tangent to $\odot O$. What are the values of x and y?

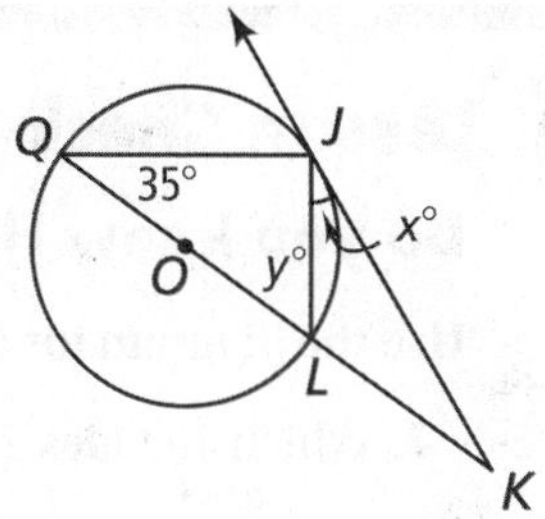

b. Reasoning In part (a), an inscribed angle ($\angle Q$) and an angle formed by a tangent and chord ($\angle KJL$) intercept the same arc. What is always true of these angles? Explain.

Practice **In Exercises 5 and 6, find the value of each variable. Lines that appear to be tangent are tangent.**

5.

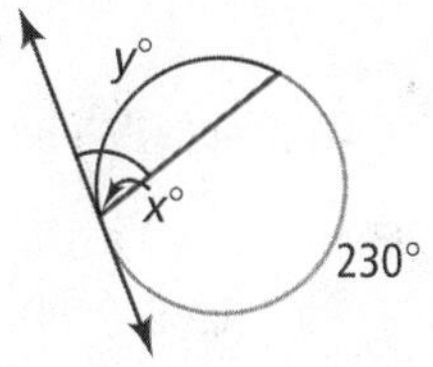

6.

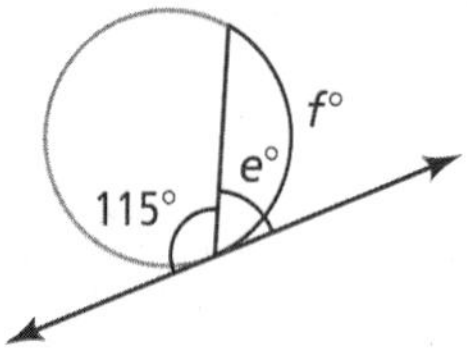

Lesson Check

Do you know HOW?

Use the diagram for Exercises 7–9.

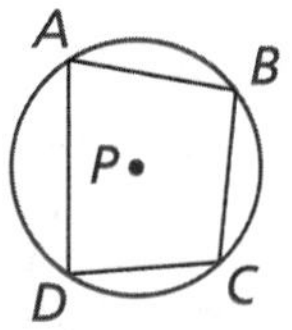

7. Which arc does $\angle A$ intercept?

8. Which angle intercepts $\overset{\frown}{ABC}$?

9. Which angles of quadrilateral *ABCD* are supplementary?

Do you UNDERSTAND?

MATHEMATICAL PRACTICES

10. Vocabulary What is the relationship between an inscribed angle and its intercepted arc?

11. Error Analysis A classmate says that $m\angle A = 90$. What is your classmate's error?

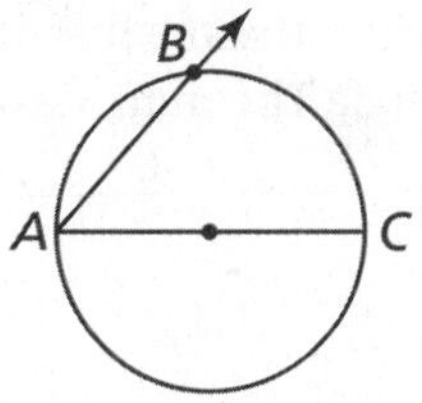

More Practice and Problem-Solving Exercises

MATHEMATICAL PRACTICES

B Apply

12. Writing A parallelogram inscribed in a circle must be what kind of parallelogram? Explain.

Find each indicated measure for $\odot O$.

13. **a.** $m\widehat{BC}$
b. $m\angle B$
c. $m\angle C$
d. $m\widehat{AB}$

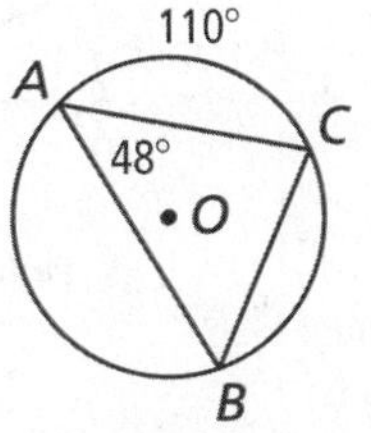

14. **a.** $m\angle A$
b. $m\widehat{CE}$
c. $m\angle C$
d. $m\angle D$
e. $m\angle ABE$

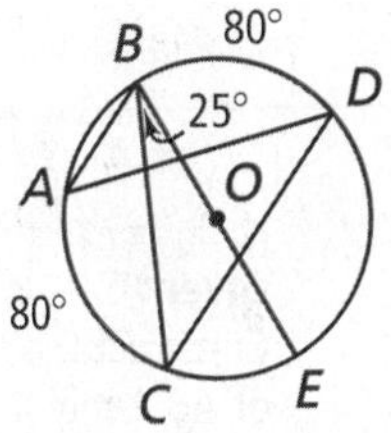

15. Think About a Plan What kind of trapezoid can be inscribed in a circle? Justify your response.

- Draw several diagrams to make a conjecture.
- How can parallel lines help?

Find the value of each variable. For each circle, the dot represents the center.

16.

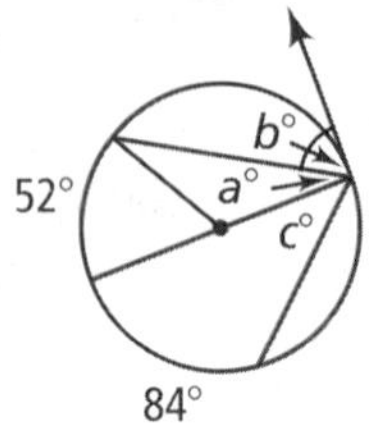

17.

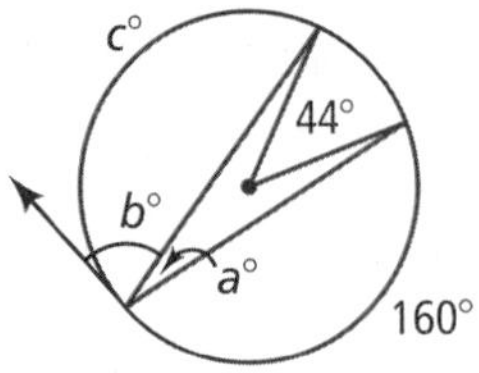

18.

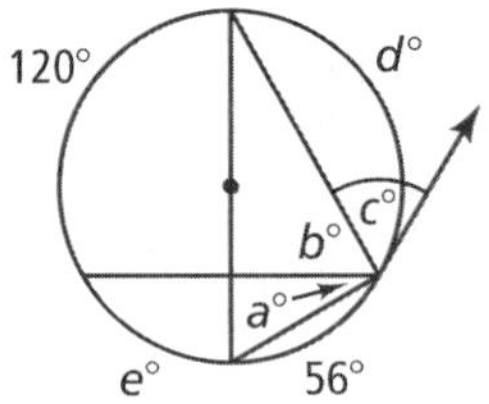

Write a proof for Exercises 19 and 20.

Proof **19.** Inscribed Angle Theorem, Case II

Given: $\odot O$ with inscribed $\angle ABC$

Prove: $m\angle ABC = \frac{1}{2} m\widehat{AC}$

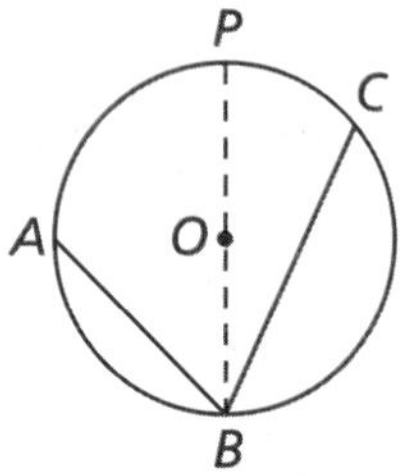

(*Hint:* Use the Inscribed Angle Theorem, Case I.)

Proof **20.** Inscribed Angle Theorem, Case III

Given: $\odot S$ with inscribed $\angle PQR$

Prove: $m\angle PQR = \frac{1}{2} m\widehat{PR}$

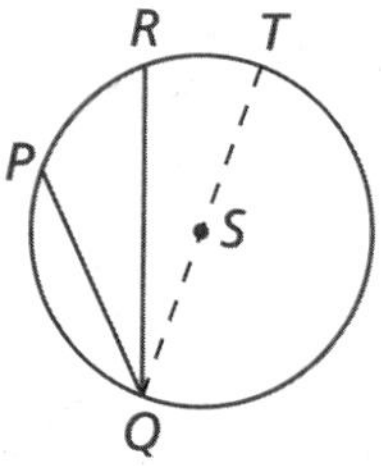

(*Hint:* Use the Inscribed Angle Theorem, Case I.)

21. Television The director of a telecast wants the option of showing the same scene from three different views.

a. Explain why cameras in the positions shown in the diagram will transmit the same scene.

b. Reasoning Will the scenes look the same when the director views them on the control room monitors? Explain.

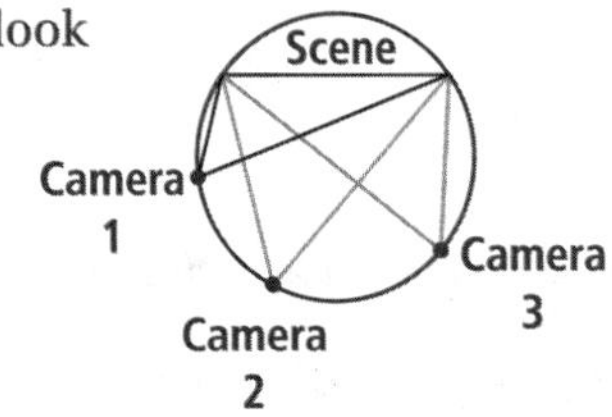

22. Reasoning Can a rhombus that is not a square be inscribed in a circle? Justify your answer.

23. Constructions The diagrams below show the construction of a tangent to a circle from a point outside the circle. Explain why $\overleftrightarrow{BC}$ must be tangent to $\odot A$. (*Hint:* Copy the third diagram and draw $\overline{AC}$.)

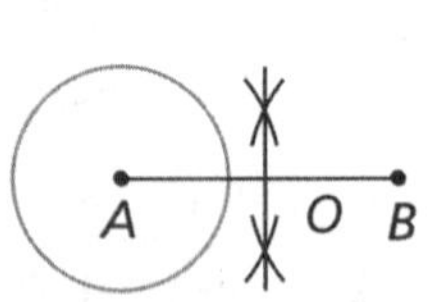

Given: $\odot A$ and point B
Construct the midpoint of $\overline{AB}$. Label the point O.

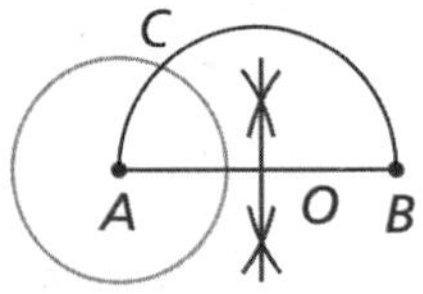

Construct a semicircle with radius OA and center O. Label its intersection with $\odot A$ as C.

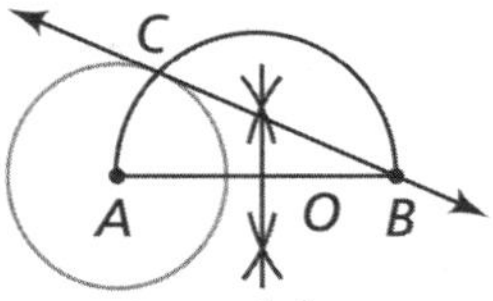

Draw $\overleftrightarrow{BC}$.

Write a proof for Exercises 24–27.

Proof **24.** Inscribed Angle Theorem, Corollary 1

Given: $\odot O$, $\angle A$ intercepts $\overset{\frown}{BC}$, $\angle D$ intercepts $\overset{\frown}{BC}$.

Prove: $\angle A \cong \angle D$

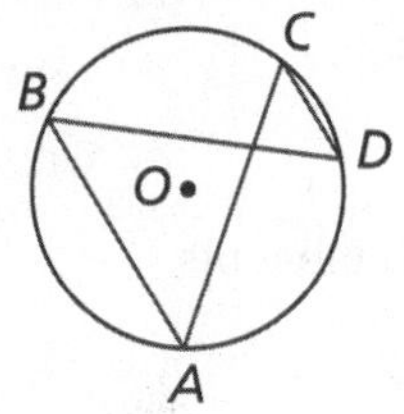

Proof **25.** Inscribed Angle Theorem, Corollary 2

Given: $\odot O$ with $\angle CAB$ inscribed in a semicircle

Prove: $\angle CAB$ is a right angle.

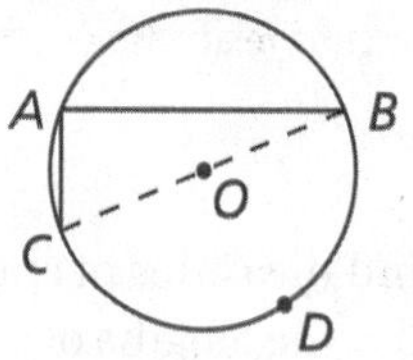

Proof **26.** Inscribed Angle Theorem, Corollary 3

Given: Quadrilateral $ABCD$ inscribed in $\odot O$

Prove: $\angle A$ and $\angle C$ are supplementary. $\angle B$ and $\angle D$ are supplementary.

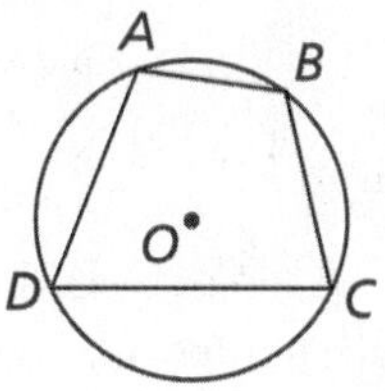

Proof **27.** Theorem 85

Given: $\overline{GH}$ and tangent ℓ intersecting $\odot E$ at H

Prove: $m\angle GHI = \frac{1}{2} m\overset{\frown}{GFH}$

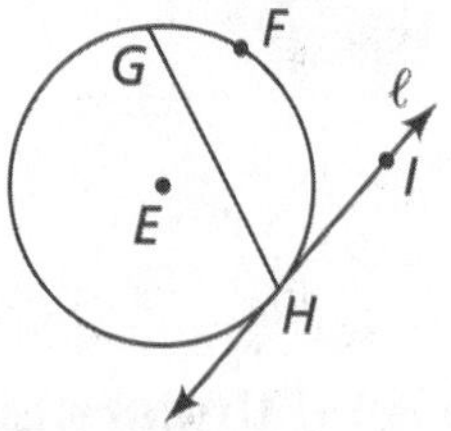

Challenge

Reasoning **Is the statement *true* or *false*? If it is true, give a convincing argument. If it is false, give a counterexample.**

28. If two angles inscribed in a circle are congruent, then they intercept the same arc.

29. If an inscribed angle is a right angle, then it is inscribed in a semicircle.

Proof **30.** Prove that if two arcs of a circle are included between parallel chords, then the arcs are congruent.

31. Constructions Draw two segments. Label their lengths x and y. Construct the geometric mean of x and y. (*Hint:* Recall a theorem about a geometric mean.)

12-6 Angle Measures and Segment Lengths

G.C.2 Identify and describe relationships among inscribed angles, radii, and chords . . .

Objectives To find measures of angles formed by chords, secants, and tangents
To find the lengths of segments associated with circles

Solve It! Write your solution to the Solve It in the space below.

Essential Understanding Angles formed by intersecting lines have a special relationship to the related arcs formed when the lines intersect a circle. In this lesson, you will study angles and arcs formed by lines intersecting either within a circle or outside a circle.

take note

Theorem 86

The measure of an angle formed by two lines that intersect inside a circle is half the sum of the measures of the intercepted arcs.

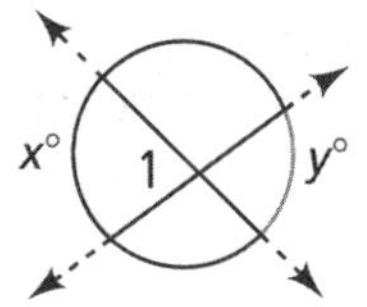

$$m\angle 1 = \tfrac{1}{2}(x + y)$$

Theorem 87

The measure of an angle formed by two lines that intersect outside a circle is half the difference of the measures of the intercepted arcs.

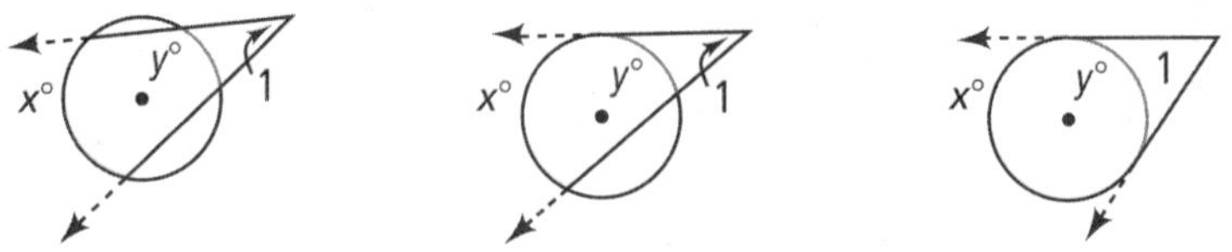

$$m\angle 1 = \tfrac{1}{2}(x - y)$$

You will prove Theorem 87 In Exercises 28 and 29.

In Theorem 86, the lines from a point outside the circle going through the circle are called secants. A **secant** is a line that intersects a circle at two points. $\overleftrightarrow{AB}$ is a secant, $\overrightarrow{AB}$ is a secant ray, and $\overline{AB}$ is a secant segment. A chord is part of a secant.

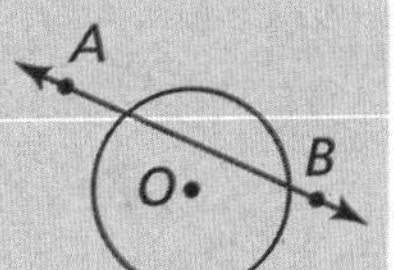

Proof Proof of Theorem 86

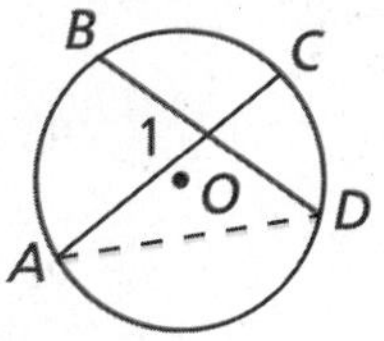

Given: $\odot O$ with intersecting chords $\overline{AC}$ and $\overline{BD}$
Prove: $m\angle 1 = \frac{1}{2}(m\widehat{AB} + m\widehat{CD})$

Begin by drawing auxiliary $\overline{AD}$ as shown in the diagram.

$m\angle BDA = \frac{1}{2}m\widehat{AB}$, and $m\angle CAD = \frac{1}{2}m\widehat{CD}$
Inscribed Angle Theorem

$m\angle 1 = m\angle BDA + m\angle CAD$
△ Exterior Angle Theorem

$m\angle 1 = \frac{1}{2}m\widehat{AB} + \frac{1}{2}m\widehat{CD}$
Substitute.

$m\angle 1 = \frac{1}{2}(m\widehat{AB} + m\widehat{CD})$
Distributive Property

ONLINE PROBLEMS Problem 1 Finding Angle Measures

Got It? What is the value of each variable?

a.
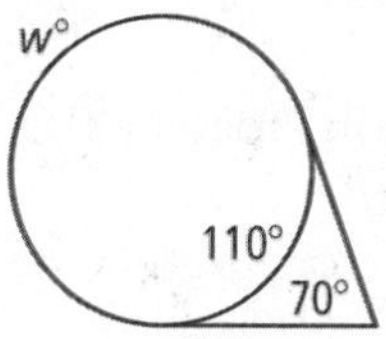

b.
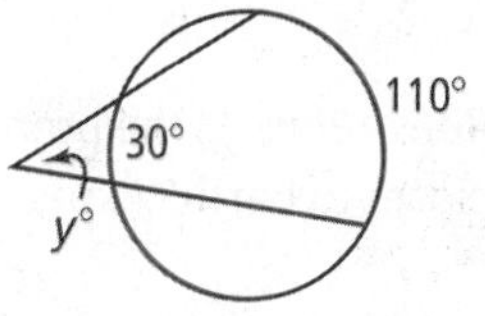

c.
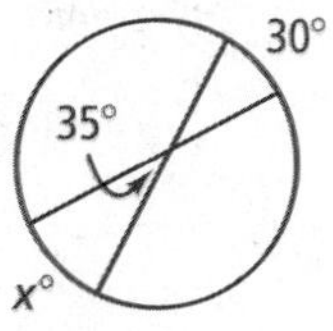

Practice **Algebra** Find the value of each variable.

1.

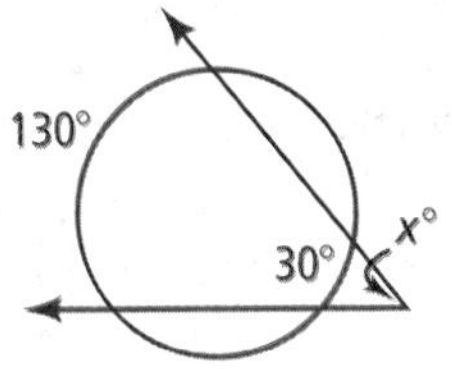

2.

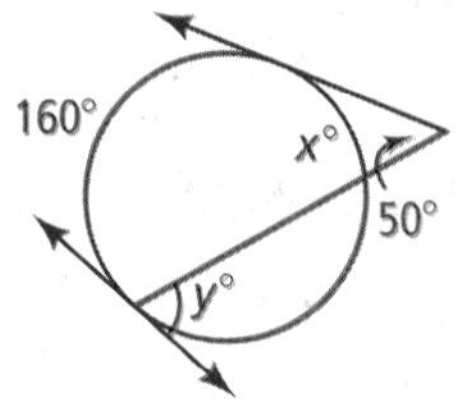

Problem 2 Finding an Arc Measure

Think

How can you represent the measures of the arcs?

Got It? a. A departing space probe sends back a picture of Earth as it crosses Earth's equator. The angle formed by the two tangents to the equator is 20°. What is the measure of the arc of the equator that is visible to the space probe?

b. **Reasoning** Is the probe or the geostationary satellite in Problem 2 closer to Earth? Explain.

Practice 3. **Algebra** Find the value of each variable.

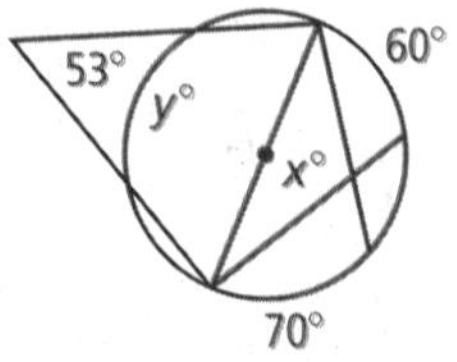

4. Photography You focus your camera on a circular fountain. Your camera is at the vertex of the angle formed by tangents to the fountain. You estimate that this angle is 40°. What is the measure of the arc of the circular basin of the fountain that will be in the photograph?

Essential Understanding There is a special relationship between two intersecting chords, two intersecting secants, or a secant that intersects a tangent. This relationship allows you to find the lengths of unknown segments.

From a given point P, you can draw two segments to a circle along infinitely many lines. For example, $\overline{PA_1}$ and $\overline{PB_1}$ lie along one such line. Theorem 88 states the surprising result that no matter which line you use, the product of the lengths $PA \cdot PB$ remains constant.

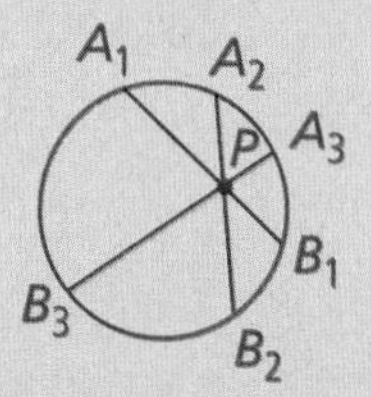

take note

Theorem 88

For a given point and circle, the product of the lengths of the two segments from the point to the circle is constant along any line through the point and circle.

I.

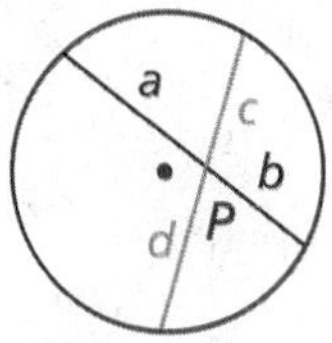

$a \cdot b = c \cdot d$

II.

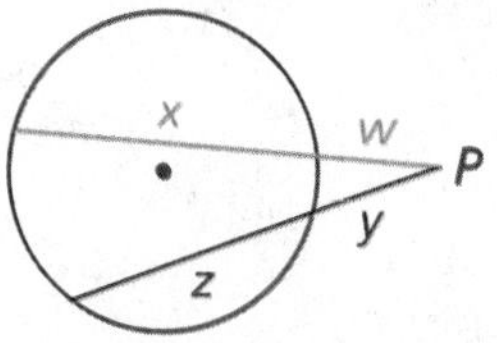

$(w + x)w = (y + z)y$

III.

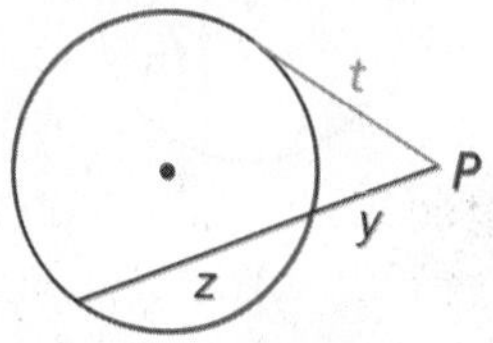

$(y + z)y = t^2$

As you use Theorem 88, remember the following.

- **Case I:** The products of the chord segments are equal.
- **Case II:** The products of the secants and their outer segments are equal.
- **Case III:** The product of a secant and its outer segment equals the square of the tangent.

Here is a proof for Case I. You will prove Case II and Case III in Exercises 30 and 31.

Proof Proof of Theorem 88, Case I

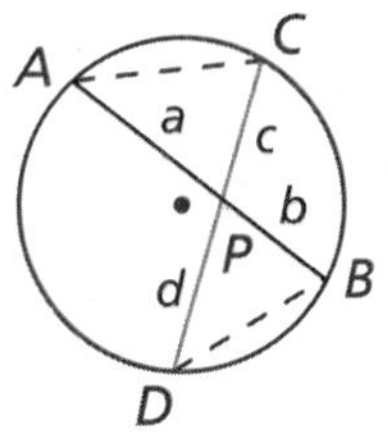

Given: A circle with chords $\overline{AB}$ and $\overline{CD}$ intersecting at P

Prove: $a \cdot b = c \cdot d$

Draw $\overline{AC}$ and $\overline{BD}$. $\angle A \cong \angle D$ and $\angle C \cong \angle B$ because each pair intercepts the same arc, and angles that intercept the same arc are congruent. $\triangle APC \sim \triangle DPB$ by the Angle-Angle Similarity Postulate. The lengths of corresponding sides of similar triangles are proportional, so $\frac{a}{d} = \frac{c}{b}$. Therefore, $a \cdot b = c \cdot d$.

ONLINE PROBLEMS Problem 3 Finding Segment Lengths

Got It? What is the value of the variable to the nearest tenth?

Plan

How can you identify the segments needed to use Theorem 88?

a.

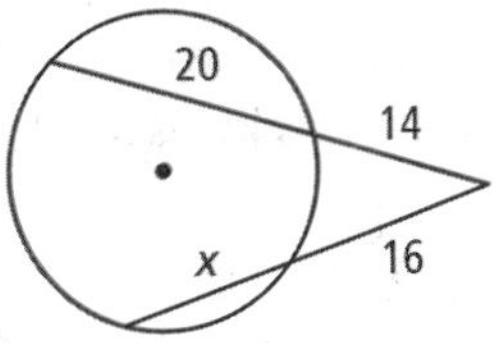

b.

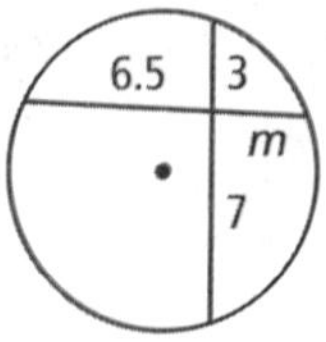

A Practice **Algebra** **Find the value of each variable using the given chord, secant, and tangent lengths. If the answer is not a whole number, round to the nearest tenth.**

5.

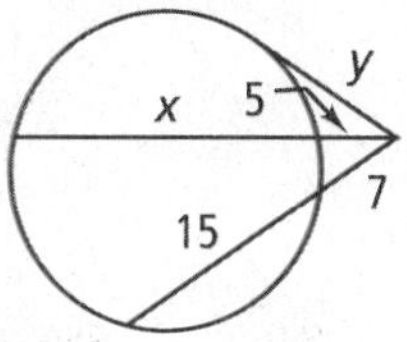

6.

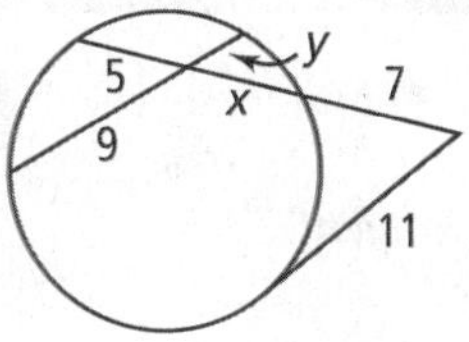

Lesson Check

Do you know HOW?

7. What is the value of x?

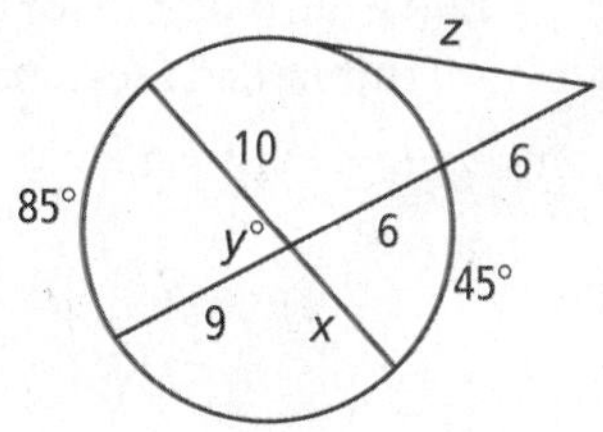

8. What is the value of y?

9. What is the value of z, to the nearest tenth?

10. The measure of the angle formed by two tangents to a circle is 80. What are the measures of the intercepted arcs?

Do you UNDERSTAND?

MATHEMATICAL PRACTICES

11. Vocabulary Describe the difference between a *secant* and a *tangent*.

12. In the diagram for Exercises 7–9, is it possible to find the measures of the unmarked arcs? Explain.

13. Error Analysis To find the value of x, a student wrote the equation $(7.5)6 = x^2$. What error did the student make?

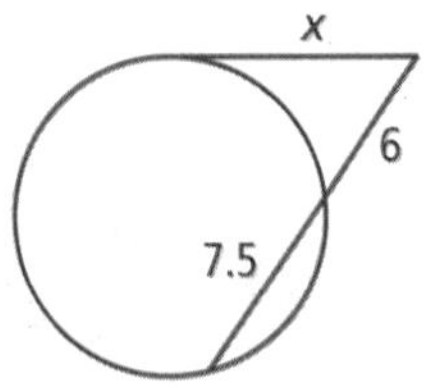

More Practice and Problem-Solving Exercises

MATHEMATICAL PRACTICES

B Apply

Algebra $\overline{CA}$ and $\overline{CB}$ are tangents to $\odot O$. Write an expression for each arc or angle in terms of the given variable.

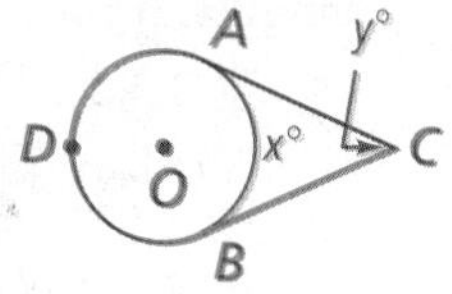

14. $m\widehat{ADB}$ using x **15.** $m\angle C$ using x **16.** $m\widehat{AB}$ using y

Find the diameter of $\odot O$. A line that appears to be tangent is tangent. If your answer is not a whole number, round it to the nearest tenth.

17.

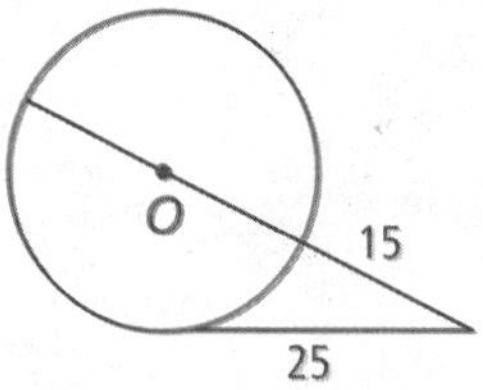

18.

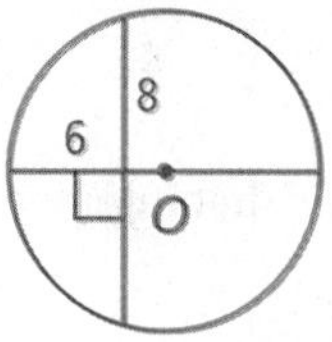

19.

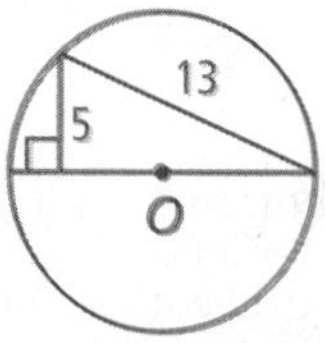

20. A circle is inscribed in a quadrilateral whose four angles have measures 85, 76, 94, and 105. Find the measures of the four arcs between consecutive points of tangency.

Wankel engine

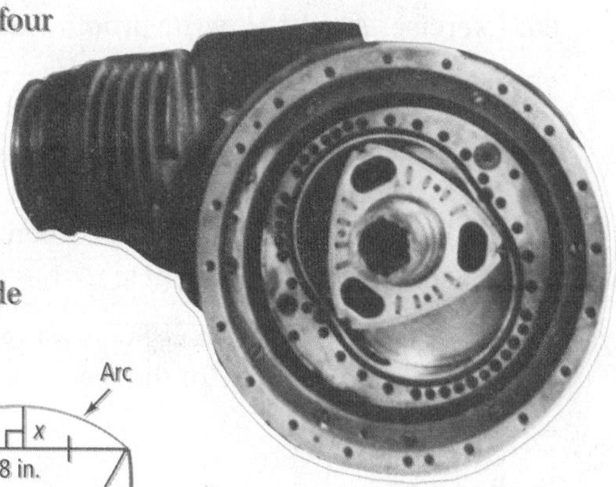

STEM **21. Engineering** The basis for the design of the Wankel rotary engine is an equilateral triangle. Each side of the triangle is a chord to an arc of a circle. The opposite vertex of the triangle is the center of the circle that forms the arc. In the diagram below, each side of the equilateral triangle is 8 in. long.

a. Use what you know about equilateral triangles and find the value of x.

b. Reasoning Copy the diagram and complete the circle with the given center. Then use Theorem 88 to find the value of x. Show that your answers to parts (a) and (b) are equal.

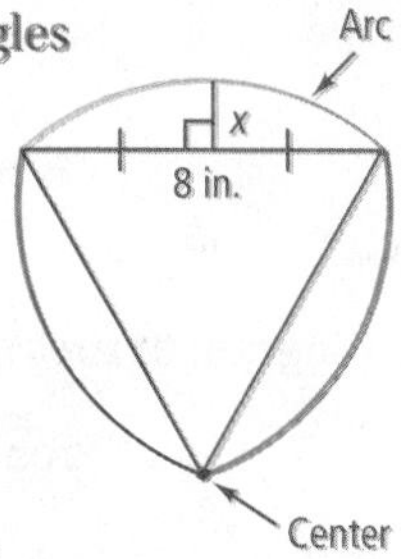

22. Think About a Plan In the diagram, the circles are concentric. What is a formula you could use to find the value of c in terms of a and b?

- How can you use the inscribed angle to find the value of c?
- What is the relationship of the inscribed angle to a and b?

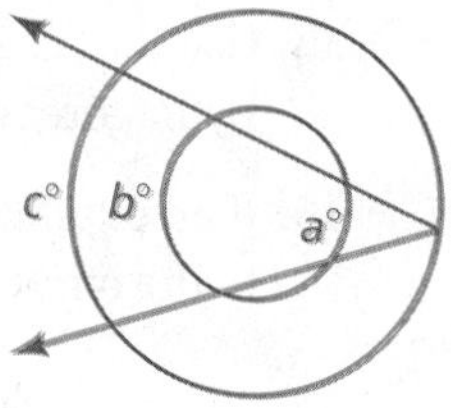

23. $\triangle PQR$ is inscribed in a circle with $m\angle P = 70$, $m\angle Q = 50$, and $m\angle R = 60$. What are the measures of $\widehat{PQ}$, $\widehat{QR}$, and $\widehat{PR}$?

24. Reasoning Use the diagram at the right. If you know the values of x and y, how can you find the measure of each numbered angle?

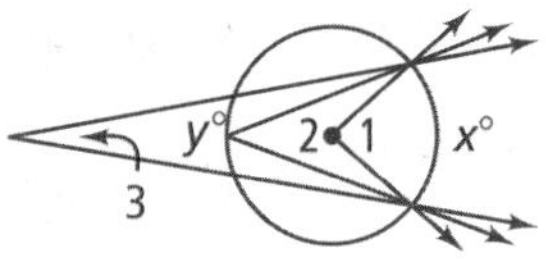

Algebra Find the values of x and y using the given chord, secant, and tangent lengths. If your answer is not a whole number, round it to the nearest tenth.

25.

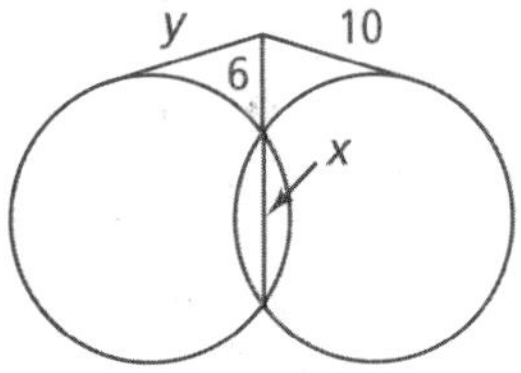

26.

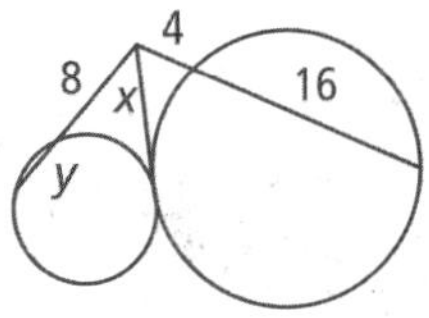

27.

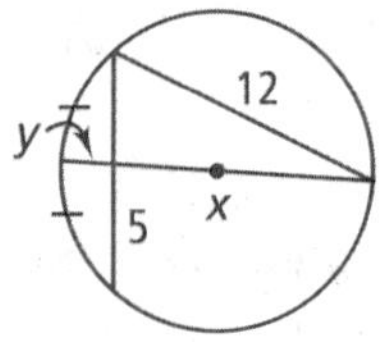

Proof 28. Prove Theorem 87 as it applies to two secants that intersect outside a circle.

Given: $\odot O$ with secants $\overline{CA}$ and $\overline{CE}$

Prove: $m\angle ACE = \frac{1}{2}(m\widehat{AE} - m\widehat{BD})$

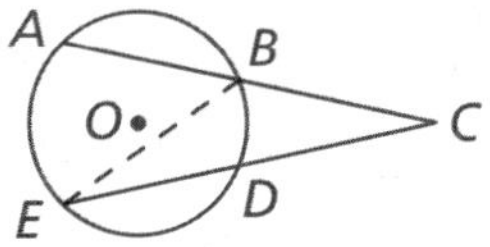

Proof 29. Prove the other two cases of Theorem 87. (See Exercise 28.)

For Exercises 30 and 31, write proofs that use similar triangles.

Proof 30. Prove Theorem 88, Case II.

Proof 31. Prove Theorem 88, Case III.

32. The diagram at the right shows a *unit circle*, a circle with radius 1.

a. What triangle is similar to $\triangle ABE$?

b. Describe the connection between the ratio for the tangent of $\angle A$ and the segment that is tangent to $\odot A$.

c. The secant ratio is $\frac{\text{hypotenuse}}{\text{length of leg adjacent to an angle}}$. Describe the connection between the ratio for the secant of $\angle A$ and the segment that is the secant in the unit circle.

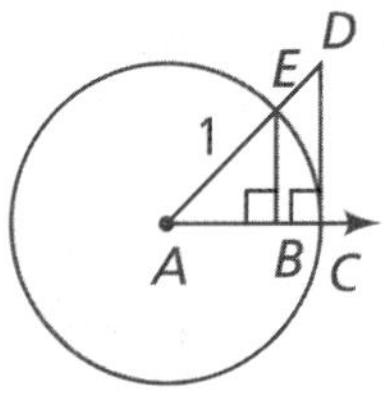

Challenge

For Exercises 33 and 34, use the diagram at the right. Prove each statement.

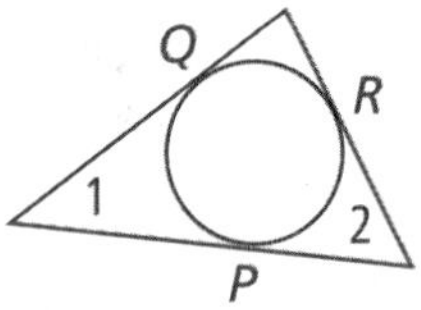

Proof 33. $m\angle 1 + m\widehat{PQ} = 180$

Proof 34. $m\angle 1 + m\angle 2 = m\widehat{QR}$

Proof 35. Use the diagram at the right and the theorems of this lesson to prove the Pythagorean Theorem.

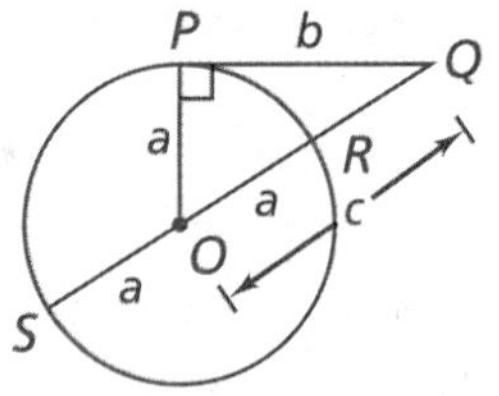

Proof 36. If an equilateral triangle is inscribed in a circle, prove that the tangents to the circle at the vertices form an equilateral triangle.

12 Chapter Review

MathXL® for School
Go to pearsonsuccessnet.com

12-1 Circles and Arcs

Quick Review

A **circle** is the set of all points in a plane equidistant from a point called the **center**. The **circumference** of a circle is $C = \pi d$ or $C = 2\pi r$. **Arc length** is a fraction of a circle's circumference. The length of $\widehat{AB} = \frac{m\widehat{AB}}{360} \cdot 2\pi r$.

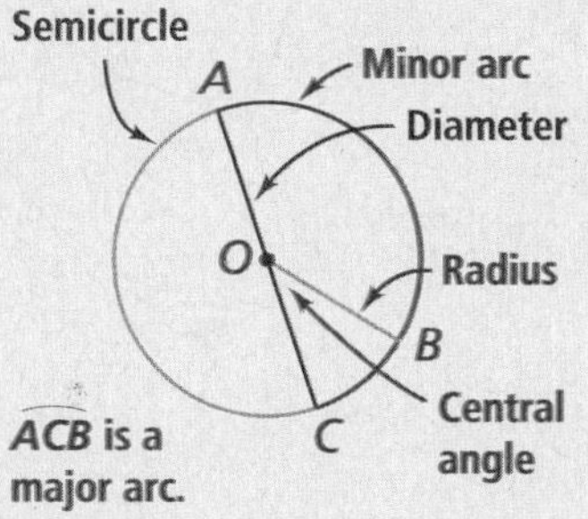

Example

A circle has a radius of 5 cm. What is the length of an arc measuring 80°?

length of $\widehat{AB} = \frac{m\widehat{AB}}{360} \cdot 2\pi r$ Use the arc length formula.

$= \frac{80}{360} \cdot 2\pi(5)$ Substitute.

$= \frac{20}{9}\pi$ Simplify.

The length of the arc is $\frac{20}{9}\pi$ cm.

Exercises

Find each measure.

1. $m\angle APD$
2. $m\widehat{AC}$
3. $m\widehat{ABD}$
4. $m\angle CPA$

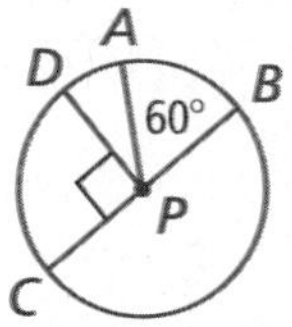

Find the length of each arc shown in red. Leave your answer in terms of π.

5. 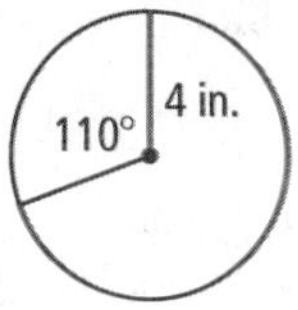

6. 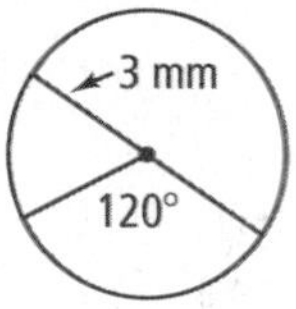

7. 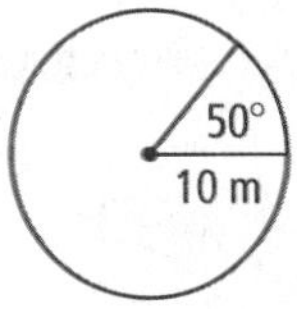

8. 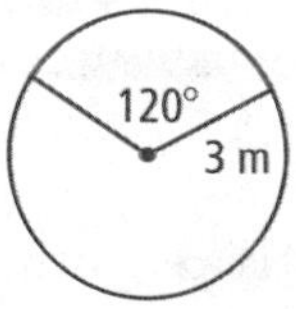

12-2 Areas of Circles and Sectors

Quick Review

The area of a circle is $A = \pi r^2$. A **sector of a circle** is a region bounded by two radii and their intercepted arc. The area of sector $APB = \frac{m\widehat{AB}}{360} \cdot \pi r^2$.

A **segment of a circle** is the part bounded by an arc and the segment joining its endpoints.

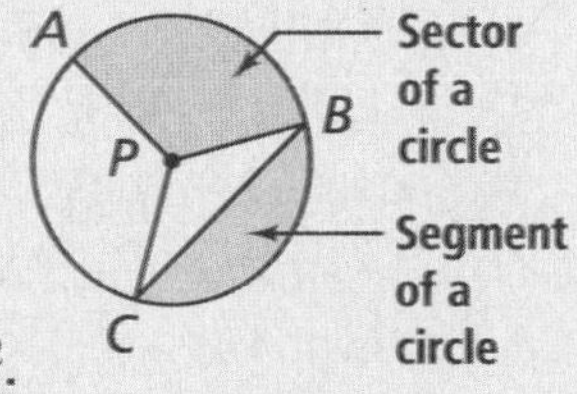

Example

What is the area of the shaded region?

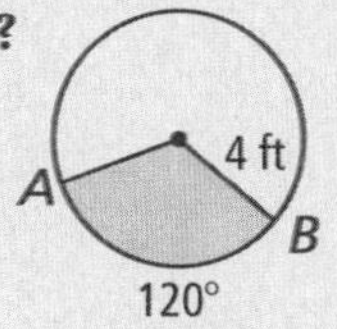

Area $= \frac{m\widehat{AB}}{360} \cdot \pi r^2$ Use the area formula.

$= \frac{120}{360} \cdot \pi(4)^2$ Substitute.

$= \frac{16\pi}{3}$ Simplify.

The area of the shaded region is $\frac{16\pi}{3}$ ft².

Exercises

What is the area of each circle? Leave your answer in terms of π.

9. 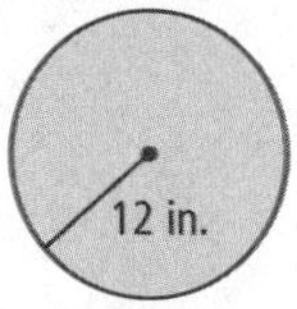

10. 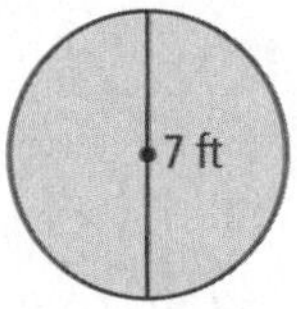

Find the area of each shaded region. Round your answer to the nearest tenth.

11. 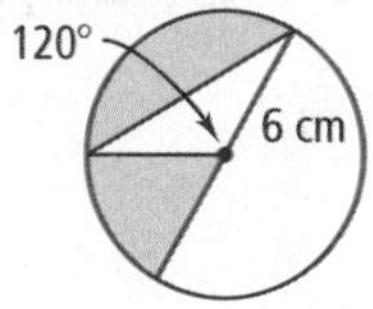

12. 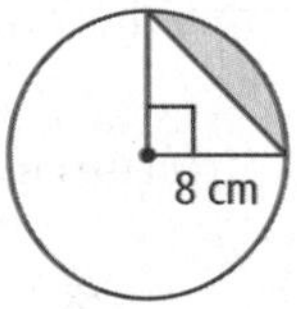

13. A circle has a radius of 20 cm. What is the area of the smaller segment of the circle formed by a 60° arc? Round to the nearest tenth.

12-3 Tangent Lines

Quick Review

A **tangent** to a circle is a line that intersects the circle at exactly one point. The radius to that point is perpendicular to the tangent. From any point outside a circle, you can draw two segments tangent to a circle. Those segments are congruent.

Example

$\overrightarrow{PA}$ and $\overrightarrow{PB}$ are tangents. Find x.

The radii are perpendicular to the tangents. Add the angle measures of the quadrilateral:

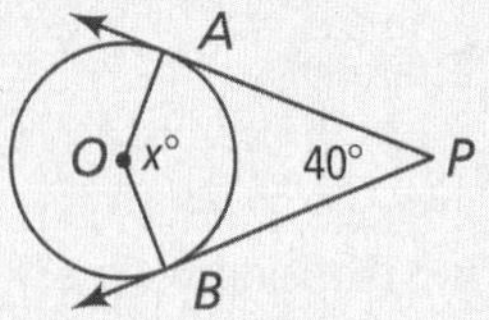

$$x + 90 + 90 + 40 = 360$$
$$x + 220 = 360$$
$$x = 140$$

Exercises

Use $\odot O$ for Exercises 14–16.

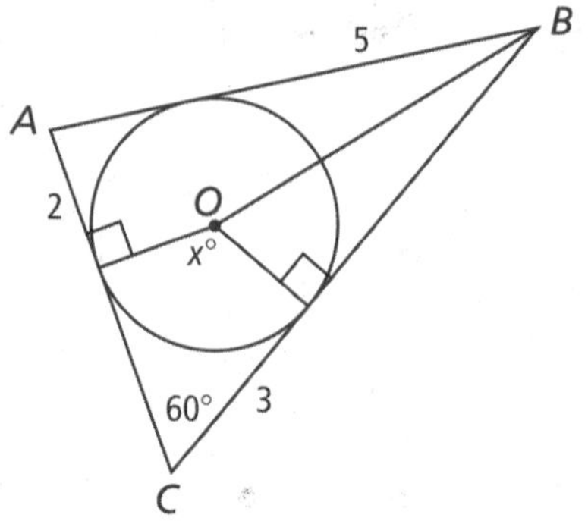

14. What is the perimeter of $\triangle ABC$?

15. $OB = \sqrt{28}$. What is the radius?

16. What is the value of x?

12-4 Chords and Arcs

Quick Review

A **chord** is a segment whose endpoints are on a circle. Congruent chords are equidistant from the center. A diameter that bisects a chord that is not a diameter is perpendicular to the chord. The perpendicular bisector of a chord contains the center of the circle.

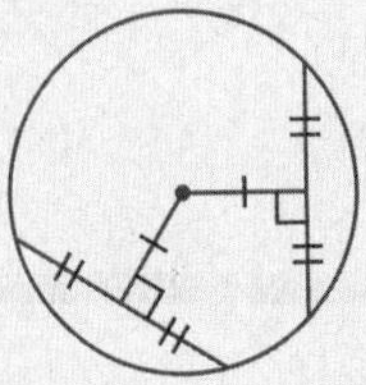

Example

Since the chord is bisected, $m\angle ACB = 90$. The radius is 13 units. So an auxiliary segment from A to B is 13 units. Use the Pythagorean Theorem.

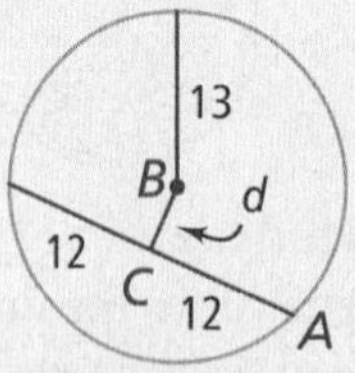

$$d^2 + 12^2 = 13^2$$
$$d^2 = 25$$
$$d = 5$$

Exercises

Use the figure below for Exercises 17–19.

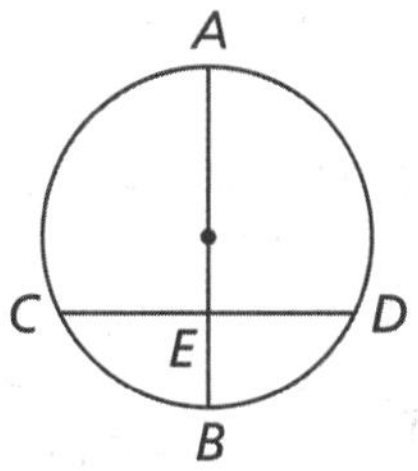

17. If $\overline{AB}$ is a diameter and $CE = ED$, then $m\angle AEC =$ __?__.

18. If $\overline{AB}$ is a diameter and is at right angles to $\overline{CD}$, what is the ratio of CD to DE?

19. If $CE = \frac{1}{2}CD$ and $m\angle DEB = 90$, what is true of $\overline{AB}$?

Use the circle below for Exercises 20 and 21.

20. What is the value of x?

21. What is the value of y?

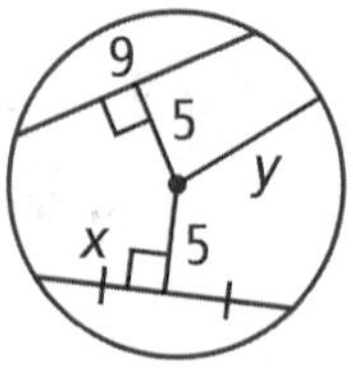

12-5 Inscribed Angles

Quick Review

An **inscribed angle** has its vertex on a circle and its sides are chords. An **intercepted arc** has its endpoints on the sides of an inscribed angle, and its other points in the interior of the angle. The measure of an inscribed angle is half the measure of its intercepted arc.

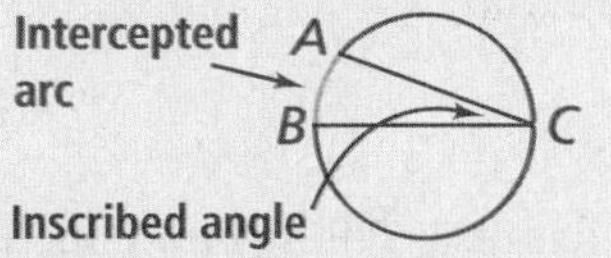

Example

What is $m\overset{\frown}{PS}$? What is $m\angle R$?

The $m\angle Q = 60$ is half of m, so $m\overset{\frown}{PS} = 120$. $\angle R$ intercepts the same arc as $\angle Q$, so $m\angle R = 60$.

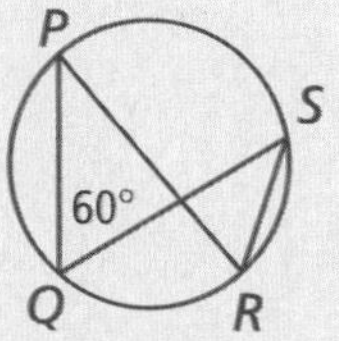

Exercises

Find the value of each variable. Line ℓ is a tangent.

22.

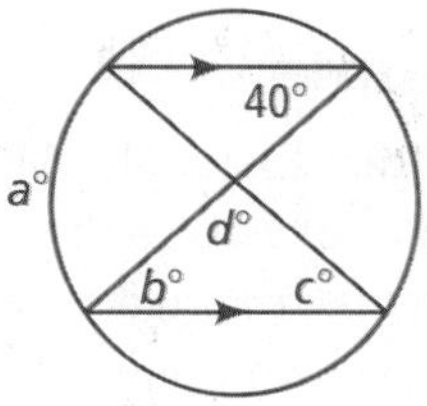

23.

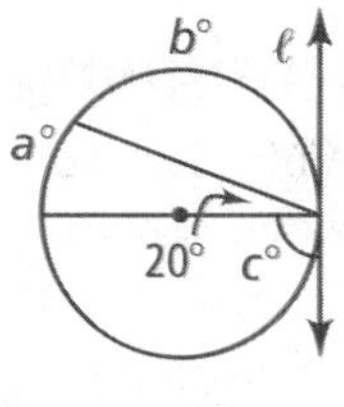

24.

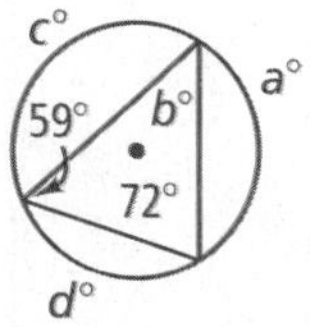

25.

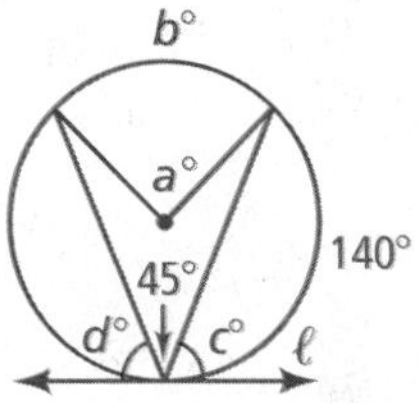

12-6 Angle Measures and Segment Lengths

Quick Review

A **secant** is a line that intersects a circle at two points. The following relationships are true:

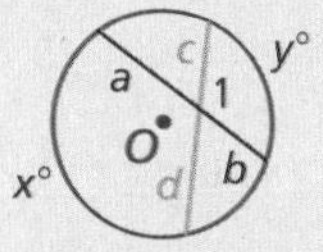

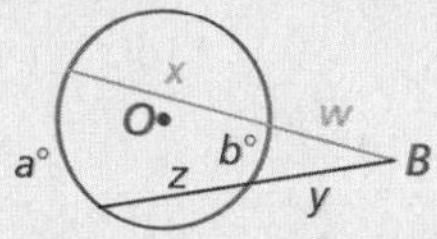

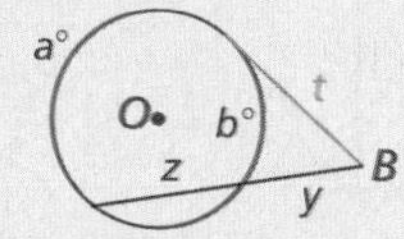

$a \cdot b = c \cdot d$

$m\angle 1 = \frac{1}{2}(x + y)$

$(w + x)w = (y + z)y$

$m\angle B = \frac{1}{2}(a - b)$

$(y + z)y = t^2$

$m\angle B = \frac{1}{2}(a - b)$

Example

What is the value of x?

$(x + 10)10 = (19 + 9)9$

$10x + 100 = 252$

$x = 15.2$

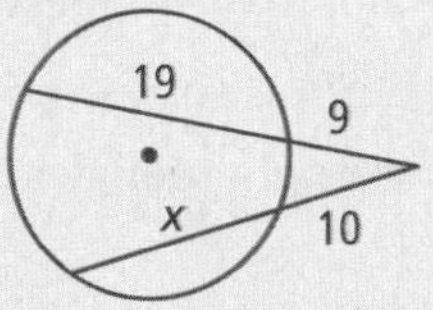

Exercises

Find the value of each variable.

26.

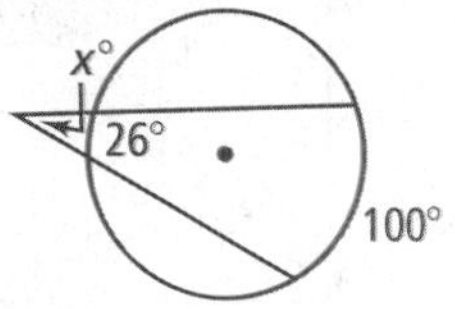

27.

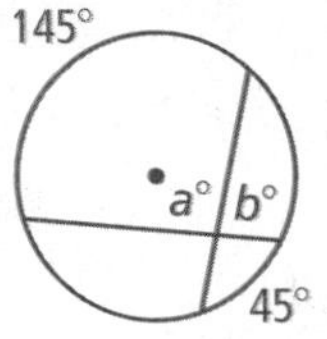

28.

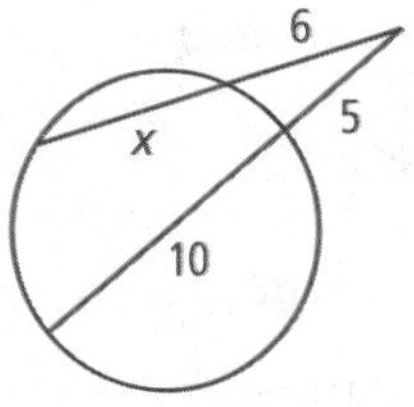

29.

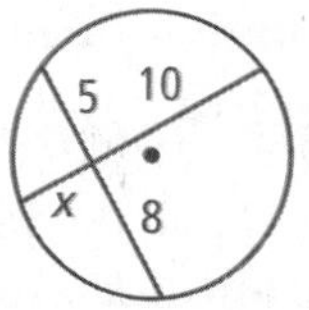

12 *Pull It* All Together

PERFORMANCE TASK

Designing a Game

ASSESSMENT

A new game on a television show will involve flat circular disks falling into slots. The diagram shows the radius of a disk and the dimensions of a slot. The disks always fall in such a way that each one rests against a side of the slot, first on one side and then on the opposite side, as shown below.

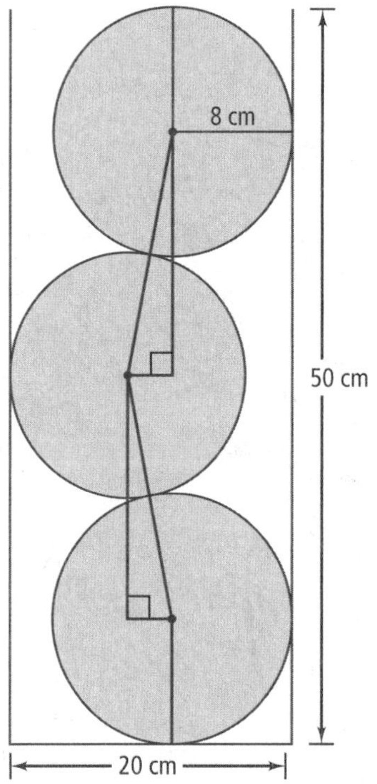

The game designer must verify that three disks will fit into a slot, without the top disk protruding from the top of the slot.

Task Description

Show that the vertical distance from the bottom of the slot to the highest point on the top disk is less than 50 cm.

- How would knowing the length of the longer leg of the right triangles in the diagram help you solve the problem?
- What are the lengths of the hypotenuse and shorter leg of the right triangles? How can you use these measurements to find the length of the longer leg?

Get Ready!

CHAPTER 13

The Pythagorean Theorem

Algebra Solve for *a*, *b*, or *c* in right $\triangle ABC$, where *a* and *b* are the lengths of the legs and *c* is the length of the hypotenuse.

1. $a = 8, b = 15, c = \blacksquare$ **2.** $a = \blacksquare, b = 4, c = 12$ **3.** $a = 2\sqrt{3}, b = 2\sqrt{6}, c = \blacksquare$

Special Right Triangles

4. Find the length of the shorter leg of a 30°–60°–90° triangle with hypotenuse $8\sqrt{5}$.

5. Find the length of the diagonal of a square whose perimeter is 24.

6. Find the height of an equilateral triangle with sides of length 8.

Area

Find the area of each figure. Leave your answer in simplest radical form.

7.

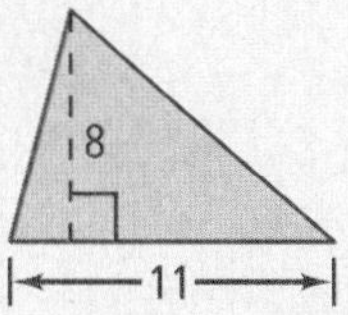

8.

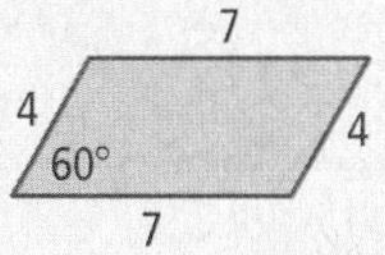

9.

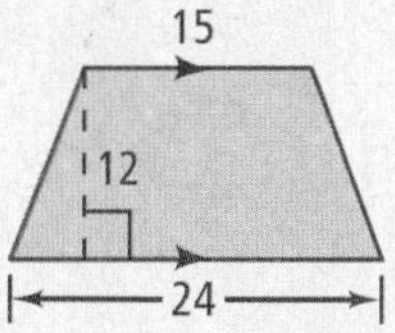

10.

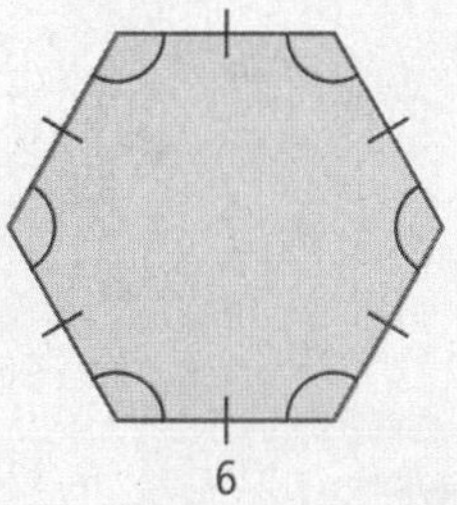

Looking Ahead Vocabulary

11. You know about the *altitude* of a triangle. What do you think is the *altitude* of a three-dimensional figure?

12. You can turn a rock over in your hands to examine its *surface*. What do you think the *surface area* of a three-dimensional figure is?

13. What does an Egyptian *pyramid* look like?

CHAPTER

13

Surface Area and Volume

Big Ideas

1 Measurement

Essential Question How do you find the surface area and volume of a solid?

Domains

- Geometric Measurement and Dimension
- Modeling with Geometry

Chapter Preview

Interactive Digital Path

Log in to **pearsonsuccessnet.com** and click on Interactive Digital Path to access the Solve Its and animated Problems.

Vocabulary

English/Spanish Vocabulary Audio Online:

English	Spanish
cone, *p. 882*	cono
cylinder, *p. 872*	cilindro
prism, *p. 867*	prisma
pyramid, *p. 879*	pirámide
sphere, *p. 911*	esfera
surface area, *pp. 868, 872, 880, 882*	área total
volume, *p. 889*	volumen

ACTIVITY LAB

Use With Lesson 13-1

Exploring the Circumference and Area of a Circle

G.GMD.1 Give an informal argument for the formulas for the circumference of a circle, area of a circle . . .

You can approximate the circumference of a circle by finding the perimeter of an inscribed regular polygon.

Activity 1

The figure at the right shows a portion of a circle of radius r with an inscribed regular n-gon.

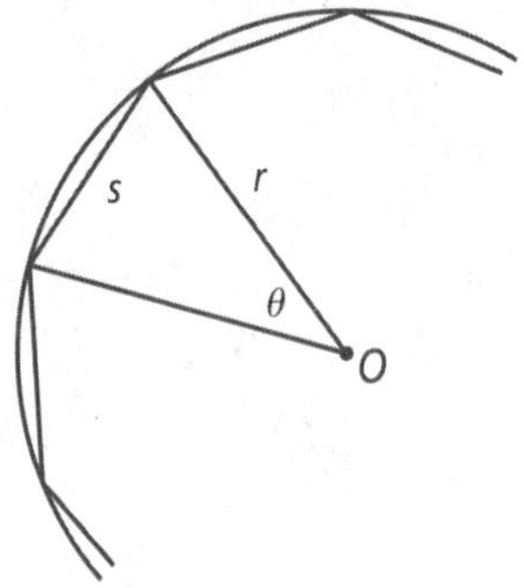

1. Find θ in terms of n.

2. Find s, the length of a side of the regular n-gon, in terms of r and n.

3. Find the perimeter of the inscribed n-gon in terms of r and n.

4. Use a graphing calculator or spreadsheet to make a table with n in one column, and $n \cdot \sin\left(\frac{180}{n}\right)$ in another column, for whole number values of n. What value does $n \cdot \sin\left(\frac{180}{n}\right)$ approach as n increases?

5. Explain how your answers to Exercises 3 and 4 show that the circumference of a circle is given by $2\pi r$.

You can use transformations to find the formula for the area of a circle.

Activity 2

Step 1 Use a compass to draw a large circle. Fold the circle horizontally and then vertically. Cut the circle into four wedges on the fold lines.

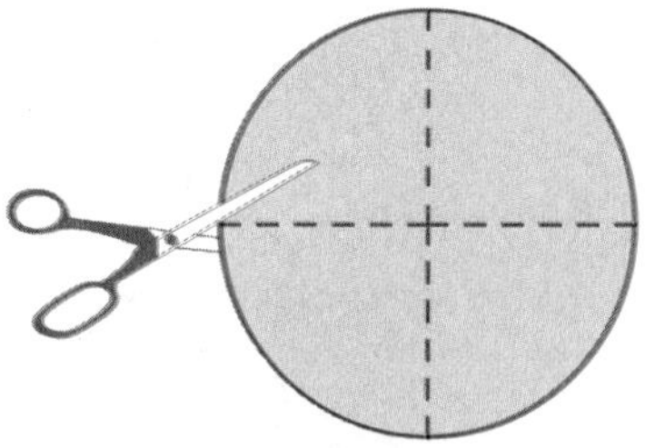

Step 2 Fold each wedge into quarters. Cut each wedge on the fold lines. You will have 16 congruent wedges.

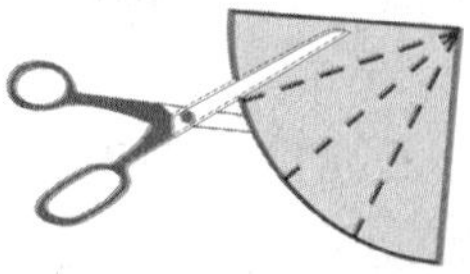

Step 3 Tape the wedges to a piece of paper to form the figure shown at the right. The figure resembles a parallelogram.

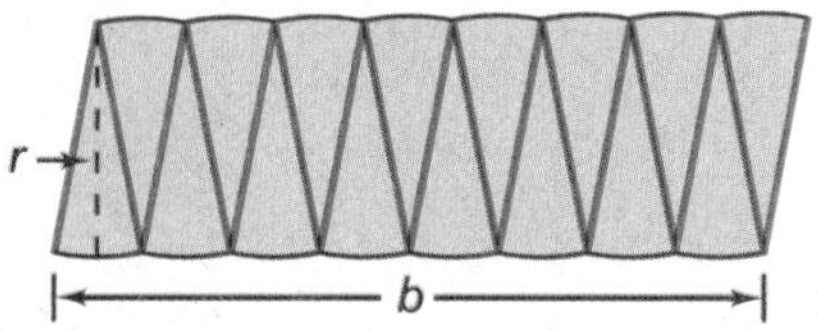

6. How does the area of the parallelogram compare with the area of the circle?

7. The base of the parallelogram is formed by arcs of the circle. Explain how the length b relates to the circumference C of the circle.

8. Explain how the length b relates to the radius r of the circle.

9. Write an expression for the area of the parallelogram in terms of r to write a formula for the area of a circle.

Exercises

In Exercises 10 and 11, use the table you made in Exercise 4.

10. A regular polygon is inscribed in a circle of radius 1 and has perimeter 6. How many sides does the polygon have?

11. A regular polygon is inscribed in a circle of radius 1 and has perimeter greater than 6.28. What is the least number of sides the polygon can have?

Repeat Steps 1 and 2 from Activity 2. Tape the wedges to a piece of paper to form another figure that resembles a parallelogram, as shown at the right.

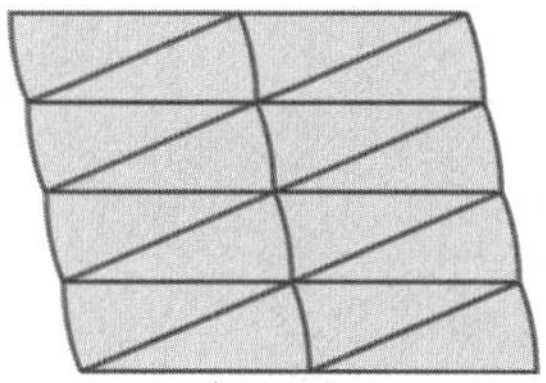

12. What are the base and height of the figure in terms of r?

13. Write an expression for the area of the figure to write a formula for the area of a circle. Is this expression the same as the one you wrote in the activity?

13-1 Surface Areas of Prisms and Cylinders

G.MG.1 Use geometric shapes . . . to describe objects. Also **N.Q.2**

Objective To find the surface area of a prism and a cylinder

Solve It! Write your solution to the Solve It in the space below.

In the Solve It, you investigated the structure of a tube. In this lesson, you will learn properties of three-dimensional figures by investigating their surfaces.

Essential Understanding To find the surface area of a three-dimensional figure, find the sum of the areas of all the surfaces of the figure.

A **prism** is a polyhedron with two congruent, parallel faces, called **bases**. The other faces are **lateral faces**. You can name a prism using the shape of its bases.

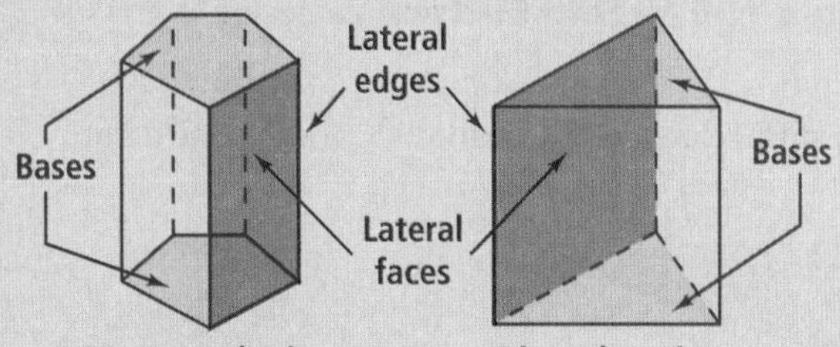

Pentagonal prism Triangular prism

An **altitude** of a prism is a perpendicular segment that joins the planes of the bases. The **height** h of a prism is the length of an altitude. A prism may be either right or oblique.

Right prisms Oblique prisms

In a **right prism**, the lateral faces are rectangles and a lateral edge is an altitude. In an **oblique prism**, some or all of the lateral faces are nonrectangular. In this book, you may assume that a prism is a right prism unless stated or pictured otherwise.

The **lateral area** (L.A.) of a prism is the sum of the areas of the lateral faces. The **surface area** (S.A.) is the sum of the lateral area and the area of the two bases.

When calculating surface areas of prisms and cylinders, the following formulas for the areas of two-dimensional figures will be useful.

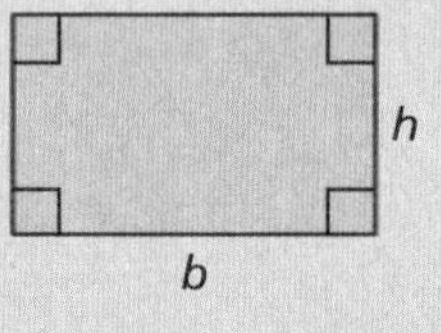

$P = 2b + 2h$

$A = bh$

Rectangle

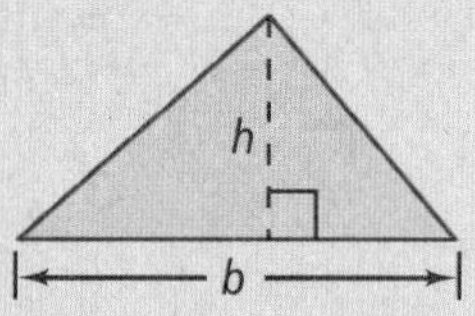

$A = \frac{1}{2}bh$

Triangle

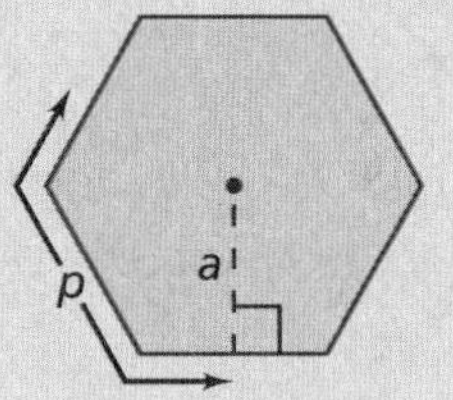

$A = \frac{1}{2}ap$

Regular Polygon

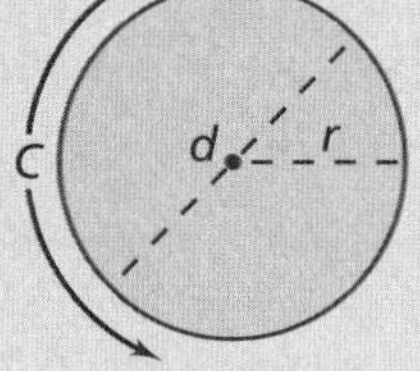

$C = \pi d$ or $C = 2\pi r$

$A = \pi r^2$

Circle

Problem 1 Using a Net to Find Surface Area of a Prism

Got It? What is the surface area of the triangular prism? Use a net.

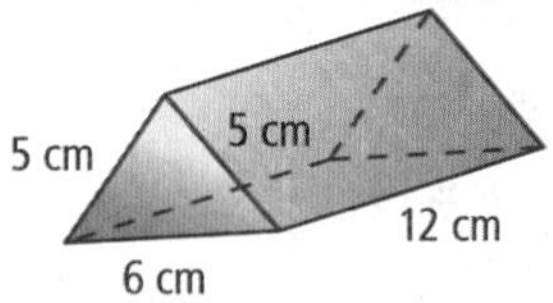

Practice 1. Use a net to find the surface area of the prism.

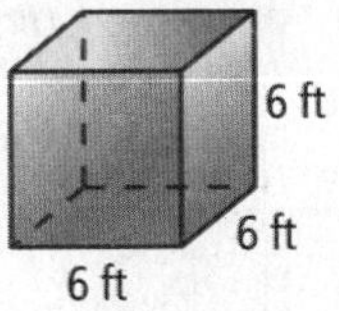

2. a. Classify the prism at the right.

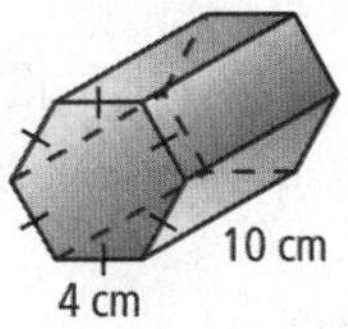

b. Find the lateral area of the prism.

c. The bases are regular hexagons. Find the sum of their areas.

d. Find the surface area of the prism.

You can find formulas for lateral and surface areas of a prism by using a net.

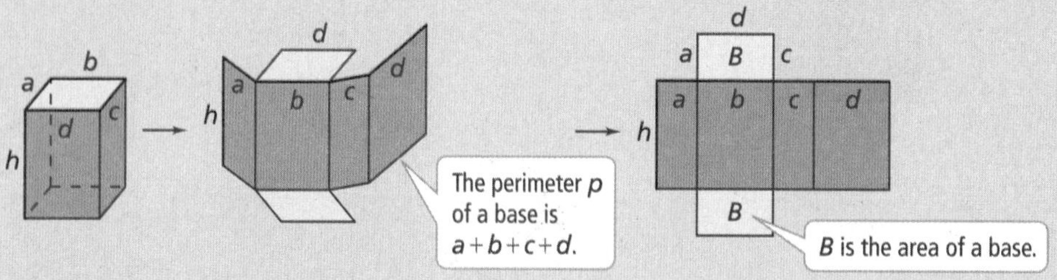

Lateral Area $= ph$ Surface Area $=$ L.A. $+ 2B$

You can use the formulas with any right prism.

take note

Theorem 89 Lateral and Surface Areas of a Prism

The lateral area of a right prism is the product of the perimeter of the base and the height of the prism.

L.A. $= ph$

The surface area of a right prism is the sum of the lateral area and the areas of the two bases.

S.A. $=$ L.A. $+ 2B$

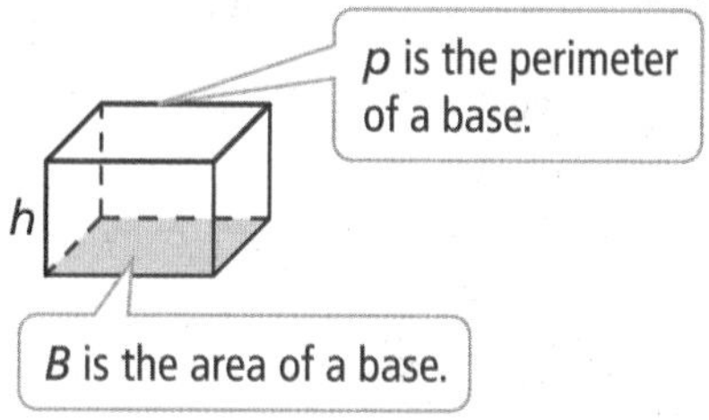

ONLINE PROBLEMS

Problem 2 Using Formulas to Find Surface Area of a Prism

Got It? **a.** What is the lateral area of the prism at the right?

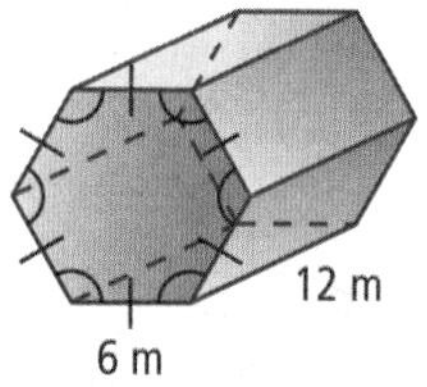

b. What is the area of a base in simplest radical form?

c. What is the surface area of the prism rounded to a whole number?

A Practice **Use formulas to find the surface area of each prism. Round your answer to the nearest whole number.**

3.

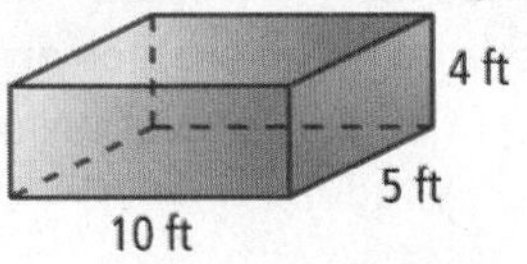

4.

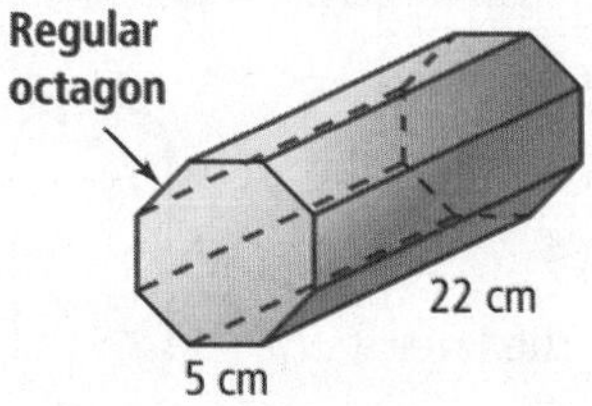

A **cylinder** is a solid that has two congruent parallel **bases** that are circles. An **altitude** of a cylinder is a perpendicular segment that joins the planes of the bases. The **height** h of a cylinder is the length of an altitude.

In a **right cylinder**, the segment joining the centers of the bases is an altitude. In an **oblique cylinder**, the segment joining the centers is not perpendicular to the planes containing the bases. In this book, you may assume that a cylinder is a right cylinder unless stated or pictured otherwise.

To find the area of the curved surface of a cylinder, visualize "unrolling" it. The area of the resulting rectangle is the **lateral area** of the cylinder. The **surface area** of a cylinder is the sum of the lateral area and the areas of the two circular bases. You can find formulas for these areas by looking at a net for a cylinder.

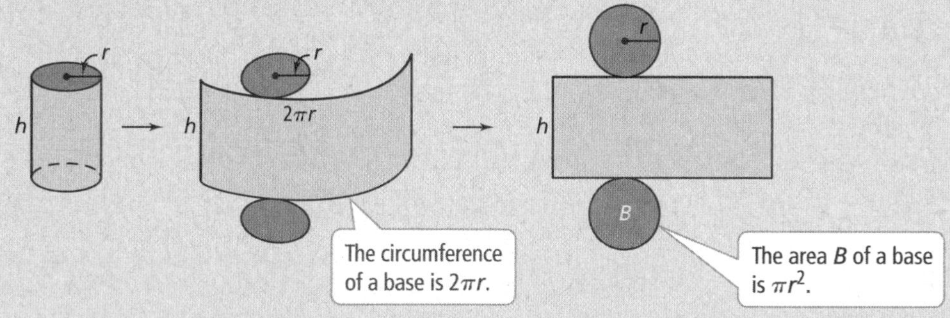

Lateral Area $= 2\pi rh$ Surface Area $= \text{L.A.} + 2\pi r^2$

take note

Theorem 90 Lateral and Surface Areas of a Cylinder

The lateral area of a right cylinder is the product of the circumference of the base and the height of the cylinder.

$\text{L.A.} = 2\pi r \cdot h$, or $\text{L.A.} = \pi dh$

The surface area of a right cylinder is the sum of the lateral area and the areas of the two bases.

$\text{S.A.} = \text{L.A.} + 2B$, or $\text{S.A.} = 2\pi rh + 2\pi r^2$

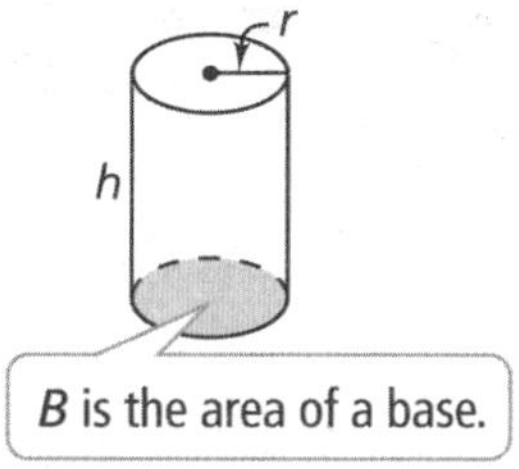

Problem 3 Finding Surface Area of a Cylinder

Got It? A cylinder has a height of 9 cm and a radius of 10 cm. What is the surface area of the cylinder in terms of π?

Think

How is finding the surface area of a cylinder like finding the surface area of a prism?

Practice Find the surface area of each cylinder in terms of π.

5.

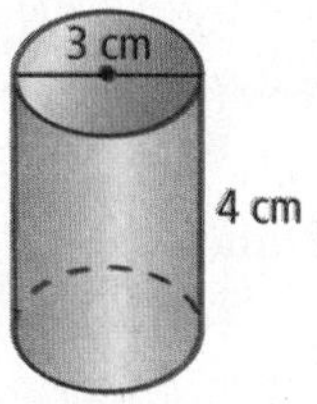

6.

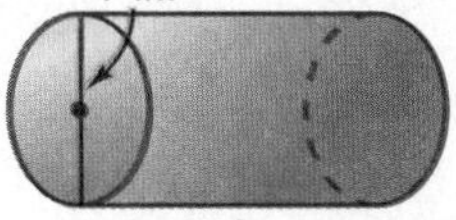

Problem 4 Finding Lateral Area of a Cylinder

Think
What is the problem asking you to find?

Got It? **a.** A smaller stencil roller has a height of 1.5 in. and the same diameter as the roller in Problem 4. What area does the smaller roller cover in one turn? Round your answer to the nearest tenth.

b. Reasoning What is the ratio of the smaller roller's height to the larger roller's height? What is the ratio of the areas the rollers can cover in one turn (smaller to larger)?

Practice **Find the lateral area of each cylinder to the nearest whole number.**

7.

8.

Lesson Check

Do you know HOW?

What is the surface area of each prism?

9.

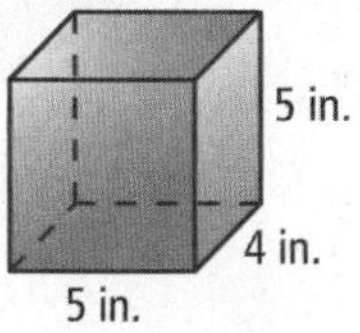

10.

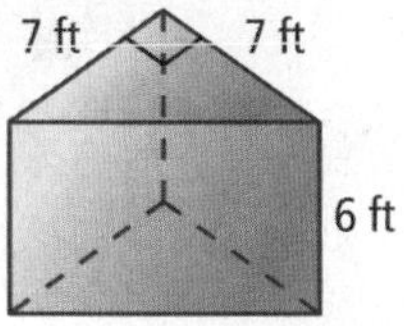

What is the surface area of each cylinder?

11.

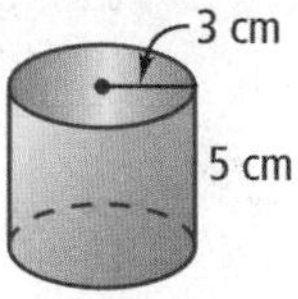

12.

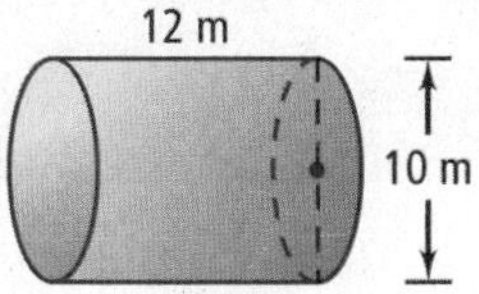

Do you UNDERSTAND?

MATHEMATICAL PRACTICES

13. Vocabulary Name the lateral faces and the bases of the prism at the right.

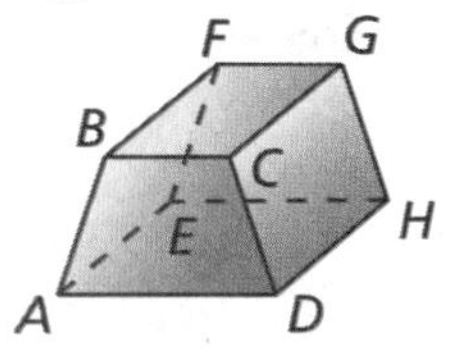

14. Error Analysis Your friend drew a net of a cylinder. What is your friend's error? Explain.

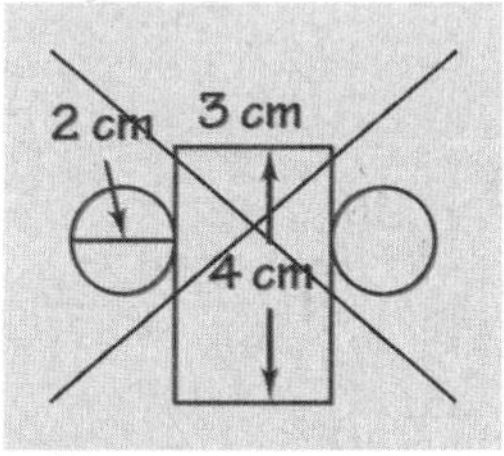

More Practice and Problem-Solving Exercises

MATHEMATICAL PRACTICES

B Apply

15. A triangular prism has base edges 4 cm, 5 cm, and 6 cm long. Its lateral area is 300 cm². What is the height of the prism?

16. Writing Explain how a cylinder and a prism are alike and how they are different.

17. Pencils A hexagonal pencil is a regular hexagonal prism, as shown at the right. A base edge of the pencil has a length of 4 mm. The pencil (without eraser) has a height of 170 mm. What is the area of the surface of the pencil that gets painted?

18. Open-Ended Draw a net for a rectangular prism with a surface area of 220 cm².

19. Consider a rectangular box with dimensions 3, 4, and 5.
  a. Find its surface area.
  b. Double each dimension and then find the new surface area.
  c. Find the ratio of the new surface area to the original surface area.
  d. Repeat parts (a)–(c) for a box with dimensions 6, 9, and 11.
  e. Make a Conjecture How does doubling the dimensions of a rectangular prism affect the surface area?

20. Think About a Plan A cylindrical bead has a square hole, as shown at the right. Find the area of the surface of the entire bead.

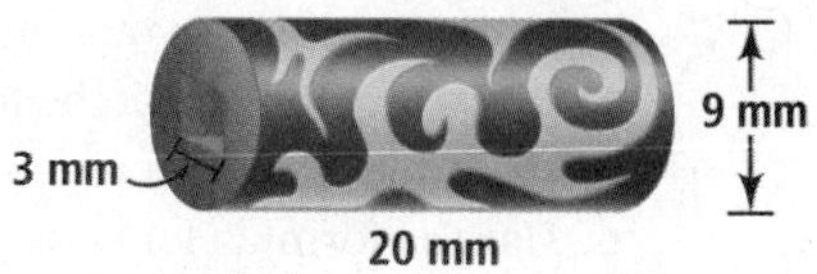

- Can you visualize the bead as a combination of familiar figures?
- How do you find the area of the surface of the inner part of the bead?

21. Estimation Estimate the surface area of a cube with edges 4.95 cm long.

22. Error Analysis Your class is drawing right triangular prisms. Your friend's paper is below. What is your friend's error?

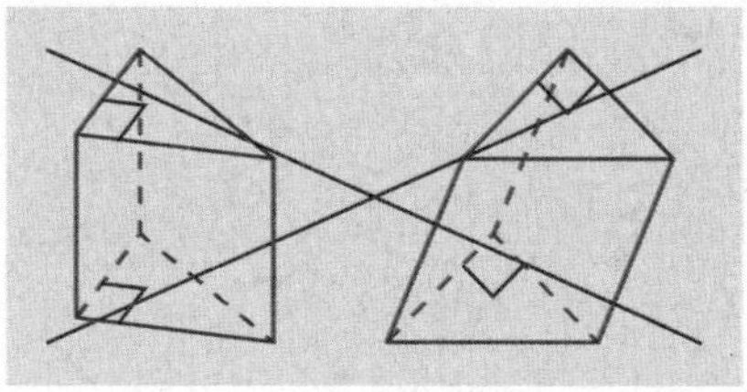

STEM **23. Packaging** A cylindrical can of cocoa has the dimensions shown at the right. What is the approximate surface area available for the label? Round to the nearest square inch.

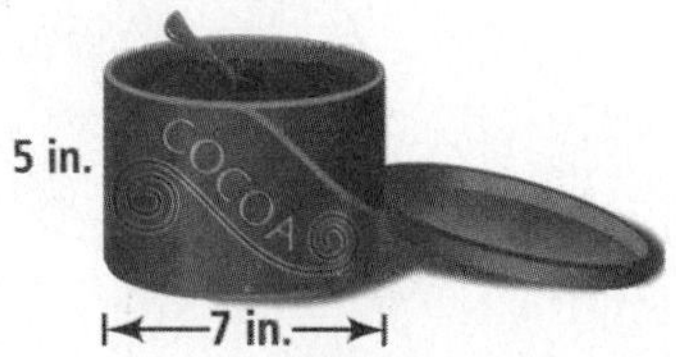

24. Pest Control A flour moth trap has the shape of a triangular prism that is open on both ends. An environmentally safe chemical draws the moth inside the prism, which is lined with an adhesive. What is the area of the trap that is lined with the adhesive?

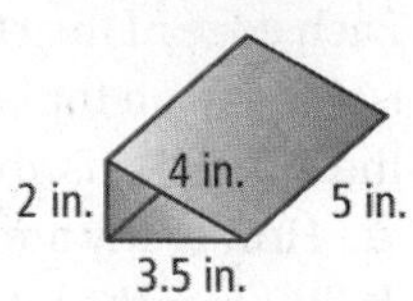

25. Suppose that a cylinder has a radius of r units, and that the height of the cylinder is also r units. The lateral area of the cylinder is 98π square units.

a. **Algebra** Find the value of r.

b. Find the surface area of the cylinder.

26. Geometry in 3 Dimensions Use the diagram at the right.

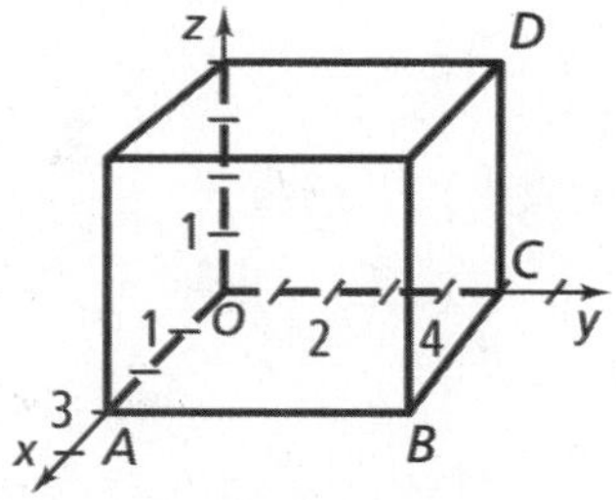

a. Find the three coordinates of each vertex A, B, C, and D of the rectangular prism.

b. Find AB.

c. Find BC.

d. Find CD.

e. Find the surface area of the prism.

Visualization Suppose you revolve the plane region completely about the given line to sweep out a solid of revolution. Describe the solid and find its surface area in terms of π.

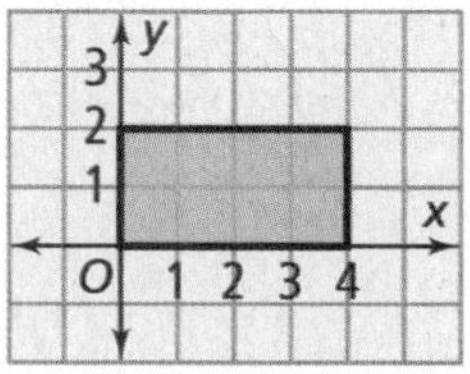

27. the y-axis

28. the x-axis

29. the line $y = 2$

30. the line $x = 4$

31. Reasoning Suppose you double the radius of a right cylinder.

a. How does that affect the lateral area?

b. How does that affect the surface area?

c. Use the formula for surface area of a right cylinder to explain why the surface area in part (b) was not doubled.

32. Packaging Some cylinders have wrappers with a spiral seam. Peeled off, the wrapper has the shape of a parallelogram. The wrapper for a biscuit container has base 7.5 in. and height 6 in.

a. Find the radius and height of the container.

b. Find the surface area of the container.

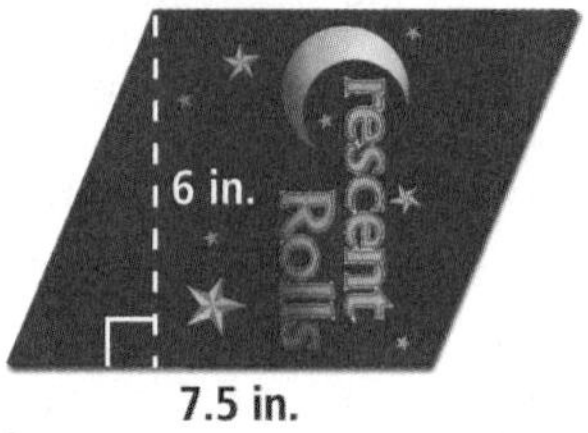

Challenge

What is the surface area of each solid in terms of π?

33.

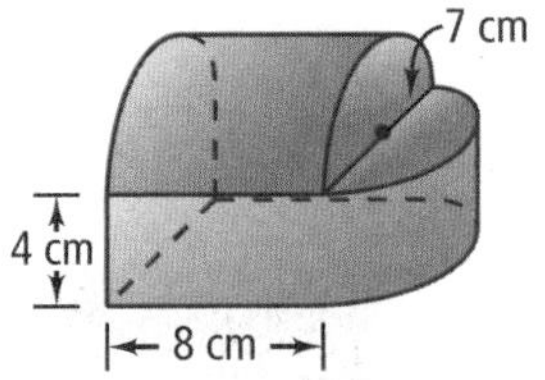

34.

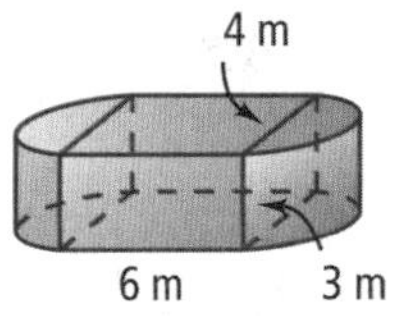

35.

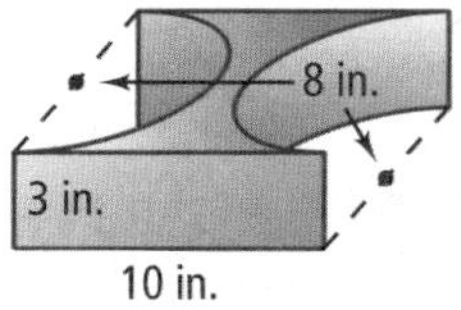

36. Each edge of the large cube at the right is 12 inches long. The cube is painted on the outside, and then cut into 27 smaller cubes. Answer these questions about the 27 cubes.

a. How many are painted on 4, 3, 2, 1, and 0 faces?

b. What is the total surface area that is unpainted?

37. Algebra The sum of the height and radius of a cylinder is 9 m. The surface area of the cylinder is 54π m^2. Find the height and the radius.

13-2 Surface Areas of Pyramids and Cones

G.MG.1 Use geometric shapes . . . to describe objects. Also **N.Q.2**

Objective To find the surface area of a pyramid and a cone

Solve It! Write your solution to the Solve It in the space below.

The Solve It involves the triangular faces of a roof and the three-dimensional figures they form. In this lesson, you will learn to name such figures and to use formulas to find their areas.

Essential Understanding To find the surface area of a three-dimensional figure, find the sum of the areas of all the surfaces of the figure.

A **pyramid** is a polyhedron in which one face (the **base**) can be any polygon and the other faces (the **lateral faces**) are triangles that meet at a common vertex (called the **vertex** of the pyramid).

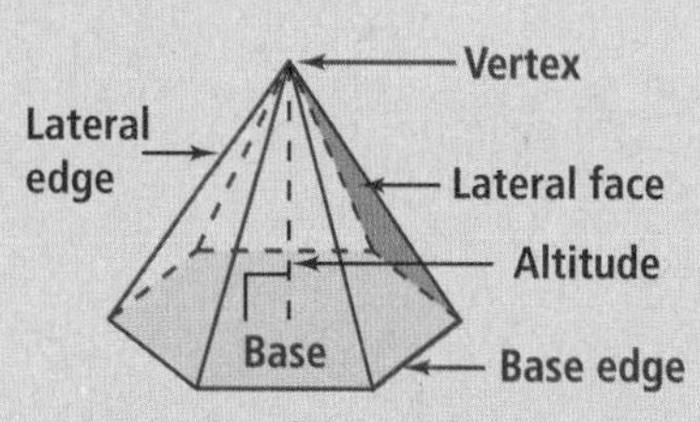

Hexagonal pyramid

You name a pyramid by the shape of its base. The **altitude** of a pyramid is the perpendicular segment from the vertex to the plane of the base. The length of the altitude is the **height** h of the pyramid.

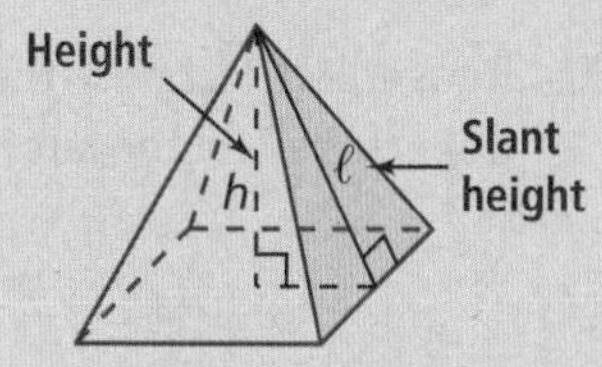

Square pyramid

A **regular pyramid** is a pyramid whose base is a regular polygon and whose lateral faces are congruent isosceles triangles. The **slant height** ℓ is the length of the altitude of a lateral face of the pyramid.

In this book, you can assume that a pyramid is regular unless stated otherwise.

The **lateral area** of a pyramid is the sum of the areas of the congruent lateral faces. You can find a formula for the lateral area of a pyramid by looking at its net.

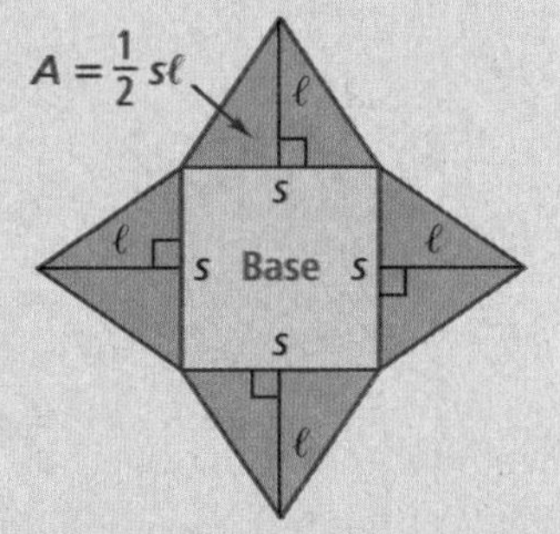

L.A. $= 4\left(\frac{1}{2}s\ell\right)$ The area of each lateral face is $\frac{1}{2}s\ell$.

$= \frac{1}{2}(4s)\ell$ Commutative and Associative Properties of Multiplication

$= \frac{1}{2}p\ell$ The perimeter p of the base is $4s$.

To find the **surface area** of a pyramid, add the area of its base to its lateral area.

take note

Theorem 91 Lateral and Surface Areas of a Pyramid

The lateral area of a regular pyramid is half the product of the perimeter p of the base and the slant height l of the pyramid.

L.A. $= \frac{1}{2}p\ell$

The surface area of a regular pyramid is the sum of the lateral area and the area B of the base.

S.A. = L.A. + B

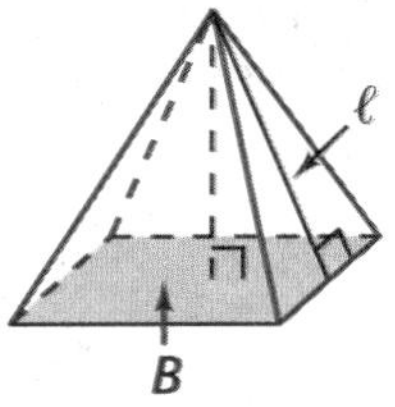

Problem 1 Finding the Surface Area of a Pyramid

Got It? **a.** A square pyramid has base edges of 5 m and a slant height of 3 m. What is the surface area of the pyramid?

b. Reasoning Suppose the slant height of a pyramid is doubled. How does this affect the lateral area of the pyramid? Explain.

A Practice Find the surface area of each pyramid to the nearest whole number.

1.

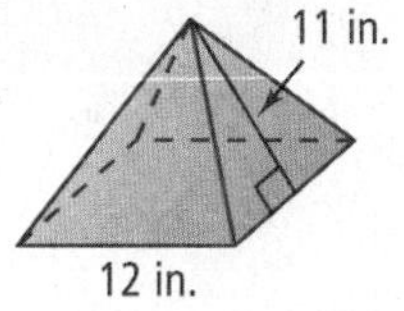

2.

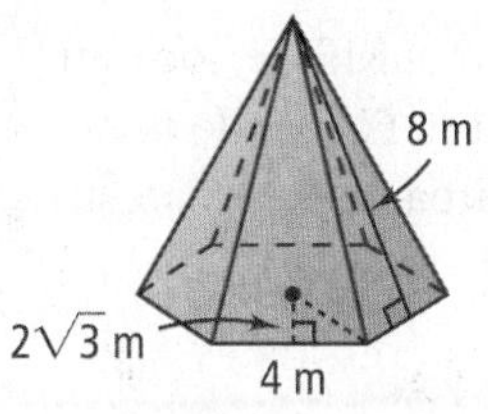

When the slant height of a pyramid is not given, you must calculate it before you can find the lateral area or surface area.

Problem 2 Finding the Lateral Area of a Pyramid

Got It? **a.** What is the lateral area of the hexagonal pyramid below? Round to the nearest square foot.

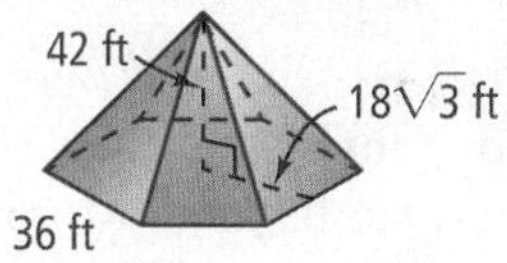

Think

What measurement do you need that is not given in the diagram?

b. Reasoning How does the slant height of a regular pyramid relate to its height? Explain.

Practice 3. Find the lateral area of the pyramid to the nearest square centimeter.

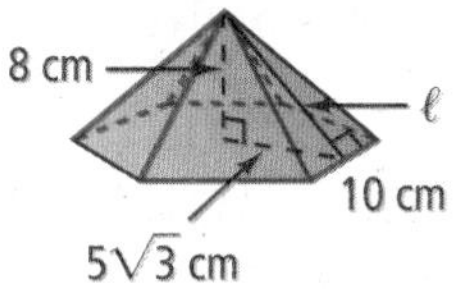

4. **Social Studies** The original height of the Pyramid of Khafre, located next to the Great Pyramid in Egypt, was about 471 ft. Each side of its square base was about 708 ft. What is the lateral area, to the nearest square foot, of a pyramid with those dimensions?

Like a pyramid, a **cone** is a solid that has one base and a vertex that is not in the same plane as the base. However, the **base** of a cone is a circle. In a **right cone**, the **altitude** is a perpendicular segment from the **vertex** to the center of the base. The **height** h is the length of the altitude. The **slant height** ℓ is the distance from the vertex to a point on the edge of the base. In this book, you can assume that a cone is a right cone unless stated or pictured otherwise.

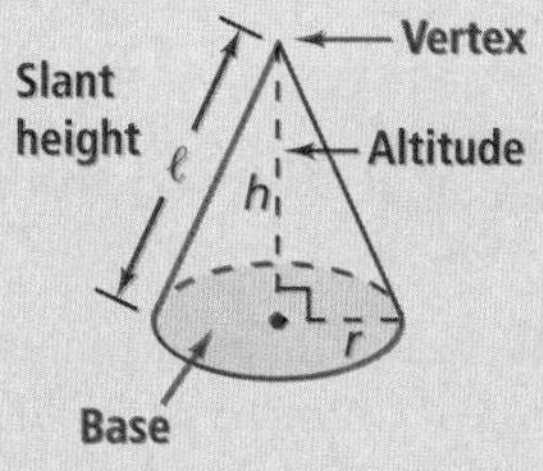

The **lateral area** is half the circumference of the base times the slant height. The formulas for the lateral area and **surface area** of a cone are similar to those for a pyramid.

take note

Theorem 92 Lateral and Surface Areas of a Cone

The lateral area of a right cone is half the product of the circumference of the base and the slant height of the cone.

$$\text{L.A.} = \frac{1}{2} \cdot 2\pi r \cdot \ell, \text{ or L.A.} = \pi r \ell$$

The surface area of a cone is the sum of the lateral area and the area of the base.

$$\text{S.A.} = \text{L.A.} + B$$

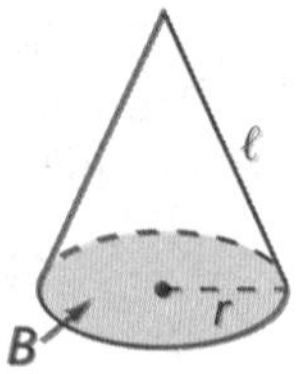

Problem 3 Finding the Surface Area of a Cone

Got It? The radius of the base of a cone is 16 m. Its slant height is 28 m. What is the surface area in terms of π?

Practice Find the surface area of each cone in terms of π.

5.

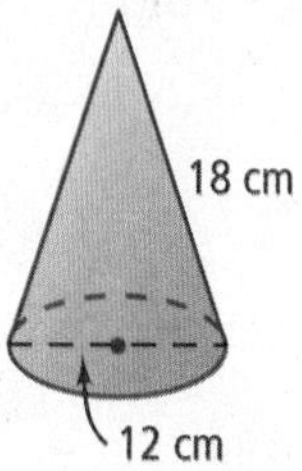

6.

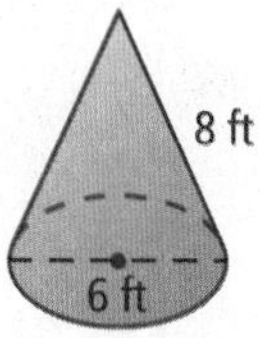

By cutting a cone and laying it out flat, you can see how the formula for the lateral area of a cone ($L.A = \frac{1}{2} \cdot C_{base} \cdot \ell$) resembles that for the area of a triangle ($A = \frac{1}{2}bh$).

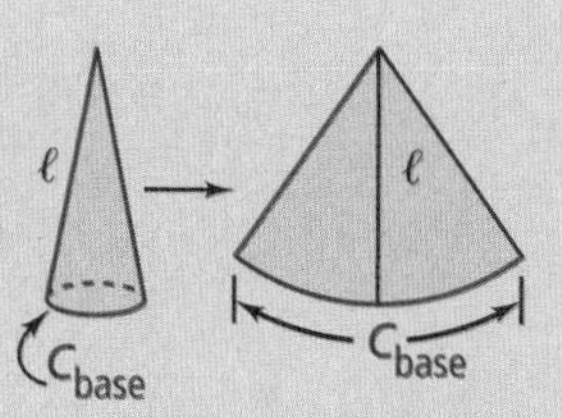

Problem 4 Finding the Lateral Area of a Cone

Think **What measurements do you need to find the lateral area?**

Got It? **a.** What is the lateral area of a traffic cone with radius 10 in. and height 28 in.? Round to the nearest whole number.

b. Reasoning Suppose the radius of a cone is halved, but the slant height remains the same. How does this affect the lateral area of the cone? Explain.

Practice Find the lateral area of each cone to the nearest whole number.

7.

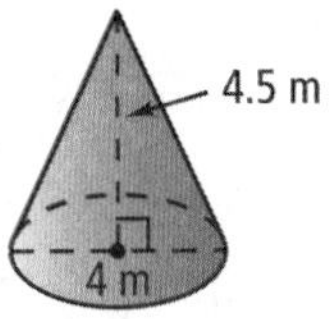

8.

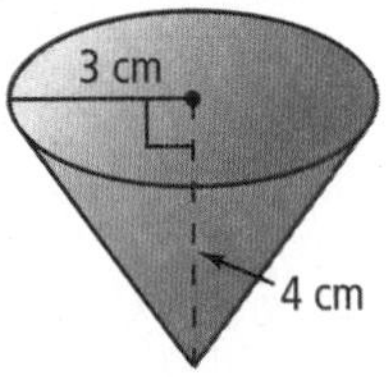

Lesson Check

Do you know HOW?

Use the diagram of the square pyramid at the right.

9. What is the lateral area of the pyramid?

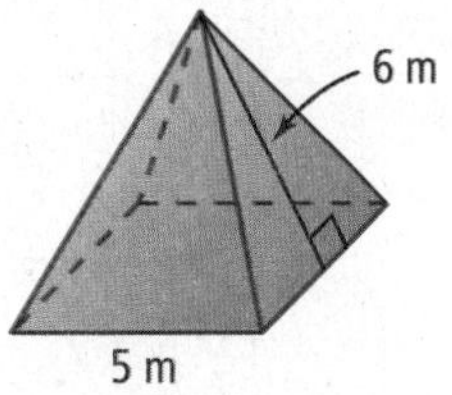

10. What is the surface area of the pyramid?

Use the diagram of the cone at the right.

11. What is the lateral area of the cone?

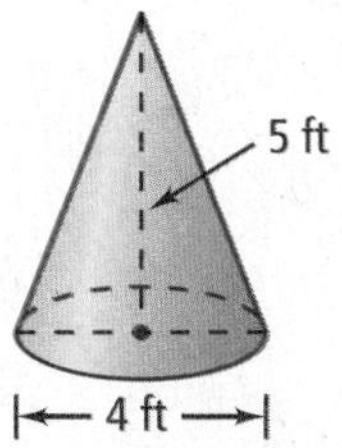

12. What is the surface area of the cone?

Do you UNDERSTAND?

MATHEMATICAL PRACTICES

13. Vocabulary How do the height and the slant height of a pyramid differ?

14. Compare and Contrast How are the formulas for the surface area of a prism and the surface area of a pyramid alike? How are they different?

15. Vocabulary How many lateral faces does a pyramid have if its base is pentagonal? Hexagonal? *n*-sided?

16. Error Analysis A cone has height 7 and radius 3. Your classmate calculates its lateral area. What is your classmate's error? Explain.

$$\begin{aligned} \text{L.A.} &= \pi r \ell \\ &= \pi(3)(7) \\ &= 21\pi \end{aligned}$$

More Practice and Problem-Solving Exercises

MATHEMATICAL PRACTICES

B Apply

17. Reasoning Suppose you could climb to the top of the Great Pyramid. Which route would be shorter, a route along a lateral edge or a route along the slant height of a side? Which of these routes is steeper? Explain your answers.

18. The lateral area of a cone is 4.8π in.^{2}. The radius is 1.2 in. Find the slant height.

19. Writing Explain why the altitude $\overline{PT}$ in the pyramid at the right must be shorter than all of the lateral edges $\overline{PA}$, $\overline{PB}$, $\overline{PC}$, and $\overline{PD}$.

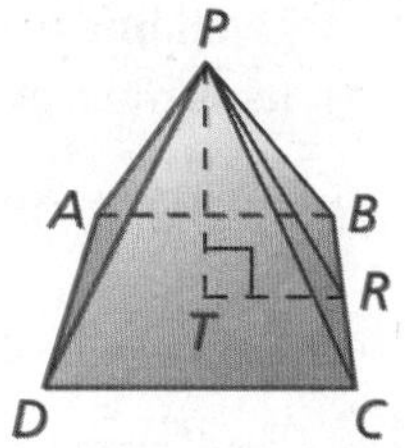

20. Think About a Plan The lateral area of a pyramid with a square base is 240 ft^2. Its base edges are 12 ft long. Find the height of the pyramid.

- What additional information do you know about the pyramid based on the given information?
- How can a diagram help you identify what you need to find?

Find the surface area to the nearest whole number.

21.

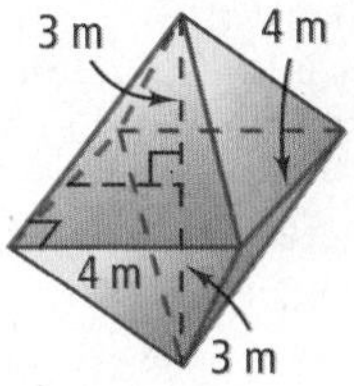

22.

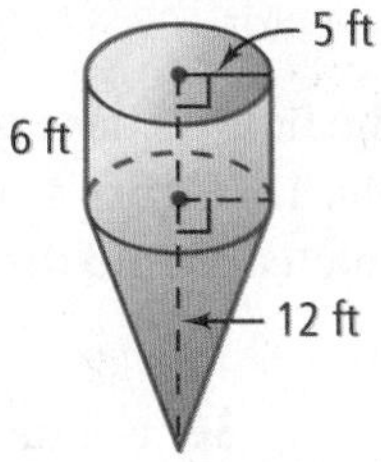

23.

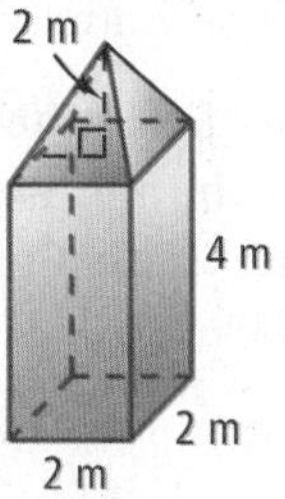

24. Open-Ended Draw a square pyramid with a lateral area of 48 cm^2. Label its dimensions. Then find its surface area.

STEM **25. Architecture** The roof of a tower in a castle is shaped like a cone. The height of the roof is 30 ft and the radius of the base is 15 ft. What is the lateral area of the roof? Round your answer to the nearest tenth.

26. Reasoning The figure at the right shows two glass cones inside a cylinder. Which has a greater surface area, the two cones or the cylinder? Explain.

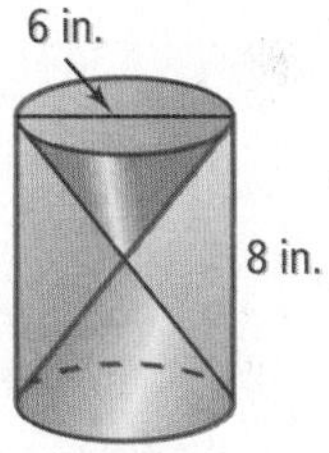

27. Writing You can use the formula S.A. $= (l + r)\,r\pi$ to find the surface area of a cone. Explain why this formula works. Also, explain why you may prefer to use this formula when finding surface area with a calculator.

28. Find a formula for the slant height of a cone in terms of the surface area and radius.

The slant height (ℓ), the height (h), the length of a side (s) of the base, the lateral area (L.A.), and the surface area (S.A.) are measurements of a square pyramid. Given two of the measurements, find the other three to the nearest tenth.

29. $s = 3$ in., S.A. $= 39$ in.^{2}

30. $h = 8$ m, $\ell = 10$ m

31. L.A. $= 118$ cm^2, S.A. $= 182$ cm^2

Visualization **Suppose you revolve the plane region completely about the given line to sweep out a solid of revolution. Describe the solid. Then find its surface area in terms of π.**

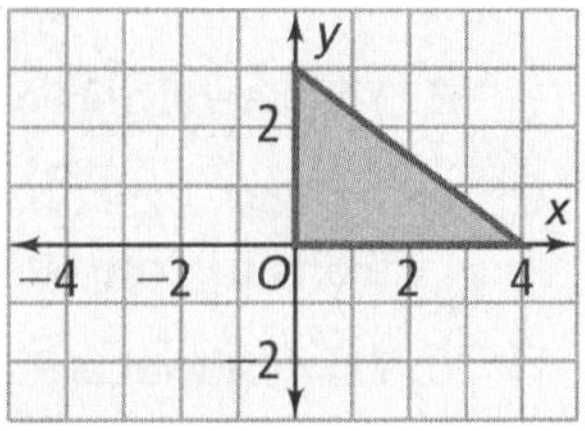

32. the y-axis

33. the x-axis

34. the line $x = 4$

35. the line $y = 3$

Challenge

36. A sector has been cut out of the disk at the right. The radii of the part that remains are taped together, without overlapping, to form the cone. The cone has a lateral area of 64π cm^2. Find the measure of the central angle of the cutout sector.

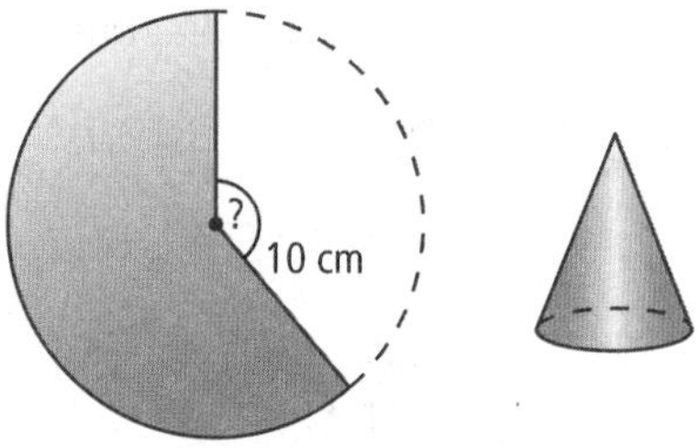

Each given figure fits inside a 10-cm cube. The figure's base is in one face of the cube and is as large as possible. The figure's vertex is in the opposite face of the cube. Draw a sketch and find the lateral and surface areas of the figure.

37. a square pyramid

38. a cone

13-3 Volumes of Prisms and Cylinders

G.GMD.3 Use volume formulas for cylinders . . . Also **G.GMD.1, G.GMD.2, G.MG.1**

Objective To find the volume of a prism and the volume of a cylinder

Solve It! Write your solution to the Solve It in the space below.

In the Solve It, you determined the volume of a box by finding how many 1 cm-by-1 cm-by-1 cm cubes the box holds.

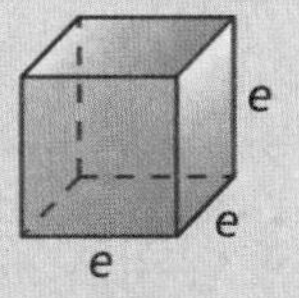

Volume is the space that a figure occupies. It is measured in cubic units such as cubic inches (in.^{3}), cubic feet (ft^3), or cubic centimeters (cm^3). The volume V of a cube is the cube of the length of its edge e, or $V = e^3$.

Essential Understanding You can find the volume of a prism or a cylinder when you know its height and the area of its base.

Both stacks of paper below contain the same number of sheets.

The first stack forms an oblique prism. The second forms a right prism. The stacks have the same height. The area of every cross section parallel to a base is the area of one sheet of paper. The stacks have the same volume. These stacks illustrate the following principle.

take note

Theorem 93 Cavalieri's Principle

If two space figures have the same height and the same cross-sectional area at every level, then they have the same volume.

The area of each shaded cross section below is 6 cm^2. Since the prisms have the same height, their volumes must be the same by Cavalieri's Principle.

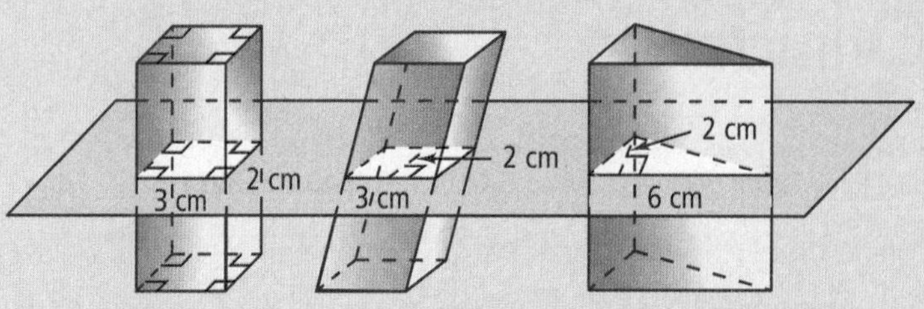

You can find the volume of a right prism by multiplying the area of the base by the height. Cavalieri's Principle lets you extend this idea to any prism.

take note

Theorem 94 Volume of a Prism

The volume of a prism is the product of the area of the base and the height of the prism.

$V = Bh$

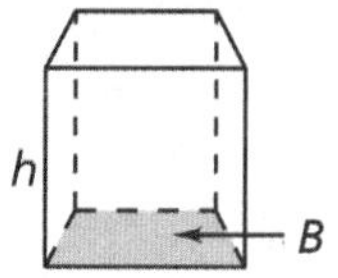

Problem 1 Finding the Volume of a Rectangular Prism

Got It? **a.** What is the volume of the rectangular prism at the right?

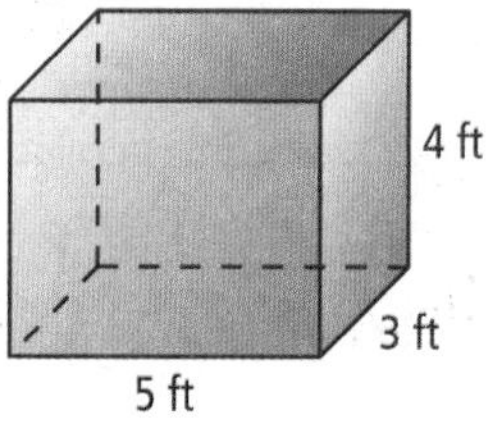

b. Reasoning Suppose the prism above is turned so that the base is 4 ft by 5 ft and the height is 3 ft. Does the volume change? Explain.

Practice 1. Find the volume of the rectangular prism.

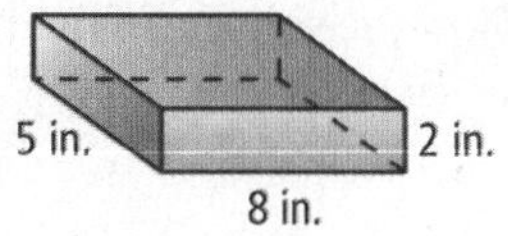

2. Find the volume of a rectangular prism with height 3.5 cm, and a square base with side length 2 cm.

Problem 2 Finding the Volume of a Triangular Prism

Think
How do you find the area of the triangular base?

Got It? a. What is the volume of the triangular prism below?

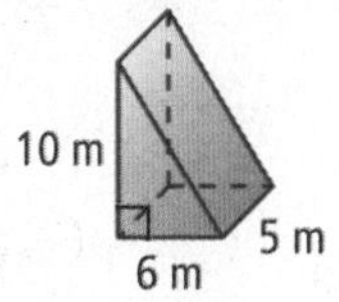

b. Reasoning Suppose the height of a prism is doubled. How does this affect the volume of the prism? Explain.

Practice 3. Find the volume of the triangular prism.

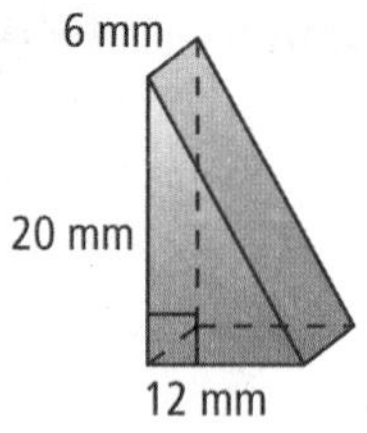

4. The base of a triangular prism is a 45°-45°-90° triangle with a leg of 5 in. The height is 1.8 in. Find the volume.

To find the volume of a cylinder, you use the same formula, $V = Bh$, that you use to find the volume of a prism. Now, however, B is the area of a circle, so you use the formula $B = \pi r^2$ to find its value.

take note

Theorem 95 Volume of a Cylinder

The volume of a cylinder is the product of the area of the base and the height of the cylinder.

$V = Bh$, or $V = \pi r^2 h$

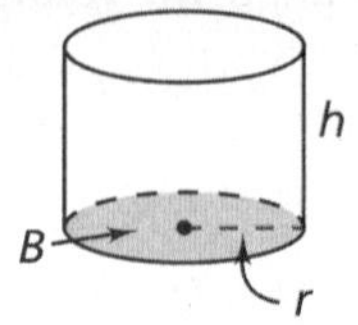

Problem 3 Finding the Volume of a Cylinder

Got It? a. What is the volume of the cylinder at the right in terms of π?

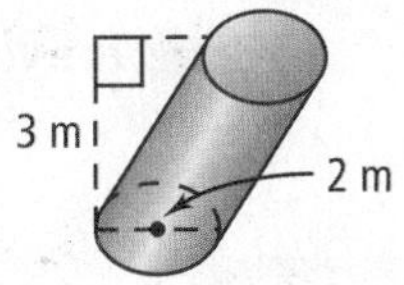

b. **Reasoning** Suppose the radius of a cylinder is halved. How does this affect the volume of the cylinder? Explain.

Practice 5. Find the volume of the cylinder in terms of π and to the nearest tenth.

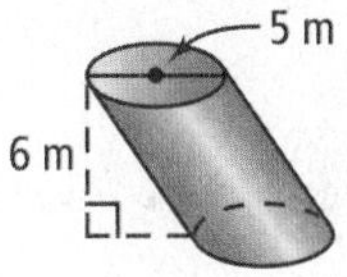

6. The diameter of a cylinder is 1 yd. Its height is 4 yd. Find the volume in terms of π and to the nearest tenth.

A **composite space figure** is a three-dimensional figure that is the combination of two or more simpler figures. You can find the volume of a composite space figure by adding the volumes of the figures that are combined.

Problem 4 Finding Volume of a Composite Figure

Got It? What is the approximate volume of the lunch box shown below? Round to the nearest cubic inch.

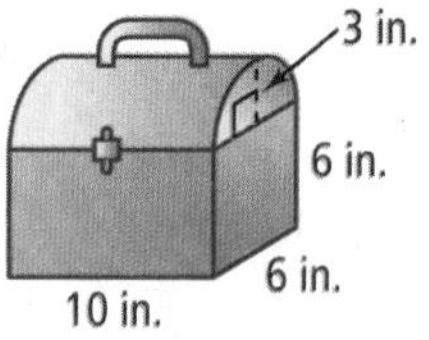

Plan

How can you find the volume by *solving a simpler problem?*

Practice 7. **Composite Figures** Use the diagram of the backpack at the right.

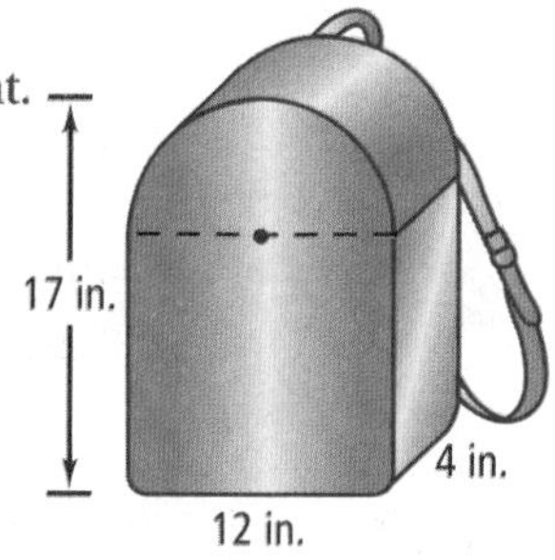

a. What two figures approximate the shape of the backpack?

b. What is the volume of the backpack in terms of π?

c. What is the volume of the backpack to the nearest cubic inch?

8. Find the volume of the composite space figure to the nearest cubic centimeter.

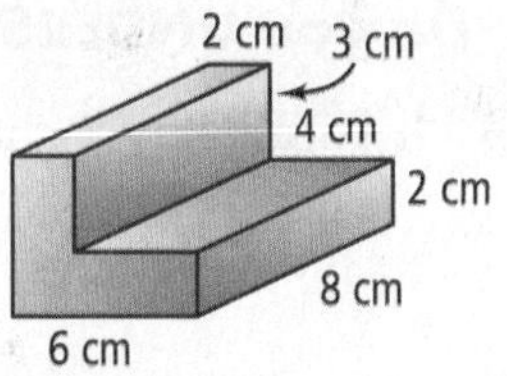

Lesson Check

Do you know HOW?

What is the volume of each figure? If necessary, round to the nearest whole number.

9.

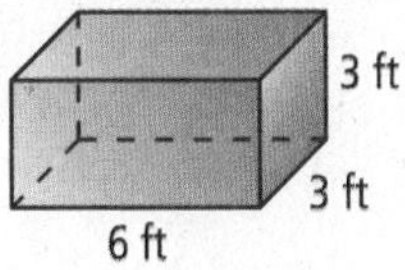

10.

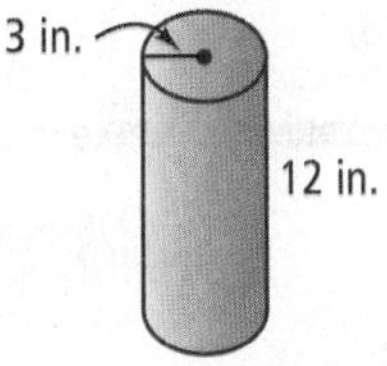

Do you UNDERSTAND?

MATHEMATICAL PRACTICES

11. Vocabulary Is the figure at the right a composite space figure? Explain.

12. Compare and Contrast How are the formulas for the volume of a prism and the volume of a cylinder alike? How are they different?

13. Reasoning How is the volume of a rectangular prism with base 2 m by 3 m and height 4 m related to the volume of a rectangular prism with base 3 m by 4 m and height 2 m? Explain.

More Practice and Problem-Solving Exercises

MATHEMATICAL PRACTICES

B Apply

14. Think About a Plan A full water bed mattress is 7 ft by 4 ft by 1 ft. If water weighs 62.4 lb/ft^3, what is the weight of the water in the mattress to the nearest pound?

- How can you determine the amount of water the mattress can hold?
- The weight of the water is in pounds per cubic feet. How can you get an answer with a unit of pounds?

15. Open-Ended Give the dimensions of two rectangular prisms that have volumes of 80 cm^3 each but also have different surface areas.

Find the height of each figure with the given volume.

16. 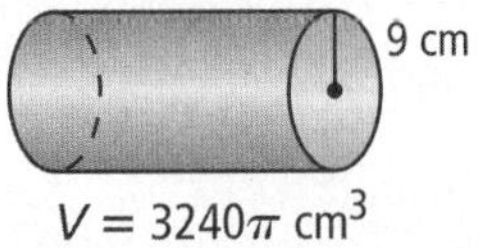

17. 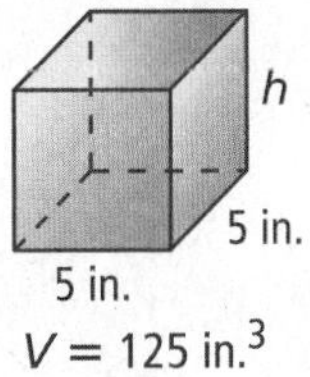

18. 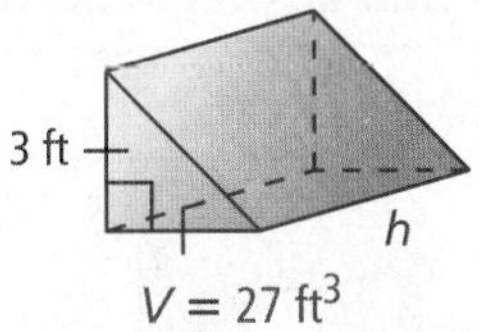

19. **Sports** A can of tennis balls has a diameter of 3 in. and a height of 8 in. Find the volume of the can to the nearest cubic inch.

20. What is the volume of the oblique prism shown at the right?

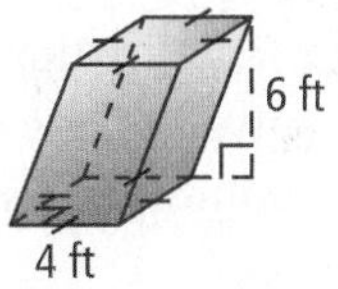

STEM 21. **Environmental Engineering** A scientist suggests keeping indoor air relatively clean as follows: For a room with a ceiling 8 ft high, provide two or three pots of flowers for every 100 ft^2 of floor space. If your classroom has an 8-ft ceiling and measures 35 ft by 40 ft, how many pots of flowers should it have?

22. **Reasoning** Suppose the dimensions of a prism are tripled. How does this affect its volume? Explain.

23. **Swimming Pool** The approximate dimensions of an Olympic-size swimming pool are 164 ft by 82 ft by 6.6 ft.
   a. Find the volume of the pool to the nearest cubic foot.
   b. If 1 $ft^3 \approx 7.48$ gal, about how many gallons does the pool hold?

24. **Writing** The figures at the right can be covered by equal numbers of straws that are the same length. Describe how Cavalieri's Principle could be adapted to compare the areas of these figures.

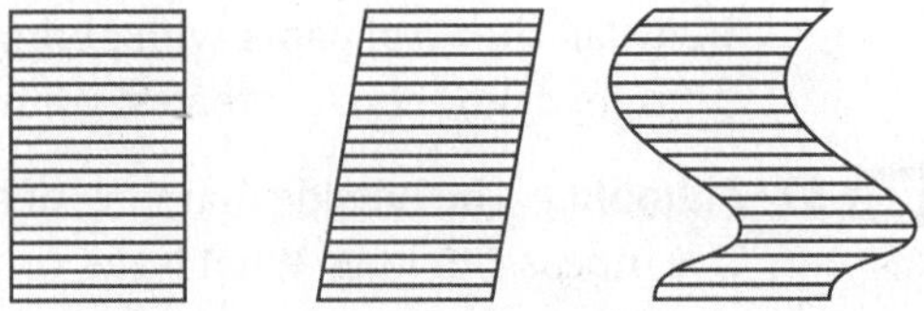

25. **Algebra** The volume of a cylinder is 600π cm^3. The radius of a base of the cylinder is 5 cm. What is the height of the cylinder?

26. **Coordinate Geometry** Find the volume of the rectangular prism at the right.

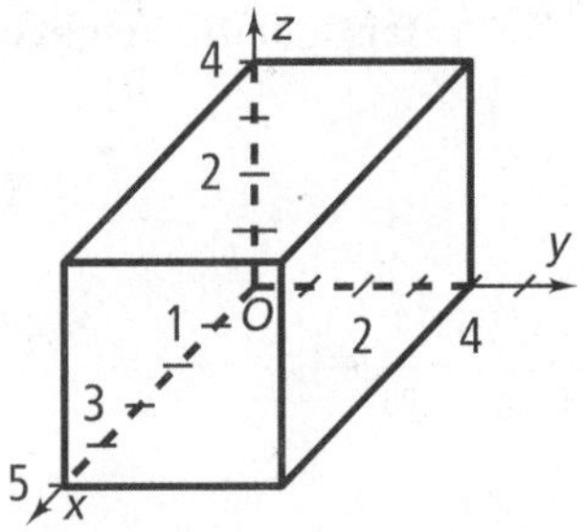

27. **Algebra** The volume of a cylinder is 135π cm^3. The height of the cylinder is 15 cm. What is the radius of a base of the cylinder?

28. **Landscaping** To landscape her 70 ft-by-60 ft rectangular backyard, your aunt is planning first to put down a 4-in. layer of topsoil. She can buy bags of topsoil at $2.50 per 3-$ft^3$ bag, with free delivery. Or, she can buy bulk topsoil for $22.00/$yd^3$, plus a $20 delivery fee. Which option is less expensive? Explain.

29. The closed box at the right is shaped like a regular pentagonal prism. The exterior of the box has base edge 10 cm and height 14 cm. The interior has base edge 7 cm and height 11 cm. Find each measurement to the nearest tenth.
   a. the outside surface area
   b. the inside surface area
   c. the volume of the material needed to make the box

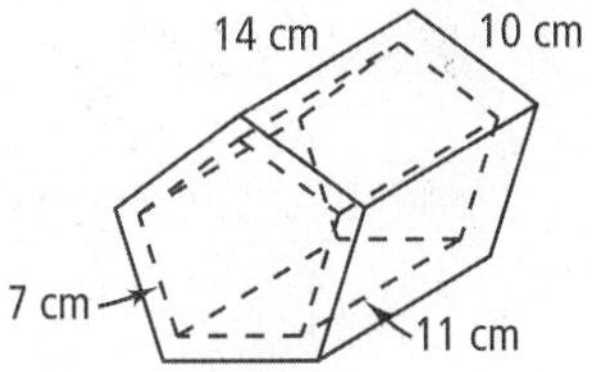

A cylinder has been cut out of each solid. Find the volume of the remaining solid. Round your answer to the nearest tenth.

30.

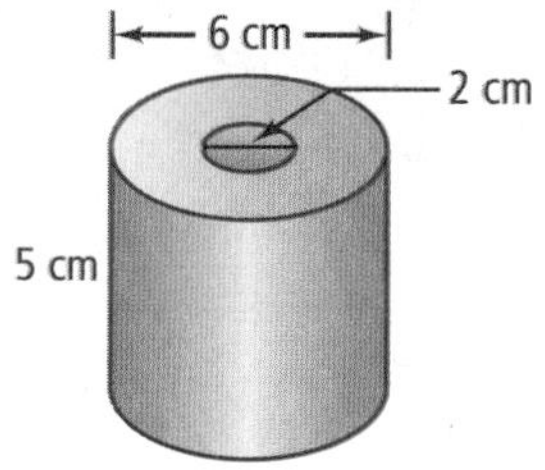

31.

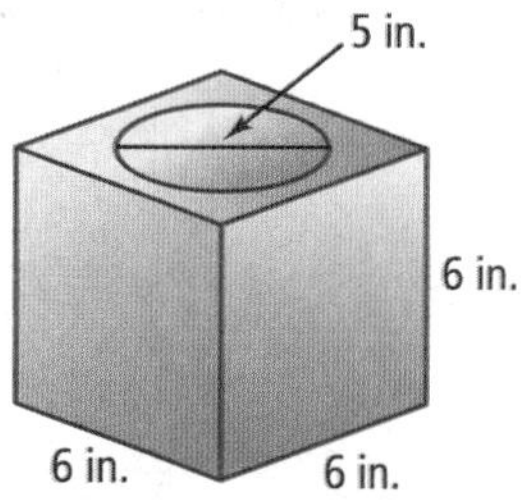

Visualization Suppose you revolve the plane region completely about the given line to sweep out a solid of revolution. Describe the solid and find its volume in terms of π.

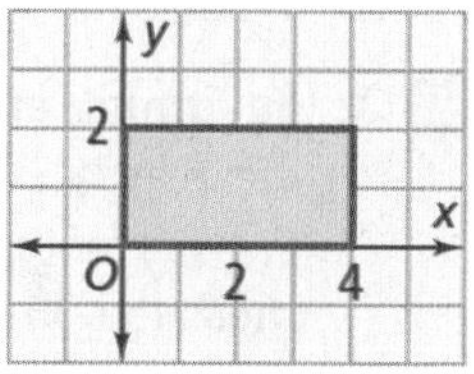

32. the x-axis

33. the y-axis

34. the line $y = 2$

35. the line $x = 5$

Challenge

36. Paper Folding Any rectangular sheet of paper can be rolled into a right cylinder in two ways.

a. Use ordinary sheets of paper to model the two cylinders. Compute the volume of each cylinder. How do they compare?

b. Of all sheets of paper with perimeter 39 in., which size can be rolled into a right cylinder with greatest volume? (*Hint:* Try making a table.)

STEM **37. Plumbing** The outside diameter of a pipe is 5 cm. The inside diameter is 4 cm. The pipe is 4 m long. What is the volume of the material used for this length of pipe? Round your answer to the nearest cubic centimeter.

38. The radius of Cylinder B is twice the radius of Cylinder A. The height of Cylinder B is half the height of Cylinder A. Compare their volumes.

ACTIVITY LAB

Use With Lesson 13-4

Finding Volume

G.GMD.1 Give an informal argument for the formulas for the . . . area of a circle, volume of a cylinder, pyramid, and cone.

Activity 1

Step 1 Draw the nets shown at the right on heavy paper.

Step 2 Cut out the nets and tape them together to make a cube and a square pyramid. Each model will have one open face.

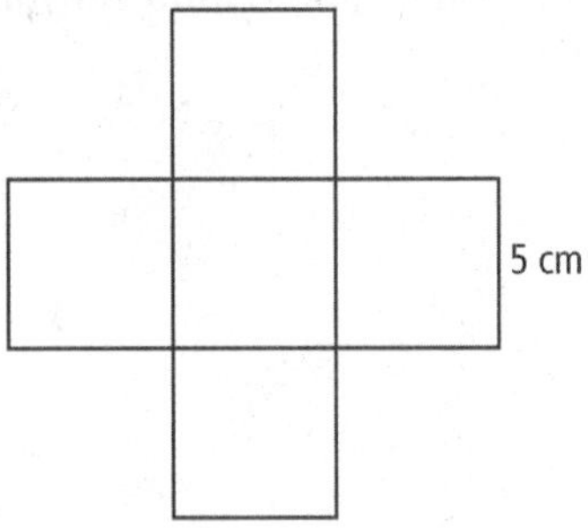

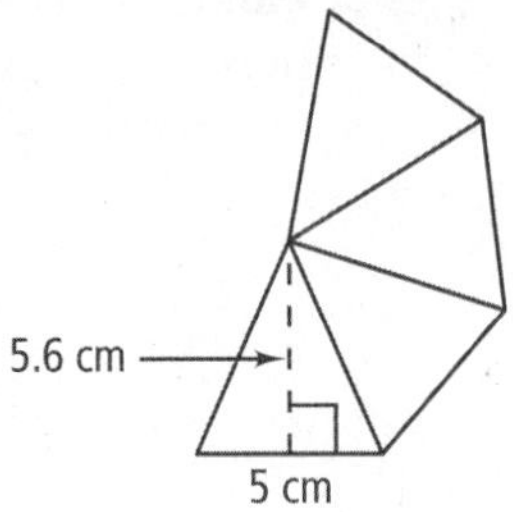

1. How do the areas of the bases of the cube and the pyramid compare?

2. How do the heights of the cube and the pyramid compare?

3. Fill the pyramid with rice or other material. Then pour the rice from the pyramid into the cube. How many pyramids full of rice does the cube hold?

4. The volume of the pyramid is what fractional part of the volume of the cube?

5. **Make a Conjecture** What do you think the formula for the volume of a pyramid is? Explain.

Activity 2

Step 1 Draw the nets shown at the right on heavy paper.

Step 2 Cut out the nets and tape them together to make a cylinder and a cone. Each model will have one open face.

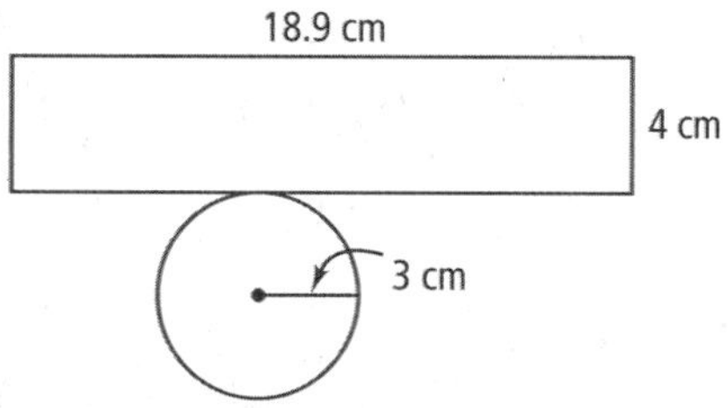

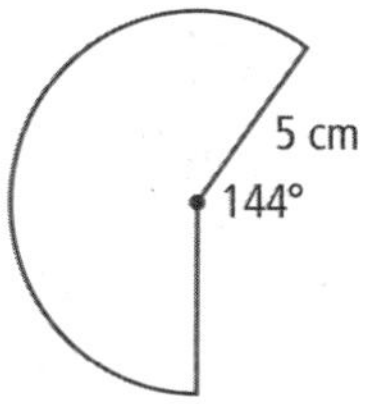

6. How do the areas of the bases of the cylinder and the cone compare?

7. How do the heights of the cylinder and the cone compare?

8. Fill the cone with rice or other material. Then pour the rice from the cone into the cylinder. How many cones full of rice does the cylinder hold?

9. What fractional part of the volume of the cylinder is the volume of the cone?

10. Make a Conjecture What do you think the formula for the volume of a cone is? Explain.

13-4 Volumes of Pyramids and Cones

G.GMD.3 Use volume formulas for . . . pyramids, cones . . . to solve problems. Also **G.GMD.1, G.GMD.2, G.MG.1**

Objective To find the volume of a pyramid and of a cone

Solve It! Write your solution to the Solve It in the space below.

In the Solve It, you analyzed the relationship between the volume of a prism and the volume of an embedded pyramid.

Essential Understanding The volume of a pyramid is related to the volume of a prism with the same base and height.

take note

Theorem 96 Volume of a Pyramid

The volume of a pyramid is one third the product of the area of the base and the height of the pyramid.

$$V = \frac{1}{3}Bh$$

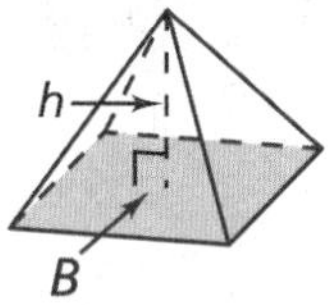

Because of Cavalieri's Principle, the volume formula is true for all pyramids. The height h of an oblique pyramid is the length of the perpendicular segment from its vertex to the plane of the base.

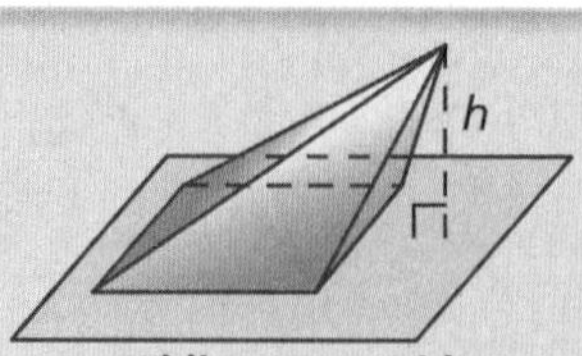

Oblique pyramid

Problem 1 Finding Volume of a Pyramid

Got It? A sports arena shaped like a pyramid has a base area of about 300,000 ft^2 and a height of 321 ft. What is the approximate volume of the arena?

A Practice

1. **Buildings** The Transamerica Pyramid Building in San Francisco is 853 ft tall with a square base that is 149 ft on each side. To the nearest thousand cubic feet, what is the volume of the Transamerica Pyramid?

2. Find the volume of the square pyramid. Round to the nearest tenth if necessary.

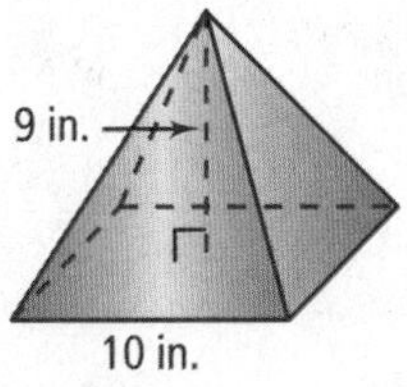

Problem 2 Finding the Volume of a Pyramid

Got It? What is the volume of a square pyramid with base edges 24 m and slant height 13 m?

Think

How is the height of the pyramid related to the slant height?

Practice **Find the volume of each square pyramid, given its slant height. Round to the nearest tenth.**

3.

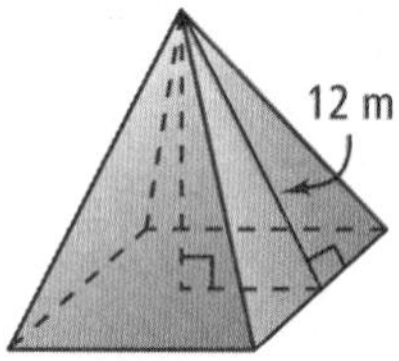

4.

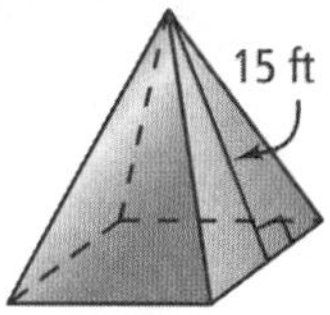

Essential Understanding The volume of a cone is related to the volume of a cylinder with the same base and height.

The cones and the cylinder have the same base and height.
It takes three cones full of rice to fill the cylinder.

take note

Theorem 97 Volume of a Cone

The volume of a cone is one third the product of the area of the base and the height of the cone.

$V = \frac{1}{3}Bh$, or $V = \frac{1}{3}\pi r^2 h$

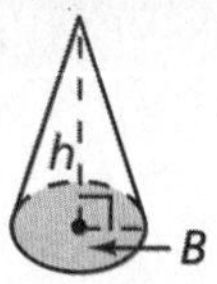

A cone-shaped structure can be particularly strong, as downward forces at the vertex are distributed to all points in its circular base.

Problem 3 Finding the Volume of a Cone

Got It? **a.** The height and radius of a child's tepee are half those of the tepee in Problem 3. What is the volume of the child's tepee to the nearest cubic foot?

b. Reasoning What is the relationship between the volume of the original tepee and the child's tepee?

Think How can you use algebra to verify your answer?

Practice STEM **5. Chemistry** In a chemistry lab you use a filter paper cone to filter a liquid. The diameter of the cone is 6.5 cm and its height is 6 cm. How much liquid will the cone hold when it is full?

STEM **6. Chemistry** This cone has a filter that was being used to remove impurities from a solution but became clogged and stopped draining. The remaining solution is represented by the shaded region. How many cubic centimeters of the solution remain in the cone?

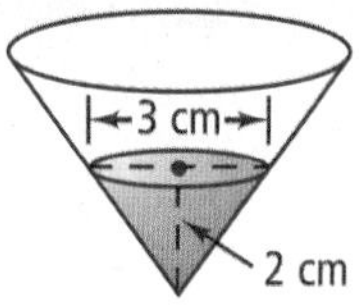

The formula for the volume of a cone applies to all cones, including oblique cones.

Problem 4 Finding the Volume of an Oblique Cone

Got it? **a.** What is the volume of the oblique cone below in terms of π and rounded to the nearest cubic meter?

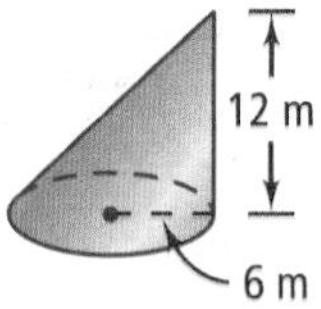

b. Reasoning How does the volume of an oblique cone compare to the volume of a right cone with the same diameter and height? Explain.

Practice Find the volume of each cone in terms of π and rounded to the nearest whole number.

7. 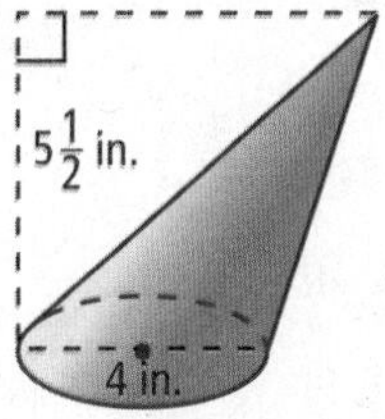

8. 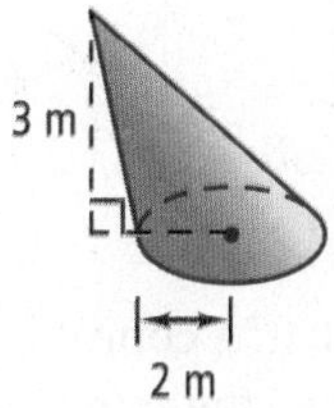

Lesson Check

Do you know HOW?

What is the volume of each figure? If necessary, round to the nearest tenth.

9. 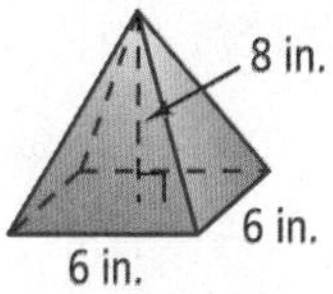

10. 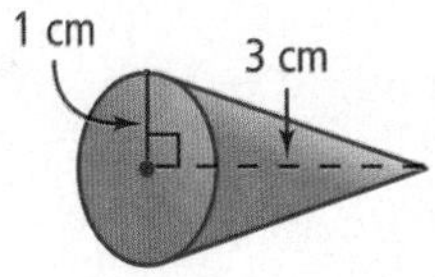

Do you UNDERSTAND?

MATHEMATICAL PRACTICES

11. Compare and Contrast How are the formulas for the volume of a pyramid and the volume of a cone alike? How are they different?

12. Error Analysis A square pyramid has base edges 13 ft and height 10 ft. A cone has diameter 13 ft and height 10 ft. Your friend claims the figures have the same volume because the volume formulas for a pyramid and a cone are the same: $V = \frac{1}{3}Bh$. What is her error?

More Practice and Problem-Solving Exercises

MATHEMATICAL PRACTICES

B Apply

13. Think About a Plan A cone with radius 1 fits snugly inside a square pyramid, which fits snugly inside a cube. What are the volumes of the three figures?

- How can you *draw a diagram* of the situation?
- What dimensions do the cone, pyramid, and cube have in common?

14. Reasoning Suppose the height of a pyramid is halved. How does this affect its volume? Explain.

15. Writing Without doing any calculations, explain how the volume of a cylinder with $B = 5\pi$ cm^2 and $h = 20$ cm compares to the volume of a cone with the same base area and height.

Find the volume to the nearest whole number.

16.

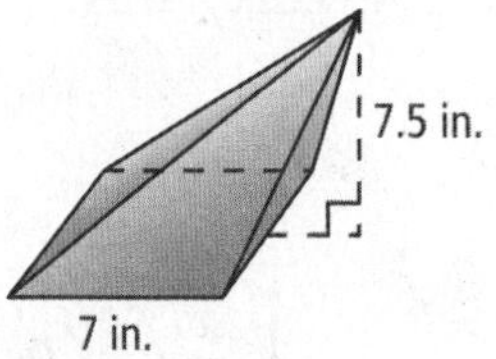

Square base

17.

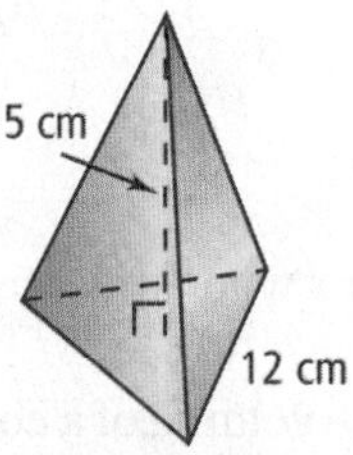

Equilateral base

18.

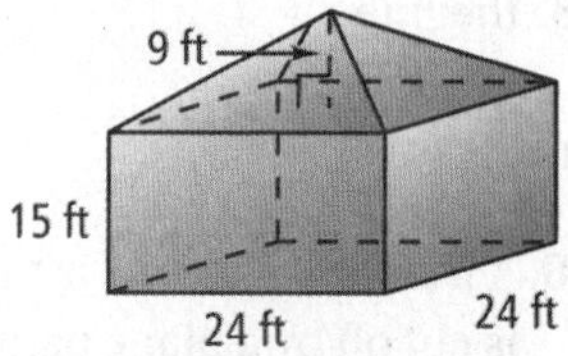

Square base

19. Writing The two cylinders pictured at the right are congruent. How does the volume of the larger cone compare to the total volume of the two smaller cones? Explain.

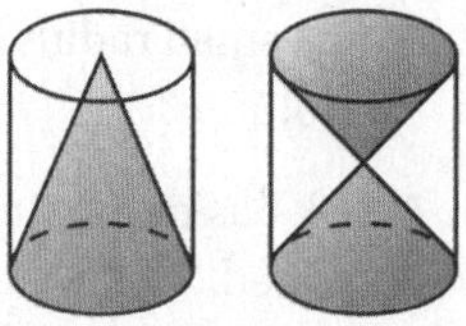

STEM 20. Architecture The Pyramid of Peace is an opera house in Astana, Kazakhstan. The height of the pyramid is approximately 62 m and one side of its square base is approximately 62 m.

a. What is its volume to the nearest thousand cubic meters?

b. How tall would a prism-shaped building with the same square base as the Pyramid of Peace have to be to have the same volume as the pyramid?

STEM 21. Hardware Builders use a plumb bob to find a vertical line. The plumb bob shown at the right combines a regular hexagonal prism with a pyramid. Find its volume to the nearest cubic centimeter.

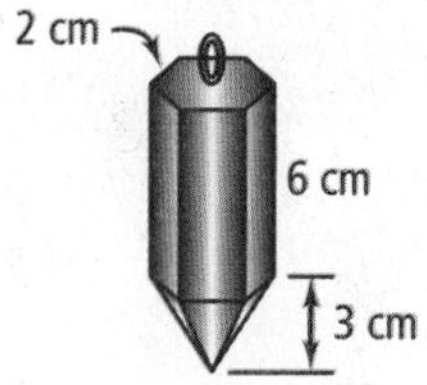

22. Reasoning A cone with radius 3 ft and height 10 ft has a volume of 30π ft^3. What is the volume of the cone formed when the following happens to the original cone?

a. The radius is doubled.

b. The height is doubled.

c. The radius and the height are both doubled.

Algebra Find the value of the variable in each figure. Leave answers in simplest radical form. The diagrams are not to scale.

23.

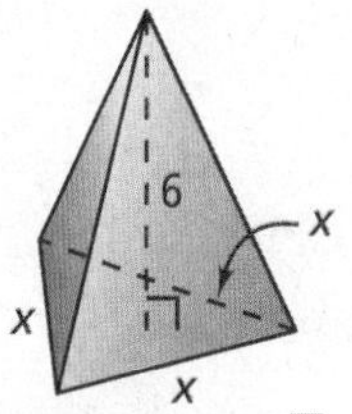

Volume $= 18\sqrt{3}$

24.

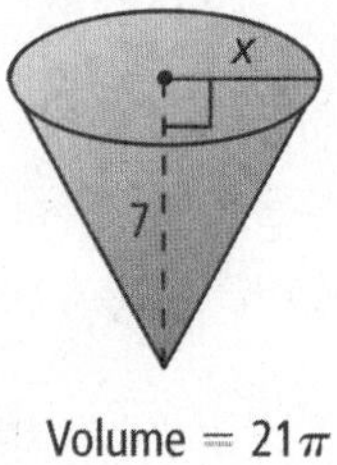

Volume $= 21\pi$

25.

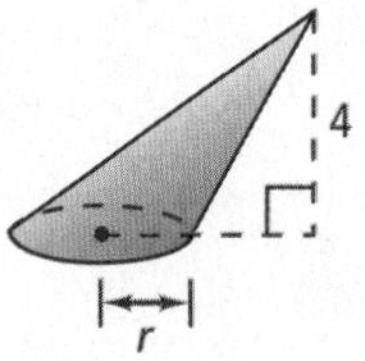

Volume $= 24\pi$

Visualization **Suppose you revolve the plane region completely about the given line to sweep out a solid of revolution. Describe the solid. Then find its volume in terms of π.**

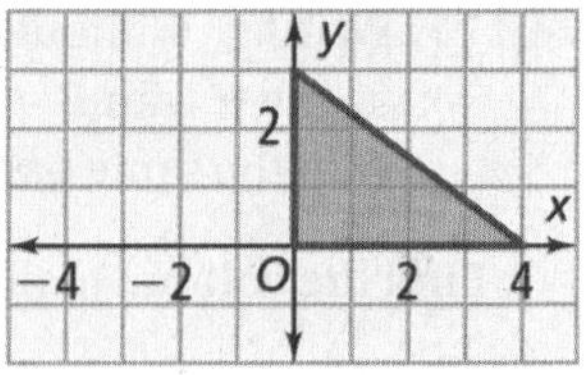

26. the y-axis

27. the x-axis

28. the line $x = 4$

29. the line $y = -1$

Challenge

30. A *frustum* of a cone is the part that remains when the top of the cone is cut off by a plane parallel to the base.

a. Explain how to use the formula for the volume of a cone to find the volume of a frustum of a cone.

b. Containers A popcorn container 9 in. tall is the frustum of a cone. Its small radius is 4.5 in. and its large radius is 6 in. What is its volume?

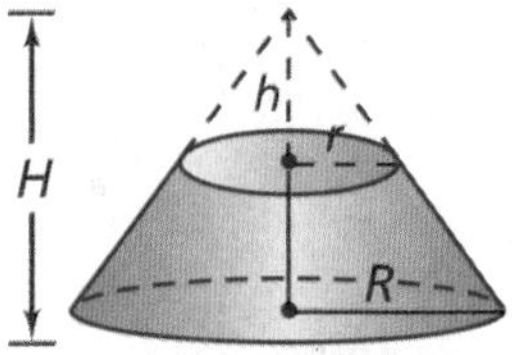

Frustum of cone

31. A disk has radius 10 m. A 90° sector is cut away, and a cone is formed.

a. What is the circumference of the base of the cone?

b. What is the area of the base of the cone?

c. What is the volume of the cone? (*Hint:* Use the slant height and the radius of the base to find the height.)

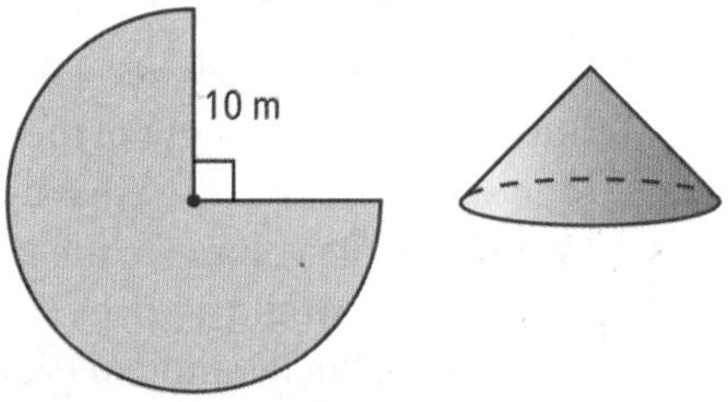

13-5 Surface Areas and Volumes of Spheres

G.GMD.3 Use volume formulas for . . . spheres to solve problems. Also **G.GMD.2, G.MG.1**

Objective To find the surface area and volume of a sphere

Solve It! Write your solution to the Solve It in the space below.

In the Solve It, you considered the sizes of objects with circular cross sections.

A **sphere** is the set of all points in space equidistant from a given point called the **center**. A **radius** is a segment that has one endpoint at the center and the other endpoint on the sphere. A **diameter** is a segment passing through the center with endpoints on the sphere.

Essential Understanding You can find the surface area and the volume of a sphere when you know its radius.

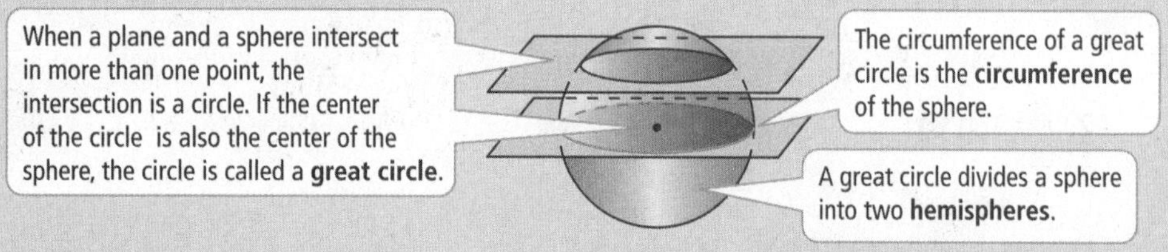

A baseball can model a sphere. To approximate its surface area, you can take apart its covering. Each of the two pieces suggests a pair of circles with radius r, which is approximately the radius of the ball. The area of the four circles, $4\pi r^2$, suggests the surface area of the ball.

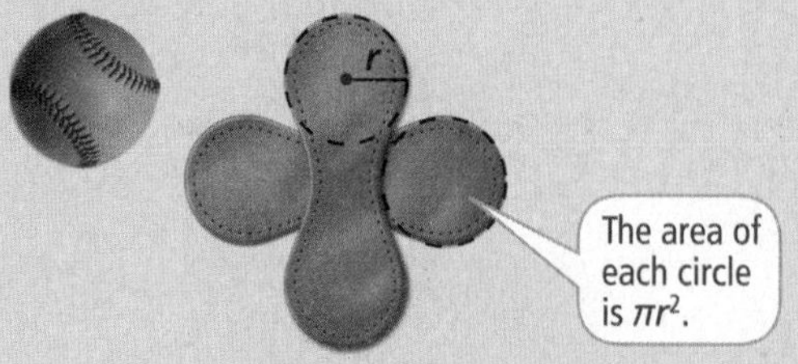

take note

Theorem 98 Surface Area of a Sphere

The surface area of a sphere is four times the product of π and the square of the radius of the sphere.

$$S.A. = 4\pi r^2$$

ONLINE PROBLEMS

Problem 1 Finding the Surface Area of a Sphere

Got It? What is the surface area of a sphere with a diameter of 14 in.? Give your answer in terms of π and rounded to the nearest square inch.

A Practice **Find the surface area of the sphere with the given diameter or radius. Leave your answer in terms of π.**

1. $d = 32$ mm

2. $r = 100$ yd

You can use spheres to approximate the surface areas of real-world objects.

Problem 2 Finding Surface Area

Got It? What is the surface area of a melon with circumference 18 in.? Round your answer to the nearest ten square inches.

Practice **Use the given circumference to find the surface area of each spherical object. Round your answer to the nearest whole number.**

3. a pincushion with $C = 8$ cm

4. a head of lettuce with $C = 22$ in.

In the previous lesson, you learned that the volume of a cone is $\frac{1}{3}\pi r^3$. You can use this with Cavalieri's Principle to find the formula for the volume of a sphere.

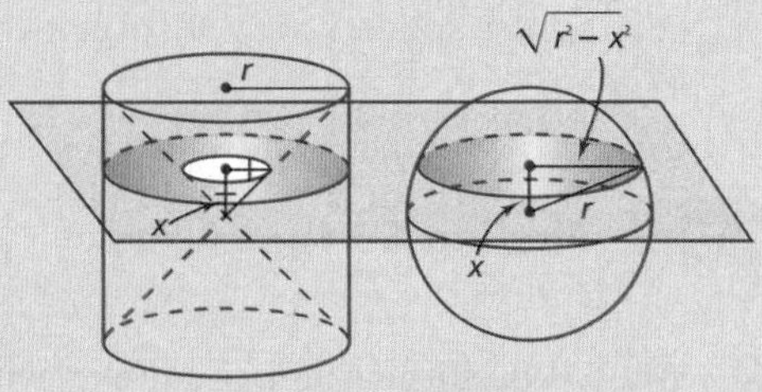

Both figures at the right have a parallel plane x units above their centers that form circular cross sections.

The area of the cross section of the cylinder minus the area of the cross section of the cone is the same as the area of the cross section of the sphere. Every horizontal plane will cut the figures into cross sections of equal area. By Cavalieri's Principle, the volume of the sphere = the volume of the cylinder − the volume of two cones.

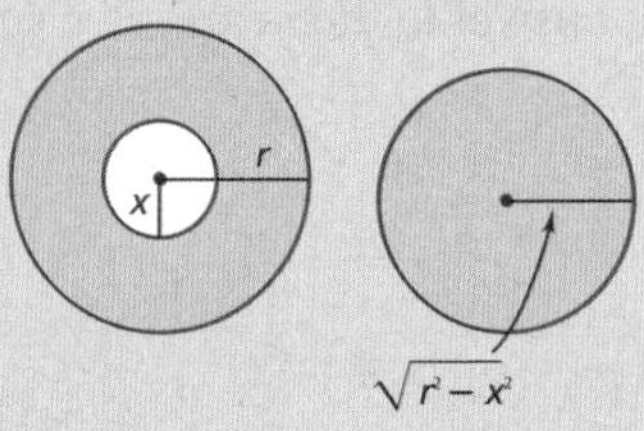

$$\begin{aligned}\text{Volume of a sphere} &= \pi r^2(2r) - 2\left(\tfrac{1}{3}\pi r^3\right)\\ &= 2\pi r^3 - \tfrac{2}{3}\pi r^3\\ &= \tfrac{4}{3}\pi r^3\end{aligned}$$

take note

Theorem 99 Volume of a Sphere

The volume of a sphere is four thirds the product of π and the cube of the radius of the sphere.

$V = \frac{4}{3}\pi r^3$

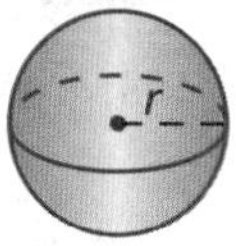

ONLINE PROBLEMS

Problem 3 Finding the Volume of a Sphere

Think

What measurement do you need to calculate the volume?

Got It? **a.** A sphere has a diameter of 60 in. What is its volume to the nearest cubic inch?

b. Reasoning Suppose the radius of a sphere is halved. How does this affect the volume of the sphere? Explain.

Practice Find the volume of each sphere. Give each answer in terms of π and rounded to the nearest cubic unit.

5.

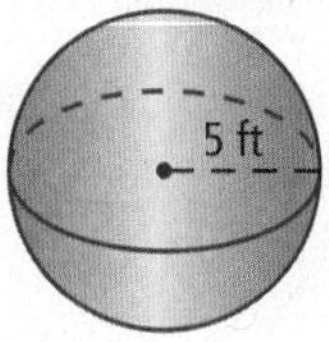

6.

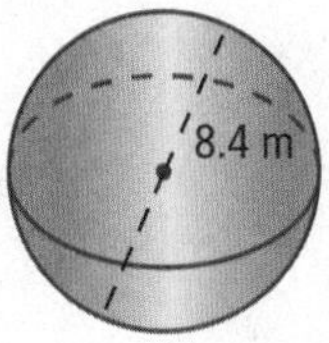

Notice that you only need to know the radius of a sphere to find its volume and surface area. This means that if you know the volume of a sphere, you can find its surface area.

Problem 4 Using Volume to Find Surface Area

Got It? The volume of a sphere is 4200 ft^3. What is its surface area to the nearest tenth?

Think

What measurement do you need to calculate the surface area?

Practice **A sphere has the volume given. Find its surface area to the nearest whole number.**

7. $V = 900 \text{ in.}^3$

8. $V = 140 \text{ cm}^3$

Lesson Check

Do you know HOW?

The diameter of a sphere is 12 ft.

9. What is its surface area in terms of π?

10. What is its volume to the nearest tenth?

11. The volume of a sphere is 80π cm^3. What is its surface area to the nearest whole number?

Do you UNDERSTAND?

MATHEMATICAL PRACTICES

12. Vocabulary What is the ratio of the area of a great circle to the surface area of the sphere?

13. Error Analysis Your classmate claims that if you double the radius of a sphere, its surface area and volume will quadruple. What is your classmate's error? Explain.

More Practice and Problem-Solving Exercises

MATHEMATICAL PRACTICES

B Apply

14. Mental Math Use $\pi \approx 3$ to estimate the surface area and volume of a sphere with radius 3 cm.

15. Open-Ended Give the dimensions of a cylinder and a sphere that have the same volume.

16. Visualization The region enclosed by the semicircle at the right is revolved completely about the x-axis.

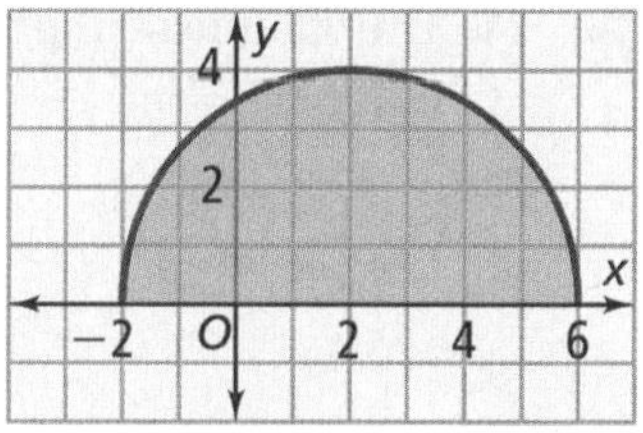

a. Describe the solid of revolution that is formed.
b. Find its volume in terms of π.
c. Find its surface area in terms of π.

17. Think About a Plan A cylindrical tank with diameter 20 in. is half filled with water. How much will the water level in the tank rise if you place a metallic ball with radius 4 in. in the tank? Give your answer to the nearest tenth.

- What causes the water level in the tank to rise?
- Which volume formulas should you use?

18. The sphere at the right fits snugly inside a cube with 6-in. edges. What is the approximate volume of the space between the sphere and the cube?

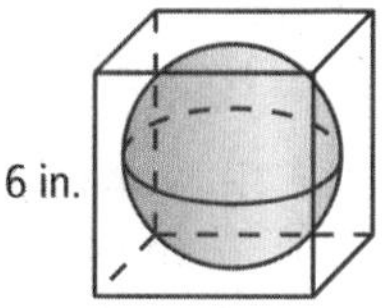

(A) 28.3 in.^{3}
(B) 76.5 in.^{3}
(C) 102.9 in.^{3}
(D) 113.1 in.^{3}

STEM **19. Meteorology** On September 3, 1970, a hailstone with diameter 5.6 in. fell at Coffeyville, Kansas. It weighed about 0.018 lb/in.^{3} compared to the normal 0.033 lb/in.^{3} for ice. About how heavy was this Kansas hailstone?

20. Reasoning Which is greater, the total volume of three spheres, each of which has diameter 3 in., or the volume of one sphere that has diameter 8 in.?

21. Reasoning How many great circles does a sphere have? Explain.

Find the volume in terms of π of each sphere with the given surface area.

22. 4π m^2 **23.** 36π in.^{2} **24.** 9π ft^2 **25.** 100π mm^2

26. 25π yd^2 **27.** 144π cm^2 **28.** 49π m^2 **29.** 225π mi^2

30. Recreation A spherical balloon has a 14-in. diameter when it is fully inflated. Half of the air is let out of the balloon. Assume that the balloon remains a sphere.
a. Find the volume of the fully inflated balloon in terms of π.
b. Find the volume of the half-inflated balloon in terms of π.
c. What is the diameter of the half-inflated balloon to the nearest inch?

31. Sports Equipment The diameter of a golf ball is 1.68 in.

a. Approximate the surface area of the golf ball.
b. **Reasoning** Do you think that the value you found in part (a) is greater than or less than the actual surface area of the golf ball? Explain.

Geometry in 3 Dimensions A sphere has center (0, 0, 0) and radius 5.

32. Name the coordinates of six points on the sphere.

33. Tell whether each of the following points is *inside, outside,* or *on the sphere*.
a. $A(0, -3, 4)$ b. $B(1, -1, -1)$ c. $C(4, -6, -10)$

34. Food An ice cream vendor presses a sphere of frozen yogurt into a cone, as shown at the right. If the yogurt melts into the cone, will the cone overflow? Explain.

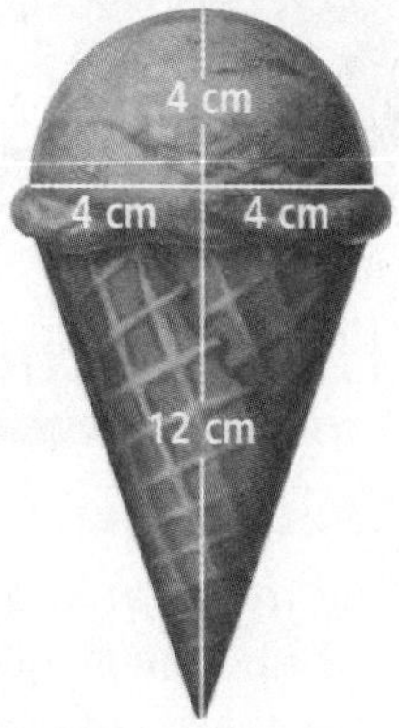

35. The surface area of a sphere is 5541.77 ft^2. What is its volume to the nearest tenth?

36. Geography The circumference of Earth at the equator is approximately 40,075 km. About 71% of Earth is covered by oceans and other bodies of water. To the nearest thousand square kilometers, how much of Earth's surface is land?

Find the surface area and volume of each figure in terms of π.

37.

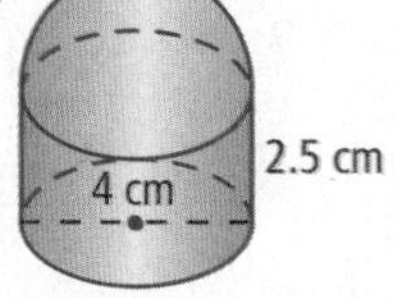

38.

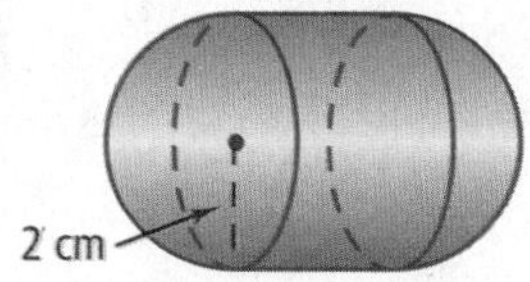

39.

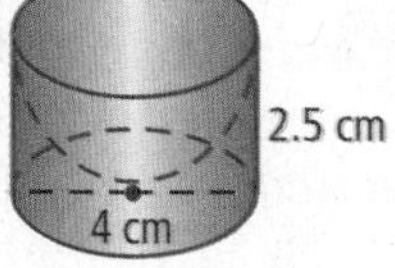

STEM **40. Astronomy** The diameter of the Earth is about 7926 mi. The diameter of the moon is about 27% of the diameter of Earth. What percent of the volume of Earth is the volume of the moon? Round your answer to the nearest whole percent.

STEM **41. Science** The density of steel is about 0.28 lb/in.^{3}. Could you lift a solid steel ball with radius 4 in.? With radius 6 in.? Explain.

42. A cube with edges 6 in. long fits snugly inside a sphere as shown at the right. A diagonal of the cube is the diameter of a sphere.

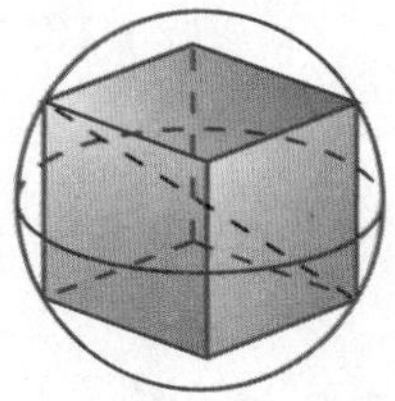

a. Find the length of the diagonal of the cube and the radius of the sphere. Leave your answer in simplest radical form.

b. What is the volume of the space between the sphere and the cube to the nearest tenth?

Challenge

Find the radius of a sphere with the given property.

43. The number of square meters of surface area equals the number of cubic meters of volume.

44. The ratio of surface area in square meters to volume in cubic meters is 1 : 5.

45. Suppose a cube and a sphere have the same volume.

a. Which has the greater surface area? Explain.

b. Writing Explain why spheres are rarely used for packaging.

46. A plane intersects a sphere to form a circular cross section. The radius of the sphere is 17 cm and the plane comes to within 8 cm of the center. Draw a sketch and find the area of the cross section, to the nearest whole number.

47. History At the right, the sphere fits snugly inside the cylinder. Archimedes (about 287–212 B.C.) requested that such a figure be put on his gravestone along with the ratio of their volumes, a finding that he regarded as his greatest discovery. What is that ratio?

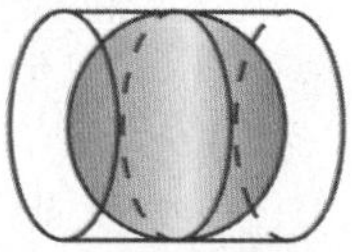

13 Chapter Review

MathXL® for School
Go to pearsonsuccessnet.com

13-1 Surface Areas of Prisms and Cylinders

Quick Review

The **lateral area of a right prism** is the product of the perimeter of the base and the height. The **lateral area of a right cylinder** is the product of the circumference of the base and the height of the cylinder. The **surface area** of each solid is the sum of the lateral area and the areas of the bases.

Example

What is the surface area of a cylinder with radius 3 m and height 6 m?

S.A. $= 2\pi rh + 2(\pi r^2)$	Use the formula for surface area of a cylinder.
$= 2\pi(3)(6) + 2\pi(3)^2$	Substitute.
$= 36\pi + 18\pi$	Simplify.
$= 54\pi$	

The surface area of the cylinder is 54π m^2.

Exercises

Find the surface area of each figure. Leave your answers in terms of π where applicable.

1. 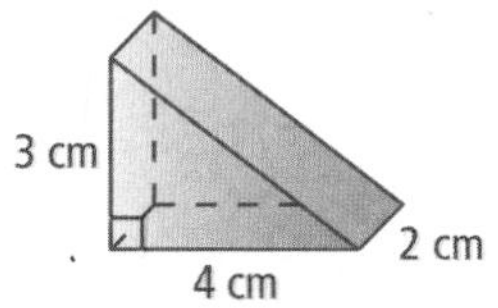

2. 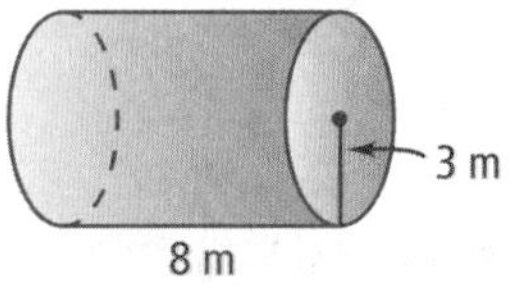

3. 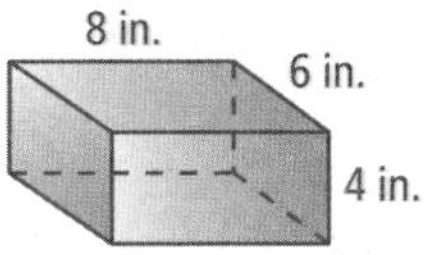

4. 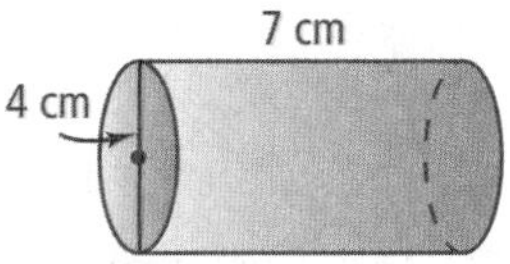

5. A cylinder has radius 2.5 cm and lateral area 20π cm^2. What is the surface area of the cylinder in terms of π?

13-2 Surface Areas of Pyramids and Cones

Quick Review

The **lateral area of a regular pyramid** is half the product of the perimeter of the base and the slant height. The **lateral area of a right cone** is half the product of the circumference of the base and the slant height. The surface area of each solid is the sum of the lateral area and the area of the base.

Example

What is the surface area of a cone with radius 3 in. and slant height 10 in.?

S.A. $= \pi r\ell + \pi r^2$	Use the formula for surface area of a cone.
$= \pi(3)(10) + \pi(3)^2$	Substitute.
$= 30\pi + 9\pi$	Simplify.
$= 39\pi$	

The surface area of the cone is 39π in.^{2}.

Exercises

Find the surface area of each figure. Round your answers to the nearest tenth.

6. 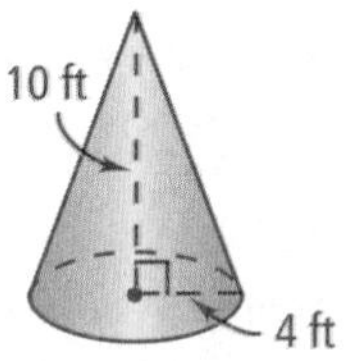

7. 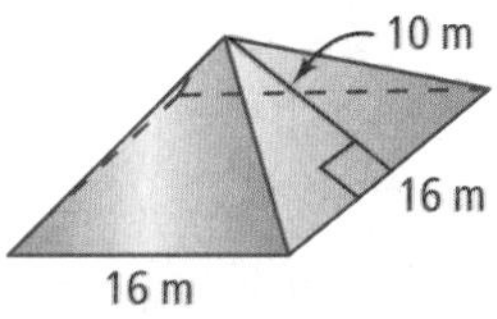

8. 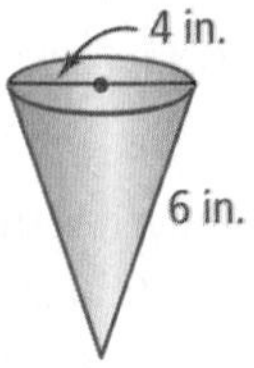

9. 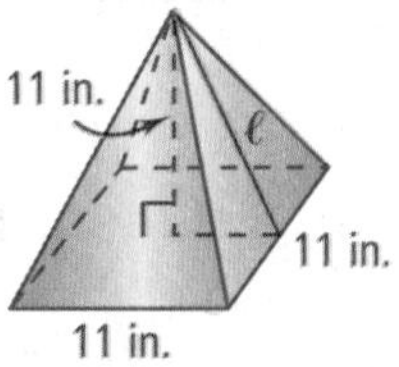

10. A cone has radius r and slant height ℓ. Find the ratio in simplest form of the lateral area of the cone to its surface area.

13-3 and 13-4 Volumes of Prisms, Cylinders, Pyramids, and Cones

Quick Review

The **volume** of a space figure is the space that the figure occupies. Volume is measured in cubic units. The **volume of a prism** and the **volume of a cylinder** are the product of the area of a base and the height of the solid. The **volume of a pyramid** and the **volume of a cone** are one third the product of the area of the base and the height of the solid.

Example

What is the volume of a rectangular prism with base 3 cm by 4 cm and height 8 cm?

$V = Bh$	Use the formula for the volume of a prism.
$= (3 \cdot 4)(8)$	Substitute.
$= 96$	Simplify.

The volume of the prism is 96 cm^3.

Exercises

Find the volume of each figure. If necessary, round to the nearest tenth.

11. 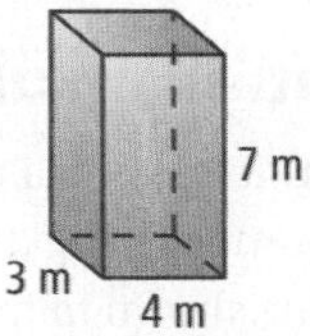

12. 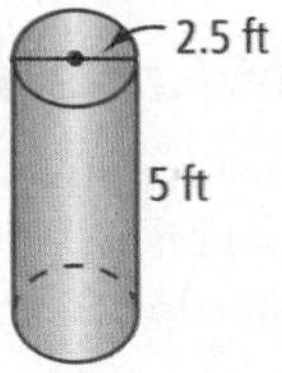

13. 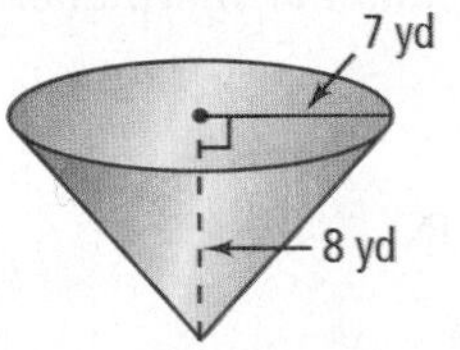

14. 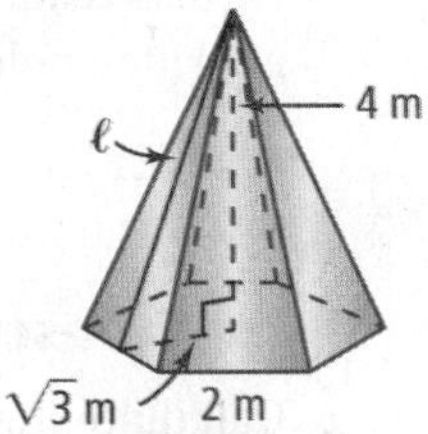

13-5 Surface Areas and Volumes of Spheres

Quick Review

The **surface area of a sphere** is four times the product of π and the square of the radius of the sphere. The **volume of a sphere** is $\frac{4}{3}$ the product of π and the cube of the radius of the sphere.

Example

What is the surface area of a sphere with radius 7 ft? Round your answer to the nearest tenth.

$S.A. = 4\pi r^2$	Use the formula for surface area of a sphere.
$= 4\pi(7)^2$	Substitute.
≈ 615.8	Simplify.

The surface area of the sphere is about 615.8 ft^2.

Exercises

Find the surface area and volume of a sphere with the given radius or diameter. Round your answers to the nearest tenth.

15. $r = 5$ in.

16. $d = 7$ cm

17. $d = 4$ ft

18. $r = 0.8$ ft

19. What is the volume of a sphere with a surface area of 452.39 cm^2? Round your answer to the nearest hundredth.

20. What is the surface area of a sphere with a volume of 523.6 m^3? Round your answer to the nearest square meter.

21. **Sports Equipment** The circumference of a lacrosse ball is 8 in. Find its volume to the nearest tenth of a cubic inch.

13 Pull It All Together

PERFORMANCE TASK

ASSESSMENT

Measuring the Immeasurable

Justin wants to measure the thickness of a paper towel, but his ruler is not the proper measuring device. He is able to take the measurements shown in the diagram.

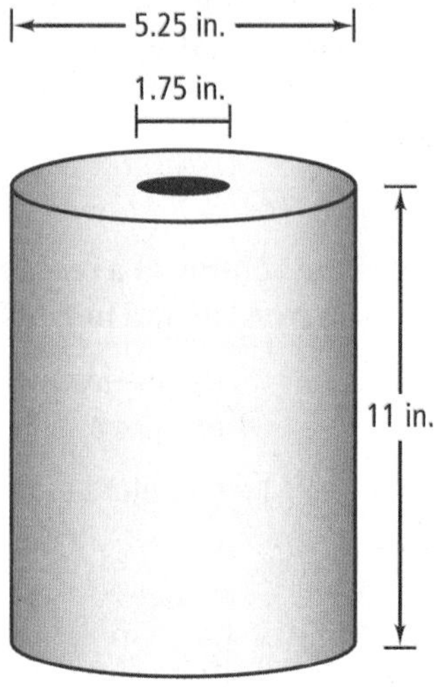

He also reads some additional information from the packaging, which is written below.

70 SHEETS PER ROLL
EACH 9.0 IN. BY 11.0 IN.

Task Description

Calculate the thickness of a paper towel.

- What is the volume of the paper towels? (Be sure to include just the towels and not the cardboard tube in the center.)
- What three-dimensional shape is formed by stretching the entire roll of paper towels flat on the floor? What is an expression for the volume of this shape?

CHAPTER 14

Get Ready!

Converting Between Percents, Fractions, and Decimals

Write two equivalent forms for each of the following.

1. 0.7875 **2.** $\frac{7}{8}$ **3.** 0.95 **4.** 60%

Simplifying Ratios

Simplify each ratio.

5. $\frac{45}{60}$ **6.** $\frac{24}{36}$ **7.** $\frac{7 \cdot 6}{4 \cdot 3}$

Evaluating Expressions

Evaluate each expression for $x = 6$ and $y = -2$.

8. $9x - 5y + 8$ **9.** $\frac{x}{y}$ **10.** $\frac{2x + y}{y^2}$

Solving Equations

Solve each equation.

11. $2n + 7 = 23$ **12.** $3(n - 2) = 8$ **13.** $\frac{5}{7}n - 12 = 15$

Looking Ahead Vocabulary

14. When you describe the likelihood that a baseball player will get a hit, you are finding an *experimental probability.* What do you think the experiment in this situation is?

15. People training to be pilots sometimes use flight simulators, machines that create a *simulation* of an actual flight. What do you suppose are some ways *simulations* could be used in a math class?

CHAPTER 14

Probability

Big Ideas

1 Probability
Essential Question: What is the difference between experimental probability and theoretical probability?

2 Data Representation
Essential Question: What is a frequency table?

3 Probability
Essential Question: What does it mean for an event to be random?

Domains

- Conditional Probability and the Rules of Probability
- Using Probability to Make Decisions

Chapter Preview

Vocabulary

English/Spanish Vocabulary Audio Online:

English	Spanish
combination, *p. 942*	combinación
conditional probability, *p. 958*	probabilidad condicional
dependent events, *p. 949*	sucesos dependientes
experimental probability, *p. 926*	probabilidad experimental
independent events, *p. 949*	sucesos independientes
mutually exclusive events, *p. 952*	sucesos mutuamente excluyentes
permutation, *p. 941*	permutación
sample space, *p. 925*	espacio de muestral
theoretical probability, *p. 927*	probabilidad teórica

Interactive Digital Path

Log in to **pearsonsuccessnet.com** and click on Interactive Digital Path to access the Solve Its and animated Problems.

14-1 Experimental and Theoretical Probability

S.CP.1 Describe events as subsets of a sample space using characteristics of the outcomes . . .

Objective To calculate experimental and theoretical probability

Solve It! Write your solution to the Solve It in the space below.

In the Solve It, you probably considered where the hour hand would be based on where the minute hand is. In the language of probability, this position would be a *favorable outcome*. An **outcome** is the possible result of a situation or experiment. An **event** may be a single outcome or a group of outcomes. For the clock, the hour hand's being about halfway between 12 and 1 or about halfway between 1 and 2 are two favorable outcomes for the event of where the hour hand may stop between 12:00 and 2:00. The set of all possible outcomes is the **sample space**.

Essential Understanding Probability is a measure of the likelihood that an event will occur.

take note

Key Concept Probability

Definition

If the outcomes in a sample space are equally likely to occur, the **probability** of an event *P*(event) is a numerical value from 0 to 1 that measures the likelihood of an event.

$$P(\text{event}) = \frac{\text{number of favorable outcomes}}{\text{number of possible outcomes}}$$

You can write the probability of an event as a ratio, decimal, or percent.

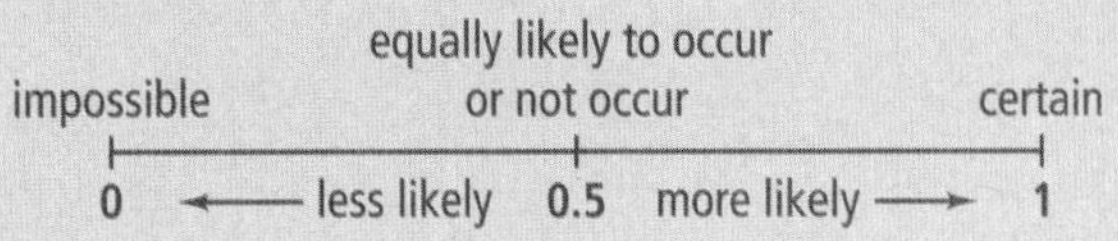

You can find probabilities by using the results of an experiment or by reasoning mathematically.

take note

Key Concept Experimental Probability

Experimental probability of an event measures the likelihood that the event occurs based on the actual results of an experiment.

$$P(\text{event}) = \frac{\text{number of times the event occurs}}{\text{number of times the experiment is done}} \begin{array}{l} \leftarrow \text{number of favorable outcomes} \\ \leftarrow \text{number of possible outcomes} \end{array}$$

ONLINE PROBLEMS

Problem 1 Calculating Experimental Probability

Got It? A park has 538 trees. You choose 40 at random and determine that 25 are maple trees. What is the experimental probability that a tree chosen at random is a maple tree? About how many trees in the park are likely to be maple trees?

A Practice **1.** A baseball player got a hit 19 times of his last 64 times at bat.

a. What is the experimental probability that the player got a hit?

b. If the player comes up to bat 200 times in a season, about how many hits is he likely to get?

2. A medical study tests a new cough medicine on 4250 people. It is effective for 3982 people. What is the experimental probability that the medicine is effective? For a group of 9000 people, predict the approximate number of people for whom the medicine will be effective.

When a sample space consists of real data, you can find the experimental probability. **Theoretical probability** describes the likelihood of an event based on mathematical reasoning.

This chapter uses *standard number cubes* to illustrate probability. A standard number cube has 6 faces with a number from 1 to 6 on each face. No number is used twice.

Problem 2 Calculating Theoretical Probability

Got It? What is the probability of getting each sum when rolling two standard number cubes?

a. 9 **b.** 2 **c.** 13

Think

How can a table of the possible results help you find each probability?

Practice **A bag contains letter tiles that spell the name of the state MISSISSIPPI. Find the theoretical probability of drawing one tile at random for each of the following.**

3. $P(\text{I})$ **4.** $P(\text{S})$

The **complement of an event** consists of all of the possible outcomes in the sample space that are not part of the event. For example, if you roll a standard number cube, the probability of rolling a number less than 3 is $P(\text{rolling} < 3) = \frac{2}{6}$, or $\frac{1}{3}$. The probability of *not* rolling a number less than 3 is $P(\text{not} < 3) = \frac{4}{6}$, or $\frac{2}{3}$.

take note

Key Concept Probability of a Complement

The sum of the probability of an event and the probability of its complement is 1.

$P(\text{event}) + P(\text{not event}) = 1 \qquad P(\text{not event}) = 1 - P(\text{event})$

ONLINE PROBLEMS

Problem 3 Using Probabilities of Events and Their Complements

Got It? A jar contains 10 red marbles, 8 green marbles, 5 blue marbles, and 6 white marbles. What is the probability that a randomly chosen marble is not red?

Think

What is another way to write *P*(not red)?

A Practice **A bag contains letter tiles that spell the name of the state MISSISSIPPI. Find the theoretical probability of drawing one tile at random for each of the following.**

5. $P(\text{not M})$

6. $P(\text{not P})$

Lesson Check

Do you know HOW?

For Exercises 7–9, use the spinner to find each theoretical probability.

7. P (an even number)

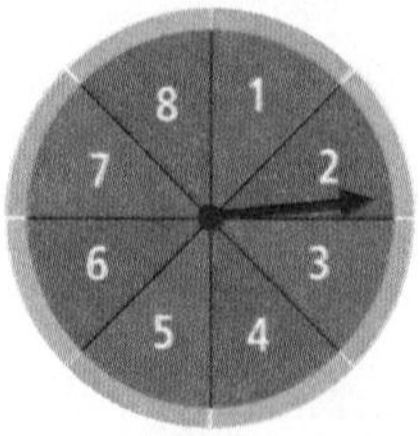

8. P(a number greater than 5)

9. P(a prime number)

Do you UNDERSTAND?

MATHEMATICAL PRACTICES

10. **Vocabulary** How are experimental and theoretical probability similar? How are they different?

11. **Open-Ended** Give an example of an impossible event.

12. **Error Analysis** Your friend says that the probability of rolling a number less than 7 on a standard number cube is 100. Explain your friend's error and find the correct probability.

More Practice and Problem-Solving Exercises

MATHEMATICAL PRACTICES

B Apply

13. **Think About a Plan** Suppose that you flip 3 coins. What is the theoretical probability of getting at least 2 heads?
    - What is the sample space of possible outcomes?
    - What are the favorable outcomes?

14. **Music** A music collection includes 10 rock CDs, 8 country CDs, 5 classical CDs, and 7 hip hop CDs.
    a. What is the probability that a CD randomly selected from the collection is a classical CD?
    b. What is the probability that a CD randomly selected from the collection is not a classical CD?

15. You are playing a board game with a standard number cube. It is your last turn and if you roll a number greater than 2, you will win the game. What is the probability that you will not win the game?

STEM 16. **Weather** If there is a 70% chance of snow this weekend, what is the probability that it will not snow?

17. **Quality Control** From 15,000 graphing calculators produced by a manufacturer, an inspector selects a random sample of 450 calculators and finds 4 defective calculators. Estimate the total number of defective calculators out of the 15,000.

18. Suppose you choose a letter at random from the word shown below. What is the probability that you will not choose a B?

PROBABILITY

A student randomly selected 65 vehicles in the student parking lot and noted the color of each. She found that 9 were black, 10 were blue, 13 were brown, 7 were green, 12 were red, and 14 were a variety of other colors. What is each experimental probability?

19. *P*(red)

20. *P*(black)

21. *P*(not blue)

22. *P*(not green)

STEM **23. Genetics** Genetics was first studied by Gregor Mendel, who experimented with pea plants. He crossed pea plants that had yellow, round seeds with pea plants that had green, wrinkled seeds. The following are the probabilities for each type of new seed.

yellow, round: 56.25%
yellow, wrinkled: 18.75%
green, round: 18.75%
green, wrinkled: 6.25%

If 2014 seeds were produced, how many of each variety would you expect?

Reasoning For Exercises 24–27, describe each of the following situations using one of the following probabilities. Explain your answer.

I. 0 **II.** between 0 and 0.5 **III.** between 0.5 and 1 **IV.** 1

24. having school on Tuesday

25. two elephants in the city zoo having the same weight

26. getting your driver's license at the age of 10

27. turning on the TV while a commercial is playing

Challenge

28. The students in a math class took turns rolling a standard number cube. The results are shown in the table at the right.

a. What is the theoretical probability of rolling the number 1 with the number cube?

b. What was the experimental probability of rolling the number 1 for the experiment in class?

Number Cube Experiment

Outcome	1	2	3	4	5	6
Times Rolled	39	40	47	42	38	44

29. Another way to express probability is with *odds*. Odds compare the number of favorable outcomes to the number of unfavorable outcomes. Odds in favor of an event are usually written as

number of favorable outcomes : number of unfavorable outcomes.

Suppose the probability of drawing a red marble from a bag of marbles is $\frac{3}{10}$.

a. What are the odds in favor of drawing a red marble?

b. What are the odds against drawing a red marble?

14-2 Probability Distributions and Frequency Tables

Prepares for **S.CP.4** Construct and interpret two-way frequency tables of data when two categories are associated with each object being classified . . . Also prepares for **S.CP.5**

Objective To make and use frequency tables and probability distributions

Solve It! Write your solution to the Solve It in the space below.

In the Solve It, you used information from the table to calculate probability. A **frequency table** is a data display that shows how often an item appears in a category.

Essential Understanding You can use data organized in tables that show frequencies to find probabilities.

take note

Key Concept Relative Frequency

Relative frequency is the ratio of the frequency of the category to the total frequency.

Problem 1 Finding Relative Frequencies

Got It? What is the relative frequency of preference for each type of music?

a. classical **b.** hip hop **c.** country

Type of Music Preferred	Frequency
Rock	10
Hip Hop	7
Country	8
Classical	5
Alternative	6
Other	4

d. Critical Thinking Without calculating the rest of the relative frequencies, what is the sum of the relative frequencies for all the types of music? Explain how you know.

Practice **Blood Drive** **The honor society at a local high school sponsors a blood drive. High school juniors and seniors who weigh over 110 pounds may donate. The table at the right indicates the frequency of donor blood type.**

Blood Drive Results

Blood Type	Frequency
O	30
A	25
B	6
AB	2

1. What is the relative frequency of blood type A?

2. The blood drive is extended for a second day, and the frequency doubles for each blood type. Do the relative frequencies for each blood type change? Explain.

You can use relative frequency to approximate the probabilities of events.

Problem 2 Calculating Probability by Using Relative Frequencies

Think **How can you use the frequency table to find the probability?**

Got It? A student conducts a probability experiment by spinning the spinner shown. Using the results in the frequency table, what is the probability of the spinner pointing at 4 on the next spin?

Spinner Result	1	2	3	4
Frequency	29	32	21	18

A Practice **Twenty-three preschoolers were asked what their favorite snacks are. The results are shown in the bar graph at the right.**

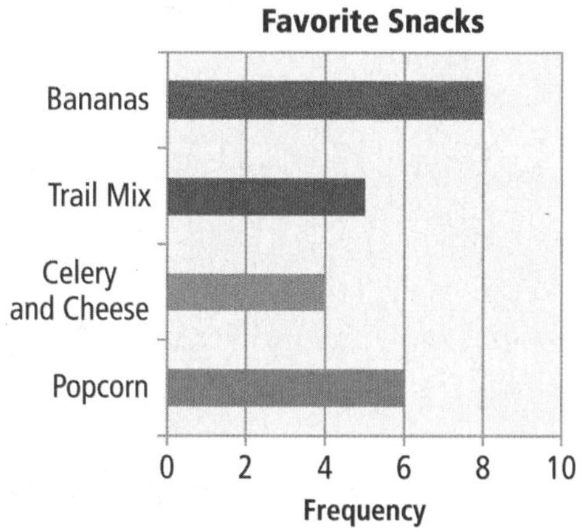

3. What is the probability that a preschooler chosen at random chose popcorn as his or her favorite snack?

4. What is the probability that a preschooler chosen at random did not choose bananas as his or her favorite snack?

A **probability distribution** shows the probability of each possible outcome. A probability distribution can be shown in a frequency table.

Problem 3 Finding a Probability Distribution

Got It? On a math test, there were 10 scores between 90 and 100, 12 scores between 80 and 89, 15 scores between 70 and 79, 8 scores between 60 and 69, and 2 scores below 60. What is the probability distribution for the test scores?

Think

How can you use relative frequencies to find the probability distribution?

Practice 5. The data collected for new students enrolled at a community college show that 26 are under the age of eighteen, 395 are between the ages of eighteen and twenty-two, 253 are between the ages of twenty-three and twenty-seven, 139 are between the ages of twenty-eight and thirty-two, and 187 are over the age of thirty-two. What is the probability distribution for these data?

Lesson Check

Do you know HOW?

Consumer Research The results of a survey show the frequency of responses for preferred music formats. What are the relative frequencies of the following formats?

Preferred Format	Frequency
CD	54
Radio	50
Blu-ray	10
MP3	28

6. CD

7. MP3

8. Blu-ray

9. Radio

10. What is the probability distribution for the music formats?

Do you UNDERSTAND?

MATHEMATICAL PRACTICES

11. Describe the sample space of possible outcomes for tossing a coin once.

12. Error Analysis A friend says that her sweepstakes ticket will either win or not win, so the theoretical probability of its winning must be 50%. Explain your friend's error.

More Practice and Problem-Solving Exercises

MATHEMATICAL PRACTICES

B Apply

13. Reasoning The possible outcomes for a spinner are 1, 2, 3, 4, 5, and 6. The outcomes are equally likely. What is a probability distribution of the possible outcomes for the spinner?

14. Text Messages The table at the right shows the number of text messages sent in one month by students at Metro High School.

a. If a student is chosen at random, what is the probability that the student sends 1500 or fewer text messages in one month?

b. If a student is chosen at random, what is the probability that the student sends more than 1500 messages in a month?

Number of Text Messages t	Number of Students
$t \leq 500$	25
$500 < t \leq 1500$	120
$1500 < t \leq 2500$	300
$t > 2500$	538

15. Computers The results of a survey of 80 households in Westville are shown at the right.

a. What is the probability distribution of the number of computers in Westville households?

b. If Westville has 15,200 households, predict the number of households that will have exactly 3 computers.

c. How many households will have either two or three computers?

Computer Survey

Number of Computers	Frequency
0	12
1	29
2	31
3	6
More than 3	2

16. Think About a Plan You can make a probability distribution table for theoretical probabilities. What is a probability distribution for four tosses of a single coin?

- What are all of the possible outcomes?
- What is the probability of each outcome?
- How can you display this in a table?

17. Employment The table below shows the number of people (in thousands) working in each occupational category, according to the U.S. Bureau of Labor Statistics.

U.S. Occupational Categories of Employed Workers

Occupational Category	Management, Professional, and Related	Service	Sales and Office	Natural Resources, Construction, Maintenance	Production, Transportation, and Material Moving
Number (thousands)	9773	2271	1456	289	177

a. Make a table showing the relative frequency for each occupational category.

b. If an employed person is randomly selected, what is the likelihood the person works in the Service category? Explain how you know.

18. a. Make a probability distribution for the sum of the faces after rolling two standard number cubes.

b. Are the probabilities theoretical or based on experimental results? Explain.

19. A student chose 100 letters at random from a page of a textbook. Partial results are in the table at the right. Make a probability distribution for the data. Include a category for all other letters not represented by the table.

Letter	Tally
a	𝍸 |||
e	𝍸 𝍸 ||||
i	𝍸 ||
n	𝍸	
o	𝍸 |||
r	||||
s	𝍸	
t	𝍸 ||||

20. Error Analysis The results of a survey about students' favorite type of pet are shown in the probability distribution below. What is wrong with this probability distribution? What information do you need to correct the probability distribution?

Favorite Pet	Dogs	Cats	Birds	Fish	Hamsters
Probability	0.36	0.34	0.15	0.08	0.12

Challenge

21. A spinner has an equal number of even and odd numbers. The relative probability of getting an outcome of an even number on any spin is 50%. Make a probability distribution for even numbers for two spins, for three spins, and for four spins. How does the probability distribution change for each additional spin?

14-3 Permutations and Combinations

S.CP.9 Use permuations and combinations to compute probabilities . . . and solve problems.

Objective To use permutations and combinations to solve problems

Solve It! Write your solution to the Solve It in the space below.

In the Solve It, you may have drawn a diagram or listed all of the different possible ways to add the samples. Sometimes there are so many possibilities that listing them all is not practical.

Essential Understanding You can use counting techniques to find all of the possible ways to complete different tasks or choose items from a list.

take note

Key Concept Fundamental Counting Principle

The **Fundamental Counting Principle** says that if event M occurs in m ways and event N occurs in n ways, then event M followed by event N can occur in $m \cdot n$ ways.

Example 4 entrees and 6 drinks give $4 \cdot 6 = 24$ possible lunch specials.

Here's Why It Works Suppose that you are choosing an outfit by first selecting blue jeans or black pants and then selecting a red, green, or blue shirt. The tree diagram shows the possible outfits you can choose. For m pant choices and n shirt choices, there are $m \cdot n$ or $2 \cdot 3 = 6$ possible outfits.

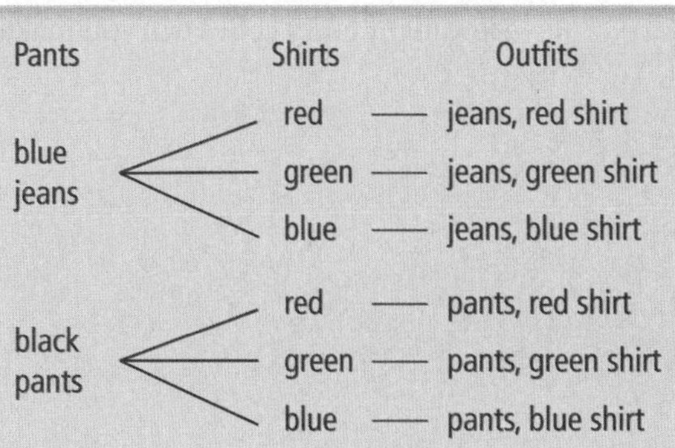

You can use the Fundamental Counting Principle for situations that involve more than two events.

Problem 1 Using the Fundamental Counting Principle

Got It? Suppose that a computer generates passwords that begin with a letter followed by 2 digits, like R38. The same digit can be used more than once. How many different passwords can the computer generate?

Letter - 26
number - 10
Number - 10
(if you can't use the same # more than once this would be 9)
= 2600

Practice

1. **Telephones** International calls require the use of a country code. Many country codes are 3-digit numbers. Country codes do not begin with a 0 or 1. There are no restrictions on the second and third digits. How many different 3-digit country codes are possible?

2. **Security** To make an entry code, you first need to choose a single-digit number and then two letters, which can repeat. How many entry codes can you make?

A **permutation** is an arrangement of items in which the order of the objects is important. You can use the Fundamental Counting Principle to find the total number of permutations. Suppose you want to find the number of ways to line up 4 friends. There are 4 ways to choose the first person, 3 ways to choose the second person, 2 ways to choose the third, and only 1 way to choose the last. So there are $4 \cdot 3 \cdot 2 \cdot 1 = 24$ permutations, or ways to arrange your friends.

You can use *factorial notation* to write $4 \cdot 3 \cdot 2 \cdot 1$ as 4! (You say this as "4 factorial.") For any positive integer n, ***n* factorial** is $n! = n(n-1)(n-2) \cdot \ldots \cdot 3 \cdot 2 \cdot 1$. Zero factorial is defined to be equal to 1.

Problem 2 Finding the Number of Permutations

Got It? In how many ways can you arrange 12 books on a shelf?

12·11·10·9·8·7·6·4·2·1 =
use factoreal sign →12! 479,001,600 way
Number use factorial mode on Calculator PRB
PRB arrow twice
= twice

Practice Find the value for each expression.

3. 6!

720

4. 9!

362,880

Suppose you want 3 songs to play from the 8 songs you have downloaded. There are 8 ways to select the first song, 7 ways to select the second song, and 6 ways to select the third song. By the Fundamental Counting Principle, this is $8 \cdot 7 \cdot 6$ ways, or 336 ways. You can express the result using factorials, as shown below.

take note

Key Concept Permutation Notation

The number of permutations of n items of a set arranged r items at a time is

$${}_nP_r = \frac{n!}{(n-r)!} \text{ for } 0 \le r \le n$$

Example $${}_8P_3 = \frac{8!}{(8-3)!} = \frac{8!}{5!} = \frac{8 \cdot 7 \cdot 6 \cdot 5 \cdot 4 \cdot 3 \cdot 2 \cdot 1}{5 \cdot 4 \cdot 3 \cdot 2 \cdot 1} = 8 \cdot 7 \cdot 6 = 336$$

Problem 3 Finding a Permutation

Got It? Twelve swimmers compete in a race. In how many possible ways can the swimmers finish first, second, and third?

Does order matter? yes

nPR

$_{12}P_3 = 1320$ $\frac{1}{1320}$ (1 guess) out of 1320

$_{12}C_3$

Practice Find the value of each expression.

5. $\frac{15!}{(15-10)!}$ $= \frac{n!}{(n-r)!}$ $_{15}P_{10} = 1.09 \times 10^{10}$

$n = 15$

$r = 10$

6. $_{10}P_6$

A **combination** is a selection of items in which order is *not* important. Suppose you select 3 different fruits to make a fruit salad. The order you select the fruits does not matter.

take note

Key Concept Combination Notation

The number of combinations of n items chosen r at a time is

$$_nC_r = \frac{n!}{r!(n-r)!} \text{ for } 0 \leq r \leq n$$

Example $_9C_4 = \frac{9!}{4!(9-4)!} = \frac{9!}{4!5!} = \frac{9 \cdot 8 \cdot 7 \cdot 6 \cdot 5 \cdot 4 \cdot 3 \cdot 2 \cdot 1}{(4 \cdot 3 \cdot 2 \cdot 1)(5 \cdot 4 \cdot 3 \cdot 2 \cdot 1)} = \frac{9 \cdot 8 \cdot 7 \cdot 6}{4 \cdot 3 \cdot 2 \cdot 1} = 126$

Problem 4 Using the Combination Formula

Got It? A service club has 8 freshmen. Five of the freshmen are to be on the clean-up crew for the town's annual picnic. How many different ways are there to choose the 5-member clean-up crew?

Think

If you are not using a calculator, how can you simplify the calculation?

Does the order matter? (no) NCr

$_8C_5 = \boxed{56}$

Use NCr if no
use NPr if yes

Practice Find the value of the expression.

7. $_{10}C_6$

8. A class has 30 students. In how many ways can committees be formed using the following numbers of students?

a. 3 students

b. 5 students

To determine whether to use the permutation formula or the combination formula, you must decide whether order is important.

Problem 5 Identifying Combinations and Permutations

Got It? A yogurt shop allows you to choose any 3 of the 10 possible mix-ins for a Just Right Smoothie. How many different Just Right Smoothies are possible?

Think Does the order matter?

nCr $_{10}C_3$ = 120

Practice **For Exercises 9–10, determine whether to use a permutation or a combination. Then solve the problem.**

9. You and your friends pick up seven movies to watch over a holiday. You have time to watch only two. In how many ways can you select the two to watch?

10. Suppose that the math team at your school competes in a regional tournament. The math team has 12 members. Regional teams are made up of 4 people. How many different regional teams are possible?

You can use permutations and combinations to help you solve probability problems.

Problem 6 Finding Probabilities

Got It? Three pool balls are randomly chosen from a set numbered from 1 to 15. What is the probability of choosing first the number 1 ball, then the number 2 ball, and then the number 3 ball?

Does order matter? yes So it's nPr

nPr = 15P3 = 2730 = 1/2730 (Probability)

Practice 11. You have a stack of 8 cards numbered 1–8. What is the probability that the first cards selected are 5 and 6?

nCr = 8C2 (2)
8C2

8C2 = 28 Probability 1/28

Does order matter no you can choose 5 & 6 or 6 & 5

12. To win a lottery, 6 numbers are drawn at random from a pool of 50 numbers. Numbers cannot repeat. You have one lottery ticket. What is the probability that you hold the winning ticket?

Does order matter no

nCr 50C6 1/15,890,700 possibility

60C6 • 28 1/1,401,788,080 possibility

Powerball

Lesson Check

Do you know HOW?

Evaluate each expression.

13. 3!

14. 0!

15. $_6P_2$

16. $_6P_3$

17. $_6C_2$

18. $_6C_3$

19. Sports How many ways can you choose 6 people to form a volleyball team out of a group of 10 players?

Do you UNDERSTAND?

MATHEMATICAL PRACTICES

20. Compare and Contrast How are combinations and permutations similar? How are they different?

21. Reasoning Your friend says that she can calculate any probability if she knows how many successful outcomes there are. Is there something else needed? Explain.

More Practice and Problem-Solving Exercises

MATHEMATICAL PRACTICES

B Apply

22. Entertainment Suppose that you and 4 friends go to a popular movie. You arrive late and cannot sit together, but you find 3 available seats in a row. How many possible ways can you and your friends sit in these seats?

23. Think About A Plan There are 8 online songs that you want to download. If you only have enough money to download 3 of the songs, how many different groups of songs can you buy?

- Does the order in which you select the songs matter? Explain.
- Should you use the permutation formula or combination formula?
- What are the values of n and r?

24. Government There are 24 members of the U.S. Senate Committee on Finance. How many possible ways are there to choose a 13-member subcommittee to review current energy legislation?

25. Music What is the probability of the youngest four members of a 15-member choir being randomly selected for a quartet (a group of four singers)?

26. What is the probability of randomly choosing a specific set of 7 books off a bookshelf holding 12 books?

27. Error Analysis A friend says that there are 6720 different ways to combine 5 out of 8 ingredients to make a stew. Explain the error and find the correct answer.

28. Reasoning Can ${}_nC_r$ ever be equal to ${}_nP_r$? Explain.

29. A 4-digit code is needed to unlock a bicycle lock. The digits 0 through 9 can be used only once in the code.

a. What is the probability that all of the digits are even?

b. Writing These types of locks are usually called combination locks. What name might a mathematician prefer? Why?

Challenge

30. *Circular permutations* are arrangements of objects in a circle or a loop. For example, the number of different ways a group of friends can sit around a table represent circular permutations. Permutations that are equivalent after a rotation of the circle are considered the same. Make a table for the regular and circular permutations of 2 out of 2, 3 out of 3, and 4 out of 4. What formula do you think could be used to find the number of circular permutations for n out of n items?

14-4 Compound Probability

S.CP.7 Apply the Addition Rule, $P(A \text{ or } B) = P(A) + P(B) - P(A \text{ and } B)$… Also S.CP.1, S.CP.2, S.CP.5

	Long sleeve	Sweater	Jacket	TOTAL
Soph	12	3	9	24
Jr	5	10	3	18
Senior	7	4	4	15
TOTAL	24	17	16	57

Objectives To identify independent and dependent events
To find compound probabilities

Solve It! Write your solution to the Solve It in the space below.

Probability ~ Freshman Sweater 0

Probability ~ Sophomore jackets $\frac{9}{24} = \frac{3}{8}$

Probability ~ long sleeve or jacket $\frac{24}{57}$ or $\frac{16}{57} = \frac{40}{57}$

If you were to find the probability of rain in both cities in the Solve It, you would be finding the probability of a *compound event.* A **compound event** is an event that is made up of two or more events.

Essential Understanding You can find the probability of compound events by using the probability of each part of the compound event.

If the occurrence of an event does not affect how another event occurs, the events are called **independent events.** If the occurrence of an event does affect how another event occurs, the events are called **dependent events.** To calculate the probability of a compound event, first determine whether the events are independent or dependent.

Problem 1 Identifying Independent and Dependent Events

Got It? You roll a standard number cube. Then you flip a coin. Are the outcomes independent or dependent events? Explain.

Indepent: Do not impact outcomes of each event

dependent: They do affect the outcomes of each event.

A Practice **Determine whether the outcomes of each trial are *independent* or *dependent* events.**

1. A card is randomly chosen from a standard deck of cards, then replaced; another card is chosen at random.

independent

2. Asking a student's age, and asking what year he or she expects to graduate.

dependent

You can find the probability that two independent events will both occur by multiplying the probabilities of each event.

take note

Key Concept **Probability of *A* and *B***

Two events *A* and *B* are independent if and only if $P(A \text{ and } B) = P(A) \cdot P(B)$.

Problem 2 Finding the Probability of Independent Events

Plan

Why are the events independent?

Got It? You roll a standard number cube and spin the spinner at the right. What is the probability that you roll a number less than 3 and the spinner lands on a vowel?

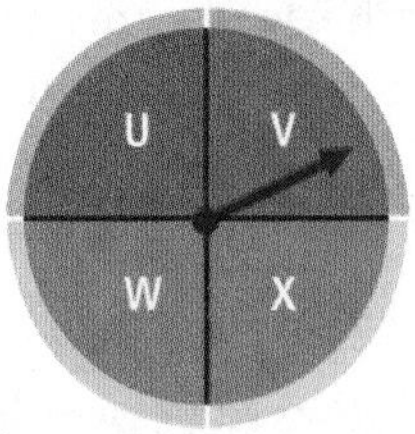

$P(A) = P(\text{less than } 3)$

$P(B) = P(\text{vowel})$

independent

$P(A) \cdot P(B) =$

$\frac{2}{6} \cdot \frac{1}{4} = \frac{2}{24} = \boxed{\frac{1}{12}}$

A Practice **You spin the spinner at the right and, without looking, you choose a tile from a set of tiles numbered from 1 to 10. Find each probability.**

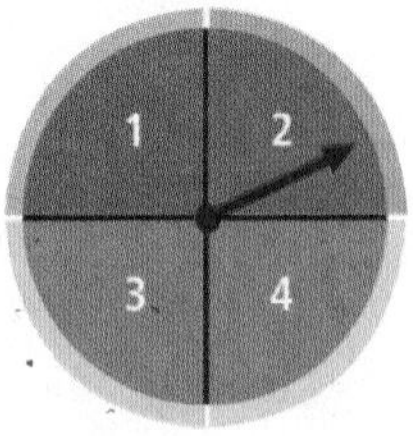

3. *P*(spinner lands on an odd number, and you choose an even number)

A, B

$\frac{2}{4} \cdot \frac{5}{10} = \frac{10}{40} = \boxed{\frac{1}{4}}$

4. P(spinner lands a number less than 4, and you choose a 9 or 10)

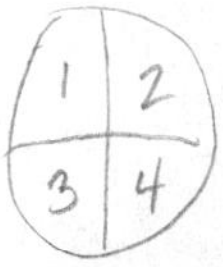

$\frac{3}{4} \cdot \frac{2}{10} = \frac{6}{40} = \boxed{\frac{3}{20}}$

You can also use the relationship $P(A \text{ and } B) = P(A) \cdot P(B)$ to test two events for independence.

Problem 3 Using Probabilities to Test for Independence

Got It? The probability that event A occurs is 0.3 and the probability that event B occurs is 0.1. There is a 25% chance that events A and B occur together. Are events A and B independent? Explain.

Plan
How can you use the given probabilities to test for independence?

$P(A) = 0.3$
$P(B) = 0.1$
$P(A \text{ and } B) = .25$

$P(A \text{ and } B) = P(A) \cdot P(B)$
$0.25 = 0.3 \cdot 0.1$
$0.25 \neq 0.03$
dependent – don't match

Practice **Use the given probabilities below to determine whether events A and B are independent.**

5. $P(A) = 0.3$, $P(B) = 0.4$, $P(A \text{ and } B) = 0.7$

6. $P(A) = \frac{2}{3}$, $P(B) = \frac{4}{5}$, $P(A \text{ and } B) = \frac{8}{15}$

$P(A) \cdot P(B) = P(A \text{ and } B)$

$\frac{2}{3} \cdot \frac{4}{5} = \frac{8}{15}$

$\frac{8}{15} = \frac{8}{15}$

if they match they are independent

Events that cannot happen at the same time are called **mutually exclusive events**. For example, you cannot roll a 2 and a 5 on a standard number cube at the same time, so the events are mutually exclusive. If events A and B are mutually exclusive, then the probability of both A and B occurring is 0. The probability that either A or B occurs is the sum of the probability of A occurring and the probability of B occurring.

take note

Key Concept Probability of Mutually Exclusive Events

If A and B are mutually exclusive events, then $P(A \text{ and } B) = 0$, and $P(A \text{ or } B) = P(A) + P(B)$.

ONLINE PROBLEMS

Problem 4 Finding the Probability of Mutually Exclusive Events

Got It? A student athlete may participate in only one sport per season. In the spring season, 15% of the athletes play baseball and 23% are on the track team. What is the probability of an athlete's either playing baseball or being on the track team?

P(a) = 15%

P(b) = 23%

chance of picking either a baseball or track player 38%

A Practice **A bag contains 3 blue chips, 6 black chips, 2 green chips, and 4 red chips. Use this information to find each probability if a chip is selected at random.**

or = + or add

7. P(green chip or red chip)

+

$\frac{2+4}{15}$ $\quad \frac{2}{15} + \frac{4}{15} = \frac{6}{15} = \frac{2}{5}$

8. P(blue, black, or red chip)

$\frac{3+6+4}{15} = \frac{13}{15}$

Overlapping events have outcomes in common. For example, for a standard number cube, the event of rolling an even number and the event of rolling a multiple of 3 overlap because a roll of 6 is a favorable outcome for both events.

take note

Key Concept Probability of Overlapping Events

If A and B are overlapping events, then $P(A \text{ or } B) = P(A) + P(B) - P(A \text{ and } B)$.

Here's Why It Works Suppose you have 7 index cards, each having one of the following letters written on it:

A B C D E F G

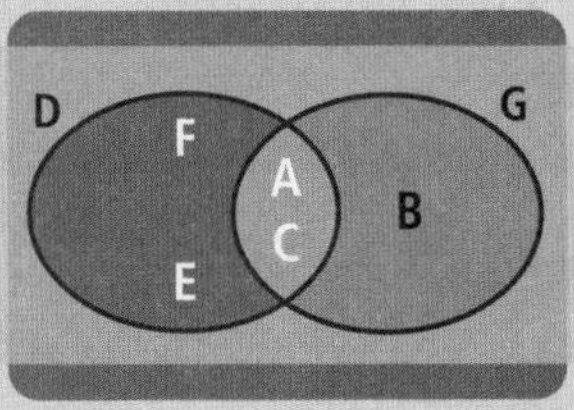

P(FACE), the probability of selecting a letter from the word FACE, is $\frac{4}{7}$.

P(CAB), the probability of selecting a letter from the word CAB, is $\frac{3}{7}$.

Consider P(FACE or CAB), the probability of choosing a letter from either the word FACE or the word CAB. These events overlap since the words have two letters in common. If you simply add P(FACE) and P(CAB), you get $\frac{4}{7} + \frac{3}{7} = \frac{4+3}{7}$. The value of the numerator should be the number of favorable outcomes, but there are only 5 distinct letters in the words FACE and CAB. The problem is that when you simply add, the letters A and C are counted twice, once in the favorable outcomes for the word FACE, and once in the favorable outcomes for the word CAB. You must subtract the number of letters that the two words have in common so they are only counted once.

$$P(\text{FACE or CAB}) = \frac{4+3-2}{7} = \frac{4}{7} + \frac{3}{7} - \frac{2}{7} = P(\text{FACE}) + P(\text{CAB}) - P(\text{AC})$$

Problem 5 Finding Probabilities of Overlapping Events

Got It? What is the probability of rolling either an odd number or a number less than 4 when rolling a standard number cube?

1 2 3 4 5 6 $\frac{4}{6} = \frac{2}{3}$

3 + 3

$P(odd) = \frac{3}{6}$ $\frac{6}{6} = 1$ It will happen no matter what

$P(\text{<four}) = \frac{3}{6}$

Practice **A set of cards contains four suits (red, blue, green, and yellow). In each suit there are cards numbered from 1 to 10. In Exercises 9 and 10, calculate the following probabilities for one card selected at random.**   4 X 10 = 40 cards

9. P (green or yellow card, or card numbered 1)

$10 + 10 + 4 - 2 = \frac{22}{40} = \frac{11}{20}$

overlapping

10. P (red or blue card, or card less than 6)

Lesson Check

Do you know HOW?

11. Suppose A and B are independent events. What is $P(A \text{ and } B)$ if $P(A) = 50\%$ and $P(B) = 25\%$?

12. Suppose A and B are mutually exclusive events. What is $P(A \text{ or } B)$ if $P(A) = 0.6$ and $P(B) = 0.25$?

13. Suppose A and B are overlapping events. What is $P(A \text{ or } B)$ if $P(A) = \frac{1}{3}$, $P(B) = \frac{1}{2}$ and $P(A \text{ and } B) = \frac{1}{5}$?

Do you UNDERSTAND?

MATHEMATICAL PRACTICES

14. Open-Ended Give an example of independent events, and an example of dependent events. Describe how the examples differ.

15. Error Analysis Your brother says that the probability that it will be cloudy tomorrow and the probability that it will rain are independent events. Explain your brother's error.

More Practice and Problem-Solving Exercises

MATHEMATICAL PRACTICES

B Apply

16. Pets In a litter of 8 kittens, there are 2 brown females, 1 brown male, 3 spotted females, and 2 spotted males. If a kitten is selected at random, what is the probability that the kitten will be female or brown?

17. Think About A Plan Suppose you are taking a test and there are three multiple-choice questions that you do not know the answers to. Each has four answer choices. Rather than leave the answers blank, you decide to guess. What is the probability that you will answer all three questions correctly?

- Is each guess independent or dependent?
- What is the probability that a random guess will answer a question when there are four answer choices?

18. Vacation In a math class, 75% of the students have visited the ocean and 50% have visited the mountains on vacation before. If 45% of the students have visited the ocean and the mountains on vacation before, what is the probability that a randomly selected student has visited the ocean or the mountains?

19. What is the probability that a standard number cube rolled three times will roll first even, then odd, and then even?

20. **Weather** Today's forecast calls for a 40% chance of rain in Chicago and a 75% chance of rain in Orlando. The probability that it will rain in both cities today is 30%. Are the events "It rains in Chicago" and "It rains in Orlando" independent? Explain.

21. **Baseball** A baseball player has a batting average of .320, so the probability that he gets a hit during a batting attempt is 0.32. The probability that he steals a base after getting on base is 0.05. If the probability that the player gets a hit and then steals a base is 0.008, are these events independent? Explain.

22. **Writing** Describe the difference between mutually exclusive and overlapping events. Give examples of each.

23. When you draw a marble out of a bag and then draw another without replacing the first, the probability of the second event is different from the probability of the first.
   a. What is the probability of drawing a red marble out of a bag containing 3 red and 7 blue marbles?
   b. What is the probability of drawing a second red marble if a red marble is drawn the first time and not replaced?
   c. What is the probability of drawing two red marbles in a row?

Challenge

Reasoning For each set of probabilities, determine if the events *A* and *B* are mutually exclusive. Explain.

24. $P(A) = \frac{1}{2}$, $P(B) = \frac{1}{3}$, $P(A \text{ or } B) = \frac{2}{3}$

25. $P(A) = \frac{1}{6}$, $P(B) = \frac{3}{8}$, $P(A \text{ and } B) = 0$

26. **Reasoning** Are mutually exclusive events dependent or independent? Explain.

14-5 Probability Models

S.CP.4 Construct and interpret two-way frequency tables of data . . . Use the two-way table as a sample space to decide if events are independent and to approximate conditional probabilities.

Objective To construct and use probability models

Solve It! Write your solution to the Solve It in the space below.

In the Solve It, the data is displayed in a *two-way frequency table.* A **two-way frequency table**, or *contingency table*, displays the frequencies of data in two different categories.

Essential Understanding You can use two-way frequency tables to organize data and identify sample spaces to approximate probabilities.

Problem 1 Using a Two-Way Frequency Table

Got It? The two-way frequency table at the right shows the number of male and female students by grade level on the prom committee. What is the probability that a member of the prom committee is a male who is a junior?

	Male	Female	Total
Juniors	3	4	7
Seniors	3	2	5
Totals	6	6	12

Practice For Exercises 1 and 2, use the two-way frequency table below to find the probability of each event.

1. P(8th-grade boy)

Attendance at Soccer Camp

	6th Graders	7th Graders	8th Graders	Total
Boys	7	6	10	23
Girls	8	7	12	27
Totals	15	13	22	50

2. P(6th-grade girl)

The probability that an event will occur, given that another event has already occurred, is called a **conditional probability**. You can write the conditional probability of event B, given that event A has already occurred, as $P(B \mid A)$. You read $P(B \mid A)$ as "the probability of event B, given event A."

Problem 2 Finding Probability

Got It? a. What is the probability that a randomly selected person is 30–45 years old, given that the person is in favor of the minimum-wage bill?

Age Group	For	Against	No Opinion	Total
18–29	310	50	20	380
30–45	200	30	10	240
45–60	120	20	30	170
Over 60	150	20	40	210
Totals	780	120	100	1000

Plan
What part of the table do you need to use?

b. Reasoning What is the probability that a randomly selected person is not 18–29, given that the person is in favor of the minimum wage bill?

Practice For Exercises 3 and 4, use the two-way frequency table below to find the probability of each event.

3. $P(\text{6th grade} \mid \text{boy})$

Attendance at Soccer Camp

	6th Graders	7th Graders	8th Graders	Total
Boys	7	6	10	23
Girls	8	7	12	27
Totals	15	13	22	50

4. $P(\text{8th grade} \mid \text{girl})$

Problem 3 Using Relative Frequencies

Got It? What is the probability that a randomly selected sales representative, who did not attend the seminar, did not see an increase in sales?

Plan
Which column should you use to solve this problem?

	Attended Seminar	Did Not Attend Seminar	Total
Increased Sales	0.48	0.02	0.5
No Increase in Sales	0.32	0.18	0.5
Totals	0.8	0.2	1

A Practice **Veterinary Medicine** For Exercises 5 and 6, use the table below. It shows the relative frequency of treatments that a veterinarian gave dogs and cats during one week.

5. When you find the probability that the treatment consists of shots only, given that the vet is treating the cat, how do you limit the sample space?

	Shots Only	Shots and Checkup	Total
Dogs	0.31	0.23	0.54
Cats	0.26	0.20	0.46
Totals	0.57	0.43	1

6. What is the probability that an animal chosen at random is a dog, given that the treatment was shots only?

Lesson Check

Do you know HOW?

Use the two-way frequency table to find the probabilities.

7. *P*(democrat and supports the issue)

	Supports the Issue	Does Not Supports the Issue	Total
Democrat	24	36	60
Republican	27	33	60
Totals	51	69	120

8. *P*(democrat | supports the issue)

Do you UNDERSTAND?

MATHEMATICAL PRACTICES

9. Error Analysis Using the table in Exercises 7 and 8, a student calculated the relative frequency of those who do not support the issue, given that they are Republican, as $\frac{33}{33 + 36} = 0.478$. What error did the student make?

10. Vocabulary What is a two-way frequency table?

11. Suppose A is a female student and B is a student who plays sports. What does $P(B \mid A)$ mean?

More Practice and Problem-Solving Exercises

MATHEMATICAL PRACTICES

B Apply

Academic Competition **The table at the right show the participants in an academic competition. Use this information for Exercises 12–16.**

	Male	Female	Total
Freshmen	3	5	8
Sophomores	6	4	10
Juniors	7	5	12
Seniors	4	6	10
Totals	20	20	40

12. What is P(female)?

13. What is P(freshman)?

14. What is P(female freshman)?

15. What is P(female | freshman)?

16. What is P(freshman | female)?

17. **Think About a Plan** The two-way table at the right shows the number of employees at a factory who have attended a safety workshop and the number who have ever been injured on the job. What is the probability that a randomly selected worker from the factory has attended the safety workshop, given that the employee has not been injured on the job?
    - Which column is needed for solving this problem?
    - Do you need the total number of workers or the total not injured?

	Injured	Not Injured	Total
Safety Workshop	3	36	39
No Safety Workshop	12	24	36
Totals	15	60	75

18. **Reasoning** Recall that two events are independent when the occurrence of one has no effect the other. The table at the right is a frequency table.
    a. Calculate $P(B)$.
    b. Calculate $P(B \mid A)$.
    c. Does the occurrence of A have any effect on the probability of B? What can you say about events A and B?
    d. Are events C and D independent? Explain.
    e. Are events C and F independent? Explain.

	B	D	F	Total
A	7	5	4	16
C	3	4	5	12
E	11	7	2	20
Total	21	16	11	48

19. **Writing** What is the sum of the probabilities of each outcome in a probability experiment? How does this relate to the relative frequencies in a contingency table? Explain and give an example.

20. Healthcare The table at the right is a relative frequency distribution for healthy people under the age of 65.

a. Copy and complete the table.

b. What is the probability of getting the flu, given that you are vaccinated?

c. What is the probability of getting the flu, given that you have not been vaccinated?

Flu Vaccines

	Got the Flu	Did Not Get the Flu	Total
Vaccinated	■	54%	60%
Not Vaccinated	■	■	■
Totals	15%	■	100%

Challenge

21. When you construct a two-way frequency table, you add across rows and down columns to find values for the totals row and column. The values in the totals column and totals row of the table are called *marginal frequencies*, and the values in the interior of the table are called *joint frequencies*. In the table below, the values 9, 3, 5, and 8 represent the joint frequencies, and the values 14, 11, 12, 13, and 25 represent the marginal frequencies.

	Exam Score ≥ 85%	Exam Score < 85%	Total
Studied more than 4 hours	9	3	12
Studied less than 4 hours	5	8	13
Totals	14	11	25

a. Why do you think the values in the interior of the table are called joint frequencies?

b. What do the marginal frequencies of the table represent?

c. If you replace the joint and marginal frequencies in a two-way frequency with the respective relative frequencies, what do the values in the totals row and column represent? Use the given table to provide an example.

14-6 Conditional Probability Formulas

S.CP.3 Understand the conditional probability of A given B as $P(A \text{ and } B)/P(B)$ ... Also S.CP.4, S.CP.5, S.CP.6

Objective To understand and calculate conditional probabilities

Solve It! Write your solution to the Solve It in the space below.

In the Solve It, you may have calculated the probability that it rains and you clean the garage and the probability that it does not rain and you clean the garage and then added the probabilities together.

Essential Understanding You can find conditional probabilities using a formula.

In the previous lesson, you found probabilities using frequency tables. For example, in the relative frequency table at the right, the probability that a sales representative had an increase in sales, given that he attended the training seminar, is $\frac{0.48}{0.8} = 0.6$.

	Attended Seminar	Did Not Attend Seminar	Total
Increased Sales	0.48	0.02	0.5
No Increase in Sales	0.32	0.18	0.5
Totals	0.8	0.2	1

With respect to probability, this would be

$$P(\text{increased sales} \mid \text{attend seminar}) = \frac{P(\text{attend seminar and had increased sales})}{P(\text{attended seminar})}.$$

This suggests an algebraic formula for finding conditional probability.

take note

Conditional Probability Formula

For any two events A and B, the probability of B occurring, given that event A has occurred, is $P(B \mid A) = \frac{P(A \text{ and } B)}{P(A)}$, where $P(A) \neq 0$.

Problem 1 Using Conditional Probabilities

Got It? Use the information in Problem 1. The probability of a volunteer's receiving the placebo and having his or her health improve was 20%. What is the conditional probability of a volunteer's health improving, given that he or she received the placebo?

A Practice 1. **Allowance** Suppose that 62% of children are given a weekly allowance, and 38% of children do household chores to earn an allowance. What is the probability that a child does household chores, given that the child gets an allowance?

Conditional probabilities are usually not reversible. $P(A \mid B) \neq P(B \mid A)$.

Problem 2 Comparing Conditional Probabilities

Got It? The same survey as the one in Problem 2 showed that 5% of the pet owners own a dog, a cat, and at least one other type of pet.

a. What is the conditional probability that a pet owner owns a cat and some other type of pet, given that he or she owns a dog?

Think

How are the sample spaces limited in each of the conditional probabilities?

b. What is the conditional probability that a pet owner owns a dog and some other type of pet, given that he or she owns a cat?

c. Critical Thinking Can you calculate the conditional probability of owning another pet for a pet owner who owns a cat and no dogs? Explain.

Practice **2.** You roll two standard number cubes. What is the probability that the sum is even, given that at least one number cube shows a 2? What is the probability that at least one number cube shows a 2, given that the sum is even?

Because $P(B \mid A) = \frac{P(A \text{ and } B)}{P(A)}$, then $P(A \text{ and B}) = P(A) \cdot P(B \mid A)$.
You can use this form of the conditional rule when you know the conditional probability. You can also combine conditional probabilities to find the probability of an event that can happen in more than one way.

Problem 3 Using a Tree Diagram

Got It? **a.** A soccer team wins 65% of its games on muddy fields and 30% of their games on dry fields. The probability of the field's being muddy for their next game is 70%. What is the probability that the team will win their next game?

b. Critical Thinking If the probability of the field's being muddy increases, how will that influence the probability that the soccer team will win their next game? Explain.

Practice **Softball Suppose that your softball team has a 75% chance of making the playoffs. Your cross-town rivals have an 80% chance of making the playoffs. Teams that make the playoffs have a 25% chance of making the finals. Use this information to find the following probabilities.**

3. *P*(your team makes the playoffs and the finals)

4. *P*(cross-town rivals make the playoffs and the finals)

If $P(B \mid A) = P(B)$, then the statement $P(A \text{ and } B) = P(A) \cdot P(B \mid A)$ simplifies to $P(A \text{ and } B) = P(A) \cdot P(B)$, which is true only if A and B are independent events. This leads to another way to test events for independence:

Two events A and B are independent events if and only if $P(A \mid B) = P(A)$ and $P(B \mid A) = P(B)$.

Problem 4 Using Conditional Probability to Test for Independence

Got It? Use the two-way frequency table and the situation given in Problem 4. Consider events A and B below. Are the events independent? Use probabilities to determine your answer.

Event A: The selected student is a junior.
Event B: The selected student does not have a part-time job.

Think
What are the sample spaces for $P(A \mid B)$ and $P(B \mid A)$?

Practice **The table shows the number of men and women at a company who are managers or team members. Use probabilities to determine whether events A and B below are independent.**

Company Positions of Men and Women

	Men	Women	Totals
Manager	5	3	8
Team Member	25	15	40
Totals	30	18	48

5. Event A: An employee is a man.
Event B: An employee is a manager.

6. Event A: An employee is a woman.
Event B: An employee is a team member.

Lesson Check

Do you know HOW?

A jar contains 10 large, red marbles; 4 small, red marbles; 6 large, blue marbles; and 5 small, blue marbles. Calculate the following conditional probabilities for choosing a marble at random.

7. $P(\text{large} \mid \text{red})$

8. $P(\text{large} \mid \text{blue})$

9. For the same jar of marbles, which of the conditional probabilities is larger, $P(\text{red} \mid \text{small})$ or $P(\text{small} \mid \text{red})$? Explain.

Do you UNDERSTAND?

MATHEMATICAL PRACTICES

10. Error Analysis Your friend says that the conditional probability of one event is 0% if it is independent of another given event. Explain your friend's error.

11. Compare and Contrast How is finding a conditional probability like finding a compound probability? How are they different?

More Practice and Problem-Solving Exercises

MATHEMATICAL PRACTICES

B Apply

12. Think About a Plan Suppose there are two stoplights between your home and school. On the many times you have taken this route, you have determined that 70% of the time you are stopped on the first light and 40% of the time you are stopped on both lights. If you are not stopped on the first light, there is a 50% chance that you are stopped on the second light. What is the probability that you make it to school without having to stop at a stoplight?

- What conditional probability are you looking for?
- How can a tree diagram help?

13. Sports There is a 40% chance that a school's basketball team will make the playoffs this year. If they make the playoffs, there is a 15% chance that they will win the championship. There is also a 30% chance that the same school's volleyball team will make the playoffs this year. If the volleyball team makes the playoffs, there is a 30% chance that they will win the championship. What is the probability that at least one of these teams will win a championship this year?

The table below shows the number of males and females at a school who are left- or right-handed. Use the table to answer each question.

	Male	Female	Totals
Left-Handed	8	6	14
Right-Handed	69	77	146
Totals	77	83	160

14. Use probabilities to determine whether events A and B are independent.

Event A: A student is female.
Event B: A student is right-handed.

15. Use probabilities to determine whether events A and B are independent.

Event A: A student is male.
Event B: A student is left-handed.

16. **Writing** Describe the advantages of using a two-way frequency table to determine whether two events are independent.

STEM **Science** **In a research study, one third of the volunteers received drug A, one third received drug B, and one third received a placebo. Out of all the volunteers, 10% received drug A and got better, 8% received drug B and got better, and 12% received the placebo and got better.**

17. What is the conditional probability of a volunteer getting better if he or she was given drug A?

18. What is the conditional probability of a volunteer getting better if he or she was given drug B?

19. What is the conditional probability of a volunteer getting better if he or she was given the placebo?

STEM 20. **Chemistry** A scientist discovered that a certain element was present in 35% of the samples she studied. In 15% of all samples, the element was found in a special compound. What is the probability that the compound is in a sample that contains the element?

21. **Music** Three students compared the music on their MP3 players. Find the probability that a randomly selected song is country, given that it is not on Student A's MP3 player. Round to the nearest hundredth.

Student	Rock	Country	R & B
A	0.10	0.02	0.03
B	0.13	0.05	0.23
C	0.10	0.01	0.33

22. **Fire Drill** A fire drill will begin at a randomly chosen time between 8:30 A.M. and 3:30 P.M. You have a math test planned for 2:05 P.M. to 3:00 P.M. If the fire drill is in the afternoon, what is the probability that it will start during the test?

Challenge

23. The table below shows the average standardized test scores for a group of students. If 35% of the students are seniors, 40% are juniors, and 25% are freshman, what is the probability that a student chosen at random will have an average score of at least 125?

	Average Score <125	Average Score Between 125 and 145	Average Score >145
Freshman	48%	37%	15%
Junior	36%	52%	12%
Senior	13%	69%	18%

14-7 Modeling Randomness

S.MD.6 Use probabilities to make fair decisions . . . Also S.MD.7

Objectives To understand random numbers
To use probabilities in decision making

Solve It! Write your solution to the Solve It in the space below.

In the Solve It, you thought of ways to select 4 people. In this lesson, you will learn ways to make a random selection and use probabilities to make decisions and solve real-world problems.

Essential Understanding You can use probability to make choices and to help make decisions based on prior experience.

A random event has no predetermined pattern or bias toward one outcome or another. You can use random number tables or randomly generated numbers using graphing calculators or computer software to help you make fair decisions. On page 979, you will find a random number table to use with this lesson.

Problem 1 Making Random Selections

Think
How can a single-digit number be represented by two digits?

Got It? A teacher wishes to choose three students from a class of 25 students to raise the school's flag. What numbers should the teacher choose based on this line from a random number table?

65358 70469 87149 89509 72176 18103 55169 79954 72002 20582

Practice **Use the lines from a random number table to select numbers to use in each problem.**

1. Choose 3 students from a list of 45 volunteers.

72749 13347 65030 26128 49067 27904 49953 74674 94617 13317

2. Choose 5 families to survey from a phone directory page with 950 names.

11873 57196 32209 67663 07990 12288 59245 83638 23642 61715

Problem 2 Making a Simulation

Got It? Suppose that to win a game, you must roll a standard number cube until all of the sides show at least one time. On average, how many times will you have to roll the number cube before each side shows at least one time? Use a random number table or a random number generator.

Think

How do you start to model a situation?

Practice **For Exercises 3 and 4, describe how to use random numbers to do a simulation for each situation.**

3. A teacher assigns students new seats randomly each week. On average, how long will it be before a student is assigned the same seat for two weeks in a row?

4. Sports A basketball player makes 80% of her free throw attempts. Find the average number of free throw attempts needed in order to make 3 free throws in a row.

In Problem 2, you figured out how many boxes of cereal on average you would expect to have to buy to collect all 6 prizes. You can use this information to make a decision about whether it is worth trying to collect all 6 prizes. Similarly, you can use the *expected value* of a situation that involves uncertainty to make a decision. *Expected value* uses theoretical probability to tell you what you can expect in the long run. If you know what *should* happen mathematically, you make better decisions in problem situations. The **expected value** is the sum of each outcome's value multiplied by its probability.

take note

Key Concept Calculating Expected Value

If A is an event that includes outcomes $A_1, A_2, A_3, \ldots$ and Value (A_n) is a quantitative value associated with each outcome, the expected value of A is given by

$$\text{Value}(A) = P(A_1) \cdot \text{Value}(A_1) + P(A_2) \cdot \text{Value}(A_2) + \ldots$$

ONLINE PROBLEMS

Problem 3 Calculating an Expected Value

Got It? **a.** How many points can you expect to get for the dartboard shown in Problem 3 if you receive these points: 30 points for white, 15 points for red, and -10 points for blue?

b. For part (a), what number of points could be set for the blue area that would result in an expected value of 0?

A Practice 5. **Games** In a game show, a contestant receives a prize that has a 5% probability of being worth \$1000 and a 95% probability of being worth \$1. What is the expected value of winning a prize?

Problem 4 Making Decisions Based on Expected Values

Got It? a. Use the information from Problem 4. Suppose the probability for the field goal was 80% and the probability for a touchdown was 30%. Which play should the coach choose?

b. Are there situations where the coach should choose a play that doesn't have the greatest expected value? Explain.

A Practice 6. **Video Games** In a video game, a player has an 80% probability of winning 1000 points if he attacks a certain monster. There is a 20% probability that he will lose 25,000 points. What is the expected value of points earned? Should the player attack the monster? Explain.

Lesson Check

Do you know HOW?

7. What are the first four numbers between 1 and 45 which would be chosen on the basis of the following line from a random number table?

81638 36566 42709 33717 59943 12027 46547

8. A basketball player can either attempt a 3-point shot (with a 25% probability of scoring) or pass to a teammate with a 50% probability of scoring 2 points. What are the expected values for each choice? Which choice should he make?

Do you UNDERSTAND?

MATHEMATICAL PRACTICES

9. Reasoning A friend says that using a random number table to pick a person at random isn't as fair as throwing a dart at the list of names. Explain your friend's error.

10. Vocabulary Explain the meaning of *expected value*. Include an example.

11. **Writing** Describe how you can use a random number generator to model the results of tossing a coin a hundred times.

More Practice and Problem-Solving Exercises

MATHEMATICAL PRACTICES

B Apply

12. **Think About A Plan** A business owner is choosing which of two potential products to develop. Developing Product A will cost $10,000, and the product has a 60% probability of being successful. Product B will cost $15,000 to develop, and it has a 30% probability of being successful. If Product A is successful, the business will gain $200,000. If product B is successful, the business will gain $450,000. Which product should the business owner choose?
    - How can the expected values of Product A and Product B help the business owner make the decision?
    - Compare the expected values. Recommend that the business owner choose the product with the greater expected value.

13. **Business** A company is deciding whether to invest in a new business opportunity. There is a 40% chance that the company will lose $25,000; a 25% chance that the company will break even; and a 35% chance that the company will make $40,000. Should company executives decide to invest in the opportunity? Explain.

14. **Finance** A stock has a 25% probability of increasing by $10 per share over the next month. The stock has a 75% probability of decreasing by $5 per share over the same period. What is the expected value of the stock's increase or decrease? Based on this information, should you buy the stock? Explain.

15. **Test Taking** You earn 1 point for each correct response on a multiple choice test and lose 0.5 point for an incorrect response. Each question has four answer choices. If a student does not know the correct answer and guesses, what is the expected value of the guess?

16. **Games** A bag contains 10 marbles; 4 are red, 5 are yellow, and 1 is blue. You draw one marble from the bag without looking. If you draw a blue marble, you win $10. If you draw a red marble, you win $5, and if you draw a yellow marble, you win $3. What is the expected value of drawing one marble? Would you play this game for $5? Explain.

17. **Writing** A polling company has been hired to survey 500 households out of a possible 2500 households. How can the 500 households be randomly selected for the survey?

Challenge

18. **Stocks** An investor is choosing between three stocks she might purchase. The potential outcomes are listed in the table.
    a. Calculate the expected value of the gain or loss for each stock.
    b. Set up a model and use a random number table to model the investment in each stock.
    c. How do the results of the random number table model compare with the expected values?
    d. Does the expected value tell you anything about the riskiness of each stock?

Potential Outcomes

	Lose $25 per Share	Gain $5 per Share	Gain $45 per Share
Stock ABC	40%	15%	45%
Stock JKL	15%	65%	20%
Stock MNO	5%	80%	15%

Random Number Table

18823	18160	93593	67294	19632	62617	86779	74024
65358	70469	87149	89509	72176	18103	55169	79954
72002	20582	25325	22451	22445	62132	81638	36566
42709	33717	59943	12027	46547	72749	13347	65030
26128	49067	27904	49953	74674	94617	13317	58697
31973	06303	94202	62287	56164	79157	98375	24558
99241	38449	46438	91579	01907	72146	05764	22400
94490	49833	09258	11873	57196	32209	67663	07990
12288	59245	83638	23642	61715	35483	84563	79956
88618	54619	24853	59783	47537	88822	47227	09262
25041	57862	19203	86103	02800	23198	70639	43757
52064	75820	50994	31050	67304	16730	29373	96700
07845	69584	70548	52973	72302	97594	92241	15204
42665	29990	57260	75846	01152	30141	35982	96088
04003	36893	51639	65625	28426	90634	32979	05449
32959	06776	72420	55622	81422	67587	93193	67479
29041	35939	80920	31801	38638	87905	37617	53135
63364	20495	50868	54130	32625	30799	94255	03514
27838	19139	82031	46143	93922	32001	05378	42457
94248	29387	32682	86235	35805	66529	00886	25875
40156	92636	95648	79767	16307	71133	15714	44142
44293	19195	30569	41277	01417	34656	80207	33362
71878	31767	40056	52582	30766	70264	86253	07179
24757	57502	51033	16551	66731	87844	41420	10084
55529	68560	50069	50652	76104	42086	48720	96632
39724	50318	91370	68016	06222	26806	86726	52832
80950	27135	14110	92292	17049	60257	01638	04460
21694	79570	74409	95087	75424	57042	27349	16229
06930	85441	37191	75134	12845	67868	51500	97761
18740	35448	56096	37910	35485	19640	07689	31027
40657	14875	70695	92569	40703	69318	95070	01541
52249	56515	59058	34509	35791	22150	56558	75286
86570	07303	40560	57856	22009	67712	19435	90250
62962	66253	93288	01838	68388	55481	00336	19271
78066	09117	62350	58972	80778	46458	83677	16125
89106	30219	30068	54030	49295	48985	01624	72881
88310	18172	89450	04987	02781	37935	76222	93595
20942	90911	57643	34009	20728	88785	81212	08214
93926	66687	58252	18674	18501	22362	37319	33201
88294	55814	67443	77285	36229	26886	66782	89931
29751	08485	49910	83844	56013	26596	20875	34568
11169	15529	33241	83594	01727	86595	65723	82322
06062	54400	80649	70749	50395	48993	77447	24862
87445	17139	43278	55031	79971	18515	61850	49101
39283	22821	44330	82225	53534	77235	42973	60190

ACTIVITY LAB

Use With Lesson 14-7

Probability and Decision Making

S.MD.7 Analyze decisions and strategies using probability concepts . . .

Understanding probability is important in areas from game playing to testing new pharmaceutical drugs.

Activity 1

Your older sister has devised a game to play with your younger brother. She says that your brother can choose who goes first. Here are the rules:

Roll a standard number cube.

Player 1 wins a point if the number cube shows an even number or a 5.

Player 2 wins a point if the number cube is a factor of 24.

1. a. In each turn, what is the probability that Player 1 scores a point? What is the probability that Player 2 scores a point?

b. What advice would you give your brother? Should he choose to be Player 1 or Player 2? Explain.

Activity 2

A pharmaceutical company tested a new formulation for eye drops on 160 people who suffered from very dry eyes. Two groups of test subjects were randomly selected. The first group received a placebo and the second group received the new eye drops. Below are the results of the testing.

Eye Drop Test Results

	Improvement	No Improvement
Group 1	48	32
Group 2	39	41

2. What is the probability that someone in Group 1 showed improvement?

3. What is the probability that someone in Group 2 showed improvement?

4. Would you advise further development on the new formulation for eye drops or for the company to drop this new medication? Justify your answer using probabilities.

14 Chapter Review

MathXL® for School
Go to pearsonsuccessnet.com

14-1 Experimental and Theoretical Probability

Quick Review

Experimental probability is based on how many successes are observed in repeated trials of an event. **Theoretical probability** describes the likelihood of an event based on what should happen mathematically. The **sample space** is the set of all possible outcomes of an experiment.

Example

There are 14 boys and 11 girls in a homeroom. If a student is selected at random, what is the probability that the student is a girl?

There are 25 possible outcomes in the sample space. Of these, 11 are girls. The probability that the student is a girl is $P(\text{girl}) = \frac{11}{25} = 0.44$.

Exercises

There are 12 math teachers, 9 science teachers, 3 music teachers, and 6 social studies teachers at a conference. If a teacher is selected at random, find each probability.

1. P(science)
2. P(not music)
3. P(reading)
4. P(not math)
5. **Bowling** Suppose you rolled 5 strikes and 7 nonstrikes in a bowling game. Based on these results, what is the experimental probability that you will roll a strike?

14-2 Probability Distributions and Frequency Tables

Quick Review

A **frequency table** shows how often an item appears in a category. The **relative frequency** of an item is the ratio of the frequency of the category to the total frequency. A **probability distribution** shows the probabilities of every possible outcome of an experiment.

Example

What is the relative frequency of sedans?

Type of Car	Frequency
Truck	3
Minivan	6
Sedan	12
Sports	2
Other	7

There are 30 cars in all, and 12 of them are sedans. So the relative frequency of sedans is $\frac{12}{30} = 0.4$.

Exercises

Use the frequency table below to find each probability.

Test Grade	Frequency
A	7
B	11
C	6
D	3
F	1

6. P(A)
7. P(B)
8. P(B or C)
9. P(grade below C)
10. P(grade above C)
11. P(grade above D)

14-3 Permutations and Combinations

Quick Review

According to the **Fundamental Counting Principle,** if event M can occur in m ways and event N can occur in n ways, then event M and event N can occur in $m \cdot n$ ways.

***n* factorial:**

$n! = n \cdot (n-1) \cdot (n-2) \cdot \ldots \cdot 3 \cdot 2 \cdot 1$

Permutation formula (order matters):

$${}_nP_r = \frac{n!}{(n-r)!}$$

Combination formula (order is not important):

$${}_nC_r = \frac{n!}{r!(n-r)!}$$

Example

How many ways can a teacher choose a group of 4 students from 15 if order does not matter?

$${}_{15}C_4 = \frac{15!}{4!(15-4)!} = 1365 \text{ ways}$$

Exercises

Evaluate each of the following.

12. 5!

13. 8!

14. $\frac{7!}{3!}$

15. $\frac{12!}{9!3!}$

16. ${}_8P_5$

17. ${}_{10}P_2$

18. ${}_9C_7$

19. ${}_{20}C_3$

20. License Plate A license plate is made up of 3 letters followed by 4 digits. How many different license plates are possible if none of the letters or digits can be repeated?

21. Music A student wants to put 3 songs on her MP3 player from a collection of 25 songs. How many different ways can she do this?

14-4 Compound Probability

Quick Review

For independent events A and B, $P(A \text{ and } B) = P(A) \cdot P(B)$. For mutually exclusive events A and B, $P(A \text{ or } B) = P(A) + P(B)$.
For overlapping events A and B,
$P(A \text{ or } B) = P(A) + P(B) - P(A \text{ and } B)$.

Example

If a classmate rolls a standard number cube, what is the probability that she rolls a prime number or an even number?

$P(\text{prime}) = \frac{3}{6} = \frac{1}{2}$ 2, 3, and 5 are prime.

$P(\text{even}) = \frac{3}{6} = \frac{1}{2}$ 2, 4, and 6 are even.

$P(\text{even and prime}) = \frac{1}{6}$ 2 is even and prime.

$P(\text{even or prime}) = \frac{1}{2} + \frac{1}{2} - \frac{1}{6} = \frac{5}{6}$

Exercises

Suppose A and B are independent events, $P(A) = 0.46$, and $P(B) = 0.25$. Find each probability.

22. $P(A \text{ and } B)$

23. $P(A \text{ or } B)$

24. A bag contains 3 red marbles, 4 green marbles, 5 blue marbles, and 4 yellow marbles. If a marble is selected at random, what is the probability that it is red or green?

25. Writing Explain why the formula $P(A \text{ or } B) = P(A) + P(B) - P(A \text{ and } B)$ can be used for any two events A and B.

14-5 Probability Models

Quick Review

A **two-way frequency** table shows data that fall into two different categories. You can use two-way frequency tables to find relative frequencies of items in different categories.

Example

What is the relative frequency of female juniors on the student council?

	Male	Female	Totals
Juniors	2	2	4
Seniors	1	3	4
Totals	3	5	8

There are 8 members, and 2 of them are female juniors. The relative frequency is $\frac{2}{8} = 0.25$.

Exercises

Studying **Use the two-way frequency table to answer each question.**

	Studied	Did Not Study	Total
Passed	19	7	26
Failed	1	4	5
Totals	20	11	31

26. Did more students choose to study or to not study for the quiz?

27. What is the relative frequency of students who studied for the quiz and passed?

28. What is the relative frequency of students who did not study and failed?

14-6 Conditional Probability Formulas

Quick Review

To find the conditional probability that dependent events A and B occur, multiply the probability that event A occurs by the probability that event B occurs, given that event A has already occurred.

$P(A \text{ and } B) = P(A) \cdot P(B|A)$

For any two events A and B with $P(A) \neq 0$,

$P(B|A) = \frac{P(A \text{ and } B)}{P(A)}$.

Example

A coach's desk drawer contains 3 blue pens, 5 black pens, and 4 red pens. What is the probability that he selects a black pen followed by a red pen, if the first pen is not replaced?

$P(\text{black, then red}) = P(\text{black}) \cdot P(\text{red, given black})$

$= \frac{5}{12} \cdot \frac{4}{11} = \frac{5}{33}$

Exercises

Solve each problem.

29. Recreation The ball bin in the gym contains 8 soccer balls, 12 basketballs, and 10 kickballs. If Coach Meyers selects 2 balls at random and does not replace the first, what is the probability that she selects 2 basketballs?

30. Tests Suppose your teacher has given 2 pop quizzes this week. Seventy percent of her class passed the first quiz, and 50% passed both quizzes. If a student is selected at random, what is the probability that he or she passed the second quiz, given that the student passed the first quiz?

31. Shopping At a shoe store yesterday, 74% of customers bought shoes, 38% bought accessories, and 55% bought both shoes and accessories. If a customer is selected at random, what is the probability that he bought accessories, given that he bought shoes?

14-7 Modeling Randomness

Quick Review

Random events have no predetermined pattern or bias toward one outcome or the other. You can use random number tables and graphing calculators to help you model random events and make fair decisions. A simulation is a probability model that can be used to make predictions about real world situations.

Example

Twenty students are assigned 2-digit numbers from 01 to 20. Use the excerpt from the random number table below to randomly select the first 3 students.

80261 53267 85048 53091 18479 06286 38323

Reading from left to right, the 2-digit numbers are:

80, 26, 15, 32, 67, 85, 04, 85, 30, 91, 18, . . .

The first 3 students are indicated by the numbers 15, 04, and 18

Exercises

Golf On average, Raymond shoots lower than 80 in 3 out of 4 rounds of golf. He conducts a simulation to predict how many times he will shoot lower than 80 in his next 5 rounds. Let 1, 2, and 3 represent shooting lower than 80, and let 4 represent shooting 80 or higher.

22113 22413 34141 12131 34432

34112 34142 24241 44231 41122

23132 13314 14133 11432 41214

34423 13332 12422 11422 33312

32. How many trials of the simulation did Raymond conduct?

33. In how many trials of the simulation did Raymond shoot lower than 80 in at least 4 of the 5 rounds?

34. According to this simulation, what is the experimental probability that Raymond will shoot lower than 80 in at least 4 of his next 5 rounds?

14

Pull It All Together

PERFORMANCE TASK

ASSESSMENT

Making Business Decisions

Loretta's Ice Cream tested two new flavors, chocolate caramel swirl and raspberry. In a survey of 100 customers, the store received the following information about the new flavors:

- Twenty-four customers like only raspberry.
- Twice as many customers like only chocolate caramel swirl as like both new flavors.
- The number of customers that like both new flavors is equal to the number of customers that do not like either new flavor.

A new flavor is served all summer if there is at least a 50% probability that a random customer likes the flavor.

Task Description

Should Loretta serve either of these new flavors all summer? Use information from the survey to justify your answer.

HONORS APPENDIX

The oval lawn behind the White House in Washington, D.C., is called *the Ellipse*. It has views of the Washington Monument, the Jefferson Memorial, the Department of Commerce, and the Old Post Office Building. The Ellipse is 616 ft long and 528 ft wide, and is in the shape of a conic section. Its shape can be modeled using the methods of this chapter.

H-1 Conic Sections and Parabolas

What you'll learn about

- Conic Sections
- Geometry of a Parabola
- Translations of Parabolas
- Reflective Property of a Parabola

... and why

Conic sections are the paths of nature: Any free-moving object in a gravitational field follows the path of a conic section.

Analytic geometry combines number and form. It is the marriage of algebra and geometry that grew from the works of Frenchmen René Descartes (1596–1650) and Pierre de Fermat (1601–1665). Their achievements allowed geometry problems to be solved algebraically and algebra problems to be solved geometrically. Analytic geometry opened the door for Newton and Leibniz to develop calculus.

In Lessons H-1 through H-3, we will learn that parabolas, ellipses, and hyperbolas are all conic sections and can all be expressed as second-degree equations. We will investigate their uses, including the reflective properties of parabolas and ellipses and how hyperbolas are used in long-range navigation.

Conic Sections

Imagine two nonperpendicular lines intersecting at a point V. If we fix one of the lines as an *axis* and rotate the other line (the *generator*) around the axis, then the generator sweeps out a **right circular cone** with **vertex** V, as illustrated in Figure 8.1. Notice that V divides the cone into two parts called **nappes**, with each nappe of the cone resembling a pointed ice-cream cone.

History of Conic Sections

Parabolas, ellipses, and hyperbolas had been studied for many years when Apollonius (c.250–175 B.C.E.) wrote his eight-volume *Conic Sections*. Apollonius, born in Perga, Asia Minor, was the first to unify these three curves as cross sections of a cone and to view the hyperbola as having two branches. Interest in conic sections was renewed in the 17th century when Galileo proved that projectiles follow parabolic paths and Johannes Kepler (1571–1630) discovered that planets travel in elliptical orbits.

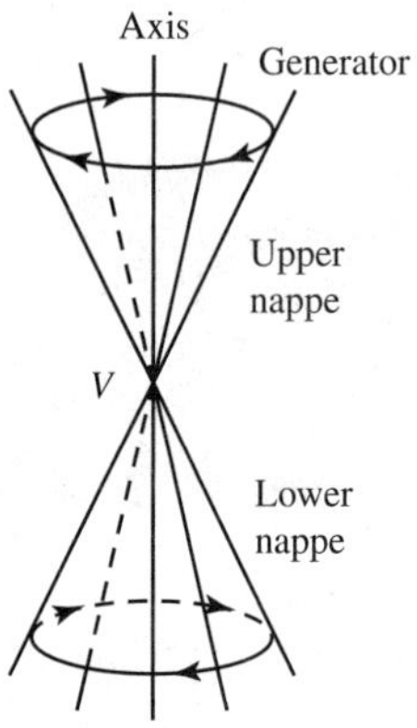

FIGURE H.1 A right circular cone (of two nappes).

A **conic section** (or **conic**) is a cross section of a cone, in other words, the intersection of a plane with a right circular cone. The three basic conic sections are the *parabola*, the *ellipse*, and the *hyperbola* (Figure H.2a).

Some atypical conics, known as **degenerate conic sections**, are shown in Figure H.2b. Because it is atypical and lacks some of the features usually associated with an ellipse, a circle is considered to be a degenerate ellipse. Other degenerate conic sections can be obtained from cross sections of a degenerate cone; such cones occur when the generator and axis of the cone are parallel or perpendicular. (See Exercise 67.)

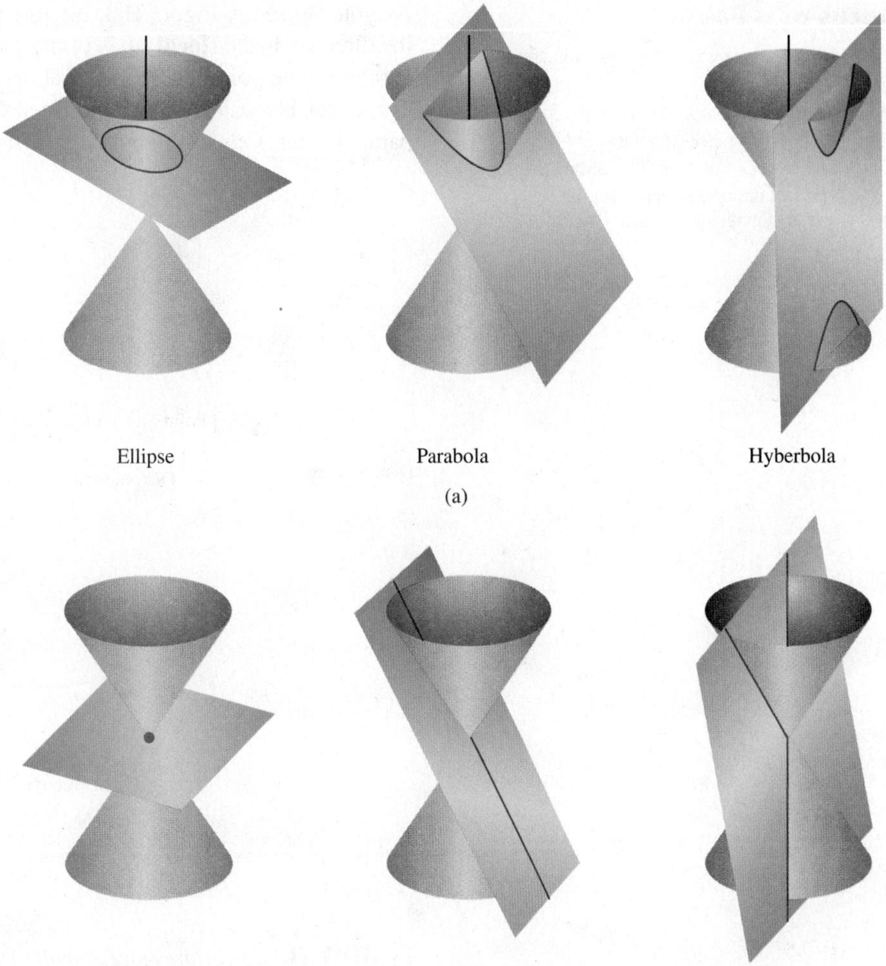

FIGURE H.2 (a) The three standard types of conic sections and (b) three degenerate conic sections.

The conic sections can be defined algebraically as the graphs of **second-degree (quadratic) equations in two variables**, that is, equations of the form

$$Ax^2 + Bxy + Cy^2 + Dx + Ey + F = 0,$$

where A, B, and C are not all zero.

Geometry of a Parabola

The graph of a quadratic function is an upward- or downward- opening parabola. We have seen the role of the parabola in free fall and projectile motion. We now investigate the geometric properties of parabolas.

A Degenerate Parabola

If the focus F lies on the directrix l, the parabola "degenerates" to the line through F perpendicular to l. Henceforth, we will assume F does not lie on l.

DEFINITION Parabola

A **parabola** is the set of all points in a plane equidistant from a particular line (the **directrix**) and a particular point (the **focus**) in the plane (Figure H.3).

Locus of a Point

Before the word *set* was used in mathematics, the Latin word *locus*, meaning "place," was often used in geometric definitions. The locus of a point was the set of possible places a point could be and still fit the conditions of the definition. Sometimes, conics are still defined in terms of loci.

As you can see in Figure H.3, the line passing through the focus and perpendicular to the directrix is the **(focal) axis** of the parabola. The axis is the line of symmetry for the parabola. The point where the parabola intersects its axis is the **vertex** of the parabola. The vertex is located midway between the focus and the directrix and is the point of the parabola that is closest to both the focus and the directrix.

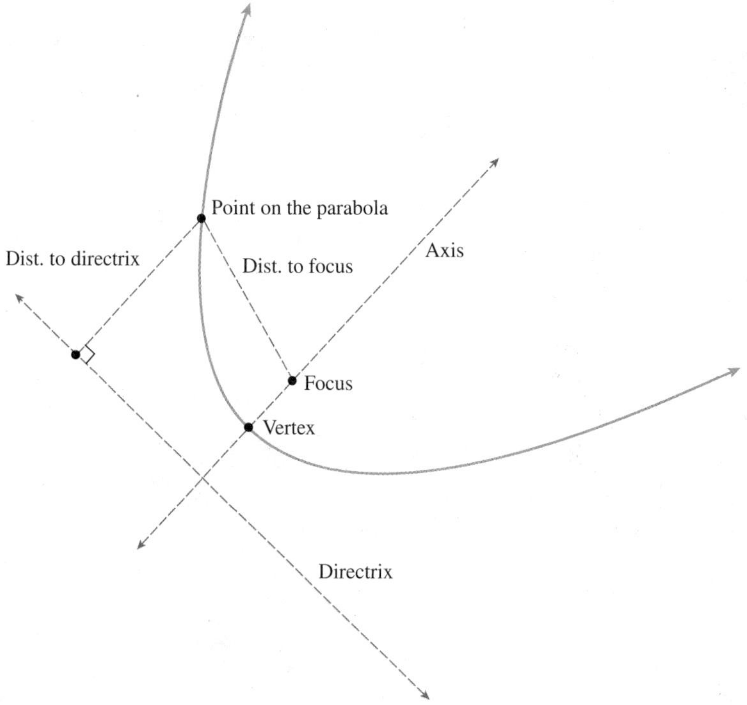

FIGURE H.3 *Structure of a Parabola.* The distance from each point on the parabola to both the focus and the directrix is the same.

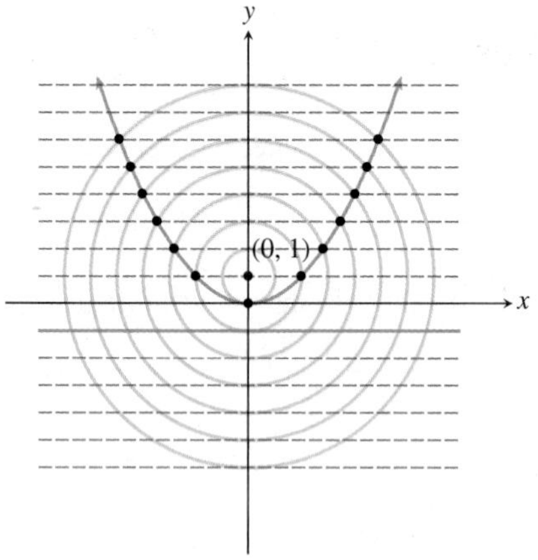

FIGURE H.4 The geometry of a parabola.

EXPLORATION 1 Understanding the Definition of Parabola

1. Prove that the vertex of the parabola with focus $(0, 1)$ and directrix $y = -1$ is $(0, 0)$ (Figure H.4).
2. Find an equation for the parabola shown in Figure H.4.
3. Find the coordinates of the points of the parabola that are highlighted in Figure H.4.

We can generalize the situation in Exploration 1 to show that an equation for the parabola with focus $(0, p)$ and directrix $y = -p$ is $x^2 = 4py$ (Figure H.5).

We must show first that a point $P(x, y)$ that is equidistant from $F(0, p)$ and the line $y = -p$ satisfies the equation $x^2 = 4py$, and then that a point satisfying the equation $x^2 = 4py$ is equidistant from $F(0, p)$ and the line $y = -p$:

Let $P(x, y)$ be equidistant from $F(0, p)$ and the line $y = -p$. Notice that

$$\sqrt{(x - 0)^2 + (y - p)^2} = \text{distance from } P(x, y) \text{ to } F(0, p), \text{ and}$$
$$\sqrt{(x - x)^2 + (y - (-p))^2} = \text{distance from } P(x, y) \text{ to } y = -p.$$

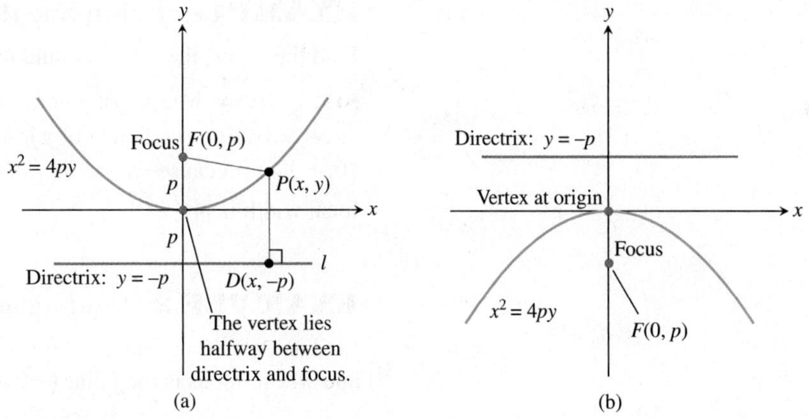

FIGURE H.5 Graphs of $x^2 = 4py$ with (a) $p > 0$ and (b) $p < 0$.

Equating these distances and squaring yields:

$$(x - 0)^2 + (y - p)^2 = (x - x)^2 + (y - (-p))^2$$

$$x^2 + (y - p)^2 = 0 + (y + p)^2 \qquad \text{Simplify.}$$

$$x^2 + y^2 - 2py + p^2 = y^2 + 2py + p^2 \qquad \text{Expand.}$$

$$x^2 = 4py \qquad \text{Combine like terms.}$$

By reversing the above steps, we see that a solution (x, y) of $x^2 = 4py$ is equidistant from $F(0, p)$ and the line $y = -p$.

The equation $x^2 = 4py$ is the **standard form** of the equation of an upward- or downward-opening parabola with vertex at the origin. If $p > 0$, the parabola opens upward; if $p < 0$, it opens downward. An alternative algebraic form for such a parabola is $y = ax^2$, where $a = 1/(4p)$. So the graph of $x^2 = 4py$ is also the graph of the quadratic function $f(x) = ax^2$.

When the equation of an upward- or downward-opening parabola is written as $x^2 = 4py$, the value p is interpreted as the **focal length** of the parabola—the *directed* distance from the vertex to the focus of the parabola. A line segment with endpoints on a parabola is a **chord** of the parabola. The value $|4p|$ is the **focal width** of the parabola—the length of the chord through the focus and perpendicular to the axis.

Parabolas that open to the right or to the left are *inverse relations* of upward- or downward-opening parabolas. Therefore, equations of parabolas with vertex $(0, 0)$ that open to the right or to the left have the standard form $y^2 = 4px$. If $p > 0$, the parabola opens to the right, and if $p < 0$, to the left (Figure H.6).

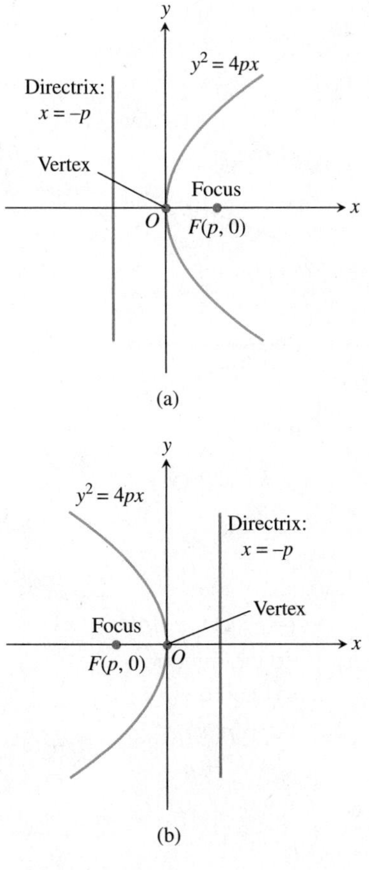

FIGURE H.6 Graph of $y^2 = 4px$ with (a) $p > 0$ and (b) $p < 0$.

Parabolas with Vertex (0, 0)

• **Standard equation**	$x^2 = 4py$	$y^2 = 4px$
• **Opens**	Upward or downward	To the right or to the left
• **Focus**	$(0, p)$	$(p, 0)$
• **Directrix**	$y = -p$	$x = -p$
• **Axis**	y-axis	x-axis
• **Focal length**	p	p
• **Focal width**	$\lvert 4p \rvert$	$\lvert 4p \rvert$

See Figures H.5 and H.6.

EXAMPLE 1 Finding the Focus, Directrix, and Focal Width

Find the focus, the directrix, and the focal width of the parabola $y = -(1/3)x^2$.

SOLUTION Multiplying both sides of the equation by -3 yields the standard form $x^2 = -3y$. The coefficient of y is $4p = -3$; thus $p = -3/4$. So the focus is $(0, p) = (0, -3/4)$. Because $-p = -(-3/4) = 3/4$, the directrix is the line $y = 3/4$. The focal width is $|4p| = |-3| = 3$. *Now try Exercise 1.*

EXAMPLE 2 Finding an Equation of a Parabola

Find an equation in standard form for the parabola whose directrix is the line $x = 2$ and whose focus is the point $(-2, 0)$.

SOLUTION Because the directrix is $x = 2$ and the focus is $(-2, 0)$, the focal length is $p = -2$ and the parabola opens to the left. The equation of the parabola in standard form is $y^2 = 4px$ or, more specifically, $y^2 = -8x$. *Now try Exercise 15.*

Translations of Parabolas

When a parabola with the equation $x^2 = 4py$ or $y^2 = 4px$ is translated horizontally by h units and vertically by k units, the vertex of the parabola moves from $(0, 0)$ to (h, k) (Figure H.7). Such a translation does not change the focal length, the focal width, or the direction the parabola opens.

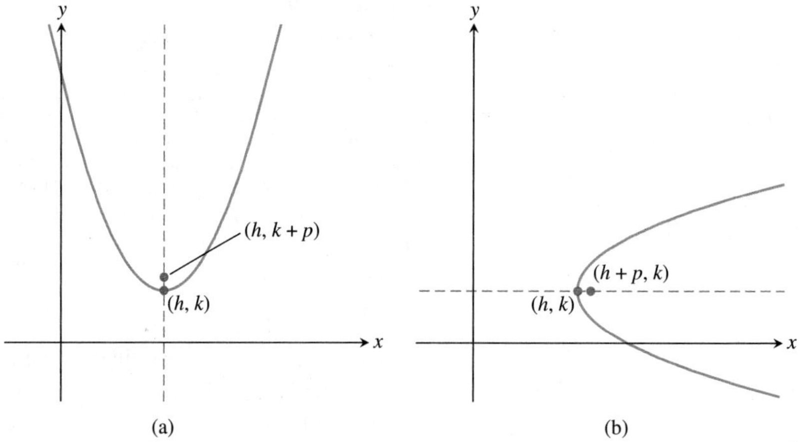

FIGURE H.7 Parabolas with vertex (h, k) and focus on (a) $x = h$ and (b) $y = k$.

Parabolas with Vertex (h, k)

• **Standard equation**	$(x - h)^2 = 4p(y - k)$	$(y - k)^2 = 4p(x - h)$
• **Opens**	Upward or downward	To the right or to the left
• **Focus**	$(h, k + p)$	$(h + p, k)$
• **Directrix**	$y = k - p$	$x = h - p$
• **Axis**	$x = h$	$y = k$
• **Focal length**	p	p
• **Focal width**	$\|4p\|$	$\|4p\|$

See Figure H.7.

EXAMPLE 3 Finding an Equation of a Parabola

Find the standard form of the equation for the parabola with vertex $(3, 4)$ and focus $(5, 4)$.

SOLUTION The axis of the parabola is the line passing through the vertex $(3, 4)$ and the focus $(5, 4)$. This is the line $y = 4$. So the equation has the form

$$(y - k)^2 = 4p(x - h).$$

Because the vertex $(h, k) = (3, 4)$, $h = 3$ and $k = 4$. The directed distance from the vertex $(3, 4)$ to the focus $(5, 4)$ is $p = 5 - 3 = 2$, so $4p = 8$. Thus the equation we seek is

$$(y - 4)^2 = 8(x - 3).$$

Now try Exercise 21.

When solving a problem like Example 3, it is a good idea to sketch the vertex, the focus, and other features of the parabola as we solve the problem. This makes it easy to see whether the axis of the parabola is horizontal or vertical and the relative positions of its features. Exploration 2 "walks us through" this process.

EXPLORATION 2 Building a Parabola

Carry out the following steps using a sheet of rectangular graph paper.

1. Let the focus F of a parabola be $(2, -2)$ and its directrix be $y = 4$. Draw the x- and y-axes on the graph paper. Then sketch and label the focus and directrix of the parabola.
2. Locate, sketch, and label the axis of the parabola. What is the equation of the axis?
3. Locate and plot the vertex V of the parabola. Label it by name and coordinates.
4. What are the focal length and focal width of the parabola?
5. Use the focal width to locate, plot, and label the endpoints of a chord of the parabola that parallels the directrix.
6. Sketch the parabola.
7. Which direction does it open?
8. What is its equation in standard form?

Sometimes it is best to sketch a parabola by hand, as in Exploration 2; this helps us see the structure and relationships of the parabola and its features. At other times, we may want or need an accurate, active graph. If we wish to graph a parabola using a function grapher, we need to solve the equation of the parabola for y, as illustrated in Example 4.

EXAMPLE 4 Graphing a Parabola

Use a function grapher to graph the parabola $(y - 4)^2 = 8(x - 3)$ of Example 3.

SOLUTION

$$(y - 4)^2 = 8(x - 3)$$

$$y - 4 = \pm\sqrt{8(x - 3)} \quad \text{Extract square roots.}$$

$$y = 4 \pm \sqrt{8(x - 3)} \quad \text{Add 4.}$$

Let $Y_1 = 4 + \sqrt{8(x - 3)}$ and $Y_2 = 4 - \sqrt{8(x - 3)}$, and graph the two equations in a window centered at the vertex, as shown in Figure H.8.

Now try Exercise 45.

Closing the Gap

In Figure H.8, we centered the graphing window at the vertex $(3, 4)$ of the parabola to ensure that this point would be plotted. This avoids the common grapher error of a gap between the two upper and lower parts of the conic section being plotted.

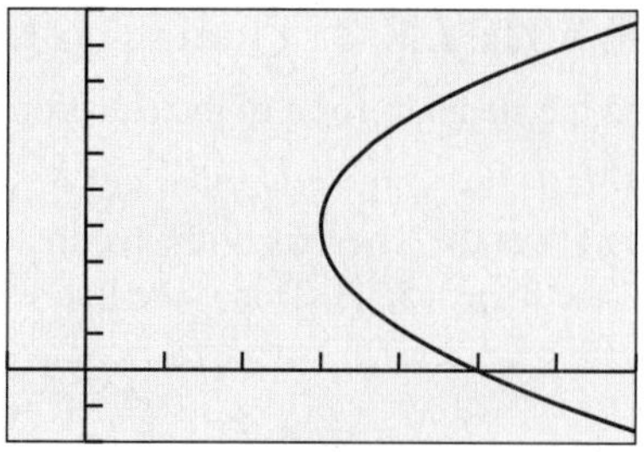

[–1, 7] by [–2, 10]

FIGURE H.8 The graphs of $Y1 = 4 + \sqrt{8(x - 3)}$ and $Y2 = 4 - \sqrt{8(x - 3)}$ together form the graph of $(y - 4)^2 = 8(x - 3)$. (Example 4)

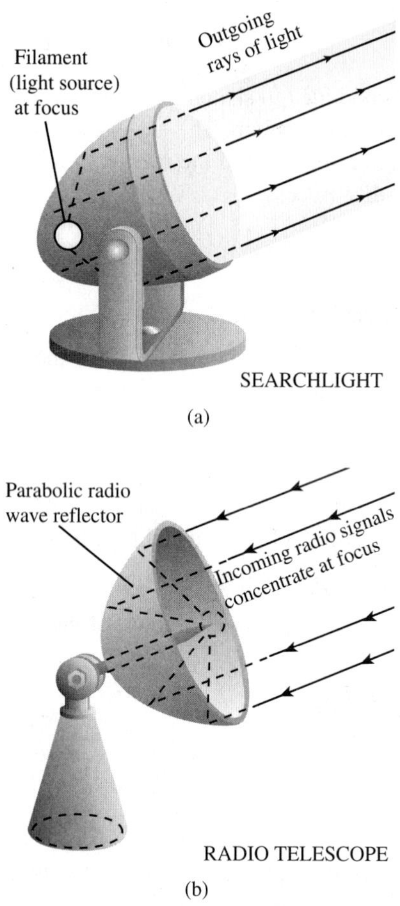

FIGURE H.9 Examples of parabolic reflectors.

EXAMPLE 5 Using Standard Forms with a Parabola

Prove that the graph of $y^2 - 6x + 2y + 13 = 0$ is a parabola, and find its vertex, focus, and directrix.

SOLUTION Because this equation is quadratic in the variable y, we complete the square with respect to y to obtain a standard form.

$$
\begin{aligned}
y^2 - 6x + 2y + 13 &= 0 \\
y^2 + 2y &= 6x - 13 && \text{Isolate the } y\text{-terms.} \\
y^2 + 2y + 1 &= 6x - 13 + 1 && \text{Complete the square.} \\
(y + 1)^2 &= 6x - 12 \\
(y + 1)^2 &= 6(x - 2)
\end{aligned}
$$

This equation is in the standard form $(y - k)^2 = 4p(x - h)$, where $h = 2$, $k = -1$, and $p = 6/4 = 3/2 = 1.5$. It follows that

- the vertex (h, k) is $(2, -1)$;
- the focus $(h + p, k)$ is $(3.5, -1)$, or $(7/2, -1)$;
- the directrix $x = h - p$ is $x = 0.5$, or $x = 1/2$.

Now try Exercise 49.

Reflective Property of a Parabola

The main applications of parabolas involve their use as reflectors of sound, light, radio waves, and other electromagnetic waves. If we rotate a parabola in three-dimensional space about its axis, the parabola sweeps out a **paraboloid of revolution**. If we place a signal source at the focus of a reflective paraboloid, the signal reflects off the surface in lines parallel to the axis of symmetry, as illustrated in Figure H.9a. This property is used by flashlights, headlights, searchlights, microwave relays, and satellite up-links.

The principle works for signals traveling in the reverse direction as well (Figure H.9b); signals arriving parallel to a parabolic reflector's axis are directed toward the reflector's focus. This property is used to intensify signals picked up by radio telescopes and television satellite dishes, to focus arriving light in reflecting telescopes, to concentrate heat in solar ovens, and to magnify sound for sideline microphones at football games.

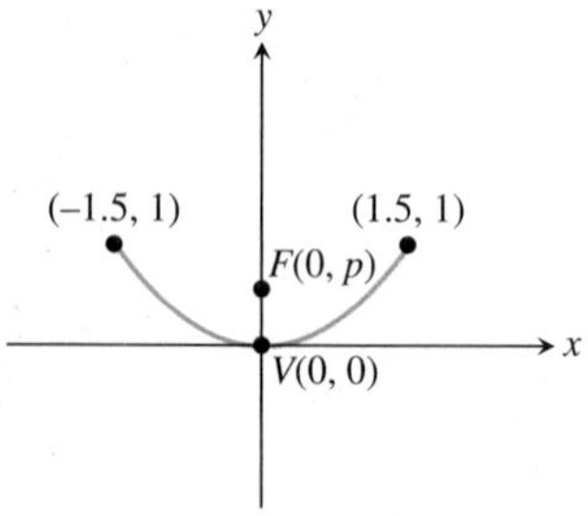

FIGURE H.10 Cross section of parabolic reflector in Example 6.

EXAMPLE 6 Studying a Parabolic Microphone

On the sidelines of each of its televised football games, the FBTV network uses a parabolic reflector with a microphone at the reflector's focus to capture the conversations among players on the field. If the parabolic reflector is 3 ft across and 1 ft deep, where should the microphone be placed?

SOLUTION

We draw a cross section of the reflector as an upward-opening parabola in the Cartesian plane, placing its vertex *V* at the origin (Figure H.10). We let the focus *F* have coordinates $(0, p)$ to yield the equation

$$x^2 = 4py.$$

Because the reflector is 3 ft across and 1 ft deep, the points $(\pm 1.5, 1)$ must lie on the parabola. The microphone should be placed at the focus, so we need to find the value of p. We do this by substituting the values we found into the equation:

$$\begin{aligned} x &= 4py \\ (\pm 1.5)^2 &= 4p(1) \\ 2.25 &= 4p \\ p &= \frac{2.25}{4} = 0.5625 \end{aligned}$$

Because $p = 0.5625$ ft, or 6.75 inches, the microphone should be placed inside the reflector along its axis and $6\frac{3}{4}$ inches from its vertex. *Now try Exercise 59.*

LESSON H-1 EXERCISES

Exercise numbers with a gray background indicate problems that the authors have designed to be solved *without a calculator.*

In Exercises 1–6, find the vertex, focus, directrix, and focal width of the parabola.

1. $x^2 = 6y$ **2.** $y^2 = -8x$

3. $(y - 2)^2 = 4(x + 3)$ **4.** $(x + 4)^2 = -6(y + 1)$

5. $3x^2 = -4y$ **6.** $5y^2 = 16x$

In Exercises 7–10, match the graph with its equation.

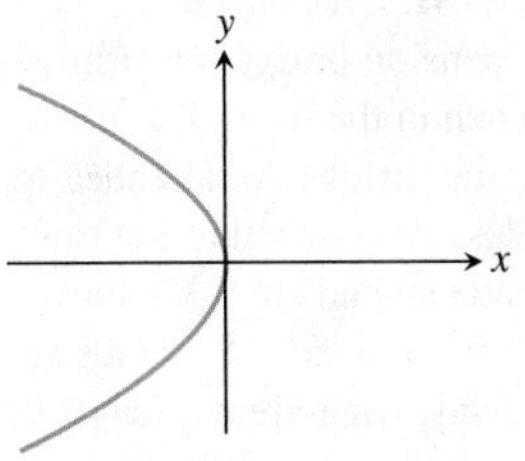

(a)

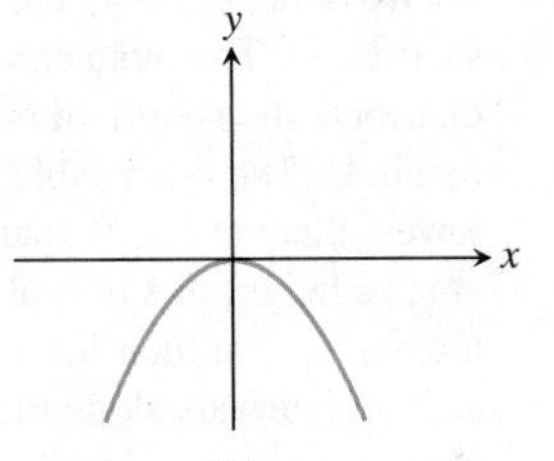

(b)

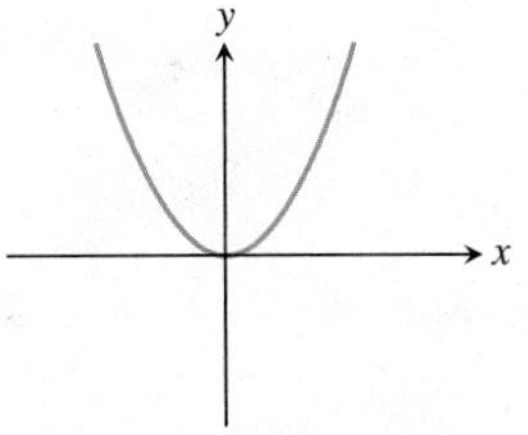

(c)

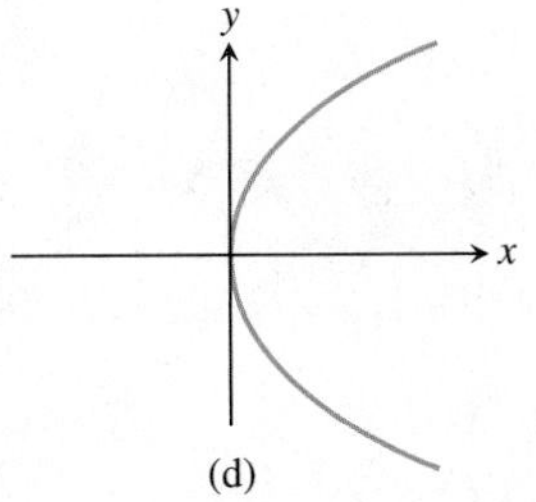

(d)

7. $x^2 = 3y$ **8.** $x^2 = -4y$

9. $y^2 = -5x$ **10.** $y^2 = 10x$

In Exercises 11–30, find an equation in standard form for the parabola that satisfies the given conditions.

11. Vertex $(0, 0)$, focus $(-3, 0)$

12. Vertex $(0, 0)$, focus $(0, 2)$

13. Vertex $(0, 0)$, directrix $y = 4$

14. Vertex $(0, 0)$, directrix $x = -2$

15. Focus $(0, 5)$, directrix $y = -5$

16. Focus $(-4, 0)$, directrix $x = 4$

17. Vertex $(0, 0)$, opens to the right, focal width $= 8$

18. Vertex $(0, 0)$, opens to the left, focal width $= 12$

19. Vertex $(0, 0)$, opens downward, focal width $= 6$

20. Vertex $(0, 0)$, opens upward, focal width $= 3$

21. Focus $(-2, -4)$, vertex $(-4, -4)$

22. Focus $(-5, 3)$, vertex $(-5, 6)$

23. Focus $(3, 4)$, directrix $y = 1$

24. Focus $(2, -3)$, directrix $x = 5$

25. Vertex $(4, 3)$, directrix $x = 6$

26. Vertex $(3, 5)$, directrix $y = 7$

27. Vertex $(2, -1)$, opens upward, focal width $= 16$

28. Vertex $(-3, 3)$, opens downward, focal width $= 20$

29. Vertex $(-1, -4)$, opens to the left, focal width $= 10$

30. Vertex $(2, 3)$, opens to the right, focal width $= 5$

In Exercises 31–36, sketch the graph of the parabola by hand.

31. $y^2 = -4x$ **32.** $x^2 = 8y$

33. $(x + 4)^2 = -12(y + 1)$

34. $(y + 2)^2 = -16(x + 3)$

35. $(y - 1)^2 = 8(x + 3)$ **36.** $(x - 5)^2 = 20(y + 2)$

In Exercises 37–48, graph the parabola using a function grapher.

37. $y = 4x^2$ **38.** $y = -\frac{1}{6}x^2$

39. $x = -8y^2$ **40.** $x = 2y^2$

41. $12(y + 1) = (x - 3)^2$ **42.** $6(y - 3) = (x + 1)^2$

43. $2 - y = 16(x - 3)^2$ **44.** $(x + 4)^2 = -6(y - 1)$

45. $(y + 3)^2 = 12(x - 2)$ **46.** $(y - 1)^2 = -4(x + 5)$

47. $(y + 2)^2 = -8(x + 1)$ **48.** $(y - 6)^2 = 16(x - 4)$

In Exercises 49–52, prove that the graph of the equation is a parabola, and find its vertex, focus, and directrix.

49. $x^2 + 2x - y + 3 = 0$

50. $3x^2 - 6x - 6y + 10 = 0$

51. $y^2 - 4y - 8x + 20 = 0$

52. $y^2 - 2y + 4x - 12 = 0$

In Exercises 53–56, write an equation for the parabola.

53.

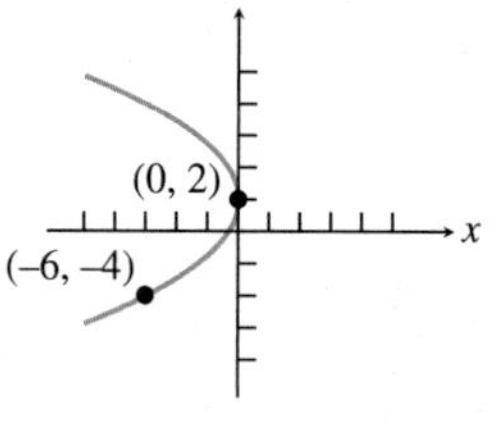

54.

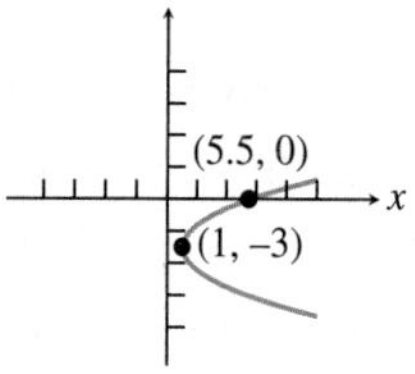

55.

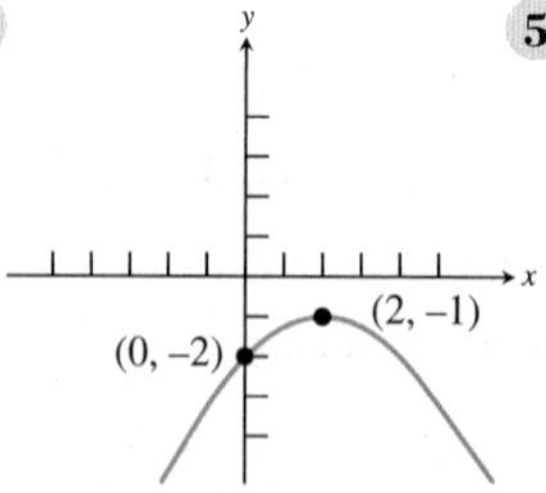

56.

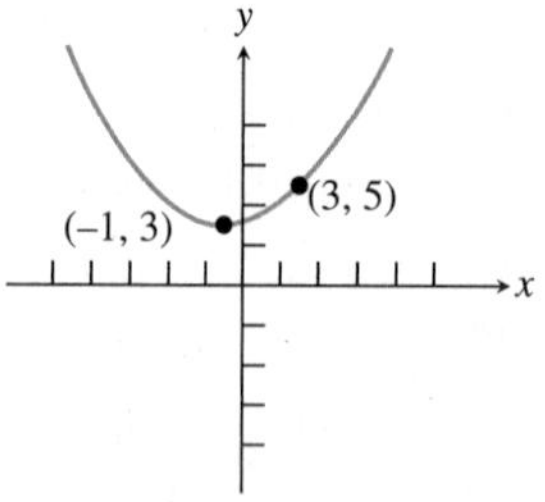

57. Writing to Learn Explain why the derivation of $x^2 = 4py$ is valid regardless of whether $p > 0$ or $p < 0$.

58. Writing to Learn Prove that an equation for the parabola with focus $(p, 0)$ and directrix $x = -p$ is $y^2 = 4px$.

59. Designing a Flashlight Mirror The mirror of a flashlight is a paraboloid of revolution. Its diameter is 6 cm and its depth is 2 cm. How far from the vertex should the filament of the lightbulb be placed for the flashlight to have its beam run parallel to the axis of its mirror?

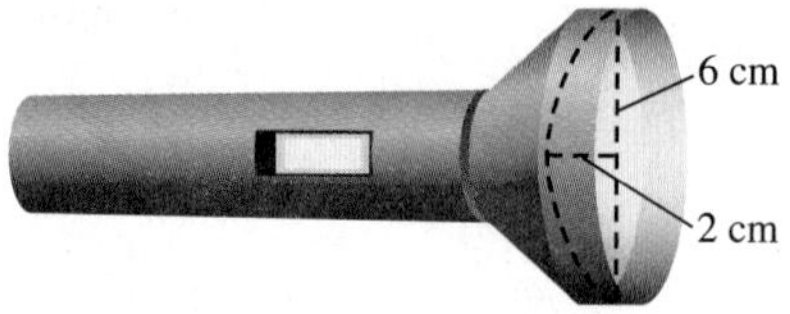

60. Designing a Satellite Dish The reflector of a television satellite dish is a paraboloid of revolution with diameter 5 ft and a depth of 2 ft. How far from the vertex should the receiving antenna be placed?

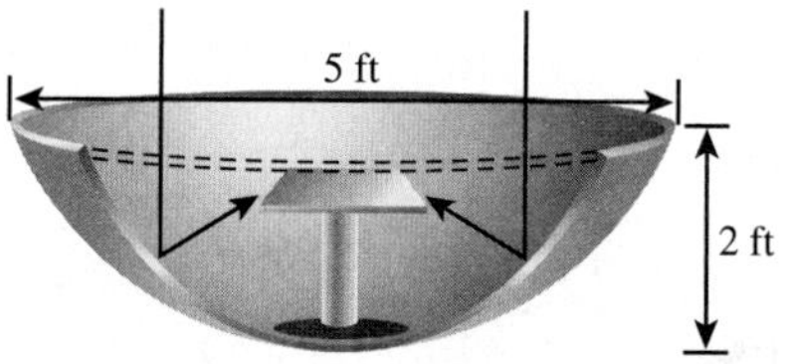

61. Parabolic Microphones The Sports Channel uses a parabolic microphone to capture all the sounds from golf tournaments throughout a season. If one of its microphones has a parabolic surface generated by the parabola $x^2 = 10y$, locate the focus (the electronic receiver) of the parabola.

62. Parabolic Headlights Stein Glass, Inc., makes parabolic headlights for a variety of automobiles. If one of its headlights has a parabolic surface generated by the parabola $x^2 = 12y$, where should its lightbulb be placed?

63. Group Activity Designing a Suspension Bridge The main cables of a suspension bridge uniformly distribute the weight of the bridge when in the form of a parabola. The main cables of a particular bridge are attached to towers that are 600 ft apart. The cables are attached to the towers at a height of 110 ft above the roadway and are 10 ft above the roadway at their lowest points. If vertical support cables are at 50-ft intervals along the level roadway, what are the lengths of these vertical cables?

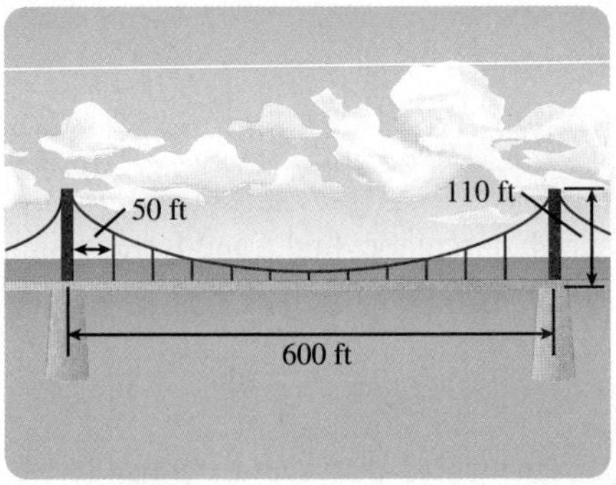

64. Group Activity Designing a Bridge Arch Parabolic arches are known to have greater strength than other arches. A bridge with a supporting parabolic arch spans 60 ft with a 30-ft-wide road passing underneath the bridge. In order to have a minimum clearance of 16 ft, what is the maximum clearance?

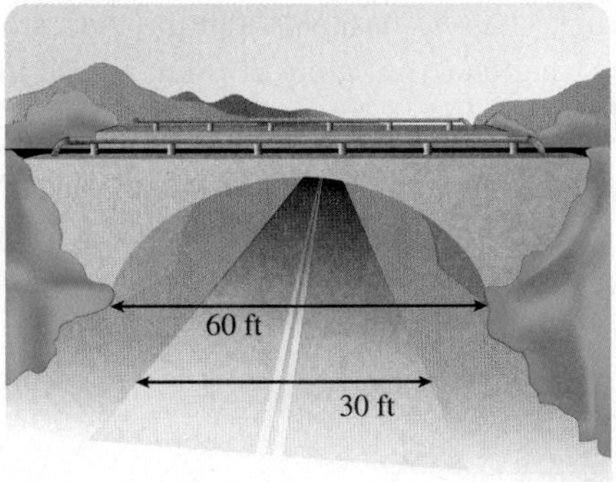

Explorations

65. Dynamically Constructing a Parabola Use a geometry software package, such as *Cabri Geometry II*™, *The Geometer's Sketchpad*®, or similar application on a handheld device, to construct a parabola geometrically from its definition. (See Figure H.3.)

(a) Start by placing a line l (directrix) and a point F (focus) not on the line in the construction window.

(b) Construct a point A on the directrix, and then the segment AF.

(c) Construct a point P where the perpendicular bisector of AF meets the line perpendicular to l through A.

(d) What curve does P trace out as A moves?

(e) Prove that your answer to part (d) is correct.

66. Constructing Points of a Parabola Use a geometry software package, such as *Cabri Geometry II*™, *The Geometer's Sketchpad*®, or similar application on a handheld device, to construct Figure H.4, associated with Exploration 1.

(a) Start by placing the coordinate axes in the construction window.

(b) Construct the line $y = -1$ as the directrix and the point $(0, 1)$ as the focus.

(c) Construct the horizontal lines and concentric circles shown in Figure H.4.

(d) Construct the points where these horizontal lines and concentric circles meet.

(e) Prove these points lie on the parabola with directrix $y = -1$ and focus $(0, 1)$.

67. Degenerate Cones and Degenerate Conics Degenerate cones occur when the generator and axis of the cone are parallel or perpendicular.

(a) Draw a sketch and describe the "cone" obtained when the generator and axis of the cone are parallel.

(b) Draw sketches and name the types of degenerate conics obtained by intersecting the degenerate cone in part (a) with a plane.

(c) Draw a sketch and describe the "cone" obtained when the generator and axis of the cone are perpendicular.

(d) Draw sketches and name the types of degenerate conics obtained by intersecting the degenerate cone in part (c) with a plane.

Extending the Ideas

68. Tangent Lines A **tangent line** of a parabola is a line that intersects but does not cross the parabola. Prove that a line tangent to the parabola $x^2 = 4py$ at the point (a, b) crosses the y-axis at $(0, -b)$.

69. Focal Chords A **focal chord** of a parabola is a chord of the parabola that passes through the focus.

(a) Prove that the x-coordinates of the endpoints of a focal chord of $x^2 = 4py$ are $x = 2p(m \pm \sqrt{m^2 + 1})$, where m is the slope of the focal chord.

(b) Using part (a), prove that the minimum length of a focal chord is the focal width $|4p|$.

70. Latus Rectum The focal chord of a parabola perpendicular to the axis of the parabola is the **latus rectum**, which is Latin for "right chord." Using the results from Exercises 68 and 69, prove:

(a) For a parabola the two endpoints of the latus rectum and the point of intersection of the axis and directrix are the vertices of an isosceles right triangle.

(b) The legs of this isosceles right triangle are tangent to the parabola.

H-2 Ellipses

What you'll learn about

- Geometry of an Ellipse
- Translations of Ellipses
- Orbits and Eccentricity
- Reflective Property of an Ellipse

... and why

Ellipses are the paths of planets and comets around the Sun, or of moons around planets.

Geometry of an Ellipse

When a plane intersects one nappe of a right circular cylinder and forms a simple closed curve, the curve is an ellipse.

DEFINITION Ellipse

An **ellipse** is the set of all points in a plane whose distances from two fixed points in the plane have a constant sum. The fixed points are the **foci** (plural of focus) of the ellipse. The line through the foci is the **focal axis**. The point on the focal axis midway between the foci is the **center**. The points where the ellipse intersects its axis are the **vertices** of the ellipse (Figure H.11).

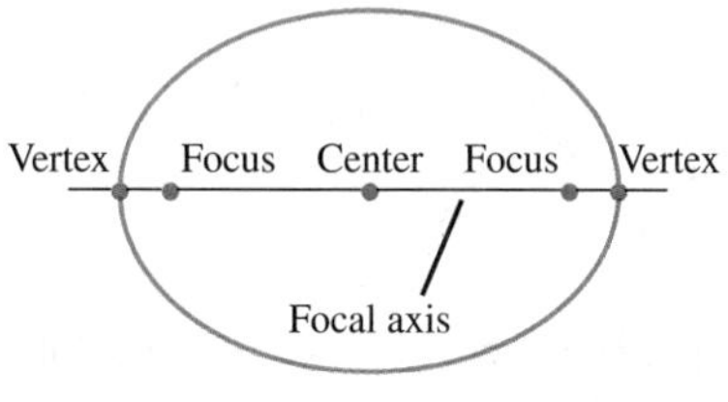

FIGURE H.11 Key points on the focal axis of an ellipse.

Figure H.12 shows a point $P(x, y)$ of an ellipse. The fixed points F_1 and F_2 are the foci of the ellipse, and the distances whose sum is constant are d_1 and d_2. We can construct an ellipse using a pencil, a loop of string, and two pushpins. Put the loop around the two pins placed at F_1 and F_2, pull the string taut with a pencil point P, and move the pencil around to trace out the ellipse (Figure H.13).

We now use the definition to derive an equation for an ellipse. For some constants a and c with $a > c \geq 0$, let $F_1(-c, 0)$ and $F_2(c, 0)$ be the foci (Figure H.14). Then an ellipse is defined by the set of points $P(x, y)$ such that

$$PF_1 + PF_2 = 2a.$$

Using the distance formula, the equation becomes

$$\sqrt{(x+c)^2 + (y-0)^2} + \sqrt{(x-c)^2 + (y-0)^2} = 2a.$$

$$\sqrt{(x-c)^2 + y^2} = 2a - \sqrt{(x+c)^2 + y^2} \quad \text{Rearrange terms.}$$

$$x^2 - 2cx + c^2 + y^2 = 4a^2 - 4a\sqrt{(x+c)^2 + y^2} + x^2 + 2cx + c^2 + y^2 \quad \text{Square.}$$

$$a\sqrt{(x+c)^2 + y^2} = a^2 + cx \quad \text{Simplify.}$$

$$a^2(x^2 + 2cx + c^2 + y^2) = a^4 + 2a^2cx + c^2x^2 \quad \text{Square.}$$

$$(a^2 - c^2)x^2 + a^2y^2 = a^2(a^2 - c^2) \quad \text{Simplify.}$$

Letting $b^2 = a^2 - c^2$, we have

$$b^2x^2 + a^2y^2 = a^2b^2,$$

which is usually written as

$$\frac{x^2}{a^2} + \frac{y^2}{b^2} = 1.$$

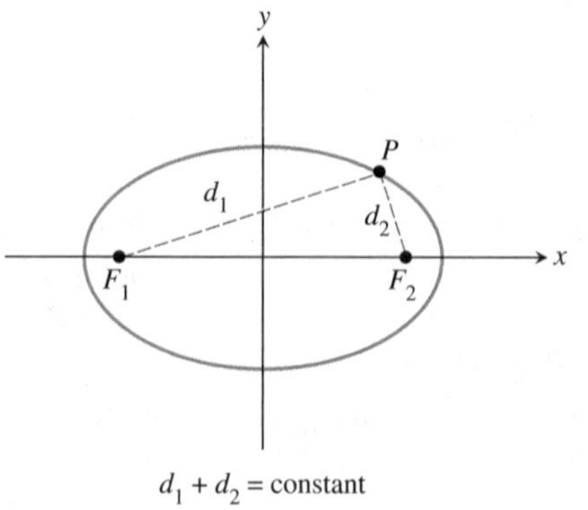

FIGURE H.12 *Structure of an Ellipse.* The sum of the distances from the foci to each point on the ellipse is a constant.

Because these steps can be reversed, a point $P(x, y)$ satisfies this last equation if and only if the point lies on the ellipse defined by $PF_1 + PF_2 = 2a$, provided that $a > c \geq 0$ and $b^2 = a^2 - c^2$. The *Pythagorean relation* $b^2 = a^2 - c^2$ can be written many ways, including $c^2 = a^2 - b^2$ and $a^2 = b^2 + c^2$.

The equation $x^2/a^2 + y^2/b^2 = 1$ is the **standard form** of the equation of an ellipse centered at the origin with the x-axis as its focal axis. An ellipse centered at the origin with the y-axis as its focal axis is the *inverse* of $x^2/a^2 + y^2/b^2 = 1$, and thus has an equation of the form

$$\frac{y^2}{a^2} + \frac{x^2}{b^2} = 1.$$

As with circles and parabolas, a line segment with endpoints on an ellipse is a **chord** of the ellipse. The chord lying on the focal axis is the **major axis** of the ellipse. The chord through the center perpendicular to the focal axis is the **minor axis** of the ellipse. The length of the major axis is $2a$ and of the minor axis is $2b$. The number a is the **semimajor axis**, and b is the **semiminor axis**.

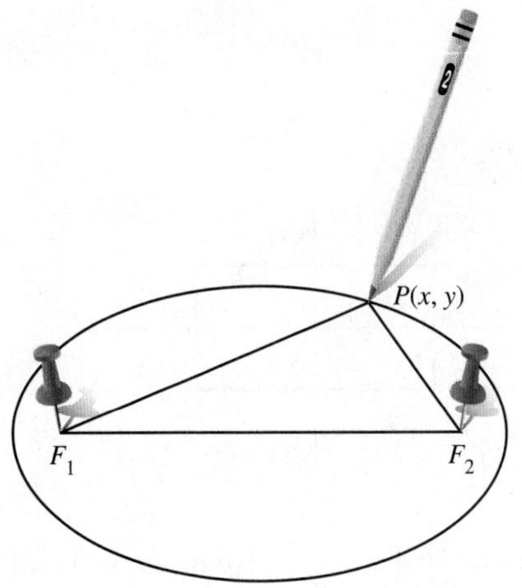

FIGURE H.13 How to draw an ellipse.

Ellipses with Center (0, 0)

• **Standard equation**	$\dfrac{x^2}{a^2} + \dfrac{y^2}{b^2} = 1$	$\dfrac{y^2}{a^2} + \dfrac{x^2}{b^2} = 1$
• **Focal axis**	x-axis	y-axis
• **Foci**	$(\pm c, 0)$	$(0, \pm c)$
• **Vertices**	$(\pm a, 0)$	$(0, \pm a)$
• **Semimajor axis**	a	a
• **Semiminor axis**	b	b
• **Pythagorean relation**	$a^2 = b^2 + c^2$	$a^2 = b^2 + c^2$

See Figure H.15.

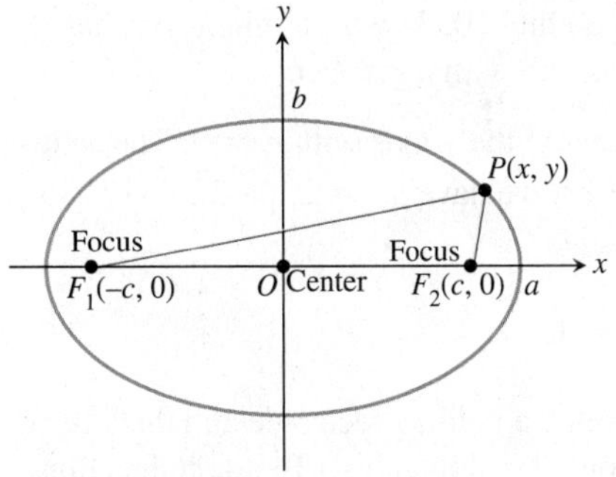

FIGURE H.14 The ellipse defined by $PF_1 + PF_2 = 2a$ is the graph of the equation $x^2/a^2 + y^2/b^2 = 1$, where $b^2 = a^2 - c^2$.

Axis Alert

For an ellipse, the word *axis* is used in several ways. The focal axis is a *line*. The major and minor axes are *line segments*. The semimajor and semiminor axes are *numbers*.

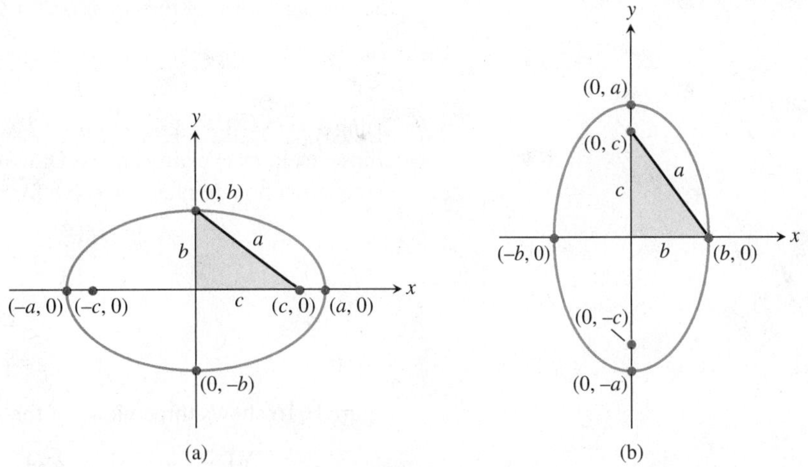

FIGURE H.15 Ellipses centered at the origin with foci on (a) the x-axis and (b) the y-axis. In each case, a right triangle illustrating the Pythagorean relation is shown.

EXAMPLE 1 Finding the Vertices and Foci of an Ellipse

Find the vertices and the foci of the ellipse $4x^2 + 9y^2 = 36$.

SOLUTION Dividing both sides of the equation by 36 yields the standard form $x^2/9 + y^2/4 = 1$. Because the larger number is the denominator of x^2, the focal axis is the x-axis. So $a^2 = 9$, $b^2 = 4$, and $c^2 = a^2 - b^2 = 9 - 4 = 5$. Thus the vertices are $(\pm 3, 0)$, and the foci are $(\pm \sqrt{5}, 0)$. *Now try Exercise 1.*

An ellipse centered at the origin with its focal axis on a coordinate axis is symmetric with respect to the origin and both coordinate axes. Such an ellipse can be sketched by first drawing a *guiding rectangle* centered at the origin with sides parallel to the coordinate axes and then sketching the ellipse inside the rectangle, as shown in the Drawing Lesson.

Drawing Lesson

How to Sketch the Ellipse $x^2/a^2 + y^2/b^2 = 1$

1. Sketch line segments at $x = \pm a$ and $y = \pm b$ and complete the rectangle they determine.
2. Inscribe an ellipse that is tangent to the rectangle at $(\pm a, 0)$ and $(0, \pm b)$.

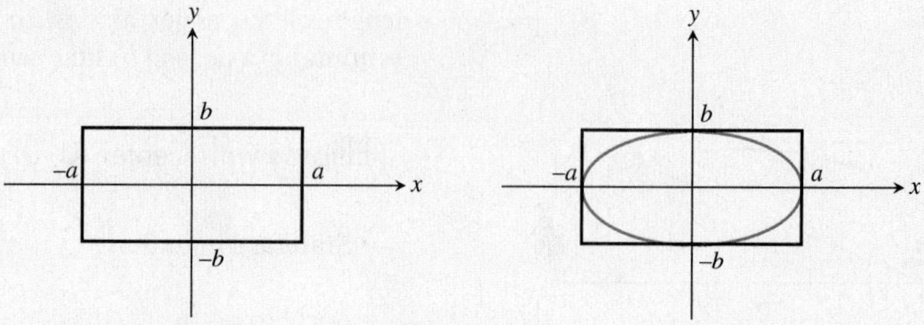

If we wish to graph an ellipse using a function grapher, we need to solve the equation of the ellipse for y, as illustrated in Example 2.

EXAMPLE 2 Finding an Equation and Graphing an Ellipse

Find an equation of the ellipse with foci $(0, -3)$ and $(0, 3)$ whose minor axis has length 4. Sketch the ellipse and support your sketch with a grapher.

SOLUTION The center is $(0, 0)$. The foci are on the y-axis with $c = 3$. The semiminor axis is $b = 4/2 = 2$. Using $a^2 = b^2 + c^2$, we have $a^2 = 2^2 + 3^2 = 13$. So the standard form of the equation for the ellipse is

$$\frac{y^2}{13} + \frac{x^2}{4} = 1.$$

Using $a = \sqrt{13} \approx 3.61$ and $b = 2$, we can sketch a guiding rectangle and then the ellipse itself, as explained in the Drawing Lesson. (Try doing this.) To graph the ellipse using a function grapher, we solve for y in terms of x.

$$\frac{y^2}{13} = 1 - \frac{x^2}{4}$$

$$y^2 = 13(1 - x^2/4)$$

$$y = \pm\sqrt{13(1 - x^2/4)}$$

Figure H.16 shows three views of the graphs of

$$Y1 = \sqrt{13(1 - x^2/4)} \quad \text{and} \quad Y2 = -\sqrt{13(1 - x^2/4)}.$$

We must select the viewing window carefully to avoid grapher failure.

Now try Exercise 17.

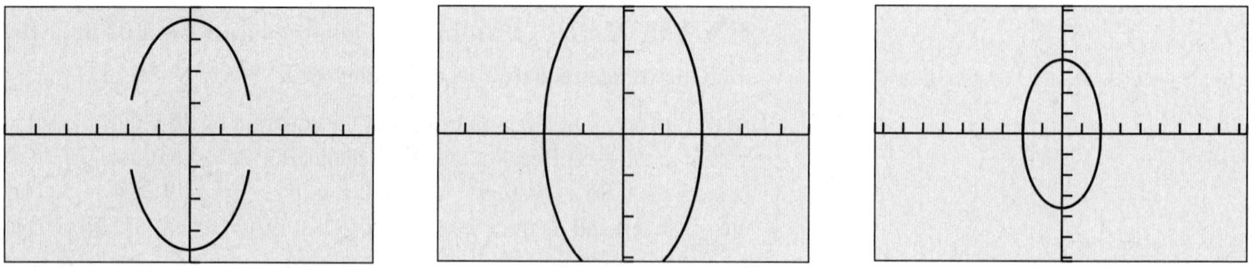

[–6, 6] by [–4, 4]
(a)

[–4.7, 4.7] by [–3.1, 3.1]
(b)

[–9.4, 9.4] by [–6.2, 6.2]
(c)

FIGURE H.16 Three views of the ellipse $y^2/13 + x^2/4 = 1$. All of the windows are square or approximately square viewing windows so we can see the true shape. Notice that the gaps between the upper and lower function branches do not occur when the grapher window includes columns of pixels whose x-coordinates are ± 2 as in (b) and (c). (Example 2)

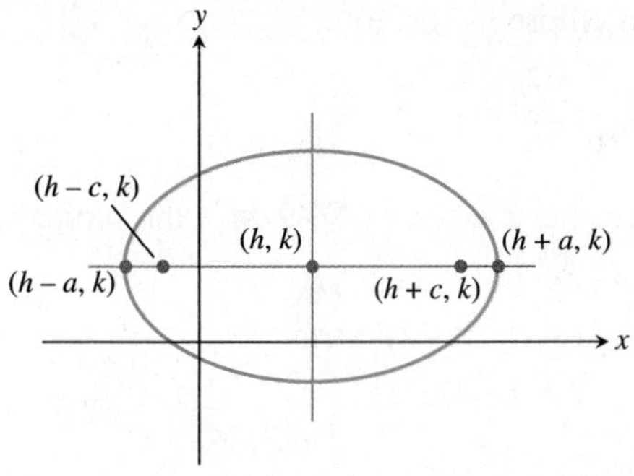

(a)

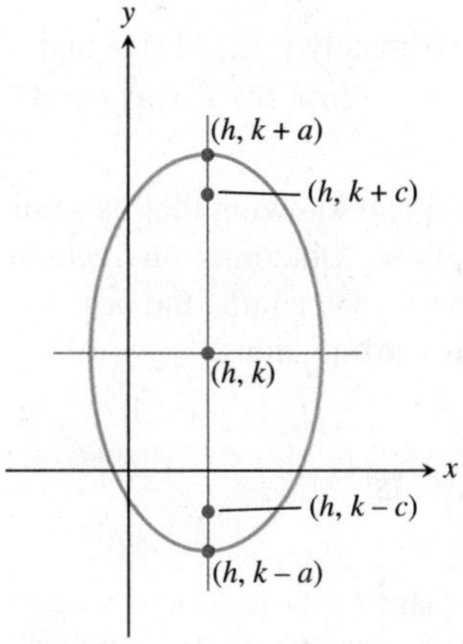

(b)

FIGURE H.17 Ellipses with center (h, k) and foci on (a) $y = k$ and (b) $x = h$.

Translations of Ellipses

When an ellipse with center $(0, 0)$ is translated horizontally by h units and vertically by k units, the center of the ellipse moves from $(0, 0)$ to (h, k), as shown in Figure H.17. Such a translation does not change the length of the major or minor axis or the Pythagorean relation.

Ellipses with Center (h, k)

• **Standard equation**	$\frac{(x-h)^2}{a^2} + \frac{(y-k)^2}{b^2} = 1$	$\frac{(y-k)^2}{a^2} + \frac{(x-h)^2}{b^2} = 1$
• **Focal axis**	$y = k$	$x = h$
• **Foci**	$(h \pm c, k)$	$(h, k \pm c)$
• **Vertices**	$(h \pm a, k)$	$(h, k \pm a)$
• **Semimajor axis**	a	a
• **Semiminor axis**	b	b
• **Pythagorean relation**	$a^2 = b^2 + c^2$	$a^2 = b^2 + c^2$

See Figure H.17.

EXAMPLE 3 Finding an Equation of an Ellipse

Find the standard form of the equation for the ellipse whose major axis has endpoints $(-2, -1)$ and $(8, -1)$, and whose minor axis has length 8.

SOLUTION Figure H.18 shows the major axis endpoints, the minor axis, and the center of the ellipse. The standard equation of this ellipse has the form

$$\frac{(x-h)^2}{a^2} + \frac{(y-k)^2}{b^2} = 1,$$

where the center (h, k) is the midpoint $(3, -1)$ of the major axis. The semimajor axis and semiminor axis are

$$a = \frac{8-(-2)}{2} = 5 \quad \text{and} \quad b = \frac{8}{2} = 4.$$

So the equation we seek is

$$\frac{(x-3)^2}{5^2} + \frac{(y-(-1))^2}{4^2} = 1,$$

$$\frac{(x-3)^2}{25} + \frac{(y+1)^2}{16} = 1.$$

Now try Exercise 31.

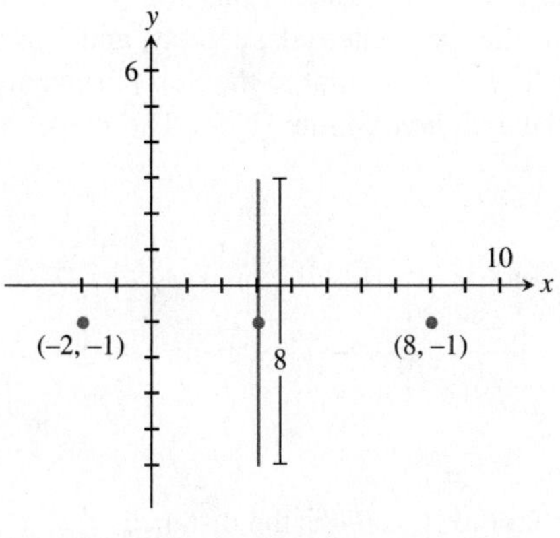

FIGURE H.18 Given information for Example 3.

EXAMPLE 4 Locating Key Points of an Ellipse

Find the center, vertices, and foci of the ellipse

$$\frac{(x+2)^2}{9} + \frac{(y-5)^2}{49} = 1.$$

SOLUTION The standard equation of this ellipse has the form

$$\frac{(y-5)^2}{49}+\frac{(x+2)^2}{9}=1.$$

The center (h, k) is $(-2, 5)$. Because the semimajor axis $a = \sqrt{49} = 7$, the vertices $(h, k \pm a)$ are

$$(h, k+a) = (-2, 5+7) = (-2, 12) \quad \text{and}$$
$$(h, k-a) = (-2, 5-7) = (-2, -2).$$

Because

$$c = \sqrt{a^2 - b^2} = \sqrt{49-9} = \sqrt{40}$$

the foci $(h, k \pm c)$ are $(-2, 5\ (-2, 5 \pm \sqrt{40})$, or approximately $(-2, 11.32)$ and $(-2, -1.32)$.

Now try Exercise 37.

With the information found about the ellipse in Example 4 and knowing that its semiminor axis $b = \sqrt{9} = 3$, we could easily sketch the ellipse. Obtaining an accurate graph of the ellipse using a function grapher is another matter. Generally, the best way to graph an ellipse using a graphing utility is to use parametric equations.

EXPLORATION 1 Graphing an Ellipse Using Its Parametric Equations

1. Use the Pythagorean trigonometry identity $\cos^2 t + \sin^2 t = 1$ to prove that the *parametrization* $x = -2 + 3\cos t$, $y = 5 + 7\sin t$, $0 \le t \le 2\pi$ will produce a graph of the ellipse $(x+2)^2/9 + (y-5)^2/49 = 1$.
2. Graph $x = -2 + 3\cos t$, $y = 5 + 7\sin t$, $0 \le t \le 2\pi$ in a square viewing window to support part 1 graphically.
3. Create parametrizations for the ellipses in Examples 1, 2, and 3.
4. Graph each of your parametrizations in part 3 and check the features of the obtained graph to see whether they match the expected geometric features of the ellipse. Revise your parametrization and regraph until all features match.
5. Prove that each of your parametrizations is valid.

Orbits and Eccentricity

Kepler's First Law of Planetary Motion, published in 1609, states that the path of a planet's orbit is an ellipse with the Sun at one of the foci. Asteroids, comets, and other bodies that orbit the Sun follow elliptical paths. The closest point to the Sun in such an orbit is the *perihelion*, and the farthest point is the *aphelion* (Figure H.19). The shape of an ellipse is related to its *eccentricity*.

DEFINITION Eccentricity of an Ellipse

The **eccentricity** of an ellipse is

$$e = \frac{c}{a} = \frac{\sqrt{a^2 - b^2}}{a},$$

where a is the semimajor axis, b is the semiminor axis, and c is the distance from the center of the ellipse to either focus.

A New e

Try not to confuse the eccentricity e with the natural base e used in exponential and logarithmic functions. The context should clarify which meaning is intended.

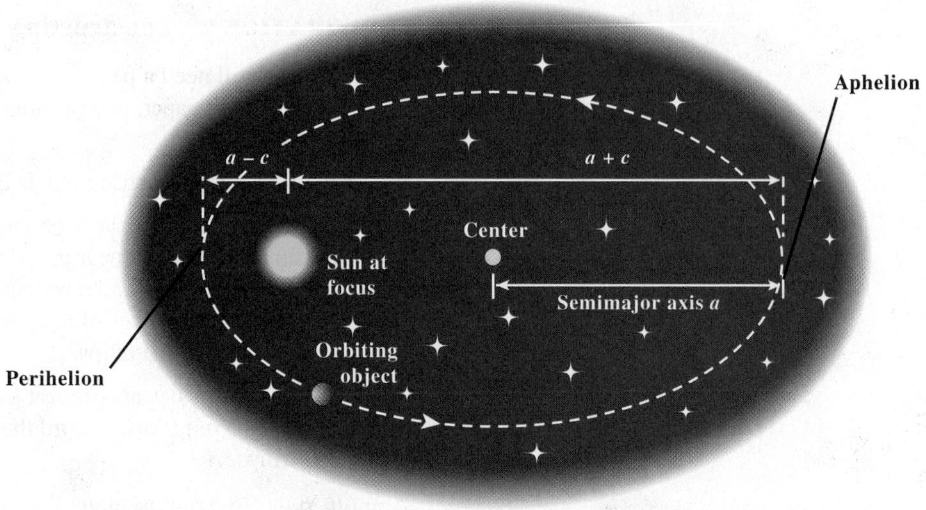

FIGURE H.19 Many celestial objects have elliptical orbits around the Sun.

The noun *eccentricity* comes from the adjective *eccentric*, which means off-center. Mathematically, the eccentricity is the ratio of c to a. The larger c is, compared to a, the more off-center the foci are.

In any ellipse, $a > c \geq 0$. Dividing this inequality by a shows that $0 \leq e < 1$. So the eccentricity of an ellipse is between 0 and 1.

Ellipses with highly off-center foci are elongated and have eccentricities close to 1; for example, the orbit of Halley's comet has eccentricity $e \approx 0.97$. Ellipses with foci near the center are almost circular and have eccentricities close to 0; for instance, Venus's orbit has an eccentricity of 0.0068.

What happens when the eccentricity $e = 0$? In an ellipse, because a is positive, $e = c/a = 0$ implies that $c = 0$ and thus $a = b$. In this case, the ellipse *degenerates* into a circle. Because the ellipse is a circle when $a = b$, it is customary to denote this common value as r and call it the radius of the circle.

Surprising things happen when an ellipse is nearly but not quite a circle, as in the orbit of our planet, Earth.

EXAMPLE 5 Analyzing Earth's Orbit

Earth's orbit has a semimajor axis $a \approx 149.598$ Gm (gigameters) and an eccentricity of $e \approx 0.0167$. Calculate and interpret b and c.

SOLUTION Because $e = c/a$, $c = ea \approx 0.0167 \times 149.598 = 2.4982866$ and

$$b = \sqrt{a^2 - c^2} \approx \sqrt{149.598^2 - 2.4982866^2} \approx 149.577.$$

The semiminor axis $b \approx 149.577$ Gm is only 0.014% shorter than the semimajor axis $a \approx 149.598$ Gm. The aphelion distance of Earth from the Sun is $a + c \approx 149.598 + 2.498 = 152.096$ Gm, and the perihelion distance is $a - c \approx 149.598 - 2.498 = 147.100$ Gm.

Thus Earth's orbit is nearly a perfect circle, but the distance between the center of the Sun at one focus and the center of Earth's orbit is $c \approx 2.498$ Gm, more than 2 orders of magnitude greater than $a - b$. The eccentricity as a percentage is 1.67%; this measures how far *off-center* the Sun is.

Now try Exercise 53.

EXPLORATION 2 Constructing Ellipses to Understand Eccentricity

Each group will need a pencil, a centimeter ruler, scissors, some string, several sheets of unlined paper, two pushpins, and a foam board or other appropriate backing material.

1. Make a closed *loop* of string that is 20 cm in circumference.
2. Place a sheet of unlined paper on the backing material, and carefully place the two pushpins 2 cm apart near the center of the paper. Construct an ellipse using the loop of string and a pencil as shown in Figure H.13. Measure and record the resulting values of a, b, and c for the ellipse, and compute the ratios $e = c/a$ and b/a for the ellipse.
3. On separate sheets of paper repeat step 2 three more times, placing the push-pins 4, 6, and 8 cm apart. Record the values of a, b, c and the ratios e and b/a for each ellipse.
4. Write your observations about the ratio b/a as the eccentricity ratio e increases. Which of these two ratios measures the shape of the ellipse? Which measures how off-center the foci are?
5. Plot the ordered pairs $(e, b/a)$, determine a formula for the ratio b/a as a function of the eccentricity e, and overlay this function's graph on the scatter plot.

Reflective Property of an Ellipse

Because of their shape, ellipses are used to make reflectors of sound, light, and other waves. If we rotate an ellipse in three-dimensional space about its focal axis, the ellipse sweeps out an **ellipsoid of revolution**. If we place a signal source at one focus of a reflective ellipsoid, the signal reflects off the elliptical surface to the other focus, as illustrated in Figure H.20. This property is used to make mirrors for optical equipment and to study aircraft noise in wind tunnels.

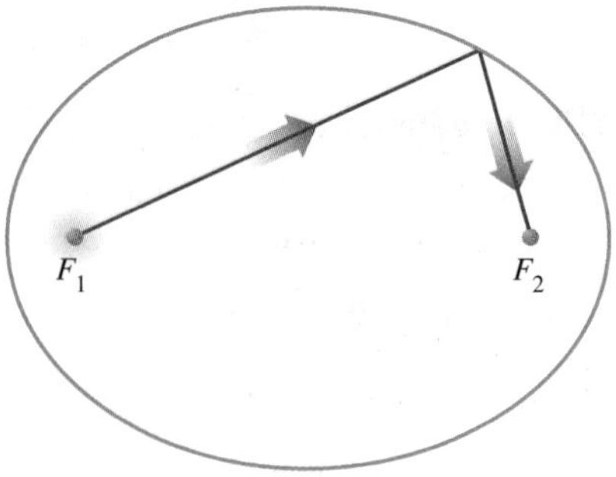

FIGURE H.20 The reflective property of an ellipse.

Ellipsoids are used in health care to avoid surgery in the treatment of kidney stones. An elliptical *lithotripter* emits underwater ultrahigh-frequency (UHF) shock waves from one focus, with the patient's kidney carefully positioned at the other focus (Figure H.21).

Whispering Galleries

In architecture, ceilings in the shape of an ellipsoid are used to create *whispering galleries*. A person whispering at one focus can be heard across the room by a person at the other focus. An ellipsoid is part of the design of the Texas state capitol; a hand clap made in the center of the main vestibule (at one focus of the ellipsoid) bounces off the inner elliptical dome, passes through the other focus, bounces off the dome a second time, and returns to the person as a distinct echo.

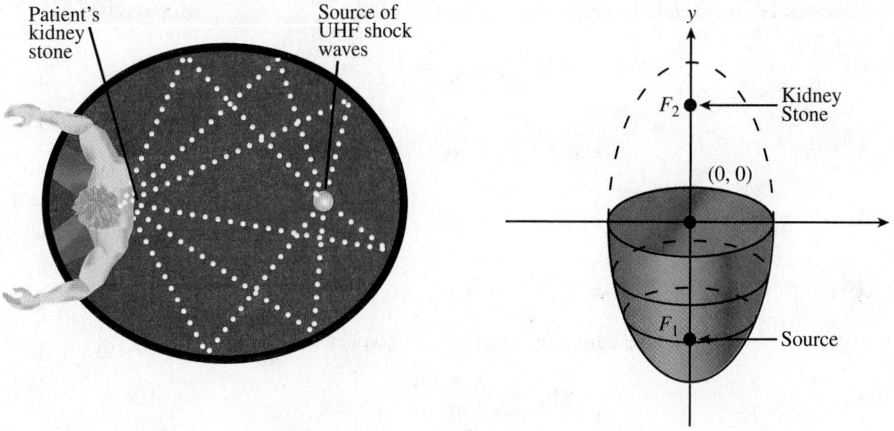

FIGURE H.21 How a lithotripter breaks up kidney stones.

EXAMPLE 6 Focusing a Lithotripter

The ellipse used to generate the ellipsoid of a lithotripter has a major axis of 12 ft and a minor axis of 5 ft. How far from the center are the foci?

SOLUTION From the given information, we know $a = 12/2 = 6$ and $b = 5/2 = 2.5$. So

$$c = \sqrt{a^2 - b^2} \approx \sqrt{6^2 - 2.5^2} \approx 5.4544.$$

The foci are about 5 ft 5.5 inches from the center of the lithotripter.

Now try Exercise 59.

LESSON H-2 EXERCISES

Exercise numbers with a gray background indicate problems that the authors have designed to be solved *without a calculator.*

In Exercises 1–6, find the vertices and foci of the ellipse.

1. $\dfrac{x^2}{16} + \dfrac{y^2}{7} = 1$ **2.** $\dfrac{y^2}{25} + \dfrac{x^2}{21} = 1$

3. $\dfrac{y^2}{36} + \dfrac{x^2}{27} = 1$ **4.** $\dfrac{x^2}{11} + \dfrac{y^2}{7} = 1$

5. $3x^2 + 4y^2 = 12$ **6.** $9x^2 + 4y^2 = 36$

In Exercises 7–10, match the graph with its equation, given that the tick marks on all axes are 1 unit apart.

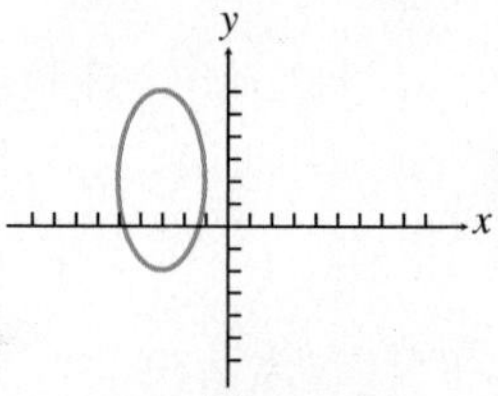

(a)

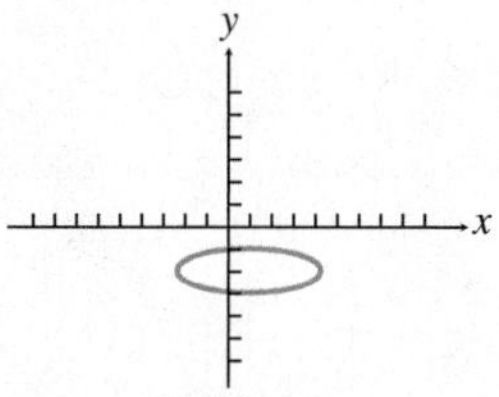

(b)

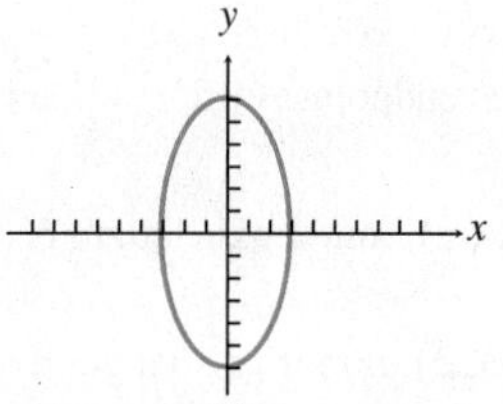

(c)

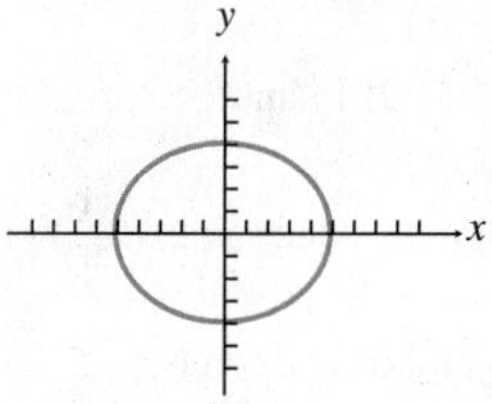

(d)

7. $\dfrac{x^2}{25} + \dfrac{y^2}{16} = 1$ **8.** $\dfrac{y^2}{36} + \dfrac{x^2}{9} = 1$

9. $\dfrac{(y-2)^2}{16} + \dfrac{(x+3)^2}{4} = 1$

10. $\dfrac{(x-1)^2}{11} + (y+2)^2 = 1$

In Exercises 11–16, sketch the graph of the ellipse by hand.

11. $\frac{x^2}{64} + \frac{y^2}{36} = 1$ **12.** $\frac{x^2}{81} + \frac{y^2}{25} = 1$

13. $\frac{y^2}{9} + \frac{x^2}{4} = 1$ **14.** $\frac{y^2}{49} + \frac{x^2}{25} = 1$

15. $\frac{(x+3)^2}{16} + \frac{(y-1)^2}{4} = 1$

16. $\frac{(x-1)^2}{2} + \frac{(y+3)^2}{4} = 1$

In Exercises 17–20, graph the ellipse using a function grapher.

17. $\frac{x^2}{36} + \frac{y^2}{16} = 1$ **18.** $\frac{y^2}{64} + \frac{x^2}{16} = 1$

19. $\frac{(x+2)^2}{5} + 2(y-1)^2 = 1$

20. $\frac{(x-4)^2}{16} + 16(y+4)^2 = 8$

In Exercises 21–36, find an equation in standard form for the ellipse that satisfies the given conditions.

21. Major axis length 6 on y-axis, minor axis length 4

22. Major axis length 14 on x-axis, minor axis length 10

23. Foci $(\pm 2, 0)$, major axis length 10

24. Foci $(0, \pm 3)$, major axis length 10

25. Endpoints of axes are $(\pm 4, 0)$ and $(0, \pm 5)$

26. Endpoints of axes are $(\pm 7, 0)$ and $(0, \pm 4)$

27. Major axis endpoints $(0, \pm 6)$, minor axis length 8

28. Major axis endpoints $(\pm 5, 0)$, minor axis length 4

29. Minor axis endpoints $(0, \pm 4)$, major axis length 10

30. Minor axis endpoints $(\pm 12, 0)$, major axis length 26

31. Major axis endpoints $(1, -4)$ and $(1, 8)$, minor axis length 8

32. Major axis endpoints $(-2, -3)$ and $(-2, 7)$, minor axis length 4

33. Foci $(1, -4)$ and $(5, -4)$, major axis endpoints $(0, -4)$ and $(6, -4)$

34. Foci $(-2, 1)$ and $(-2, 5)$, major axis endpoints $(-2, -1)$ and $(-2, 7)$

35. Major axis endpoints $(3, -7)$ and $(3, 3)$, minor axis length 6

36. Major axis endpoints $(-5, 2)$ and $(3, 2)$, minor axis length 6

In Exercises 37–40, find the center, vertices, and foci of the ellipse.

37. $\frac{(x+1)^2}{25} + \frac{(y-2)^2}{16} = 1$ **38.** $\frac{(x-3)^2}{11} + \frac{(y-5)^2}{7} = 1$

39. $\frac{(y+3)^2}{81} + \frac{(x-7)^2}{64} = 1$ **40.** $\frac{(y-1)^2}{25} + \frac{(x+2)^2}{16} = 1$

In Exercises 41–44, graph the ellipse using a parametric grapher.

41. $\frac{y^2}{25} + \frac{x^2}{4} = 1$ **42.** $\frac{x^2}{30} + \frac{y^2}{20} = 1$

43. $\frac{(x+3)^2}{12} + \frac{(y-6)^2}{5} = 1$ **44.** $\frac{(y+1)^2}{15} + \frac{(x-2)^2}{6} = 1$

In Exercises 45–48, prove that the graph of the equation is an ellipse, and find its vertices, foci, and eccentricity.

45. $9x^2 + 4y^2 - 18x + 8y - 23 = 0$

46. $3x^2 + 5y^2 - 12x + 30y + 42 = 0$

47. $9x^2 + 16y^2 + 54x - 32y - 47 = 0$

48. $4x^2 + y^2 - 32x + 16y + 124 = 0$

In Exercises 49 and 50, write an equation for the ellipse.

49.

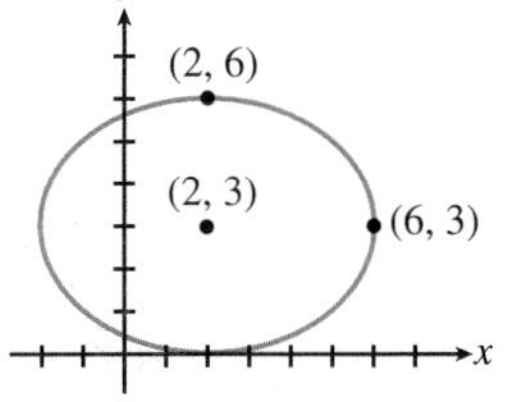

50.

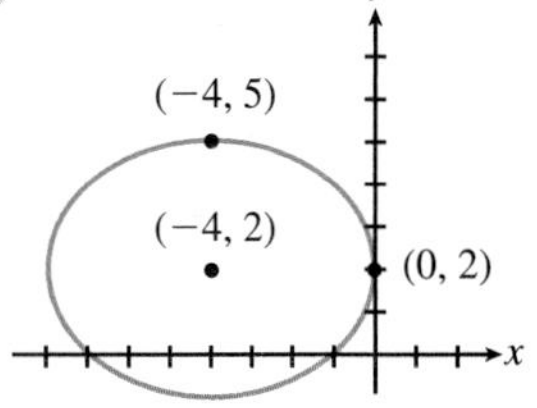

51. Writing to Learn Prove that an equation for the ellipse with center $(0, 0)$, foci $(0, \pm c)$, and semimajor axis $a > c \geq 0$ is $y^2/a^2 + x^2/b^2 = 1$, where $b^2 = a^2 - c^2$. [*Hint*: Refer to derivation at the beginning of the lesson.]

52. Writing to Learn Dancing Among the Stars Using the data in Table H.1, prove that the object with the most eccentric orbit sometimes is closer to the Sun than the planet with the least eccentric orbit.

Table H.1 Semimajor Axes and Eccentricities of the Planets and Pluto

Object	Semimajor Axis (Gm)	Eccentricity
Mercury	57.9	0.2056
Venus	108.2	0.0068
Earth	149.6	0.0167
Mars	227.9	0.0934
Jupiter	778.3	0.0485
Saturn	1427	0.0560
Uranus	2869	0.0461
Neptune	4497	0.0050
Pluto	5900	0.2484

Source: Shupe, et al., National Geographic Atlas of the World (rev.6th ed.). Washington, DC: National Geographic Society, 1992, plate 116, and other sources.

53. The Moon's Orbit The Moon's apogee (farthest distance from Earth) is 252,710 miles, and perigee (closest distance to Earth) is 221,463 miles. Assuming the Moon's orbit of Earth is elliptical with Earth at one focus, calculate and interpret a, b, c, and e.

54. Hot Mercury Given that the diameter of the Sun is about 1.392 Gm, how close does Mercury get to the Sun's surface?

55. Saturn Find the perihelion and aphelion distances of Saturn.

56. Venus and Mars Write equations for the orbits of Venus and Mars in the form $x^2/a^2 + y^2/b^2 = 1$.

57. Sungrazers One comet group, known as the sungrazers, passes within a Sun's diameter (1.392 Gm) of the solar surface. What can you conclude about $a - c$ for orbits of the sungrazers?

58. Halley's Comet The orbit of Halley's comet is 36.18 AU long and 9.12 AU wide. What is its eccentricity?

59. Lithotripter For an ellipse that generates the ellipsoid of a lithotripter, the major axis has endpoints $(-8, 0)$ and $(8, 0)$. One endpoint of the minor axis is $(0, 3.5)$. Find the coordinates of the foci.

60. Lithotripter (Refer to Figure H.21.) A lithotripter's shape is formed by rotating the portion of an ellipse below its minor axis about its major axis. If the length of the major axis is 26 in. and the length of the minor axis is 10 in., where should the shock-wave source and the patient be placed for maximum effect?

Group Activities In Exercises 61 and 62, solve the system of equations algebraically and support your answer graphically.

61. $\dfrac{x^2}{4} + \dfrac{y^2}{9} = 1$

$x^2 + y^2 = 4$

62. $\dfrac{x^2}{9} + y^2 = 1$

$x - 3y = -3$

63. Group Activity Consider the system of equations

$$x^2 + 4y^2 = 4$$
$$y = 2x^2 - 3$$

(a) Solve the system graphically.

(b) If you have access to a grapher that also does symbolic algebra, use it to find the exact solutions to the system.

64. Writing to Learn Look up the adjective *eccentric* in a dictionary and read its various definitions. Notice that the word is derived from *ex-centric*, meaning "out-of-center" or "off-center." Explain how this is related to the word's everyday meanings as well as its mathematical meaning for ellipses.

Explorations

65. Area and Perimeter The area of an ellipse is $A = \pi ab$, but the perimeter cannot be expressed so simply:

$$P \approx \pi(a + b)\left(3 - \frac{\sqrt{(3a + b)(a + 3b)}}{a + b}\right)$$

(a) Prove that, when $a = b = r$, these become the familiar formulas for the area and perimeter (circumference) of a circle.

(b) Find a pair of ellipses such that the one with greater area has smaller perimeter.

66. Pendulum Velocity vs. Position As a pendulum swings toward and away from a motion detector, its distance (in meters) from the detector is given by the position function $x(t) = 3 + \cos(2t - 5)$, where t represents time (in seconds). The velocity (in m/sec) of the pendulum is given by $y(t) = -2 \sin(2t - 5)$.

(a) Using parametric mode on your grapher, plot the (x, y) relation for velocity versus position for $0 \le t \le 2\pi$.

(b) Write the equation of the resulting conic in standard form, in terms of x and y, and eliminating the parameter t.

67. Pendulum Velocity vs. Position A pendulum that swings toward and away from a motion detector has a distance (in feet) from the detector of $x(t) = 5 + 3\sin(\pi t + \pi/2)$ and a velocity (in ft/sec) of $y(t) = 3\pi \cos(\pi t + \pi/2)$, where t represents time (in seconds).

(a) Prove that the plot of velocity versus position (distance) is an ellipse.

(b) Writing to Learn Describe the motion of the pendulum.

Extending the Ideas

68. Prove that a nondegenerate graph of the equation

$$Ax^2 + Cy^2 + Dx + Ey + F = 0$$

is an ellipse if $AC > 0$.

69. Writing to Learn The graph of the equation

$$\frac{(x - h)^2}{a^2} + \frac{(y - k)^2}{b^2} = 0$$

is considered to be a degenerate ellipse. Describe the graph. How is it like a full-fledged ellipse, and how is it different?

H-3 Hyperbolas

> **What you'll learn about**
> - Geometry of a Hyperbola
> - Translations of Hyperbolas
> - Eccentricity and Orbits
> - Reflective Property of a Hyperbola
> - Long-Range Navigation
>
> **... and why**
>
> The hyperbola is the least-known conic section, yet it is used in astronomy, optics, and navigation.

Geometry of a Hyperbola

When a plane intersects both nappes of a right circular cylinder, the intersection is a hyperbola. The definition, features, and derivation for a hyperbola closely resemble those for an ellipse. As you read on, you may find it helpful to compare the nature of the hyperbola with the nature of the ellipse.

DEFINITION Hyperbola

A hyperbola is the set of all points in a plane whose distances from two fixed points in the plane have a constant *difference*. The fixed points are the **foci** of the hyperbola. The line through the foci is the **focal axis**. The point on the focal axis midway between the foci is the **center**. The points where the hyperbola intersects its focal axis are the **vertices** of the hyperbola (Figure H.22).

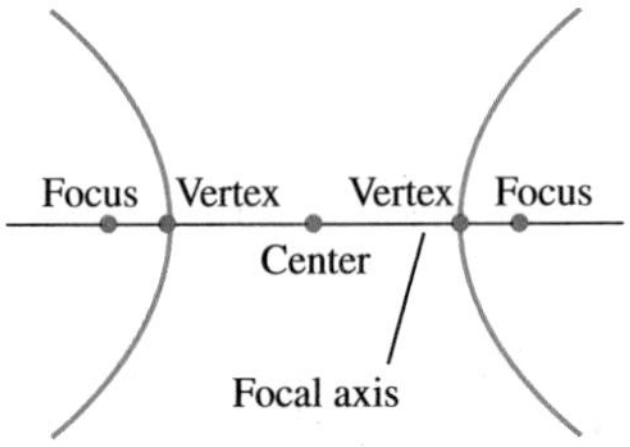

FIGURE H.22 Key points on the focal axis of a hyperbola.

Figure H.23 shows a hyperbola centered at the origin with its focal axis on the x-axis. The vertices are at $(-a, 0)$ and $(a, 0)$, where a is some positive constant. The fixed points $F_1(-c, 0)$ and $F_2(c, 0)$ are the foci of the hyperbola, with $c > a$.

Notice that the hyperbola has two *branches*. For a point $P(x, y)$ on the right-hand branch, $PF_1 - PF_2 = 2a$. On the left-hand branch, $PF_2 - PF_1 = 2a$. Combining these two equations gives us

$$PF_1 - PF_2 = \pm 2a.$$

Using the distance formula, the equation becomes

$$\sqrt{(x+c)^2 + (y-0)^2} - \sqrt{(x-c)^2 + (y-0)^2} = \pm 2a.$$

$$\sqrt{(x-c)^2 + y^2} = \pm 2a + \sqrt{(x+c)^2 + y^2} \qquad \text{Rearrange terms.}$$

$$x^2 - 2cx + c^2 + y^2 = 4a^2 \pm 4a\sqrt{(x+c)^2 + y^2} + x^2 + 2cx + c^2 + y^2 \qquad \text{Square.}$$

$$\mp a\sqrt{(x+c)^2 + y^2} = a^2 + cx \qquad \text{Simplify.}$$

$$a^2(x^2 + 2cx + c^2 + y^2) = a^4 + 2a^2cx + c^2x^2 \qquad \text{Square.}$$

$$(c^2 - a^2)x^2 - a^2y^2 = a^2(c^2 - a^2) \qquad \text{Multiply by } -1 \text{ and simplify.}$$

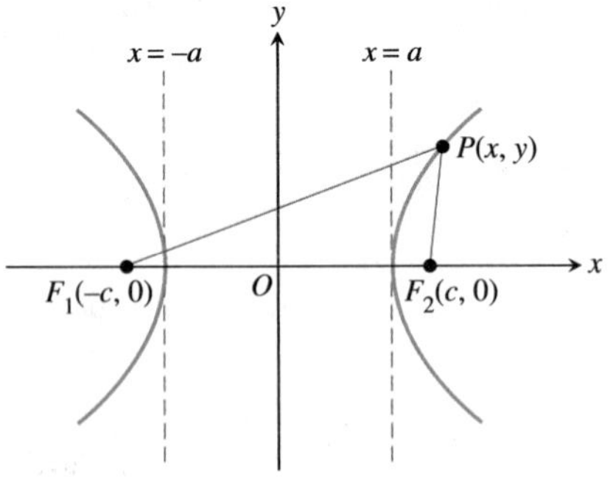

FIGURE H.23 *Structure of a Hyperbola.* The difference of the distances from the foci to each point on the hyperbola is a constant.

Letting $b^2 = c^2 - a^2$, we have

$$b^2x^2 - a^2y^2 = a^2b^2,$$

which is usually written as

$$\frac{x^2}{a^2} - \frac{y^2}{b^2} = 1.$$

Because these steps can be reversed, a point $P(x, y)$ satisfies this last equation if and only if the point lies on the hyperbola defined by $PF_1 - PF_2 = \pm 2a$, provided that

$c > a > 0$ and $b^2 = c^2 - a^2$. The *Pythagorean relation* $b^2 = c^2 - a^2$ can be written many ways, including $a^2 = c^2 - b^2$ and $c^2 = a^2 + b^2$.

The equation $x^2/a^2 - y^2/b^2 = 1$ is the **standard form** of the equation of a hyperbola centered at the origin with the x-axis as its focal axis. A hyperbola centered at the origin with the y-axis as its focal axis is the *inverse relation* of $x^2/a^2 - y^2/b^2 = 1$, and thus has an equation of the form

$$\frac{y^2}{a^2} - \frac{x^2}{b^2} = 1.$$

As with other conics, a line segment with endpoints on a hyperbola is a **chord** of the hyperbola. The chord lying on the focal axis connecting the vertices is the **transverse axis** of the hyperbola. The length of the transverse axis is $2a$. The line segment of length $2b$ that is perpendicular to the focal axis and that has the center of the hyperbola as its midpoint is the **conjugate axis** of the hyperbola. The number a is the **semitransverse axis**, and b is the **semiconjugate axis**.

The hyperbola

$$\frac{x^2}{a^2} - \frac{y^2}{b^2} = 1$$

has two *asymptotes*. These asymptotes are slant lines that can be found by replacing the 1 on the right-hand side of the hyperbola's equation by a 0:

$$\underbrace{\frac{x^2}{a^2} - \frac{y^2}{b^2} = 1}_{\text{hyperbola}} \rightarrow \underbrace{\frac{x^2}{a^2} - \frac{y^2}{b^2} = 0}_{\text{Replace 1 by 0.}} \rightarrow \underbrace{y = \pm\frac{b}{a}x}_{\text{asymptotes}}$$

Naming Axes

The word "transverse" comes from the Latin *trans vertere*: to go across. The transverse axis "goes across" from one vertex to the other. The conjugate axis is the transverse axis for the *conjugate hyperbola*, defined in Exercise 67.

A hyperbola centered at the origin with its focal axis one of the coordinate axes is symmetric with respect to the origin and both coordinate axes. Such a hyperbola can be sketched by drawing a rectangle centered at the origin with sides parallel to the coordinate axes, followed by drawing the asymptotes through opposite corners of the rectangle, and finally sketching the hyperbola using the central rectangle and asymptotes as guides, as shown in the Drawing Lesson.

Drawing Lesson

How to Sketch the Hyperbola $x^2/a^2 - y^2/b^2 = 1$

1. Sketch line segments at $x = \pm a$ and $y = \pm b$, and complete the rectangle they determine.
2. Sketch the asymptotes by extending the rectangle's diagonals.
3. Use the rectangle and asymptotes to guide your drawing.

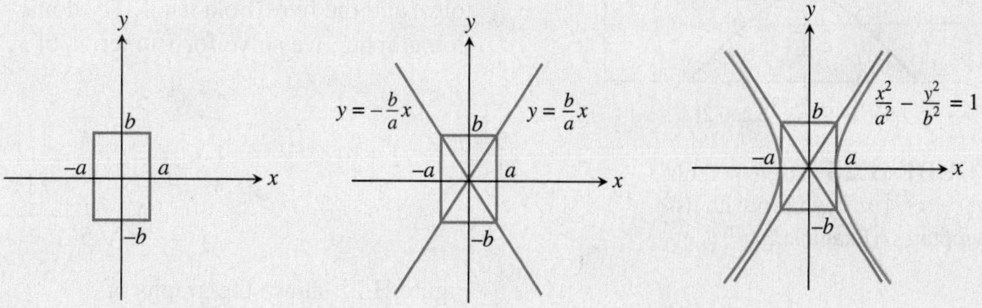

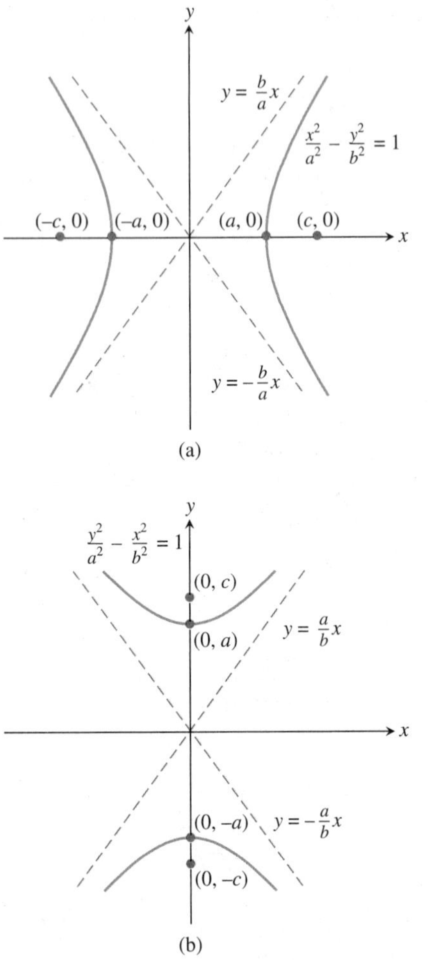

FIGURE H.24 Hyperbolas centered at the origin with foci on (a) the x-axis and (b) the y-axis.

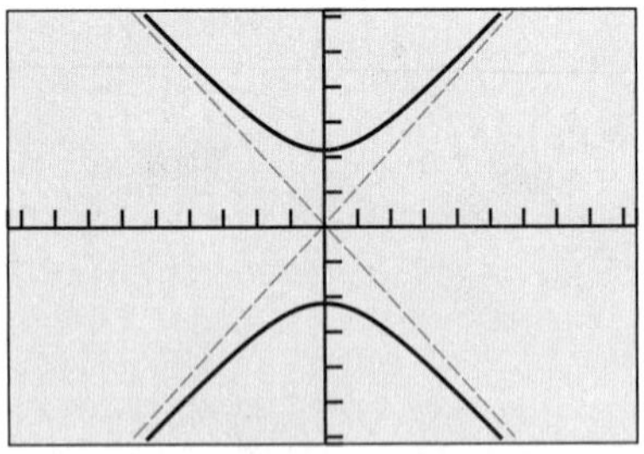

[−9.4, 9.4] by [−6.2, 6.2]

FIGURE H.25 The hyperbola $y^2/5 - x^2/4 = 1$, shown with its asymptotes. (Example 2)

Hyperbolas with Center (0, 0)

• **Standard equation**	$\frac{x^2}{a^2} - \frac{y^2}{b^2} = 1$	$\frac{y^2}{a^2} - \frac{x^2}{b^2} = 1$
• **Focal axis**	x-axis	y-axis
• **Foci**	$(\pm c, 0)$	$(0, \pm c)$
• **Vertices**	$(\pm a, 0)$	$(0, \pm a)$
• **Semitransverse axis**	a	a
• **Semiconjugate axis**	b	b
• **Pythagorean relation**	$c^2 = a^2 + b^2$	$c^2 = a^2 + b^2$
• **Asymptotes**	$y = \pm \frac{b}{a}x$	$y = \pm \frac{a}{b}x$

See Figure H.24.

EXAMPLE 1 Finding the Vertices and Foci of a Hyperbola

Find the vertices and the foci of the hyperbola $4x^2 - 9y^2 = 36$.

SOLUTION Dividing both sides of the equation by 36 yields the standard form $x^2/9 - y^2/4 = 1$. So $a^2 = 9$, $b^2 = 4$, and $c^2 = a^2 + b^2 = 9 + 4 = 13$. Thus the vertices are $(\pm 3, 0)$, and the foci are $(\pm\sqrt{13}, 0)$. *Now try Exercise 1.*

If we wish to graph a hyperbola using a function grapher, we need to solve the equation of the hyperbola for y, as illustrated in Example 2.

EXAMPLE 2 Finding an Equation and Graphing a Hyperbola

Find an equation of the hyperbola with foci $(0, -3)$ and $(0, 3)$ whose conjugate axis has length 4. Sketch the hyperbola and its asymptotes, and support your sketch with a grapher.

SOLUTION The center is $(0, 0)$. The foci are on the y-axis with $c = 3$. The semiconjugate axis is $b = 4/2 = 2$. Thus $a^2 = c^2 - b^2 = 3^2 - 2^2 = 5$. The standard form of the equation for the hyperbola is

$$\frac{y^2}{5} - \frac{x^2}{4} = 1.$$

Using $a = \sqrt{5} \approx 2.24$ and $b = 2$, we can sketch the central rectangle, the asymptotes, and the hyperbola itself. Try doing this. To graph the hyperbola using a function grapher, we solve for y in terms of x.

$$\frac{y^2}{5} = 1 + \frac{x^2}{4} \qquad \text{Add } \frac{x^2}{4}$$

$$y^2 = 5(1 + x^2/4) \qquad \text{Multiply by 5.}$$

$$y = \pm\sqrt{5(1 + x^2/4)} \qquad \text{Extract square roots.}$$

Figure H.25 shows the graphs of

$$y_1 = \sqrt{5(1 + x^2/4)} \quad \text{and} \quad y_2 = -\sqrt{5(1 + x^2/4)},$$

together with the asymptotes of the hyperbola

$$y_3 = \frac{\sqrt{5}}{2}x \quad \text{and} \quad y_4 = -\frac{\sqrt{5}}{2}x.$$

Now try Exercise 17.

In Example 2, because the hyperbola had a vertical focal axis, selecting a viewing rectangle was easy. When a hyperbola has a horizontal focal axis, we try to select a viewing window to include the two vertices in the plot and thus avoid gaps in the graph of the hyperbola.

Translations of Hyperbolas

When a hyperbola with center $(0, 0)$ is translated horizontally by h units and vertically by k units, the center of the hyperbola moves from $(0, 0)$ to (h, k), as shown in Figure H.26. Such a translation does not change the length of the transverse or conjugate axis or the Pythagorean relation.

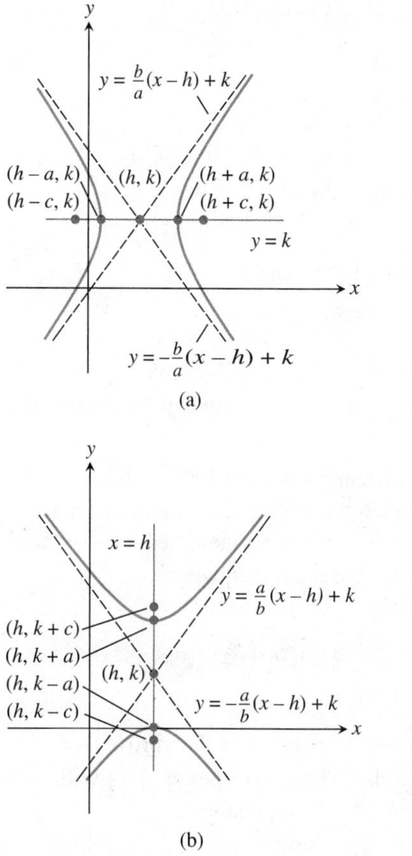

FIGURE H.26 Hyperbolas with center (h, k) and foci on (a) $y = k$ and (b) $x = h$.

Hyperbolas with Center (h, k)

• **Standard equation**	$\frac{(x-h)^2}{a^2} - \frac{(y-k)^2}{b^2} = 1$	$\frac{(y-k)^2}{a^2} - \frac{(x-h)^2}{b^2} = 1$
• **Focal axis**	$y = k$	$x = h$
• **Foci**	$(h \pm c, k)$	$(h, k \pm c)$
• **Vertices**	$(h \pm a, k)$	$(h, k \pm a)$
• **Semitransverse axis**	a	a
• **Semiconjugate axis**	b	b
• **Pythagorean relation**	$c^2 = a^2 + b^2$	$c^2 = a^2 + b^2$
• **Asymptotes**	$y = \pm\frac{b}{a}(x - h) + k$	$y = \pm\frac{a}{b}(x - h) + k$

See Figure H.26.

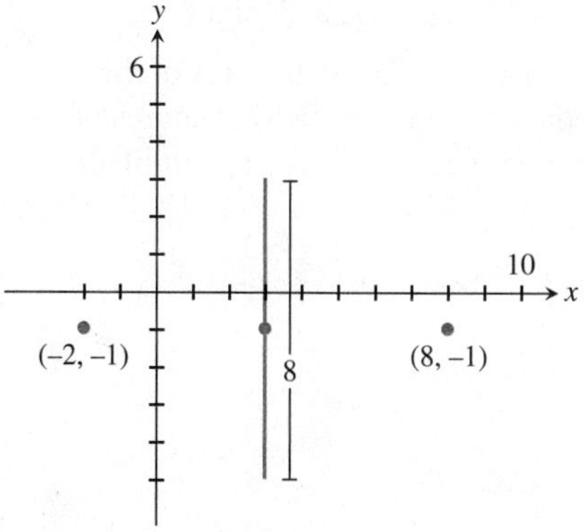

FIGURE H.27 Given information for Example 3.

EXAMPLE 3 Finding an Equation of a Hyperbola

Find the standard form of the equation for the hyperbola whose transverse axis has endpoints $(-2, -1)$ and $(8, -1)$ and whose conjugate axis has length 8.

SOLUTION Figure H.27 shows the transverse axis endpoints, the conjugate axis, and the center of the hyperbola. The standard equation of this hyperbola has the form

$$\frac{(x-h)^2}{a^2} - \frac{(y-k)^2}{b^2} = 1,$$

where the center (h, k) is the midpoint $(3, -1)$ of the transverse axis. The semitransverse axis and semiconjugate axis are

$$a = \frac{8 - (-2)}{2} = 5 \quad \text{and} \quad b = \frac{8}{2} = 4.$$

So the equation we seek is

$$\frac{(x-3)^2}{5^2} - \frac{(y-(-1))^2}{4^2} = 1,$$

$$\frac{(x-3)^2}{25} - \frac{(y+1)^2}{16} = 1.$$

Now try Exercise 31.

EXAMPLE 4 Locating Key Points of a Hyperbola

Find the center, vertices, and foci of the hyperbola

$$\frac{(x+2)^2}{9} - \frac{(y-5)^2}{49} = 1.$$

SOLUTION The center (h, k) is $(-2, 5)$. Because the semitransverse axis $a = \sqrt{9} = 3$, the vertices are

$$(h + a, k) = (-2 + 3, 5) = (1, 5) \quad \text{and}$$
$$(h - a, k) = (-2 - 3, 5) = (-5, 5).$$

Because $c = \sqrt{a^2 + b^2} = \sqrt{9 + 49} = \sqrt{58}$, the foci $(h \pm c, k)$ are $(-2 \pm \sqrt{58}, 5)$, or approximately $(5.62, 5)$ and $(-9.62, 5)$. *Now try Exercise 39.*

With the information found about the hyperbola in Example 4 and knowing that its semiconjugate axis $b = \sqrt{49} = 7$, we could easily sketch the hyperbola. Obtaining an accurate graph of the hyperbola using a function grapher is another matter. Often, the best way to graph a hyperbola using a graphing utility is to use parametric equations.

EXPLORATION 1 Graphing a Hyperbola Using Its Parametric Equations

1. Use the Pythagorean trigonometry identity $\sec^2 t - \tan^2 t = 1$ to prove that the parametrization $x = -1 + 3/\cos t$, $y = 1 + 2 \tan t$ $(0 \le t \le 2\pi)$ will produce a graph of the hyperbola $(x + 1)^2/9 - (y - 1)^2/4 = 1$.
2. Using Dot graphing mode, graph $x = -1 + 3/\cos t$, $y = 1 + 2 \tan t$ $(0 \le t \le 2\pi)$ in a square viewing window to support part 1 graphically. Switch to Connected graphing mode, and regraph the equation. What do you observe? Explain.
3. Create parametrizations for the hyperbolas in Examples 1, 2, 3, and 4.
4. Graph each of your parametrizations in part 3 and check the features of the obtained graph to see whether they match the expected geometric features of the hyperbola. If necessary, revise your parametrization and regraph until all features match.
5. Prove that each of your parametrizations is valid.

Eccentricity and Orbits

DEFINITION Eccentricity of a Hyperbola

The **eccentricity** of a hyperbola is

$$e = \frac{c}{a} = \frac{\sqrt{a^2 + b^2}}{a},$$

where a is the semitransverse axis, b is the semiconjugate axis, and c is the distance from the center to either focus.

For a hyperbola, because $c > a$, the eccentricity $e > 1$. In Lesson H-2 we learned that the eccentricity of an ellipse satisfies the inequality $0 \le e < 1$ and that, for $e = 0$, the ellipse is a circle.

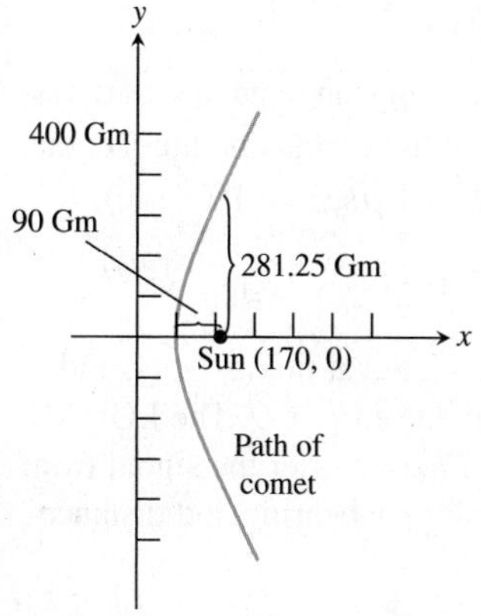

FIGURE H.28 The graph of one branch of $x^2/6400 - y^2/22{,}500 = 1$. (Example 5)

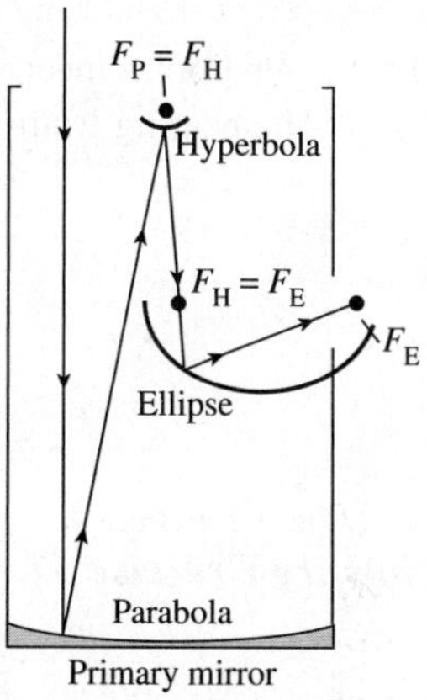

FIGURE H.29 Cross section of a reflecting telescope.

Kepler's First Law of Planetary Motion says that a planet's orbit is elliptical with the Sun at one focus. Since 1609, astronomers have generalized Kepler's Law; the current theory states: A celestial body that travels within the gravitational field of a much more massive body follows a path that closely approximates a conic section that has the more massive body as a focus. Two bodies that do not differ greatly in mass (such as Earth and the Moon, or Pluto and its moon Charon) actually revolve around their balance point, or *barycenter*. In theory, a comet can approach the Sun from interstellar space, make a partial loop about the Sun, and then leave the solar system, returning to deep space; such a comet follows a path that is one branch of a hyperbola.

EXAMPLE 5 Analyzing a Comet's Orbit

A comet following a hyperbolic path about the Sun has a perihelion distance of 90 Gm. When the line from the comet to the Sun is perpendicular to the focal axis of the orbit, the comet is 281.25 Gm from the Sun. Calculate a, b, c, and e. What are the coordinates of the center of the Sun if we coordinatize space so that the hyperbola is given by

$$\frac{x^2}{a^2} - \frac{y^2}{b^2} = 1?$$

SOLUTION The perihelion distance is $c - a = 90$. When $x = c$, $y = \pm b^2/a$ (see Exercise 74). So $b^2/a = 281.25$, or $b^2 = 281.25a$. Because $b^2 = c^2 - a^2$, we have the system

$$c - a = 90 \quad \text{and} \quad c^2 - a^2 = 281.25a,$$

which yields the equation:

$$\begin{aligned} (a + 90)^2 - a^2 &= 281.25a \\ a^2 + 180a + 8100 - a^2 &= 281.25a \\ 8100 &= 101.25a \\ a &= 80 \end{aligned}$$

Therefore, $a = 80$ Gm, $b = 150$ Gm, $c = 170$ Gm, and $e = 17/8 = 2.125$ (Figure H.28). If the comet's path is the branch of the hyperbola with positive x-coordinates, then the Sun is at the focus $(c, 0) = (170, 0)$. *Now try Exercise 55.*

Reflective Property of a Hyperbola

Like other conics, a hyperbola can be used to make a reflector of sound, light, and other waves. If we rotate a hyperbola in three-dimensional space about its focal axis, the hyperbola sweeps out a **hyperboloid of revolution**. If a signal is directed toward a focus of a reflective hyperboloid, the signal reflects off the hyperbolic surface to the other focus. In Figure H.29 light reflects off a primary parabolic mirror toward the mirror's focus $F_P = F_H$, which is also the focus of a small hyperbolic mirror. The light is then reflected off the hyperbolic mirror, toward the hyperboloid's other focus $F_H = F_E$, which is also the focus of an elliptical mirror. Finally the light is reflected into the observer's eye, which is at the second focus of the ellipsoid F_E.

Reflecting telescopes date back to the 1600s when Isaac Newton used a primary parabolic mirror in combination with a flat secondary mirror, slanted to reflect the light out the side to the eyepiece. French optician G. Cassegrain was the first to use a hyperbolic secondary mirror, which directed the light through a hole at the vertex of the primary mirror (see Exercise 64). Today, reflecting telescopes such as the Hubble Space Telescope have become quite sophisticated and must have nearly perfect mirrors to focus properly.

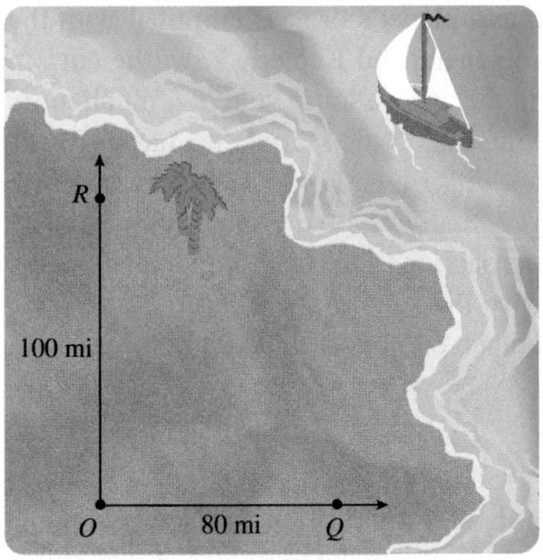

FIGURE H.30 Strategically located LORAN transmitters O, Q, and R. (Example 6)

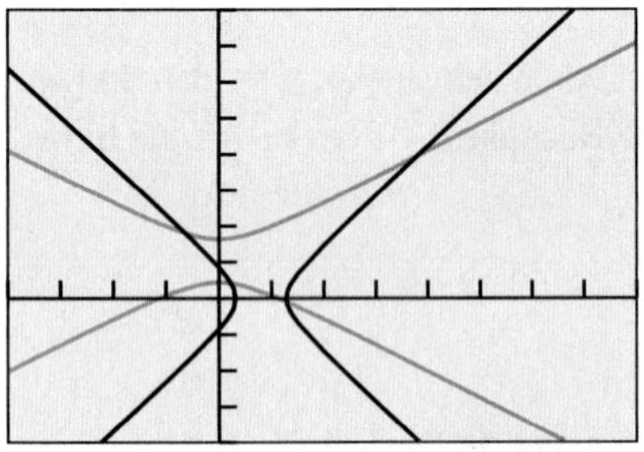

[–200, 400] by [–200, 400]

FIGURE H.31 Graphs for Example 6.

Long-Range Navigation

Hyperbolas and radio signals are the basis of the LORAN (long-range navigation) system. Example 6 illustrates this system using the definition of hyperbola and the fact that radio signals travel 980 ft per microsecond (1 microsecond = 1 μsec = 10^{-6} sec).

EXAMPLE 6 Using the LORAN System

Radio signals are sent simultaneously from transmitters located at points O, Q, and R (Figure H.30). R is 100 mi due north of O, and Q is 80 mi due east of O. The LORAN receiver on sloop *Gloria* receives the signal from O 323.27 μsec after the signal from R, and 258.61 μsec after the signal from Q. What is the sloop's bearing and distance from O?

SOLUTION The *Gloria* is at a point of intersection between two hyperbolas: one with foci O and R, the other with foci O and Q.

The hyperbola with foci $O(0, 0)$ and $R(0, 100)$ has center $(0, 50)$ and transverse axis

$$2a = (323.27\ \mu\text{sec})(980\ \text{ft}/\mu\text{sec})(1\ \text{mi}/5280\ \text{ft}) \approx 60\ \text{mi}.$$

Thus $a \approx 30$ and $b = \sqrt{c^2 - a^2} \approx \sqrt{50^2 - 30^2} = 40$, yielding the equation

$$\frac{(y-50)^2}{30^2} - \frac{x^2}{40^2} = 1.$$

The hyperbola with foci $O(0, 0)$ and $Q(80, 0)$ has center $(40, 0)$ and transverse axis

$$2a = (258.61\ \mu\text{sec})(980\ \text{ft}/\mu\text{sec})(1\ \text{mi}/5280\ \text{ft}) \approx 48\ \text{mi}.$$

Thus $a \approx 24$ and $b = \sqrt{c^2 - a^2} \approx \sqrt{40^2 - 24^2} = 32$, yielding the equation

$$\frac{(x-40)^2}{24^2} - \frac{y^2}{32^2} = 1.$$

The *Gloria* is at point P where upper and right-hand branches of the hyperbolas meet (Figure H.31). Using a grapher we find that $P \approx (187.09, 193.49)$. The bearing from point O is

$$\theta \approx 90° - \tan^{-1}\left(\frac{193.49}{187.09}\right) \approx 44.04°,$$

and the distance from point O is

$$d \approx \sqrt{187.09^2 + 193.49^2} \approx 269.15.$$

So the *Gloria* is about 187.1 mi east and 193.5 mi north of point O on a bearing of roughly 44°, and the sloop is about 269 mi from point O. ***Now try Exercise 57.***

LESSON H-3 EXERCISES

xercise numbers with a gray background indicate problems that e authors have designed to be solved *without a calculator*.

Exercises 1–6, find the vertices and foci of the hyperbola.

1. $\frac{x^2}{16} - \frac{y^2}{7} = 1$ **2.** $\frac{y^2}{25} - \frac{x^2}{21} = 1$

3. $\frac{y^2}{36} - \frac{x^2}{13} = 1$ **4.** $\frac{x^2}{9} - \frac{y^2}{16} = 1$

5. $3x^2 - 4y^2 = 12$ **6.** $9x^2 - 4y^2 = 36$

Exercises 7–10, match the graph with its equation.

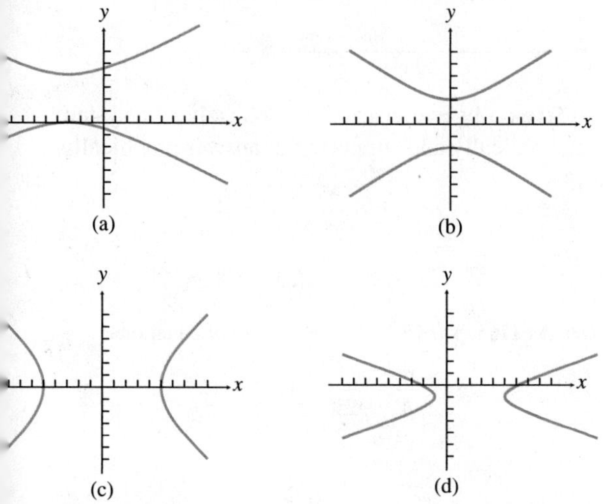

7. $\frac{x^2}{25} - \frac{y^2}{16} = 1$ **8.** $\frac{y^2}{4} - \frac{x^2}{9} = 1$

9. $\frac{(y-2)^2}{4} - \frac{(x+3)^2}{16} = 1$

10. $\frac{(x-2)^2}{9} - (y+1)^2 = 1$

Exercises 11–16, sketch the graph of the hyperbola by hand.

11. $\frac{x^2}{49} - \frac{y^2}{25} = 1$ **12.** $\frac{y^2}{64} - \frac{x^2}{25} = 1$

13. $\frac{y^2}{25} - \frac{x^2}{16} = 1$ **14.** $\frac{x^2}{169} - \frac{y^2}{144} = 1$

15. $\frac{(x+3)^2}{16} - \frac{(y-1)^2}{4} = 1$

16. $\frac{(x-1)^2}{2} - \frac{(y+3)^2}{4} = 1$

Exercises 17–22, graph the hyperbola using a function grapher.

17. $\frac{x^2}{36} - \frac{y^2}{16} = 1$ **18.** $\frac{y^2}{64} - \frac{x^2}{16} = 1$

19. $\frac{x^2}{4} - \frac{y^2}{9} = 1$ **20.** $\frac{y^2}{16} - \frac{x^2}{9} = 1$

21. $\frac{x^2}{4} - \frac{(y-3)^2}{5} = 1$ **22.** $\frac{(y-3)^2}{9} - \frac{(x+2)^2}{4} = 1$

In Exercises 23–38, find an equation in standard form for the hyperbola that satisfies the given conditions.

23. Foci $(\pm 3, 0)$, transverse axis length 4

24. Foci $(0, \pm 3)$, transverse axis length 4

25. Foci $(0, \pm 15)$, transverse axis length 8

26. Foci $(\pm 5, 0)$, transverse axis length 3

27. Center at $(0, 0)$, $a = 5$, $e = 2$, horizontal focal axis

28. Center at $(0, 0)$, $a = 4$, $e = 3/2$, vertical focal axis

29. Center at $(0, 0)$, $b = 5$, $e = 13/12$, vertical focal axis

30. Center at $(0, 0)$, $c = 6$, $e = 2$, horizontal focal axis

31. Transverse axis endpoints $(2, 3)$ and $(2, -1)$, conjugate axis length 6

32. Transverse axis endpoints $(5, 3)$ and $(-7, 3)$, conjugate axis length 10

33. Transverse axis endpoints $(-1, 3)$ and $(5, 3)$, slope of one asymptote 4/3

34. Transverse axis endpoints $(-2, -2)$ and $(-2, 7)$, slope of one asymptote 4/3

35. Foci $(-4, 2)$ and $(2, 2)$, transverse axis endpoints $(-3, 2)$ and $(1, 2)$

36. Foci $(-3, -11)$ and $(-3, 0)$, transverse axis endpoints $(-3, -9)$ and $(-3, -2)$

37. Center at $(-3, 6)$, $a = 5$, $e = 2$, vertical focal axis

38. Center at $(1, -4)$, $c = 6$, $e = 2$, horizontal focal axis

In Exercises 39–42, find the center, vertices, and the foci of the hyperbola.

39. $\frac{(x+1)^2}{144} - \frac{(y-2)^2}{25} = 1$

40. $\frac{(x+4)^2}{12} - \frac{(y+6)^2}{13} = 1$

41. $\frac{(y+3)^2}{64} - \frac{(x-2)^2}{81} = 1$

42. $\frac{(y-1)^2}{25} - \frac{(x+5)^2}{11} = 1$

In Exercises 43–46, graph the hyperbola using a parametric grapher in Dot graphing mode.

43. $\frac{y^2}{25} - \frac{x^2}{4} = 1$ **44.** $\frac{x^2}{30} - \frac{y^2}{20} = 1$

45. $\frac{(x+3)^2}{12} - \frac{(y-6)^2}{5} = 1$

46. $\frac{(y+1)^2}{15} - \frac{(x-2)^2}{6} = 1$

In Exercises 47–50, graph the hyperbola, and find its vertices, foci, and eccentricity.

47. $4(y-1)^2 - 9(x-3)^2 = 36$

48. $4(x-2)^2 - 9(y+4)^2 = 1$

49. $9x^2 - 4y^2 - 36x + 8y - 4 = 0$

50. $25y^2 - 9x^2 - 50y - 54x - 281 = 0$

In Exercises 51 and 52, write an equation for the hyperbola.

51.

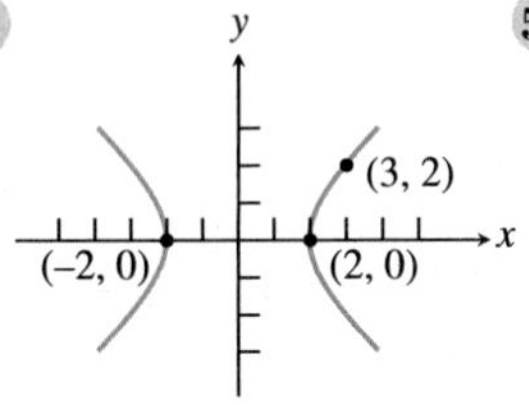

52.

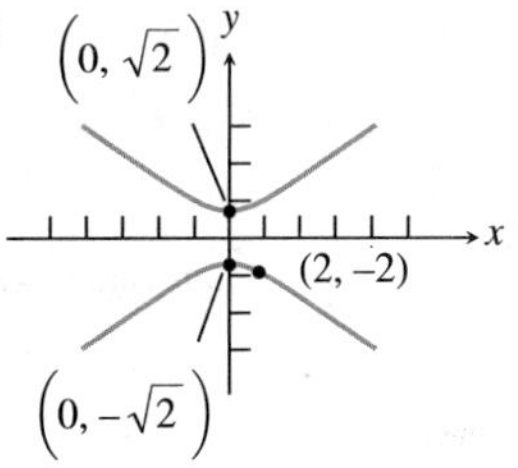

53. **Writing to Learn** Prove that an equation for the hyperbola with center $(0, 0)$, foci $(0, \pm c)$, and semitransverse axis a is $y^2/a^2 - x^2/b^2 = 1$, where $c > a > 0$ and $b^2 = c^2 - a^2$. [*Hint*: Refer to derivation at the beginning of the lesson.]

54. **Degenerate Hyperbolas** Graph the degenerate hyperbola.

(a) $\dfrac{x^2}{4} - y^2 = 0$ **(b)** $\dfrac{y^2}{9} - \dfrac{x^2}{16} = 0$

55. **Rogue Comet** A comet following a hyperbolic path about the Sun has a perihelion of 120 Gm. When the line from the comet to the Sun is perpendicular to the focal axis of the orbit, the comet is 250 Gm from the Sun. Calculate a, b, c, and e. What are the coordinates of the center of the Sun if the center of the hyperbolic orbit is (0, 0) and the Sun lies on the positive x-axis?

56. **Rogue Comet** A comet following a hyperbolic path about the Sun has a perihelion of 140 Gm. When the line from the comet to the Sun is perpendicular to the focal axis of the orbit, the comet is 405 Gm from the Sun. Calculate a, b, c, and e. What are the coordinates of the center of the Sun if the center of the hyperbolic orbit is (0, 0) and the Sun lies on the positive x-axis?

57. **Long-Range Navigation** Three LORAN radio transmitters are positioned as shown in the figure, with R due north of O and Q due east of O. The cruise ship *Princess Ann* receives simultaneous signals from the three transmitters. The signal from O arrives 323.27 μsec after the signal from R, and 646.53 μsec after the signal from Q. Determine the ship's bearing and distance from point O.

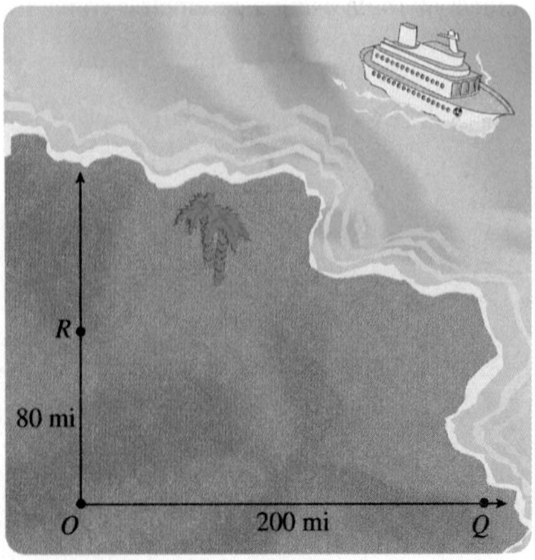

58. **Gun Location** Observers are located at positions A, B, and C with A due north of B. A cannon is located somewhere in the first quadrant as illustrated in the figure. A hears the sound of the cannon 2 sec before B, and C hears the sound 4 sec before B. Determine the bearing and distance of the cannon from point B. (Assume that sound travels at 1100 ft/sec.)

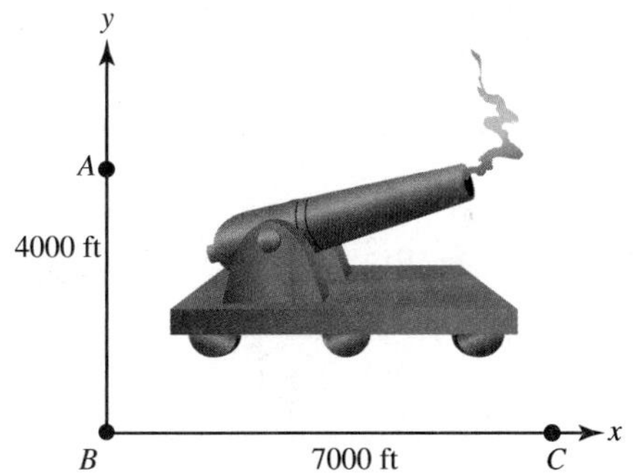

Group Activities In Exercises 59 and 60, solve the system of equations algebraically and support your answer graphically.

59. $\dfrac{x^2}{4} - \dfrac{y^2}{9} = 1$

$x - \dfrac{2\sqrt{3}}{3}y = -2$

60. $\dfrac{x^2}{4} - y^2 = 1$

$x^2 + y^2 = 9$

61. **Group Activity** Consider the system of equations

$$\frac{x^2}{4} - \frac{y^2}{25} = 1$$
$$\frac{x^2}{25} + \frac{y^2}{4} = 1.$$

(a) Solve the system graphically.

(b) If you have access to a grapher that also does symbolic algebra, use it to find the the exact solutions to the system.

62. **Writing to Learn Escape of the Unbound** When NASA launches a space probe, the probe reaches a speed sufficient for it to become unbound from Earth and escape along a hyperbolic trajectory. Look up *escape speed* in an astronomy textbook or on the Internet, and write a paragraph in your own words about what you find.

Explorations

63. **Constructing Points of a Hyperbola** Use a geometry software package, such as *Cabri Geometry II*™, *The Geometer's Sketchpad*®, or a similar application on a handheld device, to carry out the following construction.

(a) Start by placing the coordinate axes in the construction window.

(b) Construct two points on the x-axis at $(\pm 5, 0)$ as the foci.

(c) Construct concentric circles of radii $r = 1, 2, 3, \ldots, 12$ centered at these two foci.

(d) Construct the points where these concentric circles meet and have a difference of radii of $2a = 6$, and overlay the conic that passes through these points if the software has a conic tool.

(e) Find the equation whose graph includes all of these points.

64. Cassegrain Telescope A Cassegrain telescope as described in the section has the dimensions shown in the figure. Find the standard form for the equation of the hyperbola centered at the origin with the x-axis as the focal axis.

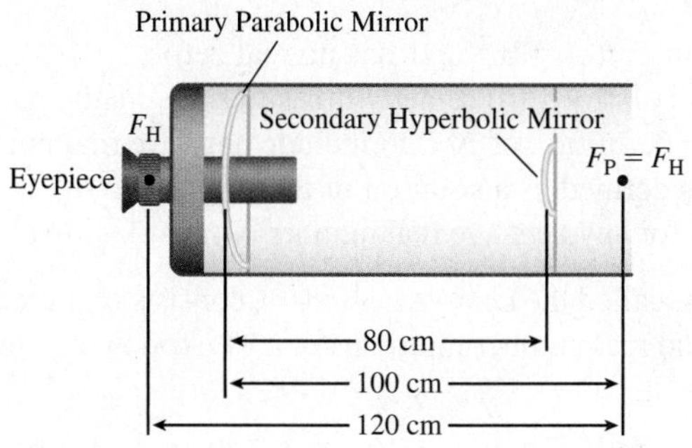

Extending the Ideas

65. Prove that a nondegenerate graph of the equation

$$Ax^2 + Cy^2 + Dx + Ey + F = 0$$

is a hyperbola if $AC < 0$.

66. Writing to Learn The graph of the equation

$$\frac{(x-h)^2}{a^2} - \frac{(y-k)^2}{b^2} = 0$$

is considered to be a degenerate hyperbola. Describe the graph. How is it like a full-fledged hyperbola, and how is it different?

67. Conjugate Hyperbolas The hyperbolas

$$\frac{(x-h)^2}{a^2} - \frac{(y-k)^2}{b^2} = 1 \text{ and } \frac{(y-k)^2}{b^2} - \frac{(x-h)^2}{a^2} = 1$$

obtained by switching the order of subtraction in their standard equations are **conjugate hyperbolas**. Prove that these hyperbolas have the same asymptotes and that the conjugate axis of each of these hyperbolas is the transverse axis of the other hyperbola.

68. Focal Width of a Hyperbola Prove that for the hyperbola

$$\frac{x^2}{a^2} - \frac{y^2}{b^2} = 1,$$

if $x = c$, then $y = \pm b^2/a$. Why is it reasonable to define the **focal width** of such hyperbolas to be $2b^2/a$?

69. Writing to Learn Explain how the standard form equations for the conics are related to

$$Ax^2 + Bxy + Cy^2 + Dx + Ey + F = 0.$$

H-4 Complex Numbers

What you'll learn about

- Complex Numbers
- Operations with Complex Numbers
- Complex Conjugates and Division
- Complex Solutions of Quadratic Equations

... and why

The zeros of polynomials are complex numbers.

Complex Numbers

Figure H.32 shows that the function $f(x) = x^2 + 1$ has no real zeros, so $x^2 + 1 = 0$ has no real-number solutions. To remedy this situation, mathematicians in the 17th century extended the definition of $\sqrt{a}$ to include negative real numbers a. First the number $i = \sqrt{-1}$ is defined as a solution of the equation $i^2 + 1 = 0$ and is the **imaginary unit**. Then for any negative real number $\sqrt{a} = \sqrt{|a|} \cdot i$.

The extended system of numbers, called the *complex numbers*, consists of all real numbers and sums of real numbers and real number multiples of i. The following are all examples of complex numbers:

$$-6, \quad 5i, \quad \sqrt{5}, \quad -7i, \quad \frac{5}{2}i + \frac{2}{3}, \quad -2 + 3i, \quad 5-3i, \quad \frac{1}{3} + \frac{4}{5}i.$$

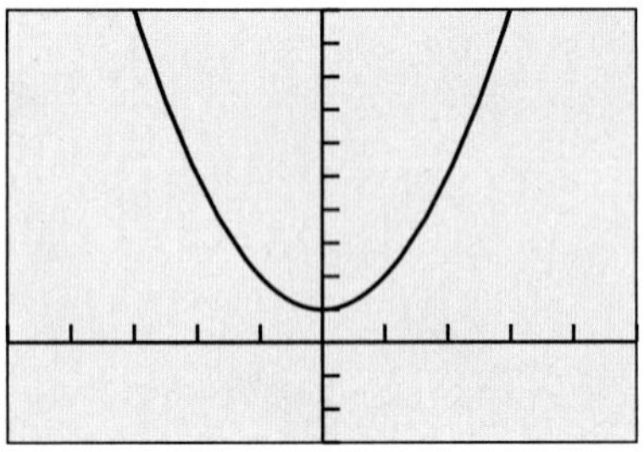

[–5, 5] by [–3, 10]

FIGURE H.32 The graph of $f(x) = x^2 + 1$ has no x-intercepts.

Historical Note

René Descartes (1596–1650) coined the term imaginary in a time when negative solutions to equations were considered *false*. Carl Friedrich Gauss (1777–1855) gave us the term complex number and the symbol i for $\sqrt{-1}$. Today practical applications of complex numbers abound.

DEFINITION Complex Number

A **complex number** is any number that can be written in the form

$$a + bi,$$

where a and b are real numbers. The real number a is the **real part**, the real number b is the **imaginary part**, and $a + bi$ is the **standard form**.

A real number a is the complex number $a + 0i$, so *all real numbers are also complex numbers*. If $a = 0$ and $b \neq 0$, then $a + bi$ becomes bi, and is an **imaginary number**. For instance, $5i$ and $-7i$ are imaginary numbers.

Two complex numbers are **equal** if and only if their real and imaginary parts are equal. For example,

$$x + yi = 2 + 5i \quad \text{if and only if} \quad x = 2 \text{ and } y = 5.$$

Operations with Complex Numbers

Adding complex numbers is done by adding their real and imaginary parts separately. Subtracting complex numbers is also done using the same parts.

DEFINITION Addition and Subtraction of Complex Numbers

If $a + bi$ and $c + di$ are two complex numbers, then

Sum: $(a + bi) + (c + di) = (a + c) + (b + d)i,$

Difference: $(a + bi) - (c + di) = (a - c) + (b - d)i.$

EXAMPLE 1 Adding and Subtracting Complex Numbers

(a) $(7 - 3i) + (4 + 5i) = (7 + 4) + (-3 + 5)i = 11 + 2i$

(b) $(2 - i) - (8 + 3i) = (2 - 8) + (-1 - 3)i = -6 - 4i$

Now try Exercise 3.

The **additive identity** for the complex numbers is $0 = 0 + 0i$. The **additive inverse** of $a + bi$ is $-(a + bi) = -a - bi$ because

$$(a + bi) + (-a - bi) = 0 + 0i = 0.$$

Many of the properties of real numbers also hold for complex numbers. These include:

- Commutative properties of addition and multiplication,
- Associative properties of addition and multiplication, and
- Distributive properties of multiplication over addition and subtraction.

Using these properties and the fact that $i^2 = -1$, complex numbers can be multiplied by treating them as algebraic expressions.

EXAMPLE 2 Multiplying Complex Numbers

$$\begin{aligned}(2 + 3i) \cdot (5 - i) &= 2(5 - i) + 3i(5 - i) \\ &= 10 - 2i + 15i - 3i^2 \\ &= 10 + 13i - 3(-1) \\ &= 13 + 13i\end{aligned}$$

Now try Exercise 9.

We can generalize Example 2 as follows:

$$\begin{aligned}(a + bi)(c + di) &= ac + adi + bci + bdi^2 \\ &= (ac - bd) + (ad + bc)i\end{aligned}$$

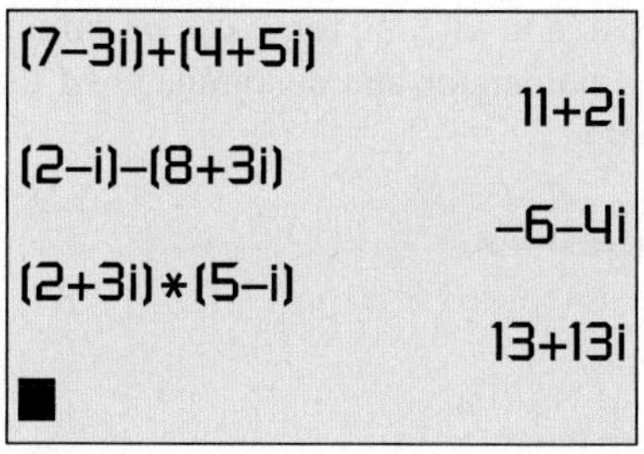

FIGURE H.33 Complex number operations on a grapher. (Examples 1 and 2)

Many graphers can perform basic calculations on complex numbers. Figure H.33 shows how the operations of Examples 1 and 2 look on some graphers.

We compute positive integer powers of complex numbers by treating them as algebraic expressions.

EXAMPLE 3 Raising a Complex Number to a Power

If $z = \frac{1}{2} + \frac{\sqrt{3}}{2}i$, find z^2 and z^3.

SOLUTION

$$\begin{aligned}z^2 &= \left(\frac{1}{2} + \frac{\sqrt{3}}{2}i\right)\left(\frac{1}{2} + \frac{\sqrt{3}}{2}i\right) \\ &= \frac{1}{4} + \frac{\sqrt{3}}{4}i + \frac{\sqrt{3}}{4}i + \frac{3}{4}i^2 \\ &= \frac{1}{4} + \frac{2\sqrt{3}}{4}i + \frac{3}{4}(-1) \\ &= -\frac{1}{2} + \frac{\sqrt{3}}{2}i\end{aligned}$$

$$\begin{aligned}z^3 = z^2 \cdot z &= \left(-\frac{1}{2} + \frac{\sqrt{3}}{2}i\right)\left(\frac{1}{2} + \frac{\sqrt{3}}{2}i\right) \\ &= -\frac{1}{4} - \frac{\sqrt{3}}{4}i + \frac{\sqrt{3}}{4}i + \frac{3}{4}i^2 \\ &= -\frac{1}{4} + 0i + \frac{3}{4}(-1) \\ &= -1\end{aligned}$$

FIGURE H.34 The square and cube of a complex number. (Example 3)

Figure H.34 supports these results numerically. *Now try Exercise 27.*

Example 3 demonstrates that $1/2 + (\sqrt{3}/2)i$ is a cube root of -1 and a solution of $x^3 + 1 = 0$.

Complex Conjugates and Division

The product of the complex numbers $a + bi$ and $a - bi$ is a positive real number:

$$(a + bi) \cdot (a - bi) = a^2 - (bi)^2 = a^2 + b^2.$$

We introduce the following definition to describe this special relationship.

DEFINITION Complex Conjugate

The **complex conjugate** of the complex number $z = a + bi$ is

$$\bar{z} = \overline{a + bi} = a - bi.$$

The **multiplicative identity** for the complex numbers is $1 = 1 + 0i$. The **multiplicative inverse**, or **reciprocal**, of $z = a + bi$ is

$$z^{-1} = \frac{1}{z} = \frac{1}{a + bi} = \frac{1}{a + bi} \cdot \frac{a - bi}{a - bi} = \frac{a}{a^2 + b^2} - \frac{b}{a^2 + b^2} i.$$

In general, a quotient of two complex numbers, written in fraction form, can be simplified as we just simplified $1/z$—by multiplying the numerator and denominator of the fraction by the complex conjugate of the denominator.

EXAMPLE 4 Dividing Complex Numbers

Write the complex number in standard form.

(a) $\dfrac{2}{3 - i}$ **(b)** $\dfrac{5 + i}{2 - 3i}$

SOLUTION Multiply the numerator and denominator by the complex conjugate of the denominator.

(a)
$$\frac{2}{3 - i} = \frac{2}{3 - i} \cdot \frac{3 + i}{3 + i} = \frac{6 + 2i}{3^2 + 1^2} = \frac{6}{10} + \frac{2}{10} i = \frac{3}{5} + \frac{1}{5} i$$

(b)
$$\frac{5 + i}{2 - 3i} = \frac{5 + i}{2 - 3i} \cdot \frac{2 + 3i}{2 + 3i} = \frac{10 + 15i + 2i + 3i^2}{2^2 + 3^2} = \frac{7 + 17i}{13} = \frac{7}{13} + \frac{17}{13} i$$

Now try Exercise 33.

Complex Solutions of Quadratic Equations

Recall that the solutions of the quadratic equation $ax^2 + bx + c = 0$, where a, b, and c are real numbers and $a \neq 0$, are given by the quadratic formula

$$x = \frac{-b \pm \sqrt{b^2 - 4ac}}{2a}.$$

The radicand $b^2 - 4ac$ is the **discriminant**, and tells us whether the solutions are real numbers. In particular, if $b^2 - 4ac < 0$, the solutions involve the square root of a negative number and so lead to complex-number solutions. In all, there are three cases, which we now summarize:

Discriminant of a Quadratic Equation

For a quadratic equation $ax^2 + bx + c = 0$, where a, b, and c are real numbers and $a \neq 0$,

- If $b^2 - 4ac > 0$, there are two distinct real solutions.
- If $b^2 - 4ac = 0$, there is one repeated real solution.
- If $b^2 - 4ac < 0$, there is a complex conjugate pair of solutions.

EXAMPLE 5 Solving a Quadratic Equation

Solve $x^2 + x + 1 = 0$.

SOLUTION

Solve Algebraically

Using the quadratic formula with $a = b = c = 1$, we obtain

$$x = \frac{-(1) \pm \sqrt{(1)^2 - 4(1)(1)}}{2(1)} = \frac{-(1) \pm \sqrt{-3}}{2} = -\frac{1}{2} \pm \frac{\sqrt{3}}{2}i.$$

So the solutions are $-1/2 + (\sqrt{3}/2)i$ and $-1/2 - (\sqrt{3}/2)i$, a complex conjugate pair.

Confirm Numerically

Substituting $-1/2 + (\sqrt{3}/2)i$ into the original equation, we obtain

$$\left(-\frac{1}{2} + \frac{\sqrt{3}}{2}i\right)^2 + \left(-\frac{1}{2} + \frac{\sqrt{3}}{2}i\right) + 1$$
$$= \left(-\frac{1}{2} - \frac{\sqrt{3}}{2}i\right) + \left(-\frac{1}{2} + \frac{\sqrt{3}}{2}i\right) + 1 = 0.$$

By a similar computation we can confirm the second solution.

Now try Exercise 41.

LESSON H-4 EXERCISES

Exercise numbers with a gray background indicate problems that the authors have designed to be solved *without a calculator*.

In Exercises 1–8, write the sum or difference in the standard form $a + bi$ without using a calculator.

1. $(2 - 3i) + (6 + 5i)$

2. $(2 - 3i) + (3 - 4i)$

3. $(7 - 3i) + (6 - i)$

4. $(2 + i) - (9i - 3)$

5. $(2 - i) + (3 - \sqrt{-3})$

6. $(\sqrt{5} - 3i) + (-2 + \sqrt{-9})$

7. $(i^2 + 3) - (7 + i^3)$

8. $(\sqrt{7} + i^2) - (6 - \sqrt{-81})$

In Exercises 9–16, write the product in standard form without using a calculator.

9. $(2 + 3i)(2 - i)$ **10.** $(2 - i)(1 + 3i)$

11. $(1 - 4i)(3 - 2i)$ **12.** $(5i - 3)(2i + 1)$

13. $(7i - 3)(2 + 6i)$ **14.** $(\sqrt{-4} + i)(6 - 5i)$

15. $(-3 - 4i)(1 + 2i)$ **16.** $(\sqrt{-2} + 2i)(6 + 5i)$

In Exercises 17–20, write the expression in the form bi, where b is a real number.

17. $\sqrt{-16}$ **18.** $\sqrt{-25}$

19. $\sqrt{-3}$ **20.** $\sqrt{-5}$

In Exercises 21–24, find the real numbers x and y that make the equation true.

21. $2 + 3i = x + yi$ **22.** $3 + yi = x - 7i$

23. $(5 - 2i) - 7 = x - (3 + yi)$

24. $(x + 6i) = (3 - i) + (4 - 2yi)$

In Exercises 25–28, write the complex number in standard form.

25. $(3 + 2i)^2$ **26.** $(1 - i)^3$

27. $\left(\frac{\sqrt{2}}{2} + \frac{\sqrt{2}}{2}i\right)^4$ **28.** $\left(\frac{\sqrt{3}}{2} + \frac{1}{2}i\right)^3$

In Exercises 29–32, find the product of the complex number and its conjugate.

29. $2 - 3i$ **30.** $5 - 6i$

31. $-3 + 4i$ **32.** $-1 - \sqrt{2}i$

In Exercises 33–40, write the expression in standard form without using a calculator.

33. $\frac{1}{2 + i}$ **34.** $\frac{i}{2 - i}$

35. $\frac{2 + i}{2 - i}$ **36.** $\frac{2 + i}{3i}$

37. $\frac{(2 + i)^2(-i)}{1 + i}$ **38.** $\frac{(2 - i)(1 + 2i)}{5 + 2i}$

39. $\frac{(1 - i)(2 - i)}{1 - 2i}$ **40.** $\frac{(1 - \sqrt{2}i)(1 + i)}{(1 + \sqrt{2}i)}$

In Exercises 41–44, solve the equation.

41. $x^2 + 2x + 5 = 0$ **42.** $3x^2 + x + 2 = 0$

43. $4x^2 - 6x + 5 = x + 1$ **44.** $x^2 + x + 11 = 5x - 8$

Explorations

45. Group Activity The Powers of i

(a) Simplify the complex numbers $i, i^2, \ldots, i^8$ by evaluating each one.

(b) Simplify the complex numbers $i^{-1}, i^{-2}, \ldots, i^{-8}$ by evaluating each one.

(c) Evaluate i^0.

(d) Writing to Learn Discuss your results from (a)–(c) with the members of your group, and write a summary statement about the integer powers of i.

46. Writing to Learn Describe the nature of the graph of $f(x) = ax^2 + bx + c$ when a, b, and c are real numbers and the equation $ax^2 + bx + c = 0$ has nonreal complex solutions.

Extending the Ideas

47. Prove that the difference between a complex number and its conjugate is a complex number whose real part is 0.

48. Prove that the product of a complex number and its complex conjugate is a complex number whose imaginary part is zero.

49. Prove that the complex conjugate of a product of two complex numbers is the product of their complex conjugates.

50. Prove that the complex conjugate of a sum of two complex numbers is the sum of their complex conjugates.

51. Writing to Learn Explain why $-i$ is a solution of $x^2 - ix + 2 = 0$ but i is not.

H-5 Solving Inequalities Algebraically and Graphically

What you'll learn about

- Solving Absolute Value Inequalities
- Solving Quadratic Inequalities
- Approximating Solutions to Inequalities
- Projectile Motion

... and why

These techniques are involved in using a graphing utility to solve inequalities in this textbook.

Solving Absolute Value Inequalities

The methods for solving inequalities parallel the methods for solving equations. Here are two basic rules we apply to solve absolute value inequalities.

Solving Absolute Value Inequalities

Let u be an algebraic expression in x and let a be a real number with $a \geq 0$.

1. If $|u| < a$, then u is in the interval $(-a, a)$. That is,

$$|u| < a \quad \text{if and only if} \quad -a < u < a.$$

2. If $|u| > a$, then u is in the interval $(-\infty, -a)$ or (a, ∞), that is,

$$|u| > a \quad \text{if and only if} \quad u < -a \text{ or } u > a.$$

The inequalities $<$ and $>$ can be replaced with $\leq$ and $\geq$, respectively. See Figure H.35.

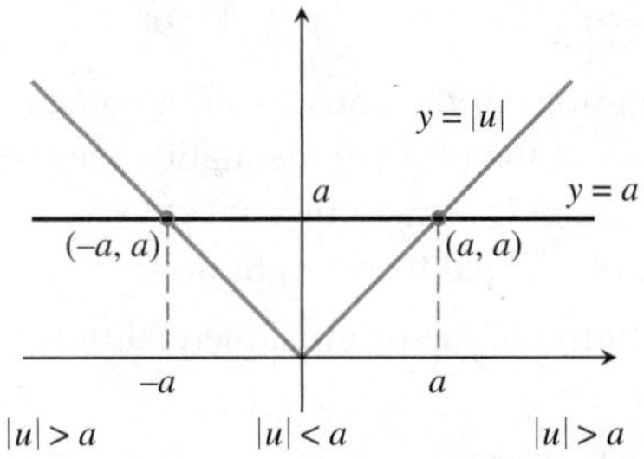

FIGURE H.35 The solution of $|u| < a$ is represented by the portion of the number line where the graph of $y = |u|$ is below the graph of $y = a$. The solution of $|u| > a$ is represented by the portion of the number line where the graph of $y = |u|$ is above the graph of $y = a$.

EXAMPLE 1 Solving an Absolute Value Inequality

Solve $|x - 4| < 8$.

SOLUTION

$|x - 4| < 8$	Original inequality
$-8 < x - 4 < 8$	Equivalent double inequality.
$-4 < x < 12$	Add 4.

As an interval the solution is $(-4, 12)$.

Figure H.36 shows that points on the graph of $y = |x - 4|$ are below the points on the graph of $y = 8$ for values of x between -4 and 12.

Now try Exercise 3.

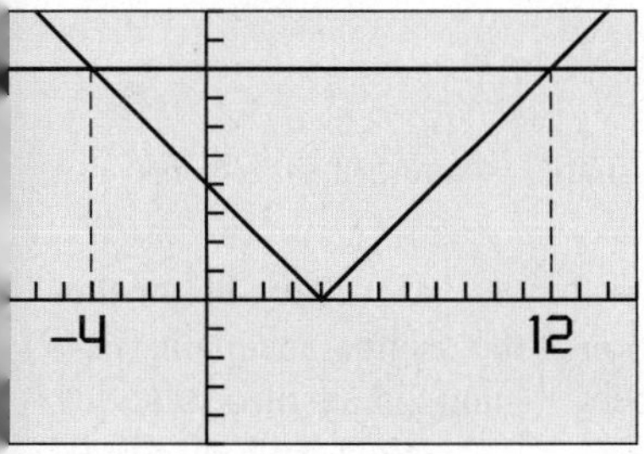

[–7, 15] by [–5, 10]

FIGURE H.36 The graphs of $y = |x - 4|$ and $y = 8$. (Example 1)

EXAMPLE 2 Solving Another Absolute Value Inequality

Solve $|3x - 2| \geq 5$.

SOLUTION The solution of this absolute value inequality consists of the solutions of both of these inequalities.

$3x - 2 \leq -5$	or	$3x - 2 \geq 5$	
$3x \leq -3$	or	$3x \geq 7$	Add 2.
$x \leq -1$	or	$x \geq \frac{7}{3}$	Divide by 3.

(continued)

The solution consists of all numbers that are in either one of the two intervals $(-\infty, -1]$ or $[7/3, \infty)$, which may be written as $(-\infty, -1] \cup [7/3, \infty)$. The notation "$\cup$" is read as "union."

Figure H.37 shows that points on the graph of $y = |3x - 2|$ are above or on the points on the graph of $y = 5$ for values of x to the left of and including -1 and to the right of and including 7/3. *Now try Exercise 7.*

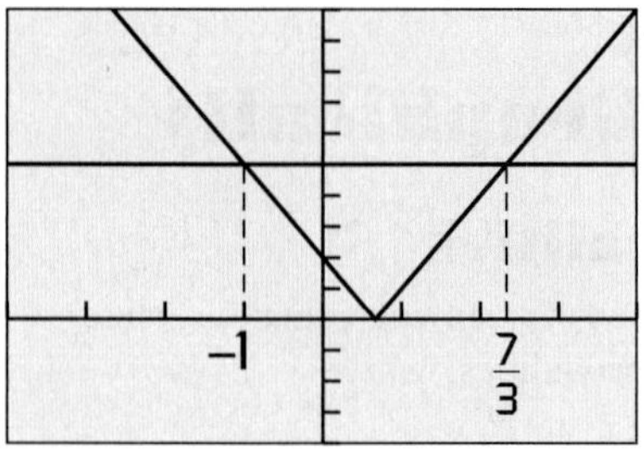

[–4, 4] by [–4, 10]

FIGURE H.37 The graphs of $y = |3x - 2|$ and $y = 5$. (Example 2)

Union of Two Sets

The **union of two sets A and B**, denoted by $A \cup B$, is the set of all objects that belong to A or B or both.

Solving Quadratic Inequalities

To solve a quadratic inequality such as $x^2 - x - 12 > 0$ we begin by solving the corresponding quadratic equation $x^2 - x - 12 = 0$. Then we determine the values of x for which the graph of $y = x^2 - x - 12$ lies above the x-axis.

EXAMPLE 3 Solving a Quadratic Inequality

Solve $x^2 - x - 12 > 0$.

SOLUTION First we solve the corresponding equation $x^2 - x - 12 = 0$.

$$
\begin{aligned}
x^2 - x - 12 &= 0 \\
(x - 4)(x + 3) &= 0 && \text{Factor.} \\
x - 4 = 0 \quad \text{or} \quad x + 3 &= 0 && ab = 0 \Rightarrow a = 0 \text{ or } b = 0 \\
x = 4 \quad \text{or} \quad x &= -3 && \text{Solve for } x.
\end{aligned}
$$

The solutions of the corresponding quadratic equation are -3 and 4, and they are not solutions of the original inequality because $0 > 0$ is false. Figure H.38 shows that the points on the graph of $y = x^2 - x - 12$ are above the x-axis for values of x to the left of -3 and to the right of 4.

The solution of the original inequality is $(-\infty, -3) \cup (4, \infty)$.

Now try Exercise 11.

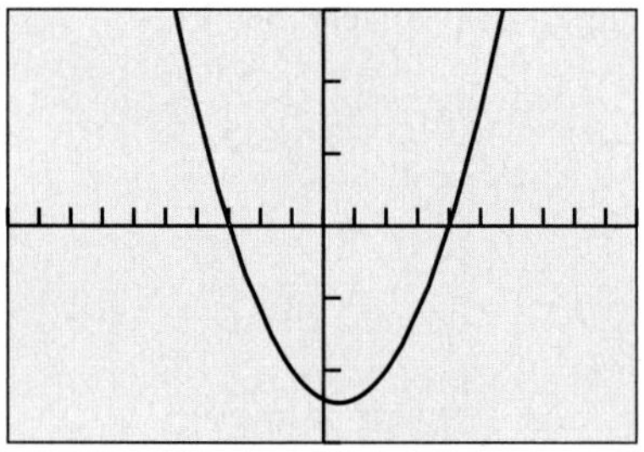

[–10, 10] by [–15, 15]

FIGURE H.38 The graph of $y = x^2 - x - 12$ appears to cross the x-axis at $x = -3$ and $x = 4$. (Example 3)

In Example 4, the quadratic inequality involves the symbol $\le$. In this case, the solutions of the corresponding quadratic equation are also solutions of the inequality.

EXAMPLE 4 Solving Another Quadratic Inequality

Solve $2x^2 + 3x \le 20$.

SOLUTION First we subtract 20 from both sides of the inequality to obtain $2x^2 + 3x - 20 \le 0$. Next, we solve the corresponding quadratic equation $2x^2 + 3x - 20 = 0$.

$$
\begin{aligned}
2x^2 + 3x - 20 &= 0 \\
(x + 4)(2x - 5) &= 0 && \text{Factor.} \\
x + 4 = 0 \quad \text{or} \quad 2x - 5 &= 0 && ab = 0 \Rightarrow a = 0 \text{ or } b = 0 \\
x = -4 \quad \text{or} \quad x &= \frac{5}{2} && \text{Solve for } x.
\end{aligned}
$$

The solutions of the corresponding quadratic equation are -4 and $5/2 = 2.5$. You can check that they are also solutions of the inequality.

Figure H.39 shows that the points on the graph of $y = 2x^2 + 3x - 20$ are below the x-axis for values of x between -4 and 2.5. The solution of the original inequality is $[-4, 2.5]$. We use square brackets because the numbers -4 and 2.5 are also solutions of the inequality. *Now try Exercise 9.*

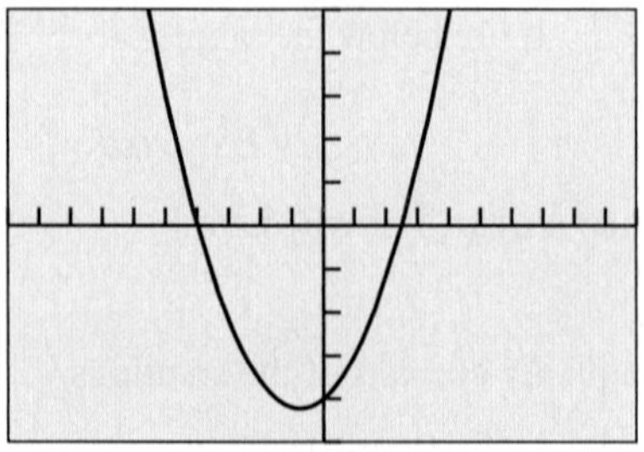

[–10, 10] by [–25, 25]

FIGURE H.39 The graph of $y = 2x^2 + 3x - 20$ appears to be below the x-axis for $-4 < x < 2.5$. (Example 4)

In Examples 3 and 4 the corresponding quadratic equation factored. If this doesn't happen we will need to approximate the zeros of the quadratic equation if it has any. Then we write the endpoints of any intervals accurate to two decimal places as illustrated in Example 5.

EXAMPLE 5 Solving a Quadratic Inequality Graphically

Solve $x^2 - 4x + 1 \geq 0$ graphically.

SOLUTION We can use the graph of $y = x^2 - 4x + 1$ in Figure H.40 to determine that the solutions of the equation $x^2 - 4x + 1 = 0$ are about 0.27 and 3.73. Thus, the solution of the original inequality is $(-\infty, 0.27] \cup [3.73, \infty)$. We use square brackets because the zeros of the quadratic equation are solutions of the inequality even though we only have approximations to their values.

Now try Exercise 21.

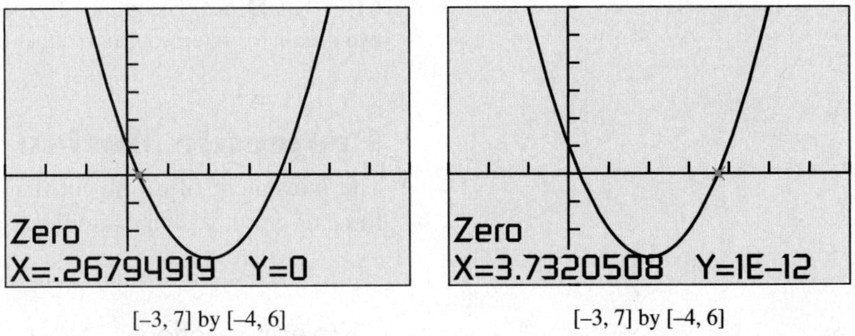

FIGURE H.40 This figure suggests that $y = x^2 - 4x + 1$ is zero for $x \approx 0.27$ and $x \approx 3.73$. (Example 5)

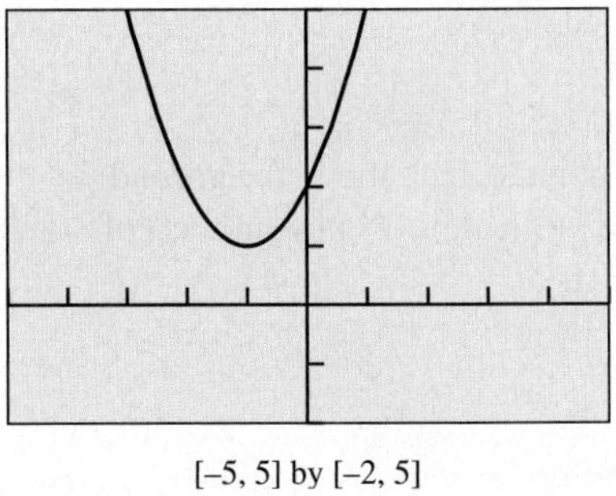

FIGURE H.41 The values of $y = x^2 + 2x + 2$ are never negative. (Example 6)

EXAMPLE 6 Showing That a Quadratic Inequality Has No Solution

Solve $x^2 + 2x + 2 < 0$.

SOLUTION Figure P.48 shows that the graph of $y = x^2 + 2x + 2$ lies above the x-axis for all values for x. Thus, the inequality $x^2 + 2x + 2 < 0$ has *no* solution.

Now try Exercise 25.

Figure H.41 also shows that the solution of the inequality $x^2 + 2x + 2 > 0$ is the set of all real numbers or, in interval notation, $(-\infty, \infty)$. A quadratic inequality can also have exactly one solution (see Exercise 31).

Approximating Solutions to Inequalities

To solve the inequality in Example 7 we approximate the zeros of the corresponding graph. Then we determine the values of x for which the corresponding graph is above or on the x-axis.

EXAMPLE 7 Solving a Cubic Inequality

Solve $x^3 + 2x^2 - 1 \geq 0$ graphically.

SOLUTION We can use the graph of $y = x^3 + 2x^2 - 1$ in Figure H.42 to show that the solutions of the corresponding equation $x^3 + 2x^2 - 1 = 0$ are approximately -1.62, -1, and 0.62. The points on the graph of $y = x^3 + 2x^2 - 1$ are above the x-axis for values of x between -1.62 and -1, and for values of x to the right of 0.62.

The solution of the inequality is $[-1.62, -1] \cup [0.62, \infty)$. We use square brackets because the zeros of $y = x^3 + 2x^2 - 1$ are also solutions of the inequality.

Now try Exercise 27.

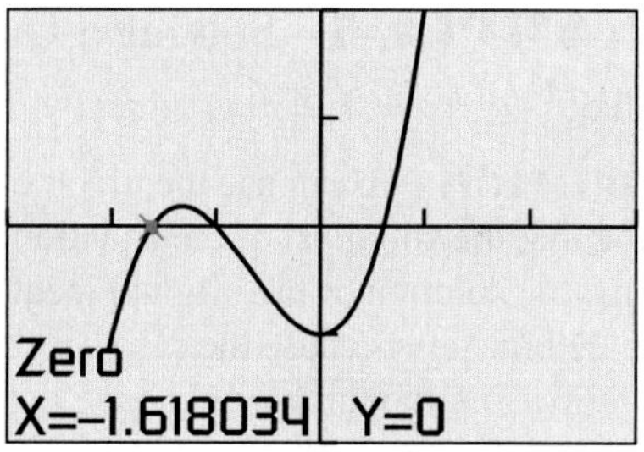

[–3, 3] by [–2, 2]

FIGURE H.42 The graph of $y = x^3 + 2x^2 - 1$ appears to be above the x-axis between the two negative x-intercepts and to the right of the positive x-intercept. (Example 7)

Projectile Motion

The movement of an object that is propelled vertically, but then subject only to the force of gravity, is an example of **projectile motion**.

Projectile Motion

Suppose an object is launched vertically from a point s_0 feet above the ground with an initial velocity of v_0 feet per second. The vertical position s (in feet) of the object t seconds after it is launched is

$$s = -16t^2 + v_0t + s_0.$$

EXAMPLE 8 Finding Height of a Projectile

A projectile is launched straight up from ground level with an initial velocity of 288 ft/sec.

(a) When will the projectile's height above ground be 1152 ft?

(b) When will the projectile's height above ground be at least 1152 ft?

SOLUTION Here $s_0 = 0$ and $v_0 = 288$. So, the projectile's height is $s = -16t^2 + 288t$.

(a) We need to determine when $s = 1152$.

$$s = -16t^2 + 288t$$

$$1152 = -16t^2 + 288t \quad \text{Substitute } s = 1152.$$

$$16t^2 - 288t + 1152 = 0 \quad \text{Add } 16t^2 - 288t.$$

$$t^2 - 18t + 72 = 0 \quad \text{Divide by 16.}$$

$$(t - 6)(t - 12) = 0 \quad \text{Factor.}$$

$$t = 6 \text{ or } t = 12 \quad \text{Solve for } t.$$

The projectile is 1152 ft above ground twice; the first time at $t = 6$ sec on the way up, and the second time at $t = 12$ sec on the way down (Figure H.43).

(b) The projectile will be at least 1152 ft above ground when $s \geq 1152$. We can see from Figure H.43 together with the algebraic work in (a) that the solution is [6, 12]. This means that the projectile is at least 1152 ft above ground for times between $t = 6$ sec and $t = 12$ sec, including 6 and 12 sec.

In Exercise 32 we ask you to use algebra to solve the inequality $s = -16t^2 + 288t \geq 1152$. *Now try Exercise 33.*

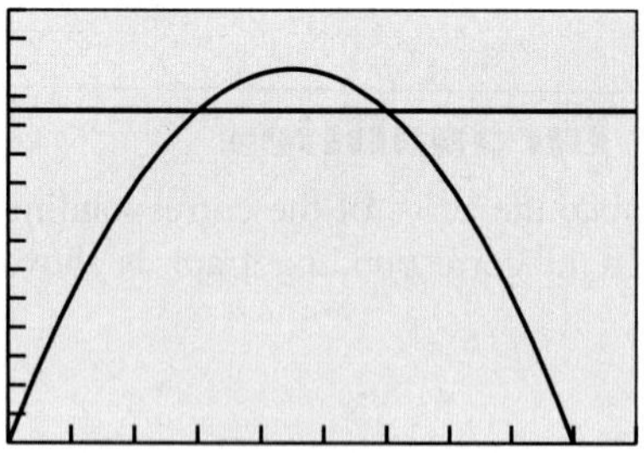

[0, 20] by [0, 1500]

FIGURE H.43 The graphs of $s = -16t^2 + 288t$ and $s = 1152$. We know from Example 8a that the two graphs intersect at (6, 1152) and (12, 1152).

LESSON H-5 EXERCISES

In Exercises 1–8, solve the inequality algebraically. Write the solution in interval notation and draw its number line graph.

1. $|x + 4| \geq 5$ **2.** $|2x - 1| > 3.6$

3. $|x - 3| < 2$ **4.** $|x + 3| \leq 5$

5. $|4 - 3x| - 2 < 4$ **6.** $|3 - 2x| + 2 > 5$

7. $\left|\frac{x + 2}{3}\right| \geq 3$ **8.** $\left|\frac{x - 5}{4}\right| \leq 6$

In Exercises 9–16, solve the inequality. Use algebra to solve the corresponding equation.

9. $2x^2 + 17x + 21 \leq 0$ **10.** $6x^2 - 13x + 6 \geq 0$

11. $2x^2 + 7x > 15$ **12.** $4x^2 + 2 < 9x$

13. $2 - 5x - 3x^2 < 0$ **14.** $21 + 4x - x^2 > 0$

15. $x^3 - x \geq 0$ **16.** $x^3 - x^2 - 30x \leq 0$

In Exercises 17–26, solve the inequality graphically.

17. $x^2 - 4x < 1$ **18.** $12x^2 - 25x + 12 \geq 0$

19. $6x^2 - 5x - 4 > 0$ **20.** $4x^2 - 1 \leq 0$

21. $9x^2 + 12x - 1 \geq 0$ **22.** $4x^2 - 12x + 7 < 0$

23. $4x^2 + 1 > 4x$ **24.** $x^2 + 9 \leq 6x$

25. $x^2 - 8x + 16 < 0$ **26.** $9x^2 + 12x + 4 \geq 0$

In Exercises 27–30, solve the cubic inequality graphically.

27. $3x^3 - 12x + 2 \geq 0$ **28.** $8x - 2x^3 - 1 < 0$

29. $2x^3 + 2x > 5$ **30.** $4 \leq 2x^3 + 8x$

31. Group Activity Give an example of a quadratic inequality with the indicated solution.

(a) All real numbers **(b)** No solution

(c) Exactly one solution **(d)** $[-2, 5]$

(e) $(-\infty, -1) \cup (4, \infty)$ **(f)** $(-\infty, 0] \cup [4, \infty)$

32. Revisiting Example 8 Solve the inequality $-16t^2 + 288t \geq 1152$ algebraically and compare your answer with the result obtained in Example 10.

33. Projectile Motion A projectile is launched straight up from ground level with an initial velocity of 256 ft/sec.

(a) When will the projectile's height above ground be 768 ft?

(b) When will the projectile's height above ground be at least 768 ft?

(c) When will the projectile's height above ground be less than or equal to 768 ft?

34. Projectile Motion A projectile is launched straight up from ground level with an initial velocity of 272 ft/sec.

(a) When will the projectile's height above ground be 960 ft?

(b) When will the projectile's height above ground be more than 960 ft?

(c) When will the projectile's height above ground be less than or equal to 960 ft?

35. Writing to Learn Explain the role of equation solving in the process of solving an inequality. Give an example.

36. Travel Planning Barb wants to drive to a city 105 mi from her home in no more than 2 h. What is the lowest average speed she must maintain on the drive?

37. Connecting Algebra and Geometry Consider the collection of all rectangles that have length 2 in. less than twice their width.

(a) Find the possible widths (in inches) of these rectangles if their perimeters are less than 200 in.

(b) Find the possible widths (in inches) of these rectangles if their areas are less than or equal to 1200 in.^{2}.

38. Boyle's Law For a certain gas, $P = 400/V$, where P is pressure and V is volume. If $20 \leq V \leq 40$, what is the corresponding range for P?

39. Cash-Flow Planning A company has current assets (cash, property, inventory, and accounts receivable) of \$200,000 and current liabilities (taxes, loans, and accounts payable) of \$50,000. How much can it borrow if it wants its ratio of assets to liabilities to be no less than 2? Assume the amount borrowed is added to both current assets and current liabilities.

Explorations

40. Constructing a Box with No Top An open box is formed by cutting squares from the corners of a regular piece of cardboard (see figure) and folding up the flaps.

(a) What size corner squares should be cut to yield a box with a volume of 125 in.^{3}?

(b) What size corner squares should be cut to yield a box with a volume more than 125 in.^{3}?

(c) What size corner squares should be cut to yield a box with a volume of at most 125 in.^{3}?

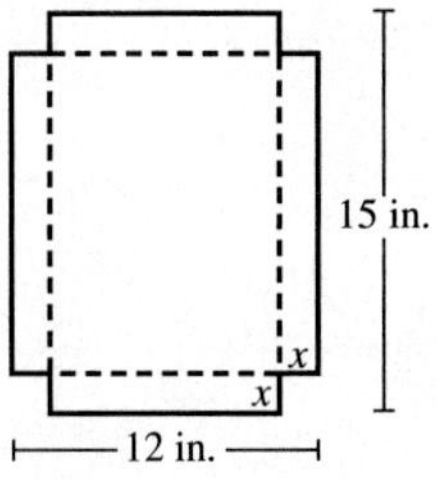

Extending the Ideas

In Exercises 41 and 42, use a combination of algebraic and graphical techniques to solve the inequalities.

41. $|2x^2 + 7x - 15| < 10$ **42.** $|2x^2 + 3x - 20| \geq 10$

H-6 Complex Zeros and the Fundamental Theorem of Algebra

What you'll learn about

- Two Major Theorems
- Complex Conjugate Zeros
- Factoring with Real Number Coefficients

... and why

These topics provide the complete story about the zeros and factors of polynomials with real number coefficients.

Two Major Theorems

A polynomial function of degree n has at most n real zeros. Figure H.44 shows that the polynomial function $f(x) = x^2 + 2x + 5$ of degree 2 has no real zeros. (Why?) A little arithmetic, however, shows that the complex number $-1 + 2i$ is a zero of f:

$$\begin{aligned} f(-1 + 2i) &= (-1 + 2i)^2 + 2(-1 + 2i) + 5 \\ &= (-3 - 4i) + (-2 + 4i) + 5 \\ &= 0 + 0i \\ &= 0 \end{aligned}$$

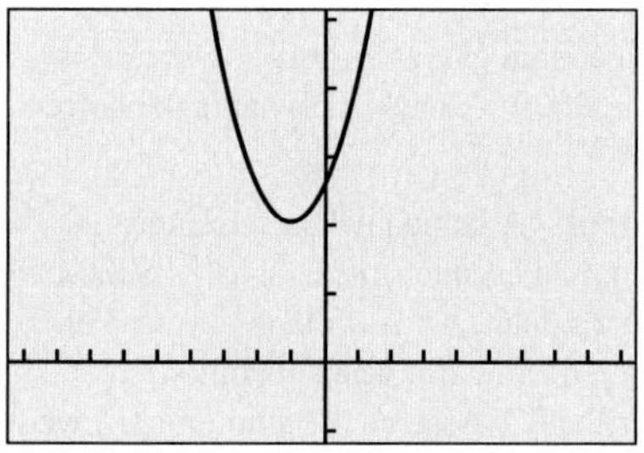

[–9.4, 9.4] by [–2, 10]

FIGURE H.44 The graph of $f(x) = x^2 + 2x + 5$ has no x-intercepts, so f has no real zeros.

The quadratic formula shows that $-1 \pm 2i$ are the two zeros of f and can be used to find the complex zeros for any polynomial function of degree 2. In this section we will learn about complex zeros of polynomial functions of higher degree and how to use these zeros to factor polynomial expressions.

THEOREM 100 Fundamental Theorem of Algebra

A polynomial function of degree n has n complex zeros (real and nonreal). Some of these zeros may be repeated.

The Factor Theorem, which states that a polynomial function $f(x)$ has a factor $x - k$ if and only if $f(k) = 0$, extends to the complex zeros of a polynomial function. Thus, k is a complex zero of a polynomial if and only if $x - k$ is a factor of the polynomial, even if k is not a real number. We combine this fact with the Fundamental Theorem of Algebra to obtain the following theorem.

THEOREM 101 Linear Factorization Theorem

If $f(x)$ is a polynomial function of degree $n > 0$, then $f(x)$ has precisely n linear factors and

$$f(x) = a(x - z_1)(x - z_2)\cdots(x - z_n)$$

where a is the leading coefficient of $f(x)$ and $z_1, z_2, \ldots, z_n$ are the complex zeros of $f(x)$. The z_i are not necessarily distinct numbers; some may be repeated.

The Fundamental Theorem of Algebra and the Linear Factorization Theorem are *existence theorems*. They tell us of the existence of zeros and linear factors, but not how to find them.

One connection is lost going from real zeros to complex zeros. If k is a *nonreal* complex zero of a polynomial function $f(x)$, then k is *not* an x-intercept of the graph of f. The other connections hold whether k is real or nonreal:

Fundamental Polynomial Connections in the Complex Case

The following statements about a polynomial function f are equivalent if k is a complex number:

1. $x = k$ is a solution (or root) of the equation $f(x) = 0$.
2. k is a zero of the function f.
3. $x - k$ is a factor of $f(x)$.

EXAMPLE 1 Exploring Fundamental Polynomial Connections

Write the polynomial function in standard form, and identify the zeros of the function and the x-intercepts of its graph.

(a) $f(x) = (x - 2i)(x + 2i)$

(b) $f(x) = (x - 5)(x - \sqrt{2}i)(x + \sqrt{2}i)$

(c) $f(x) = (x - 3)(x - 3)(x - i)(x + i)$

SOLUTION

(a) The quadratic function $f(x) = (x - 2i)(x + 2i) = x^2 + 4$ has two zeros: $x = 2i$ and $x = -2i$. Because the zeros are not real, the graph of f has no x-intercepts.

(b) The cubic function

$$\begin{aligned} f(x) &= (x - 5)(x - \sqrt{2}i)(x + \sqrt{2}i) \\ &= (x - 5)(x^2 + 2) \\ &= x^3 - 5x^2 + 2x - 10 \end{aligned}$$

has three zeros: $x = 5$, $x = \sqrt{2}i$, and $x = -\sqrt{2}i$. Of the three, only $x = 5$ is an x-intercept.

(c) The quartic function

$$\begin{aligned} f(x) &= (x - 3)(x - 3)(x - i)(x + i) \\ &= (x^2 - 6x + 9)(x^2 + 1) \\ &= x^4 - 6x^3 + 10x^2 - 6x + 9 \end{aligned}$$

has four zeros: $x = 3$, $x = 3$, $x = i$, and $x = -i$. There are only three distinct zeros. The real zero $x = 3$ is a repeated zero of multiplicity two. Due to this even multiplicity, the graph of f touches but does not cross the x-axis at $x = 3$, the only x-intercept.

Figure H.45 supports our conclusions regarding x-intercepts.

Now try Exercise 1.

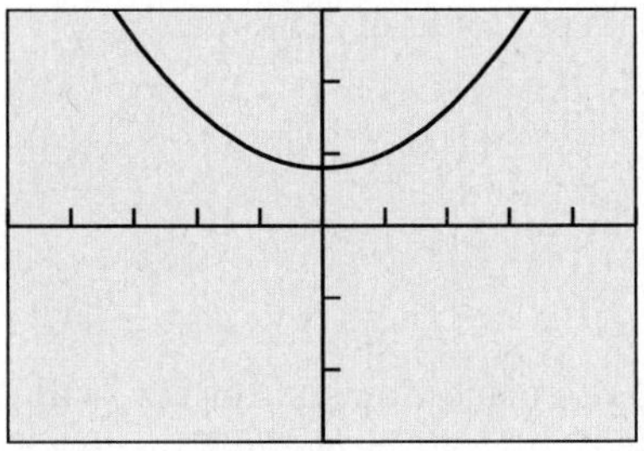

[–5, 5] by [–15, 15]
(a)

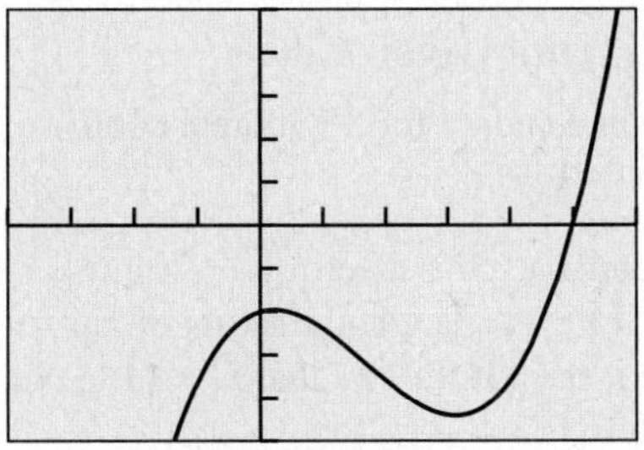

[–4, 6] by [–25, 25]
(b)

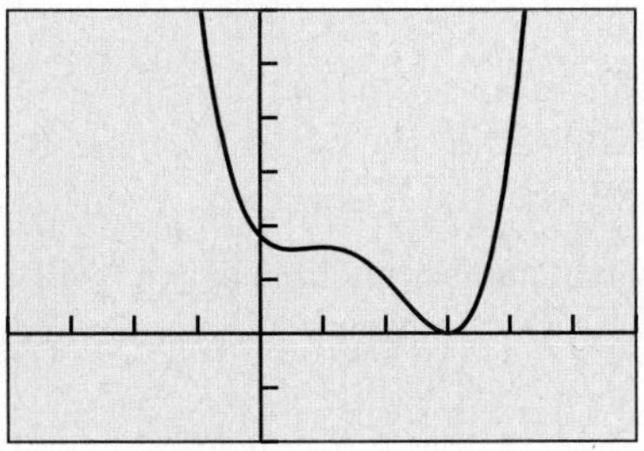

[–4, 6] by [–10, 30]
(c)

FIGURE H.45 The graphs of (a) $y = x^2 + 4$, (b) $y = x^3 - 5x^2 + 2x - 10$, and (c) $y = x^4 - 6x^3 + 10x^2 - 6x + 9$. (Example 1)

Complex Conjugate Zeros

In Lesson H-4 we saw that, for quadratic equations $ax^2 + bx + c = 0$ with real coefficients, if the discriminant $b^2 - 4ac$ is negative, the solutions are a conjugate pair of complex numbers. This relationship generalizes to polynomial functions of higher degree in the following way:

THEOREM 102 Complex Conjugate Zeros

Suppose that $f(x)$ is a polynomial function with *real coefficients*. If a and b are real numbers with $b \neq 0$ and $a + bi$ is a zero of $f(x)$, then its complex conjugate $a - bi$ is also a zero of $f(x)$.

EXPLORATION 1 What Can Happen if the Coefficients Are Not Real?

1. Use substitution to verify that $x = 2i$ and $x = -i$ are zeros of $f(x) = x^2 - ix + 2$. Are the conjugates of $2i$ and $-i$ also zeros of $f(x)$?
2. Use substitution to verify that $x = i$ and $x = 1 - i$ are zeros of $g(x) = x^2 - x + (1 + i)$. Are the conjugates of i and $1 - i$ also zeros of $g(x)$?
3. What conclusions can you draw from parts 1 and 2? Do your results contradict the theorem about complex conjugate zeros?

EXAMPLE 2 Finding a Polynomial from Given Zeros

Write a polynomial function of minimum degree in standard form with real coefficients whose zeros include -3, 4, and $2 - i$.

SOLUTION Because -3 and 4 are real zeros, $x + 3$ and $x - 4$ must be factors. Because the coefficients are real and $2 - i$ is a zero, $2 + i$ must also be a zero. Therefore, $x - (2 - i)$ and $x - (2 + i)$ must both be factors of $f(x)$. Thus,

$$\begin{aligned} f(x) &= (x + 3)(x - 4)[x - (2 - i)][x - (2 + i)] \\ &= (x^2 - x - 12)(x^2 - 4x + 5) \\ &= x^4 - 5x^3 - 3x^2 + 43x - 60 \end{aligned}$$

is a polynomial of the type we seek. Any nonzero real number multiple of $f(x)$ will also be such a polynomial. *Now try Exercise 7.*

EXAMPLE 3 Finding a Polynomial from Given Zeros

Write a polynomial function of minimum degree in standard form with real coefficients whose zeros include $x = 1, x = 1 + 2i, x = 1 - i$.

SOLUTION Because the coefficients are real and $1 + 2i$ is a zero, $1 - 2i$ must also be a zero. Therefore, $x - (1 + 2i)$ and $x - (1 - 2i)$ are both factors of $f(x)$. Likewise, because $1 - i$ is a zero, $1 + i$ must be a zero. It follows that $x - (1 - i)$ and $x - (1 + i)$ are both factors of $f(x)$. Therefore,

$$\begin{aligned} f(x) &= (x - 1)[x - (1 + 2i)][x - (1 - 2i)][x - (1 + i)][x - (1 - i)] \\ &= (x - 1)(x^2 - 2x + 5)(x^2 - 2x + 2) \\ &= (x^3 - 3x^2 + 7x - 5)(x^2 - 2x + 2) \\ &= x^5 - 5x^4 + 15x^3 - 25x^2 + 24x - 10 \end{aligned}$$

is a polynomial of the type we seek. Any nonzero real number multiple of $f(x)$ will also be such a polynomial. *Now try Exercise 13.*

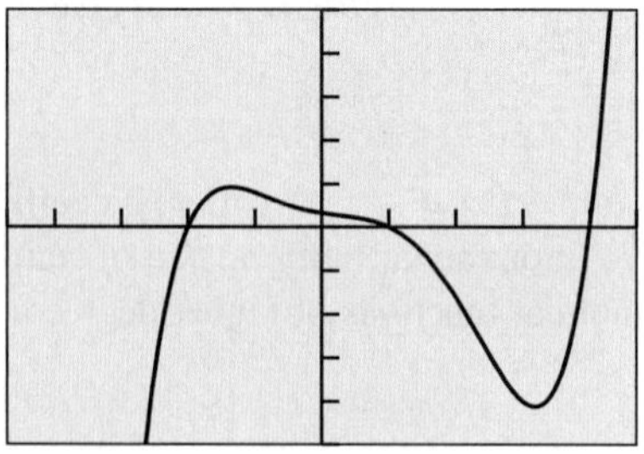

[–4.7, 4.7] by [–125, 125]

FIGURE H.46 $f(x) = x^5 - 3x^4 - 5x^3 + 5x^2 - 6x + 8$ has three real zeros. (Example 4)

EXAMPLE 4 Factoring a Polynomial with Complex Zeros

Find all zeros of $f(x) = x^5 - 3x^4 - 5x^3 + 5x^2 - 6x + 8$, and write $f(x)$ in its linear factorization.

SOLUTION Figure H.46 suggests that the real zeros of f are $x = -2$, $x = 1$, and $x = 4$.

Using synthetic division we can verify these zeros and show that $x^2 + 1$ is a factor of f. So $x = i$ and $x = -i$ are also zeros. Therefore,

$$\begin{aligned} f(x) &= x^5 - 3x^4 - 5x^3 + 5x^2 - 6x + 8 \\ &= (x + 2)(x - 1)(x - 4)(x^2 + 1) \\ &= (x + 2)(x - 1)(x - 4)(x - i)(x + i). \end{aligned}$$

Now try Exercise 29.

Synthetic division can be used with complex number divisors in the same way it is used with real number divisors.

EXAMPLE 5 Finding Complex Zeros

The complex number $z = 1 - 2i$ is a zero of $f(x) = 4x^4 + 17x^2 + 14x + 65$. Find the remaining zeros of $f(x)$, and write it in its linear factorization.

SOLUTION We use synthetic division to show that $f(1 - 2i) = 0$:

$$\begin{array}{r|rrrrr} 1 - 2i & 4 & 0 & 17 & 14 & 65 \\ & & 4 - 8i & -12 - 16i & -27 - 26i & -65 \\ \hline & 4 & 4 - 8i & 5 - 16i & -13 - 26i & 0 \end{array}$$

Thus $1 - 2i$ is a zero of $f(x)$. The conjugate $1 + 2i$ must also be a zero. We use synthetic division on the quotient found above to find the remaining quadratic factor:

$$\begin{array}{r|rrrr} 1 + 2i & 4 & 4 - 8i & 5 - 16i & -13 - 26i \\ & & 4 + 8i & 8 + 16i & 13 + 26i \\ \hline & 4 & 8 & 13 & 0 \end{array}$$

Finally, we use the quadratic formula to find the two zeros of $4x^2 + 8x + 13$:

$$\begin{aligned} x &= \frac{-8 \pm \sqrt{64 - 208}}{8} \\ &= \frac{-8 \pm \sqrt{-144}}{8} \\ &= \frac{-8 \pm 12i}{8} \\ &= -1 \pm \frac{3}{2}i \end{aligned}$$

Thus the four zeros of $f(x)$ are $1 - 2i$, $1 + 2i$, $-1 + (3/2)i$, and $-1 - (3/2)i$. Because the leading coefficient of $f(x)$ is 4, we obtain

$$f(x) = 4[x - (1 - 2i)][x - (1 + 2i)]\left[x - \left(-1 + \tfrac{3}{2}i\right)\right]\left[x - \left(-1 - \tfrac{3}{2}i\right)\right].$$

If we wish to remove fractions in the factors, we can distribute the 4 to get

$$f(x) = [x - (1 - 2i)][x - (1 + 2i)][2x - (-2 + 3i)][2x - (-2 - 3i)].$$

Now try Exercise 33.

Factoring with Real Number Coefficients

Let $f(x)$ be a polynomial function with real coefficients. The Linear Factorization Theorem tells us that $f(x)$ can be factored into the form

$$f(x) = a(x - z_1)(x - z_2) \cdots (x - z_n),$$

where z_i are complex numbers. Recall, however, that nonreal complex zeros occur in conjugate pairs. The product of $x - (a + bi)$ and $x - (a - bi)$ is

$$\begin{aligned}[x - (a + bi)][x - (a - bi)] &= x^2 - (a - bi)x - (a + bi)x + (a + bi)(a - bi) \\ &= x^2 - 2ax + (a^2 + b^2).\end{aligned}$$

So the quadratic expression $x^2 - 2ax + (a^2 + b^2)$, whose coefficients are real numbers, is a factor of $f(x)$. Such a quadratic expression with real coefficients but no real zeros is **irreducible over the reals**. In other words, if we require that the factors of a polynomial have real coefficients, the factorization can be accomplished with linear factors and irreducible quadratic factors.

Factors of a Polynomial with Real Coefficients

Every polynomial function with real coefficients can be written as a product of linear factors and irreducible quadratic factors, each with real coefficients.

EXAMPLE 6 Factoring a Polynomial

Write $f(x) = 3x^5 - 2x^4 + 6x^3 - 4x^2 - 24x + 16$ as a product of linear and irreducible quadratic factors, each with real coefficients.

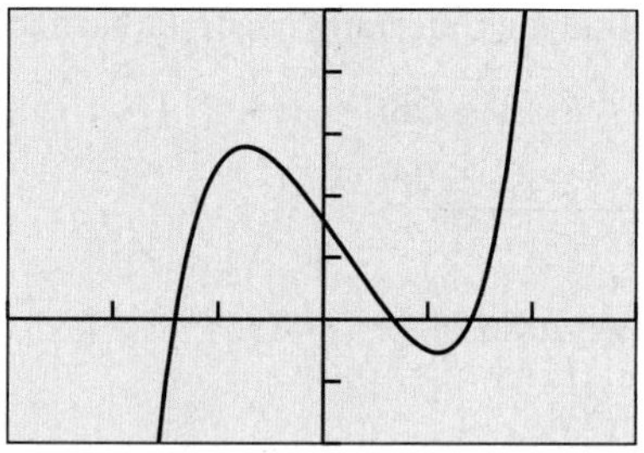

[–3, 3] by [–20, 50]

FIGURE H.47 $f(x) = 3x^5 - 2x^4 + 6x^3 - 4x^2 - 24x + 16$ has three real zeros. (Example 6)

SOLUTION The Rational Zeros Theorem provides the candidates for the rational zeros of f (see page Z7 for the text of the Rational Zeros Theorem). The graph of f in Figure H.47 suggests which candidates to try first. Using synthetic division, we find that $x = 2/3$ is a zero. Thus,

$$\begin{aligned}f(x) &= \left(x - \frac{2}{3}\right)(3x^4 + 6x^2 - 24) \\ &= \left(x - \frac{2}{3}\right)(3)(x^4 + 2x^2 - 8) \\ &= (3x - 2)(x^2 - 2)(x^2 + 4) \\ &= (3x - 2)(x - \sqrt{2})(x + \sqrt{2})(x^2 + 4)\end{aligned}$$

Because the zeros of $x^2 + 4$ are complex, any further factorization would introduce nonreal complex coefficients. We have taken the factorization of f as far as possible, subject to the condition that *each factor has real coefficients.*

Now try Exercise 37.

We have seen that if a polynomial function has real coefficients, then its nonreal complex zeros occur in conjugate pairs. *Because a polynomial of odd degree has an odd number of zeros, it must have at least one zero that is real.*

Polynomial Function of Odd Degree

Every polynomial function of odd degree with real coefficients has at least one real zero.

The function $f(x) = 3x^5 - 2x^4 + 6x^3 - 4x^2 - 24x + 16$ in Example 6 fits the conditions of this theorem, so we know immediately that we are on the right track in searching for at least one real zero.

LESSON H-6 EXERCISES

Exercise numbers with a gray background indicate problems that the authors have designed to be solved *without a calculator.*

In Exercises 1–4, write the polynomial in standard form, and identify the zeros of the function and the x-intercepts of its graph.

1. $f(x) = (x - 3i)(x + 3i)$

2. $f(x) = (x + 2)(x - \sqrt{3}i)(x + \sqrt{3}i)$

3. $f(x) = (x - 1)(x - 1)(x + 2i)(x - 2i)$

4. $f(x) = x(x - 1)(x - 1 - i)(x - 1 + i)$

In Exercises 5–12, write a polynomial function of minimum degree in standard form with real coefficients whose zeros include those listed.

5. i and $-i$

6. $1 - 2i$ and $1 + 2i$

7. 1, $3i$, and $-3i$

8. -4, $1 - i$, and $1 + i$

9. 2, 3, and i

10. -1, 2, and $1 - i$

11. 5 and $3 + 2i$

12. -2 and $1 + 2i$

In Exercises 13–16, write a polynomial function of minimum degree in standard form with real coefficients whose zeros and their multiplicities include those listed.

13. 1 (multiplicity 2), -2 (multiplicity 3)

14. -1 (multiplicity 3), 3 (multiplicity 1)

15. 2 (multiplicity 2), $3 + i$ (multiplicity 1)

16. -1 (multiplicity 2), $-2 - i$ (multiplicity 1)

In Exercises 17–20, match the polynomial function graph to the given zeros and multiplicities.

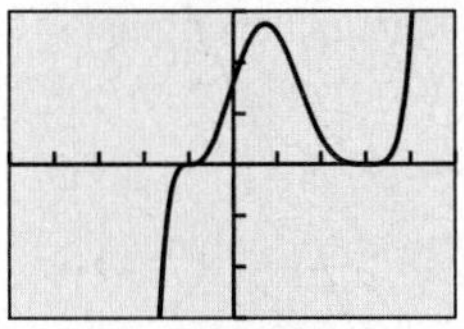

[–5, 5] by [–150, 150]

(a)

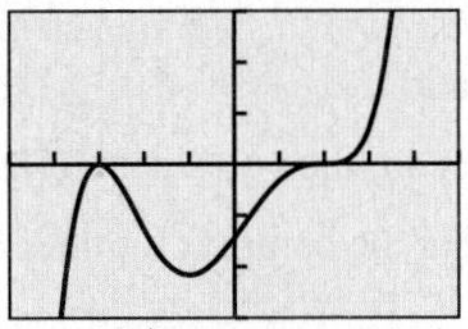

[–5, 5] by [–150, 150]

(b)

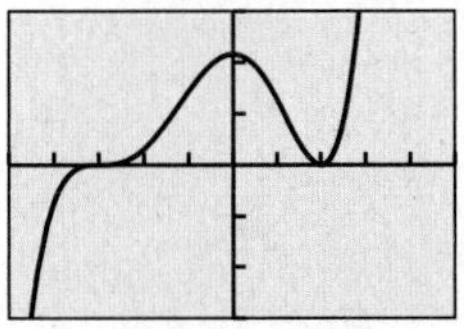

[–5, 5] by [–150, 150]

(c)

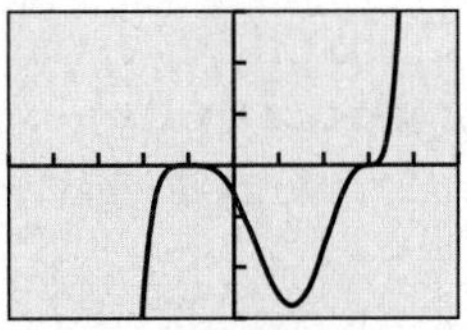

[–5, 5] by [–150, 150]

(d)

17. -3 (multiplicity 2), 2 (multiplicity 3)

18. -3 (multiplicity 3), 2 (multiplicity 2)

19. -1 (multiplicity 4), 3 (multiplicity 3)

20. -1 (multiplicity 3), 3 (multiplicity 4)

In Exercises 21–26, state how many complex and real zeros the function has.

21. $f(x) = x^2 - 2x + 7$

22. $f(x) = x^3 - 3x^2 + x + 1$

23. $f(x) = x^3 - x + 3$

24. $f(x) = x^4 - 2x^2 + 3x - 4$

25. $f(x) = x^4 - 5x^3 + x^2 - 3x + 6$

26. $f(x) = x^5 - 2x^2 - 3x + 6$

In Exercises 27–32, find all of the zeros and write a linear factorization of the function.

27. $f(x) = x^3 + 4x - 5$

28. $f(x) = x^3 - 10x^2 + 44x - 69$

29. $f(x) = x^4 + x^3 + 5x^2 - x - 6$

30. $f(x) = 3x^4 + 8x^3 + 6x^2 + 3x - 2$

31. $f(x) = 6x^4 - 7x^3 - x^2 + 67x - 105$

32. $f(x) = 20x^4 - 148x^3 + 269x^2 - 106x - 195$

In Exercises 33–36, using the given zero, find all of the zeros and write a linear factorization of $f(x)$.

33. $1 + i$ is a zero of $f(x) = x^4 - 2x^3 - x^2 + 6x - 6$.

34. $4i$ is a zero of $f(x) = x^4 + 13x^2 - 48$.

35. $3 - 2i$ is a zero of $f(x) = x^4 - 6x^3 + 11x^2 + 12x - 26$.

36. $1 + 3i$ is a zero of $f(x) = x^4 - 2x^3 + 5x^2 + 10x - 50$.

In Exercises 37–42, write the function as a product of linear and irreducible quadratic factors all with real coefficients.

37. $f(x) = x^3 - x^2 - x - 2$

38. $f(x) = x^3 - x^2 + x - 6$

39. $f(x) = 2x^3 - x^2 + 2x - 3$

40. $f(x) = 3x^3 - 2x^2 + x - 2$

41. $f(x) = x^4 + 3x^3 - 3x^2 + 3x - 4$

42. $f(x) = x^4 - 2x^3 + x^2 - 8x - 12$

In Exercises 43 and 44, use *Archimedes' Principle,* which states that when a sphere of radius r with density d_S is placed in a liquid of density $d_L = 62.5$ lb/ft^3, it will sink to a depth h where

$$\frac{\pi}{3}(3rh^2 - h^3)d_L = \frac{4}{3}\pi r^3 d_S.$$

Find an approximate value for h if:

43. $r = 5$ ft and $d_S = 20$ lb/ft^3.

44. $r = 5$ ft and $d_S = 45$ lb/ft^3.

In Exercises 45–48, answer yes or no. If yes, include an example. If no, give a reason.

45. Writing to Learn Is it possible to find a polynomial of degree 3 with real number coefficients that has -2 as its only real zero?

46. Writing to Learn Is it possible to find a polynomial of degree 3 with real coefficients that has $2i$ as its only nonreal zero?

47. Writing to Learn Is it possible to find a polynomial $f(x)$ of degree 4 with real coefficients that has zeros -3, $1 + 2i$, and $1 - i$?

48. Writing to Learn Is it possible to find a polynomial $f(x)$ of degree 4 with real coefficients that has zeros $1 + 3i$ and $1 - i$?

In Exercises 49 and 50, find the unique polynomial with real coefficients that meets these conditions.

49. Degree 4; zeros at $x = 3$, $x = -1$, and $x = 2 - i$; $f(0) = 30$

50. Degree 4; zeros at $x = 1 - 2i$ and $x = 1 + i$; $f(0) = 20$

51. Sally's distance D from a motion detector is given by the data in Table H.2.

(a) Find a cubic regression model, and graph it together with a scatter plot of the data.

(b) Describe Sally's motion.

(c) Use the cubic regression model to estimate when Sally changes direction. How far is she from the motion detector when she changes direction?

Table H.2 Motion Detector Data

t (sec)	D (m)	t (sec)	D (m)
0.0	3.36	4.5	3.59
0.5	2.61	5.0	4.15
1.0	1.86	5.5	3.99
1.5	1.27	6.0	3.37
2.0	0.91	6.5	2.58
2.5	1.14	7.0	1.93
3.0	1.69	7.5	1.25
3.5	2.37	8.0	0.67
4.0	3.01		

52. Jacob's distance D from a motion detector is given by the data in Table H.3.

(a) Find a quadratic regression model, and graph it together with a scatter plot of the data.

(b) Describe Jacob's motion.

(c) Use the quadratic regression model to estimate when Jacob changes direction. How far is he from the motion detector when he changes direction?

Table H.3 Motion Detector Data

t (sec)	D (m)	t (sec)	D (m)
0.0	4.59	4.5	1.70
0.5	3.92	5.0	2.25
1.0	3.14	5.5	2.84
1.5	2.41	6.0	3.39
2.0	1.73	6.5	4.02
2.5	1.21	7.0	4.54
3.0	0.90	7.5	5.04
3.5	0.99	8.0	5.59
4.0	1.31		

Explorations

53. Group Activity The Powers of 1 + *i*

(a) Selected powers of $1 + i$ are displayed in Table H.4. Find a pattern in the data, and use it to extend the table to power 7, 8, 9, and 10.

(b) Compute $(1 + i)^7$, $(1 + i)^8$, $(1 + i)^9$, and $(1 + i)^{10}$ using the fact that $(1 + i)^6 = -8i$.

(c) Compare your results from parts (a) and (b) and reconcile, if needed.

Table H.4 Powers of 1 + *i*

Power	Real Part	Imaginary Part
0	1	0
1	1	1
2	0	2
3	−2	2
4	−4	0
5	−4	−4
6	0	−8

54. Group Activity The Square Roots of *i*
Let a and b be real numbers such that $(a + bi)^2 = i$.

(a) Expand the left-hand side of the given equation.

(b) Think of the right-hand side of the equation as $0 + 1i$, and separate the real and imaginary parts of the equation to obtain two equations.

(c) Solve for a and b.

(d) Check your answer by substituting them in the original equation.

(e) What are the two square roots of i?

55. Verify that the complex number i is a zero of the polynomial $f(x) = x^3 - ix^2 + 2ix + 2$.

56. Verify that the complex number $-2i$ is a zero of the polynomial $f(x) = x^3 - (2 - i)x^2 + (2 - 2i)x - 4$.

Extending the Ideas

In Exercises 57 and 58, verify that $g(x)$ is a factor of $f(x)$. Then find $h(x)$ so that $f = g \cdot h$.

57. $g(x) = x - i$; $f(x) = x^3 + (3 - i)x^2 - 4ix - 1$

58. $g(x) = x - 1 - i$; $f(x) = x^3 - (1 + i)x^2 + x - 1 - i$

59. Find the three cube roots of 8 by solving $x^3 = 8$.

60. Find the three cube roots of −64 by solving $x^3 = -64$.

H-7 Graphs of Rational Functions

What you'll learn about

- Rational Functions
- Transformations of the Reciprocal Function
- Limits and Asymptotes
- Analyzing Graphs of Rational Functions
- Exploring Relative Humidity

... and why

Rational functions are used in calculus and in scientific applications such as inverse proportions.

Rational Functions

Rational functions are ratios (or quotients) of polynomial functions.

DEFINITION Rational Functions

Let f and g be polynomial functions with $g(x) \neq 0$. Then the function given by

$$r(x) = \frac{f(x)}{g(x)}$$

is a **rational function**.

The domain of a rational function is the set of all real numbers except the zeros of its denominator. Every rational function is continuous on its domain.

EXAMPLE 1 Finding the Domain of a Rational Function

Find the domain of f and use limits to describe its behavior at value(s) of x not in its domain.

$$f(x) = \frac{1}{x-2}$$

SOLUTION The domain of f is all real numbers $x \neq 2$. The graph in Figure H.48 strongly suggests that f has a vertical asymptote at $x = 2$. As x approaches 2 from the left, the values of f decrease without bound. As x approaches 2 from the right, the values of f increase without bound. Using the correct notation, we write

$$\lim_{x \to 2^-} f(x) = -\infty \quad \text{and} \quad \lim_{x \to 2^+} f(x) = \infty.$$

The tables in Figure H.49 support this visual evidence numerically.

Now try Exercise 1.

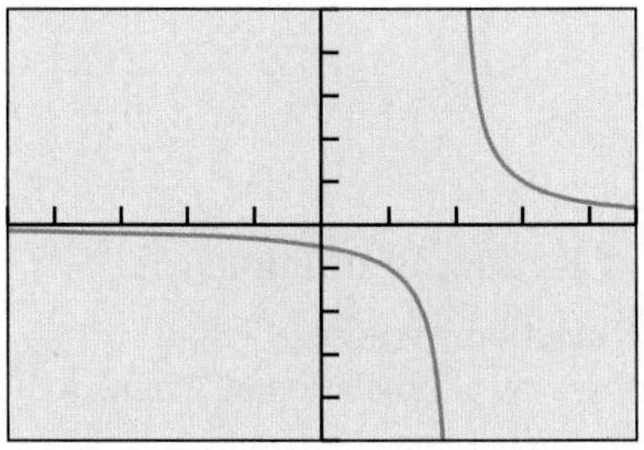

[–4.7, 4.7] by [–5, 5]

FIGURE H.48 The graph of $f(x) = 1/(x-2)$. (Example 1)

(a)

X	Y1	
2	ERROR	
2.01	100	
2.02	50	
2.03	33.333	
2.04	25	
2.05	20	
2.06	16.667	

Y1 = 1/(X–2)

(b)

X	Y1	
2	ERROR	
1.99	–100	
1.98	–50	
1.97	–33.33	
1.96	–25	
1.95	–20	
1.94	–16.67	

Y1 = 1/(X–2)

FIGURE H.49 Table of values for $f(x) = 1/(x-2)$ for values of x (a) to the right of 2, and (b) to the left of 2. (Example 1)

The line $y = b$ is a *horizontal asymptote* of the graph of f if

$$\lim_{x \to -\infty} f(x) = b \quad \text{or} \quad \lim_{x \to \infty} f(x) = b.$$

The line $x = a$ is a *vertical asymptote* of the graph of f if

$$\lim_{x\to a^-} f(x) = \pm\infty \quad \text{or} \quad \lim_{x\to a^+} f(x) = \pm\infty.$$

We can see from Figure H.48 that $\lim_{x\to-\infty} 1/(x-2) = \lim_{x\to\infty} 1/(x-2) = 0$, so the line $y = 0$ is a horizontal asymptote of the graph of $f(x) = 1/(x-2)$. Because $\lim_{x\to2^-} f(x) = -\infty$ and $\lim_{x\to2^+} f(x) = \infty$, the line $x = 2$ is a vertical asymptote of $f(x) = 1/(x-2)$.

Transformations of the Reciprocal Function

One of the simplest rational functions is the reciprocal function

$$f(x) = \frac{1}{x},$$

which is one of the basic functions. It can be used to generate many other rational functions.

Here is what we know about the reciprocal function.

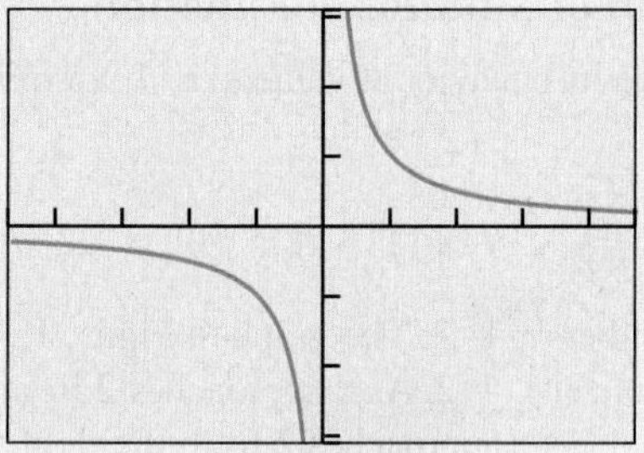

[–4.7, 4.7] by [–3.1, 3.1]

FIGURE H.50 The graph of $f(x) = 1/x$.

BASIC FUNCTION The Reciprocal Function

$f(x) = \dfrac{1}{x}$

Domain: $(-\infty, 0) \cup (0, \infty)$

Range: $(-\infty, 0) \cup (0, \infty)$

Continuity: All $x \neq 0$

Decreasing on $(-\infty, 0)$ and $(0, \infty)$

Symmetric with respect to origin (an odd function)

Unbounded

No local extrema

Horizontal asymptote: $y = 0$

Vertical asymptote: $x = 0$

End behavior: $\lim_{x\to-\infty} f(x) = \lim_{x\to\infty} f(x) = 0$

EXPLORATION 1 Comparing Graphs of Rational Functions

1. Sketch the graph and find an equation for the function g whose graph is obtained from the reciprocal function $f(x) = 1/x$ by a translation of 2 units to the right.
2. Sketch the graph and find an equation for the function h whose graph is obtained from the reciprocal function $f(x) = 1/x$ by a translation of 5 units to the right, followed by a reflection across the x-axis.
3. Sketch the graph and find an equation for the function k whose graph is obtained from the reciprocal function $f(x) = 1/x$ by a translation of 4 units to the left, followed by a vertical stretch by a factor of 3, and finally a translation 2 units down.

The graph of any nonzero rational function of the form

$$g(x) = \frac{ax + b}{cx + d}, \ c \neq 0$$

can be obtained through transformations of the graph of the reciprocal function. If the degree of the numerator is greater than or equal to the degree of the denominator, we can use polynomial division to rewrite the rational function.

EXAMPLE 2 Transforming the Reciprocal Function

Describe how the graph of the given function can be obtained by transforming the graph of the reciprocal function $f(x) = 1/x$. Identify the horizontal and vertical asymptotes and use limits to describe the corresponding behavior. Sketch the graph of the function.

(a) $g(x) = \dfrac{2}{x + 3}$ **(b)** $h(x) = \dfrac{3x - 7}{x - 2}$

SOLUTION

(a) $g(x) = \dfrac{2}{x + 3} = 2\left(\dfrac{1}{x + 3}\right) = 2f(x + 3)$

The graph of g is the graph of the reciprocal function shifted left 3 units and then stretched vertically by a factor of 2. So the lines $x = -3$ and $y = 0$ are vertical and horizontal asymptotes, respectively. Using limits we have $\lim_{x \to \infty} g(x) = \lim_{x \to -\infty} g(x) = 0$, $\lim_{x \to -3^+} g(x) = \infty$, and $\lim_{x \to -3^-} g(x) = -\infty$. The graph is shown in Figure H.51a.

(b) We begin with polynomial division:

$$\begin{array}{r} 3 \\ x - 2 \overline{)3x - 7} \\ \underline{3x - 6} \\ -1 \end{array}$$

So, $h(x) = \dfrac{3x - 7}{x - 2} = 3 - \dfrac{1}{x - 2} = -f(x - 2) + 3.$

Thus the graph of h is the graph of the reciprocal function translated 2 units to the right, followed by a reflection across the x-axis, and then translated 3 units up. (Note that the reflection must be executed before the vertical translation.) So the lines $x = 2$ and $y = 3$ are vertical and horizontal asymptotes, respectively. Using limits we have $\lim_{x \to \infty} h(x) = \lim_{x \to -\infty} h(x) = 3$, $\lim_{x \to 2^+} g(x) = -\infty$, and $\lim_{x \to 2^-} g(x) = \infty$. The graph is shown in Figure H.51b.

Now try Exercise 5.

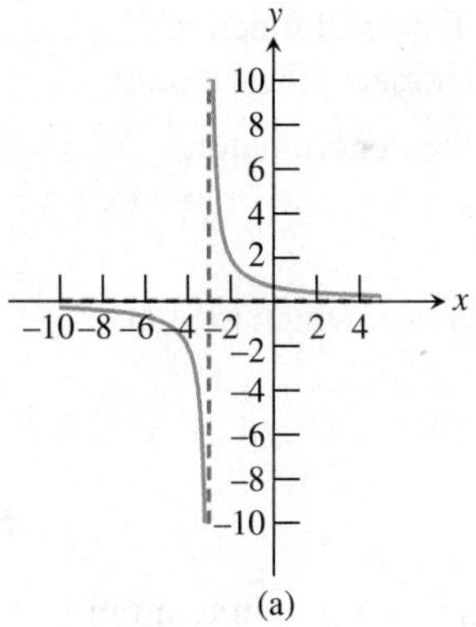

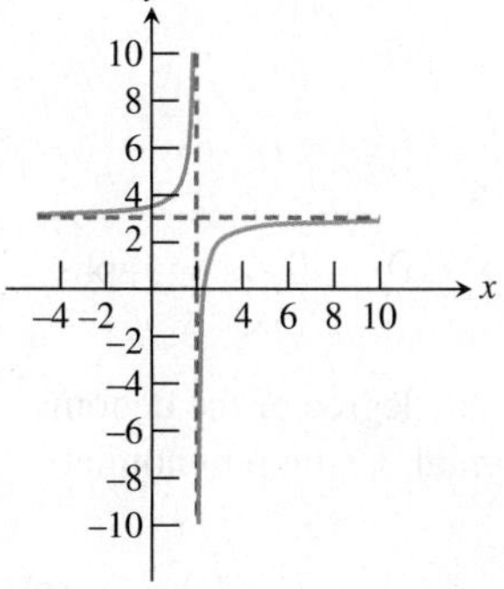

FIGURE H.51 The graphs of (a) $g(x) = 2/(x + 3)$ and (b) $h(x) = (3x - 7)/(x - 2)$, with asymptotes shown in red.

Limits and Asymptotes

In Example 2 we found asymptotes by translating the known asymptotes of the reciprocal function. In Example 3, we use graphing and algebra to find an asymptote.

EXAMPLE 3 Finding Asymptotes

Find the horizontal and vertical asymptotes of $f(x) = (x^2 + 2)/(x^2 + 1)$. Use limits to describe the corresponding behavior of f.

SOLUTION

Solve Graphically

The graph of f in Figure H.52 suggests that

$$\lim_{x \to \infty} f(x) = \lim_{x \to -\infty} f(x) = 1$$

and that there are no vertical asymptotes. The horizontal asymptote is $y = 1$.

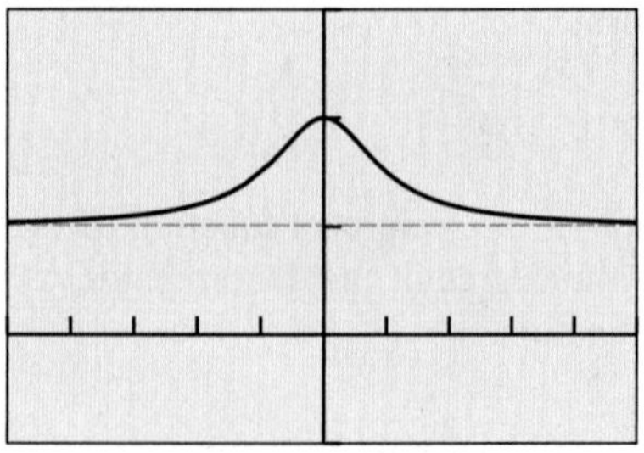

[–5, 5] by [–1, 3]

FIGURE H.52 The graph of $f(x) = (x^2 + 2)/(x^2 + 1)$ with its horizontal asymptote $y = 1$.

Solve Algebraically

Because the denominator $x^2 + 1 > 0$, the domain of f is all real numbers. So there are no vertical asymptotes. Using polynomial long division, we find that

$$f(x) = \frac{x^2 + 2}{x^2 + 1} = 1 + \frac{1}{x^2 + 1}.$$

When the value of $|x|$ is large, the denominator $x^2 + 1$ is a large positive number, and $1/(x^2 + 1)$ is a small positive number, getting closer to zero as $|x|$ increases. Therefore,

$$\lim_{x \to \infty} f(x) = \lim_{x \to -\infty} f(x) = 1,$$

so $y = 1$ is indeed a horizontal asymptote. *Now try Exercise 19.*

Example 3 shows the connection between the end behavior of a rational function and its horizontal asymptote. We now generalize this relationship and summarize other features of the graph of a rational function:

Graph of a Rational Function

The graph of $y = f(x)/g(x) = (a_n x^n + \cdots)/(b_m x^m + \cdots)$ has the following characteristics:

1. **End behavior asymptote:**

   If $n < m$, the end behavior asymptote is the horizontal asymptote $y = 0$.

   If $n = m$, the end behavior asymptote is the horizontal asymptote $y = a_n/b_m$.

   If $n > m$, the end behavior asymptote is the quotient polynomial function $y = q(x)$, where $f(x) = g(x)q(x) + r(x)$. There is no horizontal asymptote.
2. **Vertical asymptotes:** These occur at the real zeros of the denominator, provided that the zeros are not also zeros of the numerator of equal or greater multiplicity.
3. ***x*-intercepts:** These occur at the real zeros of the numerator, which are not also zeros of the denominator.
4. ***y*-intercept:** This is the value of $f(0)$, if defined.

It is a good idea to find all of the asymptotes and intercepts when graphing a rational function. If the end behavior asymptote of a rational function is a slant line, we call it a **slant asymptote**, as illustrated in Example 4.

EXAMPLE 4 Graphing a Rational Function

Find the asymptotes and intercepts of the function $f(x) = x^3/(x^2 - 9)$ and graph the function.

SOLUTION The degree of the numerator is greater than the degree of the denominator, so the end behavior asymptote is the quotient polynomial. Using polynomial long division, we obtain

$$f(x) = \frac{x^3}{x^2 - 9} = x + \frac{9x}{x^2 - 9}.$$

So the quotient polynomial is $q(x) = x$, a slant asymptote. Factoring the denominator,

$$x^2 - 9 = (x - 3)(x + 3),$$

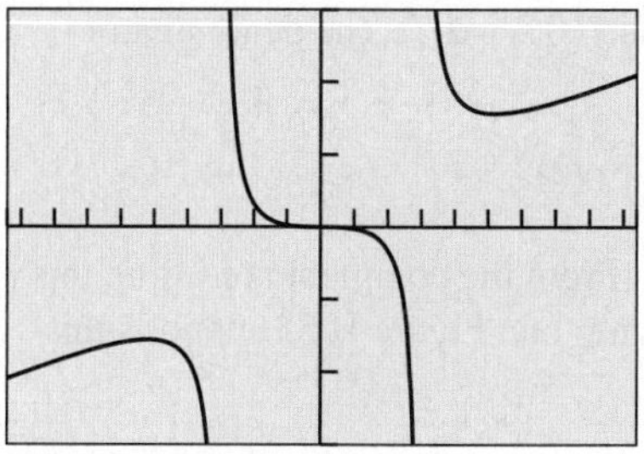

[–9.4, 9.4] by [–15, 15]

(a)

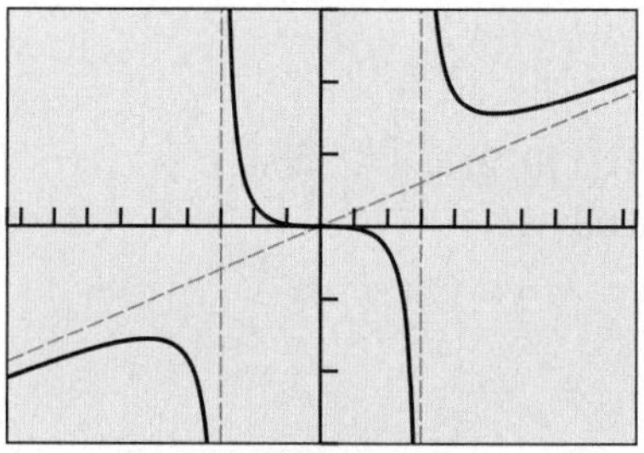

[–9.4, 9.4] by [–15, 15]

(b)

FIGURE H.53 The graph of $f(x) = x^3/(x^2 - 9)$ (a) by itself and (b) with its asymptotes. (Example 4)

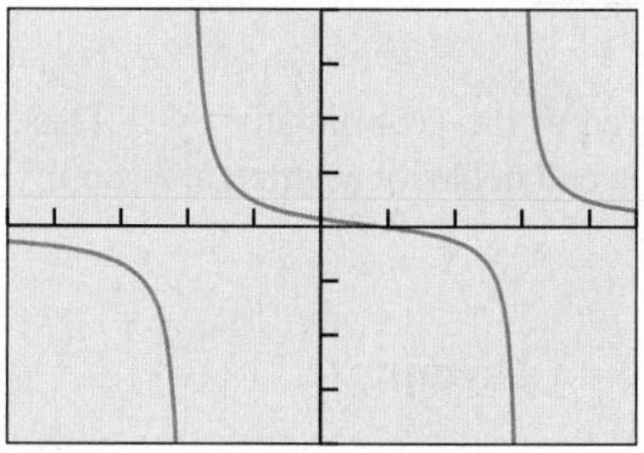

[–4.7, 4.7] by [–4, 4]

FIGURE H.54 The graph of $f(x) = (x - 1)/(x^2 - x - 6)$. (Example 5)

shows that the zeros of the denominator are $x = 3$ and $x = -3$. Consequently, $x = 3$ and $x = -3$ are the vertical asymptotes of f. The only zero of the numerator is 0, so $f(0) = 0$, and thus we see that the point (0, 0) is the only x-intercept and the y-intercept of the graph of f.

The graph of f in Figure H.53a passes through (0, 0) and suggests the vertical asymptotes $x = 3$ and $x = -3$ and the slant asymptote $y = q(x) = x$. Figure H.53b shows the graph of f with its asymptotes overlaid. *Now try Exercise 29.*

Analyzing Graphs of Rational Functions

Because the degree of the numerator of the rational function in Example 5 is less than the degree of the denominator, we know that the graph of the function has $y = 0$ as a horizontal asymptote.

EXAMPLE 5 Analyzing the Graph of a Rational Function

Find the intercepts and asymptotes, use limits to describe the behavior at the vertical asymptotes, and analyze and draw the graph of the rational function

$$f(x) = \frac{x - 1}{x^2 - x - 6}.$$

SOLUTION The numerator is zero when $x = 1$, so the x-intercept is 1. Because $f(0) = 1/6$, the y-intercept is 1/6. The denominator factors as

$$x^2 - x - 6 = (x - 3)(x + 2),$$

so there are vertical asymptotes at $x = -2$ and $x = 3$. From the comment preceding this example we know that the horizontal asymptote is $y = 0$. Figure H.54 supports this information and allows us to conclude that

$$\lim_{x \to -2^-} f(x) = -\infty, \ \lim_{x \to -2^+} f(x) = \infty, \ \lim_{x \to 3^-} f(x) = -\infty, \text{ and } \lim_{x \to 3^+} f(x) = \infty.$$

Domain: $(-\infty, -2) \cup (-2, 3) \cup (3, \infty)$
Range: All reals
Continuity: All $x \neq -2, 3$
Decreasing on $(-\infty, -2)$, $(-2, 3)$, and $(3, \infty)$
Not symmetric
Unbounded
No local extrema
Horizontal asymptotes: $y = 0$
Vertical asymptotes: $x = -2, x = 3$
End behavior: $\lim_{x \to -\infty} f(x) = \lim_{x \to \infty} f(x) = 0$ *Now try Exercise 39.*

The degrees of the numerator and denominator of the rational function in Example 6 are equal. Thus, we know that the graph of the function has $y = 2$, the quotient of the leading coefficients, as its end behavior asymptote.

EXAMPLE 6 Analyzing the Graph of a Rational Function

Find the intercepts, analyze, and draw the graph of the rational function

$$f(x) = \frac{2x^2 - 2}{x^2 - 4}.$$

SOLUTION The numerator factors as

$$2x^2 - 2 = 2(x^2 - 1) = 2(x + 1)(x - 1),$$

(continued)

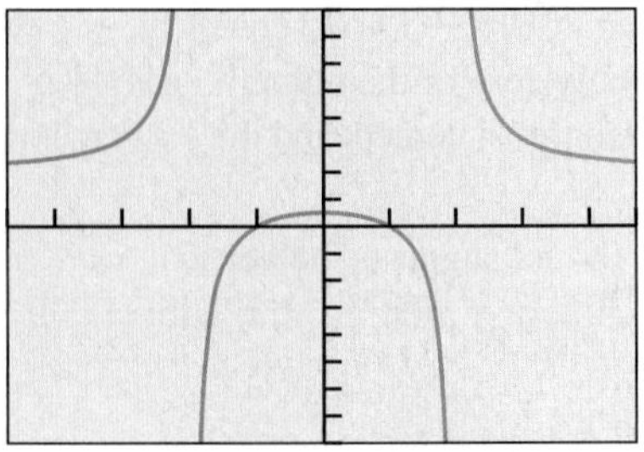

[–4.7, 4.7] by [–8, 8]

FIGURE H.55 The graph of $f(x) = (2x^2 - 2)/(x^2 - 4)$. It can be shown that f takes on no value between 1/2, the y-intercept, and 2, the horizontal asymptote. (Example 6)

so the x-intercepts are -1 and 1. The y-intercept is $f(0) = 1/2$. The denominator factors as

$$x^2 - 4 = (x + 2)(x - 2),$$

so the vertical asymptotes are $x = -2$ and $x = 2$. From the comment preceding this example we know that $y = 2$ is the horizontal asymptote. Figure H.55 supports this information and allows us to conclude that

$$\lim_{x \to -2^-} f(x) = \infty, \lim_{x \to -2^+} f(x) = -\infty, \lim_{x \to 2^-} f(x) = -\infty, \lim_{x \to 2^+} f(x) = \infty.$$

Domain: $(-\infty, -2) \cup (-2, 2) \cup (2, \infty)$
Range: $(-\infty, 1/2] \cup (2, \infty)$
Continuity: All $x \neq -2, 2$
Increasing on $(-\infty, -2)$ and $(-2, 0]$; decreasing on $[0, 2)$ and $(2, \infty)$
Symmetric with respect to the y-axis (an even function)
Unbounded
Local maximum of 1/2 at $x = 0$
Horizontal asymptotes: $y = 2$
Vertical asymptotes: $x = -2, x = 2$
End behavior: $\lim_{x \to -\infty} f(x) = \lim_{x \to \infty} f(x) = 2$ *Now try Exercise 41.*

In Examples 7 and 8 we will investigate the rational function

$$f(x) = \frac{x^3 - 3x^2 + 3x + 1}{x - 1}.$$

The degree of the numerator of f exceeds the degree of the denominator by 2. Thus, there is no horizontal asymptote. We will see that the end behavior asymptote is a polynomial of degree 2.

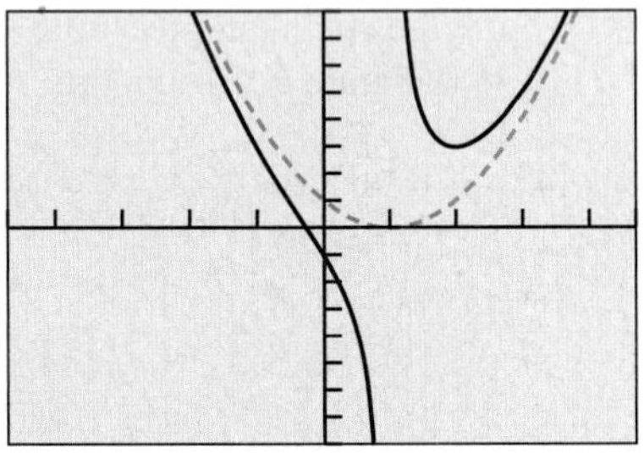

[–4.7, 4.7] by [–8, 8]

FIGURE H.56 The graph of $f(x) = (x^3 - 3x^2 + 3x + 1)/(x - 1)$ as a solid black line and its end behavior asymptote $y = x^2 - 2x + 1$ as a dashed blue line. (Examples 7 and 8)

EXAMPLE 7 Finding an End Behavior Asymptote

Find the end behavior asymptote of

$$f(x) = \frac{x^3 - 3x^2 + 3x + 1}{x - 1}$$

and graph it together with f in two windows:

(a) one showing the details around the vertical asymptote of f,

(b) one showing a graph of f that resembles its end behavior asymptote.

SOLUTION The graph of f has a vertical asymptote at $x = 1$. Divide $x^3 - 3x^2 + 3x + 1$ by $x - 1$ to show that

$$f(x) = \frac{x^3 - 3x^2 + 3x + 1}{x - 1} = x^2 - 2x + 1 + \frac{2}{x - 1}.$$

The end behavior asymptote of f is $y = x^2 - 2x + 1$.

(a) The graph of f in Figure H.56 shows the details around the vertical asymptote. We have also overlaid the graph of its end behavior asymptote as a dashed line.

(b) If we draw the graph of $f(x) = (x^3 - 3x^2 + 3x + 1)/(x - 1)$ and its end behavior asymptote $y = x^2 - 2x + 1$ in a large enough viewing window, the two graphs will appear to be identical (Figure H.57). *Now try Exercise 47.*

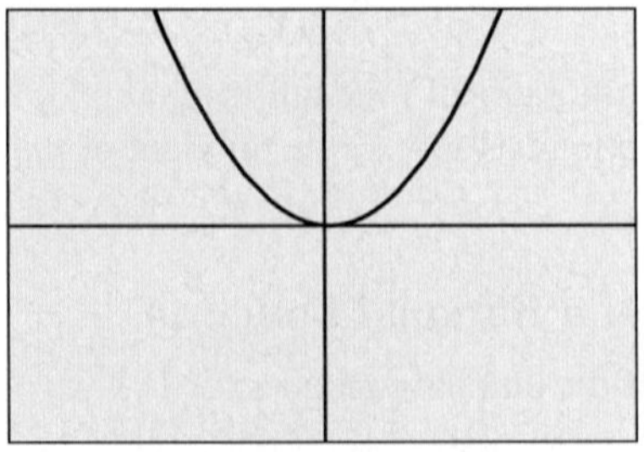

[–40, 40] by [–500, 500]

FIGURE H.57 The graphs of $f(x) = (x^3 - 3x^2 + 3x + 1)/(x - 1)$ and its end behavior asymptote $y = x^2 - 2x + 1$ appear to be identical. (Example 7)

EXAMPLE 8 Analyzing the Graph of a Rational Function

Find the intercepts, analyze, and draw the graph of the rational function

$$f(x) = \frac{x^3 - 3x^2 + 3x + 1}{x - 1}.$$

SOLUTION f has only one x-intercept and we can use the graph of f in Figure H.56 to show that it is about -0.26. The y-intercept is $f(0) = -1$. The vertical asymptote is $x = 1$ as we have seen. We know that the graph of f does not have a horizontal asymptote, and from Example 7 we know that the end behavior asymptote is $y = x^2 - 2x + 1$. We can also use Figure H.56 to show that f has a local minimum of 3 at $x = 2$. Figure H.56 supports this information and allows us to conclude that

$$\lim_{x\to 1^-} f(x) = -\infty \text{ and } \lim_{x\to 1^+} f(x) = \infty.$$

Domain: All $x \neq 1$
Range: All reals
Continuity: All $x \neq 1$
Decreasing on $(-\infty, 1)$ and $(1, 2]$; increasing on $[2, \infty)$
Not symmetric
Unbounded
Local minimum of 3 at $x = 2$
No horizontal asymptotes; end behavior asymptote: $y = x^2 - 2x + 1$
Vertical asymptote: $x = 1$
End behavior: $\lim_{x\to -\infty} f(x) = \lim_{x\to\infty} f(x) = \infty$

Now try Exercise 55.

Exploring Relative Humidity

The phrase *relative humidity* is familiar from everyday weather reports. **Relative humidity** is the ratio of constant vapor pressure to saturated vapor pressure. So, relative humidity is inversely proportional to saturated vapor pressure.

LESSON H-7 EXERCISES

Exercise numbers with a gray background indicate problems that the authors have designed to be solved *without a calculator.*

In Exercises 1–4, find the domain of the function f. Use limits to describe the behavior of f at value(s) of x not in its domain.

1. $f(x) = \frac{1}{x + 3}$
2. $f(x) = \frac{-3}{x - 1}$
3. $f(x) = \frac{-1}{x^2 - 4}$
4. $f(x) = \frac{2}{x^2 - 1}$

In Exercises 5–10, describe how the graph of the given function can be obtained by transforming the graph of the reciprocal function $g(x) = 1/x$. Identify the horizontal and vertical asymptotes and use limits to describe the corresponding behavior. Sketch the graph of the function.

5. $f(x) = \frac{1}{x - 3}$
6. $f(x) = -\frac{2}{x + 5}$
7. $f(x) = \frac{2x - 1}{x + 3}$
8. $f(x) = \frac{3x - 2}{x - 1}$
9. $f(x) = \frac{5 - 2x}{x + 4}$
10. $f(x) = \frac{4 - 3x}{x - 5}$

In Exercises 11–14, evaluate the limit based on the graph of f shown.

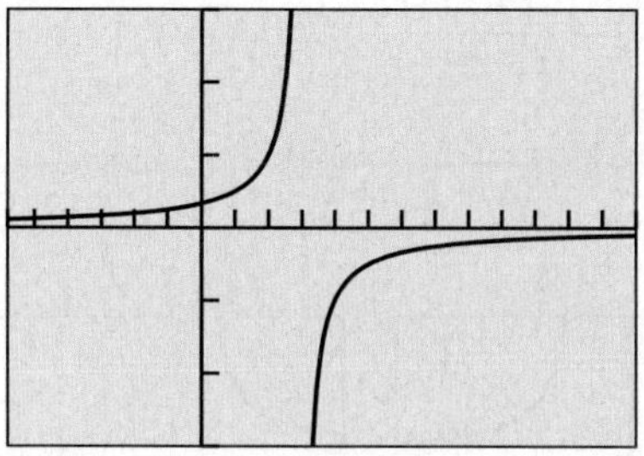

[–5.8, 13] by [–3, 3]

11. $\lim_{x\to 3^-} f(x)$
12. $\lim_{x\to 3^+} f(x)$
13. $\lim_{x\to\infty} f(x)$
14. $\lim_{x\to -\infty} f(x)$

In Exercises 15–18, evaluate the limit based on the graph of f shown.

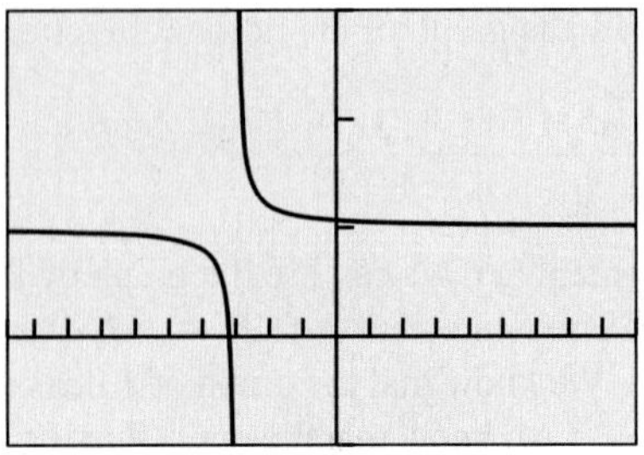

[–9.8, 9] by [–5, 15]

15. $\lim_{x \to -3^+} f(x)$

16. $\lim_{x \to -3^-} f(x)$

17. $\lim_{x \to -\infty} f(x)$

18. $\lim_{x \to \infty} f(x)$

In Exercises 19–22, find the horizontal and vertical asymptotes of $f(x)$. Use limits to describe the corresponding behavior.

19. $f(x) = \dfrac{2x^2 - 1}{x^2 + 3}$

20. $f(x) = \dfrac{3x^2}{x^2 + 1}$

21. $f(x) = \dfrac{2x + 1}{x^2 - x}$

22. $f(x) = \dfrac{x - 3}{x^2 + 3x}$

In Exercises 23–30, find the asymptotes and intercepts of the function, and graph the function.

23. $g(x) = \dfrac{x - 2}{x^2 - 2x - 3}$

24. $g(x) = \dfrac{x + 2}{x^2 + 2x - 3}$

25. $h(x) = \dfrac{2}{x^3 - x}$

26. $h(x) = \dfrac{3}{x^3 - 4x}$

27. $f(x) = \dfrac{2x^2 + x - 2}{x^2 - 1}$

28. $g(x) = \dfrac{-3x^2 + x + 12}{x^2 - 4}$

29. $f(x) = \dfrac{x^2 - 2x + 3}{x + 2}$

30. $g(x) = \dfrac{x^2 - 3x - 7}{x + 3}$

In Exercises 31–36, match the rational function with its graph. Identify the viewing window and the scale used on each axis.

31. $f(x) = \dfrac{1}{x - 4}$

32. $f(x) = -\dfrac{1}{x + 3}$

33. $f(x) = 2 + \dfrac{3}{x - 1}$

34. $f(x) = 1 + \dfrac{1}{x + 3}$

35. $f(x) = -1 + \dfrac{1}{4 - x}$

36. $f(x) = 3 - \dfrac{2}{x - 1}$

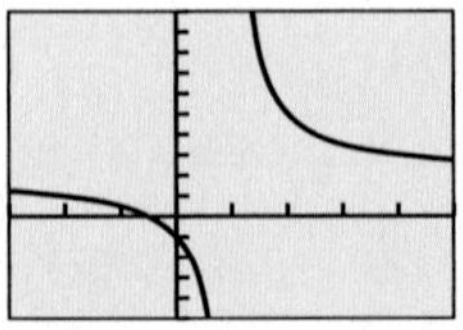

(a)

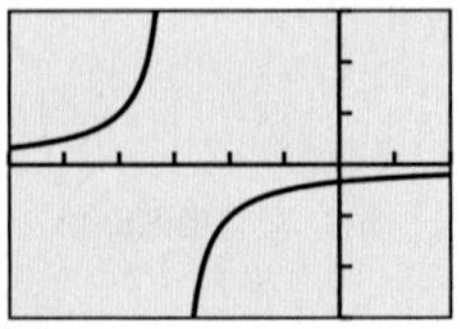

(b)

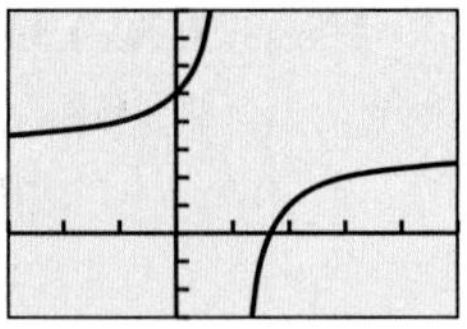

(c)

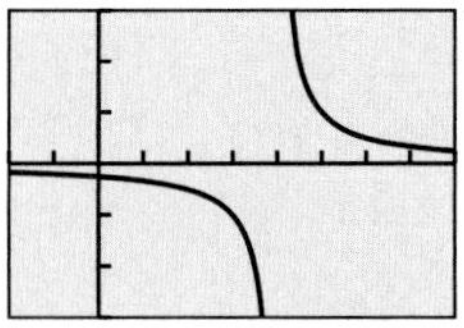

(d)

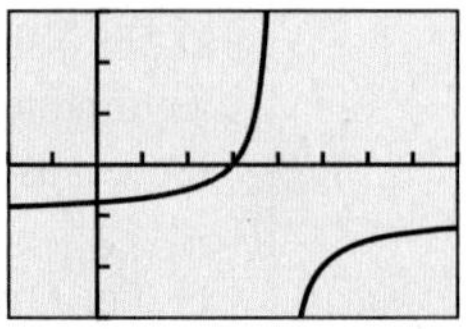

(e)

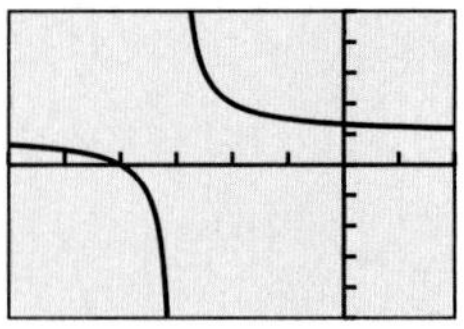

(f)

In Exercises 37–44, find the intercepts and asymptotes, use limits to describe the behavior at the vertical asymptotes, and analyze and draw the graph of the given rational function.

37. $f(x) = \dfrac{2}{2x^2 - x - 3}$

38. $g(x) = \dfrac{2}{x^2 + 4x + 3}$

39. $h(x) = \dfrac{x - 1}{x^2 - x - 12}$

40. $k(x) = \dfrac{x + 1}{x^2 - 3x - 10}$

41. $f(x) = \dfrac{x^2 + x - 2}{x^2 - 9}$

42. $g(x) = \dfrac{x^2 - x - 2}{x^2 - 2x - 8}$

43. $h(x) = \dfrac{x^2 + 2x - 3}{x + 2}$

44. $k(x) = \dfrac{x^2 - x - 2}{x - 3}$

In Exercises 45–50, find the end behavior asymptote of the given rational function f and graph it together with f in two windows:

(a) One showing the details around the vertical asymptote(s) of f.

(b) One showing a graph of f that resembles its end behavior asymptote.

45. $f(x) = \dfrac{x^2 - 2x + 3}{x - 5}$

46. $f(x) = \dfrac{2x^2 + 2x - 3}{x + 3}$

47. $f(x) = \dfrac{x^3 - x^2 + 1}{x + 2}$

48. $f(x) = \dfrac{x^3 + 1}{x - 1}$

49. $f(x) = \dfrac{x^4 - 2x + 1}{x - 2}$

50. $f(x) = \dfrac{x^5 + 1}{x^2 + 1}$

In Exercises 51–56, find the intercepts, analyze, and graph the given rational function.

51. $f(x) = \dfrac{3x^2 - 2x + 4}{x^2 - 4x + 5}$

52. $g(x) = \dfrac{4x^2 + 2x}{x^2 - 4x + 8}$

53. $h(x) = \dfrac{x^3 - 1}{x - 2}$

54. $k(x) = \dfrac{x^3 - 2}{x + 2}$

55. $f(x) = \dfrac{x^3 - 2x^2 + x - 1}{2x - 1}$

56. $g(x) = \dfrac{2x^3 - 2x^2 - x + 5}{x - 2}$

In Exercises 57–62, find the intercepts, vertical asymptotes, and end behavior asymptote, and graph the function together with its end behavior asymptote.

57. $h(x) = \dfrac{x^4 + 1}{x + 1}$

58. $k(x) = \dfrac{2x^5 + x^2 - x + 1}{x^2 - 1}$

59. $f(x) = \dfrac{x^5 - 1}{x + 2}$

60. $g(x) = \dfrac{x^5 + 1}{x - 1}$

61. $h(x) = \dfrac{2x^3 - 3x + 2}{x^3 - 1}$

62. $k(x) = \dfrac{3x^3 + x - 4}{x^3 + 1}$

Explorations

63. Group Activity *Work in groups of two.* Compare the functions $f(x) = \dfrac{x^2 - 9}{x - 3}$ and $g(x) = x + 3$.

(a) Are the domains equal?

(b) Does f have a vertical asymptote? Explain.

(c) Explain why the graphs appear to be identical.

(d) Are the functions identical?

64. Group Activity Explain why the functions are identical or not. Include the graphs and a comparison of the functions' asymptotes, intercepts, and domain.

(a) $f(x) = \dfrac{x^2 + x - 2}{x - 1}$ and $g(x) = x + 2$

(b) $f(x) = \dfrac{x^2 - 1}{x + 1}$ and $g(x) = x - 1$

(c) $f(x) = \dfrac{x^2 - 1}{x^3 - x^2 - x + 1}$ and $g(x) = \dfrac{1}{x - 1}$

(d) $f(x) = \dfrac{x - 1}{x^2 + x - 2}$ and $g(x) = \dfrac{1}{x + 2}$

65. Boyle's Law This ideal gas law states that the volume of an enclosed gas at a fixed temperature varies inversely as the pressure.

(a) Writing to Learn Explain why Boyle's Law yields both a rational function model and a power function model.

(b) Which power functions are also rational functions?

(c) If the pressure of a 2.59-L sample of nitrogen gas at a temperature of 291 K is 0.866 atm, what would the volume be at a pressure of 0.532 atm if the temperature does not change?

66. Light Intensity Aileen and Malachy gathered the data in Table 2.19 using a 75-watt lightbulb and a Calculator-Based Laboratory™ (CBL™) with a light-intensity probe.

(a) Draw a scatter plot of the data in Table H.5.

(b) Find an equation for the data assuming it has the form $f(x) = k/x^2$ for some constant k. Explain your method for choosing k.

(c) Superimpose the regression curve on the scatter plot.

(d) Use the regression model to predict the light intensity at distances of 2.2 m and 4.4 m.

Table H.5 Light-Intensity Data for a 75-W Lightbulb

Distance (m)	Intensity (W/m^2)
1.0	6.09
1.5	2.51
2.0	1.56
2.5	1.08
3.0	0.74

Extending the Ideas

In Exercises 67–70, graph the function. Express the function as a piecewise-defined function without absolute value, and use the result to confirm the graph's asymptotes and intercepts algebraically.

67. $h(x) = \dfrac{2x - 3}{|x| + 2}$

68. $h(x) = \dfrac{3x + 5}{|x| + 3}$

69. $f(x) = \dfrac{5 - 3x}{|x| + 4}$

70. $f(x) = \dfrac{2 - 2x}{|x| + 1}$

71. Describe how the graph of a nonzero rational function

$$f(x) = \frac{ax + b}{cx + d},\ c \neq 0$$

can be obtained from the graph of $y = 1/x$. (*Hint:* Use long division.)

72. Writing to Learn Let $f(x) = 1 + 1/(x - 1/x)$ and $g(x) = (x^3 + x^2 - x)/(x^3 - x)$. Does $f = g$? Support your answer by making a comparative analysis of all of the features of f and g, including asymptotes, intercepts, and domain.

H-8 Solving Inequalities in One Variable

What you'll learn about

- Polynomial Inequalities
- Rational Inequalities
- Other Inequalities
- Applications

... and why

Designing containers as well as other types of applications often require that an inequality be solved.

Polynomial Inequalities

A polynomial inequality takes the form $f(x) > 0$, $f(x) \geq 0$, $f(x) < 0$, $f(x) \leq 0$ or $f(x) \neq 0$, where $f(x)$ is a polynomial. There is a fundamental connection between inequalities and the positive or negative sign of the corresponding expression $f(x)$:

- To solve $f(x) > 0$ is to find the values of x that make $f(x)$ *positive.*
- To solve $f(x) < 0$ is to find the values of x that make $f(x)$ *negative.*

If the expression $f(x)$ is a product, we can determine its sign by determining the sign of each of its factors. Example 1 illustrates that a polynomial function changes sign only at its real zeros of odd multiplicity.

EXAMPLE 1 Finding Where a Polynomial Is Zero, Positive, or Negative

Let $f(x) = (x + 3)(x^2 + 1)(x - 4)^2$. Determine the real number values of x that cause $f(x)$ to be **(a)** zero, **(b)** positive, **(c)** negative.

SOLUTION We begin by verbalizing our analysis of the problem:

(a) The real zeros of $f(x)$ are -3 (with multiplicity 1) and 4 (with multiplicity 2). So $f(x)$ is zero if $x = -3$ or $x = 4$.

(b) The factor $x^2 + 1$ is positive for all real numbers x. The factor $(x - 4)^2$ is positive for all real numbers x except $x = 4$, which makes $(x - 4)^2 = 0$. The factor $x + 3$ is positive if and only if $x > -3$. So $f(x)$ is positive if $x > -3$ and $x \neq 4$.

(c) By process of elimination, $f(x)$ is negative if $x < -3$.

This verbal reasoning process is aided by the following **sign chart**, which shows the x-axis as a number line with the real zeros displayed as the locations of potential sign change and the factors displayed with their sign value in the corresponding interval:

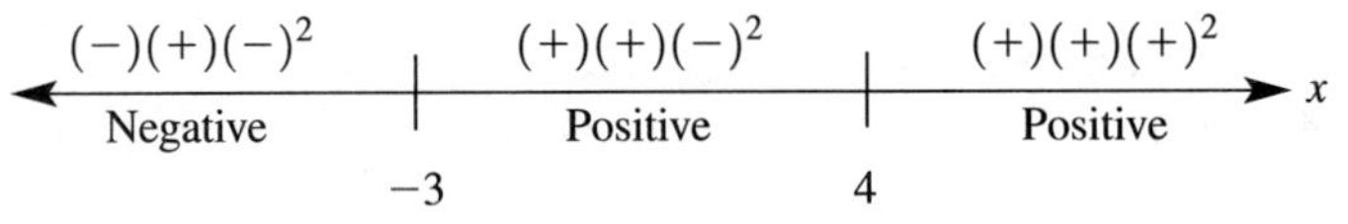

Figure H.58 supports our findings because the graph of f is above the x-axis for x in $(-3, 4)$ or $(4, \infty)$, is on the x-axis for $x = -3$ or $x = 4$, and is below the x-axis for x in $(-\infty, -3)$. *Now try Exercise 1.*

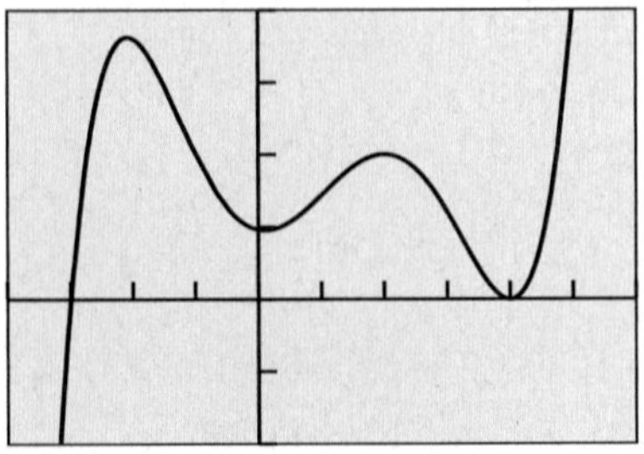

[–4, 6] by [–100, 200]

FIGURE H.58 The graph of $f(x) = (x + 3)(x^2 + 1)(x - 4)^2$. (Example 1)

Our work in Example 1 allows us to report the solutions of four polynomial inequalities:

- The solution of $(x + 3)(x^2 + 1)(x - 4)^2 > 0$ is $(-3, 4) \cup (4, \infty)$.
- The solution of $(x + 3)(x^2 + 1)(x - 4)^2 \geq 0$ is $[-3, \infty)$.
- The solution of $(x + 3)(x^2 + 1)(x - 4)^2 < 0$ is $(-\infty, -3)$.
- The solution of $(x + 3)(x^2 + 1)(x - 4)^2 \leq 0$ is $(-\infty, -3] \cup \{4\}$.

Example 1 illustrates some important general characteristics of polynomial functions and polynomial inequalities. The polynomial function $f(x) = (x + 3)(x^2 + 1)(x - 4)^2$ in Example 1 and Figure H.58—

- changes sign at its real zero of odd multiplicity $(x = -3)$;

- touches the x-axis but does not change sign at its real zero of even multiplicity ($x = 4$);
- has no x-intercepts or sign changes at its nonreal complex zeros associated with the irreducible quadratic factor $(x^2 + 1)$.

The real zeros and their multiplicity together with the end behavior of a polynomial function give us sufficient information about the polynomial to sketch its graph well enough to obtain a correct sign chart, as shown in Figure H.59.

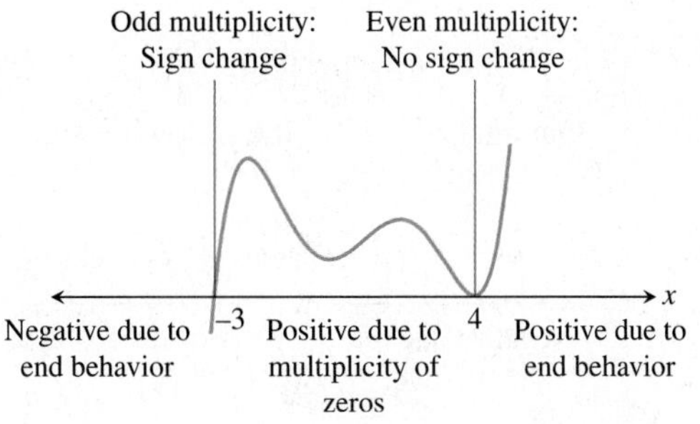

FIGURE H.59 The sign chart and graph of $f(x) = (x + 3)(x^2 + 1)(x - 4)^2$ overlaid.

EXPLORATION 1 Sketching a Graph of a Polynomial from Its Sign Chart

Use your knowledge of end behavior and multiplicity of real zeros to create a sign chart and sketch the graph of the function. Check your sign chart using the factor method of Example 1. Then check your sketch using a grapher.

1. $f(x) = 2(x - 2)^3(x + 3)^2$
2. $f(x) = -(x + 2)^4(x + 1)(2x^2 + x + 1)$
3. $f(x) = 3(x - 2)^2(x + 4)^3(-x^2 - 2)$

So far in this section all of the polynomials have been presented in factored form and all of the inequalities have had zero on one of the sides. Examples 2 and 3 show us how to solve polynomial inequalities when they are not given in such a convenient form.

Worth Trying

You may wish to make a table or graph for the function f in Example 2 to support the analytical approach used.

EXAMPLE 2 Solving a Polynomial Inequality Analytically

Solve $2x^3 - 7x^2 - 10x + 24 > 0$ analytically.

SOLUTION Let $f(x) = 2x^3 - 7x^2 - 10x + 24$. The Rational Zeros Theorem yields several possible rational zeros of f for factoring purposes:

$$\pm 1, \pm 2, \pm 3, \pm 4, \pm 6, \pm 8, \pm 12, \pm 24, \pm\frac{1}{2}, \pm\frac{3}{2}$$

A table or graph of f can suggest which of these candidates to try. In this case, $x = 4$ is a rational zero of f, as the following synthetic division shows:

$$\begin{array}{r|rrrr} 4 & 2 & -7 & -10 & 24 \\ & & 8 & 4 & -24 \\ \hline & 2 & 1 & -6 & 0 \end{array}$$

The synthetic division lets us start the factoring process, which can then be completed using basic factoring methods:

$$\begin{aligned} f(x) &= 2x^3 - 7x^2 - 10x + 24 \\ &= (x - 4)(2x^2 + x - 6) \\ &= (x - 4)(2x - 3)(x + 2) \end{aligned}$$

So the zeros of f are 4, 3/2, and -2. They are all real and all of multiplicity 1, so each will yield a sign change in $f(x)$. Because the degree of f is odd and its leading coefficient is positive, the end behavior of f is given by

$$\lim_{x \to \infty} f(x) = \infty \quad \text{and} \quad \lim_{x \to -\infty} f(x) = -\infty.$$

Our analysis yields the following sign chart:

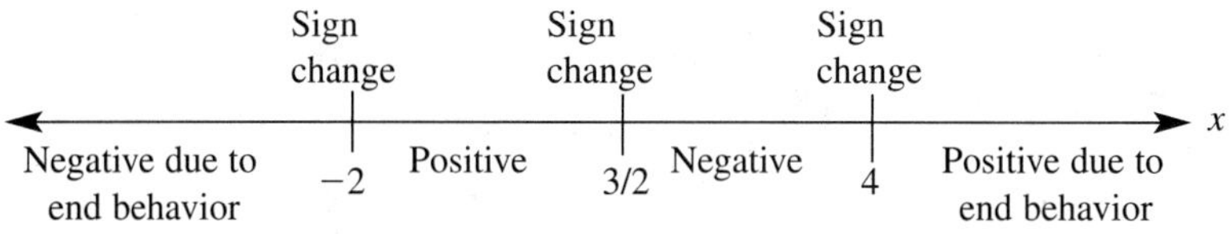

The solution of $2x^3 - 7x^2 - 10x + 24 > 0$ is $(-2, 3/2) \cup (4, \infty)$.

Now try Exercise 11.

EXAMPLE 3 Solving a Polynomial Inequality Graphically

Solve $x^3 - 6x^2 \le 2 - 8x$ graphically.

SOLUTION First we rewrite the inequality as $x^3 - 6x^2 + 8x - 2 \le 0$. Then we let $f(x) = x^3 - 6x^2 + 8x - 2$ and find the real zeros of f graphically as shown in Figure H.60. The three real zeros are approximately 0.32, 1.46, and 4.21. The solution consists of the x-values for which the graph is on or below the x-axis. So the solution of $x^3 - 6x^2 \le 2 - 8x$ is approximately $(-\infty, 0.32] \cup [1.46, 4.21]$.

The end points of these intervals are accurate to two decimal places. We use square brackets because the zeros of the polynomial are solutions of the inequality even though we only have approximations of their values. *Now try Exercise 13.*

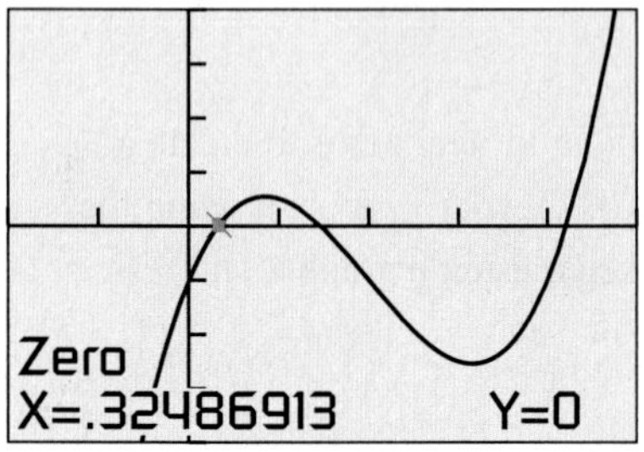

[–2, 5] by [–8, 8]

FIGURE H.60 The graph of $f(x) = x^3 - 6x^2 + 8x - 2$, with one of three real zeros highlighted. (Example 3)

When a polynomial function has no sign changes, the solutions of the associated inequalities can look a bit unusual, as illustrated in Example 4.

EXAMPLE 4 Solving a Polynomial Inequality with Unusual Answers

(a) The inequalities associated with the strictly positive polynomial function $f(x) = (x^2 + 7)(2x^2 + 1)$ have unusual solution sets. We use Figure H.61a as a guide to solving the inequalities:

- The solution of $(x^2 + 7)(2x^2 + 1) > 0$ is $(-\infty, \infty)$, all real numbers.
- The solution of $(x^2 + 7)(2x^2 + 1) \ge 0$ is also $(-\infty, \infty)$.
- The solution set of $(x^2 + 7)(2x^2 + 1) < 0$ is empty. We say an inequality of this sort has no solution.
- The solution set of $(x^2 + 7)(2x^2 + 1) \le 0$ is also empty, so the inequality has no solution.

(continued)

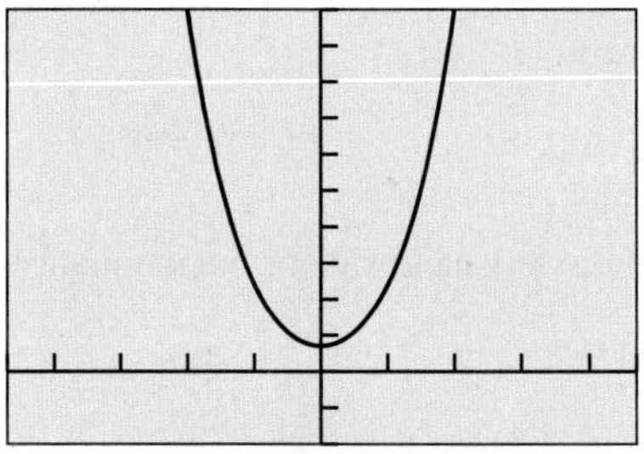

[–4.7, 4.7] by [–20, 100]

(a)

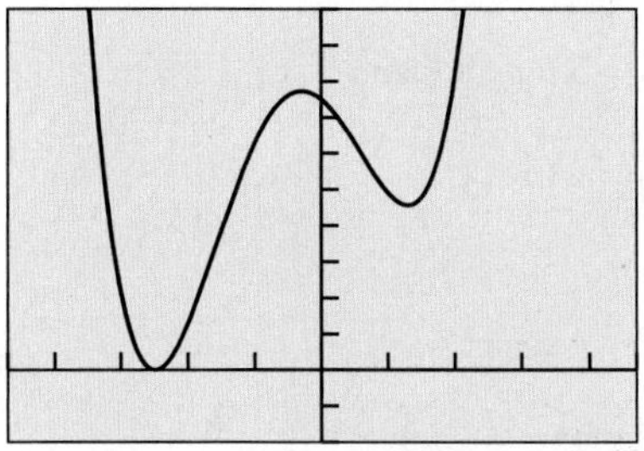

[–4.7, 4.7] by [–20, 100]

(b)

FIGURE H.61 The graphs of (a) $f(x) = (x^2 + 7)(2x^2 + 1)$ and (b) $g(x) = (x^2 - 3x + 3)(2x + 5)^2$. (Example 4)

(b) The inequalities associated with the nonnegative polynomial function $g(x) = (x^2 - 3x + 3)(2x + 5)^2$ also have unusual solution sets. We use Figure H.61b as a guide to solving the inequalities:

- The solution of $(x^2 - 3x + 3)(2x + 5)^2 > 0$ is $(-\infty, -5/2) \cup (-5/2, \infty)$, all real numbers except $x = -5/2$, the lone real zero of g.
- The solution of $(x^2 - 3x + 3)(2x + 5)^2 \geq 0$ is $(-\infty, \infty)$, all real numbers.
- The inequality $(x^2 - 3x + 3)(2x + 5)^2 < 0$ has no solution.
- The solution of $(x^2 - 3x + 3)(2x + 5)^2 \leq 0$ is the single number $x = -5/2$.

Now try Exercise 21.

Rational Inequalities

A polynomial function $p(x)$ is positive, negative, or zero for all real numbers x, but a rational function $r(x)$ can be positive, negative, zero, or *undefined*. In particular, a rational function is undefined at the zeros of its denominator. Thus when solving rational inequalities we modify the kind of sign chart used in Example 1 to include the real zeros of both the numerator and the denominator as locations of potential sign change.

EXAMPLE 5 Creating a Sign Chart for a Rational Function

Let $r(x) = (2x + 1)/((x + 3)(x - 1))$. Determine the real number values of x that cause $r(x)$ to be **(a)** zero, **(b)** undefined. Then make a sign chart to determine the real number values of x that cause $r(x)$ to be **(c)** positive, **(d)** negative.

SOLUTION

(a) The real zeros of $r(x)$ are the real zeros of the numerator $2x + 1$. So $r(x)$ is zero if $x = -1/2$.

(b) $r(x)$ is undefined when the denominator $(x + 3)(x - 1) = 0$. So $r(x)$ is undefined if $x = -3$ or $x = 1$.

These findings lead to the following sign chart, with three points of potential sign change:

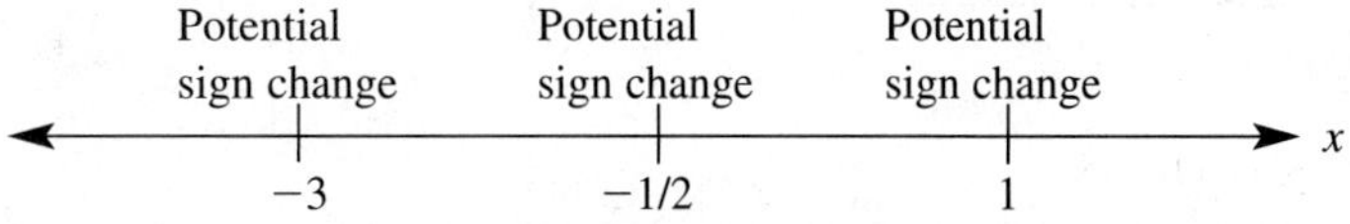

Analyzing the factors of the numerator and denominator yields:

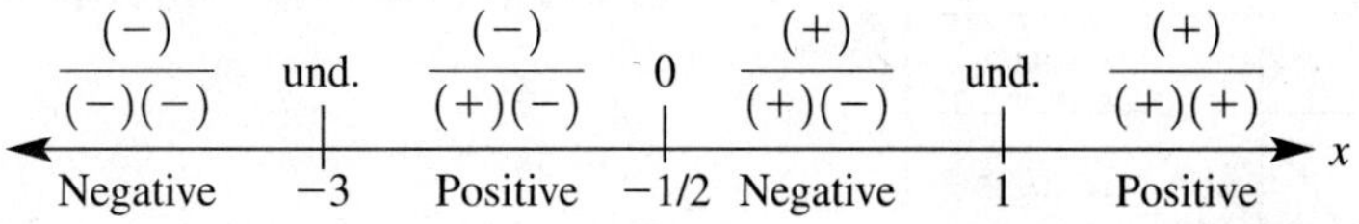

(c) So $r(x)$ is positive if $-3 < x < -1/2$ or $x > 1$, and the solution of $(2x + 1)/((x + 3)(x - 1)) > 0$ is $(-3, -1/2) \cup (1, \infty)$.

(d) Similarly, $r(x)$ is negative if $x < -3$ or $-1/2 < x < 1$, and the solution of $(2x + 1)/((x + 3)(x - 1)) < 0$ is $(-\infty, -3) \cup (-1/2, 1)$.

Figure H.62 supports our findings because the graph of r is above the x-axis for x in $(-3, -1/2) \cup (1, \infty)$ and is below the x-axis for x in $(-\infty, -3) \cup (-1/2, 1)$.

Now try Exercise 25.

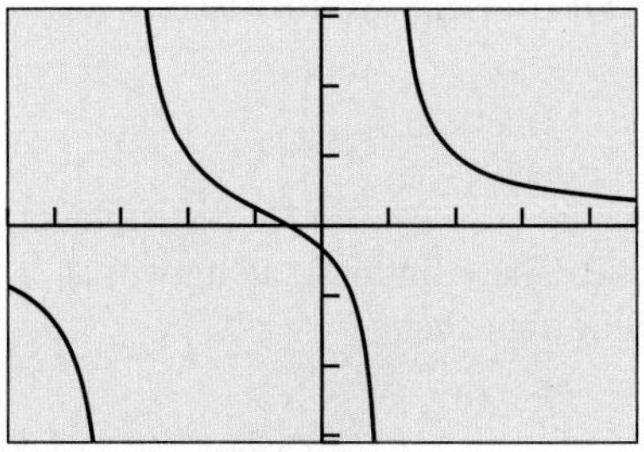

[–4.7, 4.7] by [–3.1, 3.1]

FIGURE H.62 The graph of $r(x) = (2x + 1)/((x + 3)(x - 1))$. (Example 5)

EXAMPLE 6 Solving a Rational Inequality by Combining Fractions

Solve $\dfrac{5}{x+3} + \dfrac{3}{x-1} < 0$.

SOLUTION We combine the two fractions on the left-hand side of the inequality using the least common denominator $(x + 3)(x - 1)$:

$$\frac{5}{x+3} + \frac{3}{x-1} < 0 \qquad \text{Original inequality}$$

$$\frac{5(x-1)}{(x+3)(x-1)} + \frac{3(x+3)}{(x+3)(x-1)} < 0 \qquad \text{Use LCD to rewrite fractions.}$$

$$\frac{5(x-1) + 3(x+3)}{(x+3)(x-1)} < 0 \qquad \text{Add fractions.}$$

$$\frac{5x - 5 + 3x + 9}{(x+3)(x-1)} < 0 \qquad \text{Distributive property}$$

$$\frac{8x + 4}{(x+3)(x-1)} < 0 \qquad \text{Simplify.}$$

$$\frac{2x + 1}{(x+3)(x-1)} < 0 \qquad \text{Divide both sides by 4.}$$

This inequality matches Example 5d. The solution is $(-\infty, -3) \cup (-1/2, 1)$.
Now try Exercise 49.

Other Inequalities

The sign chart method can be adapted to solve other types of inequalities, and we can support our solutions graphically as needed or desired.

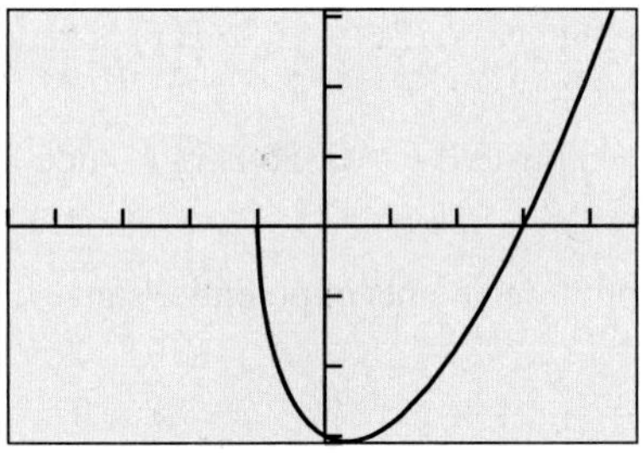

[–4.7, 4.7] by [–3.1, 3.1]

FIGURE H.63 The graph of $f(x) = (x - 3)\sqrt{x + 1}$. (Example 7)

EXAMPLE 7 Solving an Inequality Involving a Radical

Solve $(x - 3)\sqrt{x + 1} \geq 0$.

SOLUTION Let $f(x) = (x - 3)\sqrt{x + 1}$. Because of the factor $\sqrt{x + 1}$, $f(x)$ is undefined if $x < -1$. The zeros of f are 3 and -1. These findings, along with a sign analysis of the two factors, lead to the following sign chart:

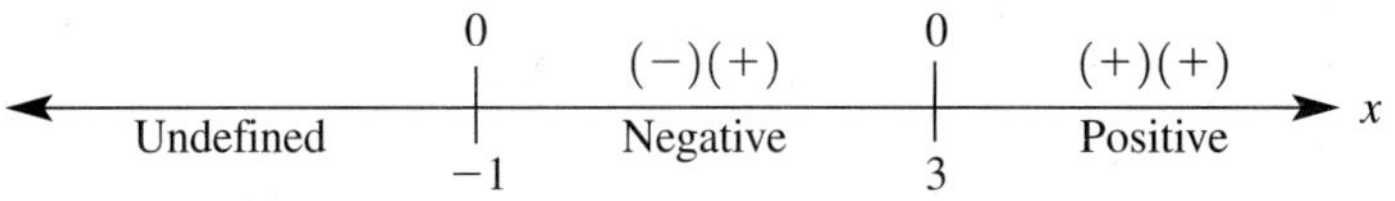

The solution of $(x - 3)\sqrt{x + 1} \geq 0$ is $\{-1\} \cup [3, \infty)$. The graph of f in Figure H.63 supports this solution.
Now try Exercise 43.

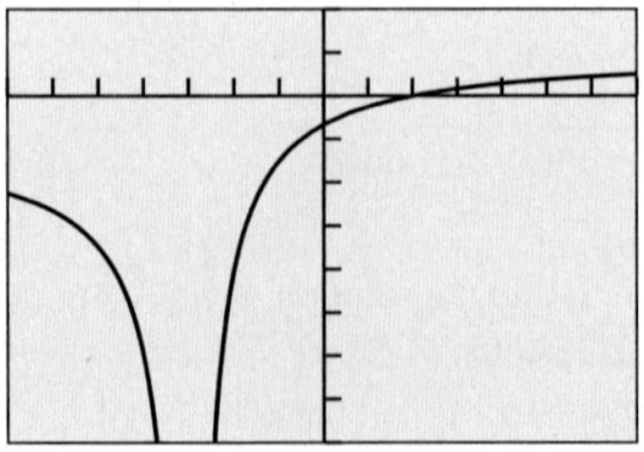

[–7, 7] by [–8, 2]

FIGURE H.64 The graph of $f(x) = (x - 3)/|x + 3|$. (Example 8)

EXAMPLE 8 Solving an Inequality Involving Absolute Value

Solve $\dfrac{x - 2}{|x + 3|} \leq 0$.

SOLUTION Let $f(x) = (x - 2)/|x + 3|$. Because $|x + 3|$ is in the denominator, $f(x)$ is undefined if $x = -3$. The only zero of f is 2. These findings, along with a sign analysis of the two factors, lead to the following sign chart:

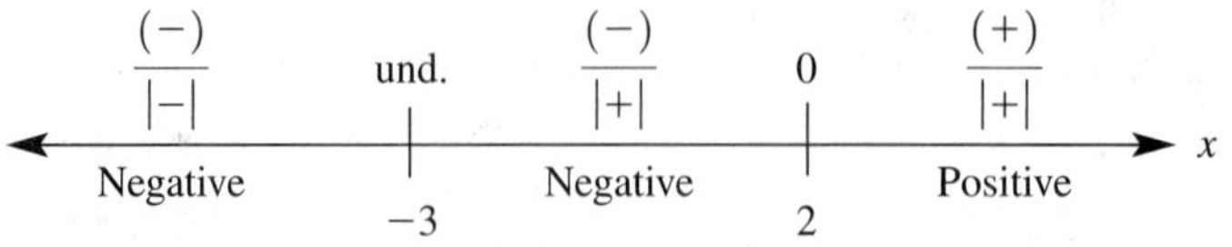

The solution of $(x - 2)/|x + 3| \leq 0$ is $(-\infty, -3) \cup (-3, 2]$. The graph of f in Figure H.64 supports this solution.
Now try Exercise 53.

Applications

EXAMPLE 9 Designing a Box—Revisited

Dixie Packaging Company has contracted with another firm to design boxes with a volume of *at least* 600 in.^{3}. Squares are still to be cut from the corners of a 20-in. by 25-in. piece of cardboard, with the flaps folded up to make an open box. What size squares should be cut from the cardboard?

SOLUTION

Model

The volume V of the box is given by

$$V(x) = x(25 - 2x)(20 - 2x),$$

where x represents both the side length of the removed squares and the height of the box. To obtain a volume of at least 600 in.^{3}, we solve the inequality

$$x(25 - 2x)(20 - 2x) \geq 600.$$

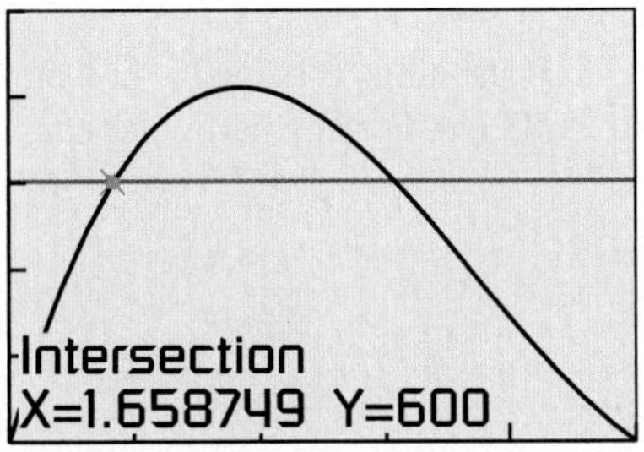

[0, 10] by [0, 1000]

FIGURE H.65 The graphs of $y_1 = x(25 - 2x)(20 - 2x)$ and $y_2 = 600$. (Example 9)

Solve Graphically

Because the width of the cardboard is 20 in., $0 \leq x \leq 10$, and we set our window accordingly. In Figure H.65, we find the values of x for which the cubic function is on or above the horizontal line. The solution is the interval $[1.66, 6.16]$.

Interpret

Squares with side lengths between 1.66 in. and 6.16 in., inclusive, should be cut from the cardboard to produce a box with a volume of at least 600 in.^{3}.

Now try Exercise 59.

EXAMPLE 10 Designing a Juice Can—Revisited

Stewart Cannery will package tomato juice in 2-liter (2000 cm^3) cylindrical cans. Find the radius and height of the cans if the cans have a surface area that is less than 1000 cm^2.

SOLUTION

Model

Recall that the surface area S is given by

$$S(r) = 2\pi r^2 + \frac{4000}{r}.$$

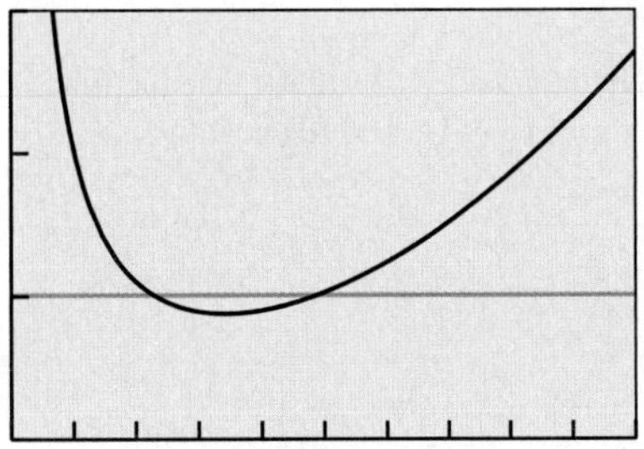

[0, 20] by [0, 3000]

FIGURE H.66 The graphs of $y_1 = 2\pi x^2 + 4000/x$ and $y_2 = 1000$. (Example 10)

The inequality to be solved is

$$2\pi r^2 + \frac{4000}{r} < 1000.$$

Solve Graphically

Figure H.66 shows the graphs of $y_1 = S(r) = 2\pi r^2 + 4000/r$ and $y_2 = 1000$. Using grapher methods we find that the two curves intersect at approximately $r \approx 4.619\ldots$ and $r \approx 9.654\ldots$. (We carry all the extra decimal places for greater accuracy in a computation below.) So the surface area is less than 1000 cm^3 if

$$4.62 < r < 9.65.$$

The volume of a cylindrical can is $V = \pi r^2 h$ and $V = 2000$. Using substitution we see that $h = 2000/(\pi r^2)$. To find the values for h we build a double inequality for $2000/(\pi r^2)$.

$$\begin{array}{lll}
4.62 < r & < 9.65 & \text{Original inequality} \\
4.62^2 < r^2 & < 9.65^2 & 0 < a < b \Rightarrow a^2 < b^2. \\
\pi \cdot 4.62^2 < \pi r^2 & < \pi \cdot 9.65^2 & \text{Multiply by } \pi. \\
\dfrac{1}{\pi \cdot 4.62^2} > \dfrac{1}{\pi r^2} & > \dfrac{1}{\pi \cdot 9.65^2} & 0 < a < b \Rightarrow \dfrac{1}{a} > \dfrac{1}{b}. \\
\dfrac{2000}{\pi \cdot 4.62^2} > \dfrac{2000}{\pi r^2} & > \dfrac{2000}{\pi \cdot 9.65^2} & \text{Multiply by 2000.} \\
\dfrac{2000}{\pi(4.619\ldots)^2} > h & > \dfrac{2000}{\pi(9.654\ldots)^2} & \text{Use the extra decimal places now.} \\
29.83 > h & > 6.83 & \text{Compute.}
\end{array}$$

Interpret

The surface area of the can will be less than 1000 cm^3 if its radius is between 4.62 cm and 9.65 cm and its height is between 6.83 cm and 29.83 cm. For any particular can, h must equal $2000/(\pi r^2)$. ***Now try Exercise 61.***

LESSON H-8 EXERCISES

Exercise numbers with a gray background indicate problems that the authors have designed to be solved *without a calculator.*

In Exercises 1–6, determine the x values that cause the polynomial function to be **(a)** zero, **(b)** positive, and **(c)** negative.

1. $f(x) = (x + 2)(x + 1)(x - 5)$

2. $f(x) = (x - 7)(3x + 1)(x + 4)$

3. $f(x) = (x + 7)(x + 4)(x - 6)^2$

4. $f(x) = (5x + 3)(x^2 + 6)(x - 1)$

5. $f(x) = (2x^2 + 5)(x - 8)^2(x + 1)^3$

6. $f(x) = (x + 2)^3(4x^2 + 1)(x - 9)^4$

In Exercises 7–12, complete the factoring if needed, and solve the polynomial inequality using a sign chart. Support graphically.

7. $(x + 1)(x - 3)^2 > 0$

8. $(2x + 1)(x - 2)(3x - 4) \le 0$

9. $(x + 1)(x^2 - 3x + 2) < 0$

10. $(2x - 7)(x^2 - 4x + 4) > 0$

11. $2x^3 - 3x^2 - 11x + 6 \ge 0$

12. $x^3 - 4x^2 + x + 6 \le 0$

In Exercises 13–20, solve the polynomial inequality graphically.

13. $x^3 - x^2 - 2x \ge 0$

14. $2x^3 - 5x^2 + 3x < 0$

15. $2x^3 - 5x^2 - x + 6 > 0$

16. $x^3 - 4x^2 - x + 4 \le 0$

17. $3x^3 - 2x^2 - x + 6 \ge 0$

18. $-x^3 - 3x^2 - 9x + 4 < 0$

19. $2x^4 - 3x^3 - 6x^2 + 5x + 6 < 0$

20. $3x^4 - 5x^3 - 12x^2 + 12x + 16 \ge 0$

In Exercises 21–24, solve the following inequalities for the given function $f(x)$.

(a) $f(x) > 0$ **(b)** $f(x) \ge 0$ **(c)** $f(x) < 0$ **(d)** $f(x) \le 0$

21. $f(x) = (x^2 + 4)(2x^2 + 3)$

22. $f(x) = (x^2 + 1)(-2 - 3x^2)$

23. $f(x) = (2x^2 - 2x + 5)(3x - 4)^2$

24. $f(x) = (x^2 + 4)(3 - 2x)^2$

In Exercises 25–32, determine the real values of x that cause the function to be **(a)** zero, **(b)** undefined, **(c)** positive, and **(d)** negative.

25. $f(x) = \dfrac{x - 1}{((2x + 3)(x - 4))}$

26. $f(x) = \dfrac{(2x - 7)(x + 1)}{(x + 5)}$

27. $f(x) = x\sqrt{x + 3}$

28. $f(x) = x^2|2x + 9|$

29. $f(x) = \dfrac{\sqrt{x + 5}}{(2x + 1)(x - 1)}$

30. $f(x) = \dfrac{x - 1}{(x - 4)\sqrt{x + 2}}$

31. $f(x) = \dfrac{(2x + 5)\sqrt{x - 3}}{(x - 4)^2}$

32. $f(x) = \dfrac{3x - 1}{(x + 3)\sqrt{x - 5}}$

Exercises 33–44, solve the inequality using a sign chart. Support aphically.

33. $\dfrac{x-1}{x^2-4} < 0$ **34.** $\dfrac{x+2}{x^2-9} < 0$

35. $\dfrac{x^2-1}{x^2+1} \le 0$ **36.** $\dfrac{x^2-4}{x^2+4} > 0$

37. $\dfrac{x^2+x-12}{x^2-4x+4} > 0$ **38.** $\dfrac{x^2+3x-10}{x^2-6x+9} < 0$

39. $\dfrac{x^3-x}{x^2+1} \ge 0$ **40.** $\dfrac{x^3-4x}{x^2+2} \le 0$

41. $x|x-2| > 0$ **42.** $\dfrac{x-3}{|x+2|} < 0$

43. $(2x-1)\sqrt{x+4} < 0$ **44.** $(3x-4)\sqrt{2x+1} \ge 0$

Exercises 45–54, solve the inequality.

45. $\dfrac{x^3(x-2)}{(x+3)^2} < 0$ **46.** $\dfrac{(x-5)^4}{x(x+3)} \ge 0$

47. $x^2 - \dfrac{2}{x} > 0$ **48.** $x^2 + \dfrac{4}{x} \ge 0$

49. $\dfrac{1}{x+1} + \dfrac{1}{x-3} \le 0$ **50.** $\dfrac{1}{x+2} - \dfrac{2}{x-1} > 0$

51. $(x+3)|x-1| \ge 0$ **52.** $(3x+5)^2|x-2| < 0$

53. $\dfrac{(x-5)|x-2|}{\sqrt{2x-3}} \ge 0$ **54.** $\dfrac{x^2(x-4)^3}{\sqrt{x+1}} < 0$

55. Writing to Learn Write a paragraph that explains two ways to solve the inequality $3(x-1)+2 \le 5x+6$.

56. Company Wages Pederson Electric charges $25 per service call plus $18 per hour for repair work. How long did an electrician work if the charge was less than $100? Assume the electrician rounds the time to the nearest quarter hour.

57. Connecting Algebra and Geometry Consider the collection of all rectangles that have lengths 2 in. less than twice their widths. Find the possible widths (in inches) of these rectangles if their perimeters are less than 200 in.

58. Planning for Profit The Grovenor Candy Co. finds that the cost of making a certain candy bar is $0.13 per bar. Fixed costs amount to $2000 per week. If each bar sells for $0.35, find the minimum number of candy bars that will earn the company a profit.

59. Designing a Cardboard Box Picaro's Packaging Plant wishes to design boxes with a volume of *not more than* 100 in.^{3}. Squares are to be cut from the corners of a 12-in. by 15-in. piece of cardboard (see figure), with the flaps folded up to make an open box. What size squares should be cut from the cardboard?

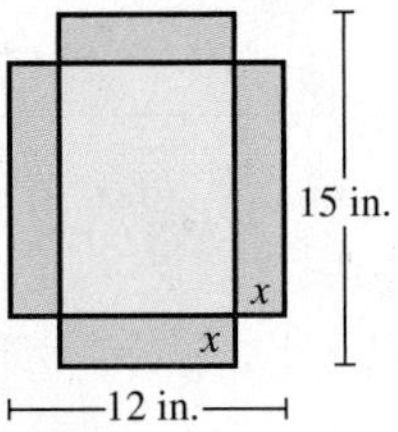

60. Cone Problem Beginning with a circular piece of paper with a 4-inch radius, as shown in (a), cut out a sector with an arc of length x. Join the two radial edges of the remaining portion of the paper to form a cone with radius r and height h, as shown in (b). What length of arc will produce a cone with a volume greater than 21 in.^{3}?

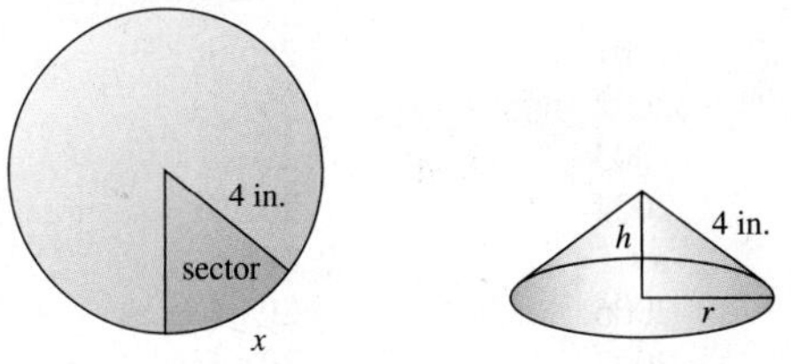

(a) (b)

61. Design a Juice Can Flannery Cannery packs peaches in 0.5-L cylindrical cans.

(a) Express the surface area S of the can as a function of the radius x (in cm).

(b) Find the dimensions of the can if the surface is less than 900 cm^2.

(c) Find the least possible surface area of the can.

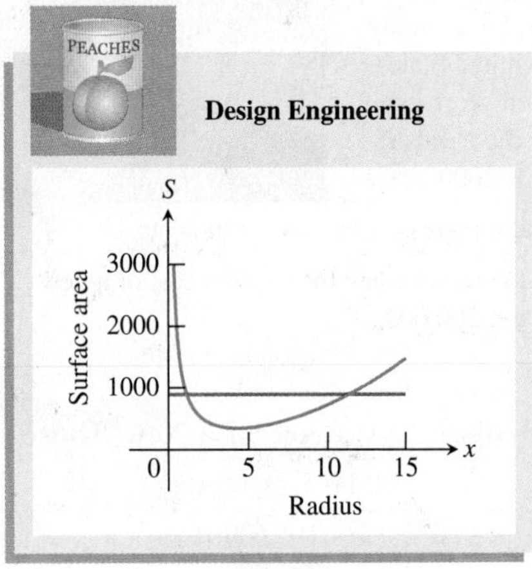

62. Resistors The total electrical resistance R of two resistors connected in parallel with resistances R_1 and R_2 is given by

$$\frac{1}{R} = \frac{1}{R_1} + \frac{1}{R_2}.$$

One resistor has a resistance of 2.3 ohms. Let x be the resistance of the second resistor.

(a) Express the total resistance R as a function of x.

(b) Find the resistance in the second resistor if the total resistance of the pair is at least 1.7 ohms.

63. The Growing of America Table H.6 shows the midyear (July 1) U.S. population estimates in millions of persons for the years 2001 through 2008. Let x be the number of years since July 1, 2000.

Table H.6 U.S. Population (in millions)

Year	Population
2001	285.0
2002	287.7
2003	290.2
2004	292.9
2005	295.6
2006	298.4
2007	301.3
2008	304.1

Source: U.S. Census Bureau, www.census.gov (June 2009).

(a) Find the linear regression model for the U.S. population in millions since the middle of 2000.

(b) Use the model to predict when the U.S. population will reach 315 million.

64. Single-Family House Cost The midyear median sales prices of new, privately owned one-family houses sold in the United States are given for selected years in Table H.7. Let x be the number of years since July 1, 2000.

(a) Find the quadratic regression model for the data.

(b) Use the model to predict when the median cost of a new home returned to \$200,000.

Table H.7 Median Sales Price of a New House

Year	Price (dollars)
2003	195,000
2004	221,000
2005	240,900
2006	246,500
2007	247,900
2008	232,100

Source: U.S. Census Bureau, www.census.gov (June 2009)

Explorations

In Exercises 65 and 66, find the vertical asymptotes and intercepts of the rational function. Then use a sign chart and a table of values to sketch the function by hand. Support your result using a grapher. (*Hint:* You may need to graph the function in more than one window to see different parts of the overall graph.)

65. $f(x) = \dfrac{(x-1)(x+2)^2}{(x-3)(x+1)}$ **66.** $g(x) = \dfrac{(x-3)^4}{x^2+4x}$

Extending the Ideas

67. Group Activity Looking Ahead to Calculus Let $f(x) = 3x - 5$.

(a) Assume x is in the interval defined by $|x - 3| < 1/3$. Give a convincing argument that $|f(x) - 4| < 1$.

(b) Writing to Learn Explain how (a) is modeled by the figure below.

(c) Show how the algebra used in (a) can be modified to show that if $|x - 3| < 0.01$, then $|f(x) - 4| < 0.03$. How would the figure below change to reflect these inequalities?

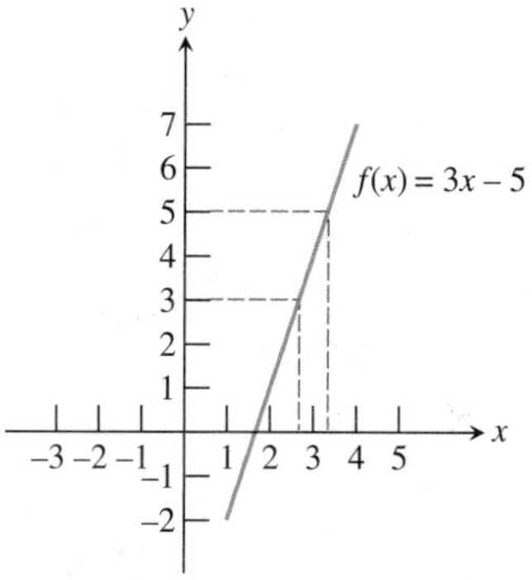

68. Writing to Learn Boolean Operators The Test menu of many graphers contains inequality symbols that can be used to construct inequality statements, as shown in (a). An answer of 1 indicates the statement is true, and 0 indicates the statement is false. In (b), the graph of $Y_1 = (x^2 - 4 \geq 0)$ is shown using Dot mode and the window $[-4.7, 4.7]$ by $[-3.1, 3.1]$. Experiment with the Test menu, and then write a paragraph explaining how to interpret the graph in(b).

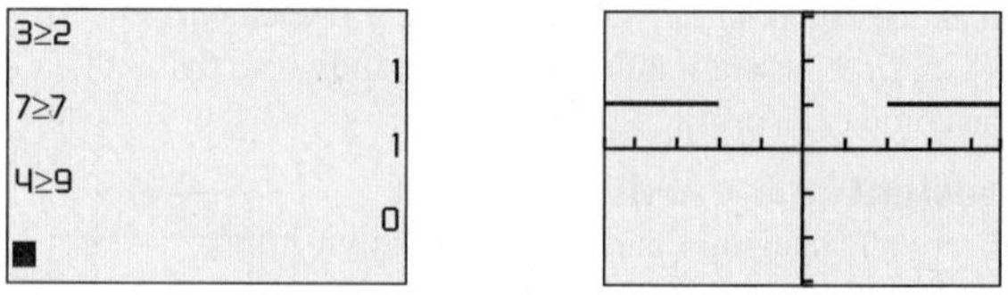

(a)

[–4.7, 4.7] by [–3.1, 3.1]

(b)

H-9 Trigonometric Functions of Acute Angles

What you'll learn about

- Right Triangle Trigonometry
- Two Famous Triangles
- Evaluating Trigonometric Functions with a Calculator
- Applications of Right Triangle Trigonometry

... and why

The many applications of right triangle trigonometry gave the subject its name.

Right Triangle Trigonometry

Recall that geometric figures are **similar** if they have the same shape even though they may have different sizes. Having the same shape means that the angles of one are congruent to the angles of the other and their corresponding sides are proportional. Similarity is the basis for many applications, including scale drawings, maps, and **right triangle trigonometry**, which is the topic of this section.

Two triangles are similar if the angles of one are congruent to the angles of the other. For two *right* triangles we need only know that an acute angle of one is equal to an acute angle of the other for the triangles to be similar. Thus a single acute angle θ of a right triangle determines six distinct ratios of side lengths. Each ratio can be considered a function of θ as θ takes on values from 0° to 90° or from 0 radians to $\pi/2$ radians. We wish to study these functions of acute angles more closely.

To bring the power of coordinate geometry into the picture, we will often put our acute angles in **standard position** in the xy-plane, with the vertex at the origin, one ray along the positive x-axis, and the other ray extending into the first quadrant. (See Figure H.67.)

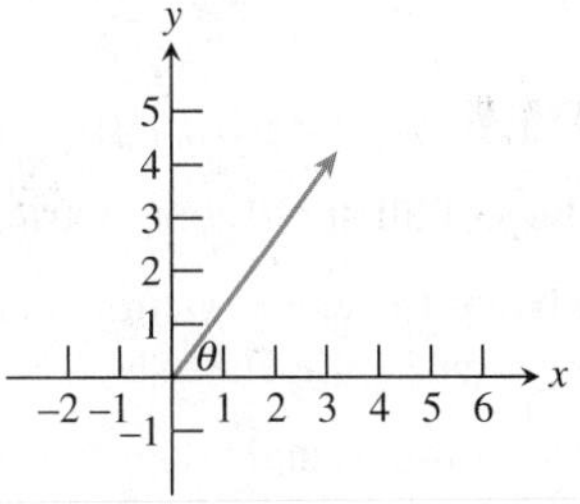

FIGURE H.67 An acute angle θ in **standard position**, with one ray along the positive x-axis and the other extending into the first quadrant.

The six ratios of side lengths in a right triangle are the six *trigonometric functions* (often abbreviated as *trig functions*) of the acute angle θ. We will define them here with reference to the right ΔABC as labeled in Figure H.68. The abbreviations *opp*, *adj*, and *hyp* refer to the lengths of the side opposite θ, the side adjacent to θ, and the hypotenuse, respectively.

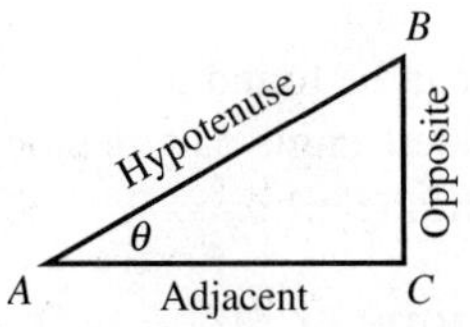

FIGURE H.68 The triangle referenced in our definition of the trigonometric functions.

DEFINITION Trigonometric Functions

Let θ be an acute angle in the right ΔABC (Figure H.68). Then

$$\textbf{sine }(\theta) = \sin\theta = \frac{opp}{hyp} \qquad \textbf{cosecant }(\theta) = \csc\theta = \frac{hyp}{opp}$$

$$\textbf{cosine }(\theta) = \cos\theta = \frac{adj}{hyp} \qquad \textbf{secant }(\theta) = \sec\theta = \frac{hyp}{adj}$$

$$\textbf{tangent }(\theta) = \tan\theta = \frac{opp}{adj} \qquad \textbf{cotangent }(\theta) = \cot\theta = \frac{adj}{opp}$$

Function Reminder

Both $\sin \theta$ and $\sin(\theta)$ represent a function of the variable θ. Neither notation implies multiplication by θ. The notation $\sin(\theta)$ is just like the notation $f(x)$, while the notation $\sin \theta$ is a widely accepted shorthand. The same note applies to all six trigonometric functions.

EXPLORATION 1 Exploring Trigonometric Functions

There are twice as many trigonometric functions as there are triangle sides that define them, so we can already explore some ways in which the trigonometric functions relate to each other. Doing this Exploration will help you learn which ratios are which.

1. Each of the six trig functions can be paired to another that is its reciprocal. Find the three pairs of reciprocals.
2. Which trig function can be written as the quotient $\sin \theta/\cos \theta$?
3. Which trig function can be written as the quotient $\csc \theta/\cot \theta$?
4. What is the (simplified) product of all six trig functions multiplied together?
5. Which two trig functions must be less than 1 for any acute angle θ? [*Hint:* What is always the longest side of a right triangle?]

Two Famous Triangles

Evaluating trigonometric functions of particular angles used to require trig tables or slide rules; now it requires only a calculator. However, the side ratios for some angles that appear in right triangles can be found *geometrically*. Every student of trigonometry should be able to find these special ratios without a calculator.

EXAMPLE 1 Evaluating Trigonometric Functions of 45°

Find the values of all six trigonometric functions for an angle of 45°.

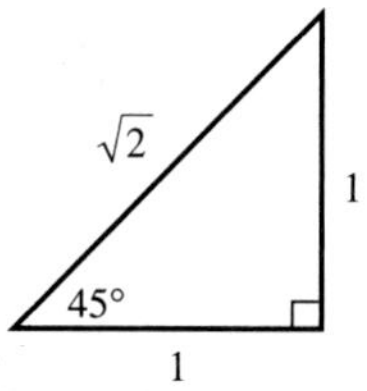

FIGURE H.69 An isosceles right triangle. (Example 1)

SOLUTION A 45° angle occurs in an *isosceles right triangle*, with angles 45°–45°–90° (see Figure H.69).

Since the size of the triangle does not matter, we set the length of the two equal legs to 1. The hypotenuse, by the Pythagorean Theorem, is $\sqrt{1+1} = \sqrt{2}$. Applying the definitions, we have

$$\sin 45° = \frac{opp}{hyp} = \frac{1}{\sqrt{2}} \text{ or } \frac{\sqrt{2}}{2} \qquad \csc 45° = \frac{hyp}{opp} = \frac{\sqrt{2}}{1}$$

$$\cos 45° = \frac{adj}{hyp} = \frac{1}{\sqrt{2}} \text{ or } \frac{\sqrt{2}}{2} \qquad \sec 45° = \frac{hyp}{adj} = \frac{\sqrt{2}}{1}$$

$$\tan 45° = \frac{opp}{adj} = \frac{1}{1} = 1 \qquad \cot 45° = \frac{adj}{opp} = \frac{1}{1} = 1$$

Now try Exercise 1.

Whenever two sides of a right triangle are known, the third side can be found using the Pythagorean Theorem. All six trigonometric functions of either acute angle can then be found. We illustrate this in Example 2 with another well-known triangle.

EXAMPLE 2 Evaluating Trigonometric Functions of 30°

Find the values of all six trigonometric functions for an angle of 30°.

SOLUTION A 30° angle occurs in a **30°–60°–90°** triangle, which can be constructed from an equilateral (60°–60°–60°) triangle by constructing an altitude to any side. Since size does not matter, start with an equilateral triangle with sides 2 units long. The altitude splits it into two congruent 30°–60°–90° triangles, each with hypotenuse 2 and smaller leg 1. By the Pythagorean Theorem, the longer leg has length $\sqrt{2^2 - 1^2} = \sqrt{3}$. (See Figure H.70.)

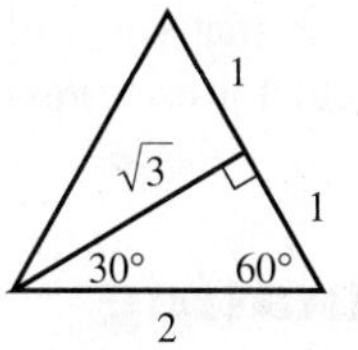

FIGURE H.70 An altitude to any side of an equilateral triangle creates two congruent 30°–60°–90° triangles. If each side of the equilateral triangle has length 2, then the two 30°–60°–90° triangles have sides of length 2, 1, and $\sqrt{3}$. (Example 2)

We apply the definitions of the trigonometric functions to get:

$$\sin 30° = \frac{opp}{hyp} = \frac{1}{2} \qquad \csc 30° = \frac{hyp}{opp} = \frac{2}{1} = 2$$

$$\cos 30° = \frac{adj}{hyp} = \frac{\sqrt{3}}{2} \qquad \sec 30° = \frac{hyp}{adj} = \frac{2}{\sqrt{3}} \text{ or } \frac{2\sqrt{3}}{3}$$

$$\tan 30° = \frac{opp}{adj} = \frac{1}{\sqrt{3}} \text{ or } \frac{\sqrt{3}}{3} \qquad \cot 30° = \frac{adj}{opp} = \frac{\sqrt{3}}{1}$$

Now try Exercise 3.

EXPLORATION 2 Evaluating Trigonometric Functions of 60°

1. Find the values of all six trigonometric functions for an angle of 60°. Note that most of the preliminary work has been done in Example 2.
2. Compare the six function values for 60° with the six function values for 30°. What do you notice?
3. We will eventually learn a rule that relates trigonometric functions of any angle with trigonometric functions of the *complementary* angle. (Recall from geometry that 30° and 60° are complementary because they add up to 90°.) Based on this exploration, can you predict what that rule will be? [*Hint:* The "co" in cosine, cotangent, and cosecant actually comes from "complement."]

Example 3 illustrates that knowing one trigonometric ratio in a right triangle is sufficient for finding all the others.

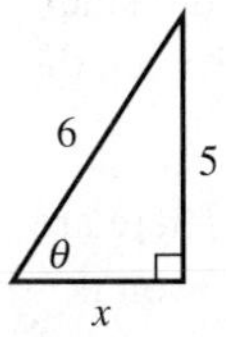

FIGURE H.71 How to create an acute angle θ such that $\sin \theta = 5/6$. (Example 3)

A Word About Radical Fractions

There was a time when $\frac{5\sqrt{11}}{11}$ was considered "simpler" than $\frac{5}{\sqrt{11}}$ because it was easier to approximate, but today they are just equivalent expressions for the same irrational number. With technology, either form leads easily to an approximation of 1.508. We leave the answers in exact form here because we want you to practice problems of this type without a calculator.

EXAMPLE 3 Using One Trigonometric Ratio to Find Them All

Let θ be an acute angle such that $\sin \theta = 5/6$. Evaluate the other five trigonometric functions of θ.

SOLUTION Sketch a triangle showing an acute angle θ. Label the opposite side 5 and the hypotenuse 6. (See Figure H.71.) Since $\sin \theta = 5/6$, this must be our angle! Now we need the other side of the triangle (labeled x in the figure).

From the Pythagorean Theorem it follows that $x^2 + 5^2 = 6^2$, so $x = \sqrt{36 - 25} = \sqrt{11}$. Applying the definitions,

$$\sin \theta = \frac{opp}{hyp} = \frac{5}{6} \qquad \csc \theta = \frac{hyp}{opp} = \frac{6}{5} = 1.2$$

$$\cos \theta = \frac{adj}{hyp} = \frac{\sqrt{11}}{6} \qquad \sec \theta = \frac{hyp}{adj} = \frac{6}{\sqrt{11}} \text{ or } \frac{6\sqrt{11}}{11}$$

$$\tan \theta = \frac{opp}{adj} = \frac{5}{\sqrt{11}} \text{ or } \frac{5\sqrt{11}}{11} \qquad \cot \theta = \frac{adj}{opp} = \frac{\sqrt{11}}{5}$$

Now try Exercise 9.

Evaluating Trigonometric Functions with a Calculator

Using a calculator for the evaluation step enables you to concentrate all your problem-solving skills on the modeling step, which is where the real trigonometry occurs. The danger is that your calculator will try to evaluate what you ask it to evaluate, even if you ask it to evaluate the wrong thing. If you make a mistake, you might be lucky and see an error message. In most cases you will unfortunately see an answer that you will assume is correct but is actually wrong. We list the most common calculator errors associated with evaluating trigonometric functions.

Common Calculator Errors When Evaluating Trig Functions

1. **Using the Calculator in the Wrong Angle Mode (Degrees/Radians)** This error is so common that everyone encounters it once in a while. You just hope to recognize it when it occurs. For example, suppose we are doing a problem in which we need to evaluate the sine of 10 degrees. Our calculator shows us this screen (Figure H.72):

```
sin(10)
                 -.5440211109
```

FIGURE H.72 Wrong mode for finding sin $(10°)$.

   Why is the answer negative? Our first instinct should be to check the mode. Sure enough, it is in radian mode. Changing to degrees, we get sin $(10) = 0.1736481777$, which is a reasonable answer. (That still leaves open the question of why the sine of 10 radians is negative, but that is a topic for the next section.) We will revisit the mode problem later when we look at trigonometric graphs.

2. **Using the Inverse Trig Keys to Evaluate cot, sec, and csc** There are no buttons on most calculators for cotangent, secant, and cosecant. The reason is because they can be easily evaluated by finding reciprocals of tangent, cosine, and sine, respectively. For example, Figure H.73 shows the correct way to evaluate the cotangent of 30 degrees.

```
(tan(30))^-1
                  1.732050808
```

FIGURE H.73 Finding cot $(30°)$.

   There is also a key on the calculator for "TAN^{-1}"—but this is *not* the cotangent function! Remember that an exponent of -1 on a *function* is *never* used to denote a reciprocal; it is always used to denote the *inverse function*. We will study the inverse trigonometric functions in a later section, but meanwhile you can see that it is a bad way to evaluate cot (30) (Figure H.74).

```
tan^-1(30)
                  88.09084757
```

FIGURE H.74 This is not cot $(30°)$.

3. **Using Function Shorthand That the Calculator Does Not Recognize** This error is less dangerous because it usually results in an error message. We will often abbreviate powers of trig functions, writing (for example) "$\sin^3 \theta - \cos^3 \theta$" instead of the more cumbersome "$(\sin(\theta))^3 - (\cos(\theta))^3$." The calculator does not recognize the shorthand notation and interprets it as a syntax error.

4. **Not Closing Parentheses** This general algebraic error is easy to make on calculators that automatically open a parenthesis pair whenever you type a function key. Check your calculator by pressing the SIN key. If the screen displays "sin (" instead of just "sin" then you have such a calculator. The danger arises because the calculator will automatically *close* the parenthesis pair at the end of a command if you have forgotten to do so. That is fine if you *want* the parenthesis at the end of the command, but it is bad if you want it somewhere else. For example, if you want "sin (30)" and you type "sin (30", you will get away with it. But if you want "sin (30) + 2" and you type "sin (30 + 2", you will not (Figure H.75).

```
sin(30)
                           .5
sin(30+2
                 .5299192642
sin(30)+2
                          2.5
```

FIGURE H.75 A correct and incorrect way to find sin $(30°) + 2$.

It is usually impossible to find an "exact" answer on a calculator, especially when evaluating trigonometric functions. The actual values are usually irrational numbers with nonterminating, nonrepeating decimal expansions. However, you can find some exact answers if you know what you are looking for, as in Example 4.

EXAMPLE 4 Getting an "Exact Answer" on a Calculator

Find the exact value of cos 30° on a calculator.

SOLUTION As you see in Figure H.76, the calculator gives the answer 0.8660254038. However, if we recognize 30° as one of our special angles (see Example 2 in this lesson), we might recall that the exact answer can be written in terms of a square root. We square our answer and get 0.75, which suggests that the exact value of cos 30° is $\sqrt{3/4} = \sqrt{3}/2$. *Now try Exercise 25.*

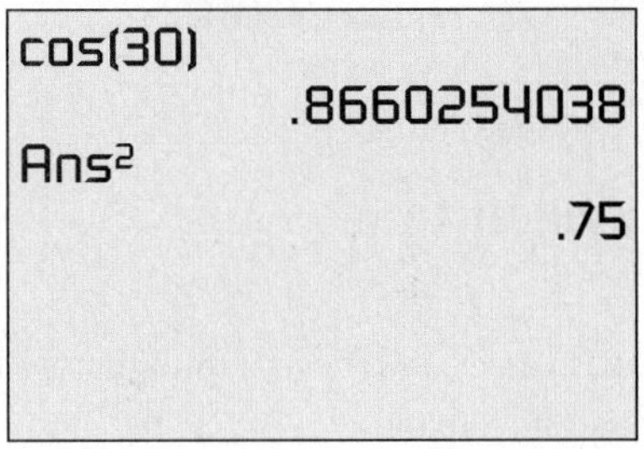

FIGURE H.76 (Example 4)

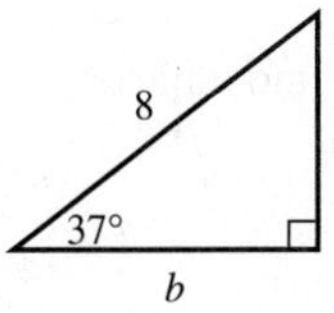

FIGURE H.77 (Example 5)

Applications of Right Triangle Trigonometry

A triangle has six "parts," three angles and three sides, but you do not need to know all six parts to determine a triangle up to congruence. In fact, three parts are usually sufficient. The trigonometric functions take this observation a step further by giving us the means for actually *finding* the rest of the parts once we have enough parts to establish congruence. Using some of the parts of a triangle to solve for all the others is **solving a triangle**.

EXAMPLE 5 Solving a Right Triangle

A right triangle with a hypotenuse of 8 includes a 37° angle (Figure H.77). Find the measures of the other two angles and the lengths of the other two sides.

SOLUTION Since it is a right triangle, one of the other angles is 90°. That leaves $180° - 90° - 37° = 53°$ for the third angle.

Referring to the labels in Figure H.77, we have

$$\sin 37° = \frac{a}{8} \qquad \cos 37° = \frac{b}{8}$$

$$a = 8 \sin 37° \qquad b = 8 \cos 37°$$

$$a \approx 4.81 \qquad b \approx 6.39$$

Now try Exercise 55.

The real-world applications of triangle solving are many, reflecting the frequency with which one encounters triangular shapes in everyday life.

A Word About Rounding Answers

Notice in Example 6 that we rounded the answer to the nearest integer. In applied problems it is illogical to give answers with more decimal places of accuracy than can be guaranteed for the input values. An answer of 729.132 feet implies razor-sharp accuracy, whereas the reported height of the building (340 feet) implies a much less precise measurement. (So does the angle of 65°.) Indeed, an engineer following specific rounding criteria based on "significant digits" would probably report the answer to Example 6 as 730 feet. We will not get too picky about rounding, but we will try to be sensible.

EXAMPLE 6 Finding the Height of a Building

From a point 340 feet away from the base of the Peachtree Center Plaza in Atlanta, Georgia, the angle of elevation to the top of the building is 65°. (See Figure H.78.) Find the height h of the building.

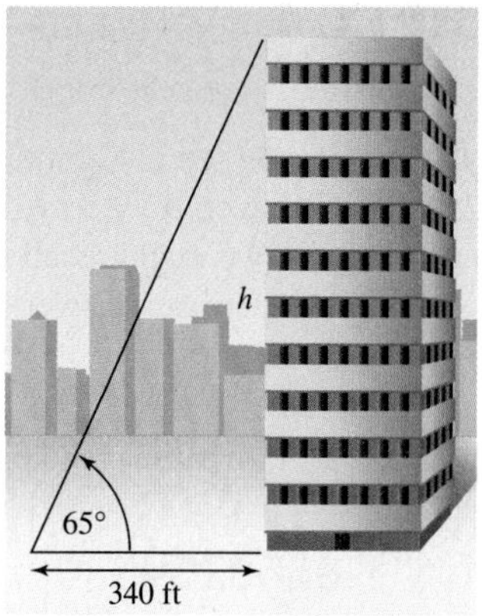

FIGURE H.78 (Example 6)

SOLUTION We need a ratio that will relate an angle to its opposite and adjacent sides. The tangent function is the appropriate choice.

$$\tan 65° = \frac{h}{340}$$
$$h = 340 \tan 65°$$
$$h \approx 729 \text{ feet}$$

Now try Exercise 61.

LESSON H-9 EXERCISES

Exercise numbers with a gray background indicate problems that the authors have designed to be solved *without a calculator.*

In Exercises 1–8, find the values of all six trigonometric functions of the angle θ.

1.

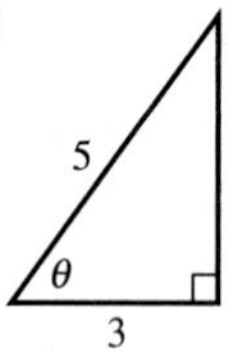

2.

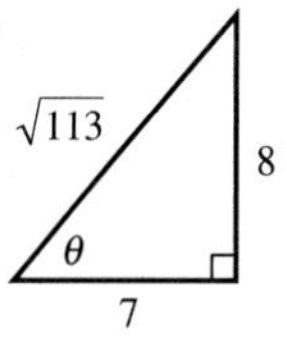

3.

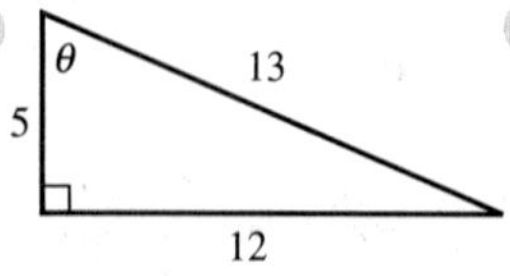

4.

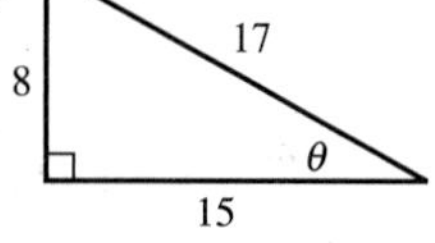

5.

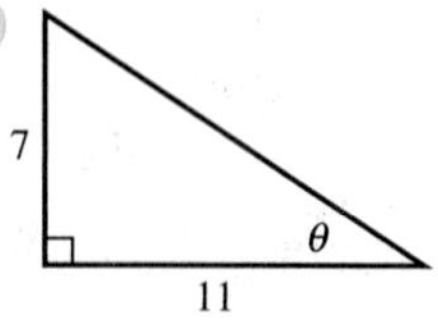

6.

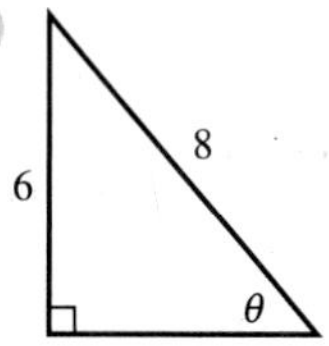

7.

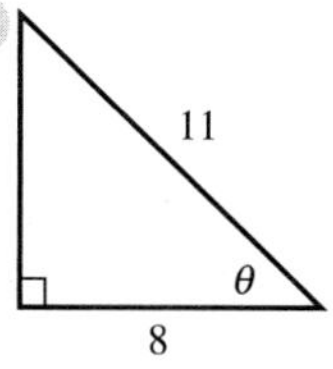

8.

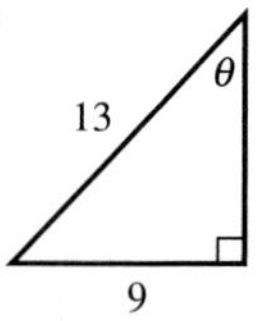

In Exercises 9–18, assume that θ is an acute angle in a right triangle s isfying the given conditions. Evaluate the remaining trigonometric functions.

9. $\sin \theta = \frac{3}{7}$

10. $\sin \theta = \frac{2}{3}$

11. $\cos \theta = \frac{5}{11}$

12. $\cos \theta = \frac{5}{8}$

13. $\tan \theta = \frac{5}{9}$

14. $\tan \theta = \frac{12}{13}$

15. $\cot \theta = \frac{11}{3}$

16. $\csc \theta = \frac{12}{5}$

17. $\csc \theta = \frac{23}{9}$

18. $\sec \theta = \frac{17}{5}$

In Exercises 19–24, evaluate *without* using a calculator.

19. $\sin\left(\frac{\pi}{3}\right)$

20. $\tan\left(\frac{\pi}{4}\right)$

21. $\cot\left(\frac{\pi}{6}\right)$

22. $\sec\left(\frac{\pi}{3}\right)$

23. $\cos\left(\frac{\pi}{4}\right)$

24. $\csc\left(\frac{\pi}{3}\right)$

In Exercises 25–28, evaluate using a calculator. Give an exact value, not an approximate answer. (See Example 4.)

25. $\sec 45°$

26. $\sin 60°$

27. $\csc\left(\frac{\pi}{3}\right)$

28. $\tan\left(\frac{\pi}{3}\right)$

In Exercises 29–40, evaluate using a calculator. Be sure the calculator is in the correct mode. Give answers correct to three decimal places.

29. $\sin 74°$

30. $\tan 8°$

31. $\cos 19°23'$

32. $\tan 23°42'$

33. $\tan\left(\frac{\pi}{12}\right)$

34. $\sin\left(\frac{\pi}{15}\right)$

35. $\sec 49°$

36. $\csc 19°$

37. $\cot 0.89$

38. $\sec 1.24$

39. $\cot\left(\frac{\pi}{8}\right)$

40. $\csc\left(\frac{\pi}{10}\right)$

In Exercises 41–48, find the acute angle θ that satisfies the given equation. Give θ in both degrees and radians. You should do these problems without a calculator.

41. $\sin\theta = \frac{1}{2}$

42. $\sin\theta = \frac{\sqrt{3}}{2}$

43. $\cot\theta = \frac{1}{\sqrt{3}}$

44. $\cos\theta = \frac{\sqrt{2}}{2}$

45. $\sec\theta = 2$

46. $\cot\theta = 1$

47. $\tan\theta = \frac{\sqrt{3}}{3}$

48. $\cos\theta = \frac{\sqrt{3}}{2}$

In Exercises 49–54, solve for the variable shown.

49.

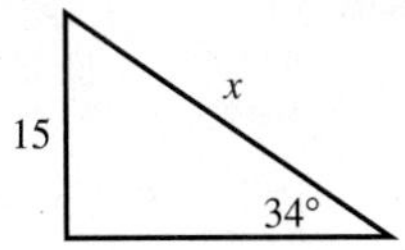

50.

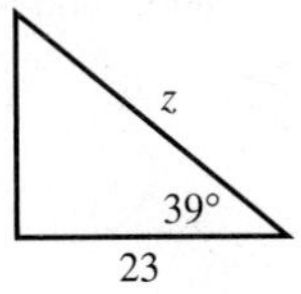

51.

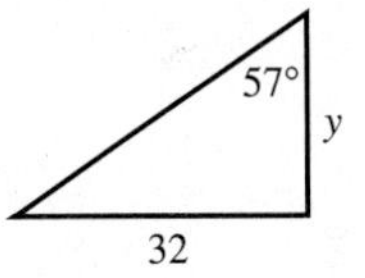

52.

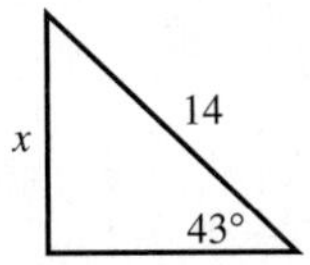

53.

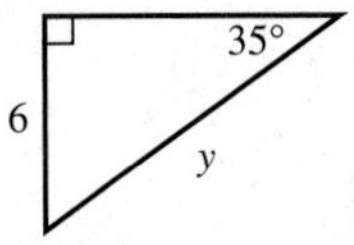

54.

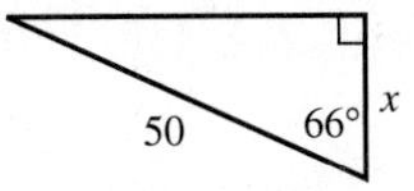

In Exercises 55–58, solve the right ΔABC for all of its unknown parts.

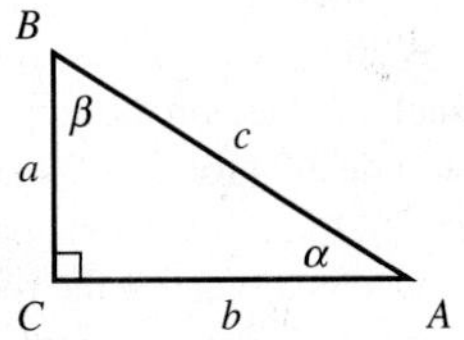

55. $\alpha = 20°$; $a = 12.3$

56. $\alpha = 41°$; $c = 10$

57. $\beta = 55°$; $a = 15.58$

58. $a = 5$; $\beta = 59°$

59. Writing to Learn What is $\lim_{\theta\to 0} \sin\theta$? Explain your answer in terms of right triangles in which θ gets smaller and smaller.

60. Writing to Learn What is $\lim_{\theta\to 0} \cos\theta$? Explain your answer in terms of right triangles in which θ gets smaller and smaller.

61. Height A guy wire from the top of the transmission tower at WJBC forms a 75° angle with the ground at a 55-foot distance from the base of the tower. How tall is the tower?

62. Height Kirsten places her surveyor's telescope on the top of a tripod 5 feet above the ground. She measures an 8° elevation above the horizontal to the top of a tree that is 120 feet away. How tall is the tree?

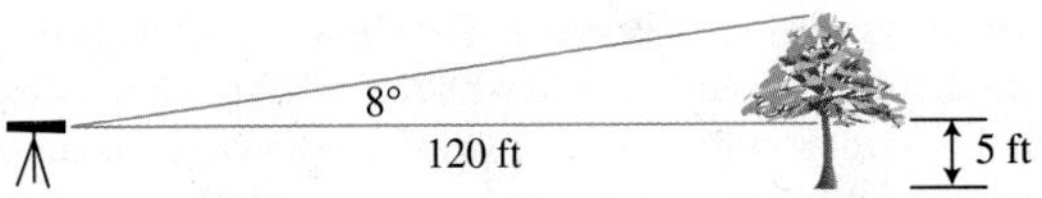

63. Group Activity Area For locations between 20° and 60° north latitude a solar collector panel should be mounted so that its angle with the horizontal is 20 greater than the local latitude. Consequently, the solar panel mounted on the roof of Solar Energy, Inc., in Atlanta (latitude 34°) forms a 54° angle with the horizontal. The bottom edge of the 12-ft-long panel is resting on the roof, and the high edge is 5 ft above the roof. What is the total area of this rectangular collector panel?

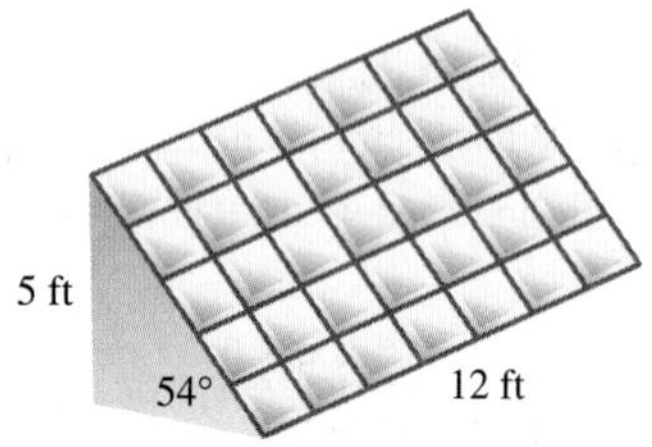

64. Height The Chrysler Building in New York City was the tallest building in the world at the time it was built. It casts a shadow approximately 130 feet long on the street when the Sun's rays form an 82.9° angle with the Earth. How tall is the building?

65. Distance DaShanda's team of surveyors had to find the distance AC across the lake at Montgomery County Park. Field assistants positioned themselves at points A and C while DaShanda set up an angle-measuring instrument at point B, 100 feet from C in a perpendicular direction. DaShanda measured $\angle ABC$ as $75°12'42''$. What is the distance AC?

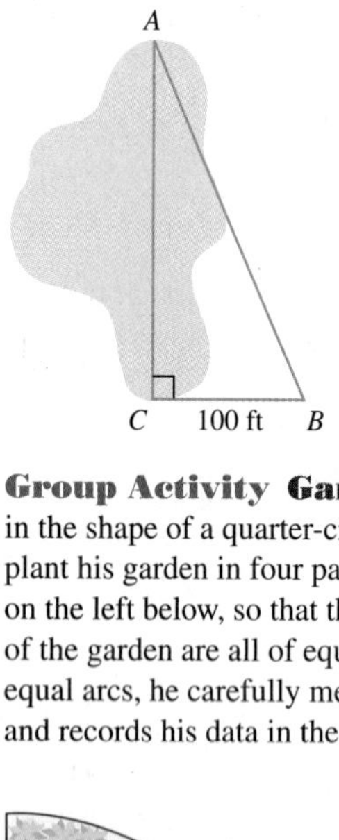

66. Group Activity Garden Design Allen's garden is in the shape of a quarter-circle with radius 10 ft. He wishes to plant his garden in four parallel strips, as shown in the diagram on the left below, so that the four arcs along the circular edge of the garden are all of equal length. After measuring four equal arcs, he carefully measures the widths of the four strips and records his data in the table shown at the right below.

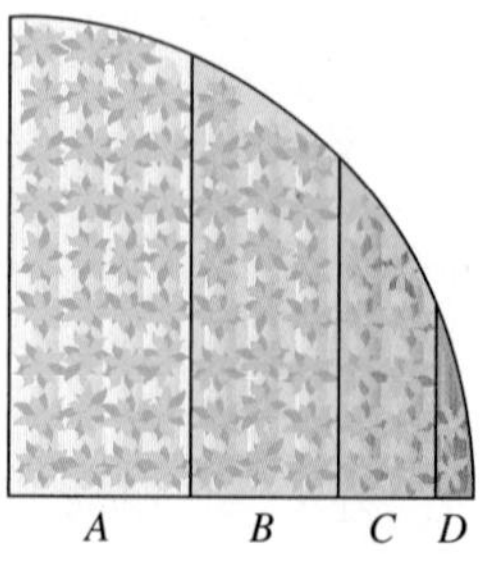

Strip	Width
A	3.827 ft
B	3.344 ft
C	2.068 ft
D	0.761 ft

Explorations

67. Mirrors In the figure, a light ray shining from point A to point P on the mirror will bounce to point B in such a way that the *angle of incidence* α will equal the *angle of reflection* β. This is the *law of reflection* derived from physical experiments. Both angles are measured from the *normal line*, which is perpendicular to the mirror at the point of reflection P. If A is 2 m farther from the mirror than is B, and if $\alpha = 30°$ and , what is the length PB?

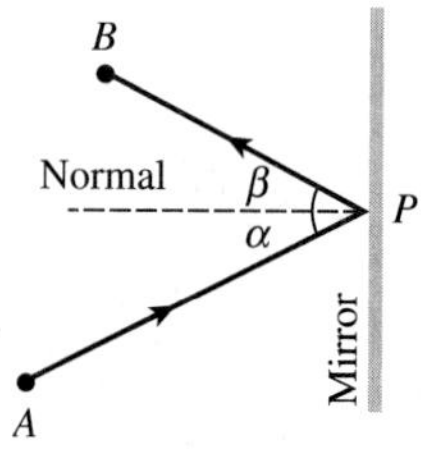

68. Pool On the pool table shown in the figure, where along the portion CD of the railing should you direct ball A so that it will bounce off CD and strike ball B? Assume that A obeys the law of reflection relative to rail CD.

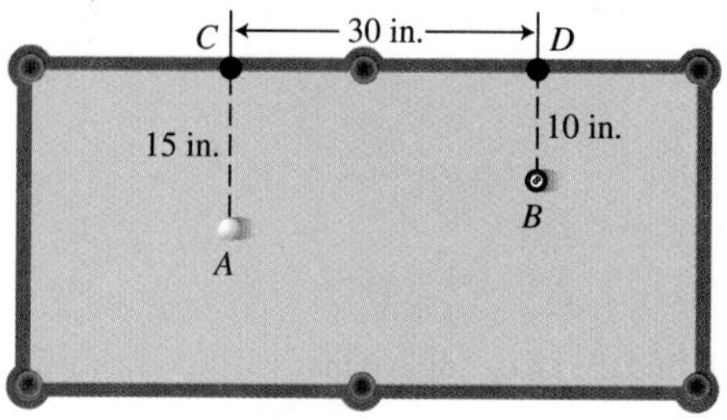

Extending the Ideas

69. Using the labeling of the triangle below, prove that if θ is an acute angle in any right triangle, $(\sin \theta)^2 + (\cos \theta)^2 = 1$.

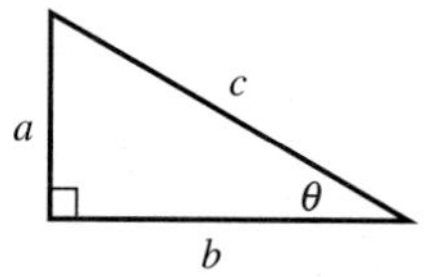

70. Using the labeling of the triangle below, prove that the area of the triangle is equal to $(1/2)\, ab \sin \theta$. [*Hint:* Start by drawing the altitude to side b and finding its length.]

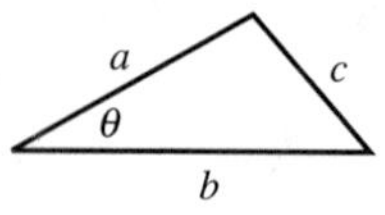

H-10 Fundamental Identities

What you'll learn about

- Identities
- Basic Trigonometric Identities
- Pythagorean Identities
- Cofunction Identities
- Odd-Even Identities
- Simplifying Trigonometric Expressions
- Solving Trigonometric Equations

... and why

Identities are important when working with trigonometric functions in calculus.

We are now moving into the analytic phase of our study of trigonometric functions. Once the transition is made from triangle ratios to functions and their graphs, one is on analytic soil. But our primary applications of trigonometry so far have been computational; we have not made full use of the properties of the functions to study the connections among the trigonometric functions themselves. In this chapter we will shift our emphasis more toward theory and proof, exploring where the properties of these special functions lead us, often with no immediate concern for real-world relevance at all. We hope in the process to give you an appreciation for the rich and intricate tapestry of interlocking patterns that can be woven from the six basic trigonometric functions—patterns that will take on even greater beauty later on when you can view them through the lens of calculus.

Identities

As you probably realize by now, the symbol "=" means several different things in mathematics.

1. $1 + 1 = 2$ means *equality of real numbers.* It is a true sentence.
2. $2(x - 3) = 2x - 6$ signifies *equivalent expressions.* It is a true sentence.
3. $x^2 + 3 = 7$ is an *open sentence,* because it can be true or false, depending on whether x is a solution to the equation.
4. $(x^2 - 1)/(x + 1) = x - 1$ is an *identity.* It is a true sentence (very much like (2) above), but with the important qualification that *x must be in the domain of both expressions.* If either side of the equality is undefined, the sentence is meaningless. Substituting -1 into both sides of the equation in (3) gives a sentence that is mathematically false (i.e., $4 = 7$), whereas substituting -1 into both sides of the identity in (4) gives a sentence that is meaningless.

Statements like "$\tan\theta = \sin\theta/\cos\theta$" and "$\csc\theta = 1/\sin\theta$" are trigonometric **identities** because they are true for all values of the variable for which both sides of the equation are defined. The set of all such values is called the **domain of validity** of the identity. We will spend much of this chapter exploring trigonometric identities, their proofs, their implications, and their applications.

Basic Trigonometric Identities

Some trigonometric identities follow directly from the definitions of the six basic trigonometric functions. These *basic identities* consist of the *reciprocal identities* and the *quotient identities.*

Basic Trigonometric Identities

Reciprocal Identities

$$\csc\theta = \frac{1}{\sin\theta} \qquad \sec\theta = \frac{1}{\cos\theta} \qquad \cot\theta = \frac{1}{\tan\theta}$$

$$\sin\theta = \frac{1}{\csc\theta} \qquad \cos\theta = \frac{1}{\sec\theta} \qquad \tan\theta = \frac{1}{\cot\theta}$$

Quotient Identities

$$\tan\theta = \frac{\sin\theta}{\cos\theta} \qquad \cot\theta = \frac{\cos\theta}{\sin\theta}$$

EXPLORATION 1 **Making a Point About Domain of Validity**

1. $\theta = 0$ is in the domain of validity of exactly three of the basic identities. Which three?
2. For exactly two of the basic identities, one side of the equation is defined at $\theta = 0$ and the other side is not. Which two?
3. For exactly three of the basic identities, both sides of the equation are undefined at $\theta = 0$. Which three?

Pythagorean Identities

Recall that, for any real number t, the numbers $(\cos t)^2$ and $(\sin t)^2$ always sum to 1. This is clearly true for the quadrantal angles that wrap to the points $(\pm 1, 0)$ and $(0, \pm 1)$, and it is true for any other t because $\cos t$ and $\sin t$ are the (signed) lengths of legs of a reference triangle with hypotenuse 1 (Figure H.79). No matter what quadrant the triangle lies in, the Pythagorean Theorem guarantees the following identity: $(\cos t)^2 + (\sin t)^2 = 1$.

If we divide each term of the identity by $(\cos t)^2$, we get an identity that involves tangent and secant:

$$\frac{(\cos t)^2}{(\cos t)^2} + \frac{(\sin t)^2}{(\cos t)^2} = \frac{1}{(\cos t)^2}$$

$$1 + (\tan t)^2 = (\sec t)^2$$

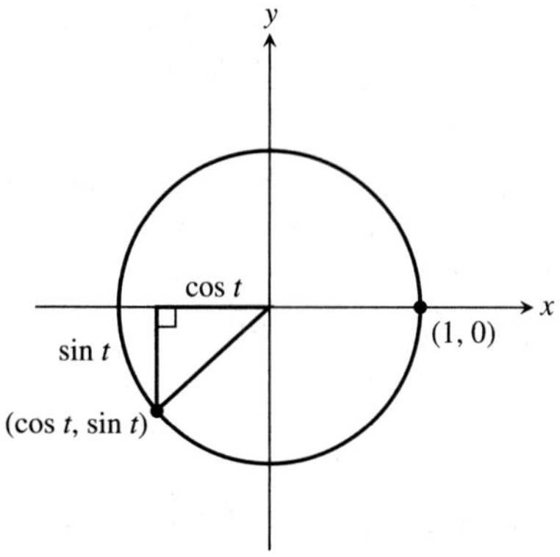

FIGURE H.79 By the Pythagorean Theorem, $(\cos t)^2 + (\sin t)^2 = 1$.

If we divide each term of the identity by $(\sin t)^2$, we get an identity that involves cotangent and cosecant:

$$\frac{(\cos t)^2}{(\sin t)^2} + \frac{(\sin t)^2}{(\sin t)^2} = \frac{1}{(\sin t)^2}$$

$$(\cot t)^2 + 1 = (\csc t)^2$$

These three identities are called the *Pythagorean identities*, which we restate using the shorthand notation for powers of trigonometric functions.

Pythagorean Identities

$$\cos^2\theta + \sin^2\theta = 1$$
$$1 + \tan^2\theta = \sec^2\theta$$
$$\cot^2\theta + 1 = \csc^2\theta$$

EXAMPLE 1 Using Identities

Find $\sin\theta$ and $\cos\theta$ if $\tan\theta = 5$ and $\cos\theta > 0$.

SOLUTION We could solve this problem by the reference triangle techniques, but we will show an alternate solution here using only identities.

First, we note that $\sec^2\theta = 1 + \tan^2\theta = 1 + 5^2 = 26$, so $\sec\theta = \pm\sqrt{26}$.
Since $\sec\theta = \pm\sqrt{26}$, we have $\cos\theta = 1/\sec\theta = 1/\pm\sqrt{26}$.
But $\cos\theta > 0$, so $\cos\theta = 1/\sqrt{26}$.

Finally,

$$\tan\theta = 5$$

$$\frac{\sin\theta}{\cos\theta} = 5$$

$$\sin\theta = 5\cos\theta = 5\left(\frac{1}{\sqrt{26}}\right) = \frac{5}{\sqrt{26}}$$

Therefore, $\sin\theta = \frac{5}{\sqrt{26}}$ and $\cos\theta = \frac{1}{\sqrt{26}}$. *Now try Exercise 1.*

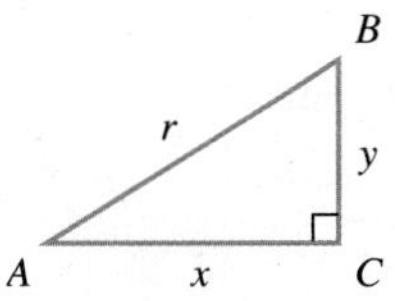

FIGURE H.80 Angles A and B are complements in right ΔABC.

If you find yourself preferring the reference triangle method, that's fine. Remember that combining the power of geometry and algebra to solve problems is one of the themes of this book, and the instinct to do so will serve you well in calculus.

Cofunction Identities

If C is the right angle in right ΔABC, then angles A and B are complements. Notice what happens if we use the usual triangle ratios to define the six trigonometric functions of angles A and B (Figure H.80).

Angle A:	$\sin A = \frac{y}{r}$	$\tan A = \frac{y}{x}$	$\sec A = \frac{r}{x}$
	$\cos A = \frac{x}{r}$	$\cot A = \frac{x}{y}$	$\csc A = \frac{r}{y}$
Angle B:	$\sin B = \frac{x}{r}$	$\tan B = \frac{x}{y}$	$\sec B = \frac{r}{y}$
	$\cos B = \frac{y}{r}$	$\cot B = \frac{y}{x}$	$\csc B = \frac{r}{x}$

Do you see what happens? In every case, the value of a function at A is the same as the value of its cofunction at B. This always happens with complementary angles; in fact, it is this phenomenon that gives a "co" function its name. The "co" stands for "complement."

Cofunction Identities

$$\sin\left(\frac{\pi}{2} - \theta\right) = \cos\theta \qquad \cos\left(\frac{\pi}{2} - \theta\right) = \sin\theta$$

$$\tan\left(\frac{\pi}{2} - \theta\right) = \cot\theta \qquad \cot\left(\frac{\pi}{2} - \theta\right) = \tan\theta$$

$$\sec\left(\frac{\pi}{2} - \theta\right) = \csc\theta \qquad \csc\left(\frac{\pi}{2} - \theta\right) = \sec\theta$$

Although our argument on behalf of these equations was based on acute angles in a triangle, these equations are genuine identities, valid for all real numbers for which both sides of the equation are defined. We could extend our acute-angle argument to produce a general proof, but it will be easier to wait and use the identities of Lesson H-12. We will revisit this particular set of fundamental identities in that section.

Odd-Even Identities

We have seen that every basic trigonometric function is either odd or even. Either way, the usual function relationship leads to another fundamental identity.

Odd-Even Identities

$$\sin(-x) = -\sin x \qquad \cos(-x) = \cos x \qquad \tan(-x) = -\tan x$$

$$\csc(-x) = -\csc x \qquad \sec(-x) = \sec x \qquad \cot(-x) = -\cot x$$

EXAMPLE 2 Using More Identities

If $\cos\theta = 0.34$, find $\sin(\theta - \pi/2)$.

SOLUTION This problem can best be solved using identities.

$$\begin{aligned} \sin\left(\theta - \frac{\pi}{2}\right) &= -\sin\left(\frac{\pi}{2} - \theta\right) && \text{Sine is odd.} \\ &= -\cos\theta && \text{Cofunction identity} \\ &= -0.34 \end{aligned}$$

Now try Exercise 7.

Simplifying Trigonometric Expressions

In calculus it is often necessary to deal with expressions that involve trigonometric functions. Some of those expressions start out looking fairly complicated, but it is often possible to use identities along with algebraic techniques (e.g., factoring or combining fractions over a common denominator) to *simplify* the expressions before dealing with them. In some cases the simplifications can be dramatic.

EXAMPLE 3 Simplifying by Factoring and Using Identities

Simplify the expression $\sin^3 x + \sin x \cos^2 x$.

SOLUTION

Solve Algebraically

$$\begin{aligned} \sin^3 x + \sin x \cos^2 x &= \sin x (\sin^2 x + \cos^2 x) \\ &= \sin x (1) && \text{Pythagorean identity} \\ &= \sin x \end{aligned}$$

Support Graphically

We recognize the graph of $y = \sin^3 x + \sin x \cos^2 x$ (Figure H.81a) as the sam èe as the graph of $y = \sin x$ (Figure H.81b).

Now try Exercise 13.

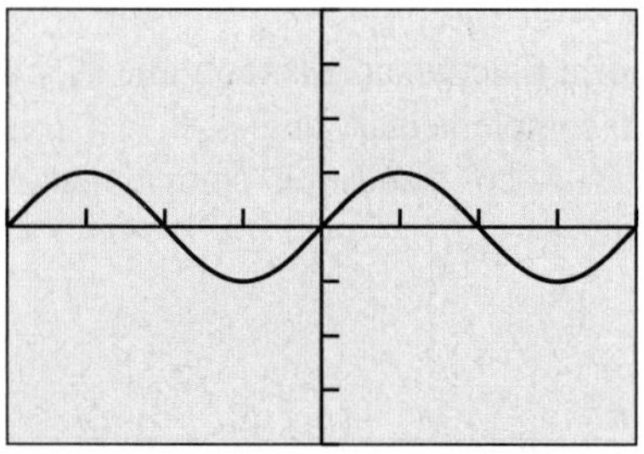

$[-2\pi, 2\pi]$ by $[-4, 4]$

(a)

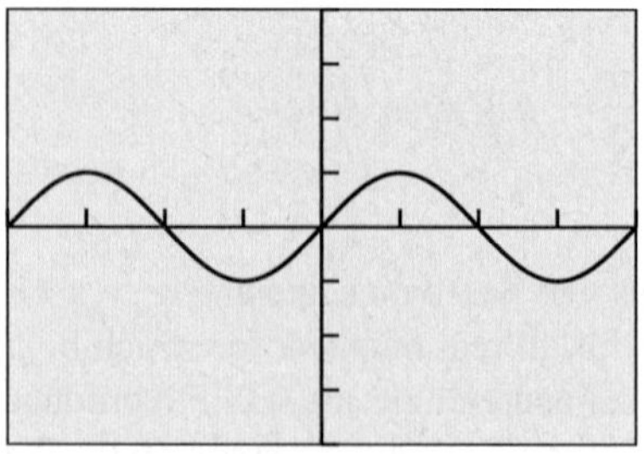

$[-2\pi, 2\pi]$ by $[-4, 4]$

(b)

FIGURE H.81 Graphical support of the identity $\sin^3 x + \sin x \cos^2 x = \sin x$. (Example 3)

EXAMPLE 4 Simplifying by Expanding and Using Identities

Simplify the expression $[(\sec x + 1)(\sec x - 1)]/\sin^2 x$.

SOLUTION

Solve Algebraically

$$\begin{aligned} \frac{(\sec x + 1)(\sec x - 1)}{\sin^2 x} &= \frac{\sec^2 x - 1}{\sin^2 x} && (a+b)(a-b) = a^2 - b^2 \\ &= \frac{\tan^2 x}{\sin^2 x} && \text{Pythagorean identity} \\ &= \frac{\sin^2 x}{\cos^2 x} \cdot \frac{1}{\sin^2 x} && \tan x = \frac{\sin x}{\cos x} \\ &= \frac{1}{\cos^2 x} \\ &= \sec^2 x \end{aligned}$$

Support Graphically

The graphs of $y = \dfrac{(\sec x + 1)(\sec x - 1)}{\sin^2 x}$ and $y = \sec^2 x$ appear to be identical, as expected (Figure H.82).

Now try Exercise 25.

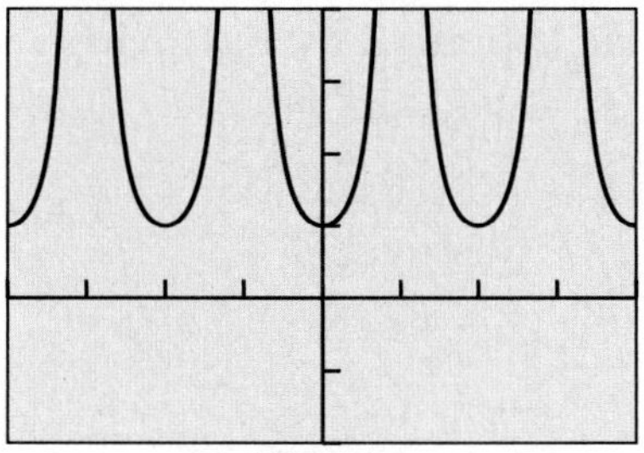

$[-2\pi, 2\pi]$ by $[-2, 4]$

(a)

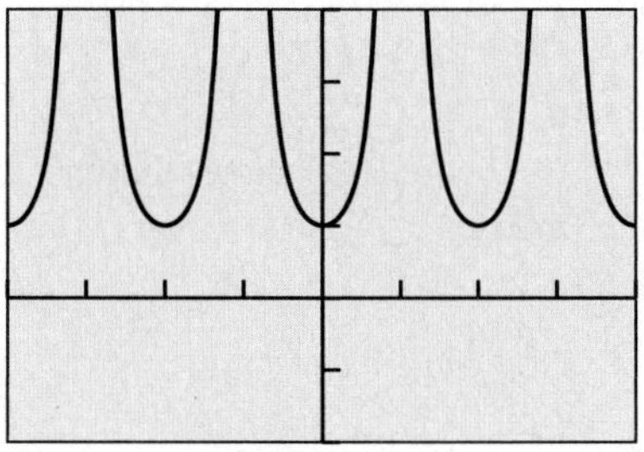

$[-2\pi, 2\pi]$ by $[-2, 4]$

(b)

FIGURE H.82 Graphical support of the identity $(\sec x + 1)(\sec x - 1)/\sin^2 x = \sec^2 x$. (Example 4)

EXAMPLE 5 Simplifying by Combining Fractions and Using Identities

Simplify the expression $\dfrac{\cos x}{1 - \sin x} - \dfrac{\sin x}{\cos x}$.

SOLUTION

$$\frac{\cos x}{1 - \sin x} - \frac{\sin x}{\cos x}$$

$$= \frac{\cos x}{1 - \sin x} \cdot \frac{\cos x}{\cos x} - \frac{\sin x}{\cos x} \cdot \frac{1 - \sin x}{1 - \sin x} \qquad \text{Rewrite using common denominator.}$$

$$= \frac{(\cos x)(\cos x) - (\sin x)(1 - \sin x)}{(1 - \sin x)(\cos x)}$$

$$= \frac{\cos^2 x - \sin x + \sin^2 x}{(1 - \sin x)(\cos x)}$$

$$= \frac{1 - \sin x}{(1 - \sin x)(\cos x)} \qquad \text{Pythagorean identity}$$

$$= \frac{1}{\cos x}$$

$$= \sec x$$

(We leave it to you to provide the graphical support.) *Now try Exercise 37.*

We will use these same simplifying techniques to prove trigonometric identities in Lesson H-11.

Solving Trigonometric Equations

The equation-solving capabilities of calculators have made it possible to solve trigonometric equations without understanding much trigonometry. This is fine, to the extent that solving equations is our goal. However, since understanding trigonometry is also a goal, we will occasionally pause in our development of identities to solve some trigonometric equations with paper and pencil, just to get some practice in using the identities.

EXAMPLE 6 Solving a Trigonometric Equation

Find all values of x in the interval $[0, 2\pi)$ that solve $\cos^3 x/\sin x = \cot x$.

SOLUTION

$$\frac{\cos^3 x}{\sin x} = \cot x$$

$$\frac{\cos^3 x}{\sin x} = \frac{\cos x}{\sin x}$$

$$\cos^3 x = \cos x \qquad \text{Multiply both sides by } \sin x.$$

$$\cos^3 x - \cos x = 0$$

$$(\cos x)(\cos^2 x - 1) = 0$$

$$(\cos x)(-\sin^2 x) = 0 \qquad \text{Pythagorean identity}$$

$$\cos x = 0 \quad \text{or} \quad \sin x = 0$$

(continued)

We reject the possibility that $\sin x = 0$ because it would make both sides of the original equation undefined.

The values in the interval $[0, 2\pi)$ that solve $\cos x = 0$ (and therefore $\cos^3 x/\sin x = \cot x$) are $\pi/2$ and $3\pi/2$. *Now try Exercise 51.*

EXAMPLE 7 Solving a Trigonometric Equation by Factoring

Find all solutions to the trigonometric equation $2 \sin^2 x + \sin x = 1$.

SOLUTION Let $y = \sin x$. The equation $2y^2 + y = 1$ can be solved by factoring:

$$\begin{aligned} 2y^2 + y &= 1 \\ 2y^2 + y - 1 &= 0 \\ (2y - 1)(y + 1) &= 0 \\ 2y - 1 = 0 \quad &\text{or} \quad y + 1 = 0 \\ y = \frac{1}{2} \quad &\text{or} \quad y = -1 \end{aligned}$$

So, in the original equation, $\sin x = 1/2$ or $\sin x = -1$. Figure H.83 shows that the solutions in the interval $[0, 2\pi)$ are $\pi/6$, $5\pi/6$, and $3\pi/2$.

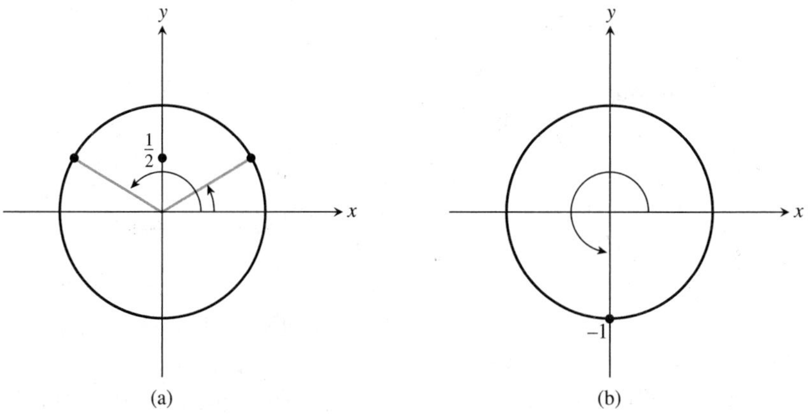

FIGURE H.83 (a) $\sin x = 1/2$ has two solutions in $[0, 2\pi)$: $\pi/6$ and $5\pi/6$. (b) $\sin x = -1$ has one solution in $[0, 2\pi)$: $3\pi/2$. (Example 7)

To get *all* real solutions, we simply add integer multiples of the period, 2π, of the periodic function $\sin x$:

$$x = \frac{\pi}{6} + 2n\pi \text{ or } x = \frac{5\pi}{6} + 2n\pi \text{ or } x = \frac{3\pi}{2} + 2n\pi$$

$$(n = 0, \pm 1, \pm 2, \dots)$$

Now try Exercise 57.

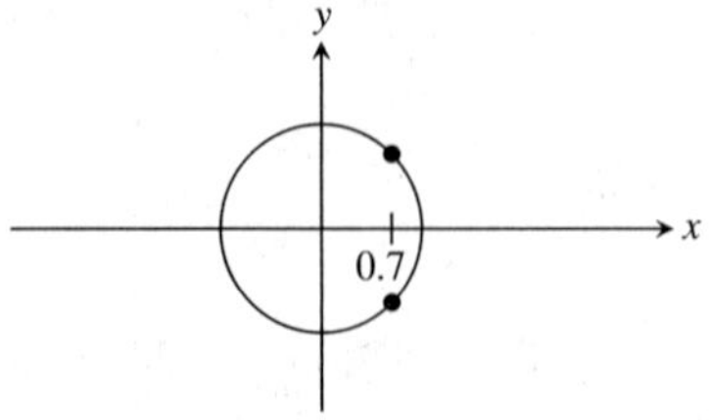

FIGURE H.84 There are two points on the unit circle with x-coordinate 0.7. (Example 8)

You might try solving the equation in Example 7 on your grapher for the sake of comparison. Finding *all* real solutions still requires an understanding of periodicity, and finding *exact* solutions requires the savvy to divide your calculator answers by π. It is likely that anyone who knows that much trigonometry will actually find the algebraic solution to be easier!

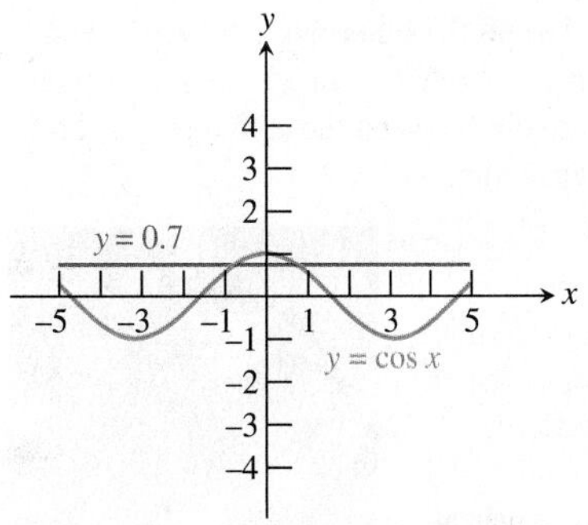

FIGURE H.85 Intersecting the graphs of $y = \cos x$ and $y = 0.7$ gives two solutions to the equation $\cos t = 0.7$. (Example 8)

EXAMPLE 8 Solving a Trig Equation with a Calculator

Find all solutions to the equation $\cos t = 0.7$, using a calculator where needed.

SOLUTION Figure H.84 shows that there are two points on the unit circle with an x-coordinate of 0.7. We do not recognize this value as one of our special triangle ratios, but we can use a graphing calculator to find the smallest positive and negative values for which $\cos x = 0.7$ by intersecting the graphs of $y = \cos x$ and $y = 0.7$ (Figure H.85).

The two values are predictably opposites of each other: $t \approx \pm 0.7954$. Using the period of cosine (which is 2π), we get the complete solution set: $\{\pm 0.7954 + 2n\pi \mid n = 0, \pm 1, \pm 2, \pm 3, \ldots\}$. *Now try Exercise 63.*

LESSON H-10 EXERCISES

Exercise numbers with a gray background indicate problems that the authors have designed to be solved *without a calculator.*

In Exercises 1–4, evaluate without using a calculator. Use the Pythagorean identities rather than reference triangles. (See Example 1.)

1. Find $\sin\theta$ and $\cos\theta$ if $\tan\theta = 3/4$ and $\sin\theta > 0$.

2. Find $\sec\theta$ and $\csc\theta$ if $\tan\theta = 3$ and $\cos\theta > 0$.

3. Find $\tan\theta$ and $\cot\theta$ if $\sec\theta = 4$ and $\sin\theta < 0$.

4. Find $\sin\theta$ and $\tan\theta$ if $\cos\theta = 0.8$ and $\tan\theta < 0$.

In Exercises 5–8, use identities to find the value of the expression.

5. If $\sin\theta = 0.45$, find $\cos(\pi/2 - \theta)$.

6. If $\tan(\pi/2 - \theta) = -5.32$, find $\cot\theta$.

7. If $\sin(\theta - \pi/2) = 0.73$, find $\cos(-\theta)$.

8. If $\cot(-\theta) = 7.89$, find $\tan(\theta - \pi/2)$.

In Exercises 9–16, use basic identities to simplify the expression.

9. $\tan x \cos x$ **10.** $\cot x \tan x$

11. $\sec y \sin(\pi/2 - y)$ **12.** $\cot u \sin u$

13. $\dfrac{1 + \tan^2 x}{\csc^2 x}$ **14.** $\dfrac{1 - \cos^2\theta}{\sin\theta}$

15. $\cos x - \cos^3 x$ **16.** $\dfrac{\sin^2 u + \tan^2 u + \cos^2 u}{\sec u}$

In Exercises 17–22, simplify the expression to either 1 or -1.

17. $\sin x \csc(-x)$

18. $\sec(-x)\cos(-x)$

19. $\cot(-x)\cot(\pi/2 - x)$

20. $\cot(-x)\tan(-x)$

21. $\sin^2(-x) + \cos^2(-x)$

22. $\sec^2(-x) - \tan^2 x$

In Exercises 23–26, simplify the expression to either a constant or a basic trigonometric function. Support your result graphically.

23. $\dfrac{\tan(\pi/2 - x)\csc x}{\csc^2 x}$

24. $\dfrac{1 + \tan x}{1 + \cot x}$

25. $(\sec^2 x + \csc^2 x) - (\tan^2 x + \cot^2 x)$

26. $\dfrac{\sec^2 u - \tan^2 u}{\cos^2 v + \sin^2 v}$

In Exercises 27–32, use the basic identities to change the expression to one involving only sines and cosines. Then simplify to a basic trigonometric function.

27. $(\sin x)(\tan x + \cot x)$

28. $\sin\theta - \tan\theta\cos\theta + \cos(\pi/2 - \theta)$

29. $\sin x \cos x \tan x \sec x \csc x$

30. $\dfrac{(\sec y - \tan y)(\sec y + \tan y)}{\sec y}$

31. $\dfrac{\tan x}{\csc^2 x} + \dfrac{\tan x}{\sec^2 x}$

32. $\dfrac{\sec^2 x \csc x}{\sec^2 x + \csc^2 x}$

In Exercises 33–38, combine the fractions and simplify to a multiple of a power of a basic trigonometric function (e.g., $3\tan^2 x$).

33. $\dfrac{1}{\sin^2 x} + \dfrac{\sec^2 x}{\tan^2 x}$ **34.** $\dfrac{1}{1 - \sin x} + \dfrac{1}{1 + \sin x}$

35. $\dfrac{\sin x}{\cot^2 x} - \dfrac{\sin x}{\cos^2 x}$ **36.** $\dfrac{1}{\sec x - 1} - \dfrac{1}{\sec x + 1}$

37. $\dfrac{\sec x}{\sin x} - \dfrac{\sin x}{\cos x}$ **38.** $\dfrac{\sin x}{1 - \cos x} + \dfrac{1 - \cos x}{\sin x}$

In Exercises 39–46, write each expression in factored form as an algebraic expression of a single trigonometric function (e.g., $(2\sin x + 3)(\sin x - 1)$).

39. $\cos^2 x + 2\cos x + 1$ **40.** $1 - 2\sin x + \sin^2 x$

41. $1 - 2\sin x + (1 - \cos^2 x)$

42. $\sin x - \cos^2 x - 1$ **43.** $\cos x - 2\sin^2 x + 1$

44. $\sin^2 x + \dfrac{2}{\csc x} + 1$

45. $4\tan^2 x - \dfrac{4}{\cot x} + \sin x \csc x$

46. $\sec^2 x - \sec x + \tan^2 x$

In Exercises 47–50, write each expression as an algebraic expression of a single trigonometric function (e.g., $2 \sin x + 3$).

47. $\dfrac{1 - \sin^2 x}{1 + \sin x}$

48. $\dfrac{\tan^2 \alpha - 1}{1 + \tan \alpha}$

49. $\dfrac{\sin^2 x}{1 + \cos x}$

50. $\dfrac{\tan^2 x}{\sec x + 1}$

In Exercises 51–56, find all solutions to the equation in the interval $[0, 2\pi)$. You do not need a calculator.

51. $2 \cos x \sin x - \cos x = 0$

52. $\sqrt{2} \tan x \cos x - \tan x = 0$

53. $\tan x \sin^2 x = \tan x$

54. $\sin x \tan^2 x = \sin x$

55. $\tan^2 x = 3$

56. $2 \sin^2 x = 1$

In Exercises 57–62, find all solutions to the equation. You do not need a calculator.

57. $4 \cos^2 x - 4 \cos x + 1 = 0$

58. $2 \sin^2 x + 3 \sin x + 1 = 0$

59. $\sin^2 \theta - 2 \sin \theta = 0$

60. $3 \sin t = 2 \cos^2 t$

61. $\cos(\sin x) = 1$

62. $2 \sin^2 x + 3 \sin x = 2$

In Exercises 63–68, find all solutions to the trigonometric equation, using a calculator where needed.

63. $\cos x = 0.37$

64. $\cos x = 0.75$

65. $\sin x = 0.30$

66. $\tan x = 5$

67. $\cos^2 x = 0.4$

68. $\sin^2 x = 0.4$

In Exercises 69–74, make the suggested trigonometric substitution, and then use Pythagorean identities to write the resulting function as a multiple of a basic trigonometric function.

69. $\sqrt{1 - x^2}$, $x = \cos \theta$

70. $\sqrt{x^2 + 1}$, $x = \tan \theta$

71. $\sqrt{x^2 - 9}$, $x = 3 \sec \theta$

72. $\sqrt{36 - x^2}$, $x = 6 \sin \theta$

73. $\sqrt{x^2 + 81}$, $x = 9 \tan \theta$

74. $\sqrt{x^2 - 100}$, $x = 10 \sec \theta$

Explorations

75. Write all six basic trigonometric functions entirely in terms of $\sin x$.

76. Write all six basic trigonometric functions entirely in terms of $\cos x$.

77. **Writing to Learn** Graph the functions $y = \sin^2 x$ and $y = -\cos^2 x$ in the standard trigonometric viewing window. Describe the apparent relationship between these two graphs and verify it with a trigonometric identity.

78. **Writing to Learn** Graph the functions $y = \sec^2 x$ and $y = \tan^2 x$ in the standard trigonometric viewing window. Describe the apparent relationship between these two graphs and verify it with a trigonometric identity.

79. **Orbit of the Moon** Because its orbit is elliptical, the distance from the Moon to the Earth in miles (measured from the center of the Moon to the center of the Earth) varies periodically. On Friday, January 23, 2009, the Moon was at its apogee (farthest from the Earth). The distance of the Moon from the Earth each Friday from January 23 to March 27 is recorded in Table H.8.

Table H.8 Distance from Earth to Moon

Date	Day	Distance
Jan 23	0	251,966
Jan 30	7	238,344
Feb 6	14	225,784
Feb 13	21	240,385
Feb 20	28	251,807
Feb 27	35	236,315
Mar 6	42	226,101
Mar 13	49	242,390
Mar 20	56	251,333
Mar 27	63	234,347

Source: The World Almanac and Book of Facts 2009.

(a) Draw a scatter plot of the data, using "day" as x and "distance" as y.

(b) Use your calculator to do a sine regression of y on x. Find the equation of the best-fit sine curve and superimpose its graph on the scatter plot.

(c) What is the approximate number of days from apogee to apogee? Interpret this number in terms of the orbit of the moon.

(d) Approximately how far is the Moon from the Earth at perigee (closest distance)?

(e) Since the data begin at apogee, perhaps a cosine curve would be a more appropriate model. Use the sine curve in part (b) and a cofunction identity to write a cosine curve that fits the data.

80. **Group Activity** Divide your class into six groups, each assigned to one of the basic trigonometric functions. With your group, construct a list of five different expressions that can be simplified to your assigned function. When you have finished, exchange lists with your "cofunction" group to check one another for accuracy.

Extending the Ideas

81. Prove that $\sin^4 \theta - \cos^4 \theta = \sin^2 \theta - \cos^2 \theta$.

82. Find all values of k that result in $\sin^2 x + 1 = k \sin x$ having an infinite solution set.

83. Use the cofunction identities and odd-even identities to prove that $\sin(\pi - x) = \sin x$.
[*Hint*: $\sin(\pi - x) = \sin(\pi/2 - (x - \pi/2))$.]

84. Use the cofunction identities and odd-even identities to prove that $\cos(\pi - x) = -\cos x$.
[*Hint*: $\cos(\pi - x) = \cos(\pi/2 - (x - \pi/2))$.]

85. Use the identity in Exercise 89 to prove that in any ΔABC, $\sin(A + B) = \sin C$.

86. Use the identities in Exercises 89 and 90 to find an identity for simplifying $\tan(\pi - x)$.

H-11 Proving Trigonometric Identities

What you'll learn about

- A Proof Strategy
- Proving Identities
- Disproving Non-Identities
- Identities in Calculus

... and why

Proving identities gives you excellent insights into the way mathematical proofs are constructed.

A Proof Strategy

We now arrive at the best opportunity in the precalculus curriculum for you to try your hand at constructing analytic proofs: trigonometric identities. Some are easy and some can be quite challenging, but in every case the *identity itself* frames your work with a beginning and an ending. The proof consists of filling in what lies between.

The strategy for proving an identity is very different from the strategy for solving an equation, most notably in the very first step. Usually the first step in solving an equation is to write down the equation. If you do this with an identity, however, you will have a beginning and an ending—with no proof in between! With an identity, you begin by writing down *one function* and end by writing down *the other*. Example 1 will illustrate what we mean.

EXAMPLE 1 Proving an Algebraic Identity

Prove the algebraic identity $\dfrac{x^2 - 1}{x - 1} - \dfrac{x^2 - 1}{x + 1} = 2.$

SOLUTION We prove this identity by showing a sequence of expressions, each one easily seen to be equivalent to its preceding expression:

$$\frac{x^2 - 1}{x - 1} - \frac{x^2 - 1}{x + 1} = \frac{(x + 1)(x - 1)}{x - 1} - \frac{(x + 1)(x - 1)}{x + 1} \quad \text{Factoring difference of squares}$$

$$= (x + 1)\left(\frac{x - 1}{x - 1}\right) - (x - 1)\left(\frac{x + 1}{x + 1}\right) \quad \text{Algebraic manipulation}$$

$$= (x + 1)(1) - (x - 1)(1) \quad \text{Reducing fractions}$$

$$= x + 1 - x + 1 \quad \text{Algebraic manipulation}$$

$$= 2$$

Notice that the first thing we wrote down was the expression on the left-hand side (LHS), and the last thing we wrote down was the expression on the right-hand side (RHS). The proof would have been just as legitimate going from RHS to LHS, but it is more natural to move from the more complicated side to the less complicated side. Incidentally, the margin notes on the right, called "floaters," are included here for instructional purposes and are not really part of the proof. A good proof should consist of steps for which a knowledgeable reader could readily supply the floaters.

Now try Exercise 1.

These, then, are our first general strategies for proving an identity:

General Strategies I

1. The proof begins with the expression on one side of the identity.
2. The proof ends with the expression on the other side.
3. The proof in between consists of showing a sequence of expressions, each one easily seen to be equivalent to its preceding expression.

Proving Identities

Trigonometric identity proofs follow General Strategies I. We are told that two expressions are equal, and the object is to prove that they are equal. We do this by changing one expression into the other by a series of intermediate steps that follow the important rule that *every intermediate step yields an expression that is equivalent to the first.*

The changes at every step are accomplished by algebraic manipulations or identities, but the manipulations or identities should be sufficiently obvious as to require no additional justification. Since "obvious" is often in the eye of the beholder, it is usually safer to err on the side of including too many steps than too few.

By working through several examples, we try to give you a sense for what is appropriate as we illustrate some of the algebraic tools that you have at your disposal.

EXAMPLE 2 Proving an Identity

Prove the identity: $\tan x + \cot x = \sec x \csc x$.

SOLUTION We begin by deciding whether to start with the expression on the right or the left. It is usually best to start with the more complicated expression, as it is easier to proceed from the complex toward the simple than to go in the other direction. The expression on the left is slightly more complicated because it involves two terms.

$$\begin{aligned}
\tan x + \cot x &= \frac{\sin x}{\cos x} + \frac{\cos x}{\sin x} && \text{Basic identities} \\
&= \frac{\sin x}{\cos x} \cdot \frac{\sin x}{\sin x} + \frac{\cos x}{\sin x} \cdot \frac{\cos x}{\cos x} && \text{Setting up common denominator} \\
&= \frac{\sin^2 x + \cos^2 x}{\cos x \cdot \sin x} \\
&= \frac{1}{\cos x \cdot \sin x} && \text{Pythagorean identity} \\
&= \frac{1}{\cos x} \cdot \frac{1}{\sin x} && \text{(A step you could choose to omit)} \\
&= \sec x \csc x && \text{Basic identities}
\end{aligned}$$

(Remember that the "floaters" are not really part of the proof.)

Now try Exercise 13.

The preceding example illustrates three general strategies that are often useful in proving trigonometric identities.

General Strategies II

1. Begin with the more complicated expression and work toward the less complicated expression.
2. If no other move suggests itself, convert the entire expression to one involving sines and cosines.
3. Combine fractions by combining them over a common denominator.

EXAMPLE 3 Identifying and Proving an Identity

Match the function

$$f(x) = \frac{1}{\sec x - 1} + \frac{1}{\sec x + 1}$$

with one of the following. Then confirm the match with a proof.

(i) $2 \cot x \csc x$ **(ii)** $\dfrac{1}{\sec x}$

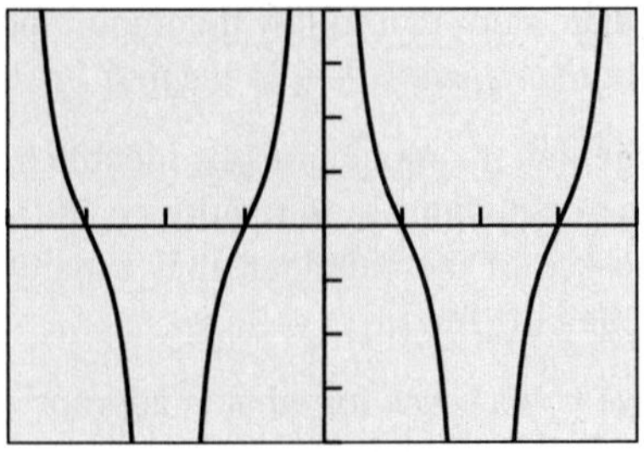

$[-2\pi, 2\pi]$ by $[-4, 4]$

$f(x) = \dfrac{1}{\sec x - 1} + \dfrac{1}{\sec x + 1}$

(a)

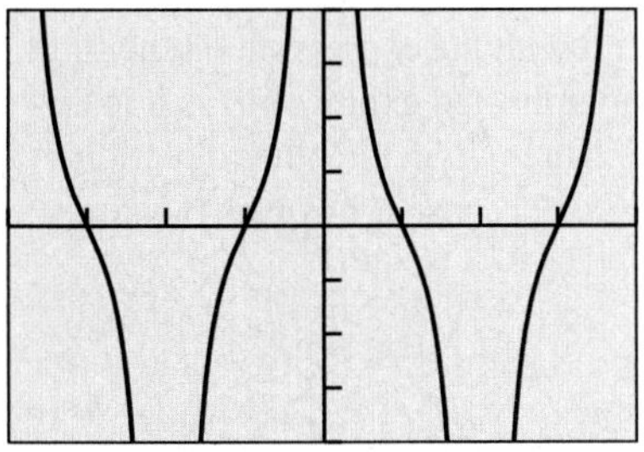

$[-2\pi, 2\pi]$ by $[-4, 4]$

$y = 2 \cot x \csc x$

(b)

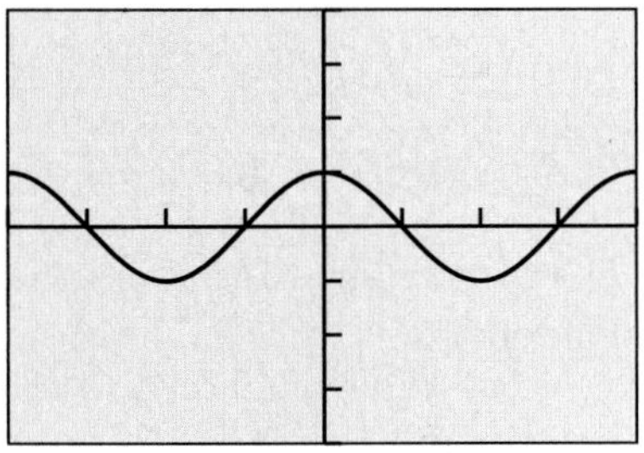

$[-2\pi, 2\pi]$ by $[-4, 4]$

$y = \dfrac{1}{\sec x}$

(c)

FIGURE H.86 A grapher can be useful for identifying possible identities. (Example 3)

SOLUTION Figures H.86a, b, and c show the graphs of the functions $y = f(x)$, $y = 2 \cot x \csc x$, and $y = 1/\sec x$, respectively. The graphs in (a) and (c) show that $f(x)$ is not equal to the expression in (ii). From the graphs in (a) and (b), it appears that $f(x)$ is equal to the expression in (i). To confirm, we begin with the expression for $f(x)$.

$$\frac{1}{\sec x - 1} + \frac{1}{\sec x + 1}$$

$$= \frac{\sec x + 1}{(\sec x - 1)(\sec x + 1)} + \frac{\sec x - 1}{(\sec x - 1)(\sec x + 1)} \qquad \text{Common denominator}$$

$$= \frac{\sec x + 1 + \sec x - 1}{\sec^2 x - 1}$$

$$= \frac{2 \sec x}{\tan^2 x} \qquad \text{Pythagorean identity}$$

$$= \frac{2}{\cos x} \cdot \frac{\cos^2 x}{\sin^2 x} \qquad \text{Basic identities}$$

$$= \frac{2 \cos x}{\sin x} \cdot \frac{1}{\sin x}$$

$$= 2 \cot x \csc x$$

Now try Exercise 55.

The next example illustrates how the algebraic identity $(a + b)(a - b) = a^2 - b^2$ can be used to set up a Pythagorean substitution.

EXAMPLE 4 Setting up a Difference of Squares

Prove the identity: $\cos t/(1 - \sin t) = (1 + \sin t)/\cos t$.

SOLUTION The left-hand expression is slightly more complicated, as we can handle extra terms in a numerator more easily than in a denominator. So we begin with the left.

$$\frac{\cos t}{1 - \sin t} = \frac{\cos t}{1 - \sin t} \cdot \frac{1 + \sin t}{1 + \sin t} \qquad \text{Setting up a difference of squares}$$

$$= \frac{(\cos t)(1 + \sin t)}{1 - \sin^2 t}$$

$$= \frac{(\cos t)(1 + \sin t)}{\cos^2 t} \qquad \text{Pythagorean identity}$$

$$= \frac{1 + \sin t}{\cos t}$$

Now try Exercise 39.

Notice that we kept $(\cos t)(1 + \sin t)$ in factored form in the hope that we could eventually eliminate the factor $\cos t$ and be left with the numerator we need. It is always a good idea to keep an eye on the "target" expression toward which your proof is aimed.

General Strategies III

1. Use the algebraic identity $(a + b)(a - b) = a^2 - b^2$ to set up applications of the Pythagorean identities.
2. Always be mindful of the "target" expression, and favor manipulations that bring you closer to your goal.

In more complicated identities (as in word ladders) it is sometimes helpful to see if both sides can be manipulated toward a common intermediate expression. The proof can then be reconstructed in a single path.

EXAMPLE 5 Working from Both Sides

Prove the identity: $\cot^2 u/(1 + \csc u) = (\cot u)(\sec u - \tan u)$.

SOLUTION Both sides are fairly complicated, but the left-hand side looks as though it needs more work. We start on the left.

$$\begin{aligned}
\frac{\cot^2 u}{1 + \csc u} &= \frac{\csc^2 u - 1}{1 + \csc u} && \text{Pythagorean identity} \\
&= \frac{(\csc u + 1)(\csc u - 1)}{\csc u + 1} && \text{Factor} \\
&= \csc u - 1
\end{aligned}$$

At this point it is not clear how we can get from this expression to the one on the right-hand side of our identity. However, we now have reason to believe that the right-hand side must simplify to $\csc u - 1$, so we try simplifying the right-hand side.

$$\begin{aligned}
(\cot u)(\sec u - \tan u) &= \left(\frac{\cos u}{\sin u}\right)\left(\frac{1}{\cos u} - \frac{\sin u}{\cos u}\right) && \text{Basic identities} \\
&= \frac{1}{\sin u} - 1 && \text{Distribute the product.} \\
&= \csc u - 1
\end{aligned}$$

Now we can reconstruct the proof by going through $\csc u - 1$ as an intermediate step.

$$\begin{aligned}
\frac{\cot^2 u}{1 + \csc u} &= \frac{\csc^2 u - 1}{1 + \csc u} \\
&= \frac{(\csc u + 1)(\csc u - 1)}{\csc u + 1} \\
&= \csc u - 1 && \text{Intermediate step} \\
&= \frac{1}{\sin u} - 1 \\
&= \left(\frac{\cos u}{\sin u}\right)\left(\frac{1}{\cos u} - \frac{\sin u}{\cos u}\right) \\
&= (\cot u)(\sec u - \tan u)
\end{aligned}$$

Now try Exercise 41.

Disproving Non-Identities

Obviously, not every equation involving trigonometric expressions is an identity. How can we spot a non-identity before embarking on a futile attempt at a proof? Try the following exploration.

EXPLORATION 1 Confirming a Non-Identity

Prove or disprove that this is an identity: $\cos 2x = 2 \cos x$.

1. Graph $y = \cos 2x$ and $y = 2 \cos x$ in the same window. Interpret the graphs to make a conclusion about whether or not the equation is an identity.
2. With the help of the graph, find a value of x for which $\cos 2x \neq 2 \cos x$.
3. Does the existence of the x-value in part (2) *prove* that the equation is *not* an identity?

4. Graph $y = \cos 2x$ and $y = \cos^2 x - \sin^2 x$ in the same window. Interpret the graphs to make a conclusion about whether or not $\cos 2x = \cos^2 x - \sin^2 x$ is an identity.

5. Do the graphs in part (4) *prove* that $\cos 2x = \cos^2 x - \sin^2 x$ is an identity? Explain your answer.

Exploration 1 suggests that we can use graphers to help confirm a *non-identity*, since we only have to produce a single value of x for which the two compared expressions are defined but unequal. On the other hand, we cannot use graphers to prove that an equation *is* an identity, since, for example, the graphers can never prove that two irrational numbers are equal. Also, graphers cannot show behavior over infinite domains.

Identities in Calculus

In most calculus problems where identities play a role, the object is to make a complicated expression simpler for the sake of computational ease. Occasionally it is actually necessary to make a *simple* expression *more complicated* for the sake of computational ease. Each of the following identities (just a sampling of many) represents a useful substitution in calculus wherein the expression on the right is simpler to deal with (even though it does not look that way). We prove one of these identities in Example 6 and leave the rest for the exercises or for future sections.

1. $\cos^3 x = (1 - \sin^2 x)(\cos x)$
2. $\sec^4 x = (1 + \tan^2 x)(\sec^2 x)$
3. $\sin^2 x = \frac{1}{2} - \frac{1}{2}\cos 2x$
4. $\cos^2 x = \frac{1}{2} + \frac{1}{2}\cos 2x$
5. $\sin^5 x = (1 - 2\cos^2 x + \cos^4 x)(\sin x)$
6. $\sin^2 x \cos^5 x = (\sin^2 x - 2\sin^4 x + \sin^6 x)(\cos x)$

EXAMPLE 6 Proving an Identity Useful in Calculus

Prove the following identity:

$\sin^2 x \cos^5 x = (\sin^2 x - 2\sin^4 x + \sin^6 x)(\cos x)$.

SOLUTION We begin with the expression on the left.

$$\begin{aligned}\sin^2 x \cos^5 x &= \sin^2 x \cos^4 x \cos x\\ &= (\sin^2 x)(\cos^2 x)^2(\cos x)\\ &= (\sin^2 x)(1 - \sin^2 x)^2(\cos x)\\ &= (\sin^2 x)(1 - 2\sin^2 x + \sin^4 x)(\cos x)\\ &= (\sin^2 x - 2\sin^4 x + \sin^6 x)(\cos x)\end{aligned}$$

Now try Exercise 51.

LESSON H-11 EXERCISES

Exercise numbers with a gray background indicate problems that the authors have designed to be solved *without a calculator.*

In Exercises 1–4, prove the algebraic identity by starting with the LHS expression and supplying a sequence of equivalent expressions that ends with the RHS expression.

1. $\dfrac{x^3 - x^2}{x} - (x - 1)(x + 1) = 1 - x$
2. $\dfrac{1}{x} - \dfrac{1}{2} = \dfrac{2 - x}{2x}$
3. $\dfrac{x^2 - 4}{x - 2} - \dfrac{x^2 - 9}{x + 3} = 5$
4. $(x - 1)(x + 2) - (x + 1)(x - 2) = 2x$

In Exercises 5–10, tell whether or not $f(x) = \sin x$ is an identity.

5. $f(x) = \dfrac{\sin^2 x + \cos^2 x}{\csc x}$
6. $f(x) = \dfrac{\tan x}{\sec x}$
7. $f(x) = \cos x \cdot \cot x$
8. $f(x) = \cos(x - \pi/2)$
9. $f(x) = (\sin^3 x)(1 + \cot^2 x)$
10. $f(x) = \dfrac{\sin 2x}{2}$

In Exercises 11–51, prove the identity.

11. $(\cos x)(\tan x + \sin x \cot x) = \sin x + \cos^2 x$
12. $(\sin x)(\cot x + \cos x \tan x) = \cos x + \sin^2 x$
13. $(1 - \tan x)^2 = \sec^2 x - 2 \tan x$
14. $(\cos x - \sin x)^2 = 1 - 2 \sin x \cos x$
15. $\dfrac{(1 - \cos u)(1 + \cos u)}{\cos^2 u} = \tan^2 u$
16. $\tan x + \sec x = \dfrac{\cos x}{1 - \sin x}$
17. $\dfrac{\cos^2 x - 1}{\cos x} = -\tan x \sin x$
18. $\dfrac{\sec^2 \theta - 1}{\sin \theta} = \dfrac{\sin \theta}{1 - \sin^2 \theta}$
19. $(1 - \sin \beta)(1 + \csc \beta) = 1 - \sin \beta + \csc \beta - \sin \beta \csc \beta$
20. $\dfrac{1}{1 - \cos x} + \dfrac{1}{1 + \cos x} = 2 \csc^2 x$
21. $(\cos t - \sin t)^2 + (\cos t + \sin t)^2 = 2$
22. $\sin^2 \alpha - \cos^2 \alpha = 1 - 2 \cos^2 \alpha$
23. $\dfrac{1 + \tan^2 x}{\sin^2 x + \cos^2 x} = \sec^2 x$
24. $\dfrac{1}{\tan \beta} + \tan \beta = \sec \beta \csc \beta$
25. $\dfrac{\cos \beta}{1 + \sin \beta} = \dfrac{1 - \sin \beta}{\cos \beta}$
26. $\dfrac{\sec x + 1}{\tan x} = \dfrac{\sin x}{1 - \cos x}$
27. $\dfrac{\tan^2 x}{\sec x + 1} = \dfrac{1 - \cos x}{\cos x}$
28. $\dfrac{\cot v - 1}{\cot v + 1} = \dfrac{1 - \tan v}{1 + \tan v}$
29. $\cot^2 x - \cos^2 x = \cos^2 x \cot^2 x$
30. $\tan^2 \theta - \sin^2 \theta = \tan^2 \theta \sin^2 \theta$
31. $\cos^4 x - \sin^4 x = \cos^2 x - \sin^2 x$
32. $\tan^4 t + \tan^2 t = \sec^4 t - \sec^2 t$
33. $(x \sin \alpha + y \cos \alpha)^2 + (x \cos \alpha - y \sin \alpha)^2 = x^2 + y^2$
34. $\dfrac{1 - \cos \theta}{\sin \theta} = \dfrac{\sin \theta}{1 + \cos \theta}$
35. $\dfrac{\tan x}{\sec x - 1} = \dfrac{\sec x + 1}{\tan x}$
36. $\dfrac{\sin t}{1 + \cos t} + \dfrac{1 + \cos t}{\sin t} = 2 \csc t$
37. $\dfrac{\sin x - \cos x}{\sin x + \cos x} = \dfrac{2 \sin^2 x - 1}{1 + 2 \sin x \cos x}$
38. $\dfrac{1 + \cos x}{1 - \cos x} = \dfrac{\sec x + 1}{\sec x - 1}$
39. $\dfrac{\sin t}{1 - \cos t} + \dfrac{1 + \cos t}{\sin t} = \dfrac{2(1 + \cos t)}{\sin t}$
40. $\dfrac{\sin A \cos B + \cos A \sin B}{\cos A \cos B - \sin A \sin B} = \dfrac{\tan A + \tan B}{1 - \tan A \tan B}$
41. $\sin^2 x \cos^3 x = (\sin^2 x - \sin^4 x)(\cos x)$
42. $\sin^5 x \cos^2 x = (\cos^2 x - 2 \cos^4 x + \cos^6 x)(\sin x)$
43. $\cos^5 x = (1 - 2 \sin^2 x + \sin^4 x)(\cos x)$
44. $\sin^3 x \cos^3 x = (\sin^3 x - \sin^5 x)(\cos x)$
45. $\dfrac{\tan x}{1 - \cot x} + \dfrac{\cot x}{1 - \tan x} = 1 + \sec x \csc x$
46. $\dfrac{\cos x}{1 + \sin x} + \dfrac{\cos x}{1 - \sin x} = 2 \sec x$
47. $\dfrac{2 \tan x}{1 - \tan^2 x} + \dfrac{1}{2 \cos^2 x - 1} = \dfrac{\cos x + \sin x}{\cos x - \sin x}$
48. $\dfrac{1 - 3 \cos x - 4 \cos^2 x}{\sin^2 x} = \dfrac{1 - 4 \cos x}{1 - \cos x}$
49. $\cos^3 x = (1 - \sin^2 x)(\cos x)$
50. $\sec^4 x = (1 + \tan^2 x)(\sec^2 x)$
51. $\sin^5 x = (1 - 2 \cos^2 x + \cos^4 x)(\sin x)$

In Exercises 52–57, match the function with an equivalent expression from the following list. Then confirm the match with a proof. (The matching is not one-to-one.)

(a) $\sec^2 x \csc^2 x$ **(b)** $\sec x + \tan x$ **(c)** $2 \sec^2 x$

(d) $\tan x \sin x$ **(e)** $\sin x \cos x$

52. $\dfrac{1 + \sin x}{\cos x}$

53. $(1 + \sec x)(1 - \cos x)$

54. $\sec^2 x + \csc^2 x$

55. $\dfrac{1}{1 + \sin x} + \dfrac{1}{1 - \sin x}$

56. $\dfrac{1}{\tan x + \cot x}$

57. $\dfrac{1}{\sec x - \tan x}$

Explorations

In Exercises 58–63, identify a simple function that has the same graph. Then confirm your choice with a proof.

58. $\sin x \cot x$

59. $\cos x \tan x$

60. $\dfrac{\sin x}{\csc x} + \dfrac{\cos x}{\sec x}$

61. $\dfrac{\csc x}{\sin x} - \dfrac{\cot x \csc x}{\sec x}$

62. $\dfrac{\sin x}{\tan x}$

63. $(\sec^2 x)(1 - \sin^2 x)$

64. Writing to Learn Let θ be any number that is in the domain of all six trig functions. Explain why the natural logarithms of all six basic trig functions of θ sum to 0.

65. If A and B are complementary angles, prove that $\sin^2 A + \sin^2 B = 1$.

66. Group Activity If your class contains $2n$ students, write the two expressions from n different identities on separate pieces of paper. (If your class contains an odd number of students, invite your teacher to join you for this activity.) You can use the identities from Exercises 11–51 in this section or from other textbooks, but be sure to write them all in the variable x. Mix up the slips of paper and give one to each student in your class. Then see how long it takes you as a class, without looking at the book, to pair yourselves off as identities. (This activity takes on an added degree of difficulty if you try it without calculators.)

Extending the Ideas

In Exercises 67–72, confirm the identity.

67. $\sqrt{\dfrac{1 - \sin t}{1 + \sin t}} = \dfrac{1 - \sin t}{|\cos t|}$

68. $\sqrt{\dfrac{1 + \cos t}{1 - \cos t}} = \dfrac{1 + \cos t}{|\sin t|}$

69. $\sin^6 x + \cos^6 x = 1 - 3 \sin^2 x \cos^2 x$

70. $\cos^6 x - \sin^6 x = (\cos^2 x - \sin^2 x)(1 - \cos^2 x \sin^2 x)$

71. $\ln |\tan x| = \ln |\sin x| - \ln |\cos x|$

72. $\ln |\sec \theta + \tan \theta| + \ln |\sec \theta - \tan \theta| = 0$

73. Writing to Learn Let $y_1 = [\sin (x + 0.001) - \sin x]/0.001$ and $y_2 = \cos x$.

(a) Use graphs and tables to decide whether $y_1 = y_2$.

(b) Find a value for h so that the graph of $y_3 = y_1 - y_2$ in $[-2\pi, 2\pi]$ by $[-h, h]$ appears to be a sinusoid. Give a convincing argument that y_3 is a sinusoid.

74. Hyperbolic Functions The *hyperbolic trigonometric functions* are defined as follows:

$$\sinh x = \frac{e^x - e^{-x}}{2} \quad \cosh x = \frac{e^x + e^{-x}}{2} \quad \tanh x = \frac{\sinh x}{\cosh x}$$

$$\operatorname{csch} x = \frac{1}{\sinh x} \quad \operatorname{sech} x = \frac{1}{\cosh x} \quad \coth x = \frac{1}{\tanh x}$$

Confirm the identity.

(a) $\cosh^2 x - \sinh^2 x = 1$

(b) $1 - \tanh^2 x = \operatorname{sech}^2 x$

(c) $\coth^2 x - 1 = \operatorname{csch}^2 x$

75. Writing to Learn Write a paragraph to explain why

$$\cos x = \cos x + \sin (10\pi x)$$

appears to be an identity when the two sides are graphed in a decimal window. Give a convincing argument that it is not an identity.

H-12 Sum and Difference Identities

What you'll learn about

- Cosine of a Difference
- Cosine of a Sum
- Sine of a Difference or Sum
- Tangent of a Difference or Sum
- Verifying a Sinusoid Algebraically

... and why

These identities provide clear examples of how different the algebra of functions can be from the algebra of real numbers.

Cosine of a Difference

There is a powerful instinct in all of us to believe that all functions obey the following law of additivity:

$$f(u + v) = f(u) + f(v)$$

In fact, very few do. If there were a hall of fame for algebraic blunders, the following would probably be the first two inductees:

$$(u + v)^2 = u^2 + v^2$$
$$\sqrt{u + v} = \sqrt{u} + \sqrt{v}$$

So, before we derive the true sum formulas for sine and cosine, let us clear the air with the following exploration.

EXPLORATION 1 Getting Past the Obvious but Incorrect Formulas

1. Let $u = \pi$ and $v = \pi/2$.
   Find $\sin(u + v)$. Find $\sin(u) + \sin(v)$.
   Does $\sin(u + v) = \sin(u) + \sin(v)$?
2. Let $u = 0$ and $v = 2\pi$.
   Find $\cos(u + v)$. Find $\cos(u) + \cos(v)$.
   Does $\cos(u + v) = \cos(u) + \cos(v)$?
3. Find your own values of u and v that will confirm that $\tan(u + v) \neq \tan(u) + \tan(v)$.

We could also show easily that

$$\cos(u - v) \neq \cos(u) - \cos(v) \quad \text{and} \quad \sin(u - v) \neq \sin(u) - \sin(v).$$

As you might expect, there *are* formulas for $\sin(u \pm v)$, $\cos(u \pm v)$, and $\tan(u \pm v)$, but Exploration 1 shows that they are not the ones our instincts would suggest. In a sense, that makes them all the more interesting. We will derive them all, beginning with the formula for $\cos(u - v)$.

Figure H.87a on the next page shows angles u and v in standard position on the unit circle, determining points A and B with coordinates $(\cos u, \sin u)$ and $(\cos v, \sin v)$, respectively. Figure H.87b shows the triangle ABO rotated so that the angle $\theta = u - v$ is in standard position. The angle θ determines point C with coordinates $(\cos\theta, \sin\theta)$.

The chord opposite angle θ has the same length in both circles, even though the coordinatization of the endpoints is different. Use the distance formula to find the length in each case, and set the formulas equal to each other:

$$AB = CD$$
$$\sqrt{(\cos v - \cos u)^2 + (\sin v - \sin u)^2} = \sqrt{(\cos\theta - 1)^2 + (\sin\theta - 0)^2}$$

Square both sides to eliminate the radical and expand the binomials to get

$$\cos^2 u - 2\cos u\cos v + \cos^2 v + \sin^2 u - 2\sin u\sin v + \sin^2 v = \cos^2\theta - 2\cos\theta + 1 + \sin^2\theta$$
$$(\cos^2 u + \sin^2 u) + (\cos^2 v + \sin^2 v) - 2\cos u\cos v - 2\sin u\sin v = (\cos^2\theta + \sin^2\theta) + 1 - 2\cos\theta$$
$$2 - 2\cos u\cos v - 2\sin u\sin v = 2 - 2\cos\theta$$
$$\cos u\cos v + \sin u\sin v = \cos\theta$$

Finally, since $\theta = u - v$, we can write

$$\cos(u - v) = \cos u \cos v + \sin u \sin v.$$

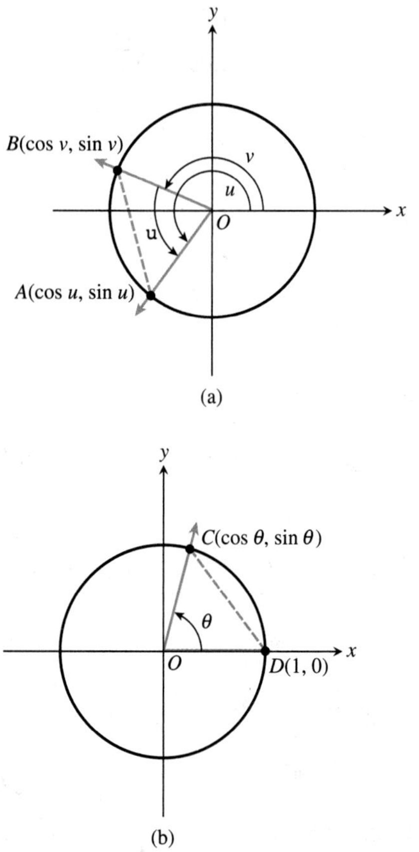

FIGURE H.87 Angles u and v are in standard position in (a), while angle $\theta = u - v$ is in standard position in (b). The chords shown in the two circles are equal in length.

EXAMPLE 1 Using the Cosine-of-a-Difference Identity

Find the exact value of cos 15° without using a calculator.

SOLUTION The trick is to write cos 15° as $\cos(45° - 30°)$; then we can use our knowledge of the special angles.

$$\begin{aligned} \cos 15° &= \cos(45° - 30°) \\ &= \cos 45° \cos 30° + \sin 45° \sin 30° && \text{Cosine difference identity} \\ &= \left(\frac{\sqrt{2}}{2}\right)\left(\frac{\sqrt{3}}{2}\right) + \left(\frac{\sqrt{2}}{2}\right)\left(\frac{1}{2}\right) \\ &= \frac{\sqrt{6} + \sqrt{2}}{4} \end{aligned}$$

Now try Exercise 5.

Cosine of a Sum

Now that we have the formula for the cosine of a difference, we can get the formula for the cosine of a sum almost for free by using the odd-even identities.

$$\begin{aligned} \cos(u + v) &= \cos(u - (-v)) \\ &= \cos u \cos(-v) + \sin u \sin(-v) && \text{Cosine difference identity} \\ &= \cos u \cos v + \sin u(-\sin v) && \text{Odd-even identities} \\ &= \cos u \cos v - \sin u \sin v \end{aligned}$$

We can combine the sum and difference formulas for cosine as follows:

Cosine of a Sum or Difference

$$\cos(u \pm v) = \cos u \cos v \mp \sin u \sin v$$

(Note the sign switch in either case.)

We pointed out in Lesson H-10 that the cofunction identities would be easier to prove with the results of Lesson H-12. Here is what we mean.

EXAMPLE 2 Confirming Cofunction Identities

Prove the identities **(a)** $\cos((\pi/2) - x) = \sin x$ and **(b)** $\sin((\pi/2) - x) = \cos x$.

SOLUTION

(a) $$\begin{aligned} \cos\left(\frac{\pi}{2} - x\right) &= \cos\left(\frac{\pi}{2}\right)\cos x + \sin\left(\frac{\pi}{2}\right)\sin x && \text{Cosine sum identity} \\ &= 0 \cdot \cos x + 1 \cdot \sin x \\ &= \sin x \end{aligned}$$

(b) $$\begin{aligned} \sin\left(\frac{\pi}{2} - x\right) &= \cos\left(\frac{\pi}{2} - \left(\frac{\pi}{2} - x\right)\right) && \sin\theta = \cos((\pi/2) - \theta) \text{ by previous proof} \\ &= \cos(0 + x) \\ &= \cos x \end{aligned}$$

Now try Exercise 41.

Sine of a Difference or Sum

We can use the cofunction identities in Example 2 to get the formula for the sine of a sum from the formula for the cosine of a difference.

$$\begin{aligned} \sin(u+v) &= \cos\left(\frac{\pi}{2}-(u+v)\right) && \text{Cofunction identity} \\ &= \cos\left(\left(\frac{\pi}{2}-u\right)-v\right) && \text{A little algebra} \\ &= \cos\left(\frac{\pi}{2}-u\right)\cos v + \sin\left(\frac{\pi}{2}-u\right)\sin v && \text{Cosine difference identity} \\ &= \sin u \cos v + \cos u \sin v && \text{Cofunction identities} \end{aligned}$$

Then we can use the odd-even identities to get the formula for the sine of a difference from the formula for the sine of a sum.

$$\begin{aligned} \sin(u-v) &= \sin(u+(-v)) && \text{A little algebra} \\ &= \sin u \cos(-v) + \cos u \sin(-v) && \text{Sine sum identity} \\ &= \sin u \cos v + \cos u(-\sin v) && \text{Odd-even identities} \\ &= \sin u \cos v - \cos u \sin v \end{aligned}$$

We can combine the sum and difference formulas for sine as follows:

Sine of a Sum or Difference

$$\sin(u \pm v) = \sin u \cos v \pm \cos u \sin v$$

(Note that the sign does *not* switch in either case.)

EXAMPLE 3 Using the Sum/Difference Formulas

Write each of the following expressions as the sine or cosine of an angle.

(a) $\sin 22° \cos 13° + \cos 22° \sin 13°$

(b) $\cos\frac{\pi}{3}\cos\frac{\pi}{4} + \sin\frac{\pi}{3}\sin\frac{\pi}{4}$

(c) $\sin x \sin 2x - \cos x \cos 2x$

SOLUTION The key in each case is recognizing which formula applies. (Indeed, the real purpose of such exercises is to help you remember the formulas.)

(a) $\sin 22° \cos 13° + \cos 22° \sin 13°$ — Recognizing sine of sum formula

$= \sin(22° + 13°)$

$= \sin 35°$

(b) $\cos\frac{\pi}{3}\cos\frac{\pi}{4} + \sin\frac{\pi}{3}\sin\frac{\pi}{4}$ — Recognizing cosine of difference formula

$= \cos\left(\frac{\pi}{3}-\frac{\pi}{4}\right)$

$= \cos\frac{\pi}{12}$

(c) $\sin x \sin 2x - \cos x \cos 2x$ — Recognizing *opposite* of cos sum formula

$= -(\cos x \cos 2x - \sin x \sin 2x)$

$= -\cos(x + 2x)$ — Applying formula

$= -\cos 3x$

Now try Exercise 19.

If one of the angles in a sum or difference is a quadrantal angle (that is, a multiple of 90° or of $\pi/2$ radians), then the sum-difference identities yield single-termed expressions. Since the effect is to reduce the complexity, the resulting identity is called a **reduction formula**.

EXAMPLE 4 Proving Reduction Formulas

Prove the reduction formulas:

(a) $\sin(x + \pi) = -\sin x$

(b) $\cos\left(x + \dfrac{3\pi}{2}\right) = \sin x$

SOLUTION

(a)
$$\begin{aligned}\sin(x + \pi) &= \sin x \cos \pi + \cos x \sin \pi \\ &= \sin x \cdot (-1) + \cos x \cdot 0 \\ &= -\sin x\end{aligned}$$

(b)
$$\begin{aligned}\cos\left(x + \frac{3\pi}{2}\right) &= \cos x \cos \frac{3\pi}{2} - \sin x \sin \frac{3\pi}{2} \\ &= \cos x \cdot 0 - \sin x \cdot (-1) \\ &= \sin x\end{aligned}$$

Now try Exercise 23.

Tangent of a Difference or Sum

We can derive a formula for $\tan(u \pm v)$ directly from the corresponding formulas for sine and cosine, as follows:

$$\tan(u \pm v) = \frac{\sin(u \pm v)}{\cos(u \pm v)} = \frac{\sin u \cos v \pm \cos u \sin v}{\cos u \cos v \mp \sin u \sin v}$$

There is also a formula for $\tan(u \pm v)$ that is written entirely in terms of tangent functions:

$$\tan(u \pm v) = \frac{\tan u \pm \tan v}{1 \mp \tan u \tan v}$$

We will leave the proof of the all-tangent formula to the exercises.

EXAMPLE 5 Proving a Tangent Reduction Formula

Prove the reduction formula: $\tan(\theta - (3\pi/2)) = -\cot\theta$.

SOLUTION We can't use the all-tangent formula (Do you see why?), so we convert to sines and cosines.

$$\begin{aligned}\tan\left(\theta - \frac{3\pi}{2}\right) &= \frac{\sin(\theta - (3\pi/2))}{\cos(\theta - (3\pi/2))} \\ &= \frac{\sin\theta\cos(3\pi/2) - \cos\theta\sin(3\pi/2)}{\cos\theta\cos(3\pi/2) + \sin\theta\sin(3\pi/2)} \\ &= \frac{\sin\theta\cdot 0 - \cos\theta\cdot(-1)}{\cos\theta\cdot 0 + \sin\theta\cdot(-1)} \\ &= -\cot\theta\end{aligned}$$

Now try Exercise 39.

Verifying a Sinusoid Algebraically

Recall that the function $f(x) = 2\sin x + 5\cos x$ is a sinusoid. We solved graphically, concluding that $f(x) \approx 5.39\sin(x + 1.19)$. We now have a way of solving this kind of problem algebraically, with exact values for the amplitude and phase shift. Example 6 illustrates the technique.

EXAMPLE 6 **Expressing a Sum of Sinusoids as a Sinusoid**

Express $f(x) = 2 \sin x + 5 \cos x$ as a sinusoid in the form $f(x) = a \sin (bx + c)$.

SOLUTION Since $a \sin (bx + c) = a (\sin bx \cos c + \cos bx \sin c)$, we have

$$\begin{aligned} 2 \sin x + 5 \cos x &= a (\sin bx \cos c + \cos bx \sin c) \\ &= (a \cos c) \sin bx + (a \sin c) \cos bx. \end{aligned}$$

Comparing coefficients, we see that $b = 1$ and that $a \cos c = 2$ and $a \sin c = 5$. We can solve for a as follows:

$$\begin{aligned} (a \cos c)^2 + (a \sin c)^2 &= 2^2 + 5^2 \\ a^2 \cos^2 c + a^2 \sin^2 c &= 29 \\ a^2(\cos^2 c + \sin^2 c) &= 29 \\ a^2 &= 29 \qquad \text{Pythogorean identity} \\ a &= \pm\sqrt{29} \end{aligned}$$

If we choose a to be positive, then $\cos c = 2/\sqrt{29}$ and $\sin c = 5/\sqrt{29}$. We can identify an acute angle c with those specifications as either $\cos^{-1}(2/\sqrt{29})$ or $\sin^{-1}(5/\sqrt{29})$, which are equal. So, an exact sinusoid for f is

$$\begin{aligned} f(x) &= 2 \sin x + 5 \cos x \\ &= a \sin (bx + c) \\ &= \sqrt{29} \sin (x + \cos^{-1}(2/\sqrt{29})) \text{ or } \sqrt{29} \sin (x + \sin^{-1}(5/\sqrt{29})) \end{aligned}$$

Now try Exercise 43.

LESSON H-12 EXERCISES

Exercise numbers with a gray background indicate problems that the authors have designed to be solved *without a calculator.*

In Exercises 1–10, use a sum or difference identity to find an exact value.

1. $\sin 15°$
2. $\tan 15°$
3. $\sin 75°$
4. $\cos 75°$
5. $\cos \dfrac{\pi}{12}$
6. $\sin \dfrac{7\pi}{12}$
7. $\tan \dfrac{5\pi}{12}$
8. $\tan \dfrac{11\pi}{12}$
9. $\cos \dfrac{7\pi}{12}$
10. $\sin \dfrac{-\pi}{12}$

In Exercises 11–22, write the expression as the sine, cosine, or tangent of an angle.

11. $\sin 42° \cos 17° - \cos 42° \sin 17°$
12. $\cos 94° \cos 18° + \sin 94° \sin 18°$
13. $\sin \dfrac{\pi}{5} \cos \dfrac{\pi}{2} + \sin \dfrac{\pi}{2} \cos \dfrac{\pi}{5}$
14. $\sin \dfrac{\pi}{3} \cos \dfrac{\pi}{7} - \sin \dfrac{\pi}{7} \cos \dfrac{\pi}{3}$
15. $\dfrac{\tan 19° + \tan 47°}{1 - \tan 19° \tan 47°}$
16. $\dfrac{\tan(\pi/5) - \tan(\pi/3)}{1 + \tan(\pi/5)\tan(\pi/3)}$
17. $\cos \dfrac{\pi}{7} \cos x + \sin \dfrac{\pi}{7} \sin x$
18. $\cos x \cos \dfrac{\pi}{7} - \sin x \sin \dfrac{\pi}{7}$
19. $\sin 3x \cos x - \cos 3x \sin x$
20. $\cos 7y \cos 3y - \sin 7y \sin 3y$
21. $\dfrac{\tan 2y + \tan 3x}{1 - \tan 2y \tan 3x}$
22. $\dfrac{\tan 3\alpha - \tan 2\beta}{1 + \tan 3\alpha \tan 2\beta}$

In Exercises 23–30, prove the identity.

23. $\sin\left(x - \dfrac{\pi}{2}\right) = -\cos x$
24. $\tan\left(x - \dfrac{\pi}{2}\right) = -\cot x$
25. $\cos\left(x - \dfrac{\pi}{2}\right) = \sin x$
26. $\cos\left[\left(\dfrac{\pi}{2} - x\right) - y\right] = \sin(x + y)$

27. $\sin\left(x + \frac{\pi}{6}\right) = \frac{\sqrt{3}}{2}\sin x + \frac{1}{2}\cos x$

28. $\cos\left(x - \frac{\pi}{4}\right) = \frac{\sqrt{2}}{2}(\cos x + \sin x)$

29. $\tan\left(\theta + \frac{\pi}{4}\right) = \frac{1 + \tan\theta}{1 - \tan\theta}$

30. $\cos\left(\theta + \frac{\pi}{2}\right) = -\sin\theta$

In Exercises 31–34, match each graph with a pair of the following equations. Use your knowledge of identities and transformations, not your grapher.

(a) $y = \cos(3 - 2x)$

(b) $y = \sin x \cos 1 + \cos x \sin 1$

(c) $y = \cos(x - 3)$

(d) $y = \sin(2x - 5)$

(e) $y = \cos x \cos 3 + \sin x \sin 3$

(f) $y = \sin(x + 1)$

(g) $y = \cos 3 \cos 2x + \sin 3 \sin 2x$

(h) $y = \sin 2x \cos 5 - \cos 2x \sin 5$

31.
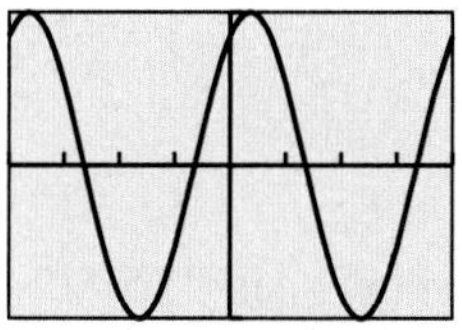
$[-2\pi, 2\pi]$ by $[-1, 1]$

32.
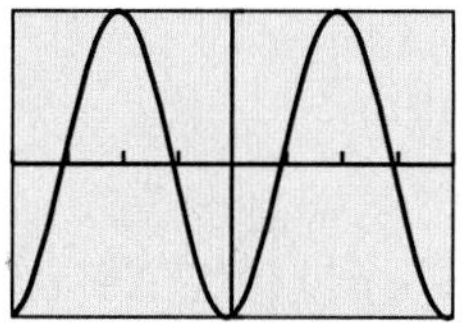
$[-2\pi, 2\pi]$ by $[-1, 1]$

33.
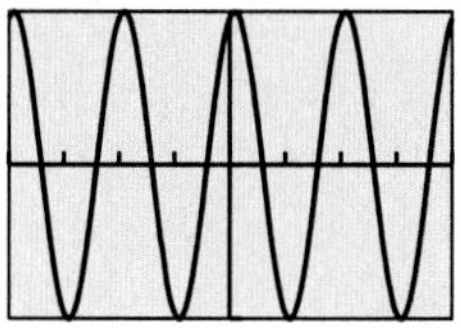
$[-2\pi, 2\pi]$ by $[-1, 1]$

34.
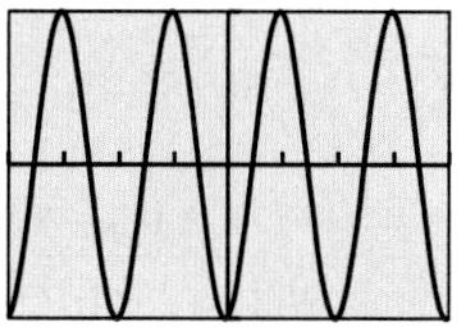
$[-2\pi, 2\pi]$ by $[-1, 1]$

In Exercises 35 and 36, use sum or difference identities (and not your grapher) to solve the equation exactly.

35. $\sin 2x \cos x = \cos 2x \sin x$

36. $\cos 3x \cos x = \sin 3x \sin x$

In Exercises 37–42, prove the reduction formula.

37. $\sin\left(\frac{\pi}{2} - u\right) = \cos u$

38. $\tan\left(\frac{\pi}{2} - u\right) = \cot u$

39. $\cot\left(\frac{\pi}{2} - u\right) = \tan u$

40. $\sec\left(\frac{\pi}{2} - u\right) = \csc u$

41. $\csc\left(\frac{\pi}{2} - u\right) = \sec u$

42. $\cos\left(x + \frac{\pi}{2}\right) = -\sin x$

In Exercises 43–46, express the function as a sinusoid in the form $y = a \sin(bx + c)$.

43. $y = 3 \sin x + 4 \cos x$

44. $y = 5 \sin x - 12 \cos x$

45. $y = \cos 3x + 2 \sin 3x$

46. $y = 3 \cos 2x - 2 \sin 2x$

In Exercises 47–55, prove the identity.

47. $\sin(x - y) + \sin(x + y) = 2 \sin x \cos y$

48. $\cos(x - y) + \cos(x + y) = 2 \cos x \cos y$

49. $\cos 3x = \cos^3 x - 3 \sin^2 x \cos x$

50. $\sin 3u = 3 \cos^2 u \sin u - \sin^3 u$

51. $\cos 3x + \cos x = 2 \cos 2x \cos x$

52. $\sin 4x + \sin 2x = 2 \sin 3x \cos x$

53. $\tan(x + y)\tan(x - y) = \frac{\tan^2 x - \tan^2 y}{1 - \tan^2 x \tan^2 y}$

54. $\tan 5u \tan 3u = \frac{\tan^2 4u - \tan^2 u}{1 - \tan^2 4u \tan^2 u}$

55. $\frac{\sin(x + y)}{\sin(x - y)} = \frac{(\tan x + \tan y)}{(\tan x - \tan y)}$

Explorations

56. Prove the identity $\tan(u + v) = \frac{\tan u + \tan v}{1 - \tan u \tan v}$.

57. Prove the identity $\tan(u - v) = \frac{\tan u - \tan v}{1 + \tan u \tan v}$.

58. **Writing to Learn** Explain why the identity in Exercise 62 cannot be used to prove the reduction formula $\tan(x + \pi/2) = -\cot x$. Then prove the reduction formula.

59. **Writing to Learn** Explain why the identity in Exercise 57 cannot be used to prove the reduction formula $\tan(x - 3\pi/2) = -\cot x$. Then prove the reduction formula.

60. **An Identity for Calculus** Prove the following identity, which is used in calculus to prove an important differentiation formula.

$$\frac{\sin(x + h) - \sin x}{h} = \sin x\left(\frac{\cos h - 1}{h}\right) + \cos x \frac{\sin h}{h}$$

61. **An Identity for Calculus** Prove the following identity, which is used in calculus to prove another important differentiation formula.

$$\frac{\cos(x + h) - \cos x}{h} = \cos x\left(\frac{\cos h - 1}{h}\right) - \sin x \frac{\sin h}{h}$$

62. **Group Activity** Place 24 points evenly spaced around the unit circle, starting with the point $(1, 0)$. Using only your knowledge of the special angles and the sum and difference identities, work with your group to find the exact coordinates of all 24 points.

Extending the Ideas

In Exercises 63–66, assume that A, B, and C are the three angles of some ΔABC. (Note, then, that $A + B + C = \pi$.) Prove the following identities.

63. $\sin(A + B) = \sin C$

64. $\cos C = \sin A \sin B - \cos A \cos B$

65. $\tan A + \tan B + \tan C = \tan A \tan B \tan C$

66. $\cos A \cos B \cos C - \sin A \sin B \cos C - \sin A \cos B \sin C - \cos A \sin B \sin C = -1$

67. Writing to Learn The figure shows graphs of $y_1 = \cos 5x \cos 4x$ and $y_2 = -\sin 5x \sin 4x$ in one viewing window. Discuss the question, "How many solutions are there to the equation $\cos 5x \cos 4x = -\sin 5x \sin 4x$ in the interval $[-2\pi, 2\pi]$?" Give an algebraic argument that answers the question more convincingly than the graph does. Then support your argument with an *appropriate* graph.

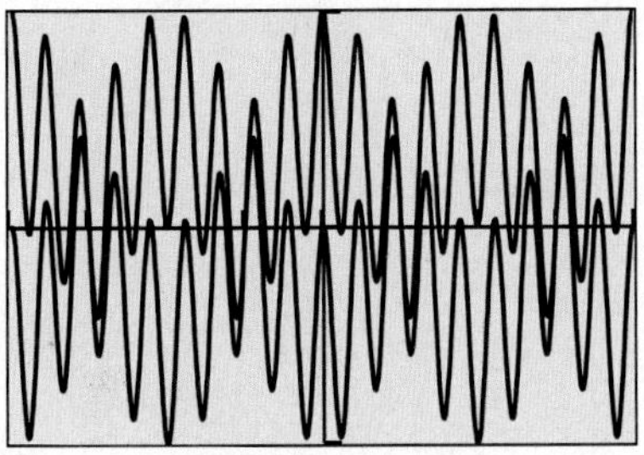

$[-2\pi, 2\pi]$ by $[-1, 1]$

68. Harmonic Motion Alternating electric current, an oscillating spring, or any other harmonic oscillator can be modeled by the equation

$$x = a \cos\left(\frac{2\pi}{T} t + \delta\right),$$

where T is the time for one period and δ is the phase constant. Show that this motion can also be modeled by the following sum of cosine and sine, each with zero phase constant:

$$a_1 \cos\left(\frac{2\pi}{T}\right)t + a_2 \sin\left(\frac{2\pi}{T}\right)t,$$

where $a_1 = a \cos \delta$ and $a_2 = -a \sin \delta$.

69. Magnetic Fields A magnetic field B can sometimes be modeled as the sum of an incident and a reflective field as

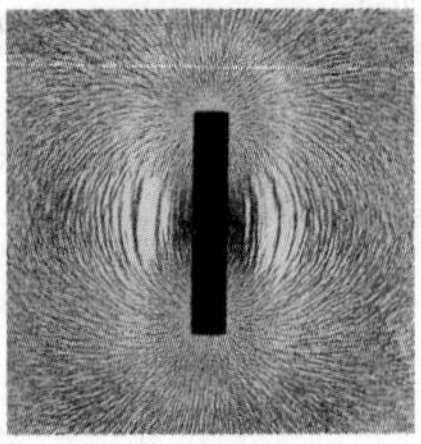

$$B = B_{in} + B_{ref},$$

where $B_{in} = \frac{E_0}{c} \cos\left(\omega t - \frac{\omega x}{c}\right)$, and

$$B_{ref} = \frac{E_0}{c} \cos\left(\omega t + \frac{\omega x}{c}\right).$$

Show that $B = 2\frac{E_0}{c} \cos \omega t \cos \frac{\omega x}{c}$.

H-13 Multiple-Angle Identities

What you'll learn about

- Double-Angle Identities
- Power-Reducing Identities
- Half-Angle Identities
- Solving Trigonometric Equations

... and why

These identities are useful in calculus courses.

Double-Angle Identities

The formulas that result from letting $u = v$ in the angle sum identities are called the *double-angle identities.* We will state them all and prove one, leaving the rest of the proofs as exercises. (See Exercises 1–4.)

Double-Angle Identities

$$\sin 2u = 2 \sin u \cos u$$

$$\cos 2u = \begin{cases} \cos^2 u - \sin^2 u \\ 2\cos^2 u - 1 \\ 1 - 2\sin^2 u \end{cases}$$

$$\tan 2u = \frac{2 \tan u}{1 - \tan^2 u}$$

There are three identities for $\cos 2u$. This is not unusual; indeed, there are plenty of other identities one could supply for $\sin 2u$ as well, such as $2 \sin u \sin (\pi/2 - u)$. We list the three identities for $\cos 2u$ because they are all *useful* in various contexts and therefore worth memorizing.

EXAMPLE 1 Proving a Double-Angle Identity

Prove the identity: $\sin 2u = 2 \sin u \cos u$.

SOLUTION

$$\begin{aligned} \sin 2u &= \sin (u + u) \\ &= \sin u \cos u + \cos u \sin u && \text{Sine of a sum } (v = u) \\ &= 2 \sin u \cos u \end{aligned}$$

Now try Exercise 1.

Power-Reducing Identities

One immediate use for two of the three formulas for $\cos 2u$ is to derive the *power-reducing identities.* Some simple-looking functions like $y = \sin^2 u$ would be quite difficult to handle in certain calculus contexts were it not for the existence of these identities.

Power-Reducing Identities

$$\sin^2 u = \frac{1 - \cos 2u}{2}$$

$$\cos^2 u = \frac{1 + \cos 2u}{2}$$

$$\tan^2 u = \frac{1 - \cos 2u}{1 + \cos 2u}$$

We will also leave the proofs of these identities as exercises. (See Exercises 37 and 38.)

EXAMPLE 2 **Proving an Identity**

Prove the identity: $\cos^4 \theta - \sin^4 \theta = \cos 2\theta$.

SOLUTION

$$\begin{aligned} \cos^4 \theta - \sin^4 \theta &= (\cos^2 \theta + \sin^2 \theta)(\cos^2 \theta - \sin^2 \theta) \\ &= 1 \cdot (\cos^2 \theta - \sin^2 \theta) && \text{Pythagorean identity} \\ &= \cos 2\theta && \text{Double-angle identity} \end{aligned}$$

Now try Exercise 15.

EXAMPLE 3 **Reducing a Power of 4**

Rewrite $\cos^4 x$ in terms of trigonometric functions with no power greater than 1.

SOLUTION

$$\begin{aligned} \cos^4 x &= (\cos^2 x)^2 \\ &= \left(\frac{1 + \cos 2x}{2}\right)^2 && \text{Power-reducing identity} \\ &= \left(\frac{1 + 2\cos 2x + \cos^2 2x}{4}\right) \\ &= \frac{1}{4} + \frac{1}{2}\cos 2x + \frac{1}{4}\left(\frac{1 + \cos 4x}{2}\right) && \text{Power-reducing identity} \\ &= \frac{1}{4} + \frac{1}{2}\cos 2x + \frac{1}{8} + \frac{1}{8}\cos 4x \\ &= \frac{1}{8}(3 + 4\cos 2x + \cos 4x) \end{aligned}$$

Now try Exercise 39.

Half-Angle Identities

The power-reducing identities can be used to extend our stock of "special" angles whose trigonometric ratios can be found without a calculator. As usual, we are not suggesting that this algebraic procedure is any more practical than using a calculator, but we are suggesting that this sort of exercise helps you to understand how the functions behave. In Exploration 1, for example, we use a power-reducing formula to find the exact values of $\sin(\pi/8)$ and $\sin(9\pi/8)$ without a calculator.

EXPLORATION 1 **Finding the Sine of Half an Angle**

Recall the power-reducing formula $\sin^2 u = (1 - \cos 2u)/2$.

1. Use the power-reducing formula to show that $\sin^2(\pi/8) = (2 - \sqrt{2})/4$.
2. Solve for $\sin(\pi/8)$. Do you take the positive or negative square root? Why?
3. Use the power-reducing formula to show that $\sin^2(9\pi/8) = (2 - \sqrt{2})/4$.
4. Solve for $\sin(9\pi/8)$. Do you take the positive or negative square root? Why?

A little alteration of the power-reducing identities results in the *half-angle identities*, which can be used directly to find trigonometric functions of $u/2$ in terms of trigonometric functions of u. As Exploration 1 suggests, there is an unavoidable ambiguity of sign involved with the square root that must be resolved in particular cases by checking the quadrant in which $u/2$ lies.

Did We Miss Two ± Signs?

You might have noticed that all of the half-angle identities have unresolved ± signs except for the last two. The fact that we can omit them on the last two identities for tan $u/2$ is a fortunate consequence of two facts: (1) sin u and tan $(u/2)$ always have the same sign (easily observed from the graphs of the two functions in Figure H.88), and (2) $1 \pm \cos u$ is never negative.

Half-Angle Identities

$$\sin\frac{u}{2} = \pm\sqrt{\frac{1-\cos u}{2}}$$

$$\cos\frac{u}{2} = \pm\sqrt{\frac{1+\cos u}{2}}$$

$$\tan\frac{u}{2} = \begin{cases} \pm\sqrt{\dfrac{1-\cos u}{1+\cos u}} \\ \dfrac{1-\cos u}{\sin u} \\ \dfrac{\sin u}{1+\cos u} \end{cases}$$

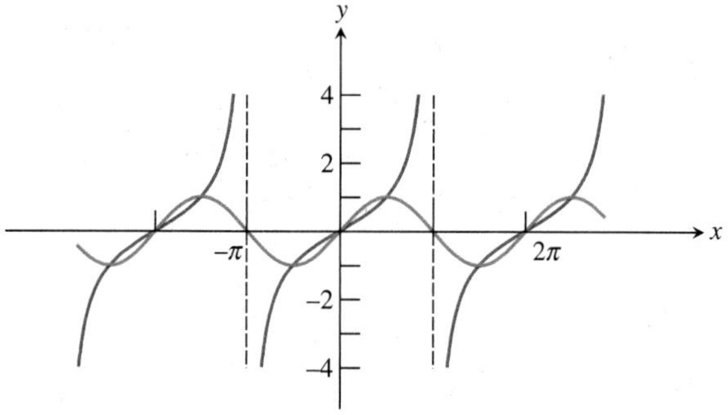

FIGURE H.88 The functions sin u and tan $(u/2)$ always have the same sign.

Solving Trigonometric Equations

New identities always provide new tools for solving trigonometric equations algebraically. Under the right conditions, they even lead to exact solutions. We assert again that we are not presenting these algebraic solutions for their practical value (as the calculator solutions are certainly sufficient for most applications and unquestionably much quicker to obtain), but rather as ways to observe the behavior of the trigonometric functions and their interwoven tapestry of identities.

EXAMPLE 4 Using a Double-Angle Identity

Solve algebraically in the interval $[0, 2\pi)$: $\sin 2x = \cos x$.

SOLUTION

$$\begin{aligned} \sin 2x &= \cos x \\ 2\sin x\cos x &= \cos x \\ 2\sin x\cos x - \cos x &= 0 \\ \cos x\,(2\sin x - 1) &= 0 \\ \cos x = 0 \quad &\text{or} \quad 2\sin x - 1 = 0 \\ \cos x = 0 \quad &\text{or} \quad \sin x = \frac{1}{2} \end{aligned}$$

The two solutions of $\cos x = 0$ are $x = \pi/2$ and $x = 3\pi/2$. The two solutions of $\sin x = 1/2$ are $x = \pi/6$ and $x = 5\pi/6$. Therefore, the solutions of $\sin 2x = \cos x$ are

$$\frac{\pi}{6}, \frac{\pi}{2}, \frac{5\pi}{6}, \frac{3\pi}{2}.$$

We can **support** this result **graphically** by verifying the four x-intercepts of the function $y = \sin 2x - \cos x$ in the interval $[0, 2\pi)$ (Figure H.89).

Now try Exercise 23.

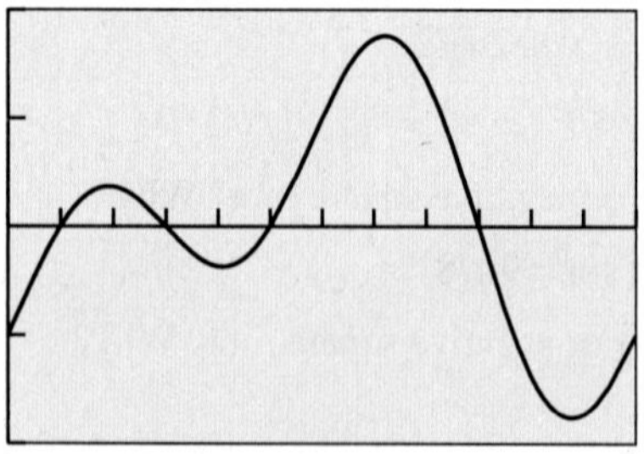

$[0, 2\pi]$ by $[-2, 2]$

FIGURE H.89 The function $y = \sin 2x - \cos x$ for $0 \le x \le 2\pi$. The scale on the x-axis shows intervals of length $\pi/6$. This graph supports the solution found algebraically in Example 4.

EXAMPLE 5 Using Half-Angle Identities

Solve $\sin^2 x = 2\sin^2(x/2)$.

SOLUTION The graph of $y = \sin^2 x - 2\sin^2(x/2)$ in Figure H.90 suggests that this function is periodic with period 2π and that the equation $\sin^2 x = 2\sin^2(x/2)$ has three solutions in $[0, 2\pi)$.

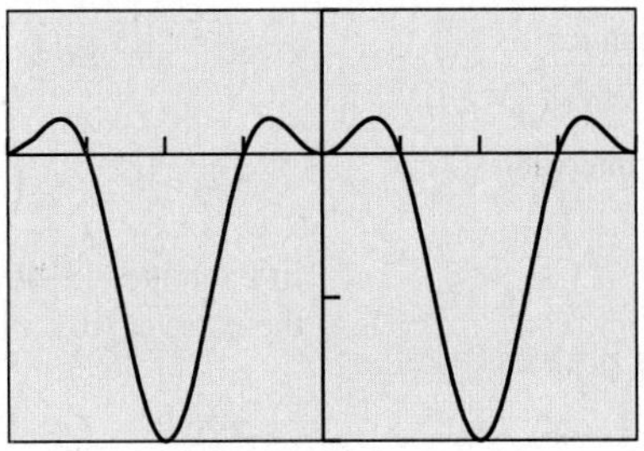

$[-2\pi, 2\pi]$ by $[-2, 1]$

FIGURE H.90 The graph of $y = \sin^2 x - 2\sin^2(x/2)$ suggests that $\sin^2 x = 2\sin^2(x/2)$ has three solutions in $[0, 2\pi)$. (Example 5)

Solve Algebraically

$$\sin^2 x = 2\sin^2\frac{x}{2}$$

$$\sin^2 x = 2\left(\frac{1 - \cos x}{2}\right) \quad \text{Half-angle identity}$$

$$1 - \cos^2 x = 1 - \cos x \quad \text{Convert to all cosines.}$$

$$\cos x - \cos^2 x = 0$$

$$\cos x(1 - \cos x) = 0$$

$$\cos x = 0 \quad \text{or} \quad \cos x = 1$$

$$x = \frac{\pi}{2} \quad \text{or} \quad \frac{3\pi}{2} \quad \text{or} \quad 0$$

The rest of the solutions are obtained by periodicity:

$$x = 2n\pi, \quad x = \frac{\pi}{2} + 2n\pi, \quad x = \frac{3\pi}{2} + 2n\pi, \quad n = 0, \pm 1, \pm 2, \ldots$$

Now try Exercise 43.

LESSON H-13 EXERCISES

Exercise numbers with a gray background indicate problems that the authors have designed to be solved *without a calculator.*

In Exercises 1–4, use the appropriate sum or difference identity to prove the double-angle identity.

1. $\cos 2u = \cos^2 u - \sin^2 u$ **2.** $\cos 2u = 2\cos^2 u - 1$

3. $\cos 2u = 1 - 2\sin^2 u$ **4.** $\tan 2u = \dfrac{2\tan u}{1 - \tan^2 u}$

In Exercises 5–10, find all solutions to the equation in the interval $[0, 2\pi)$.

5. $\sin 2x = 2\sin x$ **6.** $\sin 2x = \sin x$

7. $\cos 2x = \sin x$ **8.** $\cos 2x = \cos x$

9. $\sin 2x - \tan x = 0$ **10.** $2\cos^2 x + \cos x = \cos 2x$

In Exercises 11–14, write the expression as one involving only $\sin\theta$ and $\cos\theta$.

11. $\sin 2\theta + \cos\theta$ **12.** $\sin 2\theta + \cos 2\theta$

13. $\sin 2\theta + \cos 3\theta$ **14.** $\sin 3\theta + \cos 2\theta$

In Exercises 15–22, prove the identity.

15. $\sin 4x = 2\sin 2x\cos 2x$ **16.** $\cos 6x = 2\cos^2 3x - 1$

17. $2\csc 2x = \csc^2 x\tan x$ **18.** $2\cot 2x = \cot x - \tan x$

19. $\sin 3x = (\sin x)(4\cos^2 x - 1)$

20. $\sin 3x = (\sin x)(3 - 4\sin^2 x)$

21. $\cos 4x = 1 - 8\sin^2 x\cos^2 x$

22. $\sin 4x = (4\sin x\cos x)(2\cos^2 x - 1)$

In Exercises 23–30, solve algebraically for exact solutions in the interval $[0, 2\pi)$. Use your grapher only to support your algebraic work.

23. $\cos 2x + \cos x = 0$ **24.** $\cos 2x + \sin x = 0$

25. $\cos x + \cos 3x = 0$ **26.** $\sin x + \sin 3x = 0$

27. $\sin 2x + \sin 4x = 0$ **28.** $\cos 2x + \cos 4x = 0$

In Exercises 29 and 30, use a graphing calculator to find all exact solutions in the interval $[0, \pi)$. [*Hint:* All solutions are rational multiples of π.]

29. $\sin 2x - \cos 3x = 0$ **30.** $\sin 3x + \cos 2x = 0$

In Exercises 31–36, use half-angle identities to find an exact value without a calculator.

31. $\sin 15°$ **32.** $\tan 195°$

33. $\cos 75°$ **34.** $\sin(5\pi/12)$

35. $\tan(7\pi/12)$ **36.** $\cos(\pi/8)$

37. Prove the power-reducing identities:

(a) $\sin^2 u = \dfrac{1 - \cos 2u}{2}$ **(b)** $\cos^2 u = \dfrac{1 + \cos 2u}{2}$

38. **(a)** Use the identities in Exercise 37 to prove the power-reducing identity $\tan^2 u = \dfrac{1 - \cos 2u}{1 + \cos 2u}$.

(b) Writing to Learn Explain why the identity in part (a) does not imply that $\tan u = \sqrt{\dfrac{1 - \cos 2u}{1 + \cos 2u}}$.

In Exercises 39–42, use the power-reducing identities to prove the identity.

39. $\sin^4 x = \dfrac{1}{8}(3 - 4\cos 2x + \cos 4x)$

40. $\cos^3 x = \left(\dfrac{1}{2}\cos x\right)(1 + \cos 2x)$

41. $\sin^3 2x = \left(\dfrac{1}{2}\sin 2x\right)(1 - \cos 4x)$

42. $\sin^5 x = \left(\dfrac{1}{8}\sin x\right)(3 - 4\cos 2x + \cos 4x)$

In Exercises 43–46, use the half-angle identities to find all solutions in the interval $[0, 2\pi)$. Then find the general solution.

43. $\cos^2 x = \sin^2\left(\dfrac{x}{2}\right)$ **44.** $\sin^2 x = \cos^2\left(\dfrac{x}{2}\right)$

45. $\tan\left(\dfrac{x}{2}\right) = \dfrac{1 - \cos x}{1 + \cos x}$ **46.** $\sin^2\left(\dfrac{x}{2}\right) = \cos x - 1$

Explorations

47. Connecting Trigonometry and Geometry In a regular polygon all sides are the same length and all angles are equal in measure.

(a) If the perpendicular distance from the center of the polygon with n sides to the midpoint of a side is R, and if the length of the side of the polygon is x, show that

$$x = 2R\tan\frac{\theta}{2}$$

where $\theta = 2\pi/n$ is the central angle subtended by one side.

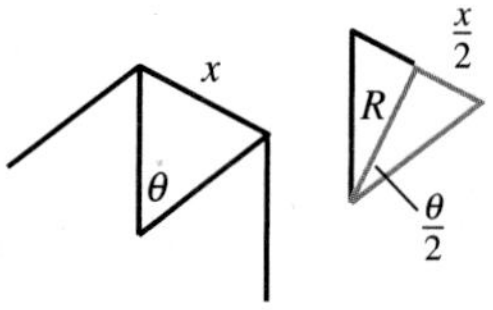

Regular polygon with n sides

(b) If the length of one side of a regular 11-sided polygon is approximately 5.87 and R is a whole number, what is the value of R?

48. Connecting Trigonometry and Geometry A rhombus is a quadrilateral with equal sides. The diagonals of a rhombus bisect the angles of the rhombus and are perpendicular bisectors of each other. Let $\angle ABC = \theta$, d_1 = length of AC, and d_2 = length of BD.

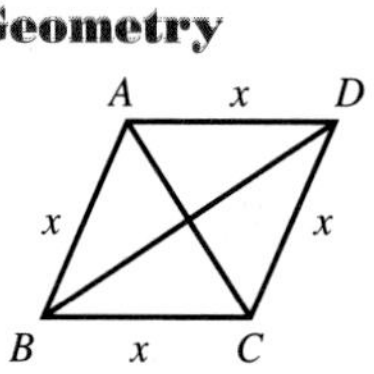

(a) Show that $\cos\dfrac{\theta}{2} = \dfrac{d_2}{2x}$ and $\sin\dfrac{\theta}{2} = \dfrac{d_1}{2x}$.

(b) Show that $\sin\theta = \dfrac{d_1 d_2}{2x^2}$.

49. Group Activity Maximizing Volume The ends of a 10-foot-long water trough are isosceles trapezoids as shown in the figure. Find the value of θ that maximizes the volume of the trough and the maximum volume.

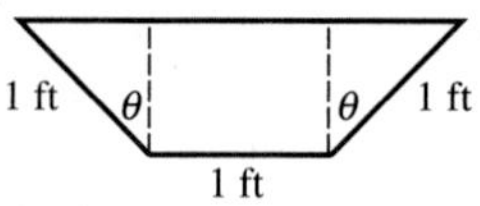

50. Group Activity Tunnel Problem A rectangular tunnel is cut through a mountain to make a road. The upper vertices of the rectangle are on the circle $x^2 + y^2 = 400$, as illustrated in the figure.

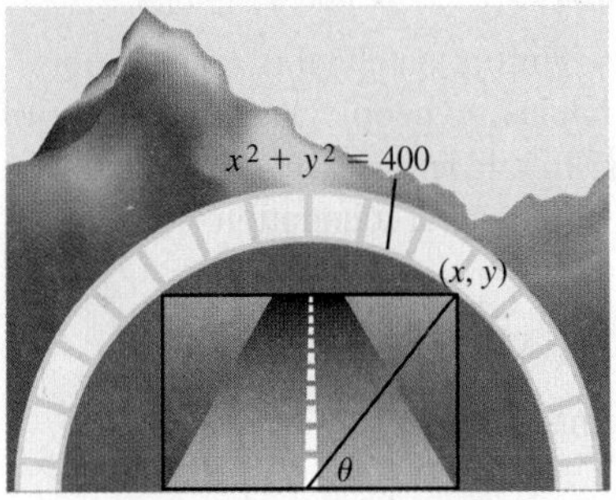

(a) Show that the cross-sectional area of the end of the tunnel is $400 \sin 2\theta$.

(b) Find the dimensions of the rectangular end of the tunnel that maximizes its cross-sectional area.

xtending the Ideas

Exercises 51–55, prove the double-angle formulas.

51. $\csc 2u = \dfrac{1}{2} \csc u \sec u$

52. $\cot 2u = \dfrac{\cot^2 u - 1}{2 \cot u}$

53. $\sec 2u = \dfrac{\csc^2 u}{\csc^2 u - 2}$

54. $\sec 2u = \dfrac{\sec^2 u}{2 - \sec^2 u}$

55. $\sec 2u = \dfrac{\sec^2 u \csc^2 u}{\csc^2 u - \sec^2 u}$

56. Writing to Learn Explain why

$$\sqrt{\frac{1 - \cos 2x}{2}} = |\sin x|$$

is an identity but

$$\sqrt{\frac{1 - \cos 2x}{2}} = \sin x$$

is not an identity.

57. Hawaiian Sunset Table H.9 gives the time of day for sunset in Honolulu, HI, on the first day of each month of 2009.

Table H.9 Sunset in Honolulu, 2009

Date	Day	Time	18:30 +
Jan 1	1	18:01	−29
Feb 1	32	18:22	−8
Mar 1	60	18:36	6
Apr 1	91	18:46	16
May 1	121	18:57	27
Jun 1	152	19:10	40
Jul 1	182	19:17	47
Aug 1	213	19:10	40
Sep 1	244	18:47	17
Oct 1	274	18:19	−11
Nov 1	305	17:55	−35
Dec 1	335	17:48	−42

Source: www.timeanddate.com

The second column gives the date as the day of the year, and the fourth column gives the time as the number of minutes past 18:30.

(a) Enter the numbers in column 2 (day) into list L1 and the numbers in column 4 (minutes past 18:30) into list L2. Make a scatter plot with x-coordinates from L1 and y-coordinates from L2.

(b) Using sine regression, find the regression curve through the points and store its equation in Y1. Superimpose the graph of the curve on the scatter plot. Is it a good fit?

(c) Make a new column showing the *residuals* (the difference between the actual y-value at each point and the y-value predicted by the regression curve) and store them in list L3. Your calculator might have a list called RESID among the NAMES in the LIST menu, in which case the command RESID → L3 will perform this operation. You could also enter L2 − Y1(L1) → L3.

(d) Make a scatter plot with x-coordinates from L1 and y-coordinates from L3. Find the sine regression curve through *these* points and superimpose it on the scatter plot.

(e) Writing to Learn Interpret what the two regressions seem to indicate about the periodic behavior of sunset as a function of time. This is not an unusual phenomenon in astronomical data, and it kept astronomers baffled for centuries.

H-14 Probability

What you'll learn about

- Sample Spaces and Probability Functions
- Determining Probabilities
- Venn Diagrams and Tree Diagrams
- Conditional Probability
- Binomial Distributions

... and why

Everyone should know how mathematical the "laws of chance" really are.

Sample Spaces and Probability Functions

Most people have an intuitive sense of probability. Unfortunately, this sense is not often based on a foundation of mathematical principles, so people become victims of scams, misleading statistics, and false advertising. In this lesson, we want to build on your intuitive sense of probability and give it a mathematical foundation.

EXAMPLE 1 Testing Your Intuition About Probability

Find the probability of each of the following events.

(a) Tossing a head on one toss of a fair coin

(b) Tossing two heads in a row on two tosses of a fair coin

(c) Drawing a queen from a standard deck of 52 cards

(d) Rolling a sum of 4 on a single roll of two fair dice

(e) Guessing all 6 numbers in a state lottery that requires you to pick 6 numbers between 1 and 46, inclusive

SOLUTION

(a) There are two equally likely outcomes: $\{T, H\}$. The probability is 1/2.

(b) There are four equally likely outcomes: $\{TT, TH, HT, HH\}$. The probability is 1/4.

(c) There are 52 equally likely outcomes, 4 of which are queens. The probability is 4/52, or 1/13.

(d) By the Multiplication Principle of Counting (Section H.91), there are $6 \times 6 = 36$ equally likely outcomes. Of these, three $\{(1, 3), (3, 1), (2, 2)\}$ yield a sum of 4 (Figure 9.2). The probability is 3/36, or 1/12.

(e) There are ${}_{46}C_6 = 9{,}366{,}819$ equally likely ways that 6 numbers can be chosen from 46 numbers without regard to order. Only one of these choices wins the lottery. The probability is $1/9{,}366{,}819 \approx 0.00000010676$. *Now try Exercise 5.*

FIGURE H.91 A sum of 4 on a roll of two dice. (Example 1d)

Notice that in each of these cases we first counted the number of possible outcomes of the experiment in question. The set of all possible outcomes of an experiment is the **sample space** of the experiment. An **event** is a subset of the sample space. Each of our sample spaces consisted of a finite number of **equally likely outcomes**, which enabled us to find the probability of an event by counting.

Is Probability Just for Games?

Probability theory got its start in letters between Blaise Pascal (1623–1662) and Pierre de Fermat (1601–1665) concerning games of chance, but it has come a long way since then. Modern mathematicians like David Blackwell (1919), the first African-American to receive a fellowship to the Institute for Advanced Study at Princeton, have greatly extended both the theory and the applications of probability, especially in the areas of statistics, quantum physics, and information theory. Moreover, the work of John Von Neumann (1903–1957) has led to a separate branch of modern discrete mathematics that really is about games, called game theory.

Probability of an Event (Equally Likely Outcomes)

If E is an event in a finite, nonempty sample space S of equally likely outcomes, then the **probability** of the event E is

$$P(E) = \frac{\text{the number of outcomes in } E}{\text{the number of outcomes in } S}.$$

The hypothesis of equally likely outcomes is critical here. Many people guess wrongly on the probability in Example 1d because they figure that there are 11 possible outcomes for the sum on two fair dice: $\{2, 3, 4, 5, 6, 7, 8, 9, 10, 11, 12\}$ and that 4 is one of them. (That reasoning is correct so far.) The reason that 1/11 is not the probability of rolling a sum of 4 is that all those sums are *not equally likely*.

On the other hand, we can *assign* probabilities to the 11 outcomes in this smaller sample space in a way that is consistent with the number of ways each total can occur. The table below shows a **probability distribution**, in which each outcome is assigned a unique probability by a *probability function.*

Outcome	Probability
2	1/36
3	2/36
4	3/36
5	4/36
6	5/36
7	6/36
8	5/36
9	4/36
10	3/36
11	2/36
12	1/36

We see that the outcomes are not equally likely, but we can find the probabilities of events by adding up the probabilities of the outcomes in the event, as in the following example.

EXAMPLE 2 Rolling the Dice

Find the probability of rolling a sum divisible by 3 on a single roll of two fair dice.

SOLUTION The event E consists of the outcomes $\{3, 6, 9, 12\}$. To get the probability of E we add up the probabilities of the outcomes in E (see the table of the probability distribution):

$$P(E) = \frac{2}{36} + \frac{5}{36} + \frac{4}{36} + \frac{1}{36} = \frac{12}{36} = \frac{1}{3}.$$

Now try Exercise 7.

Notice that this method would also have worked just fine with our 36-outcome sample space, in which every outcome has probability 1/36. In general, it is easier to work with sample spaces of equally likely events because it is not necessary to write out the probability distribution. When outcomes do have unequal probabilities, we need to know what probabilities to assign to the outcomes.

Not every function that assigns numbers to outcomes qualifies as a probability function.

Empty Set

A set with no elements is the *empty set*, denoted by $\varnothing$.

DEFINITION Probability Function

A **probability function** is a function P that assigns a real number to each outcome in a sample space S subject to the following conditions:

1. $0 \leq P(O) \leq 1$ for every outcome O;

2. the sum of the probabilities of all outcomes in S is 1;

3. $P(\varnothing) = 0$.

The probability of any event can then be defined in terms of the probability function.

Random Variables

A more formal treatment of probability would distinguish between an *outcome* in a sample space and a *number* that is associated with that outcome. For example, an outcome in Example 2 is really something like , to which we associate the number $2 + 1 = 3$. A function that assigns a number to an outcome is called a **random variable**. A different random variable might assign the number $2 \cdot 1 = 2$ to this outcome of the dice. Another random variable might assign the number 21

Probability of an Event (Outcomes Not Equally Likely)

Let S be a finite, nonempty sample space in which every outcome has a probability assigned to it by a probability function P. If E is any event in S, the **probability** of the event E is the sum of the probabilities of all the outcomes contained in E.

EXAMPLE 3 Testing a Probability Function

Is it possible to weight a standard 6-sided die in such a way that the probability of rolling each number n is exactly $1/(n^2 + 1)$?

SOLUTION The probability distribution would look like this:

Outcome	Probability
1	1/2
2	1/5
3	1/10
4	1/17
5	1/26
6	1/37

This is not a valid probability function, because $1/2 + 1/5 + 1/10 + 1/17 + 1/26 + 1/37 \neq 1$.

Now try Exercise 9a.

Determining Probabilities

It is not always easy to determine probabilities, but the arithmetic involved is fairly simple. It usually comes down to multiplication, addition, and (most importantly) counting. Here is the strategy we will follow:

Strategy for Determining Probabilities

1. Determine the sample space of all possible outcomes. When possible, choose outcomes that are equally likely.
2. If the sample space has equally likely outcomes, the probability of an event E is determined by counting:

$$P(E) = \frac{\text{the number of outcomes in } E}{\text{the number of outcomes in } S}$$

3. If the sample space does not have equally likely outcomes, determine the probability function. (This is not always easy to do.) Check to be sure that the conditions of a probability function are satisfied. Then the probability of an event E is determined by adding up the probabilities of all the outcomes contained in E.

EXAMPLE 4 Choosing Chocolates, Sample Space I

Sal opens a box of a dozen chocolate cremes and generously offers two of them to Val. Val likes vanilla cremes the best, but all the chocolates look alike on the outside. If four of the twelve cremes are vanilla, what is the probability that both of Val's picks turn out to be vanilla?

SOLUTION The experiment in question is the selection of two chocolates, without regard to order, from a box of 12. There are ${}_{12}C_2 = 66$ outcomes of this experiment, and all of them are equally likely. We can therefore determine the probability by counting.

The event E consists of all possible pairs of 2 vanilla cremes that can be chosen, without regard to order, from 4 vanilla cremes available. There are ${}_4C_2 = 6$ ways to form such pairs.

Therefore, $P(E) = 6/66 = 1/11$.

Now try Exercise 25.

Many probability problems require that we think of events happening in succession, often with the occurrence of one event affecting the probability of the occurrence of another event. In these cases, we use a law of probability called the Multiplication Principle of Probability.

Multiplication Principle of Probability

Suppose an event A has probability p_1 and an event B has probability p_2 under the assumption that A occurs. Then the probability that both A and B occur is $p_1 p_2$.

If the events A and B are **independent**, we can omit the phrase "under the assumption that A occurs," since that assumption would not matter.

As an example of this principle at work, we will solve the *same problem* as that posed in Example 4, this time using a sample space that appears at first to be simpler, but which consists of events that are not equally likely.

EXAMPLE 5 Choosing Chocolates, Sample Space II

Sal opens a box of a dozen chocolate cremes and generously offers two of them to Val. Val likes vanilla cremes the best, but all the chocolates look alike on the outside. If four of the twelve cremes are vanilla, what is the probability that both of Val's picks turn out to be vanilla?

Ordered or Unordered?

Notice that in Example 4 we had a sample space in which order was disregarded, whereas in Example 5 we have a sample space in which order matters. (For example, *UV* and *VU* are distinct outcomes.) The order matters in Example 5 because we are considering the probabilities of two events (first draw, second draw), one of which affects the other. In Example 4, we are simply counting unordered combinations.

SOLUTION As far as Val is concerned, there are two kinds of chocolate cremes: vanilla (V) and unvanilla (U). When choosing two chocolates, there are four possible outcomes: *VV*, *VU*, *UV*, and *UU*. We need to determine the probability of the outcome *VV*.

Notice that these four outcomes are *not equally likely*! There are twice as many U chocolates as V chocolates. So we need to consider the distribution of probabilities, and we may as well begin with $P(VV)$, as that is the probability we seek.

The probability of picking a vanilla creme on the first draw is 4/12. The probability of picking a vanilla creme on the second draw, *under the assumption that a vanilla creme was drawn on the first*, is 3/11. By the Multiplication Principle, the probability of drawing a vanilla creme on both draws is

$$\frac{4}{12} \cdot \frac{3}{11} = \frac{1}{11}.$$

Since this is the probability we are looking for, we do not need to compute the probabilities of the other outcomes. However, you should verify that the other probabilities would be:

$$P(VU) = \frac{4}{12} \cdot \frac{8}{11} = \frac{8}{33}$$

$$P(UV) = \frac{8}{12} \cdot \frac{4}{11} = \frac{8}{33}$$

$$P(UU) = \frac{8}{12} \cdot \frac{7}{11} = \frac{14}{33}$$

Notice that $P(VV) + P(VU) + P(UV) + P(UU) = (1/11) + (8/33) + (8/33) + (14/33) = 1$, so the probability function checks out. *Now try Exercise 33.*

Venn Diagrams and Tree Diagrams

We have seen many instances in which geometric models help us to understand algebraic models more easily, and probability theory is yet another setting in which this is true. **Venn diagrams**, associated mainly with the world of set theory, are good for visualizing

John Venn

John Venn (1834–1923) was an English logician and clergyman, just like his contemporary, Charles L. Dodgson. Although both men used overlapping circles to illustrate their logical syllogisms, it is Venn whose name lives on in connection with these diagrams. Dodgson's name barely lives on at all, and yet he is far the more famous of the two: under the pen name Lewis Carroll, he wrote *Alice's Adventures in Wonderland* and *Through the Looking Glass*.

Addition Principle of Probability

A more careful look at the Venn diagram in Figure H.93 will suggest the following general formula for events A and B in a sample space:

$$P(A \text{ or } B) = P(A) + (B) - P(A \text{ and } B)$$

If A and B do not happen to intersect, this reduces to $P(A \text{ or } B) = P(A) + (B)$. In this case, we call A and B **mutually exclusive** events.

relationships among events within sample spaces. **Tree diagrams** are good for visualizing the Multiplication Principle of Probability.

EXAMPLE 6 Using a Venn Diagram

In a large high school, 54% of the students are girls and 62% of the students play sports. Half of the girls at the school play sports.

(a) What percentage of the students who play sports are boys?

(b) If a student is chosen at random, what is the probability that it is a boy who does not play sports?

SOLUTION To organize the categories, we draw a large rectangle to represent the sample space (all students at the school) and two overlapping regions to represent "girls" and "sports" (Figure H.92). We fill in the percentages (Figure H.93) using the following logic:

- The overlapping (green) region contains half the girls, or $(0.5)(54\%) = 27\%$ of the students.
- The yellow region (the rest of the girls) then contains $(54 - 27)\% = 27\%$ of the students.
- The blue region (the rest of the sports players) then contains $(62 - 27)\% = 35\%$ of the students.
- The white region (the rest of the students) then contains $(100 - 89)\% = 11\%$ of the students. These are boys who do not play sports.

We can now answer the two questions by looking at the Venn diagram.

(a) We see from the diagram that the ratio of *boys* who play sports to *all students* who play sports is $\frac{0.35}{0.62}$, which is about 56.45%.

(b) We see that 11% of the students are boys who do not play sports, so 0.11 is the probability.

Now try Exercises 27a–d.

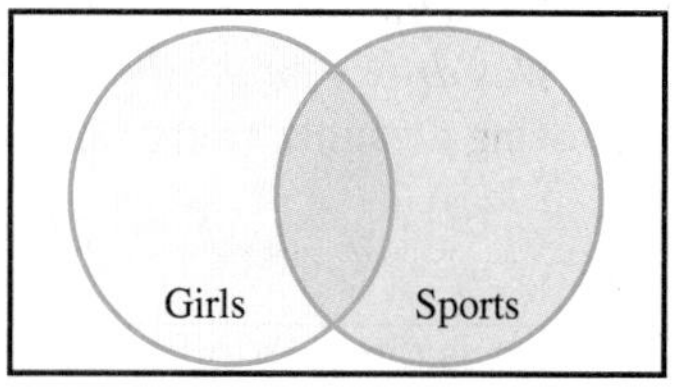

FIGURE H.92 A Venn diagram for Example 6. The overlapping region common to both circles represents "girls who play sports." The region outside both circles (but inside the rectangle) represents "boys who do not play sports."

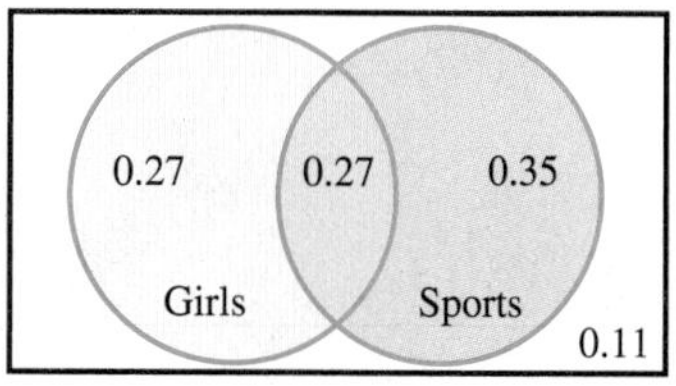

FIGURE H.93 A Venn diagram for Example 6 with the probabilities filled in.

EXAMPLE 7 Using a Tree Diagram

Two identical cookie jars are on a counter. Jar A contains 2 chocolate chip and 2 peanut butter cookies, while jar B contains 1 chocolate chip cookie. We select a cookie at random. What is the probability that it is a chocolate chip cookie?

SOLUTION It is tempting to say 3/5, since there are 5 cookies in all, 3 of which are chocolate chip. Indeed, this would be the answer if all the cookies were in the same jar. However, the fact that they are in different jars means that the 5 cookies are *not equally likely outcomes*. That lone chocolate chip cookie in jar B has a much

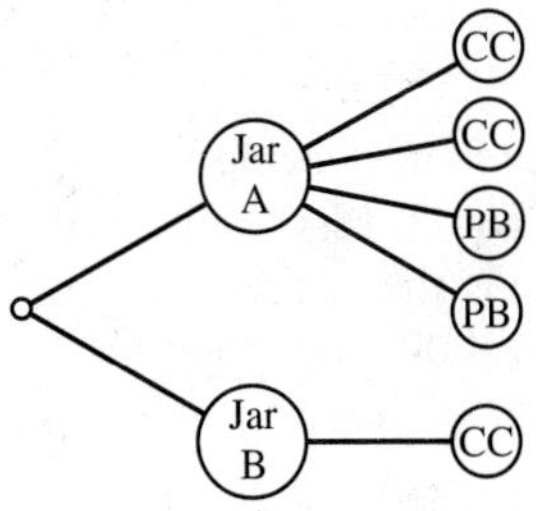

FIGURE H.94 A tree diagram for Example 7.

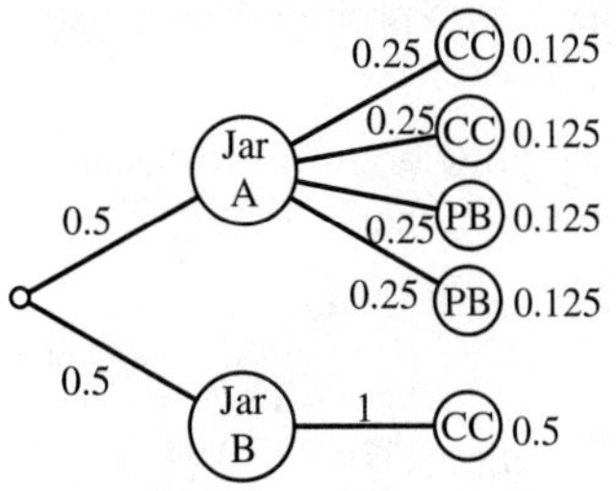

FIGURE H.95 The tree diagram for Example 7 with the probabilities filled in. Notice that the five cookies are not equally likely to be drawn. Notice also that the probabilities of the five cookies do add up to 1.

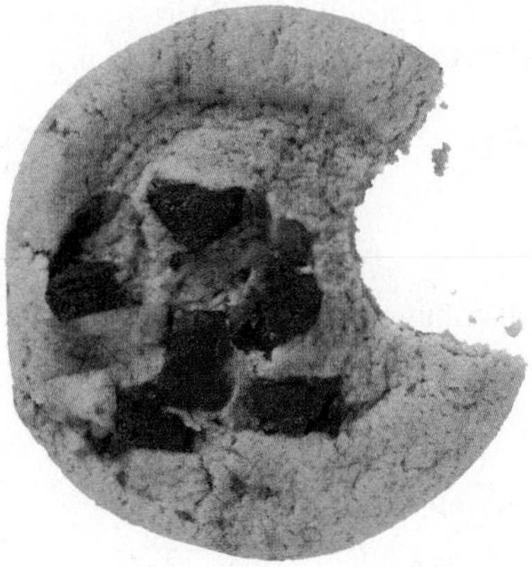

better chance of being chosen than any of the cookies in jar A. We need to think of this as a two-step experiment: first pick a jar, then pick a cookie from that jar.

Figure H.94 gives a visualization of the two-step process. In Figure H.95, we have filled in the probabilities along each branch, first of picking the jar, then of picking the cookie. The probability at the *end* of each branch is obtained by multiplying the probabilities from the root to the branch. (This is the Multiplication Principle.) Notice that the probabilities of the 5 cookies (as predicted) are not equal.

The event "chocolate chip" is a set containing three outcomes. We add their probabilities together to get the correct probability:

$P(\text{chocolate chip}) = 0.125 + 0.125 + 0.5 = 0.75$ *Now try Exercise 29.*

Conditional Probability

The probability of drawing a chocolate chip cookie in Example 7 is an example of **conditional probability**, since the "cookie" probability is **dependent** on the "jar" outcome. A convenient symbol to use with conditional probability is $P(A|B)$, pronounced "P of A given B," meaning "the probability of the event A, given that event B occurs." In the cookie jars of Example 7,

$$P(\text{chocolate chip} \mid \text{jar } A) = \frac{2}{4} \quad \text{and} \quad P(\text{chocolate chip} \mid \text{jar } B) = 1$$

(In the tree diagram, these are the probabilities along the *branches* that come out of the two jars, not the probabilities at the *ends* of the branches.)

The Multiplication Principle of Probability can be stated succinctly with this notation as follows:

$$P(A \text{ and } B) = P(A) \cdot P(B \mid A)$$

This is how we found the numbers at the ends of the branches in Figure H.95.

As our final example of a probability problem, we will show how to use this formula in a different but equivalent form, sometimes called the **conditional probability formula**:

Conditional Probability Formula

If the event B depends on the event A, then $P(B \mid A) = \dfrac{P(A \text{ and } B)}{P(A)}$.

EXAMPLE 8 Using the Conditional Probability Formula

Suppose we have drawn a cookie at random from one of the jars described in Example 7. Given that it is chocolate chip, what is the probability that it came from jar A?

SOLUTION By the formula,

$$P(\text{jar } A \mid \text{chocolate chip}) = \frac{P(\text{jar } A \text{ and chocolate chip})}{P(\text{chocolate chip})}$$

$$= \frac{(1/2)(2/4)}{0.75} = \frac{0.25}{0.75} = \frac{1}{3}$$

Now try Exercise 31.

EXPLORATION 1 Testing Positive for HIV

As of the year 2003, the probability of an adult in the United States having HIV/AIDS was 0.006 (source: *2004 CIA World Factbook*). The ELISA test is used to detect the virus antibody in blood. If the antibody is present, the test reports positive with probability 0.997 and negative with probability 0.003. If the antibody is not present, the test reports positive with probability 0.015 and negative with probability 0.985.

1. Draw a tree diagram with branches to nodes "antibody present" and "antibody absent" branching from the root. Fill in the probabilities for North American adults (age 15–49) along the branches. (Note that these two probabilities must add up to 1.)
2. From the node at the end of each of the two branches, draw branches to "positive" and "negative." Fill in the probabilities along the branches.
3. Use the Multiplication Principle to fill in the probabilities at the ends of the four branches. Check to see that they add up to 1.
4. Find the probability of a positive test result. (Note that this event consists of two outcomes.)
5. Use the conditional probability formula to find the probability that a person with a positive test result actually *has* the antibody, i.e., $P(\text{antibody present} \mid \text{positive})$.

You might be surprised that the answer to part 5 is so low, but it should be compared with the probability of the antibody being present *before* seeing the positive test result, which was 0.006. Nonetheless, that is why a positive ELISA test is followed by further testing before a diagnosis of HIV/AIDS is made. This is the case with many diagnostic tests.

Binomial Distributions

It is not always easy to determine a probability distribution for a sample space with unequal probabilities. An interesting exception for those who have studied the Binomial Theorem is the binomial distribution.

Talking the Talk

Notice that the probabilities in Example 9 are associated with the random variable that *counts the number of 3's* on four rolls of a fair die. For this random variable, then, $P(4) \approx 0.00077$, $P(0) \approx 0.48225$, and $P(2) \approx 0.01929$.

EXAMPLE 9 Repeating a Simple Experiment

We roll a fair die four times. Find the probability that we roll:

(a) All 3's. **(b)** No 3's. **(c)** Exactly two 3's.

SOLUTION

(a) We have a probability 1/6 of rolling a 3 each time. By the Multiplication Principle, the probability of rolling a 3 all four times is $(1/6)^4 \approx 0.00077$.

(b) There is a probability 5/6 of rolling something other than 3 each time. By the Multiplication Principle, the probability of rolling a non-3 all four times is $(5/6)^4 \approx 0.48225$.

(c) The probability of rolling two 3's followed by two non-3's (again by the Multiplication Principle) is $(1/6)^2(5/6)^2 \approx 0.01929$. However, that is not the only outcome we must consider. In fact, the two 3's could occur *anywhere* among the four rolls, in exactly $\binom{4}{2} = 6$ ways. That gives us 6 outcomes, each with probability $(1/6)^2(5/6)^2$. The probability of the event "exactly two 3's" is therefore $\binom{4}{2}(1/6)^2(5/6)^2 \approx 0.11574$. *Now try Exercise 47.*

Did the form of those answers look a little familiar? Watch what they look like when we let $p = 1/6$ and $q = 5/6$:

$$P(\text{four 3's}) = p^4$$
$$P(\text{no 3's}) = q^4$$
$$P(\text{two 3's}) = \binom{4}{2} p^2 q^2$$

You can probably recognize these as three of the terms in the expansion of $(p + q)^4$. This is no coincidence. In fact, the terms in the expansion

$$(p + q)^4 = p^4 + 4p^3q^1 + 6p^2q^2 + 4p^1q^3 + q^4$$

give the exact probabilities of 4, 3, 2, 1, and 0 threes (respectively) when we toss a fair die four times! That is why this is called a *binomial probability distribution*. The general theorem follows.

Binomial Probabilities on a Calculator

Your calculator might be programmed to find values for the binomial probability distribution function (binompdf). The solutions to Example 10 in one calculator syntax, for example, could be obtained by:

(a) binompdf(20, .9, 20) (20 repetitions, 0.9 probability, 20 successes)

(b) binompdf(20, .9, 18) (20 repetitions, 0.9 probability, 18 successes)

(c) 1 − binomcdf(20, .9, 17) (1 minus the *cumulative* probability of 17 or fewer successes)

Check your owner's manual for more information.

THEOREM 103 Binomial Distribution

Suppose an experiment consists of n independent repetitions of an experiment with two outcomes, called "success" and "failure." Let $P(\text{success}) = p$ and $P(\text{failure}) = q$. (Note that $q = 1 - p$.)

Then the terms in the binomial expansion of $(p + q)^n$ give the respective probabilities of exactly $n, n - 1, \ldots, 2, 1, 0$ successes. The distribution is shown below:

Number of successes out of n independent repetitions	Probability
n	p^n
$n - 1$	$\binom{n}{n-1} p^{n-1} q$
$\vdots$	$\vdots$
r	$\binom{n}{r} p^r q^{n-r}$
$\vdots$	$\vdots$
1	$\binom{n}{1} p q^{n-1}$
0	q^n

EXAMPLE 10 Shooting Free Throws

Suppose Michael makes 90% of his free throws. If he shoots 20 free throws, and if his chance of making each one is independent of the other shots (an assumption you might question in a game situation), what is the probability that he makes

(a) All 20? **(b)** Exactly 18? **(c)** At least 18?

SOLUTION We could get the probabilities of all possible outcomes by expanding $(0.9 + 0.1)^{20}$, but that is not necessary in order to answer these three questions. We just need to compute three specific terms.

(a) $P(20 \text{ successes}) = (0.9)^{20} \approx 0.12158$

(b) $P(18 \text{ successes}) = \binom{20}{18}(0.9)^{18}(0.1)^2 \approx 0.28518$

(c)
$$\begin{aligned} P(\text{at least 18 successes}) &= P(18) + P(19) + P(20) \\ &= \binom{20}{18}(0.9)^{18}(0.1)^2 + \binom{20}{19}(0.9)^{19}(0.1) + (0.9)^{20} \\ &\approx 0.6769 \end{aligned}$$

Now try Exercise 49.

LESSON H-14 EXERCISES

Exercise numbers with a gray background indicate problems that the authors have designed to be solved *without a calculator.*

In Exercises 1–8, a red die and a green die have been rolled. What is the probability of the event?

1. The sum is 9. **2.** The sum is even.

3. The number on the red die is greater than the number on the green die.

4. The sum is less than 10.

5. Both numbers are odd.

6. Both numbers are even.

7. The sum is prime. **8.** The sum is 7 or 11.

9. Writing to Learn Alrik's gerbil cage has four compartments, A, B, C, and D. After careful observation, he estimates the proportion of time the gerbil spends in each compartment and constructs the table below.

Compartment	A	B	C	D
Proportion	0.25	0.20	0.35	0.30

(a) Is this a valid probability function? Explain.

(b) Is there a problem with Alrik's reasoning? Explain.

10. (Continuation of Exercise 9) Suppose Alrik determines that his gerbil spends time in the four compartments A, B, C, and D in the ratio 4:3:2:1. What proportions should he fill in the table above? Is this a valid probability function?

The maker of a popular chocolate candy that is covered in a thin colored shell has released information about the overall color proportions in its production of the candy, which is summarized in the following table.

Color	Brown	Red	Yellow	Green	Orange	Tan
Proportion	0.3	0.2	0.2	0.1	0.1	0.1

In Exercises 11–16, a single candy of this type is selected at random from a newly opened bag. What is the probability that the candy has the given color(s)?

11. Brown or tan **12.** Red, green, or orange

13. Red **14.** Not red

15. Neither orange nor yellow **16.** Neither brown nor tan

A peanut version of the same candy has all the same colors except tan. The proportions of the peanut version are given in the following table.

Color	Brown	Red	Yellow	Green	Orange
Proportion	0.3	0.2	0.2	0.2	0.1

In Exercises 17–22, a candy of this type is selected at random from each of two newly opened bags. What is the probability that the two candies have the given color(s)?

17. Both are brown.

18. Both are orange.

19. One is red, and the other is green.

20. The first is brown, and the second is yellow.

21. Neither is yellow.

22. The first is not red, and the second is not orange.

Exercises 23–32 concern a version of the card game "bid Euchre" that uses a pack of 24 cards, consisting of ace, king, queen, jack, 10, and 9 in each of the four suits (spades, hearts, diamonds, and clubs). In bid Euchre, a hand consists of 6 cards. Find the probability of each event.

23. Euchre A hand is all spades.

24. Euchre All six cards are from the same suit.

25. Euchre A hand includes all four aces.

26. Euchre A hand includes two jacks of the same color (called the right and left bower).

27. Using Venn Diagrams A and B are events in a sample space S such that $P(A) = 0.6$, $P(B) = 0.5$, and $P(A \text{ and } B) = 0.3$.

(a) Draw a Venn diagram showing the overlapping sets A and B and fill in the probabilities of the four regions formed.

(b) Find the probability that A occurs but B does not.

(c) Find the probability that B occurs but A does not.

(d) Find the probability that neither A nor B occurs.

(e) Are events A and B independent? (That is, does $P(A \mid B) = P(A)$?)

28. Using Venn Diagrams A and B are events in a sample space S such that $P(A) = 0.7$, $P(B) = 0.4$, and $P(A \text{ and } B) = 0.2$.

(a) Draw a Venn diagram showing the overlapping sets A and B and fill in the probabilities of the four regions formed.

(b) Find the probability that A occurs but B does not.

(c) Find the probability that B occurs but A does not.

(d) Find the probability that neither A nor B occurs.

(e) Are events A and B independent? (That is, does $P(A \mid B) = P(A)$?)

In Exercises 29 and 30, it will help to draw a tree diagram.

29. Piano Lessons If it rains tomorrow, the probability is 0.8 that John will practice his piano lesson. If it does not rain tomorrow, there is only a 0.4 chance that John will practice. Suppose that the chance of rain tomorrow is 60%. What is the probability that John will practice his piano lesson?

30. Predicting Cafeteria Food If the school cafeteria serves meat loaf, there is a 70% chance that they will serve peas. If they do not serve meat loaf, there is a 30% chance that they will serve peas anyway. The students know that meat loaf will be served exactly once during the 5-day week, but they do not know which day. If tomorrow is Monday, what is the probability that

(a) The cafeteria serves meat loaf?

(b) The cafeteria serves meat loaf and peas?

(c) The cafeteria serves peas?

31. Conditional Probability There are two precalculus sections at West High School. Mr. Abel's class has 12 girls and 8 boys, while Mr. Bonitz's class has 10 girls and 15 boys. If a West High precalculus student chosen at random happens to be a girl, what is the probability she is from Mr. Abel's class? [*Hint*: The answer is not 12/22.]

32. **Group Activity Conditional Probability** Two boxes are on the table. One box contains a normal coin and a two-headed coin; the other box contains three normal coins. A friend reaches into a box, removes a coin, and shows you one side: a head. What is the probability that it came from the box with the two-headed coin?

33. **Renting Cars** Floppy Jalopy Rent-a-Car has 25 cars available for rental—20 big bombs and 5 midsize cars. If two cars are selected at random, what is the probability that both are big bombs?

34. **Defective Calculators** Dull Calculators, Inc., knows that a unit coming off an assembly line has a probability of 0.037 of being defective. If four units are selected at random during the course of a workday, what is the probability that none of the units are defective?

35. **Causes of Death** The government designates a single cause for each death in the United States. The resulting data indicate that 45% of deaths are due to heart and other cardiovascular disease and 22% are due to cancer.

    (a) What is the probability that the death of a randomly selected person will be due to cardiovascular disease or cancer?

    (b) What is the probability that the death will be due to some other cause?

36. **Yahtzee** In the game of *Yahtzee*, on the first roll five dice are tossed simultaneously. What is the probability of rolling five of a kind (which is Yahtzee!) on the first roll?

37. **Writing to Learn** Explain why the following statement cannot be true. The probabilities that a computer salesperson will sell zero, one, two, or three computers in any one day are 0.12, 0.45, 0.38, and 0.15, respectively.

38. **HIV Testing** A particular test for HIV, the virus that causes AIDS, is 0.7% likely to produce a false positive result—a result indicating that the human subject has HIV when in fact the person is not carrying the virus. If 60 individuals who are HIV-negative are tested, what is the probability of obtaining at least one false result?

39. **Graduate School Survey** The Earmuff Junction College Alumni Office surveys selected members of the class of 2000. Of the 254 who graduated that year, 172 were women, 124 of whom went on to graduate school. Of the male graduates, 58 went on to graduate school. What is the probability of the given event?

    (a) The graduate is a woman.

    (b) The graduate went on to graduate school.

    (c) The graduate was a woman who went on to graduate school.

40. **Indiana Jones and the Final Exam** Professor Indiana Jones gives his class a list of 20 study questions, from which he will select 8 to be answered on the final exam. If a given student knows how to answer 14 of the questions, what is the probability that the student will be able to answer the given number of questions correctly?

    (a) All 8 questions

    (b) Exactly 5 questions

    (c) At least 6 questions

41. **Graduation Requirement** To complete the kinesiology requirement at Palpitation Tech you must pass two classes chosen from aerobics, aquatics, defense arts, gymnastics, racket sports, recreational activities, rhythmic activities, soccer, and volleyball. If you decide to choose your two classes at random by drawing two class names from a box, what is the probability that you will take racket sports and rhythmic activities?

42. **Writing to Learn** During July in Gunnison, Colorado, the probability of at least 1 hour a day of sunshine is 0.78, the probability of at least 30 minutes of rain is 0.44, and the probability that it will be cloudy all day is 0.22. Write a paragraph explaining whether this statement could be true.

In Exercises 43–50, ten dimes dated 1990 through 1999 are tossed. Find the probability of each event.

43. **Tossing Ten Dimes** Heads on the 1990 dime only

44. **Tossing Ten Dimes** Heads on the 1991 and 1996 dimes only

45. **Tossing Ten Dimes** Heads on all 10 dimes

46. **Tossing Ten Dimes** Heads on all but one dime

47. **Tossing Ten Dimes** Exactly two heads

48. **Tossing Ten Dimes** Exactly three heads

49. **Tossing Ten Dimes** At least one head

50. **Tossing Ten Dimes** At least two heads

Explorations

51. **Empirical Probability** In real applications, it is often necessary to approximate the probabilities of the various outcomes of an experiment by performing the experiment a large number of times and recording the results. Barney's Bread Basket offers five different kinds of bagels. Barney records the sales of the first 500 bagels in a given week in the table shown below:

Type of Bagel	Number Sold
Plain	185
Onion	60
Rye	55
Cinnamon Raisin	125
Sourdough	75

    (a) Use the observed sales number to approximate the probability that a random customer buys a plain bagel. Do the same for each other bagel type and make a table showing the approximate probability distribution.

    (b) Assuming independence of the events, find the probability that three customers in a row all order plain bagels.

    (c) **Writing to Learn** Do you think it is reasonable to assume that the orders of three consecutive customers actually are independent? Explain.

52. **Straight Poker** In the original version of poker known as "straight" poker, a 5-card hand is dealt from a standard deck of 52 cards. What is the probability of the given event?

(a) A hand will contain at least one king.

(b) A hand will be a "full house" (any three of one kind and a pair of another kind).

53. **Married Students** Suppose that 23% of all college students are married. Answer the following questions for a random sample of eight college students.

(a) How many would you expect to be married?

(b) Would you regard it as unusual if the sample contained five married students?

(c) What is the probability that five or more of the eight students are married?

54. **Group Activity Investigating an Athletic Program** A university widely known for its track and field program claims that 75% of its track athletes get degrees. A journalist investigates what happened to the 32 athletes who began the program over a 6-year period that ended 7 years ago. Of these athletes, 17 have graduated and the remaining 15 are no longer attending any college. If the university's claim is true, the number of athletes who graduate among the 32 examined should have been governed by binomial probability with $p = 0.75$.

(a) What is the probability that exactly 17 athletes should have graduated?

(b) What is the probability that 17 or fewer athletes should have graduated?

(c) If you were the journalist, what would you say in your story on the investigation?

Extending the Ideas

55. **Expected Value** If the outcomes of an experiment are given numerical values (such as the total on a roll of two dice, or the payoff on a lottery ticket), we define the **expected value** to be the sum of all the numerical values times their respective probabilities.

For example, suppose we roll a fair die. If we roll a multiple of 3, we win \$3; otherwise we lose \$1. The probabilities of the two possible payoffs are shown in the table below:

Value	Probability
+3	2/6
−1	4/6

The expected value is

$$3 \times (2/6) + (-1) \times (4/6) = (6/6) - (4/6) = 1/3.$$

We interpret this to mean that we would win an average of 1/3 dollar per game in the long run.

(a) A game is called *fair* if the expected value of the payoff is zero. Assuming that we still win \$3 for a multiple of 3, what should we pay for any other outcome in order to make the game fair?

(b) Suppose we roll *two* fair dice and look at the total under the original rules. That is, we win \$3 for rolling a multiple of 3 and lose \$1 otherwise. What is the expected value of this game?

56. **Expected Value** (Continuation of Exercise 55) Gladys has a personal rule never to enter the lottery (picking 6 numbers from 1 to 46) until the payoff reaches 4 million dollars. When it does reach 4 million, she always buys ten different \$1 tickets.

(a) Assume that the payoff for a winning ticket is 4 million dollars. What is the probability that Gladys holds a winning ticket? (Refer to Example 1 of this section for the probability of any ticket winning.)

(b) Fill in the probability distribution for Gladys's possible payoffs in the table below. (Note that we subtract \$10 from the \$4 million, since Gladys has to pay for her tickets even if she wins.)

Value	Probability
−10	
+3,999,990	

(c) Find the expected value of the game for Gladys.

(d) **Writing to Learn** In terms of the answer in part (b), explain to Gladys the long-term implications of her strategy.

HONORS APPENDIX Review Exercises

Exercise numbers with a gray background indicate problems that the authors have designed to be solved *without a calculator.*

H-1 Conic Sections and Parabolas

Find the vertex, focus, directrix, and focal width of the parabola, and sketch the graph.

1. $y^2 = 12x$ **2.** $x^2 = -8y$

3. $(x + 2)^2 = -4(y - 1)$ **4.** $(y + 2)^2 = 16x$

Identify the conic. Then complete the square to write the conic in standard form, and sketch the graph.

5. $x^2 - 6x - y - 3 = 0$

6. $x^2 + 2x + 4y - 7 = 0$

7. $3x^2 - 6x - 4y - 9 = 0$

Find the equation for the conic in standard form.

8. Parabola: vertex $(0, 0)$, focus $(2, 0)$

9. Parabola: vertex $(0, 0)$, opens downward, focal width $= 12$

10. Parabola: vertex $(-3, 3)$, directrix $y = 0$

11. Parabola: vertex $(1, -2)$, opens to the left, focal length $= 2$

H-2 Ellipses

Identify the type of conic. Find the center, vertices, and foci of the conic, and sketch its graph.

12. $\dfrac{y^2}{8} + \dfrac{x^2}{5} = 1$ **13.** $\dfrac{x^2}{25} + \dfrac{y^2}{36} = 1$

14. $\dfrac{(x - 2)^2}{16} + \dfrac{(y + 1)^2}{7} = 1$

15. $\dfrac{y^2}{36} + \dfrac{(x + 6)^2}{20} = 1$

Identify the conic. Then complete the square to write the conic in standard form, and sketch the graph.

16. $\dfrac{(x - 2)^2}{4} + y^2 = 1$

17. $\dfrac{y^2}{3} + x^2 = 1$

18. $x^2 + 4x + 3y^2 - 5 = 0$

Identify the conic. Solve the equation for *y* and graph it.

19. $3x^2 - 8xy + 6y^2 - 5x - 5y + 20 = 0$

20. $10x^2 - 8xy + 6y^2 + 8x - 5y - 30 = 0$

Find the equation for the conic in standard form.

21. Ellipse: center $(0, 0)$, foci $(\pm 12, 0)$, vertices $(\pm 13, 0)$

22. Ellipse: center $(0, 0)$, foci $(0, \pm 2)$, vertices $(0, \pm 6)$

23. Ellipse: center $(0, 2)$, semimajor axis $= 3$, one focus is $(2, 2)$.

24. Ellipse: center $(-3, -4)$, semimajor axis $= 4$, one focus is $(0, -4)$.

H-3 Hyerbolas

Identify the type of conic. Find the center, vertices, and foci of the conic, and sketch its graph.

25. $\dfrac{y^2}{16} - \dfrac{x^2}{49} = 1$ **26.** $\dfrac{x^2}{49} - \dfrac{y^2}{9} = 1$

27. $\dfrac{(x + 3)^2}{18} - \dfrac{(y - 5)^2}{28} = 1$

28. $\dfrac{(y - 3)^2}{9} - \dfrac{(x - 7)^2}{12} = 1$

Identify the conic. Then complete the square to write the conic in standard form, and sketch the graph.

29. $x^2 - y^2 - 2x + 4y - 6 = 0$

30. $2x^2 - 3y^2 - 12x - 24y + 60 = 0$

31. $12x^2 - 4y^2 - 72x - 16y + 44 = 0$

Find the equation for the conic in standard form.

32. Hyperbola: center $(0, 0)$, foci $(0, \pm 6)$, vertices $(0, \pm 5)$

33. Hyperbola: center $(0, 0)$, vertices $(\pm 2, 0)$, asymptotes $y = \pm 2x$

34. Hyperbola: center $(2, 1)$, vertices $(2 \pm 3, 1)$, one asymptote is $y = (4/3)(x - 2) + 1$

35. Hyperbola: center $(-5, 0)$, one focus is $(-5, 3)$, one vertex is $(-5, 2)$.

H-4 Complex Numbers

Perform the indicated operation, and write the result in the standard form *a* + *bi* without using a calculator.

36. $(3 + i) - (8i - 6)$

37. $(4 + 3i)(7 + 6i)$

38. $(3 - 2i) + (-2 + 5i)$ **39.** $(5 - 7i) - (3 - 2i)$

40. $(1 + 2i)(3 - 2i)$ **41.** $(1 + i)^3$

42. $(1 + 2i)^2(1 - 2i)^2$ **43.** i^{29}

44. $\sqrt{-16}$ **45.** $\dfrac{2 + 3i}{1 - 5i}$

H-5 Solving Inequalities Algebraically and Graphically

Solve each inequality.

46. $\dfrac{3x - 5}{4} \le -1$ **47.** $|2x - 5| < 7$

48. $|3x + 4| \ge 2$ **49.** $4x^2 + 3x > 10$

50. $2x^2 - 2x - 1 > 0$ **51.** $9x^2 - 12x - 1 \le 0$

52. $x^3 - 9x \le 3$ **53.** $4x^3 - 9x + 2 > 0$

54. $\left|\dfrac{x + 7}{5}\right| > 2$ **55.** $2x^2 + 3x - 35 < 0$

56. $4x^2 + 12x + 9 \ge 0$ **57.** $x^2 - 6x + 9 < 0$

H-6 Complex Zeros and the Fundamental Theorem of Algebra

Find all the real zeros of the function, finding exact values when possible. Identify each zero as rational or irrational. State the number of nonreal complex zeros.

58. $f(x) = x^4 - 10x^3 + 23x^2$

59. $k(t) = t^4 - 7t^2 + 12$

60. $h(x) = x^3 - 2x^2 - 8x + 5$

61. $k(x) = x^4 - x^3 - 14x^2 + 24x + 5$

Find all of the zeros and write a linear factorization of the function.

62. $f(x) = 2x^3 - 9x^2 + 2x + 30$

63. $f(x) = 5x^3 - 24x^2 + x + 12$

64. $f(x) = 6x^4 + 11x^3 - 16x^2 - 11x + 10$

65. $f(x) = x^4 - 8x^3 + 27x^2 - 50x + 50$, given that $1 + 2i$ is a zero.

Write the function as a product of linear and irreducible quadratic factors all with real coefficients.

66. $f(x) = x^3 - x^2 - x - 2$

67. $f(x) = 9x^3 - 3x^2 - 13x - 1$

68. $f(x) = 2x^4 - 9x^3 + 23x^2 - 31x + 15$

69. $f(x) = 3x^4 - 7x^3 - 3x^2 + 17x + 10$

H-7 Graphs of Rational Functions

Describe how the graph of the given function can be obtained by transforming the graph of the reciprocal function $f(x) = 1/x$. Identify the horizontal and vertical asymptotes.

70. $f(x) = \dfrac{-x + 7}{x - 5}$

71. $f(x) = \dfrac{3x + 5}{x + 2}$

Find the asymptotes and intercepts of the function, and graph it.

72. $f(x) = \dfrac{x^2 + x + 1}{x^2 - 1}$

73. $f(x) = \dfrac{2x^2 + 7}{x^2 + x - 6}$

74. $f(x) = \dfrac{x^2 - 4x + 5}{x + 3}$

75. $g(x) = \dfrac{x^2 - 3x - 7}{x + 3}$

Find the intercepts, analyze, and graph the given rational function.

76. $f(x) = \dfrac{x^3 + x^2 - 2x + 5}{x + 2}$

77. $f(x) = \dfrac{-x^4 + x^2 + 1}{x - 1}$

78. **Breaking Even** Midtown Sporting Goods has determined that it needs to sell its soccer shinguards for \$5.25 a pair in order to be competitive. It costs \$4.32 to produce each pair of shinguards, and the weekly overhead cost is \$4000.

(a) Express the average cost that includes the overhead of producing one shinguard as a function of the number x of shinguards produced each week.

(b) Solve algebraically to find the number of shinguards that must be sold each week to make \$8000 in profit. Support your work graphically.

79. **Deer Population** The number of deer P at any time t (in years) in a federal game reserve is given by

$$P(t) = \frac{800 + 640t}{20 + 0.8t}.$$

(a) Find the number of deer when t is 15, 70, and 100.

(b) Find the horizontal asymptote of the graph of $y = P(t)$.

(c) According to the model, what is the largest possible deer population?

H-8 Solving Inequalities in One Variable

Solve the inequality algebraically, and support graphically.

80. $2x^3 + 3x^2 - 17x - 30 < 0$

81. $3x^4 + x^3 - 36x^2 + 36x + 16 \geq 0$

82. $\dfrac{x + 3}{x^2 - 4} \geq 0$

83. $\dfrac{x^2 - 7}{x^2 - x - 6} < 1$

84. $(2x - 1)^2|x + 3| \leq 0$

85. $\dfrac{(x - 1)|x - 4|}{\sqrt{x + 3}} > 0$

86. **Industrial Design** Johnson Cannery will pack peaches in 1-L cylindrical cans. Let x be the radius of the base of the can in centimeters.

(a) Express the surface area S of the can as a function of x.

(b) Find the radius and height of the can if the surface area is 900 cm^2.

(c) What dimensions are possible for the can if the surface area is to be less than 900 cm^2?

87. **Industrial Design** Gilman Construction is hired to build a rectangular tank with a square base and no top. The tank is to hold 1000 ft^3 of water. Let x be a length of the base.

(a) Express the outside surface area S of the tank as a function of x.

(b) Find the length, width, and height of the tank if the outside surface area is 600 ft^2.

(c) What dimensions are possible for the tank if the outside surface area is to be less than 600 ft^2?

H-9 Trigonometric Functions of Acute Angles

Solve the right triangle *ABC*.

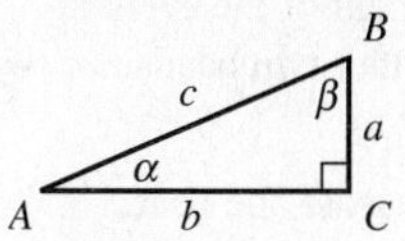

88. $\alpha = 35°, c = 15$

89. $b = 8, c = 10$

90. $\beta = 48°, a = 7$

91. $\alpha = 28°, c = 8$

92. $b = 5, c = 7$

93. $a = 2.5, b = 7.3$

94. Height of Building The angle of elevation of the top of a building from a point 100 m away from the building on level ground is 78°. Find the height of the building.

95. Height of Tree A tree casts a shadow 51 ft long when the angle of elevation of the Sun (measured with the horizon) is 25°. How tall is the tree?

96. Traveling Car From the top of a 150-ft building Flora observes a car moving toward her. If the angle of depression of the car changes from 18° to 42° during the observation, how far does the car travel?

97. Finding Distance A lighthouse L stands 4 mi from the closest point P along a straight shore (see figure). Find the distance from P to a point Q along the shore if $\angle PLQ = 22°$.

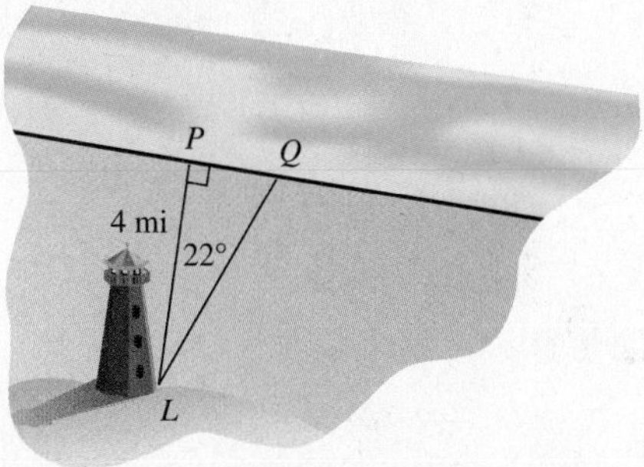

H-10 and H-11 Proving Fundamental Trigonometric Identities

Write the expression as the sine, cosine, or tangent of an angle.

98. $2 \sin 100° \cos 100°$

99. $\dfrac{2 \tan 40°}{1 - \tan^2 40°}$

Simplify the expression to a single term. Support your answer graphically.

100. $(1 - 2\sin^2\theta)^2 + 4\sin^2\theta\cos^2\theta$

101. $1 - 4\sin^2 x \cos^2 x$

Prove the identity.

102. $\cos 3x = 4\cos^3 x - 3\cos x$

103. $\cos^2 2x - \cos^2 x = \sin^2 x - \sin^2 2x$

104. $\tan^2 x - \sin^2 x = \sin^2 x \tan^2 x$

105. $2\sin\theta\cos^3\theta + 2\sin^3\theta\cos\theta = \sin 2\theta$

106. $\csc x - \cos x \cot x = \sin x$

107. $\dfrac{\tan\theta + \sin\theta}{2\tan\theta} = \cos^2\left(\dfrac{\theta}{2}\right)$

108. $\dfrac{1 + \tan\theta}{1 - \tan\theta} + \dfrac{1 + \cot\theta}{1 - \cot\theta} = 0$

109. $\sin 3\theta = 3\cos^2\theta\sin\theta - \sin^3\theta$

110. $\cos^2\left(\dfrac{t}{2}\right) = \dfrac{1 + \sec t}{2\sec t}$

111. $\dfrac{\tan^3\gamma - \cot^3\gamma}{\tan^2\gamma + \csc^2\gamma} = \tan\gamma - \cot\gamma$

112. $\dfrac{\cos\phi}{1 - \tan\phi} + \dfrac{\sin\phi}{1 - \cot\phi} = \cos\phi + \sin\phi$

113. $\dfrac{\cos(-z)}{\sec(-z) + \tan(-z)} = 1 + \sin z$

114. $\sqrt{\dfrac{1 - \cos y}{1 + \cos y}} = \dfrac{1 - \cos y}{|\sin y|}$

H-12 Sum and Difference Identities

Prove the identity.

115. $\tan\left(u + \dfrac{3\pi}{4}\right) = \dfrac{\tan u - 1}{1 + \tan u}$

116. $\dfrac{1}{4}\sin 4\gamma = \sin\gamma\cos^3\gamma - \cos\gamma\sin^3\gamma$

117. $\tan\dfrac{1}{2}\beta = \csc\beta - \cot\beta$

118. $\arctan t = \dfrac{1}{2}\arctan\dfrac{2t}{1 - t^2}, \quad -1 < t < 1$

Use a grapher to conjecture whether the equation is likely to be an identity. Confirm your conjecture.

119. $\sec x - \sin x \tan x = \cos x$

120. $(\sin^2\alpha - \cos^2\alpha)(\tan^2\alpha + 1) = \tan^2\alpha - 1$

Write the expression in terms of sin *x* and cos *x* only.

121. $\sin 3x + \cos 3x$

122. $\sin 2x + \cos 3x$

123. $\cos^2 2x - \sin 2x$

124. $\sin 3x - 3\sin 2x$

H-13 Multiple-Angle Identities

Find the general solution without using a calculator. Give exact answers.

125. $\sin 2x = 0.5$

126. $\cos x = \dfrac{\sqrt{3}}{2}$

127. $\tan x = -1$

128. $2 \sin^{-1} x = \sqrt{2}$

129. $\tan^{-1} x = 1$

130. $2 \cos 2x = 1$

Solve the equation graphically. Find all solutions in the interval $[0, 2\pi)$.

131. $\sin^2 x - 3 \cos x = -0.5$

132. $\cos^3 x - 2 \sin x - 0.7 = 0$

133. $\sin^4 x + x^2 = 2$

134. $\sin 2x = x^3 - 5x^2 + 5x + 1$

Find all solutions in the interval $[0, 2\pi)$ without using a calculator. Give exact answers.

135. $2 \cos x = 1$

136. $\sin 3x = \sin x$

137. $\sin^2 x - 2 \sin x - 3 = 0$

138. $\cos 2t = \cos t$

139. $\sin (\cos x) = 1$

140. $\cos 2x + 5 \cos x = 2$

H-14 Probability

List the elements of the sample space.

141. Spinners A game spinner on a circular region divided into 6 equal sectors numbered 1–6 is spun.

142. Rolling Dice A red die and a green die are rolled.

143. Code Words A two-digit code is selected from the digits $\{1, 3, 6\}$, where no digits are to be repeated.

144. Production Line A product is inspected as it comes off the production line and is classified as either defective or nondefective.

In Exercises 145-148, a penny, a nickel, and a dime are tossed.

145. List all possible outcomes.

146. List all outcomes in the event "two heads or two tails."

147. List all outcomes in the complement of the event in Exercise 146 (i.e., the event "neither two heads nor two tails.")

148. Find the probability of tossing at least one head.

Solve each problem.

149. Coin Toss A fair coin is tossed six times. Find the probability of the event "HHTHTT."

150. Coin Toss A fair coin is tossed five times. Find the probability of obtaining two heads and three tails.

151. Coin Toss A fair coin is tossed four times. Find the probability of obtaining one head and three tails.

152. Assembly Line In a random check on an assembly line, the probability of finding a defective item is 0.003. Find the probability of a nondefective item occurring 10 times in a row.

153. Success or Failure An experiment has only two possible outcomes—success (S) or failure (F)—and repetitions of the experiment are independent events. If $P(S) = 0.5$, find the probability of obtaining three successes and one failure in four repetitions.

Postulates and Theorems

Postulates

Postulate 1
Same-Side Interior Angles Postulate
If a transversal intersects two parallel lines, then same-side interior angles are supplementary.

Postulate 2
Side-Side-Side (SSS) Postulate
If three sides of one triangle are congruent to the three sides of another triangle, then the two triangles are congruent.

Postulate 3
Side-Angle-Side (SAS) Postulate
If two sides and the included angle of one triangle are congruent to two sides and the included angle of another triangle, then the two triangles are congruent.

Postulate 4
Angle-Side-Angle (ASA) Postulate
If two angles and the included side of one triangle are congruent to two angles and the included side of another triangle, then the two triangles are congruent.

Postulate 5
Angle-Angle Similarity (AA ~) Postulate
If two angles of one triangle are congruent to two angles of another triangle, then the triangles are similar.

Postulate 6
If two figures are congruent, then their areas are equal.

Postulate 7
Arc Addition Postulate
The measure of the arc formed by two adjacent arcs is the sum of the measures of the two arcs.

Theorems

Theorem 1
Vertical Angles Theorem
Vertical angles are congruent.

Theorem 2
Congruent Supplements Theorem
If two angles are supplements of the same angle (or of two congruent angles), then the two angles are congruent.

Theorem 3
Congruent Complements Theorem
If two angles are complements of the same angle (or of two congruent angles), then the two angles are congruent.

Theorem 4
All right angles are congruent.

Theorem 5
If two angles are congruent and supplementary, then each is a right angle.

Theorem 6
Alternate Interior Angles Theorem
If a transversal intersects two parallel lines, the alternate interior angles are congruent.

Theorem 7
Corresponding Angles Theorem
If a transversal intersects two parallel lines, then corresponding angles are congruent.

Theorem 8
Alternate Exterior Angles Theorem
If a transversal intersects two parallel lines, then alternate exterior angles are congruent.

Theorem 9
Converse of the Corresponding Angles Theorem
If two lines and a transversal form corresponding angles that are congruent, then the two lines are parallel.

Theorem 10
Converse of the Alternate Interior Angles Theorem
If two lines and a transversal form alternate interior angles that are congruent, then the two lines are parallel.

Theorem 11
Converse of the Same-Side Interior Angles Postulate
If two lines and a transversal form same-side interior angles that are congruent, then the two lines are parallel.

Theorem 12
Converse of the Alternate Exterior Angles Theorem
If two lines and a transversal form alternate exterior angles that are congruent, then the two lines are parallel.

Theorem 13
If two lines are parallel to the same line, then they are parallel to each other.

Theorem 14
In a plane, if two lines are perpendicular to the same line, then they are parallel to each other.

Theorem 15
Perpendicular Transversal Theorem
In a plane, if a line is perpendicular to one of two parallel lines, then it is perpendicular to the other.

Theorem 16
Third Angles Theorem
If two angles of one triangle are congruent to two angles of another triangle, than the third angles are congruent.

Theorem 17
Angle-Angle-Side (AAS) Theorem
If two angles and a nonincluded side of one triangle are congruent to two angles and a nonincluded side of another triangle, then the two triangles are congruent.

Theorem 18
Isosceles Triangle Theorem
If two sides of a triangle are congruent, then the angles opposite those sides are congruent.

Corollary
If a triangle is equilateral, then the triangle is equiangular.

Theorem 19
Converse of the Isosceles Triangle Theorem
If two angles of a triangle are congruent, then the sides opposite the angles are congruent.

Corollary
If a triangle is equiangular, then it is equilateral.

Theorem 20
If a line bisects the vertex angle of an isosceles triangle, then the line is also the perpendicular bisector of the base.

Theorem 21
Hypotenuse-Leg (HL) Theorem
If the hypotenuse and a leg of one right triangle are congruent to the hypotenuse and a leg of another right triangle, then the triangles are congruent.

Theorem 22
Triangle Midsegment Theorem
If a line segment joins the midpoints of two sides of a triangle, then the segment is parallel to the third side and is half as long.

Theorem 23
Perpendicular Bisector Theorem
If a point is on the perpendicular bisector of a line segment, then it is equidistant from the endpoints of the segment.

Theorem 24
Converse of the Perpendicular Bisector Theorem
If a point is equidistant from the endpoints of a line segment, then it is on the perpendicular bisector of the segment.

Theorem 25
Angle Bisector Theorem
If a point is on the bisector of an angle, then the point is equidistant from the sides of the angle.

Theorem 26
Converse of the Angle Bisector Theorem
If a point in the interior of an angle is equidistant from the sides of the angle, then the point is on the angle bisector

Theorem 27
Concurrency of Perpendicular Bisectors Theorem
The perpendicular bisectors of the sides of a triangle are concurrent at a point equidistant from the vertices.

Theorem 28
Concurrency of Angle Bisectors Theorem
The bisectors of the angles of a triangle are concurrent at a point equidistant from the sides of the triangle.

Theorem 29
Concurrency of Medians Theorem
The medians of a triangle are concurrent at a point that is two-thirds the distance from each vertex to the midpoint of the opposite side.

Theorem 30
Concurrency of Altitudes Theorem
The lines that contain the altitudes of a triangle are concurrent.

Theorem 31
If two sides of a triangle are not congruent, then the larger angle lies opposite the longer side.

Theorem 32
If two angles of a triangle are not congruent, then the longer side lies opposite the larger angle.

Theorem 33
Triangle Inequality Theorem
The sum of the lengths of any two sides of a triangle is greater than the length of the third side.

Theorem 34
The Hinge Theorem (SAS Inequality Theorem)
If two sides of one triangle are congruent to two sides of another triangle and the included angles are not congruent, then the longer third side is opposite the larger included angle.

Theorem 35
Converse of the Hinge Theorem (SSS Inequality)
If two sides of one triangle are congruent to two sides of another triangle and the third sides are not congruent, then the larger included angle is opposite the longer third side.

Theorem 36
Polygon Angle-Sum Theorem
The sum of the measures of the angles of an n-gon is $(n - 2)180$.

Corollary
The measure of each angle of a regular n-gon is $\frac{(n-2)180}{n}$.

Theorem 37
The sum of the measures of the exterior angles of a polygon, one at each vertex, is 360.

Theorem 38
If a quadrilateral is a parallelogram, then its opposite sides are congruent.

Theorem 39
If a quadrilateral is a parallelogram, then its consecutive angles are supplementary.

Theorem 40
If a quadrilateral is a parallelogram, then its opposite angles are congruent.

Theorem 41
If a quadrilateral is a parallelogram, then its diagonals bisect each other.

Theorem 42
If three (or more) parallel lines cut off congruent segments on one transversal, then they cut off congruent segments on every transversal.

Theorem 43
If both pairs of opposite sides of a quadrilateral are congruent, then the quadrilateral is a parallelogram.

Theorem 44
If an angle of a quadrilateral is supplementary to both of its consecutive angles, then the quadrilateral is a parallelogram.

Theorem 45
If both pairs of opposite angles of a quadrilateral are congruent, then the quadrilateral is a parallelogram.

Theorem 46
If the diagonals of a quadrilateral bisect each other, then the quadrilateral is a parallelogram.

Theorem 47
If one pair of opposite sides of a quadrilateral is both congruent and parallel, then the quadrilateral is a parallelogram.

Theorem 48
If a parallelogram is a rhombus, then its diagonals are perpendicular.

Theorem 49
If a parallelogram is a rhombus, then each diagonal bisects a pair of opposite angles.

Theorem 50
If a parallelogram is a rectangle, then its diagonals are congruent.

Theorem 51
If the diagonals of a parallelogram are perpendicular, then the parallelogram is a rhombus.

Theorem 52
If one diagonal of a parallelogram bisects a pair of opposite angles, then the parallelogram is a rhombus.

Theorem 53
If the diagonals of a parallelogram are congruent, then the parallelogram is a rectangle.

Theorem 54
If a quadrilateral is an isosceles trapezoid, then each pair of base angles is congruent.

Theorem 55
If a quadrilateral is an isosceles trapezoid, then its diagonals are congruent.

Theorem 56
Trapezoid Midsegment Theorem
If a quadrilateral is a trapezoid, then

(1) the midsegment is parallel to the bases,and

(2) the length of the midsegment is half the sum of the lengths of the bases.

Theorem 57
If a quadrilateral is a kite, then its diagonals are perpendicular.

Theorem 58
Side-Angle-Side Similarity (SAS ~) Theorem
If an angle of one triangle is congruent to an angle of a second triangle, and the sides that include the two angles are proportional, then the triangles are similar.

Theorem 59
Side-Side-Side Similarity (SSS ~) Theorem
If the corresponding sides of two triangles are proportional, then the triangles are similar.

Theorem 60
The altitude to the hypotenuse of a right triangle divides the triangle into two triangles that are similar to the original triangle and to each other.

Corollary 1
The length of the altitude to the hypotenuse of a right triangle is the geometric mean of the lengths of the segments of the hypotenuse.

Corollary 2
The altitude to the hypotenuse of a right triangle separates the hypotenuse so that the length of each leg of the triangle is the geometric mean of the length of the hypotenuse and the length of the segment of the hypotenuse adjacent to the leg.

Theorem 61
Side-Splitter Theorem
If a line is parallel to one side of a triangle and intersects the other two sides, then it divides those sides proportionally.

Converse
If a line divides two sides of a triangle proportionally, then it is parallel to the third side.

Corollary
If three parallel lines intersect two transversals, then the segments intercepted on the transversals are proportional.

Theorem 62
Triangle-Angle-Bisector Theorem
If a ray bisects an angle of a triangle, then it divides the opposite side into two segments that are proportional to the other two sides of the triangle.

Theorem 63
Pythagorean Theorem
If a triangle is a right triangle, then the sum of the squares of the lengths of the legs is equal to the square of the length of the hypotenuse.

Theorem 64
Converse of the Pythagorean Theorem
If the sum of the squares of the lengths of two sides of a triangle is equal to the square of the length of the third side, then the triangle is a right triangle.

Theorem 65
If the square of the length of the longest side of a triangle is greater than the sum of the squares of the lengths of the other two sides, then the triangle is obtuse.

Theorem 66
If the square of the length of the longest side of a triangle is less than the sum of the squares of the lengths of the other two sides, then the triangle is acute.

Theorem 67
45°-45°-90° Triangle Theorem
In a 45°-45°-90° triangle, both legs are congruent and the length of the hypotenuse is $\sqrt{2}$ times the length of a leg.

Theorem 68
30°-60°-90° Triangle Theorem
In a 30°-60°-90° triangle, the length of the hypotenuse is twice the length of the shorter leg. The length of the longer leg is $\sqrt{3}$ times the length of the shorter leg.

hypotenuse = 2 • shorter leg longer leg 5 $\sqrt{3}$ • shorter leg.

Theorem 69
Area of a Regular Polygon
The area of a regular polygon is half the product of the apothem and the perimeter.

Theorem 70

Circumference of a Circle

The circumference of a circle is π times the diameter.

$C = \pi d$ or $C = 2\pi r$

Theorem 71

Arc Length

The length of an arc of a circle is the product of the ratio $\frac{\text{measure of the arc}}{360}$ and the circumference of the circle.

length of $\overset{\frown}{AB} = \frac{m\overset{\frown}{AB}}{360} \cdot 2\pi r$ or

length of $\overset{\frown}{AB} = \frac{m\overset{\frown}{AB}}{360} \cdot \pi d$

Theorem 72

Area of a Circle

The area of a circle is the product of π and the square of the radius.

$A = \pi r^2$

Theorem 73

Area of a Sector of a Circle

The area of a sector of a circle is the product of the ratio $\frac{\text{measure of the arc}}{360}$ and the area of the circle.

Area of sector $AOB = \frac{m\overset{\frown}{AB}}{360} \cdot \pi r^2$

Theorem 74

If a line is tangent to a circle, then the line is perpendicular to the radius at the point of tangency.

Theorem 75

If a line in the plane of a circle is perpendicular to a radius at its endpoint on the circle, then the line is tangent to the circle.

Theorem 76

If two segments are tangent to a circle from a point outside the circle, then the two segments are congruent.

Theorem 77

Within a circle or in congruent circles, congruent central angles have congruent arcs.

Converse

Within a circle or in congruent circles, congruent arcs have congruent central angles.

Theorem 78

Within a circle or in congruent circles, congruent central angles have congruent chords.

Converse

Within a circle or in congruent circles, congruent chords have congruent central angles.

Theorem 79

Within a circle or in congruent circles, congruent chords have congruent arcs.

Converse

Within a circle or in congruent circles, congruent arcs have congruent chords.

Theorem 80

Within a circle or in congruent circles, chords equidistant from the center (or centers) are congruent.

Converse

Within a circle or in congruent circles, congruent chords are equidistant from the center (or centers).

Theorem 81

In a circle, if a diameter is perpendicular to a chord, it bisects the chord and its arc.

Theorem 82

In a circle, if a diameter bisects a chord (that is not a diameter), it is perpendicular to the chord.

Theorem 83

In a circle, the perpendicular bisector of a chord contains the center of the circle.

Theorem 84

Inscribed Angle Theorem

The measure of an inscribed angle is half the measure of its intercepted arc.

Corollary 1

Two inscribed angles that intercept the same arc are congruent.

Corollary 2

An angle inscribed in a semicircle is a right angle.

Corollary 3

The opposite angles of a quadrilateral inscribed in a circle are supplementary.

Theorem 85

The measure of an angle formed by a tangent and a chord is half the measure of the intercepted arc.

Theorem 86

The measure of an angle formed by two lines that intersect inside a circle is half the sum of the measures of the intercepted arcs.

Theorem 87

The measure of an angle formed by two lines that intersect outside a circle is half the difference of the measures of the intercepted arcs.

Theorem 88

For a given point and circle, the product of the lengths of the two segments from the point to the circle is constant along any line through the point and circle.

Theorem 89

Lateral and Surface Areas of a Prism

The lateral area of a right prism is the product of the perimeter of the base and the height of the prism.

$L.A. = ph$

The surface area of a right prism is the sum of the lateral area and the areas of the two bases.

$S.A. = L.A. + 2B$

Theorem 90

Lateral and Surface Areas of a Cylinder

The lateral area of a right cylinder is the product of the circumference of the base and the height of the cylinder.

$L.A. = 2\pi rh$, or $L.A. = \pi dh$

The surface area of a right cylinder is the sum of the lateral area and areas of the two bases.

$S.A. = L.A. + 2B$, or $S.A. = \pi rh + 2\pi r^2$

Theorem 91

Lateral and Surface Areas of a Pyramid

The lateral area of a regular pyramid is half the product of the perimeter p of the base and the slant height ℓ of the pyramid.

$L.A. = \frac{1}{2}p\ell$

The surface area of a regular pyramid is the sum of the lateral area and the area B of the base.

$S.A. = L.A. + B$

Theorem 92

Lateral and Surface Areas of a Cone

The lateral area of a right cone is half the product of the circumference of the base and the slant height of the cone.

$L.A. = \frac{1}{2} \cdot 2\pi r\ell$ or $L.A. = \pi r\ell$

The surface area of a right cone is the sum of the lateral area and the area of the base.

$S.A. = L.A. + B$

Theorem 93

Cavalieri's Principle

If two space figures have the same height and the same cross-sectional area at every level, then they have the same volume.

Theorem 94

Volume of a Prism

The volume of a prism is the product of the area of the base and the height of the prism.

$V = Bh$

Theorem 95

Volume of a Cylinder

The volume of a cylinder is the product of the area of the base and the height of the cylinder.

$V = Bh$, or $V = \pi r^2 h$

Theorem 96

Volume of a Pyramid

The volume of a pyramid is one third the product of the area of the base and the height of the pyramid.

$V = \frac{1}{3}Bh$

Theorem 97

Volume of a Cone

The volume of a cone is one third the product of the area of the base and the height of the cone.

$V = \frac{1}{3}Bh$ or $V = \frac{1}{3}\pi r^2 h$

Theorem 98

Surface Area of a Sphere

The surface area of a sphere is four times the product of π and the square of the radius of the sphere.

$V = 4\pi r^2$

Theorem 99

Volume of a Sphere

The volume of a sphere is four thirds the product of π and the cube of the radius of the sphere.

$V = \frac{4}{3}\pi r^3$

Theorem 100

Fundamental Theorem of Algebra

A polynomial function of degree n has n complex zeros (real and nonreal). Some of these zeros may be repeated.

Theorem 101

Linear Factorization Theorem

If $f(x)$ is a polynomial function of degree $n > 0$, then $f(x)$ has precisely n linear factors and

$$f(x) = a(x - z_1)(x - z_2)\cdots(x - z_n)$$

where a is the leading coefficient of $f(x)$ and $z_1, z_2, \ldots, z_n$ are the complex zeros of $f(x)$. The z_i are not necessarily distinct numbers; some may be repeated.

Theorem 102

Complex Conjugate Zeros

Suppose that $f(x)$ is a polynomial function with real coefficients. If a and b are real numbers with $b \neq 0$ and $a + bi$ is a zero of $f(x)$, then its complex conjugate $a - bi$ is also a zero of $f(x)$.

Theorem 103

Binomial Distribution

Suppose an experiment consists of n independent repetitions of an experiment with two outcomes, called "success" and "failure." Let $P(\text{success}) = p$ and $P(\text{failure}) = q$. (Note that $q = 1 - p$.)

Then the terms in the binomial expansion of $(p + q)^n$ give the respective probabilities of exactly $n, n - 1, \ldots, 2, 1, 0$ successes. The distribution is shown below:

Number of successes out of n independent repetitions	Probability
n	p^n
$n - 1$	$\binom{n}{n-1}p^{n-1}q$
$\vdots$	$\vdots$
r	$\binom{n}{r}p^r q^{n-r}$
$\vdots$	$\vdots$
1	$\binom{n}{1}pq^{n-1}$
0	q^n

Additional Postulates, Theorems, and Formulas

Distance Formula

The distance between two points $A(x_1, y_1)$ and $B(x_2, y_2)$ is

$$d = \sqrt{(x_2 - x_1)^2 + (y_2 - y_1)^2}$$

Triangle Angle-Sum Theorem

The sum of the measures of the angles of a triangle is 180.

Triangle Exterior Angle Theorem

The measure of each exterior angle of a triangle equals the sum of the measures of its two remote interior angles.

$$m\angle 1 = m\angle 2 + m\angle 3$$

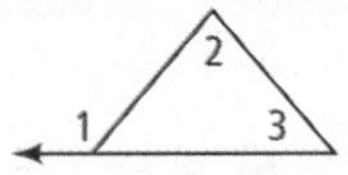

Corollary

The measure of an exterior angle of a triangle is greater than the measure of each of its remote interior angles.

Ruler Postulate

Every point on a line can be paired with a real number. This makes a one-to-one correspondence between the points on the line and the real numbers.

Segment Addition Postulate

If three points A, B, and C are collinear and B is between A and C, then $AB + BC = AC$.

Midpoint Formula

The coordinates of the midpoint of a segment are the average of the x-coordinates and the average of the y-coordinates of the endpoints.

Factor Theorem

A polynomial function $f(x)$ has a factor $x - k$ if and only if $f(k) = 0$.

Rational Zeros Theorem

Suppose f is a polynomial function of degree $n \geq 1$ of the form

$$f(x) = a_n x^n + a_{n-1}x^{n-1} + \cdots + a_0,$$

with every coefficient an integer and $a_0 \neq 0$. If $x = p/q$ is a rational zero of f, where p and q have no common integer factors other than ± 1, then

- p is an integer factor of the constant coefficient a_0, and
- q is an integer factor of the leading coefficient a_n.

Visual **Glossary**

English / Spanish

A

Absolute value function (p. 335) A function of the form $f(x) = |mx + b| + c$, where $m \neq 0$, is an absolute value function.

Función de valor absoluto (p. 335) Una función de la forma $f(x) = |mx + b| + c$, donde $m \neq 0$, es una función de valor absoluto.

Example $f(x) = |3x - 2| + 3$
$f(x) = |2x|$

Absolute value of a complex number (p. 188) The absolute value of a complex number is its distance from the origin on the complex number plane. In general, $|a + bi| = \sqrt{a^2 + b^2}$.

Valor absoluto de un número complejo (p. 188) El valor absoluto de un número complejo es la distancia a la que está del origen en el plano de números complejo. Generalmente, $|a + bi| = \sqrt{a^2 + b^2}$.

Example $|3 - 4i| = \sqrt{3^2 + (-4)^2} = 5$

Adjacent arcs (p. 798) Adjacent arcs are on the same circle and have exactly one point in common.

Arcos adyacentes (p. 798) Los arcos adyacentes están en el mismo círculo y tienen exactamente un punto en común.

Example

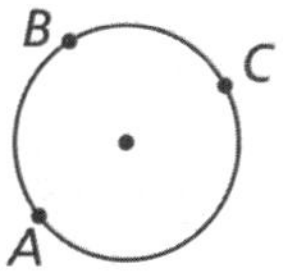

$\overset{\frown}{AB}$ and $\overset{\frown}{BC}$ are adjacent arcs.

Alternate interior (exterior) angles (p. 414) Alternate interior (exterior) angles are nonadjacent interior (exterior) angles that lie on opposite sides of the transversal.

Ángulos alternos internos (externos) (p. 414) Los ángulos alternos internos (externos) son ángulos internos (externos) no adyacentes situados en lados opuestos de la transversal.

Example

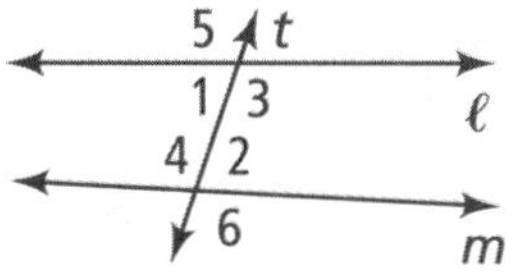

$\angle 1$ and $\angle 2$ are alternate interior angles, as are $\angle 3$ and $\angle 4$. $\angle 5$ and $\angle 6$ are alternate exterior angles.

Altitude *See* **cone; cylinder; parallelogram; prism; pyramid; trapezoid.**

Altura *Ver* **cone; cylinder; parallelogram; prism; pyramid; trapezoid.**

Altitude of a triangle (p. 555) An altitude of a triangle is the perpendicular segment from a vertex to the line containing the side opposite that vertex.

Altura de un triángulo (p. 555) Una altura de un triángulo es el segmento perpendicular que va desde un vértice hasta la recta que contiene el lado opuesto a ese vértice.

Example

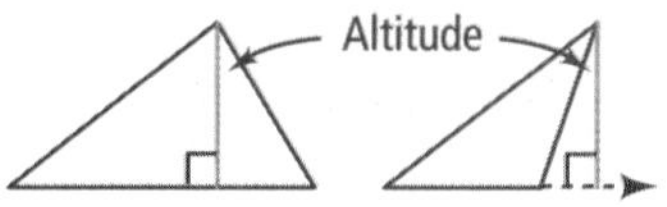

English	Spanish
Angle of elevation or depression (p. 777) An angle of elevation (depression) is the angle formed by a horizontal line and the line of sight to an object above (below) the horizontal line.	**Ángulo de elevación o depresión (p. 777)** Un ángulo de elevación (depresión) es el ángulo formado por una línea horizontal y la recta que va de esa línea a un objeto situado arriba (debajo) de ella.

Example

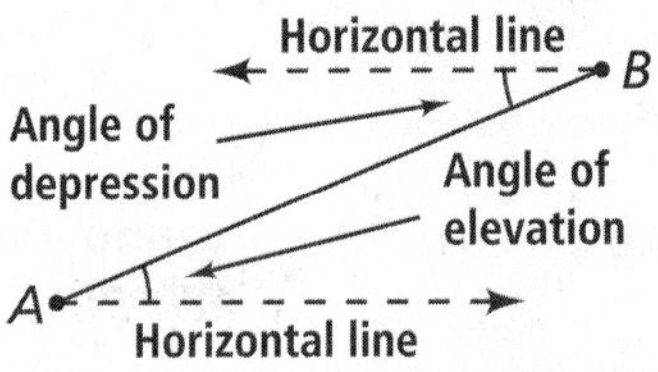

Apothem (p. 784) The apothem of a regular polygon is the distance from the center to a side.	**Apotema (p. 784)** La apotema de un polígono regular es la distancia desde el centro hasta un lado.

Example

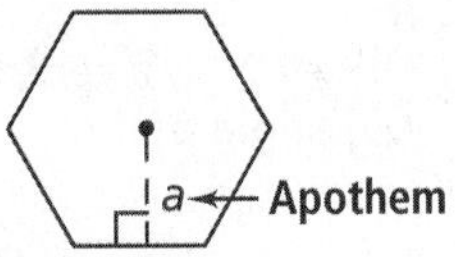

Arc length (p. 801) The length of an arc of a circle is the product of the ratio $\frac{\text{measure of the arc}}{360}$ and the circumference of the circle.	**Longitud de un arco (p. 801)** La longitud del arco de un círculo es el producto del cociente $\frac{\text{medida del arco}}{360}$ por la circunferencia del círculo.

Example

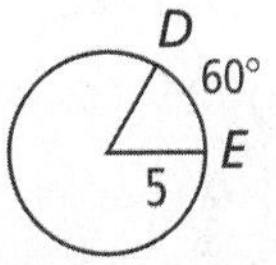

Length of $\widehat{DE} = \frac{60}{360} \cdot 2\pi(5) = \frac{5\pi}{3}$

Axis of symmetry (p. 115, 335) The line that divides a parabola into two mpatching halves.	**Eje de simetría (pp. 115, 335)** El eje de simetría es la línea que divide una parábola en dos mitades exactamente iguales.

Example

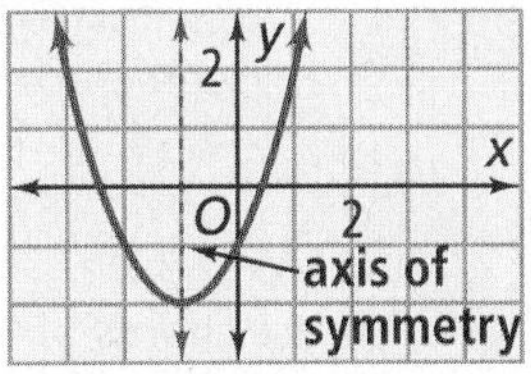

B

Base(s) *See* **cone; cylinder; isosceles triangle; parallelogram; prism; pyramid; trapezoid.**	**Base(s)** *Ver* **cone; cylinder; parallelogram; prism; pyramid; trapezoid; triangle.**
Base angles *See* **trapezoid; isosceles triangle.**	**Ángulos de base** *Ver* **trapezoid; isosceles triangle.**
Binomial (p. 49) A polynomial of two terms.	**Binomio (p. 49)** Polinomio compuesto de dos términos.

Example $3x + 7$ is a binomial.

Visual **Glossary**

English

Boundary (p. 346) A boundary of the graph of a linear inequality is a line in the coordinate plane. It separates the solutions of the inequality from the nonsolutions. Points of the line itself may or may not be solutions.

Spanish

Límite (p. 346) Un límite de la gráfica de una desigualdad lineal es una línea en el plano de coordenadas. Ésta separa las soluciones de la desigualdad de las no soluciones. Las soluciones pueden ser o no puntos de la línea.

C

Center *See* **circle; dilation; regular polygon; sphere.**

Centro *Ver* **circle; dilation; regular polygon; sphere.**

Central angle of a circle (p. 797) A central angle of a circle is an angle whose vertex is the center of the circle.

Ángulo central de un círculo (p. 797) Un ángulo central de un círculo es un ángulo cuyo vértice es el centro del círculo.

Example

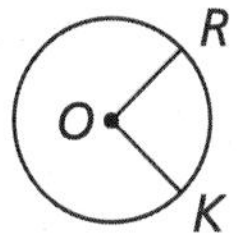

$\angle ROK$ is a central angle of $\odot O$.

Centroid of a triangle (p. 553) The centroid of a triangle is the point of concurrency of the medians of the triangle.

Centroide de un triángulo (p. 553) El centroide de un triángulo es el punto de intersección de sus medianas.

Example P is the centroid of $\triangle ABC$.

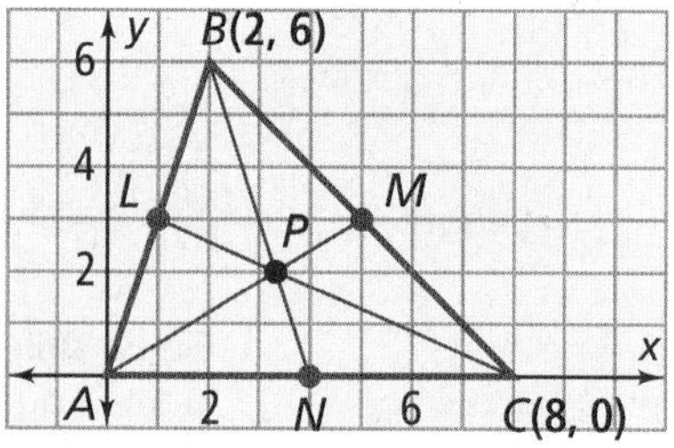

Chord (p. 828) A chord of a circle is a segment whose endpoints are on the circle.

Cuerda (p. 828) Una cuerda de un círculo es un segmento cuyos extremos son dos puntos del círculo.

Example

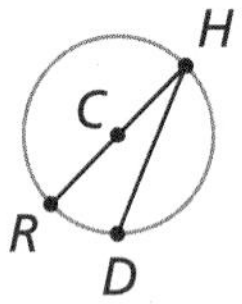

$\overline{HD}$ and $\overline{HR}$ are chords of $\odot C$.

English	Spanish

Circle (p. 797) A circle is the set of all points in a plane that are a given distance, the *radius*, from a given point, the *center*. The standard form for an equation of a circle with center (h, k) and radius r is $(x - h)^2 + (y - k)^2 = r^2$.

Círculo (p. 797) Un círculo es el conjunto de todos los puntos de un plano situados a una distancia dada, el *radio*, de un punto dado, el *centro*. La fórmula normal de la ecuación de un círculo con centro (h, k) y radio r es $(x - h)^2 + (y - k)^2 = r^2$.

Example

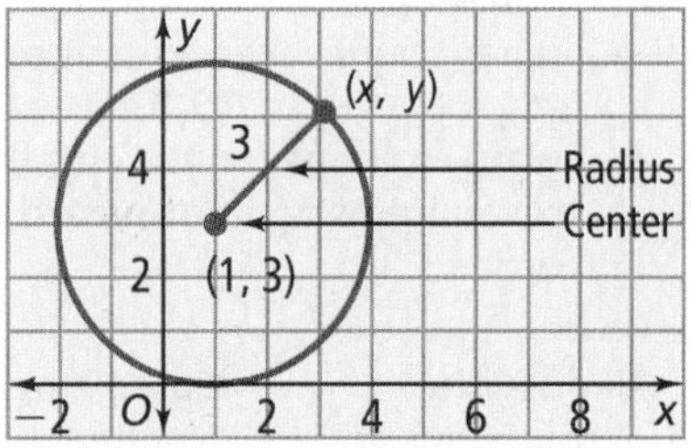

The equation of the circle whose center is (1, 3) and whose radius is 3 is $(x - 1)^2 + (y - 3)^2 = 9$.

Circumcenter of a triangle (p. 545) The circumcenter of a triangle is the point of concurrency of the perpendicular bisectors of the sides of the triangle.

Circuncentro de un triángulo (p. 545) El circuncentro de un triángulo es el punto de intersección de las bisectrices perpendiculares de los lados del triángulo.

Example

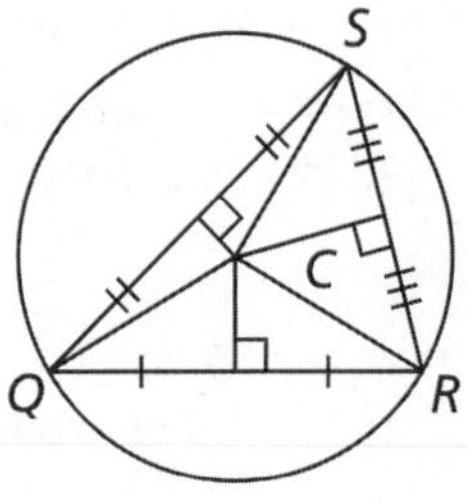

$QC = SC = RC$

C is the circumcenter.

Circumference (p. 800) The circumference of a circle is the distance around the circle. Given the radius r of a circle, you can find its circumference C by using the formula $C = 2\pi r$.

Circunferencia (p. 800) La circunferencia de un círculo es la distancia alrededor del círculo. Dado el radio r de un círculo, se puede hallar la circunferencia C usando la fórmula $C = 2\pi r$.

Example

$$C = 2\pi r = 2\pi(4) = 8\pi$$

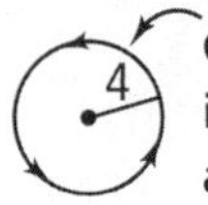

Circumference is the distance around the circle.

Circumscribed about (p. 545) A circle is circumscribed about a polygon if the vertices of the polygon are on the circle. A polygon is circumscribed about a circle if all the sides of the polygon are tangent to the circle.

Circunscritoa (p. 545) Un círculo está circunscrito a un polígono si los vértices del polígono están en el círculo. Un polígono está circunscrito a un círculo si todos los lados del polígono son tangentes al círculo.

Example

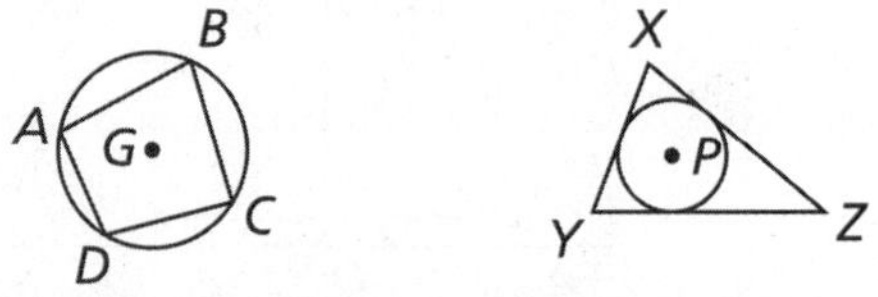

⊙G is circumscribed about $ABCD$.

$\triangle XYZ$ is circumscribed about ⊙P.

English | Spanish

Combination (p. 942) Any unordered selection of r objects from a set of n objects is a combination. The number of combinations of n objects taken r at a time is ${}_nC_r = \frac{n!}{r!(n-r)!}$ for $0 \le r \le n$.

Combinación (p. 942) Cualquier selección no ordenada de r objetos tomados de un conjunto de n objetos es una combinación. El número de combinaciones de n objetos, cuando se toman r objetos cada vez, es ${}_nC_r = \frac{n!}{r!(n-r)!}$ para $0 \le r \le n$.

Example The number of combinations of seven items taken four at a time is ${}_7C_4 = \frac{7!}{4!(7-4)!} = 35$. There are 35 ways to choose four items from seven items without regard to order.

Complement of an event (p. 928) All possible outcomes that are not in the event. P(complement of event) = 1 − P(event)

Complemento de un suceso (p. 928) Todos los resultados posibles que no se dan en el suceso. P(complemento de un suceso) = 1 − P(suceso)

Example The complement of rolling a 1 or a 2 on a standard number cube is rolling a 3, 4, 5, or 6.

Completing the square (p. 168) A method of solving quadratic equations. Completing the square turns every quadratic equation into the form $x^2 = c$.

Completar el cuadrado (p. 168) Método para solucionar ecuaciones cuadráticas. Cuando se completa el cuadrado, se transforma la ecuación cuadática a la formula $x^2 = c$.

Example $x^2 + 6x - 7 = 9$ is rewritten as $(x + 3)^2 = 25$ by completing the square.

Complex conjugates (p. 192) Number pairs of the form $a + bi$ and $a - bi$ are complex conjugates.

Conjugados complejos (p. 192) Los pares de números de la forma $a + bi$ y $a - bi$ son conjugados complejos.

Example The complex number $2 - 3i$ and $2 + 3i$ are complex conjugates.

Complex number (p. 188) Complex numbers are the real numbers and the imaginary numbers.

Número complejo (p. 188) Los números complejos son los números reales y los números imaginarios.

Example $6 + i$, 7, $2i$

Complex number plane (p. 188) The complex number plane is identical to the coordinate plane except each ordered pair (a, b) represents the complex number $a + bi$. The horizontal axis is the Real axis. The vertical axis is the Imaginary axis.

Plano de números complejos (p. 188) El plano de los números complejos es idéntico al plano de coordenadas, a excepción de que cada par ordenado (a, b) representa el número complejo $a + bi$. El eje horizontal es el eje real. El eje vertical es el eje imaginario.

Example

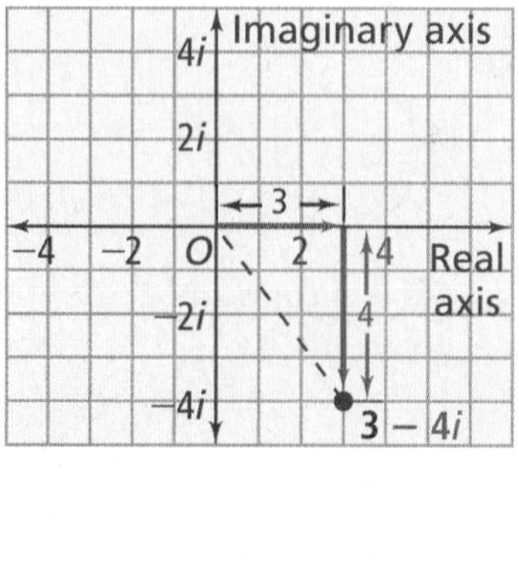

English	Spanish

Composite function (p. 289) A composite function is a combination of two functions such that the output from the first function becomes the input for the second function.

Función compuesta (p. 289) Una función compuesta es la combinación de dos funciones. La cantidad de salida de la primera función es la cantidad de entrada de la segunda función.

Example $f(x) = 2x + 1$, $g(x) = x^2 - 1$

$$(g \circ f)(x) = g(f(5)) = g(2(5) + 1)$$
$$= g(11) = 11^2 - 1$$
$$= 120$$

Composite space figures (p. 894) A composite space figure is the combination of two or more figures into one object.

Figuras geométricas compuestas (p. 894) Una figura geométrica compuesta es la combinación de dos o más figuras en un mismo objeto.

Example

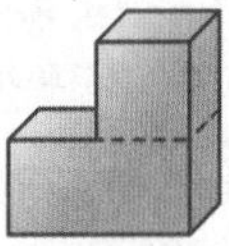

Compound event (p. 949) An event that consists of two or more events linked by the word *and* or the word *or*.

Suceso compuesto (p. 949) Suceso que consiste en dos o más sucesos unidos por medio de la palabra *y* o la palabra *o*.

Example Rolling a 5 on a standard number cube and then rolling a 4 is a compound event.

Compound inequality (p. 311) You can join two inequalities with the word *and* or the word *or* to form a compound inequality.

Desigualdad compuesta (p. 311) Puedes unir dos desigualdades por medio de la palabra *y* o la palabra *o* para formar una desigualdad compuesta.

Example $-1 < x$ and $x \leq 3$
$x < -1$ or $x \geq 3$

Concentric circles (p. 800) Concentric circles lie in the same plane and have the same center.

Círculos concéntricos (p. 800) Los círculos concéntricos están en el mismo plano y tienen el mismo centro

Example

The two circles both have center *D* and are therefore concentric.

Concurrent lines (p. 545) Concurrent lines are three or more lines that meet in one point. The point at which they meet is the *point of concurrency.*

Rectas concurrentes (p. 545) Las rectas concurrentes son tres o más rectas que se unen en un punto. El punto en que se unen es el *punto de concurrencia.*

Example

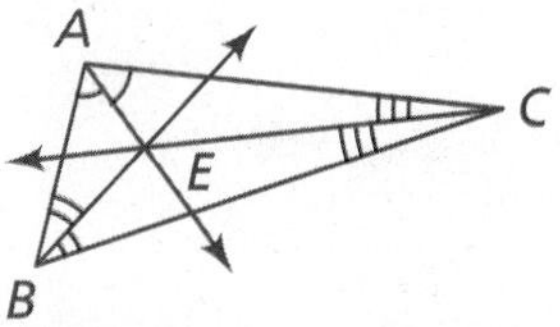

Point *E* is the point of concurrency of the bisectors of the angles of $\triangle ABC$. The bisectors are concurrent.

English | Spanish

Conditional probability (p. 958) A conditional probability contains a condition that may limit the sample space for an event. The notation $P(B \mid A)$ is read "the probability of event B, given event A." For any two events A and B in the sample space, $P(B \mid A) = \frac{P(A \text{ and } B)}{P(A)}$.

Probabilidad condicional (p. 958) Una probabilidad condicional contiene una condición que puede limitar el espacio muestral de un suceso. La notación $P(B \mid A)$ se lee "la probabilidad del suceso B, dado el suceso A". Para dos sucesos cualesquiera A y B en el espacio muestral, $P(B \mid A) = \frac{P(A \text{ y } B)}{P(A)}$.

Example
$$= \frac{P(\text{departs and arrives on time})}{P(\text{departs on time})}$$
$$= \frac{0.75}{0.83}$$
$$\approx 0.9$$

Cone (p. 882) A cone is a three-dimensional figure that has a circular *base*, a *vertex* not in the plane of the circle, and a curved lateral surface, as shown in the diagram. The *altitude* of a cone is the perpendicular segment from the vertex to the plane of the base. The *height* is the length of the altitude. In a *right cone*, the altitude contains the center of the base. The *slant height* of a right cone is the distance from the vertex to the edge of the base.

Cono (p. 882) Un cono es una figura tridimensional que tiene una *base* circular, un *vértice* que no está en el plano del círculo y una superficie lateral curvada (indicada en el diagrama). La *altura* de un cono es el segmento perpendicular desde el vértice hasta el plano de la base. La *altura*, por extensión, es la longitude de la altura. Un *cono recto* es un cono cuya altura contiene el centro de la base. La *longitude de la generatriz* de un cono recto es la distancia desde el vértice hasta el borde de la base.

Example

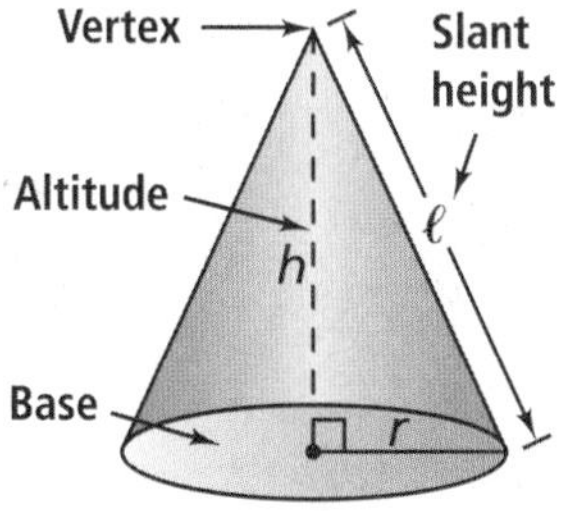

Right cone

Congruence transformation (p. 516) *See* **isometry**.

Transformación de congruencia (p. 516) *Ver* **isometry**.

Congruent circles (p. 797) Congruent circles are circles whose radii are congruent.

Círculos congruentes (p. 797) Los círculos congruentes son círculos cuyos radios son congruentes.

Example

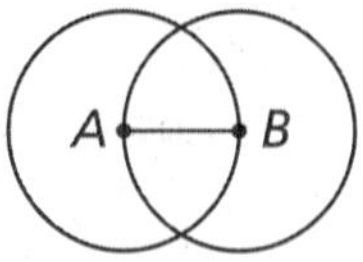

$\odot A$ and $\odot B$ have the same radius, so $\odot A \cong \odot B$.

English | Spanish

Congruent polygons (p. 451) Congruent polygons are polygons that have corresponding sides congruent and corresponding angles congruent.

Polígonos congruentes (p. 451) Los polígonos congruentes son polígonos cuyos lados correspondientes son congruentes y cuyos ángulos correspondientes son congruentes.

Example

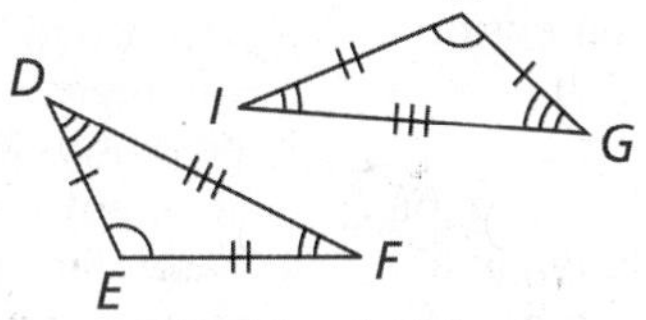

$\triangle DEF \cong \triangle GHI$

Consecutive angles (p. 601) Consecutive angles of a polygon share a common side.

Ángulos consecutivos (p. 601) Los ángulos consecutivos de un polígono tienen un lado común.

Example

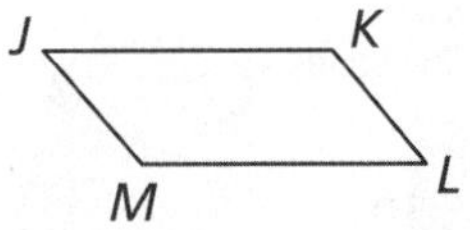

In ▱*JKLM*, $\angle J$ and $\angle M$ are consecutive angles, as are $\angle J$ and $\angle K$. $\angle J$ and $\angle L$ are *not* consecutive.

Coordinate proof (p. 649) *See* **proof.**

Prueba de coordenadas (p. 649) *Ver* **proof.**

Corollary (p. 489) A corollary is a theorem that can be proved easily using another theorem.

Corolario (p. 489) Un corolario es un teorema que se puede probar fácilmente usando otro teorema.

Example **Theorem:** If two sides of a triangle are congruent, then the angles opposite those sides are congruent.
Corollary: If a triangle is equilateral, then it is equiangular.

Corresponding angles (p. 414) Corresponding angles lie on the same side of the transversal *t* and in corresponding positions relative to ℓ and *m*.

Ángulos correspondientes (p. 414) Los ángulos correspondientes están en el mismo lado de la transversal *t* y en las correspondientes posiciones relativas a ℓ y *m*.

Example

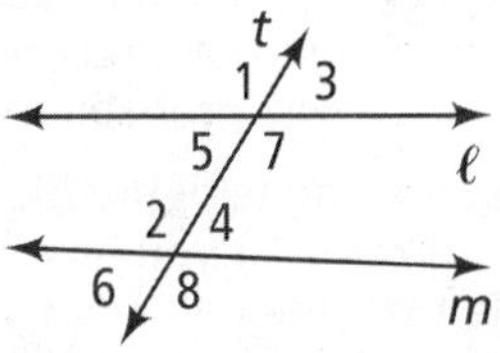

$\angle 1$ and $\angle 2$ are corresponding angles, as are $\angle 3$ and $\angle 4$, $\angle 5$ and $\angle 6$, and $\angle 7$ and $\angle 8$.

English | Spanish

Cross Products Property (p. 670) The product of the extremes of a proportion is equal to the product of the means.

Propiedad de los productos cruzados (p. 670) El producto de los extremos de una proporción es igual al producto de los medios.

Example If $\frac{x}{3} = \frac{12}{21}$, then $21x = 3 \cdot 12$

Cylinder (p. 872) A cylinder is a three-dimensional figure with two congruent circular *bases* that lie in parallel planes. An *altitude* of a cylinder is a perpendicular segment that joins the planes of the bases. Its length is the *height* of the cylinder. In a *right cylinder*, the segment joining the centers of the bases is an altitude. In an *oblique cylinder*, the segment joining the centers of the bases is not perpendicular to the planes containing the bases.

Cilindro (p. 872) Un cilindro es una figura tridimensional con dos *bases* congruentes circulares en planos paralelos. Una *altura* de un cilindro es un segmento perpendicular que une los planos de las bases. Su longitud es, por extensión, la *altura* del cilindro. En un *cilindro recto*, el segmento que une los centros de las bases es una altura. En un *cilindro oblicuo*, el segmento que une los centros de las bases no es perpendicular a los planos que contienen las bases.

Example

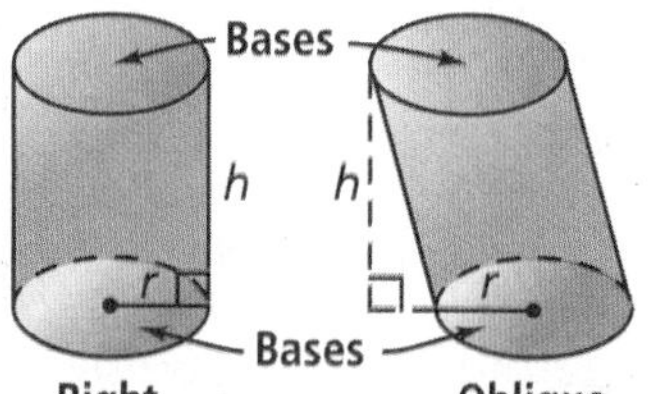

D

Degree of a monomial (p. 47) The sum of the exponents of the variables of a monomial.

Grado de un monomio (p. 47) La suma de los exponentes de las variables de un monomio.

Example $-4x^3y^2$ is a monomial of degree 5.

Degree of a polynomial (p. 48) The highest degree of any term of the polynomial.

Grado de un polinomio (p. 48) El grado de un polinomio es el grado mayor de cualquier término del polinomio.

Example The polynomial $P(x) = x^6 + 2x^3 - 3$ has degree 6.

Dependent events (p. 949) When the outcome of one event affects the probability of a second event, the events are dependent events.

Sucesos dependientes (p. 949) Dos sucesos son dependientes si el resultado de un suceso afecta la probabilidad del otro.

Example You have a bag with marbles of different colors. If you pick a marble from the bag and pick another without replacing the first, the events are dependent events.

Diameter of a circle (p. 797) A diameter of a circle is a segment that contains the center of the circle and whose endpoints are on the circle. The term *diameter* can also mean the length of this segment.

Diámetro de un circulo (p. 797) Un diámetro de un círculo es un segmento que contiene el centro del cíírculo y cuyos extremos estan en el círculo. El término *diámetro* tambien puedi referirse a la longitud de este segmento.

English	Spanish

Diameter of a sphere (p. 911) The diameter of a sphere is a segment passing through the center, with endpoints on the sphere.

Diametro de una esfera (p. 911) El diametro de unaesfera es un segmento que contiene el centro de la esfera y the sphere. cuyos extremos estan en la esfera.

Example

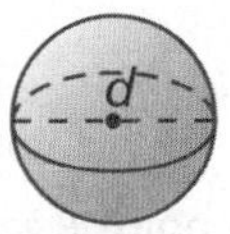

Difference of squares (p. 96) A difference of two squares is an expression of the form $a^2 - b^2$. It can be factored as $(a + b)(a - b)$.

Diferencia de dos cuadrados (p. 96) La diferencia de dos cuadrados es una expresión de la forma $a^2 - b^2$. Se puede factorizar como $(a + b)(a - b)$.

Example $25a^2 - 4 = (5a + 2)(5a - 2)$
$m^6 = 1 = (m^3 + 1)(m^3 - 1)$

Dilation (p. 723) A dilation is a transformation that has *center* C and *scale factor n*, where $n > 0$, and maps a point R to R' in such a way that R' is on $\overrightarrow{CR}$ and $CR' = n \cdot CR$. The center of a dilation is its own image. If $n > 1$, the dilation is an *enlargement*, and if $0 < n < 1$, the dilation is a *reduction*.

Dilatacion (p. 723) Una dilatacion, o *transformacion de semejanza*, tiene *centro* C y *factor de escala n* para $n > 0$, y asocia un punto R a R' de tal modo que R' esta en $\overrightarrow{CR}$ y $CR' = n \cdot CR$. El centro de una dilatacion es su propia imagen. Si $n > 1$, la dilatacion es un *aumento*, y si $0 < n < 1$, la a *reduction*. dilatacion es una *reduccion*.

Example

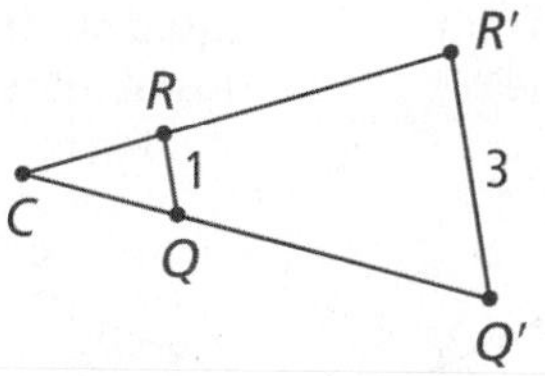

$\overline{R'Q'}$ is the image of $\overline{RQ}$ under a dilation with center C and scale factor 3.

Directrix (p. 222) The directrix of a parabola is the fixed line used to define a parabola. Each point of the parabola is the same distance from the focus and the directrix.

Directriz (p. 222) La directriz de una parábola es la recta fija con que se define una parábola. Cada punto de la parábola está a la misma distancia del foco y de la directriz.

Example

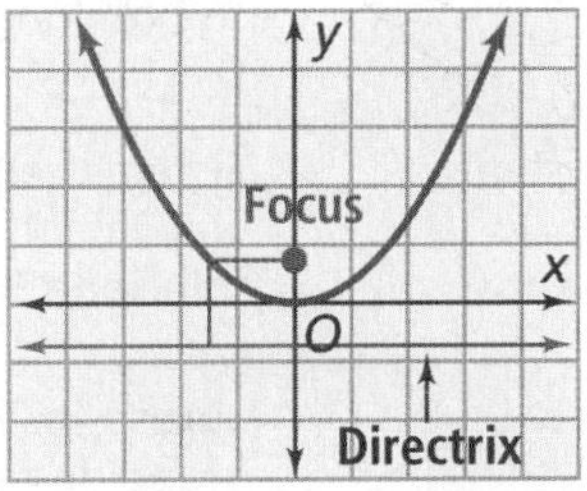

Discriminant (p. 181) The discriminant of a quadratic equation of the form $ax^2 + bx + c = 0$ is $b^2 - 4ac$. The value of the discriminant determines the number of solutions of the equation.

Discriminante (p. 181) El discriminante de una ecuación cuadrática $ax^2 + bx + c = 0$ es $b^2 - 4ac$. El valor del discriminante determina el número de soluciones de la ecuación.

Example The discriminant of $2x^2 + 9x - 2 = 0$ is 97.

English	Spanish

Distance from a point to a line (p. 540) The distance from a point to a line is the length of the perpendicular segment from the point to the line.

Distancia desde un punto hasta una recta (p. 540) La distancia desde un punto hasta una recta es la longitud del segmento perpendicular que va desde el punto hasta la recta.

Example

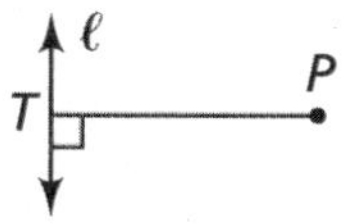

The distance from point *P* to a line ℓ is *PT*.

E

Enlargement (p. 724) *See* **dilation.**

Aumento (p. 724) *Ver* **dilation.**

Equiangular triangle or polygon (p. 594) An equiangular triangle (polygon) is a triangle (polygon) whose angles are all congruent.

Triángulo o polígono equiángulo (p. 594) Un triángulo (polígono) equiángulo es un triángulo (polígono) cuyos ángulos son todos congruentes.

Example

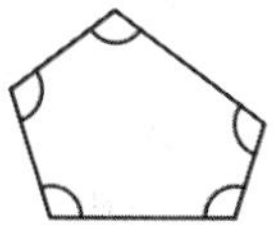

Each angle of the pentagon is a 108° angle.

Equidistant (p. 537) A point is equidistant from two objects if it is the same distance from the objects.

Equidistante (p. 537) Un punto es equidistante de dos objetos si la distancia entre el punto y los objetos es igual.

Example

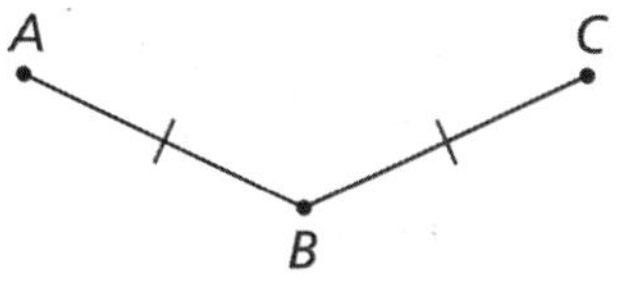

Point *B* is equidistant from points *A* and *C*.

Equilateral triangle or polygon (p. 594) An equilateral triangle (polygon) is a triangle (polygon) whose sides are all congruent.

Triángulo o polígono equilátero (p. 594) Un triángulo (polígono) equilátero es un triángulo (polígono) cuyos lados son todos congruentes.

Example

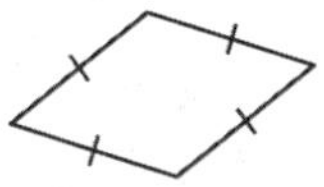

Each side of the quadrilateral is 1.2 cm long.

Equivalent systems (p. 357) Equivalent systems are systems that have the same solution(s).

Sistemas equivalentes (p. 357) Sistemas equivalentes son sistemas que tienen la misma solución o las mismas soluciones.

Event (p. 925) Any group of outcomes in a situation involving probability.

Suceso (p. 925) En la probabilidad, cualquier grupo de resultados.

Example When rolling a number cube, there are six possible outcomes. Rolling an even number is an event with three possible outcomes, 2, 4, and 6.

English	Spanish
Expected value (p. 974) The average value you can expect for a large number of trials of an experiment; the sum of each outcome's value multiplied by its probability.	**Valor esperado (p. 974)** El valor promedio que se puede esperar para una cantidad grande de pruebas en un experimento; la suma de los valores de los resultados multiplicados cada uno por su probabilidad.

Example In a game, a player has a 25% probability of earning 10 points by spinning an even number and a 75% probability of earning 5 points by spinning an odd number.
expected value =
$0.25(10) + 0.75(5) = 6.25$

Experimental probability (p. 926) The ratio of the number of times an event actually happens to the number of times the experiment is done. $P(\text{event}) = \frac{\text{number of times an event happens}}{\text{number of times the experiment is done}}$	**Probabilidad experimental (p. 926)** La razón entre el número de veces que un suceso sucede en la realidad y el número de veces que se hace el experimento. $P(\text{suceso}) = \frac{\text{número de veces que sucede un suceso}}{\text{número de veces que se hace el experimento}}$

Example A baseball player's batting average shows how likely it is that a player will get a hit, based on previous times at bat.

Extended proportion (p. 678) *See* **proportion.**	**Proporción extendida (p. 678)** *Ver* **proportion.**
Extended ratio (p. 669) *See* **ratio.**	**Razón extendida (p. 669)** *Ver* **ratio.**
Extremes of a proportion (p. 670) In the proportion $\frac{a}{b} = \frac{c}{d}$, a and d are the extremes.	**Valores extremos de una proporción (p. 670)** En la proporción $\frac{a}{b} = \frac{c}{d}$, a y d son los valores extremos.

Example The product of the extremes of $\frac{x}{4} = \frac{x+3}{2}$ is $2x$.

F

Factor by grouping (p. 102) A method of factoring that uses the Distributive Property to remove a common binomial factor of two pairs of terms.	**Factor común por agrupación de términos (p. 102)** Método de factorización que aplica la propiedad distributiva para sacar un factor común de dos pares de términos en un binomio.

Example The expression $7x(x - 1) + 4(x - 1)$ can be factored as $(7x + 4)(x - 1)$.

Flow proof (p. 431) *See* **proof.**	**Prueba de flujo (p. 431)** *Ver* **proof.**
Focal length (p. 222) The focal length of a parabola is the distance between the vertex and the focus.	**Distancia focal (p. 222)** La distancia focal de una parábola es la distancia entre el vértice y el foco.
Focus (plural: foci) of a parabola (p. 222) A parabola is the set of all points in a plane that are the same distance from a fixed line and a fixed point not on the line. The fixed point is the focus of the parabola.	**Foco de una parabola (p. 222)** Una parábola es el conjunto de todos los puntos en un plano con la misma distancia desde una línea fija y un punto fijo que no permanece en la línea. El punto fijo es el foco de la parábola.

English	Spanish

Frequency table (p. 932) A table that groups a set of data values into intervals and shows the frequency for each interval.

Tabla de frecuencias (p. 932) Tabla que agrupa un conjunto de datos en intervalos y muestra la frecuencia de cada intervalo.

Example

Interval	Frequency
0–9	5
10–19	8
20–29	4

Fundamental Counting Principle (p. 939) If there are m ways to make the first selection and n ways to make the second selection, then there are $m \cdot n$ ways to make the two selections.

Principio fundamental de Conteo (p. 939) Si hay m maneras de hacer la primera selección y n maneras de hacer la segunda selección, quiere decir que hay $m \cdot n$ maneras de hacer las dos selecciones.

Example For 5 shirts and 8 pairs of shorts, the number of possible outfits is $5 \cdot 8 = 40$.

G

Geometric mean (p. 701) The geometric mean is the number x such that $\frac{a}{x} = \frac{x}{b}$, where a, b, and x are positive numbers.

Media geométrica (p. 701) La media geométrica es el número x tanto que $\frac{a}{x} = \frac{x}{b}$, donde a, b y x son números positivos.

Example The geometric mean of 6 and 24 is 12.

$$\frac{6}{x} = \frac{x}{24}$$
$$x^2 = 144$$
$$x = 12$$

Great circle (p. 911) A great circle is the intersection of a sphere and a plane containing the center of the sphere. A great circle divides a sphere into two *hemispheres*.

Círculo máximo (p. 911) Un círculo máximo es la intersección de una esfera y un plano que contiene el centro de la esfera. Un círculo máximo divide una esfera en dos *hemisferios*.

Example

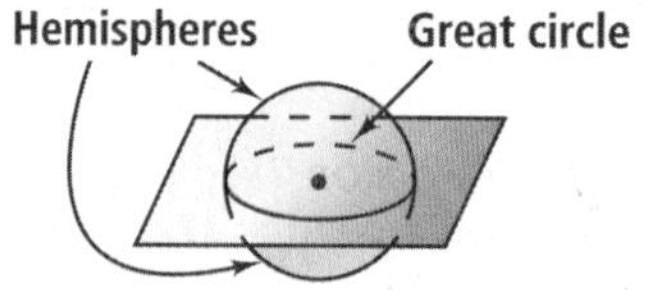

Greatest integer function (pp. 277, 343) The greatest integer function corresponds each input x to the greatest integer less than or equal to x.

Función del entero mayor (pp. 277, 343) La función del entero mayor relaciona cada entrada x con el entero mayor que es menor oigual a x.

H

Half-plane (p. 346) A half-plane is the set of points in a coordinate plane that are on one side of the boundary of the graph of a linear inequality.

Semiplano (p. 346) Un semiplano es el conjunto de puntos de un plano de coordenadas que están a un lado del límite de la gráfica de desigualdad lineal.

English	Spanish
Height *See* **cone; cylinder; parallelogram; prism; pyramid; trapezoid.**	**Altura** *Ver* **cone; cylinder; parallelogram; prism; pyramid; trapezoid.**
Hemisphere (p. 911) *See* **great circle.**	**Hemisferio (p. 911)** *Ver* **great circle.**
Hypotenuse (p. 495) *See* **right triangle.**	**Hipotenusa (p. 495)** *Ver* **right triangle.**

I

Identity (p. 302) An equation that is true for every value of the variable is an identity.	**Identidad (p. 302)** Una ecuación que es verdadera para cada valor de la variable es una identidad.
Imaginary number (p. 188) An imaginary number is any number of the form $a + bi$, where a and b are real numbers and $b \neq 0$.	**Número imaginario (p. 188)** Un número imaginario es cualquier número de la forma $a + bi$, donde a y b son números reales y $b \neq 0$.

Example $2 + 3i$, $7i$, i

Imaginary unit (p. 186) The imaginary unit i is the complex number whose square is -1.	**Unidad imaginaria (p. 186)** La unidad imaginaria i es el número complejo cuyo cuadrado es -1.
Incenter of a triangle (p. 548) The incenter of a triangle is the point of concurrency of the angle bisectors of the triangle.	**Incentro de un triángulo (p. 548)** El incentro de un triángulo es el punto donde concurren las tres bisectrices de los ángulos del triángulo.

Example

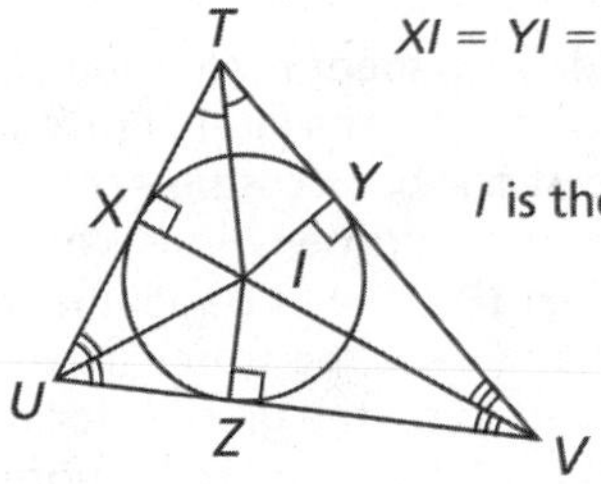

$XI = YI = ZI$

I is the incenter.

Independent events (p. 949) When the outcome of one event does not affect the probability of a second event, the two events are independent	**Sucesos independientes (p. 949)** Cuando el resultado de un suceso no altera la probabilidad de otro, los dos sucesos son independientes.

Example The results of two rolls of a number cube are independent. Getting a 5 on the first roll does not change the probability of getting a 5 on the second roll.

Index (p. 32) With a radical sign, the index indicates the degree of the root.	**Índice (p. 32)** Con un signo de radical, el índice indica el grado de la raíz.

Example index 2 index 3 index 4
$\sqrt{16}$ $\sqrt[3]{16}$ $\sqrt[4]{16}$

English | Spanish

Indirect measurement (p. 694) Indirect measurement is a way of measuring things that are difficult to measure directly.

Medición indirecta (p. 694) La medición indirecta es un modo de medir cosas difíciles de medir directamente.

Example By measuring the distances shown in the diagram and using proportions of similar figures, you can find the height of the taller tower. $\frac{196}{540} = \frac{x}{1300} \rightarrow x \approx 472$ ft

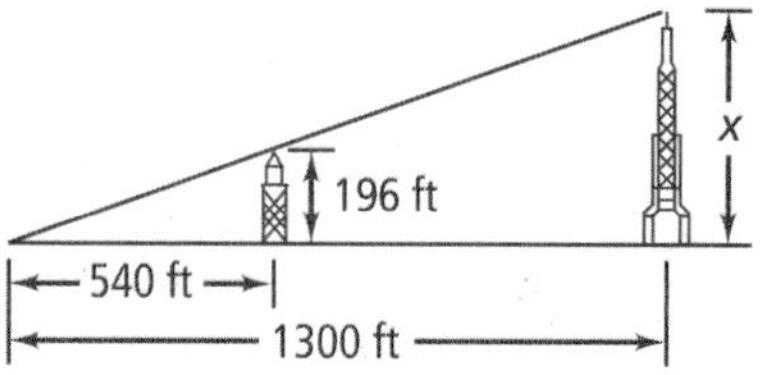

Indirect proof (p. 562) *See* **indirect reasoning; proof.**

Prueba indirecta (p. 562) *Ver* **indirect reasoning; proof.**

Indirect reasoning (p. 562) Indirect reasoning is a type of reasoning in which all possiblities are considered and then all but one are proved false. The remaining possibility must be true.

Razonamiento indirecto (p. 562) Razonamiento indirecto es un tipo de razonamiento en el que se consideran todas las posibilidades y se prueba que todas son falsas, a excepción de una. La posibilidad restante debe ser verdadera.

Example Eduardo spent more than $60 on two books at a store. Prove that at least one book costs more than $30.
Proof: Suppose neither costs more than $30. Then he spent no more than $60 at the store. Since this contradicts the given information, at least one book costs more than $30.

Inscribed angle (p. 839) An angle is inscribed in a circle if the vertex of the angle is on the circle and the sides of the angle are chords of the circle.

Ángulo inscrito (p. 839) Un ángulo está inscrito en un círculo si el vértice del ángulo está en el círculo y los lados del ángulo son cuerdas del círculo.

Example

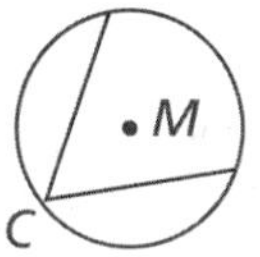

$\angle C$ is inscribed in $\odot M$.

Inscribed in (p. 548) A circle is inscribed in a polygon if the sides of the polygon are tangent to the circle. A polygon is inscribed in a circle if the vertices of the polygon are on the circle.

Inscrito en (p. 548) Un círculo está inscrito en un polígono si los lados del polígono son tangentes al círculo. Un polígono está inscrito en un círculo si los vértices del polígono están en el círculo.

Example

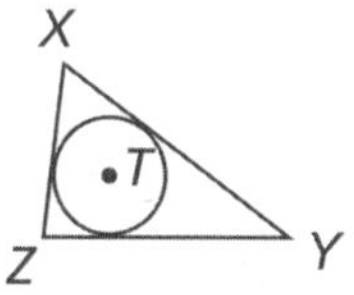

$\odot T$ is inscribed in $\triangle XYZ$.

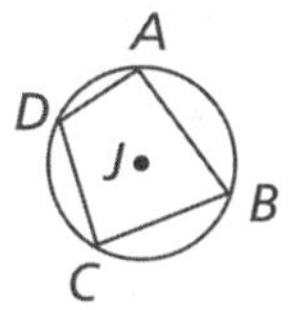

ABCD is inscribed in $\odot J$.

English	Spanish

Intercepted arc (p. 839) An intercepted arc is an arc of a circle having endpoints on the sides of an inscribed angle, and its other points in the interior of the angle.

Arco interceptor (p. 839) Un arco interceptor es un arco de un círculo cuyos extremos están en los lados de un ángulo inscrito y los punto restantes están en el interior del ángulo.

Example

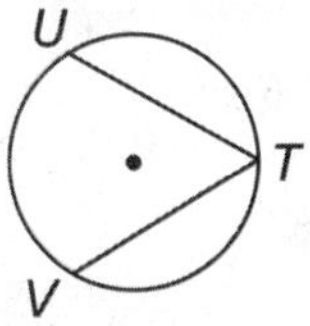

$\widehat{UV}$ is the intercepted arc of inscribed $\angle T$.

Inverse function (p. 290) If function f pairs a value b with a then its inverse, denoted f^{-1}, pairs the value a with b. If f^{-1} is also a function, then f and f^{-1} are inverse functions.

Funcion inversa (p. 290) Si la función f empareja un valor b con a, entonces su inversa, cuya notación es f^{-1}, empareja el valor a con b. Si f^{-1} también es una función, entonces f y f^{-1} son funciones inversas.

Example If $f(x) = x + 3$, then $f^{-1}(x) = x - 3$.

Inverse operations (p. 300) Inverse operations are operations that undo each other.

Operaciones inversas (p. 300) Operaciones inversas son operaciones que se cancelan mutuamente.

Isometry (p. 511) An isometry, also known as a *congruence transformation,* is a transformation in which an original figure and its image are congruent.

Isometría (p. 511) Una isometría, conocida también como una *transformación de congruencia*, es una transformación en donde una figura original y su imagen son congruentes.

Isosceles trapezoid (p. 636) An isosceles trapezoid is a trapezoid whose nonparallel opposite sides are congruent.

Trapecio isósceles (p. 636) Un trapecio isosceles es un trapecio cuyos lados opuestos no paralelos son congruentes.

Example

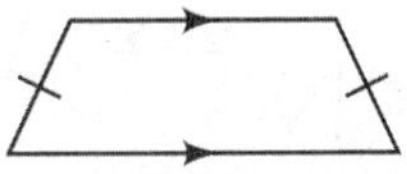

Isosceles triangle An isosceles triangle is a triangle that has at least two congruent sides. If there are two congruent sides, they are called *legs*. The *vertex angle* is between them. The third side is called the *base* and the other two angles are called the *base angles*.

Triángulo isósceles Un triángulo isósceles es un triángulo que tiene por lo menos dos lados congruentes. Si tiene dos lados congruentes, éstos se llaman *catetos*. Entre ellos se encuentra el *ángulo del vértice*. El tercer lado se llama *base* y los otros dos ángulos se llaman *ángulos de base*.

Example

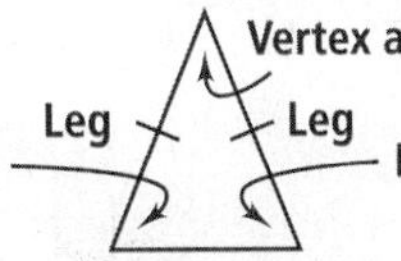

English — L — Spanish

Lateral area (pp. 868, 872, 880) The lateral area of a prism or pyramid is the sum of the areas of the lateral faces. The lateral area of a cylinder or cone is the area of the curved surface.

Área lateral (pp. 868, 872, 880) El área lateral de un prisma o pirámide es la suma de las áreas de sus caras laterals. El área lateral de un cilindro o de un cono es el área de la superficie curvada.

Example

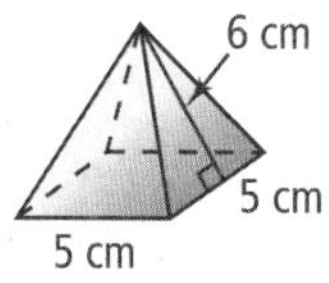

$$\text{L.A. of pyramid} = \frac{1}{2}p\ell = \frac{1}{2}(20)(6) = 60 \text{ cm}^2$$

Lateral face *See* **prism; pyramid.**

Cara lateral *Ver* **prism; pyramid.**

Leg *See* **isosceles triangle; right triangle; trapezoid.**

Cateto *Ver* **isosceles triangle; right triangle; trapezoid.**

Linear equation (p. 319) A linear equation in two variables is an equation that can be written in the form $ax + by = c$. *See also* **Standard form of a linear equation.**

Ecuación lineal (p. 319) Una ecuación lineal de dos variables es una ecuación que se puede escribir de la forma $ax + by = c$. *Ver también* **Standard form of a linear equation.**

Example $y = 2x + 1$ can be written as $-2x + y = 1$.

Linear function (p. 319) A function whose graph is a line is a linear function. You can represent a linear function with a linear equation.

Función lineal (p. 319) Una función cuya gráfica es una recta es una función lineal. La función lineal se representa con una ecuación lineal.

Example

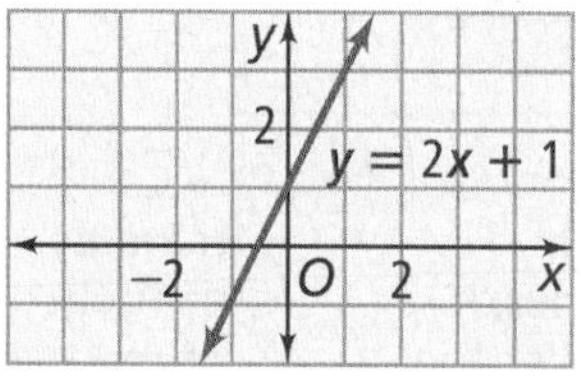

Linear inequality (p. 346) A linear inequality is an inequality in two variables whose graph is a region of the coordinate plane that is bounded by a line.

Desigualdad lineal (p. 346) Una desigualdad lineal es una desigualdad de dos variables cuya gráfica es una región del plano de coordenadas delimitado por una recta.

Example

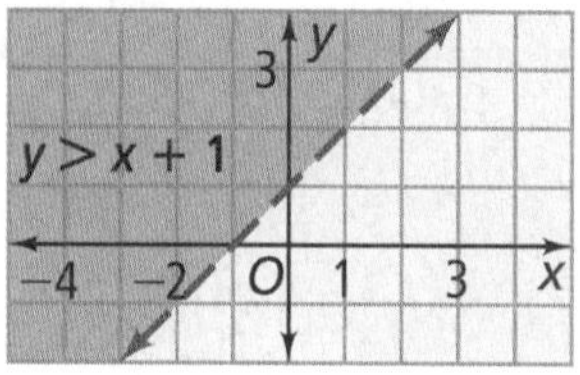

Literal equation (p. 303) A literal equation is an equation that uses more than one letter as a variable.

Ecuación literal (p. 303) Una ecuación literal es una ecuación en la cual más de una letra expresa una variable.

English — M — Spanish

Major arc (p. 797) A major arc of a circle is an arc that is larger than a semicircle.

Arco mayor (p. 797) Un arco mayor de un círculo es cualquier arco más grande que un semicírculo.

Example

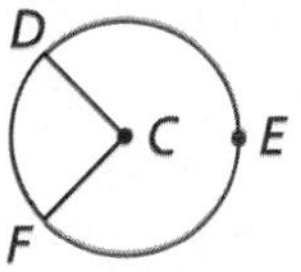

$\widehat{DEF}$ is a major arc of $\odot C$.

Matrix (p. 379) A matrix is a rectangular array of numbers written within brackets.

Matriz (p. 379) Una matriz es un conjunto de números encerrados en corchetes y dispuestos en forma de rectángulo.

Example

$$A = \begin{bmatrix} 1 & -2 & 0 & 10 \\ 9 & 7 & -3 & 8 \\ 2 & -10 & 1 & -6 \end{bmatrix}$$

The number 2 is the element in the third row and first column. A is a 3×4 matrix.

Matrix element (p. 379) Every item listed in a matrix is an element of the matrix. An element is identified by its position in the matrix.

Elemento matricial (p. 379) Cada cifra de una matriz es un elemento de la matriz. El elemento se identifica según la posición que ocupa en la matriz.

Example

$$A = \begin{bmatrix} 1 & -2 & 0 & 10 \\ 9 & 7 & -3 & 8 \\ 2 & -10 & 1 & -6 \end{bmatrix}$$

Element a_{21} is 9, the element in the second row and first column.

Maximum (p. 116) The *y*-coordinate of the vertex of a parabola that opens downward.

Valor máximo (p. 116) La coordenada *y* del vértice en una parábola que se abre hacia abajo.

Example

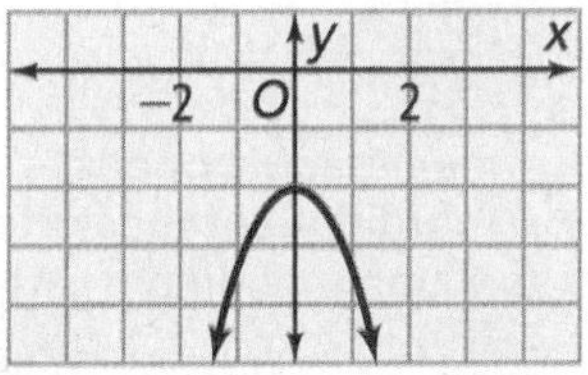

Since the parabola opens downward, the *y*-coordinate of the vertex is the function's maximum value.

Means of a proportion (p. 670) In the proportion $\frac{a}{b} = \frac{c}{d}$, b and c are the means.

Valores medios de una proporción (p. 670) En la proporción $\frac{a}{b} = \frac{c}{d}$, b y c son los valores medios.

Example The product of the means of $\frac{x}{4} = \frac{x+3}{2}$ is $4(x + 3)$ or $4x + 12$.

English | Spanish

Median of a triangle (p. 553) A median of a triangle is a segment that has as its endpoints a vertex of the triangle and the midpoint of the opposite side.

Mediana de un triángulo (p. 553) Una mediana de un triángulo es un segmento que tiene en sus extremos el vértice del triángulo y el punto medio del lado opuesto.

Example

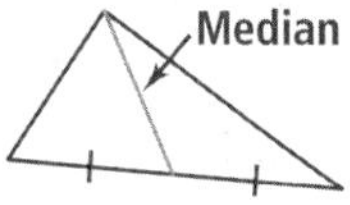

Midsegment of a trapezoid (p. 638) The midsegment of a trapezoid is the segment that joins the midpoints of the nonparallel opposite sides of a trapezoid.

Segmento medio de un triángulo (p. 638) Un segmento medio de un triángulo es un segmento que une los puntos medios de dos lados del triángulo.

Example

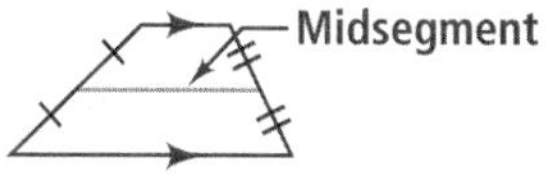

Midsegment of a triangle (p. 529) A midsegment of a triangle is a segment that joins the midpoints of two sides of the triangle.

Segmento medio de un triángulo (p. 529) Un segmento medio de un triángulo es un segmento que une los puntos medios de dos lados del triángulo.

Example

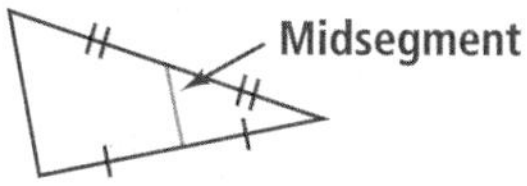

Minimum (p. 116) The *y*-coordinate of the vertex of a parabola that opens upward.

Valor mínimo (p. 116) La coordenada *y* del vértice en una parábola que se abre hacia arriba.

Example

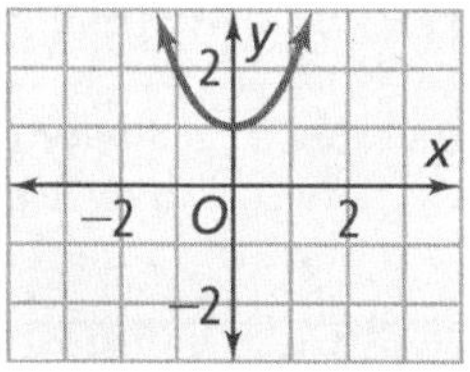

Since the parabola opens upward, the *y*-coordinate of the vertex is the function's minimum value.

Minor arc (p. 797) A minor arc is an arc that is smaller than a semicircle.

Arco menor (p. 797) Un arco menor de un círculo es un arco más corto que un semicírculo.

Example

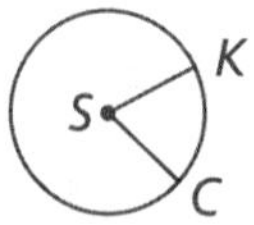

$\widehat{KC}$ is a minor arc of $\odot S$.

Monomial (p. 47) A real number, a variable, or a product of a real number and one or more variables with whole-number exponents.

Monomio (p. 47) Número real, variable o el producto de un número real y una o más variables con números enteros como exponentes.

Example 9, *n*, and $-5xy^2$ are examples of monomials.

English	Spanish

English | **Spanish**

Mutually exclusive events (p. 952) When two events cannot happen at the same time, the events are mutually exclusive. If A and B are mutually exclusive events, then $P(A \text{ or } B) = P(A) + P(B)$.

Sucesos mutuamente excluyentes (p. 952) Cuando dos sucesos no pueden ocurrir al mismo tiempo, son mutuamente excluyentes. Si A y B son sucesos mutuamente excluyentes, entonces $P(A \text{ o } B) = P(A) + P(B)$.

Example Rolling an even number E and rolling a multiple of five M on a standard number cube are mutually exclusive events.

$$P(E \text{ or } M) = P(E) + P(M)$$
$$= \frac{3}{6} + \frac{1}{6}$$
$$= \frac{4}{6}$$
$$= \frac{2}{3}$$

N

Natural base exponential function (p. 253) A natural base exponential function is an exponential function with base e.

Función exponencial con base natural (p. 253) Ua función exponencial con base natural es una función exponencial con base e.

***n* factorial (p. 941)** The product of the integers from n down to 1, for any positive integer n. You write n factorial as $n!$. The value of $0!$ is defined to be 1.

***n* factorial (p. 941)** Producto de todos los enteros desde n hasta 1, de cualquier entero positivo n. El factorial de n se escribe $n!$. El valor de $0!$ se define como 1.

Example $4! = 4 \cdot 3 \cdot 2 \cdot 1 = 24$

O

Oblique cylinder or prism *See* **cylinder; prism.**

Cilindro oblicuo o prisma *Ver* **cylinder; prism.**

Opposite angles (p. 600) Opposite angles of a quadrilateral are two angles that do not share a side.

Ángulos opuestos (p. 600) Los ángulos opuestos de un cuadrilátero son dos ángulos que no comparten lados.

Example

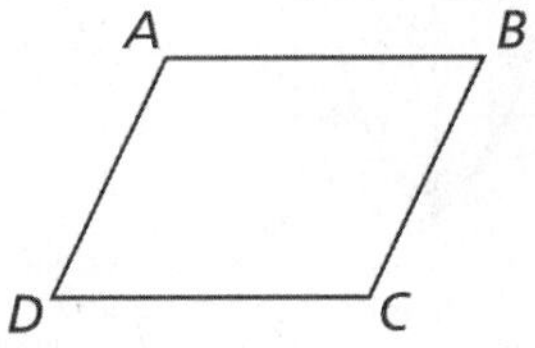

$\angle A$ and $\angle C$ are opposite angles, as are $\angle B$ and $\angle D$.

Opposite sides (p. 600) Opposite sides of a quadrilateral are two sides that do not share a vertex.

Lados opuestos (p. 600) Los lados opuestos de un cuadrilátero son dos lados que no tienen un vértice en común.

Example

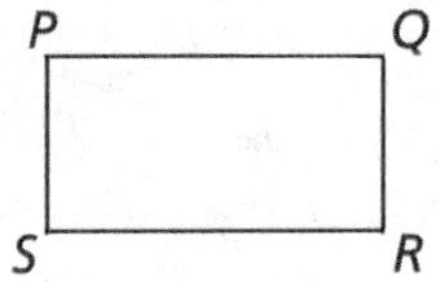

$\overline{PQ}$ and $\overline{SR}$ are opposite sides, as are $\overline{PS}$ and $\overline{QR}$.

English | Spanish

Orthocenter of a triangle (p. 556) The orthocenter of a triangle is the point of concurrency of the lines containing the altitudes of the triangle.

Ortocentro de un triángulo (p. 556) El ortocentro de un triángulo es el punto donde se intersecan las alturas de un triángulo.

Example

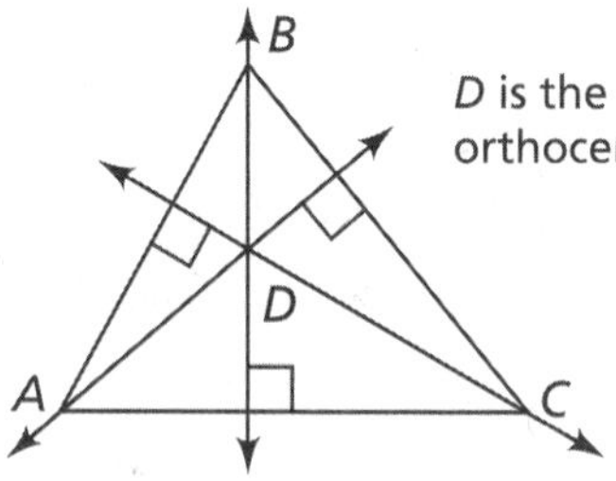

D is the orthocenter.

Outcome (p. 925) The result of a single trial in a probability experiment.

Resultado (p. 925) Lo que se obtiene al hacer una sola prueba en un experimento de probabilidad.

Example The outcomes of rolling a number cube are 1, 2, 3, 4, 5, and 6.

Overlapping events (p. 953) Events that have at least one common outcome. If *A* and *B* are overlapping events, then $P(A \text{ or } B) = P(A) + P(B) - P(A \text{ and } B)$.

Sucesos traslapados (p. 953) Sucesos que tienen por lo menos un resultado en común. Si A y B son sucesos traslapados, entonces $P(A \text{ ó } B) = P(A) + P(B) - P(A \text{ y } B)$.

Example Rolling a multiple of 3 and rolling an odd number on a number cube are overlapping events.

$$P(\text{multiple of 3 or odd}) = P(\text{multiple of 3}) + P(\text{odd}) - P(\text{multiple of 3 and odd})$$
$$= \frac{1}{3} + \frac{1}{2} - \frac{1}{6}$$
$$= \frac{2}{3}$$

P

Parabola (p. 115) The graph of a quadratic function.

Parábola (p. 115) La gráfica de una función cuadrática.

Example

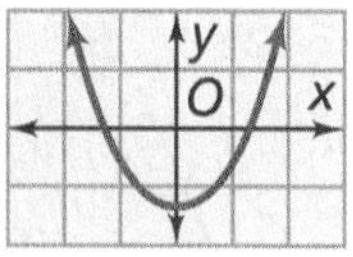

Paragraph proof (p. 405) *See* **proof.**

Prueba de párrafo (p. 405) *Ver* **proof.**

Parallel lines (p. 412) Two lines are parallel if they lie in the same plane and do not intersect. The symbol ∥ means "is parallel to."

Rectas paralelas (p. 412) Dos rectas son paralelas si están en el mismo plano y no se cortan. El símbolo ∥ significa "es paralelo a".

Example $\ell \parallel m$

The red symbols indicate parallel lines.

English

Spanish

Parallelogram (p. 600) A parallelogram is a quadrilateral with two pairs of parallel sides. You can choose any side to be the *base*. An *altitude* is any segment perpendicular to the line containing the base drawn from the side opposite the base. The *height* is the length of an altitude.

Paralelogramo (p. 600) Un paralelogramo es un cuadrilátero con dos pares de lados paralelos. Se puede escoger cualquier lado como la *base*. Una *altura* es un segmento perpendicular a la recta que contiene la base, trazada desde el lado opuesto a la base. La *altura*, por extensión, es la longitud de una altura.

Example

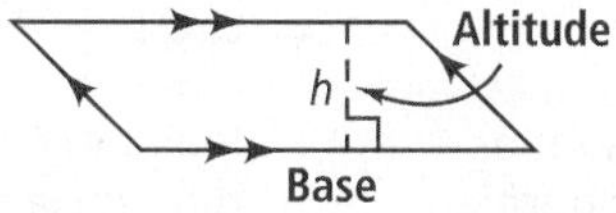

Parallel planes (p. 412) Parallel planes are planes that do not intersect.

Planos paralelos (p. 412) Planos paralelos son planos que no se cortan.

Example

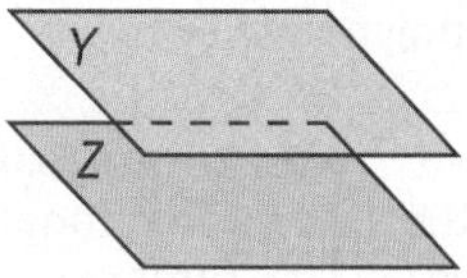

Planes *Y* and *Z* are parallel.

Parent function (pp. 115, 325) A family of functions is a group of functions with common characteristics. A parent function is the simplest function with these characteristics.

Función elemental (pp. 115, 325) Una familia de funciones es un grupo de funciones con características en común. La función elemental es la función más simple que reúne esas características.

Example $y = x$ is the parent function for the family of linear equations of the form $y = mx + b$.

Perfect square trinomial (p. 93) Any trinomial of the form $a^2 + 2ab + b^2$ or $a^2 - 2ab + b^2$.

Cuadrado perfecto (p. 93) Número cuya raíz cuadrada es un número entero.

Example $(x + 3)^2 = x^2 + 6x + 9$

Permutation (p. 941) An arrangement of some or all of a set of objects in a specific order. You can use the notation $_nP_r$ to express the number of permutations, where n equals the number of objects available and r equals the number of selections to make.

Permutación (p. 941) Disposición de algunos o de todos los objetos de un conjunto en un orden determinado. El número de permutaciones se puede expresar con la notación $_nP_r$, donde n es igual al número total de objetos y r es igual al número de selecciones que han de hacerse.

Example How many ways can you arrange 5 objects 3 at a time?

$$_3P_5 = \frac{5!}{(5-3)!} = \frac{5!}{2!} = \frac{5 \cdot 4 \cdot 3 \cdot 2 \cdot 1}{2 \cdot 1} = 60$$

There are 60 ways to arrange 5 objects 3 at a time.

Pi (p. 800) Pi (π) is the ratio of the circumference of any circle to its diameter. The number π is irrational and is approximately 3.14159.

Pi (p. 800) Pi (π) es la razón de la circunferencia de cualquier círculo a su diámetro. El número π es irracional y se aproxima a $\pi \approx 3.14159$.

Example

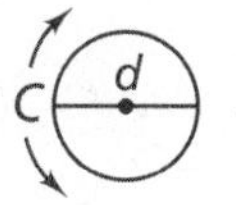

$\pi = \frac{C}{d}$

English	Spanish
Piecewise function (pp. 274, 343) A piecewise function has different rules for different parts of its domain.	**Función de fragmentos (pp. 274, 343)** Una función de fragmentos tiene reglas diferentes para diferentes partes de su dominio.
Point of concurrency (p. 545) *See* **concurrent lines.**	**Punto de concurrencia (p. 545)** *Ver* **concurrent lines.**
Point of tangency (p. 818) *See* **tangent to a circle.**	**Punto de tangencia (p. 818)** *Ver* **tangent to a circle.**
Polynomial (p. 48) A monomial or the sum or difference of two or more monomials. A quotient with a variable in the denominator is not a polynomial.	**Polinomio (p. 48)** Un monomio o la suma o diferencia de dos o más monomios. Un cociente con una variable en el denominador no es un polinomio.

Example $2x^2$, $3x + 7$, 28, and $-7x^3 - 2x^2 + 9$ are all polynomials.

English	Spanish
Prism (p. 867) A prism is a polyhedron with two congruent and parallel faces, which are called the *bases*. The other faces, which are parallelograms, are called the *lateral faces*. An *altitude* of a prism is a perpendicular segment that joins the planes of the bases. Its length is the *height* of the prism. A *right prism* is one whose lateral faces are rectangular regions and a lateral edge is an altitude. In an *oblique prism*, some or all of the lateral faces are nonrectangular.	**Prisma (p. 867)** Un prisma es un poliedro con dos caras congruentes paralelas llamadas *bases*. Las otras caras son paralelogramos llamados *caras laterales*. La *altura* de un prisma es un segmento perpendicular que une los planos de las bases. Su longitud es también la *altura* del prisma. En un *prisma rectangular*, las caras laterales son rectangulares y una de las aristas laterales es la altura. En un *prisma oblicuo*, algunas o todas las caras laterales no son rectangulares.

Example

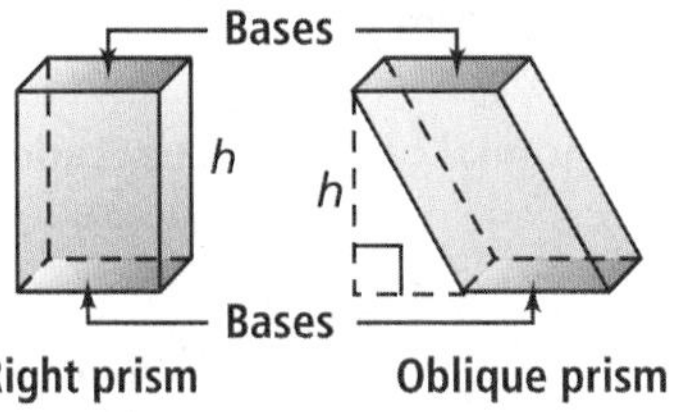

English	Spanish
Probability (p. 925) How likely it is that an event will occur (written formally as *P*(event)).	**Probabilidad (p. 925)** La posibilidad de que un suceso ocurra, escrita formalmente *P*(suceso).

Example You have 4 red marbles and 3 white marbles. The probability that you select one red marble, and then, without replacing it, randomly select another red marble is $P(\text{red}) = \frac{4}{7} \cdot \frac{3}{6} = \frac{2}{7}$.

English	Spanish

Probability distribution (p. 935) A probability distribution is a function that tells the probability of each outcome in a sample space.

Distribución de probabilidades (p. 935) Una distribución de probabilidades es una función que señala la probabilidad de que cada resultado ocurra en un espacio muestral.

Example

Roll	Fr.	Prob.
1	5	0.125
2	9	0.225
3	7	0.175
4	8	0.2
5	8	0.2
6	3	0.075

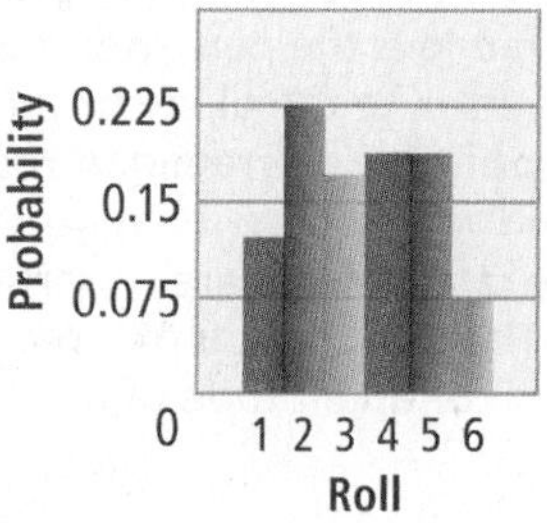

The table and graph both show the experimental probability distribution for the outcomes of 40 rolls of a standard number cube.

Proof (p. 398) A proof is a convincing argument that uses deductive reasoning. A proof can be written in many forms. In a *two-column proof*, the statements and reasons are aligned in columns. In a *paragraph proof*, the statements and reasons are connected in sentences. In a *flow proof*, arrows show the logical connections between the statements. In a *coordinate proof*, a figure is drawn on a coordinate plane and the formulas for slope, midpoint, and distance are used to prove properties of the figure. An *indirect proof* involves the use of indirect reasoning.

Prueba (p. 398) Una prueba es un argumento convincente en el cual se usa el razonamiento deductivo. Una prueba se puede escribir de varias maneras. En una *prueba de dos columnas*, los enunciados y las razones se alinean en columnas. En una *prueba de párrafo*, los enunciados y razones están unidos en oraciones. En una *prueba de flujo*, hay flechas que indican las conexiones lógicas entre enunciados. En una *prueba de coordenadas*, se dibuja una figura en un plano de coordenadas y se usan las fórmulas de la pendiente, punto medio y distancia para probar las propiedades de la figura. Una *prueba indirecta* incluye el uso de razonamiento indirecto.

Example

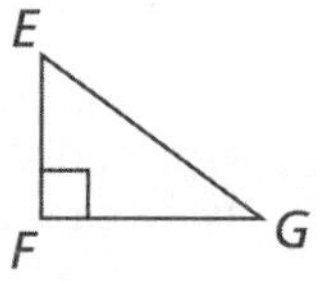

Given: $\triangle EFG$, with right angle $\angle F$
Prove: $\angle E$ and $\angle G$ are complementary.

Paragraph Proof: Because $\angle F$ is a right angle, $m\angle F = 90$. By the Triangle Angle-Sum Theorem, $m\angle E + m\angle F + m\angle G = 180$. By substitution, $m\angle E + 90 + m\angle G = 180$. Subtracting 90 from each side yields $m\angle E + m\angle G = 90$. $\angle E$ and $\angle G$ are complementary by definition.

Proportion (p. 670) A proportion is a statement that two ratios are equal. An *extended proportion* is a statement that three or more ratios are equal.

Proporción (p. 670) Una proporción es un enunciado en el cual dos razones son iguales. Una *proporción extendida* es un enunciado que dice que tres razones o más son iguales.

Example $\frac{x}{5} = \frac{3}{4}$ is a proportion.
$\frac{9}{27} = \frac{3}{9} = \frac{1}{3}$ is an extended proportion.

English	Spanish
Pure imaginary number (p. 188) If $a = 0$ and $b \neq 0$, the number $a + bi$ is a pure imaginary number.	**Número imaginario puro (p. 188)** Si $a = 0$ y $b \neq 0$, el número $a + bi$ es un número imaginario puro.
Pyramid (p. 879) A pyramid is a polyhedron in which one face, the *base*, is a polygon and the other faces, the *lateral faces*, are triangles with a common vertex, called the *vertex* of the pyramid. An *altitude* of a pyramid is the perpendicular segment from the vertex to the plane of the base. Its length is the *height* of the pyramid. A *regular pyramid* is a pyramid whose base is a regular polygon and whose lateral faces are congruent isosceles triangles. The *slant height* of a regular pyramid is the length of an altitude of a lateral face.	**Pirámide (p. 879)** Una pirámide es un poliedro en donde una cara, la *base*, es un polígono y las otras caras, las *caras laterales*, son triángulos con un vértice común, llamado el *vértice* de la pirámide. Una *altura* de una pirámide es el segmento perpendicular que va del vértice hasta el plano de la base. Su longitude es, por extensión, la *altura* de la pirámide. Una *pirámide regular* es una pirámide cuya base es un polígono regular y cuyas caras laterales son triángulos isósceles congruentes. La *apotema* de una pirámide regular es la longitude de la altura de la cara lateral.

Example

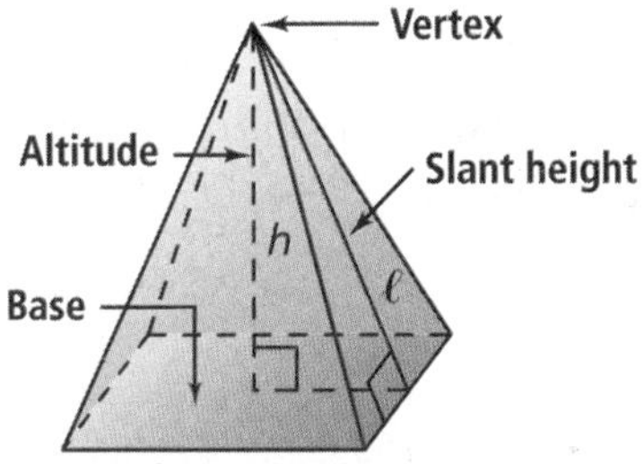

English	Spanish
Pythagorean triple (p. 746) A Pythagorean triple is a set of three nonzero whole numbers *a*, *b*, and *c*, that satisfy the equation $a^2 + b^2 = c^2$.	**Tripleta de Pitágoras (p. 746)** Una tripleta de Pitágoras es un conjunto de tres números enteros positivos *a*, *b*, and *c* que satisfacen la ecuación $a^2 + b^2 = c^2$.

Example The numbers 5, 12, and 13 form a Pythagorean triple because $5^2 + 12^2 = 13^2 = 169$.

Q

English	Spanish
Quadratic equation (p. 148) A quadratic equation is one that can be written in the standard form $ax^2 + bx + c = 0$, where $a \neq 0$.	**Ecuación cuadrática (p. 148)** Ecuación que puede expresarse de la forma normal como $ax^2 + bx + c = 0$, en la que $a \neq 0$.

Example $4x^2 + 9x - 5 = 0$

English	Spanish
Quadratic formula (p. 176) If $ax^2 + bx + c = 0$ and $a \neq 0$, then $x = \frac{-b \pm \sqrt{b^2 - 4ac}}{2a}$.	**Fórmula cuadrática (p. 176)** Si $ax^2 + bx + c = 0$ y $a \neq 0$, entonces $x = \frac{-b \pm \sqrt{b^2 - 4ac}}{2a}$.

Example $2x^2 + 10x + 12 = 0$

$$x = \frac{-b \pm \sqrt{b^2 - 4ac}}{2a}$$

$$x = \frac{-10 \pm \sqrt{10^2 - 4(2)(12)}}{2(2)}$$

$$x = \frac{-10 \pm \sqrt{4}}{4}$$

$$x = \frac{-10 + 2}{4} \text{ or } \frac{-10 - 2}{4}$$

$$x = -2 \text{ or } -3$$

English | Spanish

Quadratic function (p. 115) A function of the form $y = ax^2 + bx + c$, where $a \neq 0$. The graph of a quadratic function is a parabola, a U-shaped curve that opens up or down.

Función cuadrática (p. 115) La función $y = ax^2 + bx + c$, en la que $a \neq 0$. La gráfica de una función cuadrática es una parábola, o curva en forma de U que se abre hacia arriba o hacia abajo.

Example $y = 5x^2 - 2x + 1$ is a quadratic function.

Quadratic parent function (p. 115) The simplest quadratic function $f(x) = x^2$ or $y = x^2$.

Función cuadrática madre (p. 115) La función cuadrática más simple $f(x) = x^2$ ó $y = x^2$.

Example $y = x^2$ is the parent function for the family of quadratic equations of the form $y = ax^2 + bx + c$.

R

Radicand (p. 32) The expression under the radical sign is the radicand.

Radicando (p. 32) La expresión que aparece debajo del signo radical es el radicando.

Example The radicand of the radical expression $\sqrt{x+2}$ is $x + 2$.

Radian Measure (p. 815) The radian measure of a central angle of a circle is the ratio of the length of the intercepted arc to the radius of the circle. One radian is the measure of a central angle that intercepts an arc with length equal to the radius of the circle. On a unit circle, the radian measure of a central angle is the length of the arc it intercepts.

Medida en radianes (p. 815) La medida en radianes de un ángulo central de un círculo es la razón de la longitud del arco interceptado al radio del círculo. Un radián es la medida de un ángulo central que intercepta un arco con una longitud igual al radio del círculo. En un círculo unitario, la medida en radianes de un ángulo central es la longitud del arco que este intercepta.

Radius of a circle (p. 797) A radius of a circle is any segment with one endpoint on the circle and the other endpoint at the center of the circle. *Radius* can also mean the length of this segment.

Radio de un círculo (p. 797) Un radio de un círculo es cualquier segmento con extremo en el círculo y el otro extremo en el centro del círculo. *Radio* también se refeiere a la longitud de este segmento.

Radius of a regular polygon (p. 784) The radius of a regular polygon is the distance from the center to a vertex.

Radio de un polígono regular (p. 784) El radio de un polígono regular es la distancia desde el centro hasta un vértice.

Example

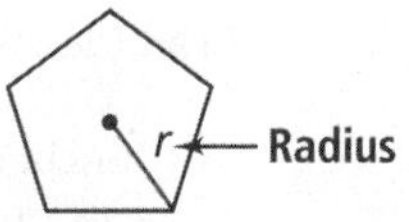

Radius of a sphere (p. 911) The radius of a sphere is a segment that has one endpoint at the center and the other endpoint on the sphere.

Radio de una esfera (p. 911) El radio de una esfera es un segmento con un extremo en el centro y otro en la esfera.

Example

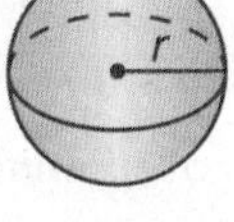

English	Spanish

Ratio (p. 667) A ratio is the comparison of two quantities by division.

Razón (p. 667) Una razón es la comparación de dos cantidades por medio de una división.

Example $\frac{5}{7}$ and 7 : 3 are ratios.

Rectangle (p. 619) A rectangle is a parallelogram with four right angles.

Rectángulo (p. 619) Un rectángulo es un paralelogramo con cuatro ángulos rectos.

Example

Reduction (p. 724) *See* **dilation.**

Reducción (p. 724) *Ver* **dilation.**

Reflection (p. 328) A reflection flips the graph of a function across a line, such as the *x*- or *y*-axis. Each point on the graph of the reflected function is the same distance from the line of reflection as is the corresponding point on the graph of the original function.

Reflexión (p. 328) Una reflexión voltea la gráfica de una función sobre una línea, como el eje de las *x* o el eje de las *y*. Cada punto de la gráfica de la función reflejada está a la misma distancia del eje de reflexión que el punto correspondiente en la gráfica de la función original.

Example

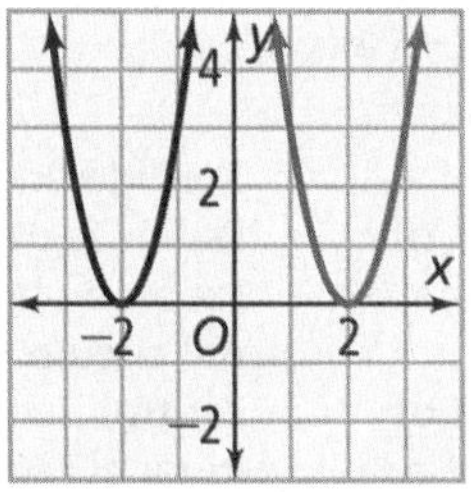

Regular polygon (p. 594) A regular polygon is a polygon that is both equilateral and equiangular. Its *center* is the point that is equidistant from its vertices.

Polígono regular (p. 594) Un polígono regular es un polígono que es equilateral y equiangular. Su *centro* es el punto equidistante de sus vértices.

Example

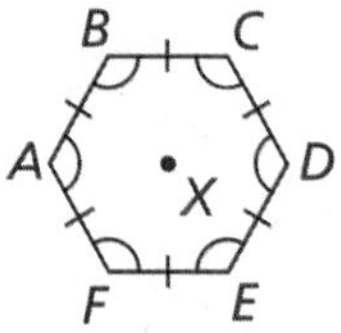

ABCDEF is a regular hexagon. Point *X* is its center.

Regular pyramid (p. 879) *See* **pyramid.**

Pirámide regular (p. 879) *Ver* **pyramid.**

Relative frequency (p. 932) The ratio of the number of times an event occurs to the total number of events in the sample space.

Frecuencia relativa (p. 932) La razón del número de veces que ocurre un evento al número de eventos en el espacio muestral.

Example

Archery Results

Scoring Region	Yellow	Red	Blue	Black	White
Arrow Strikes	52	25	10	8	5

$$\text{Relative frequency of spinning 1} = \frac{\text{frequency of spinning 1}}{\text{total frequencies}} = \frac{29}{100}$$

English | Spanish

Rhombus (p. 619) A rhombus is a parallelogram with four congruent sides.

Example

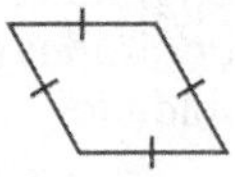

Rombo (p. 619) Un rombo es un paralelogramo de cuatro lados congruentes.

Right cone (p. 882) *See* **cone.**

Cono recto (p. 882) *Ver* **cone.**

Right cylinder (p. 862) *See* **cylinder.**

Cilindro recto (p. 862) *Ver* **cylinder.**

Right prism (p. 858) *See* **prism.**

Prisma rectangular (p. 858) *Ver* **prism.**

Right triangle (p. 546) A right triangle contains one right angle. The side opposite the right angle is the *hypotenuse* and the other two sides are the *legs*.

Triángulo rectángulo (p. 546) Un triángulo rectángulo contiene un ángulo recto. El lado opuesto del ángulo recto es la *hipotenusa* y los otros dos lados son los *catetos*.

Root of the equation (p. 148) A solution of an equation.

Ráiz de la ecuación (p. 148) Solucion de una ecuación.

Row operation (p. 381) A row operation on an augmented matrix is any of the following: switch two rows, multiply a row by a constant, add one row to another.

Operación de fila (p. 381) Una operación de fila en una matriz ampliada es cualquiera de las siguientes opciones: el intercambio de dos filas, la multiplicación de una fila por una constante o la suma de dos filas.

S

Same-side interior angles (p. 414) Same-side interior angles lie on the same side of the transversal t and between ℓ and m.

Example

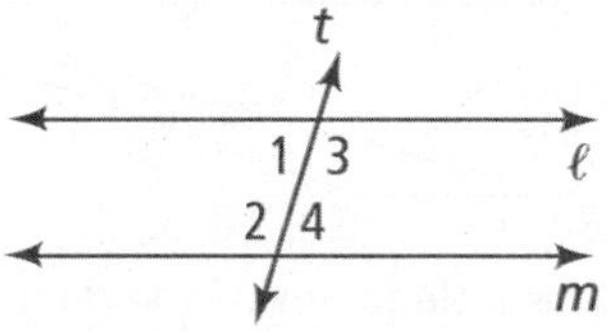

$\angle 1$ and $\angle 2$ are same-side interior angles, as are $\angle 3$ and $\angle 4$.

Ángulos internos del mismo lado (p. 414) Los ángulos internos del mismo lado están situados en el mismo lado de la transversal t y dentro de ℓ y m.

Sample space (p. 925) The part of a population that is surveyed.

Example Let the set of all males between the ages of 19 and 34 be the population. A random selection of 900 males between those ages would be a sample of the population.

Muestra (p. 925) Porción que se estudia de una población.

English	Spanish
Scale (p. 682) A scale is the ratio of any length in a scale drawing to the corresponding actual length. The lengths may be in different units.	**Escala (p. 682)** Una escala es la razón de cualquier longitud en un dibujo a escala en relación a la longitud verdadera correspondiente. Las longitudes pueden expresarse en distintas unidades.
Scale drawing (p. 682) A scale drawing is a drawing in which all lengths are proportional to corresponding actual lengths.	**Dibujo a escala (p. 682)** Un dibujo a escala es un dibujo en el que todas las longitudes son proporcionales a las longitudes verdaderas correspondientes.

Example

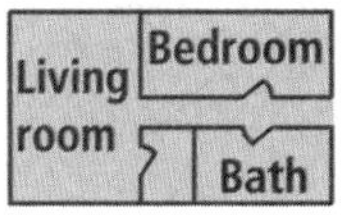

Scale:
1 in. = 30 ft

Scale factor (pp. 678, 723) A scale factor is the ratio of corresponding linear measurements of two similar figures.	**Factor de escala (pp. 678, 723)** El factor de escala es la razón de las medidas lineales correspondientes de dos figuras semejantes.

Example

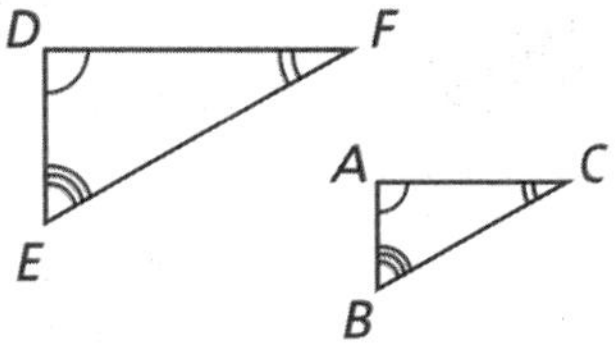

$\triangle ABC \sim \triangle DEF$

$\frac{AB}{DE} = \frac{BC}{EF} = \frac{CA}{FD}$

Scale factor of a dilation (p. 723) The scale factor of a dilation is the ratio of the distances from the center of dilation to an image point and to its preimage point.	**Factor de escala de dilatación (p. 723)** El factor de escala de dilatación es la razón de las distancias desde el centro de dilatación hasta un punto de la imagen y hasta un punto de la preimagen

Example

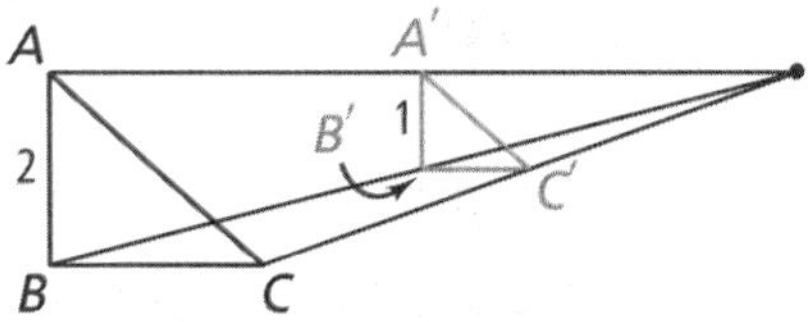

The scale factor of the dilation that maps $\triangle ABC$ to $\triangle A'B'C'$ is $\frac{1}{2}$.

Secant (p. 849) A secant is a line, ray, or segment that intersects a circle at two points.	**Secante (p. 849)** Una secante es una recta, semirrecta o segmento que corta un cículo en dos puntos.

Example

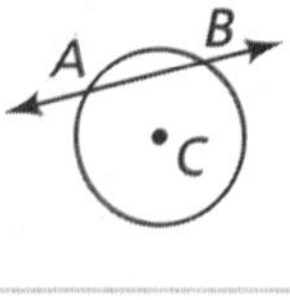

$\overleftrightarrow{AB}$ is a secant of $\odot C$.

Sector of a circle (p. 809) A sector of a circle is the region bounded by two radii and their intercepted arc.	**Sector de un círculo (p. 809)** Un sector de un círculo es la región limitada por dos radios y el arco abarcado por ellos.

Example

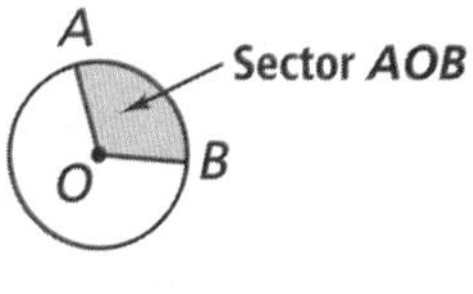

English

Segment of a circle (p. 810) A segment of a circle is the part of a circle bounded by an arc and the segment joining its endpoints.

Example

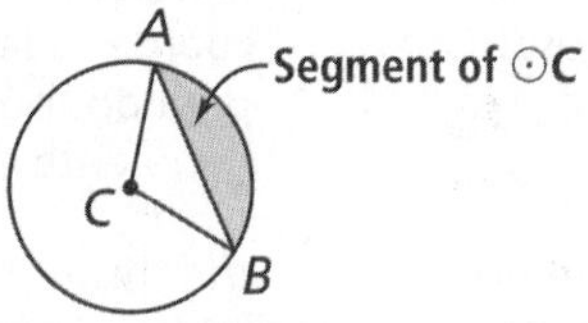

Spanish

Segmento de un círculo (p. 810) Un segmento de un círculo es la parte de un círculo bordeada por un arco y el segmento que une sus extremos.

Semicircle (p. 797) A semicircle is half a circle.

Semicírculo (p. 797) Un semicírculo es la mitad de un círculo.

Example

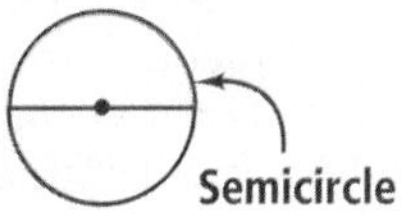

Similar figures (pp. 678, 733) Similar figures are two figures that have the same shape, but not necessarily the same size.

Figuras semejantes (pp. 678, 733) Los figuras semejantes son dos figuras que tienen la misma forma pero no necesariamente el mismo tamaño.

Example

Similar polygons (p. 678) Similar polygons are polygons having corresponding angles congruent and the lengths of corresponding sides proportional. You denote similarity by ~.

Polígonos semejantes (p. 678) Los polígonos semejantes son polígonos cuyos ángulos correspondientes son congruentes y las longitudes de los lados correspondientes son proporcionales. El símbolo ~ significa "es semejante a".

Example

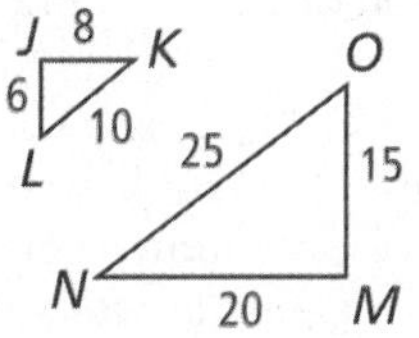

$\triangle JKL \sim \triangle MNO$

Scale factor $= \frac{2}{5}$

Similarity transformation (p. 733) A composition of a rigid motion and a dilation.

Transformación de semejanza (p. 733) Una transfomación que contiene un movimiento rígido y una dilatación.

Sine ratio (p. 768) *See* **trigonometric ratios.**

Razón seno (p. 768) *Ver* **trigonometric ratios.**

Skew lines (p. 412) Skew lines are lines that do not lie in the same plane.

Rectas cruzadas (p. 412) Las rectas cruzadas son rectas que no están en el mismo plano.

Example

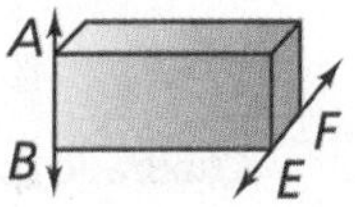

$\overleftrightarrow{AB}$ and $\overleftrightarrow{EF}$ are skew.

Slant height *See* **cone; pyramid.**

Generatriz (cono) o apotema (pirámide) *Ver* **cone; pyramid.**

English	Spanish

Slope (p. 317) The slope of a non-vertical line is the ratio of the vertical change to the horizontal change between points. You can calculate slope by finding the ratio of the difference in the y-coordinates to the difference in the x-coordinates for any two points on the line. The slope of a vertical line is undefined.

Pendiente (p. 317) La pendiente de una línea no vertical es la razón del cambio vertical al cambio horizontal entre puntos. Puedes calcular la pendiente al hallar la razón de la diferencia de la coordenada y y la diferencia de la coordenada x para dos puntos cualesquiera de la línea. La pendiente de una línea vertical es indefinida.

Example The slope of the line through points $(-1, -1)$ and $(1, -2)$ is $\frac{-2-(-1)}{1-(-1)} = \frac{-1}{2} = -\frac{1}{2}$.

Slope-intercept form (p. 319) The slope-intercept form of an equation of a line is $y = mx + b$, where m is the slope and b is the y-intercept.

Forma pendiente-intercepto (p. 319) La forma pendienteintercepto de una ecuación lineal es $y = mx + b$, donde m es la pendiente y b es el intercepto en y.

Example $y = 8x + 2$
$y = -x + 1$
$y = -\frac{1}{2}x - 14$

Solution of an equation (p. 300) A solution of an equation is a number that makes the equation true.

Solución de una ecuación (p. 300) Una solución de una ecuación es cualquier número que haga verdadera la ecuación.

Example The solution of $2x - 7 = -12$ is $x = -2.5$.

Sphere (p. 911) A sphere is the set of all points in space that are a given distance r, the *radius*, from a given point C, the *center*. A *great circle* is the intersection of a sphere with a plane containing the center of the sphere. The *circumference* of a sphere is the circumference of any great circle of the sphere.

Esfera (p. 911) Una esfera es el conjunto de los puntos del espacio que están a una distancia dada r, el *radio*, de un punto dado C, el *centro*. Un *círculo máximo* es la intersección de una esfera y un plano que contiene el centro de la esfera. La *circunferencia* de una esfera es la circunferencia de cualquier círculo máximo de la esfera.

Example

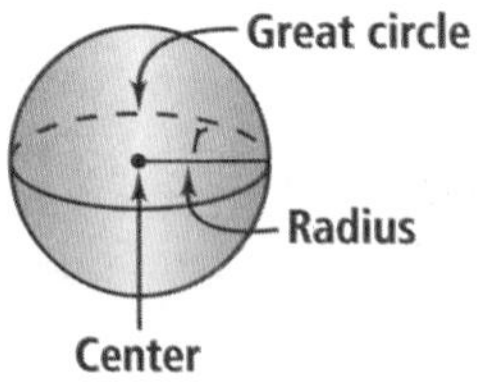

Square (p. 619) A square is a parallelogram with four congruent sides and four right angles.

Cuadrado (p. 619) Un cuadrado es un paralelogramo con cuatro lados congruentes y cuatro ángulos rectos.

Example

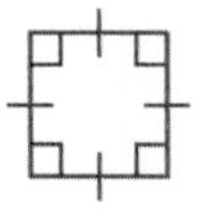

English

Spanish

Square root function (p. 263) A square root function is a function that can be written in the form $f(x) = a\sqrt{x-h} + k$, where $a \neq 0$. The domain of a square root function is all real numbers $x \geq h$.

Función de raíz cuadrada (p. 263) Una función de raíz cuadrada es una función que puede ser expresada como $f(x) = a\sqrt{x-h} + k$, donde $a \neq 0$. El dominio de una función de raíz cuadrada son todos los números reales tales que $x \geq h$.

Example $f(x) = 2\sqrt{x-3} + 4$

Standard form of a polynomial (p. 48) The form of a polynomial that places the terms in descending order by degree.

Forma normal de un polinomio (p. 48) Cuando el grado de los término de un de un polinomio disminuye de izquierda a derecha, está en forma normal, o en orden descendente.

Example $15x^3 + x^2 + 3x + 9$

Standard form of a quadratic equation (p. 148) The standard form of a quadratic equation is $ax^2 + bx + c = 0$, where $a \neq 0$.

Forma normal de una ecuación cuadrática (p. 148) Cuando una ecuación cuadrática se expresa de forma $ax^2 + bx + c = 0$, donde $a \neq 0$.

Example $-x^2 + 2x - 9 = 0$

Standard form of a quadratic function (p. 115) The standard form of a quadratic function is $f(x) = ax^2 + bx + c$, where $a \neq 0$.

Forma normal de una función cuadrática (p. 115) La forma normal de una función cuadrática es $f(x) = ax^2 + bx + c$, donde $a \neq 0$.

Example $f(x) = 2x^2 - 5x + 2$

Standard form of an equation of a circle (p. 232) The standard form of an equation of a circle with center (h, k) and radius r is $(x-h)^2 + (y-k)^2 = r^2$.

Forma normal de la ecuación de un círculo (p. 232) La forma normal de la ecuación de un círculo con un centro (h, k) y un radio r es $(x-h)^2 + (y-k)^2 = r^2$.

Example In $(x+5)^2 + (y+2)^2 = 48$, $(-5, -2)$ is the center of the circle.

Step function (pp. 277, 343) A step function pairs every number in an interval with a single value. The graph of a step function can look like the steps of a staircase.

Función escalón (pp. 277, 343) Una función escalón empareja cada número de un intervalo con un solo valor. La gráfica de una función escalón se puede parecer a los peldaños de una escalera.

Surface area (pp. 868, 872, 880) The surface area of a prism, cylinder, pyramid, or cone is the sum of the lateral area and the areas of the bases. The surface area of a sphere is four times the area of a great circle.

Área (pp. 868, 872, 880) El área de un prisma, pirámide, cilindro o cono es la suma del área lateral y las áreas de las bases. El área de una esfera es igual a cuatro veces el área de un círculo máximo.

Example

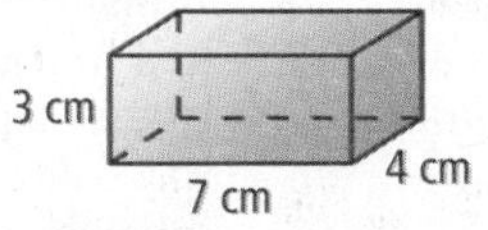

$$\begin{aligned} \text{S.A. of prism} &= \text{L.A.} + 2B \\ &= 66 + 2(28) \\ &= 122 \text{ cm}^2 \end{aligned}$$

English	Spanish

T

Tangent to a circle (p. 818) A tangent to a circle is a line, segment, or ray in the plane of the circle that intersects the circle in exactly one point. That point is the *point of tangency*.

Tangente de un círculo (p. 818) Una tangente de un círculo es una recta, segmento o semirrecta en el plano del círculo que corta el círculo en exactamente un punto. Ese punto es el *punto de tangencia*.

Example

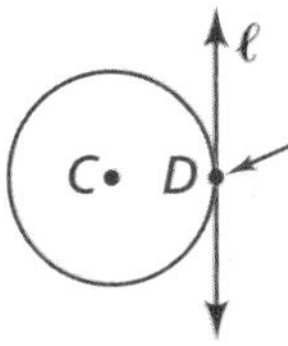

Line ℓ is tangent to $\odot C$. Point D is the point of tangency.

Test point (p. 346) A test point is a point that you pick on one side of the boundary of the graph of a linear inequality. If the test point makes the inequality true, then all points on that side of the boundary are solutions of the inequality. If the test point makes the inequality false, then all points on the other side are solutions.

Punto de prueba (p. 346) Un punto de prueba es un punto que escoges a un lado del límite de la gráfica de una desigualdad lineal. Si el punto de prueba hace que la desigualdad sea verdadera, entonces todos los puntos en ese límite son soluciones de la desigualdad. Si el punto de prueba hace que la desigualdad sea falsa, entonces todos los puntos del otro lado del límite son soluciones.

Theorem (p. 402) A theorem is a conjecture that is proven.

Teorema (p. 402) Un teorema es una conjetura que se demuestra.

Example The theorem "Vertical angles are congruent" can be proven by using postulates, definitions, properties, and previously stated theorems.

Theoretical probability (p. 927) The ratio of the number of favorable outcomes to the number of possible outcomes if all outcomes have the same chance of happening.

$$P(\text{event}) = \frac{\text{number of favorable outcomes}}{\text{number of possible outcomes}}$$

Probabilidad teórica (p. 927) Si cada resultado tiene la misma probabilidad de darse, la probabilidad teórica de un suceso se calcula como la razón del número de resultados favorables al número de resultados posibles.

$$P(\text{suceso}) = \frac{\text{numero de resultados favorables}}{\text{numero de resultados posibles}}$$

Example In tossing a coin, the events of getting heads or tails are equally likely. The likelihood of getting heads is $P(\text{heads}) = \frac{1}{2}$.

Transformation (p. 325) A transformation of a function $y = af(x - h) + k$ is a change made to at least one of the values a, h, and k. The four types of transformations are dilations, reflections, rotations, and translations.

Transformación (p. 325) Una transformación de una función $y = af(x - h) + k$ es un cambio que se le hace a por lo menos uno de los valores a, h y k. Hay cuatro tipos de transformaciones: dilataciones, reflexiones, rotaciones y traslaciones.

Example $g(x) = 2(x - 3)^2$ is a transformation of $f(x) = x^2$.

English | Spanish

Transversal (p. 414) A transversal is a line that intersects two or more lines at distinct points.

Transversal (p. 414) Una transversal es una línea que interseca dos o más líneas en puntos precisos.

Example

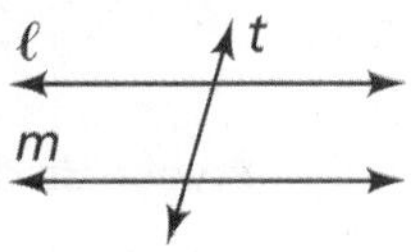

t is a transversal of ℓ and m.

Translation (p. 325) A translation shifts the graph of the parent function horizontally, vertically, or both without changing its shape or orientation.

Traslación (p. 325) Una traslación desplaza la gráfica de la función madre horizontalmente, verticalmente o en ambas direcciones, sin cambiar su forma u orientación.

Example

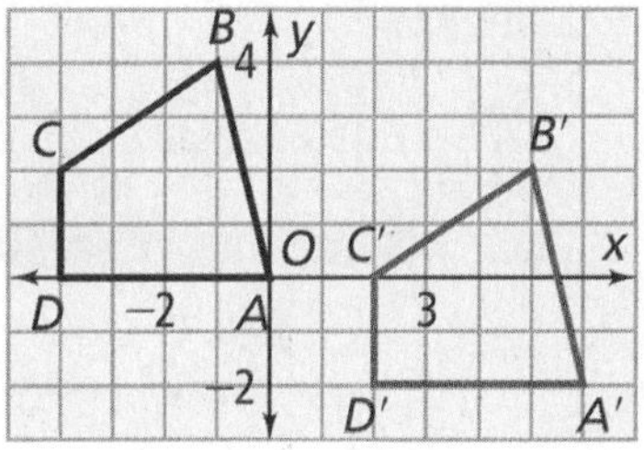

Trapezoid (p. 636) A trapezoid is a quadrilateral with exactly one pair of parallel sides, the *bases*. The nonparallel sides are called the *legs* of the trapezoid. Each pair of angles adjacent to a base are *base angles* of the trapezoid. An *altitude* of a trapezoid is a perpendicular segment from one base to the line containing the other base. Its length is called the *height* of the trapezoid.

Trapecio (p. 636) Un trapecio es un cuadrilátero con exactamente un par de lados paralelos, las *bases*. Los lados no paralelos se llaman los *catetos* del trapecio. Cada par de ángulos adyacentes a la base son los *ángulos de base* del trapecio. Una *altura* del trapecio es un segmento perpendicular que va de una base a la recta que contiene la otra base. Su longitud se llama, por extensión, la *altura* del trapecio.

Example

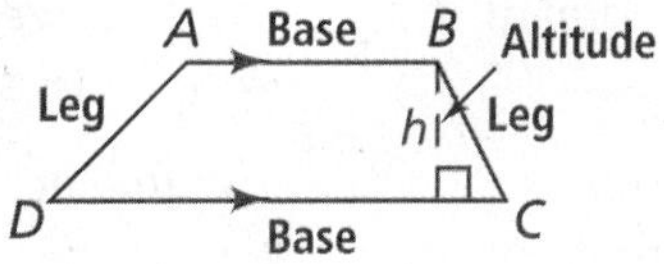

In trapezoid $ABCD$, $\angle ADC$ and $\angle BCD$ are one pair of base angles, and $\angle DAB$ and $\angle ABC$ are the other.

Trigonometric ratios (p. 768) In right $\triangle ABC$ with acute $\angle A$,

$$\text{sine } \angle A = \sin A = \frac{\text{leg opposite } \angle A}{\text{hypotenuse}}$$

$$\text{cosine } \angle A = \cos A = \frac{\text{leg adjacent to } \angle A}{\text{hypotenuse}}$$

$$\text{tangent } \angle A = \tan A = \frac{\text{leg opposite } \angle A}{\text{leg adjacent to } \angle A}$$

Razones trigonométricas (p. 768) En un triángulo rectángulo $\triangle ABC$ con ángulo agudo $\angle A$,

$$\text{seno } \angle A = \text{sen } A = \frac{\text{cateto opuesto a } \angle A}{\text{hipotenusa}}$$

$$\text{coseno } \angle A = \cos A = \frac{\text{cateto adyecente a } \angle A}{\text{hipotenusa}}$$

$$\text{tangente } \angle A = \tan A = \frac{\text{cateto opuesto a } \angle A}{\text{cateto adyecente a } \angle A}$$

Example

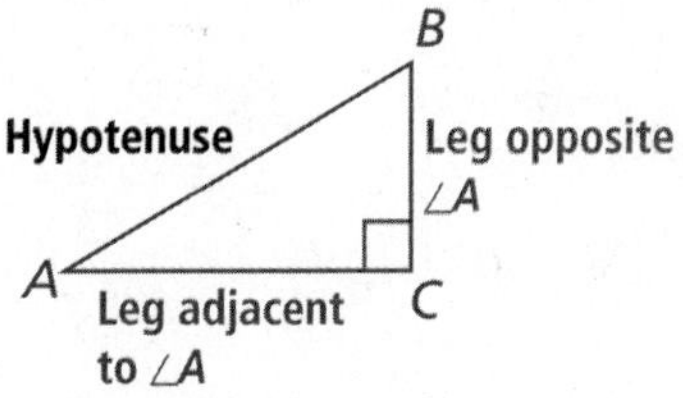

English	Spanish

Trinomial (p. 49) A polynomial of three terms.

Trinomio (p. 49) Polinomio compuesto de tres términos.

Example $3x^2 + 2x - 5$

Two-column proof (p. 398) *See* **proof.**

Prueba de dos columnas (p. 398) *Ver* **proof.**

Two-way frequency table (p. 957) A table that displays frequencies in two different categories.

Tabla de frecuencias de doble entrada (p. 957) Una tabla de frecuencias que contiene dos categorías de datos.

Example

	Male	Female	Totals
Juniors	3	4	7
Seniors	3	2	5
Totals	6	6	12

V

Vertex of a parabola (p. 116) The highest or lowest point on a parabola. The axis of symmetry intersects the parabola at the vertex.

Vértice de una parabola (p. 116) El punto más alto o más bajo de una parábola. El punto de intersección del eje de simetría y la parábola.

Example

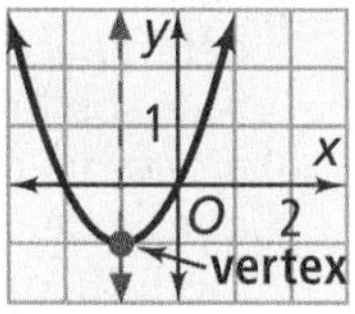

Vertex *See* **cone; pyramid.** The plural form of *vertex* is *vertices*.

Vértice *Ver* **cone; pyramid.**

Vertex angle (p. 486) *See* **isosceles triangle.**

Ángulo del vértice (p. 486) *Ver* **isosceles triangle.**

Vertical compression (p. 328) A vertical compression reduces all *y*-values of a function by the same factor between 0 and 1.

Compresión vertical (p. 328) Una compresión vertical reduce todos los valores de *y* de una función por el mismo factor entre 0 y 1.

Vertical stretch (p. 328) A vertical stretch multiplies all *y*-values of a function by the same factor greater than 1.

Estiramiento vertical (p. 328) Un estiramiento vertical multiplica todos los valores de *y* por el mismo factor mayor que 1.

Volume (p. 889) Volume is a measure of the space a figure occupies.

Volumen (p. 889) El volumen es una medida del espacio que ocupa una figura.

English	Spanish

X

x-intercept, y-intercept (p. 319) The point at which a line crosses the *x*-axis (or the *x*-coordinate of that point) is an *x*-intercept. The point at which a line crosses the *y*-axis (or the *y*-coordinate of that point) is a *y*-intercept.

Intercepto en x, intercepto en y (p. 319) El punto donde una recta corta el eje *x* (o la coordenada *x* de ese punto) es el intercepto en *x*. El punto donde una recta cruza el eje *y* (o la coordenada *y* de ese punto) es el intercepto en *y*.

Example

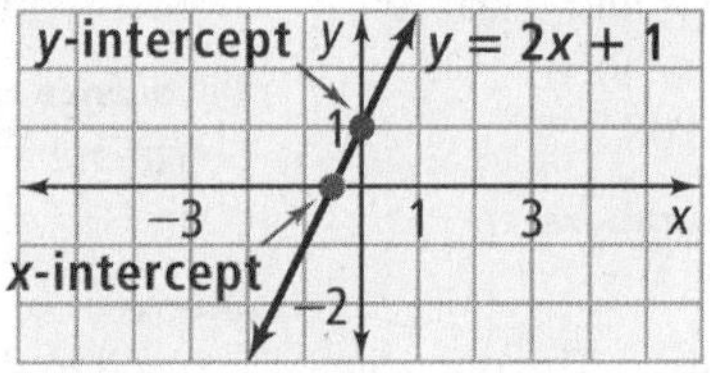

The *x*-intercept of $y = 2x + 1$ is $\left(-\frac{1}{2}, 0\right)$ or $-\frac{1}{2}$

The *y*-intercept of $y = 2x + 1$ is (0, 1) or 1.

Z

Zero of a function (p. 148) An *x*-intercept of the graph of a function.

Cero de una función (p. 148) Intercepto *x* de la gráfica de una función.

Example The zeros of $y = x^2 - 4$ are ± 2.

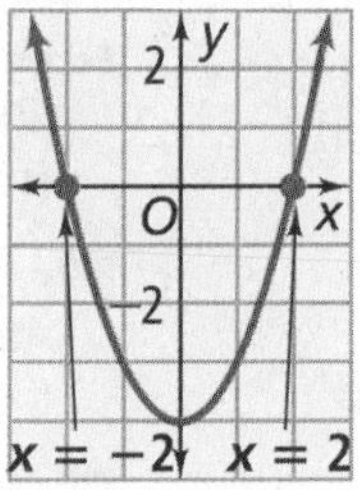

Zero-Product Property (p. 158) For all real numbers *a* and *b*, if $ab = 0$, then $a = 0$ or $b = 0$.

Propiedad del producto cero (p. 158) Para todos los números reales *a* y *b*, si $ab = 0$, entonces $a = 0$ ó $b = 0$.

Example $x(x + 3) = 0$
$x = 0$ or $x + 3 = 0$
$x = 0$ or $x - 3$

Visual **Glossary**

Appendix Glossary

A

Acute angle An angle whose measure is between 0° and 90°, p. H67.

Addition principle of probability $P(A \text{ or } B) = P(A) + P(B) - P(A \text{ and } B)$. If A and B are mutually exclusive events, then $P(A \text{ or } B) = P(A) + P(B)$, p. H108.

Additive identity for the complex numbers $0 + 0i$ is the complex number zero, p. H33.

Additive inverse of a complex number The opposite of $a + bi$, or $-a - bi$, p. H33.

Aphelion The farthest point from the Sun in a planet's orbit, p. H16.

B

Binomial probability In an experiment with two possible outcomes, the probability of one outcome occurring k times in n independent trials is

$$P(E) = \frac{n!}{k!(n-k)!}p^k(1-p)^{n-k},$$

where p is the probability of the outcome occurring once, p. H111.

Branches The two separate curves that make up a hyperbola, p. H22.

C

Center The central point in a circle, ellipse, hyperbola, or sphere, pp. H12, H22.

Chord of a conic A line segment with endpoints on the conic, pp. H5, H13, H23.

Cofunction identity An identity that relates the sine, secant, or tangent to the cosine, cosecant, or cotangent, respectively, p. H77.

Complements or complementary angles Two angles of positive measure whose sum is 90°, p. H77.

Complex conjugates Complex numbers $a + bi$ and $a - bi$, p. H34.

Complex number An expression $a + bi$, where a (the real part) and b (the imaginary part) are real numbers, p. H32.

Conditional probability The probability of an event A given that an event B has already occurred $(P(A|B))$, p. H109.

Cone See *Right circular cone.*

Conic section (or conic) A curve obtained by intersecting a double-napped right circular cone with a plane, p. H2.

D

Dependent event An event whose probability depends on another event already occurring, p. H109.

Difference identity An identity involving a trigonometric function of $u - v$, pp. H92–H94.

Difference of complex numbers $(a + bi) - (c + di) = (a - c) + (b - d)i$, p. H32.

Directrix of a parabola, ellipse, or hyperbola A line used to determine the conic, p. H3.

Discriminant For the equation $ax^2 + bx + c$, the expression $b^2 - 4ac$; for the equation $Ax^2 + Bxy + Cy^2 + Dx + Ey + F = 0$, the expression $B^2 - 4AC$, pp. H34.

Domain of validity of an identity The set of values of the variable for which both sides of the identity are defined, p. H75.

Double-angle identity An identity involving a trigonometric function of $2u$, p. H98.

E

Eccentricity A nonnegative number that specifies how off-center the focus of a conic is, pp. H16–H17, H26.

Ellipse The set of all points in the plane such that the sum of the distances from a pair of fixed points (the foci) is a constant, p. H12.

Ellipsoid of revolution A surface generated by rotating an ellipse about its major axis, p. H18.

Empty set A set with no elements, p. H105.

End behavior asymptote of a rational function A polynomial that the function approaches as $|x| \to \infty$, p. H52.

Equal complex numbers Complex numbers whose real parts are equal and whose imaginary parts are equal, p. H32.

Equally likely outcomes Outcomes of an experiment that have the same probability of occurring, p. H104.

Event A subset of a sample space, p. H104.

F

Focal axis The line through the focus and perpendicular to the directrix of a conic, pp. H4, H12, H22.

Focal length of a parabola The *directed distance* from the vertex to the focus, p. H5.

Focal width of a parabola The length of the chord through the focus and perpendicular to the axis, p. H5.

Focus, foci See *Ellipse, Hyperbola, Parabola.*

Fundamental Theorem of Algebra A polynomial function of degree $n > 0$ has n complex zeros (counting multiplicity), p. H42.

H

Half-angle identity Identity involving a trigonometric function of $u/2$, p. H100.

Hyperbola A set of points in a plane, the absolute value of the difference of whose distances from two fixed points (the foci) is a constant, p. H22.

Hyperboloid of revolution A surface generated by rotating a hyperbola about its transverse axis, p. H27.

Hypotenuse Side opposite the right angle in a right triangle, p. H67.

I

Identity An equation that is always true throughout its domain, p. H75.

Imaginary unit The complex number $i = \sqrt{-1}$, p. H32.

Independent events Events A and B such that $P(A \text{ and } B) = P(A)P(B)$, p. H107.

Irreducible quadratic over the reals A quadratic polynomial with real coefficients that cannot be factored using real coefficients, p. H46.

L

Linear factorization theorem A polynomial $f(x)$ of degree $n > 0$ has the factorization $f(x) = a(x - z_1)(x - z_2)\cdots(x - z_n)$ where the z_i are the zeros of f, p. H42.

M

Major axis The line segment through the foci of an ellipse with endpoints on the ellipse, p. H13.

Minor axis The perpendicular bisector of the major axis of an ellipse with endpoints on the ellipse, p. H13.

Multiplication principle of probability If A and B are independent events, then $P(A \text{ and } B) = P(A) \cdot P(B)$. If A depends on B, then $P(A \text{ and } B) = P(A \mid B) \cdot P(B)$, p. H107.

Multiplicative inverse of a complex number The reciprocal of $a + bi$, or $\frac{1}{a + bi} = \frac{a}{a^2 + b^2} - \frac{b}{a^2 + b^2}i$, p. H34.

N

Nappe See *Right circular cone.*

O

Odd-even identity For a basic trigonometric function f, an identity relating $f(x)$ to $f(-x)$ p. H78.

Opens upward or downward A parabola $y = ax^2 + bx + c$ opens upward if $a > 0$ and opens downward if $a < 0$, p. H6.

Opposite See *Additive inverse of a complex number.*

Outcomes The various possible results of an experiment, p. H104.

P

Parabola The graph of a quadratic function, or the set of points in a plane that are equidistant from a fixed point (the focus) and a fixed line (the directrix), p. H3.

Paraboloid of revolution A surface generated by rotating a parabola about its line of symmetry, p. H8.

Perihelion The closest point to the Sun in a planet's orbit, p. H16.

Probability distribution The collection of probabilities of outcomes in a sample space assigned by a probability function, p. H105.

Probability of an event in a finite sample space of equally likely outcomes The number of outcomes in the event divided by the number of outcomes in the sample space, p. H104.

Probability function A function P that assigns a real number to each outcome O in a sample space satisfying: $0 \le P(O) \le 1$, $P(\varnothing) = 0$, and the sum of the probabilities of all outcomes is 1, p. H105.

Product of complex numbers $(a + bi)(c + di) = (ac - bd) + (ad + bc)i$, pp. H33.

Projectile motion The movement of an object that is subject only to the force of gravity, p. H40.

Pythagorean identities $\sin^2\theta + \cos^2\theta = 1$, $1 + \tan^2\theta = \sec^2\theta$, and $1 + \cot^2\theta = \csc^2\theta$, p. H76.

Q

Quotient identities $\tan\theta = \frac{\sin\theta}{\cos\theta}$ and $\cot\theta = \frac{\cos\theta}{\sin\theta}$, p. H75.

Quotient of complex numbers
$\frac{a+bi}{c+di} = \frac{ac+bd}{c^2+d^2} + \frac{bc-ad}{c^2+d^2}i$, pp. H34.

R

Random variable A function that assigns real-number values to the outcomes in a sample space, p. H105.

Rational function Function of the form $\frac{f(x)}{g(x)}$, where $f(x)$ and $g(x)$ are polynomials and $g(x)$ is not the zero polynomial, p. H49.

Reciprocal identity An identity that equates a trigonometric function with the reciprocal of another trigonometric function, p. H75.

Right angle A 90° angle, p. H67.

Right circular cone The surface created when a line is rotated about a second line that intersects but is not perpendicular to the first line, p. H2.

S

Sample space Set of all possible outcomes of an experiment, p. H104.

Second-degree equation in two variables
$Ax^2 + Bxy + Cy^2 + Dx + Ey + F = 0$, where A, B, and C are not all zero, p. H3.

Semimajor axis The distance from the center to a vertex of an ellipse, p. H13.

Semiminor axis The distance from the center of an ellipse to a point on the ellipse along a line perpendicular to the major axis, p. H13.

Slant asymptote An end behavior asymptote that is a slant line, p. H52.

Solve a triangle To find one or more unknown sides or angles of a triangle, p. H71.

Standard form:

equation of an ellipse $\frac{(x-h)^2}{a^2} + \frac{(y-k)^2}{b^2} = 1$ or $\frac{(y-k)^2}{a^2} + \frac{(x-h)^2}{b^2} = 1$, p. H12.

equation of a hyperbola
$\frac{(x-h)^2}{a^2} - \frac{(y-k)^2}{b^2} = 1$ or
$\frac{(y-k)^2}{a^2} - \frac{(x-h)^2}{b^2} = 1$, p. H23.

equation of a parabola $(x-h)^2 = 4p(y-k)$ or $(y-k)^2 = 4p(x-h)$, p. H5.

Standard form of a complex number $a + bi$, where a and b are real numbers, p. H32.

Standard position (angle) An angle positioned on a rectangular coordinate system with its vertex at the origin and its initial side on the positive x-axis, p. H67.

Sum identity An identity involving a trigonometric function of $u + v$, p. H91.

Sum of complex numbers $(a + bi) + (c + di) = (a + c) + (b + d)i$, p. H32.

T

Transverse axis The line segment whose endpoints are the vertices of a hyperbola, p. H23.

Tree diagram A visualization of the *Multiplication Principle of Probability*, p. H108.

U

Union of two sets *A* and *B* The set of all elements that belong to A or B or both, p. H38.

V

Venn diagram A visualization of the relationships among events within a sample space, p. H107.

Vertex of a cone See *Right circular cone.*

Vertex of a parabola The point of intersection of a parabola and its line of symmetry, p. H4.

Vertical asymptote The line $x = a$ is a vertical asymptote of the graph of the function f if
$\lim_{x\to a^+} f(x) = \pm\infty$ or
$\lim_{x\to a^-} f(x) = \pm\infty$, p. H52.

Vertices of an ellipse The points where the ellipse intersects its focal axis, p. H12.

Vertices of a hyperbola The points where a hyperbola intersects the line containing its foci, p. H22.

Index

A

B

C

F

Index

J

K

L

Index

Index

Q

R

S

T

U

V

W

X

Y

Z

Acknowledgments

Staff Credits

The people who made up the High School Mathematics team—representing composition services, core design digital and multimedia production services, digital product development, editorial, editorial services, manufacturing, marketing, and production management—are listed below.

Patty Fagan, Suzanne Finn, Matt Frueh, Cynthia Harvey, Linda Johnson, Roshni Kutty, Cheryl Mahan, Eve Melnechuk, Cynthia Metallides, Hope Morley, Michael Oster, Wynnette Outland, Brian Reardon, Matthew Rogers, Ann-Marie Sheehan, Kristen Siefers, Richard Sullivan, Susan Tauer, Mark Tricca, Oscar Vera, Paula Vergith

Additional Credits: Emily Bosak, Olivia Gerde, Alyse McGuire, Stephanie Mosely

Illustration

Jeff Grunewald: 497, 599, 614, 658, 676, 686, 687, 694, 706, 714, 715, 718; **Stephen Durke:** 433, 443, 453, 462, 476, 483, 493, 510, 536, 539, 543, 547, 548, 552, 568, 577, 579, 581, 586, 706, 764, 774, 777, 778, 783, 804, 805, 806, 814; **Phil Guzy:** 753, 776, 800, 804, 805, 877, 878, 904, 911, 919; **Rob Schuster:** 258, 370, 377

Technical Illustration

Aptara, Inc.; Datagrafix, Inc.; GGS Book Services

Photography

Every effort has been made to secure permission and provide appropriate credit for photographic material. The publisher deeply regrets any omission and pledges to correct errors called to its attention in subsequent editions.

Unless otherwise acknowledged, all photographs are the property of Pearson Education, Inc.

108, Kyla Brown; **315,** Richard Wahlstrom Workbook/Jupiter Images/Getty Images; **409,** Jenny Thompson/Fotolia; **416,** Kevin Fleming/Corbis; **428,** photo courtesy of Frank Adelstein, Ithaca, NY; **436,** Robert Llewellyn/Corbis; **480,** Viktor Kitaykin/iStockphoto; **490,** John Wells/Photo Researchers, Inc; **501,** Image Source Black/Jupiter Images; **521 l,** M.C. Escher's "Symmetry E56" © 2009 The M.C. Escher Company-Holland. All rights reserved. www.mcescher.com; **521 r,** M.C. Escher's "Symmetry E18" © 2009 The M.C. Escher Company-Holland. All rights reserved. www.mcescher.com; **535,** Joseph Sohm/Visions of America, LLC/Alamy Images; **595 l,** Laurie Strachan/Alamy Images; **595 r,** BestShot/iStockphoto; **608,** Esa Hiltula/Alamy Images; **620 t,** Claro Cortes IV/Reuters/Landov LLC; **620 b,** Michael Jenner/Alamy Images; **634,** Rodney Raschke/Active Photo Service; **644,** Colin Underhill/Alamy Images; **706,** ©James L. Amos/Corbis; **714,** Victor R. Boswell Jr./Contributor National Geographic/Getty Images; **790,** Dennis Marsico/Corbis; **826,** Clive Streeter/©DK Images; **846,** Vario Images GmbH & Co.KG/Alamy Images; **851,** Melvyn Longhurst/Alamy; **855,** dpa/Corbis; **876,** Ron Chapple Stock/Alamy; **918,** Stephen Sweet/Alamy; **H1,** © Shutterstock; **H10,** © Tony Roberts/Corbis; **H27,** © NASA; **H66,** © BrandX Pictures; **H82,** © Digital Vision; **H97,** © NASA; **H109,** © PhotoDisc/ Getty Royalty Free.

Chapter 1: Whole chapter taken from Chapter 10 of *Pearson High School Math 2014 Common Core Integrated Math 2 Write-In Student Edition Volume 2.*

Chapter 2: Whole chapter taken from Chapter 11 of *Pearson High School Math 2014 Common Core Integrated Math 2 Write-In Student Edition Volume 2.*

Chapter 3: Whole chapter taken from Chapter 12 of *Pearson High School Math 2014 Common Core Integrated Math 2 Write-In Student Edition Volume 2.*

Chapter 4: Whole chapter taken from Chapter 14 of *Pearson High School Math 2014 Common Core Integrated Math 2 Write-In Student Edition Volume 2.*

Chapter 5: Whole chapter taken from Chapter 2 of *Pearson High School Math 2014 Common Core Integrated Math 3 Write-In Student Edition Volume 1.*

Chapter 6: Lessons 1-2 taken from Chapter 1, Lessons 6-7 of *Pearson High School Math 2014 Common Core Integrated Math 2 Write-In Student Edition Volume 1.* Lessons 3-6 taken from Chapter 2, Lessons 1-4 of *Pearson High School Math 2014 Common Core Integrated Math 2 Write-In Student Edition Volume 1.*

Chapter 7: Whole chapter taken from Chapter 3 of *Pearson High School Math 2014 Common Core Integrated Math 2 Write-In Student Edition Volume 1.*

Chapter 8: Whole chapter taken from Chapter 4 of *Pearson High School Math 2014 Common Core Integrated Math 2 Write-In Student Edition Volume 1.*

Chapter 9: Whole chapter taken from Chapter 5 of *Pearson High School Math 2014 Common Core Integrated Math 2 Write-In Student Edition Volume 1.*

Chapter 10: Whole chapter taken from Chapter 6 of *Pearson High School Math 2014 Common Core Integrated Math 2 Write-In Student Edition Volume 1.*

Chapter 11: Whole chapter taken from Chapter 7 of *Pearson High School Math 2014 Common Core Integrated Math 2 Write-In Student Edition Volume 1.*

Chapter 12: Whole chapter taken from Chapter 8 of *Pearson High School Math 2014 Common Core Integrated Math 2 Write-In Student Edition Volume 2.*

Chapter 13: Whole chapter taken from Chapter 9 of *Pearson High School Math 2014 Common Core Integrated Math 2 Write-In Student Edition Volume 1.*

Chapter 14: Whole chapter taken from Chapter 13 of *Pearson High School Math 2014 Common Core Integrated Math 2 Write-In Student Edition Volume 2.*

Honors Appendix: Lessons 1-3 taken from Chapter 8, Sections 1-3 of *Precalculus: Graphical, Numerical, Algebraic, Eighth Edition.* Lessons 4-5 taken from Chapter P, Sections 6-7 of *Precalculus: Graphical, Numerical, Algebraic, Eighth Edition.* Lessons 6-8 taken from Chapter 2, Sections 5, 6, 8 of *Precalculus: Graphical, Numerical, Algebraic, Eighth Edition.* Lesson 9 taken from Chapter 4, Section 2 of *Precalculus: Graphical, Numerical, Algebraic, Eighth Edition.* Lessons 10-13 taken from Chapter 5, Sections 1-4 of *Precalculus: Graphical, Numerical, Algebraic, Eighth Edition.* Lesson 14 taken from Chapter 9, Section 3 of *Precalculus: Graphical, Numerical, Algebraic, Eighth Edition.*